This volume is dedicated to all students of Management Accounting—past, present, and future.

AUTHORS

CECILY A. RAIBORN

Dr. Cecily A. Raiborn is Professor of Accounting at Loyola University–New Orleans. She received her Ph.D. from Louisiana State University in 1975. Professor Raiborn teaches cost, managerial, intermediate, and advanced accounting at the undergraduate level, and financial and managerial accounting, cost management, and performance measurement at the graduate level. Her research interests include cost management, international, quality, and ethics issues. She has published articles in accounting, law, and ethics journals including *Management Accounting, Advances in Management Accounting, Journal of Accounting Case Research, Labor Law Journal,* and *Journal of Business Ethics.* She serves on the editorial board of *Advances in Management Accounting.* In 1991, she received the AICPA/Louisiana CPA Society Outstanding Educator Award. Her interests outside the classroom include travelling, reading, water activities, fishing, decorating, and cooking.

BRENDA M. MALLOUK

Brenda Mallouk is known for her energetic teaching style and her popularity with students. Currently, she is a member of the accounting faculty at the University of Toronto. She is also involved in professional accounting education. Brenda Mallouk has authored many books and articles in the field of accounting and education. Her research work has appeared in conference proceedings and journals. Her research interests include cost control, teaching methodology, and management control issues. In addition to her teaching experience at the University of Toronto, she has taught extensively in Central America, the Caribbean, and the People's Republic of China. She is actively involved on many university committees and has received several Excellence in Teaching Awards at the University of Toronto. Her passion is travelling to exotic locales.

GARY SPRAAKMAN

Gary Spraakman is an associate professor of management accounting at the Atkinson Faculty of Liberal and Professional Studies, York University. He has a Ph.D. in accounting from Concordia University. Prior to pursuing his Ph.D. studies, he worked as a senior consultant at Coopers and Lybrand and as a manager at The Molson Companies and Alberta Social Services. He received his faculty's major teaching excellence award, which is adjudicated by the alumni association. Gary's research focus is management accounting, broadly from historical accounting, to questioning theory, to information technology, to innovation. Recently, he published academic articles in *Critical Perspectives on Accounting,* the *Journal of Management Accounting Research* and the *Accounting Historians Journal,* and teaching cases in the *Journal of Accounting Case Research* and other publications.

JESSE T. BARFIELD

Dr. Jesse T. Barfield is a Professor of Accounting at Loyola University–New Orleans. He received his Ph.D. from Louisiana State University in 1971. He earned an undergraduate degree in accounting and a masters in accounting at Florida State University. He has practiced as a CPA and is licensed to practice in Florida and Louisiana. His research and professional interests include managerial and cost accounting, total quality management, and quality assessments for managers. He teaches accounting, quality management, and auditing in Loyola's undergraduate program and also teaches graduate courses in the MBA and MQM programs. He was chosen by the Loyola CBA undergraduates to receive the 1998 Award for Outstanding Teaching. He has published in the *Journal of Accountancy, Management Accounting, The Florida Certified Public Accountant,* and *The Louisiana CPA.*

MICHAEL R. KINNEY

Dr. Michael Kinney is a native of the rural, sandhills area of Nebraska and received a BA degree from Hastings College, Hastings, Nebraska in 1978. Following graduation, Professor Kinney worked as an insurance agent and broker and later as a commodity futures broker. He returned to graduate school in 1984, earning an MS in accounting from the University of Wyoming and a Ph.D. from the University of Arizona. Professor Kinney joined the faculty of accounting at Texas A&M in 1989, and is currently the Price Waterhouse Teaching Excellence Professor of accounting. He teaches undergraduate courses in cost and management accounting and graduate courses in management control systems, corporate tax, and tax strategies. He has received numerous teaching awards including the outstanding teacher of the Texas A&M College of Business from the College of Business Honors Society (twice), and Delta Iota Chapter's Beta Alpha Psi teaching excellence award in accounting (twice). Professor Kinney also received the Southwest Chapter of the Academy of International Business' Distinguished Paper Award for international research. Professor Kinney has authored and co-authored numerous articles in accounting, taxation, and finance. Professor Kinney is married with four children, and he spends his free time sailing the Gulf of Mexico.

BRIEF TABLE OF CONTENTS

TABLE OF CONTENTS

TABLE OF CONTENTS

TABLE OF CONTENTS

TABLE OF CONTENTS

TABLE OF CONTENTS

TABLE OF CONTENTS

TABLE OF CONTENTS

TABLE OF CONTENTS

TABLE OF CONTENTS

Accounting is often referred to as the *language of business.* However, managers must be able to communicate their information needs to accountants and understand the resulting answers. This text provides a context for dialogue among all the business disciplines and emphasizes the practical rather than the theoretical. Thus, it stresses the techniques and procedures of greatest managerial importance. The perspective taken by *Managerial Accounting* is that managers and accountants must have a common understanding of the organizational role of accounting information. They need to understand what techniques are available to provide that information, what details are needed to perform the techniques, and the benefits and limitations of the information provided by the various techniques in response to managers' needs. This integrated approach to information flow will create an atmosphere of trust, sharing, and cooperation.

We believe that it is critical for readers to understand that accounting is a cross-functional discipline that provides information useful to all management areas. It is also essential that readers recognize that managerial accounting information is necessary in all types of organizations (manufacturing, service, and not-for-profit), regardless of their size. Substantial effort has been taken to illustrate all of these enterprise types, in both domestic and international operations. Rapid changes in the global business environment, such as the introduction of profit-making operations into those countries that were previously communist, will create new demands for management information, and this information will be prepared in the international language of business: accounting.

AUDIENCE

This text is primarily directed toward students who have a basic familiarity with the informational content of financial statements.

Learning Objectives

Each chapter provides an orderly framework for the material to be covered. Marginal annotations indicate the text coverage of the learning objectives.

PEDAGOGY

This text is very student-oriented. The following text features have been designed to promote an ease of learning and provide a high interest level.

On Site Openers

Each chapter begins with a vignette about a relevant aspect of a real-world organization. These openers show students how the chapter topics affect an operating business on a daily basis. The On Sites feature organizations such as Ganong Bros. Ltd., Dell Computer, Petro-Canada, Bright Pearl Seafood Restaurant Inc., Air Canada, WestJet, Riscky's Barbeque, Canadian National Railway, National Bank, and more.

Key Terms

When a new term is introduced within a chapter, it is listed in boldface type, indicated in a margin annotation, and defined at that point. All key terms in each chapter are presented at the end of the chapter with page references for the definition. Additionally, a complete end-of-text glossary is provided.

News Notes

News Notes in the chapters provide selections from the popular business press and reflect the contemporary world of business activity. Two themes (general business and international) are used to illustrate how managerial accounting concepts affect business. There are more than 60 references to organizations such as the Bank of Montreal, Celestica, Dell Computer, Royal & SunAlliance, Canadian Tire, Levi Strauss & Co., PeopleSoft, and Wal-Mart.

Internet Links

Web site addresses for many real-world companies are listed on the book's Web site: **www.raiborn.nelson.com**

Site Analysis

This chapter section continues the discussion of the On Site company's reaction to, or resolution of, the opening topic.

Chapter Summary

A summary of the most important concepts in each chapter is provided to promote student retention.

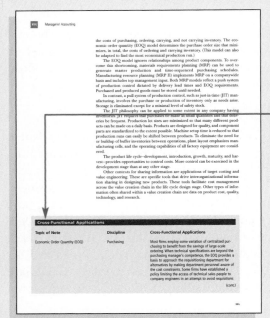

Cross-Functional Applications

These strategies follow the Chapter Summary and indicate how some tools presented in the chapter are applicable to business disciplines such as economics, finance, human resources, management, and marketing, as well as to nonbusiness disciplines such as engineering, law, operations research, and public administration. For example, the applications in the chapter on capital budgeting (10) indicate that capital budgets assist economists in planning an optimum production function, help financial managers analyze and predict profitability and cash flows, and aid lawyers in lease agreement negotiations.

Solution Strategies

In this section, students are provided with all relevant formulas and major computational formats from the chapter. These strategies may be used as guides to work end-of-chapter materials or to refresh one's memory.

Demonstration Problem

At the end of appropriate chapters, a demonstration problem and solution are given so that students can check their understanding of chapter computations before doing end-of-chapter assignments.

End-of-Chapter Materials

Each chapter contains a variety of end-of-chapter materials at different levels of difficulty. Materials include self-test questions (with answers), questions, exercises, problems, cases, ethics and quality discussions, communications activities, projects and Using the Internet questions. Students are encouraged to do the self-test questions on their own to signal their comprehension of the chapter content. If their test scores are low, students may want to reread the chapter before proceeding. Some of the end-of-chapter materials are specifically designed to provide the opportunity for students to use their writing skills and/or to emphasize the needs of different individuals in an organization (for instance, the marketing manager, finance officer, production supervisor, or human resource manager). Many of the ethics and quality discussions are taken from the popular business press and relate to actual business situations. Some of the discussion questions provide a reference to an article that could help in answering the question or provide greater information about a situation. Students are encouraged to use the Internet to gather information.

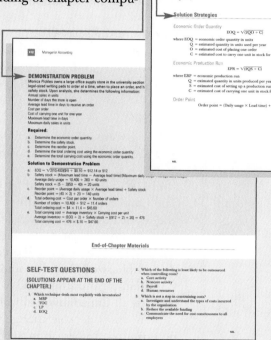

The ethics and quality items provide the dual benefit of indicating that choices are important to an organization's current and future existence as well as providing an additional avenue for written expression and logical thought.

Numerical end-of-chapter materials that are computer-solvable are indicated with a **spreadsheet icon**.

Supplementary Learning Objectives

In addition to the learning objectives in the chapter, additional learning objectives are provided to correspond to the additional parts of Chapters 1, 7, 11, and 13 that appear on the book's Web site:
- Web Chapter 1: The Strategic Context
- Web Chapter 7: Controlling Costs

- Web Chapter 11: Responsibility Accounting and Transfer Pricing in Decentralized Operations
- Web Chapter 13: Measuring and Rewarding Performance

If there are additional learning objectives for the chapter, they are indicated at the end of the chapter, before "End-of-Chapter Materials." For example, the first chapter has two additional learning objectives: How did management accounting develop? How does information technology affect management accounting? For the full text, see **www.raiborn.nelson.com**

End-of-Text Appendices

Appendix A is a brief overview of the various ethical theories to help students analyze ethics situations and answer the chapter ethics discussion questions. Appendix B provides present and future value tables of $1 and an ordinary annuity of $1.

Glossary

The end-of-text glossary includes all of the key terms in the text and their definitions. Key term definitions are shown in the margin where the terms appear in the text.

MAJOR CHANGES IN THE FIRST CANADIAN EDITION

The Canadian authors gathered comments from Canadian adopters and reviewers and made numerous changes to increase the U.S. text's teachability, student orientation, and relevance to the Canadian marketplace. The basic management accounting techniques and practices were kept within a sharpened strategic context that emphasized Canadian and global organizations. The underlying belief was that Canadian organizations had to compete globally, or at least that global competition affected all Canadian organizations.

The most notable change was to set the textbook within the context of a computerized or information technology-intensive organization. This change recognizes that management accounting is only a part of an organization's numerous computerized information systems. In other words, management accounting in terms of budgeting and control is just one of numerous systems maintained and used by medium-sized and larger firms. The textbook discusses enterprise resource planning (ERP) systems, which are a means of integrating all systems through a common relational database. From a practical point of view, students should understand how management accounting is part of an ERP system.

The Canadian authors recognize that the introduction of information technology and ERP systems is a major change from past management accounting textbooks, but one for which the Canadian adopters and reviewers have been supportive. It is critical for readers to undertand that accounting is a cross-functional discipline that provides information useful to all management areas.

ORGANIZATION

- Chapter 1 sets the stage for future chapters by first carefully and thoroughly defining management accounting and then explaining how it is a part of control. This chapter also explains strategy and how management accounting assists with implementing strategy. The importance of the value creation chain in implementing strategy is discussed, along with how management accounting relates to both the value creation chain and strategy. The chapter then addresses the enterprise resource planning (ERP) systems environment in which businesses operate. ERP is followed up in other chapters. In summary, Chapter 1 is designed to help students understand the numerous forces that must be considered by businesspeople today and how those forces affect management accounting and decision making.

- Chapter 2 provides an introduction to basic cost terminology and cost flows. This chapter allows students to understand the varying but basic informational needs of managers and how that information can be captured, analyzed, and used in an organization with a well-designed cost management system.

- Chapter 3 discusses cost behaviour and cost–volume–profit analysis. This chapter discusses the basic and traditional management accounting techniques and practices. It includes a discussion of variable and absorption costing methodology.

- Chapter 4 provides a basic discussion of two important traditional costing systems: job order costing and process costing.

- Chapter 5 discusses the basic management accounting technique of standard costs. This topic is discussed for both a service and a manufacturing operation.

- Chapter 6 discusses the contemporary techniques of activity-based costing and activity-based management.

- Chapter 7 is a new chapter that focuses on managing costs in a changing workplace. This chapter includes contemporary and relevant techniques for controlling costs.

- Chapter 8 discusses relevant revenues and costs. In decision making, it is important to understand which costs are relevant and which are irrelevant.

- Chapter 9 discusses traditional budgeting and the behavioural consequences that may result from the use of various budgeting techniques. The chapter also examines the role of continuous budgeting and discusses the recommendations of the European organization, the Beyond Budgeting Round Table group.

- Chapter 10 looks at capital investment and return measurements. The Canadian method of capital budgeting and its tax implications are discussed using an example in the chapter appendix.

- Chapter 11 covers management accounting in decentralized organizations. It includes a discussion of transfer pricing and how it can be used to set prices.

- Chapter 12 is an entirely new chapter. It discusses both cost management systems and performance measurement systems, and comments on the advantages of integrating these two systems with an ERP system. It brings management accounting into circa 2004.

- Chapter 13 covers the processes of measuring and rewarding performance.

PEDAGOGY

- The theme of each chapter-opening vignette is often carried through the chapter using a fictitious company within a related industry. Because of the need to maintain confidentiality of proprietary information, the On Site company's actual data are not used, but example data are reflective of reality.

- The end-of-chapter materials include discussion questions on both ethics and quality. Many of these questions address actual business situations. The quality discussion questions focus on the impact of introducing (or choosing not to introduce) quality techniques on company costs, employee and customer behaviour, and production/service processes.
- Many of the end-of-chapter items ask the student to act as if he or she had a particular position at the firm. This approach promotes analysis and discussion from alternative perspectives. There are typically at least two exercises for each key concept in the chapter.
- Journal entries are, in many places, presented separately in chapter appendices. This placement allows instructors to include or exclude this accounting process information without interrupting the flow of materials in each of the chapters.

INSTRUCTOR SUPPORT MATERIALS

The text is accompanied by the following full range of support materials for the instructor:

Instructor's Solutions Manual

This volume, prepared by the authors, has been independently reviewed and checked for accuracy. It contains complete solutions to each question, exercise, problem, and case in the text, as well as suggested answers for the ethics and quality discussions and the communications activities.

Solution Transparency Acetates

Acetates are provided from the solutions manual for all numerical end-of-chapter materials.

Test Bank

The test bank, which has been prepared by Jean Pai, University of Manitoba, contains more than one thousand multiple-choice, short exercise, and short discussion questions with related solutions.

Computerized Test Bank

A computerized version of the test bank includes editing and word-processing features that allow test customization through the addition, deletion, and scrambling of test selections.

Instructor's Manual

This manual, developed by Shelley Lukasewich, contains sample syllabi, a listing of chapter learning objectives and terminology, chapter lecture outlines, and some exam multiple-choice questions for use as additional test material or for quizzes.

Microsoft® PowerPoint® Teaching Transparency Slides

Microsoft® PowerPoint® files, prepared by Professor Connie Reed, University of Toronto, provide entertaining and informative graphics and text for full-colour electronic presentations.

Instructor's CD-ROM

The Instructor's CD-ROM contains the Instructor's Solutions Manual, the Test Bank, the Computerized Test Bank, the Instructor's Manual, and the Microsoft® Teaching Transparency Slides.

Web Resources

This text's supporting Web site at **www.raiborn.nelson.com** provides downloadable versions of key instructor supplements, as well as Web Links, Web Cases, Check Figures, Internet Exercises, Test Yourself Questions, Supplementary Learning Objectives, Microsoft® Excel® spreadsheets, and more.

STUDENT SUPPORT MATERIALS

Students are also provided with a comprehensive support package to enhance their learning experience.

Study Guide

The student study guide, prepared by Wendy L. Schultz, University of Manitoba, contains chapter learning objectives, chapter overviews, detailed chapter notes, and self-test questions.

Spreadsheet Applications for Managerial Accounting

Spreadsheet applications are available on **www.raiborn.nelson.com** and allow students to use Microsoft® Excel® spreadsheets to solve the many in-text problems (which have been indicated with a spreadsheet icon).

Student Solutions Manual

The Student Solutions Manual contains solutions to the odd-numbered Exercises and Problems in the text.

Practice Sets

Four practice sets are available for the text:

- Pennsylvania Containers: An Activity-Based Costing Case illustrates activity-based costing using a manufacturing company that produces garbage dumpsters and customized trash receptacles (ISBN 0-538-88522-X).
- California Car Company: An Active Learning Costing Case provides a hands-on way for students to learn about the manufacturing process and the advantages of activity-based costing (ISBN 0-324-18450-6). An accompanying instructor's manual is available by contacting your sales representative.
- Peachtree® Accounting Software and Practice Set includes payroll transactions for a merchandising business operated as a proprietorship. It includes business documents, and it can be solved manually or with Peachtree® Software (ISBN 0-324-14980-8).
- SunBlaze Inc. depicts a manufacturing business operated as a corporation that uses a job order cost system (ISBN 0-324-00279-3).

ACKNOWLEDGMENTS

We would like to thank the many people who have helped us during the revision of this text. The constructive comments and suggestions made by the following reviewers were instrumental in developing, rewriting, and improving the quality and readability of this book.

Philip Beaulieu	University of Calgary
Hilary Becker	Carleton University
Carole Bowman	Sheridan College
Ted Carney	Humber College
Anthony Moung Yin Chan	Ryerson University
Suzanne Coombs	Kwantlen University College
Angela Downey	University of Lethbridge
D.H. Drury	McGill University
Fathi Elloumi	Athabasca University
Michael Favere-Marchesi	Simon Fraser University
Ilene Gilborn	Mount Royal College
Rob Harvey	Algonquin College
Jeffrey Kantor	University of Windsor
Valerie Kinnear	Mount Royal College
Glen Kobussen	University of Saskatchewan
Michael Maingot	University of Ottawa
R.C. Nichols	British Columbia Institute of Technology
Mary Oxner	St. Francis Xavier University
Paul Roy	York University
Wendy Schultz	University of Manitoba
Shu-Lun Wong	Memorial University

Many others have contributed directly or indirectly to this project: Surenda P. Agrawal, University of Memphis; Uday Chandra, University of Oklahoma; Robert C. Elmore, Tennessee Technological University; Micah Frankel, California State University–Hayward; Ronald W. Halsac, Community College of Allegheny County–Pittsburgh; George A. Heyman, Oakton Community College; Jerry Joseph, Indiana University of Pennsylvania; Celina L. Jozsi, University of South Florida; Shelley Lukasewich; Noel McKeon, Florida Community College; Paul H. Mihalek, University of Hartford; Liz Mulig, University of Texas–Tyler; Sandra Pelfrey, Oakland University; Paulette A. Ratliff, University of Oklahoma; Barbara Reider, University of Alaska–Anchorage; Jack M. Ruhl, Western Michigan University; Marilyn Sagrillo, University of Wisconsin–Green Bay; Catherine Seguin, University of Toronto; Ann E. Selk, University of Wisconsin–Green Bay; P. K. Sen, SUNY–Buffalo; Thomas J. Stoffel, University of St. Thomas; Glenys Sylvestre, University of Regina; Gerald A. Thalmann, North Central College; Kiran Verma, University of Massachusetts–Boston.

Special mention must be given to Barbara Reider at the University of Alaska–Anchorage, Rochelle Gordon, Lawrence Chung, Ambrus Kecskés, Christina Kim, Amy Nimjeh, and Joel Ridenour, as well as to the many other individuals who provided information related to the On Sites and Site Analyses. Sincere appreciation and heartfelt thanks go to Zippora Goldberg for her kindness, understanding, and generous support.

Special thanks must also be made to the Institute of Management Accountants and the Certified General Accountants Association of Canada. These organizations have been extremely generous in granting their permission to use numerous problems and excerpts from their publications. Permission has been received from the Institute of Certified Management Accountants to use questions and/or unofficial answers from past CMA examinations. We also want to acknowledge the many publishers who granted permission for use of their materials as On Site/Site Analysis/News Note excerpts.

The authors would like to thank Gilda Serrao for her assistance in typing portions of the manuscript, Vicky Faclaris for editing assistance, and Karen Wong for research assistance.

The authors would like to thank everyone at Nelson who has toiled long hours to help both of us with this project. We would especially like to thank our families and friends, who have encouraged and supported us in this endeavour.

Brenda Mallouk
Gary Spraakman

Chapter 1

LEARNING OBJECTIVES

After reading this chapter, you should be able to answer the following questions:

1 **What**
is the definition of management accounting?

2 **How**
does management accounting form part of the management control system?

3 **What**
is strategy and what is the role of management accounting in strategy?

4 **How**
does management accounting facilitate the accomplishment of strategy through the value creation chain?

5 **What**
is new with management accounting?

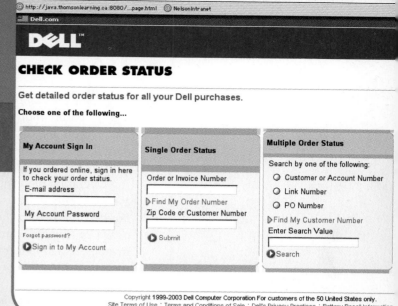

www.dell.com

Dell Computer Corporation

Management accounting serves management in a global environment, as exemplified by **DELL COMPUTER**.

Dell has been very successful in optimizing its value creation chain,[1] which is its set of processes and activities that convert inputs into PCs and other products and services at the lowest possible cost. A large part of this success has resulted from Dell's strategic decisions to contract out or outsource various activities and processes where it is not able to meet world-class standards itself. Dell outsources almost everything—from sales to manufacturing to research and development. However, Dell invested significantly in Web site procedures and systems for dealing with suppliers, which were linked to its customers using the Internet and its organizational know-how and systems. Dell's network of linked suppliers makes it possible for the company to tailor PC products efficiently to fit the needs of individual buyers, whether for home use or for a global company.

Dell was quick to benefit from Web-based sales and customer service operations. No traditional distribution network stands between it and its customers. Customers are served by a telephone or an on-line order taker who actually works for a division of a telephone company. More frequently, the orders are placed by the customer through Dell's Web page. Once placed by telephone or Internet, the order is sent to a coordinator—actually an employee who works for another company—who in turn passes the order to the relevant Dell assembly plant from among five around the world. At the same time, the coordinator directs the suppliers to ship the parts to the selected plant. The coordinator also directs the parcel courier to the respective plant at the predetermined time for pickup and then delivery of the finished product to the customer. In addition, Dell allows customers to track the status of their orders with the Internet.

Dell depends on its ability to optimize its procedures and systems and its relationships with employees, suppliers, investors, and customers. The clarity of this approach for implementing its strategy is reflected in Dell's above-average financial performance.

*F*or the company to continue to prosper as a corporate giant, Dell Computer Corporation's managers increasingly need to understand the company's markets and customer desires. Such knowledge is more difficult for Dell to obtain now than in the past since, like many other businesses, the company now operates globally and thus deals with many different customers and competitors.

Operating globally creates two primary considerations for an organization. First, the managers must understand the factors that influence the various international business markets so that the locations in which the company has the strengths and desire to compete can be identified. Second, a company must devise a business strategy, or a long-term, dynamic plan that fulfills organizational goals and objectives through satisfaction of customer needs or wants within the company's acknowledged operating markets.

This first chapter introduces management accounting for use in both traditional and the new global organizations, and shows how, as an organizational control, management accounting assists with the implementation of an organization's strategy. The chapter links strategy creation and implementation to control and management accounting. To help readers fully understand how management accounting assists with implementing strategy, the value creation chain is used to explain the organization as a series of processes and activities that create value for customers. The main point is that the value creation chain underlies both strategy and management accounting. Also, the history of management accounting and its partner, information technology, are discussed on the Web page for Chapter 1 to provide a more insightful understanding of management accounting in global organizations such as Dell.

In other words, this chapter defines and explains management accounting and the organizational context within which it functions. It deals with how management accounting fits with management per se, strategy, controls, activities, and information technology.

The other chapters will address the techniques and systems of management accounting, which will be more understandable once the context is already understood. There are two overriding themes. First, management accounting assists managers with developing and implementing strategy. Second, management accounting is increasingly computerized as a component of enterprise resource planning systems. Chapter 2 introduces and defines basic terminology for management accounting. Chapter 3 describes some very basic management accounting analytical techniques, cost–volume–profit analysis and variable costs. Chapter 4 explains two traditional costing systems, job costing and process costing. Standard costs—another necessary concept for management accounting analysis—are discussed in Chapter 5. Activity-based management and activity-based costing are the main topics for Chapter 6. Within the framework of managing costs, the innovative Chapter 7 provides a number of contemporary techniques. Chapter 8 provides a means of assessing the relevance of various costs for making different decisions. Budgeting is the main topic for Chapter 9, while capital budgeting, and responsibility accounting and transfer pricing are the main topics for Chapters 10 and 11, respectively. Chapter 12 is groundbreaking in providing new material on both cost management and performance measurement systems. Chapter 13 concludes the book by discussing approaches for measuring and rewarding performance.

MANAGEMENT ACCOUNTING DEFINED

Before proceeding, management accounting needs to be defined. Other important terms will be defined in this and the other chapters. **Management accounting** is defined as the gathering and application of information used to plan, make decisions, evaluate performance, and control an organization. This definition makes clear that management accounting deals with the use of information, which may be financial or nonfinancial (i.e., operational). The definition also makes clear that the information is for managers to use for their work in terms of planning, decision making, performance evaluation, and in general the control of the activities that occur in an organization.

Management accounting has two-way interactions with other organizational units. The management accounting unit gathers information from other units about their activities. The management accounting unit also provides information to other units to allow them to manage their activities, particularly for coordination among units. For example, the management accounting unit would gather sales information from sales units and then provide that information to the production unit, and vice versa.

Management accounting gathers two time-based types of information: "expected" and "what happened." "Expected" information includes what might or should be. For example, standards and budgets specify information in terms of what should exist in the future. "What happened" information reports what has already taken place, as with financial accounting statements reporting events that have already occurred. More will be said about each of these types of information in this and other chapters of the book.

Management accounting can be understood more precisely when it is compared to financial accounting.

Financial Accounting

Financial accounting focuses on external users and is generally required for obtaining loans, preparing tax returns, and reporting to the investment community on how well or poorly the business is performing. The information used in financial accounting must comply with generally accepted accounting principles (GAAP). Financial accounting information is usually quite aggregated and relates to the entire organization. In some cases, a regulatory agency (such as a provincial securities commission) or an industry commission (such as in banking or insurance) may prescribe specific financial accounting practices.

Management Accounting

In contrast to financial accounting, management accounting can be applied in all types of organizations to provide information for internal users. Exhibit 1-1 details the differences between financial and management accounting.

Managers are often concerned with individual parts or segments of the business rather than with the organization as a whole. Therefore, management accounting information often focuses on particular segmental aspects of an entity rather than the big picture of financial accounting. Management accounting is flexible because it is not regulated by any organization or regulatory body. Often, management accountants provide forecasted, qualitative, and nonmonetary information. For instance, a manager debating whether to sell a piece of land now or in three years is not likely to use the land's historical cost to make the decision. Instead, he or she

LEARNING OBJECTIVE 1

What is the definition of management accounting?

management accounting
the gathering and application of information used to plan, make decisions, evaluate performance, and control an organization

financial accounting
generation of accounting information for external reporting

[Handwritten margin notes: management accounting deals with segments as opposed to the whole organization which financial accounting focuses on. Management accounting is flexible and does not have to conform to GAAP or any other regulatory body.]

EXHIBIT 1-1

Financial and Management
Accounting Differences

	Financial	**Management**
Primary users	External	Internal
Primary organizational focus	Whole (aggregated)	Parts (segmented)
Information characteristics	Must be:	May be:
	Historical	Forecasted
	Quantitative	Quantitative or qualitative
	Monetary	Monetary or nonmonetary
	Accurate	Timely and, at a minimum, a reasonable estimate
Overriding criteria	Generally accepted accounting principles	Situational relevance (usefulness)
	Consistency	Benefits in excess of costs
	Verifiability/Objectivity	Flexibility
Recordkeeping	Formal	Combination of formal and informal

will need estimates about expected changes in land prices for the next three years as well as information about expected events, such as the possibility that a shopping centre will be built on property adjoining the land.

A primary criterion for internal information is that it serves management's needs. A related criterion is the cost/benefit consideration that information should be developed and provided only if the cost of producing it is less than the benefit gained from using the information.

Cost Accounting

cost accounting
tools and methods applied to determine the cost of making products or performing services

Cost accounting bridges the financial accounting and management accounting functions as shown in Exhibit 1-2. As part of financial accounting, cost accounting provides product cost measurements for inventories and cost of goods sold on the financial statements. As part of management accounting, cost accounting provides some of the quantitative, cost-based information managers need to assess product profitability, prepare budgets, and make investment decisions. Cost accounting measurements often depend on classification of costs as product or period costs. These topics will be elaborated upon in a later chapter.

For students interested in pursuing management accounting as a profession, there are three Canadian accounting designations: CA, CGA, and CMA. Only the CMA specializes in management accounting. The CGA allows for a specialty in management accounting. The CA has no focus on management accounting. All three designations require the prospective candidate to have a university degree and to complete postgraduate courses in order to qualify.

EXHIBIT 1-2

Financial, Management, and
Cost Accounting Overlap

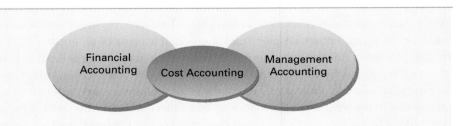

MANAGEMENT ACCOUNTING: A COMPONENT OF MANAGEMENT CONTROL

In the context of an entire organization, management accounting is one of many **controls** that ensure, with varying degrees of success, that employees (and managers) do what is required. The control problem is that employees do not always do what the organization requires (i.e., "individuals are sometimes unable or unwilling to act in the organization's best interest, and a set of controls must be implemented to guard against undesirable behaviour and to encourage desirable actions"[2]). There are two reasons why employees and even managers might not do what would be deemed appropriate by the organization. First, employees may not always understand what is expected or how best to perform jobs, as they may lack the necessary ability, training, or information. Controls are needed to compensate for personal limitations. Second, employees may lack goal congruence with the organization. In other words, the organization may want the employees to undertake certain activities, but the employees may prefer to undertake a different set of activities. For example, a retail organization may want sales personnel to be friendly and polite to all customers; this may be difficult for poorly trained employees who are paid minimum wage rates. Controls are needed to ensure that only appropriate activities are being performed.

There are three approaches to control or influence the behaviour of employees: specify appropriate activities, specify appropriate results, and recruit or develop appropriate personnel. These controls relate to management accounting information in numerous ways.

Specific action controls attempt to ensure that employees perform certain **activities** and/or do not perform others. Undesirable activities can be precluded with behavioural constraints such as locks, separate rooms, fences, and the separation of duties. The physical controls prevent entry to areas, while the separation of duties has a similar effect over activities. Action control specifies the appropriate activities to be undertaken, via work rules, policies and procedures, and codes of conduct. Activities are, in effect, preprogrammed, and the managerial accounting information reporting on the activities would be nonfinancial.

The results approach to control is less specific. Instead of specifying activities through action controls, a result control specifies what must be accomplished, leaving the selection of activities to the employees and managers. This type of control is particularly reasonable when the overseeing manager does not know the most appropriate activities under unseen circumstances (such as a salesperson being unobservable). Results accountability can be accomplished through setting expectations for performance (e.g., for sales, costs, and profits) with standards, budgets, and management by objectives, which will be discussed in subsequent chapters. Briefly, standards include expectations about what should be produced in terms of quantity and/or quality. An example of a quantitative measure would be the number of purchase orders to be processed by a clerk; the qualitative measure would be the number of errors per, say, 1,000 purchase orders processed, with lower numbers of errors indicating higher quality. Budgets are commitments that are equated to dollars of sales, costs, profits, or profitability. Management accounting information reporting on the results could be financial or nonfinancial.

The third approach to control is personnel. The control is placed on getting employees to do what the organization desires without using action or result controls. To control via personnel, the capabilities of employees can be upgraded

control
exertion of managerial influence on operations so that they will conform to plans

activities
repetitive actions, movements, or work sequences performed to fulfill a business function

[handwritten margin note:] 3 approaches to control
→ specify appropriate activities
→ specify appropriate results
→ recruit and develop appropriate personnel

through selective hiring of only those who are likely to do what the organization desires. Relatedly, the employees and managers are more likely to do what the organization desires if communication is effective. This can be ensured by clarification of what is desired and by detailed coordination of employees and managers. Finally, personnel control can be accomplished by creating an organizational culture that compels or forces employees to do what is organizationally correct. Personnel control does not require management accounting information.

Management accounting is a control. It is used to specify and monitor activities and results. Nevertheless, there are other controls that need to be carefully considered when developing management accounting practices. These other controls include financial accounting, management information systems, employee and manager performance evaluation systems, and **organizational culture**. For example, an organization with a strong culture of performance will not be as dependent on management accounting for ensuring activity performance as will an organization whose culture considers performance to be onerous.

organizational culture
the set of basic assumptions about the organization, its goals, and its business practices; describes an organization's norms in internal and external, as well as formal and informal, transactions

LEARNING OBJECTIVE   **3**

What is strategy and what is the role of management accounting in strategy?

strategy
a long-term dynamic plan that fulfills organizational goals and objectives through satisfaction of customer needs or wants within the company's acknowledged operating markets

MANAGEMENT ACCOUNTING: IMPLEMENTING STRATEGY

To understand how management accounting assists an organization in effectively implementing its strategy, we must first understand **strategy**. What follows is a brief primer on strategy, particularly on the basic terms and components.

An organization should begin its strategy formulation with a mission statement. The mission statement should (1) clearly state what the organization wants to accomplish and (2) express how that organization uniquely meets its targeted customers' needs with its products and services. This statement may change over time. Molson is an example of a Canadian organization that has retained its beer focus for more than 200 years, although it has had varying degrees of success through investments in other businesses from time to time. Seagram (originally established in Canada) has had a changing mission. Seagram had been in the "spirits and wine" business, but refocused itself when it acquired Universal Studios (film and music) and entered the "entertainment" business. Then Seagram merged with the French company Vivendi, to form Vivendi Universal.[3] Vivendi started as a water-treatment company, but expanded into the media business. The merger of Vivendi and Seagram transformed the merged organization into a global media giant, Vivendi Universal, which was expected to bring together media and the Internet. That strategic focus required Seagram's original profitable spirits and wine business to be divested from Vivendi Universal. Unfortunately, the strategic vision (or dream) of convergence did not materialize. Vivendi had to sell many of its businesses, including its publishing unit. At the time of writing, Vivendi Universal consisted of the following business units: music, games, film, pay-TV, telecoms, and the Internet.[4]

Strategy links an organization's mission to its actual activities. In other words, activities implement strategy. Strategy can also be defined as follows:

> Strategy is the art of creating value. It provides the intellectual frameworks, conceptual models, and governing ideas that allow an organization's managers to identify opportunities for bringing value to customers and for delivering value at a profit. In this respect, strategy is the way a company defines its business and links together with the only two resources that really matter in today's economy: knowledge and relationships or an organization's competencies and its customers.[5]

An organization's strategy tries to match its internal skills and resources to the opportunities found in the external environment.[6] Although small organizations may have a single strategy, larger organizations often have an overall entity strategy as well as individual strategies for each business unit (such as a division). The business units' strategies should flow from the overall strategy to ensure that effective and efficient resource allocations are made, an overriding corporate culture is developed, and organizational direction is enhanced. Senior management needs to question the appropriateness of a strategy.[7] Profitability by product line should be compared to that of major competitors. This comparability should extend to product line sales, prices, and customers. It should include determination of the product line source of the organization's profits.

Management accounting serves managers in designing, implementing, and evaluating the organization's strategy by providing information about expectations of what a strategy will accomplish and cost, and the strategy's actual past performance.

Strategy should dominate the activities within an organization. All activities should support the strategy. Exhibit 1-3 provides an example of how one company has restructured its purchasing function around its strategy.

Organizational Structure

Organizational structure is designed to implement the organization's strategy. The structure must be appropriate for doing the job of implementing strategy, or in other words, structure follows strategy.[8] An organization should be understood as being composed of people, resources, and commitments that are acquired and

organizational structure
the way in which authority and responsibility for making decisions is distributed in an organization

---

EXHIBIT 1-3
Strategic Purchasing

With the exception of labour, most corporate expenditures, including long-term capital investments, flow through the purchasing department. Large contracts most certainly have a significant purchasing input. Capital projects may not originate within purchasing, but they certainly make their way there. With all that flowing through the purchasing department, it is no wonder that opportunities exist for cost savings.

Strategic sourcing involves a fundamental re-examination of corporate purchasing behaviour. It consists of a total analysis of current purchasing activities and the systematic application of a select number of business drivers to the input stream, ranging from rate negotiations to long-term **strategic alliances**. It eliminates the "three bids and a buy" mentality and entrenches a mentality that requires a true understanding of the needs of internal customers and of the dynamics of the marketplace. Fundamentally, it requires a deeper understanding and stricter adherence to the processes that drive the corporation.

The results of the strategic sourcing initiative to date have exceeded expectations. The savings from 1998 to 2002 were as follows.

strategic alliance
an agreement involving two or more firms with complementary core competencies to jointly contribute to the value creation chain

	Annual Recurring Savings	Annual One-Time Savings	Total Annual Savings
1998	10.4	7.2	17.6
1999	15.2	5.4	20.6
2000	30.2	3.7	33.9
2001	29.7	38.5	68.2
2002 (target)	22.7	0	22.7

Source: Reprinted from an article appearing in the February 2003 issue of *CMA Management* magazine by Robert Lepine and Ken Rawson, with permission of Certified Management Accountants of Canada.

goal
a desired result or condition that is expressed in qualitative terms

objective
a quantitatively expressed result that can be achieved during a preestablished period or by a specified date; should logically measure progress in achieving goals

authority
the right (usually by virtue of position or rank) to use resources to accomplish a task or achieve an objective; can be delegated or assigned to others

responsibility
the obligation to accomplish a task or achieve an objective; cannot be delegated to others

centralization
an organizational structure in which top management makes most decisions and controls most activities of the organizational units from the organization's central headquarters

decentralization
the downward delegation by top management of authority and decision making to the individuals who are closest to internal processes and customers

empowerment
all practices that are designed to give workers the training, authority, and responsibility they need to manage their own jobs and make decisions about their work

arranged to achieve results specified by the strategy via goals and objectives. **Goals** are desired results expressed in qualitative terms. For example, in profit-oriented organizations, one typical goal is to maximize shareholder wealth. Goals are also likely to be formulated for other major stakeholders such as customers, employees, and suppliers. In contrast, **objectives** are quantitatively expressed results that can be achieved during a preestablished period or by a specified date. Objectives should logically measure progress in achieving goals. For example, Coca-Cola had a goal of being the soft-drink sponsor of a recent Summer Olympic Games and reportedly spent $40 million for that right. The objective following from that goal was to emphasize the drink's "universal appeal" and thus, the company had daily themes for each of the 17 days. Coca-Cola developed 100 different commercials to fit the daily themes and paid approximately $62 million for television advertising time during the Games' telecast.[9]

Management accounting provides information for setting the goals and objectives. Subsequently, management accounting provides information on the organization's success with accomplishing those goals and objectives. Of course, there is more data precision with objectives than with goals.

The organizational structure reflects the way in which authority and responsibility for making decisions is distributed in an organization. The right—usually by virtue of position or rank—to use resources to accomplish an activity or to achieve an objective is called **authority**. The obligation to accomplish an activity or achieve an objective is called **responsibility**. The organizational structure normally evolves from its mission, goals, and managerial responsibilities.

Management accounting information is prepared in order to help managers carry out their responsibilities. At the same time, management accounting reports on how well these managers have fulfilled their responsibilities.

A continuum of feasible structures reflects the extent of authority and responsibility of managers and employees. At one end of the continuum is **centralization**, in which all authority for making decisions is retained by top management. Centralized firms often have difficulty diversifying operations because top management might lack the necessary and critical industry-specific knowledge. If higher-level management insists on maintaining all authority, then the people who deal directly with the issues (whether problems or opportunities), who have the most relevant information, and who can best foresee the consequences are not making the decisions.

At the other end of the continuum is **decentralization**, in which the authority for making decisions is distributed to various personnel, including lower-level managers and, possibly, line employees. In today's fast-changing and competitive operating environment, implementation of a decentralized organizational structure in a large firm is almost imperative and typically cost-beneficial. However, for decentralization to work effectively, there must be employee **empowerment**, which means that employees are given the authority and responsibility to make their own decisions about their work. A decision to decentralize is also a decision to use responsibility accounting, which will be discussed in Chapter 11.

Most organizations operate at some point on the continuum rather than at either end. Thus, a decision about where a new division will be located might be made by top management; when the new division is completed, the division manager might be empowered to make ongoing operating decisions. Long-term strategic decisions about the division might be made by the division manager in conjunction with top management. For both centralized and decentralized organi-

Line workers who oversee highly complex automated machinery generally have the greatest knowledge of how to solve problems or increase the productivity of their equipment. Empowerment allows those individuals to exercise that knowledge to the company's benefit.

zations, management accounting practices need to be designed to provide appropriate information to managers who make decisions.

Core Competencies

A **core competency** is any critical function or activity in which one organization has a higher proficiency than its competitors. Core competencies are the roots of competitiveness and competitive advantage. "Core competencies are different for every organization; they are, so to speak, part of an organization's personality."[10] Technological innovation, engineering, product development, and after-sale service are some examples of core competencies. For instance, the Japanese electronics industry is viewed as having a core competency in the miniaturization of electronics. Bell Canada Enterprises and Disney believe that they have core competencies in communications and entertainment, respectively.

core competency
any critical function or activity in which one organization has a higher proficiency than its competitors; the roots of competitiveness and competitive advantage

Generic Strategies

In determining its strategy or strategies to meet the needs of targeted customers, an organization may choose differentiation or cost leadership.[11] A company deciding to compress its competitive scope focuses on a specific market segment to the exclusion of others. Many companies producing or selling luxury goods (such as Rolex watches) adopt this strategy. The same approach has, however, been adopted by some nonluxury entities, such as Harvey's hamburger restaurants, which allow the customer to select from a range of toppings.

A company choosing a **differentiation** strategy distinguishes its product or service from that of competitors by adding enough value (including quality and/or features) that customers are willing to pay a higher price. Differentiation can be "based on the product itself, the delivery system by which it is sold, the marketing approach, or other factors."[12]

Competition may also be avoided by establishing a position of **cost leadership**, that is by becoming the low-cost producer/provider and, therefore, being able to charge low prices that emphasize cost efficiencies. In this strategy, competitors

differentiation
a competitive strategy in which an organization distinguishes its products or services from those of competitors by adding enough value (including quality and/or features) that customers are willing to pay a higher price

cost leadership
a competitive strategy in which an organization becomes the low-cost producer/provider and is thus able to charge low prices that emphasize cost efficiencies

cannot compete on price and must differentiate their products/services from the cost leader. Wal-Mart excels at cost leadership, which is only possible with extensive information systems and control over its multitude of suppliers who are located around the world.

A final factor affecting strategy is the environment in which the organization operates. An **environmental constraint** is any limitation on strategy caused by external cultural, fiscal (such as taxation structures), legal/regulatory, or political situations and by competitive market structures. Because environmental constraints cannot be directly controlled by an organization's management, these factors tend to have long-run rather than short-run effects. Managerial actions and organizational culture influence the firm and may work to affect the operating environment through numerous activities, including attempts to change laws.

The food industry provides many excellent examples of the influence of culture as one environmental constraint on organizational strategy. Many companies have recognized that culture may affect strategy because products and services that sell well in one locale may not be appropriate in another locale. For instance, Coca-Cola has not attempted to sell its fermented milk drink in Canada and, although sales of pigs' feet, oxtails, and pork ears may be popular staples in many Hispanic, Haitian, and Jamaican diets, these items are not available at most local Canadian grocery stores.

environmental constraint
any limitation on strategy caused by external cultural, fiscal (such as taxation structures), legal/regulatory, or political situations or by competitive market structures; tends to have long-run rather than short-run effects

Management Accounting Provides Information

Management accounting provides information important in designing, implementing, and evaluating strategies. In designing a strategy, management accounting provides information on prospective customers such as their numbers, locations, spending patterns, and profitability. These data provide the basis for detailed forecasts and plans upon which to make decisions about whether to pursue the strategy. Once the strategy is implemented, management accounting provides information for effectively accomplishing the strategy, and then for evaluating its success and its effectiveness among competitors.

Management accounting provides both financial and nonfinancial or operational data for designing, implementing, and assessing strategies. A particularly important focus of management accounting is on costs involved with strategies, including unit costs and total costs, as well as the costs for organizational units.

An article in *The Globe and Mail* provided a vivid example of the role performed by management accounting with strategy.[13] With the prospect of a recession and expected higher travel costs, many organizations are intent on reducing those costs as much as possible. With existing strategies, management accounting can identify travel costs and compare them over time and between organizations, providing management with reference points when making decisions on how to regulate travel and economize on travel costs. The use of travel in accomplishing the organization's strategy must also be considered. The most common techniques for travel cost control range from greater use of discount airlines to demanding that employees book their own trips electronically. Other techniques include establishing guidelines for all aspects of travel; requiring travellers to book in advance and stay over Saturday night to lower airline fares; booking airline flights through consolidators (firms that buy discounted air seats in bulk); and cutting administrative costs by equipping travellers with electronic tools for filing expense accounts and for making travel reservations (which are still vetted and finalized by the corporate travel agency).

MANAGEMENT ACCOUNTING'S CONTRIBUTION TO THE VALUE CREATION CHAIN

Strategic management involves organizational planning for deployment of resources to create value for customers and shareholders. The strategic management of resources is concerned with the following issues:[14]

- how to deploy resources to support strategies
- how resources are used in, or recovered from, change processes
- how customer value and shareholder value will serve as guides to the effective use of resources
- how resources are to be deployed and redeployed over time

These areas cannot be measured by financial accounting because they often relate to nonmonetary information and measurements. Thus, management accounting provides the necessary estimates to help managers address these issues and focus on strategic objectives.

The foundation of the strategic management of resources is the **value creation chain (VCC)**[15] or the set of processes and activities that convert inputs into products and services that have value to the organization's customers. The value creation chain includes both internal and supplier processes. Managers can use the value creation chain to determine which activities create customer value as reflected in product/service prices and thus, revenues earned. By reducing or eliminating activities that do not add value within the value creation chain, organizations can become more efficient and effective.

value creation chain
the set of processes and activities that convert inputs into products and services that have value to the organization's customers

For their contributions to the value creation chain, employees are compensated and suppliers earn revenues. Successful organizations will gain the cooperation of everyone in the value creation chain and communicate a perspective that today's competition is more between value creation chains than between individual businesses. Once this concept is accepted, members of the value creation chain become aware that information must be shared among all entities in the chain.

Exhibit 1-4 presents a simple model of the VCC. It reflects that organizations can either undertake the activities themselves or, like Dell Computer Corporation, outsource to suppliers.

The VCC in Exhibit 1-4 is premised on the belief that value is created for customers in goods and services by activities. Although organizations are accountable for many activities, Exhibit 1-4 divides those activities into five major categories that apply to an organization conducting all activities itself or largely outsourcing the required activities to create value. The exhibit also recognizes that one set of activities in creating value includes the interaction required from the customer in obtaining the good or service, for example, whether physically or via the Internet. The stages of the VCC are briefly defined.

- **Sourcing:** obtaining raw or crudely produced materials in order to add value at later stages. A dairy or producer of milk must obtain raw milk from farmers.
- **Enhancing:** making basic products from raw materials. The conversion of crude oil into gasoline and other petroleum products is an example of enhancing.
- **Aggregating:** putting together various enhanced products to produce a complex product. An automobile is an example of aggregating, as it is the production

---

Sourcing ⟶ Enhancing ⟶ Aggregating ⟶ Disseminating ⟵ Interacting

EXHIBIT 1-4

The Value Creation Chain

Source: Robert J. Fong and Gary Spraakman, *Fusion: The Creation of Innovation*, forthcoming.

result of assembling numerous parts or products. A Dell computer is another example, as the company assembles parts from suppliers into a custom computer for the customer order.

- **Disseminating:** distributing products or services to customers or consumers. Disseminating includes wholesale and retail activities.
- **Interacting:** the only stage conducted by the customer. It is the activities undertaken by the customer in obtaining the good or service being produced by the value creation chain. We drive to a movie theatre and wait in line to see a movie; or we rent a video or DVD to see a movie at home; or, soon, we will download a movie to see it at home.

The VCC can be demonstrated with an automotive assembly operation such as that of General Motors of Canada, which, according to the VCC, operates at the "aggregating" and "disseminating" stages. General Motors' aggregating would consist of assembling cars from parts and subassemblies acquired from suppliers such as Magna International who have "enhanced" or produced parts or subassemblies from raw materials or less processed parts that were obtained by "sourcing" from suppliers of more basic components. Once General Motors has assembled the cars, it must "disseminate" those cars through its dealer network, which interfaces directly with customers, the car buyers. The "interacting" stage comprises the activities that the customers undertake in acquiring a car.

In contrast to General Motors, Wal-Mart's strategy is focused on the disseminating stage. Explicitly, Wal-Mart has pursued a strategy of converging product lines such as men's clothing, drugs and toiletries, automotive, food, etc. It offers customers a wide range of products from its outlets at the lowest possible prices. Wal-Mart influences and exerts control over suppliers at the aggregating and enhancing stages, but it does not perform those activities.

Dell has perfected its VCC in its strategy of delivering PCs and servers. In 2001, Dell started selling network switches. Now it is applying that VCC to printers, electronic storage, and handheld computers.[16] Dell's VCC, or "Dellification," is simple: sell directly to customers to cut out costly intermediaries, buy components in huge volumes to get the lowest prices, force suppliers to locate within a few miles of Dell's facilities so parts can be delivered only hours before they are needed, and use information technology to reduce costs and improve customer service.

Regardless of their VCC stage, organizations require management accounting information in order to manage relationships required with their activities. Customer information is necessary to determine which products and services are desired and how many units of each must be produced, and to project demand levels for existing and future products and services. Information on the effectiveness of supplier relationships (e.g., on-time deliveries) is necessary for acquiring the parts, materials, and services needed in producing goods and services that create value for customers.

Managers require management information so they may plan, control, evaluate performance, and make VCC decisions. In planning, managers describe outcomes they hope to achieve in the future. Managers exert control by acting to bring operations into compliance with the plans. Performance is evaluated by measuring actual outcomes against plans, past performance levels, and other performance benchmarks. Managers make decisions in the process of executing plans and controlling operations.

It was noted that a value creation chain is the set of all activities that convert materials into products and services for the final consumer. In this regard, **vertical integration** is a measure of the extent to which the value creation chain resides

vertical integration
the extent to which the value creation chain resides within a single firm

within a single organization. Organizations that are highly vertically integrated have more in-house links to the value creation chain than links to other firms. Firms with low vertical integration depend on their suppliers or customers to contribute more links to the value creation chain. The very successful Dell Computer Corporation has low vertical integration, as it contracts out most activities. One of the most significant choices managers make for their organizations is the role to be played in the value creation chain in which they are located. Many of the headlines in the financial press today relate to value creation chain role decisions. For example, decisions involving strategic alliances, restructuring, outsourcing, and mergers are driven by value creation chain considerations. To remain competitive, firms must monitor not only their own costs and quality, but also the operations of suppliers, customers, and competitors.

Outsourcing

In the present business environment, **outsourcing** is an integral part of strategy. Virtually any process or activity in the value creation chain required to generate a product or service can be outsourced. For example, marketing and sales, accounting, engineering, manufacturing, customer service, and product distribution have all been outsourced. In the accounting domain, the payroll function is increasingly being outsourced, as is financial accounting and all aspects of information technology. By outsourcing processes and activities, organizations can concentrate

outsourcing
contracting with outside manufacturers or vendors for necessary goods or services rather than producing the goods or performing the services in-house

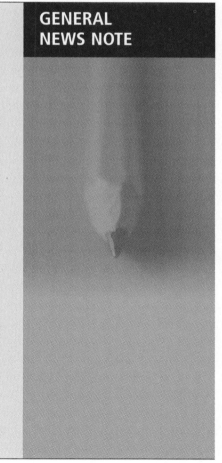

BMO Employs Supply Chain Management

GENERAL NEWS NOTE

Buying supplies just got easier at the BANK OF MONTREAL, as it rolls out a new online procurement system powered and hosted by Oracle. According to Karen Rubin, vice president of strategic sourcing at the Toronto-based institution, the bank is targeting all buying across the organization for efficiencies, vendor consolidation, better pricing and relationship management. "We expect the chief savings to come through process improvement and automation and we're beginning to unearth those as we slog through the enterprise business unit by business unit," said Steve Pare, team leader, e-procurement at BMO.

BMO, which buys more than $US1.2 billion in goods and services annually, had already consolidated its vendors and wanted to become more efficient in its purchasing by introducing an end-to-end technology solution that covered everything from catalogue, order, receipt and payment. "We wanted to work smarter and faster with existing suppliers," said Rubin. The bank needed an integrated system. It selected Oracle iProcurement, part of the Oracle Applications Suite. iProcurement standardizes purchasing processes and allows users to serve themselves and search catalogues to order items. The bank also implemented Oracle Accounts Payable, Oracle Fixed Assets and Oracle Internet Expense.

The new system will allow BMO to better understand its suppliers and where its money goes, especially when it comes to small-ticket items. That should, in turn, allow the bank to fine tune its purchasing processes across its 30 different business units and leverage more savings. For example, Rubin notes, the bank has 1,200 branches and they are always buying flowers for customers. "We've never been able to get at that dollar value to make it a worthwhile sourcing exercise. Now we'll have consolidated capabilities to get that information and maybe do a deal with [a supplier] that we couldn't have done before." Testing started with the 50-person network and systems groups, "We were able to ramp up all our processes," Rubin explained. Pare said the bank didn't want to "bite off too much at one time." Now it's ready to commence rollout across the organization and into its U.S. subsidiary, Harris Bank.

Source: Jim Middlemiss, "BMO Employs Supply Chain Management," *Bank Systems & Technology*, August 2001, pp. 2–3.

their resources on strategically important functions. The outsourcing decision should be made only after proper analysis. Managers should, with the assistance of management accounting, compare the cost of manufacturing a product component internally with the cost of purchasing it from outside suppliers (or from another division at a specific transfer price).

Relevant management accounting information for an insource/outsource decision includes both quantitative and qualitative factors, some of which are shown in Exhibit 1-5. Many of the quantitative factors, such as incremental production cost per unit and the purchase price quoted by the supplier, are known with a high degree of certainty. Other factors, such as the opportunity cost associated with production facilities, must be estimated. The qualitative factors should be evaluated by more than one employee so that personal biases do not cloud valid business judgment.

These additional considerations indicate that there are many potential long-run effects of what are often regarded as short-run decisions. Managers should take a long-range perspective for insource/outsource decisions. They need to recognize that when an activity is outsourced, some degree of control is given up. Thus, the organization's management should carefully evaluate the viability of activities to be outsourced. Because of nonmonetary considerations, corporate management may make a decision not to outsource, even though the costs would be less. The activity or function may be considered too critical to the organization's long-term viability (e.g., product research and development); the organization may be pursuing a core competency relative to this function; or issues such as product/service quality, time of delivery, flexibility of use, or reliability of supply cannot be resolved to the company's satisfaction. In such instances, the company's management may want to reevaluate its activities relative to this function to determine how to perform the function at a lower cost than that quoted by an outside organization.

EXHIBIT 1-5

Insource/Outsource Considerations

Relevant Quantitative Factors

Incremental production costs for each unit

Unit cost of purchasing from outside supplier (price less any discounts available plus shipping, etc.)

Availability of production capacity to manufacture components

Opportunity costs of using facilities for production rather than for other purposes

Availability of storage space for units and raw materials

Relevant Qualitative Factors

Relevant net advantage given uncertainty of estimates (costs, risks, and so forth)

Reliability of source(s) of supply

Ability to assure quality when units are purchased from outside

Nature of the work to be subcontracted (such as the importance of the part to the whole)

Availability of suppliers

Impact on customers and markets

Future bargaining position with supplier(s)

Perceptions regarding possible future price changes

Perceptions about current product prices (Are the prices appropriate or—as may be the case with international suppliers—is product dumping involved?)

Strategic and competitive importance of component to long-run organizational success

If outsourcing is chosen, the organization should, with the aid of management accounting information, prepare a comprehensive list of criteria for selecting suppliers or vendors, and these criteria must be communicated to the potential suppliers. Although monetary considerations may be important, corporate management generally recognizes that some nonmonetary needs, such as those mentioned above, are even more critical.

After a supplier has been selected, there must be regular monitoring and evaluation of performance. Again, financial accounting information may be important and is easily assessed (e.g., the invoices received from the supplier are not for the amount originally quoted per unit of product or service). But other performance criteria must also be evaluated with management accounting, such as whether the supplier shipped defective parts or whether goods were late.

In making outsourcing decisions, a company should first define its primary reasons for outsourcing. Some of the more common reasons for outsourcing are indicated in Exhibit 1-6. By outsourcing noncore competencies, an organization can further develop its core competencies and devote additional resources to those skills or expertise that represent potential sources of competitive advantage.

EXHIBIT 1-6
Top Ten Reasons to Outsource

1. Improve organizational focus.
2. Gain access to world-class capabilities.
3. Accelerate the benefits of re-engineering.
4. Share risks.
5. Free non-capital resources.
6. Make capital funds available.
7. Reduce operating costs.
8. Obtain cash infusion.
9. Obtain resources not available internally.
10. Eliminate a function that is difficult to manage.

Source: Composite of the Outsourcing Institute survey of 1,200 companies, member experiences, and published research; reported in "Outsourcing: Redefining the Corporation of the Future." From a paid advertising section prepared for *Fortune* magazine's December 12, 1994, issue. Reprinted by permission of *Fortune* Magazine.

RECENT DEVELOPMENTS AND THEIR IMPACT ON MANAGEMENT ACCOUNTING

LEARNING OBJECTIVE 5

What is new with management accounting?

A discipline such as management accounting evolves over time based on the needs and demands of its users. Its evolution is also influenced by the profession of management accounting or, in other words, the practitioners of management accounting.

The demand for management accounting is being influenced by the needs of its organizational users. With globalization, these organizations are either expanding globally or being affected by global competitors. The global economy encompasses the international trade of goods and services, movement of labour, and flows of capital and information.[17] The world has essentially become smaller through improved modes of communication and transportation as well as trade agreements that promote, rather than hinder, the international movement of goods and services among countries. The overall result is more complexity because of global considerations. Management accounting is being called upon to provide additional information for managers to plan, make decisions, evaluate performance, and control organizations within a complex business environment.

GENERAL NEWS NOTE

Virtual Manufacturing

The Internet is bringing a major change to manufacturing economics. It is the key element that differentiates virtual manufacturing from mere contract manufacturing and other forms of outsourcing. It fosters an intimate degree of partnership among all companies involved and enables the operation of a smooth, efficient, and integrated corporation.

Cisco Systems, a leading example of how a global company can leverage the power of a networked supply chain and virtual manufacturing partners, saves $75 million U.S. annually through its networked supply chain. Cisco's supply chain starts with the customer—more than 80 percent of Cisco product orders are now placed via the Internet—translating to $45 million U.S. in business per day. Supply partners fulfill more than half of these orders. Cisco entrusts most production to virtual manufacturers operating 37 factories around the globe—each of which is linked to Cisco via the Internet. Cisco's partners not only make all the components and perform 90 percent of the sub-assembly work, they even do 55 percent of the final assembly. Cisco partners regularly ship finished Cisco networking gear to end customers without a Cisco employee ever touching the product. The end result is an estimated savings of between $500 and $800 million U.S. in a recent year.

One of Cisco's partners is Celestica, of Toronto, a global leader in the electronics manufacturing services industry. With over 18,000 employees worldwide—over 4,500 in their Toronto manufacturing and design facility—Celestica provides a broad range of services including design, prototyping, assembly, testing, product assurance, supply chain management, worldwide distribution, and after-sales service to its customers.

Cisco is one of Celestica's largest customers, providing expertise in the manufacturing of various technically demanding products, ranging from modem-type components to complex router systems. The Web-enabled systems linking Celestica to Cisco provide a wealth of information, from shop floor data and demand changes to engineering specifications. This close link between Cisco and Celestica provides various business efficiencies through cumulative learning—Celestica's expertise in manufacturing allows it to pinpoint productivity gains in a variety of areas of mutual benefit, thus enabling Cisco to stay close to product development.

Source: Reprinted from an article appearing in the February 2000 issue of *CMA Management* magazine by Mike Ansley, with permission of Certified Management Accountants of Canada.

These same globally affected organizations are also influenced by information technology in terms of computerized transaction processing and electronic telecommunication such as that done with the Internet, intranet, and extranet. Management accounting has had to change in order to "fit" within this new context. The first step has been to change from manual and then mainframe accounting systems to enterprise resource planning (ERP) systems. ERP systems provide management accounting with accounting information as well as a wide range of processing activities and operational information. ERP systems integrate all information systems, enabling management accounting access to a range of data previously impossible to obtain. The second step, made possible by ERP systems, has been a general shift to manage at the activity level rather than at the more abstract level of financial transactions. This greater level of detail with activities has resulted in increased complexity. Management accounting has its focus on activities, and it can be most effective when it is used with ERP systems to incorporate the activity level for costing and performance measurements. ERP systems allow management accounting to deal with the complexity of global competition with management at the detailed activity level.

The example of Dell Computer Corporation highlights the new environment for management accounting. Improved differentiation and lower costs must exist together. These apparently conflicting demands must be accomplished. Management accounting managers must be constantly on the outlook for improving product or service quality while at the same time reducing costs. Information technology is an integral component of this new environment.

In this new context of information technology and activities, one additional event has had an impact on management accounting: a crisis of confidence that has been epitomized by the demise of Texas-based Enron. Public accounting firm Arthur Andersen shredded tonnes of paper related to the firm's audit work at Enron. Arthur Andersen, which had 85,000 audit and consulting employees in Canada, the U.S., and worldwide, has become virtually a shell of its former self. Nevertheless, billions of dollars in claims are being sought by aggrieved shareholders and ex-staffers of Enron.[18] The U.S. Justice department has charged Arthur Andersen with criminal intent in conjunction with destroying the Enron documents. Although our governments have made minor responses to the same problems in Canada (such as with Nortel), the U.S. appears to be headed toward major reforms that could include an independent accounting board, a more muscular Securities and Exchange Commission, CEO/CFO certification, auditor independence, and more outside directors.[19] For example, on January 15, 2003, the U.S. Securities and Exchange Commission (SEC) adopted new rules from the Sarbanes–Oxley Act of 2002 pertaining to the use of non-GAAP financial information, insider trading during pension fund blackout periods, and disclosure requirements relating to corporate codes of ethics and audit committee financial experts.

Despite the great demand for management accounting information, the lack of credibility that stigmatizes public accountants could easily be transferred to management accounting. Thus, it behooves those users and preparers of management accounting to be credible and honest in all reporting and use of management accounting information. Granted, management accounting information is only used internally, but credible and honest information is necessary for planning, making decisions, evaluating performance, and controlling organizations—activities that all have external effects.

More than ever, adherence to ethical standards is required. In contrast to laws, **ethical standards** represent beliefs about moral and immoral behaviours. Because beliefs are inherently personal, some differences in moral perspectives exist among individuals. However, the moral perspective is generally more homogeneous within a given society than it is across societies. In a business context, ethical standards are norms for individual conduct in making decisions and engaging in business transactions.

ethical standards
norms that represent beliefs about moral and immoral behaviours; norms for individual conduct in making decisions and engaging in business transactions

Managers in global businesses are very aware that legal and ethical standards differ from one country to another. Although, in general, both legal and ethical standards for business conduct are higher in most industrialized and economically developed countries, the standards and their enforcement vary greatly from one industrialized country to another. Therefore, because of varying standards of ethical behaviour and varying international laws, a company should develop internal norms for conduct, such as a code of ethics, to ensure that behaviour is consistent in all of its geographical operating segments.

Appendix A provides a primer for assessing behaviour for ethicalness. That discussion will provide subject content and thereby assist students in satisfactorily completing the "Ethics and Quality Discussion" questions at the end of each chapter.

The Best Little Factory in Texas

Last year Dell wrung $1 billion out of its costs—half from manufacturing. Dell executives vow to cut another $1 billion this year. Visit the Topfer Manufacturing Center in Austin (named after former vice chairman Mort Topfer), and it's hard to conceive how Dell could be any more efficient.

Workers already scuttle about in the 200,000-square-foot plant like ants on a hot plate. Gathered in cramped six-person "cells," they assemble computers from batches of parts that arrive via a computer-directed conveyor system overhead.

If a worker encounters a problem, that batch can instantly be shifted to another cell, avoiding the stoppages that plague conventional assembly lines.

Dell is constantly tinkering with factory layout and product design to move computers through at a higher velocity. So far they've done extraordinarily well: Dell has increased production by a third over the past two years while cutting manufacturing space in half. Workers in the six-person cells now assemble 18 units an hour, double the pace of a couple of years ago.

Can Dell keep it up? John Egan, the manager of the Topfer factory, explains how. Guiding a reporter through the crowded plant, the former manager of an IBM circuit-board factory points to places where Dell can shave off a few seconds of assembly time or move completed products out the door a couple of minutes faster.

A robot is being tested to pack computers into cartons, eliminating a human-staffed line doing the same thing, freeing up space for more assembly cells. Elsewhere Dell plans to combine the tasks of downloading software and testing computers, eliminating a step—and valuable seconds of worker time. Subtle changes in product design simplify assembly or reduce the number of people needed to complete a product.

Other gains are harder to quantify. Dell builds each unit to order, for example, so flexibility is essential. Every change on the factory floor that allows workers to adapt to sudden shifts in demand reduces the excess capacity of people and plant space Dell must maintain to get products out on time. Dell's purchasing managers are working equally hard with suppliers to watch parts inventories on an hour-by-hour basis, making sure Dell has just enough parts to meet expected demand without clogging the system with excess inventory.

Dell's vice chairman, Kevin Rollins, says the company has tripled production per square foot over the past five years and will triple it again over the next five years. "That's the way the world works," he says, without a trace of doubt.

Source: Daniel Fisher, "The Best Little Factory in Texas," *Forbes*, June 10, 2002. Reprinted by permission of *Forbes* Magazine © 2003 Forbes Inc.

CHAPTER SUMMARY

Strategy should be based on a mission statement that indicates what the organization wants to accomplish. Goals and objectives should flow from that statement. Strategy options may be constrained by internal or external factors. Organizational structure indicates the distribution of authority and responsibility in the entity. Core competencies indicate the organization's internal strengths and capabilities and, thus, help select appropriate business functions to do internally or to out-source. Management style and organizational culture provide a foundation for normal business practices and protocol for interactions among employees, customers, and suppliers.

Management practices today are increasingly recognizing the need to develop systems for managing costs and activities through the value creation chain. The value creation chain consists of all processes both internal and external to the firm. The external processes are provided by vendors, and possibly customers. The more a firm relies on outsourcing, the greater is the need to have systems in place to manage the costs and activities of its vendors.

Managers perform numerous functions including planning, controlling, and decision making. Control includes, but is much broader than, management accounting. Controls are needed to encourage employees and managers to perform appropriate actions and to discourage inappropriate actions. There are three approaches or alternatives to influence the behaviour of employees and managers—actions, results, and personnel.

Management accounting is defined as the gathering and application of information used to plan, make decisions, evaluate, and control an organization. Management accountants provide information for managers' planning, controlling, performance evaluation, and decision-making needs. Management accounting, accordingly, uses certain types of information to control organizations. Management accounting is only one of numerous alternatives for controlling organizations. Management accounting is used as organizations become complex because of large-scale operations or uncertainty. The greater the complexity, the more developed will be the management accounting. Simpler organizations can be operated satisfactorily with only financial accounting and managers' general understanding of operations. With greater complexity, there is a need for management accounting to assist managers in understanding operations.

Information technology in the form of enterprise resource planning (ERP) systems and other systems for dealing with suppliers and customers can greatly enhance the ability of managers. Management accounting, as part of ERP systems, can be much more valuable in assisting with the management of complex and global organizations.

Cross-Functional Applications

Topic of Note	Discipline	Cross-Functional Applications
Centralization, Decentralization	Transportation and Logistics Management	These concepts are used in management to describe not only the distribution of authority and responsibility throughout the organization but also the proximity of the distribution system to the customer. Decentralized distribution is most proximate to the customer and often more expensive than a centralized system, due to the economies of scale inherent in centralized processes.

(cont.)

Cross-Functional Applications

Topic of Note	Discipline	Cross-Functional Applications
	Financial Accounting	A major concern for the design of a general ledger accounting system is whether to centralize the process at a home office and have the various branches report data there, or decentralize the process in branch offices and integrate it through a common database. Decentralization often brings the branch manager closer to the information needed to make tactical decisions.
	Economics	Centralization or decentralization of the factors of production always implies a shift in the economies of scale. Centralization will increase the economies of scale, spreading the committed fixed cost over a greater number of units and thus lowering the unit cost. This spreading of fixed cost will reach a limit as centralization increases, and inefficiency caused by too many units will create diseconomies of scale.

Key Terms

Activities (p. 7)
Authority (p. 10)
Centralization (p. 10)
Control (p. 7)
Core competency (p. 11)
Cost accounting (p. 6)
Cost leadership (p. 11)
Decentralization (p. 10)
Differentiation (p. 11)
Empowerment (p. 10)
Environmental constraint (p. 12)
Ethical standards (p. 19)

Financial accounting (p. 5)
Goal (p. 10)
Management accounting (p. 5)
Objective (p. 10)
Organizational culture (p. 8)
Organizational structure (p. 9)
Outsourcing (p. 15)
Responsibility (p. 10)
Strategy (p. 8)
Strategic alliance (p. 9)
Value creation chain (p. 13)
Vertical integration (p. 14)

Supplementary Learning Objectives on the Web

W1-1: How did management accounting develop?
W1-2: How does information technology affect management accounting?

End-of-Chapter Materials

SELF-TEST QUESTIONS

(SOLUTIONS APPEAR AT THE END OF THE CHAPTER.)

1. Which of the following does the definition of management accounting not include?
   a. planning
   b. making decisions
   c. ordering inventory
   d. controlling

2. All of the following except one is an object of control. Which is not an object of control?
   a. specific actions
   b. profits
   c. results
   d. personnel

3. The value creation chain consists of:
   a. activities
   b. dollars
   c. assets
   d. liabilities

4. What should not be outsourced?
   a. human resource functions
   b. internal audit activities
   c. core functions
   d. manufacturing functions

5. If outsourcing is chosen, the company should first
   a. hire a lawyer to negotiate the contract
   b. prepare a comprehensive list of criteria for selecting the supplier
   c. analyze costs and benefits from outsourcing
   d. undertake a competitive analysis

6. What is not new in management accounting?
   a. enterprise resource planning systems
   b. globalization
   c. public confidence
   d. controls

7. What basically exists between management and financial accounting?
   a. an enterprise resource planning system
   b. cost accounting
   c. controls
   d. strategy

8. What is not a control?
   a. an accounting report
   b. an expectation
   c. a reporting relationship
   d. a calculator

9. Which of the following does not relate to management accounting?
   a. internal
   b. historical
   c. timely
   d. flexible

10. Strategy is primarily concerned with
    a. creating value
    b. expansion
    c. customers
    d. employees

QUESTIONS

1. What is the role of information in decision making?

2. Why would operating in a global (rather than a strictly domestic) marketplace create a need for additional information? Discuss some of the additional information you think managers would need and why such information would be valuable.

3. Discuss the validity of the following statement: "Only large companies (such as those that are publicly held and listed on a major stock exchange) have the opportunity to operate in a global marketplace."

4. Why is an effective management information system a key element of an effective management control system?

5. Why do managers require both internal and external information to manage effectively?

6. Why would an organization have multiple control systems in place?

7. Why is cost control different from cost minimization?

8. How is managerial accounting related to financial accounting? To cost accounting?

9. Why is the choice of organizational structure a cost management decision?

10. Why is a mission statement important to an organization?

11. What is organizational strategy? Why would each organization have a unique strategy or set of strategies?

12. Distinguish between goals and objectives. What goals do you hope to achieve by taking this course? What objectives can you establish to measure the degree to which you achieve these stated goals?

13. Differentiate between authority and responsibility. Can you have one without the other? Explain.

14. In what types of organizations or under what organizational conditions would centralization be a more useful structure than decentralization? When would decentralization be more useful than centralization?

15. What is a core competency and how do core competencies impact the feasible set of alternative organizational strategies?

16. Why are many organizations relying more on outsourcing now than in the past?

17. Define each of the two generic strategies an organization may pursue, and discuss the attributes of each type of strategy.

18. Define and differentiate among the primary management functions. Provide several examples of instances in which a manager would need different information in order to perform these functions.

19. Are the financial implications of strategic planning more important in a business than in a not-for-profit organization? Why or why not?

20. Why would employee empowerment generally require group as well as individual performance measurements?

21. "Most organizations determine product or service price by adding a reasonable profit margin to costs incurred." Is this statement true or false? Provide a rationale for your answer.

22. What is the value creation chain of an organization and how does it interface with strategic resource management?

23. Why is it especially necessary to achieve a balance between short-term and long-term considerations in today's business environment?

24. *Outsourcing* is a term often heard in business today. Discuss the factors that contribute to an increased reliance on outsourcing and the types of activities that are frequently outsourced.

25. What are the major risks associated with outsourcing and what types of activities should never be considered for outsourcing?

26. Strategic alliances are popular today for exploiting new market opportunities. What are strategic alliances and why are managers using this organizational structure so frequently today?

27. How does the exchange of information by firms in a value creation chain increase the opportunities for the value creation chain to become more competitive?

EXERCISES

1. (LO 1) The following words and phrases describe or are associated with either financial or managerial accounting. Indicate for each item whether it is more closely associated with financial (F) or management (M) accounting.

a.	Verifiable	h.	Focus is on organizational segments
b.	Historical	i.	Cost/benefit analysis
c.	Relevant	j.	Focus is on serving external users
d.	Internally focused	k.	Emphasis is on timeliness
e.	*CICA Handbook*	l.	Emphasis is on consistency
f.	Forecasted	m.	Future oriented
g.	Formal	n.	Flexible

2. (LO 3) Match the following lettered items on the left with the appropriate numbered description on the right.

a. Authority	1. A target expressed in quantitative terms
b. Core competency	2 The right to use resources to accomplish something
c. Goal	3. A process that an organization does better than other organizations
d. Objective	4. A process of choosing among alternatives
e. Responsibility	5. A desired result, expressed qualitatively
f. Decision making	6. The obligation to accomplish something
g. Effectiveness	7. A measure of success of an endeavour
h. Planning	8. The process of determining long-term and short-term strategy
i. Efficiency	9. A measure of output achieved relative to resources consumed

3. (LO 3) Match the following lettered items on the left with the appropriate numbered description on the right.

a. Strategy	1. Basic assumptions about an organization, its goals, and its practices
b. Outsourcing	2. A long-term plan related to organizational goals and objectives
c. Value creation chain	3. The way in which authority and responsibility are distributed in an organization
d. Organizational culture	4. The attribute of being the low-cost producer or service provider
e. Cost leadership	5. The process of contracting with external parties to provide inputs or services
f. Differentiation	6. The processes of an organization and its suppliers to convert inputs into products and services
g. Organizational structure	7. The attribute of avoiding competition by distinguishing a product or service from that of competitors

4. (LO 3) Obtain a copy of your university or college's mission statement. Draft a mission statement for this class that supports the university or college's mission statement.
   a. How does your mission statement reflect the goals and objectives of the university or college's mission statement?
   b. How can you measure the successful accomplishment of your objectives?
   c. Is there a difference between the effective and the efficient accomplishment of your objectives? Provide the rationale for your answer.

5. (LO 3) Early this year, you started a house-cleaning service and now have twenty customers. Because of other obligations (including classes), you have had to hire three employees.
   a. What types of business activities would you empower these employees to handle and why?
   b. What types of business activities would you keep for yourself and why?

6. (LO 3) As part of a team, make a list of the core competencies of your university or college and explain why you believe these items to be core competencies. Make an appointment with a professor, and, without sharing your list, ask what he or she believes the core competencies are and why. Prepare a written report contrasting the two lists, and explain the basis of the differences.

7. (LO 4) You are the manager of an exclusive jewellery store that sells primarily on credit. The majority of your customers use the store's credit card rather than a bank or other major credit card.
   a. What would you consider to be the primary benefits of outsourcing the store's accounts collection function?
   b. What would you consider to be the primary risks of outsourcing the store's accounts collection function?

8. (LO 3) Choose a company that might utilize each of the following strategies relative to its competitors and discuss the benefits that might be realized from that strategy.
   a. Differentiation
   b. Cost leadership

9. (LO 3) You are the manager of the local Toys Я Us store. Make a list of 10 factors that you believe to be critical to your organization. How would each of your key variables impact your strategic planning?

10. (LO 3) You are the manager of a small restaurant in your hometown.
    a. What information would you want to have in making the decision whether to add chicken fajitas and Boston clam chowder to your menu?
    b. Why would each of the above information items be significant?

11. (LO 5) The 2003 annual report of Calgary Oil Company (headquartered in Calgary) was slightly untraditional in that the opening "letter" to shareholders was given not only in English, but also in German, French, Spanish, Japanese, and Chinese.
    a. Discuss the costs and benefits to a Canadian-based company in taking the time to provide such translations.
    b. What additional information would you want to have to assess how such translations are related to Calgary Oil's strategic plans?

12. (LO 2) As the marketing manager for a small copying company, you have requested that your boss purchase a new high-speed, colour copier that collates up to 50 sets of copies. The current colour copier operates at approximately one-third the speed of the new one and only collates 25 sets of copies.
    a. How might you present the costs and benefits of this purchase to your boss?
    b. What additional information might you request from the marketing manager if you were the accounting or finance manager?

13. (LO 3) In their annual reports, companies provide brief descriptions of their most important contracts. These descriptions include strategic alliances. Select a large, publicly traded company and obtain a copy of its most recent annual report. Review the portions of the annual report that discuss strategic alliances. (Annual reports can be found on the Internet at www.sedar.com)

    Required:
    Based on your review, prepare an oral report in which you discuss the following points:
    a. motivations for establishing strategic alliances,
    b. the extent to which strategic alliances are used to conduct business, and
    c. the relative financial success of the strategic alliances.

14. (LO 4) Following are descriptions of four companies. Based on the descriptions given, discuss the relative extent to which each company might benefit from conducting value creation chain cost analysis as a tool to become more cost competitive.
    a. Car dealer. This firm is a typical Ford dealership that handles the entire Ford/Mercury/Lincoln product line.
    b. Small manufacturing company. This small company manufactures ceramic lawn furniture that is sold through a wholesaling firm to lawn and garden retail stores.
    c. Large manufacturer of paper products. This firm makes hundreds of household and commercial products from a variety of stock and custom inputs.

d.   Large personal computer company. This firm manufactures no components; instead, it purchases all required components in large volume. The components are custom-assembled into products sold to mail-order customers. The firm competes principally on the basis of price.

CASES

1.   You have owned Lee Construction for 15 years and employ 100 employees. Business has been profitable, but you are concerned that the locale in which your business is based may soon experience a downturn in growth. One way you have decided to help prepare for such an event is to engage in a higher level of strategic planning, beginning with a mission statement for your company.
a.   How does a mission statement add strength to the strategic planning process?
b.   Who should be involved in developing a mission statement and why?
c.   What factors should be considered in the development of a mission statement? Why are these factors important?
d.   Prepare a mission statement for Lee Construction and discuss how your mission statement will provide benefits to tactical as well as strategic planning.

2.   Successful business organizations appear to be those that have clearly defined long-range goals and a well-planned strategy to reach those goals. These successful organizations understand their markets as well as their internal strengths and weaknesses. These organizations take advantage of this knowledge to grow, through internal development or acquisitions, in a consistent and disciplined manner.
a.   Discuss the need for long-range goals for business organizations.
b.   Discuss how long-range goals are set.
c.   Define the concepts of strategic planning and management control. Discuss how they relate to each other and contribute to progress toward the attainment of long-range goals.

   (CMA adapted)

3.   Dell Computer Corporation has a straightforward business strategy: "Eliminate middlemen and don't build PCs until you have firm orders in hand." (Silvia Ascarelli, "Dell Finds U.S. Strategy Works in Europe," *Wall Street Journal,* February 3, 1997.)
a.   Dell is gaining a large European market share using its uniquely American strategy. Provide some reasons why a U.S. strategy might not be accepted by overseas customers.
b.   Dell once tried to enter the retail sales market instead of relying on direct sales. Research Dell's attempt at a different strategic approach and discuss its outcome.
c.   Although strategic planning is essential to Dell's success, why would short-term planning also be tremendously important to this company?

4.   Outsourcing is a frequently used method of cost-cutting or of eliminating organizational activities that are not viewed as core competencies. However, outsourcing also creates new costs and, sometimes, new problems.
a.   Discuss some of the benefits and drawbacks of outsourcing the following activities in a large, publicly held corporation: (1) accounting; (2) data processing; (3) regulatory compliance; (4) research and development; and (5) travel arrangements.
b.   What effect might outsourcing each of the activities in part (a) have on the organization's corporate culture?
c.   In the summer of 2002, the City of Toronto was faced with a strike by some of its unions over the issue of outsourcing. Obtain information about this "confrontation" and its settlement. How would you have reacted as (1) the lead negotiator for the City of Toronto and (2) the president of one of the unions?

5.   Four common organizational constraints involve monetary capital, intellectual capital, technology, and organizational structure. Additionally, the environment in which the organization operates may present one or more types of constraints (cultural, fiscal, legal/regulatory, or political).

   a.   Discuss whether each of these constraints might or might not be influential in the following types of organizations:

      i.   City Hall in a major metropolitan city

      ii.   A franchised quick-copy business

      iii.   A newly opened firm of lawyers, all of whom recently graduated from law school

      iv.   An international oil exploration and production company

Explain the rationale for each of your answers.

   b.   For each of the previously listed organizations, discuss your perceptions of which of the constraints would be most critical and why.

   c.   For each of the previously listed organizations, discuss your perceptions of whether human or structural capital would be most important and why.

6.   Canada provides an ethnically, racially, and culturally diverse workplace. It has been argued that this plurality may be a competitive handicap for Canadian businesses. For example, communicating may be difficult because some workers do not speak English; motivating workers may be complicated because workers have diverse work ethics; and work scheduling may be difficult because of differing religions and ethnic holidays. Conversely, it has been argued that Japan has a competitive advantage because its population is much more homogeneous.

   a.   What are the advantages of a pluralistic society in the global marketplace?

   b.   On balance, does Canada's plurality give it a competitive advantage or place it at a competitive disadvantage? Discuss.

7.   You have recently come into a very large inheritance and have decided to buy an existing business or open a new one. Given your interests, you have narrowed your choices to the following:

- Purchase the existing cable company in your regional area
- Purchase an airline that operates in most areas of the country
- Open a plant to manufacture and sell hot sauce domestically and in Central and South America
- Buy franchises for and open 15 locations of a fast-food restaurant in areas of the former Soviet Union

   a.   Discuss the competitive influences that will impact each of your potential businesses.

   b.   How would product/service differentiation or cost leadership work in each of your potential businesses?

   c.   Which business would you open and why?

8.   Strategic alliances are important parts of the value creation chain. In many organizations, suppliers are beginning to provide more and more input into customer activities. For example, in 1997 Chrysler announced that supplier ideas were expected to result in approximately $325 million in cost savings and, thus, increased profits.

   a.   In Canada, when would a strategic alliance be considered illegal?

   b.   What would you perceive to be the primary reasons for pursuing a strategic alliance?

   c.   You are the manager of a catalogue company that sells flowers and plants. With whom would you want to establish strategic alliances? What issues might you want to specify prior to engaging in the alliance?

ETHICS AND QUALITY DISCUSSIONS

1.   Mission statements are supposed to indicate what an organization does and why it exists. Some of them, however, are simply empty words, with little or no substance and with few people using them to guide activities.

   a.   Why does an organization need a mission statement? Or does it?

   b.   How might a mission statement help an organization in its pursuit of ethical behaviour from employees?

c. How might a mission statement help an organization in its pursuit of production of quality products and provision of high customer service?

2. Broadstreet Deli and Bakery is known countrywide for its excellent bread and dough-nuts. Sales have been falling, however, because of small but continuous price increases. The increases have been warranted because of increased costs for ingredients. The vice-president of marketing wants to substitute low-grade animal fat for 95% of the vegetable shortening currently used and reduce the selling prices of the products to their old levels. She does not, however, want to change the slogan on the package ("Made with Pure Vegetable Shortening") since some vegetable shortening will still be used.

a. From a strategic viewpoint, do you believe that this is a wise decision? Discuss the rationale for your answer.

b. You are the marketing manager for the bakery. How would you react to this proposal?

3. Today, many companies are outsourcing noncore competencies. Some companies are even becoming "virtual" organizations, like Amazon.com, which is a bookless, storeless bookstore. (Note: The July 7, 1997, *Forbes* article "The Plug-And-Play Economy" may provide a useful starting point.)

a. How might product quality be improved through outsourcing?
b. How might product quality be reduced through outsourcing?
c. How might customer service be improved through outsourcing?
d. How might customer service be reduced through outsourcing?

4. Strategic alliances and joint ventures are being used with increasing frequency to exploit market opportunities. For example, according to a consulting organization, 55% of Canada's fastest-growing companies are involved in an average of three alliances. From the perspective of controlling the quality of production, discuss how a strategic alliance is significantly different from a typical vendor/customer relationship.

5. According to Curtis C. Verschoor, in "Canadian Study Shows Wide Support for Corporate Responsibility," *Strategic Finance*, April 2002, pp. 20–22, the Canadian Democracy and Corporate Accountability Commission conducted a public opinion poll in the fall of 2000, which found that a substantial majority of shareholders [74%] agreed with the statement: "Executives have a responsibility to take into account the impact their decisions have on employees, local communities, and the country as well as making profits." This contrasts with the popular view that shareholders are con-cerned about financial returns almost to the exclusion of social responsibility.

Required:
Compare and contrast the view found with this research and the "popular view" for firms in your community.

COMMUNICATIONS ACTIVITIES

1. "Many companies have taken advantage of the Internet by strategically deploying new resources. Some of the advantages and benefits that have frequently been attributed to the Internet include enhanced ease of doing business, reduced transaction time, more extensive customer relationships, and access to a larger market of buyers and sellers.... For customers, the value proposition is enhanced because they can now do business with a simple keystroke, any time of the day, anywhere in the world. They can produce made-to-measure products at the best prices within a shorter time. In addition, they can obtain personalized comprehensive information about products and services. This value proposition is unprecedented. Strategic deployment of the Internet encompasses and impacts the three dimensions of the value proposition of every company: product attributes, cost, and production times."

Source: Hugues Boisvert, "Reinventing the @nterprise," *CMA Magazine*, April 2001, pp. 30–33.

Prepare a five-minute oral presentation in which you identify your business major and discuss how the Internet has affected the value creation chain of an organization that you understand. The organization could be one where you work or worked or one that you have followed as an investor or as a family member of an employee.

2. Find the latest annual report for a major Canadian company. Read the annual report and review the financial data presented. Use the textual information to identify the firm's basic strategy for a specific product line or organizational segment. (Frequently, the Management Report is useful for this purpose.) Write a brief essay describing the corporate strategy and the information that managers will need to be successful in competing with such a strategy.

PROJECTS

1. Your organization produces a variety of electronic products and has decided to locate a new production facility in Eastern Europe. The new facility will produce motherboards for the organization's line of PCs and also supply electronic components to a variety of consumer product manufacturers in Canada, the U.S. and Europe. Production processes in the new facility will be highly automated, using very sophisticated production equipment. The vice president of manufacturing is assigned the responsibility of plant oversight. This person maintains an office and staff in Paris; she is a native-born, French-speaking citizen of Canada.

   The criteria to be used in selecting the location of the new plant are the subject of the project. Your class should be divided into teams, preferably of four members each. One member of each team should represent each of the following functional areas: marketing, manufacturing, finance, and accounting. Each team member should develop a list discussing the important criteria for determining the location of the new production site. The individual members' lists should then be discussed by the teams and coordinated into five- to ten-minute oral presentations.

2. Obtain the annual reports of three companies and compare their organization charts. Which companies have treasurers and/or controllers? To whom do these individuals report, and who reports to them? Does there appear to be anything unusual about the lines of responsibility?

USING THE INTERNET

1. Use Google or another search engine to investigate the strategies that IBM has followed since 1975. Divide the strategies into different but meaningful periods, and explain your justification. These different strategic periods should emphasize different products or services. Describe these strategic periods with a four- or five-page report.

2. Use Google or another search engine to understand how Dell Computer and Wal-Mart use information technology to competitive advantage. This requires an understanding of the current strategy of each organization. You will need about five or six pages to describe the strategies of the two companies and how those strategies are reinforced by information technology.

SOLUTIONS TO SELF-TEST QUESTIONS

1. c, 2. b, 3. a, 4. c, 5. b, 6. d, 7. b, 8. d, 9. b, 10. a.

ENDNOTES

1. "Value creation chain" will be used instead of the more common "value chain" to emphasize that processes and activities must create value.

2. Kenneth A. Merchant, "The Control Function of Management," *Sloan Management Review,* Summer 1982, pp. 43–55.

3. Devin Leonard, "Mr. Messier is Ready for His Close-Up," *Fortune* (Asia), September 3, 2001, pp. 26–33.

4. http://finance.vivendiuniversal.com/finance/strategy/businessunits.cfm

5. Richard Normann and Rafael Ramirez, "From Value Chain to Value Constellation: Designing Interactive Strategy," *Harvard Business Review,* July–August 1993, p. 65.

6. Thomas S. Bateman and Scott A. Snell, *Management: Building Competitive Advantage,* Chicago: Irwin, 1996, p. 117.

7. Richard Koch, *The Financial Times Guide to Management and Finance,* London: Financial Times/Pitman Publishing, 1994, p. 39.

8. Alfred D. Chandler, Jr., *Strategy and Structure,* Boston: MIT Press, 1962.

9. Associated Press, "100 Different Ads, Most Running Only Once, Is Coke's Plan," *New Orleans Times-Picayune,* July 16, 1996, p. C2.

10. Peter F. Drucker, "The Information Executives Truly Need," *Harvard Business Review,* January–February 1995, p. 60.

11. Michael Porter, *Competitive Advantage: Creating and Sustaining Superior Performance,* New York: Free Press, 1985, p. 17.

12. Richard J. Palmer, "Strategic Goals and Objectives and the Design of Strategic Management Accounting," *Advances in Management Accounting,* Vol. 1, 1992, p. 187.

13. Douglas McArthur, "Business Travel: Companies Crack the Whip on Travel Spending," *The Globe and Mail,* January 17, 2001, p. 1.

14. Adopted from W.P. Birkett, "Management Accounting and Knowledge Management," *Management Accounting,* November 1995, pp. 44–48.

15. The value creation chain is also known as the value chain.

16. Andrew Park, Faith Keenan, and Cliff Edwards, "Whose Lunch Will Dell Eat Next?" *Business Week,* August 12, 2002, pp. 66–67.

17. Paul Krugman, *Peddling Prosperity,* quoted by Alan Farnham in "Global—or Just Globaloney," *Fortune,* June 27, 1994, p. 98,

18. Joseph Weber, "Commentary: The Heavy Hand of Justice," *Business Week,* April 1, 2002, pp. 32–33.

19. Dan Carney and Amy Barrett, "Let the Reforms Begin," *Business Week,* July 22, 2002, pp. 26–31.

Chapter 2

Cost Terminology and Cost Flows

LEARNING OBJECTIVES

After reading this chapter, you should be able to answer the following questions:

1 What is the relationship between cost objects and direct costs?

2 What product cost categories exist and what items comprise these categories?

3 How does the conversion process work in manufacturing and service companies?

4 What assumptions do accountants make about cost behaviour and why are these assumptions necessary?

5 How can mixed costs be analyzed using the high–low method and least-squares regression analysis? (Appendix 2A)

6 How are predetermined overhead rates developed and how does the selection of a capacity measure affect overhead application?

7 How is underapplied or overapplied overhead accounted for at year-end and why are these accounting techniques appropriate?

8 Why are separate predetermined overhead rates generally more useful than combined rates?

9 How is cost of goods manufactured calculated? Cost of goods sold?

ON SITE

www.risckys.com/bbq.asp

Riscky's Barbeque

Jim Riscky's grandmother began selling smoked meats in 1927 as a way to dispose of inventory from her husband's butcher shop at the end of the week. In time, the butcher shop became a family-owned supermarket that continued grandmom's sideline barbecue business. When Jim Riscky's father was killed in an accident, the 33-year-old took over the family enterprise and started a barbecue restaurant. Jim rapidly realized that the profit margin on barbecue was much higher than it could ever be on groceries. He began to convert the old supermarket to the centre of a catering business that supplied barbecue and fixings to many of the major events in the area.

Today, **RISCKY'S BARBEQUE** has 10 locations. Other Riscky's restaurant locations have different themes, such as Riscky Rita's with spicy western-style food and Riscky's Steakhouse. Because cost control is so important in the restaurant business, Jim Riscky relies on a centralized commissary operation to prepare or process food items (such as barbecue, baked beans, potato salad, and vegetables) that can travel easily to the various restaurant sites. This organizational characteristic allows Riscky to control his direct labour and overhead costs to a much greater extent than if each restaurant were independently responsible for cooking food that is more easily prepared in mass quantities.

Even with investor offers of financing, Jim Riscky has resisted taking his operations to locations outside his home base. He understands that long-distance locations do not currently fit into his organizational strategy. He says, "the centralized preparation location is one secret to the success of my restaurants. I can have large amounts of food prepared on a daily basis and yet retain such consistently high quality that customers cannot tell if the food was prepared on- or off-site. Thus, I only do business in the local area."

SOURCE: Interview with Jim Riscky. (www.risckys.com/bbq.asp) Reprinted by permission of Riscky's Barbeque.

*C*ost is a major factor both in achieving strategic success through competing effectively and in operating profitably. It is of interest to everyone. A student is concerned about the cost of a Saturday-night dinner and movie. Parents are concerned about the cost of their child's postsecondary education. University administrators are concerned about the costs associated with equipping and operating new computer labs. Jim Riscky is concerned about the costs of ingredients, equipment, and product quality assurance.

However, simply referring to the cost is inappropriate because numerous conditions must be specified before the cost can be determined. Is the student considering a fast-food or a four-star restaurant? Will the child want to attend a public or private school, in the home city or away? Are the computer labs going to be open beyond normal class hours and how will they be staffed? At Riscky's, how many meals are to be prepared and what does it cost the company to prepare and serve each meal?

To be strategically effective, managers must be able to understand and communicate about costs using common management accounting terms. **Cost** is an often-used word and reflects a monetary measure of the resources given up to acquire a good or service. But the term cost is seldom used without a preceding adjective to specify the type of cost being considered. Different types of costs are used in different situations. For instance, an asset's historical or acquisition cost is used to prepare a balance sheet, but its replacement cost is used to estimate its insurance value.

Before being able to communicate information to others effectively, accountants must clearly understand the differences among the various types of costs, their computations, and their usage. This chapter provides the terminology that is necessary to understand and articulate cost and management accounting information. The chapter also presents cost flows and accumulation in a production environment.

COMPONENTS OF PRODUCT COST

A **cost object** is anything to which management desires to attach costs or to which costs are related. A cost object can be a product or service, a department, a division, or a territory. Any cost that is clearly traceable to the cost object is called a **direct cost**. Costs that cannot be traced are **indirect** (or common) **costs** and these costs can only be **allocated**, or assigned, to cost objects by the use of one or more appropriate drivers, predictors, or arbitrarily chosen bases. Different cost objects may be designated for different decisions. As the cost object changes, the costs that are direct and indirect to it may also change. For instance, if a production division is specified as the cost object, the production division manager's salary is direct. If instead the cost object is a sales territory and the production division operates in more than one territory, the production division manager's salary is indirect.

Costs can also be classified as either period or product costs. **Period costs** are incurred in the nonproduction area. They are related to business functions such as selling and administration, while **product costs** are all the costs incurred to produce a product or provide a service. These costs are either direct or indirect to a particular cost object. Product costs are also called inventoriable costs and include the costs of direct material, direct labour, and manufacturing overhead (a set of indirect costs).

Direct Material

Any readily identifiable, physical part of a product that is clearly, conveniently, and economically traceable to that product is a **direct material**. Direct materials may be

---

cost
a monetary measure of the resources given up to acquire a good or service

LEARNING OBJECTIVE **1**

What is the relationship between cost objects and direct costs?

cost object
anything to which costs attach or are related

direct cost
a cost that is clearly, conveniently, and economically traceable to a particular cost object

indirect cost
a cost that cannot be clearly traced to a particular cost object

allocate
assign indirect or overhead costs based on the use of a cost driver, a predictor, or an arbitrary method

period cost
a cost that is incurred during an accounting period to support the activities of the company; the cost of resources consumed during the period

product cost
a cost associated with making or acquiring inventory or providing a service

direct material
a readily identifiable, physical part of a product that is clearly, conveniently, and economically traceable to that product

purchased raw materials or manufactured components.[1] Direct materials cost should theoretically include the cost of all materials used in manufacturing a product or performing a service. For example, the cost of the tomato paste, corn syrup, vinegar, molasses, food starch, flavouring, salt, and water would theoretically make up the direct materials cost for Riscky's barbecue sauce.

Because direct costs are so expensive to record, management may decide that the benefit of treating an insignificant cost as direct is not worth the clerical cost involved. Such costs are treated and classified as indirect costs. For instance, most accountants would agree that the costs of the flavouring, salt, and water are neither economically traceable nor monetarily significant to the sauce's production cost. Thus, these costs would probably be deemed indirect materials and therefore would be included as part of overhead.

Similarly in a service business, some materials that could be traced to a cost object may have such an insignificant cost that they are not considered direct. For instance, a marketing firm needs to separately accumulate costs of each advertising campaign for each of its clients. When dummy boards, or mock-ups, of possible ads are created, artists use a variety of coloured pens and pencils for design purposes. The firm would probably not attempt to trace the costs of these items to a particular advertising campaign. The costs would be too insignificant and thus would be charged to overhead.

Managers try to keep the cost of raw materials at the very lowest price and in some cases try to form partnerships with their suppliers.

Rick George, Suncor's president and chief executive officer, said costs from subcontractors and other suppliers will be the single largest source of savings in cutting the cash operating cost of a barrel (of oil) to $9 by the end of 2003 from the current $10.50. He said, "We're looking for partners and suppliers who want to work with us for a very long time. We're looking for suppliers who want to help us reduce those costs."[2]

The International News Note on page 36 shows the same theme in the automobile industry.

To remain competitive in the parts business, companies will have to know their cost structures and understand why and how they exist. This means that companies will have to review their costs on a continuous basis.

Direct Labour

Direct labour refers to the individuals who work specifically on a cost object (i.e., manufacturing a product or performing a service). Their labour transforms raw materials or supplies into finished goods or completed services. Another perspective on direct labour is that it directly *adds* value to the final product or service. The food preparer and the chef at Riscky's represent direct labour.

Direct labour cost consists of wages or salaries paid to employees who work directly on a cost object (usually on a product or in the performance of a service). Direct labour cost should include basic compensation, production efficiency bonuses, and the employer's share of employment taxes. In addition, when a company's operations are relatively stable, direct labour cost should include all employer-paid insurance costs, holiday and vacation pay, and pension and other retirement benefits.

Even though direct labour cost is clearly traceable to a particular cost object, a given cost must also be conveniently and economically traceable to the product or

LEARNING OBJECTIVE **2**

What product cost categories exist and what items comprise these categories?

direct labour
the time spent by individuals who work specifically on manufacturing a product or performing a service and whose efforts are conveniently and economically traceable to that product or service; can also be viewed as the cost of the direct labour time

Price Reductions Demanded

Supplier price cuts are demanded by auto makers on a regular basis. Generally, suppliers give in: the average annual supplier price reduction over the next few years is expected to be about 3.3%.

Historically there have been two schools of supplier management in the automotive industry. The US-based auto makers over the years gained a reputation for focusing on price reductions from suppliers and the slumping automotive market in recent years has intensified some of that pressure. Japanese car makers like Honda and Toyota, however, became known for building long-term, close-knit relationships with top suppliers under the keiretsu system, which had original equipment manufacturers owning a percentage of their top suppliers.

In keiretsu, suppliers are considered family members and, although price reductions may be requested, Japanese auto companies would try to make certain that those reductions would not produce significant financial harm to the suppliers.

Given the history of a relationship in which car makers have long been able to dictate pricing to their suppliers through collective purchasing power, suppliers have had no choice but to adopt cost-cutting measures of their own. The knock-on effect of their actions is being felt down the supplier chain to the smallest component makers.

Japanese auto makers want long-term supplier relationships. They select suppliers as a person would a mate. The Japanese are equally tough on price but are committed to maintaining supplier continuity. So if Toyota or Honda finds that Green's [a supplier] price exceeds the target cost, both sides look for savings.

When it comes to selecting suppliers, the Big 3 choose on the basis of lowest price and annual price reductions, says Neil DeKoker, president of the Original Equipment Suppliers Association. "They look globally for the lowest parts prices from the lowest cost countries."

Sources: David Hannon, "The Automotive Buy—Suppliers: Friend or Foe?," *Purchasing*, Boston, Feb. 6, 2003; Brian Milligan, "Automakers Keep Demanding Price Cuts From Suppliers," *Purchasing*, March 9, 2000, pp. 87–89; Jeremy Grant, "Supplier Industry: Parts Companies Feel Knock-on Effect," FT.com London, March 3, 2003; Robert Sherefkin and Amy Wilson, "Why the Big 3 Can't Be Japanese," *Automotive News*, Detroit, Feb. 10, 2003.

service to be considered direct. As with some materials, some labour costs that should theoretically be considered direct are treated as indirect for two reasons.

First, it might be cost inefficient to trace the labour costs. For example, some employee fringe benefits should conceptually be treated as direct labour cost, but many companies do not have stable workforces and cannot develop a reasonable estimate of fringe benefit costs. Thus, the time, effort, and cost of trying to trace the fringe benefit costs might not be worth the additional accuracy that would be provided. In contrast, when fringe benefit costs are extremely high (such as for professional staff in a service organization), tracing them to products and services may provide more useful management information.

Second, erroneous information about product or service costs might result from handling such costs in the theoretically correct manner. An assumed payroll for one week for the six production workers who make barbecue sauce at Riscky's commissary can illustrate this possibility. If each of these employees earns $8 per hour, their overtime pay would be $12 per hour (time-and-a-half). One week prior to a holiday, the employees worked a total of 300 hours, including 60 hours of overtime to complete all the orders. Of the total employee labour payroll of $2,640 only $2,400 would be classified as direct labour cost. The remaining $240 (60 hours × $4 per hour) would be considered overhead.

Barbecue sauce production is scheduled based on the expected current demand. If the $4 per hour overtime premium were assigned to the sauce produced during the overtime hours, the labour cost for this sauce would appear to be 50% greater than that for sauce manufactured during regular working hours. Since scheduling is random, the sauce made during overtime hours should not be forced to bear the overtime charges. Therefore, amounts incurred for costs such as overtime or shift premiums are usually considered overhead rather than direct labour cost and are allocated to all products made by Riscky's commissary.

There are occasions, however, when allocating costs such as overtime to overhead (all units) is not appropriate. If a catering request by a customer is to be scheduled during overtime hours or comes in as a rush request that requires overtime be worked, then the overtime or shift premiums incurred should be considered direct labour and be attached to the particular job that created the costs.

Direct labour cost in proportion to total product cost has been slowly declining in many industries, especially over the past 25 years. Now, in many highly automated production environments, it is not uncommon to find that direct labour accounts for a very small proportion of total cost at many manufacturers. Eventually, managers may find that almost all direct labour cost is replaced with a new cost of production—the cost of robots and other fully automated machinery. Thus, although labour may still be an essential element of production in some industries, managers should avoid overestimating the importance of labour cost in a technically advanced setting.

At Dell Computer Corporation, a robot that can pack computers into cartons is currently being tested in order to eliminate a human-staffed line. This will free up space for more assembly cells. Elsewhere, Dell plans to combine the tasks of downloading software and testing computers, eliminating a step. Subtle changes in product design simplify assembly or reduce the number of people needed to complete a product.[3]

Overhead

Overhead is any manufacturing or production cost that is not directly or conveniently traceable to manufacturing a product or providing a service. Overhead is considered indirect and, accordingly, does not include direct material and direct labour. Manufacturing overhead costs are essential to the process of converting raw materials into finished goods. "The greatest part of most companies' costs (other than those for purchased materials) typically occurs in overhead categories. In manufacturing, more than two-thirds of all nonmaterial costs tend to be indirect or overhead expenses."[4] Direct labour cost has become a progressively smaller proportion of product cost in recent years and overhead has become a much larger portion; therefore, it requires much more attention than in the past.

At the Chrysler plant in Illinois, the use of robots and better production processes has eliminated more than 1,000 jobs in the new factory.[5] At Pirelli Tire, a new production process has been designed to cut the cost of its products by 25%, while raising the quality and lowering costs by as much as 15% for some models. Pirelli's new technology, called a modular integrated robotized system, or MIRS, is an automated process that allows for high-speed production in an area about one-fifth the floor space required for traditional tire-making methods, thus creating minifactories that can be located next to car manufacturing plants. Through the use of robots and specialized software, Pirelli says that it will be able to reduce the steps in manufacturing a tire from 14 to just three, while cutting the lead time from six days to just 72 minutes.[6]

The sum of direct materials, direct labour, and overhead costs comprises total product cost.[7] According to generally accepted accounting principles, product costs are inventoriable until the products are sold or otherwise disposed of.

overhead
the expenses of a business such as rent, insurance, and utilities consumed in the production of a product or consumed in the supplying of a service

LEARNING OBJECTIVE **3**

How does the conversion process work in manufacturing and service companies?

Stage of Production

Production processing or conversion can be viewed as existing in three stages: (1) work not started (raw materials), (2) work in process, and (3) finished work. The stages of production in a manufacturing firm and some costs associated with each stage are illustrated in Exhibit 2-1. In the first stage of processing, the cost incurred reflects the prices paid for raw materials and/or supplies. As work progresses through the second stage, accrual-based accounting requires that costs related to the conversion of raw materials or supplies be accumulated and attached to the product. These costs include wages paid to people producing the goods as well as overhead charges. The total costs incurred in stages 1 and 2 are equal to the total production cost of finished goods in stage 3.

Cost accounting provides the means for accumulating the processing costs and allocating the costs to the goods produced. The primary accounts involved in the cost accumulation process are (1) Raw Materials, (2) Work in Process, and (3) Finished Goods. These accounts relate to the three stages of production shown in Exhibit 2-1 and form a common database for cost, management, and financial accounting.

Service firms, ordinarily, do not have the same degree of cost complexity as manufacturers. The work-not-started stage of processing normally consists of the cost of supplies necessary for performing services. Supplies are inventoried until they are placed into a work-in-process stage. At that point, labour and overhead are added to achieve finished results. Developing the cost of services is extremely important and useful in service-oriented businesses. For instance, cost accounting is very useful in hospitals that need to accumulate the costs incurred by patients in their hospital stays, in architectural firms that need to accumulate the costs incurred for designs and models of individual projects, and in legal firms that need to accumulate all costs incurred for a legal case until it is completed.

The product and service costs accumulated in the inventory accounts are composed of three cost components—direct materials, direct labour, and manufacturing overhead. Each of these components was discussed in the preceding section of this chapter. Precise classification of some costs into one of these categories may be difficult and judgment may be required in the classification process.

Prime and Conversion Costs

The total cost of direct materials and direct labour is referred to as **prime cost** because these costs are most convincingly associated with and traceable to a specific

prime cost
the total cost of direct materials and direct labour; so called because these costs are most convincingly associated with and traceable to a specific product

---

EXHIBIT 2-1

Stages of Production

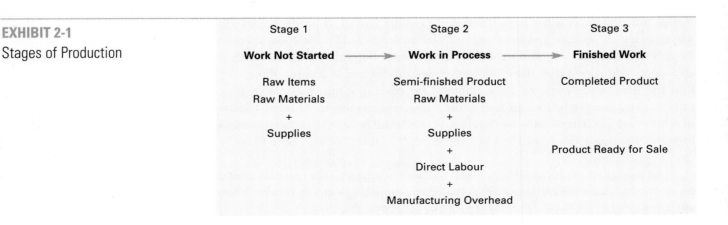

Stage 1	Stage 2	Stage 3
Work Not Started ⟶	**Work in Process** ⟶	**Finished Work**
Raw Items	Semi-finished Product	Completed Product
Raw Materials	Raw Materials	
+	+	
Supplies	Supplies	
	+	Product Ready for Sale
	Direct Labour	
	+	
	Manufacturing Overhead	

product. **Conversion cost** is defined as the sum of direct labour and manufacturing overhead that is directly or indirectly necessary for transforming direct (raw) materials and purchased parts into a saleable finished product. Because direct labour is included as part of both prime cost and conversion cost, prime cost plus conversion cost does not sum to product cost, as direct labour would be double-counted. Exhibit 2-2 shows the typical components of product cost for a manufacturing company in terms of prime and conversion costs.

conversion cost
the sum of direct labour and manufacturing overhead that is directly or indirectly necessary for transforming direct (raw) materials and purchased parts into a saleable finished product

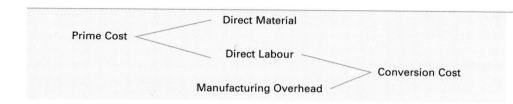

EXHIBIT 2-2
Components of Product Cost

COST BEHAVIOUR

A cost may change from a prior period because of changes in activity. The way a cost responds to a change in activity is known as its cost behaviour. For Riscky's Barbeque, activity measures can include sales; production volume; machine hours; the number of purchase orders sent; or the number of grocery stores and restaurants selling Riscky products, meals using barbecue sauce, or other Riscky products. The way a *total* (rather than unit) cost reacts to a change in activity reflects that cost's behaviour pattern. Every cost will change if enough time passes or if extreme shifts in activity occur. Therefore, for **cost behaviour** information to be properly identified, analyzed, and used, a time frame must be specified to indicate how far into the future a cost should be examined, and a particular range of activity must be assumed. The time frame generally encompasses the operating cycle or a year, whichever is longer. The assumed activity range usually reflects the company's normal operating range and is referred to as the **relevant range**.

To understand how costs will behave under various conditions, accountants need to find the underlying cost driver for cost changes. A **cost driver** is an activity or occurrence that has a direct cause–effect relationship with a cost. For example, a production volume has a direct effect on the total cost of raw materials used and so can be said to drive that cost. A change in production volume causes a similar change in the cost of raw materials.

In most situations, the cause–effect relationship is less clear because costs are commonly affected by multiple factors. For example, quality assurance costs are affected by volume of production, quality of materials used, skill level of workers, and level of automation. Although determining which factor actually caused a specific change in quality assurance cost might be difficult, managers could choose any one of these factors to predict that cost, if they were confident about the factor's relationship with cost changes. When a change in an activity measure is accompanied by a consistent, observable change in a cost item, that activity measure is a **predictor**. To be used as a predictor, the activity measure need only change with the cost in a foreseeable manner.

In contrast to a cost driver, a predictor does not necessarily cause the change in the related item; the two items simply need to change in the same manner. The difference between a cost driver and a predictor is important. A cost driver reflects the actual cause–effect relationship; a predictor reflects a possible relationship or

LEARNING OBJECTIVE   4

What assumptions do accountants make about cost behaviour and why are these assumptions necessary?

cost behaviour
the manner in which a cost responds to a change in a related level of activity

relevant range
the specified range of activity over which a variable cost remains constant per unit and a fixed cost remains fixed in total

cost driver
a factor that has a direct cause–effect relationship to a cost

predictor
an activity measure that is accompanied by a consistent, observable change in a cost item

perhaps even a totally random occurrence that simply seems to be related. However, managers often use both cost drivers and predictors to estimate how changes in activity will influence cost behaviour.

Variable and Fixed Costs

Cost behaviour patterns will be referred to throughout the text because they are so helpful in many management accounting situations requiring analysis and decision making. The two types of cost behaviours are variable and fixed. The respective total cost and unit cost definitions for variable and fixed cost behaviours are presented in Exhibit 2-3.

Variable Cost

variable cost
a cost that varies in total in direct proportion to changes in activity

A cost that varies in total in direct proportion to changes in activity is classified as a **variable cost**. The costs of materials, wages, and sale commissions are examples. Variable costs can be extremely important in the total profit picture of a company, because every time a product is produced and/or sold or a service is rendered and/or sold, a corresponding amount of that variable cost is incurred. Variable costs are constant per unit; consequently, the total variable cost varies in direct proportion to the changes in activity. [8]

When direct labour cost is treated as a variable cost, in an economic downturn there are numerous layoffs. However, this may not be the case everywhere. For example, in Japan, many workers have lifelong employment contracts; thus, companies often treat direct labour costs as fixed. Because of a downturn in the Japanese economy, some companies are trying to modify this situation and trade these fixed costs for variable ones. This can be seen in the News Note on page 41.

Fixed Cost

fixed cost
a cost that remains constant in total within a specified range of activity

In contrast, a cost that remains constant in total within the relevant range of activity is a **fixed cost**. Many fixed costs are incurred to provide a firm with production capacity. Fixed costs include depreciation,[9] property taxes, and insurance. On a per-unit basis, a fixed cost varies inversely with changes in activity: the per-unit fixed cost decreases with increases in activity and increases with decreases in activity. In other words with increased activity, the fixed costs are spread over more units and thus fixed costs per unit are lower.

When the manufacturers can't sell as many vehicles as they can build, the fixed costs of the assembly plants drive up the cost of each vehicle. Thus, the auto makers use incentives so they can sell more cars and thus keep production up and unit costs

EXHIBIT 2-3

Comparative Total and Unit Cost Behaviour Definitions

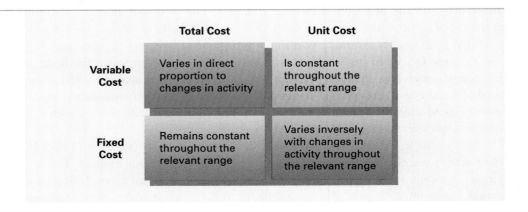

	Total Cost	Unit Cost
Variable Cost	Varies in direct proportion to changes in activity	Is constant throughout the relevant range
Fixed Cost	Remains constant throughout the relevant range	Varies inversely with changes in activity throughout the relevant range

Lifetime Contracts Make Labour Cost Fixed

Recent business publications contend that Japan's current economic woes are compounded by the inability of companies to reduce their workforces due to lifetime employment practices.

Most Japanese companies understand the nature of their current problem. The typical Japanese company still views almost all of its costs, including labour, as fixed. To steer their way through the current recession, however, Japanese companies must focus on reducing all costs, which means changing their view on the fixed nature of personnel expenses.

However if there was any question about whether Japan's tradition of lifetime employment could survive into the new millennium, it's being answered now. The recession of 1998 struck the Japanese electronics industry hard, with most manufacturers reporting losses—or at least big drops in profits—at the close of the fiscal year ending in March [1999]. The top five semiconductor makers were all in the red. And they are all mulling layoffs, even if they opt not to use that word.

Konosuke Matsushita was an originator of the lifetime-employment system. But now, the company he founded is offering to pay employees as much as 40 months' salary to quit the firm.

The job cuts, particularly those at Matsushita, have shaken the confidence of many Japanese, because the latest job-cutters include some of the most faithful practitioners of the custom of guaranteeing employees a job for life at blue-chip companies. Japanese media are treating Matsushita's move as symbolic of lifetime employment's demise.

Sources: Douglas T. Shinsato, "Japan Tries to Get the Size Right," *Wall Street Journal,* June 28, 1993, p. A16; Yoshiko Hara, "Japan Says Sayonara to Lifetime Employment," *Electronic Engineering Times,* Manhasset; September 27, 1999, p. 168; Todd Zaun and Peter Landers, "Job Cutbacks Take a Heavy Toll on Japan—A Spate of Layoffs Weakens Economy and Tradition of Lifetime Employment," *Wall Street Journal,* August 3, 2001, p. A5.

down.[10] General Motors Corp. and Ford Motor Co. are launching new marketing programs in the U.S. and Canada that feature zero-percent financing as well as cash rebates in hopes of clearing dealers' inventories of remaining models.[11]

In the long run, however, even fixed costs will not remain constant. Business will increase or decrease sufficiently that production capacity may be added or sold. Alternatively, management may decide to "trade" fixed and variable costs for one

Many automobile manufacturers use zero-percent financing or cash back rebates to help dealers clear their inventories.

another. For example, if a company installs new highly computerized equipment rather than employing labourers, an additional large fixed cost for depreciation is generated and the variable cost of hourly production workers is eliminated.

Some companies hire other firms, such as IBM, to do their data processing. This process of "outsourcing" can create another type of cost. In such cases, there is a trade-off of costs. Oftentimes, substantial fixed costs are eliminated and are replaced by a variable cost. Whether a company exchanges variable for fixed, or fixed for mixed costs (a combination of fixed and variable costs), shifting costs from one type of cost behaviour to another changes the basic cost structure of the company and can have a significant impact on profits.

Although direct materials and direct labour are generally variable in relation to production volume, overhead costs may be variable, mixed, or fixed. Variable overhead includes the cost of indirect materials and indirect labour paid on an hourly basis, such as wages for forklift operators, material handlers, and others who support the production, assembly, or service process. Also included in variable overhead are the costs of oil and grease used for machine maintenance, paper towels used in the manufacturing-area restrooms, and the variable portion of utility charges (or any other mixed cost) for the manufacturing area. Depreciation calculated using the units-of-production method is a variable manufacturing overhead cost.

Fixed manufacturing overhead comprises costs such as straight-line depreciation on manufacturing plant assets, and insurance and property taxes on production/service-providing assets. Fixed indirect manufacturing labour cost includes salaries for production supervisors, janitorial workers, shift superintendents, and service managers. The fixed portion of mixed costs (such as maintenance and utilities) incurred in the manufacturing area is also part of fixed manufacturing overhead. Investments in new equipment may create significantly large fixed overhead costs but may also improve product or service quality—and thus reduce another overhead cost: that of poor quality. This is borne out by the following example.

Alwin Thompson is passionate about his products. His big fascination is fruit pies: "Just look at those cherries. You don't get many pies like that anymore," he says, surveying his products in the sampling room of Inter Link Foods' Blackburn bakery. Mr. Thompson founded Inter Link Foods in 1994. "If you make 40 products you will not do any of them efficiently," he says. He now concentrates on making a handful of core "quality" products at low unit cost and high volume. When he first bought the bakery, it was making a lot of products for the catering trade and losing money. It operated old machinery and much of the work was done by hand. Inter Link swiftly rationalized the product line and invested in automation. Many products were dropped in order to concentrate on a narrow range of "mainstream" cakes and pastries for sale to the big supermarkets as "own-label" products and "in-store baked items." As a result, productivity has been improved.[12]

Mixed Costs

mixed cost
a cost that has both a variable and a fixed component; it does not fluctuate in direct proportion to changes in activity, nor does it remain constant with changes in activity

Some costs are not strictly variable or fixed; they are a combination of both. This type of cost is called a **mixed cost.** It is said to have both a variable and a fixed component. This type of cost does not fluctuate in direct proportion to changes in activity, nor does it remain constant with changes in activity. Electricity is a good example of a mixed cost. Electricity bills are commonly computed as a flat charge (the fixed component) for basic service plus a stated rate for each kilowatt hour (kwh) of electricity used (the variable component). Exhibit 2-4 shows a graph for

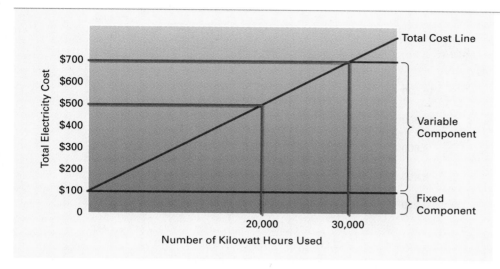

EXHIBIT 2-4
Graph of a Mixed Cost

Riscky's electricity charge, which consists of a flat rate of $100 per month plus $0.02 per kwh. If Riscky's uses 20,000 kwh of electricity in a month, its total electricity bill is $500 [$100 + ($0.02 × 20,000)]. If the company uses 30,000 kwh, the electricity bill is $700. Management accountants generally separate mixed costs into their variable and fixed components so that the behaviour of these costs is more readily apparent and can be analyzed in greater detail.

Step Cost

Another type of cost shifts upward or downward when activity changes by a certain interval or "step." A **step cost** can be variable or fixed. Step variable costs have small steps, and step fixed costs have large steps. For example, as shown in Exhibit 2-5, if Riscky's purchasing agent buys tomato paste in lots of less than 2,000 litres, the price per litre is $1.10. If tomato paste is purchased in lots between 2,000 and 10,000 litres, the price falls to $0.95 per litre. Quantities over 10,000 litres may be purchased for only $0.85 per litre. Therefore, if Riscky's Barbeque buys 4,000 litres, it will pay $3,800 for its purchases; if it buys 11,000 litres, the price will be $9,350. In contrast, as shown in Exhibit 2-6, at Riscky's, the salary cost for a delivery person

step cost
a variable or fixed cost that shifts upward or downward when activity changes by a certain interval or step

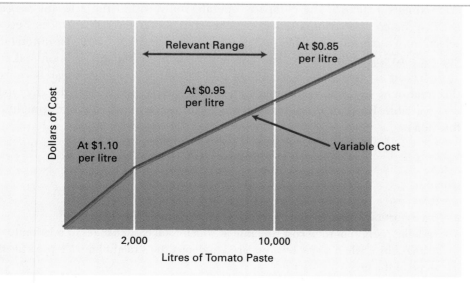

EXHIBIT 2-5
Step Variable Cost

EXHIBIT 2-6

Step Fixed Cost

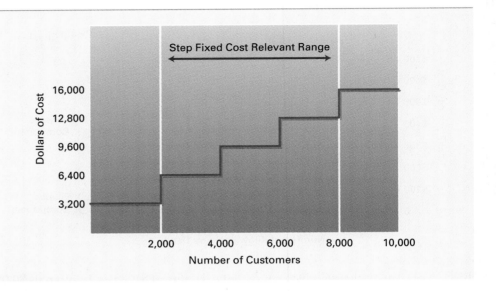

who can service 2,000 customers per month is $3,200 per month. If delivery volume increases from the current 8,000 customers to 10,000 customers, Riscky's will need five drivers rather than the four that are presently employed. An additional 2,000 customers will result in an additional step fixed cost of $3,200.

Although all costs do not strictly conform to the categories just described, the categories represent the types of cost behaviour typically encountered in business. Managers who understand cost behaviour can better estimate total costs at various levels of activity. When step variable or step fixed costs exist, accountants must choose a specific relevant range of activity that will allow step variable costs to be treated as variable and step fixed costs to be treated as fixed.

Separating mixed costs and specifying a relevant range for step costs allows accountants to treat their perceptions of the cost behaviours that occur in the relevant range as if they were fact. A variable cost is assumed to be perfectly linear and equal to the average variable unit cost within the relevant range, while a fixed cost is assumed to be constant in total within the relevant range. These treatments of variable and fixed costs are justified for two reasons. First, the assumed conditions approximate reality; if the company operates only within the relevant range of activity, the cost behaviours reflect the expected and actual cost patterns. Second, selection of a constant variable cost per unit and a constant fixed cost in total provides a convenient, stable measurement for use in planning and decision making.

All costs are treated by accountants as linear rather than curvilinear. Because of this treatment, the general formula for a straight line is used to describe any type of cost (variable, fixed, or mixed) within a relevant range of activity. The straight-line formula is:

$$y = a + bx$$

where

y = total cost

a = fixed portion of total cost

b = variable portion of total cost (the rate at which total cost changes in relation to changes in x; when a graph is prepared to depict the straight line, b represents the slope of the line)

x = activity base (or cost driver) to which y is being related

Exhibit 2-7 illustrates the use of the straight-line formula for each type of cost behaviour. An entirely variable cost is represented as $y = \$0 + bx$. Zero is shown as the value for a because there is no fixed cost. A purely fixed cost is formulated as $y = a + \$0x$. Zero is the b-term in the formula since no cost component varies with activity. A mixed cost has formula values for both the a and b unknowns.

Since mixed costs contain amounts for both values, mixed costs must be separated into their variable and fixed components before separate overhead rates (fixed and variable) can be calculated. The simplest method of separation is the **high–low method.**

High–Low Method

The high–low method is a cost estimation technique for separating a mixed cost into its variable and fixed components. The high–low method uses activity and cost information from an actual set of cost observations to calculate the variable and fixed cost estimates. The highest and lowest activity levels are selected from the data set if these two levels are within the relevant range. The reason for selecting the high and low activity levels rather than high and low costs is that the analysis is undertaken to estimate how costs change in relation to activity changes. Activities cause costs to change; costs do not cause activities to change.

LEARNING OBJECTIVE 5

How can mixed costs be analyzed using the high–low method and least-squares regression analysis? (Appendix 2A)

high–low method
a technique for separating mixed costs that uses actual observations of a total cost at the highest and lowest levels of activity and calculates the change in both activity and cost; the levels chosen must be within the relevant range

EXHIBIT 2-7

Uses of the Straight-Line Cost Formula

Variable Cost

To explain or predict a variable cost such as indirect materials when the cost per unit is $2:

$$y = \$0 + \$2x$$

where y = total indirect materials cost
x = number of units produced

Fixed Cost

To explain or predict a fixed cost such as building rent of $80,000 per year:

$$y = \$80,000 + \$0x$$

where y = total annual building rent

Mixed Cost

To explain or predict a mixed cost such as repairs and maintenance when the fixed element is $14,000 per year and the variable element is $0.60 per machine hour

$$y = \$14,000 + \$0.60x$$

where y = total annual repairs and maintenance cost
x = number of machine hours incurred

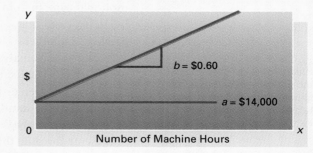

A nonrepresentative point that falls outside of the relevant range of activity or that is a distortion of normal costs within the relevant range is known as an **outlier**. These outliers should be disregarded when analyzing mixed costs under the high–low method.

The high–low method is used to develop an equation that predicts the unknown values of a dependent variable (*y*-term) from the known values of one or more independent variables (*x*-term). An **independent variable** is an amount that, when changed, will cause consistent, observable changes in another variable. A **dependent variable** is an unknown amount that can be predicted by the use of one or more independent variables.

Total mixed cost increases or decreases with changes in activity. The change in cost is equal to the change in activity multiplied by the unit variable cost; the fixed cost element does not fluctuate with changes in activity. The variable cost per unit of activity reflects the average change in cost for each additional unit of activity. Finding the changes in activity and cost simply involves subtracting the observation values of activity and cost at the lowest level of activity from the observation values of activity and cost at the highest level of activity. These differences are then used to calculate the *b*-term in the $y = a + bx$ formula as follows:

$$b = \frac{\text{Cost at Highest Activity Level} - \text{Cost at Lowest Activity Level}}{\text{Highest Activity Level} - \text{Lowest Activity Level}}$$

$$= \frac{\text{Change in the Total Cost}}{\text{Change in Activity Level}}$$

The *b*-term represents the unit variable cost per measure of activity. At either the lowest or the highest level of activity, the *b*-value can be multiplied by the activity level to determine the amount of total variable cost contained in the total mixed cost at either the highest or lowest level of activity.

Since a mixed cost has both a variable (*b*) and a fixed component (*a*), the latter is found by subtracting total variable cost from total cost: $y - bx = a$. Either the highest or the lowest level of activity can be used to determine the fixed portion of the mixed cost. Both activity levels are assumed to be on the same straight line and, thus, fixed cost would be constant at all activity levels within the relevant range.

The high–low method is illustrated in Exhibit 2-8 using assumed cups of coffee served and utility cost information for Riscky Rita's Restaurant. The restaurant's normal operating range of activity is between 8,000 and 11,600 cups of coffee per month. For Riscky Rita's Restaurant, the variable cost is $0.10 per cup of coffee and the fixed cost is $569 per month.

Note that the July data for Riscky Rita's Restaurant are outside the relevant range; this unusually high activity was analyzed and found to be caused by a promotional campaign in which Riscky Rita's gave cups of coffee to those who passed by, in order to make the community aware of a new brand of coffee that has just become available.

Regression analysis is another technique used to separate mixed costs into their variable and fixed cost elements. Regression (discussed in Appendix 2A) often results in a better estimate of the cost formula than does the high–low method. Performing it by hand is tedious; however, many software packages are available to do regression analysis. Regression analysis often results in a more reliable estimate of the cost formula than does the high–low method. Unlike the high–low method, this method uses all of the data points to calculate the cost formula.

Regardless of which method is used to separate mixed costs, it is important to recognize the following three points. First, high–low and regression are simply cost estimation techniques; neither provides exact costs of future activities. Second, the appropriateness of the cost formula depends on the validity of the activity measure chosen to predict the variable cost. The activity base selected should be logically related to the incurrence of overhead cost and should reflect significant correlation. (**Correlation** is a statistical measure of the strength of the relationship between two variables.) Third, when significant changes are occurring in a business (such as the introduction of new production techniques or new product lines or expansion into

correlation
a statistical measure of the strength of the relationship between two variables

---

EXHIBIT 2-8
High–Low Analysis of Utility Cost

The following information on cups of coffee and utility cost is available from the prior year:

Month	Level of Activity in Cups of Coffee	Utility Cost
January	11,300	$1,712
February	11,400	1,716
March	9,000	1,469
April	11,500	1,719
May	11,200	1,698
June	10,100	1,691
July	14,200	2,589

Step 1: Select the highest and lowest levels of activity within the relevant range and obtain the costs associated with those levels. These levels and costs are 11,500 and 9,000 cups of coffee and $1,719 and $1,469, respectively. (The July data is considered an outlier and thus is omitted from the analysis.)

Step 2: Calculate the change in activity level and the change in cost.

	Cups of Coffee	Associated Utility Cost
High activity (April)	11,500	$1,719
Low activity (March)	9,000	1,469
Changes	2,500	$ 250

Step 3: Determine the relationship of cost change to activity change to find the variable cost element.

$$b = \frac{\text{Change in total cost}}{\text{Change in activity level}} = \frac{\$250}{2,500} = \$0.10 \text{ per cup}$$

Step 4: Compute total variable cost (TVC) at either level of activity.

Highest level of activity: TVC = $0.10(11,500) = $1,150
or
Lowest level of activity: TVC = $0.10(9,000) = $900

Step 5: Subtract total variable cost from total cost at either level of activity to determine fixed cost.

Highest level of activity: $a = \$1,719 - \$1,150$
$= \$569$

Lowest level of activity: $a = \$1,469 - \$900$
$= \$569$

Step 6: Substitute the fixed and variable cost values in the straight-line formula to get an equation that can be used to estimate total cost at any level of activity within the relevant range.

$y = \$569 + \$0.10x$ (where x = number of cups of coffee)

new locales), historical information may not be very useful in attempting to predict future costs.

As has been discussed earlier, overhead costs are essential to the conversion process but simply cannot be traced directly to output. Overhead is any manufacturing or production cost that is indirect to manufacturing a product or providing a service and, accordingly, does not include direct material and direct labour. It does include indirect material and indirect labour as well as any and all other costs incurred in the production area. The greater part of most companies' costs (other than those for purchased materials) typically occurs in overhead categories. Even in manufacturing, more than two-thirds of all nonmaterial costs tend to be indirect or overhead expenses.

Overhead

Direct material and direct labour are easily traced to a product or service. Overhead, on the other hand, cannot be directly traced to products and must be allocated to the products manufactured or services rendered during that time.

LEARNING OBJECTIVE 6

How are predetermined overhead rates developed and how does the selection of a capacity measure affect overhead application?

DEVELOPING AND USING PREDETERMINED OVERHEAD RATES

The amount of overhead for a year is not known with certainty until the end of the year, when all of the invoices have been received. Businesses cannot wait until year-end to find out the amount of overhead to charge to the products that are currently being produced. Companies calculate a predetermined overhead rate which they use to calculate the cost of goods produced.

To illustrate the setting of predetermined overhead rates, an analysis of the hypothetical past data for the individual overhead costs for Red River Barbeque (a fictitious company intended to be similar to Riscky's Barbeque) will be used. The data for 2004 has generated the information shown in Exhibit 2-9. This information is used to illustrate the calculation of the predetermined overhead rates. The company's activity base is kilograms of barbecue smoked. Its contemplated range of activity for the upcoming year is between 1,000,000 and 1,500,000 kilograms of barbecue.

All cost factors are presented in terms of the a (fixed) and b (variable) values of the straight-line formula. Note that the information in Exhibit 2-9 indicates that both supervision and equipment maintenance contract costs increase at an activity level of 1,400,000 kilograms of barbecue. These costs are said to be step-fixed or long-term variable costs.

Variable Overhead Rate

Variable overhead (VOH) changes proportionately in total with some measure of volume or activity. A **predetermined overhead rate** should be computed for each variable overhead cost pool. The information needed for these computations can be taken from any level of activity that is within the relevant range. The total cost for each cost pool is then divided by the level of activity on which the estimate was based to determine a per unit cost of the activity. Variable manufacturing overhead is applied to production using the result of multiplying the related activity base by the cost per unit of the activity.

Since VOH is constant per unit at all activity levels within the relevant range, the activity level chosen for estimating total variable cost is unimportant. Red River

predetermined overhead rate
a budgeted constant charge per unit of activity used to assign overhead costs to production or services

The formulas are based on kilograms of barbecue smoked as the independent variable (x).

	a = Fixed Cost	b = Variable Cost
Purely Variable Costs		
Indirect materials		$0.11
Indirect labour:		
Support workers		0.07
Idle time		0.02
Fringe benefits		0.03
Total variable cost per kilogram		$0.23
Purely Fixed Costs		
Supervision[1]	$ 90,000	
Depreciation	100,000	
Maintenance contract[2]	30,000	
Insurance	4,256	
Total fixed cost	$224,256	
Mixed Costs		
Utilities[3]	6,832	0.01
Total costs for x < 1,400,000 kilograms	$231,088	$0.24

[1]Supervision is expected to be $120,000 when $x \geq$ 1,400,000 kilograms.
[2]Equipment maintenance contract will increase to $36,000 when x $\geq$ 1,400,000 kilograms.
[3]Utilities are a mixed cost—partially variable and partially fixed. Thus, the variable portion of utilities will be shown in the listing of variable costs and the fixed amount in the listing of fixed costs.

EXHIBIT 2-9

Red River Barbeque
Analysis of Overhead Costs

Barbeque estimates $121,000 of indirect materials cost for 1,100,000 kilograms of barbecue. This is based on the predetermined variable overhead rate for indirect materials of $0.11 per kilogram. Correspondingly, if the indirect materials cost is truly variable, the company would estimate a total cost of $154,000 for 1,400,000 kilograms (1,400,000 × $0.11).

The activity measure selected to apply overhead to production should provide a logical relationship between the measure and the overhead cost incurrence. The activity measure that generally first comes to mind is production volume. However, unless a company makes only one type of output (such as Red River Barbeque), production volume is not really a feasible activity measure for any overhead cost. If multiple products or services are produced, overhead costs are incurred because of numerous factors, including the differing nature of the items, product variety, and product complexity.

The concept of homogeneity (uniform common attribute of all items included in a set) underlies all cost allocation. Some measure of activity that is common to all costs in a given cost pool must be used to allocate overhead to heterogeneous (unlike) products. The most frequently used volume-based allocation measures include direct labour hours, direct labour dollars, machine hours, production orders, and production-related physical measures such as kilograms and litres. In addition, companies often use only a single total overhead cost pool or two overhead cost pools (total variable and total fixed). Alternatively, some companies apply overhead to products separately in each department and develop predetermined departmental overhead rates for this purpose.

As technology and the manufacturing environment change, companies must recognize that they may need to change their cost information systems. Using a less-than-appropriate allocation base and a minimal number of cost pools can result in poor managerial information. The failure of traditional labour-based allocation systems, with a small number of cost pools, to assign costs accurately is becoming more apparent as companies automate, increase the number and variety of product lines, and incur higher overhead costs than ever before.

A new production environment is emerging in which innovative manufacturing methods—based on computer-driven, automated machinery and information technology—are changing a number of accounting practices. For example, using direct labour to allocate overhead costs in highly automated plants results in extremely large overhead rates because the costs are applied over an ever-decreasing number of labour hours (or dollars). When automated plants allocate overhead on the basis of direct labour, managers are frequently concerned about the high rates per labour-hour. On occasion, some managers have concluded that the way to reduce overhead is to reduce labour. This conclusion is erroneous. The overhead charge is high because labour is low; further reducing labour will simply increase the overhead rate. This is because a reduction in labour hours means that the denominator is lower, however the numerator remains the same. In situations where there is a mixture of lower-paid labourers and highly skilled labourers who are paid high hourly rates, direct labour cost is the best base to use.

If only a single type of activity base is to be used for overhead allocations in highly automated plants, machine hours are a more appropriate base than either direct labour hours or direct labour dollars. However, machine hours and overhead costs should be accumulated by machine type to develop a predetermined overhead rate per machine. In this way, overhead can be assigned in a cause-and-effect manner to products as they move through the various machine processes.

Many companies are looking at multiple cost pools and new activity measures for overhead allocation, including number or time of machine setups, number of different parts, material handling time, and quantity of product defects.[13] But regardless of how many cost pools are created or which activity base is chosen, the method of overhead application is the same. In a typical cost system, overhead is assigned to Work in Process Inventory, using the predetermined rate multiplied by the actual quantity of the activity base. For simplicity, at this time, separate cost pools for variable and fixed overhead will be assumed, as will a single activity measure for allocating each.

The 2005 predetermined rate for Red River Barbeque is computed on the basis of variable overhead costs and the planned production volume for 2005. At Red River Barbeque, the estimated production volume (kilograms of barbecue smoked) for 2005 is set at 1,372,800 kilograms. At that level of activity, it is estimated that the variable overhead cost will amount to $329,472. Dividing this cost estimate by the production volume estimate gives the predetermined variable overhead rate of $0.24 per kilogram, as follows:

$$\text{Predetermined VOH rate} = \text{Estimated VOH cost} \div \text{Estimated output in kilograms}$$
$$= \$329,472 \div 1,372,800$$
$$= \$0.24$$

Based on this estimate of production, overhead will be assigned to the Work in Process Inventory account as production occurs in fiscal 2005.

The computation produces the necessary information for product costing purposes, but it does not provide the detail needed by managers to plan or control each of the individual variable overhead costs. For these purposes, managers need individual costs per type of activity resource consumption, as shown in Exhibit 2-10.

Estimated indirect materials	$151,008 ÷ 1,372,800 =	0.11
Estimated indirect labour		
Support workers	$ 96,096 ÷ 1,372,800 =	0.07
Idle time	$ 27,456 ÷ 1,372,800 =	0.02
Fringe benefits	$ 41,184 ÷ 1,372,800 =	0.03
Estimated utilities	$ 13,728 ÷ 1,372,800 =	0.01
Total variable manufacturing overhead rate		$0.24

* based on 1,372,800 kg

EXHIBIT 2-10

Detailed Predetermined Variable Overhead Rate Calculation*
(Total Estimated Variable Overhead = $329,472)

This information allows the actual and the estimated costs of each type to be compared. Any significant variations from the estimated amounts can be investigated and their causes determined.

Remember that predetermined overhead rates are always calculated in advance of the year of application. So the 2005 rate for Red River Barbeque was computed in 2004, on the basis of estimated variable overhead costs and production volume for 2005. Some companies use two separate accounts to record overhead while others use only a single account. If actual and applied accounts are separated, the applied account is a contra account to the actual overhead account and is closed against it at year-end. The alternative is to maintain one general ledger account that is debited for actual overhead costs and credited for applied overhead. This method is used throughout the text.

Manufacturing overhead may be recorded in a single overhead account or in separate accounts for the variable and fixed components. If separate rates are used to apply variable and fixed overhead, the general ledger would most commonly contain separate variable and fixed overhead accounts. When separate accounts are used, mixed costs must be separated into their variable and fixed components or assigned to either the variable or fixed overhead general ledger account. More and more companies are automating, thus overhead costs represent a larger part of product cost. As a result of this there is great benefit to separating overhead costs according to their behaviour. Benefits of these separations are thought to be greater than the time and effort expended to make the separation.

Fixed Overhead Rate

Fixed manufacturing overhead (FOH) is that portion of total overhead that remains constant in total with changes in activity within the relevant range. For product costing purposes, all fixed manufacturing overhead costs must be estimated and assigned to appropriate cost pools to calculate the numerator of the predetermined fixed manufacturing overhead rate. Exhibit 2-11 shows the predetermined fixed overhead rate for 1,372,800 kilograms of barbecue.

Since fixed overhead is constant in total, it varies inversely on a per-unit basis with changes in activity. Therefore, a different unit cost is associated with each different level of activity. For this reason, calculating the predetermined FOH rate per unit requires that a specific activity level be chosen for the denominator. The level of activity selected is usually the firm's expected activity. **Expected annual capacity** is a short-run concept representing the anticipated level of activity of the firm for the upcoming year. If actual results are close to expected results (in both dollars and volume), this measure of **capacity** (either according to production volume or

expected annual capacity
a short-run concept representing the anticipated level of activity for the upcoming year

capacity
a measure of production volume or of some other cost driver related to plant production capability during a period

Supervision	$ 90,000
Depreciation	100,000
Maintenance contract	30,000
Insurance	4,256
Utilities	6,832
Total fixed costs	$231,088
Fixed cost on a per kilogram basis ($231,088 ÷ 1,372,800)*	$ 0.17

*rounded

ideal capacity
see *theoretical capacity*

theoretical capacity
the estimated absolute maximum
potential production activity that
could occur in a production facility
during a specific time frame

practical capacity
the activity level that could be
achieved during normal working
hours given unused capacity and
ongoing, regular operating interruptions, such as holidays, downtime,
and start-up time

normal capacity
a firm's long-run average activity
(over five to ten years), which gives
effect to historical and estimated
future production levels and to
cyclical and seasonal fluctuations

volume of some other specified cost driver) should result in product costs that most closely reflect actual costs. Except where otherwise indicated throughout the text, the expected annual capacity level has been chosen as the level at which to calculate the predetermined fixed manufacturing overhead rate because it is believed to be the most prevalent practice.[14]

Companies may choose to use an activity level other than expected annual capacity to compute their predetermined fixed overhead rates. Alternative measurement bases include **ideal** or **theoretical capacity**, **practical capacity**, and **normal capacity**.

The estimated maximum productive activity that could occur in an organization during a specified time frame is the ideal or theoretical capacity. This measure assumes that all production factors are maximum and operating perfectly; as such, it disregards realities such as machinery breakdowns and reduced or halted plant operation on holidays.

Reducing theoretical capacity by factors such as unused resources and ongoing, regular operating interruptions (such as holidays, downtime, and start-up time) provides the practical capacity that could be efficiently achieved during normal working hours.

Sometimes managers wish to consider historical and estimated future production levels as well as cyclical and seasonal fluctuations in the computation of a predetermined fixed overhead rate. In such an instance, a normal capacity measure that encompasses the long-run (five to ten years) average activity of the firm may be used. This measurement represents a reasonably attainable level of activity, but does not provide estimates that are most similar to actual historical costs. Distortions of cost could arise if activity levels varied significantly within the long-run period.

Practical capacity should be used as the relevant capacity level because it reveals the cost of unused resources. The concept of unused resources makes a distinction between the cost of resources available for manufacturing and the cost of resources actually used for that purpose. It highlights the fact that some capacity is idle.

By using the practical capacity available in determining the fixed (overhead) rate, the cost of each unit produced contains only the cost of the resource used and, unlike the cost computed (expected activity), does not include the cost of unused resources. Hence, each identical item of production is assigned the same cost, regardless of the number of such items produced or the number of changes in the product mix.[15]

The fixed overhead costs for Red River Barbeque were given in Exhibit 2-11. In that exhibit, the cost per kilogram was calculated; however, because Red River Barbeque is highly automated, the company's accountant has determined that fixed costs are more appropriately related to barbecue smoking hours (BSH) than to production volume (kilograms). In one hour, 12 kilograms of barbecue can be smoked. Therefore, to produce the estimated 1,372,800 kilograms of barbecue during 2005 will require 114,400 BSH (1,372,800 kilograms ÷ 12 kilograms per hour). Based on these figures, the predetermined fixed overhead rate is calculated as $2.02 per BSH:

FOH costs for 2005 ÷ BSH to produce 1,372,800 kilograms of barbecue
$$= \$231,088^* \div 114,400$$
$$= \$2.02 \text{ per BSH}$$

*From Exhibit 2–11

OVERHEAD APPLICATION

Once the predetermined variable and fixed manufacturing overhead rates have been calculated, they are used throughout the year to apply (or assign) overhead to Work in Process Inventory. Production overhead (both variable and fixed) is assigned to goods being transferred from one processing department to another or as goods are transferred to Finished Goods Inventory so that a complete product cost can be obtained. Additionally, overhead must be applied at the end of each period so that the Work in Process Inventory account contains costs for all three product elements (direct materials, direct labour, and manufacturing overhead).

Applied overhead is the amount of manufacturing overhead assigned to Work in Process Inventory as a result of the occurrence of the activity that was used to develop the application rate. Application is based on the predetermined overhead rates and the actual level of activity. For example, assume that during January 2005, Red River Barbeque produces 108,000 kilograms of barbecue and its smoking equipment operates for 9,100 hours. The previously calculated rates of $0.24 for variable manufacturing overhead and $2.02 for fixed manufacturing overhead result in the following applications to Work in Process Inventory: $25,920 of variable production overhead (108,000 kilograms × $0.24 per kilogram) and $18,382 of fixed production overhead (9,100 BSH × $2.02 per BSH). The journal entry to record the application of overhead is:

applied overhead
the amount of overhead assigned to Work in Process Inventory as a result of the occurrence of the activity that was used to develop the application rate; the result of multiplying the quantity of actual activity by the predetermined rate

Work in Process Inventory	44,302	
Variable Manufacturing Overhead ($0.24 × 108,000 kg)		25,920
Fixed Manufacturing Overhead ($2.02 × 9,100 BSH)		18,382
To apply manufacturing overhead to production in January.		

Underapplied and Overapplied Manufacturing Overhead

Although companies may be able to estimate future overhead costs and expected activity with some degree of accuracy, it simply is not humanly possible to project future events precisely. Thus, actual overhead incurred during the period probably never equals applied overhead. The difference between the two amounts represents *underapplied* or *overapplied* overhead.

Variable or Fixed Manufacturing Overhead	
Actual Overhead costs	Applied Overhead costs

If the ending balance in the above account is a debit, then the overhead is **under-applied**, which means that the amount of overhead applied to Work in Process

underapplied overhead
overhead applied to Work in Process Inventory that is less than actual overhead incurred for a period

overapplied overhead
overhead applied to Work in Process Inventory that is greater than actual overhead incurred for a period

Inventory is less than the actual overhead incurred. If the ending balance is a credit, then the overhead is **overapplied**, which means that the amount of overhead applied to Work in Process Inventory is greater than the actual overhead incurred.

It is important to note that the incurrence of actual manufacturing overhead costs does not affect the process of overhead application. Actual manufacturing overhead costs may be recorded in the accounts on a daily, weekly, or monthly basis. Those overhead costs are created because activity takes place in the production area of the company. The application of predetermined overhead is based on the predetermined overhead rate multiplied by the actual quantity of the cost driver. Thus, applied overhead is the amount of overhead assigned to Work in Process Inventory as a result of incurring the activity that was used to develop the application rate.

The manufacturing overhead accounts used for recording actual and applied overhead amounts are temporary accounts. Any balances in these accounts must be closed at year-end because the amounts belong to the period in which overhead was incurred.

LEARNING OBJECTIVE   7

How is underapplied or overapplied overhead accounted for at year-end and why are these accounting techniques appropriate?

Disposition of Underapplied and Overapplied Overhead

In a typical costing system, actual overhead costs are debited to the variable and fixed overhead general ledger accounts and credited to the various sources of overhead costs. (These entries are presented in a subsequent section of this chapter.) Applied overhead is debited to Work in Process Inventory using the predetermined rates and actual levels of activity, and credited to the variable and fixed overhead general ledger accounts. Applied overhead is added to actual direct materials and direct labour costs in the computation of cost of goods manufactured. The end-of-period balance in each overhead general ledger account represents underapplied (debit) or overapplied (credit) overhead.

Variable or Fixed Manufacturing Overhead		Work in Process Inventory		
Actual OH costs	Applied OH costs	DM	✓✓✓	
XXX*	YYY	DL	✓✓✓	
		Applied OH costs	YYY	

*Offsetting these debits are credits to various sources of overhead costs, such as Accumulated Depreciation, Accounts Payable, Supplies Inventory, and Wages Payable.

Disposition of underapplied or overapplied overhead depends on the materiality (significance) of the amount involved. If the amount of the variance is immaterial (small), it is closed to Cost of Goods Sold in a manufacturing firm or to Cost of Services Rendered in a service firm. When underapplied overhead is closed (debit balance), it causes Cost of Goods Sold (or Cost of Services Rendered) to increase since not enough overhead was applied to production during the year. Alternatively, closing overapplied overhead (credit balance) causes Cost of Goods Sold (or Cost of Services Rendered) to decrease because too much overhead was applied to production during the year. The journal entry to close an immaterial (small) amount of overapplied variable overhead is:

Variable Manufacturing Overhead	xxxx	
Cost of Goods Sold		xxxx
To close overapplied variable manufacturing overhead		
to cost of goods sold.		

If the amount of underapplied or overapplied overhead is significant (large), it should be allocated among the accounts containing applied overhead (Work in Process Inventory, Finished Goods Inventory, and Cost of Goods Sold or Cost of Services Rendered). Allocation to the accounts is based on the relative ending account balances. A significant amount of underapplied or overapplied overhead means that the balances in these accounts are quite different from what they would have been had actual overhead costs been assigned to production. The underapplied or overapplied amount is allocated among the affected accounts so that their balances conform more closely to actual costs as required for external reporting by generally accepted accounting principles.

Exhibit 2-12 uses year-end hypothetical amounts for Red River Barbeque to illustrate the technique of prorating overapplied variable overhead among the necessary accounts. Had the amount been underapplied, the accounts debited and credited in the journal entry would have been reversed. The calculation would be the same if the overhead were fixed rather than variable.

If predetermined overhead rates are based on valid cost drivers, those rates provide a rational and systematic way for accountants to assign overhead costs to products for external financial statement preparation. Separate cost pools as well as separate variable and fixed overhead rates should be used to obtain the most

LEARNING OBJECTIVE 8

Why are separate predetermined overhead rates generally more useful than combined rates?

EXHIBIT 2-12

Prorating Overapplied Variable Overhead at 2006 Year-End

Variable Manufacturing Overhead Balance

Actual manufacturing overhead incurred	$73,400
Applied variable manufacturing overhead	94,400
Overapplied variable manufacturing overhead	$21,000

Variable Manufacturing Overhead

Actual	73,400	Applied	94,400
		Balance	21,000

Steps to Follow:

1. Calculate the ratio of the balances of each of the affected accounts to their total amount.

Account	Account Balance	Proportion	Percentage
Work in Process Inventory	$ 58,500	$ 58,500 ÷ $390,000	15%
Finished Goods Inventory	97,500	$ 97,500 ÷ $390,000	25%
Cost of Goods Sold	234,000	$234,000 ÷ $390,000	60%
Total	$390,000		100%

2. Multiply the overapplied variable manufacturing overhead amount by the percentages to determine the amount of the adjustment needed for each of the affected accounts.

Account	Percentage	×	Overapplied VOH	=	Adjustment
Work in Process Inventory	15%	×	$21,000	=	$3,150
Finished Goods Inventory	25%	×	$21,000	=	5,250
Cost of Goods Sold	60%	×	$21,000	=	12,600
	100%				$21,000

3. Prepare the journal entry to close the variable manufacturing overhead account and assign the adjustment amount to appropriate accounts:

Variable Manufacturing Overhead	21,000	
Work in Process Inventory		3,150
Finished Goods Inventory		5,250
Cost of Goods Sold		12,600
To prorate overapplied variable manufacturing overhead.		

refined information for planning, controlling, and decision making. In spite of this fact, some companies may (and commonly do) choose to use combined overhead rates rather than separate ones for variable and fixed overhead.

COMBINED OVERHEAD RATES

Combined overhead rates are traditionally used in businesses for three reasons: clerical ease, clerical cost savings, and absence of any formal requirement to separate overhead costs by cost behaviour. The process of computing a combined predetermined overhead rate is essentially the same as that of computing separate rates. The difference is that only one type of activity can be selected for the cost pool (rather than different activities for the variable and fixed components as was shown for Red River Barbeque). Once the activity base is chosen, management specifies the level of activity at which costs are to be estimated. Variable and fixed costs are computed for that activity using the appropriate cost formulas, and the costs are totalled and divided by the activity level to yield a single overhead application rate.

Assume that Red River Barbeque decides to use a combined predetermined manufacturing overhead rate based on expected production volume rather than on barbecue smoking hours. With the previously specified 1,372,800 kilograms of barbecue as its expected activity level, the company's combined predetermined overhead rate is calculated as follows:

Total estimated VOH at 1,372,800 kilograms of barbecue (from Exhibit 2-10)	$ 329,472
Total estimated FOH (from Exhibit 2-11)	231,088
Total estimated overhead cost	$ 560,560
Divided by expected activity in kilograms of barbecue	÷1,372,800
Predetermined overhead rate per kilogram (rounded)*	$ 0.41

*Rounded from ($0.40833). Note that the single rate is equal to the sum of the variable and fixed rates ($0.24 + $0.17).

For each kilogram of barbecue produced by Red River Barbeque in 2005, the company's Work in Process Inventory account will be charged with $0.41 of overhead. If Red River Barbeque produces 108,000 kilograms of barbecue in January, the journal entry to record $44,280 (108,000 × $0.41) of overhead that would be added to the Work in Process Inventory account would be:

Work in Process Inventory	44,280	
Manufacturing Overhead		44,280
To apply January overhead to production.		

Although the use of a combined overhead rate achieves the necessary function of assigning overhead costs to production, it reduces a manager's ability to determine the causes of underapplied or overapplied overhead. Exhibit 2-13 provides an example in which the overapplied overhead is solely related to fixed costs—a fact not observable from the combined rate.

When companies use a single overhead application rate, the rate can be related to a particular cost pool (such as machine-related overhead) or to overhead costs in general. As more cost pools are combined, the underlying cause–effect relationships between activities and costs are blurred. This factor may contribute to an inability to reduce costs, improve productivity, or discover the causes of underapplied or overapplied overhead. The lack of detailed information hinders man-

EXHIBIT 2-13

Use of a Single Predetermined Manufacturing OH Rate

| Actual 2006 production volume | 1,378,800 |
| Actual 2006 barbecue smoking hours | 114,900 |

Assume that actual 2006 manufacturing overhead costs were exactly as estimated by Red River Barbeque.

Variable ($0.24 per kilogram × 1,378,800)	$330,912
Fixed (From Exhibit 2-9)	231,088
Total actual overhead	$562,000

Applied 2006 manufacturing overhead using a single rate:

1,378,800 kilograms × $0.40833* per kilogram = $563,005

Actual OH − Applied OH = $562,000 − $563,005 = $1,005 overapplied overhead

Compare the above to that below where separate predetermined overhead rates are used for the same production level:

Variable (1,378,800 kilograms × $0.24 each)	$330,912	(same as actual)
Fixed (114,900 BSH** × $2.02 per BSH)	232,098	($1,010*** greater than actual)
Total	$563,010	

*Presented earlier as a rounded number ($0.41)

** BSH stands for barbecue smoking hour

***Difference due to rounding

agers' abilities to plan operations, control costs, and make decisions. Thus, although some clerical cost savings may be achieved, the ultimate costs of poor information are probably significantly greater than the savings generated.

Using separate departmental and cost pool activity bases is superior to using a combined plantwide base. Since most companies produce a wide variety of products or perform a wide variety of services, different activity measures should be used to calculate overhead rates for different departments and for different types of overhead costs. Machine hours may be the most appropriate activity base for many costs in a department that is highly automated. Direct labour hours may be the best basis for assigning the majority of overhead costs in a labour-intensive department. In the quality control area, the number of defects may provide the best allocation base. Using separate bases for overhead computations allows management to accumulate and apply costs for distinct homogeneous groups of activities. Separate rates will provide better information for planning, control, performance evaluation, and decision making.

ACCUMULATION OF PRODUCT COSTS

Product costs are accumulated for inventory purposes and expensed to Cost of Goods Sold. All product costs flow through Work in Process Inventory to Finished Goods Inventory and, ultimately, to Cost of Goods Sold. The perpetual inventory control system continuously provides current inventory and cost of goods sold information for financial statement preparation and for inventory planning, cost control, and decision making. The costs of maintaining a perpetual inventory system have fallen significantly as computerized production, bar coding, and information processing have become more pervasive. This text will assume that all companies discussed use the perpetual inventory method.

The following hypothetical information for Red River Barbeque is used to illustrate the flow of product costs in a manufacturing organization. The June 1, 2006, inventory account balances for the company are as follows: Raw Materials (all direct), $2,500; Work in Process, $6,000; and Finished Goods, $9,000. The company uses separate variable and fixed accounts to record the incurrence of manufacturing overhead. Such separation of information improves the accuracy of tracking and controlling costs. Manufacturing overhead costs are transferred at the end of the month to the Work in Process Inventory account. The following transactions, keyed to the journal entries in Exhibit 2-14, represent Red River Barbeque's activity for the month of June.

During June, Red River Barbeque's purchasing agent bought $85,000 of raw materials on account (entry 1), and $81,600 of materials was transferred into the production area; of these, $69,000 represented direct materials and $12,600 represented indirect materials (entry 2). Production wages for the month totalled $18,800; direct labour accounted for $5,000 of that amount (entry 3). The June salaries for production supervisors were $7,500 (entry 4). The total utility cost for June was $1,870; analyzing this cost indicated that $1,200 of this amount was variable and $670 was fixed (entry 5). Contract maintenance of $2,692 was paid (entry 6). Red River also recorded depreciation on the manufacturing assets of $8,333 (entry 7), and recorded the expiration of $355 of prepaid insurance on the manufacturing assets (entry 8). Red River recorded applied manufacturing overhead of $46,600; of that amount, variable manufacturing overhead was $27,600 (entry 9). During June, $122,150 of goods were completed and transferred to Finished Goods Inventory (entry 10). Items that were sold during the month of June are transferred from Finished Goods Inventory. The cost of these items amounted to $120,150. (entry 11) to Cost of Goods Sold. Sales on account in the amount of $242,000 were recorded during the month (entry 12); Underapplied overhead was closed to Cost of Goods Sold (entry 13).

As illustrated in the T-accounts in Exhibit 2-15, the perpetual inventory system provides detailed information about the cost of raw materials used, goods completed, and goods sold. From this information, financial statements can be prepared.

<table>
<tr><td>**LEARNING OBJECTIVE   9**</td></tr>
</table>

How is cost of goods manufactured calculated? Cost of goods sold?

cost of goods manufactured
the total manufacturing costs attached to units produced during an accounting period

cost of goods manufactured statement
the total cost of the goods that were completed and transferred to Finished Goods Inventory during the period

COST OF GOODS MANUFACTURED AND SOLD

In merchandising businesses, cost of goods sold (CGS) is presented as the beginning merchandise inventory plus purchases minus ending merchandise inventory. Manufacturing businesses cannot use such a simplistic approach to calculate cost of goods sold. The production costs incurred during the period relate both to goods that were completed and to goods that are still in process. **Cost of goods manufactured (CGM)** represents the total production cost of the goods that were completed and transferred to Finished Goods Inventory during the period. A manufacturer prepares a **cost of goods manufactured statement** as a preliminary step to the presentation of cost of goods sold. This amount does not include the cost of work still in process at the end of the period. The cost of goods manufactured statement allows managers to see the relationships among the various production costs and to know the results of the cost flows through the inventory accounts. It is prepared only as an internal statement and is not provided to external parties.

Using the information from Exhibit 2-15, a cost of goods manufactured statement is presented in Exhibit 2-16 and a cost of goods sold schedule is presented in Exhibit 2-17 on page 61. The cost of goods manufactured statement reflects the manufacturing activity as summarized in the Work in Process Inventory (WIP) account. The statement starts with the calculation of the cost of raw materials used in the production process during the period. This figure is calculated as beginning raw materials inventory plus raw materials purchased during the period minus the ending balance of raw materials inventory. Direct labour cost is determined from payroll records of the period and is added to the cost of direct materials used. Variable and fixed overhead are added to the prime costs of direct materials used and direct labour incurred to arrive at the total current period manufacturing costs.

EXHIBIT 2-14

Flow of Product Costs Through the Accounts

(1) Raw Materials Inventory	85,000	
Accounts Payable		85,000
To record cost of raw materials purchased on account.		
(2) Work in Process Inventory	69,000	
Variable Manufacturing Overhead	12,600	
Raw Materials Inventory		81,600
To record transfer of direct and indirect materials.		
(3) Work in Process Inventory	5,000	
Variable Manufacturing Overhead	13,800	
Salaries and Wages Payable		18,800
To accrue manufacturing wages for direct and indirect labour.		
(4) Fixed Manufacturing Overhead	7,500	
Salaries and Wages Payable		7,500
To accrue production supervisors' salaries.		
(5) Variable Manufacturing Overhead	1,200	
Fixed Manufacturing Overhead	670	
Utilities Payable		1,870
To record mixed manufacturing utility cost in its variable and fixed proportions.		
(6) Fixed Manufacturing Overhead	2,692	
Cash		2,692
To record payments for contract maintenance for the period.		
(7) Fixed Manufacturing Overhead	8,333	
Accumulated Depreciation = Manufacturing Equipment		8,333
To record depreciation on manufacturing assets for the period.		
(8) Fixed Manufacturing Overhead	355	
Prepaid Manufacturing Insurance		355
To record expiration of prepaid insurance on manufacturing assets.		
(9) Work in Process Inventory	46,600	
Variable Manufacturing Overhead		27,600
Fixed Manufacturing Overhead		19,000
To record the transfer of predetermined fixed and variable overhead costs to Work in Process Inventory.		
(10) Finished Goods Inventory	122,150	
Work in Process Inventory		122,150
To record the transfer of work completed during the period.		
(11) Cost of Goods Sold	120,150	
Finished Goods Inventory		120,150
To record cost of goods sold for the period.		
(12) Accounts Receivable	242,000	
Sales		242,000
To record the sale of goods on account during the period.		
(13) Cost of Goods Sold	550	
Fixed Manufacturing Overhead		550
To close underapplied fixed manufacturing overhead to cost of goods sold.		

EXHIBIT 2-15

Cost Flow Overview—
T Accounts

Raw Materials Inventory

Beginning balance	2,500	Raw material	(2)	81,600
Purchase	(1) 85,000			
	87,500			
Ending balance	5,900			

Salaries and Wages Payable

	Direct & indirect	(3)	18,800
	Supervisors	(4)	7,500

Variable Manufacturing Overhead

Indirect material	(2)	12,600	Applied variable	(9)	27,600
Indirect labour	(3)	13,800			
Variable utilities	(5)	1,200			
		27,600			

Fixed Manufacturing Overhead

Supervisor salaries	(4)	7,500	Applied fixed	(9)	19,000
Fixed utilities	(5)	670			
Fixed maintenance	(6)	2,692	Close		
Depreciation	(7)	8,333	underapplied		
Insurance	(8)	355	fixed overhead	(13)	550
		19,550			19,550

Accounts Payable

	Purchase	(1)	85,000

Utilities Payable

	Variable and		
	fixed overhead	(5)	1,870

Accounts Receivable

Credit Sales	(12) 242,000		

Accumulated Depreciation—Manufacturing Equipment

	Depreciation	(7)	8,333

Work in Process Inventory

Beginning balance	6,000	Complete	(10) 122,150
Direct material	(2) 69,000			
Direct labour	(3) 5,000			
Applied overhead				
(variable and				
fixed)	(9) 46,600			
	126,600			
Ending balance	4,450			

Finished Goods Inventory

Beginning balance	9,000	Sold	(11) 120,150
Complete	(10) 122,150		
	131,150		
Ending balance	11,000		

Cost of Goods Sold

Sold	(11) 120,150		
Close			
underapplied			
fixed overhead	(13)	550	
	120,700		

Sales

	Sold	(12) 242,000	

Prepaid Factory Insurance

	Expired		
	insurance	(8)	355

Cash

	Maintenance	(6)	2,692

Adding the beginning Work in Process Inventory cost to total current period manufacturing costs provides a subtotal amount that is referred to as "total costs to account for." The value of ending Work in Process Inventory is subtracted from this subtotal to provide the Cost of Goods Manufactured during the period.

To calculate the Cost of Goods Sold, the Cost of Goods Manufactured (CGM) is added to the beginning balance of Finished Goods (FG) Inventory to determine the cost of goods available for sale during the period. The ending Finished Goods Inventory is then deducted from the cost of goods available for sale during the period to arrive at the **cost of goods sold**. (The cost of goods sold amount may need to be adjusted by any under/overapplied overhead as is shown in this case.) In a perpetual inventory system, the actual amount of ending Finished Goods Inventory, which is arrived at by taking a physical inventory, can be compared to the amount that is listed in the finished goods inventory account at the end of the period. Any differences can be attributed to losses that might have arisen from theft, breakage, evaporation, or accounting errors. Major differences between the amount of inventory shown in the accounting records and the actual amount of inventory on hand should be investigated.

cost of goods sold
the cost of the products or services sold during the period

Red River Barbeque
Cost of Goods Manufactured Statement
For Month Ended June 30, 2005

Manufacturing costs for the period:		
Raw Materials Used:		
Beginning raw materials balance	$2,500	
Plus: Purchases of raw materials	85,000	
Raw materials available for use	$87,500	
Less: Ending raw materials balance	5,900	
Total raw materials used	$81,600	
Less: Indirect materials	12,600	
Total direct materials used		$ 69,000
Direct Labour		5,000
Variable manufacturing overhead applied		27,600
Fixed manufacturing overhead applied		19,000
Total current period manufacturing costs		120,600
Plus: Beginning work in process inventory, June 1, 2005		6,000
Total costs to account for		$126,600
Less: Ending work in process inventory, June 30, 2005		4,450
Cost of goods manufactured		$122,150

EXHIBIT 2-16

Cost of Goods Manufactured Statement

Red River Barbeque
Schedule of Cost of Goods Sold
For Month Ended June 30, 2005

Beginning Balance of Finished Goods Inventory, June 1, 2005	$ 9,000
Plus: Cost of Goods Manufactured	122,150
Cost of Goods Available for Sale	$131,150
Less: Ending Balance of Finished Goods Inventory, June 30, 2005	11,000
Cost of Goods Sold	$120,150
Plus: Underapplied Fixed Overhead	550
Cost of Goods Sold	$120,700

EXHIBIT 2-17

Schedule of Cost of Goods Sold

Riscky's Barbeque

With his "gimme" hat pulled down, shirttail flapping, and grease on his jeans from crawling under a piece of restaurant equipment, Jim Riscky doesn't look much like a CEO. But his willingness to understand and tinker with every detail of his varied enterprises is the secret to the success of Riscky's Barbeque.

To maintain profitability in his restaurants, Jim Riscky must understand what his costs are and how they will behave under alternative conditions. By purchasing meat in large quantities, he can control a significant direct material cost. Less control can be maintained over the cost of direct labour because of the minimum wage rate. Overhead costs are controlled through the use of the centralized commissary and, additionally, through relatively low-cost, but high-traffic, restaurant locations.

Riscky's business philosophy is easy: "The best way to see if something works is to try it—to not be afraid to change things. Some people may find it hard to operate that way, but I find it's usually cheaper to try something and carefully watch it in operation than to spend a lot of time planning. To me, time is money and the worrying before implementation just seems excessively costly."

Source: Interview with Jim Riscky. Reprinted by permission of Riscky's Barbeque.

APPENDIX 2A

Least-Squares Regression Analysis

How can mixed costs be analyzed using the high–low method and least-squares regression analysis?

least-squares regression analysis a statistical technique for mathematically determining the cost line of a mixed cost that best fits the data set by considering all representative data points; allows the user to investigate the relationship between or among dependent and independent variables

The chapter illustrates the high–low method of separating mixed costs into their variable and fixed elements. A potential weakness of the high–low method is that outliers may be inadvertently used in the calculation. Outliers are not representative of actual costs and are generally not good predictors of future costs. Thus, a cost formula derived from outlier data will probably not be very useful.

This appendix introduces a statistical technique known as **least-squares regression analysis**, another method of mixed cost analysis. The least-squares method makes it possible to mathematically determine the cost formula of a mixed cost by considering the best fit to all representative data points rather than only two points. (Outliers should be excluded from the set of data points.)

Like the high–low method, least-squares separates the variable and fixed cost elements of any type of mixed cost. When multiple independent variables exist, least-squares regression also helps managers to select the independent variable that has the strongest correlation with—and thus is the best predictor of—the dependent variable. For example, least-squares can be used by managers trying to decide if machine hours, direct labour hours, or number of parts per product best explains and predicts changes in a certain manufacturing overhead cost pool.

All chapter examples assume that a linear relationship exists between the independent and dependent variables. Thus, each one-unit change in an independent variable produces a specific unit change in the dependent variable. When only one independent variable is used to predict the dependent variable, the process is known as **simple regression** analysis. In **multiple regression**, two or more independent variables are used.

Simple linear regression employs the same straight-line formula $(y = a + bx)$ used in the high–low method. First, the available data set consisting of the actual values of the independent variable (x) and actual values of the dependent variable (y) is analyzed for outliers, which are eliminated from consideration. Next, a **regression line** is mathematically developed that represents the line that best fits the data observations. This line minimizes the sum of the squares of the vertical deviations between it and the actual observation points.

Exhibit 2-18 graphically illustrates least-squares regression. Graph A of the exhibit presents a set of actual observations. These observed values from the data set are designated as y values. Graph B indicates that many lines could be drawn through the data set, but most would provide a poor fit. The y values are used, along with the actual activity levels (x values), to mathematically determine the regression line of best fit. This regression line represents values computed for the dependent variable for all actual activity levels. The dependent values that comprise the regression line are designated as y_c values.

The vertical line segments from the actual observation points (y values) to the regression line (y_c values) in Graph B of Exhibit 2-18 are called deviations. The amount of a deviation is determined by subtracting the y_c value at an activity level from its related y value. Deviations above the regression line are positive amounts, while deviations below the line are negative. By squaring the deviations, the negative signs are eliminated. The positive sum of the squared deviations $[(y - y_c)^2]$ can be mathematically manipulated to yield the regression line of best fit. This regression line minimizes the sum of the squared deviations (hence, the name least-squares). The least-squares regression line can then be used to estimate cost formula values for fixed (a) and variable (b) terms. This equation can then be used by the cost analyst to make predictions and analyses.

The Riscky Rita's Restaurant data for cups of coffee and utility cost from Exhibit 2-8 are used here to illustrate the calculation of the least-squares regression

simple regression
regression analysis using only one independent variable to predict the dependent variable

multiple regression
regression analysis using two or more independent variables

regression line
a line that represents the cost formula for a set of cost observations fit to those observations in a mathematically determined manner

---

EXHIBIT 2-18

Illustration of Least-Squares Regression Line

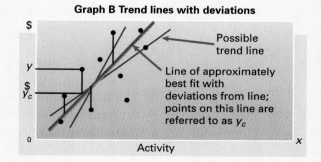

Graph A Assumed set of data points

Graph B Trend lines with deviations

line. The equations necessary to compute b and a values using the method of least squares are as follows:[16]

$$b = \frac{\Sigma xy - n\bar{x}\bar{y}}{\Sigma x^2 - n\bar{x}^2}$$

$$a = \bar{y} - bx$$

where
x = mean (or arithmetic average) of the independent variable
y = mean (or arithmetic average) of the dependent variable
n = number of observations

The Riscky Rita's Restaurant data must be restated in an appropriate form for substitution into the equations for b and a. Because of the magnitude of the x values, calculations are made for each 100 cups of coffee to avoid working with extremely large numbers. At the completion of the calculations, the resulting values are converted to a per-unit b value by dividing by 100. These restatements are as follows:

x	y	xy	x^2
113	$ 1,712	$ 193,456	12,769
114	1,716	195,624	12,996
90	1,469	132,210	8,100
115	1,719	197,685	13,225
112	1,698	190,176	12,544
101	1,691	170,791	10,201
645	$10,005	$1,079,942	69,835

(Note that the outlier for July of 12,200 cups of coffee has once again been ignored.) The mean value for the data in the x-column is 107.5 (or 645 ÷ 6) and the mean value for the data in the y-column is $1,667.50 (or $10,005 ÷ 6).

Substituting appropriate amounts into the formulas yields the b (variable) and a (fixed) cost values. The b value is calculated first, since it is used to compute a.

$$b = \frac{\Sigma xy - n\bar{x}\bar{y}}{\Sigma x^2 - n\bar{x}^2}$$

$$= \frac{\$1,079,942 - 6(107.5)(\$1,667.50)}{69,835 - 6(107.5)(107.5)}$$

$$= \frac{\$4,404.50}{497.5} = \$8.85 \text{ per hundred or } \$0.09 \text{ per cup of coffee}$$

$$a = \bar{y} - b\bar{x}$$
$$= \$1,667.50 - \$8.85(107.5)$$
$$= \$1,667.50 - \$951.38$$
$$= \$716.12$$

Thus, the cost formula under least-squares regression is:

Total utility cost = $716.12 + $0.09 per cup of coffee

Notice that the least-squares method gives a different cost formula than did the high–low method demonstrated in Exhibit 2-8. Regression information yields more reliable results—a characteristic that is very important to managers seeking to understand and control costs based on changes in activity. Because of the many computer packages that are able to do least-squares regression quickly and accurately, it has become virtually costless to do this type of analysis using a variety of possibilities as the independent variable.

CHAPTER SUMMARY

This chapter is premised on the belief that managers must understand their organizations' costs if they are to achieve strategic successes. Accordingly, it introduces terminology used by managers and management accountants and presents the flow of costs in a manufacturing environment.

Direct costs are so defined because they are traceable to a specific cost object. Although indirect costs cannot be explicitly traced to a cost object, allocation techniques can be used to assign such costs to related cost objects. Materials and labour may be directly or indirectly related to particular products, but manufacturing overhead costs are indirect and must be allocated to the products produced.

Variable costs are constant per unit but fluctuate in total with changes in activity levels within the relevant range. Fixed costs are constant in total as activity levels change within the relevant range, but vary inversely on a per-unit basis with changes in activity levels. The relevant range is generally the company's normal operating range. Step variable costs have small steps and are treated as variable costs; step fixed costs have large steps and are treated as fixed costs. Mixed costs have both a variable and a fixed element.

A predictor is an activity measure that changes in a consistent, observable way with changes in a cost. A cost driver is an activity measure that has a direct causal effect on a cost.

If separate variable and fixed manufacturing overhead rates are to be calculated, mixed costs must be separated into their variable and fixed components. One technique that can be used to make this separation is the high–low method. The high–low method uses two points of actual activity data (the highest and lowest) to determine the change in cost and activity. Dividing the cost change by the activity change gives the per-unit variable cost portion of the mixed cost. Fixed cost is found by subtracting total variable cost from total cost at either the high or the low level of activity.

All mixed costs must be separated into their variable and fixed elements using either regression analysis or the high–low method.

Given the overhead cost formulas, accountants can calculate predetermined overhead rates by dividing estimated overhead costs by a selected level of activity. Such rates assign overhead cost to goods or services based on the actual quantity of activity used to produce the goods or services. The use of predetermined rates eliminates the delays and distortions that occur when actual manufacturing overhead is applied. Separate rates computed according to cost behaviour yield costs that best reflect the resources sacrificed to make a product or perform a service.

Since unit variable costs remain constant over the relevant range of activity, total variable overhead can be divided by any level of activity to compute the predetermined rate. The predetermined fixed overhead rate is computed as estimated fixed overhead at a specific level of activity divided by that level of activity. Most companies select the expected annual capacity level as the activity measure.

Using predetermined rates normally results in either underapplied or overapplied overhead at year-end. If the total amount of underapplied or overapplied overhead is small, it is closed to Cost of Goods Sold or Cost of Services Rendered. If the amount is large, it is allocated to Work in Process Inventory, Finished Goods Inventory, and Cost of Goods Sold/Services Rendered.

A Cost of Goods Manufactured Statement discloses the total cost of the goods completed and transferred to finished goods during the period. This statement provides the necessary information to prepare the cost of goods sold section of a manufacturer's income statement. The cost of goods manufactured computation is prepared for internal management information and is presented on a statement that supports the cost of goods sold computation on the income statement.

Cross-Functional Applications

Topic of Note	Discipline	Cross-Functional Applications
Predetermined Overhead (POR)	Accounting	Using predetermined OH rates allows timely financial statement valuations, provides stable product costs, and assists managers in making plans, controlling costs, and solving problems.
	Business Law	Many purchase/sale agreements, where future selling prices cannot be accurately determined, are tied to POR. Since direct costs are traceable, it is only the overhead component of total cost that must be estimated in such contractual pricing arrangements.
	Economics	POR represents estimates that economists can use to structure cost models and analyze and predict the impact of marginal costs on overall efficiency. These models can be used to make routine decisions such as order size or outsourcing to clarify management's view of the playing field.
	Finance	Using POR helps in estimating costs for future periods and provides more timely knowledge of gross profit margins.
	Management	POR estimates are used by management to plan the flow of costs and control the cost drivers. POR helps in OH cost analysis and control. Production or sales activities can be simulated before they are actually incurred. This serves to focus management's attention on the most critical activities/cost drivers.
	Marketing	Marketers must use POR to estimate costs and profitability. Underestimating overhead cost will have a negative impact on profits, and overestimating overhead cost will reduce competitive advantage along price or quality lines.

Key Terms

Allocate (p. 34)
Applied overhead (p. 53)
Capacity (p. 51)
Conversion cost (p. 39)

Correlation (p. 47)
Cost (p. 34)
Cost behaviour (p. 39)
Cost driver (p. 39)

Cost object (p. 34)
Cost of goods manufactured (p. 58)
Cost of goods manufactured statement (p. 58)
Cost of goods sold (p. 61)
Dependent variable (p. 46)
Direct cost (p. 34)
Direct labour (p. 35)
Direct material (p. 34)
Expected annual capacity (p. 51)
Fixed cost (p. 40)
High–low method (p. 45)
Ideal capacity (see *theoretical capacity*) (p. 52)
Independent variable (p. 46)
Indirect cost (p. 34)
Least-squares regression analysis (p. 62)
Mixed cost (p. 42)
Multiple regression (p. 63)

Normal capacity (p. 52)
Outlier (p. 46)
Overhead (p. 37)
Overapplied overhead (p. 54)
Period cost (p. 34)
Practical capacity (p. 52)
Predetermined overhead rate (p. 48)
Predictor (p. 39)
Prime cost (p. 38)
Product cost (p. 34)
Regression analysis (p. 46)
Regression line (p. 63)
Relevant range (p. 39)
Simple regression (p. 63)
Step cost (p. 43)
Theoretical capacity (p. 52)
Underapplied overhead (p. 53)
Variable cost (p. 40)

Solution Strategies

High–Low Method (example using assumed amounts)

	(Independent Variable) Activity	(Dependent Variable) Associated Total Cost	=	Total Variable Cost (Rate × Activity)	+	Total Fixed Cost
High level of activity	28,000	$36,000	=	$22,400	+	13,600
Low level of activity	18,000	28,000	=	14,400	+	13,600
Differences	10,000	8,000				

$0.80 variable cost per unit of activity

Flexible Budget (at any activity level within the relevant range)

$$y = a + bx$$

or

Total cost = Total fixed cost + (Variable cost per unit of activity × Level of activity)

Predetermined Overhead Rate

Predetermined OH rate = Total estimated manufacturing overhead ÷ Estimated level of activity

(Should be separated into variable and fixed rates and by related cost pools)

Underapplied and Overapplied Manufacturing Overhead

Variable/Fixed Manufacturing Overhead	XXX	
Various accounts		XXX

Actual overhead is debited to the Overhead General
Ledger account and credited to the sources of
the overhead costs.

Work in Process Inventory*	YYY	
Variable/Fixed Manufacturing Overhead		YYY

Applied overhead is debited to WIP Inventory and
credited to the Overhead General Ledger account.

*Can be debited directly to Cost of Services Rendered (CSR) in a service company

A debit balance in Variable or Fixed Manufacturing Overhead at the end of the
period is underapplied overhead; a credit balance is overapplied overhead. An
immaterial underapplied or overapplied balance in the OH account is closed at the
end of the period to CGS or CSR; a material amount is prorated to WIP Inventory,
FG Inventory, and CGS or CSR.

Flow of Costs

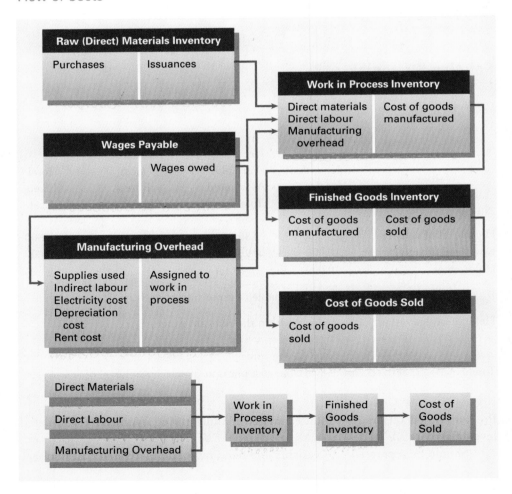

Cost of Goods Manufactured Statement

Cost of Goods Manufactured		
Manufacturing Cost for the Period		
Raw materials		
Beginning raw materials balance	XX	
Plus: Purchases of direct raw materials	+ XX	
Raw materials available for use	XXX	
Less: Ending direct raw materials balance	− XX	
Total raw materials used		XXX
Direct labour		+XX
Variable manufacturing overhead		+XX
Fixed manufacturing overhead		+ XXX
Total current period manufacturing costs		XXX
Plus: Beginning work in process inventory		+ XX
Total costs to account for		XXXX
Less: Ending work in process inventory		− XX
Cost of Goods Manufactured		XXXX

Cost of Goods Sold Schedule

Beginning Finished Goods Inventory	XX
Plus: Cost of Goods Manufactured	+XXXX
Cost of Goods Available for Sale	XXXX
Less: Ending Finished Goods Inventory	− XX
Cost of Goods Sold	XXXX

DEMONSTRATION PROBLEM

Seguin Company Ltd. had the following account balances as of April 1, 2006.

Raw materials (direct and indirect)	$19,300
Work in Process Inventory	43,000
Finished Goods Inventory	28,000
Prepaid Insurance	9,600

Transactions during April were:

- Purchased $92,000 of raw materials on account.
- Issued $80,000 of raw materials, of which $57,000 were direct to the product.
- Manufacturing payroll of $54,000 was accrued; $37,000 was for direct labour and the rest was for supervisors.
- Utility costs were accrued at $4,900; of these costs, $1,000 were fixed.
- Property taxes on the factory building were accrued in the amount of $1,500.
- Prepaid insurance in the amount of $800 on the manufacturing equipment expired in April.
- Straight-line depreciation on manufacturing equipment was $10,000.
- Predetermined overhead of $58,150 ($24,900 variable and $33,250 fixed) was applied to Work in Process Inventory.
- Transferred finished products from Work in Process Inventory to Finished Goods Inventory.
- Sales on account totalled $230,000.
- Cost of goods sold was $151,000.
- Selling and administrative costs were $43,575 (credit "Various Accounts").
- Ending Work in Process Inventory is $24,500; Ending Indirect Materials Inventory is $2,500; and Ending Direct Materials Inventory $28,800.

Required:

a. Journalize the transactions for April.
b. Prepare a cost of goods manufactured statement for April. (Any under- or overapplied overhead is written off to Cost of Goods Sold.)
c. Prepare an income statement, including a detailed schedule of cost of goods sold.

Solution to Demonstration Problem

a.	(1)	Raw Materials Inventory	92,000	
		Accounts Payable		92,000
		To record purchases of raw materials.		
	(2)	Work in Process Inventory	57,000	
		Variable Manufacturing Overhead	23,000	
		Raw Materials Inventory		80,000
		To record issuance of raw materials from the storeroom.		
	(3)	Work in Process Inventory	37,000	
		Fixed Manufacturing Overhead	17,000	
		Salaries and Wages Payable		54,000
		To record manufacturing payroll.		
	(4)	Variable Manufacturing Overhead	3,900	
		Fixed Manufacturing Overhead	1,000	
		Utilities Payable		4,900
		To record the utilities cost.		
	(5)	Fixed Manufacturing Overhead	1,500	
		Property Taxes Payable		1,500
		To accrue property taxes on manufacturing.		
	(6)	Fixed Manufacturing Overhead	800	
		Prepaid Insurance		800
		To record expired insurance on manufacturing equipment.		
	(7)	Fixed Manufacturing Overhead	10,000	
		Acc. Depreciation—Manufacturing Equipment		10,000
		To record depreciation on manufacturing equipment.		
	(8)	Work in Process Inventory	58,150	
		Variable Manufacturing Overhead		24,900
		Fixed Manufacturing Overhead		33,250
		To apply overhead to work in process.		
	(9)	Finished Goods Inventory	170,650*	
		Work in Process Inventory		170,650
		To record cost of goods transferred from Work in Process Inventory to Finished Goods Inventory.		

* from cost of goods manufactured statement

	(10)	Cost of Goods Sold	151,000	
		Finished Goods Inventory		151,000
		To record cost of goods sold.		
	(11)	Accounts Receivable	230,000	
		Sales		230,000
		To record sales on account.		
	(12)	Selling and Administrative Expenses	43,575	
		Various Accounts		43,575
		To record selling and administrative expenses.		
	(13)	Fixed Manufacturing Overhead	2,950	
		Variable Manufacturing Overhead		2,000
		Cost of Goods Sold		950
		To close under- and overapplied overhead.		

Posting of the Journal Entries

Raw Materials Inventory			
Bal	19,300	(2)	80,000
(1)	92,000		
Bal	31,300		

Work in Process Inventory			
Bal	43,000	(9)	170,650
(2)	57,000		
(3)	37,000		
(8)	58,150		
	195,150		
Bal	24,500		

Finished Goods Inventory			
Bal	28,000	(10)	151,000
(9)	170,650		
	198,650		
Bal	47,650		

Prepaid Insurance			
Bal	9,600	(6)	800
Bal	8,800		

Accumulated Depreciation		
	(7)	10,000

Various Payables		
	(1)	92,000
	(3)	54,000
	(4)	4,900
	(5)	1,500
	Bal	152,400

Fixed Manufacturing Overhead			
(3)	17,000	(8)	33,250
(4)	1,000		
(5)	1,500		
(6)	800		
(7)	10,000		
	30,300		
(13)	2,950		

Variable Manufacturing Overhead			
(2)	23,000	(8)	24,900
(4)	3,900		
	26,900	(13)	2,000

Cost of Goods Sold			
(10)	151,000	(13)	950

Accounts Receivable		
(11)	230,000	

Sales		
	(11)	230,000

Selling Admin. Expenses		
(12)	43,575	

b.

Seguin Company Ltd.
Cost of Goods Manufactured Statement
For the Month Ended April 30, 2006

Raw Materials		
Beginning raw materials, April 1, 2005		$ 19,300
Plus: Purchases of raw materials		92,000
Raw materials available for use		$111,300
Less: Indirect materials used	$23,000	
Ending balance indirect materials	2,500	25,500
Total direct materials		$ 85,800
Less: Ending direct materials inventory		28,800
Total direct materials used		$ 57,000
Direct labour		37,000
Variable manufacturing overhead applied	$24,900	
Fixed manufacturing overhead applied	33,250	58,150
Total current period manufacturing costs		$152,150
Plus: Beginning Work in Process Inventory		43,000
Total cost to account for		$195,150
Less: Ending Work in Process Inventory		24,500
Cost of goods manufactured this period*		$170,650

*Under- and overapplied overhead is written off to cost of goods sold.

c.

Seguin Company Ltd.
Schedule of Cost of Goods Sold
For the Month Ended April 30, 2006

Beginning Finished Goods Inventory, April 1, 2006	$ 28,000
Plus: Cost of Goods Manufactured in April, 2006	170,650
Cost of Goods Available for Sale	$198,650
Less: Ending Finished Goods Inventory, April 30, 2006	47,650
Cost of Goods Sold	$151,000
Less: Overapplied Overhead	950
Cost of goods sold	$150,050

Seguin Company Ltd.
Income Statement
For the Month Ended April 30, 2006

Sales	$230,000
Less: Cost of Goods Sold	150,050
Gross Profit	$ 79,950
Selling and Administrative Expenses	43,575
Profit (Loss) from Operations (before taxes)	$ 36,375

End-of-Chapter Materials

SELF-TEST QUESTIONS

(SOLUTIONS APPEAR AT THE END OF THE CHAPTER.)

Questions 1 through 3 are based on the following information pertaining to Forrest Ltd.'s manufacturing operations:

Inventories	January 1, 2005	December 31, 2005
Raw materials	$20,000	$30,000
Work in process	40,000	25,000
Finished goods	28,000	35,000
Additional information for 2005:		
Raw materials purchased		$100,000
Direct manufacturing labour payroll		80,000
Direct manufacturing labour rate per hour		10
Manufacturing overhead rate per direct labour-hour		8

1. For 2005, what was the prime cost?
   a. $80,000
   b. $100,000
   c. $170,000
   d. $180,000

2. For 2005, what was the conversion cost?
   a. $80,000
   b. $144,000
   c. $165,000
   d. $180,000

3. For 2005, what was the cost of goods manufactured?
   a. $205,000
   b. $234,000
   c. $249,000
   d. $274,000

(Self-Test Questions 1–3 are adapted by the author from *Management Accounting* examinations published by the Certified General Accountants Association of Canada © CGA-Canada, 1999, used by permission.)

Use the following information to answer Questions 4 and 5:
The following information pertains to Spectra Ltd.'s manufacturing operations:

Inventories	March 1, 2006	March 31, 2006
Raw materials	$36,000	$30,000
Work in process	18,000	12,000
Finished goods	54,000	72,000
Additional information for the month of March 2006:		
Raw materials purchased	$84,000	

Direct labour cost
incurred $60,000

Direct labour rate
per hour   7.50

Manufacturing
overhead rate per
direct labour-hour   10.00

4. What was the prime cost for the month of March 2006?
   a. $ 90,000
   b. $120,000
   c. $144,000
   d. $150,000

5. What was the conversion cost for the month of March 2006?
   a. $ 90,000
   b. $140,000
   c. $144,000
   d. $170,000

(Self-Test Questions 4–5 are adapted by the author from *Management Accounting* examinations published by the Certified General Accountants Association of Canada © CGA-Canada, 2000, used by permission.)

6. Basic Black Company has 30 full-time employees. Actual time for each employee for the last period was as follows:

Billable time for clients	2,000 hours
Vacation time	200 hours
Professional development	175 hours
Unbillable time	0 hours
Sick leave	125 hours

   Demand for the company's services is at 100% of the time available. Each employee is paid a salary of $75,000 per year. John Black, the CEO, believes that clients should be charged for employee benefits. What should be the total actual indirect-cost rate per billable hour?
   a. $4.17
   b. $5.83
   c. $7.50
   d. $9.17

Use the following information to answer Questions 7 and 8.

Brash Ltd. manufactures flowerpots. It expects to sell 40,000 flowerpots in 2006. At the start of fiscal 2006, the company had beginning inventory of raw materials suffi-cient to produce 48,000 units. Beginning inventory of fin-ished units totalled 4,000 with a target ending inventory of 5,000 units. The flowerpots sell for $6.00 and the company has no work in process inventory. Direct materials costs for each flowerpot total $2.00 and direct labour is $1.00. Manufacturing overhead is $0.40 per unit.

7. What will be the amount of Cost of Goods Sold for 2006?
   a. $122,400
   b. $136,000
   c. $139,000
   d. $149,600

8. What will be the total costs incurred for direct materials, direct manufacturing labour, and manufacturing overhead, respectively, for 2006?
   a $0; $40,000; $16,000
   b. $0; $41,000; $16,000
   c. $80,000; $40,000; $16,000
   d. $82,000; $41,000; $16,400

9. The following information relates to the Glow By Jabot Ltd.

Finished goods, beginning inventory, January 1, 2006	$15,000
Finished goods, ending inventory, December 31, 2006	9,500
Cost of goods sold	56,000
Sales	125,000
Operating expenses	25,000

   What is Glow By Jabot's Cost of Goods Manufactured for 2006?
   a. $31,500
   b. $50,500
   c. $56,500
   d. $61,500

10. David Faber Inc. had the following activities and costs during 2006:

Direct materials:	
Beginning inventory	$ 50,000
Purchases	154,000
Ending inventory	26,000
Direct manufacturing labour	40,000
Manufacturing overhead	30,000
Work in process, beginning inventory	2,000
Work in process, ending inventory	10,000
Finished goods, beginning inventory	60,000
Finished goods, ending inventory	40,000

    What is the cost of raw materials used by Faber Inc. in 2006?
    a. $24,000
    b. $128,000
    c. $178,000
    d. $204,000

(Self-Test Questions 6–10 are adapted by the author from *Management Accounting* examinations published by the Certified General Accountants Association of Canada © CGA-Canada, 2001, used by permission.)

QUESTIONS

1. Why must the word *cost* be accompanied by an adjective to be meaningful?

2. With respect to a specific cost object, what is the difference between a direct cost and an indirect cost?

3. What is a product cost? What are the three general categories of product costs?

4. What specific costs are usually included in direct labour cost?

5. Over the past decade or so, which product cost category has been growing most rapidly? Why?

6. What is meant by the term *conversion cost* and what product cost(s) does the term include?

7. "Prime costs and conversion costs are components of product cost; therefore, the sum of these two cost categories is equal to product cost." Is this statement true or false? Explain.

8. At year-end, where on the balance sheet would the costs appear for products that had been placed into production but were not finished?

9. Why is the relevant range important to managers?

10. How do predictors and cost drivers differ? Why is the distinction important?

11. What is the distinction between a fixed cost and a variable cost?

12. What is a mixed cost? How do mixed costs behave with changes in the activity measure?

13. What is a step cost? Explain the distinction between a step fixed and a step variable cost.

14. What are the two major types of overhead cost? Which of these categories has been increasing in recent years?

15. Why is it necessary to separate mixed costs into their variable and fixed cost elements for product costing purposes?

16. Why must a particular level of activity be specified to calculate a predetermined fixed overhead rate? Why is such specificity not required to calculate a predetermined variable overhead rate?

17. What is the primary criterion for selecting an overhead application base? Explain.

18. Why do some companies use multiple cost pools, rather than a single cost pool, to allocate overhead costs?

19. What are the four capacity measures that may be used for overhead application? Which capacity measure do you think will result in the greatest underapplication of overhead? Why?

20. Why may overhead for a given period be underapplied? What are the alternative methods for disposing of the underapplied overhead?

21. What is included on the Cost of Goods Manufactured Statement? Why is it said that this statement shows the flow of costs in a manufacturing company?

22. Describe the difference between Cost of Goods Manufactured and Cost of Goods Sold.

23. (Appendix 2A) How does the least-squares regression method improve upon the high–low method for separating mixed costs into their fixed and variable components?

24. (Appendix 2A) Differentiate between an independent and a dependent variable.

EXERCISES

1. (LO 1, 2, 4, 7, 8, 9; Terminology) Your cousin is taking managerial accounting at another university and has asked for your help with this exercise. Match the numbered definitions with the lettered terms. Definitions may be used more than once or not at all.

   a. Cost of goods manufactured
   b. Applied overhead
   c. Overhead
   d. Conversion cost
   e. Mixed cost
   f. Dependent cost
   g. Indirect cost
   h. Product cost
   i. Period cost
   j. Direct cost
   k. Prime cost
   l. Outsourcing
   m. Cost driver

   1. The sum of direct labour and manufacturing overhead
   2. A cost outside the production area
   3. A factor that causes a cost to be incurred
   4. A cost that has both a variable and a fixed component
   5. Buying rather than internally making
   6. The sum of direct materials and direct labour costs
   7. A cost that cannot be traced to a particular cost object
   8. Any unknown cost that needs to be predicted
   9. The total cost of products finished during the period
   10. A cost that is clearly traceable to a particular object
   11. The total of all costs that are not traceable to a particular object
   12. Expenses and losses
   13. Overhead assigned to Work in Process

2. (LO 2; Product cost category) Classify the following manufacturing costs incurred in manufacturing potato chips as direct materials, direct labour, or manufacturing overhead.
   a. Hourly wages of a packaging machine operator
   b. Wages of maintenance and clean-up personnel
   c. Potato costs
   d. Cooking oil costs (considered to be significant)
   e. Seasoning costs (considered to be significant)
   f. Packaging material costs
   g. Packing carton costs
   h. Heating and energy costs
   i. Potato storage costs
   j. Production supervisor's salary

3. (LO 2; Product cost category) Chancellor Canoe Company manufactures aluminum canoes. The following are some costs incurred in the manufacturing process in 2006:

   Material Costs

Aluminum	$371,000
Oil and grease for equipment	6,000
Chrome rivets to assemble canoes	3,600
Wooden ribbing and braces	18,400

   Labour Costs

Equipment operators	$120,000
Equipment mechanics	54,000
Manufacturing supervisors	28,000

Required:

a. What is the direct material cost for 2006?

b. What is the direct labour cost for 2006?

c. What are the indirect labour and indirect materials costs for 2006?

4. (LO 2; Direct labour cost) Gina's Finest Ltd. is a catering operation that operates two shifts. The company pays a late-shift premium of 10% and an overtime premium of 50%. Labour premiums are included in service overhead.

The May 2006 manufacturing payroll is as follows:

Total wages for May for 7,000 hours	$66,000
Normal hourly wage for early-shift employees	$ 8
Total regular hours worked, split evenly between the early and late shifts	5,000

All overtime was worked by the early shift during May.

Required:

a. How many overtime hours were worked in May?

b. How much of the total labour cost should be charged to direct labour? To service overhead?

c. What amount of service overhead was for late-shift premiums? For overtime premiums?

5. (LO 3; Prime cost and conversion cost) The accounting records of Carlton Ltd., a small construction company, showed the following construction and operating costs for the year 2006:

Direct materials	$718,000
Direct labour	421,000
Indirect materials	102,000
Indirect labour	129,000
Construction utilities	103,000
Selling and administrative expenses	317,000

Required:

a. What amount of prime cost was incurred in 2006?

b. What amount of conversion cost was incurred in 2006?

c. What was total product cost for 2006?

6. (LO 4; Cost behaviour, product cost category) Classify the following manufacturing costs incurred in the production of bicycles as direct materials, direct labour, or manufacturing overhead. Indicate whether each cost is most likely fixed, mixed, or variable. Use number of units produced as the activity measure.

a. Manufacturing supervision

b. Aluminum tubing

c. Rims

d. Emblem

e. Gearbox

f. Crew supervisor's salary

g. Fenders

h. Inventory clerk's salary

i. Inspector's salary

j. Handlebars

k. Metalworkers' wages (assume wages are hourly)

l. Roller chain

m. Spokes (assume costs are considered significant)

n. Paint (assume costs are considered significant)

7. (LO 4; Cost behaviour) Indicate whether each of the following items is a variable (V), fixed (F), or mixed (M) cost with respect to production volume, and whether it is a product or service cost or a period cost. If some items have alternative answers, indicate the alternatives and the reasons for them.

a. Hourly wages of forklift operators who move materials along the assembly line
b. Hand soap used in manufacturing-area restrooms
c. Utility costs incurred at manufacturing company headquarters
d. Drafting paper used in an architectural firm
e. Cost of company labels attached to shirts made by the firm
f. Wages of quality control inspectors at a manufacturing plant
g. Insurance premiums on raw materials warehouses
h. Salaries of staff auditors in an accounting firm
i. Cost of clay to make pottery
j. Wages of carpenters in a construction company

8. (LO 4; Direct versus indirect costs) Atkinson College at York University has six departments: Accounting, Finance, International Business, Management, Marketing, and Decision Sciences. The following costs are incurred in the Accounting Department:
a. Accounting faculty salaries
b. Department chairperson's salary
c. Cost of computer time of campus mainframe used by members of the department
d. Cost of equipment purchased by the department from allocated government funds
e. Cost of travel by department faculty paid from externally generated funds contributed directly to the department
f. Cost of secretarial salaries (secretaries are shared by the entire college)
g. Depreciation allocation of the college building cost for the number of offices used by department faculty
h. Cost of periodicals and books purchased by the department
Required:
The dean has asked you, a new faculty member with a fresh outlook, to indicate whether each of the above costs is direct or indirect to the Accounting Department.

9. (LO 4; Cost behaviour) Sender Incorporated produces croquet sets. The company incurred the following costs to produce 2,000 sets last month:

Wooden cases (1 per set)	$ 4,000
Balls (6 per set)	6,000
Mallets	12,000
Wire hoops (12 per set including extras)	4,800
Straight-line depreciation	2,400
Supervisors' salaries	4,400
Total	$33,600

Required:
The firm's accountant has requested that you assist her by answering the following:
a. What did each croquet set component cost? What did each croquet set cost?
b. What type of behaviour would you expect each of these costs to exhibit?
c. This month the company expects to produce 2,500 sets. Would you expect each type of cost to increase or decrease relative to last month? Why? What will be the total cost of 2,500 sets?

10. (LO 4; Cost behaviour) Smielauskas Printers Ltd. pays $200 per month for a photocopy machine maintenance contract. In addition, variable charges average $0.04 per page copied.
Required:
a. Determine the total cost and the cost per page if the company makes the following number of photocopies (pages):
i. 1,000
ii. 2,000
iii. 4,000
b. Why is the cost per page different in each of the above three cases?

11. (LO 5; High–low method) Sammy Brady Appliances Ltd. incurred the following expenses for utilities during the first six months of 2006:

Month	Sales Volume	Utilities
January	$60,000	$600
February	35,000	350
March	40,000	400
April	50,000	450
May	30,000	150
June	42,500	425

Required:
a. Using the high–low method, develop a formula for utilities expense.
b. Describe any unusual features of your solution in part (a). Give a probable explanation for the result.

12. (LO 5; High–low method) The owner of the Winters Fishery Restaurant wants to estimate a cost function for its supplies expense. The restaurant has been operating for six months and has had the following activity (customer volume) and costs:

Month	Customer Volume	Supplies ($)
March	3,400	6,100
April	3,100	5,850
May	3,400	6,200
June	3,600	6,400
July	3,000	5,500
August	2,800	5,400

Required:
a. In a restaurant, what types of supplies are in the variable expense category? The fixed expense category?
b. Using the high–low method, estimate the cost equation for supplies expense.
c. What amount of supplies expense would the company expect to incur in a month in which 3,300 customers were served?

13. (LO 6; Under/overapplied overhead) Colin Powell Company is a large boat repair company. The company maintains two departments—the repair department and the painting department. The repair department is labour intensive with little or no automation, however the painting department is primarily operated through the use of robots that are programmed for individual jobs. For each department, the company uses the most logical base to determine the overhead application rate.

Budgeted data for fiscal 2006 included:

	Repair	Painting
Estimated overhead	$435,000	$965,900
Estimated direct labour costs	$275,600	$ 31,650
Estimated machine-hours	1,875 MH*	217,600 MH*

*MH stands for "machine-hours"

Required:
a. Assuming that the company desires profits of 12% of costs, determine the total estimated bill for a boat that is expected to require the following:

	Repair	Painting
Direct materials	$275	$ 85
Direct labour—Mechanic (8 h @ $15/h)	$120	
Machine Programmer (0.5 h @ $24/h)		$ 12
Machine-hours	0.5 MH	3 MH

b. By how much did the repair department under- or overapply its overhead in 2006, if the actual results for the department in 2006 were:

	Dollars	**Hours**
Overhead	$442,250	
Direct labour	274,920	
Machine-hours		1,831 MH

14. (LO 6; Overhead application) The IT department at Hong Kong Corporation was set up with the intent that the facilities would be used by production department A approximately 60% of the time and by production department B approximately 40% of the time.

The IT department's budgeted costs for February are:

Variable	$245 per processing hour
Fixed	$258,000 per month

The IT Department's actual results for February were:

Department A Usage	630 processing hours
Department B Usage	315 processing hours
Total costs of the IT Department for the month	$489,525.

Based on the above results, management allocated the costs of the IT Department as follows:

$489,525 ÷ 945 hours = $518.016 per hour

Costs charged to department A	630 hours × $518.016/hour = $326,350
Costs charged to department B	315 hours × $518.016/hour = $163,175

Required:

a. As the manager of department A, what objections would you have to the method of cost allocation used?

b. How should the costs have been allocated?

15. (LO 6; Under/overapplied overhead) Brooke Corporation opened for business on January 1, 2005. Paul Martin, the newly hired controller, was asked to establish a pre-determined overhead rate to use in applying overhead to the various jobs. After consulting with various individuals in the accounting department, he came up with the following estimated data for 2005.

Supervision	$ 50,000
Indirect labour	115,000
Inspection	70,000
Maintenance	35,000
Indirect material	25,000
Heat, light, power	20,000
Depreciation	35,000
Miscellaneous manufacturing overhead	10,000
Total manufacturing overhead	$360,000
Direct labour hours	144,000

At the end of fiscal 2005, the first year of operations, the following results were recorded:

Supervision	$ 51,000
Indirect labour	99,000
Inspection	73,000
Maintenance	39,000
Indirect material	20,000
Heat, light, power	18,000
Depreciation	35,000
Miscellaneous manufacturing overhead	3,000
Total manufacturing overhead	$338,000
Direct labour hours	121,500

Required:

a.   Compute the predetermined overhead rate.

b.   Determine the over- or underapplied overhead for the year.

c.   Explain the causes for over- or underapplied overhead.

16. (LO 6; Predetermined OH rates and underapplied/overapplied OH) Letterman Glassworks had the following information in its Work in Process Inventory account for June 2006:

Work in Process Inventory			
Beginning Balance	5,000	Transferred Out	167,500
Materials added	75,000		
Labour (10,000 DLHs)	45,000		
Applied Overhead	60,000		
Ending Balance	17,500		

All workers are paid the same rate per hour. Manufacturing overhead is applied to Work in Process Inventory on the basis of direct labour hours. The only work left in process at the end of the month had a total of 1,430 direct labour hours accumulated to date.

Required:

a.   What is the total predetermined overhead rate per direct labour-hour?

b.   What amounts of material, labour, and overhead are included in the ending Work in Process Inventory balance?

c.   If actual total overhead for June is $61,350, what is the amount of underapplied or overapplied overhead?

17. (LO 6; Selecting capacity measure) Ambrus Paper Supply Company manufactures recycled paper. The company has decided to use predetermined manufacturing overhead rates to apply manufacturing overhead to its products. To set such rates, the company has gathered the following estimated data:

Variable manufacturing overhead at 12,000 machine-hours	$72,000
Variable manufacturing overhead at 14,000 machine-hours	84,000
Fixed manufacturing overhead at all levels between 12,000 and 20,000 machine-hours	72,000

Practical capacity is 20,000 machine-hours; expected capacity is 75% of practical capacity.

Required:

a.   What is the company's predetermined variable manufacturing overhead rate?

b.   Compute the company's fixed manufacturing overhead rate based on expected capacity. Using practical capacity, compute the company's predetermined fixed manufacturing overhead rate.

c.   If the company incurred a total of 13,500 machine-hours during a period, what would be the total amount of applied manufacturing overhead, assuming fixed manufacturing overhead was applied based on expected capacity? Practical capacity?

d.   If actual manufacturing overhead during the period was $155,000, what was the amount of underapplied or overapplied manufacturing overhead, assuming fixed manufacturing overhead was applied based on expected capacity? Practical capacity? (Use your answers to parts (a) and (b).)

e.   Based on your answers to parts (c) and (d), explain why most firms use expected capacity as the manufacturing overhead allocation base. What is the benefit of using practical capacity?

18. (LO 6, 7; Predetermined overhead; under/overapplied overhead) Michael Baldwin is the newly hired manager of the production department at the Genoa City Company. The company allocates manufacturing overhead on a predetermined basis using direct labour cost as a base.

The accounting department has prepared the following analysis of actual results compared to estimated figures for fiscal 2006.

	Estimated	Actual
Sales (units)	20,000	18,000
Production (units)	20,000	19,000
Direct materials	$ 50,000	$ 46,400
Direct labour	36,000	45,750
Supplies	2,000	1,400
Building Depreciation	2,000	2,000
Salaries		
Manager	13,000	15,000
Assistant Manager	10,000	10,750
Total manufacturing cost	$113,000	$121,300

Additional information:

There were no beginning or ending inventories of work in process.

Required:

If the company prorates any under- or overapplied manufacturing overhead to the inventory accounts and to cost of goods sold, how much manufacturing overhead will be allocated to cost of goods sold? What is the impact of this allocation on the cost of goods sold?

19. (LO 6, 7; Overhead application with multiple rates) Nijmeh Technologies has determined that a single overhead application rate no longer results in a reasonable allocation of overhead to its diverse products. Accordingly, the company has restructured its overhead application. It has established six cost pools and identified appropriate cost drivers. The new cost pools, allocation bases and rates are as follows:

Cost Pool	Application Rate
Setup costs	$37 per setup
Machine costs	$15 per machine-hour
Labour-related costs	$ 7 per direct labour-hour
Material handling costs received	$ 1 per kilogram of material
Quality costs	$80 per customer return
Other costs	$ 4 per machine-hour

During 2005, the company experienced the following volume for each cost application base:

Setups	300
Machine-hours	9,000
Direct labour hours	8,000
Kilograms of material received	100,000
Customer returns	250

Required:

a. Determine the amount of overhead applied in 2005.
b. Assume that the company incurred $362,000 in actual overhead costs in 2005. Compute the company's underapplied or overapplied overhead.
c. Why are more firms adopting multiple application rates to apply overhead?

20. (LO 7; Disposition of underapplied/overapplied OH) Rose Reed Research Services Company has an overapplied overhead balance of $31,000 at the end of 2006. Selected account balances at year-end are:

Work in Process Inventory	$ 27,000
Finished Goods Inventory	60,000
Cost of Goods Sold	213,000

Required:

a. Prepare the necessary journal entries to close the overapplied overhead balance assuming that:
  i.   the amount is material.
  ii. the amount is immaterial.
b. Which approach is the better choice, and why?

21. (LO 7; Cost predictors) The following are graphical representations of the relationships among four different costs and production volume. Briefly discuss for each cost

Graph A	Graph B	Graph C	Graph D
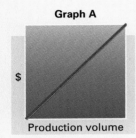	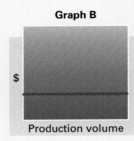	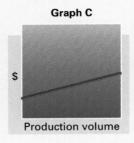	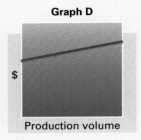

why production volume is, or is not, a good predictor for the cost. Also, identify a specific cost item that may be represented by each graph.

22. (LO 9; CGM and CGS) Brandon Walker Machine Shop had the following inventory balances at the beginning and end of September 2006:

	01/09/06	30/09/06
Raw Materials Inventory	$ 16,000	$ 18,000
Work in Process Inventory	94,000	72,000
Finished Goods Inventory	36,000	22,000

All raw materials are direct to the production process. The following information is available about manufacturing costs incurred during September:

Cost of raw materials used	$ 94,000
Direct labour costs	181,000
Manufacturing overhead	258,000

Required:
As the company accountant, you have been asked to
a.   Calculate the cost of goods manufactured for September.
b.   Determine the cost of goods sold for September.

23. (LO 3, 9; Cost of services rendered) The following information is related to the Painless Animal Clinic for April 2006, the firm's first month in operation:

Veterinary salaries for April	$23,000
Assistants' salaries for April	7,200
Medical supplies purchased in April	3,200
Utilities for month (80% related to animal treatment)	900
Office salaries for April (50% of time spent in animal treatment)	3,400
Medical supplies at April 30	1,800
Depreciation on medical equipment for April	2,100
Building rental (80% related to animal treatment)	1,700

Required:
Compute the cost of services rendered.

24. (LO 9; CGM and CGS) The December 2006 cost of goods sold at Mark Haines Custom Mirrors amounted to $900,000. The December 31 work in process was 80% of the December 1 work in process. Overhead was 100% of direct labour cost. During December, $220,000 of raw materials were purchased. All raw materials are direct to the production process. Other December information follows:

	December 1	December 31
Raw Materials Inventory	$108,000	$ 95,400
Work in Process Inventory	180,000	?
Finished Goods Inventory	419,000	411,200

Required:
a.   Prepare the December cost of goods manufactured statement.
b.   What was the amount of prime cost incurred in December?
c.   What was the amount of conversion cost incurred in December?
d.   Prepare a cost of goods sold schedule for December.

25. (LO 6, 7, 9; CGM; CGS; Journal entries for over/underapplied overhead) You are presented with the following selected account balances for the Lily Simon Co. Ltd.:

	January 1, 2006	December 31, 2006
Raw materials inventory	$14,500	$28,350
Work in process	59,700	23,850
Finished goods	17,680	?
Accrued payroll	10,000	7,500
Accounts payable	12,000	?
Accounts receivable	18,000	22,000
Accumulated depreciation	7,500	10,000
Prepaid insurance	4,000	3,000
Overhead applied	—	60,000
Miscellaneous credits	—	12,000

Additional information:
a. The Accounts Payable account is used only for the purchase of direct and indirect materials. The Miscellaneous Credits account is used for all other liabilities except payroll.
b. All sales are on account. The selling price per unit of $25 has remained unchanged for the last two years.
c. The FIFO method is used for computing cost of goods sold.
d. Indirect materials issued: $12,000.
e. Payment of accounts payable during the year: $55,000.
f. Wages paid to employees during the year: $155,000.
g. 15,000 units were completed during the year.
h. 8,200 units remain in finished goods inventory at the end of the year.
i. Collection of accounts receivable during the year: $200,000.
j. All of the accounts mentioned (other than Sales and Accounts Receivable) are related to production.
k. Materials and supplies purchased: $59,000.
l. Manufacturing overhead is applied at a predetermined overhead rate of 80% of direct labour cost.

Required:
Calculate the following:
   i.   Direct material used
   ii.   Direct labour cost
   iii.   Cost of goods manufactured
   iv.   Cost of goods sold
   v.   Balance of accounts payable at December 31
   vi.   Sales during 2006

(Adapted by the author from *Management Accounting* examinations, published by the Certified General Accountants Association of Canada © CGA-Canada, 1994, used by permission.)

PROBLEMS

1. (LO 1, 2; Period versus product costs) One of your co-workers (at the manufacturing firm where you are employed) feels that it does not matter if a cost is classified as a period or product cost. She maintains that, as long as the cost is included in one of the financial statements, how it is classified will have no impact on the operating results of the company.

She is aware that some members of the accounting department have been debating how a particular expenditure of $150,000 should be classified. Some feel that it should be a period cost, whereas others feel it should be a product cost.
Required:
a. Briefly define period costs and product costs.
b. Explain to your co-worker why it is or is not important to classify the $150,000 expenditure properly as either a period or product cost. Include in your

discussion the specific circumstances under which your co-worker's assertion might be correct or incorrect.

(Adapted by the author from *Management Accounting* examinations, published by the Certified General Accountants Association of Canada © CGA-Canada, 1995, used by permission.)

2. (LO 1, 2; Cost classification, cost object) Elton, a painter, incurred the following costs during September 2005 when he painted three houses. He spent $600 on paint, $50 on paint thinner, and $65 on brushes. He also bought two pair of coveralls for $12 each; he wears coveralls only while he works. During the first week of September, Elton placed a $10 ad for his business in the classifieds. Elton had to hire an assistant for one of the painting jobs; he paid her $8 per hour, and she worked 25 hours.

Being a very methodical person, Elton keeps detailed records of his mileage to and from each painting job. The average operating cost per kilometre for his van is $0.25. He found a $15 receipt in his van for a map that he purchased in September; he uses it to find addresses when he is first contacted to give an estimate on a painting job. He also had road toll receipts for $6 for a painting job he did. Elton charges his customers for travel costs related to painting their homes.

Near the end of September, Elton decided to go camping, and he turned down a job on which he had bid $1,800. He called the homeowner long-distance (at a cost of $3.60) to explain his reasons for declining the job.

Required:
Using the following headings, you are asked to indicate how each of the September costs incurred by Elton would be classified. Assume that the cost object is a house-painting job.

Cost   Variable   Fixed   Direct   Indirect   Period   Product

3. (LO 1, 2; Cost flows, prime costs and conversion costs) Abbott Contractors had the following inventory balances at the beginning and end of May 2005:

	May 1	May 31
Raw Materials	$16,900	$21,700
Work in Process	32,100	29,600
Finished Goods	25,800	22,600

During May, the company purchased $90,000 of raw materials. All raw materials are considered direct materials. Total labour payroll for the month was $78,000. Direct labour employees were paid $9 per hour and worked 6,800 hours in May. Total manufacturing overhead charges for the period were $109,300. Mr. Abbott, the company president, has asked for your help.

Required:
a. Determine the prime cost added to production during May.
b. Determine the conversion cost added to production in May.
c. Determine the cost of goods manufactured in May.
d. Determine the cost of goods sold in May.

4. (LO 3, 4; Cost behaviour) A company's cost structure may contain many different cost behaviour patterns. Descriptions of several different costs follow.
   1. Cost of raw materials, where the cost decreases by $0.06 per unit for each of the first 150 units purchased, after which it remains constant at $2.75 per unit.
   2. City water bill, which is computed as follows:

First 750,000 litres or less	$1,000 flat fee
Next 15,000 litres	$0.002 per litre used
Next 15,000 litres	$0.005 per litre used
Next 15,000 litres	$0.008 per litre used
Etc.	Etc.

   3. Rent on a manufacturing building donated by the city, where the agreement provides for a fixed-fee payment, unless 250,000 labour hours are worked, in which case no rent needs to be paid.
   4. Cost of raw materials used.
   5. Electricity bill—a flat fixed charge of $250 plus a variable cost after 150,000 kilowatt hours are used.

6. Salaries of maintenance workers if one maintenance worker is needed for every 1,000 hours or less of machine time.
7. Depreciation of equipment using the straight-line method.
8. Rent on a manufacturing building donated by the province, where the agreement provides for a monthly rental of $100,000 less $1 for each labour-hour worked in excess of 200,000 hours. However, a minimum rental payment of $20,000 must be made each month.
9. Rent on a machine that is billed at $1,000 for up to 500 hours of machine time. After 500 hours of machine time, an additional charge of $1 per hour is paid up to a maximum charge of $2,500 per period.

Required:
Identify, by letter, the graph below that illustrates each of the cost behaviour patterns. Graphs may be used more than once. On each graph, the vertical axis represents cost and the horizontal axis represents level of activity or volume.

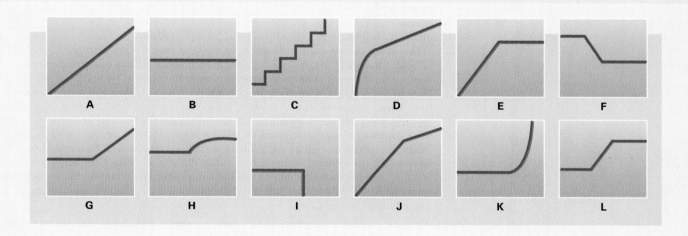

Source: Material from the Uniform CPA Examination Questions and Unofficial Answers, Copyright by the American Institute of Certified Public Accountants, Inc., is adapted with permission.

5. (LO 4; Cost behaviour) Tom Costello has been elected to handle the local Grande Theatre summer play. He is trying to determine the price to charge Grande Theatre members for attendance at this year's presentation of "My Fair Lady." He has developed the following cost estimates associated with the play:
    *   Cost of printing invitations will be $260 for 100 to 500; cost to print between 500 and 600 will be $280.
    *   Cost of readying and operating the theatre for three evenings will be $1,000 if attendance is below 500; this cost rises to $1,200 if attendance is 500 or above.
    *   Postage to mail invitations will be $0.30 each.
    *   Cost of building stage sets will be $1,215.
    *   Cost of printing up to 1,000 programs will be $250.
    *   Cost of security will be $110 per night plus $30 per hour; five hours will be needed each night.
    *   Costumes will be donated by several local businesses.

The Grande Theatre has 200 members, and each member is allowed two guests. Ordinarily, only 75% of the members attend the summer offering, and each member brings the two allowed guests. The play will be presented from 8 to 11 p.m. Invitations are mailed to those members who call to say they plan to come and also to each of the guests they specify.

Required:
a. Indicate the type of behaviour exhibited by all the items Tom needs to consider.
b. If the ordinary attendance occurs, what will be the total cost of the summer offering of the play?

c.   If the ordinary attendance occurs, what will be the cost per person attending?

d.   If 90% of the members attend and each invites two guests, what will be the total cost of the play? The cost per person? What primarily causes the difference in the cost per person?

6. (LO 4; Cost behaviour) Celestial Delights prepares dinners for several airlines, and sales average 300,000 meals per month. The significant costs of each dinner prepared are for the meat, vegetables, plastic trays, and utensils. (No desserts are provided, because passengers are more calorie-conscious than in the past.) The company prepares meals in batches of 1,000. The following data are shown in the company's accounting records for April 2005:

Cost of meat for 1,000 dinners	$900
Cost of vegetables for 1,000 dinners	360
Cost of plastic trays and utensils for 1,000 dinners	120
Direct labour cost for 1,000 dinners	950

Overhead charges total $1,200,000 per month; these are considered fully fixed for purposes of cost estimation.

Required:

Company management has asked you to address the following:

a.   What is the cost per dinner based on average sales and April prices?

b.   If sales increase to 400,000 dinners per month, what will the cost per dinner be (assuming that cost behaviour patterns remain the same as in April)?

c.   If sales are 400,000 dinners per month but the company does not want the cost per dinner to exceed its current level (based on part (a)), what amount can the company pay for meat, assuming all other costs are the same as in April?

d.   The company's major competitor has bid a price of $10.96 per dinner to the airlines. The profit margin in the industry is 100% of total cost. If Celestial Delights is to retain the airlines' business, how many dinners must the company produce each month to reach the bid price of the competitor and maintain the 100% profit margin? Assume April cost patterns will not change and dinners must be produced in batches of 1,000.

7. (LO 5; Appendix 2A) Irving Enterprises has compiled the following data to analyze its utility costs in an attempt to improve cost control:

Month	Machine-Hours	Utility Cost
January	200	$150
February	325	220
March	400	240
April	410	245
May	525	310
June	680	395
July	820	420
August	900	450

Required:

a.   Determine the *a* and *b* values for the utility cost formula using the high–low method.

b.   Determine the *a* and *b* values for the utility cost formula using least-squares regression analysis.

c.   Assuming September's machine-hours are expected to be 760, what is the expected utility cost for September based on your answer to part (a)? Based on your answer to part (b)? Why do these answers differ?

d.   Which of the answers—part (a) or part (b)—is preferable, and why?

e.   As a manager, what questions might you ask about the data just compiled?

8. (LO 6; Capacity measures and underapplied/overapplied OH) Lawrence Chung Enterprises makes only one product. It has a theoretical capacity of 50,000 units annually. Practical capacity is 80% of theoretical capacity, and normal capacity is 80% of practical capacity. The firm is expecting to produce 36,000 units next year. The company president, John Bennett, has estimated the following manufacturing overhead costs for the coming year:

Indirect materials	$ 2.00 per unit
Indirect labour	$144,000 plus $2.50 per unit
Utilities for the plant	$ 6,000 plus $0.04 per unit
Repairs and maintenance for the plant	$ 20,000 plus $0.34 per unit
Material handling costs	$ 16,000 plus $0.12 per unit
Depreciation on plant assets	$ 0.06 per unit
Rent on plant building	$ 50,000 per year
Insurance on plant building	$ 12,000 per year

Required:

a. Determine the cost formula for total manufacturing overhead.

b. Assume that Chung produces 35,000 units during the year and that actual costs are exactly as estimated. Calculate the over- or underapplied overhead for each possible measurement base. Chung uses separate overhead rates for fixed and variable overhead.

c. Which information determined in part (b) would be the most beneficial to management, and why?

9. (LO 6, 7, 9; Flow of costs) After preparing for your managerial accounting exam, you confidently turn to your roommate and declare, "I think I've finally figured out how product costs flow through the various accounts and how they are reflected on income statements and balance sheets."

On hearing this wonderful news, your roommate responds, "Hey, if you really want to test your understanding of product costing, try working a problem my old prof gave me." After rummaging for 15 minutes through various files, folders, and shelves, your roommate slaps a sheet of paper in front of you and explains that the sheet contains information pertaining to one year of operations for the Peterson Manufacturing Company. The sheet contains the following information:

Beginning inventory, direct material	$ 20,000
Ending inventory, direct material	40,000
Direct material used	400,000
Sales	900,000
Beginning Work in Process Inventory	100,000
Ending Work in Process Inventory	160,000
Cost of products completed during the year	800,000
Actual manufacturing overhead costs incurred	190,000
Selling and administrative expenses	140,000
Beginning Finished Goods Inventory	200,000
Ending Finished Goods Inventory	170,000
Beginning balance—Property, Plant and Equipment	450,000
Ending balance—Property, Plant and Equipment	480,000

Applied manufacturing overhead is 60% of direct labour cost.

Required:

Compute the following:

a. Cost of direct materials purchased.

b. Cost of direct labour.

c. Applied manufacturing overhead.

d. Cost of Goods Sold before closing underapplied or overapplied manufacturing overhead.

e. Net income or net loss before closing underapplied or overapplied manufacturing overhead.

10. (LO 6, 9; CGM, Overhead and CGS) Chretien Inc. produces Canadian flags for department stores. The raw materials account includes both direct and indirect materials. The account balances at the beginning and end of July 2006 are as follows:

	July 1	July 31
Raw Materials Inventory	$18,000	$16,700
Work in Process Inventory	24,500	19,200
Finished Goods Inventory	8,000	9,200

During the month, the firm purchased $92,000 of raw materials; direct materials consumption in July was $47,900. Manufacturing payroll costs for July were $95,000, of which 87% was related to direct labour. Manufacturing overhead charges for depreciation, insurance, utilities, and maintenance were $69,400 for the month.

Required:
a. Determine total actual overhead for July.
b. Prepare a cost of goods manufactured statement.
c. Prepare a schedule of the cost of goods sold.

11. (LO 8, 9; CGM; journal entries) Newman Ltd. manufactures a single product—mailboxes. The following data represent transactions and balances for December 2005, the company's first month of operations.

Direct materials purchased on account	$124,000
Direct materials issued to production	93,000
Direct labour payroll accrued	67,000
Manufacturing insurance expired	1,800
Manufacturing utilities accrued	8,100
Manufacturing depreciation recorded	7,900
Ending work in process (6,000 units)	18,000
Sales on account ($12 per unit)	324,000
Ending finished goods	3,000 units

Required:
As a consulting accountant, you have been asked to address the following:
a. How many units were sold in December? How many units were completed?
b. What was the total cost of goods manufactured in December?
c. What was the per unit cost of goods manufactured in December?
d. Prepare the journal entries to record the flow of costs in the company for December using the perpetual inventory system.

12. (LO 9; CGM and CGS) Lotsa Pull began business in late December of last year and makes home vacuum cleaners. The following data are taken from the firm's accounting records that pertain to its first year of operation.

Direct materials purchased on account	$213,000
Direct materials issued to production	192,000
Direct labour payroll accrued	114,000
Indirect labour payroll paid	45,300
Manufacturing insurance expired	2,700
Manufacturing utilities paid	8,900
Manufacturing depreciation recorded	18,700
Ending work in process inventory	32,000
Ending finished goods inventory (80 units)	12,800
Sales on account ($210 per unit)	442,050

Required:
a. How many units did the company sell in its first year? How many units were manufactured in the first year?
b. What was the total cost of goods manufactured?
c. What was the per unit cost of goods manufactured?
d. What was the cost of goods sold in the first year?
e. Did the company post a positive gross profit in its first year of operations?

13. (LO 9; Missing figures) Rosemary Pierre, the chief accountant, is looking at the following situations:

	Case 1	Case 2	Case 3
Sales	$9,300	$?	$112,000
Direct materials used	1,200	?	18,200
Direct labour	?	4,900	?
Prime cost	3,700	?	?
Conversion cost	4,800	8,200	49,300
Manufacturing overhead	?	?	17,200
Cost of goods manufactured	6,200	14,000	?

Beginning work in process	500	900	5,600
Ending work in process	?	1,200	4,200
Beginning finished goods	?	1,900	7,600
Ending finished goods	1,200	?	?
Cost of goods sold	?	12,200	72,200
Gross profit	3,500	?	?
Operating expenses	?	3,500	18,000
Net income (loss)	2,200	4,000	?

Required:

For each of the above cases, compute the missing figures.

14. (LO 2, 3, 7, 9; Calculating the numbers for the Cost of Goods Sold Statement) Last night, the sprinkler system at Plant A was accidentally set off. The ensuing deluge destroyed most of the cost records in Plant A for the month just completed (May). The plant manager has come to you in a panic—he has to complete his report for head office by the end of today. He wants you to give him the numbers that he needs for his report. He can provide you with some fragments of information that he has been able to salvage:

Raw Materials		
Beginning 25,000	
Ending 55,000	

Work in Process		
Beginning 15,000	

Finished Goods		
	400,000 Withdrawals in May
Ending 50,000	

Cost of Goods Sold	

Manufacturing Overheads*		
Beginning 0	

Accrued Wages Payable		
	10,000 Beginning
	20,000 Ending

*(Variable and fixed combined)

Other information:
a. Total direct materials requisitions for the month were $180,000.
b. A total of 10,000 direct labour-hours were worked during the month at an average wage of $15 hour.
c. Overhead is applied to production at $10 per direct labour-hour.
d. On May 31, there was one job, #XL235, left in Work in Process. It included $4,000 of direct materials. Twenty direct labour-hours had been worked on this job to date (the job was started on May 30).
e. Actual manufacturing overhead expenses for May were $95,000.

Required:

Compute the following:
i. Material purchases during May.
ii. Cost of Work in Process Inventory at the end of May.
iii. Amount paid to labour force in May.
iv. Cost of goods sold in May.
v. Over/underapplied overhead in May.
vi Cost of goods transferred from Work in Process to Finished Goods in May.
vii Cost of Finished Goods Inventory at the beginning of May.

(CGA adapted)

CASES

1. Some of the costs incurred by businesses are designated "direct labour costs." As used in practice, the term *direct labour cost* has a wide variety of meanings. Unless the meaning intended in a given context is clear, misunderstanding and confusion are likely. A user who does not understand the elements included in direct labour cost may interpret the numbers incorrectly and poor management decisions may result.

   In addition to understanding the conceptual definition of direct labour cost, management accountants must understand how direct labour cost should be measured.
   Required:
   a. Distinguish between direct labour and indirect labour.
   b. Discuss why some nonproductive labour (such as coffee breaks and personal time) can be and often is treated as direct labour, while other nonproductive time (such as downtime or training) is treated as indirect labour.
   c. Following are three labour cost categories used by a company and some costs it has included in each category:
      - Direct labour: Included in the company's direct labour cost are cost production efficiency bonuses and certain benefits for direct labour workers such as Employment Insurance (employer's portion), group life insurance, vacation pay, and workers' compensation.
      - Manufacturing overhead: Included in the company's overhead are costs for wage-continuation plans (short-term and long-term disability) in the event of illness, the company-sponsored cafeteria, the human resources department, and recreational facilities.
      - Direct labour or manufacturing overhead depending on the situation: Included in this category are maintenance expenses, overtime premiums, and shift premiums.

      Explain the rationale used by the company in classifying these costs in the three categories.
   d. The two aspects of measuring direct labour costs are (1) the quantity of labour effort that is to be included (the types of hours to be counted) and (2) the unit price by which each of these quantities is multiplied to arrive at monetary cost. Why are these considered separate and distinct aspects of measuring labour cost?

   (CMA adapted)

2. Larry King Company experienced a flood on May 21 of the current year that destroyed the company's work in process inventory. For the purposes of submitting an insurance claim, the company needs an estimate of the inventory value. Management found the following information in some records that were salvaged:

Direct labour-hours from May 1 to May 20	1,750
Raw Materials Inventory, May 1	$1,000
Work in Process Inventory, May 1	5,000
Accounts payable, May 1	5,500
Accounts payable, May 20	8,000
Direct labour hourly rate	6
Estimated fixed manufacturing overhead, May 1 to May 20	3,500
Estimated variable manufacturing overhead, May 1 to May 20	5,250

   On May 22, the company took a physical inventory and found $2,500 of raw materials on hand. The accounts payable account is used only for purchases of raw materials. Payments made on account from May 1 through May 20 were $6,500.
   Required:
   a. Determine the value of the Work in Process Inventory that was destroyed by the flood if $16,000 of goods had been transferred to Finished Goods from May 1 to May 20.
   b. What other information might the insurance company require? How would management determine or estimate this information?

3. Roger Martin Inc.'s main business is the publication of books and magazines. Glenn Whyte is the production manager of the Moncton plant, which manufactures paper used in all of Martin's publications. The Moncton plant has no sales staff and limited contact with outside customers since most of its sales are to other divisions of Martin. As a consequence, the Moncton plant is evaluated by merely comparing its expected costs to its actual costs to determine how well costs were controlled.

Whyte perceives the accounting reports that he receives to be the result of a historical number-generating process that provides little information that is useful in performing his job. Consequently, the entire accounting process is perceived as a negative motivational device that does not reflect how hard or effectively he works as a production manager. In discussions with Hope Brady, controller of the Moncton plant, Whyte said, "I think the cost reports are misleading. I know I've had better production over a number of operating periods, but the cost reports still say I have excessive costs. Look, I'm not an accountant; I'm a production manager. I know how to get a good quality product out. Over a number of years, I've even cut the raw materials used to do it. The cost reports don't show any of this; they're always negative, no matter what I do. There's no way you can win with accounting or the people at headquarters who use these reports."

Brady gave Whyte little consolation when she stated that the accounting system and the cost reports generated by headquarters are just part of the corporate game and almost impossible for an individual to change. "Although these reports are used to evaluate your division and are the means headquarters uses to determine whether you have done the job they want, you shouldn't worry too much. You haven't been fired yet! Besides, these cost reports have been used by Martin for the last fifteen years."

From discussions with the operations people at other Martin divisions, Whyte knows that the turnover of production managers at the company was high, even though relatively few were fired. A typical comment was: "The accountants may be quick with numbers, but they don't know anything about production. I wound up completely ignoring the cost reports. No matter what they say about not firing people, negative cost reports mean negative evaluations. I'm better off working for another company."

A copy of the most recent cost report for the Moncton plant follows:

Moncton Plant Cost Report
For the Month of November 2005
(in thousands)

	Expected Cost	Actual Cost	Excess Cost
Raw materials	$ 400	$ 437	$37
Direct labour	560	540	(20)
Manufacturing overhead	100	134	34
Total	$1,060	$1,111	$51

Required:
a. Discuss Glenn Whyte's perceptions of:
   i. The business role of Hope Brady, controller.
   ii. Corporate headquarters' reasons for issuing cost reports.
   iii. Himself, as a production manager.
b. How could the cost report be changed to make it more useful to Mr. Whyte?

(CMA)

4. Moss Manufacturing has just completed a major change in its quality control (QC) process. Previously, products were reviewed by QC inspectors at the end of each major process, and the company's ten QC inspectors were charged as direct labour to the operation or job. In an effort to improve efficiency and quality, the company purchased a computerized video QC system for $250,000. The system consists of a minicomputer, 15 video cameras, other peripheral hardware, and software.

The new system uses cameras stationed by QC engineers at key points in the production process. Each time an operation changes or there is a new operation, the cameras are moved, and a new master picture is loaded into the computer by a QC engineer. The camera takes pictures of the units in process, and the computer compares them with the picture of a "good" unit. Any differences are sent to a QC engineer, who removes the bad units and discusses the flaws with the production supervisors. The new system has replaced the ten QC inspectors with two QC engineers.

The operating costs of the new QC system, including the salaries of the two QC engineers, have been included as manufacturing overhead in calculating the company's plantwide manufacturing overhead rate, which is based on direct labour dollars.

The company's president is confused. His vice president of production has told him how efficient the new system is, yet there is a large increase in the manufacturing overhead rate. The computation of the rate before and after automation is as follows:

	Before	After
Estimated overhead	$1,900,000	$2,100,000
Estimated direct labour cost	1,000,000	700,000
Estimated overhead rate	190%	300%

"Three hundred percent," lamented the president. "How can we be competitive with such a high manufacturing overhead rate?"

Required:

a. i. Define manufacturing overhead, and cite three examples of costs typically included in manufacturing overhead.

    ii. Explain why companies develop manufacturing overhead rates.

b. Explain why the increase in the overhead rate should not have a negative financial impact on Moss Manufacturing.

c. Explain, in the greatest detail possible, how Moss Manufacturing could change its overhead accounting system to eliminate confusion over product costs.

(CMA)

5. Small businesses are usually the first organizations to feel the effects of a recessionary economy and are generally the last to recover. Two major reasons for small business financial difficulties are managerial inexperience and inadequate financing or financial management.

Small business managers frequently have problems in planning and controlling profits including revenue generation and cost reduction activities. These important financial methods are especially critical during a recessionary time period. The financial problems of small businesses are further compounded when there are poor accounting records and inexperience in the management of money.

Required:

a. Profit planning is critical for the planning and controlling of profits of a small business. Identify key features that need to be considered when developing a profit plan.

b. The management accountant can help assure that good accounting records exist in an organization. Discuss the key features that form the basis for a good accounting system that will support management decisions.

c. Explain how the management accountant can assist an organization in adopting measures to assure appropriate money management.

ETHICS AND QUALITY DISCUSSIONS

1. You are the chief financial officer for a small manufacturing company that has applied for a bank loan. In speaking with the bank loan officer, you are told that two minimum criteria for granting loans are (1) a 40% gross profit and (2) income of at least 15% of sales. Looking at the last four months' income statements, you find that gross profit has been between 30% and 33% and income has ranged from 18% to 24% of sales. You discuss these relationships with the company president, who suggests that some of the product costs included in Cost of Goods Sold be moved to the selling, general, and administrative categories so that the income statement will conform to the bank's criteria.

Required:

a. Which types of product costs might most easily be reassigned to period cost classifications?

b. Since the president is not suggesting that any expenses be kept off the income statement, do you see any ethical problems with the request? Discuss.

c. Write a short memo to convince the banker to lend the company the funds in spite of its noncompliance with the loan criteria.

2. A cost of operating any organization in the contemporary business environment is computer software. Most software can be purchased on either a per-unit basis (making it a variable cost) or a site-licence basis (making it a fixed cost). You are the manager of Manley Marketing, a company that engages in a great deal of market research. You have asked the company to acquire a copy of a statistical analysis package that would cost $400 per package for each of the twenty people in your department. Alternatively, the software company will give a site licence at a cost of $12,000. The package is essential to the organization's ability to perform research, but the controller does not have funds in the budget for twenty copies. Therefore, the controller purchases four copies and tells you to duplicate the other necessary copies. You resist, saying that to do so would violate the copyright law, which allows only one copy to be made for backup purposes.

Required:

a. Since the fixed cost for the site licence exceeds the cost for 20 copies, can you think of any reason to incur that $12,000 cost? Discuss.

b. Assume you are currently working on a marketing research project for Triton Publishing Company. Proper analysis requires the use of this software package. Is the cost of the software a direct or an indirect cost to the Triton project? If direct, what amount do you believe could be attached to the project? If indirect, should the cost be allocated to the project in some way? If so, how?

c. How would you handle this situation? What might be the consequences of your actions?

3. Assigning overhead costs to products is necessary to more accurately estimate the cost of producing a product or performing a service. One product that takes on an exceptional number of additional charges for overhead is an aspirin dose (two units) in a cosmetics hospital. Following is an estimate of why a patient is charged $7 for a dose of aspirin. Some costs are referred to as "shared and shifted costs"; others are called overhead. In all cases, this simply means that these costs are not covered by revenue dollars elsewhere and so must be covered for the hospital to do all of the things a hospital charges for—including administering aspirin.

Peterborough Cosmetics Hospital Product Costing Sheet

	Unit	Unit Cost	Total Units	Total Cost
Raw Material				
Aspirin	each	$ 0.006	2	$0.012
Direct Labour				
Physician	hour	60.000	0.0084	0.500
Pharmacist	hour	30.000	0.0200	0.600
Nurse	hour	20.000	0.0056	0.112
Indirect Labour				
Orderly	hour	12.000	0.0167	0.200
Recordkeeping	hour	12.000	0.0167	0.200
Supplies				
Cup	each	0.020	1	0.020
Shared and Shifted Costs				
Unreimbursed Medical Costs		0.200	1	0.200
Indigent Care		0.223	1	0.223
Uncollectible Receivables		0.084	1	0.084
Malpractice Insurance*		0.034	2	0.068
Excess Bed Capacity		0.169	1	0.169
Other Operating Costs		0.056	1	0.056

Other Administrative Costs	0.112	1	0.112
Excess Time Elements	0.074	1	0.074
Product Cost			$2.630
Hospital Overhead Costs @ 32.98%			0.867
Full Cost (Including Overhead)			$3.497
Profit (@ 100%)			3.497
Price (Per Dose)			$6.994

*Note that the dose is charged twice for malpractice insurance—once for each aspirin!
Source: Based on David W. McFadden, "The Legacy of the $7 Aspirin," *Management Accounting* (April 1990), p. 39. Adapted with permission of the Institute of Management Accountants, Montvale, N.J., USA. Web site: www.imanet.org.

Required:
a. Discuss the reasons why such cost shifting is necessary.
b. What other kinds of costs might be included in the additional overhead charge at the rate of 32.98%?
c. Discuss the ethical implications of shifting costs—such as those for uncollectible receivables and excess bed capacity—to a patient receiving a dose of aspirin.
d. Are you willing to accept the way the hospital estimates its $7 charge for a dose of aspirin, knowing what costs are considered in developing such a charge if you are a customer or the hospital administrator? Discuss the reasons behind your answers.

COMMUNICATIONS ACTIVITIES

1. To explain or predict the behaviour of costs, accountants often use factors that change in a consistent pattern with the costs in question.
    Required:
    What are some factors you might select to predict or explain the behaviour of the following costs?
    a. Inspection costs
    b. Equipment maintenance
    c. Salesperson's travel expenses
    d. Indirect manufacturing labour

2. The following summary numbers have been taken from Number One Landscaping Ltd. The firm produces and sells a variety of plants, sod, and other landscaping products.

Prevention costs	$ 600,000
Appraisal costs	200,000
Internal failure costs	400,000
External failure costs	600,000
Total quality costs	$1,800,000

    The company is now actively seeking to identify ways to reduce total quality costs. The company's current strategy is to increase spending in one or more quality cost categories in hopes of achieving greater spending cuts in other quality cost categories.
    Required:
    Write a memorandum to the president of Number One Landscaping Ltd. and discuss ways to reduce spending on quality-related costs. Your memo should address
    a. Which of the spending categories are more susceptible to control by management?
    b. Why it is more logical for the company to increase spending in the prevention cost and appraisal cost categories than in the failure cost categories?
    c. Which cost category is the most likely target for spending reductions?

3. Many firms are turning to robotics to manufacture in repetitive situations. They feel that costs will be reduced and products will be superior.
   Required:
   Discuss the following with respect to the above statements.
   a. Why is determining the cost to manufacture a product quite a different activity from determining how to control such costs?
   b. Does the advancement of technology appear to make costs more difficult to control? Discuss.
   c. For many production costs, why should "number of units produced" not be considered a cost driver even though it may certainly be a valid cost predictor?

PROJECTS

1. Choose one of the following projects or one of your own:
   a. Mowing the lawn
   b. Changing the oil in the car
   c. Preparing a meal or a dessert
   d. Cleaning your dorm room or apartment
   Required:
   Determine the cost of goods produced or the cost of services rendered, estimating as well as you can the cost of materials, cost of labour (assume a pay scale of $7.50 per hour for all labour time), and overhead cost. Based on your estimated cost, what would you consider to be a reasonable sale price for your product or service? Justify your answer.

2. It is well known that obtaining a university education is an expensive undertaking. Consider your university education to be a cost object, and as completely as possible, identify all costs you and/or your parents have incurred for your education. Separate the costs you identified into two categories: direct and indirect. Last, estimate the total direct and total indirect costs of your education.

3. Invite to your class an alumnus who has worked in the controller's function in a given manufacturing industry for 20 years or more. Ask this individual to discuss changes in how overhead is applied to production that he or she has observed during his or her career. Specifically ask the individual to address the following points:
   a. How technology has affected the amount of overhead cost incurred relative to the amount of other product costs incurred;
   b. How technology has affected the application of overhead to production; and
   c. Any changes that have occurred in the way overhead costs have been recorded and accounted for over the years.

4. You and three of your classmates have decided to form a new business venture. The business will provide a variety of in-house and on-site computer training programs. Your clients will be local businesses and individuals who want to enhance their understanding of and ability to use computer software applications.

   As a first step in the financial management of the new business, you have decided it is necessary to develop a quantitative financial plan that will cover all aspects of the start-up of the business. For example, this plan should include the financing of and expenditures for acquiring a business site and necessary equipment, training employees, and so on.

   Your business partnership team must explicitly state any assumptions that need to be made in developing the financial plan, including the size and scope of the business. Your team may divide the planning effort among the members in any optimal way. At the conclusion of the planning process, a written report must be prepared by the team. At a minimum, the report must contain the following:
   - estimates of the service volume or other measures that were used as the basis for the financial plan;
   - important assumptions that were made about the business and its clients;

- a description of all resources that need to be acquired according to the financial plan;
- estimates of all start-up expenditures;
- a plan for obtaining the financial resources needed to meet the expenditures.

5. Consider WestJet airline. There are no fax machines and martinis at the gate, and no meals during the flight. If connecting to another airline, passengers retrieve their baggage and carry it to the connecting flight. "We try to maximize our resources and find efficiencies wherever we turn," says WestJet's director of sales and marketing.

> We manage a turnaround of about half an hour. The Canadian industry average is an hour or more. Everyone helps out to make the turnaround as fast as possible. Our captains go back in the cabin and tidy up between flights.

Source: "The Little Airline That Could," *Canadian Business*, Toronto, April 1997, pp. 34-40.

Required:

Obtain current financial statements of several prominent airline carriers. Use the financial statements as a basis to write a report that answers the following questions.
a. What are the major costs incurred by airline companies?
b. Which major costs are likely to be fixed and which are likely to be variable?
c. Based on your answers to parts (a) and (b), why do airlines strive to have quick turnarounds for flights?

(This project is best suited to be accomplished in teams. Optimally, each team should have three members: one to examine marketing costs, one to examine financing costs, and one to examine the costs of service provision including costs of plant and equipment.)

USING THE INTERNET

1. Using the Internet, find an article about costs.
    Required:
    Make a list of the costs you find and define as many different types as you can from the article.

2. Visit www.cbsc.org for information on overhead application.
    Once at the site, click on
    1. English,
    2. Popular Business Topics,
    3. Financial Planning, and
    4. Profit Pricing for Cost of A Service.
    Required:
    Write a report on how overhead is applied.

SOLUTIONS TO SELF-TEST QUESTIONS

1. c: Prime cost = Direct materials used + Direct labour
    = ($20,000 + $100,000 − $30,000) + $80,000
    = $90,000 + $80,000
    = $170,000

2. b: Conversion cost = Direct labour + Manufacturing overhead
    = $80,000 + [($80,000 ÷ 10) × 8]
    = $80,000 + $64,000
    = $144,000

3. c: Cost of goods manufactured
    = Beginning work in process + Direct materials used + Direct labour + Manufacturing overhead − Ending work in process
    = $40,000 + $90,000 + $80,000 + $64,000 − $25,000
    = $249,000

4. d: Prime cost = Direct materials + Direct labour

Direct materials ($84,000 + $36,000 − $30,000) =	$ 90,000
Direct labour =	60,000
Prime cost =	$150,000

5. b: Conversion cost = Direct labour + Manufacturing overhead

Manufacturing overhead [($60,000 ÷ $7.50) × $10.00]	$ 80,000
Direct labour	60,000
	$140,000

6. c: (200 + 175 + 125) ÷ (2,000 + 200 + 175 + 125) × $75,000 = $15,000
$15,000 ÷ 2,000 = $7.50

7. b: 40,000 × ($2.00 + $1.00 + $0.40) = $136,000

8. d: (40,000 + 5,000 − 4,000) × $2.00 = $82,000
(40,000 + 5,000 − 4,000) × $1.00 = $41,000
(40,000 + 5,000 − 4,000) × $0.40 = $16,400

9. b: $56,000 + $9,500 − $15,000 = $50,500

10. c: $50,000 + $154,000 − $26,000 = $178,000

ENDNOTES

1. Outside processing cost may also be considered a direct material cost. For example, a furniture manufacturer may want a special plastic laminate on tables. Rather than buying the necessary equipment, the manufacturer may send the tables to another company that specializes in this process. The amount paid for this process may be considered a direct material cost by the manufacturer.

2. Patrick Brethour, "Suncor To Squeeze Suppliers To Cut Costs," *The Globe and Mail*, June 18, 2002, p. B5.

3. Daniel Fisher, "The Best Little Factory in Texas," *Forbes*, New York, June 10, 2002, Vol. 169, Issue 13, p. 110.

4. James Brian Quinn et al., "Beyond Products: Services-Based Strategy," *Harvard Business Review* (March/April, 1990), p. 65.

5. "Robots Cut Jobs at Jeep Factory," *Star Tribune*, Minneapolis, Minn. April 30, 2001, p. 07D.

6. Deborah Ball, "Pirelli Unveils New Tire-Making Process," *Wall Street Journal*, Brussels, Dec. 3, 1999, p. 3.

7. This definition of product cost is traditionally accepted and is also referred to as absorption costing. Another product costing method, called variable costing, excludes the fixed manufacturing overhead component from inventories. Absorption and variable costing are discussed in Appendix 3A.

8. An accountant's view of a variable cost is, in fact, a slight distortion of reality. Variable costs usually increase at a changing rate until a range of activity is reached in which the average variable cost rate per unit becomes fairly constant. Within this range, the slope of the cost line becomes less steep because the firm benefits from operating efficiencies such as price discounts on materials, improved worker skills, and increased productivity. Beyond this range, the slope becomes quite steep as the firm enters an activity range in which some operating inefficiencies (such as worker crowding and material shortages) cause the average variable cost rate to trend sharply higher. Because of the curves on each end of the graph, accountants choose as the relevant range that range of activity in which the variable costs per unit are constant.

9. Section 3060 of the *CICA Handbook* uses the term *amortization*. In practice, however, the term *depreciation* is still used, therefore *depreciation* will be used in this text.

10. Al Haas, "Falling Prices Make It a Vintage Year for Used-Car Buying," *The (New Orleans) Times-Picayune*, July 3, 1998, p. F1.

11. Tony Van Alpen (Detroit AP), "Car Incentives Back As Dealers Clear Backlog," *Toronto Star*, July 3, 2002.

12. Sheila James, "Taking a Small but Toothsome Slice of the Bakery Market," *Financial Times*, London, Oct. 5, 1999, p. 35.

13. Use of such nontraditional activity measures to allocate overhead and the resultant activity-based costs are discussed in Chapter 6.

14. Although many firms use expected activity to compute their predetermined fixed overhead rates, this choice of activity level may not be the most effective for planning and control purposes because it ignores the effects of unused capacity. This issue is discussed further in Chapter 5 in regard to standard cost variances.

15. Marinus DeBruine and Parvez R. Sopariwala, "The Use of Practical Capacity for Better Management Decisions," *Journal of Cost Management*, Spring 1994, pp. 26–27.

16. These equations are derived from mathematical computations beyond the scope of this text but are found in many statistics books. The symbol Σ means "the summation of."

Chapter 3

Cost–Volume–Profit Analysis

LEARNING OBJECTIVES

After reading this chapter, you should be able to answer the following questions:

1 **How** is the breakeven point computed and what does it represent?

2 **How** can cost–volume–profit (CVP) analysis be used by a company?

3 **How** do costs, revenues, and contribution margin interact with changes in an activity base (volume)?

4 **How** are breakeven and profit–volume graphs prepared?

5 **How** does cost–volume–profit (CVP) analysis differ in single-product and multiproduct firms?

6 **What** are the underlying assumptions of CVP analysis and how do these assumptions create a short-run managerial perspective?

7 **How** are the margin of safety and operating leverage concepts used in business?

8 **What** are cost accumulation and cost presentation approaches to product costing? (Appendix 3A)

9 **How** do changes in sales and/or production levels affect net income as computed under absorption and variable costing? (Appendix 3A)

ON SITE

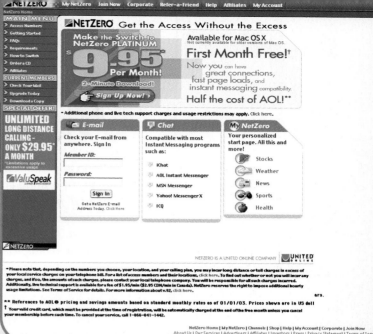

http://www.netzero.com

NetZero

NETZERO was started in 1998 to provide free and value-priced Internet connectivity. It has since become United Online, Inc. after a merger with Juno Online Services on September 25, 2001. NetZero ceased to trade as a separate public company as of September 26, 2001.

Like all newcomers, NetZero sought to grow rapidly while maximizing the return on every dollar it spent. Accordingly, in 20 months, NetZero acquired 5 million registered users and as of the quarter ended June 2000 had more than $18.7 million in revenues, while squeezing out a 4.7% gross margin. Six months later, the company's cost per thousand ad impressions was chopped in half to $3, while revenue increased threefold to about $3 as well. Thus, NetZero was able to achieve one of its greatest challenges: breaking even at the gross margin level.

NetZero also managed to turn one of its major (fixed) costs, telecommunications, into variable costs by contracting with numerous national providers.

Since consumers were offered free Internet access, NetZero sought revenues from advertising. NetZero minimized the risks associated with this critical dependency by generating revenues from numerous sources in the event that any major customer might jump ship. Subscribers were attracted by NetZero software distributed to consumers via promotional agreements with software and hardware manufacturers and a multitude of other sponsors. A multitude of subscribers attracts advertisers. Additionally, a carefully cultivated brand image helped NetZero establish the brand equity cachet that serious advertising sponsors sought.

The merger with Juno also benefited the newly created United Online through the elimination of redundancies and creation of synergies via economies of scale. The rejuvenated firm hopes to take AOL head-on.

SOURCE: Adapted from *NetZero 2000 Annual Report*, http://www.netzero.com/investors; *United Online Overview*, http://www.irconnect.com/untd and company executives.

*B*reakeven point—does the term ring a bell? It should. That's the magic number that tells you when your revenue will cover your expenses. Although entrepreneurs often fail to realize the significance of recognizing and reaching the breakeven point, understanding what it takes to break even is critical to making any business profitable.

Incorporating accurate and thorough breakeven analysis as a routine part of your financial planning will keep you abreast of how your business is really faring. Determining how much business is needed to keep the door open will help improve your cash flow management and your bottom line.[1]

To be strategically successful, managers must ensure that their organizations are achieving the right combination and volume of products and selling prices that will generate enough revenue to cover all variable and fixed costs. This is a problem faced by all organizations. Covering costs is a matter of operational survival regardless of whether you manage Chapters-Indigo Bookstores or the Toronto Raptors, are a promoter of a concert to be held at the National Arts Centre, or are a physician with your own practice. The first part of this chapter discusses methodology for calculating an organization's breakeven point. At breakeven, a company experiences neither profits nor losses on its operating activities. As a manager, promoter, or physician, however, you would most likely not want to operate at a volume level that simply covers costs; you would want to make profits. Knowing the breakeven level of operations provides a point of reference from which you would be better able to plan for volume goals that should generate income rather than produce losses.

The latter part of the chapter looks at cost accumulation and cost presentation of data. The method of accumulation specifies which manufacturing cost components are recorded as part of the product cost. The method of presentation focuses on how costs are shown on external financial statements or internal management reports. Accumulation and presentation procedures are accomplished using one of two methods: absorption or variable costing. Each method uses the same basic data but structures and processes it differently.

LEARNING OBJECTIVE **1**

How is the breakeven point computed and what does it represent?

breakeven point
that level of activity, in units or dollars, at which total revenues equal total costs

THE BREAKEVEN POINT

The level of activity, in units or dollars, at which total revenues equal total costs is called the **breakeven point (BEP)**. Although most business managers hope to do better than just break even, the breakeven point is an important point of reference by which the manager can judge either the company's level of risk of not exceeding the BEP or the company's level of comfort in exceeding the BEP. Managers make this determination by comparing the magnitude of the company's current or planned sales with the BEP. Finding the breakeven point requires an understanding of an organization's revenue and cost functions.

Basic Assumptions

Certain assumptions are made about cost behaviour so that cost information can be used in accounting computations. The following list summarizes these simplifying assumptions about revenue and cost functions.

- *Relevant range*: A primary assumption is that the company is operating within the relevant range of activity specified in determining the revenue and cost information used in each of the following assumptions.[2]
- *Revenue*: Total revenue fluctuates in direct proportion to units sold. Revenue per unit is assumed to remain constant, and fluctuations in per-unit revenue for factors such as quantity discounts are ignored.

- *Variable costs:* Total variable costs fluctuate in direct proportion to the level of activity or volume. On a per-unit basis, variable costs are assumed to remain constant within the relevant range. This assumed variable cost behaviour is the same as assumed revenue behaviour. Variable production costs include direct material, direct labour, and variable overhead; variable selling costs include charges for items such as commissions and shipping. Variable administrative costs may exist in areas such as purchasing.
- *Fixed costs:* Total fixed costs remain constant within the relevant range; thus, per-unit fixed costs decrease as volume increases and increase as volume decreases. Fixed costs include both fixed manufacturing overhead and fixed selling and administrative expenses.
- *Mixed costs*: Mixed costs must be separated into their variable and fixed elements before they can be used in CVP analysis. Any method (such as high–low or regression analysis) that validly separates these costs in relation to one or more predictors may be used.

Because these basic assumptions treat selling prices and costs as known and constant, any analysis based on these assumptions is valid for only the short term. Long-range planning must recognize the possibilities of price and cost fluctuations.

An important amount in breakeven and CVP analysis is **contribution margin (CM)**, which can be defined on either a per-unit or total basis. On a per-unit basis, contribution margin (CM) is equal to unit selling price minus per-unit variable production, selling, and administrative costs ($R - VC = CM$). Contribution margin reflects the revenue remaining after all variable costs have been covered. Contribution margin per unit is constant, because both revenue and variable costs per unit have been defined as being constant. Total contribution margin fluctuates in direct proportion to sales volume.

contribution margin
selling price per unit minus all variable production, selling, and administrative costs per unit

To illustrate computation of the breakeven point, the fiscal 2005 income statement information for Aspinall Computer Corporation is presented in Exhibit 3-1 on page 104. The current relevant range of production and sales for the company is between 10,000 and 30,000 SCSI drives. The costs given in the exhibit are costs for all product elements.

A DVD is installed after undergoing testing by Patrick Aspinall, the expert.

EXHIBIT 3-1

Aspinall Computer Corporation
Income Statement for 2005

	Total	Contribution Per Unit	Contribution Margin Ratio Percentage
Sales (15,000 units)		$6,750,000	$ 450	100%
Variable costs:				
Production	$4,725,000		$ 315	70
Selling	270,000		18	4
Total variable cost		(4,995,000)	$(333)	(74)
Contribution margin		$1,755,000	$ 117	26%
Fixed costs:				
Production	$ 550,000			
Selling and administrative expenses	700,000			
Total fixed costs		(1,250,000)		
Profit before Income Taxes		$ 505,000		

Mathematical Approach to CVP Analysis

This approach uses an algebraic equation to calculate the breakeven point. However, the answer to the equation is not always acceptable and may need to be rounded to a whole number. For instance, partial units cannot be sold, and some items may be sold only in specified lot sizes.

Algebraic breakeven computations use an equation representing the income statement. This equation groups costs by behaviour and shows the relationships among revenue, volume, variable cost, fixed cost, and profit as follows:

$$R(X) - VC(X) - FC = PBT$$

where

R = revenue (selling price) per unit
X = number of units sold or to be sold
$R(X)$ = total revenue
VC = variable cost per unit
$VC(X)$ = total variable cost
FC = fixed cost
PBT = profit before tax

Since the equation represents an income statement, profit (P) can be set equal to zero so that the formula indicates a breakeven situation. At the point where P = $0, total revenues are equal to total costs and the breakeven point (BEP) in units can be found by solving the equation for X.

$$R(X) - VC(X) - FC = \$0$$
$$R(X) - VC(X) = FC$$
$$(R - VC)(X) = FC$$
$$X = FC \div (R - VC)$$

Breakeven volume is equal to total fixed cost divided by the difference between revenue per unit and variable cost per unit. Since revenue minus variable cost equals contribution margin, the formula can be abbreviated as follows:

$$(R - VC)X = FC$$
$$(CM)X = FC$$
$$X = FC \div CM$$

where
CM = contribution margin per unit.

For Aspinall Computer Corporation, Exhibit 3-1 indicates a unit selling price of $450, a unit variable cost of $333, and total fixed costs of $1,250,000. The contribution margin is $117 per unit ($450 − $333). Substituting these values into the equation yields the following breakeven point:

$$\$450X - \$333X = \$1,250,000$$
$$\$117X = \$1,250,000$$
$$X = \$1,250,000 \div \$117$$
$$X = 10,684 \text{ units*}$$

*This answer is rounded up from 10,683.76.

As mentioned, the breakeven point can be expressed either in units or in dollars of revenue. One way to convert a unit breakeven point to dollars is to multiply the breakeven point in units by the selling price per unit. For Aspinall Computer Corporation, the breakeven point in sales dollars is $4,807,800 (10,684 units × $450 per unit).

Another method of computing the breakeven point in sales dollars requires the computation of a contribution margin ratio. The **contribution margin ratio (CM%)** is calculated as contribution margin divided by revenue and indicates what proportion of revenue remains after variable costs have been covered. The contribution margin ratio represents that portion of the revenue dollar remaining to go toward covering fixed costs and increasing profits. The contribution margin ratio can be computed with either per-unit or total cost information; thus, if unit selling price and unit variable cost are not known, the breakeven point can still be calculated. Dividing total fixed cost by the CM ratio gives the breakeven point in sales dollars.

$$X_\$ = FC \div CM \text{ ratio}$$

where

$X_\$$ = breakeven point in sales dollars
CM% = contribution margin ratio or (R − VC) ÷ R

The contribution margin ratio for Aspinall Computer Corporation is given in Exhibit 3-1 as 26% ($117 ÷ $450). Thus, based on the CM ratio, the company's breakeven point in dollars equals $1,250,000 ÷ 0.26 = $4,807,692—virtually the same amount shown in the earlier calculation (rounding caused the slight difference). The company's breakeven point in units can be determined by dividing the BEP in sales dollars by the unit selling price $4,807,692 ÷ $450 = 10,684 (rounded up from 10,683.76).

Another measure that can be used is the **variable cost (VC) ratio.** This is found by subtracting the CM ratio from 100 percent, and it represents the variable cost proportion of each revenue dollar.

Knowledge of the BEP can help managers plan for future operations. Managers want to earn profits, not just cover costs. Substituting an amount other than zero for the profit (P) term converts the breakeven formula to cost–volume–profit analysis.

contribution margin ratio
contribution margin divided by revenue; indicates what proportion of selling price remains after variable costs have been covered

variable cost ratio
100% minus the CM ratio; represents the variable cost proportion of each revenue dollar

cost–volume–profit analysis
the process of examining the relationships among revenues, costs, and profits for a relevant range of activity and for a particular time period

USING COST–VOLUME–PROFIT ANALYSIS

LEARNING OBJECTIVE 2

How can cost–volume–profit (CVP) analysis be used by a company?

Cost–volume–profit (CVP) analysis is the process of examining the relationships among revenues, costs, and profits for a relevant range of activity and for a particular time period. This technique is applicable in all economic sectors (manufacturing, wholesaling, retailing, and service industries) because the same types of managerial functions are performed in all types of organizations.

When known amounts are used for selling price per unit, variable cost per unit, volume of units, and fixed costs, the algebraic equation given in the previous section can be solved to give the amount of profit generated under specified conditions. A more frequent and significant application of CVP analysis is to set a desired target profit and focus on the relationships between that target and specified income statement amounts to find an unknown. Volume is a common unknown because managers want to achieve a particular level of profit and need to know what quantity of sales must be generated for this objective to be accomplished. Managers may want to use CVP analysis to determine how high variable cost can go (given fixed costs, selling price, and volume) and still provide a given profit level. Variable cost may be increased or decreased by modifying product design specifications, the manufacturing process, or the grade of material.

Profits may be stated as either a fixed or a variable amount and on either a before-tax or an after-tax basis. The following examples continue to use the Aspinall Computer Corporation data using different amounts of target profit.

Fixed Amount of Profit Before Tax

If the desired profit is stated as a before-tax amount, it is treated in CVP analysis simply as an additional cost to be covered. The following equation yields before-tax profit in units:

$$R(X) - VC(X) - FC = PBT$$
$$R(X) - VC(X) = FC + PBT$$
$$X = (FC + PBT) \div (R - VC)$$
$$X = (FC + PBT) \div CM$$

where PBT = profit before tax.

If sales dollars are desired, the formula is as follows:

$$R(X) = (FC + PBT) \div CM\%$$

Assume that Aspinall Computer Corporation wants to generate a before-tax profit of $622,000. To do so, the company must sell 16,000 units, which will generate $7,200,000 of revenue. These calculations are shown in Exhibit 3-2.

Fixed Amount of Profit After Tax

Both production costs and income taxes are important factors in analyzing organizational profitability. Income taxes represent a significant influence on business

EXHIBIT 3-2

CVP Analysis—Fixed Amount of Profit Before Tax

PBT desired = $622,000

In Units:

$$R(X) - VC(X) = FC + PBT$$
$$CM(X) = FC + PBT$$
$$(\$450X - \$333X) = \$1,250,000 + \$622,000$$
$$X = \$1,872,000 \div \$117$$
$$X = 16,000 \text{ units}$$

In Sales Dollars:

$$\text{Sales} = (FC + PBT) \div CM \text{ ratio}$$
$$= \$1,872,000 \div 0.26$$
$$= \$7,200,000$$

decision making. Managers need to be aware of the income tax effects when choosing a target profit amount.

A company desiring a particular amount of after-tax net income must first determine the equivalent amount on a before-tax basis, given the applicable tax rate. The CVP formulas needed to calculate a desired after-tax net income amount are as follows:

$$R(X) - VC(X) - FC = PBT$$
$$[(PBT)(TR)] = \text{Tax Expense}$$

Thus, the profit after tax (PAT) is equal to the profit before tax minus the applicable tax. Defined as such, PAT can be integrated into the original before-tax CVP formula above:

$$PBT - (PBT)(TR) = PAT$$
$$PBT(1 - TR) = PAT$$
$$PBT = PAT \div (1 - TR)$$

where
PBT = fixed amount of profit before tax
PAT = fixed amount of profit after tax
 TR = tax rate

Assume that Aspinall Computer Corporation wants to earn $444,000 of profit after taxes and the company's marginal tax rate is 30%. The number of units and dollars of sales needed are calculated in Exhibit 3-3.

Rather than specifying a fixed amount of profit to be earned, managers may state profit as a variable amount. Then, as units sold or sales dollars increase, profit will increase proportionally. Variable profit may be stated on either a before-tax or an after-tax basis and either as a percentage of revenues or a per-unit amount. If the variable amount is stated as a percentage, it is convenient to convert that percentage into a per-unit amount. When variable profit is used, the CVP formula must be adjusted to recognize that the profit is related to volume of activity.

EXHIBIT 3-3

CVP Analysis—Fixed Amount of Profit After Tax

PAT desired = $444,000; tax rate = 30%

In Units:

$$PBT = PAT \div (1 - \text{Tax Rate})$$
$$= \$444,000 \div (1 - 0.30)$$
$$= \$444,000 \div 0.70$$
$$= \$634,286 \text{ necessary profit before income tax (rounded)}$$
$$R(X) - VC(X) = FC + PBT$$
$$CM(X) = FC + PBT$$
$$\$117X = \$1,250,000 + \$634,286 \text{ (rounded)}$$
$$\$117X = \$1,884,286$$
$$X = \$1,884,286 \div \$117$$
$$= 16,106 \text{ units (rounded)}$$

In Sales Dollars:

$$\text{Sales} = (FC + PBT) + CM \text{ ratio}$$
$$= (\$1,250,000 + \$634,286) \div 0.26$$
$$= \$1,884,286 \div 0.26$$
$$= \$7,247,254 \text{ (rounded)}$$

Variable Amount of Profit Before Tax

Managers may want desired profit to be equal to a specified variable amount of sales. The CVP formula for computing the unit volume of sales necessary to earn a specified variable rate or per-unit profit before income tax is as follows:

$$R(X) - VC(X) - FC = P_uBT(X)$$

where P_uBT = profit per unit before income tax.

Solving for X (or volume) gives the following:

$$R(X) - VC(X) - P_uBT(X) = FC$$
$$CM(X) - P_uBT(X) = FC$$
$$X(CM - P_uBT) = FC$$
$$X = FC \div (CM - P_uBT)$$

The variable profit is treated in the CVP formula as if it were an additional variable cost to be covered. If the profit is viewed in this manner, the original contribution margin and contribution margin ratio are effectively adjusted downward to reflect the desired net margin or profit per unit.

When the desired profit is set as a percentage of selling price, that percentage cannot exceed the contribution margin ratio. If it does, an infeasible problem is created, because the "adjusted" contribution margin is negative. In such a case, the variable cost percentage plus the desired profit percentage would exceed 100% of the selling price—a condition that cannot occur.

Assume that Patrick Aspinall, the president of Aspinall Computer Corporation, wants to know what level of sales (in units and dollars) would be required to earn an 8% before-tax profit on sales. The calculations in Exhibit 3-4 provide the answer.

EXHIBIT 3-4

CVP Analysis—Variable Amount of Profit Before Tax

P_uBT desired = 8% on sales revenues
P_uBT per unit = 0.08($450)
= $36

In Units:

$$(R(X) - VC(X)) - P_uBT(X) = FC$$
$$CM(X) - P_uBT(X) = FC$$
$$(\$450X - \$333X) - \$36X = \$1,250,000$$
$$X = \$1,250,000 \div (\$117 - \$36)$$
$$= \$1,250,000 \div \$81$$
$$= 15,433 \text{ units (rounded)}$$

In Sales Dollars:
The following relationships exist:

	Per Unit	Percent of Sales
Selling price	$450	100%
Variable costs	(333)	(74%)
Variable profit before income tax	(36)	(8%)
"Adjusted" contribution margin	$ 81	18%

Sales = FC ÷ "Adjusted" CM ratio*
= $1,250,000 ÷ 0.18
= $6,944,444**

* Note that it is not necessary to have per-unit data; all computations can be made with percentage information only.
**15,433 units @ $450 selling price = $6,944,850. Difference due to rounding.

Variable Amount of Profit After Tax

Adjusting the CVP formula to determine the return on sales on an after-tax basis involves stating profits in relation to both the volume and the tax rate. The algebraic manipulations are as follows:

$$(R(X) - VC(X) - FC = P_uBT(X)$$
$$[P_uBT(X)](TR) = \text{Tax Expense}$$

$$P_uBT(X) - [P_uBT(X)](TR) = P_uAT(X)$$
$$P_uBT(X)(1 - TR) = P_uAT(X)$$
$$P_uBT(X) = P_uAT(X) \div (1 - TR)$$

$$R(X) - VC(X) - FC = P_uBT(X)$$
$$R(X) - VC(X) - P_uBT(X) = FC$$
$$CM(X) - P_uBT(X) = FC$$
$$X(CM - P_uBT) = FC$$
$$X = FC \div (CM - P_uBT)$$

where
P_uBT = desired profit per unit before tax
P_uAT = desired profit per unit after tax

Assume that Aspinall Computer Corporation wishes to earn a profit after tax of 14% of revenue and has a 30% tax rate. The necessary sales in units and dollars are computed in Exhibit 3-5.

EXHIBIT 3-5

CVP Analysis—Variable Amount of Profit After Tax

$$P_uAT \text{ desired} = 14\% \text{ of revenue}$$
$$= 0.14(\$450)$$
$$= \$63$$
$$\text{Tax rate} = 30\%$$

In Units:

$$P_uBT(X) = [\$63 \div (1 - 0.30)](X)$$
$$= (\$63 \div 0.70)X$$
$$= \$90X$$
$$R(X) - VC(X) - P_uBT(X) = FC$$
$$CM(X) - P_uBT(X) = FC$$
$$\$450X - \$333X - \$90X = \$1,250,000$$
$$\$27X = \$1,250,000$$
$$X = \$1,250,000 \div \$27$$
$$= 46,297 \text{ units (rounded)}$$

Note that the necessary number of units (46,297 units) is beyond the current maximum of Aspinall's relevant range of activity (30,000 units). Thus, it is highly unlikely that such a high rate of profit could be generated under the current cost structure.

In Sales Dollars:

	Per Unit	Percent of Sales
Selling price	$450	100
Variable costs	(333)	(74)
Variable profit before taxes	(90)	(20)
"Adjusted" contribution margin	$ 27	6%

$$\text{Sales} = FC \div \text{"Adjusted" CM ratio}$$
$$= \$1,250,000 \div 0.06$$
$$= \$20,833,333 \text{ (rounded)}*$$

*46,297 units @ $450 selling price = $20,833,650. The difference between the answer in units and the answer in sales dollars results from rounding in both the unit answer and the contribution margin percentage answer.

All the previous illustrations of CVP analysis were made using a variation of the formula approach. Solutions were not accompanied by mathematical proofs. The income statement model is an effective means of developing and presenting solutions and/or proofs for solutions to CVP applications.

The answers provided by breakeven and CVP analysis are valid only in relation to specific selling prices and cost relationships. Changes in the company's selling price or cost structure will cause changes in the breakeven point and in the sales needed for the company to achieve a desired profit figure.

THE INCOME STATEMENT APPROACH

The income statement approach to CVP analysis allows the preparation of pro forma statements. Income statements can be used to prove the accuracy of computations made using the formula approach to CVP analysis, or the statements can be prepared to determine the impact of various sales levels on profits either before or after tax. Since the formula and income statement approaches are based on the same relationships, each should be able to prove the other.[3] Exhibit 3-6 proves each of the computations made in Exhibits 3-2 through 3-5 for Aspinall Computer Corporation. The answers provided by breakeven or cost–volume–profit analysis are valid only in relation to specific selling prices and cost relationships. Changes that occur in the company's selling price or cost structure will cause a change in the breakeven point or in the sales needed to obtain a desired profit figure. How revenue and cost changes will affect a company's breakeven point or sales volume required to realize desired profits can be determined through incremental analysis.

EXHIBIT 3-6

Income Statement Approach to
CVP—Proof of Computations

Previous computations:

Exhibit 3-1—Breakeven point: 10,684 units
Exhibit 3-2—Fixed profit ($622,000) before tax: 16,000 units
Exhibit 3-3—Fixed profit ($444,000) after tax: 16,106 units
Exhibit 3-4—Variable profit (8% of revenues) before tax: 15,433 units
Exhibit 3-5—Variable profit (14% of revenues) after tax: 46,297 units

R = $450 per unit; VC = $333 per unit; FC = $1,250,000;
Tax rate = 30% for Exhibits 3-4 and 3-5

	Basic Breakeven Data	Ex. 3-2	Ex. 3-3	Ex 3-4	Ex. 3-5
Units sold	10,684[3]	16,000	16,106[3]	15,433[3]	46,297[3]
Sales	$ 4,807,800	$ 7,200,000[5]	$ 7,247,254	$ 6,944,850	$ 20,833,333[2]
Total variable costs	(3,557,772)	(5,328,000)	(5,363,298)	(5,139,189)	(15,416,901)
Contribution margin	$ 1,250,028	$ 1,872,000	$ 1,883,956	$ 1,805,661	$ 5,416,432
Total fixed costs	(1.250,000)	(1,250,000)	(1,250,000)	(1,250,000)	1,250,000)
Profit Before Income Taxes	$ 28[1]	$ 622,000	$ 633,956	$ 555,661[4]	$ 4,166,432
Income Taxes (30%)			(190,187)		(1,249,930)
Profit After Income Taxes (NI)			$ 443,769		$ 2,916,502[6]

[1] Difference due to rounding
[2] Rounded ($450 × 46,297 = $20,833,650)
[3] Rounded
[4] Desired profit before tax = 8% on revenue; 0.08 × $555,588 (difference due to rounding)
[5] Rounded ($450 × 16,106 = $7,247,700)
[6] Desired profit after tax = 14% of revenue; (0.14 × $20,833,333) = $2,916,667 (Difference due to rounding)

INCREMENTAL ANALYSIS FOR SHORT-RUN CHANGES

LEARNING OBJECTIVE 3

How do costs, revenues, and contribution margin interact with changes in an activity base (volume)?

The breakeven point may increase or decrease, depending on the particular changes that occur in the revenue and cost factors. Other things being equal, the breakeven point will increase if there is an increase in the total fixed cost, a decrease in selling price per unit, or an increase in variable costs. A decrease in selling price, an increase in variable costs, or a combination of the two will cause a decrease in unit contribution margin. These relationships are illustrated in Exhibit 3-7. The breakeven point will decrease if there is a decrease in total fixed cost or an increase in unit (or percentage) contribution margin. A change in the breakeven point will also cause a shift in total profits or losses at any level of activity.

Incremental analysis is a process focusing only on factors that change from one course of action or decision to another. As related to CVP situations, incremental analysis is based on changes occurring in revenues, costs, and/or volume. The following are some examples of changes that may occur in a company and the incremental computations that can be used to determine the effects of those changes on the breakeven point or profits.

incremental analysis
a technique used in decision analysis that compares alternatives by focusing on the differences in their projected revenues and costs

We continue to use the basic facts presented for Aspinall Computer Corporation in Exhibit 3-1. All of the following examples use before-tax information to simplify the computations. After-tax analysis would require the application of a $(1 - \text{tax rate})$ factor to all profit figures.

Case 1

The company wishes to earn a before-tax profit of $702,000. How many units does it need to sell?

Since the breakeven point is known, answering this question requires simply determining how many units above the breakeven point are needed to generate before-tax profits of $702,000. Each dollar of contribution margin generated by product sales goes first to cover fixed costs and then to produce profits. Thus, after the breakeven point is reached, each dollar of contribution margin is a dollar of profit. To achieve $702,000 in desired profit requires Aspinall Computer

---

EXHIBIT 3-7

Effects of Changes From Original Data

Original Data: (from Exhibit 3-1)

Revenue per unit	$450
Variable cost per unit	333
Contribution margin per unit	$117
Fixed costs	= $1,250,000
Breakeven point	= 10,684 units

If fixed costs increase to $2,340,000, BEP rises to 20,000 units

$$\$117X = \$2,340,000$$
$$X = \$2,340,000 \div \$117$$
$$X = 20,000$$

If revenue per unit falls to $433, BEP rises to 12,500 units

$$\$433 - \$333 = \$100 \text{ new CM}$$
$$\$100X = \$1,250,000$$
$$X = 12,500$$

If variable costs rise to $340, BEP rises to 11,364 units

$$\$450 - \$340 = \$110 \text{ new CM}$$
$$\$110X = \$1,250,000$$
$$X = 11,364 \text{ (rounded)}$$

Corporation to sell 6,000 units over the breakeven point (10,684 units), with each drive providing $117 of contribution margin:

$$\$702,000 \div \$117 = 6,000 \text{ units above BEP}$$
$$\therefore \text{Total units} = 10,684 + 6,000 = 16,684$$

Case 2

Aspinall Computer Corporation estimates that it can sell an additional 40 units if it spends $4,200 more on advertising. Should the company incur this extra fixed cost?

The contribution margin from the additional units must first cover the additional fixed cost before profits can be generated.

Increase in contribution margin	
40 units × $117 CM per unit	$ 4,680
Less: Increase in fixed cost	(4,200)
Equals: Net incremental benefit	$ 480

Since the net incremental benefit is $480, the advertising campaign would result in an additional profit and, thus, should be undertaken.

Case 3

The company estimates that, if the selling price of each unit is reduced to $440, an additional 1,000 units per year can be sold. Should the company reduce the prices of the units? Current sales volume, given in Exhibit 3-1, is 15,000 units.

If the selling price (SP) is reduced, the contribution margin per unit will decrease to $107 per drive ($440 SP − $333 VC). Sales volume is estimated to increase to 16,000 units (15,000 + 1,000).

Total new contribution margin	
(16,000 units × $107 CM per unit)	$ 1,712,000
Less: Total fixed costs (unchanged)	(1,250,000)
Equals: New profit before taxes	$ 462,000
Less: Current profit before taxes (from Exhibit 3-1)	(505,000)
Equals: Reduction in profit before taxes	$ (43,000)

Based on the above computation, the company will have less profit before taxes than is currently being generated; therefore, the company should not reduce its selling price. It is possible, however, that the reduction in price might increase sales by more than 1,000 units, and this might make the reduction worthwhile.

Case 4

Aspinall Computer Corporation has the opportunity on a one-time basis to sell 5,000 units to a foreign company. This sale will not disturb existing Canadian sales. The foreign company is offering to pay $375 per drive. The drives will be packaged and sold using the foreign company's own logo. Packaging costs will increase by $10.00 per unit. If the order is accepted, an additional $10,000 will be incurred by Aspinall to ship the product, but no other variable selling costs will be incurred by the company. Should Aspinall Computer Corporation make this sale?

The new total variable cost per drive is $343 ($333 total current variable costs + $10.00 additional variable packaging costs). The $375 selling price minus the $343 new total variable cost provides a contribution margin of $32 per drive sold to the foreign company.

Total contribution margin provided by	
this sale (5,000 units × $32 CM per drive)	$160,000
Less: Additional fixed cost related to this sale	10,000
Net incremental benefit	$150,000

The total contribution margin generated by the sale not only covers the additional fixed cost of the shipping, but also provides a net incremental benefit or profit to the firm; therefore, the deal should be made.

These are just a few examples of changes that might occur in a company's revenue and cost structure. In most situations, a complete income statement need not be prepared to determine the effects of changes. The contribution margin or incremental approach will often be sufficient to decide on the monetary merits of proposed or necessary changes. In making decisions, however, management must also consider the qualitative and long-run effects of the changes.

The contribution approach is often used to evaluate alternative pricing strategies in economic downturns. In such times, companies must recognize the reality that they will be unable to sell a normal volume of goods at normal prices. With this understanding, they can choose to maintain normal prices and sell a lower volume of goods, or reduce prices and attempt to maintain market share and normal volume.

> For the past year we have seen this in the automobile industry. To keep market share they [auto makers] discounted products and offered zero-percent financing on many vehicles. This resulted in lower gross profit but it does keep the factories operating.
>
> In 2001, the North American car industry [was] expected to run at only 80% of capacity, meaning a number of manufacturers [were] operating in the sub-80% range, where it is hard to be profitable.[4]

Solutions to breakeven problems are determined in this chapter using an algebraic formula. In some situations, however, information is clearer when presented in a more visual format, such as a graph. A breakeven graph may be used to graphically depict the relationships among revenues, variable costs, fixed costs, and profits (or losses). A breakeven graph can be prepared to graph the relationships among revenue, volume, and the various costs. The breakeven point on a breakeven graph is located at the point where the total cost and total revenue lines cross. The following steps are necessary in preparing a **breakeven graph**.

Step 1   Label the x-axis as volume and the y-axis as dollars. Plot the variable cost line as a linear function with a slope equal to total variable cost per unit. Next, plot the revenue line with a slope equal to the unit sales price. The area between the variable cost and revenue lines represents total contribution margin at each level of volume. The result of this step is shown in Exhibit 3-8.

Step 2:   To graph total cost, add a line parallel to the total variable cost line. The distance between the total and variable cost lines is the amount of fixed cost. The total cost line is above and to the left of the total variable cost line. The breakeven point is located where the revenue and total cost lines intersect. If exact readings could be taken on the graph shown in Exhibit 3-9, the breakeven point for Aspinall Computer Corporation would be shown as $4,807,800 of sales and 10,684 units (both figures are rounded).

LEARNING OBJECTIVE 4

How are breakeven and profit–volume graphs prepared?

breakeven graph
a graphical depiction of the relationships among revenues, variable costs, fixed costs, and profits (or losses)

EXHIBIT 3-8

Step One in Breakeven Graph
Preparation

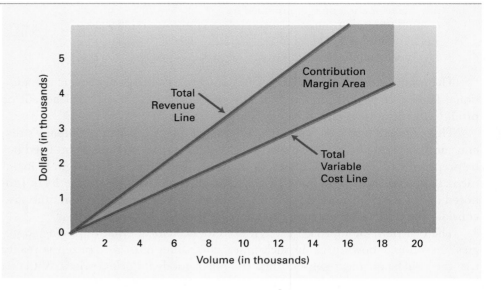

EXHIBIT 3-9

Breakeven Graph

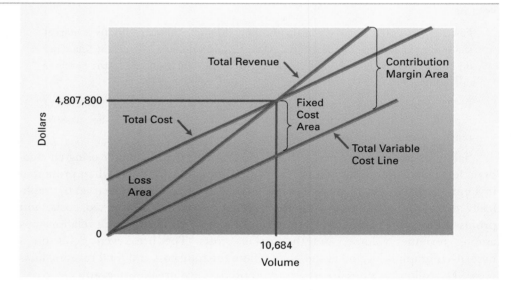

The format of the above breakeven graph allows the following important observations to be made.

1. Contribution margin is created by the excess of revenues over variable costs. If variable costs are greater than revenues, no quantity of volume will allow a profit to be made.
2. Total contribution margin is equal to total fixed cost plus profit or minus loss.
3. Before profits can be generated, contribution margin must exceed fixed costs.

Another method of visually presenting income statement information is the **profit–volume (PV) graph**, which reflects the amount of profit or loss at each sales level. The horizontal axis on the PV graph represents unit sales volume, and the vertical axis represents dollars. Amounts shown above the horizontal axis are positive and represent profits, while amounts shown below the horizontal axis are negative and represent losses.

profit–volume graph
a graphical presentation of the profit or loss associated with each level of sales

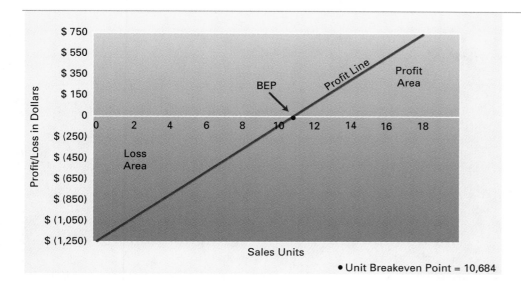

EXHIBIT 3-10
Profit–Volume Graph

To draw the graph, first locate two points: total fixed costs and breakeven point. Total fixed costs are shown on the vertical axis as a negative amount (or below the sales volume line). If no units were sold, fixed costs would still be incurred, and a loss would result. The location of the breakeven point may be determined either by use of a breakeven graph or algebraically. The breakeven point in units is shown on the horizontal axis because there is no profit or loss at that point. With these two points plotted, a line is drawn that passes between them and extends through the breakeven point. This line can be used to read, from the vertical axis, the amount of profit or loss for any sales volume. This line represents total contribution margin, and its slope is determined by the unit contribution margin. The line shows that no profit is earned until the contribution margin covers the fixed costs.

The PV graph for Aspinall Computer Corporation is shown in Exhibit 3-10 above. Total fixed costs are $1,250,000 and the breakeven point is 10,684 units. The profit line reflects the original Exhibit 3-1 income statement data that, at sales of 15,000 SCSI drives, the company earns a profit of $505,000.

Although graphic approaches to breakeven point, cost–volume–profit analysis, and profit–volume relationships provide detailed visual displays, they may not yield precise answers to questions asked by mangers. Such solutions must be found using an algebraic formula approach because exact numerical points cannot always be read from the graphs.

CVP ANALYSIS IN A MULTIPRODUCT ENVIRONMENT

LEARNING OBJECTIVE 5

How does cost–volume–profit (CVP) analysis differ in single-product and multiproduct firms?

The breakeven point for many companies is influenced by the mix of products sold. For example, the daily breakeven attendance at the National Arts Centre depends on how many tickets are sold in the various price ranges for each performance. Likewise, the breakeven point for an Air Canada overseas flight will be influenced by the number of first-class, business-class, and economy-class tickets sold for the flight.

Companies typically produce and sell a variety of products or services. To perform CVP analysis in a multiproduct company, it is necessary to assume a constant product sales mix or an average contribution margin ratio. The constant mix assumption can be referred to as the "bag" or "package" assumption. This analogy

Only the best quality parts are used at Aspinall Computer Corporation.

compares the sales mix to a bag or package of items that are sold together. For example, whenever some of Product A is sold, specified quantities of Products B and C are also sold.

Use of the constant sales mix assumption allows the computation of a weighted average contribution margin ratio. The CM ratio is *weighted* on the basis of the quantity of each item included in the bag. The contribution margin ratio of the item that makes up the largest proportion of the bag has the greatest impact on the average contribution margin of the bag mix. Without the assumptions of a constant sales mix, the breakeven point cannot be calculated, nor can CVP analysis be used effectively.[5]

The Aspinall Computer Corporation example continues. Because of the success of the SCSI drives, company management has decided to produce DVD drives. Vice president of marketing Ambrus Kesckes estimates that, for every five SCSI drives sold, the company will sell two DVD drives. Therefore, the "bag" of products has a 5:2 ratio. The company will incur an additional $150,000 in fixed costs related to plant assets (depreciation, insurance, and so on) to support a higher relevant range of production and additional licensing fees. Exhibit 3-11 provides relevant company information and shows the breakeven computations.

The weighted average contribution margin ratio is calculated by multiplying the sales mix percentage (relative to sales dollars)* by the CM ratio** for each product and summing the results. According to the note in Exhibit 3-11, the relationship of dollars of SCSI drive sales to dollars of DVD drive sales is 90% to 10%. Based on this information, the CM ratio for the "bag" of products is computed by multiplying these percentages by the contribution margin ratios of the respective individual products (also from Exhibit 3-9) and adding the results as follows:

SCSI drives	$90\% \times 26\%$ =	0.234
DVD drives	$10\% \times 20\%$ =	0.020
Total CM ratio		0.254

*For SCSI drives this is calculated as $2,250 ÷ $2,500, which is 90%, and for DVD drives as $250 ÷ $2,500, which is 10%.

**The contribution margin ratio for SCSI drives is calculated as $585 ÷ $2,250, which is 26% and for DVDs as $50 ÷ $250, which is 20%.

EXHIBIT 3-11

CVP Analysis—Multiple Products

Product cost information	SCSI Drives		DVD	
Selling price	$450	100%	$125	100%
Total variable cost	(333)	(74%)	(100)	(80%)
Contribution margin	$117	26%	$ 25	20%

Total Fixed Costs ($1,250,000 previous + $150,000 additional new costs) = $1,400,000

	SCSI Drives	DVD	Per Bag Total	Per Bag Percent
Number of products per bag	5	2		
Revenue per product	$450	$125		
Total revenue per "bag"	$2,250	$250	$2,500	100.0%
Variable cost per unit	(333)	(100)		
Total variable cost per "bag"	(1,665)	(200)	(1,865)	(74.6)%
Contribution margin—product	$117	$ 25		
Contribution margin—"bag"	$ 585	$ 50	$ 635	25.4%

BEP in *units* (where B = "bags" of products)

$$CM(B) = FC$$
$$\$2,500 - \$1,865 = 1,400,000$$
$$\$635B = \$1,400,000$$
$$B = 2,205 \text{ bags to break even (rounded)}$$

Note: Each bag is made up of 5 SCSI drives; thus, it will take 11,025 (5 × 2,205) SCSI drives and 4,410 (2 × 3,205) DVD drives to break even, assuming the constant 5:2 sales mix.

BEP in *sales dollars* (where CM ratio = Weighted average CM for each "bag" of products):

$$B_\$ = FC \div CM \text{ ratio}$$
$$B_\$ = \$1,400,000 \div 0.254$$
$$B_\$ = \$5,511,811 \text{ (rounded)}$$

Note: The breakeven sales dollars also represent the assumed constant sales mix of $2,205 of sales of SCSI drives to $250 of sales of DVD drives to represent a 90% ($2,250 ÷ $2,500) to 10% ($250 ÷ $2,500) ratio. Thus, the company must have approximately $4,960,630 ($5,511,811 × 90%) of sales of SCSI drives and $551,181 ($5,511,811 × 10%) in sales of DVDs to break even.

Proof of the above computations using the income statement approach is shown below:

	SCSI Drives	DVD Drives	Total
Sales	$ 4,960,630	$ 551,181	$5,511,811[1]
Variable costs[2]	(3,670,866)	(440,945)	(4,111,811)
Contribution margin	$ 1,289,764	$ 110,236	$ 1,400,000
Fixed costs			(1,400,000)
Income before income taxes			$ 0

[1]From Exhibit 3-11.

[2]These amounts are determined by taking the previously calculated variable cost percentages of 74% for SCSI drives and 80% for DVDs (Exhibit 3-11).

Any shift in the proportion of sales mix of products will change the weighted average contribution margin and the breakeven point. If the sales mix shifts toward products with lower contribution margins, there will be an increase in the BEP; furthermore, there will be a decrease in profits unless there is a corresponding increase in total revenues. A shift toward higher-margin products without a corresponding decrease in revenues will cause increased profits and a lower breakeven point.

To break even at the level indicated, Aspinall Computer Corporation must sell the products in exactly the relationships specified in the original sales mix. If sales are at the specified level but not in the specified mix, the company will experience either a profit or a loss, depending on whether the mix is shifted toward the product with the higher or lower contribution margin ratio.

LEARNING OBJECTIVE   6

What are the underlying assumptions of CVP analysis and how do these assumptions create a short-run managerial perspective?

UNDERLYING ASSUMPTIONS OF CVP ANALYSIS

The CVP model is a useful planning tool that can provide information on how profits are affected when changes are made in the costing system or in sales levels. Like any model, however, it reflects reality but does not duplicate it. Cost–volume–profit analysis is a tool that focuses on the short run, partially because of the assumptions that underlie the computations. Although these assumptions are necessary, they limit the results' accuracy. These assumptions follow; some of them were also provided at the beginning of the chapter.

1. All variable cost and revenue behaviour patterns are constant per unit and linear within the relevant range.
2. Total contribution margin (total revenue – total variable cost) is linear within the relevant range and increases proportionally with output. This assumption follows directly from assumption 1.
3. Total fixed cost is a constant amount within the relevant range.
4. Mixed costs can be accurately separated into their fixed and variable elements. Such accuracy is particularly unrealistic, but estimates can be developed from the high–low method or regression analysis (discussed in Chapter 2 and Appendix 2A).
5. Sales and production are equal; thus, there is no material fluctuation in inventory levels. This assumption is necessary because of the allocation of fixed costs to inventory at potentially different rates each year.
6. There will be no capacity additions during the period under consideration. If such additions were made, fixed (and possibly variable) costs would change. Any changes in fixed or variable costs would invalidate assumptions 1 to 3.
7. In a multiproduct firm, the sales mix will remain constant. If this assumption were not made, no useful weighted average contribution margin could be computed for the company for purposes of CVP analysis.
8. There is no inflation, or inflation affects all cost factors equally, or if factors are affected unequally, the appropriate effects are incorporated into the CVP figures.
9. Labour productivity, production technology, and market conditions will not change. If any of these changes occured, costs would change correspondingly, and it is possible that selling prices would change. Such changes would invalidate assumptions 1 to 3.

The nine assumptions are the traditional ones associated with cost–volume–profit analysis and reflect a basic disregard of possible (and probable) future changes. Accountants generally assume that cost behaviour, once classified, remains constant over periods of time as long as operations remain within the relevant range and in the absence of evidence to the contrary. Thus, for example, once a cost is determined to be fixed, it is fixed next year, the year after, and from then on.

As mentioned in Chapter 2, however, it may be more realistic to regard fixed costs as long-term variable costs. Companies can, over the long run and through managerial decisions, lay off supervisors and sell plant and equipment items.

Alternatively, companies may grow and increase their fixed investments in people, plant, and equipment. Fixed costs are not fixed forever. In many companies, some costs considered to be fixed "have been the most variable and rapidly increasing costs."[6] Part of this cost "misclassification" problem has occurred because of improper specification of cost drivers. As companies become less focused on production and sales volumes as cost drivers, they will begin to recognize that fixed costs only exist under a short-term reporting period perspective.

In addition, certain costs may arise that are variable in the first year of providing a product or service to a customer but will not recur in future years. Customer acquisition costs for a pure-play Internet operation is $82 per customer. On-line customer acquisition costs may continue to rise in the short term but they should eventually drop as on-line companies become more recognized by buyers. It is a fact that pure-play Internet companies spend 20% to 40% more than those companies that do not have Internet presence.[7]

Differing current and future period costs are very important concerns in various service businesses. Getting new customers requires a variety of one-time costs for things such as advertising, mailing, and checking customers' credit histories.

As companies and customers become more familiar with one another, services can be provided more efficiently or higher prices can be charged for the trusted relationship. Failure to consider such changes in costs can provide a very distorted picture of how profits are generated and, therefore, can lead to an improper analysis of the relationships of costs, volume, and profits.

MARGIN OF SAFETY AND OPERATING LEVERAGE

LEARNING OBJECTIVE **7**

How are the margin of safety and operating leverage concepts used in business?

The breakeven point is the lowest level of sales volume at which an organization would want to operate. As sales increase from that point, managers become less concerned about whether decisions will cause the company to lose money. Thus, when making decisions about various business opportunities, managers often consider the company's **margin of safety** and **operating leverage**.

Margin of Safety

The margin of safety is the excess of a company's estimated (budgeted) or actual sales over its breakeven point. It is the amount that sales can drop before reaching the breakeven point and thus provides a measure of the amount of "cushion" from losses. It helps management to determine how close to the danger level the company is operating and provides an indication of risk. The lower the margin of safety, the more carefully management must watch sales figures and control costs so that a net loss will not be generated. At low margins of safety, managers are less likely to take advantage of opportunities that could send the company into a loss position.

The margin of safety can be expressed as units, dollars, or a percentage. The following formulas are applicable:

Margin of safety in units = Estimated units − Breakeven units
Margin of safety in dollars = Estimated (Actual) sales dollars − Breakeven sales dollars
Margin of safety percentage = Margin of safety in units or dollars ÷ Estimated (Actual) sales in units or dollars

The breakeven point for Aspinall Computer Corporation (using the original, single-product data from page 104) is 10,684 SCSI drives or $4,807,800 of sales. The income statement for the company presented in Exhibit 3-1 shows actual sales for

margin of safety
the excess of the estimated (budgeted) or actual sales of a company over its breakeven point; can be calculated in units or sales dollars, or as a percentage

operating leverage
a factor that reflects the relationship of a company's variable and fixed costs; measures the change in profits expected to result from a specified percentage change in sales

2005 of 15,000 SCSI drives and sales revenue of $6,750,000. The margin of safety for Aspinall Computer Corporation is calculated in Exhibit 3-12 below. The margin is high, since the company is operating far above its breakeven point.

Operating Leverage

Another measure that is closely related to the margin of safety and also provides useful management information is the company's degree of operating leverage. The relationship of a company's variable and fixed costs is reflected in its operating leverage. Typically, highly labour-intensive organizations, such as McDonald's and Pizza Pizza, have high variable costs and low fixed costs and thus have a low operating leverage and a relatively low breakeven point. (An exception to this rule is sports teams, which are highly labour-intensive but have labour costs that are fixed rather than variable.) Companies with a low operating leverage can show a profit even when they experience wide swings in volume levels. Many companies choose to outsource certain of their functions. For example, BP Amoco PLC is contracting out the accounting services at its Canadian petroleum subsidiary, a U.S.$200 million agreement. This is the largest business process outsourcing deal in Canada and the first of its kind in the oilpatch. PricewaterhouseCoopers will look after the accounting and associated information technology for BP Amoco, the largest natural gas producer in Canada.[8] This philosophy allows companies to eliminate some fixed costs and, therefore, reduce the probability of losses if business volume declines.

Conversely, organizations that are highly capital-intensive, such as Air Canada, have a cost structure that includes very high fixed costs. Such a structure reflects high operating leverage. Because fixed costs are high, the breakeven point is relatively high; if selling prices are predominantly set by the market, volume has the primary impact on profitability. As companies become more automated, they will face this type of cost structure and will be increasingly dependent on volume to add profits.

Companies with high operating leverage have high contribution margin ratios. Although such companies have to establish fairly high sales volumes initially to cover fixed costs, once those costs are covered, each unit sold after breakeven produces large profits. Thus, a small increase in sales can have a major impact on a company's profits. Also, as discussed in the News Note on page 121, companies attempt to manage their levels of operating leverage as economic conditions change.

The **degree of operating leverage** (DOL) indicates how sensitive the company is to sales increases and decreases by measuring how a percentage change in sales affects company profits. The computation for the degree of operating leverage is:

degree of operating leverage
a measure of how a percentage change in sales will affect profits; calculated at a specified sales level as contribution margin divided by income before tax

$$\text{Degree of operating leverage} = \text{Contribution margin} \div \text{Profit before tax}$$

The calculation assumes that fixed costs do not increase when sales increase.

EXHIBIT 3-12
Margin of Safety

In units:	15,000 actual − 10,684 BEP = 4,316 SCSI drives
In sales dollars:	$6,750,000 actual − $4,807,800 BEP = $1,942,200
In percentage:	(15,000 − 10,684) ÷ 15,000 = 0.288, or 29% rounded
	or
	($6,750,000 − $4,807,800) ÷ $6,750,000 = 0.288 or 29% (rounded)

Managing Operating Leverage

GENERAL NEWS NOTE

Electronics manufacturer Celestica Inc. will cut 10 percent to 15 percent of its workforce—as many as 6,000 jobs—as it copes with falling revenue and a continuing industrywide slowdown, the company said on July 17, 2002.

Celestica, which manufactures equipment sold by major telecommunication companies such as Lucent Technologies Inc. and computer companies such as International Business Machines Corp., said it is reducing its manufacturing capacity to deal with a slump in the worldwide telecom sector.

Celestica, which is controlled by conglomerate Onex Corp., has also been on an efficiency drive for much of the last year.

"Over the past 15 months, we have rebalanced our manufacturing footprint and have been focused on driving greater efficiency from our operations.

We [Celestica] have made significant progress on these initiatives, resulting in stable profitability, and as a result believe that we can undertake this action without compromising our growth opportunities or limiting our customers' potential growth needs."[9]

Assume that Aspinall Computer Corporation is currently selling 12,000 SCSI drives. Using the basic facts from Exhibit 3-1, Exhibit 3-13 provides the income statement that reflects this sales level. As shown in this exhibit, the company has an operating leverage factor of 9.12 at this level of sales. If the company increases sales by 20%, the change in profits is equal to the degree of operating leverage multiplied by the percentage change in sales, or 182%! If sales decrease by the same 20%, there is a negative 182% impact on profits.

The degree of operating leverage decreases the further a company moves from its breakeven point. When the margin of safety is small, the degree of operating leverage is large. In fact, at breakeven, the degree of operating leverage is infinite, because any increase from zero is an infinite percentage change. If a company is operating close to the breakeven point, each percentage increase in sales can make a dramatic impact on net income. As the company moves away from breakeven sales, the margin of safety increases, but the degree of operating leverage declines.

EXHIBIT 3-13

Degree of Operating Leverage

	12,000 Drives Current	14,400 Drives 20% Increase	9,600 Drives 20% Decrease
Sales	$ 5,400,000	$ 6,480,000	$ 4,320,000
Variable costs ($333 per drive)	3,996,000	(4,795,200)	(3,196,800)
Contribution margin	$ 1,404,000	$ 1,684,800	$ 1,123,200
Fixed costs	(1,250,000)	(1,250,000)	(1,250,000)
Profit before tax	$ 154,000	$ 434,800	$ (126,800)

Degree of operating leverage:

Contribution margin ÷ Profit before tax

[($1,404,000 ÷ $154,000)]   9.12

[($1,684,800 ÷ $434,800)]   3.87

[$1,123,200 ÷ $(126,800)]   Can't be calculated

Profit increase at 14,400 drives = $434,800 − $154,000
= $280,800 or 182% of original income

Profit decrease at 9,600 drives = $(126,800) − $154,000
= $(280,800) or −182% of original income

SITE ANALYSIS

United Online

The mission of United Online is to provide consumers with a high-quality Internet access experience that fits both their needs and their budgets through the company's two subsidiaries—NetZero and Juno Online. The company set out to get to breakeven as quickly as possible, and it was successful in reaching that point at the gross margin level. The strategy of the combined company under the banner of United Online has been successful by the company's own account. The company offers Internet services in more than 5,000 cities across the United States and in Canada. The headquarters of the company is in Westlake Village, California. It also has offices in New York City and Hyderabad, India.

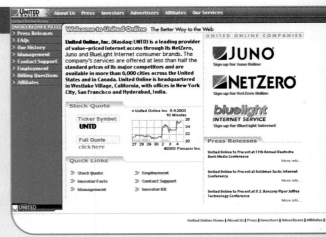

The third-quarter performance (March 2002) was driven by strong consumer demand for NetZero and Juno value-priced Internet services, operating leverage from the company's efficient cost structure, and outstanding execution delivered by all 430 United Online employees worldwide. The company feels that the combination of NetZero and Juno to create this new company is clearly an example of a merger that has worked.

United Online has far to go before it stops growing. On June 6, 2002, to further diversify its revenue stream and expand its business model, United entered into an agreement with CNM Network, Inc. to offer value-priced long distance telephone plans under the NetZero brand.

Brian Woods, executive vice-president and chief marketing officer of United Online, said, "Offering users a high-quality, affordable long distance service as a complement to our value-priced ISP services further solidifies NetZero's position as a highly attractive alternative to the higher priced services that are currently available."

On May 30, 2002, the company announced the launch of high-speed Internet service—in addition to its established dial-up service—through Comcast Cable Communications Inc.

In the third quarter ended March 2002, United boasted revenues of $50.9 million and 1.6 million paying subscribers: quite a performance for a firm whose foundations were built on free Internet access. The company intends to grow its pay subscriber base by 70,000 to 90,000 subscribers, resulting in 1.67 million to 1.69 million pay subscribers by June 30, 2002.

While its business model has had to adapt to the constant flux of the dynamic new economy, United Online remains firmly positioned in the value corner of the market, fearing little competition to its rather unique value-approach pricing method. Media megalith AOL Time Warner is suffering under burdensome debt and a slumping advertising market. United Online has come a long way from its free-lunch offer that drew salivating consumers in droves. Whether it will be able to survive next to its more powerful peers, only time will tell.

Source: Adapted from *United Online Overview*, www.irconnect.com/untd.
Reprinted by permission of United Online, Inc.

APPENDIX 3A

Absorption and Variable Costing

Knowing the cost to produce a product or provide a service is important to all businesspeople. But, as discussed in Chapter 2, cost may be defined in a variety of ways. A company's costing system and inventory measurement method provide necessary, but not sufficient, information for determining product cost. Two additional dimensions must be considered: cost accumulation and cost presentation. The method of presentation focuses on how costs are shown on external financial statements or internal management reports. Accumulation and presentation procedures use either absorption or variable costing. These methods are discussed and contrasted. The methods use the same basic data but structure and process these data differently.

The most common approach to product costing is **absorption costing**, which is also known as full costing. This approach treats the costs of all manufacturing components (direct material, direct labour, variable manufacturing overhead, and fixed manufacturing overhead) as inventoriable or product costs. Exhibit 3-14 depicts the absorption costing model.

An organization incurs costs for direct material (DM), direct labour (DL), variable manufacturing overhead (VOH) and fixed manufacturing overhead (FOH) to produce products. However, when one thinks about the costs of production, it can be said that direct material (DM), direct labour (DL), and variable manufacturing overhead (VOH) are incurred when goods are produced or services are rendered. Since total DM, DL, and VOH costs increase with each additional product made or unit of service rendered, these costs are considered product costs and are inventoried until the product or service is sold. Fixed manufacturing overhead (FOH) cost, on the other hand, may be incurred even when production or service facilities are idle. Although total FOH cost does not vary with units of production or level of service, this cost provides the basic capacity necessary for production or service to occur. Because production could not take place without the incurrence of fixed manufacturing overhead, absorption costing considers this cost to be inventoriable.

LEARNING OBJECTIVE   **8**

What are cost accumulation and cost presentation approaches to product costing?

absorption costing
a cost accumulation method that treats the costs of all manufacturing components (direct materials, direct labour, variable overhead, and fixed overhead) as inventoriable or product costs; also known as full costing

EXHIBIT 3-14
Absorption Costing Model

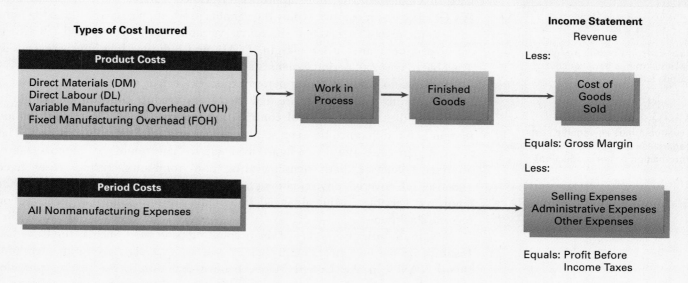

Thus, when absorption costing is used, the financial statements show the Work in Process Inventory, Finished Goods Inventory, and Cost of Goods Sold accounts as including variable per-unit production costs as well as a per-unit allocation of fixed manufacturing overhead. Absorption costing also presents expenses on an income statement according to their functional classifications. A **functional classification** is a grouping of costs that were all incurred for the same basic purpose. Functional classifications include categories such as cost of goods sold, selling expenses, and administrative expenses.

The actual Work in Process Inventory cost that is transferred to Finished Goods Inventory is computed as follows:

Direct materials	$xxx
Direct labour	xxx
Variable manufacturing overhead	xxx
Fixed manufacturing overhead	xxx
Production cost for period	$xxx
Plus: Beginning Work in Process	xxx
Total cost to account for this period	$xxx
Less: Ending Work In Process*	xxx
Cost of Goods Manufactured	$xxx

* Calculation of this amount is covered in a later chapter.

Variable costing, also known as **direct costing**,[10] is a cost accumulation method that includes only variable production costs (direct material, direct labour, and variable manufacturing overhead) as inventoriable or product costs. Thus, variable costing defines product costs solely as costs of *actual production*. Since fixed manufacturing overhead will be incurred even if there is no production, variable costing proponents believe that this cost does not qualify as a product cost. Under this method the fixed manufacturing overhead costs are therefore treated as period costs (expenses) and are charged against revenue as incurred. Variable costing is illustrated in Exhibit 3-15.

A variable costing income statement and management report separates costs by cost behaviour (variable and fixed), although it may also present expenses by functional classifications within the behavioural categories. Under variable costing, Cost of Goods Sold is more appropriately called *Variable* Cost of Goods Sold (VCGS), because it comprises only the variable production costs related to the units sold. Remember that revenue (R) minus variable cost of goods sold (VCGS) is called **product contribution margin** (PCM), and indicates how much revenue is available to cover all period expenses and to provide net income.

Variable nonmanufacturing period expenses (such as a sales commission set at 10% of product selling price) are deducted from product contribution margin to determine the amount of **total contribution margin** (TCM). Total contribution margin is the difference between total revenues and total variable expenses. This amount represents the dollar figure available to "contribute" to the coverage of all fixed expenses, both manufacturing and nonmanufacturing. After fixed expenses are covered, any remaining contribution margin provides income to the company. Variable costing financial statements are also known as contribution income statements.

Major authoritative bodies of the accounting profession, such as the Canadian Institute of Chartered Accountants (CICA) and the Financial Accounting Standards Board (FASB) in the United States, believe that absorption costing provides

functional classification
a grouping of costs incurred for the same basic purpose

variable costing
a cost accumulation method that includes only variable production costs (direct materials, direct labour, and variable manufacturing overhead) as product or inventoriable costs and treats fixed manufacturing overhead as a period cost; also known as direct costing

direct costing
see *variable costing*

product contribution margin
revenue minus variable cost of goods sold

total contribution margin
revenue minus all variable costs regardless of the area of incurrence (production or nonproduction)

EXHIBIT 3-15
Variable Costing Model

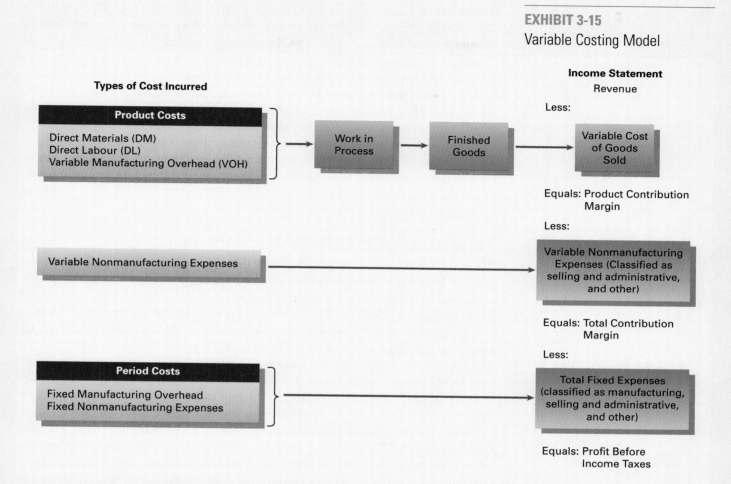

external parties with the most informative picture of earnings. The rationale for this position reflects the importance of the matching concept in that absorption costing expenses all product costs in the period that the related revenue is recognized.

Cost behaviour (relative to changes in activity) cannot be observed from an absorption costing income statement. Managers attempting to use absorption costing information for internal decision making find that combining costs into functional classifications obscures important cost behaviour patterns Therefore, although companies must prepare external statements using absorption costing, internal reports are also often prepared to show cost behaviours to facilitate management analysis and decision making. Cost behaviour is extremely important for a variety of managerial activities including cost–volume–profit analysis, relevant costing, and budgeting.[11] Whether the perspective is of the short run or long run, one of the preeminent concerns of all firms is generation of revenues in excess of all costs.

Two basic differences can be seen between absorption and variable costing. The first difference is in the way fixed overhead (FOH) is treated for product costing purposes. Under absorption costing, FOH is considered a product cost; under variable costing, it is considered a period cost. Absorption costing advocates contend that products cannot be made without the capacity provided by fixed manufacturing costs and so these costs are product costs. Variable costing advocates contend that fixed manufacturing costs would be incurred whether or not production occurs and, therefore, cannot be product costs because they are not caused by production. The second difference is in the presentation of costs on the income statement. Absorption costing classifies expenses by function, whereas variable costing categorizes expenses first by behaviour and then may further classify them by function.

Even with their differences, the two costing methods have some underlying similarities. First, both methods use the same basic cost information. Second, the treatment of direct material, direct labour, and variable manufacturing overhead is the same under absorption and variable costing; these costs are always considered product costs. Third, selling and administrative expenses are considered period costs under both costing methods. Fourth, there are no differences among accounts other than in Work in Process Inventory, Finished Goods Inventory, and the expense accounts under the two methods.

Absorption and Variable Costing Illustrations

Aspinall Computer Corporation is a small drive-production company. Data for this product are used to compare absorption and variable costing procedures and presentations. Exhibit 3-16 gives the production costs per unit, the annual budgeted nonmanufacturing costs, and other basic operating data for the company. All costs are assumed to remain constant over the three years 2003 through 2005 and, for simplicity, the company is assumed to have no Work in Process Inventory at the end of a period. Actual costs are assumed to equal the budgeted costs for the years presented. The bottom section of Exhibit 3-17 compares actual unit production with actual unit sales to determine the change in inventory for each of the three years.

Since the company began operations in 2003, there is no beginning Finished Goods Inventory. The next year, 2004, also has a zero beginning inventory because all units produced in 2003 were also sold in 2003. In 2004 and 2005, production and sales quantities differ, which is a common situation because production frequently "leads" sales so that inventory can be stockpiled for a later period. The illustration purposefully has no beginning inventory and equal cumulative units of production and sales for the three years to demonstrate that, regardless of whether absorption or variable costing is used, the cumulative income before taxes will be the same

---

EXHIBIT 3-16

Basic Data for 2003, 2004, and 2005

Sales price per unit	$ 6.00
Direct material cost per unit	$ 2.040
Direct labour	1.500
Variable manufacturing overhead	0.180
Total variable manufacturing cost per unit	$ 3.720
Fixed overhead based on expected activity level of 30,000 units	$16,020
Fixed overhead applied per unit = $16,020 ÷ 30,000	$ 0.534
Total absorption cost per unit:	
Variable manufacturing cost	$ 3.720
Fixed manufacturing overhead	0.534
Total absorption cost per unit	$ 4.254
Estimated (budgeted) nonmanufacturing expenses:	
Variable selling expenses per unit	$ 0.24
Fixed selling and administrative expenses	$2,340.00
Total Estimated (budgeted) nonmanufacturing expenses = ($0.24 per unit sold + $2,340)	

	2003	2004	2005	Total
Actual units made	30,000	29,000	31,000	90,000
Actual units sold	30,000	27,000	33,000	90,000
Change in Finished Goods Inventory	0	+2,000	−2,000	0

EXHIBIT 3-17

What Happened Over the Three Years?

Absorption Costing Presentation

	2003	2004	2005	Total
Sales ($6 per unit)	$ 180,000	$ 162,000	$ 198,000	$ 540,000
CGS ($4.254 per unit)	(127,620)	(114,858)	(140,382)	(382,860)
Gross Margin	$ 52,380	$ 47,142	$ 57,618	$ 157,140
Deduct: Underapplied Fixed Overhead*		(534)		(534)
Add: Overapplied Fixed Overhead*			534	534
Adjusted Gross Margin	$ 52,380	$ 46,608	$ 58,152	$ 157,140
Operating Expenses				
Selling and Administrative	(9,540)	(8,820)	(10,260)	(28,620)
Income Before Income Taxes	$ 42,840	$ 37,788	$ 47,892	$ 128,520

*Underapplied overhead means that the cost of goods sold is too low and thus the gross margin is overstated; therefore, it must be deducted from the gross margin. In the case of overapplied overhead the opposite happens.

Variable Costing Presentation

	2003	2004	2005	Total
Sales ($6 per unit)	$ 180,000	$ 162,000	$ 198,000	$ 540,000
Variable CGS ($3.72 per unit)	(111,600)	(100,440)	(122,760)	(334,800)
Product Contribution Margin	$ 68,400	$ 61,560	$ 75,240	$ 205,200
Variable Selling Expenses ($0.24 × units sold)	(7,200)	(6,480)	(7,920)	(21,600)
Total Contribution Margin	$ 61,200	$ 55,080	$ 67,320	$ 183,600
Fixed Expenses				
Manufacturing	$ 16,020	$ 16,020	$ 16,020	$ 48,060
Selling and Administrative	2,340	2,340	2,340	7,020
Total Fixed Expenses	$ (18,360)	$ (18,360)	$ (18,360)	$ (55,080)
Income Before Income Taxes	$ 42,840	$ 36,720	$ 48,960	$ 128,520

EXHIBIT 3-18

Absorption and Variable Costing Income Statements for 2003, 2004, and 2005

($128,520 in Exhibit 3-18) under these conditions. Also, for any particular year in which there is no change in inventory levels from the beginning of the year to the end of the year, both methods will result in the same net income. An example of this occurs in 2003, as is demonstrated in Exhibit 3-18.

Because all actual production and operating costs are assumed to be equal to the budgeted costs for the years 2003 through 2005, the only item that requires an adjustment is the under- and overapplied overhead, which occurs in years 2004 and 2005. The amounts are immaterial (not significant) and are reflected as adjustments to the gross margins for 2004 and 2005 in Exhibit 3-18.

The underapplied fixed overhead occurs because the units produced were different from the number of units that were budgeted. In 2003 the budgeted and the actual production are equal. For 2004, the underapplied fixed overhead of $534 is calculated as the difference between the applied fixed overhead and the actual fixed overhead. (Actual fixed overhead $16,020 minus applied fixed overhead [$0.534 × 29,000 units] $15,486 = $534). In 2005 the production was greater than the estimated amount (the amount used to set the fixed overhead rate), and therefore the fixed overhead is overapplied. Variable costing does not have over- or underapplied fixed overhead because all fixed manufacturing overhead is not applied to units produced but is written off in its entirety as a period expense.

In Exhibit 3-18, income before tax for 2004 for absorption costing exceeds that of variable costing by $1,068. This difference is caused by the positive change in inventory (2,000 units shown in Exhibit 3-18, to which the absorption costing method applies the predetermined fixed manufacturing overhead to each unit (2,000 units × $0.534 = $1,068). This $1,068 is the fixed manufacturing overhead added to absorption costing inventory and therefore not expensed in 2004. Critics of absorption costing refer to this phenomenon as one that creates illusory or phantom profits. Phantom profits are temporary absorption-costing profits caused by producing more inventory than is sold. When sales increase to eliminate the previously produced inventory, the phantom profits disappear. In contrast, all fixed manufacturing overhead, including the $1,068, is expensed in its entirety in variable costing.

Exhibit 3-17 shows that in 2005 inventory decreased by 2,000 drives. This decrease, multiplied by the predetermined fixed overhead ($0.534) applied, explains the $1,068 by which 2005 absorption costing income falls short of variable costing income in Exhibit 3-18. This is because the fixed manufacturing overhead written off in absorption costing through the cost of goods sold at $0.534 per drive for all units sold in excess of production (33,000 − 31,000 = 2,000) results in the $1,068 by which absorption costing income is lower than variable costing income in 2005.

Variable costing income statements are more useful internally for short-term planning, controlling, and decision making than absorption costing statements. To carry out their functions, managers need to understand and be able to project how different costs will change in reaction to changes in activity levels. Variable costing, through its emphasis on cost behaviour, provides that necessary information.

The income statements in Exhibit 3-18 show that absorption and variable costing tend to provide different income figures in some years. Comparing the two sets of statements illustrates that the difference in income arises solely from which production component costs are included in or excluded from product cost for each method. If no beginning or ending inventories exist, cumulative total income under both methods will be identical. For Aspinall Computer Corporation over the three-year period, 90,000 drives are produced and 90,000 are sold. Thus, all the costs incurred (whether variable or fixed) are expensed in one year or another under either method. The income difference in each year is caused solely by the timing of the expensing of fixed manufacturing overhead.

LEARNING OBJECTIVE   9

How do changes in sales and/or production levels affect net income as computed under absorption and variable costing?

COMPARISON OF THE TWO APPROACHES

Variable costing income statements are more useful internally for planning, controlling, and decision making than absorption costing statements are. This benefit exists because, to carry out their various functions effectively, mangers need to understand and be able to project how different costs will change in reaction to changes in activity levels. "Systems designed mainly to value inventory for financial and tax statements are not giving managers the accurate and timely information they need to promote operating efficiencies and measure product costs."[12]

Absorption and variable costing provide different income figures when sales are not equal to production. These income differences arise solely from what components are included in or excluded from the product cost under each of the two methods rather than from the method of presentation. That is, the differences are caused by including fixed manufacturing overhead as a product cost under absorption costing but considering it a period cost under variable costing.

When sales equal production, no differences will occur in net income under each of the two methods. However when production and sales differ, there will be a difference in profit under the two methods.

Under variable costing, when production is greater than sales, inventory is being accumulated for sales in the next period. Under variable costing, the cost of the unsold inventory is made up of direct material, direct labour, and variable manufacturing costs. All fixed manufacturing costs are written off in the period in which they were incurred. Thus, total expenses under variable costing will be higher than those under absorption costing and lead to a lower net income in that period.

Under absorption costing when production is greater than sales, the cost of the unsold inventory is made up of direct material, direct labour, variable manufacturing overhead, and fixed manufacturing overhead. Because of the inclusion of fixed manufacturing overhead, the cost of the unsold inventory is valued higher under this method than under variable costing; therefore, because some of the fixed manufacturing overhead is included in the unsold inventory, this method will show a greater net income than under variable costing in the period.

The amount of fixed factory overhead included in product cost under absorption costing will ultimately be taken into account in computing net income when the products are sold. Product sales, however, may take place in a time period different from the one in which the costs are actually incurred.

Exhibit 3-19 summarizes the differences between absorption and variable costing according to four categories: composition of product cost, structure of the chart of accounts, process of accumulating costs, and format of the income statement. Although four categories are presented, only two real differences exist between the methods. The primary difference lies in the treatment of fixed manufacturing overhead. Fixed overhead is a product cost for absorption costing and a period cost for variable costing. The other difference is that absorption costing requires different charts of accounts, processes of accumulating costs, and formats for income statements.

Information must be gathered and recorded somewhat differently under these two costing methods. Thus, the accounting process is affected, although maintaining two sets of accounting records is unnecessary. Often, the accounting system is kept on a variable costing basis, and working paper entries are made at year-end to convert the internal information to an appropriate external format.

Because absorption costing uses a process of deferring and releasing fixed overhead costs to and from inventory, income manipulation is possible under absorption costing by adjusting production of inventory relative to sales. For this reason, some people believe that variable costing might be more useful for external purposes than absorption costing. For internal reporting, keeping the accounting records on a variable costing basis will allow managers to have information available about the behaviour of various product and period costs. This information can be used in computing the breakeven point and analyzing a variety of cost–volume–profit relationships.

EXHIBIT 3-19

Differences Between Absorption and Variable Costing

Absorption Costing	Variable Costing
(1) Composition of Product Cost	
Fixed manufacturing overhead is attached, in separate measurable amounts, to units produced. Only if the firm sells all inventory produced in a period as well as all inventory on hand at the beginning of the period will all previously incurred fixed manufacturing overhead be recognized on the income statement as part of Cost of Goods Sold.	Fixed manufacturing overhead is recognized as a period cost (expense) when it is incurred. It does not attach in separate measurable amounts to the units produced. Each period, all fixed manufacturing overhead incurred is recognized on the income statement as an expense, but not through Cost of Goods Sold.
(2) Structure of the Chart of Accounts	
Costs are classified according to functional categories such as production, selling, and administrative.	Costs are classified according to both types of cost behaviour (fixed or variable) and functional categories (manufacturing and non-manufacturing). Mixed costs are separated into their fixed and variable components.
(3) Process of Accumulating Costs	
Costs are assigned to functional categories without analysis of behaviour. All manufacturing costs are considered product costs. All nonmanufacturing costs are considered period costs.	Costs are classified and accumulated by cost behaviour. Only variable manufacturing costs are considered product costs. Fixed manufacturing costs are considered period costs. All nonmanufacturing costs are considered period costs.
(4) Format of the Income Statement	
Costs are presented on the income statement by functional categories, which allows gross margin to be highlighted. The various functional categories present costs without regard to cost behaviour. Nonmanufacturing period costs are deducted from gross margin to determine income before taxes.	Costs are presented on the income statement separately by cost behaviour, which allows the contribution margin to be highlighted. Fixed costs are deducted from the contribution margin to determine income before taxes. Costs may be further categorized by functional classifications.

CHAPTER SUMMARY

Management planning for strategic success includes planning for price, volume, fixed and variable costs, contribution margins, and breakeven points. The interrelationships of these factors are studied when applying breakeven and cost–volume–profit (CVP) analysis. Management should understand these interrelationships and combine them effectively and efficiently for strategic success.

The breakeven point (BEP) is that quantity of sales volume at which the company will experience zero profit or loss. Total contribution margin (sales minus all variable costs) is equal to total fixed costs at the BEP. The BEP can be calculated using a cost–volume–profit formula that reflects basic income statement relationships. The BEP will change if the company's selling price(s) or costs change.

Since most companies want to operate above breakeven, CVP analysis extends the BEP computation by introducing a desired profit factor. A company can determine the sales necessary to generate a desired amount of profit by adding the desired profit to fixed costs and dividing that total by the contribution margin or contribution margin ratio. Profit can be stated as a fixed or a variable amount on a before- or after-tax basis. After fixed costs are covered, each dollar of contribution margin generated by company sales will produce a dollar of before-tax profit.

In a multiproduct firm, all breakeven and cost–volume–profit analyses are performed using an assumed constant sales mix of products or services. This sales mix is referred to as the "bag" assumption. Use of the "bag" assumption requires the computation of a weighted average contribution margin (and, thus, contribution margin ratio) for the "bag" of products being sold by the company. Answers to breakeven or CVP computations are in units or dollars of "bags" of products; these "bag" amounts can be converted to individual products by using the sales mix relationship.

CVP analysis is short-range in focus because it assumes linearity of all functions. Managers need to include in their considerations the effects of changes in both current and future costs to make better, more realistic decisions. Although CVP analysis provides one way for a manager to reduce the risk of uncertainty, the model is based on several assumptions that limit its ability to reflect reality.

The margin of safety (MS) of a firm indicates how far (in units, sales dollars, or a percentage) a company is operating from its breakeven point. A company's degree of operating leverage (DOL) shows what percentage change in profit would occur given a specified percentage change in sales from the current level.

This chapter provides a number of management accounting or more specifically management tools for planning profitability. These tools are crucial for strategic success, which requires profitability.

Two methods by which a business can determine product costs are absorption and variable costing. Under absorption costing, all manufacturing costs, both variable and fixed, are treated as product costs. The absorption costing income statement reflects a full production cost approach for cost of goods sold, computes gross margin, and classifies nonmanufacturing costs according to functional areas rather than by cost behaviour.

Variable costing computes product costs by including only the variable costs of production (direct material, direct labour, and variable manufacturing overhead). Fixed manufacturing overhead is considered to be a period expense in the period of occurrence under variable costing. The variable costing income statement presents cost of goods sold as comprising only the variable production cost per unit, shows product and total contribution margin figures, and classifies costs according to their cost behaviour (variable or fixed). Variable costing provides management with better information for internal purposes than absorption costing.

Net income determined under absorption costing differs from that determined under variable costing for any period in which production and sales volumes differ. This difference between the two income amounts reflects the amount of fixed manufacturing overhead that is either attached to, or released from, inventory in absorption costing as opposed to being immediately expensed in variable costing. Thus it stands to reason that the inventory value will also be different under each of these methods.

Cross-Functional Applications

Topic of Note	Discipline	Cross-Functional Applications
Cost–Volume–Profit Analysis (CVP)	Marketing	In a competitive environment, especially for price-sensitive products, CVP analysis guides market researchers in decisions involving pricing policies, promotional strategies, and product line assortment. Pricing policies can be a decisive competitive advantage; however, the marketer must have a clear understanding of the profitability per unit of product sold prior to implementing price changes, discounts, coupons, trade-ins, etc. The contribution margin format of an income statement assists marketers in targeting their promotional budgets toward products that yield the greatest contribution to overall profits. Product line and merchandising decisions involving the introduction or culling of products from the assortment offered are heavily influenced by CVP analysis.
	Microeconomics	CVP analysis originated as an economic theory of the great economist Alfred Marshall and it still remains a major concept of price formation in the marketplace. Economists use the concept to verify research on price formations determined by other quantifiable theories such as supply–demand equilibrium, utility–preference theory, and value-added models.
	Production Management	CVP analysis guides production cost decisions concerning the use of analysis (CVP) technology or manufacturing processes to spread fixed costs over the (continued) production run. Routine, short-run decisions may be determined by production managers based on production capacity and the impact of the short run on reducing the fixed production cost per unit.
	Research and Development (R&D)	It is pointless for a design engineer to develop a product that is not saleable in the marketplace in quantities necessary to assure an acceptable profit. Engineers must work within the constraints of CVP analysis to make decisions concerning cost/quality of materials, assortment of features in the product design, as well as processing, storing, and packaging. Most engineering schools currently recommend managerial accounting as a business elective to develop a practical appreciation of cost constraints in research, design, and environmental and manufacturing engineering.

(cont.)

Cross-Functional Applications

Topic of Note	Discipline	Cross-Functional Applications
	Public Administration	Both federal and provincial legislative bodies have governmental operation committees that are under great public pressure to produce public services and transfer payment activities more efficiently. Public administrators are currently using CVP analysis to make outsourcing decisions. In the area of transfer payments, comparative studies of the cost of administration between large insurance and public entities influence organizational decisions in government.
	Accounting	Breakeven and CVP analysis show relationships among all profitability factors in the relevant range and help managers to seek the best combination of those factors, determine the sales volume needed to meet desired profit figures, and explain how taxes will affect desired profits.
	Finance	Financial managers use CVP analysis to assist in the projection of costs, profitability and cash flows, budgets, and pro forma (future projection) financial statements and incorporate CVP information to estimate operational, cash, and capital equipment needs, as well as the resources available to meet them.
Absorption versus Variable Costing*	Accounting	Users of cost information need to understand the differences in product costing methods and how those differences will affect analysis. In variable costing, costs are separated into their fixed and variable elements, making decision making easier.
	Marketing	Variable and absorption costing provide different definitions of product cost and, thus, may help in deciding on selling prices for special orders.
	Economics	Absorption costing focuses on short-run profits rather than long-run profit contributions; variable costing provides managers with costs that are close to the economist's notion of marginal costs and, thus, improves decision making.
	Management	Variable costing provides information necessary for effective operational planning, controlling, and decision making; however, strict reliance on variable costing information might lead to underpricing and lowered profits.
	Finance	Users should compare the information from both absorption and variable costing to standard industry-related financial statement guidelines for normal cost and profit ranges to determine if the company's basic costs and expense structures are reasonable; estimations of a firm's value are generally made by analysts using external financial statements based on absorption costing.

* Appendix 3A

Key Terms

Absorption costing (p. 123)
Breakeven graph (p. 113)
Breakeven point (p. 102)
Contribution margin (p. 103)
Contribution margin ratio (p. 105)
Cost–volume–profit analysis
 (p. 105)
Degree of operating leverage
 (p. 120)
Direct costing (p. 124)

Functional classification (p. 124)
Incremental analysis (p. 111)
Margin of safety (p. 119)
Operating leverage (p. 119)
Product contribution margin
 (p. 124)
Profit–volume graph (p. 114)
Total contribution margin (p. 124)
Variable cost ratio (p. 105)
Variable costing (p. 124)

Solution Strategies

Cost–Volume–Profit

CVP problems can be solved by using a numerator/denominator approach. All numerators and denominators and the type of problem to which each relates are listed below. The formulas relate to both single-product and multiproduct firms, but results for multiproduct firms are per bag and must be converted to units of individual products.

Problem Situation	Numerator	Denominator
Simple BEP in units	FC	CM
Simple BEP in dollars	FC	CM%
CVP with fixed profits in units	FC + P	CM
CVP with fixed profit in dollars	FC + P	CM%
CVP with variable profit in units	FC	$CM - P_u$
CVP with variable profit in dollars	FC	$CM\% - P_u\%$

where
 FC = fixed cost
 CM = contribution margin per unit
 CM% = contribution margin percentage
 P = total profit (on a before-tax basis)
 P_u = profit per unit (on a before-tax basis)
 $P_u\%$ = profit percentage per unit (on a before-tax basis)

   To convert after-tax profit to before-tax profit, divide after-tax profit by $(1 - \text{tax rate})$.

Margin of Safety

   Margin of safety in units = Actual units − Breakeven units
   Margin of safety in dollars = Actual sales \$ − Breakeven sales \$
   Margin of safety percentage = Margin of safety in units or dollars ÷ Estimated
                    (Actual) sales in units or dollars

Degree of Operating Leverage

Degree of operating leverage = Contribution margin ÷ Profit before tax

Predicted additional profit = Degree of operating leverage × Percent change in sales × Current profit

Absorption versus Variable Costing

1. Which method is being used: absorption or variable?
   a. If absorption:
      • What is the fixed overhead application rate?
      • What capacity was used in the denominator in determining the fixed manufacturing overhead application rate?
      • What is the cost per unit of product? (DM + DL + VOH + FOH)
   b. If variable:
      • What is the cost per unit of product? (DM + DL + VOH)
      • What is the total manufacturing overhead? Assign to the income statement as a period cost.
2. What is the relationship of production to sales? If:
   a. Production = Sales
      Absorption costing income = Variable costing income
   b. Production > Sales
      Absorption costing income > Variable costing income
   c. Production < Sales
      Absorption costing income < Variable costing income
3. How is the difference in income measured?
   Dollar difference between absorption costing income and variable costing income = FOH application rate × Change in inventory units.
4. How are dollar differences in fixed costs used to explain profit differences?

Profit Impacts—Why?	
Production = Sales	Income is the same under both methods
Production > Sales	Fixed costs are hidden in ending inventory under absorption costing so profit is greater under absorption costing than under variable costing where the total fixed cost incurred in the period is written off in the period.
Production < Sales	Profit under variable costing is greater than under absorption costing because cost of sales contains fixed costs from the prior period under absorption costing.

Note: The effects of the relationships presented here are based on two qualifying assumptions:
(1) that unit costs are constant over time, and
(2) that any fixed cost variances are written off when incurred rather than being prorated to inventory balances.

DEMONSTRATION PROBLEMS

Problem 1

Dotto Corporation, a small manufacturer run by CEO Norma Dotto, makes and sells jar lid openers. Cost information for one unit is as follows:

Direct material	$ 1.00
Direct labour	0.50
Variable manufacturing overhead	0.25
Variable selling expenses	0.05
Total variable costs	$ 1.80
Total fixed manufacturing expenses	$194,400

Each lid opener sells for $4.50. Current annual production and sales volume is 150,000 lid openers. A predetermined fixed manufacturing overhead rate can be computed based on this activity level.

Required:

a.   Compute the unit contribution margin and contribution margin ratio for Dotto Corporation's product.
b.   Compute the breakeven point in units for Dotto Corporation, using contribution margin.
c.   Compute the breakeven point in sales dollars for Dotto Corporation, using contribution margin ratio.
d.   If Dotto Corporation wants to earn $43,200 of before-tax profits, how many openers will it have to sell?
e.   If Dotto Corporation wants to earn $40,500 after taxes and is subject to a 25% tax rate, how many units will it have to sell?
f.   If Dotto Corporation's fixed manufacturing costs increased by $7,560, how many units would it need to sell to break even? (Use original data.)
g.   Dotto Corporation can sell an additional 12,000 openers overseas for $3.50. Variable costs will increase by $0.20 for shipping expenses, and fixed manufacturing costs will increase by $25,000 because of the purchase of a new machine. This is a one-time-only sale and will not affect domestic sales this year or in the future. Should Dotto Corporation sell the additional units?

Problem 2

TabbyWorld makes and sells scratch posts for cats. Cost information for one scratch post is as follows:

Direct material	$ 2.00
Direct labour	1.00
Variable manufacturing overhead	0.50
Variable selling expenses	0.10
Total variable costs	$ 3.60
Total fixed manufacturing expenses	$388,800

Each scratch post sells for $9. Current annual production and sales volume is 75,000 posts. The company uses this activity level to set the predetermined fixed manufacturing overhead rate.

Required:

a.   Compute the contribution margin and contribution margin ratio for TabbyWorld's product.
b.   Compute the breakeven point in units for TabbyWorld, using contribution margin.
c.   Compute the breakeven point in sales dollars for TabbyWorld, using contribution margin ratio.
d.   What is TabbyWorld's margin of safety in units? In sales dollars?
e.   What is TabbyWorld's degree of operating leverage? If sales increase by 20%, by how much will before-tax profit increase?
f.   If TabbyWorld wants to earn $43,200 of before-tax profits, how many posts will it have to sell?
g.   If TabbyWorld wants to earn $40,500 after taxes and is subject to a 25% tax rate, how many units will it have to sell?
h.   If TabbyWorld's fixed manufacturing costs increased by $7,560, how many units would it need to sell to break even? (Use original data.)
i.   TabbyWorld can sell an additional 6,000 scratch posts overseas for $8.50. Variable costs will increase by $0.30 for shipping expenses, and fixed manufacturing costs will increase by $25,000 because of the purchase of a new machine. This is a one-time-only sale and will not affect domestic sales this year or in the future. Should TabbyWorld sell the additional units?

j.   (Appendix 3A) What is the absorption cost per unit?
k.   (Appendix 3A) What is the variable cost per unit?

Solutions to Demonstration Problems

Problem 1

a.   CM = Selling price − Variable cost = $4.50 − $1.80 = $2.70
CM% = Selling price − Variable cost ÷ Selling price = $2.70 ÷ $4.50 = 60%
b.   BEP = Fixed cost ÷ CM = $194,400 ÷ $2.70 = 72,000
c.   BEP = Fixed cost ÷ CM% = $194,400 ÷ 60% = $324,000
(Note: This answer is also equal to 72,000 units × $4.50 per unit selling price.)
d.   BEP = (FC + Desired profit) ÷ CM = ($194,400 + $43,200) ÷ $2.70 = 88,000 units
e.   Profit after tax ÷ (1 − Tax rate) = Profit before tax $40,500 ÷ 0.75 = $54,000
BEP = (FC + Desired profit) ÷ CM = ($194,400 + $54,000) ÷ $2.70 = 92,000 units
f.   Additional units to break even = Increase in FC ÷ CM = $7,560 ÷ $2.70 = 2,800;
New BEP = 72,000 + 2,800 = 74,800 units
g.   New CM for these units = $3.50 − $2.00 = $1.50; 12,000 × $1.50 = $18,000, which is $7,000 below the additional $25,000 fixed costs. Dotto Corporation should not sell the additional units.

Problem 2

a.   CM = Selling price − Variable cost = $9.00 − $3.60 = $5.40
CM% = (Selling price − Variable cost) ÷ Selling price = $5.40 ÷ $9.00 = 60%
b.   BEP = Fixed cost ÷ CM = $388,800 ÷ $5.40 = 72,000
c.   BEP = Fixed cost ÷ CM% = $388,800 ÷ 0.6 = $648,000
(Note: This answer is also equal to 72,000 units × $9 per unit selling price.)
d.   Margin of safety = Current units of sales − Breakeven sales = 75,000 − 72,000 = 3,000 units
Current revenues = Current sales volume × Unit selling price = 75,000 × $9 = $675,000
Margin of safety = Current revenues − Breakeven revenues = $675,000 − $648,000 = $27,000
e.   Current CM = 75,000 × $5.40 = $405,000;
Current before-tax profit = $405,000 − $388,800 = $16,200
Degree of operating leverage = $405,000 ÷ $16,200 = 25
Increase in income = 25 × 20% = 500%
Proof: 75,000 × 1.2 = 90,000 units; 90,000 × $5.40 = $486,000 CM − $388,800 FC = $97,200 PBT; ($16,200 current PBT × 500%) + $16,200 = $97,200
f.   BEP = (FC + Desired Profit) ÷ CM = ($388,800 + $43,200) ÷ $5.40 = 80,000 units
g.   Profit after tax ÷ (1 − Tax rate) = Profit before tax
$40,500 ÷ 0.75 = $54,000
BEP = (FC + Desired Profit) ÷ CM = ($388,800 + $54,000) ÷ $5.40 = 82,000 units
h.   Additional units to break even = Increase in FC ÷ CM = $7,560 ÷ $5.40 = 1,400;
New BEP = 72,000 + 1,400 = 73,400
i.   New CM for these units = $8.50 − $3.90 = $4.60; 6,000 × $4.60 = 27,600, which is $2,600 above the additional $25,000 fixed cost. Yes, TabbyWorld should sell the additional units.
j.   (Appendix 3A) Absorption cost = $3.60 + ($388,800 ÷ 75,000) = $3.60 + ≈ $5.18 = $8.78
k.   (Appendix 3A) Variable cost = $3.60

End-of-Chapter Materials

SELF-TEST QUESTIONS

(SOLUTIONS APPEAR AT THE END OF THE CHAPTER.)

1. The difference between the sales price and the total variable costs is:
   a. gross operating profit
   b. net profit
   c. the breakeven point
   d. the contribution margin
   e. cost–volume–profit analysis

   (IMA adapted)

Questions 2–5 are based on the following information. Treat each question independently.

Glow by Jabot Inc., an independent division of Jabot Cosmetics Inc., produces the best-selling perfume stick. The income statement for this division is reproduced below. The operating results are for fiscal 2005, a year in which Glow by Jabot had sales of 1,800 units. Glow by Jabot's manufacturing capacity is 3,000 units per year.

Glow by Jabot Inc.
Income Statement
For the Year Ended May 31, 2005

Sales		$900,000
Variable costs		
Manufacturing	$315,000	
Selling and administrative expenses	180,000	
Total variable costs		$495,000
Contribution margin		$405,000
Fixed costs		
Manufacturing	$ 90,000	
Selling	112,500	
Administration	45,000	
Total fixed costs		$247,500
Net income before income taxes		$157,500
Income taxes (32%)		50,400
Net income		$107,100

2. The breakeven volume in units (perfume sticks) for 2005 is:
   a. 420 units
   b. 1,100 units
   c. 495 units
   d. 550 units
   e. None of the above

3. If the sales volume is estimated to be 2,100 units (perfume sticks) in 2006, and if the prices and costs stay at the same levels and amounts for 2005, the after-tax net income that Glow by Jabot can expect for 2006 is:
   a. $153,000
   b. $110,250
   c. $283,500
   d. $184,500
   e. None of the above

4. Triton Publishers, a large magazine publisher, wishes to run a contest and would like to purchase 1,500 perfume sticks at $450 per stick. Assuming that all of Glow by Jabot's costs would be at the same levels and prices as in 2005, what net income after taxes would Glow by Jabot make if it took this order and rejected some business from regular customers so as not to exceed capacity?
   a. $297,500
   b. $252,000
   c. $239,700
   d. $256,500
   e. None of the above

5. Assume that Glow by Jabot estimates that the per-unit selling price will decline by 10% in 2006 and that variable costs will increase $40 per unit. There will be no change in fixed costs. What sales volume in dollars would be required to earn an after-tax net income of $107,100 in 2006?
   a. $1,140,000
   b. $825,000
   c. $1,500,000
   d. $1,350,000
   e. None of the above

6. Fenmore Ltd. presents you with the following information and asks you to calculate its operating leverage.

Revenue	$1,000,000
Variable costs	350,000
Contribution margin	$ 650,000
Fixed costs	210,000
Profit before taxes	$ 440,000

   a. 0.8
   b. 2.27
   c. 1.48
   d. 0.48
   e. None of the above

Use the following information to answer Questions 7 and 8.

Hilary Becker Ltd. is a manufacturer of fishing equipment. The company has just launched a new salmon "lure" with the following primary costs: $5 of raw materials and $10 of direct labour. Applied overhead is 100% of direct labour. Assume that 35% of overhead is variable. All costs are based on an expected level of production and sales of 10,000 units.

7. If Hilary Becker Ltd. requires a minimum contribution margin of 30% for all of its products, what should be the minimum selling price of the new lure?
   a. $21.43
   b. $26.43
   c. $30.71
   d. $35.71
   e. None of the above

8. If the selling price of the new lure is set at $28, how many units must be sold to generate an income of $10,000?
   a. 3,333
   b. 6,842
   c. 7,895
   d. 15,384
   e. None of the above

(Appendix 3A) Questions 9 and 10 are based on information taken from Paul Williams Investigation Corporation's records for the fiscal year ended November 30, 2005.

Direct materials used	$300,000
Direct labour	100,000
Variable manufacturing overhead	50,000
Fixed manufacturing overhead	80,000
Selling and administrative costs (variable)	40,000
Selling and administrative costs (fixed)	20,000

9. If Paul Williams Investigation Corporation uses variable costing, the inventoriable costs for the 2004–2005 fiscal year are:
   a. $400,000
   b. $450,000
   c. $490,000
   d. $530,000
   e. None of the above

   (IMA adapted)

10. Using absorption costing, inventoriable costs are:
    a. $400,000
    b. $450,000
    c. $530,000
    d. $590,000
    e. None of the above

    (IMA adapted)

QUESTIONS

1. Since managers in commercial entities aspire to make a profit, why do these managers care about the breakeven point?

2. Why does contribution margin fluctuate in direct proportion to sales volume?

3. How is breakeven analysis related to CVP?

4. If the variable costs that are associated with a product increase per unit but selling price and fixed costs remain constant, what will happen to (a) contribution margin, and (b) breakeven point? Explain.

5. What do you think are the three most fundamental CVP assumptions? Why should managers who use CVP analysis keep these assumptions in mind when using the answers provided by the model?

6. What effect would specifying the quality of a product be likely to have on each of the CVP factors?

7. Tony Soprano, the president of Tony's Waste Management Ltd., has just been informed that his business is operating at 4% above the breakeven point. What should his course of action be and why?

8. Why is it necessary to consider qualitative factors when solving problems using CVP?

9. Why is the perspective of managers using CVP a short-term one, and what are the implications of such a perspective?

10. What is a breakeven graph? How is it similar to and different from a profit–volume graph?

11. What is the bag assumption and why is it necessary in a multiproduct company?

12. In allocating a scarce production resource in a multiproduct corporation whose goal is to maximize the total corporate contribution margin, why would management not simply produce the product that generates the highest contribution margin per unit?

13. Why are some direct costs irrelevant to the decision to eliminate a product line?

14. What is meant by the term *incremental* as it applies to costs and revenues?

15.* For each of the terms that follow, indicate whether the term would be found on an absorption costing income statement (A), a variable costing income statement (V), or both (B).
    a. Cost of goods sold
    b. Contribution margin
    c. Gross margin
    d. Selling expenses
    e. Variable expenses
    f. Administrative expenses
    g. Fixed expenses

16.* Which of the following statements are true?
   a. Net income under absorption costing is a function of both sales volume and production volume.
   b. Net income under absorption costing is a function of sales volume only.
   c. Net income under variable costing is a function of both sales volume and production volume.
   d. Net income under variable costing is a function of sales volume only.

17.* Which of the following are defined as product costs when absorption costing is used? When variable costing is used?
   a. Direct material
   b. Variable manufacturing overhead
   c. Selling expenses
   d. Direct labour
   e. Fixed manufacturing overhead
   f. Administrative expenses

18.* Which approach (variable or absorption) classifies costs by behaviour? Which classifies costs by functional categories? Are these mutually exclusive?

19.* What is the difference between absorption and variable costing in the treatment of fixed manufacturing overhead? Why is this difference important?

* Appendix 3A

EXERCISES

1. (LO 1; BEP) Margaret White Co. has the following revenue and cost functions:
Revenue = $15 per unit
Fixed costs = $400,000
Variable costs = $11 per unit
Required:
Determine the breakeven point, both in units and in dollars.

2. (LO 1; BEP) The following information is available for Sam Goldberg Ltd.
   a. Total fixed costs are $45,000, and the unit contribution margin is $9.
   b. Unit selling price is $8, unit variable cost is $5, and total fixed costs are $48,000.
   c. Unit selling price is $12, contribution margin is 25% of revenue, and total fixed costs are $30,000.
   d. Unit variable cost is 80% of the unit selling price, total fixed costs are $48,000, and unit selling price is $12.
   e. Unit variable cost is $5, contribution margin per unit is $3, and total fixed costs are $24,000. Compute total sales at the breakeven volume in addition to total number of units.
   Required:
   For each of the above situations determine how many units must be sold for the company to break even.

3. (LO 2; CVP with before-tax profit) Radford Corporate Supplies Ltd. is planning to make and sell 10,000 computer disk trays. Fixed costs are $40,000, and variable costs are 60% of the selling price.
   Required:
   Your neighbour, Alison Baird, who works for the firm, wants you to help her determine what the selling price must be for the company to earn $10,000 of before-tax profit on the trays.

4. (LO 2; CVP with after-tax profit) Domestic Steel, Inc., manufactures furnace air filters that sell for $1,000. The unit costs are:

Direct material	$375
Direct labour	250
Variable manufacturing overhead	130
Variable selling expense	45

Annual fixed manufacturing overhead is $100,000 and fixed selling and administrative expenses are $120,000. The company is in a 30% tax bracket.
Required:
Determine how many furnace air filters the company needs to make and sell to earn $140,000 in after-tax profit.

5. (LO 2; CVP analysis) Joanne Steinman has learned about the CVP model but has not yet gained confidence in using it.
    Required:
    You have been asked to help her compute the number of units that must be sold and the total sales in each of the following situations:
    a. The company's profit goal is $40,000. Total fixed costs are $80,000, unit contribution margin is $5, and unit selling price is $8.
    b. The company's profit goal is $25,000 after tax, and its tax rate is 40%. Unit variable cost is $6, unit contribution margin is $4, and total fixed costs are $40,000.
    c. The company's after-tax profit goal is $54,000, and the tax rate is 40%. Unit variable cost is 70% of the $10 unit selling price, and total fixed costs are $60,000.
    d. The company's after-tax profit goal is $30,000, and the tax rate is 50%. Unit contribution margin is $3, unit variable cost is 70% of the unit selling price, and total fixed costs are $60,000.
    e. The company's after-tax profit goal is $40,000 and the tax rate is 50%. Unit variable cost is $9, unit contribution margin is 25% of selling price, and total fixed costs are $25,000.

6. (LO 2; CVP analysis) Exotic Rugs has annual sales of $2,000,000, variable expenses of 60% of sales, and fixed expenses of $80,000 monthly.
    Required:
    How much will sales have to increase so that Exotic Rugs will have before-tax profit of 20% of sales?

7. (LO 2, 3; BEP) Triton Publishing Ltd. publishes paperback cartoon books. The following operational data relate to a typical month:

Unit sales price	$10.00
Unit variable cost	4.60
Fixed costs	16,200
Current volume of books	3,200

    The company is considering an expansion that would increase monthly fixed costs by $5,400. If it does expand, production and sales will increase by 2,000 books.
    Required:
    As the company's newest employee and the only employee who has had a course in managerial accounting, you have been asked to do the following:
    a. Without considering the expansion, calculate the firm's breakeven point and its monthly before-tax profit.
    b. Recalculate the breakeven point in books and Triton's monthly before-tax profit assuming that the company undertakes the expansion.

8. (LO 3; CVP in alternative cost structures) Nicol Walker Ltd., a large, diversified corporation, is considering the acquisition of two firms that manufacture electric razors. Victor Ltd. has a variable unit cost of $11 and total fixed costs of $2,500,000. Brandon Ltd. has a variable unit cost of $14 and total fixed costs of $500,000. The wholesale price for the electric razors is $16, and each firm has an annual capacity of 800,000 razors.
    Required:
    Which firm would you recommend that the corporation acquire if the estimated demand for electric razors is:
    a. 400,000 units per year?
    b. 600,000 units per year?
    c. 800,000 units per year?

9. (LO 4; CVP graph, PV graph) Yun Candy Co. makes and sells boxes of Cajun candies. The firm's income statement for fiscal 2005 follows:

Sales (25,000 boxes @ $12)		$300,000
Variable costs		
Production (25,000 @ $3)	$75,000	
Sales commissions (25,000 @ $1.20)	30,000	(105,000)
Contribution margin		$195,000
Fixed costs		
Production	$58,000	
General, selling, and administrative	20,000	(78,000)
Profit before tax		$117,000

Required:
a.   Prepare a cost–volume–profit graph for Yun Candy Co.
b.   Prepare a profit–volume graph for Yun Candy Co.

10. (LO 5; Multiproduct BEP) William Chan Ltd. sells flags and sun visors at the entrances to local sporting events. The firm sells two flags for each sun visor. A flag sells for $3 and costs $1. A sun visor sells for $1.50 and costs $1. The company's monthly fixed costs are $4,500.
Required:
Calculate the number of flags that the company will sell at the breakeven point (BEP). Prove your answer.

11. (LO 5; Multiproduct CVP) David Rosenberg Golf World manufactures two types of golf carts, which are sold to golfers throughout the country. The compact cart is sold for an average price of $2,000 per unit; variable manufacturing costs are $1,800 per unit. The standard-size cart is sold for an average price of $3,500 per unit; variable manufacturing costs are $3,000 per unit. Total fixed costs are estimated to be $360 million per year.
Required:
a.   Determine the breakeven volume for the company if the expected sales mix is one-third compact carts and two-thirds standard carts.
b.   Because of a battery shortage, the management team expects the sales mix to shift to 50% compact carts and 50% standard carts. Determine the breakeven volume based on the new sales mix, and explain why your answer differs from the one you gave in part (a).
c.   It is expected that if the firm produced more than 50% compact carts, fixed costs would increase by $65 million. Determine the breakeven volume based on a sales mix of 60% compact carts and 40% standard carts.

12. (LO 7; BEP, margin of safety) Abe Carver has a street lunch vending business in which he sells quiche and a can of pop as a package for $3. The variable costs of each package lunch are $1.20. His annual fixed costs are $27,000.
Required:
a.   What is his breakeven point in revenue and number of lunches?
b.   If the business is currently selling 18,000 lunches annually, what is Carver's margin of safety in units, percentage, and dollars?

13. (LO 7; CVP, margin of safety) Sanjay Gupta Tool and Die Company is considering acquiring new equipment to set up a production line to produce a newly designed locking wrench. Demand for this wrench is estimated at 100,000 units a year, and the selling price is to be $10. One production line being considered uses primarily manual labour. Estimated variable production cost per unit on this line is $7, and total fixed production cost for the line is $150,000. The other possible production line is more automated; its estimated variable production cost per unit is $3, and total fixed production cost for the line is $630,000.
Required:
a.   Which production line would you recommend that the firm use? What is the margin of safety for each production line?
b.   If the demand were estimated to be 120,000 units, would your recommendation change?

c. If the demand were estimated to be 150,000 units, would your recommendation change?

d. Assume that the firm has an after-tax profit goal of $60,000. If the tax rate is 40% and estimated demand is 100,000 units, what will the selling price have to be for both production lines?

14. (LO 7; Margin of safety, operating leverage) Picante Hot Sauce Inc. sells its small bottle of pepper sauce for $2.90. Variable costs are $0.52 per bottle, and fixed costs are $288,000 annually. The firm is currently selling 320,000 bottles annually.

Required:

a. What is the company's margin of safety in units?

b. Calculate the degree of operating leverage.

c. If the company can increase sales by 25%, by what percentage will its income increase? Prove your answer.

15. (LO 9; Appendix 3A, product cost under AC and VC) The Alison Ground Electric Company is considering switching to variable costing. In an effort to better understand the significance of the possible change, the management team has asked that ending inventories be costed on both an absorption and a variable costing basis. Production for the year was 200,000 units, of which 25,000 units remained in ending inventory. Additional information concerning production follows:

Direct material costs	$600,000
Direct labour costs	450,000
Manufacturing overhead costs	600,000

Manufacturing overhead has not been separated into fixed and variable components, but the fixed manufacturing overhead rate approximates $6 per direct labour hour. The current direct labour rate is $10 per hour.

Required:

As consultant to the team, you have been asked to calculate the total costs to be assigned to ending inventory under both absorption and variable costing.

16. (LO 9; Appendix 3A, product cost under AC & VC) The Blue Suede Shoe Company produced 100,000 pairs of shoes and sold 70,000 in its first year of operations. There was no Work in Process Inventory at year-end. Its costs for that year were as follows:

Direct materials	$ 400,000
Direct labour	300,000
Variable manufacturing overhead	150,000
Variable selling and administrative expenses	210,000
Fixed manufacturing overhead	250,000
Fixed selling and administrative expense	175,000
Total	$1,485,000

Required:

a. Compute the cost of one unit of product if the company uses variable costing.

b. Compute the cost of one unit of product if the company uses absorption costing.

17. (LO 9; Appendix 3A, missing information) Shortly after the end of its first year of operations, thieves stole or destroyed nearly all cost and production records of the Fred Shearer Products Company, a producer of high-quality burglar alarms. Having been hired to piece together the fragments of the records that were salvaged from the scene, you have determined the following regarding the first-year operations:

Production in units	?
Sales in units	9,500
Total sales	$109,250
Gross margin	54,625
Total fixed manufacturing overhead costs incurred	22,500
Total selling and administrative costs	38,000
Variable production costs (per unit)	3.50

Required:

a. How many units were produced in the first year?

b. From the previous information, prepare an income statement using absorption costing.

18. (LO 9; Appendix 3A absorption costing) Josiah Bartlett Corporation has been in operation for two years. It is a privately held firm and produces no external financial information. It employs the variable costing method for preparing internal financial statements. Selected information from its first two years of operations follows:

	2005	2006
Litres of product produced	500,000	500,000
Litres of product sold	450,000	525,000
Fixed production costs	$2,000,000	$2,000,000
Variable production costs	2,500,000	2,500,000
Net income (variable costing)	500,000	1,600,000

Required:
a. Had the company used absorption costing in fiscal 2005, how much net profit would it have reported?
b. Had the company used absorption costing in both years, how much net profit would it have reported in fiscal 2006?

PROBLEMS

1. (LO 1, 2, 3; BEP, CVP before and after tax) High School Traditions operates a shop that makes and sells class rings for local high schools. Operating statistics follow:

Average selling price per ring	$ 250
Variable costs per ring	
Rings and stones	$ 90
Sales commissions	18
Variable manufacturing overhead	8
Annual fixed costs	
Selling expenses	$42,000
Administrative expenses	56,000
Production expenses	30,000

The company's tax rate is 30%.

Required:
a. What is the firm's breakeven point in rings? In revenue?
b. How much revenue is needed to yield $140,000 before-tax profit?
c. How much revenue is needed to yield an after-tax profit of $120,000?
d. How much revenue is needed to yield an after-tax profit of 20% of revenue?
e. The firm's marketing manager believes that by spending an additional $12,000 in advertising and lowering the price by $20 per ring, he can increase the number of rings sold by 25%. He is currently selling 2,200 rings. Should he make these changes?

2. (LO 3; Breakeven analysis) The company for which you work as a managerial accountant engages independent agents to sell the company's products. These agents are currently being paid a commission of 15% based on sales price but are asking for an increase to 20% of sales made during the coming year. You had already prepared the following pro forma income statement for the company based on the 15% commission.

Forrester Creations Corporation
Pro Forma Income Statement
For the Year Ending April 30, 2005

Sales		$1,000,000
Cost of goods sold (all variable)		600,000
Gross profit		$ 400,000
Selling and administrative:		
Variable (commission only)	$150,000	
Fixed	10,000	160,000
Income before taxes		$ 240,000
Income tax expense (25%)		60,000
Net income		$ 180,000

Management wants to examine the possibility of employing the company's own sales-people. They believe they will need a sales manager at an annual salary of $60,000 and three salespeople at an annual salary of $30,000 each plus a commission of 5% of sales. All other fixed costs as well as the variable cost percentages would remain the same as in the above pro forma income statement.

Required:

a.   Based on the pro forma income statement above, what is the breakeven point in sales dollars for Forrester Creations Corporation for the year ending April 30, 2005?

b.   If Forrester Creations Corporation employed its own salespeople, what would be the breakeven point in sales dollars for the year ending April 30, 2005?

c.   What would be the volume of sales dollars required for the year ending April 30, 2005, to yield the same net income as projected in the pro forma income statement if Forrester Creations Corporation continued to use the independent sales agents and agreed to their demand for a 20% sales commission?

d.   Compute the estimated sales volume in sales dollars that would generate an iden-tical net income for the year ending April 30, 2005, regardless of whether Forrester Creations Corporation employs its own salespeople or continues to use the independent sales agents and pays them a 20% commission.

3.   (LO 2, 3; Contribution analysis) Because of the opportunities created for competition by the merger between Air Canada and Canadian Airlines, Onexa Air is about to introduce a daily round-trip flight on the Toronto-to-Vancouver route. Onexa offers only one class of seats on all its flights, comfort class, which provides lots of leg room. No other airline offers this kind of seat. Onexa is in the process of determining how it should price its round-trip tickets. The following information is available.

Seating capacity per plane	360
Maximum expected demand for seats on any flight	300
Food and beverage service cost for a round trip per passenger	
(no additional charge to passenger)	$ 40
Commission to travel agents paid by Onexa on each	
ticket (assume all tickets are booked by travel agents)	8% of fare
Fuel costs for a round-trip flight	$ 24,000
Fixed annual lease costs allocated to a round trip flight	$ 100,000
Fixed ground services costs (maintenance, check-in,	
baggage handling) allocated to a round-trip flight	$ 10,000
Fixed flight crew salaries allocated to a round-trip flight	$ 8,000

For simplicity, assume that fuel costs are *not* affected by the actual number of passen-gers on a flight.

The market research group at Onexa segments the market into two groups, business travellers and pleasure travellers, and provides the following information on the effect of different price levels on the estimated demand for seats on any given flight:

	Price Charged	Number of Seats Expected to be Sold
Business travellers	$ 500	200
	$2,000	190
Pleasure travellers	$ 500	100
	$2,000	20

Assume these prices are the only choices available to Onexa. The market research team offers one additional piece of information: pleasure travellers usually begin their travel in one week, spend at least a weekend at their destination, and return in a fol-lowing week. Business travellers usually begin and complete their travel within the same week and do not stay over a weekend.

Required:

a. Prepare an analysis of the total contribution margin that would be obtained from each of the two types of travellers at each of the two fares.

b. Explain the key factor or factors that should be considered in determining which fare or fares to charge.

c. If Onexa wishes to charge different prices for the two types of travellers, explain how it might achieve such a policy.

4. (LO 3; CVP analysis) The following income statement for Hall Company shows the results for fiscal 2005.

Hall Company
Income Statement
Year Ended December 31, 2005

Sales (90,000 units @ $4.00)			$360,000
Cost of goods sold:			
Direct materials		$90,000	
Direct labour		90,000	
Manufacturing overhead:			
Variable	$18,000		
Fixed	80,000	98,000	278,000
Gross margin (profit)			$ 82,000
Selling expenses:			
Variable:			
Sales commissions[1]	$18,000		
Shipping	3,600	$21,600	
Fixed:			
Advertising		40,000	$61,600
Administrative expenses:			
Variable	$ 4,500		
Fixed	20,400	24,900	86,500
Net profit (loss)			$ (4,500)

[1]Based on sales dollars, not physical units.

Required:

Answer the following *independent* questions.

a. Assuming the relationship between advertising dollars spent and sales achieved remains constant, how much may advertising be increased to bring production and sales to 130,000 units and earn a target net income of 5% of sales?

b. For 2005, a mail-order firm is willing to buy 60,000 units of product "if the price is right." Assume that the present market of 90,000 units at $4 each will not be disturbed. Hall will not pay any sales commissions on these 60,000 units. Variable administration costs will continue at the same rate. The mail-order firm will pick up the units directly at the Hall factory. However, Hall must refund $24,000 of the total sales price as a promotional and advertising allowance for the mail-order firm. In addition, special packaging will increase manufacturing costs on these 60,000 units by $0.10 per unit. At what unit price must the mail-order firm's business be quoted for Hall to break even on total operations in 2005?

c. The president suspects that a fancy new package will aid consumer sales and ultimately, Hall's sales. Present packaging costs per unit are all variable and consist of $0.05 for direct materials and $0.04 for direct labour; new packaging costs will be $0.30 and $0.13 for direct materials and direct labour, respectively. Assuming no other changes in cost behaviour, how many units must be sold to earn a net income of $20,000?

(Problems 1–4 adapted by the author from *Management Accounting examinations,* published by the Certified General Accountants Association of Canada © CGA-Canada, used by permission. #1 © 1994, #2 and 4 © 2001, #3 © 2000.)

5. (LO 3; CVP analysis, contribution approach) G. Spraakman and Son, Ltd. builds custom-made pleasure boats that range in price from $10,000 to $250,000. For the past 30 years, Mr. Spraakman, Sr. has determined the selling price of each boat by estimating the cost of material, labour, and a prorated portion of overhead. He adds 20% to estimated costs for profits.

For example, a recent price quotation was determined as follows:

Direct materials	$ 50,000
Direct labour	80,000
Manufacturing overhead	20,000
	$150,000
Plus 20%	30,000
Selling price	$180,000

The overhead figure was determined by estimating total overhead for the year and allocating it at 25% of direct labour costs.

If a customer rejected the price and business was slow, Mr. Spraakman, Sr. might be willing to reduce his markup to as little as 5% over estimated costs. Thus, average markup for the year was estimated at 15%. Mr. Spraakman, Jr. has just completed a managerial accounting course that dealt with pricing, and he believes that the firm could use some of the techniques discussed in the course. The course emphasized the contribution margin approach to pricing and Mr. Spraakman, Jr. feels that such an approach would be helpful in determining an appropriate price for the boats.

Total overhead, which includes selling and administrative expenses for the year, has been estimated at $1,500,000 of which $900,000 is fixed and the remainder is variable in direct proportion to direct labour.

Required:
a. Assume the customer rejected the $180,000 quotation and also rejected a $157,500 (5% markup) quotation during a slack period. The customer countered with a $150,000 offer.
   i. What is the minimum selling price Mr. Spraakman, Sr. could have quoted without reducing or increasing company net income?
   ii. What is the difference in company net income for the year between accepting or rejecting the customer's offer?
b. Identify and briefly explain one advantage and one disadvantage of the contribution approach to pricing compared to the approach previously used by G. Spraakman and Son, Ltd.

6. (LO 4; Profit–volume graph) The Senior Citizens Club has enlisted your help in developing a presentation for a group of local business executives who have previously given generously to support the club's efforts. An investigation reveals that each member pays dues of $8 per month, monthly variable costs per member are $1, and the club's monthly fixed expenses are $2,100. Most of the club's workers are volunteers.
Required:
a. Prepare a breakeven graph for the club.
b. Prepare a profit–volume graph for the club.
c. Which graph would you recommend that the club use in its presentation?

7. (LO 5; Multiproduct CVP) Della Computers Ltd. manufactures three types of computers, all of which are sold at wholesale to dealers throughout the world. Laptop models manufactured by Della sell at an average price of $2,200, and variable costs per unit total $1,900. Standard-size Della computers sell at an average price of $3,700, and variable costs per unit equal $3,000. Luxury models manufactured by Della sell at an average price of $6,000, and the variable costs per unit are $5,000. Fixed costs for the company are estimated at $1,080,000,000.
Required:
a. The company's marketing department estimates that next year's unit sales mix will be 30% laptop, 50% standard, and 20% luxury. What is the breakeven point in units for the firm?

b. If the company has an after-tax profit goal of $1 billion and the tax rate is 50%, how many units of each type of computer must be sold for the goal to be reached?

c. Assume the sales mix shifts to 50% laptop, 40% standard, and 10% luxury. How does this mix affect your answer to part (b)?

d. If the company sold more luxury computers and fewer laptop computers, how would your answers to parts (a) and (b) change?

8. (LO 5; Multiproduct company) Enchanting Sounds makes portable CD players, CDs, and batteries, which follow a normal sales mix pattern of 1:3:6. The following are the company's costs:

	CD Players	CDs	Batteries
Variable product costs	$ 62	$1.20	$0.22
Variable selling expenses	14	0.50	0.10
Variable administrative expenses	3	0.05	0.03
Selling prices	140	5.00	0.50
Annual fixed manufacturing overhead	$110,000		
Annual fixed selling expenses	60,000		
Annual fixed administrative expenses	16,290		

The firm is in a 40% income tax bracket. As the new owner of the firm, you are interested in fine-tuning the performance of the company and need to devote some attention to the questions listed below.

Required:

a. What is the annual dollar breakeven point?

b. How many CD players, CDs, and batteries are expected to be sold at the breakeven point?

c. If the firm desires a before-tax profit of $114,640, how much total revenue is required and how many units of each item must be sold?

d. If the firm desires an after-tax profit of $103,176, how much total revenue is required and how many units of each item must be sold?

9. (LO 5; Multiproduct company) The Arts & Crafts Emporium makes carved wooden mallard ducks and ducklings. For every duck the firm sells, it sells two ducklings. Information on the two products is as follows:

	Ducks	Ducklings
Selling price	$12	$6
Variable cost	4	4
Contribution margin	$ 8	$2

Monthly fixed costs are $12,000. You have just purchased the firm.

Required:

a. What is the average contribution margin ratio?

b. What is the breakeven point? At the breakeven point, identify the total units of each product sold and sales dollars of each product.

c. If the company wants to earn $24,000 in before-tax profit per month, how many ducks and how many ducklings must it sell?

d. The company, which is in a 40% tax bracket, specifies $9,000 of after-tax profit as its objective. You believe that the mix has changed to five ducklings for every duck. How much total revenue is needed, and in what product proportions, to achieve this profit objective?

10. (LO 5, 6; Multiproduct CVP, incremental analysis) Alan Guiliford owns a travel agency. He receives commission revenue based on the total dollar volume of business he generates for various client firms in the travel and entertainment industries. His rates of commission currently are 20% of total hotel fees, 15% of total car rental fees, and 10% of airline ticket fees. Alan is your friend and has asked for your help. Data for a normal month's operations are as follows:

Costs		Fees Generated for Clients	
Advertising	$1,000	Hotel fees	$10,800
Rent	800	Car rental fees	3,600
Utilities	300	Airline ticket fees	14,200
Other expenses	1,400		$28,600

Required:

a. Given the stated commission percentages, what is Alan's normal total monthly commission? The normal monthly before-tax profit?

b. Alan can increase the amount of hotel fees he generates by 40% if he spends an additional $200 on advertising. Should he do this?

c. Connie Reed has offered to merge her bookings with Alan's and become his employee. She would receive a base salary of $600 a month plus 20% of the commissions on client fees she generates, which, for a normal month, are

Hotel fees	$5,000
Car rental fees	2,000
Airline ticket fees	2,000

Should Alan accept the proposal?

d. Use the information in part (c). During Connie's first month, she generated $10,000 of total fees, but they were as follows:

Hotel fees	$3,000
Car rental fees	2,000
Airline ticket fees	5,000

Will Alan be pleased? Why or why not?

11. (LO 3, 7; Margin of safety) The Judith Poë Corporation produces children's golf clubs. The company has received a large order from a retail establishment for 10,000 golf clubs that is willing to pay $26 each. This sale will have no impact on present sales.

Ray Guitar, the sales manager, noted that the unit cost of goods sold, based on present production of 50,000 units, was $26.60. No marketing or administrative costs will be incurred with this order. This offer was $0.60 below the present cost as shown below.

Judith Poë Corporation
Income Statement
For the Year Ended December 31, 2006

Sales	$1,850,000
Cost of goods sold	1,330,000
Gross Profit	$ 520,000
Marketing and administrative expenses	250,000
Income before taxes	$ 270,000

Required:

a. What advice would you give the company on accepting the order given the following facts:

i. Poë will save $0.30 per unit because the chain will be attaching its own brand name labels.

ii. Of the total cost of goods sold, the variable cost of goods is $1,006,400 and variable marketing and administrative costs are $146,000. The remainder of the cost of good sold is fixed.

b. Based on the information in part (a):

i. Calculate the breakeven point in units for fiscal 2006.

ii. Calculate the margin of safety under the present sales level.

12. (LO 3, 7; CVP analysis, operating leverage) Gilda Serrao Ltd. has decided to introduce a new product, which can be manufactured by either a capital-intensive method or a labour-intensive method. The manufacturing method will not affect the quality of the product. The estimated manufacturing costs by the two methods are as follows.

	Capital- Intensive	Labour- Intensive
Raw materials	$5.00	$5.60
Direct labour	(0.5 h @ $12/h) $6.00	(0.8 h @ $9/h) $7.20
Variable overhead	(0.5 h @ $6/h) $3.00	(0.8 h @ $6/h) $4.80
Directly traceable incremental Fixed manufacturing costs	$2,440,000	$1,320,000

Gilda's market research department has recommended an introductory unit sales price of $30. The incremental selling expenses are estimated to be $500,000 annually plus $2 for each unit sold regardless of manufacturing method.

Required:

a. Calculate the estimated breakeven point in annual unit sales of the new product if Gilda Serrao Ltd. uses the
   i.   capital-intensive manufacturing method
   ii. labour-intensive manufacturing method
b. Determine the annual unit sales volume at which Gilda Serrao Ltd. would be indifferent between the two manufacturing methods.
c. Serrao's management must decide which manufacturing method to employ. One factor it must consider is operating leverage.
   i.   Explain operating leverage and the relationship between operating leverage and business risk.
   ii. Explain the circumstances under which Gilda Serrao Ltd. should employ each of the two manufacturing methods.
d. Identify the business factors other than operating leverage that Gilda Serrao Ltd. must consider before selecting the capital-intensive or labour-intensive manufacturing method.

(IMA adapted)

13. (LO 3, 4, 6, 7; Graphs, margin of safety, operating leverage) You are considering acquiring one of two local firms (VPI and TECH) that manufacture slip rings. VPI employs a considerable amount of labour in its manufacturing processes, and its salespeople all work on commission. TECH employs the latest technology in its manufacturing operations, and its salespeople are all salaried.

You have obtained the following financial information concerning the two firms:

	VPI		TECH	
	2004	2005	2004	2005
Sales	$100,000	$160,000	$100,000	$140,000
Expenses including taxes	88,000	137,200	88,000	111,200
Net Income	$ 12,000	$ 22,800	$ 12,000	$ 28,800

After examining cost data, you determine that the fixed costs for VPI are $10,000, while the fixed costs for TECH are $50,000. The tax rate for both firms is 40%.

Required:

a. Determine breakeven sales for each of the firms in 2004 and 2005.
b. Determine the relative operating leverage for each firm in 2004 and 2005.
c. Suppose you could acquire either firm for $200,000 and you want an after-tax return of 12% on your investment. Determine what sales level for each firm would allow you to reach your goal.
d. Assuming the demand for slip rings fluctuates widely, comment on the relative positions of the firms.
e. Prepare a profit–volume graph for each firm.

14. (LO 9; Appendix 3A, AC and VC) David Roost Corporation is a manufacturer of a synthetic element. David Roost, president of the company, has been eager to get the operating results for the fiscal year just completed. He was surprised when the income statement revealed that income before taxes had dropped to $885,000 from $900,000

even though sales volume had increased 100,000 kg. This drop in net income had occurred even though Roost had implemented the following changes during the past 12 months to improve the profitability of the company.

- Due to a 10% increase in production costs, the sales price of the company's product was increased by 12%. This action took place on December 1, 2005.
- The managers of the selling and administrative departments were given strict instructions to spend no more in fiscal 2005 than in fiscal 2004.

Roost's accounting department prepared and distributed to top management the comparative income statements presented below. The accounting staff also prepared related financial information that is presented in the schedule following the income statements to assist management in evaluating the company's performance. Roost uses the FIFO inventory method for finished goods.

David Roost Corporation
Statements of Operating Income
For the Years Ended November 30, 2004 and 2005
($000 omitted)

	2004		2005	
Sales revenue		$9,000		$11,200
Cost of goods sold	$7,200		$8,320	
Manufacturing overhead variance	(600)		495	
Adjusted cost of goods sold		6,600		8,815
Gross margin		$2,400		$ 2,385
Selling and administrative expenses		1,500		1,500
Income before taxes		$ 900		$ 885

David Roost Corporation
Selected Operating and Financial Data
For 2004 and 2005

	2004	2005
Sales price	$10/kg	$11.20 kg
Material cost	$1.50/kg	$1.65 kg
Direct labour cost	$2.50/kg	$2.75 kg
Variable overhead cost	$1.00/kg	$1.10 kg
Fixed overhead cost	$3.00/kg	$3.30 kg
Fixed overhead costs	$3,000,000	$3,300,000
Selling and administrative (all fixed)	$1,500,000	$1,500,000
Sales volume (in units)	900,000 kg	1,000,000 kg
Beginning inventory (in units)	300,000 kg	600,000 kg

Required:

a. Explain to David Roost why the company's net income decreased in the current fiscal year despite the sales price and sales volume increases.

b. A member of Roost's accounting department has suggested that the company adopt variable (direct) costing for internal reporting purposes.
   i. Prepare an operating income statement before taxes for the year ended November 30, 2005, for Roost Corporation using the variable (direct) costing method.
   ii. Present a numerical reconciliation of the difference in income before taxes using the absorption costing method as currently employed by Roost and the variable (direct) costing method as proposed.

c. Identify and discuss the advantages and disadvantages of using the variable (direct) costing method for internal reporting purposes.

(IMA adapted)

15. (LO 8; Appendix 3A, AC and VC) The following information concerns the first four years of operation at Basic Black Ltd.:

Cost per unit:	
Direct materials	$ 4.50
Direct labour	2.00
Variable production costs	0.60
Fixed production costs:	
($200,000 ÷ 400,000 units expected volume)	0.50
Total	$ 7.60
Selling price per unit	$11.00
Other expenses:	
Variable selling expense per unit	0.60
Other fixed expenses	200,000

Production and sales data in units:

Year	1	2	3	4
Production	360,000	400,000	420,000	400,000
Sales	300,000	410,000	420,000	450,000

Required:
Prepare income statements under absorption costing and variable costing methods for each of the four years. Charge any variances to Cost of Goods Sold.

16. (LO 8; Appendix 3A, product costs under VC and AC, CM, GM) Golf-Go Equipment Company produces and sells electric golf carts. The company uses a costing system based on actual costs. Selected accounting and production information for fiscal 2005 follows:

Net income (under absorption costing)	$400,000
Sales	$3,400,000
Fixed manufacturing overhead cost incurred	$600,000
Variable selling and administrative costs	$400,000
Fixed selling and administrative costs	$500,000
Net income (under variable costing)	$310,000
Units produced	2,000
Units sold	?

Golf-Go had no Work in Process Inventory at either the beginning or end of fiscal 2005. The company also did not have any Finished Goods Inventory at the beginning of the fiscal year.

Required:
Compute each of the following:
a.   number of units sold
b.   cost of one unit under variable costing
c.   cost of one unit under absorption costing
d.   total contribution margin under variable costing
e.   gross margin under absorption costing

17. (LO 8, 9; Appendix 3A, converting AC to VC) Jay Leno Ltd. has been recording inventory on an absorption costing basis. There are plans to convert to a variable costing basis for internal reporting purposes. To get an impression of the overall impact of the change, the management team would like to see the effect on the company's income figures since its inception three years ago. Data for the last three years follow:

	2004	2005	2006
Absorption costing income	$80,000	$110,000	$200,000
Fixed manufacturing costs	$50,000	$ 54,000	$ 70,000
Units produced	5,000	6,000	7,000
Units sold	4,000	5,000	7,000

Required:
Calculate the variable costing income for each of the three years. Assume the fixed manufacturing overhead application rate is based on actual units produced. If necessary, use a FIFO cost flow assumption.

18. (LO 8, 9; Appendix 3A, missing numbers, VC income statement) The following information was taken from the cost records of Reed Incorporated for 2005. For 2005, the company had no units in Finished Goods Inventory at the beginning of the year, and no units in Work in Process Inventory at either the beginning or end of the year. Reed uses variable costing.

	Variable Costs	**Fixed Costs**
Direct materials	$3 per unit	
Direct labour	5 per unit	
Manufacturing overhead	2 per unit	$200,000
Selling and administrative expenses	2 per unit	350,000

The product contribution margin in 2005 was $8 per unit, and net income was $200,000.

Required:
a. What was the company's sales price per unit?
b. What were total revenues?
c. How many units were sold?
d. Prepare a variable costing income statement for fiscal 2005.

19. (LO 9; Appendix 3A, VC and absorption costing) As a member of the board of directors of MJ Company, you are reviewing the following income statement for the year ended December 31, 2005, the company's first year of operations. During this first year, MJ was able to sell all 100,000 units that it produced. However, it had a maximum production capacity of 400,000 units.

MJ Company
Income Statement (Absorption Costing)
Year ended December 31, 2005

Sales (100,000 @ $50.00)		$5,000,000
Cost of goods sold:		
Variable (100,000 @ $10.00)	$1,000,000	
Fixed	4,000,000	5,000,000
Gross profit		0
General and administrative expenses (all fixed)		500,000
Net loss		$ (500,000)

You and the other members of the board of directors are concerned about this loss. One of the consultants who helped start up the company proposes that she take over as president and be paid a bonus based on 50% of any profits the company makes while she is president. The board of directors agrees to these terms.

The new president decides that production should be increased in 2006 to 300,000 units. Sales for 2006 remain at the same level as for 2005, that is, 100,000 units. At the end of the year, MJ's income statement, prepared on the same basis as the year before, shows income before the president's bonus of $2,166,667. The president receives a bonus in accordance with the agreement.

Required:
a. Prepare, in *good form,* the income statement of MJ for the year ended December 31, 2006, which shows a net income after the president's bonus. Ignore income taxes.
b. Explain fully why you have concerns about the profits and the bonus paid to the president in 2006.
c. Under variable costing, indicate what the net income (loss) would be for each of the two years, that is, 2005 and 2006.
d. At what sales level, compared to production, would the president be indifferent to the product costing approach used to determine her bonus? Explain fully.
e. At what sales level, compared to production, would the president prefer variable costing to absorption costing? Explain fully.

CASES

1. Kalifo Company manufactures a line of electric garden tools that are sold in general hardware stores. The company's controller, Amber Moore, has just received the sales

forecast for the coming year for Kalifo's three products: weeders, hedge clippers, and leaf blowers. Kalifo has experienced considerable variations in sales volumes and variable costs over the past two years, and Moore believes the forecast should be carefully evaluated from a cost–volume–profit viewpoint. The preliminary forecast information for 2005 is as follows:

	Weeders	Hedge Clippers	Blowers
Unit sales	50,000	50,000	100,000
Unit selling price	$28	$36	$48
Variable manufacturing cost per unit	13	12	25
Variable selling cost per unit	5	4	6

For 2005, Kalifo's fixed manufacturing overhead is estimated at $2,000,000, and the company's fixed selling and administrative expenses are forecasted to be $600,000. Kalifo has an effective tax rate of 40%.

Required:

a. Determine Kalifo Company's forecasted net profit for 2005.

b. Assuming the sales mix remains as budgeted, determine how many units of each product Kalifo Company must sell to break even in 2005.

c. Determine the total dollar sales Kalifo Company must have in 2005 to earn an after-tax profit of $450,000.

d. After preparing the original estimates, Kalifo Company determined that the variable manufacturing cost of leaf blowers would increase 20% and the variable selling cost of hedge clippers would increase $1 per unit. However, Kalifo has decided not to change the selling price of either product. In addition, Kalifo has learned that its leaf blower has been perceived as the best value on the market; so it can expect to sell three times as many leaf blowers as any other product. Under these circumstances, determine how many units of each product Kalifo Company would have to sell to break even in 2005.

e. Explain the limitations of cost–volume–profit analysis that Amber Moore should consider when evaluating Kalifo Company's 2005 forecast.

(CMA adapted)

2. Seacoast Airline is a small local carrier that flies among the Atlantic provinces. All seats are economy, and the following data are available:

Average full passenger fare	$150
Number of seats per plane	120
Average load factor (seats occupied)	70%
Average variable cost per passenger	$40
Fixed operating costs per month	$1,800,000

Required:

a. What is the breakeven point in passengers and revenues?

b. What is the breakeven point in number of flights?

c. If Seacoast raises its average full passenger fare to $200, it is estimated that the load factor will decrease to 55%. What will be the breakeven point in number of flights?

d. The cost of fuel is a significant variable cost to any airline. If fuel charges increase $8 per barrel, it is estimated that variable cost per passenger will rise to $60. In this case, what will be the new breakeven point in passengers and in number of flights? (Refer to original data.)

e. Seacoast Airline has experienced an increase in variable cost per passenger to $50 and an increase in total fixed costs to $2,000,000. The company has decided to raise the average fare to $180. What number of passengers is needed to generate an after-tax profit of $600,000 if the tax rate is 40%?

f. Seacoast is considering offering a discounted fare of $120, which the company feels would increase the load factor to 80%. Only the additional seats would be sold at the discounted fare. Additional monthly advertising costs would be $100,000. How much before-tax profit would the discounted fare provide Seacoast if the company has 40 flights per day, 30 days per month? (Use the original data.)

g. Seacoast has an opportunity to obtain a new route. The company feels it can sell seats at $175 on the route, but the load factor would be only 60%. The company would fly the route 20 times per month. The increase in fixed costs for additional crew, additional planes, landing fees, maintenance, and so on, would total $100,000 per month. Variable cost per passenger would remain at $40.

   i.   Should the company obtain the route?

   ii.   How many flights would Seacoast need to earn pre-tax profit of $57,500 per month on this route?

   iii.   If the load factor could be increased to 75%, how many flights would the company need in order to earn before-tax profit of $57,500 per month on this route?

   iv.   What qualitative factors should Seacoast consider in making its decision about acquiring this route?

3. (Appendix 3A) The Daniels Tool & Die Corporation has been in existence for a little over three years. The company's sales have increased each year as its reputation has been building. The company manufactures dies to its customers' specifications. Manufacturing overhead is applied to the jobs based on direct labour hours; the absorption (full) costing method is used. Overapplied or underapplied overhead is treated as an adjustment to Cost of Goods Sold. The company's income statements for the last two years are as follows:

Daniels Tool & Die Corporation
Comparative Income Statements
For the Years 2005 and 2006

	2005	2006
Sales	$840,000	$1,015,000
Cost of goods sold		
Finished goods inventory, January 1	$ 25,000	$ 18,000
Cost of goods manufactured	548,000	657,600
Total available	$573,000	$ 675,600
Finished goods inventory, December 31	18,000	14,000
Cost of goods sold before overhead adjustment	$555,000	$ 661,600
Underapplied manufacturing overhead	36,000	14,400
Cost of goods sold	$591,000	$ 676,000
Gross profit	$249,000	$ 339,000
Selling expenses	$ 82,000	$ 95,000
Administrative expenses	70,000	75,000
Total operating expenses	$152,000	$ 170,000
Operating income	$ 97,000	$ 169,000

Daniels Tool & Die Corporation
Other Information

	12/31/04	12/31/05	12/31/06
Raw Material Inventory	$22,000	$30,000	$10,000
Work in Process Inventory:			
Costs	$40,000	$48,000	$64,000
Direct labour hours	1,335	1,600	2,100
Finished Goods Inventory:			
Costs	$25,000	$18,000	$14,000
Direct labour hours	1,450	1,050	820

Daniels used the same predetermined overhead rate in applying overhead to production orders in both 2005 and 2006. The rate was based on the following estimates:

Fixed manufacturing overhead	$25,000
Variable manufacturing overhead	$155,000
Direct labour hours	25,000
Direct labour costs	$150,000

Actual direct labour hours expended were 20,000 in 2005 and 23,000 in 2006. Raw materials put into production were $292,000 in 2005 and $370,000 in 2006. Actual fixed overhead was $42,300 for 2005 and $37,400 for 2006, and the planned direct labour rate was the direct labour rate achieved.

For both years, all of the reported administrative costs were fixed, while the variable portion of the reported selling expenses resulted from a commission of 5% of sales revenue.

Required:

a. For the year ended December 31, 2006, prepare a revised income statement for the company using the variable costing method. Be sure to include the contribution margin on your statement.

b. Prepare a numerical reconciliation of the difference in operating income between the 2006 income statement prepared on the basis of absorption costing and the revised 2006 income statement prepared on the basis of variable costing.

c. Describe both the advantages and disadvantages of using variable costing.

4. (Appendix 3A) James P. Znajda Optics Inc. specializes in manufacturing lenses for large telescopes and cameras used in space exploration. Because the specifications for the lenses are determined by the customer and vary considerably. manufacturing overhead is applied to each of the orders on the basis of direct labour hours. The company uses the absorption (full) costing method. Znajda Optics Inc.'s predetermined overhead rates for 2005 and 2006 were based on the following estimates:

Direct labour hours	32,500	44,000
Direct labour cost	$325,000	$462,000
Fixed manufacturing overhead	$130,000	$176,000
Variable manufacturing overhead	$162,500	$198,000

Jack Sheriton, Znajda's controller, would like to use variable costing for internal reporting purposes, since he believes statements based on variable costing are more appropriate for use in making product decisions. To explain the benefits of variable costing to the other members of Znajda's management team, Sheriton plans to convert the company's income statement from absorption costing to variable costing. He has gathered the following information for this purpose:

James P. Znajda Optics Inc.
Comparative Income Statements
For the years 2005 and 2006

	2005	2006
Net sales	$1,140,000	$1,520,000
Cost of goods sold		
Finished goods inventory on January 1	$ 16,000	$ 25,000
Cost of goods manufactured	720,000	976,000
Total available for sale	$ 736,000	$1,001,000
Finished goods inventory on December 31	25,000	14,000
Cost of goods sold before overhead adjustment	$ 711,000	$ 987,000
Overhead adjustment	12,000	7,000
Cost of goods sold	$ 723,000	$ 994,000
Gross profit	$ 417,000	$ 526,000
Selling expense	$ 150,000	$ 190,000
Administrative expense	160,000	187,000
Total operating expenses	$ 310,000	$ 377,000
Operating income	$ 107,000	$ 149,000

Znajda's actual manufacturing data for the two years are as follows:

	2005	2006
Direct labour hours	30,000	42,000
Direct labour cost	$300,000	$435,000
Raw materials used	$140,000	$210,000
Fixed manufacturing overhead	$132,000	$175,000

The company's actual inventory balances were:

	12/31/04	12/31/05	12/31/06
Raw Material Inventory	$32,000	$36,000	$18,000
Work in Process Inventory:			
Costs	44,000	34,000	60,000
Direct labour hours	1,800	1,400	2,500
Finished Goods Inventory:			
Costs	16,000	25,000	14,000
Direct labour hours	700	1,080	550

For both years, all administrative costs were fixed, while a portion of the selling expense resulting from an 8% commission on net sales was variable. Znajda reports any overapplied or underapplied overhead as an adjustment to Cost of Goods Sold.

Required:

a. For the year ended December 31, 2006, prepare the revised income statement for Znajda Optics, Inc. using the variable costing method. Be sure to include the contribution margin on the revised income statement.

b. Describe two advantages of using variable costing rather than absorption costing.

(CMA adapted)

5. Mulder rolled over in his bed. The shrill ringing of the telephone was not something he wanted to hear. He and Scully had just finished one of their toughest cases earlier that morning and he had hoped to get a few more hours of sleep. He picked up the phone. It was Scully. Naturally, she was bringing the unwelcome news that Skinner wanted to see both of them right away. Mulder dragged himself out of bed, showered and dressed, and went directly to headquarters.

When he got there, Scully was waiting. They both went into Skinner's office. Skinner looked concerned and confused. He explained that the recent discovery of fossilized life in a meteorite from Mars was stirring up all kinds of interest in the search for extraterrestrial lifeforms. He had been asked to plan a mission to Mars to look for more specific signs of life, using a top secret fleet of alien space vessels assembled from wreckage over the last 50 years.

"That doesn't sound too tough," said Mulder. "Why the confused look?"

Skinner turned. "It's quite simple really," he replied. "I've been assured that funding will not be a problem but I must provide an accurate estimate of the costs and a description of the research the team would perform once it reached Mars. My problem right now is that in starting to get cost estimates from the various departments, I've discovered that many mission configurations with different numbers of astronauts are possible, but I'd like to understand the nature of each cost and have a graphical presentation of them for my presentation to my superiors.

"I might just send the mission commander on a low-cost basis, but I'd really like to send others because I believe we will get more useful information."

Skinner provided Mulder and Scully with the following information:

Mission commander (1 required)	$250,000
Mission specialists (0 to 20 required), each	$100,000
Spaceship rental (capacity 3 astronauts), each	$500,000
Mission distance (return)	500 million
Time spent on Mars	1 year
Cost of oxygen, food, other consumables	$100 per day per astronaut

Skinner also explained that, although they haven't actually flown the ships, they have managed to translate some of the logs and discovered the times for various trips undertaken by the previous owners. The information is as follows:

Distance (km)	Trip Time (days)
20,000,000	21.5
40,000,000	44.2
100,000,000	106.3
150,000,000	155.6
30,000,000	35.1
1,000,000,000	975.5
400,000,000	413.8
5,000,000	5.9
600,000,000	583.7

Required:

a.   Using the high–low method, determine the expected round trip flight time for the flight to Mars.

b.   Draw a graph in which you have plotted the data provided in the above table. Include the line that represents the equation that results from the high–low calculations performed in part (a).

c.   For each cost identified in the information provided by Skinner, state the nature of the cost, and draw a graph showing the cost. In each case, use the number of mission specialists as the cost driver. (Use a spreadsheet for all parts of this question.)

Adapted from work by Stephen Mills, NBV Business Systems

ETHICS AND QUALITY DISCUSSIONS

1.   The president of a large automotive firm is speaking at a conference and has been asked to specify the breakeven point for his firm in either units or sales dollars. The president of the firm replies that this is not possible because of the many variables that have to be taken into consideration in determining a breakeven point. The questioner replies that the president is being evasive and expresses doubt that the shareholders of the firm are being adequately served by a management team that does not even know the firm's breakeven point. You are in the audience and the person next to you asks you to answer the following:

a.   What are some of the variables that the president of the firm has in mind?

b.   How could the person who asked the question have reached the stated conclusion about the management team of the firm?

2.   Rumsfield Chemical Company's new president has learned that, for the past four years, the company has been dumping its industrial waste into the local river and falsifying reports to authorities about the levels of suspected cancer-causing materials in that waste. His plant manager says that there is no proof that the waste causes cancer, and there are only a few fishing towns within a hundred kilometres downstream. If the company has to treat the substance to neutralize its potentially injurious effects and then transport it to a legal dumpsite, the company's variable and fixed costs will rise to a level that might make the firm uncompetitive. If the company loses its competitive advantage, 10,000 local employees could become unemployed, and the town's economy could collapse.

a.   What kinds of variable and fixed costs can you think of that would increase (or decrease) if the waste were treated rather than dumped? How would these costs affect product contribution margin?

b.   What are the ethical conflicts the president faces?

c.   What rationalizations can you detect that have been devised by plant employees?

d.   What options and suggestions can you offer the president?

3.   Assume that, as a service to your community, you have agreed to serve on a community board that is investigating the possibility of opening a daycare centre

and preschool for area children. You are the financial expert on the board. Details follow:

The Community Club plans to open a childcare centre that will operate five days a week, 50 weeks each year, and charge $25 per week for each child. It has been determined that $20,000 must be spent to upgrade the facilities in the club building to meet provincial standards. These facilities have an estimated life of five years.

Supplies for each child are estimated to cost $0.50 per day, and food is estimated to cost $0.75 per day. Each year $1,000 must be spent on new equipment for the centre. For every 10 children, one paraprofessional must be included on the staff. Annual salaries for professionals and paraprofessionals are $9,000 and $4,000 respectively.

Due to space limitations in the facility, only 60 children can be accepted. This would require a staff of three professionals and six paraprofessionals.

Required:

a. Prepare a schedule showing the first year's cash financial results of operating the centre with 20, 40, and 60 children.

b. Discuss some of the problems (including ethical ones) of employing financial analysis in this type of problem.

4. Lily Simon is a sales representative for a heavy construction equipment manufacturer. She is compensated by a moderate fixed salary plus an 8% bonus on sales. Simon is aware that some of the higher-priced items earn the company a lower contribution margin and some of the lower-priced items earn the company a higher contribution margin. She learned this information from the variable costing financial statements produced by the company for management-level employees. One of Simon's best friends is a manager at the company.

Simon has recently started pushing sales of the high-priced items (to the exclusion of lower-priced items) by generously entertaining receptive customers and offering them gifts through the company's promotion budget. She feels that management has not given her adequate raises in the 20 years she has been with the company, and now she is too old to find a better job. As Simon's best friend and as a manager of the company, you are being asked to contemplate the following:

a. Are Simon's actions legal?

b. What are the ethical issues involved in the case from Simon's standpoint?

c. Are there ethical issues in the case from company management's standpoint?

d. What do you believe Simon should do? Why?

5. In Japan, the decision to stop production of a product or to close down a plant has different cost consequences than in the United States. One principal difference is that Japanese managers are much less likely to fire workers who are displaced by an event such as a plant closing. Japanese managers simply try to move the displaced workers to active plants. However, this concept of permanent or lifetime employment can be awkward to manage when economic times become difficult and prudent financial management suggests that activities, including employment, be scaled back to cut costs. Several years ago, one Japanese company found the following unique solution:

Nissan Motor Co., as a sign that its severe slump may be worsening, is taking the unusual step of loaning some of its idle factory workers to a rival auto maker.

Nissan said it will assign 250 of its production employees to work for six months at factories run by Isuzu Motors Ltd., a 37% owned affiliate of General Motors Corp.

Nissan's spokesman, Koji Okuda, called the move an attempt to deal with the company's sharp drop in auto output in Japan. In May, Nissan's Japanese auto production fell 26% from a year earlier. "Demand is low," Mr. Okuda said. "We have to adjust our operations."[13]

As an economic journalist of a large international publication, you have been asked to contemplate the following issues.

a. What specific types of costs might Nissan have considered relevant in its decision to lend employees to Isuzu?

b. Why would Isuzu be interested in hiring, on a temporary basis, workers of Nissan?

c. What were the likely impacts of this arrangement on the quality of the output at Isuzu? The quality of output at Nissan?

COMMUNICATIONS ACTIVITIES

1. Which of the following dimensions of product costing would be affected by a switch from absorption to variable costing; the product costing system, the measurement method, cost accumulation, or financial statement presentation? Why and how?

2. The normal preparation of sushi requires a highly paid chef to prepare a cylinder of rice that is topped with a sliver of raw fish. A new machine has been developed that produces perfectly formed sushi. The cost of the machines range from $75,000 to $125,000.

   Assume that you are an adviser to a restaurant that currently serves sushi.

   a. How would the purchase of a sushi machine change the restaurant's cost structure?

   b. Discuss whether the new machine would likely affect the revenues as well as the costs of the restaurant.

   c. How might the machine affect the quality of sushi?

3. Your neighbour, Tim Allen, wants to do some home improvements but finds that the power drill he owns is ill-equipped for the job. You are vice president of the Zoomby Corporation, which manufactures the Zoomby Power Drill 2000. Tim knows that you can purchase tools from the company at "cost plus 10%"—a tremendous discount from what he would have to pay in a retail store.

   Discuss the variety of ways in which Zoomby could compute "cost" in selling tools to company employees and which one or ones would be the most appropriate.

PROJECTS

1. This team project involves a class debate on the relative merits of variable and absorption costing. The class should be divided into teams of two and each team should be prepared to debate the issue orally. All teams should be asked to submit evidence of sources they have identified and notes of the arguments they have constructed for both sides of the issue.

   In preparing for the debate, students should be encouraged to search for materials to support their arguments. A voluminous amount of literature exists and many materials should be easily obtained.

2. Invite an accountant from a local business that has used variable costing to your class. Ask the accountant to demonstrate and explain the reconciliation of the variable costing data to an absorption format for external reporting. Also, ask for an explanation of the reconciliation required for purposes of computing income tax obligations.

3. Find a series of annual income statements for two companies. One company should be in a highly capital-intensive industry (with high fixed costs) such as steel production. The other company should have comparably low fixed costs and high variable costs (as do certain service firms). For the two companies, try to answer the following questions:

   a. In which company is annual change in net income more sensitive to annual change in revenues?

   b. Discuss your perception of the differences in risk of owning shares in the two companies because of differences in their cost structures.

USING THE INTERNET

1. Go to the annual report for Sun-Rype Products Ltd. at www.sun-rype.com and look in the notes to the financial statements to find out how fixed manufacturing overhead is treated at the company.

2. Go to www.businesstools.org/breakeven/breakeven.html. At this site, you will find some very interesting information about breakeven analysis. There are tools that can be used to find contribution margin per unit, contribution margin ratio, and other interesting facts about breakeven analysis.

3 Go to www.dinkytown.net/java/BreakEven.html. You will find a breakeven calculator and definitions used in breakeven analysis. Practise using the calculator to see how the system works.

SOLUTIONS TO SELF-TEST QUESTIONS

1. d: Sales revenue – Total variable costs = Contribution margin

2. b: Breakeven Sales Units are equal to Sales = Variable Costs + Fixed Costs
   $$\$500x = \$275^1x + \$247,500$$
   $$\$225x = \$247,500$$
   $$x = 1,100 \text{ units}$$
   $^1\$495,000 \div 1,800 \text{ units}$

3. a: Contribution margin = ($405,000 ÷ $900,000) = 45%
   Total contribution margin = $1,050,000 × 0.55 = $472,500
   Sales = 2,100 × $500 = $1,050,000
   CM = 0.45 × $1,050,000 = $472,500
   PBT = $472,500 − $247,500 = $225,000
   NI = 0.68 × $225,000 = $153,000

4. c: Unit cost of sales = $275 (55% of $500)
   Total cost of sales = $825,000 ($275 × 3,000 sticks)
   S = (1,500 × $450) + (1,500 × $500) = $1,425,000
   CGS = (3,000 × $275) = $825,000
   CM = $1,425,000 − $825,000 = $600,000
   PBT = $600,000 − $247,500 = $352,500
   NI = 0.68 × $352,500 = $239,700

5. d: Variable cost will increase from $275 to $315 and selling price will decrease from $500 to $450.
   $$\$450x = \$247,500 + 315x + \$157,500^1$$
   $$\$135x = \$405,000$$
   $$x = 3,000 \text{ units}$$
   S = 3,000 units × $450 = $1,350,000
   $^1\$107,100 \div 0.68$

6 c: The operating leverage is 1.48 computed as follows:
   Operating leverage = Contribution margin ÷ Profit before taxes
   Operating leverage = $650,000 ÷ $440,000 = 1.48

7. b: Selling price − [$5 + $10 + 0.35 ($10)] = 0.30 of selling price
   Selling price − $18.50 = 0.30 of selling price
   0.70 of selling price = $18.50
   Selling price = $26.43

8. c: Contribution margin = $28.00 − $18.50 = $9.50
   Total contribution margin should be equal to fixed costs plus desired income.
   Total contribution margin should be equal to [($0.65 × $10.00) × 10,000] + 10,000.
   Number of units sold × $9.50 = $75,000
   Number of units sold = 7,895 (rounded)

9. b: Capitalize to inventory only the variable costs for variable costing.
   Total inventoriable costs = $450,000 ($300,000 + $100,000 + $50,000)

10. c: All costs of production are capitalized to inventory.
    Total inventoriable costs = $530,000 ($300,000 + $100,000 + $50,000 + $80,000)

ENDNOTES

1. Kevin D. Thompson, "Planning for Profit," *Black Enterprise*, pp. 93–94. Copyright April 1993, The Earl Graves Publishing Co. Inc., 130 Fifth Avenue, New York, NY 10011.

2. Relevant range is the range of activity over which a variable cost will remain constant per unit and a fixed cost will remain constant in total.

3. The income statement approach can readily be adapted to computerized spreadsheet format, which can be used to obtain results quickly for many different combinations of the CVP factors.

4. Robert L. Simison, "US Auto Makers Brace for Disappointing 2001—Globalization Dents Domestic," *Asian Wall Street Journal,* January 8, 2001.

5. Once the constant percentage contribution margin in a multiproduct firm is determined, all situations regarding income points can be treated the same as they were earlier in the chapter—remembering that the answers reflect the bag assumption.

6. Robin Cooper and Robert S. Kaplan, "How Cost Accounting Distorts Product Costs," *Management Accounting,* April 1998, p. 27.

7. Matt Hamblen, *Computerworld,* Framingham, August 21, 2000, p. 48.

8. Ian McKinnon and Carol Howes, "BP Amoco Outsources Accounting," *Financial Post,* January 12, 2000, p. C11.

9. David Paddon, Canadian Press, reprinted in the *Toronto Star,* July 18, 2002, p. D4.

10. Direct costing is, however, a misnomer for variable costing. All variable manufacturing costs, whether direct or indirect, are considered product costs under variable costing.

11. Relevant costing is covered in Chapter 8 and budgeting is discussed in Chapter 9.

12. Robert S. Kaplan, "One Cost System Isn't Enough," *Harvard Business Review,* January–February 1988, p. 61.

13. Michael Williams, "Nissan Will Loan Workers to Rival Amid Low Demand," *Wall Street Journal,* June 24, 1994, p. A4.

Chapter 4

Costing Systems

LEARNING OBJECTIVES

After completing this chapter, you should be able to answer the following questions:

1 What
production situations are appropriate for a job order costing system and why?

2 How
are costs accumulated in a job order product costing system using specialized documents?

3 What
production situations are appropriate for a process costing system and why?

4 Why
are equivalent units of production used in process costing?

5 How
are equivalent units of production, unit costs, and inventory values computed using the weighted average method of process costing?

6 How
is a cost of production report prepared under the weighted average method of process costing?

7 What
is the effect of multidepartmental processing on the computation of equivalent units of production?

8 How
is a cost of production report prepared in a multidepartmental processing operation?

9 How
are equivalent units of production, unit costs, and inventory values computed using the FIFO method of process costing? (Appendix 4A)

10 How
is a cost of production report prepared under the FIFO method of process costing? (Appendix 4A)

11 How
do normal and abnormal losses of units differ and how is each treated in the calculation of equivalent units of production? (Appendix 4B)

ON SITE

www.ganong.com

Ganong Bros. Ltd.

The name "**GANONG**" whets appetites across Canada and around the world wherever these fine chocolates are available. Ganong candies and chocolates have enlivened many a Christmas morning and special occasion since 1873, when two brothers embarked on an experiment in candy making in St. Stephen, New Brunswick. The company introduced the wrapped chocolate bar in 1906 and invented the milk chocolate bar by 1910. Ganong also invented a worldwide phenomenon— the wrapped chocolate cream bar.

It was Arthur D. Ganong, president from 1917 to 1957, and his head of manufacturing, George Ensor, who actually came up with the idea to wrap snack-sized portions of chocolate in cellophane. The two men enjoyed spending warm spring days fishing, and they soon discovered that warm weather wreaked havoc on the unwrapped chocolate pieces they had stashed in their pockets. They began wrapping the chocolate soon after, but it took a while before they realized that they could make some money from the idea. "It finally dawned on them that, if this was a convenience food for them, why wouldn't it be a convenience food for others?" says the current president, David Ganong.

Although the actual name of the first chocolate bar to hit the shelves in 1910 is debated within the company, Mr. Ganong says he knows it was chocolate on the outside with a sweet centre.[1]

Boxed chocolates represent only about a quarter of his company's business, says Mr. Ganong, just the fourth president—all of whom have been family members—since the firm's formation in 1873.

The rest is divided among three other categories: the fast-developing business of fruit snacks; bagged candies, such as jujubes and peppermints; and bulk candy products and chocolate bars, such as Chicken Bones, Ganong's signature hard candy with a chocolate centre.[2]

No one makes Chicken Bones like Ganong. "We do take the extra time and cost to put a layer of clear, hard candy around the outside of it after all the colour and flavour is inside," Mr. Ganong said. "It gives it this really wonderful shine that a Ganong Chicken Bone has. The appearance, because of the hard candy on the outside, is really spectacular."

There is also substance, beyond the looks. "The chocolate centre of a Ganong Chicken Bone is a special, rich, bitter flavour that blends perfectly with the cinnamon candy jacket," he said.[3]

Tradition. Quality. Innovation. They are Ganong hallmarks and part of its heritage. It's what sets Ganong apart. Among the thousands of privately owned companies in Canada, Ganong has a certain distinction. Its name is not only synonymous with fine chocolate, but it's also recognized as a good business.

The *National Post* said in 1999 that Ganong is one of "Canada's 50 Best Managed Private Companies." The *Post* says that's because of "the high importance placed on hiring, training, and motivating staff. The second link is timing: beating the competition to the punch on both the creative and delivery fronts."

Therein lies the key to Ganong's continued success as one of the country's pre-eminent candy and chocolate makers. Take tradition mixed with the never-ending pursuit of quality, add good, talented people, and beat the competition with the best product. It works every time.[4]

SOURCES: *National Post*, December 15, 1999; Gordon Pitts, "Ganong Boss Aims for Sweet Spot," B4 Cdn Business, *The Globe and Mail*, March 3, 2003; Chuck Brown, "Make No Bones About These Chicken Bones," *New Brunswick Telegraph Journal*, November 25, 2002; Ganong Bros. Web site www.ganong.com (reprinted by permission of Ganong.)

To compute the cost of products, it is necessary to decide on (1) the product costing system, and (2) the valuation method to be used. The costing system defines the cost object and the method of assigning costs to production. The valuation method specifies how the costs will be measured. Companies must have both a cost system and a valuation method. These activities are necessary for strategic success. This chapter will introduce the two primary cost systems—job order and process. Three valuation methods can be used—actual, normal, and standard. This chapter discusses the first two valuation methods. The third, standard costing, will be discussed in a later chapter.

There are thousands of printers throughout the world, from Helsinki to Auckland, from Vladivostok to Capetown, from Beirut to Hong Kong. No two print jobs are identical, no two print shops are the same, and the needs of no two print customers are exact counterparts.

The basic economic problem of printers is pricing their conversion service for hundreds of different jobs using technology that is [constantly] shifting. Printers try to predict the cost of a job in order to mark it up for pricing.... Many hours of effort are devoted to job cost predictions.[5]

Building a specialized product to order is not what could be called mass manufacturing! But, like making any other product, it requires converting raw materials to a finished product through the use of direct labour and manufacturing overhead. Since each order is substantially different from any other order, it would be very difficult to develop a set of costs for this process. Thus, in these situations, a method of cost accounting called job order costing is used to record the conversion process.

JOB ORDER COSTING SYSTEM

Product costing is concerned with (1) cost identification, (2) cost management, and (3) product cost assignment. In a **job order costing system**, costs are accumulated individually by job—defined as a single unit[6] or a group of like units identifiable as being produced to distinct customer specifications.

Each **job** in a job costing system is treated as a unique "cost entity" or cost object. Job order costing is useful in companies like Dell Computer Corporation, which concentrates on direct selling to customers on the Internet. The company configures computers to meet each customer's needs. The use of job order costing allows the costs and profits of each job to be known.

LEARNING OBJECTIVE 1

What production situations are appropriate for a job order costing system and why?

job order costing system
a product costing method used by entities that produce limited quantities of custom-made goods or services that conform to specifications designated by the purchaser

job
a single unit or group of like units identifiable as being produced to distinct customer specifications

Made to Measure

Even with the proliferation of off-the-rack clothing and shirt sales galore, there is obviously still a thriving market for custom-sewn cotton shirts.

"I'd [Christy Allen] say we sell an average of 20 custom shirts a month. They range from $100 to $250. Lots of customers need this to get a nice fit—like weightlifters. Then, there are people who just like to have this nice custom fit as opposed to what's on the shelf."

"This appeals to people who want the best," he [Italo D'Alessio] said. "Word of mouth is how they find me. And it's the fit that brings them back. I take seven measurements on the collar alone."[7]

GENERAL NEWS NOTE

The above News Note describes a company that uses a job order costing system.

Costs of different jobs are maintained in separate subsidiary ledger accounts and are not added together or commingled in the ledger accounts. The logic of separating costs for individual jobs is shown by the following example. During March, Dan Ondrack, an artist, made drawings and three small to-scale clay models, each for a different customer. When completed, one of the models will be 33 metres high, the second one will be 12 metres, and the third will be 27 metres. To total all of Ondrack's business costs for March and to divide them by the three projects would produce a meaningless average cost for each project. This type of average cost per job would be equally meaningless in any other entity that manufactures products or provides services geared to unique customer specifications. Since job results are heterogeneous and distinctive in nature, the costs of those jobs are, logically, not averageable.

Exhibit 4-1 on page 168 provides the Work in Process control and subsidiary ledger accounts for Ondrack's job order product costing system. Note that the ending balance of the Work in Process Control account is the sum of the three subsidiary ledger accounts.

The usual production costs of direct materials, direct labour, and manufacturing overhead are accumulated for each job. The typical job order inventory accounts use actual direct materials and actual direct labour cost combined with predetermined overhead rates multiplied by some actual cost driver (such as direct labour hours, cost or quantity of materials used, or number of materials requisitions). This method is called normal costing and is used because actual direct material and actual direct labour costs are fairly easy to identify and can be associated with a particular job.[8]

Manufacturing overhead costs are not usually traceable to specific jobs and must be allocated to production. For example, Ondrack's electricity cost during March is related to all jobs worked on during that month. It would be difficult, if not impossible, to accurately determine which jobs created the need for what amount of electricity. To help ensure the proper recording of costs, the amounts appearing in the subsidiary ledger accounts are periodically compared and reconciled to the Work in Process Inventory control account in the general ledger.

The output of a given job can be a single unit or multiple similar or dissimilar units. For example, Ondrack's output is a clay model of each customer's contracted-for project. If a job's output is a single product, the total costs accumulated for the job are assigned to the individual unit. When multiple outputs result, a unit cost may only be computed if the units are similar. In such a case, the total accumulated job cost is averaged over the number of units produced to determine a cost per unit. If the output consisted of dissimilar units (for instance, if all Ondrack's three

EXHIBIT 4-1

Separate Subsidiary Ledger
Accounts for Jobs

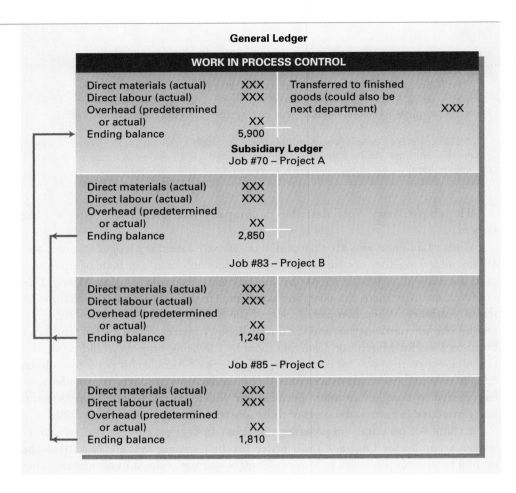

General Ledger

WORK IN PROCESS CONTROL

Direct materials (actual)	XXX	Transferred to finished		
Direct labour (actual)	XXX	goods (could also be		
Overhead (predetermined		next department)		XXX
or actual)	XX			
Ending balance	5,900			

Subsidiary Ledger
Job #70 – Project A

Direct materials (actual)	XXX	
Direct labour (actual)	XXX	
Overhead (predetermined		
or actual)	XX	
Ending balance	2,850	

Job #83 – Project B

Direct materials (actual)	XXX	
Direct labour (actual)	XXX	
Overhead (predetermined		
or actual)	XX	
Ending balance	1,240	

Job #85 – Project C

Direct materials (actual)	XXX	
Direct labour (actual)	XXX	
Overhead (predetermined		
or actual)	XX	
Ending balance	1,810	

projects were for the same customer), no cost per unit could be determined, although it is still possible to know the total cost of the job.

These basic facts about the nature of a job order costing system provide the necessary foundation to account for individual jobs.

LEARNING OBJECTIVE 2

How are costs accumulated in a job order product costing system using specialized documents?

JOB ORDER COSTING: DETAILS AND DOCUMENTS

A job can be categorized by its stage of existence in its production life cycle. There are three basic stages of production: (1) agreed-upon but not yet started, (2) jobs in process, and (3) completed jobs. Since job order costing is used by companies making products according to user specifications, unique raw materials may be required. Raw materials are often not acquired until a job is agreed upon. The materials acquired, although often separately distinguishable and related to specific jobs, are accounted for in a single general ledger control account (Raw Materials Inventory) with subsidiary ledger backup. The materials may, however, be designated in the storeroom (and possibly in the subsidiary records) as being "held for use in Job XX." Such designations should keep the materials from being used on a job other than the one for which they were acquired.

Materials Requisitions

When materials are needed for a job, a materials requisition form is prepared so that the materials can be released from the warehouse and sent to the production area. A **materials requisition form** (shown in Exhibit 4-2) is a source document that indicates the types and quantities of materials to be placed into production or used in performing a service. The form provides a way to track responsibility for materials cost and links materials to specific jobs. Materials requisitions release warehouse personnel from further responsibility for the issued materials and assign responsibility to the department that issued the requisition. As materials are issued, their costs are released from Raw Materials Inventory and, if the materials are direct to the job, are sent to Work in Process Inventory. If the Raw Materials Inventory account also contains indirect materials, those costs are assigned to Overhead when the indirect materials are issued. The journal entry will be

Work in Process Inventory (Direct Materials)	XXX	
Manufacturing Overhead (Indirect Materials)	XXX	
Raw Material Inventory		XXX

To put direct and indirect materials into production.

> **materials requisition form**
> a source document that indicates the types and quantities of materials to be placed into production or used in performing a service; causes materials and their costs to be released from the raw materials warehouse and sent to Work in Process Inventory

Completed materials requisition forms are important documents in the audit trail of company records because they provide the ability to verify the flow of materials from the warehouse to the department and job that received the materials. Such documents are usually prenumbered and come in multicopy sets so that completed copies can be maintained in the warehouse and the department, and with each job.

When direct materials are first issued to production, a job moves from the first stage of its production life cycle into the second—jobs in process. In this state, it is necessary to begin the process of cost accumulation using the primary accounting document in a job order system—the job order cost sheet (also called a job cost record).

Job Order Cost Sheet

The source document that provides virtually all financial information about a particular job is the **job order cost sheet**, as shown in Exhibit 4-3 on page 170. The set of all job order cost sheets for uncompleted jobs composes the Work in Process Inventory subsidiary ledger. The total costs contained in all job order cost sheets for uncompleted jobs should reconcile to the Work in Process Inventory control account balance in the general ledger, as shown in Exhibit 4-1.

The top portion of a job order cost sheet includes a job number, a description of the task, customer identification, various scheduling information, delivery instructions, and contract price. The remainder of the form details actual costs for

> **job order cost sheet**
> a source document that provides virtually all the financial information about a particular job; the set of all job order cost sheets for uncompleted jobs composes the Work in Process Inventory subsidiary ledger

Date _____

Job Number _____   Department _____

Authorized by _____   Issued by _____

Received by _____   Inspected by _____

Item No.	Part No.	Description	Unit of Measure	Quantity Required	Quantity Issued	Unit Cost	Total Cost

EXHIBIT 4-2
Materials Requisition Form

EXHIBIT 4-3

Job Order Cost Sheet

Job Number: ___186___

Customer Name and Address

Calgary Museum of Natural History

3497 Azores Blvd.

Calgary, Alta.

Contract Agreement Date:	3/25/05
Scheduled Starting Date:	4/5/05
Agreed Completion Date:	3/1/06
Actual Completion Date:	
Delivery Instructions:	Crate and deliver to museum

Description of Job:

Signs as per attached illustrations

Contract Price: $182,521

Department A—Art

Direct Materials (Est. $10,900)			Direct Labour (Est. $3,969)			Overhead based on					
						# of Requisitions (@ $15)			# of DLH (@ $8)		
Date	Source	Amount	Date	Source	Amount	Date	Source	Amount	Date	Source	Amount
4/5	MR# 630	$ 35	4/9	wk ended	$368	4/30	2 MRs	$30	4/30	45 DLH	$360
4/21	MR# 637	125	4/23	wk ended	981						

Department B—Moulding
(same format as above but with different OH rates

Department C—Welding
(same format as above but with different OH rates

SUMMARY

	Art Dept.		Moulding Dept.		Welding Dept.	
	Actual	Estimated (Budget)	Actual	Estimated (Budget)	Actual	Estimated (Budget)
Direct Materials	$11,034	$10,900	$23,176	$24,500	$22,639	$17,640
Direct Labour	3,890	3,969	22,985	24,118	3,421	3,310
Overhead (Req.)	193	180	4,987	4,804	2,995	2,940
Overhead (DLH)	1,029	1,056	3,952	3,783	1,347	1,460
Totals	$16,146	$16,105	$55,100	$57,205	$30,402	$25,350

		Actual	Estimated (Budgeted)
Final Costs:	Art Dept.	$ 16,146	$16,105
	Moulding Dept.	55,100	57,205
	Welding Dept.	30,402	25,350
	Total	$101,648	$98,660

materials and labour and applied overhead costs. The form might also include estimated cost information.

Exhibit 4-3 illustrates a job order cost sheet for Exhibits International, Inc. The company has been contracted to produce signs for the Calgary Museum of Natural History. Direct materials and direct labour costs are assigned to jobs, and the amounts are indicated on the job order cost sheet as work on the job is performed. Direct materials information is gathered from the materials requisition forms, while direct labour information is found on employee time sheets or employee labour tickets. (Employee time sheets are discussed in the next section.)

At Exhibits International, overhead is applied to production using two predetermined overhead rates. The first rate is based on the number of materials requisitions, and the second is based on direct labour hours. Exhibits International's management has found that these two activity bases better reflect the incurrence of costs than would a single base. Using the number of materials requisitions reflects management's determination that numerous parts create substantially more of some types of overhead support costs, such as warehousing and purchasing. Direct labour hours provides a reasonable allocation base for overhead costs such as electricity, indirect labour, and indirect materials.

Employee Time Sheets

An **employee time sheet** or **time ticket** (Exhibit 4-4) indicates, for each employee, what jobs were worked on during the day and the amount of time employees worked on them. These time sheets are most reliable if the employee fills them out as the day progresses. As work arrives at an employee station, it is accompanied by a tag specifying its job order number. The times that work was started and stopped are noted on the time sheet.[9] These time sheets should be collected and reviewed by supervisors to ensure that the information is as accurate as possible.

In today's highly automated factories, employee time sheets may not be extremely useful or necessary documents. However, machine time can be tracked in the same way as human labour through the use of machine clocks or counters. As jobs are transferred from one machine to another, the clock or counter can be

employee time sheet (time ticket)
a source document that indicates, for each employee, what jobs were worked on during the day and for what amounts of time

---

EXHIBIT 4-4
Employee Time Sheet

For Week Ending _____

Department _____

Employee Name _____

Employee I.D. Number _____

| Type of Work | | Job Number | Start Time | Stop Time | Day (circle) | Total Hours |
Code	Description					
					M T W Th F S	
					M T W Th F S	
					M T W Th F S	
					M T W Th F S	
					M T W Th F S	
					M T W Th F S	

_____   _____
Employee Signature   Supervisor Signature (for overtime)

reset to mark the start and stop times. Machine times can then be equated to employee–operator time. Another convenient way to track employee time is through bar coding. Using bar coding also provides the ability to trace machine depreciation to specific products by using a time-related depreciation measure (such as depreciation per hour of use).

Transferring employee time sheet (or an alternative source document) information to the job order cost sheet requires a knowledge of employee labour rates. Wage rates are found in the employees' personnel files. The employee time spent on the job is multiplied by the employee's wage rate. The amounts are summed to find total direct labour cost for the period, and the summation is recorded on the cost sheet. Time sheet information is also used for payroll preparation. All indirect labour costs are charged to manufacturing overhead. The journal entry to record the information follows:

Work in Process Inventory (Direct Labour)	XXX	
Manufacturing Overhead (Indirect Labour)	XXX	
Wages Payable		XXX
To record direct and indirect labour.		

Time sheets are filed and retained because they are basic documents that can be referenced to satisfy various future information needs. If total actual labour costs for the job differ significantly from the original estimate, the manager responsible for labour cost control can be asked to clarify the reasons underlying the situation.

cost-plus job
a job being billed at cost plus a specified profit margin

In addition, if a job is being billed at cost plus a specified profit margin (a **cost-plus job**), the number of hours worked may be checked by the buyer. This situation is quite common and especially important when dealing with government contracts. Hours not worked directly on the contracted job cannot be arbitrarily or incorrectly charged to the cost-plus job without the potential for detection.

Lastly, time sheets provide information on overtime hours. Under the *Employment Standards Act*, overtime must be paid at a time-and-a-half rate to all non-management employees.

Overhead

Actual overhead incurred during production is included in an overhead control account. If actual overhead is applied to jobs, the cost accountant will wait until the end of the period and divide actual overhead incurred by some related measure of activity or cost driver. Actual overhead would be applied to jobs by multiplying the actual overhead rate by the actual measure of activity associated with each job.

More commonly, overhead is applied to job order cost sheets by using one or more annualized predetermined overhead application rates. Overhead is assigned to jobs by multiplying the predetermined rate times the actual measure of the activity base that was incurred during the period and was associated with each job. If predetermined rates are used, overhead is applied at the end of the period or at completion of production, whichever is earlier. Overhead is applied at the end of each period so that the Work in Process Inventory account contains costs for all three product elements (direct materials, direct labour, and overhead). When jobs are completed during a period, overhead is applied to Work in Process Inventory so that a complete product cost can be transferred to Finished Goods Inventory. The journal entry to apply overhead is as follows:

Work in Process Inventory	XXX	
Manufacturing Overhead		XXX
To apply overhead to work in process.		

Completion of Production

When a job is completed, its total cost is transferred to the Finished Goods Inventory account.

Finished Goods Inventory	XXX	
Work in Process Inventory		XXX
To transfer completed goods to		
finished goods inventory.		

Job cost sheets for completed jobs are removed from the WIP subsidiary ledger and are transferred to a Finished Goods file. They serve as a subsidiary ledger for that account. When goods are sold, the cost shown on the job order cost sheet is transferred to Cost of Goods Sold.

Cost of Goods Sold	XXX	
Finished Goods Inventory		XXX
To record sale of goods.		

Job cost sheets for sold jobs are kept in a company's permanent files. A completed job cost sheet provides management with a historical summary of total costs and if appropriate, the cost per finished unit for a given job. The cost per unit may be helpful for planning and control purposes as well as for bidding on future contracts. If a job was exceptionally profitable, management might decide to pursue additional similar jobs. If a job was unprofitable, the job cost sheet may provide indications of areas in which cost control was lax. Such indications are more readily determinable if the job cost sheet presents the original estimated cost information.

The News Note below discusses how technology can improve efficiency and profitability.

In any job order product costing system, the individual job is the focal point. The next section presents a comprehensive job order costing illustration using Exhibits International, Inc., the company introduced earlier.

JOB ORDER COST ILLUSTRATION

Exhibits International, Inc. normally sets selling prices at cost plus 85%. The sales price ($182,521) of the sign is established by multiplying the total estimated (budgeted) cost information shown in Exhibit 4-3 ($98,660) by 185%. This sales price

GENERAL NEWS NOTE

Impact of Technology

The ability of Johnson [president of His Life Woodworks] to visualize and develop designs for large custom projects helps the company get business, but that custom emphasis creates problems because all of the details have to be tracked.

"Custom woodworks is a progressive experience. The customer is never done making up his/her mind. There's so much freedom to add, change and remove things."

His Life Woodworks uses BusinessMaster, an operations management program that is designed to improve purchasing, order entry, inventory control, production scheduling, job costing, etc.

"Implementing the system and getting controls in place showed us how low we were pricing our goods, and why we weren't making any money." Ultimately, you know which jobs you'll lose money on, and you can make the difficult choice to turn them down, Brim [the vice president] says. "Now we have valid information to decide whether we want to do that kind of work anymore."

Source: Adapted from Karl D. Forth, "Breaking Down Barriers to Growth," *Chartwell Communications, Inc.*, Volume 74, Issue 4, pp. 40–46, March 2002.

was agreed to by the Calgary Museum of Natural History in a contract dated March 25, 2005. Exhibits International's managers scheduled the job to begin on April 5 and be completed by March 1 of the following year. The job is assigned the number 186 for identification purposes.

The following journal entries illustrate the flow of costs for the Art Department of Exhibits International, Inc. during April 2005. Several jobs were worked on in the Art Department during that month, including Job #186. Although costs would be accounted for individually for each job worked on during the month, only the detail for Job #186 is shown.

In entries 1, 2, and 4 (following), Work in Process Inventory—Art Dept. has been debited twice to highlight the costs associated with Job #186 versus those associated with other jobs. In practice, the Work in Process control account for a given department would be debited only once for total costs assigned to it. The details for posting to the individual job cost records would be presented in the journal entry explanations.

1. During April 2005, materials requisition forms #628–641 indicated that $4,995 of raw materials were issued from the warehouse to the Art Department. This amount included $160 of direct materials used on Job #186 (issued on April 5 and 21) and $4,245 of direct materials used on other jobs. The remaining $590 of raw materials issued during April were indirect materials.

Work in Process Inventory—Art Dept. (Job #186)	160	
Work in Process Inventory—Art Dept. (other jobs)	4,245	
Manufacturing Overhead—Art Dept. (indirect materials)	590	
Raw Materials Inventory		4,995

To record direct and indirect materials issued per requisitions during April.

2. The April time sheets and payroll summaries of the Art Department were used to trace direct and indirect labour to that department. Total labour cost for the Art Department for April was $15,075. Job #186 required $1,349 of direct labour cost during the two biweekly pay periods of April 9 ($368) and April 23 ($981). The remaining jobs in process required $12,576 of direct labour costs. Indirect labour costs for April totalled $1,150.

Work in Process Inventory—Art Dept. (Job #186)	1,349	
Work in Process Inventory—Art Dept. (other jobs)	12,576	
Manufacturing Overhead—Art Dept. (indirect labour)	1,150	
Salaries and Wages Payable		15,075

To record salaries and wages associated with the Art Dept. during April.

3. In addition to indirect materials and indirect labour, the Art Department incurred other overhead costs during April. Repairs and maintenance costs were paid in cash. Overhead costs were also incurred for supplies, etc.; these costs have been credited to "Various other accounts." The following entry summarizes the accumulation of these other actual overhead costs for April.

Manufacturing Overhead—Art Dept.	846	
Accumulated Depreciation		285
Prepaid Insurance		50
Utilities Payable		325
Cash		110
Various other accounts		76

To record actual overhead costs of the Art Dept. during
April exclusive of indirect materials and indirect labour.

4. Exhibits International, Inc., prepares financial statements at the end of each month. To do so, Work in Process Inventory must include all production costs—direct materials, direct labour, and overhead. Exhibits International allocates overhead to the Art Department Work in Process Inventory based on two predetermined overhead rates: $15 per materials requisition and $8 per direct labour hour. In April, materials for Job #186 required two materials requisitions, and the artists had worked a total of 45 hours. The other jobs worked on during the month received total applied overhead of $1,493 (19 requisitions × $15 and 151 DLH × $8).

Work in Process Inventory—Art Dept. (Job #186)	390	
Work in Process Inventory—Art Dept. (other jobs)	1,493	
Manufacturing Overhead—Art Dept.		1,883

To apply overhead to the Art Dept. Work in Process for
April using predetermined application rates.

Notice that the amount of overhead actually incurred during April in the Art Department ($590 + $1,150 + $846 = $2,586) is not equal to the amount of overhead applied to that department's Work in Process Inventory ($1,883). This $703 difference is the underapplied overhead for the month. Because the predetermined rates are based on annual estimates, differences in actual and applied overhead will accumulate during the year. Under- or overapplied overhead will be closed at year-end, as shown earlier in Chapter 2, to either Cost of Goods Sold (if the under- or overapplied amount is immaterial) or to WIP, FG, and CGS (if significant).

The preceding summarizations indicate the types of entries that each department at Exhibits International, Inc. would make. Direct materials and direct labour data are posted to each job order cost sheet on a continuous basis (usually daily); entries are posted to the general ledger control accounts at less frequent intervals (usually monthly).

Similar entries for the other signs are made throughout the production process. Exhibit 4-3 shows the completed cost sheet for Job #186 for Exhibits International. Note that direct materials requisitions, direct labour cost, and applied overhead shown earlier in items 1, 2, and 4 are posted on the job cost sheet. Other entries are not detailed.

Job #186 will be worked on by all departments, sometimes concurrently. When the job is completed, its costs are transferred to Finished Goods Inventory. The journal entries related to completion and sale are as follows:

Finished Goods Inventory—Job #186	101,648	
Work in Process Inventory—Art Dept.		16,146
Work in Process Inventory—Moulding		55,100
Work in Process Inventory—Welding		30,402

To record transfer of completed job to finished
goods inventory.

Cost of Goods Sold—Job #186[1]	101,648	
Finished Goods Inventory—Job #186		101,648

To record the sale.

1. Under- or overapplied overhead has been disregarded for this illustration.

Accounts Receivable—Calgary Museum	182,521	
Sales		182,521

To record sale on credit.

The completed job cost sheet can be used by managers in all departments to determine how well costs were controlled. Although the Art Department experienced higher direct materials cost than estimated, direct labour in that department was under the estimated amount. In the Moulding Department, actual direct materials and direct labour costs were slightly below the estimated amount. The welding department experienced a rather substantial unfavourable difference in materials costs. Overall, costs were controlled relatively well on this job, since total costs were only 3% above the estimate.

Managers are interested in controlling costs on each job as well as by department for each time period. Actual direct materials, direct labour, and manufacturing overhead costs are accumulated in departmental accounts and are periodically compared to estimates so that managers can respond to significant deviations. Transactions must be recorded in a consistent, complete, and accurate manner to have information on actual costs available for periodic comparisons. Managers may stress different types of cost control in different types of businesses.

The Exhibits International, Inc. example assumed the use of predetermined overhead rates. Attempting to use actual overhead costs for determination of job cost is difficult because of the delayed timing of overhead information and differences in periodical activity levels. The delay in information may be critical when a job is being provided for a customer on a cost-plus basis. Atypical variations in periodic activity could cause management to make incorrect assumptions about the cost per job. A manager might mistakenly determine that a particular job's cost was significantly higher or lower than it would have been in a period of normal activity. In a cost-plus contract, incorrect assumptions about costs could result in overcharging some customers while undercharging others. Such problems are overcome by using predetermined overhead rates.

JOB ORDER COSTING TO ASSIST MANAGEMENT

Job order costing is useful to managers in planning, controlling, decision making, and evaluating performance. Knowing the costs of individual jobs will allow managers to better estimate future job costs and establish realistic selling prices.

The major difference in job costing for a service organization and a manufacturing firm is that a service organization uses an insignificant amount of direct materials on each job. In such cases, direct materials may be treated (for the sake of convenience) as part of overhead rather than accounted for separately. The accountant in the service company may only need to trace direct labour to jobs and allocate all other production costs to overhead. Allocations of these costs may be accomplished most effectively by using a predetermined rate per direct labour hour or, if wage rates are approximately equal throughout the firm, per direct labour dollar. Other alternative cost drivers may also be used as possible overhead allocation bases.

Whether the entity is a manufacturer or a service organization that tailors its output to customer specifications, company management will find that job order costing techniques will help in the managerial function.

The following example demonstrates the usefulness to managers of job order costing.

Seawind Company

The Seawind Company manufactures three types of boats built to customer specifications.[10] Before job order costing was instituted, the owner (Ronnie Trump) had no means of determining the costs associated with the production of each type of boat. When a customer provided boat specifications and asked what the selling price would be, Ronnie merely estimated costs in what he felt was a reasonable manner. In fact, during the construction process, Ronnie did not assign any costs to Work in Process Inventory; all production costs were sent to the Finished Goods Inventory account.

After implementing a job order costing system, Seawind Company had better control over its inventory, better inventory valuations for financial statements, and better information with which to prevent part stockouts (not having parts in inventory) and production stoppages. The job order costing system provided Mr. Trump with information on what work was currently in process and at what cost. From this information, Ronnie was better able to judge whether additional work could be accepted and when current work would be completed. Since job order costing assigns costs to Work in Process Inventory, balance sheet figures were more accurate. As materials were used in the production system, the use of materials requisitions to transfer goods from Raw Materials Inventory to Work in Process produced inventory records that were more current and reflective of raw materials quantities on hand. Finally, the use of a job order product costing system gave Mr. Trump an informed means by which to estimate costs and more adequately price future jobs.

Introduction to Process Costing

Job order costing is appropriate for companies making products or providing services in limited quantities that conform to customer specifications. In contrast, the mass production of candy and chocolate is totally unlike the job order production process discussed earlier in the chapter. Because the process itself differs, so must the method of accounting for that process. Ganong Bros., like many other chocolate producers, would use **process costing** to determine the product cost of its candy and chocolates. Process costing is used by manufacturers that make large quantities of homogeneous products in a continuous mass production environment to accumulate and assign costs to units of production.

There are two methods of calculating the product unit cost in a process costing system—weighted average and FIFO. The weighted average method is discussed in the main part of the chapter and the FIFO method is illustrated in Appendix 4A of this chapter. The major difference between these two methods is in the treatment of the Beginning Work in Process Inventory. This difference has an impact on the calculation of the product unit cost. Once this cost has been determined, it is used to value the department's ending Work in Process Inventory and the cost of the units transferred out of the department.

In some ways, the cost accumulation in a process costing system is similar to job order product costing procedures. In a **process costing system**, as in a job order system, costs are accumulated by cost component in each production department. As units are transferred from one department to the next, unit costs are also transferred, so that a total cost is accumulated by the end of the production. In a job order system, accumulated departmental costs are assigned to specific jobs, which may be single units or batches of units. In contrast, in a process costing system, accumulated departmental costs are assigned to all the units that flowed through the department during the period. The valuation method chosen (actual, normal, standard), affects which costs are included in the inventory accounts.

Two other differences between job order and process costing are (1) the quantity of production for which costs are being accumulated at any one time and (2) the cost object to which the costs are assigned. For example, an entrepreneur who bakes cakes and cookies for specific orders would use a job order product costing

LEARNING OBJECTIVE **3**

What production situations are appropriate for a process costing system and why?

process costing
a method of accumulating and assigning costs to units of production in companies that make large quantities of homogeneous products

process costing system
a product costing system used by companies that produce large amounts of homogeneous products through a continuous production flow

system. The costs of the direct materials, direct labour, and overhead associated with production of each baking job would be gathered and assigned to the individual jobs. The cost per cookie could be determined if all the cookies baked for the job were similar.

In contrast, bakeries such as Weston Bakeries Ltd., which makes more than two million cookies a week, would not use a job order system because volume is simply too great and the cookies are reasonably homogeneous. At Weston Bakeries Ltd., direct materials, direct labour, and overhead costs could be gathered during the period for each department and each product. Because a variety of cookies are produced in any department during a period, costs must be accumulated by and assigned to each type of cookie worked on during the period. Production does not have to be complete for costs to be assigned in a process costing system.

As shown in Exhibit 4-5, the costs of inventory components are accumulated in the accounts as the inventory flows through the production process. At the end of production, the accumulated costs must be assigned to all the units produced to determine the cost per unit for purposes of inventory measurement and calculation of cost of goods sold.

Exhibit 4-6 presents the source documents and records used to make initial cost assignments to production departments during a period. As goods are transferred from one department to the next, the related departmental costs are also transferred. The three products in the exhibit are started in Department One. Then Products A and B and their related production costs are transferred to Department Two. Additional costs in Department Two will attach to these products before they are sent to Finished Goods Inventory. Product C, however, does not have to go through Department Two, and thus its cost will consist only of materials, labour, and overhead costs from Department One.

As in job order costing, the direct material and direct labour components of product cost present relatively few problems for cost accumulation and assignment.

EXHIBIT 4-5

Flow of Costs Through Production

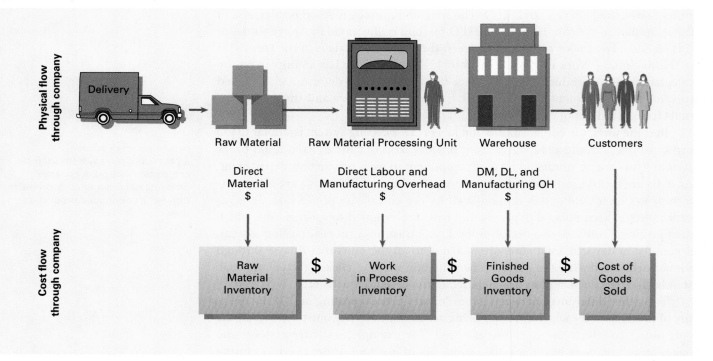

EXHIBIT 4-6

Cost Flows and Cost
Assignments

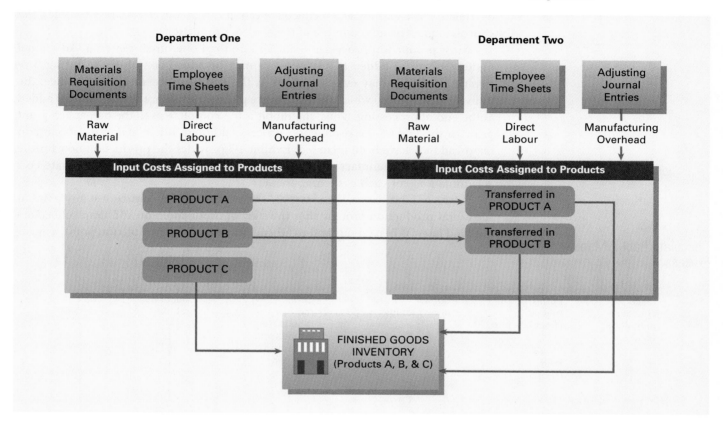

EXHIBIT 4-6

Cost Flows and Cost
Assignments

Direct material cost can be measured from the materials requisition slips and raw
material invoice prices; direct labour cost can be determined from the employee
time sheets and wage rates for the period. These costs are assigned at the end of the
period (usually weekly, biweekly, or monthly) from the departments to the units
produced. Although direct material and direct labour are easily traced to production, overhead must be allocated to units.

Either an actual overhead amount or a predetermined rate may be used to
assign overhead to products. If actual overhead is relatively constant each period
and production volume is relatively steady over time, then using actual overhead
costs provides a fairly stable production cost. If such conditions do not exist, application of actual overhead will yield fluctuating product costs, and a predetermined
overhead rate (or rates) should be used.

Accumulating Costs by Separate Cost Components

Cost assignment in any process costing environment using actual costs is an averaging process. In general, and in the simplest of situations, a product's unit cost
results from dividing a period's departmental production costs by that period's
departmental quantity of production. However, in most situations, cost components
are added at different points in the production process, and thus separate accumulations must be made for each cost component.

For a production operation to begin, some direct material must be introduced. Without any direct material, there would be no need for labour or overhead to be incurred. The material added at the start of production is 100% complete throughout the process regardless of the percentage of completion of labour and overhead. For example, when chocolate rabbits are made at Connie's Candies, the chocolate must be added in full at the start of production.

Most production processes require more than one direct material. Additional materials may be added at any point or may be added continuously during processing. Materials may even be added at the end of processing. For instance, the individual boxes into which the rabbits are placed for sale are direct material added at the end of processing. Thus, the rabbit is 0% complete as to the box at any point prior to the end of the production process, although other material, labour, and overhead may have been incurred. Exhibit 4-7 provides the production flow for the chocolate rabbit manufacturing process and illustrates the need for separate cost accumulations for each cost component.

As the exhibit shows, the material "chocolate" is 100% complete at any point in the rabbit production process after the start of production; no additional chocolate is added later. When labour and overhead reach the 95% completion point, a sugar

EXHIBIT 4-7

Chocolate Rabbit Manufacturing Process

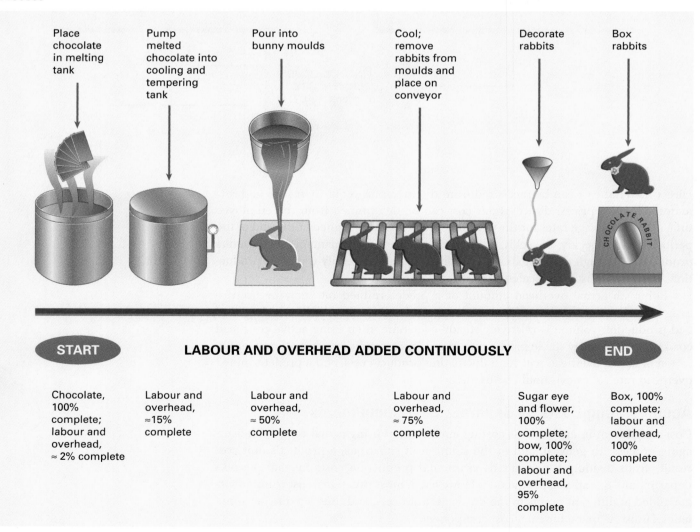

| Place chocolate in melting tank | Pump melted chocolate into cooling and tempering tank | Pour into bunny moulds | Cool; remove rabbits from moulds and place on conveyor | Decorate rabbits | Box rabbits |

START | **LABOUR AND OVERHEAD ADDED CONTINUOUSLY** | **END**

| Chocolate, 100% complete; labour and overhead, ≈ 2% complete | Labour and overhead, ≈15% complete | Labour and overhead, ≈ 50% complete | Labour and overhead, ≈ 75% complete | Sugar eye and flower, 100% complete; bow, 100% complete; labour and overhead, 95% complete | Box, 100% complete; labour and overhead, 100% complete |

eye and flower as well as a bow are added. Before the 95% point, the eyes, flowers, and bows are 0% complete; after this point, these materials are 100% complete. Last, the rabbits are boxed and are 100% complete. Thus, at the end of a period, rabbits could be anywhere in the production process. If, for example, the rabbits were 75% complete as to labour and overhead, they would be 100% complete as to chocolate, and 0% complete as to eyes, flowers, bows, and boxes.

When different components of a product are at different stages of completion, separate cost accumulations are necessary for each cost component. But a single cost accumulation can be made for multiple cost components that are at the same degree of completion. For example, separate cost accumulations would need to be made for the chocolate and the boxes. However, because the sugar eyes, sugar flowers, and bows are added at the same point, these can be viewed as one ingredient (decorations) and a single cost accumulation can be made for this. Additionally, because direct labour and overhead are incurred at the same rate in the chocolate bunny–making process, these two components may be combined and one cost accumulation can be made for "conversion" as a single category.

In a process costing environment, costs are accumulated by department and then by cost component for a single time period. Additionally, because most companies manufacture more than one type of product, costs must also be accumulated by product. For example, the candy company would accumulate the costs of producing peanut butter three-ounce rabbits separately from the costs of producing white chocolate one-pound rabbits.

Calculating Equivalent Units of Production

LEARNING OBJECTIVE 4

Why are equivalent units of production used in process costing?

After production costs have been accumulated by department and by cost component, they need to be assigned to the units produced during the period of cost accumulation. If all units were 100% complete at the end of each accounting period, units could simply be counted to obtain the denominator for cost assignment. But in most production processes, an inventory of partially completed units called Work in Process Inventory (WIP) exists at the end of each period. Any partially completed ending inventory of the current period becomes the partially completed beginning inventory of the next period. Process costing assigns costs to both fully and partially completed units by converting partially completed units to equivalent whole units or equivalent units of production.

Equivalent units of production (EUP) approximate the number of whole units of output that could have been produced during a period from the actual effort expended during that period. Using EUP is necessary because using only completed units to determine unit cost would not clearly reflect all the work accomplished during a period. For instance, if 45 partially completed units were determined to be two-thirds complete, these partially completed units would be counted as 30 whole units (45 × 2/3). To calculate equivalent units of production for a period, it is necessary to multiply the number of actual units being produced by their percentage of completion at the end of the period.

equivalent units of production an approximation of the number of whole units of output that could have been produced during a period from the actual effort expended during that period

For example, assume that Department One had no beginning Work in Process inventory. During January, Department One produced 100,000 complete units and 10,000 units that were 20% complete. These incomplete units are in ending Work in Process Inventory. The period's equivalent units of production are 102,000 [(100,000 × 100%) + (10,000 × 20%)]. This quantity is used to calculate the departmental equivalent unit product costs.

Use of equivalent units of production requires recognition of two factors related to inventory. First, units in beginning Work in Process Inventory were started last

Process costing is used for homogeneous items

period but will be completed during the current period. This two-period production sequence means that some costs for these units were incurred in the prior period and additional costs will be incurred in the current period. Second, partially completed units in the ending Work in Process Inventory were started in the current period, however these will not be completed until the next period. Thus, ending Work in Process Inventory includes all costs incurred as a result of this period's production efforts. However, to finish the units, additional costs will need to be incurred in the next period.

Qualified production personnel should inspect ending work in process units to determine what proportion of work was completed during the current period. The mathematical complement to this proportion represents the amount of work to be performed next period. Physical inspection at the end of last period provided the information about the work to be performed on the beginning inventory in the current period.

INTRODUCING WEIGHTED AVERAGE AND FIFO PROCESS COSTING

weighted average method
a method of process costing that computes an average cost per equivalent unit of production; combines beginning inventory units with current production and beginning inventory costs with current costs to compute that average

FIFO method
a method of process costing that computes an average cost per equivalent unit of production using only current production and current cost information; units and costs in beginning inventory are accounted for separately

One purpose of any costing system is to determine product costs for financial statements. When goods are transferred from Work in Process Inventory of one department to another department or to Finished Goods Inventory, a cost must be assigned to those goods. In addition, at the end of any period, a cost amount must be assigned to goods that are only partially complete and still remain in Work in Process Inventory.

As stated earlier, the alternative methods of accounting for cost flows in process costing are the **weighted average method** and the **FIFO** (first-in, first-out) **method**.

These methods relate to the way in which physical cost flows are accounted for in the production process. The weighted average method computes a single average cost per unit based on the combined beginning inventory and current period production. The FIFO method separates the prior period production and its cost (Beginning Work in Process Inventory) from the current period production and its cost so that a current period cost per unit can be calculated. Both methods result in approximately the same unit cost unless a large cost change has occurred between periods.

EUP Calculations and Cost Assignment

Exhibit 4-8 on page 184 outlines the six steps necessary to determine the costs assignable to units completed and to units still in process (Ending WIP) at the end of the period in a process costing system. Each of these steps is discussed briefly, and then a complete example is provided.

Step One. Calculate the total physical units for which the department is responsible, or the **total units to account for**. This amount is equal to the total number of whole or partial units worked on in the department during the current period—beginning WIP inventory units plus units started.

Step Two. Determine what happened to the units to account for during the period. This step also requires the use of physical units that may fit into one of two categories: (1) completed and transferred out or (2) partially completed and remaining in Ending Work in Process Inventory.[11]

At this point, verify that the total units for which the department was accountable are equal to the total units that were actually accounted for. If these amounts are not equal, any additional computations will be incorrect.

Step Three. Use one of the process costing methods (weighted average cost or FIFO) to determine the equivalent units of production for each cost component. If all materials are at the same degree of completion, a single materials computation can be made. If multiple materials are used and are placed into production at different points, multiple EUP calculations may be necessary for materials. If overhead is applied to production using direct labour as a base or if these two factors (labour and overhead) are always at the same degree of completion, a single EUP schedule can be made for conversion. If neither condition exists, separate EUP calculations must be prepared for labour and overhead.[12]

Step Four. Find the **total cost to account for**, which includes the balance in Work in Process Inventory at the beginning of the period plus all current costs for direct material, direct labour, and overhead.

Step Five. Compute the cost per equivalent unit for each cost component using either the weighted average or the FIFO equivalent units of production calculated in Step Three.

Step Six. Use the costs computed in Step Five to assign costs from the production process to the units completed and transferred out of the production process and to the units remaining in ending Work in Process Inventory. After this cost assignment is made, verify that the total costs assigned equal the total costs accountable for from Step Four.

Linda Geraldine Chocoholics Ltd. is used to demonstrate the steps involved in the computation of equivalent units of production and cost assignment for both process costing methods. Linda Geraldine Chocoholics Ltd. uses the same manufacturing process in making solid chocolate greeting cards as Connie's Candies Ltd. uses in making chocolate bunnies. At Linda Geraldine Chocoholics Ltd. the production process consists of two departments: Moulding and Packaging. Chocolate is purchased from a vendor and is the only direct material. For purposes of simplicity, any decoration on the cards is minimal and is considered part of overhead. Since the chocolate is added at the start of processing, Work in Process Inventory is 100% complete as to direct material as soon as processing has begun. Labour and

LEARNING OBJECTIVE   5

How are equivalent units of production, unit costs, and inventory values computed using the weighted average method of process costing?

total units to account for
total whole or partial physical units for which the department is responsible during the current period; beginning WIP inventory units plus units started

total cost to account for
the balance in Work in Process Inventory at the beginning of the period plus all current costs for direct material, direct labour, and overhead

EXHIBIT 4-8

Steps in Process Costing

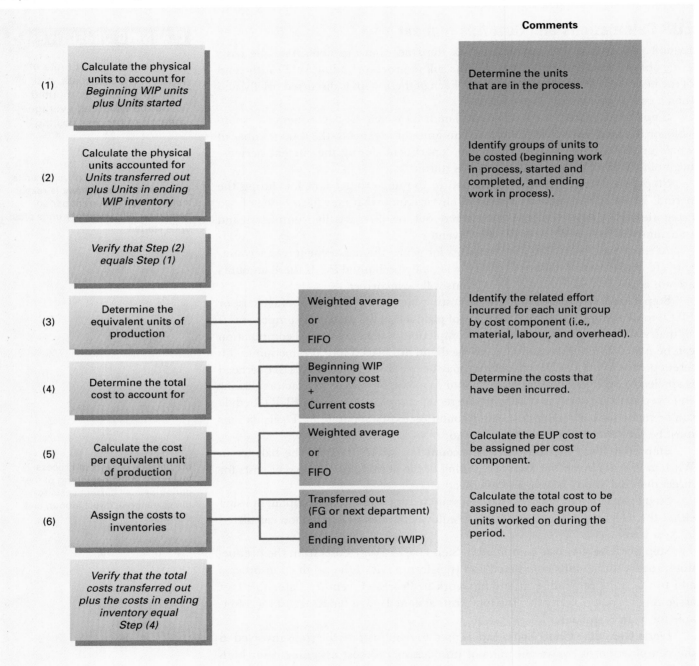

overhead are assumed to be added at the same rate throughout the production process. Exhibit 4-9 on page 185 presents information for June 2005 regarding Linda Geraldine Chocoholics Ltd.'s production inventories and costs for the Moulding Department.

Although quantities are given for both cards transferred out of and cards remaining in ending Work in Process Inventory, it is not essential to provide both

	Units
Beginning WIP inventory	
(100% complete as to direct material; 30% complete as to conversion)	12,000
Cards started during current period	115,500
Cards completed and transferred to the next department	120,700
Ending WIP inventory	
(100% complete as to direct material; 80% complete as to conversion)	6,800

Cost of beginning WIP inventory:

Direct material	$ 45,000.00	
Direct labour and overhead	4,678.60	
Total Cost of Beginning WIP Inventory	$ 49,678.60	

Current period costs:

Direct material	$334,950.00	
Direct labour and overhead	202,191.00	
Total Current Costs	$537,141.00	

EXHIBIT 4-9

Linda Geraldine Chocoholics Ltd. Production and Cost Information

Department One—Moulding for the Month of June 2005

of these figures. The number of chocolate greeting cards remaining in process at June 30 can be calculated as the total cards to account for minus the cards completed and transferred out during the period. Alternatively, the number of cards transferred out can be computed as the total cards to account for minus the cards in ending Work in Process Inventory.

Weighted Average Method

The weighted average method of computing equivalent units of production adds the units in beginning Work in Process Inventory to the new units started during the current period to determine the potential quantity of production for the period. The work performed during the period does not necessarily always result in complete whole units. The weighted average method is *not* concerned about what quantity of work was performed in the prior period on the units in beginning WIP inventory. This method focuses only on units that are *completed* in the current period

Process costing is the appropriate cost system to use in most food production environments.

and units that remain in ending inventory. Thus, this method includes the units and costs of the beginning Work in Process Inventory in the calculation of the unit cost.

The Linda Geraldine Chocoholic Ltd. information in Exhibit 4-9 is used to illustrate each step listed in Exhibit 4-8 for the Moulding Department.

Step One: Calculate the total units to account for

Units in beginning WIP Inventory	12,000
Units started during current period	115,500
Total units to account for	127,500

Step Two: Calculate the total units accounted for

Units completed and transferred out	120,700
Units in ending WIP Inventory	6,800
Total units accounted for	127,500

The units detailed in step two indicate the categories (those transferred out and those in ending WIP Inventory) to which costs will be assigned in the final step. The number of units accounted for in Step Two equals the number of units to account for in Step One.

Completed units are either (1) beginning WIP inventory units that have been completed during the current period, or (2) units started and completed during the period. They could be both. The number of **units started and completed** (S&C) equals the total units completed during the period minus the units in beginning WIP inventory.

At Linda Geraldine Chocoholics Ltd., all raw material for the cards is added at the start of the process, and conversion takes place continuously during the process. Exhibit 4-10 shows a schematic of what happened in the first department (Moulding) during the month of June. "A" represents the work completed in May; "B," "C," and "D" represent the amount of work completed during June. "E" represents the work that will be done in the month of July to complete the units started in June.

The units for conversion cost for A, B, D, and E are arrived at as follows:

A: 12,000 × 30% complete as to conversion   = 3,600
B: 12,000 × 70% (completion of units in A)   = 8,400
D: 6,800 × 80% complete as to conversion   = 5,440
E: 6,800 × 20% to be completed next period = 1,360

Step Three: Determine the equivalent units of production

At the end of the period, the units in beginning Work in Process Inventory and the units that were started and completed this period are 100% complete as to all cost components. The units in ending Work in Process Inventory are complete as

units started and completed
the total units completed during the period minus the units in beginning inventory; alternatively, units started minus units in ending inventory

EXHIBIT 4-10

Flow of Product in Department One—Moulding

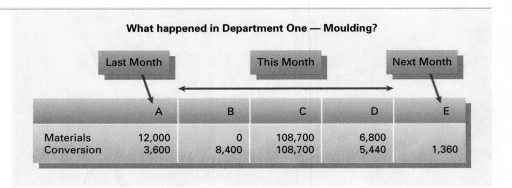

What happened in Department One — Moulding?

	Last Month	This Month		Next Month
	A	B	C	D	E
Materials	12,000	0	108,700	6,800	
Conversion	3,600	8,400	108,700	5,440	1,360

to direct material, but only 80% complete as to labour and overhead. Since labour and overhead are at the same degree of completion, a single EUP conversion calculation can be made for both of these cost components.

The weighted average computations for equivalent units of production are as follows:

	Direct Material EUP	Conversion (Direct Labour and Overhead) EUP
BWIP (whole units × % complete) (A)	12,000 × 100% = 12,000	12,000 × 30% = 3,600
BWIP completion (B)		12,000 × 70% = 8,400
Units started and completed in June (whole units × % complete) (C)	108,700 × 100% = 108,700	108,700 × 100% = 108,700
EWIP (whole units × % complete) Units started in June (D)	6,800 × 100% = 6,800	6,800 × 80% = 5,440
Equivalent Units of Production	127,500	126,140

Note that the lines labelled A, B, and C above [BWIP (12,000) and Units started and completed (108,700)] are equal to the total units completed and transferred out (120,700) given in Step Two.

Only when all product components are placed into production at the same time and at the same rate will material, labour, and overhead all be at equal percentages of completion. Generally, the cost components are at different degrees of completion and as such the completion percentage must be separately determined *for each cost component.* If the percentages of completion differ, separate EUP calculations must be made for each cost component.

The weighted average method does not distinguish between units in beginning Work in Process Inventory and units entering production during the period. In this step three, the weighted average method includes the number of whole units in beginning Work in Process Inventory and the number of units started and completed during the period. By doing so, the weighted average method treats beginning Work in Process Inventory units as though they were started and completed in the current period.

Step Four: Determine the total cost to account for

The total cost to account for equals beginning WIP inventory cost plus the additional current period costs. Note that information is provided in Exhibit 4-9 on the cost for each element of production—direct material, direct labour, and overhead. For Linda Geraldine Chocoholics Ltd., the total cost to account for is $586,819.60.

	Direct Material	Conversion	Total
Beginning WIP cost	$ 45,000.00	$ 4,678.60	$ 49,678.60
Current period costs	334,950.00	202,191.00	537,141.00
Total cost to account for	$379,950.00	$206,869.60	$586,819.60

Total cost will be assigned in Step 6 to the goods transferred out to the next department and to ending Work in Process Inventory in relation to the whole units or equivalent whole units contained in each category.

Step Five: Calculate the cost per equivalent unit of production

A cost per equivalent unit of production must be computed for each cost component for which a separate calculation of EUP is made. The weighted average method does not distinguish between units in beginning Work in Process Inventory and units started during the period, nor does it differentiate between beginning Work in Process Inventory costs and current period costs. The costs of beginning Work in Process Inventory and of the current period are summed for each cost component and averaged over that component's weighted average equivalent units of production. The calculation of unit cost for each cost component at the end of the period is as follows:

Cost per Equivalent Unit =
Beginning Work in Process Inventory Cost + Current Period Cost
÷ Total Weighted Average Equivalent Units of Production

Under the weighted average method, costs from two different periods are totalled to form the numerator of the unit cost equation, and units from two different periods are used in the denominator. This computation allows total costs to be divided by total units, which produces an average component cost per unit. The weighted average calculations for cost per EUP for material and conversion are as follows:

	Direct Material	Conversion	Total
Beginning WIP inventory costs	$ 45,000.00	$ 4,678.60	$ 49,678.60
Current period costs	334,950.00	202,191.00	537,141.00
Cost to account for (Step Four)	$379,950.00	$206,869.60	$586,819.60
Divided by EUP (Step Three)	÷ 127,500	÷ 126,140	
Cost per EUP	$ 2.98	$ 1.64	$ 4.62

The unit costs for the two product cost components (direct material and conversion) are summed to find the total production cost for all whole units completed during June. For Linda Geraldine Chocoholics Ltd., this cost is $4.62.

Step Six: Assign costs to inventories

This step assigns total production costs to units of product. Cost assignment in a department involves determining the cost of (1) goods completed and transferred out during the period and (2) the units in ending Work in Process Inventory.

Under the weighted average method, the cost of goods transferred out is found by multiplying the total number of units transferred out by the total cost per EUP (from Step Five). Because this method is based on an averaging technique that combines prior and current period work, the period in which the transferred-out units were started is not important. All units and all costs have been commingled. The total cost transferred out for Linda Geraldine Chocoholics Ltd. for June is ($4.62 × 120,700) or $557,634.

Ending Work in Process Inventory cost is calculated based on the equivalent units of production for each cost component. The equivalent units of production are multiplied by the component cost per unit computed in Step Five. The cost of ending Work in Process Inventory under the weighted average method is as follows:

Ending Work in Process Inventory:
Direct material (6,800 × 100% × $2.98) $20,264.00
Conversion (6,800 × 80% × $1.64)   8,921.60
Total cost of ending Work in Process Inventory $29,185.60

The quantities that result from multiplying whole units by the percentage of completion are equal to the equivalent units of production.

The total costs assigned to transferred-out units and units in ending Work in Process Inventory must equal the total cost to account for. For Linda Geraldine Chocoholics Ltd., total cost to account for (Step Four) was $586,819.60, which equals transferred-out cost ($557,634) plus ending work in process cost ($29,185.60).

EXHIBIT 4-11

Cost of Production Report for the Month Ended June 30, 2005 (Weighted Average Method)

Production Data

	Equivalent Units of Production		
	Whole Units	**DM**	**Conversion**
BWIP	12,000[1]	12,000	3,600
Units started	115,500		
To account for	127,500		
BWIP completed	12,000	0	8,400
S&C	108,700	108,700	108,700
Units completed	120,700		
EWIP	6,800[2]	6,800	5,440
Accounted for	127,500	127,500	126,140

Cost Data

	Total	**DM**	**Conversion**
BWIP cost	$ 49,678.60	$ 45,000.00	$ 4,678.60
Current period costs	537,141.00	334,950.00	202,191.00
Total cost to account for	$586,819.60	$379,950.00	$206,869.60
Divided by EUP		÷ 127,500	÷ 126,140
Cost per EUP	$ 4.62	$ 2.98	$ 1.64

Cost Assignment

Transferred out (120,700 × $4.62)		$557,634.00
Ending Work in Process inventory:		
Direct material		
(6,800 × 100% × $2.98)	$20,264.00	
Conversion (6,800 × 80% × $1.64)	8,921.60	
Total cost accounted for		29,185.60
		$586,819.60

[1] Fully complete as to direct material; 30% as to conversion.
[2] Fully complete as to direct material; 80% as to conversion.

The steps just discussed can be combined into a **cost of production report.** This document details all manufacturing quantities and costs, shows the computation of cost per EUP, and indicates the cost assignment to goods produced during the period. Exhibit 4-11 above shows the cost of production report for Linda Geraldine Chocoholics Ltd. under the weighted average process costing method.

Process Costing in a Multidepartmental Setting

Most companies have multiple, rather than single, department processing facilities. In a multidepartmental processing environment, goods are transferred from a predecessor department to a successor department. For example, the production of chocolate greeting cards at Linda Geraldine Chocoholics Ltd. was said to occur in two departments: Moulding and Packaging.

Manufacturing costs always follow the physical flow of goods. The costs of completed units of predecessor departments are treated as input material costs in successor departments. Such a sequential treatment requires the use of an additional cost component element called "transferred in" or "prior department cost." This element always has a percentage of completion factor of 100%, since the goods would not have been transferred out of the predecessor department if they had not been fully complete. The transferred-in element is handled the same as any other cost element in the calculations of EUP and cost per EUP.

A successor department may add additional raw material to the units that have been transferred in or may simply provide additional labour, with the corresponding incurrence of overhead. Anything added in the successor department requires

LEARNING OBJECTIVE 6

How is a cost of production report prepared under the weighted average method of process costing?

cost of production report
a document used in a process costing system; details all manufacturing quantities and costs, shows the computation of cost per equivalent unit of production (EUP), and indicates the cost assignment to goods produced during the period

LEARNING OBJECTIVE 7

What is the effect of multidepartmental processing on the computation of equivalent units of production?

its own cost element column for calculating equivalent units of production and cost per equivalent unit (unless the additional elements have the same degree of completion, in which case they can be combined).

Exhibit 4-12 provides a cost of production report for the Packaging Department at Linda Geraldine Chocoholics Ltd. Weighted average unit costs from Exhibit 4-11 are used for the units transferred in from the previous department. In this department, chocolate greeting cards are placed in cellophane-fronted cardboard boxes and sealed for customer delivery. The beginning Work in Process Inventory is assumed to be 100% complete as to transferred-in units and cost, 0% complete as to packaging, and 90% complete as to conversion. The ending Work in Process Inventory is assumed to be 100% complete as to transferred-in units and cost, 0% complete as to packaging, and 75% complete as to conversion in this department. The Packaging Department uses the weighted average process costing method.

Recording Information in the Accounts

Summary journal entries and T-accounts for Linda Geraldine Chocoholics Ltd. for June are given in Exhibit 4-13. For these entries, the following assumptions are made: sales for June were 121,000 chocolate greeting cards; all sales were on account for $10 per unit; a perpetual weighted average inventory system is in use. Assume that Linda Geraldine Chocoholics Ltd. began June with no Finished Goods Inventory.

LEARNING OBJECTIVE 8

How is a cost of production report prepared in a multidepartmental processing operation?

EXHIBIT 4-12

Multidepartmental Setting—
Packaging Department
(Weighted Average Method)

Production Data — **Equivalent Units of Production**

	Whole Units	Transferred in	DM	Conversion
BWIP	9,300[1]	9,300	0	8,370
Units transferred in	120,700			
To account for	130,000			
BWIP completed	9,300	0	9,300	930
S&C	113,100	113,100	113,100	113,100
Units completed	122,400			
EWIP	7,600[2]	7,600	0	5,700
Accounted for	130,000	130,000	122,400	128,100

Cost Data

	Total	Transferred in	DM	Conversion
BWIP cost	$ 44,930.30	$ 41,666	$ 0	$ 3,264.30
Current period costs	642,329.70	557,634	36,720	47,975.70
Total cost to account for	$687,260.00	$599,300	$36,720	$51,240.00
Divided by EUP		÷130,000	÷122,400	÷ 128,100
Cost per EUP	$ 5.31	$ 4.61	$ 0.30	$ 0.40

Cost Assignment

Transferred out (122,400 × $5.31)		$649,944
Ending Work in Process Inventory:		
Transferred in (7,600 × $4.61)	$35,036	
Conversion (7,600 × 0.75 × $0.40)	2,280	37,316
Total cost accounted for		$687,260

[1] Fully complete as to transferred-in; 0% as to direct material; 90% as to conversion.
[2] Fully complete as to transferred-in; 0% as to direct material; 75% as to conversion.

EXHIBIT 4-13

Process Costing Journal Entries
and T-Accounts

1. Work in Process Inventory—Moulding   334,950.00
        Raw Material Inventory   334,950.00
    To record issuance of direct material (chocolate)
    to production (Exhibit 4-9).

2. Work in Process Inventory—Moulding   202,191.00
        Various accounts   202,191.00
    To record labour and overhead costs
    into production (Exhibit 4-9).

3. Work in Process Inventory—Packaging   557,634.00
        Work in Process Inventory—Moulding   557,634.00
    To transfer greeting cards from the Moulding
    Department to the Packaging Department (Exhibit 4-11).

4. Work in Process Inventory—Packaging   36,720.00
        Raw Material Inventory   36,720.00
    To record issuance of direct material (boxes)
    to production (Exhibit 4-12).

5. Work in Process Inventory—Packaging   47,975.70
        Various accounts   47,975.70
    To record labour and overhead costs
    into production (Exhibit 4-12).

6. Finished Goods Inventory   649,944.00
        Work in Process Inventory—Packaging   649,944.00
    To transfer cost of completed units to finished
    goods (Exhibit 4-12).

7. Cost of Goods Sold   642,510.00
        Finished Goods Inventory   642,510.00
    To transfer cost of goods sold from finished
    goods to cost of goods sold (121,000 × $5.31)
    (cost information from Exhibit 4-12 and sales
    information from supplementary data above).

8. Accounts Receivable   1,210,000.00
        Sales   1,210,000.00
    To record June sales on account
    (121,000 × $10; information from
    supplementary data above).

LINDA GERALDINE CHOCOHOLICS LTD. T-ACCOUNTS

(Numbers in parentheses indicate the related journal entry.)

Work in Process Inventory—Moulding

Beginning balance	49,678.60	Transferred out	(3)	557,634.00
Direct material	(1) 334,950.00			
Conversion	(2) 202,191.00			
Ending balance	29,185.60			

Work in Process Inventory—Packaging

Beginning balance	44,930.30	To finished goods	(6)	649,944.00
Transferred in	(3) 557,634.00			
Direct Material	(4) 36,720.00			
Conversion	(5) 47,975.70			
Ending balance	37,316.00			

Finished Goods Inventory

Beginning balance	0	Cost of Goods Sold	(7)	642,510.00
From WIP Inventory—				
Packaging	(6) 649,944.00			
Ending balance	7,434.00			

Cost of Goods Sold

June Cost of Goods Sold	(7)	642,510.00

Ganong Bros. Ltd.

Over the years, Ganong has made candy and chocolate history. Ganong innovations have included the Chicken Bone; the first 5-cent chocolate nut bar in North America; the use of cellophane in packaging; the heart-shaped box to hold chocolates; the use of real fruit, in puree form, to make fruit snacks; and the list goes on.

David Ganong says, "At one point in time we had a 100 percent market share—and it's been a long way down from there." Finding and being successful in new markets has meant Ganong Bros. Ltd. has had to form strategic partnerships with companies such as Kerr Bros., or use the Sunkist label. Decisions like these must first be passed by the company's board of directors, with members from outside industries such as financial institutions, food production, and even beer manufacturing and marketing.

Mr. Ganong says a board of directors has been around since his grandfather's day, and he wholeheartedly endorses it. "A management team in any business can get carried away by its own ideas—and they may not necessarily be the best ideas," he says. "We've used [the board of directors] as a way to generate very, very good ideas over the years."

He acknowledges the industry is changing. Technological changes, for example, have transformed the industry. But the biggest change has come on the heels of a string of consolidations in the grocery, drug, and major retail areas. "The old days of shipping large quantities to retailers and giving them discounts have really disappeared. They want what they want—when they want it," Mr. Ganong says. In fact, in cases such as Wal-Mart, a late or incomplete shipment can mean a financial penalty or fine. "That's the way the world is. We could grumble about it if we thought it was unfair, but that's the way our customers are operating their businesses today."[13]

Ganong Bros. Limited, Canada's last family-owned chocolate maker with distribution and sales across the country, celebrated 130 years of sweet success in 2003. The historic, family-owned company celebrated throughout 2003.

Building on its reputation for innovation and excellence, Ganong introduced several new products in 2003; these treats will hit store shelves later in the year.[14]

Laura Secord Inc. is about to be acquired by Gaétan Frigon. He is negotiating with Ganong Bros. Ltd. to take over producing chocolate for the chain. David Ganong said it would add more equipment and staff to serve the future owner of Laura Secord.

"We would be very interested in operating as a supplier of substance to Laura Secord, whoever is the successful acquirer," Mr. Ganong said.[15]

APPENDIX 4A

Process Costing Using FIFO Valuation

FIFO Method

As mentioned previously, the FIFO method of determining EUP more realistically reflects the way in which most goods actually physically flow through the production system. The FIFO method does not commingle units and costs of different periods, which allows this method to focus specifically on the work performed during the current period. Equivalent units and costs of beginning Work in Process Inventory are withheld from the computation of the average unit current period cost.

LEARNING OBJECTIVE 9

How are equivalent units of production, unit costs, and inventory values computed using the FIFO method of process costing?

Steps One and Two are the same for the FIFO method as for the weighted average method because these two steps involve the use of physical units. Therefore, based on the data from Exhibit 4-9, the total units to account for and accounted for are 127,500. (These calculations are shown on page 186.)

Step Three: Determine the equivalent units of production

Under FIFO, as mentioned, the work performed in the prior period is not commingled with work of the current period. The EUP schedule for FIFO (based on Exhibit 4-10) is as follows:

	Direct Material	EUP	Conversion (Direct Labour and Overhead)	EUP
BWIP (whole units × % not completed in prior period) (B)	12,000 × 0% =	0	12,000 × 70% =	8,400
Units started and completed this period (whole units × % complete) (C)	108,700 × 100% = 108,700		108,700 × 100% = 108,700	
EWIP (whole units × % complete) (D)	6,800 × 100% =	6,800	6,800 × 80% =	5,440
EUP		115,500		122,540

Under FIFO, only the work performed on the beginning Work in Process Inventory *during the current period* is shown in the EUP schedule. This work equals the whole units in beginning Work in Process Inventory multiplied by a percentage equal to 1 minus the percentage of work done in the prior period. In the Linda Geraldine Chocoholic Ltd. example, no additional direct material is needed in June to complete the 12,000 units in beginning WIP inventory because all direct material is added at the start of the process. The beginning WIP inventory is only 30% complete as to conversion; therefore, the company needs to complete the other 70% conversion on the 12,000 beginning WIP inventory during June—or the equivalent of 8,400 units.

The remaining figures in the FIFO EUP schedule are the same as those for the weighted average method. The only difference between the weighted average and FIFO EUP computations is that under the FIFO method, the work performed in the prior period on beginning Work in Process Inventory is not included in the current period EUP. This difference is equal to the number of units in beginning Work in Process Inventory multiplied by the percentage of work performed in the prior period. A reconciliation of EUPs determined by the two methods follows.

	Direct Material	Conversion
FIFO EUP	115,500	122,540
Plus the EUP in BWIP (work done in the prior period:		
100% Direct Material; 30% Conversion)	12,000	3,600
Weighted Average EUP	127,500	126,140

Step Four: Determine the total cost to account for

This step is the same as under the weighted average method. The total cost to account for is $586,819.60.

Step Five: Calculate the cost per equivalent unit of production

Because cost determination is made on the basis of equivalent units of production, different results will be obtained for the weighted average and FIFO methods. The calculations for cost per equivalent unit reflect the difference in quantity that each method uses for beginning WIP inventory. The EUP calculation for FIFO ignores work performed on beginning Work in Process Inventory during the prior period; therefore, the FIFO cost computation per EUP also ignores prior period costs and uses only costs incurred in the current period. The FIFO cost per EUP calculation is as follows:

$$\text{Cost per Equivalent Unit} = \frac{\text{Current Period Cost}}{\text{FIFO Equivalent Units of Production}}$$

Calculations for Linda Geraldine Chocoholics Ltd. are:

	Direct Material	Conversion	Total
Current period costs	$334,950.00	$202,191.00	$537,141.00
Divided by EUP (Step Three)	÷ 115,500	÷ 122,540	
Cost per EUP	$ 2.90	$ 1.65	$ 4.55

The production cost for each whole unit produced during June under the FIFO method is $4.55. It is useful to recognize the difference between the two total cost computations. The weighted average total cost of $4.62 is the average total cost of each unit completed during June, *regardless of when production was begun*. The FIFO total cost of $4.55 is the total cost of each unit that was *both started and completed* during the current period. The $0.07 difference results from the difference in treatment of beginning Work in Process Inventory costs.

Step Six: Assign costs to inventories

This step assigns total production costs to units of product. Cost assignment in a department involves determining the cost of (1) goods completed and transferred out during the period and (2) units in ending Work in Process inventory. The FIFO method assumes that the units in beginning WIP inventory are completed first during the current period, and thus they are the first units transferred out. The remaining units transferred out during the period were both started and completed in the current period. As shown in the cost of production report in Exhibit 4-14 on page 196, the two-step computation needed to determine the cost of goods transferred out distinctly presents this FIFO logic.

The first part of the cost assignment for units transferred out relates to the units that were in beginning inventory. These units had the cost of material and some conversion costs attached to them at the start of the period. These prior period costs were not included in the cost per EUP calculations in Step Five. The costs to finish these units were incurred in the current period. To determine the total cost of producing the units in beginning WIP inventory, the cost of the beginning WIP inventory is added to the current period costs that were needed to complete the units. The second part of the cost assignment for units transferred out relates to the units started and completed in the current period. The cost of these units is computed using current period costs.

This cost assignment process for Linda Geraldine Chocoholics Ltd., which had beginning June WIP inventory of 12,000 units and 120,700 cards transferred out during the month, is as follows:

Transferred out:
(1) Beginning inventory (prior period costs)* $ 49,678.60
    Completion of beginning Work in Process Inventory
      Direct material (12,000 × 0% × $2.90)   0
      Conversion (12,000 × 70% × $1.65)   13,860.00
    Total cost of beginning Work in Process Inventory
    transferred out $ 63,538.60
(2) Units started and completed (108,700 × $4.55)   494,585.00
    Total cost of units transferred out $558,123.60

*From initial information in Exhibit 4-9 on page 185

Beginning WIP inventory of chocolate greeting cards was 100% complete as to direct material at the beginning of June; thus, no additional cost for material was added during the month. Conversion at the start of the month was only 30% complete, so 70% of the conversion work (direct labour and overhead), is performed during June at current period costs. The units started and completed are costed at the total current period FIFO cost of $4.55, because these units were fully manufactured during the current period.

The method of calculating the cost of ending Work in Process Inventory is the same under both the FIFO and weighted average methods. Although the number of equivalent units is the same under both methods, cost per unit differs. Ending Work in Process Inventory cost under FIFO is as follows:

Ending Work in Process Inventory:
    Direct material (6,800 × 100% × $2.90) $19,720.00
    Conversion (6,800 × 80% × $1.65)   8,976.00
  Total cost of ending Work in Process Inventory $28,696.00

The total cost of the units transferred out ($558,123.60) plus the cost of the ending Work in Process Inventory units ($28,696.00) equals the total cost to be accounted for ($586,819.60).

The steps discussed above are shown in the cost of production report (Exhibit 4-14) on page 196.

Cost assignment is easier for the weighted average method than for the FIFO method. However, simplicity is not the only consideration in choosing a cost flow method. The FIFO method reflects the actual physical flow of goods through production. Furthermore, when period costs do fluctuate, the FIFO method gives managers better information with which to control costs and on which to base decisions because it does not combine costs of different periods. In addition, the FIFO method focuses on current period costs, and managerial performance is usually evaluated on the basis of costs incurred only in the current period.

LEARNING OBJECTIVE   10

How is a cost of production report prepared under the FIFO method of process costing?

EXHIBIT 4-14

Cost of Production Report (FIFO Method)

Production Data		Equivalent Units of Production	
	Whole Units	DM	Conversion
BWIP	12,000[1]	12,000	3,600
Units started	115,500		
To account for	127,500		
BWIP completed	12,000	0	8,400
Started and completed	108,700	108,700	108,700
Units completed	120,700		
EWIP	6,800[2]	6,800	5,440
Accounted for	127,500	115,500	122,540

Cost Data			
	Total	DM	Conversion
BWIP cost	$ 49,678.60		
Current period costs	537,141.00	$334,950.00	$202,191.00
Total cost to account for	$586,819.60	$334,950.00	$202,191.00
Divided by EUP		÷ 115,500	÷ 122,540
Cost per EUP	$ 4.55	$ 2.90	$ 1.65

Cost Assignment

Transferred out		
Beginning Work in Process Inventory costs	$ 49,678.60	
Cost to complete:		
Conversion (8,400 × $1.65)	13,860.00	
Total cost of BWIP transferred	$ 63,538.60	
Started and completed (108,700 × $4.55)	494,585.00	$558,123.60
Ending Work in Process Inventory:		
Direct material (6,800 × 100% × $2.90)	$ 19,720.00	
Conversion (6,800 × 80% × $1.65)	8,976.00	28,696.00
Total cost accounted for		$586,819.60

[1] Fully complete as to direct material, 30% as to conversion. The quantities under EUP for this line are not included in the final EUP summation.

[2] Fully complete as to direct material, 80% as to conversion.

APPENDIX 4B

Spoiled and Lost Units

Our earlier examples assumed that there was perfect production—what went in came out of the system. However, in most production processes, some **spoilage** occurs, in which units are **spoiled** or **defective** and are not up to specification.

Loss of units occurs as a result of evaporation or leakage. For example, at Allison Baird's Chocolate Kitchen, approximately 5% of the original weight is lost in the first department, as a result of shrinkage.

Types of Lost Units

Losses in the manufacturing process can be due to either **normal spoilage** or **abnormal spoilage**. Normal losses are those that are expected to occur during the production process, that while abnormal losses generally arise because of human or machine error during the production process. At Alison Baird's Chocolate Kitchen, the weight loss that occurs during the melting process does so uniformly throughout the process.

Accounting for Lost Units

How lost units are accounted for depends on whether the loss is considered normal or abnormal. The two ways of treating normal losses are either to charge the losses to overhead or (more commonly) to include them as part of the cost of good units resulting from the process. Thus, the cost of a loss is included in Work in Process and Finished Goods Inventories and becomes an expense only when the good units are sold. This treatment has been considered appropriate because normal losses have been viewed as unavoidable costs in the production of good units.

The costs of normal **continuous losses** are calculated using the **method of neglect**. Using this method, the spoiled units are excluded in the equivalent units schedule; thus, a smaller number of equivalent units of production (EUP) results. When the cost of production is divided by a smaller EUP, the cost per equivalent unit is higher. The cost of the spoiled units is spread over the remaining units in Work in Process Inventory and over the good units transferred to the next department or to Finished Goods Inventory.

Illustrations of Lost Units

Normal Loss Charged to Good Output

At Alison Baird's Chocolate Kitchen, in Department One—Melting, where the chocolate is melted, shrinkage normally occurs. Management considers any decrease of 5% or less of the kilograms of chocolate placed into production to be normal. This example assumes the FIFO method of calculating equivalent units. The June 2005 data for Allison Baird's Chocolate Kitchen follows:

Kilograms	
Beginning WIP inventory (40% complete)	4,000
Started during month	30,000
Completed and transferred out	26,400
Ending WIP inventory (70% complete)	6,400
Lost kilograms (normal)	1,200

LEARNING OBJECTIVE 11

How do normal and abnormal losses of units differ and how is each treated in the calculation of equivalent units of production schedule?

spoilage (*spoiled unit, defective unit*) unit of product with imperfections that cannot be corrected in an economical way

normal spoilage units lost due to the nature of the manufacturing process; such losses are unavoidable and represent a product cost

abnormal spoilage units lost in production due to circumstances not inherent in the manufacturing process; these losses are not expected under normal, efficient operating conditions and are accounted for as period costs

continuous loss reductions that occur uniformly during processing

method of neglect a method of treating spoiled units in the schedule calculating equivalent units

Costs

Beginning WIP inventory:		
Material	$10,000	
Conversion	1,420	$11,420
Current period:		
Material	$68,500	
Conversion	17,094	85,594
Total costs		$97,014

As shown in Exhibit 4-15, the melting department is accountable for 34,000 kilograms of chocolate: 4,000 kilograms in beginning Work in Process Inventory plus 30,000 kilograms introduced into department during June 2005. Before the 1,200 lost units are considered, 32,800 kilograms are accounted for (26,400 transferred out and 6,400 units in ending Work in Process Inventory).

EXHIBIT 4-15

Cost of Production Report—
Normal Spoilage (FIFO)

Production Data	Equivalent Units of Production		
	Whole Units	**Material**	**Conversion**
Beginning WIP inventory (100%; 40%)	4,000		
Kilograms started	30,000		
Kilograms to account for	34,000		
Beginning WIP inventory completed (0%; 60%)	4,000	0	2,400
Kilograms started and completed	22,400	22,400	22,400
Total kilograms completed	26,400		
Ending WIP inventory (100%; 70%)	6,400	6,400	4,480
Normal shrinkage	1,200		
Kilograms accounted for	34,000	28,800	29,280

Cost Data

	Total	**Material**	**Conversion**
Beginning WIP inventory costs	$11,420		
Current costs	85,594	$68,500	$17,094
Total costs	$97,014	$68,500	$17,094
Divided by EUP		÷ 28,800	÷ 29,280
Cost per FIFO EUP	$2.9618	$2.3785	$0.5838

Cost Assignment

Transferred Out:		
Beginning WIP Inventory	$11,420.00	
Cost to complete: Conversion (2,400 × $0.5838)	1,401.12	
Total cost of beginning WIP inventory	$12,821.12	
Started and completed (22,400 × $2.9618)	66,344.32	
Total cost of kilograms transferred out		$79,165.44
Ending WIP Inventory:		
Material (6,400 × $2.378)	$15,219.20	
Conversion (4,480 × $0.5838)	2,615.42	17,834.62
Total costs accounted for		$97,000.06*

*Due to rounding

The following journal entries would have been made in this department.

Work in Process Inventory	85,594.00	
Raw Materials Inventory		68,500
Wages Payable (and/or other appropriate accounts)		17,094
To record current period costs.		
Finished Goods Inventory	79,165.44	
Work in Process Inventory		79,165.44
To record cost transferred from the department.		

Spoilage—Abnormal and Normal Spoilage

Assume, in our previous example, that management considers spoilage in excess of 3% of the kilograms placed into production—rather than 5%—to be abnormal. Since 30,000 kilograms were started in June, the maximum allowable normal shrinkage is 900 kilograms (30,000 × 3%). Because the total reduction in units in June was 1,200 kilograms, 300 kilograms are considered abnormal spoilage. Exhibit 4-16 presents the cost of production report for this new information.

EXHIBIT 4-16

Cost of Production Report—
Abnormal and Normal Spoilage

Production Data	Equivalent Units of Production		
	Whole Units	Material	Conversion
Beginning WIP inventory (100%; 40%)	4,000		
Kilograms started	30,000		
Kilograms to account for	34,000		
Beginning WIP inventory completed (0%; 60%)	4,000	0	2,400
Kilograms started and completed	22,400	22,400	22,400
Total kilograms completed	26,400		
Ending WIP inventory (100%; 70%)	6,400	6,400	4,480
Normal shrinkage	900		
Abnormal shrinkage (100%; 100%)	300	300	300
Kilograms accounted for	34,000	29,100	29,580

Cost Data

	Total	Material	Conversion
Beginning WIP inventory costs	$11,420		
Current costs	85,594	$68,500	$ 17,094
Total costs	$97,014	$68,500	$ 17,094
Divided by EUP		÷ 29,100	÷29,580
Cost per FIFO EUP	$2.9318	$2.3539	$0.57789

Cost Assignment

Transferred out:

From Beginning WIP inventory	$11,420.00	
Cost to complete: Conversion (2,400 × $0.5779)	1,386.96	
Total cost of beginning inventory	$12,806.96	
Started and completed (22,400 × $2.9318)	65,672.32	
Total cost of kilograms transferred out		$78,479.28
Ending WIP inventory:		
Material (6,400 × $2.3539)	$15,064.96	
Conversion (4,480 × $0.5779)	2,588.99	17,653.95
Abnormal loss (300 × $2.9318)		879.54
Total costs accounted for		$97,012.77*

*Due to rounding

The following journal entries would have been made in this department when both normal and abnormal spoilage exist.

Work in Process Inventory	85,594.00	
Raw Materials Inventory		68,500.00
Wages Payable (and/or other appropriate accounts)		17,094.00

To record current period costs. (from page 198)

Finished Goods Inventory	78,479.28	
Work in Process Inventory		78,479.28

To record cost transferred from the department.

Loss from Abnormal Spoilage	879.54	
Work in Process Inventory		879.54

To remove the cost of abnormal spoilage from Work in Process Inventory.

Our illustrations have used FIFO process costing. If the weighted average method were used, the difference would appear only in the treatment of beginning inventory and its cost.

Minimizing Spoilage

This chapter has assumed that there is no nonconforming production, but in reality, most businesses do produce some spoiled or defective units. Managers should always be alert for ways to minimize spoilage in a production process. The control aspect of quality implementation requires knowledge of the answers to three specific questions.

1. What does the spoilage actually cost?
2. Why does the spoilage occur?
3. How can the spoilage be controlled?

Many companies find it difficult, if not impossible, to answer the question of what spoilage (or lack of quality) costs. One cause of this difficulty is a traditional method of handling spoilage in process costing situations: spoiled units are simply excluded from the calculation of equivalent units of production. The total cost of producing both good and spoiled units is assigned solely to the good units, raising the cost of those units. Because the spoiled units are excluded from the extensions in the calculation of equivalent units, the costs of those units are effectively buried and hidden in magnitude from managers. In a job order costing environment, an estimate of spoilage cost is often added to total budgeted overhead when the predetermined overhead rate is calculated. When this occurs, spoilage cost is again hidden and ignored.

In service organizations, the cost of spoilage may be even more difficult to determine because spoilage, from a customer's viewpoint, is poor service; the customer simply may not do business with the organization again. Such a cost is not processed by the accounting system. Thus, in all instances, a potentially significant dollar amount of loss from nonconformance to requirements is unavailable for investigation as to its planning, controlling, and decision-making ramifications.

As to the second question, managers may be able to pinpoint the reasons for spoilage or poor service but those managers may have a mindset that condones lack of control. First, the managers may believe that a particular cause creates only a minimal amount of spoilage; because of this attitude, they settle for an **accepted quality level** with some tolerance for error. These error tolerances are built into the system and they become justifications for problems. Production is graded on a curve that allows for a less-than-perfect result.

accepted quality level
a predetermined level of acceptability

Incorporating error tolerances into the production system and combining such tolerances with the use of the method of neglect results in a situation in which managers do not have the information necessary to determine how much spoilage is costing the company. Therefore, although they believe that the quantity and cost of spoiled goods are minimal, the managers do not have historical or even estimated accounting amounts on which to base such a conclusion. If managers were aware of the spoilage cost, they could make more informed decisions about whether to ignore the problem causing the spoilage or try to correct its causes.

In other instances, managers may believe that spoilage is uncontrollable. In some cases, this belief is accurate. For example, when a conventional printing press converts from one job to the next, some paper and ink is wasted in the make-ready process. The amount is not large, and process analysis has proved that the cost of attempting to correct this production defect would be significantly greater than the savings resulting from the correction. But in most production situations and almost every service situation, the cause of spoiled goods or poor service is controllable. It is only necessary to determine the cause and institute corrective action.

Spoilage has often been controlled through a process of inspecting goods or, in the case of service organizations, surveying customers. Now, companies are deciding that if quality is built into a process to prevent defects, there will be less need for inspections or surveys, because spoilage and poor service will be minimized. The goal is, then, to maintain quality through process control rather than output inspection and observation.

Many companies are now implementing quality programs to minimize defects or poor service. These companies often employ statistical process control (SPC) techniques to analyze their processes for situations that are out of control and creating spoilage. SPC techniques are based on the theory that a process varies naturally over time from normal, random causes but that some variations occur that fall outside the limits of the natural variations. These uncommon or special-cause variations are typically the points at which the process produces errors, which may be defective goods or poor service. Often, these variations can be and have been eliminated by the installation of computer-integrated manufacturing systems, which have internal controls to evaluate tolerances and sense production problems.

CHAPTER SUMMARY

To be strategically successful, organizations frequently need to have a cost accounting system or a systematic way of recording and valuing costs. A cost accounting system should be compatible with the manufacturing environment in which it is used. Job order costing and process costing are traditional cost accounting systems.

Job order costing is used in companies that make a limited quantity of products or provide a limited number of services uniquely tailored to customer specifications. Job order costing is especially appropriate and useful for many service businesses, such as accounting, advertising, legal, and architectural firms. In contrast to manufacturers, many service companies often do not attempt to trace direct materials to jobs but consider them a part of overhead cost. A job order costing system considers the "job" as the cost object for which costs are accumulated. A job can consist of one or more units of output. Job costs are accumulated on a job order cost sheet.

In an actual or normal cost job order system, direct material and direct labour are traced specifically (during the period and for each department) to the individual jobs in process. Direct materials are traced through materials requisition forms; direct labour is traced through employee time sheets.

In an actual cost system, actual overhead is assigned to jobs. More commonly, however, a normal costing system is used in which overhead is applied using one or more predetermined overhead rates multiplied by the actual activity base(s) incurred. Overhead is applied to Work in Process Inventory at the end of the month or when the job is complete, whichever is earlier.

Job order costing assists management in planning, controlling, decision making, and evaluating performance. It allows managers to trace costs specifically associated with current jobs to better estimate costs for future jobs.

Process costing is used in manufacturing companies producing large quantities of homogeneous products that are manufactured on a continuous basis. It is an averaging method used to assign manufacturing costs to units of production.

Either the weighted average or the FIFO method (covered in Appendix 4A) can be used to compute equivalent units of production and assign costs in a process costing system. The difference between the two methods lies solely in the way work performed in the prior period on the beginning Work in Process Inventory is treated. Under the weighted average method, work on beginning inventory is combined with current period work, and the total costs are averaged over all units. Under the FIFO method, work performed in the last period on beginning Work in Process Inventory is not commingled with current period work, nor are costs of beginning Work in Process Inventory added to current period costs to derive unit production cost. With FIFO, current period costs are divided by current period production to generate a unit production cost related entirely to work performed in the current period.

The six basic steps necessary to derive and assign product cost under a process costing system are listed in Exhibit 4-8. Equivalent units of production must be calculated for each cost component. In multidepartmental process environments, costs must be tracked as the goods move through departments and from one department to the next. The tracking takes place through the use of a transferred-in cost component for EUP and cost per EUP computations. Other cost components include direct material, direct labour, and overhead. If different materials have different degrees of completion, each material is considered a separate cost component. If overhead is applied on a direct labour basis or is incurred at the same rate as direct labour, labour and overhead may be combined as a single cost component and referred to as conversion cost.

(Appendix 4B) Management typically specifies a certain level of shrinkage/spoilage that will be tolerated as normal. If lost units exceed that expectation, the excess is considered abnormal. Normal losses are treated as product costs and abnormal losses are treated as period costs.

Accounting for spoiled units is essential when total quality does not exist. The traditional methods of accounting for spoilage often "bury" the cost of poor quality by spreading that cost over good output. An attempt should be made to isolate the cost of spoilage. Managers who are aware of spoilage costs can make better decisions as to whether to ignore the causes of spoilage or try to correct them. Impediments to such awareness include using the method of neglect and burying the cost of spoilage in predetermined overhead rates rather than accounting for the spoilage separately. Managers may rationalize the existence of these impediments because they believe that a particular cause only creates an insignificant amount of spoilage; thus, tolerances for error are built into the system.

Cross-Functional Applications

Topic of Note	Discipline	Cross-Functional Applications
Cost of Production Report (CPR)	Production Management	The CPR provides a basis for evaluating the performance of a department or a process. Production managers can compare the quantity and cost data in the CPR with predetermined goals to ascertain whether operations are proceeding as planned. Actual

(cont.)

Cross-Functional Applications

Topic of Note	Discipline	Cross-Functional Applications
		variations from the plan often suggest problems or opportunities that can benefit the firm if they are identified early.
	Operations Research and Quality Control	When statistical process controls are combined with process costing, CPR can be used to control and improve a manufacturing process. Often, small or nondestructive sampling can predict acceptable product defects. When variation from expected operating limits occurs, researchers must study the situation to bring the process back into control. A machine in a state of disrepair could spoil excessive material and drive process costs up. This problem could be detected on a detailed CPR and corrected.
	Economics	Economists use CPRs to validate their models of cost structure. The report (CPR) will assist them in determining whether unit costs, marginal costs, and total costs are reasonable. Because economic cost models proceed from different assumptions and methods than accountants employ, the two approaches can validate one another.
	Market Research	Because cost is a key determinant in the formation of an acceptable selling price, marketers must be aware of CPR data to justify profitability per unit of sale. In addition, pricing policies are frequently related to quantity sold. For example, a small order may be priced on such CPR considerations as excessive units in ending inventory or idle plant capacity. Market share may pivot, in part, on production capacity. Marketers can use the CPR to obtain facts in both capacity and pricing decisions.
	Service Firms	Service firms, such as larger, well-established law firms, use their legal time management system (LTM) to produce cost of production reports. Lawyers are assigned an hourly billing rate related to their competency and level of responsibility. Disbursements (such as supplies or payroll of nonlegal staff) can be assigned to a materials or overhead account. Ultimately, billing hours, supplies, and overhead can be allocated to a functional department (such as litigation or legal research). A CPR can focus a service firm manager's attention on inefficiencies, savings, and profitability.
	Financial Accounting	CPR data can support the cost of goods sold information and yield a better understanding of gross margins. This, in turn, provides decision makers with more accurate information concerning cash flows related to operating activities.
Statistical Process Control (SPC)	Purchasing	When a firm's product quality depends upon a supplier's materials or subassemblies, it often insists on specific quality standards. A supplier's dependability for quality, service, and delivery time may qualify it as the firm's certified supplier. In

(cont.)

Cross-Functional Applications

Topic of Note	Discipline	Cross-Functional Applications
		addition, the two firms may share technical support as a means of preventing defects. These efforts can be reflected in the customer firm's SPC charts
	Quality Control Engineers	Quality assurance is significantly increased when SPC is combined with computer-integrated manufacturing systems. Errors and defects are minimized by monitoring the process to prevent their occurrence. Corrections can be made to faulty processes, although not all errors are correctable. Pilots in the airline industry use a variation of SPC in their flight management system to warn them of a questionable flight decision or in-flight hazard before it is too late to correct. Testing and inspection are still necessary to verify the quality conformance; however, the frequency and cost should be reduced.
	Human Resource Management	HR managers benefit from SPC by focusing their resources for training, motivation, and evaluation where they are most critically needed. Although rewards and evaluations are often left up to particular department managers in larger organizations, employee training is usually an important function of HR. SPC charts, which are often expressed in nonfinancial measurements, can be used to evaluate employee compliance with quality standards. A quality team of employees and a quality chart of desirable performance can help HR to motivate employees, especially when job evaluations and rewards are tied in.
	Design and Manufacturing Engineers	Design engineers are pressed to modify their products from many sides, especially from marketers and production managers. The SPC chart communicates a quality or safety conformity to designers. Bad designs are frequently the basis of product liability litigation. Also, the design and manufacturing engineers must review SPC charts, often adjusting them to reflect changes, such as more convenient processing methods or new technology installations.
	Marketing	Marketers, especially in high-technology markets, can use SPC charts as a promotional strategy. This could give a firm access to quality-conscious customers, perhaps even those who certify their suppliers. With the globalization of industry and mega-mergers at hand, firms are pressured to share the technical support systems, and SPC charts can coordinate that arrangement.

Key Terms

Abnormal spoilage (p. 197)

Accepted quality level (p. 200)

Continuous loss (p. 197)

Cost-plus job (p. 172)

Cost of production report (p. 189)

Defective unit (see *spoilage*) (p. 197)

Employee time sheet (time ticket) (p. 171)

Equivalent units of production (p. 181)

FIFO method (p. 182)

Job (p. 166)

Job order cost sheet (p. 169)

Job order costing system (p. 166)

Materials requisition form (p. 169)

Method of neglect (p. 197)

Normal spoilage (p. 197)

Process costing (p. 177)

Process costing system (p. 177)

Spoilage (p. 197)

Spoiled unit (see *spoilage*) (p. 197)

Total cost to account for (p. 183)

Total units to account for (p. 183)

Units started and completed (p. 186)

Weighted average method (p. 182)

Solution Strategies

Basic Journal Entries in a Job Order Costing System

Raw Material Inventory	XXX	
Accounts Payable		XXX
To record the purchase of raw materials.		
Work in Process Inventory—Dept. (Job #)	XXX	
Manufacturing Overhead	XXX	
Raw Material Inventory		XXX
To record the issuance of direct and indirect materials requisitioned for a specific job.		
Work in Process Inventory—Dept. (Job #)	XXX	
Manufacturing Overhead	XXX	
Wages Payable		XXX
To record direct and indirect labour payroll for production employees.		
Manufacturing Overhead	XXX	
Various Accounts		XXX
To record the incurrence of actual overhead costs (Account titles to be credited must be specified in an actual journal entry.)		
Work in Process Inventory—Dept. (Job #)	XXX	
Manufacturing Overhead		XXX
To apply overhead to a specific job. (This may be actual overhead or overhead applied using a predetermined rate. Predetermined overhead is applied at job completion or end of period, whichever is earlier.)		
Finished Goods Inventory (Job #)	XXX	
Work in Process Inventory		XXX
To record the transfer of completed goods from Work in Process to Finished Goods.		
Cost of Goods Sold	XXX	
Finished Goods Inventory		XXX
To record the cost of goods sold.		
Accounts Receivable	XXX	
Sales		XXX
To record the sale of goods on account.		

Steps in Process Costing Computations

1. Compute the total units to account for (in physical units):
   Beginning inventory in whole (physical) units
   + Units started (or transferred in) during period
2. Compute units accounted for (in physical units):
   Units completed and transferred out
   + Ending inventory in whole (physical) units
3. Compute equivalent units of production per cost component:
   a. Weighted average
      Beginning inventory in whole (physical) units
      + Units started and completed*
      + (Ending inventory × Percentage complete)
   b. FIFO
      (Beginning inventory × Percentage not complete at start of period)
      + Units started and completed*
      + (Ending inventory × Percentage complete)
      * Units started and completed = Units transferred − Units in beginning inventory.
4. Compute total cost to account for:
   Cost in beginning inventory
   + Cost of current period
5. Compute cost per equivalent unit per cost component:
   a. Weighted average
      Cost of component in beginning inventory
      + Cost of component for current period
      = Total cost of component
      ÷ EUP for component
   b. FIFO
      Cost of component for current period
      ÷ EUP for component
6. Assign costs to inventories:
   a. Weighted average
      1. Transferred out
         Whole units transferred × (Total cost per EUP for all components)
      2. Ending inventory
         Sum of EUP for each component × Cost per EUP for each component
   b. FIFO
      1. Transferred out:
         Beginning inventory cost
         + (Beginning inventory × Percentage not complete at beginning of
            period for each component × Cost per EUP for each component)
         + (Units started and completed × Total cost per EUP for all components)
      2. Ending inventory:
         Sum of (EUP for each component × Cost per EUP for each component)

Spoilage

Normal Loss Treatment

All good production (both fully and partially completed) absorbs the cost of the lost units through higher per-unit costs.

Abnormal Loss Treatment

The cost of lost units is assigned as a period loss.

DEMONSTRATION PROBLEM

Smoked Salmon Ltd. manufactures several smoked food items, including smoked salmon. The firm has two departments: the Smoking Department, which is highly labour-intensive, and the Packaging Department, which is highly automated. Salmon production occurs during four months of the year. Costs in the Smoking Department are accumulated in three cost pools: direct material, direct labour, and overhead. The following production and cost data relate to the November 2005 production of smoked salmon.

Production Data:

Beginning Work in Process Inventory	15,000 kilograms
(This inventory is 100% complete as to material, 60% complete as to direct labour, and 35% complete as to overhead.)	
Started this period	250,000 kilograms
Ending Work in Process Inventory	8,000 kilograms
(This inventory is 100% complete as to material, 70% complete as to direct labour, and 40% complete as to overhead.)	

Cost Data:

	Material	Direct Labour	Overhead
Beginning inventory	$ 34,000	$ 7,274	$ 7,327
Costs incurred in November	787,500	278,960	229,455

Required:

a. Use the weighted average method to determine the cost of the smoked salmon transferred to WIP Inventory—Packaging, and the cost of the packages of smoked salmon in Smoking Department—EWIP for November 2005.
b. Repeat part (a), but use the FIFO method.

Solution to Demonstration Problem

a. Weighted average method:

Step 1: Calculate total units to account for:

Beginning inventory	15,000
Units started during current period	250,000
Units to account for	265,000

Step 2: Calculate the total units accounted for:

Units completed and transferred out	257,000
Units in ending WIP inventory	8,000
Units accounted for	265,000

Step 3: Determine the equivalent units of production:

	Material	Direct Labour	Overhead
BWIP (whole units)	15,000	15,000	15,000
Units started and completed	242,000	242,000	242,000
EWIP (whole units × 100%; 70%; 40% complete)	8,000	5,600	3,200
EUP	265,000	262,600	260,200

Step 4: Determine the total cost to account for:

	Material	Direct Labour	Overhead
BWIP cost	$ 34,000	$ 7,274	$ 7,327
Current period cost	787,500	278,960	229,455
Total cost to account for	$821,500	$286,234	$236,782

Total all cost pools = $821,500 + $286,234 + $236,782 = $1,344,516

Step 5: Calculate the cost per equivalent unit of production:

	Material	Direct Labour	Overhead
Total cost	$821,500	$286,234	$236,782
Divided by EUP	÷ 265,000	÷ 262,600	÷ 260,200
Cost per EUP	$ 3.10	$ 1.09	$ 0.91

Total cost per EUP = $3.10 + $1.09 + $0.91 = $5.10

Step 6: Assign costs to EWIP Inventory and Goods Transferred Out:

Cost of goods transferred (257,000 × $5.10)		$1,310,700
Cost of ending WIP Inventory:		
Material (8,000 × $3.10)	$24,800	
Direct labour (5,600 × $1.09)	6,104	
Overhead (3,200 × $0.91)	2,912	33,816
Total cost accounted for		$1,344,516

b. FIFO method:

Step 1: Calculate total units to account for:

Beginning inventory	15,000
Units started during current period	250,000
Units to account for	265,000

Step 2: Calculate the total units accounted for:

Units completed and transferred out	257,000
Units in ending WIP inventory	8,000
Units accounted for	265,000

Step 3: Determine the equivalent units of production:

	Material	Direct Labour	Overhead
BWIP (EUP not completed in October)	0	6,000	9,750
Units started and completed	242,000	242,000	242,000
EWIP (whole units × % complete)	8,000	5,600	3,200
EUP	250,000	253,600	254,950

Step 4: Determine the total cost to account for:

	Material	Direct Labour	Overhead
BWIP cost	$ 34,000	$ 7,274	$ 7,327
Current period cost	787,500	278,960	229,455
Total cost to account for	$821,500	$286,234	$236,782

Total all cost pools = $821,500 + $286,234 + $236,782 = $1,344,516

Step 5: Calculate the cost per equivalent unit of production:

	Material	Direct Labour	Overhead
Current period cost	$787,500	$278,960	$229,455
Divided by EUP	÷ 250,000	÷ 253,600	÷ 254,950
Cost per EUP	$ 3.15	$ 1.10	$ 0.90

Total cost per EUP = $3.15 + $1.10 + $0.90 = $5.15

Step 6: Assign costs to EWIP Inventory and Goods Transferred Out:

Cost of goods transferred out:		
Beginning WIP inventory cost ($34,000 + $7,274 + $7,327)		$ 48,601
Costs to complete beginning WIP:		
Material (0 × $3.15)		0
Direct labour (6,000 × $1.10)		6,600
Overhead (9,750 × $0.90)		8,775
Total cost of beginning WIP inventory		$ 63,976
Started and completed (242,000 × $5.15)		1,246,300
Total cost of goods transferred out		$1,310,276
Cost of Ending WIP inventory:		
Material (8,000 × $3.15)	$25,200	
Direct labour (5,600 × $1.10)	6,160	
Overhead (3,200 × $0.90)	2,880	
Total cost of ending WIP Inventory		34,240
Total cost accounted for		$1,344,516

End-of-Chapter Materials

SELF-TEST QUESTIONS

(SOLUTIONS APPEAR AT END OF THE CHAPTER.)

1. The source document that provides all financial information about a particular job is:
   a.   job cost sheet
   b.   materials requisition form
   c.   time sheet
   d.   work order

2. Knowing the cost of individual jobs will allow managers to
   a.   better estimate future job costs
   b.   tailor output to customer specifications
   c.   charge the customer more
   d.   predetermine the overhead rate to charge

3. Wharton Ltd. uses weighted average process costing for the product it manufactures. All direct materials are added at the beginning of production, and conversion costs are applied evenly during production. The following data apply to the past month:

Total units in beginning WIP inventory	
(30% complete as to conversion costs)	1,500
Total units transferred to finished goods inventory	7,400
Total units in ending WIP inventory	
(60% complete as to conversion costs)	2,300

   The equivalent units of conversion costs total
   a.   7,400
   b.   8,330
   c.   8,780
   d.   9,700

4. During March, Jab Corporation's Department Two's equivalent unit product costs, computed under the weighted average method, were as follows:

Materials	$1
Conversion	3
Transferred-in	5

   Materials are introduced at the end of the process in Department Two. There were 4,000 units (40% complete as to conversion costs) in WIP at March 31. The total costs assigned to the March EWIP inventory should be
   a. $36,000
   b. $28,800
   c. $27,200
   d. $24,800

5. Amber Designer Ltd. manufactures Product X in a two-stage production cycle in Departments A and B. Materials are added at the beginning of the process in Department B. Amber uses the weighted average method. BWIP (6,000 units) for Department B was 50% complete as to conversion costs. EWIP (8,000 units) was 75% complete. During February, 12,000 units were completed and transferred out of Department B. An analysis of the costs relating to WIP

and production activity in Department B for February follows:

	Transferred-in Costs	Materials Costs	Conversion Costs
WIP, February 1:			
Costs attached	$12,000	$2,500	$1,000
Feb. activity:			
Costs added	29,000	5,500	5,000

The total cost per equivalent unit transferred out for February of Product X, rounded to the nearest penny, was
a. $2.75
b. $2.78
c. $2.82
d. $3.01

Use the following information to answer Questions 6 and 7.

Bold'N Ltd.'s costing system uses two cost categories: direct materials and conversion costs. Each product must pass through the Assembly department and the Testing department. Direct materials are added at the beginning of production. Conversion costs are allocated evenly throughout production. Data for the Assembly department for March 2005 are as follows:

Units:

Beginning work in process, 40% complete as to conversion	400 units
Units started during March	1,200 units
Ending work in process	200 units

Costs:

Beginning work in process:

Direct materials	$ 200,000
Conversion costs	200,000
Direct materials added during March	2,000,000
Conversion costs added during March	2,500,000

6. What unit cost can be inferred from the information provided regarding beginning Work in Process Inventory?
    a. $1,000
    b. $1,750
    c. $3,500
    d. $3,750

7. How many units were completed and transferred out of the Assembly department during March 2005?
    a. 200 units
    b. 1,200 units
    c. 1,400 units
    d. 1,600 units
    e. None of the above

Use the following information to answer Questions 8 and 9.

The Cutting Department is the first stage of MacKenzie Fashions Ltd.'s production cycle. Beginning Work in Process (BWIP) for this department was 80% complete as to conversion costs. Ending Work in Process (EWIP) was 50% complete. Information as to conversion costs in the Cutting Department for January is as follows:

	Units	Conversion Costs
Work in process, January 1	25,000	$ 22,000
Units started and costs incurred during January	135,000	143,000
Units completed and transferred to next department during January	100,000	

8. Using the FIFO method, what was the conversion cost of Work in Process in the Cutting Department at January 31?
    a. $33,000
    b. $38,000
    c. $39,000
    d. $45,000
    e. None of the above

9. What is the per-unit conversion cost of goods started and completed this period using the weighted average method?
    a. $1.10
    b. $1.14
    c. $1.27
    d. $1.30

10. Fashions Company has a process cost system using the FIFO cost method. All materials are introduced at the beginning of the process in Department One. The following information is available for the month of January:

Units

WIP, January 1, (40% complete as to conversion costs)	500
Started	2,000
Transferred to Department Two	2,100
WIP, January 31 (25% complete as to conversion costs)	400

What are the equivalent units of production for the month of January?

	Materials	Conversion Costs
a.	2,500	2,200
b.	2,500	1,900
c.	2,000	2,200
d.	2,000	2,000

QUESTIONS

1. In the context of job order product costing, what is a job?

2. If the costs in all of the subsidiary ledgers for all work that has been started but not yet completed were summed, the total would equal the balance in which control account? Why?

3. The sum of all costs on the job cost sheets for all the products that are sold during a period would equal the balance in which account? Would this account balance typically be determined using a perpetual or a periodic inventory system? Why?

4. What types of service organizations are likely to use job order costing?

5. Why would a change from a labour-intensive production system to a machine-driven production system likely necessitate changes in the job order costing system?

6. Describe the characteristics of a production environment in which process costing would likely be found.

7. How are job order and process costing similar? How do they differ?

8. Can a company use both job order costing and process costing for its production activities? If so, give an example. If not, explain why it would not be possible.

9. What source documents are used to provide information on raw material and direct labour usage in a process costing system? Are these different from the source documents used in job order costing? Why or why not?

10. Under what conditions is it appropriate to apply actual overhead to products in a process costing environment?

11. Why is the assignment of costs to products essentially an averaging process?

12. Is one equivalent unit computation sufficient for all of the cost categories (direct material, direct labour, and overhead)? Explain.

13. What is meant by the term *equivalent units of production* (EUP)? Why are EUP needed in process costing but not in job order costing?

14. What are the two methods used in process costing to assign an average cost to products?

15. What are the six steps involved in assigning product costs in a process costing environment? In your answer, indicate in which steps physical units are used and in which steps equivalent units are used.

16. At the end of a period, a department's total production costs are assigned to two groups of products. What are the two groups and where do their costs appear on the financial statements?

17. How are units "started and completed" calculated?

18. What is meant by the term *transferred out cost*?

19. What is the purpose of a cost of production report? Discuss the information provided to managers by this document.

20. Arrange the following terms in an equation so that each side contains two terms and the two sides are equal:

Cost of the beginning Work in Process Inventory	(BWIP)
Costs transferred out	(TO)
Cost of the ending Work in Process Inventory	(EWIP)
Costs incurred this period	(TP)

21. Arrange the following terms in an equation so that the two sides are equal, with one side representing total units to account for and the other side representing total units accounted for:

Units in the beginning Work in Process Inventory	(BI)
Units in the ending Work in Process Inventory	(EWIP)
Units started and completed	(S&C)
Units started but not completed	(SNC)
Units transferred out	(TO)

22. Under what circumstances will a department have a cost component called *transferred in*? What degree of completion will the units in this component have?

23. A company has two sequential processing departments. On the cost of production reports, will the cost per unit transferred out of the first department always be equal to the cost per unit transferred in to the second department? Why or why not?

24. A food processor transfers $56,000 of products from the Cleaning Department to the Cutting Department. What would the journal entry be for this transfer?

25. Doug Hyatt Ltd. uses a process costing system that has three sequential processing departments (Cutting, Stitching, and Finishing, respectively). What journal entry would identify the cost of goods manufactured?

26.* In a firm that uses a process costing system as both a tool to evaluate periodic cost control and to assign costs to products, would weighted average or FIFO more likely be used? Explain.

27.* In an inflationary environment (in which costs are rising from period to period), would the weighted average or FIFO method assign the higher cost to the ending Work in Process Inventory in a department? (Assume production is stable from period to period.) Explain.

28.* Does the weighted average or FIFO method provide the better picture of the actual amount of work accomplished in a period? Explain.

29.* Why does the transferred-out cost under the weighted average method include only one computation but the FIFO method includes multiple computations?

30.* How are the FIFO and weighted average methods similar and how do they differ?

31.* Why should companies design process accounting systems to capture costs of spoilage?

32.* What is meant by the method of neglect? How does the use of this method affect the cost of good production?

33.* Why is the cost of spoilage so difficult to determine in a service provider?

34.* How are statistical process control techniques used by companies to control quality-related costs?

* Relates to materials from Appendix 4A

EXERCISES

1. (LO 2; Missing numbers) The Stratychuk Auto Shop uses a job order costing system based on normal costs. Overhead is applied at the rate of 80% of direct labour costs. Jobs in process at the end of November are as shown:

	Job No. 313	Job No. 318	Job No. 340
Direct materials	$5,000	$7,000	$9,400
Direct labour	12,000	*b*	*c*
Overhead	*a*	10,000	*d*
Total	*e*	*f*	27,400

Required:
Find the values for *a* through *f*.

2. (LO 2; Total cost and sales price) The Calgary Blacksmith Shop is a small firm whose specialty is the production of custom metal products. The firm employs a job order costing system based on normal cost. Overhead is applied to production at the rate of $12 per direct labour hour. During August, the firm finished Job No. 129, a batch of metal steps for mobile homes. The total direct material and direct labour costs assigned to Job No. 129 were $14,000 and $18,000, respectively. The firm's direct labour rate is $9 per hour.

Required:
a. Compute the total cost of Job No. 129.
b. Record the journal entry to transfer the job to Finished Goods Inventory.
c. Compute the sales price of Job No. 129 if the job is priced to yield a gross margin equal to 40% of the sales price.

3. (LO 2; Journal entries) The Heather Hattery uses a perpetual inventory system. The firm maintains one inventory account for various materials that are used to make hats as well as the supplies that are used to lubricate and maintain its production machinery. For the month of August, the firm had the following transactions that affected its materials inventory account:
   • Purchased felt material on account, $80,000.
   • Issued felt for hat production, $38,000.
   • Issued lubricants for machinery maintenance, $2,000.
Required:
Record journal entries for the above three transactions.

4. (LO 2; Job costing) Forrester Creations Ltd. produces high-fashion gowns. The company uses a job order costing system. The company has no beginning or ending inventory in work in process or finished goods. Manufacturing overhead is applied at the rate of $4.50 per direct labour hour. All over- or underapplied overhead is closed to cost of goods sold. Actual results for fiscal year 2005 are:

Direct labour hours	225,000
Direct labour	$ 600,000
Indirect labour	120,000
Opening raw materials inventory	50,000
Ending raw materials inventory	250,000
Purchases of raw materials	500,000
Light, heat, and power	210,000
Indirect raw materials	37,500
Miscellaneous manufacturing overhead	240,000
Cost of goods sold	1,912,500

Required:
a. What amount of manufacturing overhead was applied to production during 2005?
b. What amount of manufacturing overhead was actually incurred during 2005?
c. Was the manufacturing overhead under- or overapplied during 2005? If so, by how much?
d. What is the amount of cost of goods sold?

5. (LO 2; Overhead application to jobs) The Welland Bridge Company constructs bridges for the large 400-series highways. In its first year of operations, the firm worked on three bridges. Each bridge is built on-site and treated as a separate job. Overhead is applied to jobs based on the number of tonnes of direct material consumed. On average, direct materials cost $50 per tonne. Some relevant information on the jobs follows:

	Bridge 1	Bridge 2	Bridge 3	Total
Direct materials	$45,000	$54,000	$135,000	$234,000
Direct labour	180,000	213,000	599,000	992,000
Manufacturing overhead				439,920

Required:
a. Compute the overhead rate per tonne of direct materials.
b. Compute the amount of overhead assigned to each bridge.
c. Compute the total costs assigned to each bridge for the first year.
d. Assuming Bridge 3 is the only one that was finished during the year, compute the year-end balance in Work in Process.

6. (LO 2; Job costing, journal entries) The following two jobs were in process on June 1, 2005, at Brenedlyn Ltd. The company uses a job order costing system.

	Job No. 43	Job No. 59
Direct (raw) materials	$1,000	$900
Direct labour	1,200	200
Manufacturing overhead applied	1,800	300

There was no opening finished goods inventory at the beginning of the month. During the month of June, Jobs No. 60 to 75 inclusive were put into process.

Direct material issued amounted to $13,000, direct labour cost incurred during the month amounted to $20,000, and actual manufacturing overhead recorded during the month amounted to $28,000. Manufacturing overhead is applied based on direct labour dollars.

The only job in process at the end of June was Job No. 75, and the costs incurred for this job were $1,150 of raw materials and $1,000 of direct labour. In addition, Job No. 73, which was 100% complete, was still on hand as of June 30. Total costs allocated to this job were $3,300.

Required:
Prepare journal entries to record
i.   cost of goods manufactured
ii. cost of goods sold
iii. closing of any over- or underapplied manufacturing overhead to cost of goods sold

7. (LO 2; Job costing) Ridge Maroni Ltd., a small manufacturer of swimwear, uses a job-order costing system. The corporate policy is to close all over- and underapplied overhead to Cost of Goods Sold. The company had the following inventory balances:

	Opening Balance January 1, 2005	Ending Balance December 31, 2005
Raw material inventory	$54,000	$39,000
Work in process	$82,500	?
Finished goods	$90,000	?

The actual data for 2005 included:

1. Overhead was applied at a rate of $4.50 per direct labour hour.
2. Purchases of materials and supplies totaled $219,000. Both are accumulated in the raw materials inventory account.
3. Of the total materials requisitions, 90% were for direct materials and 10% were for supplies.
4. Direct labour hours were 33,000 for a total cost of $264,000.
5. Work in process on December 31, 2005, consisted of units with the following costs:
   Direct materials $15,000
   Direct labour (7,500 hours) $60,000
6. At year-end, the manufacturing overhead account had a debit balance of $750.
7. Sales for the year were $744,000, with gross profit equal to 25% of sales before adjusting for under- or overapplied overhead.

Required:
a.   Calculate each of the following:
   i.   Direct materials used during 2005
   ii.   Work in process inventory, December 31, 2005
   iii. Cost of goods manufactured during 2005
   iv.   Finished goods inventory, December 31, 2005
   v.   Actual manufacturing overhead incurred during 2005
b.   There are two ways of dealing with over- or underapplied overhead. Explain each.

8. (LO 5; Total units, WA EUP) Abssy Corp. uses a weighted average process costing system. All material is added at the start of the process; labour and overhead costs are incurred evenly throughout the production process. The company's records for September contained the following information:
   Beginning Work in Process Inventory   32,000 kilograms
   Started during September   800,000 kilograms
   Transferred to finished goods   808,000 kilograms

As of September 1, the beginning inventory was 60% complete as to labour and overhead. On September 30, the ending inventory was 35% complete as to labour and overhead.

Required:

a.   Determine the total number of kilograms to account for.

b.   Determine the equivalent units of production for direct material.

c.   Determine the equivalent units of production for conversion.

9. (LO 5; Total units, WA EUP) Sam Goldberg Ltd. produces a chemical compound in which all material is added at the beginning of the production cycle. At May 1, there were 36,000 litres in beginning inventory. During May 2005, the company started 920,000 litres of raw material into production and completed 945,000 litres.

   The beginning inventory was 60% complete as to labour and 25% complete as to overhead. The ending Work in Process Inventory was 30% complete as to labour and 5% complete as to overhead. The company uses the weighted average method.

Required:

a.   Determine the total number of litres to account for.

b.   Determine the equivalent units of production for direct material.

c.   Determine the equivalent units of production for labour.

d.   Determine the equivalent units of production for conversion.

10. (LO 5; WA EUP) The following are individual situations.

a.	Units started in production	280,000
	Units transferred out	200,000
	Beginning Work in Process Inventory (60% complete)	40,000
	Ending Work in Process Inventory (75% complete)	120,000
b.	Units started in production	240,000
	Units transferred out	?
	Beginning Work in Process Inventory (25% complete)	40,000
	Ending Work in Process Inventory (60% complete)	60,000
c.	Units started in production	135,000
	Units transferred out	130,000
	Beginning Work in Process Inventory (30% complete)	15,000
	Ending Work in Process Inventory (90% complete)	?
d.	Units started in production	?
	Units transferred out	180,000
	Beginning Work in Process Inventory (20% complete)	10,000
	Ending Work in Process Inventory (70% complete)	20,000

Required:

For each of the above situations, determine the equivalent units of production using the weighted average method.

11. (LO 5; WA EUP, cost assignment) The Gilda Company produces tubes of tanning gel in a continuous flow production process. The company uses weighted average process costing to assign production costs to products. All of the gel materials are added at the beginning of the process in Department One; the plastic tubes are added in Department Two. Direct labour and overhead costs are incurred evenly throughout the process. Information on the physical unit activity and costs for April 2005 is as follows:

	Kilograms of Gel
Beginning Work in Process Inventory	42,000
Transferred out this period	150,000
Ending Work in Process Inventory	30,000

	Direct Material Cost	Conversion Cost
Beginning Work in Process Inventory	$ 6,420	$ 7,056
Incurred this period	15,180	34,944

The April beginning and ending work in process inventories are, respectively, 75% and 60% complete as to conversion.

Required:

a. Determine the equivalent units of production for direct material and conversion for April.

b. Determine the cost per equivalent unit of production for direct material and conversion for April.

c. Determine the cost of the kilograms of gel transferred out and the kilograms of gel remaining in ending Work in Process Inventory.

12. (LO 5; WA, cost assignment) On March 1, BUG-B-GONE had 12,000 litres of bug spray in work in process in Department A—the first stage of its production cycle. Costs attached to these litres were $37,160 for materials and $24,620 for conversion. Materials are added at the beginning of the process, and labour and overhead are applied evenly throughout the process. Conversion was 70% complete on March 1.

During March, 58,000 litres were started, $172,840 of material costs were incurred, and $141,780 of conversion costs were incurred. On March 31, Department A had 8,000 litres in ending work in process that were 25% complete. The company uses the weighted average method of process costing.

Required:

a. How much cost should be assigned to the litres transferred out during March?

b. How much cost should be assigned to the litres in March ending Work in Process Inventory?

13. (LO 5; Weighted average calculations; spoilage) The Regina Co. Ltd. uses a weighted average process costing system in accounting for a product that passes through two departments—A and B. In Department B, material is added only to those units that pass inspection. Inspection takes place when the product is 95% complete. A spoilage rate of 4% of finished product is considered normal.

On October 1, 2005, 3,000 units were in process in Department B and were estimated to be 40% complete. At the end of September, $25,000 of Department A costs and $13,000 of Department B costs had been assigned to these units.

During the month of October, 20,000 units were received from Department A. A total of 17,000 units was transferred to Finished Goods. At the end of October, 5,000 units were still in process and were estimated to be 70% complete.

Excerpts from Department B's Cost of Production Report for October showed the following:

Finished units (17,000 × $22.00)		$374,000
Ending inventory:		
(5,000 × $9.00)	$45,000	
(3,500 × $11.00)	38,500	83,500

Required:

What costs were charged to Department B during October?

14. (LO 5; WA calculations) Nicholas Sperry Ltd. manufactures a special type of fast-drying paint. You are attempting to verify the balances at the end of the year, which are recorded on the books of Nicholas Sperry Ltd. as follows. (A physical count revealed that the ending physical units are correct.)

	Units	Cost
Work in process		
(50% complete as to conversion costs)	450,000	$ 991,440
Finished goods	300,000	1,514,700

Materials are added at the beginning of the manufacturing process. Overhead is applied at 50% of direct labour costs. There was no beginning finished goods inventory. Additional information:

Costs

	Units	Materials	Labour
Beginning WIP (50% complete)	300,000	$ 300,000	$ 472,500
Units started	1,500,000		
Material costs		1,950,000	
Labour costs			2,992,500
Units completed	1,350,000		

Required:

Using the weighted average method, compute the following:

a.   Equivalent units of production

b.   Unit costs of production of materials, labour, and overhead

c.   Costs of the finished goods ending inventory and ending work in process inventory

(Adapted by the author from *Management Accounting examinations,* published by the Certified General Accountants Association of Canada © CGA-Canada, 2001, used by permission.)

15.   (LO 7, 8; Multidepartmental production, WA method) Donna Losell Inc. produces calendars in a two-process, two-department operation. In the Printing Department, materials are printed and cut. In the Assembly Department, the materials received from Printing are assembled into individual calendars and bound. Each department maintains its own Work in Process Inventory account, and costs are assigned using the weighted average process costing method. In Assembly, conversion costs are incurred evenly throughout the process; direct material is added at the end of the process. For November 2005, the following production and cost information was available:

Beginning inventory:

(30% complete as to conversion)		20,000 calendars
Transferred in cost	$25,000	
Conversion cost	1,114	
Transferred in during November:		80,000 calendars
Current period costs:		
Transferred in	$80,000	
Direct material	10,500	
Conversion	14,960	
Ending Work in Process Inventory:		
(80% complete as to conversion)		30,000 calendars

Required:

For the Assembly Department, compute the

a.   equivalent units of production for each cost component

b.   cost per equivalent unit for each cost component

c.   cost transferred to Finished Goods Inventory

d.   cost of Ending WIP inventory

16.   (LO 7, 8; Missing numbers, multidepartmental production, WA method) Nickel Kidman produces fruit drinks in a three-department production process (Steaming, Mixing, and Packaging). Limited information on the inventory accounts for March follows:

WIP Inventory—Steaming				WIP Inventory—Mixing		
Beg.	90,000			Beg.	300,000	
DM	270,000	?		Trans In	?	
DL	60,000			DM	?	600,000
OH	75,000			DL	?	
Ending	54,000			OH	?	
				Ending	210,000	

WIP Inventory—Packaging				Finished Goods Inventory		
Beg.	270,000			Beg.	495,000	
Trans In	?			CGM	?	1,440,000
DM	300,000			Ending	?	
DL	600,000	?				
OH	180,000					
Ending	330,000					

Required:

a.   What was the cost of goods transferred from the Steaming Department to the Mixing Department in March?

b.   What was the sum of direct material, direct labour, and overhead costs in the Mixing Department for March?

c.   What was the cost of goods manufactured for March?

17. (LO 7, 8, 13; Appendix 4A, journal entries) The Shearer Pellet Company manufactures alfalfa pellets used as animal feed. Alfalfa is processed in a two-department sequential process. The first process, dehydration, removes moisture from raw alfalfa; the second process, pelletizing, compresses the alfalfa into pellets. The following transactions occurred at Shearer Pellet in January 2005. Journalize each transaction.

    a. Alfalfa costing $200,000 was removed from Raw Material Inventory and entered into processing in the Dehydration Department.
    b. The Dehydration Department paid labour costs of $240,000; of this amount, $160,000 was considered direct.
    c. Other overhead costs amounting to $140,000 were incurred in the Dehydration Department. (Note: credit Accounts Payable.)
    d. Goods costing $660,000 were transferred from the Dehydration Department to the Pelletizing Department.
    e. Labour costs of $162,000 were incurred in the Pelletizing Department; $124,000 of this amount was considered direct.
    f. Other overhead costs incurred in the Pelletizing Department amounted to $226,000. (Note: credit Accounts Payable.)
    g. Goods costing $980,000 were transferred from the Pelletizing Department to Finished Goods Inventory.
    h. Goods costing $900,000 were sold for $1,460,000 cash.

    Required:
    Prepare journal entries for each of parts (a) to (h).

18. (LO 9; Appendix 4A, total units, FIFO EUP) Answer parts (a), (b), (c), and (d) of Exercise 9 assuming that Sam Goldberg Ltd. uses the FIFO method of process costing.

19. (LO 9; Appendix 4A, FIFO EUP) For each of the situations given in Exercise 10, determine the equivalent units of production using the FIFO method of process costing.

20. (LO 5, 9; Appendix 4A, reconciling WA and FIFO EUP) Jaylee Leno Company had 70,000 units in beginning work in process in Department 1 that were 90% complete as to material and 60% complete as to conversion. During July, 360,000 units were started in Department 1, and 395,000 units were completed and transferred to Department 2. Ending Work in Process Inventory in Department 1 on July 31 was 80% complete as to material and 45% complete as to conversion.

    Required:
    a. What are the EUP under the weighted average method?
    b. What are the EUP under the FIFO method?
    c. Reconcile the EUP calculated in parts (a) and (b).

21. (LO 9; Appendix 4A, FIFO EUP, cost assignment) Answer parts (a) and (b) of Exercise 12, assuming that BUG-B-GONE uses the FIFO method of process costing.

22. (LO 10; Appendix 4A, Multidepartmental production, FIFO method) Answer parts (a), (b), (c), and (d) of Exercise 15, assuming that Donna Losell Inc. uses the FIFO method of process costing.

23. (LO 11; Appendix 4A and 4B, normal and abnormal spoilage, FIFO) Dan Segal Corporation manufactures T-shirts on a mass-production basis. Spoilage occurs throughout the process. Normal spoilage is considered to be 0.4% or less of the materials placed into production. The following data are available for March 2005:

Beginning Work in Process Inventory (20% complete as to material; 30% complete as to conversion)	8,000 units
Started during March	180,000 units
Ending Work in Process Inventory (70% complete as to material; 80% complete as to conversion)	4,000 units
Spoiled	1,400 units

    Required:
    a. How many units were transferred out?
    b. How much normal spoilage occurred?
    c. How much abnormal spoilage occurred?

d.   What are the FIFO equivalent units of production for materials? For conversion costs?
e.   Explain how costs are associated with the normal spoilage handled.
f.   Explain how costs are associated with the abnormal spoilage handled.

PROBLEMS

1. (LO 2; Journal entries) The Shetland Publishing Company recorded the following transactions for October 2005:
    a.   Purchased materials on account, $900,000.
    b.   Issued materials into production, $700,000. Of the total materials issued, $500,000 could be traced directly to specific jobs.
    c.   Factory labour costs in the amount of $650,000 were incurred. Only $500,000 of this amount could be attributed to specific jobs.
    d.   Overhead was applied to jobs on the basis of 110% of direct labour cost.
    e.   Job #807 costing $250,000 was completed.
    f.   Job #807 was sold on account for $400,000.
    Required:
    Record all necessary journal entries to account for the previous transactions.

2. (LO 2; Journal entries) Technotronix Inc. custom manufactures robots that are used in repetitive production tasks. At the beginning of 2005, three jobs were in process. The costs assigned to the jobs as of January 1, 2005, are as follows:

	Job No. 114J	Job No. 117N	Job No. 128P
Direct materials	$200,000	$1,400,000	$100,000
Direct labour	150,000	800,000	60,000
Overhead	100,000	600,000	42,000
Total	$450,000	$2,800,000	$202,000

During the course of 2005, two more jobs were started, 133I and 134P, and the following transactions occurred:

(i) Purchases of materials	$1,200,000

(ii) Direct materials were issued to production:

Job 114J	$ 212,000
Job 117N	158,000
Job 128P	410,000
Job 133I	160,000
Job 134P	125,000

(iii)Indirect materials were issued to production	$ 111,900

(iv)Labour costs were incurred as follows:

Job 114J	$ 175,000
Job 117N	302,000
Job 128P	450,000
Job 133I	205,000
Job 134P	110,000
Indirect labour	300,000

(v) Other overhead costs were incurred	$ 500,000

(vi)Actual overhead costs were applied to jobs on the basis of machine hours. The machine hours consumed on each job were:

Job 114J	1,200
Job 117N	1,800
Job 128P	3,400
Job 133I	900
Job 134P	700

Required:
a.   Prepare the journal entries to record the previous events.

b. Assume that Jobs 114J and 117N were completed during the year. Prepare the journal entries to record the completion of these jobs.

c. Assume Job 117N was sold during the year for $3,000,000. Prepare the necessary journal entries to record the sale.

3. (LO 2; OH application rate, applied OH) Priscilla's Pottery produces a variety of finely crafted porcelain products, ranging from residential commodes to very delicate figurines. Production is sequenced in three departments. Production begins in the Sculpting Department, where clay materials are mixed and then hand-formed (some products are formed using moulds) into the required products. Next, the products go to the Glazing Department, where various protective coatings and paints are applied to the products. Lastly, the products move through the Curing Department, where they are "fired" in a kiln.

The Sculpting and Glazing Departments are very labour-intensive operations. Virtually no high-tech equipment is in use in either department.

Two years ago, the Curing Department underwent a transformation. One computer-driven kiln was installed to replace seven gas-fired kilns that were manually operated by 15 employees. Now, the entire department consists of two individuals who sequence materials into the computerized kiln, maintain the kiln, and place finished products in storage. The computerization of the Curing Department has vastly enhanced the quality of the finished products.

The company uses a job order costing system in which actual overhead costs are assigned to products using a plantwide overhead rate based on direct labour hours. For the most recent period, the total costs in each department were as follows:

	Sculpting	Glazing	Curing
Overhead:			
Indirect labour	$100,000	$ 50,000	$ 15,000
Utilities	5,000	4,000	40,000
Depreciation	20,000	8,000	90,000
Repairs & maintenance	2,000	2,500	20,000
Taxes & insurance	2,500	1,000	15,000
Total overhead	$129,500	$ 65,500	$180,000
Direct Materials	25,000	40,000	1,000
Direct labour	912,000	588,000	20,000

The actual direct labour hours worked in each department for the same period were:

	Sculpting	Glazing	Curing
Direct labour hours	114,000	84,000	2,000

Required:

a. Based on the previous information, compute the overhead application rate for the company.

b. The direct labour time expended in each department to complete two different products is as follows:

	Sculpting	Glazing	Curing
Product 1	6 h	3 h	1 h
Product 2	3 h	5 h	2 h

Compute the amount of overhead that would be applied to each product based on the rate you computed in part (a).

c. The company is considering a change in its product costing system to allow departmental application of overhead rather than plantwide application of overhead.

   i. Compute departmental overhead rates based on the departmental costs and direct labour information given earlier.

   ii. For the two products in part (b), recompute the amount of overhead that would be assigned if overhead were applied at the departmental level based on direct labour hours.

iii.   Compare the answers in part (ii) to your answers in part (b). Does this method provide a more accurate determination of costs? Why or why not?

d.   Is direct labour hours the best base for applying overhead in the Curing Department? Explain. If your answer is no, what alternative might be preferable?

4.   (LO 5; WA; two materials) Creative Cake Bakery Ltd. produces sheet cakes in mass quantities and uses a process costing system to account for its costs. The bakery production line is set up in one department. Batter is mixed first, with all necessary ingredients added at the start of production. The batter is poured into pans, baked, and cooled. The cake is then iced with a mixture of confectioners' sugar and water. The last step in the process is to let the icing harden. The cake is then moved to a display case. Icing is added when the cakes are at the 85% stage of completion.

Production and cost data for April 2005 follow. Beginning inventory consisted of 20 cakes, which were 80% complete as to labour and production overhead. The batter associated with beginning inventory had a cost of $66.10, and related conversion costs totalled $40.66. A total of 430 cakes were started during April, and 440 were completed. The ending inventory was 90% complete as to labour and production overhead. Costs for the month were batter, $1,324.40; icing, $166.50; and conversion cost, $857.34.

Required:

a.   Determine the equivalent units of production for each cost component for April for Creative Cake Bakery using the weighted average method.

b.   Calculate the cost per unit for each cost component for the bakery for April using the weighted average method.

c.   Determine the appropriate valuation for April's ending Work in Process Inventory and the units transferred to finished goods for sale.

d.   The bakery sells its cakes for $12.50 each. During April, 427 cakes were sold. What was the total gross profit margin on the sale of the cakes?

5.   (LO 5, 7; WA, two departments) The following is partial information for the month of March for Senna Company, a two-department manufacturer that uses process costing:

Department B

Work in process, beginning	12,000 units (2/3 converted)
Cost of beginning work in process:	
Transferred in from Department A	$9,500
Materials	$0
Conversion	$11,200
Units completed and transferred out during March	44,000 units
Units transferred in during March from Department A	?
Ending work in process	16,000 units (3/8 converted)
Material costs added during March	$13,200
Conversion costs added during March	$63,000

Other information:
(i)   Material is introduced at the beginning of the process in Department A, and additional material is added at the very end of the process in Department B.
(ii)   Conversion costs are incurred uniformly throughout both processes.
(iii) As the process in Department A is completed, goods are immediately transferred to Department B; as goods are completed in Department B, they are transferred to finished goods.
(iv) Unit costs of production in Department A in March were:

Materials	$0.55
Conversion	0.40
	$0.95

(v)   The company uses the weighted average method.

Required:

a.   Compute the cost of goods transferred out of Department B in March.

b.   Compute the cost of the March ending Work in Process Inventory in Department B.

6. (LO 5, 6; WA EUP, cost distribution) You are the production supervisor at Jen and Berry's. The company produces ice cream in one-litre containers and uses a weighted average process costing system to assign costs to production. All dairy ingredients are added at the beginning of the production process and pecans are added when the ice cream is 90% complete. The ice cream is put into containers in the second production department. Direct labour and overhead are incurred evenly throughout the process. For May, the company recorded the following results:

Litres in beginning inventory (40% complete)	12,000
Litres started	90,000
Litres completed (80% complete)	97,000

For the same period, total costs (beginning and current) were as follows:

Dairy ingredients	$107,100
Pecans	29,100
Conversion costs	88,880

Required:
a. Compute equivalent units of production for the dairy ingredients, pecans, and conversion.
b. Compute the cost per equivalent unit of production for each cost component.
c. Determine the cost transferred to the second production process and the cost of ending Work in Process Inventory.

7. (LO 5, 6; WA EUP, cost distribution) Western Wing Company produces a preservative used for canned food products. The company employs a weighted average process costing system. All material is introduced at the start of the process. Labour and overhead are at the same degree of completion throughout the process. The following information pertains to the company's October operations.

Unit Data

Beginning work in process (70% complete)	12,000 litres
Started this period	24,000 litres
Ending work in process (40% complete)	17,000 litres

Cost Data	Direct Material	Conversion
Beginning work in process	$ 9,500	$14,700
Incurred this period	35,600	73,080

Required:
a. Determine the total number of units to account for.
b. Compute the equivalent units of production for both material and conversion.
c. Compute the total cost to account for and total cost for both material and conversion.
d. Compute the cost per equivalent unit for material and conversion.
e. Compute the cost assigned to the goods transferred to Finished Goods Inventory and the cost of ending Work in Process Inventory.

8. (LO 6; WA, cost of production report) Ambrus Kecskés Inc. manufactures tubular steel products in a three-process operation. December information on the first process, Milling, follows:

Tonnes in process, December 1	12,000
Tonnes started in production	90,000
Tonnes in process, December 31	10,000

All material is added at the start of the process. Work in Process Inventory on December 1 was 40% complete as to labour and overhead. Work in Process Inventory on December 31 was 30% complete as to labour and overhead. A summary of costs follows:

	Beginning inventory	December
Material	$82,980	$630,000
Labour	27,290	540,000
Manufacturing overhead	23,320	357,490

Required:

Prepare a cost of production report for the Milling Department for December, assuming that Ambrus Kecskés Inc. uses a weighted average process costing system.

9. (LO 6; WA, cost of production report) Chip & Dale makes chipmunk and squirrel food. In the Mixing Department, all material is added at the beginning of the process. Labour and overhead are incurred evenly throughout the process. Unit and cost information for a recent period follows:

Beginning inventory (40% complete)	1,500 bags
Units started	56,000 bags
Ending inventory (80% complete)	800 bags

	Direct Material	Conversion
Beginning Work in Process Inventory	$ 2,440	$ 3,587
Current period costs	112,560	68,088

Required:

Prepare a cost of production report for Chip & Dale, assuming that the company employs a weighted average process costing system.

10. (LO 7, 8; WA, multidepartmental cost of production report) Alison Ground Automotive Ltd. manufactures car bumpers in a continuous two-department process. For August, company records indicate the following production results in the Machining and Finishing departments:

	Machining	Finishing
Units in beginning Work in Process Inventory	500	350
Units started or transferred in	40,000	?
Units in ending Work in Process Inventory	2,000	600

All materials are added at the beginning of production in Machining and at the end of production in Finishing. The company is highly automated and there is no separate labour category in either department. The conversion rates of completion for units in process at August 1 and 31 follow:

Machining:	August 1 (40%);	August 31 (80%)
Finishing:	August 1 (30%);	August 31 (60%)

Cost records indicate the following for the month:

	Machining		Finishing	
	Beginning	Current	Beginning	Current
Transferred in	N/A	N/A	$11,235	$?
Material	$11,140	$794,000	0	133,875
Conversion	5,105	618,450	4,533	246,432

Required:

Prepare a cost of production report for each department for August assuming that both departments use the weighted average costing method.

11. (LO 5, 6, 9, 10; Appendix 4A, WA and FIFO, cost distribution) David Letterman Company produces gourmet canned cat food. The company employs a process costing system to assign production costs to the units produced. For the second week in July, the firm had a beginning inventory of 20,000 cans that were 20% complete as to material and 50% complete as to conversion. During the week, an additional 100,000 cans were started in production. At the end of the week, 25,000 cans were still in process; these cans were 70% complete as to material and 80% complete as to conversion. Cost information follows:

	Direct Material	Conversion
Beginning Work in Process Inventory	$ 785	$ 915
Current period	15,190	8,400

Required:

a. Compute the total units to account for.
b. Determine the number of units started and completed.
c. Determine the total cost to account for.

d. Determine the equivalent units of production for each cost component based on the weighted average method.

e. Determine the cost per equivalent unit of production for each cost component based on the weighted average method.

f. Assign costs to goods transferred out and goods in ending work in process, using your answers in part (e).

g. Determine the equivalent units of production for each cost component, based on the FIFO method.

h. Based on the FIFO method, determine the cost per equivalent unit of production for each cost component.

i. Assign costs to goods transferred out and goods in ending work in process, using your answers in part (h).

12. (LO 5, 6, 9, 10; Appendix 4A, WA and FIFO, cost distribution) The Soda Factory uses a process costing system. All material is added at the start of the production process; overhead is applied on a machine hour basis and thus is not related to direct labour. Summary information for April 2005 on units and costs in the Blending Department follows:

Beginning inventory (40% complete as to labour; 35% complete as to overhead)	3,000,000 litres
Units started	15,000,000 litres
Ending Work in Process Inventory (60% complete as to labour; 70% complete as to overhead)	2,300,000 litres
Beginning Work in Process Inventory costs:	
Material	$ 390,000
Labour	285,200
Overhead	273,300
Current period costs:	
Material	$3,750,000
Labour	6,034,400
Overhead	9,593,400

Required:

a. Determine the equivalent units of production for each cost component based on the weighted average method.

b. Determine the cost per equivalent unit of production for each cost component based on the weighted average method.

c. Assign costs to goods transferred out and ending work in process using your answers to part (b).

d. Determine the equivalent units of production for each cost component based on the FIFO method.

e. Determine the cost per equivalent unit of production for each cost component based on the FIFO method.

f. Assign costs to goods transferred out and ending work in process using your answers to part (e).

g. What is the cost per equivalent unit for each cost component of the beginning inventory? Given this information, what questions would you, as plant manager, be asking and of whom?

13. (LO 10; Appendix 4A, FIFO, cost of production report) Assume that Chip & Dale (from Problem 9) uses a FIFO process costing system.

Required:

a. Prepare a cost of production report for the Mixing Department.

b. As the manager reviewing the cost of production report, what oddity would you notice about the beginning Work in Process Inventory cost per equivalent unit for conversion costs? What might explain this oddity?

14. (LO 8, 10; Appendix 4A, FIFO, multidepartmental cost of production report) Use the information in Problem 10 to prepare a cost of production report assuming that Alison Ground Automotive Ltd. uses a FIFO process costing system. Regardless of the amount calculated as the cost transferred out of Machining, assume that $1,364,055 was the amount transferred in to Finishing for the period.

15. (LO 5, 10; Appendix 4A, WA and FIFO, cost of production report) In a single-process production system, the Spookum Corporation produces wax lips for Halloween. For September 2005, the company's accounting records reflected the following:

Beginning Work in Process Inventory
    (100% complete as to Material A;
      0% complete as to Material B;
    40% complete as to Direct Labour;
    60% complete as to Manufacturing Overhead)   10,000 units
Started during the month   80,000 units
Ending Work in Process Inventory
    (100% complete as to Material A;
      0% complete as to Material B;
    30% complete as to Direct Labour;
    40% complete as to Manufacturing Overhead)   15,000 units

Cost Data	Beginning Inventory	September
Material A	$1,900	$8,000
Material B	0	37,500
Direct labour	1,195	7,550
Manufacturing overhead	1,530	9,000

Required:
a. For September, prepare a cost of production report, assuming the company uses the weighted average method.
b. Prepare a cost of production report for September, assuming the company uses the FIFO method.
c. Explain to your plant manager how the weighted average method helps disguise the apparently poor cost control in August.

16. (LO 5, 6, 9, 10; Appendix 4A, WA and FIFO) Chancer Industries, Inc. manufactures outdoor patio lights that are sold to major department stores under private labels. At the beginning of March 2005, the company had 4,000 lights in beginning Work in Process Inventory, which were 90% complete as to material and 75% complete as to conversion. During the month, 22,000 units were started; at the end of March, 5,000 remained in process. The ending Work in Process Inventory was 60% complete as to material and 40% complete as to conversion.

Actual cost data for the month were as follows:

	Material	Conversion	Total
Beginning inventory	$ 82,200	$ 31,000	$113,200
Current costs	397,800	245,000	642,800
Total costs	$480,000	$276,000	$756,000

Required:
a. Prepare EUP schedules under the weighted average and FIFO methods.
b. Prepare cost of production reports under the weighted average and FIFO methods.
c. Discuss the differences in the two reports prepared for part (b). Which would provide better information to departmental managers? Why?

17. (LO 5, 6, 9, 10; Appendix 4A, FIFO, WA). Lori Eisen Co., a baker of European breads and pastries, uses a process costing system. You are provided with the following selected information about its best-selling item for the month of November 2005.

	Physical Units	% Complete
Beginning work in process	10,000	60%
Units completed	60,000	
Ending work in process	20,000	40%

The beginning Work in Process Inventory consisted of the following:

Transferred-in costs	$10,875
Direct materials	1,750
Direct labour	1,750
Overhead applied	1,050

The actual overhead costs incurred during the month were $15,500. Costs added during November were:

Transferred-in costs	$69,125
Direct material	15,750
Direct labour	29,000
Overhead applied	?

When the process is 15% complete, 40% of the direct materials are added, with the remainder being added when the process is 50% complete. Conversion costs are incurred uniformly throughout processing. Overhead is applied on the basis of direct labour costs.

Required:

a. Is manufacturing overhead under- or overapplied during November? If so, by how much?

b. What was the cost of the units completed and transferred out to the next department during November:
    i.   under the weighted average method?
    ii. under the FIFO method?

c. What was the weighted average cost of the ending WIP inventory for November?

d. Will using the FIFO method result in a higher or lower cost per unit of ending WIP inventory for November? Why is there a difference between the FIFO and weighted average methods? Do not calculate the amount.

18. (LO 6; WA; spoilage) The Deroche Co. Ltd. uses a weighted average process costing system in accounting for its product, which moves through two manufacturing departments.

In Department 2, material is not added until the product is 95% complete. Inspection takes place when the product is 80% complete and it is expected that 3% of the units inspected will be defective.

Information for Department 2 for the month of October was as follows:

	Units	Dollars
Beginning inventory, 40% complete:	1,000	
Department 1 costs		$ 5,700
Department 2 costs		980
Received from Department 1	10,000	60,300
Department 2 costs:		
Materials		5,760
Conversion costs		25,000
Transferred to Finished Goods	9,600	
Ending inventory, 90% complete	1,050	

Required:

Prepare a cost of production report for Department 2 for the month of October.

(Problems 17–18 adapted by the author from *Management Accounting examinations,* published by the Certified General Accountants Association of Canada © CGA-Canada, 1998 (#17) and 1997 (#18), used by permission.)

CASES

1. Paul Williams Ltd. manufactures ergonomically designed furniture for computer stations. Williams' work in process inventory at May 31, 2005, consisted of the following jobs.

Job No.	Item	Units	Accumulated Cost
CC723	Computer caddy	20,000	$ 900,000
CH291	Chair	15,000	431,000
PS812	Printer stand	25,000	250,000
			$1,581,000

At May 31, 2005, the company's finished goods inventory consisted of four items.

Item	Quantity & Unit Cost	Accumulated Cost
Computer caddy	7,500 units @ $64 each	$ 480,000
Chair	19,400 units @ $35 each	679,000
Printer stand	21,000 units @ $55 each	1,155,000
Desk	11,200 units @ $102 each	1,142,400
		$3,456,400

At the end of May, the balance in the Paul Williams Ltd. materials inventory account, which includes both raw materials and purchased parts, was $668,000. Additions to, and requisitions from, the raw materials inventory during the month of May include the following:

	Raw Materials	Purchased Parts
Additions	$242,000	$396,000
Requisitions:		
Job CC723	51,000	104,000
Job CH291	3,000	10,000
Job PS812	124,000	87,000
Job DS444	65,000	187,000

Williams applies manufacturing overhead on the basis of machine hours. The company's estimated (budgeted) manufacturing overhead budget for the fiscal year ending May 31, 2005, totals $4,500,000, and the company plans to expend 900,000 machine hours during this period. Through the first 11 months of the year, a total of 830,000 machine hours were used, and total manufacturing overhead amounted to $4,274,500.

During the month of May, machine hours and direct labour hours consisted of the following:

Account	Machine Hours	Direct Labour Hours	Direct Labour Cost
CC723	12,000	11,600	$122,400
CH291	4,400	3,600	43,200
PS812	19,500	14,300	200,500
DS444	14,000	12,500	138,000
Indirect labour		3,000	29,400
Supervision			57,600
			$591,100

Listed below are the jobs that were completed and the unit sales for the month of May.

Job No.	Item	Quantity Completed
CC723	Computer caddy	20,000
CH291	Chair	15,000
DS444	Desk	5,000

Item	Quantity Shipped
Computer caddy	17,500
Chair	21,000
Printer stand	18,000
Desk	6,000

Required:

a. Is it appropriate for this company to use a job order cost system? Explain.

b. Calculate the dollar balance in Paul Williams Ltd.'s Work in Process inventory account as of May 31, 2005.

c. Calculate the dollar value of the chairs in Paul Williams Ltd.'s finished goods inventory as of May 31, 2005.

d. Explain the proper accounting treatment for overapplied or underapplied overhead balances when using a job order cost system.

2. Valport Company employs a job order cost system. Manufacturing overhead is applied on the basis of machine hours (MH) using a predetermined overhead rate. The current fiscal year rate of $15.00 per MH is based on an estimated manufacturing level of 80,000 machine hours. Valport's policy is to close the over/underapplication of manufacturing overhead to Cost of Goods Sold.

Operations for the year ended November 30, 2005, have been completed. All of the accounting entries have been made for the year except the following: application of manufacturing overhead to the jobs worked on during November; the transfer of costs from Work in Process to Finished Goods for the jobs completed in November; and the transfer of costs from Finished Goods to Cost of Goods Sold for the jobs that have been sold during November.

Summarized data that have been accumulated from the accounting records as of October 31, 2005, and for November are as follows. Jobs N11-007, N11-013, and N11-015 were completed during November 2005. All completed jobs except Job N11-013 had been turned over to customers by the close of business on November 30, 2005.

November 2005 Activity

Work in Process

Job No.	Balance 10/31/05	Direct Materials	Direct Labour	Machine Hours
N11-007	$ 87,000	$ 1,500	$ 4,500	300
N11-013	55,000	4,000	12,000	1,000
N11-015	0	25,600	26,700	1,400
D12-002	0	37,900	20,000	2,500
D12-003	0	26,000	16,800	800
Totals	$142,000	$95,000	$80,000	6,000

Operating Activity	Activity Through 10/31/2005	November 2005 Activity
Manufacturing overhead incurred		
Indirect materials	$ 125,000	$ 9,000
Indirect labour	345,000	30,000
Utilities	245,000	22,000
Depreciation	385,000	35,000
Total incurred overhead	$1,100,000	$96,000
Other items		
Material purchases*	$965,000	$98,000
Direct labour costs	845,000	80,000
Machine hours	73,000	6,000

Account Balances at Beginning of Fiscal Year December 1, 2004

Materials Inventory*	$105,000
Work in Process Inventory	60,000
Finished Goods Inventory	125,000

* Materials purchases and materials inventory consist of both direct and indirect materials. The balance of the Materials Inventory account as of November 30, 2005, is $85,000.

Required:
a. Valport Company uses a predetermined overhead rate to apply manufacturing overhead to its jobs.
   i. Explain why a business uses a predetermined overhead rate to apply manufacturing overhead to its jobs.
   ii. How much manufacturing overhead would Valport have applied to jobs through October 31, 2005?
   iii. How much manufacturing overhead would be applied to jobs by Valport during November 2005?

iv. Determine the amount by which the manufacturing overhead is over- or underapplied as of November 30, 2005. Be sure to indicate whether the overhead is over- or underapplied.

v. Over- or underapplied overhead must be eliminated at the end of the accounting period. Explain why Valport's method of closing over- or underapplied overhead to Cost of Goods Sold is acceptable in this case.

b. Determine the balance in Valport Company's Finished Goods Inventory at November 30, 2005.

c. Prepare a Statement of Cost of Goods Manufactured for Valport Company for the year ended November 30, 2005.

3. Naiman Industries manufactures moulded chairs. The company uses the weighted average method for inventory valuation. The three models of moulded chairs, which are all variations of the same design, are Standard (can be stacked), Deluxe (with arms), and Executive (with arms and padding). The company uses batch manufacturing and has a process costing system.

Naiman Industries has an extrusion operation and subsequent operations to form, trim, and finish the chairs. Plastic sheets are produced by the extrusion operation, some of which are sold directly to other manufacturers. During the forming operation, the remaining plastic sheets are moulded into chair seats and the legs are added. The Standard model is sold after this operation. During the trim operation, the arms are added to the Deluxe and Executive models and the chair edges are smoothed. Only the Executive model enters the finish operation where the padding is added. All of the units produced receive the same steps within each operation.

The May production run had a total manufacturing cost of $898,000. The units of production and direct material costs incurred were as follows:

	Units Produced	Extrusion Materials	Form Materials	Trim Materials	Finish Materials
Plastic sheets	5,000	$ 60,000			
Standard model	6,000	72,000	$24,000		
Deluxe model	3,000	36,000	12,000	$ 9,000	
Executive model	2,000	24,000	8,000	6,000	$12,000
	16,000	$192,000	$44,000	$15,000	$12,000

Manufacturing costs applied during May were:

	Extrusion Operation	Form Operation	Trim Operation	Finish Operation
Direct labour	$152,000	$60,000	$30,000	$18,000
Manufacturing overhead	240,000	72,000	39,000	24,000

Required:

a. For each product produced by Naiman Industries during May, determine the (1) unit cost and (2) total cost. Be sure to account for all costs incurred during the month, and support your answer with appropriate calculations.

b. Assume that 1,000 units of the Deluxe model remained in Work in Process Inventory at the end of the month. These units were 100% complete in the trim operation. Determine the value of the 1,000 units of the Deluxe model in Naiman Industries' Work in Process Inventory at the end of May.

(CMA adapted)

4. Fenmore Company makes rubber beach balls. Each ball passes through three separate departments before it is complete and ready for shipment to sporting goods wholesalers. The ball begins in the Moulding Department, then passes into the Vulcanizing Department, and is finished in the Packaging Department. Product costs are separately tracked by department and assigned by use of a process costing system. Overhead is applied to production in each department at a rate of 70% of the department's direct labour cost. The following information pertains to departmental operations for the second complete year of the company's existence.

WIP Inventory—Moulding		
BI	50,000	
DM	80,000	?
DL	80,000	
OH	?	
EI	25,000	

Work in Process—Vulcanizing		
BI	80,000	
Trans In	?	320,000
DM	40,000	
DL	?	
OH	?	
Ending Inventory	50,000	

WIP Inventory—Packaging		
BI	120,000	
Trans. In	?	
DM	?	
DL	20,000	?
OH	?	
Ending Inventory	90,000	

Finished Goods Inventory		
Beg.	185,000	
CGM	450,000	
		520,000
Ending Inventory	?	

Required:

a. What was the cost of goods transferred from the Moulding Department to the Vulcanizing Department for the year?

b. How much direct labour cost was incurred in the Vulcanizing Department? How much overhead?

c. How much direct material cost was charged to products passing through the Packaging Department?

d. Prepare the journal entries for all interdepartmental transfers of products, including the transfer from the Packaging Department to the Finished Goods Inventory.

5. JT Holestrom Company produces a wood-refinishing kit that sells for $17.95. The final processing of the kits occurs in the Packaging Department. An internal quilted wrap is applied at the beginning of the packaging process. A compartmentalized outside box printed with instructions and the company's name and logo is added when units are 60% through the process. Conversion costs occur evenly throughout the packaging process. The following data pertain to the activities of the Packaging Department during October.

   (i) Beginning Work in Process Inventory was 10,000 units, 40% complete as to conversion costs.

   (ii) 30,000 units were started and completed in the month.

   (iii) There were 10,000 units in ending work in process, 80% complete as to conversion costs.

   The Packaging Department's October costs were:

Quilted wrap	$80,000
Outside boxes	50,000
Direct labour	22,000
Applied overhead ($3.00 per direct labour dollar)	66,000

   The costs transferred in from prior processing were $3 per unit. The cost of goods sold for the month was $240,000, and the ending Finished Goods Inventory was $84,000. Holestrom uses the FIFO method of process costing.

   Required:

   As the controller for Holestrom Company, you have been asked to analyze the activities of the Packaging Department for October.

   a. Prepare a calculation of equivalent units of production for the October activity in the Packaging Department.

   b. Determine the cost per equivalent unit of the October production.

   c. Assuming that the actual overhead incurred during October was $5,000 more than the overhead applied, describe how the cost of the ending Work in Process Inventory would be determined. (Appendix)

   (CMA adapted)

6. Jenny Fong Corp. manufactures quality paint in a single production department. Production begins with the addition of chemicals at the beginning of the process; these

are blended and the paint is canned. Canning occurs when the mixture reaches the 90% stage of completion. The litre cans are then transferred to the Shipping Department for crating and shipment. Labour and overhead are added continuously throughout the process. Manufacturing overhead is applied at the rate of $3.00 per direct labour hour.

Prior to May, when a change in the process was implemented, work in process inventories were insignificant. The change in process enables greater production but results in substantial amounts of work in process for the first time. The company has always used the weighted average method to determine equivalent production and unit costs. Now, production management is considering changing from the weighted average method to the first-in, first-out method (FIFO).

The following data relate to actual production during May:

Units (Litres)

Work in Process Inventory, May 1 (25% complete)	4,000
Sent to Shipping Department	20,000
Started in May	21,000
Work in Process Inventory, May 31 (80% complete)	5,000

Beginning Work in Process Inventory Costs

Work in Process Inventory, May 1: 4,000 litres (25% complete)

Direct materials—chemicals	$45,600
Direct labour ($10 per hour)	6,250
Manufacturing overhead	1,875

May Costs Added

Direct materials—chemicals	$228,400
Direct materials—cans	7,000
Direct labour ($10 per hour)	35,000
Manufacturing overhead	10,500

Required:

a. Prepare a schedule of equivalent units for each cost element for May using the
   (i) weighted average method
   (ii) FIFO method

b. Calculate the cost (to the nearest cent) per equivalent unit for each element for May using the
   (i) weighted average method
   (ii) FIFO method

c. Assign the costs to the goods transferred out and to the ending Work in Process Inventory using the
   (i) weighted average method
   (ii) FIFO method

d. Discuss the advantages and disadvantages of using the weighted average method versus the FIFO method, and explain under what circumstances each method should be used. (Appendix)

(CMA adapted)

ETHICS AND QUALITY DISCUSSIONS

1. In March 2005, the Aviation Administration began investigating allegations that some maintenance supervisors for one of the large airlines had been signing off on maintenance work that actually was not performed on individual aircraft.

   a. Why could an individual airplane be considered a "job" for an airline company?

   b. One of the maintenance tasks that was allegedly not completed was the washing of a cabin head air exchanger. Assume the following facts. Some of the airline's mechanics were on strike. The task is considered routine; the plane was only one year old and in excellent condition. The plane was scheduled to depart the airport in 30 minutes on a fully booked flight; washing the exchange filter would have taken a minimum of one hour. The airline is currently having problems with on-time departures and arrivals. The plane arrived safely at its destination.

Discuss the possible perceptions and thoughts of the maintenance supervisor at the time that this maintenance should be performed.

   c. Discuss the perceptions and thoughts of the passengers at the terminal if the maintenance were performed.

   d. Discuss the ethical issues involved.

2. Dr. Lelia Sulyma is a plastic surgeon who treats both paying and nonpaying patients. In the past month, several very wealthy patients have been in for tummy tucks, face lifts, and liposuction. One patient, on whom Dr. Sulyma has worked countless hours for over a year, is a young boy who was in a motorcycle accident; the child is a pro bono case.

Required:

   a. Discuss the practical aspects of shifting some appropriately assigned overhead costs from the child's case to the wealthy patients.

   b. Discuss the ethical aspects of shifting some appropriately assigned overhead costs from the child's case to the wealthy patients.

   c. By accepting nonpaying patients who require such extensive treatment, Dr. Sulyma is not making a reasonable income from her profession. She is considering closing her practice and working only in a private for-profit hospital. Do you have any suggestions on how she might be able to continue serving both charity and wealthy patients and still earn a reasonable income?

3. McDonald's announced plans to install kitchen "McRobots." These automatons are supposed to put the "fast" back in fast food. They will cook and shake fries and then dump them in bins for scooping. They will also prepare drinks for customers.

Required:

   a. Do you foresee a fully automated McDonald's in the near future? Why or why not?

   b. Do you think computers would be better at the drive-in windows than humans? Why or why not?

   c. Do you think the use of computers will reduce the number of "rejects" (hamburgers that have been kept hot for more than 30 minutes) at McDonald's? Why or why not?

4. One of the more hotly contested political issues in recent years was whether the minimum wage should be increased (or should be increased again). Proponents of an increase in the minimum wage argue that such an increase is necessary for low-paid employees to maintain a decent standard of living. Opponents suggest that an increase in the cost of labour would cause firms to fire employees to control labour cost increases—thereby harming the very group that was intended to be the beneficiary of the wage increase.

Required:

Analyze the likely effects of an increase in the minimum wage from the perspective of

   a. its likely effects on quality

   b. ethical issues

5. Empowering workers has been an increasingly popular idea to reduce costs and raise productivity; an effort to "white-collarize" factories has been adopted by about 40% of manufacturers. In a process environment, workers are empowered to stop production lines if defects or variations are noticed. Direct labour costs are reduced and overhead costs rise. But are all workers ready for empowerment? Apparently not—some workers find it extremely stressful.

Required:

   a. As an employee, would you want to be empowered, and thus responsible for activities such as multitasking (being able to operate a variety of equipment), machine maintenance, quality, and team member discipline? Why or why not?

   b. As a manager, would you want your employees to be empowered? Why or why not?

   c. What impacts might employee empowerment have on a process environment?

6. FulRange Inc. produces complex printed circuits for stereo amplifiers. The circuits are sold primarily to major component manufacturers, and any production overruns are sold to small manufacturers at a substantial discount. The small manufacturer segment appears very profitable because the basic operating budget assigns all fixed expenses to units made for the major manufacturers, the only predictable market.

A common product defect that occurs in production is a "drift" caused by failure to maintain precise heat levels during the production process. Rejects from the 100% testing program can be reworked to acceptable levels if the defect is drift. However, in a recent analysis of customer complaints, George Wilson, the cost accountant, and the quality control engineer have ascertained that normal rework does not bring the circuits up to standard. Sampling shows that about one-half of the reworked circuits will fail after extended, high-volume amplifier operation. The incidence of failure in the reworked circuits is projected to be about 10% over one to five years' operation.

Unfortunately, there is no way to determine which reworked circuits will fail, because testing will not detect this problem. The rework process could be changed to correct the problem, but the cost/benefit analysis for the suggested change in the rework process indicates that it is not practical. FulRange's marketing analyst has indicated that this problem will have a significant impact on the company's reputation and customer satisfaction if it is not corrected. Consequently, the board of directors would interpret this problem as having serious negative implications for the company's profitability.

Wilson has included the circuit failure and rework problem in his report for the upcoming quarterly meeting of the board of directors. Due to the potentially adverse economic impact, Wilson has followed a longstanding practice of highlighting this information.

After reviewing the reports to be presented, the plant manager and her staff were upset and indicated to the controller that he should control his people better. "We can't upset the board with this kind of material. Tell Wilson to tone that down. Maybe we can get it by this meeting and have some time to work on it. People who buy those cheap systems and play them that loud shouldn't expect them to last forever."

The controller called Wilson into his office and said, "George, you'll have to bury this one. The probable failure of reworks can be referred to briefly in the oral presentation, but it should not be mentioned or highlighted in the advance material mailed to the board."

Wilson feels strongly that the board will be misinformed on a potentially serious loss of income if he follows the controller's orders. Wilson discussed the problem with the quality control engineer, who simply remarked, "That's your problem, George."

Required:
a. Discuss the ethical considerations that George Wilson should recognize in deciding how to proceed in this matter.
b. Explain what ethical responsibilities should be accepted in this situation by
   (i)   The controller
   (ii) The quality control engineer
   (iii) The plant manager and her staff
c. What should George Wilson do in this situation? Explain your answer.

(IMA adapted)

COMMUNICATIONS ACTIVITIES

1. Assume that the pedals, wheels, chain, and gears on your bicycle are the equivalent of a manufacturing process. Further assume that the bicycle is in perfect working order. Consider how many revolutions of the pedals would be required to move the bicycle a distance of 100 metres (one production run), given that the bicycle is always in the same gear. Assume that this process, repeated many times (trials), is equivalent to many production runs.

Required:

a. Even though the bicycle is in perfect working order, why will the number of revolutions required to move the bicycle a distance of 100 metres be expected to vary somewhat from one trial to the next?

b. Suppose the bicycle is in perfect working order and you conduct 100 trials in which you pedal the bicycle a distance of 100 metres. How could the resulting information be used as a statistical guide in future tests of whether the bicycle is "in control"?

2. It is interesting how process-oriented companies organize their activities. For some global industries, almost all processing steps for a given product are performed in a single location. For other industries, processing steps are distributed strategically around the globe. Consider the following industries: chemicals, pharmaceuticals, and lumber production.

    Required:

    Prepare a short paper that addresses the following questions:

    a. What factors are likely to drive the decision to scatter production activities geographically?

    b. What factors are likely to limit the extent to which a company in one of the three industries mentioned above can geographically distribute activities?

3. Distinguish between job order and process cost accounting. For each system, give at least two examples of industries for which the specified system would be appropriate. Explain why.

PROJECTS

1. Make a list of the prominent manufacturing businesses in your area and indicate whether each would more likely use process costing or job order costing. Identify the reasons each business was so classified.

2. Choose a product that is manufactured in your area. Draft an illustration of the manufacturing process of that product and indicate the points at which you assume that the various manufacturing components would be added. By mail, by phone, or in person, contact the manufacturer to see how well your illustration portrayed the actual process.

USING THE INTERNET

1. Many companies use job costing software. Search sites on-line that offer job costing packages for manufacturers.

2. Search the Internet to identify a vendor of process costing software. Read the on-line literature provided by the vendor regarding the software.

    Required:

    a. Make a list of the products that are available.

    b. Write a report that describes the major features of the software in the areas of product costing and cost control.

3. Visit the Hershey's Web site at www.hersheys.com and take a tour of the plant to see how chocolate is processed.

SOLUTIONS TO SELF-TEST QUESTIONS

1. a: Job cost sheet.

2. a: Helps to better estimate future jobs.

3. c: The average cost method of process costing commingles prior-period (BWIP) and current costs. It does not consider the degree of completion of BWIP when computing EUP.

	Units	% Complete	CC EUP
Completed	7,400	100	7,400
EWIP	2,300	60	1,380
Equivalent units			8,780

4. d: Transferred in (4,000 × $5) + $0 for material since product is only 40% complete + 40% of (4,000 × $3) = $24,800.

5. b: The total cost per equivalent unit transferred out is equal to the unit cost for transferred-in cost, material cost, and conversion cost. Transferred-in cost is by definition 100% complete. Given that materials are added at the beginning of the process in Department Two, all units are complete as to materials. Conversion costs are assumed to be uniformly incurred.

	Units	T-1	%	Mat	%	CC
Completed*	12	12	100	12	100	12
EWIP*	8	8	100	8	75	6
Equivalent units*		20		20		18

Transferred in:	($12,000 + $29,000) ÷ 20,000 EUP =	$2.05
Materials cost:	($2,500 + $5,500) ÷ 20,000 EUP =	0.40
Conversion cost:	($1,000 + $5,000) ÷ 18,000 EUP =	0.33
Total unit cost		$2.78

*in 000's

6. b:

Direct materials cost per unit	($200,000 ÷ 400)	$ 500
Conversion cost per unit	[$200,000 ÷ (400 × 0.4)]	1,250
		$1,750

7. c: 400 units + 1,200 units − 200 units = 1,400 units

8. c: Under the FIFO method, EUP for a period includes only the work done that period and excludes any work done in a prior period. The total of conversion cost EUP for the period is calculated below.

	Units	Work Done in Current Period	CC (EUP)
BWIP	25,000	20%	5,000
Started and Completed	75,000	100%	75,000
EWIP	60,000	50%	30,000
Total EUP			110,000

The total of the conversion costs for the period is given as $143,000. Dividing by total EUP of 110,000 gives a unit cost of $1.30. Thus, the conversion cost of the EWIP inventory is $39,000 ($1.30 × 30,000 EUP in EWIP).

9. c: The total of the units started last period and completed this period is 25,000. These units were 80% complete at the start of the period, at a cost of $22,000. The cost to complete was $6,500 (5,000 EUP × $1.30). The total cost of $28,500 is divided by 25,000 to obtain the unit cost. Thus the current unit cost of production is $1.30. The weighted average method would cost all units transferred out at $1.27 ($165,000 ÷ 130,000 units).

10. d: FIFO does not commingle costs. For material, there are 1,600 units complete plus the 400 that are in ending inventory. Use only B + C + D for FIFO. For conversion costs, 60% of 500 is B + 1,600 of the started are complete (100%) + 25% of Ending Inventory of 400 units = 2,000.

ENDNOTES

1. *National Post*, December 15, 1999.

2. Gordon Pitts, "Ganong Boss Aims for Sweet Spot," B4 Cdn Business, *The Globe and Mail*, March 3, 2003.

3. Chuck Brown, "Make No Bones About These Chicken Bones," *New Brunswick Telegraph Journal*, November 25, 2002

4. www.ganong.com

5. Roger V. Dickeson, "We Need Better Tools," *Printing Impressions*, Philadelphia, September 2001, pp. 116–117.

6. To eliminate the need for repetition, units should be read to mean either products or services, since job order product costing is applicable to both manufacturing and service companies. For the same reason, *produced* can mean *manufactured* or *performed*.

7. Cheryl Caswell, "Not Just Off the Cuff; Fourth-Generation Tailor Finds There's Still a Market for Custom-Made Clothing," *Charleston Daily Mail*, Charleston, W.V., November 26, 2001.

8. Although actual overhead may be assigned to jobs, such an approach would be less common because total overhead would not be known until the period was over, causing an unwarranted delay in overhead assignment.

9. One alternative to a time sheet prepared for the day is an individual time ticket for each job. These forms could be handed out by supervisors to employees as employees are assigned new jobs. Another alternative is to have supervisors maintain a record of which employees worked on what jobs for what period of time. This alternative is extremely difficult to implement, however, if a supervisor is overseeing a large number of employees or when the employees are dispersed through a large section of the plant.

10. This example is based on an article by Leonard A. Robinson and Loudell Ellis Robinson, "Steering a Boat Maker Through Cost Shoals." *Management Accounting*, January 1983, pp. 60–66. Published by Institute of Management Accountants, Montvale, N.J.

11. A third category (spoilage/breakage) does exist. It is assumed at this point that such happenings do not occur. Accounting for spoilage in process costing situations will be covered in Appendix 4B of this chapter.

12. As discussed in Chapter 2, overhead may be applied to products using a variety of traditional (direct labour hours or machine hours) or a variety of nontraditional allocation (such as number of machine set-ups, kilograms of material moved, and/or number of materials requisitions) bases. The number of equivalent unit computations that need to be made results from the number of different cost pools and overhead allocation bases established in a department or company. If there are multiple cost pools and allocation bases, a separate computation will need to be made for each cost pool that is at a different level of completion. Additionally, some highly automated manufacturers may not account for direct labour cost separately (because it is too insignificant); thus, only a single conversion cost category would exist.

13. *National Post*, December 15, 1999.

14. Canada News Wire, "Ganong Bros. Limited Celebrates 130 Sweet Years!" *Business/Financial News*, January 28, 2003.

15. Marina Strauss, "Quebecker pegged as candy man," B3, *The Globe and Mail*, September 23, 2003.

Chapter 5

Introduction to a Standard Cost System

LEARNING OBJECTIVES

After reading this chapter, you should be able to answer the following questions:

1 Why are standard cost systems used?

2 How are standards for material and labour set?

3 How are material, labour, and overhead variances calculated?

4 How can variances be used for control and performance evaluation purposes?

5 How do organizational evolution and desired level of attainability affect standard setting?

6 How are standard setting and standard usage changing in modern business?

7 What journal entries are needed in a standard cost system? (Appendix 5A)

8 What use do standard costs have in a process costing system? (Appendix 5B)

www.brightpearlseafood.com

Bright Pearl Seafood Restaurant Inc.

BRIGHT PEARL SEAFOOD RESTAURANT INC., a large restaurant specializing in Chinese cuisine, operates in downtown Toronto. The restaurant serves thousands of customers per week. The company's mission statement expresses a philosophy of producing and serving very high-quality products. It has been a winner of many awards for both service and food quality.

Production is enhanced because Bright Pearl's workforce is highly trained. Additionally, the workers are provided with tools and resources to perform effectively. Workers strive to eliminate downtime, reduce scrap, and maintain consistently high production quality.

The company operates in an area of strong competition and thus differentiates its products by focusing on providing high levels of product and service quality to its customers. In addition, this quality focus provides the underlying rationale for the company's emphasis on employee training.

Preparing dishes at the restaurant is a standardized process; each order needs to be identical to the last. Because of the substantial level of competition, price is set by the competition and Bright Pearl must exercise extreme cost control efforts. Thus, material and labour specifications must be available and adhered to for each product so that the company can meet customer expectations and remain profitable. Standard costing allows company management to understand the quality expected and costs that will be incurred in the preparation of each dish, and, more important, what impacts deviations from these standards will have on costs and profits.

SOURCE: Interview with Stephen Chan, Bright Pearl Seafood Restaurant Inc., 346-368 Spadina Avenue, Toronto, Ontario; www.brightpearlseafood.com

*T*he major goal at Bright Pearl Seafood Restaurant is to deliver outstanding customer service. To help attain this goal and have strategic success, the company establishes production standards that allow management to determine causes of variations, take corrective action, and monitor and reward performance. Performance can be evaluated by comparing actual results against a predetermined measure or criterion. Thus, standards (or benchmarks) must exist to ensure product quality and consistency, and thereby to implement strategy. Without the actual-to-standard comparison, employees and management cannot know whether expectations are met or whether problems exist. Such lack of knowledge makes managerial control impossible.

Almost all organizations develop and use some type of standards. For example, charities set a standard for the amount of annual contributions to be raised, sales managers set standards against which employee business expenses are compared, and hotels have standard lengths of time for cleaning a guest room. Because different production methods and information objectives exist in organizations, no single standard cost system is appropriate for all situations. Thus, many forms of standard cost systems are in use. Some systems use standard prices but not standard quantities; other systems (especially in service entities) use labour, but not material, standards. Traditional standard cost systems require price and quantity standards for both material and labour.

This chapter discusses a traditional standard cost system using standards for the three product cost components: direct material (DM), direct labour (DL), and manufacturing overhead (OH). The chapter examples assume the use of only one material and one labour category in production activities. The chapter provides information on why standard cost systems are used, how material and labour standards are developed, how deviations (or variances) from standard are calculated, and what information can be gained from detailed variance analysis. Innovative trends in the use of standard costing systems are also discussed. Journal entries used in a standard cost system are presented in Appendix 5A.

Why are standard cost systems used?

standards
benchmarks or norms against which actual results may be compared

standard costing system
a product costing method using unit norms for production costs

standard cost
a budgeted or estimated cost to manufacture a single unit of product or perform a single service

STANDARD COST SYSTEMS

Standards can be used with either job order or process costing systems to provide important information for managerial planning, controlling, and decision making. Standard costing assists in setting budgets and evaluating managerial performance.

A report in *Cost Management Update* states that a large percentage of companies are using standard costing. A **standard costing system** of some kind is used by 64.7% of all the survey respondents. Standard costing is favoured among all types of manufacturing firms. Of the 61 nonmanufacturing firms, roughly a third (34.4%) use standard costs, reflecting the difficulty in developing standards for unique services provided to customers. Of the firms using standard costing, about 16% report using activity-based costing (ABC discussed in Chapter 6) to develop or update cost standards.

The challenges faced by nonmanufacturing firms using **standard costs** are as varied as the types of firms represented. Allocating overhead was cited as the number one challenge in developing standards.[1]

In planning, standards are used to coordinate activities more quickly and easily than otherwise would be possible. For example, if Bright Pearl Seafood Restaurant plans to produce 20,000 spring rolls in March, management can project materials, labour, and overhead costs by reviewing the standard costs established for each of these cost elements.

Standards can also be used for motivation and control. One requirement for control is that managers be aware of differences between the actual activities and resource consumption and the expected activities and resource consumption. A standard cost system helps companies recognize **variances**—or deviations between actual and standard costs or quantities—and correct problems resulting from excess costs or usage. Actual cost systems do not provide these benefits.

variance
any difference between actual and standard costs or quantities

When the variances are significant, this is a signal for investigation. Managers, having discovered the cause, can exert influence to correct it. Suppose Bright Pearl's actual cost for raw materials for the 20,000 spring rolls was $1,000 less than expected. Management would investigate this difference to determine its cause. Several possibilities exist: the price paid for the wrappers and the filling was less than expected, or new technology or employee cross-training and team efforts made production more efficient by generating less scrap and, thus, lowered cost.

Note that the explanations of the $1,000 difference suggest that there are two possible underlying causes of the variance: one relates to raw material cost and the other relates to quantity of raw material used. These causes can exist separately or together. To evaluate performance properly, managers need to be able to determine which part of the total variance relates to which cause.

The availability of standards speeds up and improves decision making because managers have a predetermined, rigorous set of expectations upon which to base decisions, such as accepting a job at a specified price. Performance evaluation is also improved through comparing actual and standard costs of operations and highlighting significant differences.

DEVELOPMENT OF A STANDARD COST SYSTEM

Although initiated by manufacturing companies, standard cost systems are also applicable to service entities. Regardless of the type of organization, it is critical that the standards development process is handled in a knowledgeable and thorough manner.

The estimated cost to manufacture a single unit of product or to perform a single service is the standard cost. Standards are traditionally established for each component (material, labour, and overhead) of product cost. Developing a standard cost involves judgment and practicality in identifying the types of material and labour to be used and their related quantities and prices. Developing standards for

These customers are enjoying freshly made spring rolls at Bright Pearl.

overhead requires that costs have been appropriately classified according to cost behaviour, valid allocation bases have been chosen, and a reasonable level of activity has been specified.

A primary objective in manufacturing a product or performing a service is to minimize unit cost while achieving certain quality specifications. Almost all products can be manufactured with a variety of inputs (material, labour, and overhead) that would generate the same basic output. This is true even after output quality has been specified. Input choices ultimately affect the standards that are set.

Quantity and price standards can be developed once management has established the design and manufacturing process that will produce the desired output quality and has determined which input resources will be used. Standards should be developed by representatives from the following areas: management accounting, product design, industrial engineering, human resources, data processing, purchasing, and production management. It is especially important in the process of standard setting to involve managers and, to some extent, employees whose performance will be compared with the standards. Involvement helps assure credibility of the standards and helps motivate personnel to operate as closely as possible to the standards. Information from suppliers can also be useful, especially in the area of setting material price standards.

LEARNING OBJECTIVE 2

How are standards for material and labour set?

MATERIAL STANDARDS

In developing material standards, the specific direct material components used to manufacture the product or to perform the service must be identified and listed. Three things must be known about the materials: what inputs are needed, what the quality of those inputs must be, and what quantities of inputs of the specified quality are needed.

Determination of what inputs are needed is a design (recipe) specification. For example, to make a spring roll, Bright Pearl must have wrappers, pork, prawns, spring onions, ginger, bean sprouts, and carrots. Many cost–benefit trade-offs are involved in making quality decisions, so managers should consult material experts, accountants, and marketing personnel to determine which choices are most appropriate. Generally, as the grade of raw material rises, so does the cost. Decisions about material input components usually attempt to balance the interrelationships of cost, quality, quantity, and selling price.

Each spring roll is manufactured according to specifications.

Given the quality selected for each necessary component, physical quantity estimates can be made in terms of weight, size, volume, or other measures. These estimates can be based on results of engineering tests, opinions of people using the materials, and/or historical data. Information about direct material components, their specifications (including quality), and their quantities are listed on a **bill of materials**. Even companies that do not have formal standard cost systems are likely to develop a bill of materials for each of their products simply as a guide for production activity.

The example of Bright Pearl Seafood Restaurant illustrates that cost accounting can be used in businesses other than large manufacturing concerns.

We will use the firm of Margaret White Clothing Ltd. to illustrate the use of standard costing in a manufacturing operation. This firm, located in western Canada, specializes in the production of men's shirts.

Exhibit 5-1 illustrates a bill of materials for a six-button men's shirt produced by Margaret White Clothing Ltd. (MWC). Company management has chosen to view the thread used in production as an indirect material and part of variable overhead. Thus, thread is not shown on the bill of materials.

After the standard quantities of material components have been developed, prices are determined for each component. The purchasing agent is most likely to have the expertise to estimate standard prices. Prices should reflect factors such as desired quality, reliability and physical proximity of the supplier, and quantity and purchase discounts allowed. If purchasing agents are involved in setting reasonable price standards for materials, these individuals are more likely to be able to explain causes of any future variations from the standards.

When all quantity and price information has been gathered, component quantities are multiplied by unit prices to yield the total cost of each component. These totals are summed to determine the total standard material cost of one unit of product. The total standard material cost, along with other total costs, for one six-button-front shirt produced by Margaret White Clothing Ltd. is shown later, in Exhibit 5-3.

bill of materials
a document that contains information about product material components, their specifications (including quality), and the quantities needed for production

LABOUR STANDARDS

The procedures for developing labour standards are similar to those used for material standards. Each worker operation—such as bending, reaching, lifting, moving materials, cutting and sewing fabric, attaching sundry items (such as snaps and patches), and packaging—should be identified. When operations and movements are specified, activities such as setup must be considered because they are performed during the production process. All unnecessary movements by workers

Product: Six-button-front shirt		Revision Date: 3/1/05	
Product Number: Stock Keeping Unit (SKU) 312		Standard Job Size: 400	
Component ID#	**Quantity Required**	**Description of Component**	**Comments**
F-4	1.2 square metres	White cotton fabric	Highest quality
B-3	6 buttons	Bone buttons	Multicolour; imprinted with MWC logo
L-1	1 label	Label	Imprinted with MWC logo

EXHIBIT 5-1
Bill of Materials

The Beginning of Time and Motion Studies

Frederick Winslow Taylor was born in 1856 to a prominent Philadelphia family. Taylor nevertheless went to work in a steel factory, first as a machinist and then as a foreman. There he began to develop his ideas about ways to reorganize factory work to increase efficiency, minimize waste, and encourage labourers to work harder.

As a foreman, Taylor was upset when employees slacked off, and he became obsessed with finding ways to speed up their work. Beginning in 1882, Taylor and his associates began time-and-motion studies. They would break down complex manufacturing tasks into smaller motions and time these as they were performed by workers considered efficient. Using the results as a norm, and factoring in time for delays and rest, Taylor came up with a set of instructions for work to be efficiently performed. Workers were expected to meet the standard rate, with bonuses paid for faster work and penalties given for slower.

Eventually, Bethlehem Steel and other business owners hired Taylor to improve efficiency in their own shops. Shovel makers used his name as a seal of approval in their advertising. His theories laid the groundwork for the creation of the assembly line and were exported to Germany and the Soviet Union. Later, Taylor's disciples suggested that his management principles could be applied to non-industrial bureaucracies, such as government and schools.

Not everyone was happy with Taylor's ideas, however. For much of his career, Taylor was virulently opposed by workers' groups, unions, and muckraking journalists, who contended that his management system dehumanized workers.

Source: Scott Heller, "Taking Taylor's Measure: Book Weighs Cultural Impact of Efficiency Expert's Ideas," *Chronicle of Higher Education* (July 21, 1993), p. A12. This is excerpted from the condensed version. Copyright 1993, The Chronicle of Higher Education. Reprinted with permission of Scott Heller and the *Chronicle of Higher Education*.

and of materials as well as any rework activities should be disregarded when time standards are set and should be minimized or eliminated as nonvalue-added activities.

Each production operation must be converted to quantitative information to be a usable standard. Time and motion studies, discussed in the General News Note above, may be performed by the company.[2] Alternatively, times developed from industrial engineering studies or from historical data may be used.[3] Historical data, however, may incorporate past inefficiencies or may not consider recently added technologically advanced machinery or recently received worker training.

operations flow document
a listing of all tasks necessary to make a unit of product or perform a service and the time allowed for each operation

After labour tasks have been analyzed, an **operations flow document** can be prepared that lists all necessary activities and the time allowed for each. All activities should be analyzed as to their ability to add value to the product or service. Any nonvalue-added activities that are included in the operations flow document should be targeted for reduction or elimination. Exhibit 5-2 presents a simplified operations flow document that reflects the manufacturing process for a six-button shirt at Margaret White Clothing. This document shows 5.5 minutes of move time that is nonvalue-added.

Labour rate standards should reflect the wages and fringe benefits paid to employees who perform the various production tasks. All personnel doing the same job in a given department may be paid the same wage rate. Alternatively, if employees within a department performing the same or similar tasks are paid different wage rates, a weighted average rate must be computed and used as the standard. The average rate is computed as the total wage cost per hour divided by the number of workers. At some companies, to promote a team rather than an individualistic perspective, company workers receive a bonus if the entire facility meets its production and quality targets. This bonus would not be considered in determining standard cost variances for direct labour.

Product: Six-button-front shirt			Revision Date: 3/1/05	
Product Number: Stock Keeping Unit (SKU) #312			Standard Job Size: 400	
Operation ID#	**Department**	**Standard Labour Minutes per Shirt**	**Description of Task**	
27	Cutting	8.5	Align fabric for cutting (actual machine time, 6 minutes)	
29	Cutting	6.5	Cut fabric (actual machine time, 4 minutes)	
		5.5	Move to Sewing Department	
33	Sewing	7.0	Stitch fabric pieces together (actual machine time, 5.5 minutes)	
35	Sewing	3.5	Attach buttons (actual machine time, 2.0 minutes)	
37	Sewing	1.5	Attach label (actual machine time, 0.5 minutes)	

EXHIBIT 5-2

Operations Flow Document

As the composition of a labour team changes, the time needed to make a product may also change. For instance, workers who have been doing a job longer may be paid more and be able to do the job more quickly than those who were just hired. Often trade-offs must be made between rates and times for labour just as trade-offs are made between price and quality for material.

OVERHEAD STANDARDS

Management may use either a single predetermined plantwide rate or multiple departmental rates as the amount of the overhead standard cost. Additionally, the rate or rates may have separate variable and fixed components or be a combined rate.

The Cutting and Sewing departments at Margaret White Clothing rely heavily on direct labour. The predetermined variable manufacturing overhead rate for these two departments is $7 per direct labour hour. The two departments work a total of 27 (15 + 12) minutes on each shirt, so the total variable manufacturing overhead applied per shirt is $3.15 [(27 ÷ 60) × $7]. The fixed overhead rate for these two departments is $6 per machine hour. According to the operations flow document in Exhibit 5-2, the departments have a total of 18 (6 + 4 + 5.5 + 2 + 0.5) minutes of machine time. Thus, a total of $1.80 [(18 ÷ 60) × $6] of fixed manufacturing overhead will be applied to each shirt in these two departments. The costs associated with the 5.5 minutes of move time are considered part of manufacturing overhead and the overhead costs caused by move time are included in the predetermined manufacturing overhead rates.

After the bill of materials, operations flow document, and standard overhead costs have been developed, a **standard cost card** is prepared. This document (shown in Exhibit 5-3 on page 246) summarizes all the standard quantities and costs needed to complete one six-button-front SKU #312 shirt.

Standard costs and quantities are used during the period to assign costs to inventory accounts. In an actual or normal cost system, actual material and labour costs are charged to Work in Process Inventory as production occurs. In most standard cost systems, standard rather than actual costs of production are charged to

standard cost card
a document that summarizes the direct materials and direct labour standard quantities and prices needed to complete one unit of product as well as the overhead allocation bases and rates

EXHIBIT 5-3
Standard Cost Card

Product: One size fits all, six-button-front shirt   SKU Number: 312

Direct Material

Departments

ID#	Unit Cost	Total Quantity	Cutting Cost	Sewing Cost	Total Cost
F-4	$3.50 per sq. metre	1.2 sq. metres	$4.20		$4.20
B-3	$0.15 each	6 per shirt		$0.90	0.90
L-1	$0.08 each	1 per shirt		0.08	0.08
Direct Material Totals			$4.20	$0.98	$5.18

Direct Labour

ID#	Average Wage per Minute	Total Minutes	Cutting Cost	Sewing Cost	Total Cost
27	$0.16	8.5	$1.36		$1.36
29	0.16	6.5	1.04		1.04
33	0.20	7.0		$1.40	1.40
35	0.24	3.5		0.84	0.84
37	0.14	1.5		0.21	0.21
Direct Labour Totals		27.0	$2.40	$2.45	$4.85

Production Overhead

Type of Overhead	Cost Driver	Standard Time Allowed	Standard Departmental Rate	Total Cost
Variable	Direct Labour Time	27 minutes	$7.00 per DLH	$3.15
Fixed	Machine Time	18 minutes	$6.00 per MH	1.80
Overhead Total				$4.95

Total Cost = $5.18 + $4.85 + $4.95 = $14.98

Work in Process Inventory.[4] Any difference between actual and standard costs is a variance.

Because they are common input measures, direct labour hours and machine hours are used as cost drivers and referred to in the models that follow. Alternative cost drivers, such as setup time, metres of material moved, or number of defective units produced, may be more appropriately related to cost incurrence. Using these measures does not change the manner in which the calculations are made.

LEARNING OBJECTIVE 3

How are material, labour, and overhead variances calculated?

VARIANCE COMPUTATIONS

The most basic variance computation is the total difference between actual cost incurred and standard cost allowed for the period's output. This variance can be diagrammed as follows:

Actual Cost of Actual
  Production Inputs

Standard Cost of Actual
  Production Outputs

Total Variance

A total variance can be computed for each production cost element; however, total variances do not provide useful information for determining why cost differences occurred. To help managers in their control function, total variances for materials and labour are subdivided into price and quantity elements.

A **price variance** reflects the difference between what was paid and what should have been paid for inputs during the period. A **quantity variance** provides a monetary measure of the difference between the quantity of actual inputs and the standard quantity of inputs allowed for the actual output of the period. Quantity variances focus on the efficiency of results—the relationship of inputs to outputs. Quantity can be measured as metres of material, hours of direct labour time, number of setups, or any other specified and reasonable indicator of output.

The diagram used to calculate a total variance can be expanded to provide a general model indicating the subvariances:

price variance
the difference between what was paid and what should have been paid for inputs during the period

quantity variance
the difference between the quantity of actual inputs and the standard quantity of inputs for the actual output of the period multiplied by a standard price or rate

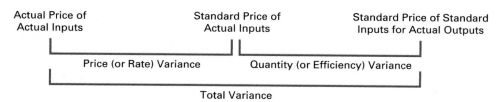

The middle column is a planned (budget) column and indicates what costs should have been incurred for actual inputs. The far-right column uses a measure of output known as the **standard quantity allowed**. This quantity measure translates actual output into the standard quantity of input that *should have been used* to achieve the actual level of output. This measurement is computed as the standard quantity allowed multiplied by the standard price of the input resources.

The diagram can be simplified using the abbreviated notations shown in Exhibit 5-4. This model progresses from the *actual* price of *actual* input on the left to the *standard* price of *standard* input allowed on the right. The middle measure of input is a hybrid of *actual* quantity and *standard* price. The price variance portion of the total variance is measured as the actual input quantity multiplied by the difference between the actual and standard prices:

standard quantity allowed
a measure of quantity that translates the actual output achieved into the standard input quantity that should have been used to achieve that output

$$\text{Price variance} = AQ\,(AP - SP)$$

The quantity variance is determined as the standard price multiplied by the difference between the *actual* quantity used and the standard quantity allowed for the *actual* output:

$$\text{Quantity variance} = SP\,(AQ - SQ)$$

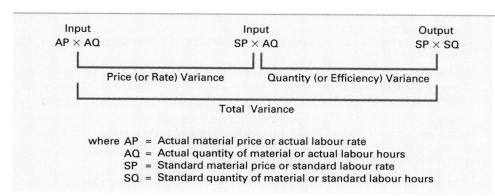

EXHIBIT 5-4
Simplified Variance Model

Production of the Six-Button-Front Shirt #312 in the Cutting Department of Margaret White Clothing Ltd. is used to illustrate variance computations. The standard costs in this department are taken from the standard cost card in Exhibit 5-3 and are repeated at the top of Exhibit 5-5. Also shown in Exhibit 5-5 are the actual quantity and cost data for the week of June 12–16, 2005. This information is used in computing the material, labour, and overhead variances for the week. Variance computations must indicate whether the variance is favourable (F) or unfavourable (U).

Material Variances

Using the model and inserting information concerning material quantities and prices provides the following computations. (Note that the standard quantity for cloth is taken from Exhibit 5-5.)

The subvariances for materials are known as the material price and material quantity variances. The **material price variance (MPV)** indicates the amount of money spent below (F for favourable) or above (U for unfavourable) the standard

material price variance
the amount of money spent below (F for favourable) or above (U for unfavourable) the standard price for the quantity of materials purchased

---

EXHIBIT 5-5

Cutting Department's Information for One Six-Button-Front Shirt

Standards for 1 Six-Button-Front Shirt SKU #312	
1.2 square metres of white cotton fabric at $3.50 per square metre	$4.20
15 minutes of labour at $9.60 per hour ($0.16 per minute)	2.40
Applied variable manufacturing overhead (based on 15 minutes of direct labour time at $7 per DLH)	1.75
Applied fixed manufacturing overhead (based on 10 minutes of machine time at $6 per machine hour (MH)*	1.00
Total standard Cutting Department cost per shirt	$9.35

Actual Data for June 12–16, 2005

Number of shirts produced	2,200
Square metres of cotton fabric used	2,730
Square metres of cotton fabric purchased	3,000
Direct labour hours incurred	500
Machine hours used	350
Actual price per square metre of cotton fabric used	$ 4.15
Average direct labour rate per hour	10.00
Total variable manufacturing overhead cost	3,360.00
Total fixed manufacturing overhead	2,875.00

Standard Quantities Allowed
Direct Material:
Standard quantity allowed for cloth = 2,200 shirts × 1.2 square metres per shirt = 2,640 square metres

Direct Labour:
Standard quantity allowed for direct labour hours = 2,200 shirts × 15 minutes per shirt = 33,000 minutes or 550 hours.

Variable Manufacturing Overhead:
Applied on the basis of direct labour hours = 2,200 shirts × 15 minutes per shirt = 33,000 minutes or 550 hours

Fixed Manufacturing Overhead:
Standard quantity allowed for machine hours = 2,200 shirts × 10 minutes per shirt = 22,000 minutes or 366 2/3 hours

*The $6 rate per machine hour is based on total expected fixed overhead of $124,800 for the year and an expected 20,800 machine hours related to the production of these shirts. This product is expected to be produced evenly at the rate of 2,496 shirts per week for 50 weeks of the year or 124,800 shirts for the year.

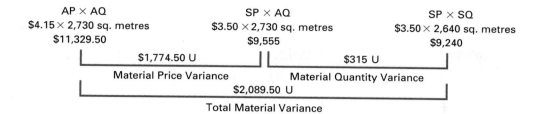

AP × AQ	SP × AQ	SP × SQ
$4.15 × 2,730 sq. metres	$3.50 × 2,730 sq. metres	$3.50 × 2,640 sq. metres
$11,329.50	$9,555	$9,240

$1,774.50 U — Material Price Variance

$315 U — Material Quantity Variance

$2,089.50 U — Total Material Variance

price for the quantity of materials purchased. For Margaret White Clothing Ltd., the actual price paid for cotton fabric was $4.15 per square metre, while the standard price was $3.50, giving an unfavourable material price variance of $1,774.50. This variance can also be calculated as [2,730 ($4.15 − $3.50) = 2,730 ($0.65) = $1,774.50]. The sign of the unfavourable variance is positive because the actual price is more than the standard price.[5]

The **material quantity variance (MQV)** indicates the cost saved (F) or expended (U) because of the difference between the actual quantity of material used and the standard quantity of material allowed for the goods produced or services rendered during the period. The company has been more efficient than expected if the actual quantity used is less than the standard quantity allowed. If a greater quantity has been used than allowed, the company has been less efficient. Margaret White Clothing Ltd. used 90 more square metres of cotton fabric than the standard allowed for the actual production of 2,200 shirts. This inefficient usage resulted in an unfavourable material quantity variance [$3.50 (2,730 − 2,640) = $3.50 (90) = $315].

The total material variance of $2,089.50 U can be calculated by taking the difference between the total actual cost of inputs ($11,329.50) and the total standard cost of the outputs ($9,240). The total variance also represents the summation of the individual material price and quantity subvariances: ($1,774.50 U + $315 U = $2,089.50 U).

material quantity variance
the cost saved (F) or expended (U) because of the difference between the actual quantity of material used and the standard quantity of material allowed for the goods produced or services rendered during the period

Point of Purchase Material Variance Model

A total variance for a cost component generally equals the sum of the price and quantity subvariances. An exception to this rule occurs when the quantity of material purchased is not the same as the quantity of material placed into production. In such cases, the general model is altered slightly to provide information more rapidly for management control purposes.

Because the material price variance relates to the purchasing (not production) function, the altered model calculates the material price variance at the point of purchase and bases that calculation on the quantity of materials *purchased* rather than the quantity of materials *used*. This variation in the model allows the material price variance to be isolated or pinpointed as close to the variance source and as quickly as possible. The material quantity variance is still computed on the basis of the actual quantity of materials used in production.

Assume that Margaret White Clothing Ltd. had purchased 3,000 square metres of cotton fabric for production of SKU #312 shirts but had only used 2,730 square metres during the week of June 12–16, 2005. The point of purchase material price variance (Material Purchase Price Variance) is calculated as shown on the next page.

AP × AQ
$4.15 × 3,000
$12,450

SP × AQ
$3.50 × 3,000
$10,500

$1,950 U

Material Price Variance

This change in the general model is shown below, with subscripts to indicate actual quantity purchased (p) and used (u).

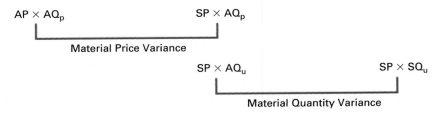

AP × AQ$_p$

SP × AQ$_p$

Material Price Variance

SP × AQ$_u$

SP × SQ$_u$

Material Quantity Variance

The material quantity variance is still calculated as presented earlier because the actual quantity of cotton fabric used in production is determined by the amount used and not by the amount purchased. Thus, the MQV would remain at $315 U. A point of purchase variance computation results in the material price and quantity variances being computed from different bases. For this reason, the above variances should not be summed; thus, no total material variance can be determined in this case.

Basing Price Variance on Purchases Rather Than Usage

Traditionally, the material price variance computation has been more commonly based on purchases than on usage. This choice allows management to calculate the variance as near as possible to the time of cost incurrence. Although a point-of-purchase calculation allows managers to see the impact of buying decisions more rapidly, such information may not be highly relevant in a just-in-time environment. Buying materials that are not needed currently requires that the materials be stored and moved—both nonvalue-added activities. Any price savings from such purchases should be measured against the additional costs of such a purchase.

Additionally, a point-of-purchase price variance may reduce a manager's ability to recognize a relationship between a favourable material price variance and an unfavourable material usage variance. If a favourable price variance results from the purchase of lower quality materials, the effects of that purchase are not known until the materials are actually used.

Labour Variances

The price and usage elements of the total labour variance are called the labour rate and labour efficiency variances. The model for computing these variances and computations for Margaret White Clothing Ltd. follow. The standard quantity is taken from Exhibit 5-5 for direct labour hours.

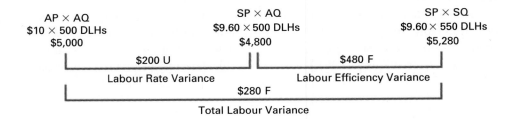

AP × AQ
$10 × 500 DLHs
$5,000

SP × AQ
$9.60 × 500 DLHs
$4,800

SP × SQ
$9.60 × 550 DLHs
$5,280

$200 U

Labour Rate Variance

$480 F

Labour Efficiency Variance

$280 F

Total Labour Variance

The **labour rate variance (LRV)** shows the difference between the actual rate or actual weighted average rate paid to the direct labour workers for the period and the standard rate for all hours actually worked during the period. The labour rate variance can also be computed as [500 × ($10 – $9.60)] = 500 ($0.40) = $200 U.

The **labour efficiency variance (LEV)** compares the number of actual direct labour hours worked with the standard hours allowed for the actual number of shirts produced. The difference is multiplied by the standard labour rate to establish a dollar value for the efficiency (F) or inefficiency (U) of the direct labour workers. The labour efficiency variance can also be calculated as [$9.60 × (500 – 550)] = $9.60 (–50) = –$480 F. The sign of the favourable variance is negative because the actual number of hours worked is *fewer than* the standard hours allowed to make the actual number of shirts.

The total labour variance ($280 F) can be determined by subtracting the total standard labour cost for the actual production ($5,280) from the total actual labour cost ($5,000). Alternatively, the total labour variance can be found by adding the labour rate and efficiency variances [$200 U + (–$480 F)].

The News Note below provides a slightly different perspective on efficiency variances. It suggests that the efficiency variance is truly composed of two elements—quality problems and efficiency problems—that should be accounted for separately.

As the News Note below points out, a company may achieve reductions in labour time and, thus, have favourable efficiency variances by producing defective or poor-quality units. For example, assume that workers who are earning $15 per hour can produce one unit of product in two hours. During a period, 1,500 units are made in 2,610 hours. The standard quantity of time allowed for production is 3,000 hours. The labour efficiency variance is $15 (2,610 – 3,000), or $5,850 F. However, 80 of the 1,500 units were defective and nonsaleable. The favourable efficiency variance of $5,850 fails to include the impact of those nonquality units. A quality variance can be computed as follows: 80 defective units × 2 hours per unit × $15 per hour or $2,400 U. Subtracting this unfavourable quality variance from the $5,850 favourable efficiency variance provides a net true efficiency variance for the

labour rate variance
the difference between the total actual direct labour wages for the period and the standard rate for all hours actually worked during the period

labour efficiency variance
the difference between the number of actual direct labour hours worked and the standard hours allowed for the actual output multiplied by the standard labour rate per hour

---

Separating Quality Problems from Efficiency Problems

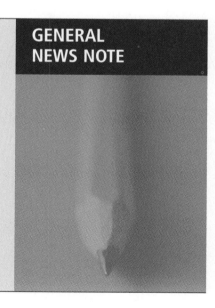

GENERAL NEWS NOTE

Historically, efficiency variances have been computed by multiplying excess inputs by the standard price. In recent years, this approach has been criticized for motivating managers to ignore quality concerns to avoid unfavourable efficiency variances. In other words, there is an incentive to produce a low-quality product by minimizing the amount of material used or the time spent in production.

An approach could be taken that separates the efficiency variance from the quality variance. Inputs consisting of conversion time or material used in defective units would be captured in the quality variance.

Separating the two variances allows production decision makers to evaluate the trade-offs between efficiency and quality. They can minimize production time to gain a favourable efficiency variance but this probably will increase the number of defective units and result in an unfavourable quality variance. Likewise, trying to minimize the number of defective units may result in investing more time and more material and therefore having an unfavourable efficiency variance.

Source: Carole Cheatham, "Updating Standard Cost Systems," *Journal of Accountancy*, December 1990, pp. 59–60.

production of 1,420 good units, or $3,450 F. This restated efficiency variance can be shown as follows:

1,420 (1,500 − 80) good units × 2 hours per unit

	= 2,840 standard hours allowed (SHA)
2,840 (1,420 × 2) SHA − 2,610 actual hours	= 230 hours less than standard (F)
230 hours × $15 standard cost per hour	= $3,450 F efficiency variance

Manufacturing Overhead Variances

The use of separate variable and fixed manufacturing overhead application rates and accounts allows the computation of separate variances for each type of overhead. These separate computations provide managers with the greatest detail as well as the greatest flexibility for control and performance evaluation purposes. Also, because of increased use of nonsimilar bases for various overhead allocations, each different cost pool for variable and fixed manufacturing overhead may require separate price and usage (quantity) computations. In the Cutting Department of Margaret White Clothing Ltd., variable and fixed manufacturing overhead calculations are based, respectively, on direct labour hours and machine hours.

As with material and labour, total variable and total fixed manufacturing overhead variances can be subdivided into specific price and quantity subvariances for each type of overhead. The overhead subvariances are referred to as follows:

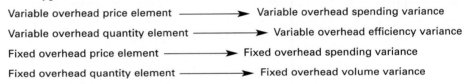

Variable Overhead

The total variable overhead (VOH) variance is the difference between actual variable manufacturing overhead costs incurred for the period and standard variable manufacturing overhead cost applied to the period's actual production or service output. The difference at year-end is the total variable manufacturing overhead variance, which is also the amount of underapplied or overapplied variable manufacturing overhead. The following diagram illustrates the computation of the total variable overhead variance.

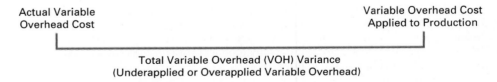

The following variable manufacturing overhead variance computations use the June 12–16, 2005, data for the Cutting Department of Margaret White Clothing Ltd. The actual variable manufacturing overhead cost for the week was $3,360 for 500 direct labour hours or $6.72 per direct labour hour; 550 standard direct labour hours were allowed for that week's production. The variable manufacturing overhead for each direct labour hour was expected to cost the company $7. The variable overhead variances for the Cutting Department are computed as shown next.

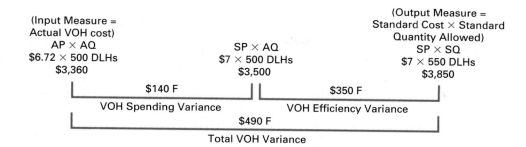

The **variable overhead spending** (or budget) **variance** is the difference between actual variable manufacturing overhead and budgeted (planned) variable manufacturing overhead based on actual input. The **variable overhead efficiency variance** is the difference between budgeted (planned) variable manufacturing overhead at the actual input activity and budgeted (planned) variable manufacturing overhead at standard input (such as DLHs) allowed. This variance quantifies the effect of using more or less actual input than the standard allowed. When actual input exceeds standard input allowed, operations appear inefficient. Excess input also means that more variable overhead is needed to support the additional input.

variable overhead spending variance
the difference between actual variable overhead and budgeted (planned) variable overhead based on actual input

variable overhead efficiency variance
the difference between budgeted (planned) variable overhead at actual input activity and budgeted variable overhead at standard input activity allowed

Fixed Overhead

The total fixed manufacturing overhead (FOH) variance is the difference between actual FOH cost incurred and standard FOH cost applied to the period's actual production. This difference is also the amount of underappplied or overapplied fixed overhead for the period. The following model shows the computation of the total fixed overhead variance.

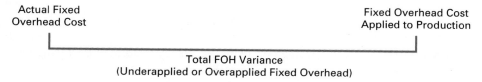

The total fixed manufacturing overhead variance is subdivided into its price and quantity elements by the insertion of budgeted (planned) fixed overhead as a middle column into the model.

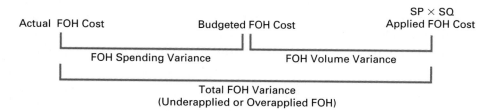

In the model, the left column is simply labelled "actual FOH cost" and is not computed as a price times quantity measure because fixed overhead is generally acquired in lump-sum amounts rather than on a per-unit input basis. The **fixed overhead spending** (or budget) **variance** is the difference between actual and planned fixed overhead. The fixed overhead **volume variance** is the difference between budgeted and applied fixed overhead. The volume variance occurs by

fixed overhead spending variance
the difference between actual and budgeted (planned) fixed overhead

volume variance
the difference between budgeted (planned) and applied fixed overhead

Overhead Variances

Bring up the topic of standard costing and you're almost certain to touch off a lively debate. Cost accountants have varying opinions on how to set them and how to interpret them.

The information systems manager and assistant controller at Howmet's Whitehall casting facility find the biggest challenge they face with standard costing is handling fixed and semi-fixed costs. Volume changes will result in different fixed costs per unit because, by definition, these costs (in total) do not change with different volumes (at least within a certain range of production). There's a danger management will mistakenly think its fixed costs have decreased due to higher volumes and underprice its parts, even when future volumes are lower.

To determine volume for standard fixed cost allocation, Whitehall's cost managers look at the various operations or capital equipment required, and use 80% of total capacity (to allow for normal downtime for maintenance and as a buffer for unforeseen breakdowns). Using practical capacity in developing fixed cost allocation rates results in cost standards that include only the cost of capacity actually used in production. Whitehall partially tracks the cost of unused capacity through efficiency percentages.

Source: Kip R. Krumwiede, "Tips From the Trenches on Standard Costing," *Cost Management Update*, Issue 106, Montvale, April 2000.

producing at a level different from that used to set the predetermined overhead rate. This topic is discussed in the News Note above.

Fixed overhead is a constant amount throughout the relevant range; thus, *the middle column is a constant figure regardless of the actual quantity of input or the standard quantity of input allowed.* This concept is a key element in computing FOH variances. The budgeted amount of fixed overhead is equal to the standard FOH rate times the estimated capacity measure used to compute the standard rate.

The Cutting Department of Margaret White Clothing Ltd. had estimated that 2,496 shirts would be produced each week, amounting to a total of 416 hours of machine time $(2,496 \times 10 \text{ minutes} = 24,960 \text{ minutes}; 24,960 \text{ minutes} \div 60 \text{ minutes} = 416 \text{ hours})$. Based on the production plan, the weekly fixed manufacturing overhead budget for the department is $2,496 (416 hours $\times$ $6).[6]

Applied fixed overhead equals the FOH application rate ($6.00) times the standard input allowed for the production achieved. In regard to fixed manufacturing overhead, the standard input allowed for the production achieved measures capacity utilization for the period. The standard input for Margaret White Clothing's Cutting Department is 10 minutes of machine time per shirt. Since 2,200 shirts were produced, the standard machine time allowed is 366 2/3 hours, as shown at the bottom of Exhibit 5-5.

Inserting the data for the Cutting Department into the model gives the following:

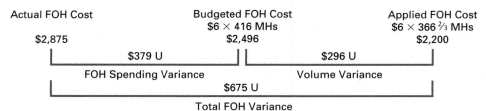

Actual FOH Cost	Budgeted FOH Cost $6 × 416 MHs	Applied FOH Cost $6 × 366 ⅔ MHs
$2,875	$2,496	$2,200

$379 U — FOH Spending Variance $296 U — Volume Variance

$675 U — Total FOH Variance

The week's actual fixed overhead cost is $2,875, while the planned amount is $2,496. The $379 unfavourable difference is the FOH spending variance, which could be related to a variety of causes such as increased rent payments or increased insurance premiums for machinery and equipment.

The FOH application rate is $6 per machine hour. This rate exists because the company expected a total of $124,800 in fixed overhead costs for the year and chose an expected annual capacity level of 20,800 machine hours. Each shirt requires 10 minutes of machine time, so the company can make six shirts in an hour. Therefore, expected capacity of shirts for the year is 124,800 shirts (20,800 hours × 6 shirts per hour) over a 50-week work-year. Had any capacity level other than 20,800 machine hours been chosen, the fixed overhead rate would have been different, even though the total amount of budgeted fixed overhead ($124,800) would have been the same. *If any level of capacity is experienced other than that which was used in determining the application rate, a volume variance will occur.* For example, if Margaret White Clothing Ltd. had chosen a yearly amount of 110,000 shirts (2,200 shirts per week) as the denominator level of activity for setting the predetermined FOH rate, there would be no volume variance for the week of June 12–16, 2005. If any number of shirts less than 2,200 had been chosen as the denominator level of activity, the volume variance would have been favourable.

The difference between the $2,496 budgeted FOH and the $2,200 applied FOH gives the $296 unfavourable volume variance for the week. This variance is also equal to the difference of 296 shirts (2,496 − 2,200) that the company expected to make but did not produce multiplied by the $1 standard fixed overhead rate per shirt.[7] The variance is unfavourable because fewer shirts were produced this week than budgeted. The $675 unfavourable total fixed manufacturing overhead variance is the underapplied balance in the fixed manufacturing overhead account for the week.

COST CONTROL AND VARIANCE RESPONSIBILITY

How can variances be used for control and performance evaluation purposes?

Cost control focuses on the variances between actual costs incurred for a period and the standard costs that should have been incurred based on actual output. To exercise any type of effective control, managers first must be provided with detailed information on the various cost components. Second, a well-designed system of cost control and variance analysis should capture variances as early as possible.

Variance analysis is the process of categorizing the nature—favourable (standard is greater than actual) or unfavourable (actual is greater than standard)—of the differences between standard and actual costs and seeking the reasons for those differences. It is important to recognize the fact that a favourable variance does not mean "good" and an unfavourable variance does not mean "bad." Given this fact, it is important to analyze all variances in order to understand what circumstances gave rise to them.

variance analysis
the process of categorizing the nature (favourable or unfavourable) of the differences between standard and actual costs and seeking the reasons for those differences

The cost control and variance analysis system should help managers determine who or what is responsible for the variance and who is best able to explain it. When variances reflect poor performance, an early measurement system may allow operational performance to be improved. The longer the reporting of a variance is delayed, the more difficult it becomes to determine its cause.

Material price and labour rate variances are not as controllable at the production or service level as are material quantity and labour efficiency variances. Price and rate standards are more dependent on outside forces, such as market competition and wage contracts, than are usage standards.

Material Variances

Material price variances are normally determined at the point of purchase. Although not always able to control prices, purchasing agents, if given adequate lead time and resources, should be able to influence prices. This influence is exerted through knowing what suppliers are available and choosing suppliers that provide the appropriate material in the most reasonable time span at the most reasonable cost. The purchasing agent can also influence material prices by purchasing in quantities that provide price discounts or by engaging in contractual arrangements such as long-term purchase contracts.

The purchasing agent is usually the person who is best able to explain why a material price variance occurs. Also, as part of the team that originally set the material price standard, the purchasing agent is usually the individual responsible for material price variances.

Material quantity variances can be determined when materials are issued or used. Such variances are considered the responsibility of the person in charge of the job or department. Materials are ordinarily requisitioned based on the number of actual units to be produced times the standard quantity per unit. When additional materials are taken out of inventory, material requisition slips of a different colour may be filled out. These colour-coded excess requisition slips allow control to occur as work is underway rather than at the end of the period or when production is completed. Monitoring requisition slips for significant excess material withdrawals alerts managers to seek causes for the excesses and, if possible, take timely corrective action.

Some production settings, such as chemical and petroleum processing, involve a continuous flow of material. In these cases, it may not be practical or reasonable to isolate quantity variances when materials are placed into production. The material quantity variance is more feasibly measured when production is complete and the total quantity of production is known. Measuring usage for relatively short time periods and reporting quantity variances after production is complete can still assist management in controlling operations. Labour efficiency variances are also more appropriately measured at the end of production in these types of manufacturing operations.

There are exceptions to the normal assignment of responsibility for material price and quantity variances. Assume that the manager in the Cutting Department at Margaret White Clothing Ltd. asks the purchasing agent to acquire, without adequate lead time, additional quantities of cotton fabric. She makes this request because the marketing manager has just told her that the demand for Six-Button-Front Style #312 shirts has unexpectedly increased. Making a spur-of-the-moment acquisition of this kind could result in paying a price higher than standard. Price variances resulting from these types of causes should be assigned to production or marketing/merchandising—for inadequate predictions—not to purchasing.

In contrast, assume the purchasing agent acquires inferior-quality cotton fabric that results in excess consumption and an unfavourable quantity variance. This quantity variance should be assigned to purchasing rather than to production. Such situations are likely to be identified from continuous, rather than end-of-period, reporting.

Labour Variances

Labour rate and labour efficiency variances are commonly identified as part of the payroll process and assigned to the person in charge of the production or service area. This assignment assumes that the manager has the ability to influence the type of labour personnel used. In many cases, however, it is very difficult to focus blame on any one individual. For instance, the Cutting Department manager could use skilled or unskilled workers to align, mark, and cut material. Using highly skilled, highly paid individuals for lower-level jobs could cause an unfavourable labour rate variance, accompanied by a favourable labour efficiency variance. Thus, as with material variances, correlations may exist between labour variances.

Sometimes a common factor may cause multiple variances. For instance, in manufacturing, the purchase of inferior-quality materials could result in a favourable material price variance, an unfavourable material quantity variance, and an unfavourable labour efficiency variance. The efficiency variance could reflect increased production time, since many units were rejected as substandard because of the inferior materials. In another common situation, the use of lower-paid, less-skilled workers results in a favourable rate variance but causes excessive material usage and decreased labour efficiency.

The probability of detecting relationships among variances is improved, but not assured, by timely variance reporting. The accounting and reporting process should highlight interrelationships of variances, and managers should be aware of the possibility of such relationships when reviewing variance reports.

Overhead Variances

The difference between actual and applied overhead is the amount of underapplied or overapplied overhead or the total overhead variance that must be explained. Control purposes differ for variable and fixed overhead because of the types of costs that make up the two categories and the ability of managers to influence those costs.

Variable Overhead

Variable overhead costs are incurred on a continual basis as work is performed and are directly related to that work. Because of this direct relationship to activity, control of VOH costs is similar to control of material and labour. Companies control variable overhead by (1) keeping actual costs in line with planned costs for the actual level of activity and (2) getting the planned output yield from the overhead resources placed into production.

Variable overhead spending variances are commonly caused by price differences—paying average actual prices that are higher or lower than the standard prices allowed. Such fluctuations often occur because price changes have not been reflected in the standard rate. For instance, average indirect labour wage rates, supply costs, or utility rates may have increased or decreased since the standard VOH rate was computed. In such instances, the standard rate should be adjusted.

If managers have no control over prices charged by external parties, they should not be held accountable for variances arising because of such price changes. In contrast, if managers could influence prices—for example through long-term purchase arrangements—such options should be investigated as to their long-term costs and benefits before a decision is made to change the standard. Waste or spoilage of resources, such as indirect materials, is another possible cause of the VOH spending variance.

The VOH efficiency variance reflects the managerial control implemented or needed in regard to the yield of output as related to input. VOH represents a variety of resources that, like direct material and direct labour, bear a known and measurable relationship to the activity base used to represent production activity. These resources are managed by monitoring and measuring their actual use in conformity with standard usage, promptly investigating any variances, and adjusting resource usage when necessary. Control of the variable overhead resource elements can only be achieved if the variance from standard for each VOH component is analyzed rather than attempting to analyze and control variable overhead in total. The cost and usage of each component of VOH could react independently of the others.

If variable manufacturing overhead is applied on the basis of direct labour hours, the signs (favourable or unfavourable) of the variable overhead and direct labour efficiency variances will be the same, because the actual and standard hours compared in the two calculations are the same. However, when alternative overhead application bases are used, the signs of these two variances may no longer be related to each other. Use of any alternative base, including those provided under activity-based costing,[8] does not affect the implementation of a standard cost system.

Fixed Overhead

Control of fixed manufacturing overhead is distinctly different from control of variable manufacturing overhead because fixed overhead may not be directly related to current activity. Since many types of fixed manufacturing costs must be committed to in lump-sum amounts before current period activity takes place, managers may have only limited ability to control FOH costs in the short run. Once managers commit to a fixed cost, it becomes unchangeable for some period of time *regardless of whether actual work takes place*. Thus, control of many fixed overhead costs must occur at the *time of commitment* rather than at the *time of production activity*.

Fixed Overhead Spending Variance

The FOH spending variance normally represents a variance in the costs of fixed overhead components, although this variance can also reflect mismanagement of resources. Control over the FOH spending variance often must take place on a transaction-by-transaction basis when managers arrange for facilities. Many fixed overhead costs are basically uncontrollable in the short run. For example, depreciation expense is based on the equipment's historical cost, salvage value, and expected life. Utility costs, which are partially fixed, are often set by rate commissions and are influenced by the size and type of the physical plant. Even a "turn-off-the-lights" program can reduce utility costs only by a limited amount. Repairs and maintenance, which are also partially fixed, can be controlled to some extent, but are highly affected by the type of operation involved. Salaries are contractual obligations that were set at the time of employment or salary review.

The information provided by a total FOH spending variance amount would not be specific enough to allow management to decide whether corrective action was possible or desirable. Individual cost variances for each component need to be reviewed. Such a review will help managers determine the actual causes of and responsibility for the several components of the total fixed overhead spending variance.

Volume Variance

In addition to controlling spending, utilizing capacity is another important aspect of managerial control. Capacity utilization is reflected in the volume variance because that computation is directly affected by the capacity level chosen to calculate the predetermined or standard fixed overhead application rate. Although utilization is controllable to some degree, the volume variance is the variance over which managers have the least influence and control, especially in the short run. But it is important that managers exercise what ability they do have to influence and control capacity utilization.

An unfavourable volume variance indicates less-than-expected utilization of capacity. If available capacity is currently being used at a level below or above that which was anticipated, managers should recognize that condition, investigate the reasons for it, and initiate appropriate action as needed. The degree of capacity utilization should always be viewed in relation to inventory and sales. If capacity is overutilized (a favourable volume variance) and inventory is stockpiling, managers should decrease capacity utilization. A favourable volume variance could, however, be due to increased sales demand with no stockpiling of inventory—in which case no adjustments should be made to reduce utilization.

If capacity is underutilized (an unfavourable volume variance) and sales are back-ordered or going unfilled, managers should try to increase capacity utilization. However, managers must understand that underutilization of capacity is not always undesirable. In a manufacturing company, it is more appropriate for managers not to produce goods that would simply end up in inventory stockpiles. Unneeded inventory production, although it serves to utilize capacity, generates substantially more costs for material, labour, and overhead, including storage and handling costs. The positive impact that such unneeded production will have on the fixed overhead volume variance is outweighed by the unnecessary costs of accumulating excess inventory.

Managers can sometimes influence capacity utilization by modifying work schedules, taking measures to relieve production constraints, eliminating non-value-added activities, and carefully monitoring the movement of resources through the production or service process. Such actions should be taken during the period rather than after the period has ended. Efforts made after work is completed may improve next period's operations but will have no impact on current work.

Expected annual capacity—rather than practical or theoretical capacity—is often selected as the denominator level of activity by which to compute the predetermined fixed manufacturing overhead application rate. Use of this base does, however, ignore an important management concern—that of unused capacity. Having but not using capacity creates additional nonvalue-added organizational costs. The only way these costs can be highlighted is through the selection of practical or theoretical capacity to compute the fixed manufacturing overhead application rate.

Rather than using the traditional fixed overhead computations, companies may want to compute fixed overhead variances in a manner that could provide additional information. This innovative process is described in Exhibit 5-6 on page 260, using Margaret White Clothing's production of the Six-Button-Front Shirt #312. In this example, the fixed manufacturing overhead rate is computed on the basis of practical capacity rather than expected annual capacity. This computation allows

EXHIBIT 5-6

Calculating a Capacity
Utilization Variance

Total fixed manufacturing overhead costs (from Exhibit 5-5)		$124,800
Total practical annual capacity of the factory in Machine Hours (MH)		25,000
Total expected annual capacity of the factory in MH (from Exhibit 5-5)		20,800

Predetermined fixed manufacturing overhead rate based on practical capacity
= $124,800 ÷ 25,000 = ≈ $4.99 per MH

Practical capacity	25,000	MH
Expected annual capacity	20,800	MH
Unused capacity	4,200	MH
Multiplied by the cost per MH	× $4.99	
Cost of unused capacity	$20,958	

If 20,000 MH are the standard hours allowed for actual production, the company would
have a capacity utilization variance of $3,992 U [(20,800 − 20,000) × $4.99].

If 21,000 MH are the standard hours allowed for actual production, the company would
have a capacity utilization variance of $998 F [(20,800 − 21,000) × $4.99].

managers to focus on the cost of unused capacity so that it can be accounted for
and, therefore, analyzed and controlled.[9]

CONVERSION COST AS AN ELEMENT IN STANDARD COSTING

Conversion cost consists of both direct labour and manufacturing overhead. The
traditional view separates the elements of product cost into three categories: direct
material, direct labour, and overhead. This practice is appropriate in labour-intensive production settings; however, in more highly automated factories, direct labour
cost generally represents an extremely small part of total product cost. In such circumstances, one worker may oversee a large number of machines and may deal
more with troubleshooting machine malfunctions than converting raw materials
into finished products. These new conditions mean that workers' wages are more
closely associated with indirect labour than direct labour.

Many companies have responded to having large overhead costs and small
direct labour costs by adapting their standard cost systems to provide for only two
elements of product cost: direct material and conversion. In these situations, conversion costs are likely to be separated into their variable and fixed components.
Conversion costs are also likely to be separated into direct and indirect categories
based on their ability to be traced to a machine rather than to a product. Overhead
may be applied by use of a variety of cost drivers, including machine hours, cost of
materials, number of production runs, number of machine setups, and throughput
time.

Variance analysis for conversion cost in automated plants normally focuses on
the following: (1) spending variances for overhead costs, (2) efficiency variances for
machinery and production costs rather than labour costs, and (3) the traditional
volume variance for production. In an automated system, managers are likely to be
able to better control not only the spending and efficiency variances but also the
volume variance. Variance analysis under a conversion cost approach is illustrated
in Exhibit 5-7. Regardless of the method by which they are computed, variances
that are significant in amount must be analyzed so that they can assist managers in
gaining production efficiencies and in controlling costs.

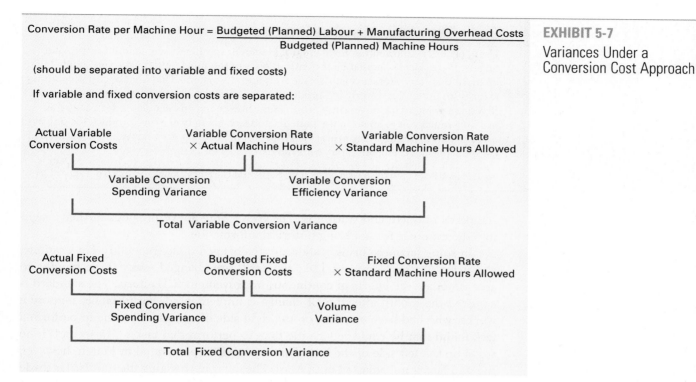

EXHIBIT 5-7
Variances Under a
Conversion Cost Approach

Conversion Rate per Machine Hour = $\dfrac{\text{Budgeted (Planned) Labour + Manufacturing Overhead Costs}}{\text{Budgeted (Planned) Machine Hours}}$

(should be separated into variable and fixed costs)

If variable and fixed conversion costs are separated:

Actual Variable Conversion Costs — Variable Conversion Rate × Actual Machine Hours — Variable Conversion Rate × Standard Machine Hours Allowed

Variable Conversion Spending Variance | Variable Conversion Efficiency Variance

Total Variable Conversion Variance

Actual Fixed Conversion Costs — Budgeted Fixed Conversion Costs — Fixed Conversion Rate × Standard Machine Hours Allowed

Fixed Conversion Spending Variance | Volume Variance

Total Fixed Conversion Variance

CONSIDERATIONS IN ESTABLISHING STANDARDS

LEARNING OBJECTIVE 5

How do organizational evolution and desired level of attainability affect standard setting?

When standards are established, appropriateness and attainability should be considered. Appropriateness, in relation to a standard, refers to the basis on which the standards are developed and how long they are expected to last. Attainability refers to the degree of difficulty or rigour that should be incurred in achieving the standard.

Appropriateness

Although standards are developed from past and current information, they should reflect technical and environmental factors expected for the period in which the standards are to be applied. Factors such as material quality, normal ordering quantities, employee wage rates (including expectations of increases in the minimum wage), degree of plant automation, facility layout, and mix of employee skills should be considered. Management should not think that standards, once set, will remain useful forever. Standards must evolve over an organization's life to reflect its changing methods and processes. Current operating performance cannot be compared against out-of-date standards because to do so would generate variances that would be illogical for planning, controlling, decision making, or evaluating performance.

To illustrate this point, suppose that Bright Pearl Seafood Restaurant Inc. had set labour time standards before initiating the modular, cross-functional teams that caused labour times to decline drastically, in part because of the elimination of many nonvalue-added labour movements. If these standards were not changed after the reorganization, consistently favourable labour efficiency variances would result. Managers should recognize that these efficiency variances would not be relevant to evaluating worker performance, determining inventory valuation, or making product pricing decisions. Rather, the new time reductions would make the

GENERAL NEWS NOTE

Don't Carry Your Mistakes Forward

Using historical information for standards is seldom specific enough and never provides targets. If you have operated inefficiently and spent too much in the past, you simply build all those costs and problems and deficiencies into the system. That kind of cost accounting is really an obstacle to improving productivity because it accepts and rewards inefficiency. If you are going to improve, you need to know how much you should be spending, not just how much you've spent in the past. That means going over every product, looking at every part, examining every process and operation, breaking each down into its individual components and then coming up with standard costs for everything you do.

Source: Jack Stack, *The Great Game of Business*, New York: Currency Doubleday, 1992, p. 101.

standards obsolete and worthless. The News Note above provides further insight into the rationale for not using historical information.

In some Japanese firms, standards are changed quite frequently. For example, at Citizen Watch Company, Ltd., standards are changed every three months to accommodate the effects of continuous improvement (CI) efforts. The standard is adjusted the month after the CI change is implemented. For instance, suppose a worker who had been standing on the right side of a production line to perform a task found that he could reduce the time to perform that task by 15 seconds if he stood on the left side of the line. This change is implemented in March, however, the standard is not adjusted until April. The delay in changing the standard is made so that the worker will have time to get used to the new procedure. By April, company management expects no labour time variance to occur from the new standard.

Citizen measures its success in meeting standards using an "achievement ratio," which is expected to be 100%, that is, no variance. If a 1% unfavourable variance occurs, a review of the process is triggered. Such a low tolerance for nonconformance is not unusual in Japanese firms and indicates how tightly Japanese production processes are controlled.[10]

Attainability

Standards provide a target level of performance and can be set at various levels of rigour. The level of rigour reflected in the standard affects motivation, and one reason for using standards is to motivate employees. Standards can be classified by their degree of rigour, ranging from easy to difficult. The classifications are similar to the levels of capacity discussed in Chapter 2: expected, practical, and theoretical.

expected standard
a standard that reflects what is actually expected to occur in a future period

Expected standards are set at a level that reflects what is actually expected to occur in the future period. Such standards anticipate future waste and inefficiencies and allow for them. As such, expected standards are not of significant value for motivation, control, or performance evaluation. Any variances from expected standards should be minimal and managers should take care that expected standards are not set to be too easy to achieve.

practical standards
standards that can be reached or slightly exceeded approximately 60% to 70% of the time with reasonable effort by workers

Standards that can be reached or slightly exceeded approximately 60% to 70% of the time with reasonable effort by workers are called **practical standards.** These standards allow for normal, unavoidable time problems or delays such as machine downtime and worker breaks. Practical standards represent an attainable challenge and have traditionally been thought to be the most effective at inducing the best worker performance and at determining how effectively and efficiently workers are performing their tasks. Both favourable and unfavourable variances result from the use of moderately rigorous standards such as these.

Standards that allow for no inefficiencies of any type are called **theoretical standards**. Theoretical standards encompass the highest level of rigour and do not allow for normal operating delays or human limitations such as fatigue, boredom, or misunderstanding. Traditionally, theoretical standards were not used because they resulted in discouraged and resentful workers who ultimately ignored the standards. Variances from theoretical standards were always unfavourable and these variances were not considered useful for constructive cost control or performance evaluation. Even in a plant that is entirely automated, there is still the possibility of human or machine failure. This traditional perspective has, however, begun to change, as the section on page 264 explains.

theoretical standards
standards that allow for no inefficiencies of any type; encompass the highest level of rigour and do not allow for normal operating delays or human limitations such as fatigue, boredom, or misunderstanding

Depending on the type of standard in effect, the acceptable ranges used to apply the management by exception principle differ. **Management by exception** allows managers to set upper and lower limits of tolerance for deviations and investigate only deviations that fall outside those tolerance ranges. This difference is especially notable for deviations on the unfavourable side. If a company uses expected standards, the ranges of acceptable variances should be extremely small, since actual cost should closely conform to the standard. In contrast, a company using theoretical standards would expect variances to fall within very wide ranges of acceptability because of the level of rigour of the standards. The News Note below, about a study of manufacturing company controllers, provides some reasons why managers are using more formalized methods of judging when to investigate variances than those used in the past.

management by exception
a technique in which managers set upper and lower limits of tolerance for deviations and investigate only deviations that fall outside those tolerance ranges

Variances large enough to fall outside the ranges of acceptability generally indicate trouble. The variances themselves, though, do not reveal the cause of the trouble or the person or group responsible. To determine causes of variances, managers must investigate problems through observation, inspection, and inquiry. Such investigations involve the time and effort of people at the operating level as well as accounting personnel. Operations personnel should be alert in spotting variances as they occur and should record the reasons for the variances to the extent that those

When to Investigate Variances

GENERAL NEWS NOTE

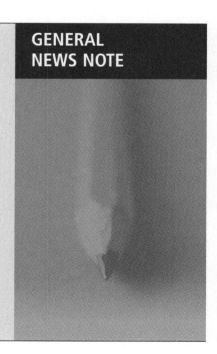

Variance investigation policies for materials and labour at large companies are moving away from pure judgment and toward the use of structured or formalized exception procedures.

One explanation is that the results are being driven by manufacturing innovations that lead to shorter production runs and shorter product life cycles. In such an environment, monthly variance reports may be so untimely as to be virtually useless. In a flexible manufacturing environment, production runs can be extremely short—only days or perhaps even hours. To provide timely feedback in an environment where the nature of operations and the products being produced change rapidly, more accounts and greater reporting frequency are required.

Another explanation relates to the increasing globalization of markets rather than to the characteristics or individual operating policies of the firm. When competing internationally, companies face more competitors, are less likely to be the lowest-cost producers, and face more uncertainties than in domestic markets. By reducing production cost surprises, intensified management accounting (in the frequency of reports and the details of variance composition) can compensate for these additional uncertainties.

Source: Bruce R. Gaumnitz and Felix P. Kollaritsch, "Manufacturing Variances: Current Practice and Trends," *Journal of Cost Management*, Spring 1991, pp. 63–64. Reprinted with permission from *The Journal of Cost Management*, © 1991, by RIA, 395 Hudson Street, New York, NY, 10014.

causes can be determined. For example, operating personnel can readily detect and report causes such as machine downtime or material spoilage.

How well a company determines the causes of variances is often proportional to how much time, effort, and money is spent in gathering information about variances during the period. Managers must be willing and able to accumulate variance information regularly and consistently to evaluate the evidence, isolate the causes, and if possible influence performance to improve the process. If variances are ignored when they occur, it is often impossible or extremely costly to determine the relevant data and to take corrective action at a later time.

LEARNING OBJECTIVE 6

How are standard setting and standard usage changing in modern business?

CHANGES IN THE USE OF STANDARDS

Sometimes, in using variances from standards for control and performance evaluation purposes, accountants (and to a certain extent businesspeople in general) believe that an incorrect measurement is employed. For example, the chapter stated that material standards often include a factor for waste and labour standards are commonly set at the expected level of attainment, even though this level allows for downtime and human error. The practice of using standards that are not aimed at the highest possible theoretical level of attainment is now being questioned in a business environment concerned with world-class operations, especially continuous improvement.

Use of Theoretical Standards for Quality Improvement

just-in-time
a philosophy about when to do something; the *when* is "as needed" and the *something* is a production, purchasing, or delivery activity

total quality management
a philosophy for organizational management and organizational change that seeks ever-increasing quality

Japanese influence on North American management philosophy and production techniques has been substantial in the recent past. **Just-in-time (JIT)** production systems and **total quality management (TQM)** concepts were both imported to this country as a result of an upsurge in Japanese productivity. These two world-class concepts are notable departures from the traditional view that ideals should not be used in standards development and application. Rather than including waste and inefficiency in the standards and then accepting additional waste and spoilage deviations under a management by exception principle, both JIT and TQM begin from the premises of zero defects, zero inefficiency, and zero downtime. Under such a system, theoretical standards become expected standards, with either no or only a minimal acceptable level of deviation from standards.

Although workers may, at first, resent the introduction of standards set at a "perfection" level, it is in their and management's best long-run interest to have such standards. When a standard permits a deviation from the ideal, managers are allowing for inefficient resource utilization. Setting standards at the tightest possible theoretical level is intended to produce the most useful information for managerial purposes as well as the highest-quality products and services at the lowest possible cost. If no inefficiencies are built into or tolerated in the system, deviations from standards should be minimized and overall organizational performance improved.

If theoretical standards are to be implemented, management must be prepared to go through a four-step "migration" process. First, teams should be established to determine where current problems lie and identify the causes of those problems. Second, if the causes relate to equipment, facility, or workers, management must be ready to invest in plant and equipment items, equipment rearrangements, or worker training so that the standards are amenable to the operations. Training is essential if workers are to perform at the high levels of efficiency demanded by theoretical standards. If the causes are related to external sources, such as poor-quality material, management must be willing to change suppliers or pay higher prices for higher-quality input. Third, because workers have now often been assigned the responsibility for quality, they must also be given the authority to react to problems, as discussed in the News Note below. "The key to quality initiatives is for employees to move beyond their natural resistance-to-change mode to a highly focused, strategic, and empowered mind-set. This shift unlocks employees' energy and creativity, and leads them to ask, "How can I do my job even better today?"[11] Fourth, requiring people to work at their maximum potential demands recognition, meaning that management must provide rewards for achievement.

Whether setting standards at the theoretical level will become the norm of North American companies cannot be determined at this time. However, the authors believe that the level of attainability for standards will move away from the expected and closer to the ideal. This conclusion reflects the current business environment in which companies most often must meet competitors head-to-head; if a company's competitor uses the highest possible standards as product norms, that company must also use such standards to compete on quality and to meet cost and, thus, profit margin objectives. Higher standards for efficiency automatically mean lower costs because of the elimination of nonvalue-added activities such as waste, idle time, and rework.

Long-Term Versus Short-Term Standards

Standards have traditionally been set after prices and quantities for the various cost elements were comprehensively investigated. These standards were almost always retained for at least one year and, sometimes, for many years. The current business environment including outsourcing, supplier contractual relationships, technology advancements, competitive niches, and enhanced product design and time-to-market considerations changes so rapidly that a standard may no longer be useful for management control purposes throughout an entire year. Company management needs to consider whether to ignore rapid changes in the environment or to incorporate those changes into the standards during a year in which significant changes occur.

Empowering Employees Is an Ethical Business Practice

GENERAL NEWS NOTE

Making employees more involved in and responsible for their work activities increases the value of those individuals not only to the organization, but also to themselves and to society as a whole. The organizational benefits gained from empowerment are that employees have a sense of ownership of and work harder toward goals they have set for themselves. Thus, employee involvement automatically promotes a higher degree of effort on the part of the work force. We avoid the basis of the Marxist critique of capitalism: the exploitation and subsequent alienation and rebellion of the worker. Problems will be solved more quickly and, therefore, the cost of errors will be reduced.

Providing training to employees for improving skills and/or decision making results in a person who is a more valuable and productive member of the company and society. Additionally, empowered employees are less likely to become bored and should experience more job satisfaction. Lastly, empowering employees provides a valuable means by which people's "timeless quest to express themselves and establish their individuality be furthered in the face of a world that is becoming more complex and more dependent on technology." The pinnacle of Maslow's hierarchy of needs is achieved as well: self-actualization.

Source: Cecily Raiborn and Dinah Payne, "TQM: Just What the Ethicist Ordered," *Journal of Business Ethics*, Vol. 15, 1996, p. 969. Reprinted with kind permission from Kluwer Academic Publishers.

Ignoring the changes is a simplistic approach that allows the same type of cost to be recorded at the same amount all year. Thus, for example, any material purchased during the year is recorded at the same standard cost regardless of when the purchase was made. This approach, although simplifying recordkeeping, eliminates any opportunity to adequately control costs or evaluate performance. Additionally, such an approach could create large differences between standard and actual costs, making standard costs unacceptable for external reporting.

Changing the standards to reflect price or quantity changes makes some aspects of management control and performance evaluation more effective and others more difficult. For instance, financial plans prepared under the original standards must be adjusted before appropriate actual comparisons can be made against them. Changing the standards also creates a problem for recordkeeping and inventory measurement. At what standard cost should a product be recorded—the standard in effect when that product was made, or the standard in effect when the financial statements are prepared? If standards are changed, they are more closely related to actual costs but many of the benefits discussed earlier in the chapter might be compromised.

Management may consider combining these two choices in the accounting system. Plans prepared by use of original and new standards can be compared; any variances reflect changes in the business environment. These variances can be designated as: uncontrollable, such as changes in the market price of raw materials; internally initiated, such as changes in standard labour time resulting from employee training or equipment rearrangement; or internally controllable, such as excess usage of material or labour time caused by the purchase of inferior materials.

The Future of Standard Costing

Critics of standard costing question the relevance of traditional variance analysis for cost control and performance appraisal in today's manufacturing and competitive environment. Nevertheless, standard costing systems continue to be widely used. This is because standard costing systems provide cost information for many other purposes besides cost control. Standard costs and variance analysis would still be required for other purposes even if they were abandoned for cost control.

For those organizations that have implemented activity-based systems, standard costing still has an important role to play in controlling the costs of unit level activities. Unit level activities can be defined as those activities that are performed each time a unit of product or service is produced.[12]

Standard Costs and Enterprise Resource Planning Systems

Although expensive to implement and operate, enterprise resource planning (ERP) systems provide a much higher level of accuracy than traditional approaches to gathering cost information. With most manufacturing processes being automated and operated with little direct labour, ERP systems have an advantage in keeping accurate record of numerous overhead cost pools at all levels in an organization. In addition, as a manufacturing facility can be used for an increasing variety of products, ERP systems are able to allocate common costs to a large number of different products. The greater capacity of ERP systems to accurately allocate costs means that ERP systems are important for developing accurate standards. Standard costs can be prepared with, for example, the sub-module mySAP.com Financials.

ERP systems address one of the major problems with standard costing, and that is complexity of the value creation chain. Complexity characterizes a value creation chain when there are multiple products and many manufacturing and testing activities. Complexity similarly exists with service organizations that have many different services and many different customers. ERP systems are able to deal with the complexity facing standard costs by allocating costs based on actual activities. This will be discussed in Chapter 12.

ERP systems—by using common charts of accounts, standard practices, and standard data definitions—are able to provide comparable data among the various parts of an organization. This standardization imposes standards across an organization. By reporting in an equivalent fashion, separate units can be compared and standards can be established based on the organizational units with superior performance. In a typical pre-ERP organization, each department or unit is a separate "fiefdom" with a tendency to resist openness. With ERP systems, openness cannot be easily avoided, and it is more difficult for inferior performers to say, "We are different and therefore we cannot be compared."

SITE ANALYSIS

Bright Pearl Seafood Restaurant Inc.

It only takes a short conversation with the managing director Stephen Chan at Bright Pearl Seafood Restaurant Inc. to understand the organization's success. He continuously emphasizes his company's dedication to two things: a quality product and an empowered workforce. Without the first, Bright Pearl could not retain its clients; without the second, the company could never produce its high-quality products. Bright Pearl's product simply has to be better; it can't compete solely on the basis of cost.

The institution of the modular team concept was a radical step for such a small organization. It required substantial training so that employees could perform multiple tasks and perform them well. Employee empowerment provided a benefit not originally considered: it took the matter of worker productivity out of the hands of company management and placed it in the work teams. "The teams are self-disciplining. If a team member is not performing up to par, the other team members either get that person 'on board' or make the comfort level such that that person would prefer not to continue." Thus, labour efficiency variances are negligible.

Bright Pearl's primary concern these days is not about standard cost variances. Costs are under control; productivity is high; workers are achieving bonuses based on team activity goals; and, best of all, employee morale is high in a work environment typically viewed as tedious. The concern of company management is an ability to remain profitable in the face of potential additional increases in costs such as labour and utilities that will affect Bright Pearl. The company knows that customers are willing to pay for a quality product and the company has "tightened its belt" to be competitive. But if costs are increased, will customers be willing to pay a higher price for their product? Chan hopes so—for the sake of the workers that his company has so carefully trained to be concerned about customer satisfaction through product quality.

Source: Interview with Stephen Chan, Managing Director, Bright Pearl Seafood Restaurant Inc.

APPENDIX 5A

Standard Cost System Journal Entries

LEARNING OBJECTIVE 7

What journal entries are needed in a standard cost system?

Journal entries for the information contained in the chapter related to Margaret White Clothing Ltd.'s Cutting Department are given in Exhibit 5-8. The material price variance in this exhibit is accounted for based on the secondary information that 3,000 square metres of cotton fabric were purchased. Note that unfavourable variances have debit balances and favourable variances have credit balances. Unfavourable variances represent excess costs, while favourable variances represent cost savings. Since standard costs are shown in Work in Process Inventory (a debit-balanced account), it is reasonable that excess costs are also debits.

Although standard cost systems are useful for internal reporting, such costs are not acceptable for external reporting unless they are substantially equivalent to those that would have resulted from using an actual cost system.[13] If standards are achievable and updated periodically, this equivalency should exist. Using standards

EXHIBIT 5-8

Journal Entries for Cutting Department, Week of June 12–16, 2005

Raw Material Inventory	10,500	
Material Price Variance	1,950	
Accounts Payable		12,450
To record the purchase of 3,000 square metres of cotton fabric at $4.15 per square metre. (From Exhibit 5-5.)		
Work in Process Inventory Cutting Dept.	9,240	
Material Quantity Variance	315	
Raw Material Inventory		9,555
To record the issuance and usage of 2,730 square metres of cotton fabric for 2,200 shirts. (From page 249.)		
Work in Process Inventory—Cutting Dept.	5,280	
Labour Rate Variance	200	
Labour Efficiency Variance		480
Wages Payable		5,000
To record the usage of 500 direct labour hours at a wage rate of $10 per DLH. (From page 250.)		
Variable Overhead—Cutting Dept.	3,360	
Various accounts		3,360
To record actual variable overhead costs. (From Exhibit 5-5.)		
Fixed Overhead—Cutting Dept.	2,875	
Various accounts		2,875
To record actual fixed overhead costs. (From Exhibit 5-5.)		
Work in Process Inventory—Cutting Dept.	6,050	
Variable Overhead—Cutting Dept.		3,850
Fixed Overhead—Cutting Dept.		2,200
To apply variable overhead at $7 per DLH and fixed overhead at $6 per MH for actual production of 2,200 shirts. (From Exhibit 5-5.) (VO = 550 hours × $7 = $3,850; FO = 366 2/3 hours × $6 = $2,200.)		
Variable Overhead—Cutting Dept.	490	
VOH Spending Variance—Cutting Dept.		140
VOH Efficiency Variance—Cutting Dept.		350
To close the variable overhead account. (From page 253.)		
FOH Spending Variance—Cutting Dept.	379	
FOH Volume Variance—Cutting Dept.	296	
Fixed Overhead—Cutting Dept.		675
To close the fixed overhead account. (From page 254.)		

for financial statements should provide fairly conservative inventory valuations because the effects of excess prices and/or inefficient operations are minimized.

If actual costs are used in financial statements, the standard cost information shown in the accounting records must be adjusted at year-end to approximate actual cost information. The nature of the year-end adjusting entries depends on whether the variance amounts are significant or not.

All manufacturing variances (material, labour, and overhead) are considered together in determining the appropriate year-end disposition. If the combined impact of these variances is considered insignificant, standard costs are approximately the same as actual costs, and the variances are closed to Cost of Goods Sold (or Cost of Services Rendered in a service organization). Unfavourable variances are closed by being credited; favourable variances are closed by being debited. In a manufacturing company, although all production of the period has not yet been sold, this treatment of insignificant variances is justified on the basis of the immateriality of the amounts involved.

Assuming that the variances are insignificant, the following journal entry is made:

Labour Efficiency Variance	480	
Cost of Goods Sold	1,985	
Material Price Variance		1,950
Material Quantity Variance		315
Labour Rate Variance		200
To close insignificant variances to Cost		
of Goods Sold.		

In contrast, if the total variance amount is significant, the overhead variances are prorated at year-end to ending inventories and Cost of Goods Sold in proportion to the relative size of those account balances. This proration disposes of the variances and presents the financial statements in a way that approximates the use of actual costing. The disposition of significant variances is similar to the disposition of large amounts of underapplied or overapplied overhead shown in Chapter 2. The material price variance based on purchases is prorated among Raw Material Inventory, Work in Process Inventory, Finished Goods Inventory, and Cost of Goods Sold or Cost of Services Rendered. All other variances occur as part of the conversion process and are prorated only to the Work in Process Inventory, Finished Goods Inventory, and Cost of Goods Sold or Cost of Services Rendered accounts.

APPENDIX 5B

Process Costing with Standard Costs

All examples in the chapter use actual historical costs to assign values to products under either the weighted average method or FIFO method. Companies may prefer to use standard rather than actual costs for inventory measurement purposes. The use of standard costs simplifies process costing and allows variances to be measured during the period. Actual costing requires that a new production cost be computed each production period. Standard costing eliminates such

LEARNING OBJECTIVE 8

What use do standard costs have in a process costing system?

recomputations, although standards do need to be reviewed (and possibly revised) at least once a year to keep the amounts current.

There are still some operations that are heavily labour-oriented. The following is an example. At Motivatit Seafood, removing the shells and meats from oysters, crabs, and crawfish must be done too gently and dexterously for machines to handle completely. Although half-shelled oysters move down an assembly line, human hands seem to do the real work. And at what pace? The best shuckers can repeat the rhythmic hammering, prying, and tossing motion at the rate of almost 500 oysters per hour, thereby setting a high standard against which to measure actual production activity.[14]

Calculations of equivalent units of production for standard process costing are identical to those for FIFO process costing. Unlike the weighted average method, both standard costing and FIFO emphasize the measurement and control of current production and current period costs. The commingling of units and costs that occurs when the weighted average method is used reduces the emphasis on current effort that standard costing is intended to represent and measure.

In a standard cost process costing system, actual costs of the current period are recorded and are compared with the standard costs of the equivalent units of production. If actual costs are less than standard, there is a favourable variance; unfavourable variances arise if actual costs are greater than the standard. Units are transferred out of a department at the standard cost of each production element.

CHAPTER SUMMARY

A standard cost is a budget for one unit of product or service output and provides a norm against which actual cost can be compared. In a traditional standard cost system, standards are computed for prices and quantities of each product component (material, labour, variable overhead, and fixed overhead). Standards should be developed by a team comprising professional staff and managers as well as employees whose performance will be evaluated by such standards. A standard cost card is used to accumulate and record specific information about the components, processes, quantities, and costs that form the standard for a product. The material and labour sections of the standard cost card are derived from the bill of materials and the operations flow document, respectively.

In a standard costing system, actual and standard costs are recorded; then, variances are computed and analyzed. Each total variance is separated into subvariances relating to price and quantity or rate and efficiency elements.

Variance analysis provides a basis for management planning, control, and performance evaluation. Using standard costs, managers can forecast what costs should be at various levels of activity and compare those forecasts with actual results. When large variances are observed, the causes should be determined and, if possible, corrective action should be taken. For this reason, variances should be recorded as early and as often in the production/service process as is feasible.

Standards should be appropriate and attainable. They should reflect current relevant technical and operational expectations. The level of rigour chosen for the standards should be based on realistic expectations and motivational effects on employees. The practical level has typically been thought to have the best motivational impact; however, some Japanese firms use theoretical standards to indicate their goals of minimum cost and zero defects. Standards are often important in implementing strategies where costs and quality must be controlled.

Some companies are changing the way standards are set and used. Traditionally, standards have included some level of waste and spoilage and, regarding fixed overhead, have been based on expected activity levels. These standards were commonly held constant for a year or longer. Recently, many firms have discovered that their standards have not been useful in implementing process, quality, or cost improvements. Thus, managers are revising standards to reflect technology advances, process improvements, and global market competitiveness.

Cross-Functional Applications

Topic of Note	Discipline	Cross-Functional Applications
Variance Analysis	Accounting	Standard costing systems permit accountants to integrate both expected and actual costs into the information system; clerical ease and efficiency is promoted in recordkeeping; variances are captured in the accounts.
	Management	Entire systems of management such as management by exception, total quality management, and contingency theory depend upon assigning responsibility to various managers and controlling performance with variance analysis (VA). VA also assists managers in strategic planning and organizational activities.
	Economics	Economic inefficiencies in a firm can be identified by comparing actual operating activities with those expected. This process can improve the measurement of marginal and incremental costs on which managers base their decisions.
	Human Resource Management	VA can identify talented managers and those who may require more training, education, or motivation. Employee training is a strain on the limited human-resources budget. VA permits employee training to be targeted and even prioritized to affect the most critical activities.
	Engineering	VA engineers, to improve their system/process efficiency, need a benchmark for their activities. In an environment where firms are closely linked in a technological sense, a common benchmark for operations is almost a necessity. Standard setting is particularly challenging for manufacturing engineers because the production process usually involves modelling people–machine relationships, which are complex in application. Despite the uncertainty, attempts are made to set reliable standards to assist in analyzing and predicting manufacturing process efficiency.
	Purchasing	VA can assist outsourcing decisions and monitor changes in outsourcing competence. As the traditional boundaries between organizations become more dynamic, it is reasonable to require suppliers to operate within the limits of customers' control requirements. JIT inventory and relationship marketing often depend upon a supplier's ability to operate within a customer's strategic standards.

(cont.)

Cross-Functional Applications

Topic of Note	Discipline	Cross-Functional Applications
	Service Industries	VA can clarify the often inexact requirements set by public law or union negotiations. When VA is combined with legal standards or union job descriptions, the performance and quality considerations can be evaluated over the long run with the same effectiveness as a production environment.
Standard Setting	Finance	Strategic financial planning depends upon acceptable and attainable standards for return on assets, investment capital, long-run profitability, and equity versus debt structure for an organization. In a rapidly changing capital market environment, financial planners must use the most updated standards to control and predict the course of their organizations in a competitive market as well as for evaluating alternative sources and uses of capital.
	Labour and Industrial Relations	Standard setting is often a major point of contention in labour management negotiations because it involves the labour cost input into a product as well as the working environment and performance evaluation of employees. Although measurements can stray from ideal standards or strategic goals by a wide margin, the important consideration is the cooperation in the process. If high standards are set in an environment of narrow, detached input, low morale and poor output are probable consequences.
	Operations Research	Methods of operational planning such as optimization roles in decision making, utility-preference modelling, scheduling, and simulation of operating systems all depend upon reliable standard setting. As a bonus, standards that are generally accepted as reliable can validate the modelling process as well.

Key Terms

Bill of materials (p. 243)
Expected standard (p. 262)
Fixed overhead spending variance (p. 253)
Just-in-time (p. 264)
Labour efficiency variance (p. 251)
Labour rate variance (p. 251)
Management by exception (p. 263)
Material price variance (p. 248)
Material quantity variance (p. 249)
Operations flow document (p. 244)
Practical standards (p. 262)
Price variance (p. 247)
Quantity variance (p. 247)

Standards (p. 240)
Standard cost (p. 240)
Standard cost card (p. 245)
Standard costing system (p. 240)
Standard quantity allowed (p. 247)
Theoretical standards (p. 263)
Total quality management (p. 264)
Variable overhead efficiency variance (p. 253)
Variable overhead spending variance (p. 253)
Variance (p. 241)
Variance analysis (p. 255)
Volume variance (p. 253)

Solution Strategies

Variances in Formula Format:

Material price variance = AQ(AP – SP)
Material quantity variance = SP(AQ – SQ)
Labour rate variance = AQ(AP – SP)
Labour efficiency variance = SP(AQ – SQ)
Variable overhead spending variance = Actual VOH – (SR × AQ)
Variable overhead efficiency variance = SR(AQ – SQ)
Fixed overhead spending variance =Actual FOH – Budgeted FOH
Fixed overhead volume variance = Budgeted FOH – (SR × SQ)

Variances in Diagram Format:

Actual Price ×
Actual Quantity Purchased | Standard Price ×
Actual Quantity Purchased

Material Price Variance
(calculated at point of purchase)

Standard Price ×
Actual Quantity Used | Standard Price ×
Standard Quantity Allowed

Material Quantity Variance

or

Actual Price ×
Actual Quantity Used | Standard Price ×
Actual Quantity Used | Standard Price ×
Standard Quantity Allowed

Material Price Variance | Material Quantity Variance

Total Material Variance

Actual Price ×
Actual Quantity
of Activity | Standard Price ×
Actual Quantity
of Activity | Standard Price ×
Standard Quantity
of Activity

Labour Rate Variance | Labour Efficiency Variance

Total Labour Variance

Actual VOH | Standard VOH Rate ×
Actual Activity | Applied VOH
(Standard VOH Rate × Standard
Quantity Allowed)

VOH Spending Variance | VOH Efficiency Variance

Total VOH Variance

Actual FOH | Budgeted FOH | Applied FOH
(Standard FOH Rate × Standard
Quantity Allowed)

FOH Spending Variance | FOH Volume Variance

Total FOH Variance

DEMONSTRATION PROBLEMS

Problem 1

Forrest Ltd. manufactures a line of swimsuits for women under the Ambrosia label. The standard variable costs of producing one swimsuit are as follows:

	Standard Quantity or Hours	Standard Price or Rate	Standard Cost
Direct materials	?	$8 per metre	$?
Direct labour	?	?	?
Variable overhead	?	$3 per direct labour hour	?
Total standard cost per suit			$63.00

In June 2005, 1,500 swimsuits were produced and all were sold. Selected information for June 2005 production follows:

	Materials Used	Direct Labour	Variable Overhead
Total standard cost for June's production	$?	$24,000	$ 4,800
Actual costs incurred	65,000	?	4,860
Materials quantity variance	1,200 U		

During June, 1,700 actual direct labour hours were incurred, and the difference between standard and actual cost per swimsuit produced was $0.42 U.

Required:

a. Total standard cost of the materials required for June production
b. Standard direct materials required per swimsuit
c. Total materials price variance
d. Standard direct labour rate per hour
e. Total actual direct labour cost incurred
f. Labour rate variance
g. Labour efficiency variance
h. Variable overhead efficiency variance
i. Variable overhead spending variance
j. Standard variable cost for one swimsuit

Problem 2

Bush Company applies fixed and variable overhead on the basis of machine hours. Below are Bush Company's results for the month just past:

Machine hours used to set the predetermined overhead rate	40,000
Variable overhead per machine-hour	$ 2.80
Actual variable overhead cost incurred	117,000
Actual fixed overhead cost incurred	302,100
Variable overhead cost applied to production	117,600
Variable overhead efficiency variance (unfavourable)	8,400
Fixed overhead budget variance (unfavourable)	2,100

Required:

a. Compute the following:
    i.   Budgeted fixed overhead
    ii. Fixed portion of the predetermined overhead rate
    iii. Standard hours allowed for units produced
    iv. Fixed overhead volume variance

v.   Fixed overhead cost applied to production
vi. Variable overhead spending variance
vii. Actual machine hours worked
viii. Underapplied or (overapplied) overhead

b.   Why is it important to separate the spending variance from the efficiency variance in variable overhead variance analysis?
c.   How would you interpret the volume variance in fixed overhead variance analysis?

(Adapted by the author from *Management Accounting examinations,* published by the Certified General Accountants Association of Canada © CGA-Canada, 2000, used by permission.)

Solutions to Demonstration Problems

Problem 1

a.   Total standard cost for swimsuits produced during June:

1,500 × $63		$94,500
Less: Standard costs of labour and overhead		
Direct labour	$24,000	
Variable overhead	4,800	28,800
Standard cost of materials used during June		$65,700

b.

Standard cost of materials used during June	$65,700
Number of swimsuits produced	1,500
Standard materials cost per swimsuit	
($65,700 ÷ 1,500)	43.80
Standard metres of direct materials per swimsuit	
($43.80 ÷ $8)	5.475 metres

c.

Actual cost of materials used	$65,000
Standard costs of materials used	65,700
Total material usage price variance	$ 700 F

Total materials variance	
Materials usage price variance	$ 700 F
Materials quantity variance	1,200 U
	$500 U

d.

Standard variable overhead cost for June	$ 4,800
Standard variable overhead rate per direct labour hour	3
Standard direct labour hours for June (4,800 ÷ 3)	1,600
Standard direct labour rate per hour (24,000 ÷ 1,600)	$ 15

or

Standard labour cost per unit	$24,000 ÷ 1,500 = $16
Standard variable overhead per unit	$63 – ($43.80 + $16) = $3.20
Standard labour hours per unit	$3.20 ÷ $3 = $1.0667
Standard labour rate per hour	$16 ÷ 1.0667 = $15

e.

Actual cost per swimsuit produced ($63.00 + $0.42)		$ 63.42
Number of swimsuits produced		× 1,500
Total actual costs of production		$95,130.00
Less: Actual cost of materials	$65,000	
Actual cost of variable overhead	4,860	69,860.00
Actual cost of direct labour		$25,270.00

f. Labour rate variance

$(AH \times AR) - (AH \times SR)$
$25,270 - (1,700 \times \$15)$
$25,270 - \$25,500$
$230 F$

g. Efficiency variance

$(AH \times SR) - (SH \times SR)$
$(1,700 \times \$15) - \$24,000$
$1,500 U$

h. Variable overhead efficiency variance

$(SH \times SR) - (AH \times SR)$
$4,800 - (1,700 \times \$3)$
$300 U$

i. Variable overhead spending variance

$(AH \times SR) - (AH \times AR)$
$5,100 - \$4,860$
$240 F$

j.

	Standard Quantity or Hours	Standard Price or Rate	Standard Cost
Direct materials	5.475 metres	$ 8 per metre	$43.80
Direct labour	1.067 hours	$15 per hour	16.00
Variable overhead	1.067 hours	$ 3 per hour	3.20
Total standard cost per swimsuit			$63.00

Problem 2

a.

i. Budgeted fixed overhead
Fixed overhead budgeted variance = $2,100
$2,100 = Actual fixed overhead − Budgeted fixed overhead
$2,100 = $302,100 − Budgeted fixed overhead
Budgeted fixed overhead = $300,000

ii. Fixed portion of predetermined overhead rate:
Budgeted fixed overhead/Machine hours to set predetermined rate
= $300,000 ÷ 40,000 hours = $7.50 per hour

iii. Standard hours allowed for production
= Applied variable overhead ÷ Variable overhead rate per hour
= $117,600 ÷ $2.80
= 42,000 hours

iv. Volume variance = Budgeted fixed overhead − $SH_A \times$ Std. FOHR
= $300,000 − (42,000 h × $7.50)
= $300,000 − $315,000
= $15,000 F

v. Fixed overhead applied = Predetermined fixed overhead × SH_A
= $7.50 × 42,000 h
= $315,000

vi. Variable overhead spending variance
Variable overhead controllable variance =
Variable overhead efficiency variance + Variable overhead spending variance
∴ Actual VOH incurred − VOH applied to production = $117,000 − $117,600 = $600 F
$600 F = $8,400 + Variable overhead spending variance
Variable overhead spending variance = $9,000 F

vii. Actual machine hours worked
Variable Overhead Spending Variance = Actual variable overhead − (AH × Standard variable overhead rate per hour)
$9,000 F = $117,000 − (AH × $2.80)
$126,000 = AH × $2.80
Actual hours = 45,000 hours

viii. Underapplied or overapplied overhead

Variable overhead spending variance	$ 9,000 F
Variable overhead efficiency variance	8,400 U
Fixed overhead budget variance	2,100 U
Fixed overhead volume variance	15,000 F
Total	$13,500 F

Overhead overapplied by $13,500

b. It is important to separate the spending variance from the efficiency variance because each measures a different aspect of the overall variable overhead variance, and each has a different cause. The spending variance measures whether the inputs were acquired at an appropriate cost or price, and the efficiency variance measures whether the inputs were used efficiently in production. In order to correct an unfavourable variance, it is necessary to identify its cause(s). Also, when evaluating performance, it is important to recognize that the two variances are often the responsibility of two different individuals.

c. The volume variance in fixed overhead variance analysis assigns a dollar value to the "cost" of operating at less than the planned activity level, or the "benefit" of operating at greater than the planned activity level.

End-of-Chapter Materials

SELF-TEST QUESTIONS

(SOLUTIONS APPEAR AT THE END OF THE CHAPTER.)

The following data apply to Questions 1 to 4.

The Cosmetics Corporation employs a standard cost system in which direct materials inventory is carried at standard cost. The organization has established the following standards for the prime costs of one Ashleanna perfume stick.

	Standard Quantity	Standard Price	Standard Cost
Direct material	8 kg	$1.80 per kg	$14.40
Direct labour	0.25 hour	$8.00 per hour	2.00
			$16.40

During November, 160,000 kg of direct material were purchased at a total cost of $304,000. The total factory wages for November were $42,000, 90% of which were for direct labour. During November, 19,000 perfume sticks were manufactured using 142,500 kg of direct material and 5,000 direct labour hours.

1. The direct material point of purchase price variance for November is:
a. $16,000 F
b. $16,000 U
c. $14,250 F
d. $14,250 U
e. $17,100 F

2. The direct material usage variance for November is:
a. $14,400 U
b. $ 1,100 F
c. $17,100 U
d. $17,100 F
e. $16,000 U

3. The direct labour rate variance for November is:
a. $2,200 F
b. $1,900 U
c. $2,000 F
d. $2,090 F
e. $2,090 U

4. The direct labour efficiency variance for November is:
a. $2,200 F
b. $2,000 F

c. $2,000 U
d. $1,800 U
e. $2,200 U

(Self-Test Questions 1–4 are IMA adapted.)

5. You are provided with the following selected information for Spectra Ltd.

Capacity machine hours	20,000
Budgeted machine hours	15,000
Actual machine hours	15,000
Standard machine hours allowed for actual production	18,000

Which of the following variances does Spectra Ltd. have?
a. An unfavourable volume variance
b. A favourable volume variance
c. No volume variance
d. A favourable variable overhead spending variance

6. Sassy Ltd. produces and sells Lipgloss. In the production of this product, the standard direct labour amounts to 5 hours at $20.00 per hour. During February, 5,000 units were produced using 26,000 direct labour hours at $21.00 per hour. What was the direct labour efficiency variance?
a. $46,000 U
b. $21,000 U
c. $20,000 U
d. $20,000 F

7. For the month of April, the manufacturing overhead volume variance at Triton Ltd. was $6,660 favourable. The organization uses a fixed overhead rate of $3.70 per direct labour hour. What does this mean for the standard direct labour hours allowed for April's output?
a. They exceeded actual hours by 1,800 hours.
b. They exceeded capacity activity by 1,800 hours.
c. They fell short of capacity activity by 1,800 hours.
d. They fell short of actual hours by 1,800 hours.

8. Squawk Box Ltd. makes and sells a single product and uses a standard cost system. During May, the company accountant, Mark Haines, budgeted $320,000 in manufacturing overhead cost at a capacity activity of 20,000 machine hours. At standard, each unit of finished product requires 4 machine hours. The following costs and activities were recorded during May:

Total actual manufacturing overhead cost incurred	$335,500
Units of product completed	4,700 units
Actual machine hours worked	21,000 machine hours

What was the amount of overhead cost that Squawk Box Ltd. applied to work in process for May?
a. $300,800
b. $315,370
c. $335,500
d. $336,000

(Self-Test Questions 5 and 8 are reprinted from *Management Accounting examinations* published by the Certified General Accountants Association of Canada © CGA-Canada, 1999 (#5) and 2000 (#8), used by permission.)

9. When a direct labour efficiency variance is prorated to inventories and cost of goods sold, the accounts affected include (more than one answer may be correct):
a. raw materials inventory
b. work in process
c. finished goods
d. accrued payroll

10. Variable overhead is applied on the basis of standard direct labour hours. If, for a given period, the direct labour efficiency variance is unfavourable, the variable overhead efficiency variance will be
a. favourable
b. unfavourable
c. zero
d. the same as the labour efficiency variance
e. indeterminable since it is not related to the labour efficiency variance.

QUESTIONS

1. Why is a standard costing system regarded as both a planning and a control tool?

2. What is a variance and what does it measure?

3. Why are standards necessary for each cost component of a product or service?

4. Describe a situation that illustrates the following statement: "Almost all products can be manufactured with a variety of inputs that would generate the same basic output."

5. Would an actual or a standard product costing system provide the better opportunity to evaluate the control of costs for a period? Explain.

6. Why should individuals other than accountants be involved in the standard setting process? Provide examples of who these additional individuals should be and what important information they might provide.

7. What is a bill of materials and how is it used in a standard cost system?

8. What is an operations flow document? How is it used in a standard cost system?

9. Why is a predetermined overhead rate considered a standard?

10. Why is the computation of the material price variance frequently based on the quantity of material purchased, rather than the quantity used, during the period?

11. What is variance analysis and why is it conducted by managers?

12. Why is a "conversion cost" category emerging in some companies to replace the traditional cost categories of direct labour and manufacturing overhead?

13. If the material price variance is computed on the basis of quantity of material purchased (point of purchase) rather than used, can a total material variance be computed? Explain your answer.

14. As the manufacturing vice president of Geraldo Controls, you have noticed that one manufacturing plant experienced several large unfavourable material quantity variances during the prior quarter. Before starting your probe of the matter, list some possible reasons for this type of variance.

15. Your manufacturing operations this period have shown a large favourable labour rate variance. Why might this have occurred? Would you expect your labour efficiency variance to be favourable or unfavourable? Why?

16. You are the supervisor of the Harvey Mail Service. Service quality in the organization is not measured relative to direct labour time. Additionally, there is a consistently large, favourable efficiency variance. Provide one positive and one negative analysis of this variance.

17. "Overhead standards should be set using the most available measurement in the production or service area, such as direct labour hours." Discuss the validity of this statement.

18. What is meant by "standard quantity allowed" when this term is used in relation to direct material? To direct labour? To overhead? Provide an example for each cost element.

19. Is fixed manufacturing overhead controlled by management on a per-unit basis? Explain your answer.

20. Of what importance is capacity utilization to managers? When managers control utilization, are they always controlling costs? Explain.

21. For the following variances, indicate (i) when each variance should be calculated and (ii) to whom responsibility for the variance should be assigned and why.
    a. Material price variance
    b. Material quantity variance
    c. Labour rate variance
    d. Labour efficiency variance
    e. Variable overhead spending variance
    f. Volume variance

22. Why is it important for managers to update standards periodically?

23. What is management by exception, and what is its role in a management control system that uses standard costing?

24. In a standard cost system, is standard cost or actual cost charged to Work in Process Inventory for direct material and direct labour? Explain. How are actual costs reflected in a standard cost system?

25. How do ERP systems impact the standard setting process within an organization?

26. How do ERP systems make organizations more transparent?

27. (Appendix 5A) If the variances incurred in a given period are not significant in amount, how are they typically closed out at the end of the period? Why is this disposition acceptable?

EXERCISES

1. (LO 1, 2, 3, 4, 5; Terminology) Match each item in the right-hand column with a term in the left-hand column.

a. Operations flow document
b. Practical standard
c. Standard
d. Theoretical standard
e. Labour rate variance
f. Overhead spending variance
g. Volume variance
h. Standard cost card
i. Variance analysts
j. Bill of materials

1. A standard that allows for no human or mechanical error
2. The difference between budgeted (estimated) and applied fixed overhead
3. A listing of tasks required to make a product
4. A document specifying the materials required for a product
5. The process of identifying causes of variances
6. A norm for a cost or a quantity
7. The difference between the actual and budgeted (estimated) overhead
8. The standard of performance that has reasonable probability of attainment
9. The difference between standard and actual labour wages
10. The document listing the standard cost of all inputs for a product

2. (LO 3; Material variances) You are the purchasing agent for The Zoo Company, which makes statues of endangered animals. Wildlife and environmental groups sell the statues at fund-raisers. In June 2005, you bought 105,600 kg of material at an average price of $2.40/kg. That month, 99,400 kg of material was used to produce 225 statues. The material standard for each statue is 420 kg of material at a standard cost of $2.25/kg.
Required:
a. Calculate the material price variance, based on quantity purchased.
b. Calculate the material quantity variance.
c. What potential reasons might you have for the price variance?

3. (LO 3; Material variances) The Waterworld Store experienced the following costs and quantities related to direct material during August 2005:

Actual quantity purchased	136,500 litres
Actual quantity used	130,500 litres
Standard quantity allowed	132,900 litres
Actual unit price per litre	$14.50
Standard unit price per litre	$13.90

Required:
a. Compute the material price variance based on (1) quantity purchased and (2) quantity used.
b. Compute the material quantity variance.
c. Why can a material price variance be computed on two different bases, but a labour rate variance cannot?

4. (LO 3; Labour variances) Alison Ground Automotive uses a standard cost system and experienced the following results related to direct labour in December:

Actual hours worked	41,250
Standard hours allowed for production	40,500
Actual direct labour rate	$7.25
Standard direct labour rate	$6.75

Required:
a. Total actual payroll
b. Labour rate variance
c. Labour efficiency variance

5. (LO 3; Labour variances) Frank Madden's Quilts makes a one-design queen-size quilt and uses a standard costing system. During February, the following direct labour hours and costs were incurred:

Standard hours	5,400
Actual hours	5,100
Standard wage rate per hour	$11.75
Actual wage rate per hour	$12.00

Required:
a. Determine total actual labour cost, standard labour cost, and the labour rate and efficiency variances.
b. Write a memo to Frank Madden about the possible causes of the rate and efficiency variances.

6. (LO 3; Labour variances) Connie Reed Cabinets builds 1.2-by-1.8 metre bookcases. Each bookcase requires 7 direct labour hours. The average standard hourly wage of workers is $9. During October, Connie Reed Cabinets built 1,200 bookcases. Direct labour time was 8,000 hours, and gross pay was $74,800.

Required:
a. Compute the labour variances.
b. Provide an explanation of the direct labour variances that is consistent with the results.

7. (LO 3; Labour variances) Silva Insurance Ltd.'s information about direct labour for September is as follows:

Efficiency variance	$17,380 U
Actual direct labour rate per hour	$ 7.50
Standard direct labour rate per hour	$ 7.90
Standard hours allowed	20,000

Required:
a. Calculate the actual hours worked during September.
b. Calculate the total payroll.
c. Calculate the labour rate variance.
d. Given the above information, Mr. Silva has asked your human resources firm, H R Sources, for some suggestions to better motivate his employees. Prepare a short memo providing some feedback to him.

8. (LO 3; Material and labour variances) Wolf Blitzer Manufacturing Co. uses a standard costing system and has provided you with the following data for its operations during May 2005:

Actual direct labour cost	$123,200
Actual variable overhead cost	$ 64,300
Standard material cost per unit	$ 7.50
Actual direct materials cost (10,000 kg)	$ 13,000
Direct materials price variance	$ 500 U
Direct labour rate variance	$ 3,200 U
Direct labour efficiency variance	$ 4,000 F
Standard variable overhead cost per direct labour hour	$8
Actual direct labour hours	7,500 h
Standard direct labour hours per unit	5 h
Actual direct materials used	9,000 kg

Required:
a. Standard direct labour rate per hour
b. Standard direct labour cost per unit
c. Number of units produced
d.. Direct material usage variance.

9. (LO 3; Material and labour variances) The Blue Noose Manufacturing Co.'s plans show estimated variable overhead is $120,000 when 30,000 direct labour hours are incurred and estimated direct labour costs are $360,000.
   For the month of April, the following are some selected variances.

Variable overhead spending variance	$ 18,000 U
Variable overhead efficiency variance	12,000 U
Materials price variance	12,000 F
Materials usage variance	7,500 U
During April, actual direct labour costs were	$419,900

The standard cost of 1 kg of material is $3.00, and 1 kg is the standard for each unit of product. In April, 75,000 units were produced and the unit materials price variance was $0.10/kg. The average wage rate exceeded the standard wage rate by $0.35.

Required:

a. Kilograms of materials purchased
b. Kilograms of material usage over standard
c. Standard hourly wage rate
d. Standard direct labour hours for the total April production

(Ex. 8–9 adapted by the author from *Management Accounting examinations,* published by the Certified General Accountants Association of Canada © CGA-Canada, 1997 (#8) and 1994 (#9), used by permission.)

10. (LO 3; Fixed overhead variances) Nicholas Sperry Co. produces briefcases. The standard variable and fixed overhead application rates per briefcase are, respectively, $0.80 and $0.50 per machine hour. Each briefcase takes 4 machine hours. During May 2005, the company had the following production statistics:

Total fixed overhead applied to production	$225,000
Actual fixed overhead	240,000
Volume variance	5,000 F
Variable overhead spending variance	10,000 F

Required:

a. Standard machine hours allowed
b. Number of briefcases produced
c. Budgeted amount of fixed overhead
d. Expected capacity in machine hours
e. Fixed overhead spending variance

11. (LO 3; Overhead variances) Joanne Steinman Manufacturing Ltd. employs a standard costing system. In the company's Montreal plant, manufacturing overhead is applied to production on the basis of machine hours. The following information from the Montreal plant pertains to October:

Standard variable manufacturing overhead rate per machine hour	$ 12
Standard fixed manufacturing overhead rate per machine hour	$ 10
Standard machine hours for month	4,200
Actual machine hours for month	4,400
Total budgeted monthly fixed manufacturing overhead	$40,000
Actual fixed manufacturing overhead	$45,000
Actual variable manufacturing overhead	$47,500

Required:

a. Total actual overhead cost
b. Total applied overhead
c. Variable overhead variances
d. Fixed overhead variances

12. (LO 3, 4; Material variances) You have just received the following information related to your company's purchases and usage of paper during October. The company runs high-volume calendar printing jobs.

Sheets of paper purchased in October	1,000,000
Sheets of paper used in October	780,000
Standard quantity allowed for good production	794,000
Actual unit purchase price per sheet	$0.037
Standard unit price per sheet	$0.039

Required:

a. Calculate the material price variance based on the quantity purchased and the material quantity variance.
b. You have asked the vice president of manufacturing to explain the difference between theoretical, practical, and expected standards. How might she explain these differences?

c.   How would using theoretical standards change the variance information calculated in part (a)? (No specific numerical calculations are necessary.)

13. (LO 3, 4; Variable overhead variances) Celine Corp. produces engraved wood plaques;
each plaque requires 15 minutes of machine time. During April, 1,800 units were manufactured. The company's predetermined variable overhead rate per machine hour is
$14. In April, $6,200 of variable overhead costs were incurred and machine time was
clocked at 410 hours.

Required:
a.   What is the total applied variable overhead for the month?
b.   Calculate the variable overhead variances.
c.   This is the sixth month in a row in which there has been a significant favourable
variable overhead efficiency variance. Provide the company accountant with an
appropriate explanation as to why so few machine hours are being used relative
to the standard.

14. (LO 3, 4; Variable overhead variances) Using the information from Exercise 8, calculate the following:
a.   Standard variable overhead cost per unit
b.   Variable overhead spending variance
c.   Variable overhead efficiency variance

15. (LO 3, 4; Variable overhead variances) Boniface Park Co. manufactures three products
(tables, chairs, and desks) and uses direct labour hours (DLH) as its overhead application base. Standard hours allowed for each product follow:

Table	10 DLH
Chair	3 DLH
Desk	12 DLH

The standard variable overhead application rate is $4 per direct labour hour.
Production for June was 100 tables, 400 chairs, and 60 desks. Actual direct labour
hours incurred were 3,020 and actual variable overhead was $11,900.
Required:
a.   Determine the total applied variable overhead for June.
b.   Calculate the variable overhead spending, efficiency, and total variances.
c.   Are direct labour hours a reasonable application base in an automated plant?
Why or why not?

16. (LO 3, 4; Fixed overhead variances) Use the information given in Exercise 15 and the
following additional information. Monthly expected capacity is 3,000 direct labour
hours. Boniface Park's fixed overhead application rate at expected annual capacity is
$2 per direct labour hour. In June, actual fixed overhead amounted to $6,100.
Required:
a.   What is the total monthly budgeted fixed overhead?
b.   What is the total applied fixed overhead for June?
c.   Compute the fixed overhead spending, volume, and total fixed overhead variance.
d.   Discuss the meaning of the fixed overhead volume variance.

17. (LO 3, 4; Overhead variances) Luste Concrete Ltd. manufactures industrial pipe. The
company uses a standard cost system and applies variable manufacturing overhead to
production using kilograms of product moved. The standard variable manufacturing
overhead rate is set at $9 per kilogram moved. The standard weight per unit is 0.75 kg.
For the year 2005, budgeted fixed manufacturing overhead is $480,000; fixed manufac-
turing overhead is applied to production using direct labour hours. The standard time
per unit is 0.5 direct labour hours. Budgeted direct labour hours for the year 2005
were 60,000. The following data pertains to the year 2005:

Number of units produced	82,000
Actual weight of units (kg)	62,300
Actual direct labour hours	42,000
Actual variable overhead cost	$582,000
Actual fixed overhead cost	$476,000

Required:
a.   The company CEO, Mark Bennett, has asked you to determine the amount of
total applied overhead, variable overhead variances, and fixed overhead variances.

b. What explanations might you offer Mr. Bennett for the variances calculated in part (a)?

18. (LO 3, 4; Overhead variances) Titanic Inc. uses a standard costing system. Standard cost data for the company's best-selling product, plastic icebergs, follow:

Direct material	$ 3
Direct labour	6
Variable overhead	4
Fixed overhead (based on expected capacity of 600,000 units)	5
Total	$18

Titanic produced 399,000 units in the year 2005. Actual variable overhead was $2,100,000 and actual fixed overhead was $4,500,000. Overhead is applied on a machine hour basis; each iceberg takes 20 minutes of machine time. Actual machine hours used for the year were 130,000.

Required:
a. All variable overhead variances
b. All fixed overhead variances
c. With the downturn in economic conditions, a lower than expected demand occurred, and Titanic Inc. only sold 100,000 units during the year. Is the volume variance a valid reflection of capacity utilization? Provide the rationale for your answer.

19. (LO 3, 4; All variances) Moose Jaw Ltd. produces Xylon and has developed the following standard costs:

Direct materials	4 kg @ $3.00/kg	$12.00
Direct labour	1.5 hours @ $16.00 per hour	24.00
Variable overhead	1.5 hours @ $10.00 per hour	15.00
Fixed overhead	1.5 hours @ $4.00 per hour	6.00
Total		$57.00

For the month of August, the following transactions took place:
i. Purchased 5,000 kg of direct materials for $15,500
ii. August's production was supposed to be 1,500 units but only 1,200 units were produced
iii. During August, 4,600 kg of materials were issued to production
iv. Direct labour payroll totalled $32,175 for 1,950 hours worked
v. Actual variable overhead was $19,000
vi. Actual fixed overhead was $10,000

Required:
a. Compute two variances for each type of manufacturing cost.
b. What does the volume variance represent?

(Reprinted from *Management Accounting examinations,* published by the Certified General Accountants Association of Canada © CGA-Canada, 1996, used by permission.)

20. (LO 3, 4; Conversion cost variances) The Prince Edward Island facilities of Spuds Inc. were automated in late 2005. As division manager, you convinced corporate headquarters to allow you to change your standard costing system. The most significant change was to combine direct labour and variable overhead into a single conversion cost pool. In its first year of implementing the new system, the following standards were set:

Variable conversion cost per machine hour		$ 12
Fixed conversion cost per machine hour (based on 80,000 budgeted machine hours)		$ 10

Data related to the actual results for the year 2005 are:

Actual machine hours worked	76,000
Standard machine hours allowed	78,000
Variable conversion costs	$904,600
Fixed conversion costs	$784,000

Required:
a. Compute the variable conversion cost variances for the year.
b. Compute the fixed conversion cost variances for the year.
c. The Prince Edward Island plant of Spuds Inc. produces goods only as they are ordered by customers. Who has the greatest control over the fixed conversion

cost volume variance and why? When should control be exercised over fixed overhead costs, and why?

21. (LO 3, 7; Calculating variances and closing) The Harrison Co. Ltd. manufactures one product, for which it has developed the following standard cost:

Materials, 5 L @ $20/L	$100
Direct labour, 2 h @ $12/h	24
Variable overhead	16
Fixed overhead	50
	$190

Normal activity of 2,400 direct labour hours was used as a denominator in arriving at the fixed overhead rate. There were no inventories on January 1, 2005. During January 2005, the following actually occurred:

i.   6,000 L of material were purchased for $119,700.
ii. 1,000 units were transferred to finished goods inventory.
iii. 5,100 L of material were issued to production.
iv. The direct labour payroll was $24,304 for 1,960 hours.
v.   Actual overhead costs totalled $16,001 variable and $58,000 fixed.
vi. 800 units were sold on account at a unit price of $250.
vii. Selling and administrative expenses totalled $25,000.

Required:
a.   Compute two variances for each element of manufacturing costs.
b.   Compute the Cost of Goods Sold assuming all variances are prorated.

22. (LO 7; Appendix 5A) The following information pertains to the operations of Judith Poë Plastics for fiscal 2005. The company manufactures exquisite pink yard flamingos.

Purchase of material (at standard cost)	$600,000
Standard cost of material issued to production	552,000
Direct labour (at standard cost)	288,000
Material price variance	3,700 U
Material quantity variance	9,100 F
Direct labour rate variance	2,100 F
Direct labour efficiency variance	3,900 U

Required:
a.   Record the journal entry for purchasing direct material on account.
b.   Record the journal entry for issuing direct material into production.
c.   Record the journal entry to accrue direct labour costs.
d.   Record the year-end journal entry to close the variance accounts, assuming the variances are not material in amount.

PROBLEMS

1. (LO 3, 4; Material and labour variances) Anne Cowan Co. manufactures electrical supply boxes and accounts for production using a standard cost system. Standard quantities and costs for one electrical supply box follow:

Direct material	2 square metres @ $2.10 per square metre
Direct labour	10 minutes @ $13.20 per hour

In May 2005, 39,600 boxes were produced. You, as the company's purchasing agent, bought 115,000 square metres of material in May at $1.70 per square metre. The May manufacturing payroll reflected $93,500 of direct labour for 6,900 hours. In May, 88,500 square metres of direct material were placed in production.

Required:
a.   Calculate the material variances, basing the price variance on quantity purchased.
b.   Calculate the labour variances.
c.   Prepare a memo to Christopher Cowan, the controller, addressing the probable cause of the price variance and how that price affected the other variances.

2. (LO 3; Material and labour variances) Katrina's Jewellery makes pendants using a variety of stock moulds. One-eighth of a kilogram of direct material and 15 minutes of

direct labour are required to produce a pendant. Direct material costs of $6.20/kg are standard, and the standard direct labour rate is $12/h.

During April, 32,000 pendants were made, and the company experienced a $744 favourable material quantity variance. The purchasing agent had purchased 800 kg of material in excess of what the company used, incurring a favourable price variance of $1,235. Total direct labour hours worked were 8,200, and a total unfavourable labour variance of $1,700 was incurred.

Required:

a. Standard quantity of material allowed
b. Actual quantity of material used
c. Actual quantity of material purchased
d. Actual price of material purchased
e. Standard hours allowed for production
f. Labour efficiency variance
g. Labour rate variance
h. Actual labour rate paid

3. (LO 3; Material variances) Assume in all cases that the material price variance is calculated on the basis of quantity purchased rather than quantity used.

	Case 1	Case 2	Case 3	Case 4
Units produced	500	9,000	g	1,760
Standard litres per unit	a	d	12.5	10.6
Standard price per litre	$0.90	e	$1.30	j
Standard litres allowed	10,000	36,000	h	k

	Case 1	Case 2	Case 3	Case 4
Actual litres purchased	b	34,900	4,900	20,000
Actual litres used	9,800	36,450	4,895	18,450
Actual price per litre	$0.92	$5.04	i	$2.55
Material price variance	$214 U	$1,396 U	$490 F	l
Material quantity variance	c	f	$26 U	$515 F

Required:

For each of the independent cases, supply the missing amounts.

4. (LO 3; Labour variances) Information for each independent case follows:

	Case 1	Case 2	Case 3	Case 4
Units produced	600	d	320	1,250
Standard hours per unit	2	0.6	g	j
Standard hours allowed	a	600	480	k
Standard rate per hour	$6	e	$5.50	$8
Actual hours worked	1,230	580	h	5,100
Actual labour cost	b	f	$1,656.80	$30,600
Labour rate variance	$246 U	$290 U	$15.20 F	l
Labour efficiency variance	c	$80 F	i	$600 U

Required:

Supply the missing amounts.

5. (LO 3, 4; Material and labour variances) Wong Corp. produces evening handbags. In June 2005, company president William Wong received the following information:

Standard metres of material allowed per handbag	1.5
Standard labour time allowed per handbag	3 hours
Standard labour rate per hour	$9
Month's production	300 handbags
Actual cost of material purchased and used ($14.90 per metre)	$7,152
Actual hours worked	880
Material quantity variance	$450 U
Labour rate variance	$2,640 U

Mr. Wong is puzzled by the information and its method of presentation.

Required:
a. Material price and labour efficiency variances
b. Standard prime (material and labour) cost to produce one handbag
c. Prepare a memo to explain to Mr. Wong the variances and the potential causes of the variances.

6. (LO 3; Direct labour variances) Alexandra MacKay Ltd. was founded several years ago by two designers who had developed several popular lines of living room, dining room, and bedroom furniture for other companies. The designers believed that their design for dinette sets could be standardized and would sell well. They formed their own company and soon had all the orders they could complete in their small plant in Moncton, New Brunswick.

From the beginning the firm was successful. The owners bought a computer and software that produced financial statements, which an employee prepared. The owners thought that the information they needed was contained in these statements.

Recently, however, the employees have been requesting raises. The owners wonder how to evaluate the employees' requests. At the suggestion of Lawrence Chung, CA, the firm's external accountant, the owners have hired a consultant to implement a standard cost system. The consultant believes that the calculation of variances will aid management in setting responsibility for labour's performance.

The supervisors believe that under normal conditions, a dinette set can be assembled with 5 h of direct labour costing $20/h. During the month, the actual direct labour wages paid to employees amounted to $127,600 for 5,800 h of work. The factory produced 1,200 dinette sets during the month.

Required:
Prepare variance computations for management's consideration.

7. (LO 3, 4; Overhead variances) Michael Sanders Ltd. makes an adjustable window screen. Standard time and costs per screen follow:

Machine time (hours)	0.20
VOH rate per machine hour	$8.50
FOH rate per machine hour	$6.50

At the end of May 2005, papers on the desk of the company's accountant, Mr. Fong, were partially ruined by a driving rain blowing through the screened windows. The following operating statistics were still legible on the accountant's report to management:

Total fixed overhead applied to production	$715,000
Actual variable overhead	937,400
Actual fixed overhead	709,000
Volume variance	13,000 F
Variable overhead spending variance	10,900 U

Mr. Fong is on vacation. Because you recently took a management accounting course paid for by Michael Sanders Ltd., you have been asked to provide the following information:

Required:
a. Standard machine hours allowed
b. Number of screens produced
c. Budgeted fixed overhead
d. Expected annual capacity in machine hours
e. Fixed manufacturing overhead spending variance
f. Fixed manufacturing overhead total variance
g. For variable overhead:
   i.   Total applied variable overhead
   ii. Total variable overhead variance
   iii. Actual machine hours incurred
   iv. Variable overhead efficiency variance
   v.   Actual variable overhead rate per machine hour
h. The president of Michael Sanders Ltd. is curious about the possible causes of the variable overhead spending variance. Who would you suggest that he call (other than the vacationing accountant) to explain the variance? Defend your answer.

8. (LO 3, 5; Overhead variances) Baldwin and Williams is a small law firm. Variable and fixed overhead are applied to legal cases as follows:

Variable overhead:

Applied on a basis of per page of documentation generated during the month at the rate of $0.22 per page

Fixed overhead:

Applied on a basis of monthly billable hours generated at the rate of $15 per hour; this rate was derived with the expectation of 1,600 billable hours per month.

During July 2005, the lawyers at Baldwin and Williams worked on a variety of cases: 198,000 pages of documentation were generated during July; total billable hours were 1,450. Actual variable and fixed overhead amounts for July were $48,650 and $25,000, respectively.

Required:
a. What is the budgeted annual fixed overhead for Baldwin and Williams?
b. Determine the variable and fixed overhead variances for the month of July.
c. Explain the variable overhead efficiency variance. In a law firm, what bases other than pages of documentation might be more useful to allocate variable overhead? Could a standard ever be set for these bases so that an efficiency variance could be calculated?

9. (LO 3, 4; Overhead variances) Lily Simon Ltd. uses a standard costing system for planning and control purposes. For August 2005, the firm expected to produce 4,000 units of product. At that level of production, expected manufacturing overhead costs are:

Variable	$ 9,600
Fixed	24,000

At standard, two machine hours are required to produce a single unit of product.
Actual results for August follow:

Units produced	4,200
Machine hours worked	8,600
Actual variable manufacturing overhead	$ 9,460
Actual fixed manufacturing overhead	$24,900

Required:
a. Calculate standard hours allowed for actual output.
b. Calculate all overhead variances.
c. For the year 2006, the firm is considering automating its current manual production process. In its standard costing system, which standards would likely be affected by such a change? Explain. What individuals would likely be consulted to assist in revising the standards?

10. (LO 3; Missing numbers, component calculations) You have been given the following information about the production of Gamma Co., and are asked to provide the plant manager with information for a meeting with the vice president of operations.

Standard Cost Card

Direct materials (DM) (6 kg @ $3/kg)	$18.00
Direct labour (DL) (0.8 h @ $5/h)	4.00
Variable overhead (VOH) (0.8 h @ $3/h)	2.40
Fixed overhead (FOH) (0.8 h @ $7/h)	5.60
	$30.00

The following is a production report for the last period of operations:

			Variances		
Costs	Total Standard Cost	Price/ Rate	Spending/ Budget	Quantity/ Efficiency	Volume
DM	$405,000	$6,900 F		$9,000 U	
DL	90,000	4,850 U		7,000 U	
VOH	54,000		$1,300 F	?	
FOH	126,000		500		$14,000 U

Required:

a.   How many units were produced last period?
b.   How many kilograms of raw material were purchased and used during the period?
c.   What was the actual cost per kilogram of raw material?
d.   How many actual direct labour hours were worked during the period?
e.   What was the actual rate paid per direct labour hour?
f.   What was the actual variable overhead cost incurred during the period?
g.   What is the total fixed cost in the company's budget?
h.   What were the denominator hours for the last period?

(Adapted by the author from *Management Accounting examinations,* published by the Certified
General Accountants Association of Canada © CGA-Canada, 2000, used by permission.)

11.   (LO 3, 4; All variances) The David Faber Company manufactures plastic and aluminum products. During the winter, substantially all production capacity is devoted to
lawn sprinklers. Because a variety of products are made throughout the year, factory
volume is measured by machine hours rather than units of product.
The company has developed the following standards for the production of a lawn
sprinkler:

Direct materials:		
Aluminum	0.2 kg @ $0.40/kg	$0.08
Plastic	1.0 kg @ $0.38/kg	0.38
Direct labour	0.3 h @ $4.00/h	1.20
Manufacturing overhead:*		
Variable	0.5 hours @ $1.60 per machine hour	0.80
Fixed	0.5 hours @ $2.20 per machine hour	1.10

*Based on an expected annual capacity of 48,000 machine hours.
During February 2005, 8,500 sprinklers were manufactured, and the following costs
were incurred and charged to production:

Materials requisitioned for production:

Aluminum	1,900 kg @ $0.40/kg	$ 760
Plastic		
Regular grade	6,000 kg @ $0.38/kg	2,280
Low grade*	3,500 kg @ $0.38/kg	1,330

Direct labour:

Regular time	2,300 h @ $4.00/h	9,200
Overtime	400 h @ $6.00/h	2,400

Manufacturing overhead:

Variable	4,340 machine hours	6,400
Fixed	4,340 machine hours	9,230
Total costs charged to production		$31,600

Material price variations are not charged to production but to a material price variance account at the time the invoice is entered. All materials are carried in inventory
at standard prices. Material purchases for February were

Aluminum	1,800 kg @ $0.48/kg	$ 864
Plastic		
Regular grade	3,000 kg @ $0.50/kg	1,500
Low grade*	6,000 kg @ $0.29/kg	1,740

*Because of plastic shortages, the company was forced to purchase lower grade plastic than called
for in the standards. This increased the number of sprinklers rejected on inspection.

Required:

a.   What is the total difference between standard and actual cost for production in
February?
b.   Compute the material and labour variances.
c.   Compute the variable and fixed overhead variances.

d. The standard material quantities already include an allowance for acceptable material scrap loss. In this situation, what is the likely cause of the material quantity variance?

e. Prepare a memo to the company president about your variance computations.

(CMA adapted)

12. (LO 4; Conversion cost variances) Lee Ltd. uses a standard costing system in its pipe manufacturing facility in Montreal. The company is automated and direct labour costs are relatively low so a conversion cost pool is used rather than separate cost pools for direct labour and overhead. For the year 2005, standards were set as follows:

Variable conversion cost rate	$14 per machine hour
Fixed conversion cost rate*	$20 per machine hour

*Based on 5,000 expected machine hours.

At standard, one machine hour is required to produce 50 metres of pipe. In the year 2005, the company produced 300,000 metres of pipe, worked 5,800 machine hours, and incurred the following costs:

Variable conversion costs	$ 75,400
Fixed conversion costs	$102,500

Required:

a. Compute the variable conversion cost and fixed conversion cost variances for the year.

b. Why is an annual computation of variances not useful to managers?

13. (LO 3, 7; All variances) Under a contract with the provincial government, ChemLabs Inc. analyzes the chemical and bacterial composition of well water in various municipalities in the interior of British Columbia. The contract price is $25.20 per test performed. The normal volume is 10,000 tests per month. Each test requires two testing kits. The standard price of each is $3.80. Direct labour time to perform the test is 10 minutes at $22.80 per hour. Overhead is allocated on the basis of direct labour hours. At normal volume, the overhead costs are as follows:

Variable overhead costs:		
Indirect labour	$18,000	
Utilities	4,000	
Labour-related costs	15,000	
Laboratory maintenance	11,000	$ 48,000
Fixed overhead costs:		
Supervisor	$30,000	
Amortization	28,000	
Base utilities	9,000	
Insurance	2,000	69,000
Total overhead		$117,000

During May 2005, 9,000 tests were performed. The records show the following actual costs and production data:

	Activity	Actual Cost
Number of test kits purchased	19,000	$70,300
Number of test kits used	18,500	
Direct labour	1,623 h	$37,646
Total overhead costs: Variable		$45,200
Fixed		$68,500

Test kits are kept in inventory at standard cost. At the end of May, no tests were in process.

Required:

a. Prepare a standard cost card for a water test.

b. Calculate the direct materials price and quantity variances and the direct labour rate and efficiency variances for May 2005, indicating whether they are favourable or unfavourable.

c. Calculate the laboratory variable overhead variances for the month, indicating whether they are favourable or unfavourable.

(CGA adapted)

14. (LO 2, 5, 6; Using standard costing) Associated Media Graphics (AMG) is a rapidly expanding company involved in the mass reproduction of instructional materials. Ralph Boston, owner and manager of AMG, has made a concentrated effort to provide a quality product at a fair price with delivery on the promised due date. Expanding sales have been attributed to this philosophy. Boston is finding it increasingly difficult to supervise the operations of AMG personally and would like to institute an organizational structure that would facilitate management control.

The loss of personal control over the operations of AMG caused Boston to look for a method of efficiently evaluating performance. Lawrence Chung, a new cost accountant, proposed the use of a standard costing system. Variances for material, labour, and manufacturing overhead could then be calculated and reported directly to Boston.

Required:
a. Assume that AMG plans to implement a standard costing system and establish standards for materials, labour, and manufacturing overhead. Identify and discuss for each of these cost components:
   i.   Who should be involved in setting the standards
   ii. The factors that should be considered in establishing the standards
b. Describe the basis for assignment of responsibility under a standard costing system.

(IMA adapted)

15. (LO 3, 4, 7; All variances, Appendix 5A) David Roost Inc. established the following standards for the year 2005 for its principal product, a kit to convert ordinary lawn mowers into mulching mowers:

Direct materials:

Mower blades	2 blades @ $13 per blade	$26
Universal adapter kit	1 kit @ $6 per kit	6

Direct labour:

Grinding process	0.5 h @ $14/h	7
Finishing and testing	0.67 h @ $12 /h	8**

Manufacturing overhead:

Variable	$8 per machine hour	4
Fixed	$12 per machine hour*	6
Total cost per kit		$57

* Based on expected production of 5,000 mulching mower kits.
**Rounded

Actual results for producing 5,400 kits in 2005 follow:

Mower blades purchased	11,300 blades @ $12.75 per blade
Mower blades used	10,900 blades
Universal adapter kits purchased	5,900 kits @ $5.60 per kit
Universal adapter kits used	5,650 kits
Actual machine hours worked	2,900 MH
Grinding process actual labour cost	$42,000 based on 2,800 DLH
Finishing and testing labour cost	$45,325 based on 3,700 DLH
Actual variable manufacturing overhead	$22,910
Actual fixed manufacturing overhead	$33,000

Required:
a. Prepare the journal entries to recognize the following:
   i.   Purchase direct materials on account.
   ii. Issue direct materials to production.

      iii. Accrue direct labour cost.

      iv. Incur manufacturing overhead cost (credit various accounts).

      v. Apply manufacturing overhead cost to production.

      vi. Close year-end balances in overhead accounts.

      vii. Transfer completed production to finished goods.

      viii. Sell 4,000 kits for $425,000.

b. Close all variances, assuming they are insignificant in amount.

c. If collectively the variances were significant in amount, how would your closing entry have differed from that shown for part (b)?

CASES

1. As part of its cost control program, Brady Company uses a standard costing system for all manufactured items. The standard cost for each item is established at the beginning of the fiscal year, and the standards are not revised until the beginning of the next fiscal year. Changes in costs, caused during the year by changes in material or labour inputs or by changes in the manufacturing process, are recognized as they occur by the inclusion of planned variances in Brady's monthly operating budgets.

    Following is the labour standard that was established for one of Brady's products, effective June 1, 2005, the beginning of the fiscal year.

Assembler A labour (5 h @ $10/h)	$ 50
Assembler B labour (3 h @ $11/h)	33
Machinist labour (2 h @ $15/h)	30
Standard cost per 100 units	$113

    The standard was based on the assumption that the labour would be performed by a team consisting of five persons with Assembler A skills, three persons with Assembler B skills, and two persons with machinist skills; this team represents the most efficient use of the company's skilled employees. The standard also assumed that the quality of material that had been used in prior years would be available for the coming year.

    For the first seven months of the fiscal year, actual manufacturing costs at Brady have been within the standards established. However, the company has received a significant increase in orders, and there is an insufficient number of skilled workers available to meet the increased production. Therefore, beginning in January, the production teams will consist of eight persons with Assembler A skills, one person with Assembler B skills, and one person with machinist skills. The reorganized teams will work more slowly than the normal teams, and as a result, only 80 units will be produced in the time in which 100 units would have normally been produced. Faulty work has never been a cause for units to be rejected in the final inspection process, and it is not expected to be a cause for rejection with the newly reorganized teams.

    Furthermore, Brady has been notified by its material supplier that a lower-quality material will be supplied beginning January 1. Normally, one unit of raw material is required for each good unit produced, and no units are lost because of defective material. Brady estimates that 6% of the units manufactured after January 1 will be rejected in the final inspection process because of defective material.

Required:

a. Determine the number of units of lower-quality material that Brady Company must put into production to produce 35,720 good finished units.

b. Without regard to your answer in part (a), assume that Brady must manufacture a total of 50,000 units in January to have sufficient good units to fill the orders received.

    i. Determine how many hours of each class of labour will be needed to manufacture a total of 50,000 units in January.

    ii. Determine the amount that should be included in Brady's January operating budget for the planned labour variance caused by the reorganization of the labour teams and the lower-quality material, and indicate how much of the planned variance can be attributed to (a) the change in material and (b) the reorganization of the labour teams.

(CMA adapted)

2. Ho-A-Yun Company produces a turbo engine component for jet aircraft manufacturers. A standard cost system has been used for years with good results.

   Unfortunately, Ho-A-Yun has recently experienced production problems. The source for its direct material went out of business. The new source produces a similar but higher-quality material. The price per kilogram from the original source had averaged $7, while the price from the new source is $7.77. The use of the new material results in a reduction of scrap. This scrap reduction reduces the actual consumption of direct material from 1.25 to 1 kg per unit. In addition, the direct labour is reduced from 24 to 22 minutes per unit because there is less scrap labour and machine setup time.

   At the same time Ho-A-Yun was changing its material source, it was also engaging in labour negotiations. The negotiations resulted in an increase of over 14% in hourly direct labour costs. The average rate rose from $12.60 per hour to $14.40 per hour. Production of the main product requires a high level of labour skill. Because of a continuing shortage in that skill area, an interim wage agreement had to be signed.

   Ho-A-Yun started using the new direct material on April 1, the same date on which the new labour agreement went into effect. Ho-A-Yun has been using standards that were set at the beginning of the calendar year. The direct material and direct labour standards for the turbo engine component are as follows:

Direct material	1.2 kg @ $6.80/kg	$ 8.16
Direct labour	20 minutes @ $12.30 per DLH	4.10
Standard prime cost per unit		$12.26

   Mr. Devereau, the management accounting supervisor, was examining a performance report that he had prepared at the close of business on April 30. The report follows.

Performance Report
Standard Cost Variance Analysis for April, 2005

Standard		Price Rate/Variance		Quantity/Efficiency Variance		Actual
DM	$ 8.16	($0.97 × 1.0)	= $0.97 U	($6.80 × 0.2)	= $1.36 F	$7.77
DL	4.10	[$2.10 × (22 ÷ 60)] =	0.77 U	[$12.30 × (2 ÷ 60)] =	0.41 U	5.28
	$12.26					$13.05

Comparison of 2005 Actual Costs

	1st Quarter Costs	April Costs	% Increase (Decrease)
DM	$ 8.75	$ 7.77	(11.2)%
DL	5.04	5.28	4.8 %
	$13.79	$13.05	(5.4)%

   Jen Hort, assistant controller, came into Devereau's office, and Devereau said, "Jen, look at this performance report! Direct material price increased 11%, and the labour rate increased over 14% during April. I expected greater variances, yet prime costs decreased over 5% from the $13.79 we experienced during the first quarter of this year. The proper message just isn't coming through."

   "This has been an unusual period," said Hort. "With all the unforeseen changes, perhaps we should revise our standards based on current conditions and start over."

   Devereau replied, "I think we can retain the current standards but expand the variance analysis. We could calculate variances for the specific changes that have occurred to direct material and direct labour before we calculate the normal price and quantity variances. What I really think would be useful to management right now is to determine the impact the changes in direct material and direct labour had in reducing our prime costs per unit from $13.79 in the first quarter to $13.05 in April; a reduction of $0.74."

Required:

a. Discuss the advantages of (i) immediately revising the standards and (ii) retaining the current standards and expanding the analysis of variances.

b. Prepare an analysis to explain the impact the new direct material source and new labour contract had on reducing Ho-A-Yun's prime costs per unit from $13.79 to $13.05. The analysis should show the changes in prime costs per unit that are caused by (i) the use of new direct materials and (ii) the new labour contract.

(This analysis should contain sufficient detail to identify the changes caused by direct material price, direct labour rate, the effect of direct material quality on material usage, and the effect of direct material quality on direct labour usage.)

(CMA adapted)

3. Fidel Goldberg, Inc. manufactures video game machines. Market saturation and technological innovations have created pricing pressures, which have resulted in declining profits. To stem the slide in profits until new products can be introduced, top management has turned its attention to both manufacturing economies and increased production. An incentive program has been developed to reward managers who contribute to an increase in the number of units produced and effect cost reductions.

The production managers have responded to the pressure of improving manufacturing in several ways, which has resulted in an increase in completed units over normal production levels. The video game machines are put together by the Assembly group, which requires parts from the Printed Circuit Boards (PCB) and Reading Heads (RH) groups. To increase production levels, the PCB and RH groups have begun to reject parts that previously would have been tested and modified to meet manufacturing standards. Preventive maintenance on machines used in the production of these parts has been postponed with only emergency repair work being performed to keep production lines moving. The Maintenance Department is concerned that there will be serious breakdowns and unsafe operating conditions.

The more aggressive Assembly group production supervisors have pressured maintenance personnel to attend to their machines at the expense of other groups. This has resulted in machine downtime in the PCB and RH groups, which, when coupled with demands for accelerated parts delivery by the Assembly group, has led to more frequent parts rejections and increased friction among departments.

Fidel Goldberg uses a standard cost system. The standard costs for video game machines are as follows:

Standards per Unit

Cost Item	Quantity	Cost	Total
Direct material			
Housing unit	1	$20	$20
Printed circuit boards	2	15	30
Reading heads	4	10	40
Direct labour			
Assembly group	2 hours	8	16
PCB group	1 hour	9	9
RH group	1.5 hours	10	15
Variable overhead	4.5 hours	2	9
Total standard cost per unit			$139

Fidel Goldberg Inc. prepares monthly reports based on standard costs. Presented next is the report for May 2005, when production and sales both reached 2,200 units.

	Budget	Actual	Variance
Units	2,000	2,200	200 F
Variable costs			
Direct material	$180,000	$220,400	$40,400 U
Direct labour	80,000	93,460	13,460 U
Variable overhead	18,000	18,800	800 U
Total variable costs	$278,000	$332,660	$54,660 U

Fidel Goldberg's top management was surprised by the unfavourable variances. Zippy Bok, the management accountant, was assigned to identify and report on the reasons for the unfavourable variances as well as the individuals or groups responsible. After her review, Bok prepared the following usage report.

Cost Item	Quantity	Actual Cost
Direct material		
Housing units	2,200 units	$ 44,000
Printed circuit boards	4,700 units	75,200
Reading heads	9,200 units	101,200
Direct labour		
Assembly	3,900 hours	31,200
Printed circuit boards	2,400 hours	23,760
Reading heads	3,500 hours	38,500
Variable overhead	9,900 hours	18,800
Total variable cost		$332,660

Bok reported that the PCB and RH groups supported the increased production levels but experienced abnormal machine downtime. This, in turn, caused idle time, which required the use of overtime to keep up with the accelerated demand for parts. The idle time was charged to direct labour. Bok also reported that the production managers of these two groups resorted to parts rejections, as opposed to testing and modification procedures formerly applied. Bok determined that the Assembly group met management's objectives by increasing production while utilizing lower than standard hours.

Required:

a. For May 2005, Fidel Goldberg's labour rate variance was $5,660 unfavourable, and the labour efficiency variance was $200 favourable. Calculate the following variances:
 i.   Material price variance
 ii. Material quantity variance
 iii. Variable overhead efficiency variance
 iv. Variable overhead spending variance

b. Using all six variances from part (a), prepare an explanation of the $54,660 unfavourable variance between budgeted and actual costs for May 2005.

c. i.   Identify and briefly explain the behavioural factors that may promote friction among the production managers and the maintenance manager.
 ii. Evaluate Zippy Bok's analysis of the unfavourable results in terms of its completeness and its effect on the behaviour of the production groups.

(CMA adapted)

4. Freeman Manufacturing produces several types of small kitchen appliances. The market has become very competitive, making effective cost control essential. Many of Freeman's products use the same purchased components, and management has been reviewing materials costs to determine if savings can be realized in this area.

Freeman uses a standard cost system in accounting for materials, and purchases are charged to inventory at the standard cost. Production is also charged at the standard cost of the materials used. When a substitute part is used in production rather than a regular part, a price variance equal to the difference in the standard costs for the materials is recognized at the time of substitution in the production process.

Part No. C88, a heavily used component, has unfavourable materials variances. Freeman knows that some of these components will be defective and fail; the accepted (normal) defective rate included in the standard allowed quantity is 5% of good units used. The original contract price for this part was $0.155 per unit, and Freeman set the standard unit cost at $0.155. Because of a recent engineering specification change that reduces manufacturing time, the contract for Part No. C88 had to be renegotiated. The results of the negotiations included an increase in the price of $0.03 per unit and a change in payment terms from n/30 to 4/10, n/30, the latter representing the vendor's recognition of current economic conditions. Freeman has a policy of taking payment discounts on all purchases. Freeman changes standard costs only once a year, and the unit price increase is currently being treated as a price variance. The activity for Part No. C88 during the month of May 2005 is shown on the next page.

Purchases of Part No. C88	300,000 units
Unit invoice price for May purchases	$0.185
Requisitions for Part No. C88	268,000 units
Substitution of Part No. B14 for C88	48,000 units
Standard cost of Part No. B14	$0.205
Defective units (C88 and B14)	19,330 units
Standard allowed quantity (good units plus 5% normal defective units) for Part No. C88 and its substitute based upon output for the month	306,600 units

The reported variances for Part No. C88 for the month of May were

Price variance	$ 9,180 U
Quantity variance	1,457 U
Total materials variances	$10,637 U

Jill Lawson, purchasing manager, claims that the unfavourable price variance is misleading and no longer measures the performance of her department. She believes her department has done a good job negotiating price concessions and purchase discounts with suppliers. In addition, Lawson notes that some price increases are due to engineering changes even though the part identification number and its standard cost have not changed.

Howard Pressberger, production manager, thinks that responsibility for the quantity variance should be shared. For example, the Production Department has no control over the quality of less expensive parts, substitutions of materials to use up otherwise obsolete stock, or engineering changes that increase the quantity of materials used.

Dale Eisen, accounting manager, has suggested that the computation of variances be changed to identify variations from standard with the causes for the variances as outlined below.

- **Economic variance**. Quantity purchased times the changes made after setting standards that were the result of negotiations based on current economic conditions.

- **Engineering change variance**. Quantity purchased times change in price due to part specifications changes.

- **Purchase price variance**. Quantity purchased times change in contract price due to changes other than part specifications or current economic conditions.

- **Substitutions variance**. Quantity substituted times the difference in standard price between parts substituted.

- **Abnormal failure rate variance**. Abnormal scrap times standard price.

- **Excess usage variance**. Standard price times the difference between the standard quantity allowed for production and actual parts used (reduced for abnormal scrap).

   Required:
   a. Compute the six material variances for Part No. C88 for May using the system recommended by Dale Eisen, indicating who would be responsible for each of the variances (round calculations to the nearest dollar).
   b. Evaluate the appropriateness of both the current and proposed methods of analyzing materials variances at Freeman Manufacturing. Include in your discussion the likely behaviour of Jill Lawson and Howard Pressberger under both methods.

(CMA adapted)

5. Sam Chu Company employs a standard costing system using absorption costing. The standards for manufacturing overhead are established at the beginning of each year by estimating the total variable and fixed manufacturing overhead costs for the year and then dividing the costs by the estimated activity base. Chu has a fairly automated manufacturing operation, and the variable overhead closely follows machine hour usage. Thus, machine hours are used to apply both variable and fixed manufacturing overhead.

The standard manufacturing overhead application rates shown below were based on an estimated manufacturing overhead for the coming year of $4,080,000 of which $1,440,000 is variable and $2,640,000 is fixed. These costs were expected to be incurred uniformly throughout the year. The total machine hours (MH) for the expected annual output, also expected to be uniform throughout the year, were estimated at 120,000 MH.

Standard Manufacturing Overhead Application Rates

Variable	$12 per MH
Fixed	22 per MH
Total	$34 per MH

Chu has reduced production in the past three months because orders have been down. In fact, manufacturing activity for the current month was 80% of what was expected. This reduced level of demand for Chu's products is expected to continue for at least the next three months.

Sara Edwards, cost accountant, has prepared some preliminary figures on manufacturing overhead for the current month at the request of Frank Paige, vice president of production, and these amounts are presented below.

Manufacturing Overhead
Preliminary Figures for the Month

Actual machine hours for the month		8,050
Standard machine hours allowed for actual output produced		8,000
Total applied manufacturing overhead		$272,000
Actual manufacturing overhead:		
Variable	$ 95,800	
Fixed	211,200	307,000
Total manufacturing overhead variance		$ 35,000 U

Edwards and Paige had the following conversation about this analysis.

Paige: "I just don't understand these numbers. I have tried to control my costs with the production cutback. I figured that my budget for one month should be about $340,000, which would give me a $33,000 favourable variance, yet you show that I have a $35,000 unfavourable variance."

Edwards: "Well, you may have done a pretty good job in controlling your costs. You really cannot take one-twelfth of your annual estimated costs to get the monthly budget to compare to your actual costs. A detailed variance analysis of manufacturing overhead would shed more light on your performance. The largest component is probably your fixed manufacturing overhead volume variance."

Paige: "Can you do that detailed variance analysis for me? What do I have to do to reduce or eliminate that fixed manufacturing overhead volume variance?"

Edwards: "Sure we can do the detailed variance analysis. I would have done it for you, but we just got these figures together now. The fixed manufacturing overhead volume variance is not that important. I'm not sure that you really can or want to reduce it under our present economic situtation."

Required:

a. Prepare a detailed variance analysis of the manufacturing overhead for Chu Company for the current month by calculating the following variances.
   i. Overhead spending variance.
   ii. Variable overhead efficiency variance.
   iii. Fixed overhead volume variance.
b. Sara Edwards also commented that the fixed manufacturing overhead volume variance is not that important and Frank Paige might not really be able to or want to reduce the fixed overhead volume variance for the month.
   i. Explain what the fixed overhead volume variance measures.
   ii. Explain how Paige could eliminate the fixed overhead volume variance.
   iii. Under the present economic conditions, would it be in Paige's best interest to eliminate the fixed overhead volume variance? Explain your answer.

ETHICS AND QUALITY DISCUSSIONS

1. Many manufacturing costs are easily controlled by use of a standard costing system and traditional variance analysis. Other organizational costs have historically been more difficult to control. Foremost among costs in this category are costs associated with legal work both by inside and outside counsel. Adding to the difficulty of controlling costs are certain practices that have evolved in the legal industry, especially those used to account for how time is spent.

   Required:
   a. What differences between legal costs and costs such as direct material and direct labour make legal costs more difficult to control?
   b. How could concepts used in standard costing for products be applied to other costs, including those incurred for legal work?
   c. Provide six suggestions as to how firms could help control their legal costs. Discuss any impacts your suggestions might have on product quality/safety, employee productivity, organizational strategy, and loss contingencies. (A loss contingency is a loss that might occur in the future that would result from a current action. For example, if an airline were to stop doing airplane maintenance, there is a high probability that some type of expensive failure would occur in the future.)

2. In today's business world, some customers treat suppliers almost like employees. Supplier representatives work in customers' factories, attend production meetings, place orders for parts, and have access to a variety of data, including sales forecasts. This environment was developed to instill harmony and create efficiencies within both customers and suppliers.

   For example, at Honeywell's Golden Valley plant, the company reduced inventory levels to those that can be measured in days rather than weeks or months, cut purchasing agents by one-fourth, and has received numerous suggestions as to part standardization so that products can retain their quality levels, but be made for less. (Note: This discussion was adapted from a January 13, 1995, *Wall Street Journal* article entitled "Strange Bedfellows: Some Companies Let Suppliers Work On Site and Even Place Orders.")

   Required:
   a. Discuss risks that customers bear when they allow suppliers to have access to critical inside information.
   b. What types of costs would customers expect to save by having representatives of suppliers on-site? Explain.
   c. How would responsibility for purchase price variances change when vendors are allowed to submit their own purchase orders?

3. Mera O'Brien was hired a month ago at the Montreal Division of the Peerless Manufacturing Company. O'Brien supervises plant production and is paid $6,500 per month. In addition, her contract calls for a percentage bonus based on cost control. The company president has defined cost control as "the ability to obtain favourable cost variances from the standards provided."

   After one month, O'Brien realized that the standards that were used at the Montreal Division were outdated. Since the last revision of standards, the Montreal Division had undergone some significant plant layout changes and installed some automated equipment, both of which reduced labour time considerably. However, by the time she realized the errors in the standards, she had received her first month's bonus cheque of $5,000.

   Required:
   a. Since the setting of the standards and the definition of her bonus arrangement were not her doing, O'Brien does not feel compelled to discuss the errors in the standards with the company president. Besides, O'Brien wants to buy a new red Porsche. Discuss the ethics of her not discussing the errors in the standards and/or the problems with the definition of cost control with the company president.

b. Assume instead that O'Brien has an elderly mother who has just been placed in a nursing home. The older O'Brien is quite ill and has no income. The younger O'Brien lives in an efficiency apartment and drives a six-year-old car so that she can send the majority of her earnings to the nursing home to provide for her mother. Discuss the ethics of her not discussing the errors in the standards and/or the problems with the definition of cost control with the company president.

c. Assume again the facts in part (b). Also assume that the company president plans to review and revise, if necessary, all production standards at the Montreal Division next year. Discuss what may occur if O'Brien does not inform the president of the problems with the standards at the current time. Discuss what may occur if O'Brien informs the president of all the facts, both professional and personal. Can you suggest a way in which she may keep a bonus and still have the standards revised? (Consider the fact that standard costs have implications for sales prices.)

4. Jack Sheriton Corporation needs to hire four factory workers who can run robotic equipment and route products through processing. All factory space is on a single floor. Labour standards have been set for product manufacturing. At this time, the company has had 10 experienced people apply for the available jobs. One of the applicants is David Sima. David is paralyzed and uses a wheelchair. He has several years' experience using the robotic equipment, but for him to use the equipment, the controls must be placed on a special panel and lowered. Willie Roberts, the human resources director, has interviewed David and has decided against hiring him because Willie does not believe David can work "up to the current labour standard."
Required:
a. How, if at all, would hiring a person with a physical disability affect labour variances (both rate and hours) if the standards had been set based on workers without physical disabilities? Provide a rationale for your answer.
b. If a supervisor has decided to hire a worker with a physical disability, how (if at all) should that worker's performance evaluations be affected? Provide a rationale for your answer.
c. What are the ethical implications of hiring people with physical disabilities in preference to those without physical disabilities? What are the ethical implications of hiring the people without physical disabilities in preference to those with physical disabilities?
d. Do you believe that the hiring of individuals with physical disabilities could come under the umbrella concept of "workplace diversity"? Why or why not?

5. Governments have instituted academic standards in English, history, math, and science. These standards specify what students should learn in what grades.
Required:
a. Assume that you have been asked to chair your province's committee to develop the math standard for Grade 6. What issues would you consider in setting the standard? (This question does not ask you to address the specific items that you believe the students should know, but rather the fundamental concepts that need to be considered before establishing the standard.)
b. Once the standard has been set, what circumstances might cause you to consider changing the standard? Why?
c. Should there be national, rather than provincial, standards for education? Discuss the rationale for your answer, including potential obstacles and how they might be overcome.

COMMUNICATIONS ACTIVITIES

1. Mark-Wright, Inc. (MWI) is a specialty frozen food processor located in eastern Canada. Since its founding in 1982, MWI has enjoyed a loyal local clientele that is willing to pay premium prices for the high quality frozen foods it prepares from specialized recipes. In the last two years, the company has experienced rapid sales growth in its operating region and has had many inquiries about supplying its products on a

national basis. To meet this growth, MWI expanded its processing capabilities, which resulted in increased production and distribution costs. Furthermore, MWI has been encountering pricing pressure from competitors outside its normal marketing region.

As MWI desires to continue its expansion, Jim Condon, CEO, has engaged a consulting firm to assist MWI in determining its best course of action. The consulting firm concluded that, while premium pricing is sustainable in some areas, if sales growth is to be achieved, MWI must make some price concessions. Also, in order to maintain profit margins, costs must be reduced and controlled. The consulting firm recommended the institution of a standard cost system to better accommodate the changes in demand that can be expected when serving an expanded market area.

Condon met with his management team and explained the recommendations of the consulting firm. Condon then assigned the task of establishing standard costs to his management team. After discussing the situation with their respective staffs, the management team met to review the matter.

Jane Morgan, purchasing manager, advised at that meeting that expanded production would necessitate obtaining basic food supplies from other than MWI's traditional sources. This would entail increased raw material and shipping costs and may result in lower quality supplies. Consequently, these increased costs would need to be made up by the processing department if current cost levels are to be maintained or reduced.

Stan Walters, processing manager, countered that the need to accelerate processing cycles to increase production, coupled with the possibility of receiving lower-grade supplies, can be expected to result in a slip in quality and a greater product rejection rate. Under these circumstances, per-unit labour utilization cannot be maintained or reduced, and forecasting future unit labour content becomes very difficult.

Susy Tseng, production engineer, advised that if the equipment is not properly maintained, and thoroughly cleaned at prescribed daily intervals, it can be anticipated that the quality and unique taste of the frozen food products will be affected. Christina Kim, vice president of sales, stated that if quality cannot be maintained, MWI cannot expect to increase sales to the levels projected.

When Condon was apprised of the problems encountered by his management team, he advised them that if an agreement could not be reached on appropriate standards, he would arrange to have them set by the consulting firm, and everyone would have to live with the results.

Required:

a. i.   Describe the major advantages of using a standard cost system.
    ii. Describe disadvantages that can result from using a standard cost system.
b. i.   Identify those who should participate in setting standards and describe the benefits of their participation in the standard-setting process.
    ii. Explain the general features and characteristics associated with the introduction and operation of a standard cost system that make it an effective tool for cost control.
c. What would be the consequences if Jim Condon has the standards set by the outside consulting firm?

(CMA adapted)

2. Some executives believe that it is extremely important to manage "by the numbers." This form of management requires that all employees with departmental or divisional responsibilities spend time understanding the company's operations and how they are reflected by the company's performance reports. Managers are then expected to make their employees aware of important signposts that can be detected in performance reports. One of the various numerical measurement systems used by companies is standard costs.

Required:

a. Discuss the characteristics that should be present in a standard cost system to encourage positive employee motivation.
b. Discuss how a standard cost system should be implemented to motivate employees positively.

c. The use of variance analysis often results in "management by exception." Discuss the meaning and behavioural implications of "management by exception." Explain how employee behaviour could be adversely affected when "actual to standard" comparisons are used as the basis for performance evaluation.

(CMA adapted)

3. Standard cost accounting is a powerful concept that is important in finance and marketing. The marketing application of the concept is to develop and manage a balanced portfolio of products. Market share and market growth can be used to classify products for portfolio purposes, and the product classifications are often extended to the organizational units that make the product. The market share/growth classifications can be depicted in the following manner.

		MARKET SHARE	
		High	Low
MARKET GROWTH RATE	High	Rising Star	Question Mark
	Low	Cash Cow	Dog

Question marks are products that show high growth rates but have relatively small market shares, such as new products that are similar to their competitors'. Rising stars are high-growth, high-market share products that tend to mature into cash cows. Cash cows are slow-growing established products that can be "milked" for cash to help the question marks and introduce new products. The dogs are low-growth, low-market share items that are candidates for elimination or segmentation.

Understanding where a product falls within this market share/growth structure is important when applying a standard cost system

Required:
a. Discuss the major advantages of using a standard cost accounting system.
b. Describe the kinds of information that are useful in setting standards and the conditions that must be present to support the use of standard costing.
c. Discuss the applicability or nonapplicability of using standard costing for a product classified as a:
   i. Cash cow
   ii. Question mark

(CMA adapted)

PROJECTS

1. Invite a representative of the accounting department of an industrial firm that uses standard costing to address your class. Ask the representative to discuss in his or her presentation the following features of his or her company's standard costing system:
   a. How standards are set for materials, labour, and overhead
   b. The frequency and nature of variance analysis
   c. The process for revising standards
   d. How the standard cost system has been affected by technological evolution.

2. In this economic downturn, WestJet Airlines continues to be very profitable. Its stock price has increased by 184% since it went public. It continues to enjoy profits while other airlines are suffering.

   WestJet enjoys a cost advantage in the airline industry that has given it a competitive edge for a number of years. Divide your class into teams and develop strategies to launch an airline that will compete against WestJet. In developing strategies, teams should employ concepts discussed in this chapter. Each team should produce a report summarizing its strategy.

USING THE INTERNET

1. To find out more information on standard costing, go to www.mamag.com, click on "fall 2000 issue," and read the article, "Management Control Systems: How SPC Enhances Budgeting and Standard Costing."

2. To find out how standard costing is used in industry, go to www.esteelman.com/steelmanu-8.htm.

3. To understand how standard costing is being used at Parker Brass, go to www.magman.com, click on "fall 2000 issue," and read the article, "Standard Costing is Alive and Well at Parker Brass."

SOLUTIONS TO SELF-TEST QUESTIONS

1. b: $(AQ \times AP) - (AQ \times SP)$

   $(160,000 \text{ kg} \times \$1.90) - (160,000 \times \$1.80) = \$16,000 \text{ U}$

2. d: $(AQ \times SP) - (SQ \times SP)$

   $(142,500 \text{ kg} \times \$1.80) - (152,000 \times \$1.80) = \$17,100 \text{ F}$

3. a: $(AH \times AR) - (AH \times SR)$

   $(5,000 \times \$7.56) - (5,000 \times \$8.00)$

   $\$37,800 - \$40,000 = \$2,200 \text{ F}$

4. c: $(AH \times SR) - (SH \times SR)$

   $(5,000 \times \$8) - (4,750 \times \$8.00)$

   $\$40,000 - \$38,000 = \$2,000 \text{ U}$

5, b: Standard hours for production attained − Budgeted machine hours = $3,000 F.

6. c: Actual hours of input, at the standard rate (26,000 × $20) $520,000

   Standard hours allowed for output, at the standard rate

   [(5,000 × 5) × $20]   500,000

   Unfavourable direct labour efficiency variance $ 20,000

7. b: Fixed overhead volume variance = $6,660 applied at $3.70 per direct labour hour

   $6,660 ÷ $3.70 = 1,800 direct labour hours

   Since the output required more hours at standard than expected, the output was greater than expected. Thus, the volume variance is favourable.

8. a: Fixed overhead application rate $320,000 ÷ 20,000 = $16.00/machine hour

   4,700 units of output at 4 machine hours each requires 4,700 × 4 = 18,800 machine hours at standard; 18,800 × $16 = $300,800

9. b and c: Proration adds to work in process and to finished goods.

10. b: Overhead is based on the direct labour hours and if this is unfavourable then the variable overhead efficiency will also be unfavourable.

ENDNOTES

1. Kip R. Krumwiede, "Results of 1999 Cost Management Survey: The Use of Standard Costing and Other Costing Practices," *Cost Management Update*, Issue No. 103, Dec. 1999/Jan. 2000.

2. In performing internal time and motion studies, observers need to be aware that employees may engage in slowdown tactics when they are being clocked. The purpose of such tactics is to have a relatively long time set as the standard, so that the employees will appear more efficient when actual results are measured.

3. An employee time sheet indicates what jobs were worked on and for what period of time. Time sheets can also be prepared for machines by use of machine clocks or counters. Bar coding is another way to track work flow through an organization.

4. The standard cost of each cost element (direct material, direct labour, variable overhead, and fixed overhead) is said to be applied to the goods produced. This terminology is the same as that used when overhead is applied to inventory based on a predetermined rate.

5. The material price and quantity variances will have to be calculated for buttons and labels as well. These calculations will not be shown in the chapter.

6. Each hour of machine time is expected to cost $6 (Exhibit 5-5).

7. $6 per hour/6 shirts per hour.

8. Activity-based costing is discussed in Chapter 6 of the text.

9. This discussion is based on the work of Robert S. Kaplan in "Flexible Budgeting in an Activity-Based Costing Framework," *Accounting Horizons*, June 1994, pp. 104–109.

10. Robin Cooper, *When Lean Enterprises Collide: Competing Through Confrontation*, Boston: Harvard Business School Press, 1995, pp. 247–248.

11. Sara Moulton, Ed Oakley, and Chuck Kremer, "How to Assure Your Quality Initiative Really Pays Off," *Management Accounting*, January 1993, p. 26.

12. Colin Drury, "Standard Costing: A Technique at Variance With Modern Management?" *Management Accounting*, London, November 1999, pp. 56–58.

13. Actual product costs should not include extraordinary charges for such items as waste, spoilage, and inefficiency. Such costs should be written off as period expenses.

14. Bruce Brumberg and Karen Alexrod, "Tastes of Louisiana," *New Orleans Times–Picayune*, September 1, 1996, pp. E-1, E-5.

Chapter 6

Activity-Based Management and Costing

LEARNING OBJECTIVES

After reading this chapter, you should be able to answer the following questions:

1 How
can reasonably accurate product and service cost information be developed?

2 What
are the differences among value-added, non-value-added, and business-value-added activities?

3 What
might cause decreased manufacturing cycle efficiency?

4 How
would the cost drivers in an activity-based costing system be developed?

5 What
distinguishes activity-based costing from conventional overhead allocation methods?

6 When
is the use of activity-based costing appropriate?

7 What
are the benefits and limitations of using activity-based costing?

www.vw.ca

The Volkswagen Saga

Massive changes in technology and competition have caused **VW** to take drastic actions to continue being profitable, including aggressive pricing and selling policies, cost cutting, and downsizing. Activity-based costing (ABC) has helped VW management make tough decisions, with a degree of clarity that otherwise would not have been possible.

An ABC pilot project was undertaken in the die-casting area at the Barrie plant. This study indicated that, overall, the area was profitable but only because two parts were making most of the profit, and five parts were making all the profit. The other 15 parts were losing money or, at best, breaking even. The pilot was so successful that the plant launched a full-scale implementation two years later.

To track progress, ABC analyses, as well as information on progress toward certain cost, quality, and cycle-time goals are shared among managers. The ABC information is used for determining product and customer profitability, pricing, budgeting, calculating cost of quality, justifying process improvement initiatives, and making outsourcing decisions. The cost and economic data provided by ABC ensure that the process improvement team concentrates on what is important and allow it to prioritize its improvement targets. VW management hopes that the activity-based costing and activity-based management (ABM) information will help the company achieve its goal of becoming the ultimate, cost-conscious, world-class, customer-focused supplier.

SOURCE: Reprinted from an article appearing in the May 1996 issue of *CMA Management* magazine by Jim Gurowka, with permission of Certified Management Accountants of Canada.

*L*ike many other companies, Volkswagen Canada has numerous, complex processes that generate a wide variety of products and services. Overhead allocations in such organizations are best made using multiple predetermined overhead rates rather than a single one. These rates should be developed and based on the underlying drivers of the overhead costs.

As global competitiveness increases, companies will need to understand the causes of costs, work harder to control costs, and be acutely aware of product line profitability. For VW Canada to meet the competition's prices and remain profitable, the most convenient method of overhead allocation no longer provides adequate product or service cost information. To overcome this deficiency, plant management piloted the implementation of a new costing system, activity-based costing (ABC), to help managers obtain the best possible estimates of product and service costs.

ABC falls under the umbrella heading of activity-based management (ABM). The simple difference between ABC and ABM has been defined as follows: ABC is about gathering cost information. ABM shows you how to do something about it.[1] This chapter defines ABM and ABC, illustrates the process of analyzing organizational activities and cost drivers, and shows how the analysis results can be used to allocate overhead costs to products and services more appropriately. The chapter also discusses the conditions under which ABC systems provide better information than traditional overhead allocations.

Over the course of the last decade, a management tool called **activity-based costing (ABC)** has become one of the more widely embraced of new management methods. Although its core lies in cost accounting, it has attracted the attention of business managers in general, and it has been the subject of articles in the Harvard Business Review, Fortune, and elsewhere in the business press. And not only is it a major theme in business, but it also has been adopted in parts of government.

In recent years, the challenge in allocated-indirect-resources has increased greatly, for several reasons. First, indirect cost as a fraction of total cost has increased (e.g., automation, the substitution of machines [indirect] for direct labourers [easily traced]). Second, there is increasing proliferation of product models and types, where complex production scheduling, parts inventories, etc., add to indirect costs (e.g., automobile models and options). Third, the reliability of the "base" that has traditionally been used to allocate direct costs is decreasing. The design of an ABC system rests on identifying the relationship between an indirect resource and the "activity" that consumes it. Once that is done, the product cost is simply the cross product of the activities that were incurred to produce that product and the cost per unit of the activity.[2]

activity-based costing
an accounting information system that identifies the various activities performed in an organization and collects costs on the basis of the underlying nature and extent of those activities

THE ABC SYSTEM

Imagine that you and three friends go to a restaurant. You order a cheeseburger and they each order an expensive prime rib. When the waiter brings the bill they say, 'Let's split the total amount evenly.' How would you feel? That is how many products and service lines 'feel' when the accountants take a large amount of indirect and support overhead expenses and allocate them to costs without any logic.[3]

A well-designed activity-based costing (ABC) system has three strategic objectives. The first is to report accurate costs that can be used to identify the source of firm profits. The second is to identify the cost of activities so that more efficient ways to perform them or produce their outputs can be identified. The final one is to identify the future need for resources so that they can be acquired more efficiently. ABC is strategically important because it allows accurate costs to be calculated. Good decisions require the accurate understanding of costs.

ABC systems necessarily model the way resources are consumed, not how they are acquired. That is, the systems relate the amount of resources consumed by activities to the outputs of those activities, not to the amount of resources acquired in the period. It is this property that allows ABC systems to report the same cost for products from period to period (assuming no change in the quantity of resources consumed and the price paid for them) even when the volume of production changes. This objective is achieved by removing the cost of unused capacity from the cost of the resources driven to the activities and then subsequently to outputs in the ABC model.[4]

DEVELOPING PRODUCT/SERVICE COST INFORMATION

Product or service costs are developed to (1) have information for financial and regulatory reporting; (2) help management make product pricing and product line expansion/contraction decisions; and (3) allow management to monitor and control operations. In many organizations, the first purpose has often overridden the other purposes for two reasons. First, external parties (such as the Securities Commissions, CICA and CCRA, and other regulatory agencies) have established rules about what should be included in or excluded from determining product cost; there have been no mandates, however, about how product costs should be determined for internal management purposes. Second, it is often easier to use the same product costing system for all three purposes. Using the mandated definitions may diminish the resulting costs' internal usefulness as summarized by the following quote: "Today's management accounting information, driven by the procedures and cycles of the organization's financial reporting system, is too late, too aggregated, and too distorted to be relevant for managers' planning and control decisions."[5]

Although it is impossible to determine exact product costs, managers should develop the best possible cost estimates. The best estimate occurs when the majority of production or service costs can be traced directly to the resulting products or services. Direct tracing requires the use of valid measures of resource

LEARNING OBJECTIVE **1**

How can reasonably accurate product and service cost information be developed?

To get from one point to another, the easiest route is the most direct one. Determining product cost is also easiest if costs incurred can be traced directly to related products.

Allocating costs to products is similar to wandering aimlessly through a mall—the costs may finally get to the right place, but oftentimes it's quicker to stop at the most convenient location.

consumption called cost drivers. Direct material and direct labour costs have always been traced easily to products because, by definition, these costs must be physically and conveniently traceable to cost objects.

If the best estimate results when the largest numbers of costs are traced directly, then the best estimate will also be obtained when the fewest costs are assigned arbitrarily. However, because overhead cannot be directly traced to individual products or services, it must be attached to products or services using a valid cost predictor (or driver) or an arbitrary method. In the past, manufacturing overhead was often attached to products using direct labour hours. Although this base may not have been the most accurate measure of resource consumption, it was generally considered a reasonable, rather than an arbitrary, allocation method.

The modern manufacturing environment is more machine-intensive, with low direct labour and high overhead costs. Attempts to use direct labour as the overhead allocation base in such an environment can lead to significant product cost distortions. Most overhead costs in these environments are machine-related: depreciation on high-cost machinery; utilities to run that machinery; and repair and maintenance to keep that machinery operating. As illustrated in Exhibit 6-1, overhead allocation rates based on direct labour can be very high and will assign primarily machine-related overhead costs to products that use high amounts of direct labour rather than to the products that are truly creating the costs to be incurred—those products that use the machine technology. The exhibit illustrates the difference in the amounts of overhead that would be applied under each of the methods. As a result, a more sophisticated method of overhead cost allocation is needed.

Machine time is often a useful overhead allocation base in the modern manufacturing environment. But even machine hours may not be adequate as the sole allocation base for overhead costs. If overhead is created by factors such as product variety, product complexity, or other cost drivers, multiple allocation bases will result in more accurate estimates of product or service cost. Because companies now have the technology to collect, process, analyze, and use a much greater quantity of information than in the past, it is possible to obtain greater accuracy in product costing by using multiple cost pools to accumulate and to rationally allocate, rather than arbitrarily assign, overhead costs.

EXHIBIT 6-1

Cost Distortions in a Machine-Intensive Environment

Overhead costs per month, primarily machine-related	$600,000
Total direct labour hours (DLH)	800
Overhead rate per DLH ($600,000 ÷ 800)	$750
Total machine hours (MH)	2,400
Overhead rate per MH ($600,000 ÷ 2,400)	$250

Product A (10,000 units per month)		**Product B (10,000 units per month)**	
Total DLH	600	**Total DLH**	200
OH assigned using DLH (600 × $750)	$450,000	OH assigned using DLH (200 × $750)	$150,000
OH per unit ($450,000 ÷ 10,000)	$45	OH per unit ($150,000 ÷ 10,000)	$15
Total MH	400	**Total MH**	2,000
OH assigned using MH (400 × $250)	$100,000	OH assigned using MH (2,000 × $250)	$500,000
OH per unit ($100,000 ÷ 10,000)	$10	OH per unit ($500,000 ÷ 10,000)	$50

ACTIVITY ANALYSIS

The development of product or service cost may be designated as an accounting function, but this task concerns all managers. Costs should be computed in a systematic and rational manner so that they are as accurate as possible and may be relied on for planning, controlling, and decision-making purposes. For example, product costs affect decisions on corporate strategy (Is it profitable to be in a particular market?), marketing (What is the relationship between product cost and product price?), production (Should a component be made or purchased?), and finance (Should money be invested in additional plant assets to manufacture this product?).

ABC, however, traces costs to the products that cause them, providing a much more accurate picture. Indirect costs are driven first to the activities and processes that occur in an organization, and then to the actual services themselves. ABC thus allocates these indirect costs more accurately and allows staff to manage activities rather than to just manage dollars.[6]

In theory, it would not matter how much it cost to make a product or perform a service if enough customers were willing to buy that item at a price that would cover a company's costs and provide a reasonable profit margin. In reality, there are two problems with this concept. First, customers usually only purchase items that provide acceptable value for the price being charged. Second, prices are often set by competitive market forces rather than by specific companies. Thus, management should be concerned about whether customers perceive selling price and value to be equal. This concern is normally addressed by ascertaining that the product meets customer quality and service expectations. Additionally, management must decide whether the company can make a reasonable profit, given external prices and internal costs. If the market price is considered a given, then cost becomes the controlling variable in profitability.

Activity-Based Management

Managers can use **activity-based management (ABM)** to help enhance customer value and organizational profits by increasing organizational efficiency and effectiveness and producing more accurate costs. ABM concepts overlap with numerous other disciplines, as shown in Exhibit 6-2.

activity-based management
a discipline that focuses on how the activities performed during the production/performance process can improve the value received by a customer and the profit achieved by providing this value

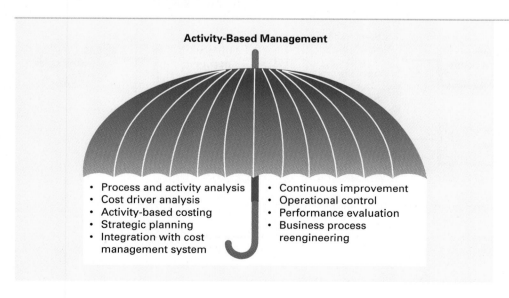

EXHIBIT 6-2

The Activity-Based Management Umbrella

Activity-Based Management

- Process and activity analysis
- Cost driver analysis
- Activity-based costing
- Strategic planning
- Integration with cost management system
- Continuous improvement
- Operational control
- Performance evaluation
- Business process reengineering

Depending on one's perspective, ABM could be viewed as part of a total quality management or business process reengineering effort. Alternatively, total quality management and business process reengineering could result from implementing activity-based management. But, most important, activity-based management should be integrated with management's strategic planning and with the organization's cost management system. Without this integration factor, activity-based management is like a book on a shelf. The book is brought down off the shelf when needed (e.g., for a process improvement project). Once the project is complete, the book can be placed back on the shelf next to the other books (improvement tools).[7] Integration into the planning process and the cost management system indicates that all the concepts under the ABM umbrella are viewed as integral parts of the organization's customer focus and long-range fiscal success (see Exhibit 6-3).

The use of activity-based management first requires an analysis of an organization's activities. An **activity** is any repetitive action, movement, or work sequence performed to fulfill a business function. Each activity should be able to be described with a verb and a noun. For example, *lift material*, *open door*, and *insert document* are all activities.

The activities performed in making or doing something can be detailed on a flowchart or grid called a **process map**. These maps should include all activities performed to accomplish a specific task or process, not just the obvious ones. For example, walking from the front desk with a change drawer and breaking open rolls of coins would not be on a typical list of Steps in Cash Register Operation. However, these activities must be performed each time a new clerk opens a register. Many activities that require significant time are not viewed as true parts of the process. By detailing all activities, process maps allow duplication, waste, and unnecessary work

activity
a repetitive action, movement, or work sequence performed to fulfill a business function

process map
a flowchart or diagram that indicates every step in making a product or providing a service

EXHIBIT 6-3

Process-Driven Improvement

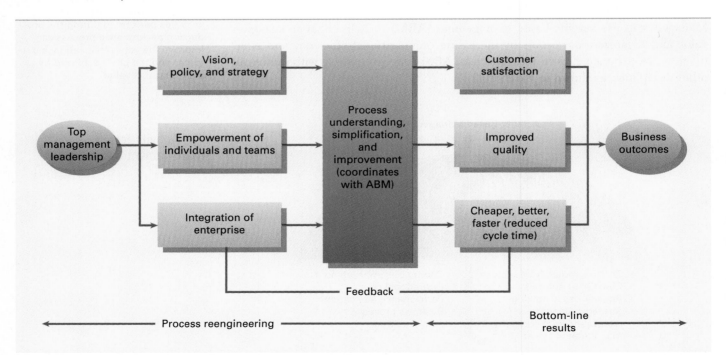

Source: Adapted from V. Daniel Hunt, *Process Mapping* (New York: Wiley, 1996) p. 31.

to be identified. These maps can also be used as benchmarking guides to assist all departments or divisions in an organization to adopt the best possible practices. Detail from a process map is included in the **value chart** shown in Exhibit 6-4. Some process maps are called value charts because they indicate the time spent in each activity from the beginning to end of a process and assess the value of each activity.

Value-Added and Non-Value-Added Activities

Activities may be value-added, non-value-added, or business-value-added. A **value-added (VA) activity** increases the worth of a product or service to customers and is one for which customers are willing to pay. VA activities are functions absolutely necessary to manufacture a product or perform a service. The time spent in these activities is the **value-added processing** (or **service**) **time**. For example, a telecommunications company in Winnipeg, Manitoba, makes a product that recognizes whether a call is being made by human voice or by data transmission (as is necessary for fax, Internet, and other modem telecommunications traffic). The manufacturing time needed to incorporate this ability into the product is value-added processing time and the time spent in making the voice/data determination is value-added service time for customers.

Other activities simply increase the time spent on a product or service but do not increase its worth to the customer. These **non-value-added (NVA) activities** create unnecessary additional costs, which, if eliminated, would decrease costs

value chart
a visual representation of the value-added and non-value-added activities and the time spent in all of these activities from the beginning to the end of a process

LEARNING OBJECTIVE 2

What are the differences among value-added, non-value-added, and business-value-added activities?

value-added activity
an activity that increases the worth of a product or service to the customer and for which the customer is willing to pay

value-added processing time
the time it takes to perform the functions necessary to manufacture a product

value-added service time
the time it takes to perform all necessary service functions for a customer

EXHIBIT 6-4
Value Chart

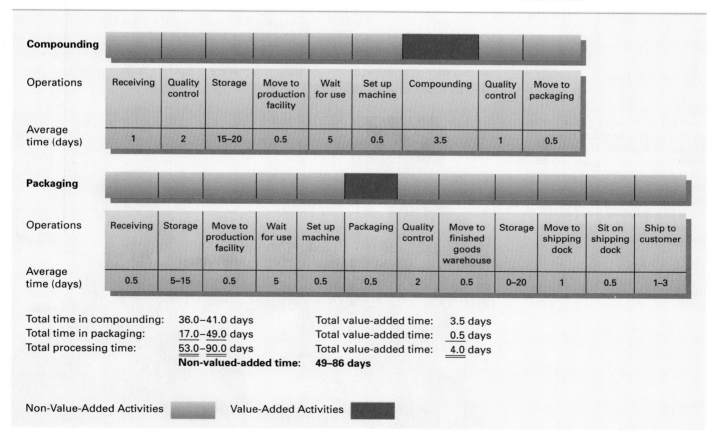

Total time in compounding: 36.0–41.0 days   Total value-added time: 3.5 days
Total time in packaging: 17.0–49.0 days   Total value-added time: 0.5 days
Total processing time: 53.0–90.0 days   Total value-added time: 4.0 days
           Non-valued-added time: **49–86 days**

Non-Value-Added Activities   Value-Added Activities

non-value-added activity
an activity that increases the time spent on a product or service but does not increase its value or worth to the customer

without affecting the product's or service's market value or quality. NVA activities exist throughout an organization and, in general, are extremely expensive.

Processing or service time may be non-value-added if activities are being performed simply to keep people and machines busy. Also, any processing time spent in unnecessarily packaging a product is non-value-added. For example, packaging a man's dress shirt into a cellophane package would most likely be viewed as non-value-added, although packaging medicines for health and safety reasons would be perceived as value-added by customers. Many companies are focusing attention on minimizing or eliminating packaging to help reduce time and cost as well as to be environmentally conscious.

Non-value-added activities also include moving and waiting. Moving products or components from one place to another constitutes **transfer time**; storage time and time spent waiting at the production operation for processing are referred to as **idle** (or wait) **time**. Although this time is non-value-added, few companies can eliminate all transfer or idle time.

transfer time
the time it takes to move products or components from one place to another (move time)

idle time
storage time and time spent waiting at a production operation for processing

inspection time
the time taken to perform quality control

Performing quality assurance activities results in **inspection time**. In most instances, quality control inspections are considered non-value-added if the concept of total quality management is adopted. Under a TQM system, the goal is zero defects by both people and machines. If this goal is being met or being strived for, inspections are simply a matter of looking for a needle in a haystack. A company, such as Motorola, with a 6 sigma achievement (incurring only 3.4 defects per million units) does not need to spend time inspecting: there is no cost–benefit justification. Alternatively, customers purchasing food or pharmaceuticals or buying seats on an airplane may view quality control inspections as very value-added.

The value chart in Exhibit 6-4 illustrates the manufacturing activities of Elyssa Corporation. Only four days of value-added production time are needed in the entire sequence; even within this sequence, as mentioned earlier, the company may question the time spent in packaging. Additionally, there is an excessive amount of time consumed in storing and moving materials. Understanding the non-value-added nature of these functions should motivate managers to minimize such activities as much as possible.

Chatting at the water cooler appears to be a good example of a non-value-added activity. However, if these individuals were lawyers discussing legal strategy for a case, the time would definitely be value-added. The perception of an activity's value to a customer is not always the same as fact ... investigate before categorizing!

Some NVA activities exist that are essential to business operations but for which customers would not willingly choose to pay. These activities are known as **business-value-added (BVA) activities**. For instance, publicly held companies must have an audit at the end of their fiscal year. Customers know that this activity must occur and that it creates costs. However, because the audit adds no direct value to companies' products or services, customers would prefer not to have to pay for this activity.

The News Note below provides one bank's classification scheme for its activities. This Note indicates that, regardless of the terminology used, there is a high degree of importance in analyzing activities.

Cycle Efficiency

In a manufacturing environment, the total **cycle time** reflects the time from the receipt of an order to completion (or delivery) of a product. Thus, total cycle time is equal to value-added processing time plus total non-value-added time. Dividing value-added processing time by total cycle time gives **manufacturing cycle efficiency (MCE)**, a measure of how well a firm's manufacturing capabilities use time resources. In a manufacturing environment, typically, cycle time efficiency at most companies is 10%. In other words, value is added to the product only 10% of the time from receipt of the parts until shipment to the customer. Waste accounts for 90% of the cycle time. A product is much like a magnet. The longer the cycle time, the more the product attracts and creates cost.[8]

In a retail environment, cycle time refers to the time from when an item is ordered to when that item is sold to a customer. Non-value-added activities in retail include shipping time from the supplier, receiving department delays for counting merchandise, and storage time between receipt and sale.

In a service company, cycle time refers to the time between the service order and service completion. All activities other than actual service performance and nonactivity (such as delays in beginning a job, unless specifically requested by the customer) are considered non-value-added *for that job*.

business-value-added activity
an activity that is necessary for the operation of a business but for which a customer would not want to pay

LEARNING OBJECTIVE 3

What might cause decreased manufacturing cycle efficiency?

cycle time
the time from when a customer places an order to the time that the product or service is delivered or, using a full life-cycle approach, the time from the conceptualization of a product or service to the time the product or service is delivered to the market/customer

manufacturing cycle efficiency
value-added production time divided by total cycle time; provides a measure of processing efficiency

Activity Analysis Takes a Customer Focus

GENERAL NEWS NOTE

ABC requires identification and classification of activities. In banking, activities are classified first as customer order-driven activities and ongoing-concern activities. The customer order-driven activities include such things as sales, services, processing, and administration. The ongoing-concern activities include areas considered as overhead such as accounting and finance, personnel, general counsel, and purchasing among others. A major effort is made to minimize the cost of these activities using the value-added, non-value-added activities analysis. These analyses have been renamed mission-related activities and nonmission-related activities analysis. Mission-related activities are defined as the things we do to satisfy the needs of our constituents, while nonmission-related activities are those things we do that increase the elapsed time of various processes, such as inspection, movement, storage, and error correction. The objective is to eliminate or at least reduce the amount of nonmission activities. A major reason for using the word mission instead of value in classifying activities is psychological. We do not want to imply that an activity, such as correcting errors, has no value. Rather, we want to convey the idea that by avoiding errors we can achieve our mission and avoid the correction activity.

Source: Republished with permission of the Institute of Management Accounting, from "ABM Lifts Bank's Bottom Line," Robert B. Sweeney and James W. Mays, *Management Accounting* March 1997; permission conveyed through Copyright Clearance Center, Inc.

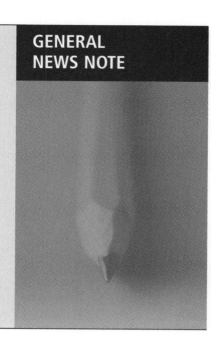

The following example illustrates non-value-added activities in a service environment. On Monday at 9:00 a.m., the telephone company is asked to install a telephone line for a customer. The job is scheduled for Tuesday at 3:30 p.m. Upon arriving at the customer's house, the service technician spends 20 minutes installing the telephone jack, 5 minutes writing an invoice, and 5 minutes chatting with the homeowner. The total cycle time is 31 hours (9:00 a.m. Monday to 4:00 p.m. Tuesday) or 1,860 minutes—of which only 20 to 25 minutes is value-added time for that particular job! (The 5 minutes spent writing the invoice could be perceived as value-added because, if a problem occurs, the invoice shows that the work was performed by a telephone company employee.) Thus, the service cycle efficiency is a mere 1.3% (25 minutes ÷ 1,860 minutes). Alternatively, if the customer did not want the line installed on Monday and asked for the delay until 3:30 p.m. on Tuesday, the total cycle time is 30 minutes and the cycle efficiency is 66 or 83% (depending on the classification of the invoice-writing time).

Non-value-added activities can be attributed to systemic, physical, and human factors. For example, a system may require that products be manufactured in large batches to minimize machinery setup costs or that service jobs be taken in order of importance. A building's layout does not always provide for the most efficient transfer of products, especially in multistorey buildings in which receiving and shipping are on the ground floor and storage and production are on other floors. People may be responsible for NVA activities because of improper skills, improper training, or a need to be sociable (as when workers discuss weekend sports events on Monday morning). Attempts to reduce non-value-added activities should focus on those activities that create the most unnecessary costs.

In a perfect environment, the manufacturing or service cycle efficiency would be 100% because all NVA time would be eliminated. Such an environment will never exist, but companies are moving toward higher cycle efficiencies. One means by which companies can move toward such an optimized environment is through the use of just-in-time (JIT) inventory, where inventory is manufactured or purchased only as it is needed or in time to be sold or used. JIT eliminates a significant portion of the idle time consumed in storage and transfer processes.

Dell Computer Corp. has also implemented JIT practices on its manufacturing floor, sequencing all production activities in such a way that in-process material continually moves toward the completed product.

At Dell's new Metric 12 facility, this process, commonly known as flow manufacturing, is complemented by a high level of automation. Hydraulic tools and conveyers lift in-process material between production areas, cutting the number of times a human touches the product by 50%. This significantly reduces the opportunity for damage and the need for product rework.

Dell also reduces the need for rework and the chance for faulty parts through its stringent quality control process. Dell has neither the time nor workforce (nor desire) to inspect incoming parts. Instead, it relies on regular on-site audits of suppliers as well as quick diagnostic tests during the assembly process. These JIT practices have allowed Dell to shrink the cycle time for its PCs, from order to shipment, to 3.5 days.

Impressive, but Keith Maxwell, vice president of procurement and manufacturing, says Dell's JIT job is not done. He is currently leading an effort to consolidate all production part inventories into a single supplier logistics centre "that will be managed by a third party. Having a single facility will allow us to deal with a single truck with multiple parts in it. It will also reduce our suppliers' costs, so they don't have to manage inventory for us."[9]

Preparing process maps or constructing value charts for each product or service would be quite time-consuming. A few such charts, however, can quickly indicate where a company is losing time through NVA activities. A cost estimate of that time can be made by totalling costs such as depreciation on storage facilities, wages for warehouse employees, and an interest charge on working capital funds that are tied up in inventory. This information allows managers to make more informed decisions about how much costs could be reduced if NVA activities were minimized or eliminated and, thus, how company profitability would be improved. Exhibit 6-5 indicates the various opportunities that exist to improve activities.

Cost Drivers

As companies engage in activities, resources are consumed and costs are incurred. All activities have one or more related cost drivers, which are factors that have direct cause-and-effect relationships to costs. For example, cost drivers for a purchasing area include the number of purchase orders, supplier contacts, and shipments received. Some cost drivers in a die-casting operation might include the size of dies, thickness of dies, number of dies to be cast per batch, and percent of changes in previously designed dies.

The number of cost drivers that can be identified is probably not the number that should be used for overhead allocation purposes. The more cost drivers and cost pools are used, the greater is the degree of accuracy of reported product costs. But the benefits provided by increased cost accuracy need to be greater than the cost of defining, accumulating, and maintaining the data.

Management should select a reasonable number of important cost drivers and be certain that the cost of measuring them is not excessive. For instance, finding

LEARNING OBJECTIVE 4

How would the cost drivers in an activity-based costing system be developed?

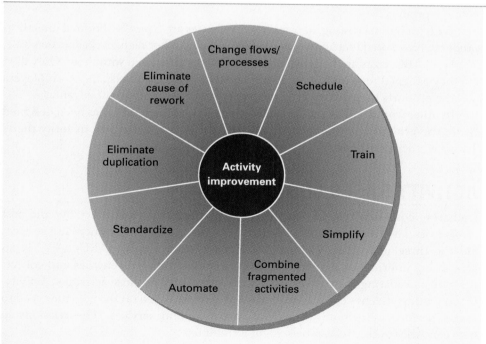

EXHIBIT 6-5

Wheel of Opportunities for Activity Improvements

Source: Lawrence S. Maisel and Eileen Morrissey, "Using Activity-Based Costing to Improve Performance," *Handbook of Cost Management 1998 Edition* (Boston: Warren, Gorham & Lamont RIA Group), p. B4-23. Reprinted from *Handbook of Cost Management*, with permission of the publisher, Research Institute of America Group.

INTERNATIONAL NEWS NOTE

Milkcom S.A./N.V. (Belgium)

Milkcom, a co-operative founded in 1963, is the biggest producer of milk cream in Belgium. It has 6,700 suppliers (of milk) and 900 people work in its production facilities with an annual turnover of $4 billion. In order to remain competitive the company decided to obtain an ISO 9002 listing. With the Vierick school (business university) an ABC system was developed for the company.

Management is able to trace their production costs much better than with conventional cost systems. With the ABC system Milkcom is able to have, for each production line and for each type of product, a bill of material and signals of any change that occurs during the production process.

Although the cost of the new system was excessive, it has been worth it according to the management. In a growing and competitive market, it is essential to know exactly how much each product type costs. This helps to continuously alter the product-mix based on the performance of each product.

Source: Gunasekaran, Marri, Yusuf, "Application of Activity-Based Costing: Some Case Experiences," *Managerial Auditing Journal*, Bradford, 1999.

and using eight cost drivers might increase organizational costs by 1% but provide enough data to reduce total costs by 10%—a net cost reduction of 9%. Adding another eight drivers to the system might reduce costs another 10% but may increase costs by 14%. Companies should use cost–benefit analysis to determine where significant cost improvements are possible. Additionally, cost drivers that are selected for use should be easy to understand, directly related to the activity being performed, and appropriate for performance measurement.

As compared to traditional cost accounting methodology, ABC provides the ability to more directly observe where, how, and why costs are incurred. ABC accomplishes this by focusing on the actual activities directly associated with providing a product.

With traditional costing, departmental expenses are typically allocated directly to products, based on direct labour hours spent or some other high-level allocation base.

With ABC, costs are first traced to the activities associated with them. Only then are they assigned to products. Inserting activities between time spent by employees and the products they deliver provides a subtle, but very important advantage.

In other words, unlike traditional costing methodology, ABC has been designed "from the ground up" to explain why costs are incurred, not just quantify them. This is a crucial difference![10]

LEARNING OBJECTIVE 5

What distinguishes activity-based costing from conventional overhead allocation methods?

ACTIVITY-BASED COSTING

Gathering costs into related cost pools, recognizing that various activity and cost levels exist, and using multiple cost drivers to assign costs to products and services are the three underlying elements of activity-based costing (ABC). ABC is an accounting information system that identifies organizational activities and collects costs by considering the underlying nature and extent of those activities. Activity-based costing attaches costs to products and services based on the activities used to make, perform, distribute, or support products and services. The relationship between ABM and ABC can be seen in Exhibit 6-6.

Overhead has traditionally been accumulated into one or two cost pools (total overhead or variable and fixed overhead), either by department or plantwide. Furthermore, one or two drivers (direct labour hours or machine hours) have typically been used to assign costs to products. Activity-based costing focuses on

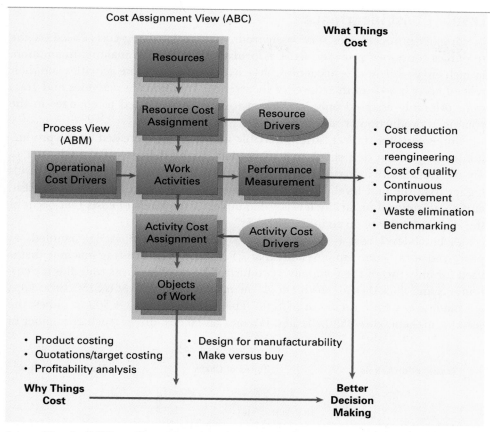

Cost Assignment View (ABC)

Source: Timothy S. White, *The 60 Minute ABC Book* (Bedford, Tex.: CAM–I, 1997), p. 19. This diagram is a slightly modified version of the CAM–I Cross, named for its development in association with the Consortium for Advanced Manufacturing–International or CAM–I.

EXHIBIT 6-6

Relationship Between AMB and ABC

resource-consuming activities as indicated in Exhibit 6-7. The ABC method of collecting cost information allows a more detailed perspective of how costs can be controlled. For example, expediting orders, correcting errors, issuing credits, and amending orders (a total of $240,000 or 40% of the department's costs) are probably non-value-added activities and candidates for elimination or reduction. These costs are buried in the traditional resource classifications.

EXHIBIT 6-7

Traditional versus ABM Focus on Sales Order Department Activities

Traditional Focus on Resources		ABM Focus on Activities	
Salaries	$460,000	Take orders	$300,000
Space	50,000	Expedite orders	70,000
Depreciation	50,000	Correct errors	60,000
Supplies	30,000	Issue credits	80,000
Other	10,000	Amend orders	30,000
	$600,000	Answer queries	20,000
		Supervise employees	40,000
			$600,000

Source: Tom Pryor, "Making New Things Familiar and Familiar Things New," *Journal of Cost Management*, Winter 1997, p. 39. Reprinted by permission of Research Institute of America Group.

Level of Cost Incurrence

In complex production or service environments, reclassifying costs based on the resources consumed provides better information for decision making. In addition, in such environments the accounting system should accumulate activities and their related costs based on their level of incurrence. Traditionally, activities and costs were primarily assessed only in relation to how they reacted to changes in the volume of production or sales.

Some costs are, in fact, strictly variable **unit-level costs** created by the production or acquisition of a single unit of product or the delivery of a single unit of service. But an activity-based system recognizes that costs may vary at activity levels higher than the unit level. These higher levels include batch, product or process, and organizational or facility levels.[11] Examples of the kinds of costs that occur at the various levels are given in Exhibit 6-8.

A **batch-level cost** is created when similar things are made, handled, or processed at the same time. Assume that VW Canada has a casting machine that is used for only two of the company's products. The machine casts thin dies for customer X and thick dies for customer Y. The machine's setup cost is $150; two setups are made a day for a total cost of $300. The first run generates 500 thin dies; the second run generates 100 thick dies. If a unit-based cost driver (such as number of

unit-level cost
a cost created by the production or acquisition of a single unit of production or the delivery of a single unit of service

batch-level cost
a cost that is created by a group of similar things made, handled, or processed at a single time

EXHIBIT 6-8
Levels of Costs

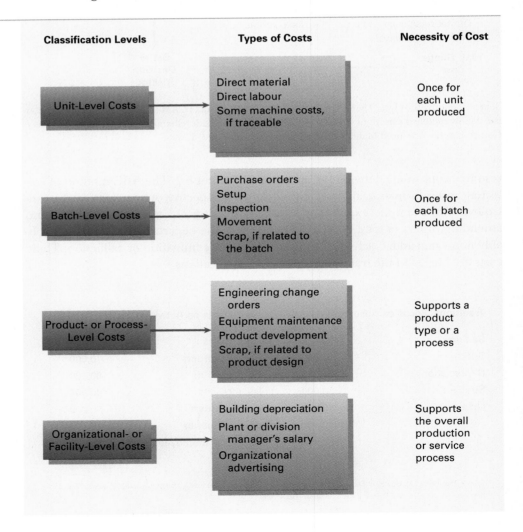

Classification Levels	Types of Costs	Necessity of Cost
Unit-Level Costs	Direct material Direct labour Some machine costs, if traceable	Once for each unit produced
Batch-Level Costs	Purchase orders Setup Inspection Movement Scrap, if related to the batch	Once for each batch produced
Product- or Process-Level Costs	Engineering change orders Equipment maintenance Product development Scrap, if related to product design	Supports a product type or a process
Organizational- or Facility-Level Costs	Building depreciation Plant or division manager's salary Organizational advertising	Supports the overall production or service process

dies cast) is used to allocate the setup cost, the setup cost per die is $0.50 ($300 ÷ 600). This method would assign the majority of the setup cost to the thin dies (500 × $0.50 = $250). However, setup is a batch-level cost, so $150 should be spread over the 500 thin dies for a cost of $0.30 per piece, and $150 should be spread over 100 thick dies for a cost of $1.50 per piece. A batch-level perspective shows the commonality of the cost to units within the batch and indicates more clearly the relationship between the activity (setup) and the driver (different casting runs).

A cost incurred in support of different products or processes is a **product- or process-level cost.** These costs are created by activities such as developing products, processing engineering change orders, or maintaining production specifications. The costs of these activities can be assigned to individual products, but the costs are independent (i.e., fixed) regardless of the number of batches or the number of units of each product produced.[12] Product- or process-level costs vary with increases in the number of products or processes that need to be sustained in an organization.

To illustrate a product- or process-level cost, assume that VW Canada's billing department revised five forms during May. Of these forms, four related to casting customers (Group One) and one was related to aluminum wheel customers (Group Two). None of the form changes related to catalytic-converter customers (Group Three). Each form revision costs $3,000 to issue. During May, the company billed 2,000 Group One customers, 3,000 Group Two customers, and 10,000 Group Three customers. If form-revision cost is treated as a unit-level cost, the total $15,000 cost would be spread over the 15,000 forms produced for a cost of $1 per unit. However, this method inappropriately assigns $10,000 of form-revision cost to Group Three, which had no form revisions for the month! Treating form-revision cost as a product- or process-level cost results in the assignment of $12,000 and $3,000 of cost, respectively, to Group One and Group Two customers. These cost amounts would be assigned not only to bills issued in the current month, but also to all Group One and Group Two customer bills produced during the entire time that the revisions are in effect, because the costs benefit all current and future issuances.

Organizational- or **facility-level costs** are incurred to support and sustain a business unit such as a department, division, or headquarters. If the unit has an identifiable output, costs may be attachable to that output in a reasonable allocation process. But if the costs incurred at this level are common to many different activities, products, or services, these costs can only be assigned arbitrarily. For instance, the salary of the organization's executive officers, cost of the annual corporate audit, and cost of shareholder meetings are companywide organizational costs. Although these costs appear to be fixed, as the organization grows, additional costs will be incurred: more executives will be added; audit costs will become more expensive; and shareholder meetings will require larger space and greater costs.

Thus, batch-level, product/process-level, and organizational/facility-level costs are all variable, but they vary with causes other than changes in production or service volume. Accounting traditionally assumed that costs that did not vary with unit-level changes in activity were fixed rather than variable. This assumption is too narrowly conceived. In contrast, activity-based systems often refer to fixed costs as being long-term variable costs. Essentially, **long-term variable costs** are step fixed costs and, rather than ignoring the steps, ABC acknowledges their existence. Professor Robert Kaplan of Harvard University refers to the Rule of One: any time there is more than one unit of a resource, that resource is variable and the appropriate cost driver simply needs to be identified. Knowledge of the driver may help to eliminate the source of a potential cost change.

product-level (or process-level) cost
a cost created by the need to implement or support a specific product

organizational-level cost
a cost incurred to support ongoing operations, which in turn provide available facilities

facility-level cost
see *organizational-level cost*

long-term variable cost
a cost that has traditionally been viewed as fixed but that will actually react to some significant change in activity; also referred to as a step fixed cost

For this reason, more accurate estimates of product or service cost can be made if costs at the unit, batch, and product/process activity levels are accumulated separately. If organizational/facility-level costs are related to a particular product or service, the costs should be assigned to that product or service. For example, the focus of BMW's Design and Engineering Centre at Gaydon, Great Britain, is on Rovers. Thus, costs of this centre should be allocated to all Rover production facilities. In the same manner, costs of the Spartanburg, USA, plant should be assigned to BMW Z3 roadsters—that facility's only output. Costs for these facilities are reasonably attachable to specific output. Use of this methodology means that cost assignment can be made relative to the activities causing the costs and that total product (or service) cost can be developed and matched with sales revenues.

In contrast, organizational- and facility-level costs may not be product- or service-related. If these costs cannot be associated with specific products or services, they should be subtracted in total from net product margin. An activity-based costing system will not normally try to assign organizational-level costs to products because the allocation base would be too arbitrary.

Exhibit 6-9 indicates how cost accumulation at the various levels can be used to determine a total unit product cost. Each product's total unit cost is multiplied by the number of units sold, and that product's cost of goods sold is subtracted from its total product revenue, yielding a net product margin. After these computations are performed for each product line, the product-line profits are summed to determine net product revenues. The unassigned organizational-level costs are subtracted to find the company profit or loss. In this model, the traditional distinction between product and period costs is not visible because the emphasis is on analyzing product profitability for internal management decision making rather than for financial statement presentation.

Two-Step Allocation

After initial recording, costs are accumulated in activity centre cost pools. An **activity centre** is any segment of the production or service process for which management wants separate information about the costs of the activities performed. In defining these centres, management should consider the following issues: geographical proximity of equipment; defined centres of managerial responsibility; magnitude of product costs; and a need to maintain a manageable number of activity centres. Costs having the same driver are accumulated in pools reflecting the appropriate level of cost incurrence (unit, batch, or product/process). If a relationship exists between a cost pool and a cost driver, then reducing or eliminating that cost driver should also reduce or eliminate the related cost.

In the past, most companies accumulated overhead using a vertical or functional approach. For example, all Sales Department costs were grouped together and separated from costs incurred in other parts of the organization. But production and service activities are horizontal by nature. A product or service flows through an organization, affecting numerous departments along the way. Gathering costs in pools reflecting the same cost drivers allows managers to better recognize these organizational cross-functional activities and focus on their cost impacts. Exhibit 6-10 on page 322 provides an example of the horizontal nature of organizational work; in this case, all activities have occurred because the Sales Department received an order from a customer.

After accumulation, costs are allocated out of the activity centre cost pools and assigned to products and services by use of an activity cost driver. An **activity cost**

activity centre
a segment of the production or service process for which management wants a separate report of the costs of activities performed

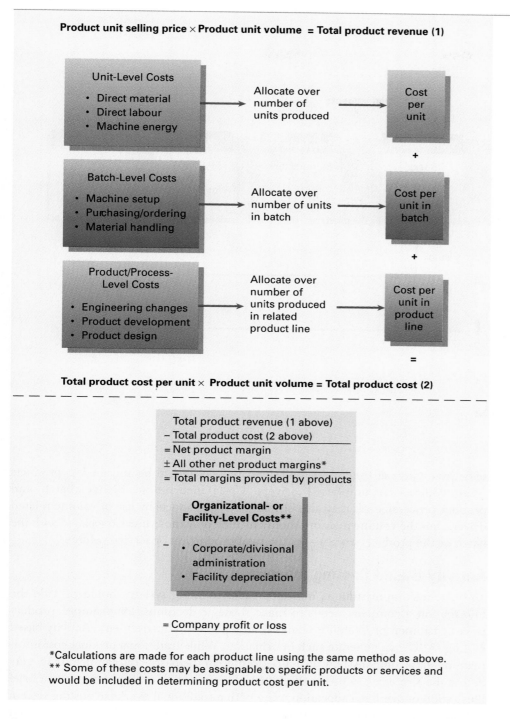

Product unit selling price × Product unit volume = Total product revenue (1)

Unit-Level Costs
- Direct material
- Direct labour
- Machine energy

→ Allocate over number of units produced → Cost per unit

+

Batch-Level Costs
- Machine setup
- Purchasing/ordering
- Material handling

→ Allocate over number of units in batch → Cost per unit in batch

+

Product/Process-Level Costs
- Engineering changes
- Product development
- Product design

→ Allocate over number of units produced in related product line → Cost per unit in product line

=

Total product cost per unit × Product unit volume = Total product cost (2)

Total product revenue (1 above)
– Total product cost (2 above)
= Net product margin
± All other net product margins*
= Total margins provided by products

Organizational- or Facility-Level Costs**
- Corporate/divisional administration
- Facility depreciation

= Company profit or loss

*Calculations are made for each product line using the same method as above.
** Some of these costs may be assignable to specific products or services and would be included in determining product cost per unit.

EXHIBIT 6-9

Determining Product Profitability and Company Profits

driver measures the demands placed on activities as well as the resources consumed by products and services; thus, an activity driver often indicates an activity's output. Exhibit 6-11 on page 323 provides some common activity cost drivers.

The process of cost assignment is the same as the overhead application process illustrated in Chapter 2. Exhibit 6-12 on page 323 illustrates this two-step process of tracing costs to products and services in an ABC system. As indicated in the exhibit, cost drivers used for the collection stage may differ from the activity drivers used for the allocation stage. Some activity centre costs are not traceable to lower levels

activity cost driver
a measure of the demands placed on activities and, thus, the resources consumed by products and services; often indicates an activity's output

EXHIBIT 6-10

Horizontal Work Activities

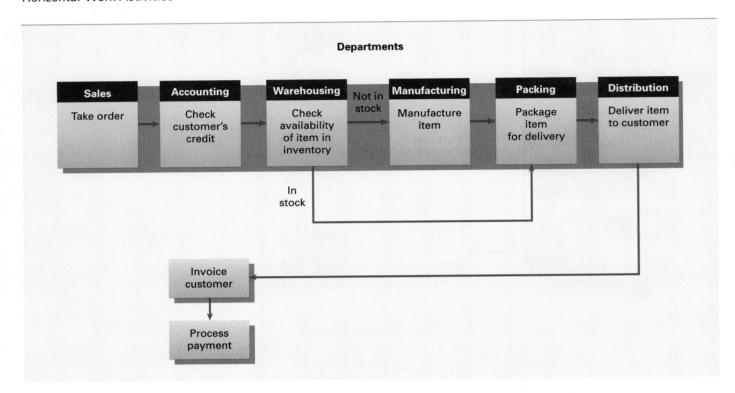

of activity. Costs at the lowest (unit) activity level should be allocated to products using volume- or unit-based drivers. Costs incurred at higher (batch and product/process) levels may also be allocated to products by use of volume-related drivers, but the volume measure should include only those units associated with the batch or the product/process—not the total production or service volume.

Activity-Based Costing Illustrated

To be of maximum value, a management accounting system should provide the information a company needs to make strategic decisions, for example, product price, customer profitability analysis, and process improvement. Activity-based costing (ABC) can generate such information. While traditional product cost information tells a company how well it performed in the past, ABC can help managers determine strategies to use in the future. The following example provides a brief illustration of overhead allocation using both a traditional overhead costing system utilizing direct labour hours as the plantwide cost driver and an activity-based costing system.

Abbott Cosmetics Ltd. manufactures three products, which vary in complexity and volume. The company manufactures 5,000 units of Product A, 2,000 units of Product B, and 1,000 units of Product C. Table 6-1 on page 324 shows the breakdown of costs for the company. Note that overhead represents 44.8% of the total production costs. The number of runs, orders, units per order, and direct labour hours for each product is shown in Table 6-2 on page 324.

EXHIBIT 6-11
Activity Drivers

Activity Centre	Activity Cost Drivers
Accounting	Reports requested; dollars expended
Personnel	Job change actions; hiring actions; training hours; counselling hours
Data processing	Reports requested; transactions processed; programming hours; program change requests
Production engineering	Hours spent in each shop; job specification changes requested; product change notices processed
Quality control	Hours spent in each shop; defects discovered; samples analyzed
Plant services	Preventive maintenance cycles; hours spent in each shop; repair maintenance actions
Material services	Dollar value of requisitions; number of transactions processed; number of personnel in direct support
Utilities	Direct usage (metered to shop); space occupied
Production shops	Fixed per-job charge; setups made; direct labour; machine hours; number of moves; material applied

Source: Republished with permission of the Institute of Management Accounting, from "Completing the Picture," Michael D. Woods, *Management Accounting*, December 1992; permission conveyed through Copyright Clearance Center, Inc.

EXHIBIT 6-12
Tracing Costs in an Activity-Based Costing System

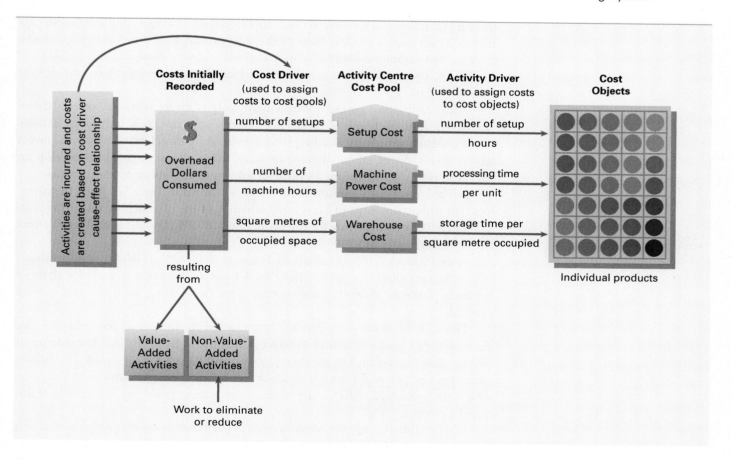

TABLE 6-1

Manufacturing Cost Proportions

Direct material	$ 900,000	30.7%
Direct labour	720,000	24.5
Overhead	1,315,340	44.8
Total	$2,935,340[1]	100.0%

[1] See information in Table 6-3.

TABLE 6-2

Annual Production Information

	Products		
	A	**B**	**C**
Number of units manufactured	5000	2,000	1,000
Number of runs	10	40	50
Number of orders	1	4	5
Number of units per order	5,000	500	200
Number of direct labour hours per unit	2	8	10
Total direct labour hours	10,000	16,000	10,000

The products vary significantly in production factors, with Product A being the simplest and least costly and Product C, the most complex and expensive. This product variation will be used to illustrate the inability of traditional costing to capture costs accurately. On the basis of the information shown in Table 6-2, calculations for both traditional and activity-based costing were done.

The following describes how activity-based costing was calculated for Abbott Cosmetics Ltd.

With traditional costing, management assigns direct material, direct labour, and overhead to each unit of production. Overhead is not broken down by activity but is assigned simply by dividing total overhead by direct machine hours, direct labour hours, direct labour dollars, or some other allocation basis to develop an overhead rate. Abbott assigned overhead using a direct labour application base.

Direct labour costs amount to $720,000, as shown in Table 6-1. Note that overhead for Abbott amounts to $1,315,340, which is 44.8% of total manufacturing cost. Therefore, the overhead rate for the company is 182.7% (Overhead dollars ÷ Direct labour dollars or $1,315,340 ÷ $720,000).

Since Product A requires 2 labour hours, or $40 of direct labour cost, overhead of $73.08 is assigned to it ($40 × 182.7%). A similar calculation is made for all three products. Table 6-3 shows the distribution of overhead using the traditional costing method.

The unit costs for each product are totalled in Table 6-3. For example, the manufacturing cost per unit of Product A is equal to $163.08. This is made up of $50 for direct material, $40 for direct labour, and $73.08 for overhead. The manufacturing cost per unit for each product will be used later to determine the price with a 40% standard markup and to illustrate pricing problems inherent in traditional costing.

ABC requires an investigation of each department to determine (a) how much time personnel actually spend on each product and (b) what factor drives costs in that department. At Abbott, extensive interviews and record analysis showed that

	A	B	C	Total
	5,000	2000	1,000	8,000
Units		**Cost per Unit**		**Total Cost**
Direct material	$ 50.00	$200.00	$250.00	$ 900,000[1]
Direct labour ($20 per hour)	40.00	160.00	200.00	720,000[2]
Overhead (182.7% of DL$)	73.08	292.32	365.40	1,315,440[3]
Manufacturing cost per unit	$163.08	$652.32	$815.40	$2,935,440[4]

[1] [($50 × 5,000) + ($200 × 2,000) + ($250 × 1,000)]
[2] [($40 × 5,000) + ($160 × 2,000) + ($200 × 1,000)]
[3] [($73.08 × 5,000) + ($292.32 × 2,000) + ($365.40 × 1,000)]
[4] [($163.08 × 5,000) + ($652.32 × 2,000) + ($815.40 × 1,000)]

TABLE 6-3

Traditional Cost Information

activities for engineering, materials handling, setup, quality assurance, and packing/shipping could be evaluated using ABC criteria. Table 6-4 shows the results of the investigation and cost calculations for each product by department or process.

	Products			
	A	B	C	Total
Engineering/order	$ 21,210	$ 21,210	$ 21,210	
× Number of orders	1	4	5	
Total Engineering Costs	$ 21,210	$ 84,840	$106,050	$ 212,100
Materials handling	$ 26.25	$ 26.25	$ 26.25	
× Number of units	5,000	2,000	1,000	
Total Materials Handling	$ 131,250	$ 52,500	$ 26,250	$ 210,000
Setup	$ 1,590	$ 1,590	$ 1,590	
× Number of runs	10	40	50	
Total Setup Costs	$ 15,900	$ 63,600	$ 79,500	$ 159,000
Quality assurance	$ 9.75	$ 9.75	$ 9.75	
× Number of units	5,000	2,000	1,000	
Total Quality Assurance	$ 48,750	$ 19,500	$ 9,750	$ 78,000
Packing/shipping	$ 46.875	$ 46.875	$ 46.875	
× Number of units	5,000	2,000	1,000	
Total Packing/Shipping	$ 234,375	$ 93,750	$ 46,875	$ 375,000
Other Overhead	$ 93,780	$ 93,780	$ 93,780	$ 281,340
Total Overhead	$ 545,265[1]	$407,970[2]	$362,205[3]	$1,315,440

[1] ($21,210 + $131,250 + $15,900 + $48,750 + $234,375 + $93,780)
[2] ($84,840 + $52,500 + $63,600 + $19,500 + $93,750 + $93,780)
[3] ($106,050 + $26,250 + $79,500 + $9,750 + $46,875 + $93,780)

TABLE 6-4

Activity-Based Cost Information

Departmental Analysis

Engineering Department—Engineering cost is driven by the number of orders for each product. For instance, one customer places one order annually for Product A, which has an engineering cost of $21,210 per order. Because there is only one order per year, the total engineering cost for Product A is $21,210. On the other end of the spectrum is Product C with an engineering cost of $106,050 for 5 orders per year, or $21,210 per order.

Materials Handling Department—The cost driver for materials handling is the number of units produced. An analysis of records for the materials handling department shows that the cost to provide parts to assembly ranges from $26,250 for Product C to $131,250 for Product A. The difference is due primarily to the greater number of units for Product A, which increases materials delivery costs.

Setup—A special team from engineering, maintenance, and production recalibrates the assembly line during production changeover (adequate records were available to separate these individuals' time on this task from other activities). Setup costs vary according to production runs. Each production run (the cost driver) requires a setup. One Product A setup, for example, costs $1,590; total setup cost, with 10 runs annually, is $15,900.

Quality Assurance Department—Each unit of production requires a quality assurance inspection. Total quality assurance for Product A is $48,750 ($9.75 per unit × 5,000 units).

Packing/Shipping—This varies from $234,375 for Product A to $46,875 for Product C.

Other Overhead—The ABC investigation revealed that the remaining processes were difficult to separate by activity. Since the product line itself was the most significant cost driver, all other activities were lumped together under "other overhead" and the cost was distributed evenly between products at the rate of $93,780 per product. This is a poor practice, but it is used here to expain the difference between the traditional method and the ABC method. A better practice is to leave the other costs unallocated. It is important to note here that under traditional costing, $1,315,440 was distributed in this fashion; however, using ABC, this non-activity-based distribution was reduced to $468,900 or 22.3% of total overhead. In other words, ABC divided 77.7% of total overhead more realistically among the five products.

In general, the value of ABC as a better overhead allocation technique is based on the percentage of overhead that is allocated by activities or cost drivers. The higher the percentage of "other overhead" not allocated by assigned activities, the more the allocation will reflect what would have been calculated using traditional methods.

Calculating Unit Costs Using ABC

The next step is a mathematical calculation of all overhead activity cost to a per-unit level.

Some of the activities identified in Table 6-4—materials handling, quality assurance, packing/shipping costs, and other overhead—are already calculated by unit. However, engineering and setup costs require further computation.

For example, the engineering cost and the setup cost per unit for Product B is calculated as shown next.

Product B Engineering Cost

$21,210.00	Engineering cost per order
× 4	Number of orders (cost driver)
$84,840.00	
÷ 2,000	Number of units produced
$ 42.42	Engineering cost per unit produced

Product B Setup Cost

$ 1,590.00	Setup cost per run
× 40	Number of runs (cost driver)
$63,600.00	
÷ 2,000	Number of units produced
$ 31.80	Setup cost per unit produced

Other Overhead—The remaining overhead is assigned by dividing the amount by the number of units of each product. For instance, dividing $93,780 by 2,000 units yields a per-unit "Other Overhead" of $46.89 for Product B (see Table 6-5).

Comparison to Traditional Cost

For comparison purposes, row 10 of Table 6-5 shows the traditional accounting unit costs given in Table 6-3 ("Manufacturing cost per unit"). The per-unit differences between traditional costing and ABC are shown in line 11. The total production cost (cost to produce all products) is the same for the two costing methods. The difference is in the cost assigned to each product, or in the division of overhead among products. For instance, Abbott Company's Product A costs $163.08 using traditional costing and $199.06 using ABC. This is a vivid example of product cross-subsidization.

The effect of ABC versus traditional costing is shown by comparing the cost and cost-based selling price differences between the two approaches. Prices for each product are calculated based on an across-the-board 40% markup of costs as shown in Table 6-6. The respective costs are simply multiplied by 1.4 (140%). For example, under traditional costing at Abbott, the price of Product A is $228.31, and under ABC, it is $278.68.

TABLE 6-5

ABC Information per Product Unit

	Product			
	A	**B**	**C**	**Total**
Units	**5,000**	**2,000**	**1,000**	**8,000**
	Per Unit Cost			**Total Cost**
1. Direct Material	$ 50.00	$200.00	$250.00	$ 900,000
2. Direct Labour ($20 per hour)	40.00	160.00	200.00	720,000
3. Engineering	4.24*	42.42	106.05	212,100
4. Materials Handling	26.25	26.25	26.25	210,000
5. Setup	3.18	31.80	79.50	159,000
6. Quality Assurance	9.75	9.75	9.75	78,000
7. Packing/Shipping	46.88*	46.88	46.88	375,000
8. Other Overhead	18.76*	46.89	93.78	281,340
9. ABC Cost per Unit	$199.06	$ 563.99	$812.21	$2,935,440
10. Traditional Cost per Unit	163.08	652.32	815.40	2,935,440
11. Difference	$ 36	$−88.33	$ −3.19	$ 0

*rounded

TABLE 6-6

Price and Markup Analysis at 40% Markup

Product A Cost		Product B Cost		Product C Cost	
Traditional	ABC	Traditional	ABC	Traditional	ABC
$163.08	$199.06	$652.32	$563.99	$815.40	$812.21

Product A Price		Product B Price		Product C Price	
$228.31	$278.68	$913.25	$789.59	$1,141.56	$1,137.09
15%[1]	ABC Markup	61.9%[2]	ABC Markup	40.5%[3]	ABC Markup

[1] [($228.31 − $199.06) ÷ $199.06]
[2] [($913.25 − $563.99) ÷ $563.99]
[3] [($1,141.56 − $812.21) ÷ $812.21]

In the bottom row is the calculated markup based on the activity-based cost and traditional price. We call this important calculation the revised ABC markup (Table 6-6). At Abbott, for Product A, the ABC markup is 15%.

Because activity-based cost accounting generates more accurate costs than traditional costing, prices based on ABC are more likely to reflect the desired markup for each individual product. Although in many industries the competitive market forces significantly influence pricing decisions, the product cost is usually an integral part of pricing decision criteria. With traditional costing, the costs that Abbott assigns for Product A are 22.1% lower [($199.06 − $163.08) ÷ $163.08] and for Product B they are 13.5% higher [($563.99 − $652.32) ÷ $652.32] than with ABC. Since traditional pricing is based on a 40% markup of traditionally calculated costs, the prices are also lower or higher by the same percentage. Abbott thinks it has a 40% markup for each of its products. Based on ABC costs for Product A, the price markup is about 15% [($228.31 − $199.06) ÷ $199.06], or 25% less than expected. Product B has a markup using ABC of 61.9% [($913.25 − $563.99) ÷ $563.99].

Abbott should be concerned that market forces will influence sales. If competitors are properly pricing their products (i.e., based on accurate costs), Abbott's products will be either over- or underpriced. Sales of the two underpriced products will probably increase, whereas the sales of the overpriced products will decrease. Over time, the product mix will change, with the company selling more of the lower-margin products (based on ABC costs), to the point of filling the available capacity with lower-margin products. The magnitude of change will depend on the markets, competitive actions, and price elasticity of the products. Abbott's revenue, profit, and profit margin will deteriorate, while total number of units sold may actually increase. At some future time, management will look at the results and ask, "What happened?"

A forward-looking attribute of ABC is that it yields better information for setting appropriate prices and determining the cost and profit impact of different product mixes. With traditional costing, a company may inappropriately assume that a particular product is contributing more profit than it actually is. The example also illustrates the importance of ABC for companies with a complex product mix, as some products may be allocated more than their fair share of overhead.

This example reflects a company operating with 45% overhead (Table 6-3, $1,315,440 ÷ $2,935,440). One should analyze the relationship between overhead level and the impact of ABC. The yardstick to measure this is the actual markup for each product ("ABC Markup" in Table 6-6). The closer the ABC markup is to the desired gross profit margin, the better.

In this scenario, if Abbott Corporation (45% overhead) uses traditional costing for pricing decisions, it could experience major changes in product demand and unexpected negative impacts on profitability.

These calculations show the impact of only a few changes in a relatively narrow product mix. Many companies deal with a more complex product mix and make such decisions numerous times each year. In our example, Product A, the under-priced and least profitable product, is more likely to increase in demand. Prices lower than competitors' create higher demand. The reverse is true for overpriced products. This demonstrates another effect of inaccurate costing and consequent pricing, that is, the probable increase in sales volume of less profitable products and decrease in sales of more profitable products.

Although even a 5% cost difference is significant when used as a basis for pricing decisions, we will use a 10% difference to postulate when it might be bene-ficial to implement ABC costing. This is because even ABC includes some "arbi-trary" allocation of overhead that is not allocated by assigned activities or cost drivers. Therefore, with overhead costs of about 15% or more of total cost, it appears that the more accurate costing with ABC would be beneficial. At overhead cost levels of less than 15% of total costs, a cost–benefit analysis would be appro-priate to further investigate the implementation benefits of the specific situation.

A cost–benefit analysis would be dependent on numerous factors. Important considerations would be the complexity of product lines and operations, size of the firm, and expected time to implement an ABC system.

In a study of 10 United Kingdom firms of varying size, the average implemen-tation cost was found to be approximately $30,000, with the implementation time varying from 20 to 52 weeks (implementation cost was correlated to implementa-tion time). Six of these firms reported no increase in operating costs of the ABC system after implementation, with seven reporting improved management infor-mation after the ABC implementation. Therefore, a company near (or below) the 15% overhead point should consider the expected increase in cost recovery through improved pricing and the estimated cost to implementation.[13]

DETERMINING WHETHER ABC IS APPROPRIATE

Not every accounting system that uses direct labour or machine hours as the cost driver provides inadequate or inaccurate cost information. Activity-based costing is a useful tool, but it is not necessarily appropriate for all companies. There are two primary assumptions that underlie ABC: (1) the costs in each cost pool are driven by homogeneous activities, and (2) the costs in each cost pool are strictly propor-tional to the activity.[14] If these assumptions are true, then ABC will be advantageous under the following conditions:

- There is significant product/service variety or complexity.
- There is a lack of commonality in the creation and use of overhead.
- There are problems with current cost allocations.
- There has been significant change in the environment in which the organization operates.

Exhibit 6-13 on page 330 illustrates a comparison of the traditional versus ABC overhead allocation.

LEARNING OBJECTIVE 6

When is the use of activity-based costing appropriate?

EXHIBIT 6-13
Traditional versus ABC
Overhead Allocations

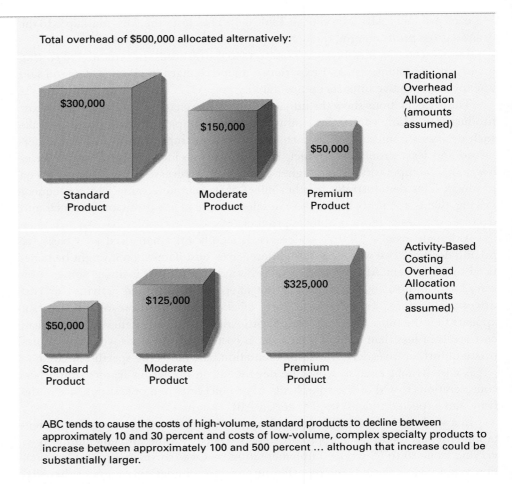

Total overhead of $500,000 allocated alternatively:

$300,000

Standard
Product

$150,000

Moderate
Product

$50,000

Premium
Product

Traditional
Overhead
Allocation
(amounts
assumed)

$50,000

Standard
Product

$125,000

Moderate
Product

$325,000

Premium
Product

Activity-Based
Costing
Overhead
Allocation
(amounts
assumed)

ABC tends to cause the costs of high-volume, standard products to decline between approximately 10 and 30 percent and costs of low-volume, complex specialty products to increase between approximately 100 and 500 percent ... although that increase could be substantially larger.

Product/Service Variety or Complexity

Two factors commonly associated with a need to consider activity-based costing are product/service variety and complexity. **Product variety** refers to the number of different types of products made. **Service variety** refers to the number of different types of services provided. The items may be variations of the same product line (such as Hallmark's different types of greeting cards or the local bank's different types of chequing accounts), or they may be in numerous product families (such as Procter & Gamble's detergents, diapers, fabric softeners, and shampoos). In either case, product/service additions cause numerous overhead costs to increase. Exhibit 6-14 illustrates the potential for increased overhead with an increase in product variety. In addition, the changes in overhead costs resulting from increased product variety show that seemingly fixed costs (such as warehousing, purchasing, and quality control) are in fact long-term variable costs.

In the quest for product variety, many companies are striving for **mass customization** of products. This production method refers to the use of a flexible manufacturing system to mass produce, relatively inexpensively, unique products for individual customers. There are four primary approaches to customization, as indicated in the News Note on page 332.

Product complexity refers to the number of components in a product or the number of processes or operations through which a product flows. Management can minimize product complexity by redesigning products and processes to standardize them and reduce the number of different components, tools, and processes

product variety
the number of different types of products produced

service variety
the number of different types of services provided

mass customization
the relatively low-cost mass production of products to the unique specifications of individual customers; requires the use of flexible manufacturing systems

product complexity
the number of components in a product or the number of processes or operations through which a product flows

EXHIBIT 6-14

Product Variety Creates
Overhead Costs

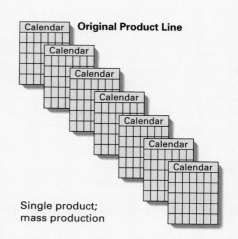

Original Product Line

Calendar

Single product;
mass production

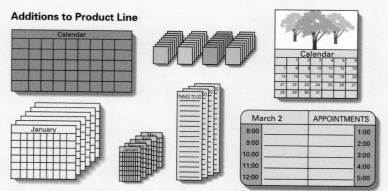

Additions to Product Line

Calendar

Original product made in mass quantities; each additional product made
in extremely limited quantities.

With which product set would the company have more?

- Inventory carrying costs?
- Purchasing costs?
- Scheduling costs?
- Setup and change-over costs?

- Expediting costs?
- Quality control costs?
- Scrap costs?
- Rework costs?

To which products do these increased costs relate?

Which product line would bear the majority of the costs?

Production overhead at P&G is significant—costs are created not only because of multiple varieties of the same type of product (detergent, diapers, etc.) but because of numerous product lines. In such a situation, using a single cost pool and driver would be efficient but highly ineffective for product cost determination.

required. Pareto analysis generally reveals that 20% of the components are used in 80% of the products. This is often referred to as the 20:80 rule. If this is the case, then companies need to consider two other factors. First, are the remaining components used in key products? If so, could equal quality be achieved by using the more common parts? If not, can the products be sold for a premium price to cover the costs associated with the use of low-volume components? Second, are the non-standard parts used in products purchased by important customers who are willing to pay a premium price for the products? If so, the benefits from the complexity

GENERAL NEWS NOTE

How Do My Customers Want My Product?

Virtually all executives today recognize the need to provide outstanding service to customers. Focusing on the customer, however, is both an imperative and a potential curse. In their desire to become customer driven, many companies have resorted to inventing new programs and procedures to meet every customer's request. But as customers and their needs grow increasingly diverse, such an approach has become a surefire way to add unnecessary cost and complexity to organizations.

Companies throughout the world have embraced mass customization in an attempt to avoid those pitfalls and provide unique value to their customers in an efficient manner.[15]

It's all about the individual—manufacturers create products for the individual and many customers purchase only enough for their appetite. But as the era of mass marketing gives way to the more customer-focused approach of "mass customization," suppliers are inviting consumers to try their hand at designing everything from eyeglasses to running shoes, makeup, and even foods.

For example, Procter & Gamble's Reflect.com Web site allows consumers to create personalized creams, shampoos, makeup, and perfumes. Clients fill out an online questionnaire that asks them about everything from their skin type to hair colour. They can then peruse a variety of products specially formulated for them. A recent press release reports that more than one million "customizations" have been created since the site was redesigned late in 2001.

"Our numbers are showing us that Reflect.com has gotten stronger and continues to grow since the launch of the new Web site," says Ginger Kent, CEO of Reflect.com. Although the site is based in the U.S., the service is available in Canada for samples, coupons, and new-product information. Consumers can register by calling a toll-free number.

Buoyed by the success of Reflect.com, P&G has extended its customization model to include coffee. It now sells custom blends of its Millstone gourmet coffee through a new Web site, PersonalBlends.com. Consumers describe their tastes in certain foods—their "Tasteprint"—and then create a name for their coffee. "Our BlendMasters create a coffee to match your Tasteprint using the highest-quality beans available," promises the Web site. "They hand-pack your coffee with your name right on the label, and ship it directly to your door."[16]

Although such customization may please some customers, it does have some drawbacks. First, there may simply be too many choices. For instance, in many provinces there are almost a hundred special licence plates that include (to name just a few) designations of birds, flowers, etc. Second, mass customization creates a tremendous opportunity for errors. And third, most companies have found that customers, given a wide variety of choices, typically make selections from a rather small percentage of the total. For instance, at Toyota, investigation of purchases revealed that 20% of the product varieties accounted for 80% of the sales.[17]

---

may be worth the cost. However, would customers be equally satisfied if more common parts were used and the product price were reduced? Parts complexity is acceptable only if it is value-added from the customer's point of view.

Process complexity may develop over time, or it may exist because of a lack of sufficient planning in product development. Processes are complex when they create difficulties for the people attempting to perform production operations (physical straining, awkwardness of motions, or wasted motions) or for the people using manufacturing machinery (multiple and/or detailed setups, lengthy transfer time between machine processes, or recalibration of instruments). Process complexity reflects numerous non-value-added activities that cause time delays and cost increases.

A company can employ simultaneous engineering to reduce both product and process complexity. **Simultaneous** (or **concurrent**) **engineering** refers to involving all the primary functional areas and personnel that contribute to a product's origi-

simultaneous engineering
an integrated approach in which all primary functions and personnel contributing to a product's origination and production are involved continuously from the beginning of a project

concurrent engineering
see simultaneous engineering

nation and production from the beginning of a project. Multifunctional teams are used to design the product by considering customer expectations, vendor capabilities, parts commonality, and production process compatibility. Such an integrated design effort is referred to as a design-for-manufacturability approach. Simultaneous engineering helps companies shorten the time to market for new products and minimize complexity and cost.

Even when simultaneous engineering is used in process development, processes may develop complexity over time. One way to overcome this type of complexity is **business process reengineering (BPR)** or process innovation and redesign. BPR's goal is to find and implement radical changes in how things are made or how tasks are performed to achieve substantial cost, service, or time reductions. Emphasizing continuous improvement, BPR ignores the way it is and looks instead for the way it should be. BPR may redesign old processes or design new ones to eliminate complexity.

> **business process reengineering**
> process innovation and redesign aimed at finding and implementing radical changes in how things are made or how tasks are performed to achieve substantial cost, service, or time reductions

> Process redesign takes a current process, improves its effectiveness, and can bring about improvements that range from 300% to 1000%. This technique is the right choice for about 70% of the business processes. [In contrast, new process design] completely ignores the present process and organizational structure. This technique takes advantage of the latest mechanization, automation, and information techniques available. New process design can lead to improvements that range from 700% to 2000%. New process design costs more and takes more time to implement than process redesign. It also has the highest degree of risk ... and is very disruptive to the organization.[18]

Many traditional cost systems were not designed to account for information such as how many different parts are used in a product, so management may not be able to identify products made with low-volume or unique components. Activity-based costing systems are more flexible and gather such details, thereby providing important information about relationships among activities and cost drivers. Armed with these data, people can focus reengineering efforts on the primary causes of process complexity and those that create the highest level of waste.

Lack of Commonality in Overhead Costs

Certain products, services, or types of customers create substantially more overhead costs than others. Although some of these additional overhead costs may be caused by product variety or process complexity, others may be related to support services. For example, some products require substantially more advertising than others; some use higher cost distribution channels; and some necessitate the use of high-technology machinery. In addition, some companies' output volumes differ significantly among their products and services. Each of these differences creates additional overhead costs. If only one or two overhead pools are used, overhead related to specific products will be spread over all products. The result will be increased costs for products that are not responsible for the increased overhead.

Problems in Current Cost Allocations

If a company has undergone one or more significant changes in its products, processes, or customer base, then managers and accountants need to investigate whether the existing cost system still provides a reasonable estimate of product or service cost. Many companies that have automated their production processes have experienced large reductions in labour cost and large increases in overhead. In such companies, using direct labour as an overhead allocation base tends to charge products made by automated equipment with insufficient overhead and products made with high proportions of direct labour with too much overhead.

Traditional cost allocations also tend to assign product costs (direct material, direct labour, and manufacturing overhead) to products and expense the majority of period costs when incurred. ABC recognizes that some period costs may be distinctly and reasonably associated with specific products and therefore should be traced and allocated to those products. This recognition changes the traditional view of product versus period cost.

Changes in Business Environment

A change in the competitive environment in which a company operates may also require better cost information. Increased competition may occur for several reasons: (1) other companies have recognized the profit potential of a particular product or service, (2) the product or service has become cost-feasible to make or perform, or (3) an industry has been deregulated. If many new companies are competing for old business, the best estimate of product or service cost must be available to management so that profit margins and prices can be reasonably set.

Changes in management strategy can also signal a need for a new cost system. For example, if management wants to begin new operations, the cost system must be capable of providing information on how costs will change. The traditional variable versus fixed cost classifications may not allow the effective development of such information. The use of ABC offers a different perspective about how the planned operational changes will affect activities and costs through its analysis of costs as short-term versus long-term variables as well as its emphasis on the use of cost drivers.

Many companies are currently engaging in continuous improvement efforts that recognize the need to eliminate non-value-added activities so as to reduce lead time, make products or perform services with zero defects, reduce product costs on an ongoing basis, and simplify products and processes. Activity-based costing, by promoting an understanding of cost drivers, allows the NVA activities to be identified and their causes eliminated or reduced—thereby enhancing operational performance.

The choice to implement activity-based costing should mean that management is willing to accept the new information and use it to plan, control, and evaluate operating activities. If this is the case, then management must have some ability to set prices relative to cost changes; accept alternative business strategies—such as eliminating or expanding product or service offerings—if the new costs should so indicate; and reduce waste where necessary, including downsizing or job restructuring. If management is powerless to institute changes for whatever reason (for example, centralized control or industry regulation), then the ABC-generated information is nothing more than an exercise in futility—and probably a fairly costly one.

Regardless of why there is a need for change in their costing systems, companies at least now have the technological capability to implement ABC systems. Introduction of the personal computer, bar coding, generic software packages, and other advanced technologies means that significantly more information can be readily and cost effectively supplied. In the past, ABC implementation would have been prohibitively expensive or technologically impossible for most companies.

This can be seen at Reichhold, Inc. Over the past five years, Reichhold, Inc. has transformed itself from a product-line focused, divisional-structured company into a customer-focused, team-based organization. Reichhold has been implementing activity-based costing to analyze the cost implications of the changes occurring in production as a result of the shift to specialty products. The implementation has been bottom up with local teams leading the process.

The company formed an ABC steering committee, which included a member of the senior management team, a business team leader, a member of the corporate manufacturing team, and several members of the financial team. The committee is responsible for overseeing ABC implementation in the United States and Canada. The company conducted pilot projects at several sites, one of which was at Weston, Ontario.

The most important contribution of ABC at the company has been the comprehensive and accurate analysis of the profitability of the company's different products. This was achieved by moving costs out of the traditional cost centres toward the activities and product lines.[19]

ABC and the Service Sector

It may appear that ABC is designed specifically for the manufacturing sector, but in reality it applies equally well to the service sector. Even within the manufacturing sector, the activities of purchasing, materials handling, and setup are in fact services supporting the manufacturing function. Within the pure service sector, the same decisions that management has in manufacturing are made by managers in service-oriented businesses. Managers need to make decisions on proper resource allocation, product offering mix and diversity, and most important, which of the many clients are profitable and worth servicing and which of them are not.

ABC is a natural fit for the banking industry because there are easily identifiable cost drivers that can be measured and priced per event. As an example, most demand deposit accounts are priced and measured based on monthly activity and usage. A business is charged a certain cost for each cheque that is written and for each item that is deposited into the business chequing account. Similarly, the concept can be applied to commercial lending transaction activities, from the initial loan review and setup to the myriad advance requests, accounting maintenance requests, and payment applications.

Some key benefits of the ABC approach are to change the way an organization thinks about its costing system and to revitalize the bank's penetration strategies and processes. ABC also forces a company to consider its activities, to seek efficiencies, and to consolidate tasks in providing services and conducting business. Considering this action for the banking industry immediately shows that this is a win–win scenario in all circumstances. The customer benefits from a higher level of customer service, and the bank benefits from a streamlined, more cost-effective approach to providing services.[20]

A recent study showed that understanding how resources are consumed can help group practices control costs. The Academy of Orthopaedic Surgeons study used an activity-based costing system to measure how resources are consumed in providing medical services. They measured resource consumption by assigning costs to each process according to how much time is spent on related work activities. The study found that an ABC business process model critically tracks how resources are consumed in providing medical services.[21]

One difference between service organizations and manufacturing organizations is that there tends to be a much higher use of time-related or duration cost drivers as opposed to transaction-based cost drivers such as the number of setups or inspections. In a manufacturing process, many costs are related to units or batches passing

Cost-Effectiveness Analysis of Intravascular Ultrasound Guided Percutaneous Coronary Intervention versus Conventional Percutaneous Coronary Intervention

Activity-based costing methodology is not strictly for the manufacturing sector. Researchers have applied ABC to determine the cost-effectiveness of applying different treatments in coronary intervention therapy.

The study involved the investigation of the cost-effectiveness of using intravascular ultrasound (IVUS) guided percutaneous coronary interventional (PCI) compared to PCI guided by coronary angiography (CAG).

Test subjects were randomized into groups using IVUS or CAG guided PCI. After 6 months, the patients were subjected to a study of related clinical investigation. The incremental costs of IVUS guided procedures and costs of reinterventions were estimated using activity-based costing versus the CAG guided PCI.

The results showed patients using the IVUS guided PCI experienced an improved clinical outcome, with lower angina levels than patients using the CAG guided group. Despite the increased cost of using IVUS due to extra procedure time, need for IVUS catheters and an increase in balloons and stents, fewer patients were found to need re-intervention, thus reducing the overall cost of the therapy compared with CAG guided PCI.[22]

through certain activities, while in a service-oriented business, costs accumulated based on time will depend on the particular case; for instance, the time for a mechanic to repair a car will depend on the particular problem with that car, or the time for a dentist to do a root canal will depend on the particulars of the patient's case and is not standard to each patient.[23]

OPERATIONAL AND STRATEGIC PLANNING AND CONTROL USING ABC

Activity-based management and costing provide many benefits for production and service organizations. The list of companies using activity-based costing is large and impressive and includes Hewlett–Packard, American Express, Caterpillar, Parker Hannifin, Harris Semiconductor, and USWEST. A recent survey by the Institute of Management Accountants of companies that were upgrading their cost management systems provided the following information: 41% of the companies surveyed were using ABC-type systems. Of the remaining 59% that were using a method other than ABC, almost one-third felt that they should also be using ABC.[24] These companies are using ABC to make both operational and strategic decisions, such as more effectively controlling costs; adjusting product, process, or marketing strategy; influencing behaviour; and evaluating performance.

To control costs, managers must understand where costs are being incurred and for what purpose. This understanding is provided by more appropriate tracing of overhead costs to products and services. Viewing fixed costs as long-term variable costs provides useful information for assessing the cost–benefit relationship of obtaining more customers or providing more goods and services. Additionally, differentiating between value-added and non-value-added activities helps managers visualize what needs to be done to control these costs, implement cost reduction activities, and plan resource utilization.

Traditional accounting systems concentrate on controlling cost incurrence, while ABC focuses on controlling the cause of the cost incurrence. Concentrating on the causes of costs makes cost reduction efforts more successful because they can be directed at specific cost drivers. It is critical, however, to understand that simply

LEARNING OBJECTIVE 7

What are the benefits and limitations of using activity-based costing?

reducing cost drivers or activities will not cause a decline in total costs unless excess resources are eliminated or reassigned to value-adding areas.

Managers who better understand the underlying cost of making a product or performing a service can obtain new insight into product or service profitability:

> Often managers can see, for the first time, the cost of nonconformance, the cost of design activities, the cost of new product launches, and the cost of administrative activities, such as processing customer orders, procurement, and handling special requests. The high cost of these activities can stimulate companies to adopt the TQM, JIT, and business process improvement programs that will produce a leaner and more responsive enterprise.[25]

This improved information can result in management decisions about expanding or contracting product variety, raising or reducing prices, and entering or leaving a market. For example, managers may decide to raise selling prices of low-volume specialty output. Or they may decide to discontinue such production because that output consumes disproportionately more resources than does high-volume output.

ABC information can even affect decisions about plant and equipment investments and highlight the benefits that can be obtained if high-technology processes are implemented. Installing computerized equipment may reduce non-value-added production activities and increase efficiency. Activity-based costing helps managers understand the effects of the various activities that are needed in the changing business environment (especially relative to technology) and provide flexibility in designing systems that are able to cope with this environment. Although activity-based costing only indirectly changes the cost accumulation process, it directly changes the cost assignment process, making it more realistic regarding how and why costs are incurred.

Activity-based costing is more than a system to generate product costs for financial statements; it is employed as a tool to improve performance through an integration with organizational strategy. One survey indicated that ABC information was used in 24% of the strategic decisions about insourcing versus outsourcing, 72% of the strategic decisions about pricing and product discontinuation, and 36% of the strategic decisions about customer profitability.[26] The News Note on page 338 provides information on the additional need to link ABC information with an organization's type of competitive strategy.

CRITICISMS OF AND CONCLUSIONS ABOUT ABC

No currently existing accounting technique or system can provide management with exact cost information for every product or with all the information needed to make consistently perfect decisions. Activity-based costing, although it can provide better information than a traditional overhead allocation process, is not a panacea for all managerial difficulties. The following points should be noted as some of this method's shortcomings.

First, implementing ABC requires a significant investment in terms of time and cost. If implementation is to be successful, substantial support is needed throughout the firm. An environment for change must be created, and creating such an environment requires overcoming a variety of individual, organizational, and environmental barriers. Individual barriers are typically related to fear of (1) the unknown or a shift in the status quo, (2) a possible loss of status, or (3) the need to learn new skills. Organizational barriers may be related to territorial, hierarchical,

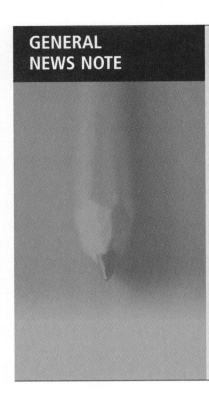

Linking ABC Information to Competitive Strategy

ABC should be linked to a company's competitive strategy regarding organizational design, new product development, product mix and pricing, and technology. Here are some examples:

- *Competing based on cost or custom design.* If a company chooses to compete based on the design of custom or low-cost products, its ABC systems should provide designers with accurate estimates of product or process costs. These costs should be available both before and during the design process. Designers should also know the costs of customization.
- *Competing based on scale economies.* If a company competes based on manufacturing scale economies and efficiencies for commodity products, its ABC systems should focus on measuring the costs of manufacturing activities and plant capacity.
- *Competing based on distribution and logistics.* If a company competes based on superior distribution and logistics, its ABC systems should focus on measuring the costs of those activities rather than manufacturing costs.

Additionally, an organization may specify quality and continuous improvement as part of its competitive strategy. ABC information can play important roles in helping a company achieve continuous improvement. It can be used to identify potential economic gains from improving quality and speed. It also can be used to measure economic progress toward improving quality and time-based performance.

Source: Michael D. Shields and Michael A. McEwen, "Implementing Activity-Based Costing Systems Successfully," *Journal of Cost Management*, Winter 1996, p. 18. Reprinted with permission from *The Journal of Cost Management*, © 1996, by RIA, 395 Hudson Street, New York, NY, 10014.

or corporate-culture issues. Environmental barriers are often built by employee groups including unions, regulatory agencies, or other stakeholders.

To overcome barriers, managers first must recognize that those barriers exist; second, managers need to investigate the causes of the barriers; and third, managers must communicate information about ABC to all concerned parties. It is essential that top management be involved with and support the implementation process. Lack of commitment or involvement by top management will make achieving meaningful progress very slow and difficult. Additionally, employees and managers must be educated in some nontraditional techniques, including new terminology, concepts, and performance measurements. Such an educational process cannot occur overnight. Assuming that top management supports the changes in the internal accounting system and employees are educated about the system, additional time will be required to analyze the activities taking place in the activity centres, trace costs to those activities, and determine the appropriate cost drivers. When the ABC system was introduced at VW Canada, for example, thousands of person-hours were spent in developing training materials and providing workshops on what ABC was, what was expected from its implementation, and why it would provide information not available from the existing accounting system.

Another shortcoming of ABC is that it does not conform specifically with generally accepted accounting principles (see Exhibit 6-15). ABC would suggest that some traditionally designated period costs, such as research and development costs and some service department costs, be allocated to products and that some traditionally designated product costs, such as factory building depreciation, not be allocated to products. Because of the differing perspectives, many companies implemented ABC as a supplemental system for internal reporting while continuing to use a more traditional system to account for product and period costs, allocate indirect costs, and prepare external financial statements. It is possible that, as ABC systems become more widely used, either the differences between GAAP and

Inventoriable Indirect Cost	GAAP	ABC
Marketing, selling, advertising, and distribution costs	E	I
Interest	E	I, E
Research and experimental costs	E	I, E
General and administrative costs	E	I
Costs of strikes	P	E
Rework labour, scrap, and spoilage	P	I
Insurance	P	I, E
Distribution and warehousing	E	I

I = inventoriable; E = expensed; P = practice varies

Source: Extracted from Richard B. Troxel, "The Relationship Between Activity-Based Costing and Generally Accepted Accounting Principles," *Handbook of Cost Management: 1998 Edition.* Boston: Warren, Gorham & Lamont/RIA Group, p. C5–10. Reprinted from *Handbook of Cost Management,* © 1998, by RIA, 395 Hudson Street, New York, NY, 10014.

EXHIBIT 6-15

Differences in Inventoriable Indirect Costs Under GAAP and ABC

ABC cost accumulation will narrow or companies will become more adept at making the appropriate adjustments at the end of a period to bring internal information into compliance with GAAP's external reporting requirements. In either event, the need for two costing systems would be eliminated.

As indicated by the following quote, another criticism that has been levelled at activity-based costing is that it does not promote total quality management and continuous improvement:

> Activity-based prescriptions for improved competitiveness usually entail steps that lead to selling more or doing less of what should not be sold or done in the first place. Indeed, activity-based cost information does nothing to change old remote-control, top-down management behaviour. Simply because improved cost information becomes available, a company does not change its commitment to mass produce output at high speed, to control costs by encouraging people to manipulate processes, and to persuade customers to buy output the company has produced to cover its costs. North American businesses will not become long-term global competitors until they change the way managers think. No cost information, not even activity-based cost management information, will do that.[27]

Companies attempting to implement ABC as a cure-all for product failures, volume declines, or financial losses will quickly recognize that the statement above is true. However, companies can implement ABC and its related management techniques in support of and in conjunction with TQM, BPR, JIT, and any other world-class methodology. The customers of these companies will be provided with the best variety, price, quality, service, and cycle time of which they are capable. Not coincidentally, they should find their businesses booming. Activity-based costing and activity-based management can effectively support continuous improvement, short lead times, and flexible manufacturing by helping managers to do the following:

- Identify and monitor significant technology costs
- Trace many technology costs directly to products
- Promote achievement of market share through use of target costing (discussed in Chapter 7)
- Identify the cost drivers that create or influence cost
- Identify activities that do not contribute to perceived customer value (i.e., non-value-added activities or waste)

- Understand the impact of new technologies on all elements of performance
- Translate company goals into activity goals
- Analyze the performance of activities across business functions
- Analyze performance problems
- Promote standards of excellence

Activity-based costing, in and of itself, does not change the amount of overhead costs incurred, but it distributes those costs in a more equitable manner. ABC does not change the cost accumulation process, but it makes that process more realistic through a reflection of how and why costs are incurred. Finally, activity-based costing does not eliminate the need for assigning indirect overhead costs to products and services, but it uses a more appropriate means of doing so than has been possible under traditional methods. In summary, ABC is an improved cost accounting tool that helps managers know how the score is kept so that they can play the game more competitively.

Activity-based costing (ABC) is a cost management method that addresses shortcomings inherent in traditional costing methods, for the handling of indirect costs (or overhead). ABC focuses on understanding the cause-and-effect relation-

SITE ANALYSIS

Volkswagen

Although the ABC information and its uses are invaluable to many functions and improvement initiatives, in the end, ABC simply helps managers and employees do their jobs better and with more certainty. It tells you not only what your organization does but also how well it is being done.

For example, the die-cast pilot project, which was discussed in the introduction to this chapter, indicated which products were profitable and which were not. Unfortunately, the two big moneymakers were in an extremely competitive market and the company was forced to reduce their prices by approximately 75%, making the profit margin close to zero. Then, two of the other three profit-producing parts were discontinued. Even the numerous improvements that had been made were not enough to turn the die-cast area around. The ABC model showed that, even under the most optimistic scenario, the die-cast area would not be profitable in the near future. Management therefore made a decision to move die-casting operations to another VW plant.

In this case, the ABC data were used to help make the toughest decision management ever has to make—the decision to close down an operation, with all its effects on employees and the community at large.

Volkswagen's experience has shown that the road to implementing activity-based management is difficult and requires a strong, dedicated leadership team to drive the project forward. The rewards of such perseverance, however, are worth it. ABC and ABM information cannot tell management what to do to improve results but, rather, point out potential opportunities, thus dramatically altering the way a company does business. As a decision-making tool, ABC and ABM information provides the most potentially valuable data that decision makers can have in their toolbox of resources.

Source: Reprinted from an article appearing in the May 1996 issue of *CMA Management* magazine by Jim Gurowka, with permission of Certified Management Accountants of Canada.

ship between resource consumption and cost expenditure, so that overhead can be traced directly to the cost object—i.e., product, process, or customer—as opposed to being arbitrarily allocated. The ability to accurately trace overhead has gained importance as overhead costs continue to rise sharply for many manufacturers.[28]

ABC and ERP

ERP systems include modules or subsystems for ABC. An ERP system is developed from the underlying activities that an organization undertakes in pursuing its value creation chain or its part of another organization's value creation chain. Activities are coded and costs are assigned to activities. Products and services are also coded, which allows their costs to be accurately calculated.

Direct costs such as material and direct labour are readily assigned with the ABC modules of ERP systems. Overhead or fixed costs are more difficult to assign. ERP systems develop cost pools at various organizational levels, to whose products and services cost drivers are subsequently assigned with consistency and accuracy.

With ERP systems, the ABC system is fully integrated with all other subsystems such as process costing, financial statements, and fixed assets. The fixed asset costs or depreciation costs are automatically recorded in cost pools and then those costs are allocated to activities and then to products and services. Similarly, those allocated costs are transferred to inventory and/or cost of goods sold, and to the financial statements, which can be produced upon demand.

CHAPTER SUMMARY

Activity-based costing (ABC) has been identified as the most suitable costing method for modern manufacturing environments and as being crucial for strategic success. It allocates overhead costs based on the actual consumption of the resources by each activity and provides direction for improving the operational performance of systems. Activity-based costing is a costing system that allocates costs to products or cost objects based on the level of activity. It adopts a two-stage process to allocate costs to products. First, costs are accumulated in relatively homogeneous activity cost pools. Second, these costs are traced to products or cost objects according to the level of activity. Activity-based management involves using activity-based costing to manage and improve the business.

In a highly competitive business environment, companies need to reduce costs to make profits. One way to reduce costs without reducing quality is to decrease the number of non-value-added organizational activities. Value is added to products only during production (manufacturing company), performance (service company), or display (retail company). Most other activities, such as inspecting, moving, storing, and waiting, are non-value-added.

Activity-based management views organizational processes as value-added and non-value-added activities. Process mapping can be used to determine all the activities that take place in the production of a product or the performance of a service. Each activity is designated as value-added or non-value-added on a value chart. Management should strive to minimize or eliminate non-value-added activities because they create unnecessary costs and longer lead times without providing extra worth for customers.

A third category of activities, known as business-value-added activities, also exists. Although customers would not want to pay for these activities, they are currently necessary to conduct business operations.

Activity-based management is also concerned with finding and selecting an appropriate number of activity cost pools and then identifying the cost drivers that best represent the firm's activities and are the underlying causes of costs. The activities chosen by management are those judged to reflect the major and most significant company processes. These activities normally overlap several functional areas and are said to occur horizontally across the firm's departmental lines. Cost drivers can also be used to evaluate the efficiency and effectiveness of the firm's activities.

Costs incurred in one area often result from activities in other areas—for instance, poor product quality or defects may be related to engineering design. Activity-based management highlights and provides feedback about relationships between and among functional areas as well as suggests areas that might benefit from process improvements or waste elimination. ABM allows and encourages the use of non-financial measures, such as lead time, as indicators of activity and performance.

Product and process variety and complexity often cause a business's costs to increase because of unobserved increases in non-value-added activities. Simultaneous engineering and business process reengineering can help firms to accelerate the time to market of new products as well as reduce design or process complexity and the related costs (both direct and indirect) of these new products and of the processes by which they are made.

Traditional costing systems often accumulate costs in one cost pool (or very few cost pools) and allocate those costs to products using one cost driver (generally related to direct labour or machine hours). Activity-based costing accumulates costs for activity centres in multiple cost pools at a variety of levels (unit, batch, product/process, and organizational/facility). ABC then allocates these costs to output using appropriate cost drivers (both volume-related and non-volume-related). Thus, costs are assigned more accurately, and managers can focus on controlling activities that create costs rather than trying to control the resulting costs themselves. Activity-based costing provides a more accurate way to assign overhead costs to products than what has been used traditionally.

Cross-Functional Applications

Topic of Note	Discipline	Cross-Functional Applications
Activity-Based Costing	Marketing	ABC can drastically affect pricing policies and as such, the marketing mix, especially in a competitive environment where bids and offers cannot be easily changed. When competitors in the industry charge extraordinarily different prices for similar products, ABC should be used to determine possible over/understatement of costs.
	Management	ABC can focus management's attention on the activities that require more control or improvement by identifying the activity that is driving excess costs. Overhead rates often obscure the actual cost driver that needs attention, especially when combined rates are used.

(cont.)

Cross-Functional Applications

Topic of Note	Discipline	Cross-Functional Applications
	Engineering	Engineers often model costs based on ideal conditions of operation by evaluating material alternatives, labour/machine usage, utilities, or efficiency of each production process. ABC shows engineers practical conditions of operation where inefficiencies exist. The difference between the two approaches suggests design or specification changes to planners.
	Economics	ABC can be used in tandem with economic models of cost structure to improve predictions or troubleshoot. Because each approach proceeds from different assumptions and measurements of cost behaviour, one system can check on the accuracy of the other.
	Management	Many medical care facilities, health insurance companies, and financial service institutions have implemented ABC in an effort to control their costs. Service industries such as medical care vary substantially in the activities that they provide for their customers. Their need is to identify and control the activity that is driving a particular cost, and ABC is useful in this matter. Also, health insurance companies are imposing their cost control standards on health care providers, which may not be relevant for management decision making.
Manufacturing Cycle	Production/ Operations Management	Non-value-added activities that lengthen the time between production start-up and completion of the product for shipment can be identified by MCE. Management can then decide whether the non-value-added activity is necessary to the company's overall objectives.
	Marketing	Short lead times create a competitive advantage associated with place utility. A marketer can build long-term relationships with customers by reducing lead times and, thus, the customers' carrying costs. Cycle efficiency is a performance measurement that can monitor flow-through time for either a manufacturer or a retailer.
	Engineering	The MCE permits engineers to compare alternative production processes or labour–equipment blends to identify which methods yield the greatest value contribution to the product.

Key Terms

Activity (p. 310)
Activity-based costing (p. 306)
Activity-based management (p. 309)
Activity centre (p. 320)
Activity cost driver (p. 321)
Batch-level cost (p. 318)
Business process reengineering
  (p. 333)
Business-value-added activity (p. 313)
Concurrent engineering (p. 332)
Cycle time (p. 313)
Facility-level cost (p. 319)
Idle time (p. 312)
Inspection time (p. 312)
Long-term variable cost (p. 319)
Manufacturing cycle efficiency
  (p. 313)

Mass customization (p. 330)
Non-value-added activity (p. 312)
Organizational-level cost (p. 319)
Process-level cost (p. 319)
Process map (p. 310)
Product complexity (p. 330)
Product-level cost (p. 319)
Product variety (p. 330)
Service variety (p. 330)
Simultaneous engineering (p. 332)
Transfer time (p. 312)
Unit-level cost (p. 318)
Value-added activity (p. 311)
Value-added processing time (p. 311)
Value-added service time (p. 311)
Value chart (p. 311)

Solution Strategies

Manufacturing Cycle Efficiency (MCE)

$$\text{MCE} = \text{Value-added processing time} \div \text{Total cycle time}$$

1. Determine the activity centres of the organization.
2. Determine activities and the efforts needed to conduct those activities—the cost drivers.
3. Determine the resources the organization consumes in conducting its activities and the level at which those resources are consumed (unit, batch, product/process, organizational/facility).
4. Allocate the resources to the activity centres based on the cost drivers.
5. Allocate unit-, batch-, and product/process-level costs to products and services based on activities and activity cost drivers involved.
6. Treat organizational/facility-level costs as nonattachable to products.

DEMONSTRATION PROBLEM

Casper Manufacturing Co. uses a traditional approach to overhead allocation. The company produces two types of products: a regular (Model R) and a programmable (Model P) thermostat. In fiscal 2005, the company incurred $300,000 of manufacturing overhead and produced 40,000 units of Model R and 20,000 units of Model P. The predetermined manufacturing overhead rate used was $10 per direct labour hour. Based on this rate, the unit cost of each model in fiscal 2005 was as follows:

	Model R	Model P
Direct material	$ 6	$10
Direct labour	5	5
Manufacturing overhead	5	5
Total	$16	$20

The market is becoming more competitive, so the firm is considering the use of activity-based costing in fiscal 2006. Analysis of the fiscal 2005 data revealed that the $300,000 of overhead could be assigned to three activities as follows:

	Setups	Materials Handling	Equipment Operations	Total
Fiscal 2005 overhead	$20,000	$60,000	$220,000	$300,000

Management determined that the following activity drivers were appropriate for each overhead category:

	Activity Driver	2005 Activity Volume
Setups	Number of setups	160 setups
Materials handling	Kilograms of material	120,000 kilograms
Equipment operations	Machine hours	40,000 MH

Activity drivers and units produced in fiscal 2005 for each product were

	Model R	Model P
Number of units	40,000	20,000
Number of setups	100	60
Kilograms of materials handled	60,000	60,000
Machine hours	14,000	26,000

Required:

a. In fiscal 2005, the company used the traditional allocation based on direct labour hours. How much total manufacturing overhead was allocated to Model R units and to Model P units?

b. For fiscal 2005, how much total manufacturing overhead would have been allocated to each model if ABC had been used? Calculate a unit cost for Model R and Model P.

c. Casper Manufacturing has a policy of setting selling prices with unit costs in mind. What direction do you think the prices of Model R and Model P will take if the company begins using activity-based costing? Why?

Solution to Demonstration Problem

a. Model R: 40,000 units × $5 $200,000
   Model P: 20,000 units × $5 100,000
   Total allocated overhead $300,000
b. Cost per setup: $20,000 ÷ 160 = $125
   Cost per kilogram: $60,000 ÷ 120,000 = $0.50
   Cost per machine hour: $220,000 ÷ 40,000 = $5.50

	Model R	
100 setups × $125		$ 12,500
60,000 kilograms × $0.50		30,000
14,000 MH × $5.50		77,000
Assignable manufacturing OH		$119,500
Divided by units		÷ 40,000
Manufacturing OH per unit		= $2.99

	Model P	
60 setups × $125		$ 7,500
60,000 kilograms × $0.50		30,000
26,000 MH × $5.50		143,000
Assignable manufacturing OH		$180,500
Divided by units		÷ 20,000
Manufacturing OH per unit		= $9.03

	Model R	**Model P**
Direct material	$ 6.00	$10.00
Direct labour	5.00	5.00
Manufacturing overhead	2.99	9.03
Total activity-based product cost	$13.99	$24.03

c. Because the cost of Model R is $13.99 under ABC and $16 under traditional costing, the price of Model R should be reduced; this pricing decision will probably make Model R more competitive and increase its sales volume. In contrast, because the cost of Model P is $20 based on the traditional approach and $24.03 using ABC, Model P's price should be raised. ABC provides more accurate costing information so that management's abilities to plan, control, solve problems, and evaluate choices should be enhanced.

End-of-Chapter Materials

SELF-TEST QUESTIONS

(SOLUTIONS APPEAR AT THE END OF THE CHAPTER.)

1. An accounting system that collects financial and operating data on the basis of the underlying nature and extent of the cost drivers is
   a. Activity-based costing
   b. Variable costing
   c. Weighted average costing
   d. FIFO costing

   (IMA adapted)

2. Cost drivers are
   a. Activities that cause costs to increase as the activity increases
   b. Accounting techniques used to control costs
   c. Accounting measurements used to evaluate whether performance is proceeding according to plan
   d. A mechanical basis—such as machine hours, computer time, size of equipment, or size of the factory—used to assign costs to activities

   (IMA adapted)

3. What is the normal effect on the numbers of cost pools and allocation bases when an activity-based cost (ABC) system replaces a traditional cost system?

	Cost Pools	Allocation Bases
a.	No effect	No effect
b.	Increase	No effect
c.	No effect	Increase
d.	Increase	Increase

   (Material from the Uniform CPA Examination Questions and Unofficial Answers, Copyright © 1994 by the American Institute of Certified Public Accountants, Inc., is reprinted by or adapted with permission.)

4. Which of the following statements about activity-based costing is not true?
   a. Activity-based costing is useful for allocating marketing and distribution costs.
   b. Activity-based costing is more likely to result in major differences from traditional cost systems if the firm manufactures only one product rather than multiple products.
   c. In activity-based costing, cost drivers are what cause costs to be incurred.
   d. Activity-based costing differs from traditional costing systems in that products are not cross-subsidized.

   (IMA adapted)

Questions 5 and 6 are based on the following information. Spectra Fashions Inc. is preparing its annual profit plan. As part of its analysis of the profitability of individual products, the controller estimates the amount of overhead that should be allocated to the individual product lines from the information given as follows:

	Ladies' Umbrellas	Men's Umbrellas
Units produced	25	25
Material moves per product line	5	15
Direct labour hours per unit	200	200
Budgeted materials handling costs	$50,000	

5. Under a costing system that allocates overhead on the basis of direct labour hours, the materials handling costs allocated to one ladies' umbrella would be
   a. $1,000
   b. $ 500
   c. $2,000
   d. $5,000

   (IMA adapted)

6. Under activity-based costing (ABC), the materials handling costs allocated to one ladies' umbrella would be
   a. $1,000
   b. $ 500
   c. $1,500
   d. $2,500

   (IMA adapted)

7. Which of the following kinds of properties should you consider when you evaluate an activity-based management system as a cost management tool?
   a. Behavioural, cultural, and technical properties
   b. Behavioural, ethical, and financial properties
   c. Cultural, ethical, and financial properties
   d. Financial, ethical, and technical properties

8. Which of the following statements best describes activity-based management?
   a. It is an approach developed in response to the competitive pressures of today's global market.
   b. It does not use activity-based costing to improve a business.
   c. It is designed to set the goals and objectives of an organization.
   d. It focuses on functional areas and products.

Use the following information to answer Questions 9 and 10.

Fine Cutlery Inc. is a manufacturer of quality carving knives. The company has always used a plantwide allocation rate for allocating manufacturing overhead to its products, but the plant manager believes that it is time to change to a better method of cost allocation. The accounting department has established the following relationships between production activities and manufacturing overhead costs.

Activity	Cost Driver	Allocation Rate
Materials handling	Number of parts	$4 per part
Assembly	Labour hours	$40 per hour
Inspection	Time spent by item at inspection station	$6 per minute

The previous plantwide allocation rate method was based on direct manufacturing labour-hours, and if that method is used, the allocation rate is $400 per labour-hour.

9. Assume that a batch of 1,000 carving knives requires 2,000 parts, 20 direct manufacturing labour-hours, and 30 minutes of inspection time. What are the indirect manufacturing costs per carving knife to produce a batch of 1,000 carving knives, assuming the previous plantwide allocation rate method is used?
   a. $ 8.00
   b. $ 9.80
   c. $800.00
   d. $980.00

10. Assume that a batch of 100 carving knives requires 200 parts, 12 direct manufacturing labour hours, and 5 minutes of inspection time. What are the indirect manufacturing costs per carving knife to produce a batch of 1,000 carving knives, assuming the activity-based method of allocation is used?
    a. $ 4.80
    b. $ 8.00
    c. $13.10
    d. $48.00

(Self-Test Questions 7–10 are reprinted from *Management Accounting examinations* published by the Certified General Accountants Association of Canada © CGA-Canada, 2001, used by permission.)

QUESTIONS

1. Why does management need product cost information?

2. Why has information developed for external uses become a primary source for internal decision making? Is this rationale valid? Explain.

3. Why is it not possible to develop totally accurate product or service costs?

4. Describe the system known as activity-based management. What cost management tools fall under the activity-based management umbrella?

5. What does a process map show and why is it useful?

6. Distinguish between a process map and a value chart.

7. Define value-added activity and non-value-added activity. Compare these types of activities and give examples of each.

8. Why is the concept of value-added activities a customer-oriented notion?

9. To what factors can non-value-added activities be attributed? Why would customers perceive these factors as not adding value?

10. What is a business-value-added activity? Why is it not always possible to eliminate this type of activity? Give an example, other than the one in the text, of a business-value-added activity that it would not be possible to eliminate.

11. Define cycle efficiency and explain how it is calculated in a manufacturing environment and in a service environment.

12. What is a cost driver and how is it used?

13. Does conventional cost accounting use cost drivers? If so, explain how. If not, explain why.

14. Why is ABM considered a process view and ABC considered a cost assignment view of an organization?

15. What are the four levels of cost drivers? Which level is the focus in traditional costing systems?

16. Briefly describe the cost accumulation and assignment process in an ABC system.

17. Why do the more traditional methods of overhead assignment overload standard products with overhead costs, and how does ABC improve overhead assignments?

18. What organizational characteristics of a company might indicate that ABC could provide improved information to the company's managers?

19. The chapter identified several underlying causes of a company's need for a new cost system. List and discuss some symptoms that might be visible reflections of these underlying causes.

20. Explain why product or service variety creates substantial overhead costs.

21. What are the primary methods of mass customization? Provide an example of each.

22. How can (a) simultaneous engineering and (b) business process reengineering help reduce process complexity?

23. Why can control in an activity-based management system be more effective than control in a conventional system?

24. Explain this comment: "Identifying non-value-added activities provides management with a distinct control opportunity."

25. Why is ABC often adopted as a stand-alone control system rather than as the main product costing system?

26. Should ABC be considered for adoption by all firms? Why or why not?

27. Can some firms expect to benefit more than others from adopting ABC? Why or why not?

28. What are the shortcomings of activity-based costing as an accounting system methodology? How might these be overcome?

29. "If a company institutes activity-based costing, its profits will rise substantially." Discuss the validity of this statement.

30. Why does the implementation of activity-based costing not reduce the amount of overhead costs incurred by an organization? How would such a reduction be achieved?

31. Are ABC systems part of ERP systems?

32. How are activities included in both ERP systems and ABC systems?

EXERCISES

1. (LO 1, 2, 3; Terminology) Match each item in the right-hand column with a term in the left-hand column.

a.	Activity-based costing	1.	Something that increases the worth of a product to a customer
b.	Value chart		
c.	Process map	2.	A measure of the demands placed on an activity
d.	Activity driver		
e.	Manufacturing cycle efficiency	3.	A measure of processing efficiency
f.	Long-term variable cost	4.	Something that increases the time and cost of production but not the worth of a product to a customer
g.	Value-added activity		
h.	Business process reengineering		
i.	Non-value-added activity	5.	A cost created by a group of things processed at a single time
j.	Batch-level cost		
		6.	Process innovation and redesign
		7.	A cost that has been traditionally viewed as fixed
		8.	A flowchart indicating all steps in producing a product or performing a service
		9.	A representation of the value-added and non-value-added activities and the time spent in these activities from the beginning to the end of a process
		10.	A system that collects costs according to the nature and extent of activities

2. (LO 1, 2, 3; Terminology) Match each item in the right-hand column with a term in the left-hand column.

    a. Activity centre
    b. Pareto principle
    c. Product complexity
    d. Transfer time
    e. Activity-based management
    f. Simultaneous engineering
    g. Mass customization
    h. Activity
    i. Idle time
    j. Product variety

    1. A process that involves all design and production personnel from the beginning of a project
    2. A methodology that focuses on activities to improve the value delivered to customers
    3. The number of components, operations, or processes needed to make a product
    4. The relatively low-cost bulk production of products to customer specifications
    5. The time spent in storage or waiting for processing
    6. The time spent moving products or components from one place to another
    7. A repetitive action performed to fulfill a business function
    8. A part of the organization for which management wants separate reporting
    9. The different types of products produced in an organization
    10. A fundamental principle often referred to as the 20:80 rule

3. (LO 2; VA and NVA activities) Baldwin and Williams opened a legal practice ten months ago. Williams, in a discussion with Lawrence Chung, an accountant, listed all the different tasks she performs during a week. Chung suggested that she list her activities as well as her partner's activities for a typical week. This list follows:

Activity	Time (hours)
Take depositions	10.4
Do legal research for cases	14.2
Make calls concerning legal cases	6.6
Travel to/from court	7.8
Litigate cases	11.9
Write correspondence	9.9
Eat lunch with clients	6.8
Eat dinner at office while watching the soaps	2.5
Contemplate litigation strategies	10.7
Play golf	3.2
Write wills for clients	4.9
Assign tasks to the firm's secretary	6.7
Fill out time sheets for client work	10.1

Required:
a. List the value-added activities and explain why they are value-added.
b. List the non-value-added activities and explain why they are non-value-added.
c. Why might it be more difficult for a small, start-up law firm to reduce the non-value-added activities listed as your answer to part (b) than it might be for a large, well-established law firm?

4. (LO 2; VA and NVA activities) Soprano Construction Company constructs beach-front vacation homes. Mr. Soprano, the CEO, has developed the following information about the average length of time it takes to complete one home:

Operation	Average Number of Days
Receive materials	1
Store materials	6
Move materials to job site	2
Measure and cut materials	7
Set up and move scaffolding	5
Wait for crew who are completing a previous job	6
Frame structure	4
Cut and frame doors and windows	3
Build gas fireplace	4
Attach siding and seal joints	5
Construct inside of home	9
Inspect home (by municipal inspectors)	1

Required:
a. What are the value-added activities and their total time?
b. What are the non-value-added activities and their total time?
c. How did you classify the inspection time? Why? Could this have been classified in another manner? Explain.

5. (LO 2; VA and NVA activities) Spectra Ltd. is investigating the costs of schedule changes in its factory. The following is a list of the activities, estimated times, and average costs required for a single schedule change.

Activity	Estimated Time	Average Cost
Review impact of orders	30 min–2 h	$ 300
Reschedule orders	15 min–24 h	800
Reschedule production orders	15 min–1 h	75
Contact production supervisor; stop production and change over; generate paperwork to return materials	5 min–2 h	45
Return excess inventory and allocate new materials	20 min–6 h	1,500
Generate new production paperwork; change routings; change bill of materials	15 min–4 h	500
Change purchasing schedule	10 min–8 h	2,100
Collect paperwork from the floor	15 min	75
Review new line schedule	15 min–30 min	100
Account for overtime premiums	3 h–10 h	1,000
Total		$6,495

Required:
a. Which of the previous activities, if any, are value-added?
b. What is the cost driver in this situation?
c. How can the cost driver be controlled and the activities eliminated?

6. (LO 2; VA and NVA activities) You are planning a weekend trip to Vancouver, British Columbia. You will be travelling by plane and will need a hotel room when you arrive. These two reservations will be made by you through 1-800 numbers. Because you are planning to stay in the city, you will take the airport shuttle service to and from your hotel and will not need a car.
Required:
a. Describe the process of preparing for this trip by listing the activities in which you would engage.
b. Indicate which of the above listed activities are value-added and which are non-value-added.
c. How might you reduce or eliminate the time spent in non-value-added activities?

7. (LO 2; VA and NVA activities) The College of Business has recently selected you as its representative on a committee to improve the preregistration process at your university.

Required:
a. Describe the activities that compose the current preregistration process.
b. Estimate the time required for the various activities listed in part (a).
c. What activities do you perceive as not adding value and why?
d. How would you improve the preregistration process?

8. (LO 2; VA & NVA activities, cycle time, cycle efficiency) Jack Sheriton is the front desk clerk at the Salem Inn. Jack performs the following functions when a guest checks into the hotel:

Function	Time (minutes)
Greet guest and ask for name	1.0
Find reservation in computer system	1.0
Ask guest to fill in card with personal information: name, address, credit card number	0.5
Wait for guest to fill in card	3.0
Answer and talk on phone to another guest	2.5
Ask guest what type of room he/she prefers and listen to response	1.5
Check computer system for this preferred room type	1.5
Obtain plastic key card and program it	0.5
Put key card in paper sleeve and write guest room number on it	1.0
Ask guest if he/she needs help with luggage	0.5
Get bellhop if help is needed	2.0
Wish guest a pleasant stay	0.5

Required:
a. Indicate whether each activity is value-added or non-value-added.
b. Calculate the cycle time and service cycle efficiency of this process.
c. Make recommendations to increase the service cycle efficiency.

9. (LO 2, 3; VA & NVA activities, cycle time, cycle efficiency) The following functions are performed in making chowder at Brady's Chowder Shoppe.

Function	Time (minutes)
Receiving ingredients	45
Moving ingredients to stockroom	15
Storing ingredients in stockroom	7,200
Moving ingredients from stockroom	15
Mixing ingredients	50
Cooking ingredients	185
Bottling ingredients	90
Moving bottled chowder to warehouse	20
Storing bottled chowder in warehouse	10,080
Moving bottled chowder from warehouse to trucks	30

Required:
a. Indicate whether each activity is value-added or non-value-added.
b. Calculate the cycle time and manufacturing cycle efficiency of this process.
c. Make some recommendations to Sean Brady, the owner, that would improve the company's manufacturing cycle efficiency.

10. (LO 4; Cost drivers) The following is a list of overhead cost pools at Williams Cosmetics Inc.
a. Equipment maintenance
b. Factory utilities
c. Factory depreciation
d. Machinery rent

e.   Quality inspection labour
f.   Computer operations
g.   Materials handling
h.   Setup
i.   Engineering changes
j.   Advertising
k.   Freight for materials
l.   Scheduling meetings
m.   Obtaining purchase order quotes
n.   Filing purchase orders
o.   Checking on overdue purchase orders

Required:
Identify a cost driver for each and explain why it is appropriate.

11. (LO 4; Cost drivers) The following activities take place at the local pizza delivery shop.
a.   Pizza oven electricity
b.   Delivery vehicle repairs, maintenance, and insurance
c.   Building insurance
d.   Plastic cups for side orders of anchovies and jalapenos
e.   Property taxes
f.   Gasoline for delivery vehicles

Required:
Determine the cost drivers for the above activities.

12. (LO 4; Cost levels) Katie's Kopies is a self-service photocopy store that has 25 photo-copy machines for customer use. A manager is always on duty to handle complaints or problems and monitor the machines.
a.   Store manager's salary
b.   Electricity expense
c.   Depreciation on the photocopy machines
d.   Property taxes on the building
e.   Order costs for purchasing paper and toner
f.   Cost of paper
g.   Cost of toner
h.   Cost of labour to place paper and toner in machines
i.   Repairs expense
j.   Insurance expense on photocopy machines
k.   Advertising and promotion expense

Required:
Determine whether each of the above costs for Katie's Kopies is a unit-level (U), batch-level (B), product/process-level (P), or organizational-level (O) cost.

13. (LO 4; Cost levels) Classify each of the following costs as being incurred at a unit level (U), batch level (B), product/process level (P), or organizational/facility level (O).
a.   Cost of printing books at a publishing house
b.   Cost of preparing payroll cheques
c.   Cost of supplies used in research and development on an existing product
d.   Salary of the vice president of marketing
e.   Cost of developing an engineering change order
f.   Depreciation on the camera at the drivers' licence office in the Ministry of Transportation
g.   Salary of guard for five-storey headquarters building
h.   Cost of paper and cover for a passport

14. (LO 5; Activity-based costing) Triton Ltd. is concerned about the profit generated by its regular paperback dictionaries. Kate Roberts, the CEO, is considering producing only the top-quality, hand-sewn dictionaries with gold-edged pages. Triton currently uses production hours to assign its $500,000 of production overhead to both types of dictionaries. Some additional data follow.

	Regular	Hand-Sewn
Direct costs	$2,500,000	$1,200,000
Number produced	1,000,000	700,000
Production hours	85,000	15,000
Square metres of space occupied	1,500	2,500
Inspection hours	5,000	25,000

The $500,000 of production overhead comprises $100,000 of utilities, $100,000 of factory/storage rent, and $300,000 of quality control inspectors' salaries.

Required:

a. How much production overhead is currently being assigned to the regular and to the hand-sewn dictionaries?

b. Determine the production overhead cost that should be assigned to each type of dictionary, using the activity driver appropriate for each type of overhead cost.

c. Should Triton Publishing stop producing the regular dictionaries? Explain.

15. (LO 4; Activity-based costing) As the manager of the five-employee Purchasing Department at Vancouver Ltd., you have decided to implement an activity-based product costing system. Annual departmental costs are $710,250 per year. Finding the best supplier takes the majority of the department's effort and creates the majority of the department's costs.

Activity	Allocation Measure	Number of People	Cost
Find best supplier	Number of telephone calls	3	$450,000
Issue purchase orders	Number of purchase orders	1	150,000
Review receiving reports	Number of receiving reports	1	110,250

During the year, the Purchasing Department makes 150,000 telephone calls, issues 10,000 purchase orders, and reviews 7,000 receiving reports. Many purchase orders are received in a single shipment.

One product manufactured by the company required the following activities in the Purchasing Department over the year: 118 telephone calls, 37 purchase orders, and 28 receiving reports.

Required:

a. What amount of Purchasing Department cost should be assigned to the manufacturing of this product?

b. If 200 units of the product are manufactured during the year, what is the Purchasing Department's cost per unit?

c. This analysis has caused you to investigate the need for such complexity in this product. After engaging in discussions with Vancouver Ltd.'s engineering design personnel and some of the company's best suppliers, it has been agreed that the number of parts in this product can be reduced and that suppliers will monitor parts supply levels on an ongoing basis. If the same type of analysis is performed for other products, you estimate that departmental costs, on average, will decrease by 25%. You have also estimated that, under the new circumstances, making 200 units of this product next year will only require 20 telephone calls, 15 purchase orders, and 8 receipts. What would be the Purchasing Department's new cost per unit for this product next year?

16. (LO 4; Activity-based costing) For the past 20 years, Williams Investigations Corp. has maintained an internal Research and Development (R&D) Department that provides services to in-house manufacturing departments. Costs of operating this department have been rising dramatically. You have suggested instituting an activity-based costing system to control costs and to charge service users for product and process development. The principal departmental expense is professional salaries. Activities in this department fall into three major categories. These categories, estimated related professional salary costs, and suggested allocation bases follow.

Activity	Salary Cost	Allocation Base
Evaluation of market opportunities	$ 600,000	Hours of professional time
Product development	1,800,000	Number of products developed
Process design	2,400,000	Number of engineering changes

In fiscal 2005, the R&D Department worked 15,000 hours evaluating market opportunities, worked on the development of 100 new products, and responded to 500 engineering-process change requests.

Required:

a. Determine the allocation rate for each activity in the R&D Department.

b. How can the rates developed in part (a) be used for evaluating output relative to costs incurred in the R&D Department?

c. How much cost would be charged to a manufacturing department that had consumed 1,000 hours of market research time, received help in developing 14 new products, and requested 75 engineering process changes?

d. What alternative does the firm have to maintaining an internal R&D department? What potential benefits and problems might arise if the company pursued this alternative?

17. (LO 4; Activity-based costing) Nicholas Sperry-Rand Plastics makes large plastic water bottles and plastic composite control panels for aircraft. Plastic bottles are relatively simple to produce and are made in large quantities. The control panels are more complicated to produce because they must be customized to individual plane types. Nicholas Sperry-Rand sells 200,000 plastic bottles annually and 5,000 control panels. A variety of information follows related to the annual production and sale of these products.

	Plastic Bottles	Control Panels
Revenues	$6,000,000	$13,000,000
Direct labour hours	2,000	53,000
Machine hours	120,000	86,250
Direct material	1,360,000	1,200,000

Labour is paid at $14 per hour. Production overhead consists of $9,500,000 of supervisors' salaries, labour fringe benefits, design and engineering, and other human-related costs and $2,500,000 of machine-related costs. Administrative costs total $1,200,000 and are allocated to individual product lines.

Required:

a. Calculate the profit or loss on each product if total overhead (production and administrative) is assigned according to direct labour hours.

b. Calculate the profit or loss on each product if total overhead (production and administrative) is assigned according to machine hours.

c. Calculate the profit or loss on each product if human-related overhead is assigned according to direct labour hours, machine-related overhead is assigned according to machine hours, and administrative overhead is assigned according to dollars of revenue.

d. Calculate the profit or loss on each product if overhead is assigned as in part (c) except that administrative overhead is deducted from total company income rather than being allocated to the individual product lines.

e. Does your answer in part (a), (b), (c), or (d) provide the best representation of the profit contributed by each product? Explain.

PROBLEMS

1. (LO 2; Value chart) You are the new controller of David Faber Ltd., a small job shop that manufactures special-order desk nameplate stands. As you review the records, you find that all the orders are shipped late, the average process time for any order is three weeks, and the time actually spent in production operations is two days. The president of the company has called you to discuss missed delivery dates.
   Required:
   Prepare a report for the executive officers in which you address
   a.   Possible causes of the problem
   b.   How a value chart could be used to address the problem

2. (LO 2, 3; VA and NVA activities, cycle efficiency) Linda Goldberg has just been elected mayor of Ottawa. She is highly concerned about deficit spending by her city. As a manager of the city's road construction workers, you have been asked to evaluate their performance in an effort to reduce costs. You noted the following activities after spending some time observing the workers.

Activity	Time (Hours)
Driving to the work location	1
Blocking off the road	2
Setting up the road stripper	3
Drinking coffee	13
Stripping the road	10
Setting up the asphalt layer machine	7
Talking to each other	4
Laying asphalt on the road	5
Unblocking the road	3
Loading equipment and leaving the area	2

   Required:
   a.   What are the value-added activities and times?
   b.   What are the non-value-added activities and times?
   c.   Calculate the cycle efficiency. Discuss the result. What suggestions can you offer the mayor regarding the road construction operations?

3. (LO 2; Cost of NVA activities) As company president, you asked Josh Lyman, the management accountant, to determine the cost of the non-value-added activities for each production run of the product as shown in the value chart in Exhibit 6-4. He gathered the following information:

Annual salary for receiving clerks	$28,000
Annual salary for quality control personnel	40,000
Annual salary for material/product handlers (movers)	19,000
Annual salary for setup personnel	26,000

   Each unit requires one square metre of storage space in a 100,000 square metre storage building. Depreciation per year on the building is $125,000, and property taxes and insurance total $35,000. Assume a 365-day year for plant assets and a 240-day year for personnel. Where a range of time is indicated, assume an average. Waiting time (all time other than production and storage time) is estimated at $50 per lot per day. Each day of delay in shipping time is estimated to cost $50 per unit per day. The average production lot size is 500 units.
   Required:
   Determine the total cost of non-value-added activities per unit.

4. (LO 4, 5; Cost drivers) Catherine Seguin Corp. makes grey metal five-drawer desks, and occasionally takes custom orders. The company's overhead costs for a month in which no custom desks are produced are as follows:

Purchasing department for raw materials and supplies (10 purchase orders per month)	$ 5,000
Setting up machines for production runs (4 times per month after maintenance checks)	1,240
Utilities (based on 3,200 machine hours)	160
Supervisors (2)	8,000
Machine and building depreciation (fixed)	5,500
Quality control and inspections (performed on random selection of desks each day; one quality control worker)	2,500
Total overhead costs	$22,400

Factory operations are highly automated and overhead is allocated to products based on machine hours. This allocation process has resulted in a manufacturing overhead allocation rate of $7 per machine hour ($22,400 ÷ 3,200 MH).

In June 2005, six orders were filled for custom desks. Selling prices were based on charges for actual direct materials, actual direct labour, and the $7 per machine hour for an estimated 200 hours of machine time. During that month, the following costs were incurred for 3,200 hours of machine time.

Purchasing department for raw materials and supplies (22 purchase orders)	$ 6,200
Setting up machines for production runs (18 times)	1,640
Utilities (based on 3,200 machine hours)	160
Supervisors (2)	8,000
Machine and building depreciation (fixed)	5,500
Quality control and inspections	2,980
Engineering design and specification costs	3,000
Total overhead costs	$27,480

Required:
a. How much of the purchasing cost is variable and how much is fixed? What types of purchasing costs would fit into each of these categories?
b. Why might the number of machine setups have increased from 4 to 18 when only six custom orders were received?
c. Why might the cost of quality control and inspections have increased?
d. Why did the engineering design and specification costs included during June not appear in the original overhead cost listing?
e. If Catherine Seguin Corp. were to adopt activity-based costing, what would you suggest as the cost drivers for each of the overhead cost items?
f. Do you think the custom orders should have been priced using an overhead rate of $7 per machine hour? Explain the reasoning behind your answer.

5. (LO 4, 5; Activity-based costing) Brash Manufacturing Ltd. has recently finished an analysis of its manufacturing labour-related costs. As vice president of finance, you are concerned about controlling these costs. The following summary presents the major categories of labour costs identified by Brash's Accounting Department.

Category	Amount
Base wages	$63,000,000
Health care benefits	10,500,000
Payroll taxes	5,040,000
Overtime	8,700,000
Training	1,875,000
Retirement benefits	6,900,000
Workplace Safety and Insurance Board (WSIB)	1,200,000

Your assistant has identified the following potential cost drivers for labour-related costs as well as their 2005 volume levels.

Potential Activity Driver	2005 Volume Level
Average number of factory employees	2,100
Number of new hires	300
Number of regular labour hours worked	3,150,000
Number of overtime hours worked	288,000
Volume of production in units	12,000,000
Number of production process changes	600
Number of production schedule changes	375
Total factory wages	$71,700,000

Required:

a. Use the appropriate activity driver to determine the per-unit cost for each labour cost pool category.

b. Based on your judgment and your calculations in part (a), which activity driver should receive the most attention from company managers in their efforts to control labour-related costs? How much of the total labour-related cost is attributable to this activity driver?

c. In the contemporary environment, many firms are asking their employees to work record levels of overtime. What activity driver does this practice suggest is a major contributor to labour-related costs? Explain.

6. (LO 4, 5; Activity-based costing) The budgeted manufacturing overhead costs of West Wing Ltd. for 2005 are as follows.

Type of Cost	Cost Amount
Electric power	$ 600,000
Work cells	3,600,000
Materials handling	1,200,000
Quality control inspections	1,200,000
Product runs (machine setups)	600,000
Total budgeted overhead costs	$7,200,000

For the last five years, the cost accounting department has been charging overhead production costs based on machine hours. The estimated capacity for fiscal 2005 is 1,200,000 machine hours.

You have recently attended a seminar on activity-based costing and believe that implementation of ABC might give the company an edge in pricing over its competitors. At your request, the production manager has provided the following data regarding expected activity for the cost drivers of the preceding budgeted overhead costs for fiscal 2005.

Type of Cost	Activity Drivers
Electric power	120,000 kilowatt hours
Work cells	720,000 square metres
Materials handling	240,000 material moves
Quality control inspections	120,000 inspections
Product runs (machine setups)	60,000 product runs

You have just received an order for 5,000 doors from a local construction company. The head of cost accounting has prepared the following cost estimate for producing the 5,000 doors.

Direct material cost	$120,000	
Direct labour cost	$360,000	
Machine hours		12,000
Direct labour hours		18,000
Electric power (kilowatt hours)		1,200
Work cells (square metres)		9,600
Number of materials handling moves		120
Number of quality control inspections		60
Number of product runs (setups)		30

Required:

a. What is the predetermined overhead rate if the traditional measure of machine hours is used?

b. What is the manufacturing cost per door under the present cost accounting system?

c. What is the manufacturing cost per door under the proposed ABC method?

d. If the prior two costing systems will result in different cost estimates, which cost accounting system is preferable as a pricing policy and why?

(Source: Reprinted by permission of Institute of Management Accountants, Montvale, N.J., USA, www.imanet.org.)

7. (LO 4; 5, 6; Activity-based costing) Edmonton Cosmetic Hospital is under increasing pressure for the charges it assesses its patients. Except for an explicit consideration of direct costs for surgery, medication, and other treatments, the current pricing system is an ad hoc one based on pricing norms for the geographical area. As the hospital controller, you have suggested that pricing would be less arbitrary if there were a tighter relationship between costs and patient charges. As a first step, you have determined that most costs can be assigned to one of the following three cost pools.

Cost pool	Amount	Activity Driver	Quantity
Professional salaries	$900,000	professional hours	30,000 hours
Building costs	450,000	square metres used	15,000 square metres
Risk management	320,000	patients served	1,000 patients

Hospital services are classified into three broad categories. The services and their volume measures follow.

Service	Professional Hours	Square Metres	Number of Patients
Surgery	6,000	1,200	200
Inpatient care	20,000	12,000	500
Outpatient care	4,000	1,800	300

Required:

a. Determine the allocation rate for each cost pool.

b. Allocate costs among the three hospital services using the allocation rates derived in part (a).

c. What bases might be used as activity cost drivers to allocate the costs of the services among the patients served by the hospital? Defend your selections.

8. (LO 4, 5, 6; Determining product cost) Poë Chemical Products has a total of $1,551,000 in overhead costs. The company's products and related statistics follow.

	Product A	Product B
Direct material (in kilograms)	93,000	127,000
Direct labour hours	20,000	25,000
Machine hours	35,000	15,000
Number of setups	200	500
Number of units produced	10,000	5,000

Additional data:

One direct labour hour costs $12, and the 220,000 kilograms of material were purchased for $363,000.

Required:

a. Assume that Poë Chemical Products uses direct labour hours to apply overhead to products. Determine the total cost for each product and the cost per unit.

b. Assume that Poë Chemical Products uses machine hours to apply overhead to products. Determine the total cost for each product and the cost per unit.

c. Determine the total cost for each product and the cost per unit, assuming that Poë Chemical Products uses the following activity centres, cost amounts, and activity drivers to apply overhead to products.

Cost pool	Cost Driver	Cost	Volume
Utilities	Number of machine hours	$500,000	50,000
Setup	Number of setups	105,000	700
Materials handling	Kilograms of material	946,000	220,000

9. (LO 4, 5, 7; Activity-based costing) Glow By Jabot Ltd. has identified activity centres to which overhead costs are assigned. The cost pool amounts for these centres and their selected cost drivers for fiscal 2005 are as follows.

Cost Pool	Cost	Cost Driver	Volume
Utilities	$487,500	Machine hours	65,000
Scheduling and setup	273,000	Setups	780
Materials handling	640,000	Kilograms of material	1,600,000
Building depreciation	457,600	Square metres occupied	35,200

The company's products and other operating statistics follow.

	Products		
	A	B	C
Direct material and labour costs	$ 40,000	$ 65,000	$ 90,000
Kilograms of materials used	500,000	300,000	800,000
Machine hours	35,000	10,000	20,000
Number of setups	130	380	270
Square metres occupied	12,000	8,300	14,900
Number of units produced	63,000	10,000	40,000
Direct labour hours	32,000	18,000	50,000

Required:
a. Determine total unit product cost. Apply overhead to products using the appropriate cost drivers for each type of cost.
b. Before installing an ABC system, Glow By Jabot Ltd. allocated manufacturing overhead to products using direct labour hours. Determine the pre-ABC total unit product cost.
c. The firm operates in a fairly noncompetitive market and product prices are set at 20% over cost. Determine the selling price for each product using the product costs determined (1) in part (a) and (2) in part (b).
d. Explain how ABC improves product cost information and, thus, determination of selling prices for Glow By Jabot Ltd.

10. (LO 4, 5, 6, 7; Activity-based costing) Count D. Cash, CMA, was not entirely convinced that his fees for different types of services were based on accurate costs. His son, Petty, who was home for the summer, had just received an A in a managerial accounting course where he learned about ABC. Petty suggested applying ABC to find more accurate costs for his father's accounting and auditing, tax, and management services. They identified the following activity centres, costs and quantities, and cost drivers.

Activity Centre	Cost	Quantity	Cost Driver
Planning and review	$ 65,240	93,200	Billable time (hours)
EDP	72,000	7,200	Computational time (hours)
Personnel	56,160	52	Number of people
Library	21,948	186	Books and periodicals purchased
Programming	56,160	4,160	Programming time (hours)
Building	87,000	15,000	Square metres
Administration	150,000	500	Number of clients
Total	$508,508		

Petty also compiled the following statistics for each of the services provided to clients during the past year.

	Accounting & Auditing	Tax	Management
Direct costs	$1,952,000	$1,610,000	$732,000
Hours of billable time	48,800	32,200	12,200
Hours of computational time	4,320	2,400	480
Number of people	30	16	6
New purchases for the library	51	99	36
Hours of programming time	1,200	520	2,440
Square metres occupied	8,800	4,875	1,325
Number of clients	170	280	50

Required:
a. Assign each of the activity costs to the three services.
b. Determine the total cost of each class of service.
c. Prior to this year, Count D. Cash applied overhead based only on professional labour hours (billable time). The overhead rate was found simply by dividing total budgeted overhead by total budgeted professional hours. Using the original information, (1) what overhead rate would Count D. Cash have used for the current year, and (2) how much overhead would have been assigned to each service area?
d. Assuming Count D. Cash bases his service prices on the cost of rendering the services, in general how would the relative prices of services differ between parts (b) and (c)?

11. (LO 4, 5, 6, 7; Activity-based costing) Cricket Components Ltd. makes three products: fax stands, organizers, and printer stands. In fiscal 2004, the company incurred $1,000,000 of manufacturing overhead costs and produced 100,000 fax stands, 10,000 organizers, and 30,000 printer stands. Using the company's overhead application rate of $10 per direct labour hour, the per unit product cost was as follows:

	Fax Stands	Organizer	Printer Stands
Direct material	$ 4.00	$15.00	$ 8.00
Direct labour	6.00	18.30	9.00
Manufacturing overhead	4.00	30.00	10.00
Total	$14.00	$63.30	$27.00

In the past few years, Cricket Components' profitability has been lagging and its overseas competition has been increasing. The company is considering implementing an activity-based costing system for 2005. In analyzing the fiscal 2004 data, you determined that the $1,000,000 of manufacturing overhead could be assigned to four basic activities: quality control, setup, materials handling, and equipment operation. Data from fiscal 2004 on the costs associated with each of the four activities follow.

	Quality Control	Setup	Materials Handling	Equipment Operation
Cost	$50,000	$50,000	$150,000	$750,000
Activity driver	Number of units produced	Number of setups	Kilograms of material used	Number of machine hours
Volume of driver	140,000	500	1,000,000	500,000

Volume measures for fiscal 2004 for each product and each activity driver were as follows:

	Fax Stands	Organizer	Printer Stands
Number of units	100,000	10,000	30,000
Number of setups	100	200	200
Kilograms of material	200,000	500,000	300,000
Number of machine hours	100,000	200,000	200,000

Required:

a. For fiscal 2005, determine the total amount of overhead allocated to each product group using their current overhead application method.

b. For fiscal 2005, determine the total overhead allocated to each product group using the activity-based costing allocation measures. Compute the cost per unit for each product group.

c. If the company sets prices based on product costs, how would the sales prices using activity-based costing differ from those using the traditional overhead allocation?

12. (LO 1, 4, 6, 7; Comprehensive) For the past five years, Judy has been running a consulting practice in which she provides two major services: general management consulting, and executive training seminars. Judy is not quite sure that she is charging appropriate fees for the different services she provides. She recently read an article about activity-based costing (ABC) that convinced her she could employ ABC to improve the accuracy of her costing. She has approached you to help determine whether the application of ABC would help. She has provided you with the following selected information concerning her consulting practice during the previous year:

Overhead Activity	Cost Pool	Quantities	Cost Driver
Planning and review	$ 300,000	60,000 hours	Billable hours
Research	48,000	200 journals	Journals purchased
General administration	600,000	300 clients	Number of clients
Building and equipment	84,000	1,200 square metres	Square metres
Clerical	85,000	17 professionals	Professional staff
	$1,117,000		

In addition, Judy provided you with the following statistics for each of the two types of services provided to clients during the year.

Overhead Activity	Management Consulting	Executive Training
Direct labour costs	$900,000	$450,000
Billable hours	45,000	15,000
Research—Journals purchased	140	60
Number of clients	120	180
Square metres	800	400
Professional staff	10	7

Required:

a. In the past, Judy divided the total overhead costs by the total billable hours to determine an average rate. To this amount she would then add the direct labour costs per hour and double this total amount to establish her average hourly charge-out rate. What was Judy's average hourly charge-out rate using this method?

b. Using ABC, what would Judy's charge-out rate be? Note that Judy will continue to add the overhead to the direct labour costs per hour on a service basis and then double this amount to set an average hourly charge-out rate.

c. After reviewing the ABC methodology described in part (b), identify *one* significant flaw in how overhead costs will be allocated by Judy in the ABC system. Discuss how this flaw would affect the average hourly charge-out rates (i.e., increase or decrease the rates) for management consulting and executive training. You do not have to calculate the new rates to answer this part of the question.

d. Identify and discuss three ways in which ABC leads to more accurate product costs.

e. Identify and discuss two limitations of ABC.

13. (LO 1, 7; Setting up the system) Last year, the accounts receivable department at Canada Hydro spent $22,500,000 to collect receivables from more than 2 million customers throughout the country. In order to better understand the nature and cost of activities of the accounts receivable department, Canada Hydro's top management has decided to perform an activity-based analysis to gather the information that will help improve the processes and make them more cost-efficient.

Required:

a. Describe the steps that Canada Hydro should follow to gather the information.

b. Identify the factors that Canada Hydro's top management should consider before carrying out an activity-based analysis of the accounts receivable department.

14. (LO 1, 7; Setting up the system) Kiddy Company manufactures bicycles. It recently received a request to manufacture 10 units of a mountain bike at a price lower than it normally accepts. Bruce, the sales manager, indicated that if the order were accepted at that price, the company could expect additional orders from the same client. Bruce believes that if Kiddy could offer this price in the market generally, sales of this bike would increase by 30%. Melany, president of Kiddy, is skeptical about accepting the order. The company has a policy of not accepting any order that does not provide a markup of 20% on full manufacturing costs. The price offered is $575 per bike.

The controller, Sanjay, has recently researched the possibility of using activity-based multiple overhead rates instead of the single rate currently in use. He has promised more accurate product costing, and Melany is curious about how this approach would affect product costing and pricing of the mountain bike.

The plantwide overhead rate is based on an expected volume of 15,000 direct labour hours and the following budgeted overhead:

Machine operating costs	$ 75,000
Rework labour	45,000
Inspection	25,000
Scrap costs	35,000
General manufacturing overhead	120,000
Total	$300,000

Expected activity for selected cost drivers for 2005 are

Machine hours	25,000
Units reworked	600
Inspection hours	500
Units scrapped	140
Direct labour hours	15,000

Estimated data for the production of one mountain bike are

Direct materials	$160
Direct labour (7.5 hours per unit)	$180
Number of machine hours	6
Number of units reworked	0.25
Number of inspection hours	0.10
Number of units scrapped	0.05

Required:

a. Using the existing single-rate method to assign overhead on a plantwide basis, determine whether or not Kiddy should accept the order for the 10 mountain bikes. Explain your decision.

b. Using activity-based costing to assign overhead, determine whether or not Kiddy should accept the order for 10 mountain bikes. Explain your decision.

15. (LO 1, 6, 7; Setting rates) Mars Company has four categories of overhead: purchasing and receiving materials, machine operating costs, materials handling, and shipping. The costs expected for these categories for the coming year are as follows:

Purchasing and receiving materials	$200,000
Machine operating costs	450,000
Materials handling	80,000
Shipping	170,000
Total	$900,000

The plant currently applies overhead using machine hours and expected annual capacity. Expected capacity is 150,000 machine hours. Robert, the financial controller, has been asked to submit a bid on job #287, on which he has assembled the following data:

Direct materials per unit	$0.35
Direct labour per unit	0.85
Applied overhead	?
Number of units produced	6,000
Number of purchases and receipts	2
Number of machine hours	1,500
Number of material moves	300
Number of kilometres to ship to the customer	2,300

Robert has been told that Arrow Company, a major competitor, is using activity-based costing and will bid on job #287 with a price of $2.95 per unit. Before submitting his bid, Robert wants to assess the effects of this alternative costing approach. He estimates that 850,000 units will be produced next year, 2,500 purchases and receipts will be made, 400,000 moves will be performed plantwide, and the delivery of finished goods will be 300,000 kilometres. The bid price policy is full manufacturing cost plus 25%.

Required:
a. Calculate the bid price per unit of job #287 using machine hours to assign overhead.
b. Using an activity-based approach, determine whether Mars or Arrow will produce the most competitive bid and obtain the contract. Show all your calculations.

(Problems 12–15 are adapted by the author from *Management Accounting examinations*, published by the Certified General Accountants Association of Canada © CGA-Canada, 1999 (#12 and 15) and 2000 (#13 and 14), used by permission.)

CASES

1. Tony Soprano has just purchased a 100,000 cubic metre commercial cold-storage warehouse as rental property. The previous owner had charged customers a flat monthly rate of $0.04 per kilogram of goods stored. The reason the warehouse was on the market was because its owner had become dissatisfied with its profitability. Despite the fact that the warehouse remained relatively full, revenues had not kept pace with operating costs. Tony asks his accountant, Stephie Demara, about using activity-based costing to better understand the causes of operational costs and to possibly revise the pricing formula. Ms. Demara determines that most costs of the warehouse can be associated with one of four activities. Those activities and their related costs, volume measures, and volume levels for fiscal 2005 follow.

Activity	Monthly Cost	Monthly Volume Measure
Send/receive goods	$6,000	Weight in kilograms—500,000
Store goods	4,000	Volume in cubic metres—80,000
Move goods	5,000	Volume in square metres—5,000
Identify goods	2,000	Number of packages—500

Required:
a. Based on the activity cost and volume data, determine the amount of cost assigned to the following customers, whose goods were all received on the first day of last month.

Customer	Weight of Order	Cubic Metres	Square Metres	Number of Packages
Lori Eisen	40,000	3,000	300	5
Paula Pressberger	40,000	2,000	200	20
Christina Kim	40,000	1,000	1,000	80

b. Determine the price to be charged to each customer under the previous owner's pricing plan.

c.   Determine the new price, assuming Tony would add a 40% markup to the cost determined in part (a).

d.   How well did the previous owner's pricing plan capture the costs incurred to provide the warehouse services? Explain.

(Source: Adapted from Harold P. Roth and Linda T. Sims, "Costing for Warehousing and Distribution," *Management Accounting*, August 1991, pp. 42–45. Adapted with permission of the Institute of Management Accountants, Montvale, N.J., USA, www.imanet.org.)

2. The following production and cost analysis for each product made by Roth and Borthick Company is for the year 2005.

Cost Component	Product A	Product B	Both Products	Cost
Units produced	10,000	10,000	20,000	
Raw materials used (units)				
Material X	50,000	50,000	100,000	$ 800,000
Material Y		100,000	100,000	$1,200,000
Labour used (hours)				
Department 1				$ 681,000
Direct labour ($375,000)	20,000	5,000	25,000	
Indirect labour				
Inspection	2,500	2,500	5,000	
Machine operations	5,000	10,000	15,000	
Setups	200	200	400	
Department 2				$ 462,000
Direct labour ($200,000)	5,000	5,000	10,000	
Indirect labour				
Inspection	2,500	5,000	7,500	
Machine operations	1,000	4,000	5,000	
Setups	200	400	600	
Machine hours used				
Department 1	5,000	10,000	15,000	$ 400,000
Department 2	5,000	20,000	25,000	$ 800,000
Power used (kwh)				$ 400,000
Department 1			1,500,000	
Department 2			8,500,000	
Other activity data				
Building occupancy				$1,000,000
Square metres occupied				
Purchasing			10,000	
Power			40,000	
Department 1			200,000	
Department 2			250,000	
Purchasing				$ 100,000
Number of purchase orders				
Material X			200	
Material Y			300	

Faye Harold, the management accountant, has just returned from a seminar on activity-based costing. To apply the concepts she has learned, she decides to analyze the costs incurred for Products A and B from an activity basis. In doing so, she specifies the following first and second allocation processes.

First Stage: Allocations to Departments

Cost Pool	Cost Object	Activity Allocation Base
Building occupancy	Departments	Square metres occupied
Purchasing	Materials	Number of purchase orders
Power	Departments	Kilowatt hours

Second Stage: Allocations to Products

Cost Pool	Cost Object	Activity Allocation Base
Departments		
Indirect labour	Products	Hours worked
Power	Products	Machine hours
Machinery related	Products	Machine hours
Building occupancy	Products	Machine hours
Materials		
Purchasing	Products	Units of material

Required:

a.   Determine the total overhead for Roth and Borthick Company.

b.   Determine the plantwide overhead rate for the company, assuming the use of direct labour hours.

c.   Determine the cost per unit for Product A and for Product B using the overhead application rate found in part (b).

d.   Using activity-based costing, determine the cost allocations to departments (first-stage allocations). Allocate in the following order: building occupancy, purchasing, and power.

e.   Using the allocations found in part (d), determine the overhead cost allocations to products (second-stage allocations).

f.   Determine the cost per unit for Product A and Product B using the overhead allocations found in part (e).

(Source: Adapted from Harold P. Roth and A. Faye Borthick, "Getting Closer to Real Product Costs," *Management Accounting*, May 1989, pp. 28-33. Adapted with permission of the Institute of Management Accountants, Montvale, N.J., USA, www.imanet.org.)

3.   Alison Baird CarryAll Company produces briefcases from leather, fabric, and synthetic materials in a single production department. The basic product is a standard briefcase made from leather and lined with fabric. CarryAll has a good market reputation because its standard briefcase is of high quality and has been produced for many years.

Last year, Alison Baird CarryAll decided to expand its product line and produce briefcases for special orders. These briefcases differ from the standard in that they vary in size, contain both leather and synthetic materials, and are imprinted with the buyer's logo. Synthetic materials are used to hold down the materials cost. To reduce labour cost per unit, most of the cutting and stitching on the specialty briefcases is done by automated machines that are used sparingly in the production of the standard briefcases. Because of these changes in the design and production of the specialty briefcases, Alison Baird CarryAll believed that they would cost less to produce than the standard briefcases. However, because they are specialty items, they were priced at $32, slightly higher than the standard briefcases, which are priced at $30.

After reviewing last month's results of operations, Alison Baird CarryAll's president became concerned about the profitability of the two product lines. The standard briefcase showed a loss while the specialty briefcases showed a greater profit margin than expected. The president is considering dropping the standard briefcase and focusing entirely on specialty items. The cost data for last month's operations follow.

	Standard		**Specialty**	
Units produced		10,000		2,500
Direct material				
Leather	1.0 square metres	$15.00	0.5 square metres	$ 7.50
Fabric	1.0 square metres	5.00	1.0 square metres	5.00
Synthetic			0.5 square metres	5.00
Total material		$20.00		$17.50
Direct labour	0.5 hours @ $12	6.00	0.25 hours @ $12	3.00
Manufacturing				
overhead	0.5 hours @ $8.98	4.49	0.25 hours @ $8.98	2.25
Cost per unit		$30.49		$22.75

Manufacturing overhead is applied using direct labour hours. The rate of $8.98 per DLH was calculated by dividing $50,500 of total overhead for the month by 5,625 direct labour hours.

Assume that the following costs and activity drivers have been identified. The purchasing department cost is $6,000, primarily created by the number of purchase orders processed. During the month, the purchasing department prepared 20 purchase orders for leather, 30 for fabric, and 50 for synthetic material.

Receiving and inspecting materials cost is $7,500. This cost is driven by the number of deliveries. During the month, 30 deliveries were made for leather, 40 for fabric, and 80 for synthetic material.

The cost of setting up the production line to produce the different types of briefcases is $10,000. A setup for production of the standard briefcases requires one hour, while setup for the specialty briefcases requires two hours. Standard briefcases are produced in batches of 200; specialty briefcases are produced in batches of 25. During the last month, there were 50 setups for the standard items and 100 setups for the specialty items.

The cost of inspecting finished goods is $8,000. All briefcases are inspected to ensure that quality standards are met. The inspection of standard briefcases takes very little time because the employees identify and correct quality problems as they do the hand-cutting and stitching. Inspection personnel indicated that, during the month, they spent 150 hours inspecting standard briefcases and 250 hours inspecting specialty cases.

Equipment-related costs are $6,000 for repairs, depreciation, and utilities. These costs are assigned to products using machine hours. A standard briefcase requires 0.5 hours of machine time, and a specialty briefcase requires 2 hours.

Plant-related costs are $13,000 for items such as property taxes, insurance, and administration. These costs are assigned to products using machine hours.

Required:

a. Using activity-based costing concepts, what overhead costs are assigned to the two product lines?

b. What is the unit cost of each type of product using activity-based costing concepts?

c. Reevaluate the president's concern about the profitability of the two product lines.

(IMA adapted)

4. Jenny Horton Corporation manufactures several types of printed circuit boards, two of which account for the majority of the company's sales. The first, a television (TV) circuit board, has been an industry standard for several years. The market for this type of board is competitive and, therefore, price sensitive. Horton plans to sell 65,000 of the TV circuit boards in fiscal 2005 for $150 per unit. The second high-volume product, a personal computer (PC) circuit board, is a recent addition to Horton's product line. The PC board incorporates the latest technology and can be sold at a premium price; the 2005 plans include the sale of 40,000 PC boards at $300 per unit.

Horton's management group is meeting to discuss how to spend sales and promotion dollars in fiscal 2005. You, the sales manager, believe that the market share for the TV board could be expanded by concentrating Horton's promotional efforts in this area. In response to this suggestion, the production manager said, "Why don't you go after a bigger market for the PC board? The cost sheets that I get show that the contribution from the PC board is more than double the contribution from the TV board.

I know we get a premium price for the PC board; selling it should help overall profitability."

The following cost and time data apply to the TV and PC boards.

	TV Board	PC Board
Direct material	$80	$140
Direct labour	1.5 hours	4 hours
Machine time	0.5 hours	1.5 hours

Variable manufacturing overhead is applied using direct labour hours. For 2005, variable manufacturing overhead is budgeted at $1,120,000 and 280,000 direct labour hours are budgeted. FOH is applied based on machine hours incurred. Hourly rates for machine time and direct labour are $10 and $14, respectively. Horton applies a materials handling charge at 10% of material cost; this charge is not included in variable manufacturing overhead. Total expenditures for materials are budgeted at $10,800,000.

Van Amberg, Horton's controller, believes that before making a decision about allocating promotional dollars to individual products it might be worthwhile to look at these products on the basis of their production activities. Van Amberg has prepared the following schedule to help the management group understand activity-based costing.

	Budgeted Cost	Cost Driver	Annual Activity for Cost Driver
Material overhead:			
Procurement	$ 400,000	Number of parts	4,000,000 parts
Production scheduling	220,000	Number of boards	110,000 boards
Packaging and shipping	440,000	Number of boards	110,000 boards
	$1,060,000		
Variable overhead:			
Machine setup	$ 446,000	Number of setups	278,750 setups
Hazardous waste disposal	48,000	Kilograms of waste	16,000 kilograms
Quality control	560,000	Number of inspections	160,000 inspections
General supplies	66,000	Number of boards	110,000 boards
	$1,120,000		
Manufacturing:			
Machine insertion	$1,200,000	Number of parts	3,000,000 parts
Manual insertion	4,000,000	Number of parts	1,000,000 parts
Wave soldering	132,000	Number of boards	110,000 boards
	$5,332,000		

Required per unit	TV board	PC Board
Parts	25	55
Machine insertions	24	35
Manual insertions	1	20
Machine setups	2	3
Hazardous waste	0.02 kg	0.35 kg
Inspections	1	2

"This information," Van Amberg explained, "can be used to calculate an activity-based cost for each TV and PC board. The only cost that remains the same for the current and the ABC cost methods is direct material cost. Cost drivers replace direct labour, machine time, and overhead costs in the current costs."

Required:

a. Using the current costing system, calculate the total gross profit (sales minus cost of goods sold) expected in fiscal 2005 for the
   1. TV board
   2. PC board

b. On the basis of activity-based costs, calculate the total gross profit expected in fiscal 2005 for the

1. TV board
2. PC board
c. Explain how the comparison of the results of the two costing methods may impact the decisions made by Horton Corporation's management group.
d. Identify at least four general advantages that are associated with activity-based costing.

(CMA)

5. Halifax Valley Architects Inc. provides a range of engineering and architectural consulting services through its three branch offices in Halifax, Saint John, and Moncton. The company allocates resources and bonuses to the three branches based on the net income reported for the period. The following presents the results from the year 2005 (dollars are in thousands).

	Halifax	Saint John	Moncton	Total
Sales	$1,500	$1,419	$1,067	$3,986
Direct material	(281)	(421)	(185)	(887)
Direct labour	(382)	(317)	(317)	(1,016)
Overhead	(710)	(589)	(589)	(1,888)
Net income	$ 127	$ 92	$ (24)	$ 195

Overhead is accumulated in one overhead pool and allocated to the branches. This pool includes rent, depreciation, taxes, etc., regardless of which office incurred the expense. This method of accumulating costs forces the offices to absorb a portion of the overhead incurred by other offices. For 2005, the overhead rate was $1.859 for every direct labour dollar incurred by an office.

Management is concerned with the results of the 2005 performance reports. During a review of overhead, it became apparent that many items of overhead were not correlated with direct labour dollars. Management decided that applying overhead based on activity-based costing and direct tracing where possible should provide a more accurate picture of branch profitability.

An analysis of the overhead revealed that the following amounts could be traced directly to the office that incurred the overhead (dollars are in thousands).

	Halifax	Saint John	Moncton	Total
Direct overhead	$180	$270	$177	$627

Activity pools and activity drivers were determined from the accounting records and staff surveys as follows.

Activity Pools		Activity Driver	Halifax	Saint John	Moncton
General admin.	$409,000	Direct labour cost	$382,413	$317,086	$317,188
Project costing	48,000	Number of time sheet entries	6,000	3,800	3,500
Accounts payable/receiving	139,000	Number of vendor invoices	1,020	850	400
Accounts receivable	47,000	Number of client invoices	588	444	96
Payroll/mail sort & delivery	30,000	Number of employees	23	26	18
Personnel recruiting	38,000	Number of new hires	8	4	7
Employee insurance processing	14,000	Insurance claims filed	230	260	180
Proposals	139,000	Number of proposals	200	250	60
Sales meetings/ sales aids	202,000	Contracted sales	1,824,439	1,399,617	571,208
Shipping	24,000	Number of projects	99	124	30

Ordering	48,000	Number of			
		purchase orders	135	110	80
Duplicating costs	46,000	Number of copies	162,500	146,250	65,000
Blueprinting	77,000	Number of blueprints	39,000	31,200	16,000
	$1,261,000				

Required:

a. What overhead costs should be assigned to each branch based on activity-based costing concepts?

b. What is the contribution of each branch before subtracting the results obtained in part (a)?

c. What is the profitability of each branch office using activity-based costing?

d. Evaluate the concerns of management regarding the traditional costing technique currently used.

(IMA)

6. Quanseh Company sells craft kits and supplies to retail outlets and through its catalogue. Some of the items are manufactured by Quanseh while others are purchased for resale. For the products it manufactures, the company currently bases its selling prices on a standard costing system that accounts for direct material, direct labour, and the associated overhead costs. In addition to these standard product costs. Quanseh incurs substantial selling costs, and Joseph, the controller, has suggested that these selling costs should be included in the product pricing structure.

After studying the costs incurred over the past two years for one of its products, skeins of knitting yarn, Joseph has selected four categories of selling costs and developed cost drivers (allocation bases) for each of these costs. The selling costs actually incurred during the past year and the cost drivers are shown below.

Cost Category	Amount	Cost Driver
Sales commissions	$ 675,000	Boxes of yarn sold to retail stores
Catalogues	295,400	Catalogues distributed
Cost of catalogue sales	105,000	Skeins sold through catalogue
Credit and collection	60,000	Number of retail orders
Total selling costs	$1,135,400	

The knitting yarn is sold to retail outlets in boxes, each containing twelve skeins of yarn; the sale of partial boxes is not permitted. Commissions are paid on sales to retail outlets but not on catalogue sales. The cost of catalogue sales includes the wages of personnel who take the catalogue orders and telephone costs. Joseph believes that the selling costs vary significantly with the size of the order; order sizes are divided into three categories as shown below.

Order Size	Catalogue Sales	Retail Sales
Small	1–10 skeins	1–10 boxes
Medium	11–20 skeins	11–20 boxes
Large	over 20 skeins	over 20 boxes

An analysis of the previous year's records produced the statistics shown in the chart below.

	Order Size			
	Small	Medium	Large	Total
Retail sales in boxes (12 skeins per box)	2,000	45,000	178,000	225,000
Catalogue sales in skeins	79,000	52,000	44,000	175,000
Number of retail orders	485	2,415	3,100	6,000
Catalogues distributed	254,300	211,300	125,200	590,800

Required:

a. Define the concept of activity-based costing and provide two examples of cost drivers that are not related to selling costs.

b. Prepare a detailed schedule showing Quanseh Company's total selling cost for each order size and the per-skein selling cost within each order size.

c.   Explain how the analysis of the selling costs for skeins of knitting yarn is likely to impact future pricing and product decisions at Quanseh Company.

(IMA adapted)

7. Coffee Bean Inc. (CBI) is a distributor and processor of a variety of different blends of coffee. The company buys coffee beans from around the world and roasts, blends, and packages them for resale. CBI currently has 15 different coffees that it offers to gourmet shops in one-kilogram bags. The major cost is raw materials; however, there is a substantial amount of manufacturing overhead in the predominantly automated roasting and packing process. The company uses relatively little direct labour.

Some of the coffees are very popular and sell in large volumes, while a few of the newer blends have very low volumes. CBI prices its coffee at standard cost, including allocated overhead, plus a markup of 30%. If prices for certain coffees are significantly higher than market, adjustments are made. The company competes primarily on the quality of its products, but customers are price conscious as well.

Data for the 2005 budget include manufacturing overhead of $3,000,000, which has been allocated on the basis of each product's standard direct labour cost. The budgeted direct labour cost for 2005 totals $600,000. Based on the sales budget and raw material standards, purchases and use of raw materials (mostly coffee beans) will total $6,000,000.

The standard prime costs for one-kilogram bags of two of the company's products appear below.

	Mauna Loa	Malaysian
Raw materials	$4.20	$3.20
Direct labour	0.30	0.30

CBI's controller believes the traditional standard costing system may be providing misleading cost information and has developed an analysis of the 2005 budgeted manufacturing overhead costs shown in the chart below.

Activity	Cost Driver	Budgeted Activity	Budgeted Cost
Purchasing	Purchase orders	1,158	$ 579,000
Materials handling	Number of setups	1,800	720,000
Quality control	Number of batches	600	144,000
Roasting	Roasting hours	96,100	961,000
Blending	Blending hours	33,600	336,000
Packaging	Packaging hours	26,000	260,000
Total manufacturing overhead cost			$3,000,000

Data regarding the 2005 production of Mauna Loa and Malaysian coffee are presented below. There will be no raw materials inventory for either of these coffees at the beginning of the year.

	Mauna Loa	Malaysian
Expected sales	100,000 kg	2,000 kg
Batch size	10,000 kg	500 kg
Setups	3 per batch	3 per batch
Purchase order size	25,000 kg	500 kg
Roasting time	1 h/100 kg	1 h/100 kg.
Blending time	0.5 h/100 kg	0.5 h/100 kg
Packaging time	0.1 h/100 kg	0.1 h/100 kg

Required:

a.   Using Coffee Bean Inc.'s current standard costing approach
   i.   Determine the company's predetermined overhead rate using direct labour cost as the single allocation base.
   ii.   Determine the standard costs and selling prices of one kilogram of Mauna Loa coffee and one kilogram of Malaysian coffee.

    b. Using the controller's analysis of budgeted manufacturing overhead, develop a new standard cost, using an activity-based costing approach, for one kilogram of
      i. Mauna Loa coffee
      ii. Malaysian coffee
    c. What are the implications of the activity-based cost of the two products with respect to the use of direct labour as a basis for allocating overhead to products and to the use of the existing standard cost system as a basis for pricing?

(IMA adapted)

ETHICS AND QUALITY DISCUSSIONS

1. An activity-based approach to management and product costing may frequently cause managers to restructure the operations of their firms. For example, given the increase in employee empowerment, many companies are eliminating entire layers of decision makers to reduce costs and get faster decisions. Companies are also consolidating certain activities such as human resources, government affairs, health, environment, and safety that were redundantly performed by various operating units.
   Required:
   a. What is the likely short-term impact on quality of eliminating a layer of decision makers?
   b. What is the likely long-term impact on quality of eliminating a layer of decision makers?
   c. How does ABM, with its cost control focus, implicitly or explicitly give consideration to effects of activities on quality?

2. Many manufacturers are deciding to no longer service small retailers. For example, some companies have policies to serve only customers who purchase $10,000 or more of their products annually. The companies defend such a policy on the basis that it allows them to better serve their larger outlets, which handle more volume and more diverse product lines.
   Required:
   a. Relate the concepts in the chapter to the decision of manufacturers to drop small customers.
   b. Are there any ethical implications of eliminating groups of customers that may be less profitable than others?
   c. Does activity-based costing adequately account for all costs that are related to a decision to eliminate a particular customer base? (Hint: Consider opportunity costs such as those related to reputation.)

3. Anne Cowan Industrial Paints Inc. has asked you to analyze and update its costing and pricing practices. The company's product line has changed over time from general paints to specialized marine coatings. Although some large orders are received, the majority of business is now generated from products designed and produced in small lot sizes to meet specifically detailed environmental and technical requirements.
       The company has experienced tremendous overhead growth, including costs in customer service, production scheduling, inventory control, and laboratory work. Manufacturing overhead has essentially doubled since the shift in product lines. Management believes that large orders are being penalized and small orders are receiving favourable cost (and therefore selling price) treatment.
   Required:
   a. Would you expect quality to increase or decrease as a result of the shift in product lines? Explain your answer.
   b. Why would the shift in product lines have caused such major increases in overhead?
   c. Is it possible that management is correct in its belief about the costs of large and small orders? If so, why, and how might the accounting system be changed to reflect the changes in the business?

4. Activity-based management implementations appear to succeed better in organizations that want to become and are striving toward becoming world-class competitors. Companies that emphasize techniques such as total quality management, employee empowerment, and benchmarking seem to view ABM as a "natural fit" and believe these types of initiatives reinforce one another. One other key to success is the commitment and support of top management to these initiatives.

   Required:
   a. How might activity-based management and activity-based costing help a company in its quest to achieve world-class status?
   b. Would it be equally as important to have top management support if a company were instituting activity-based costing rather than activity-based management? Discuss the rationale for your answer.
   c. Assume you are a member of top management in a large organization. Do you think implementation of ABM or ABC would be more valuable? Explain the rationale for your answer.

5. After discussion with production and accounting personnel, you, as the chief executive officer, have made a decision to implement activity-based management concepts. Your goal is to reduce cycle time and, thus, costs. A primary way to accomplish this goal is to install highly automated equipment in your plant; in doing so, approximately 60% of your workforce would be displaced. Your company is the major employer in the area.

   Required:
   a. Discuss the pros and cons of installing the equipment from the perspective of your (1) shareholders, (2) employees, and (3) customers.
   b. How would you explain to a worker that his or her job is non-value-added?
   c. What alternatives might you have that could accomplish the goal of reducing cycle time without creating economic havoc for the local area?

COMMUNICATIONS ACTIVITIES

1. Many companies now recognize that their cost systems are inadequate in the context of today's powerful global competition. Managers in companies selling multiple products are making important product decisions based on distorted cost information, as most cost systems designed in the past focused on inventory measurement. To elevate the level of management information, current literature suggests that companies should have as many as three cost systems for (1) inventory measurement, (2) operational control, and (3) activity-based costing.

   Required:
   a. Discuss why the traditional cost information system, which was developed to measure inventory, distorts product cost information.
   b. Identify the purpose and characteristics of each of the following cost systems:
      i. Inventory measurement
      ii. Activity-based costing
   c. i. Describe the benefits that management can obtain from using activity-based costing.
      ii. List the steps that a company using a traditional cost system would take to implement activity-based costing.

2. Explain how activity-based costing differs from traditional costing methods.

PROJECTS

1. Obtain copies of annual reports for several companies that have recently adopted activity-based costing. Typically, the adoption of such techniques is discussed in the president's letter or the management discussion and analysis section. Read these portions of the annual reports. Write a paper that describes the objectives that company

officers commonly give for adopting activity-based costing and describe any other innovative techniques that are typically adopted along with activity-based costing.

2. Invite an expert on activity-based costing systems to address your class. Ask this individual about problems and successes he or she has observed following implementation of such systems.

3. Your firm has been experiencing increased costs associated with banking activities in recent years. The corporate treasurer asked for your team's help in identifying the activities that account for the majority of the firm's banking costs. Your team met and decided that the best way to proceed was to assign one member of the team to each of the two important banking functions: cash deposits and cash payments. Each person will identify the costs associated with his or her function and the respective cost drivers. Then, each member should make recommendations about changes that could be made to reduce the overall banking costs for the firm.

USING THE INTERNET

1. ABC Technologies, Inc. is a leading vendor of activity-based costing software. From its home page at www.abctech.com, you can link to sites that profile activity-based costing case studies. In groups of three or four, select case study applications of activity-based costing from different industries. (You may have to register for a "library card" to gain access to the case studies.) Prepare a brief summary of each of the case studies by identifying the motivation for using activity-based costing and the types of activities identified in the case.

2. Go to the Internet and find five companies that use ABC software. Describe the type of company that uses this methodology.

SOLUTIONS TO SELF-TEST QUESTIONS

1. a: ABC identifies the causal relationship between the incurrence of costs and activities. It determines the cost driver for each activity and applies the cost to products on the basis of resources consumed.

2. a: A cost driver is a measure of activity, such as direct labour hours, machine hours, etc. It is a basis used to assign costs to cost objects.

3. d: In an ABC system, cost allocation is more precise than in a traditional system because activities rather than functions or department are defined as cost objects.

4. b: ABC determines the activities associated with the incurrence of costs and then accumulates a cost pool for each activity using the appropriate activity base. If a company produces only one product, then all costs are assigned to the one product. It does not matter which method is used.

5. a: $50,000 is allocated over 10,000 hours (25 × 200 hours) + (25 × 200 hours). Overhead cost per hour is $5 ($50,000 ÷ 10,000 hours), and the per-unit overhead cost of ladies' umbrellas is $1,000 ($5 × 200 direct labour hours).

6. b: ABC allocates overhead on the basis of some causal relationship between the incurrence of cost and activities. Because the moves for umbrellas constitute 25% (5 ÷ 20) of total moves, the umbrellas should absorb 25% of the total materials handling costs, or $12,500 (25% × $50,000). The remaining $37,500 is allocated to men's umbrellas. The cost per ladies' umbrella is $500 ($12,500 ÷ 25).

7. a

8. a

9. a: 20 × $400 = $8,000 per batch. $8,000 ÷ 1,000 = $8.00 per unit.

10. c: Materials handling: $4 × 200 = $800
     Assembly $40 × 12 = $480
     Inspection $6 × 5 = $30
     $1,310 ÷ 100 = $13.10 per unit.

ENDNOTES

1.   Daniel J. McConville, "Start with ABC," *Industry Week*, September 6, 1993, p. 31.

2.   Frederick W. Lindahl, *Human Resource Planning, Activity-Based Costing Implementation and Adaptation*, Human Resource Planning Society, 1996.

3.   "Strong Advocate of Activity-Based Management Explains It All to You," *Cost Management Update*, Montvale, N.J., December 2001–January 2002.

4.   Robin Cooper and Regine Slagmulder, "Activity-Based Budeting, Part 1," *Strategic Finance*, Montvale, N.J., September 2000, pp. 85–86.

5.   H. Thomas Johnson and Robert S. Kaplan, *Relevance Lost*, Boston: Harvard Business School Press, 1987, p. 1.

6.   Joseph P. Naughton–Travers, "Activity-Based Costing: The New Management Tool," *Behaviuoral Health Management*, Cleveland, March–April 2001.

7.   James Reeve, "Projects, Models and Systems—Where Is ABM Headed," *Journal of Cost Management*, Summer 1996, p. 7.

8.   Tom E. Pryor, "Activity Accounting: Key to Waste Reduction," *Accounting Systems Journal*, Fall 1989, p. 34.

9.   Tim Minahan, *Purchasing*, September 4, 1997, p. 47.

10. Michael J. Kohl and Thomas Pagano, "Learn the ABC Basics," *Credit Union Management*, Madison, September 2000.

11. This hierarchy of costs was introduced by Professor Robin Cooper in "Cost Classification in Unit-Based and Activity-Based Manufacturing Cost Systems," in the *Journal of Cost Management*, Fall 1990.

12. Robin Cooper, "Cost Classification in Unit-Based and Activity-Based Manufacturing Cost Systems," *Journal of Cost Management*, Fall 1990, p. 6.

13. Vokurka and Lummus, "At What Overhead Level Does Activity-Based Costing Pay Off?" *Production and Inventory Management Journal*, Alexandria, first quarter 2001.

14. Harold P. Roth and A. Faye Borthick, "Are You Distorting Costs by Violating ABC Assumptions?" *Management Accounting*, November 1991, p. 39.

15. Reprinted by permission of Harvard Business Review. An excerpt from "The Four Faces of Mass Customization" by James H. Gilmore and B. Joseph Pine II, January–February 1997. Copyright 1997 by the president and fellows of Harvard College.

16. S. Praskey, *Canadian Grocer*, April 2001, V. 115(3), pp. 29, 32.

17. B. Joseph Pine II, Bart Victor, and Andrew C. Boynton, "Making Mass Customization Work," *Harvard Business Review*, September–October 1993, p. 108.

18. H. James Harrington, "Process Breakthrough: Business Process Improvement," *Journal of Cost Management*, Fall 1993, pp. 36, 38.

19. Edward Blocher, Betty Wong, and Christopher T. McKittrick, "Making Bottom Up ABC Work at Reichhold Inc.," *Strategic Finance*, Montvale, N.J., April 2002.

20. Mehmet C. Kocakulah and Douglas Dickmann, "Implementing Activity-Based Costing (ABC) to Measure Commercial Loan Profitability," *The Journal of Bank Cost and Management Accounting*, Volume 14, Issue 2, San Francisco, 2001, pp. 3–15.

21. Zeller, Siegel, Kaciuba, and Lau, *Healthcare Financial Management*, Volume 53, Issue 9, September 1999, pp. 46–50.

22. Gaaster, Slothuus, Larsen, Thayssen, Haghfelt, *Scandinavian Cardiovascular Journal*, 35, 2, 2001, pp. 80–85.

23. Hilary Becker, Carleton University, 2001.

24. Cost Management Group, Institute of Management Accountants, 4th Annual Activity-Based Cost Management Survey Results, *Cost Management Update*, February 1994, p. 14.

25. Robert S. Kaplan, "In Defense of Activity-Based Cost Management," *Management Accounting*, November 1992, p. 60.

26. Dan Senson, "The Benefits of Activity-Based Cost Management to the Manufacturing Industry," *Journal of Management Accounting Research*, Fall 1995, p. 173.

27. H. Thomas Johnson, "It's Time to Stop Overselling Activity-Based Concepts," *Management Accounting*, September 1992, pp. 31, 33.

28. Needy, Bidanda, and Gulsen, "A Model to Develop, Assess and Validate an Activity-Based Costing System for Small Manufacturers," *Engineering Management Journal*, Vol. 12, No. 1, March 2000.

Chapter 7

Controlling Costs

LEARNING OBJECTIVES

After reading this chapter, you should be able to answer the following questions:

1 Why
is cost consciousness of great importance to all members of the organization?

2 How
does a company determine from whom, how much, and when to order inventory?

3 What
is materials requirements planning, and how does it affect costs?

4 What
is JIT, and how does it affect costs?

5 What
is life cycle costing?

6 How
are target costing and value engineering used to manage costs? In which life cycle stage are these tools used?

www.aircanada.ca and www.westjet.ca
Air Canada and WestJet

Immediately after the September 11, 2001, destruction of the World Trade Center in New York, airline traffic declined around the world. In Canada, AIR CANADA and WESTJET had different reactions to the decline in air travel. Air Canada, a full-service airline, suffered operating losses and asked for government assistance. WestJet, a smaller, low-fare airline, did not report losses and did not ask for government assistance. The two airlines had different cost structures.

Despite having 65% of domestic air travel, Air Canada had maintained a market share mentality. Over two years previous to September 11, 2001, Air Canada and its regional arms copied virtually every route, frequency, and fare offered by the Calgary-based WestJet, losing hundreds of millions of dollars in the process. For example, in 2000 Air Canada offered flights between Calgary and Abbotsford, B.C., after WestJet started flying between the two cities. Air Canada likely lost money as its costs were 40% higher than WestJet's.

Air Canada took the battle with WestJet a step further by launching a separate low-fare airline in 2001 called Tango, to "stimulate the market, reduce costs and, above all, to enable customers to tailor their ticket price to their own pocketbook." Tango's mandate has been made easier by the demise of Canada 3000 in the fall of 2001. Tango serves many of the same domestic and trans-border routes as Canada 3000 did in the past.

Air Canada is a high-cost airline. Tae Oum, director of the Centre for Transportation Studies at the University of British Columbia, prepared a report in 2001 for the federal government that examined Air Canada's cost-competitiveness and productivity. He concluded that Air Canada was 25% less productive than the top nine U.S. carriers, despite having an advantage in labour costs because of the lower Canadian dollar.

The connection between productivity and earning power is evident when comparing Air Canada with WestJet. Air Canada operates with roughly 136 employees per aircraft. WestJet has 64 employees per aircraft. WestJet has a highly efficient workforce that is motivated through profit-sharing to reduce costs and increase profitability. Job descriptions are less rigid at WestJet, where after landing both pilots and flight attendants clean the cabin. This cooperation contributes to a faster turnaround at the gate, and more flying time means more revenue. The result is that Air Canada and just about every other airline lost money in September 2001, whereas WestJet was profitable. In October 2001, WestJet's market valuation was close to $1 billion, much more than the market value of Air Canada.

On April 1, 2003, Air Canada formally filed for protection from its creditors in order to change itself into a "lean, more efficient, lower-cost airline." The need to cut costs was not a surprise. Air Canada management had asked the unionized workers to accept lower wages and salaries. The workers were reluctant. One of the unions for the workers responded, "Air Canada pretends that its employees are at the root of its problems. We believe that Air Canada management—and federal inaction—are the root of Air Canada's problems." Bankruptcy is always too late and too drastic a technique for reducing costs.

SOURCES: Frances Fiorino, "Bleak Vista for Air Canada," *Aviation Week & Space Technology*, Vol. 155, Issue 20, November 12, 2001, p. 15; Peter Verburg, "Prepare for Takeoff," *Canadian Business*, Vol. 73, Issue 24, December 25, 2000, pp. 94–99; Peter Verburg, "Turbulent Times," *Canadian Business*, Vol. 74, Issue 20, October 29, 2001, pp. 72–77, Guy Dixon, "Air Canada Talks Fail in Anger," *The Globe and Mail*, April 2, 2003, p. B1.

*A*ny business wanting to succeed must not only generate reasonable levels of revenues but also control the costs that generate those revenues. For airlines, there is often limited control over fares—a competitor's price on a given route must usually be matched or the organization can lose market share. It is imperative for the organization's survival to determine ways to get a handle on costs. Organizational management quickly recognizes the interaction among cost control, efficiency, and profitability.

Previous chapters presented various ways to control costs. For example, control of direct materials and direct labour costs are typically linked to the development and implementation of job and processing costing systems. Outsourcing is another way to reduce costs. ABC identifies non-value-adding costs that can be eliminated. Future chapters discuss other cost-reducing techniques. Chapter 8 introduces standards or the setting of expectations for costs. Budgeting is discussed in Chapter 9, while capital budgeting is discussed in Chapter 10. Variance analysis or the comparison of actual costs to expectations in Chapter 11 is another technique for controlling costs.

This chapter focuses on six topics related to cost control. First, the importance of cost control consciousness is discussed. The desire among members of an organization to reduce costs on an ongoing basis is necessary for the effective use of all cost control techniques. Second, this chapter discusses economic order quantity (EOQ), a technique for reducing the cost of carrying inventory. Third and fourth, the effects of material requirements planning and just-in-time are discussed as further approaches for reducing inventory and other costs. Fifth, the life cycle of products and services is discussed as to the different opportunities for reducing costs. Sixth, target costing and value engineering are discussed as methods for controlling costs.

LEARNING OBJECTIVE 1

Why is cost consciousness of great importance to all members of the organization?

cost control system
a logical structure of formal and informal activities designed to influence costs and to enable management to analyze and evaluate how well expenditures were managed during a period

COST CONTROL

Cost control is an integral part of the overall organizational decision support system. A **cost control system** should provide information to managers for planning and for determining the efficiency of activities. As indicated in Exhibit 7-1, effective control can be exercised at three points: before, during, and after an event.

Managers alone cannot control costs. They must motivate and direct subordinates to want to control costs. An organization comprises a group of individuals whose attitudes and efforts should be considered in determining how an organization's costs may be controlled. Cost control is a continuous process that requires the support of all employees at all times. Good control encompasses not only the functions shown in Exhibit 7-1 but also the ideas about cost consciousness shown

Control Point	Reason	Cost Control Methods
Before an event	Preventive; reflects planning	Expectations:[1] standards; policies concerning approval for deviations; expressions of quantitative and qualitative objectives
During an event	Corrective; ensures that the event is being pursued according to plans; allows managers to correct problems as they occur	Periodic monitoring of ongoing activities; comparison of activities and costs against expectations and standards; avoidance of excessive expenditures
After an event	Diagnostic; guides future actions	Feedback; variance analysis; responsibility reports

EXHIBIT 7-1

Functions of an Effective Cost Control System

in Exhibit 7-2. **Cost consciousness** refers to an organizationwide employee attitude toward the topics of cost understanding, cost containment, cost avoidance, and cost reduction. Each of these topics is important at a different stage of the control system.

cost consciousness
an organizationwide employee attitude toward cost understanding, cost containment, cost avoidance, and cost reduction

Cost Understanding

Control requires that a set of expectations exists. Cost control is first exercised when an expectation for that cost is prepared, which can be done only when the reasons for periodic cost changes are understood. Expectations can be compared with actual costs. Knowing that variations occurred is important, but cost control can be achieved only if managers understand why costs differed from expected amounts.

Cost Differences Related to Cost Behaviour

Costs may change from previous periods or differ from expectations for many reasons. Some costs change because of their underlying **cost behaviour**. A total variable or mixed cost increases or decreases with increases or decreases in activity level. If the current period's activity level differs from a prior period's activity level or from the expected activity level, total actual variable or mixed cost will differ from that of the prior period or the total expected cost. For example, Air Canada's food costs (on meal-hour flights) will vary almost in direct proportion with the number of passengers. Total expected costs for Air Canada will be total meals multiplied by expected cost per meal.

cost behaviour
the manner in which a cost responds to a change in a related level of activity

EXHIBIT 7-2

Cost Control System

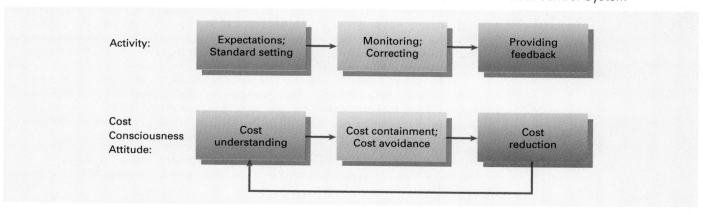

In addition to the reactions of variable costs to changes in activity levels, the following three factors can cause costs to differ from those of prior periods or from expected costs for the current period. In considering these factors, remember that an external price becomes an internal cost when a good or service is acquired.

Cost Differences Related to Quantity Purchased

A simple reason for an actual per-unit cost differing from expected is that the quantity purchased was different from what was expected. Firms are normally given quantity discounts, up to some maximum level, when bulk purchases are made. Therefore, a cost per unit may change when quantities are purchased in lot sizes different from those of previous periods or those projected. Involvement in group purchasing arrangements can make quantity discounts easier to obtain. For example in the News Note, Air Canada, which has problems with high costs as noted, joined with other airlines to form a B2B (business-to-business) buying group to improve purchasing and supply chain management. This venture is expected to reduce costs and improve performance. Air Canada has also outsourced its information technology operations to reduce costs.

Cost Differences Related to Inflation/Deflation

Fluctuations in the value of money are called general price-level changes. When the general price level changes, the prices of goods and services also change. General price-level changes affect almost all prices approximately equally and in the same direction, if all other factors are constant. An estimated cost of $150,000 might become an actual cost of $154,500 with an annual inflation rate of 3%.

Some companies include price-escalation clauses in sales contracts to cover the inflation occurring from order to delivery. Such escalators are especially prevalent in industries having production activities that require substantial time. For instance, according to Statistics Canada the consumer-price index, often used as a base for

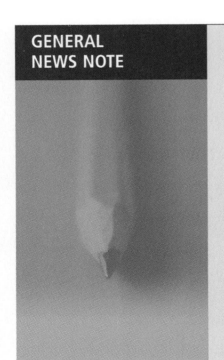

Do It Better Elsewhere!

Thirteen companies invested US$50 million in an Internet trading site project. Air Canada has brought together the collective purchasing power of its competitors to create a B2B marketplace for the airline industry. Aeroxchange will be an Internet-based trading site where the 13 companies including Air Canada, Northwest Airlines Corp., and FedEx Corp. can buy aircraft parts.

"Our objective was to create a marketplace with software that would allow us to improve our purchasing and supply chain management," said Bruce MacCoubrey, chairman of Aeroxchange and chief purchasing officer for Air Canada. Traditionally, airlines purchased parts and services through their own supplier agreements. MacCoubrey said Aeroxchange's goal is to provide better pricing for the things airlines need and ensure efficient delivery. "Our vision is to re-engineer that whole supply chain process by allowing airlines to work in a collective fashion to determine their requirements and then link up with vendors in a different way," MacCoubrey said.

At best, MacCoubrey expects that Aeroxchange will eliminate what has been an inefficient process. "The purchasing process was a largely manual interface, full of checks and balances. The whole process was not user friendly and didn't lend itself to the speed companies move at today. So one of the things that happens is people tend to avoid the purchasing process so we get a large amount of maverick spending," said MacCoubrey.

Source: Gary Hilson, "IBM, Air Canada Co-Development," *Computing Canada*, Vol. 27, Issue 17, August 10, 2001, p. 2. Reprinted by permission of *Computing Canada*, copyright © 2001, Transcontinental Media Inc.

negotiating wage and salary contracts, increased at the rate of 2.0% a year from 1991 to 2000.[2]

Cost Differences Related to Supply/Supplier Cost Adjustments

The relationship of the availability of a good or service to the demand for that item affects its selling price. If supply of an item is low but demand is high, the selling price of the item increases. The higher price often stimulates greater production, which, in turn, increases supply. In contrast, if demand falls but supply remains constant, the price falls. This lowered price should motivate lower production, which lowers supply. Therefore, price is consistently and circularly influenced by the relationship of supply to demand. Price changes for independent items are specific price-level changes, and these may move in the same or the opposite direction as a general price-level change.

Specific price-level changes may also be caused by advances in technology. As a general rule, as suppliers advance the technology of producing a good or performing a service, its cost to producing firms declines. Assuming competitive market conditions, such cost declines are often passed along to consumers of that product or service in the form of lower selling prices. To demonstrate the basic interaction of increasing technology and decreasing selling prices and costs, consider the greeting cards that play songs when they are opened. Those cards contain more computer processing power than existed in the entire world before 1950.[3]

Of course, when companies incur additional production or performance costs, they typically pass such increases on to their customers as part of specific price-level changes. Such costs may be within or outside the company's control. A cost factor that is within an organization's control is the necessity to upgrade computer systems to remain competitive. Sometimes, cost increases are caused by external factors. For instance, in November 2001, Air Canada announced it was cutting in half the special surcharge it had imposed since May of that year on all tickets to help pay for higher jet fuel prices, which had risen because of stronger demand and production constraints by OPEC producers.[4] However, with weaker demand during the summer of 2001 and the severe decline in air travel after the September 11 tragedy, jet fuel prices declined to where consumer groups were calling for removal of the surcharge. Interestingly, WestJet did not levy a surcharge. Similarly, on October 1, Canadian National Railways reduced its fuel surcharge to 2% from 4%, and then on November 1, General Motors also eliminated the 2% surcharge it paid to truckers who hauled its cars and auto parts.

The quantity of suppliers of a product or service can also affect selling prices. As the number of suppliers increases in a competitive environment, prices tend to fall. Likewise, a reduction in the number of suppliers will, all else remaining equal, cause prices to increase. A change in the number of suppliers is not the same as a change in the quantity of supply. If the supply of an item is large, one normally expects a low price; however, if there is only one supplier (or one primary supplier), the price can remain high because of supplier control. For example, with the demise in 2001 of Canada 3000, many air travellers were fearful that Air Canada would be more likely to increase air fares on transborder destinations where Canada 3000 was no longer flying.

In some cases, all other factors are not equal, and the quantity of suppliers may not affect the selling price of a good or service. Firms may unethically conspire to engage in **price fixing** or setting an item's price at a specified level. Buyers must

price fixing
a practice by which firms conspire to set a product's price at a specified level

vertical price fixing
collusion between producing businesses and their distributors to control the prices at which their products may be sold to consumers

horizontal price fixing
the practice by which competitors attempt to regulate prices through an agreement or conspiracy

cost containment
the process of attempting, to the extent possible, to minimize period-by-period increases in per-unit variable and total fixed costs

purchase the good or service at the specified price because no suppliers are offering the item at a lower price. Price fixing may be vertical or horizontal.

Vertical price fixing (also known as resale price maintenance) involves agreements by businesses and their distributors to control the prices at which products may be sold to consumers. All vertical price fixing is illegal. Companies may set suggested retail selling prices for items, but any attempts to prohibit retailers from selling below those prices are considered anticompetitive activities.

In **horizontal price fixing,** competitors attempt to regulate prices by agreeing on either a selling price or the quantity of goods that may be produced or offered for sale. Airlines, oil and credit card companies, and banks have all been accused of horizontal price fixing.

Although the preceding reasons indicate why costs change, they do not indicate what managers can do to contain the costs. Minimizing the upward trends means controlling costs. The next section discusses some concepts of cost containment.

Cost Containment

To the extent possible, managers should attempt to practise **cost containment** through minimizing period-by-period increases in per-unit variable and total fixed costs. Cost containment is generally not possible for increases resulting from inflation, tax and regulatory changes, and supply and demand adjustments because these forces occur outside the organizational structure.

However, costs that rise because of reduced competition, seasonality, and quantities purchased are subject to cost containment activities. A company should look for ways to cap upward changes in these costs. For example, purchasing agents should be aware of alternative suppliers for needed goods and services and determine which of those suppliers can provide needed items in the quantity, quality, and time desired. Comparing costs and finding new sources of supply can increase buying power and contain or reduce costs.

If bids are used to select suppliers, the purchasing agent should remember that a bid is merely the first step in negotiating. Although a low bid may eliminate some competition from consideration, additional negotiations between the purchasing agent and the remaining suppliers may result in a purchase cost lower than the bid

GENERAL NEWS NOTE

Pharmaceutical Cost Control in Canada: Does It Work?

The Canadian federal government responsibility for drug price control rests with the Patented Medicine Prices Review Board (PMPRB), an independent, quasi-judicial body. It is responsible for ensuring that prices charged by manufacturers of patented drugs are not excessive. The PMPRB reports to Parliament through the minister of health. "Excessive" is interpreted based on the following guidelines: (1) The price of an existing patented drug cannot increase by more than the Consumer Price Index (CPI). (2) The price of a new drug (in most cases) is limited so that the cost of therapy with the new drug is in the range of the costs of therapy with existing drugs in the same therapeutic class. (3) The price of a breakthrough drug is limited to the median of its prices in France, Germany, Italy, Sweden, Switzerland, Britain, and the United States. In addition, no patented drug can be priced above the highest price in this group of countries.

The PMPRB has been augmented at the provincial level by the use of generics, reference-based pricing, price freezes, and limits on markups. To a large extent, these measures have been effective in price control.

Source: Devidas Menon, "Pharmaceutical Cost Control in Canada: Does It Work?" *Health Affairs*, Vol. 20, Issue 3, May–June 2001, pp. 92–103. Republished with permission of Project Hope; Copyright Clearance Center, Inc.

Price Isn't Everything

INTERNATIONAL NEWS NOTE

All too often companies fail to operate their purchasing function in strategically consistent ways. They go after transaction price reduction instead of purchasing for maximum value or minimum total cost.

A recent example of this price mentality creating an undesirable situation was with a large multinational organization. In this case, the organization was relying heavily on the support of a technologically capable supplier to help develop a new product. The supplier invested months in this development effort—at no cost to the multinational. However, when the product moved into production and the purchasing department finally became involved in the process, the key raw materials were sent out for bids. The supplier who had helped with the development quoted a reasonable price, but it was not the lowest. As a result of purchasing's focus on price, the supplier lost the contract. The multinational obtained a lower price for the raw materials, but lost part of the technical capabilities needed for future product development. Furthermore, once into production, the alternative supplier's product fell short on a number of technical standards set during the development phase.

Source: Reprinted from an article appearing in the February 1996 issue of *CMA Management* magazine by Steven Mehltretter, with permission of Certified Management Accountants of Canada.

amount, or concessions such as faster and more reliable delivery may be obtained. Purchasing agents must remember that the supplier offering the lowest bid amount is not necessarily the best supplier to choose, as indicated in the above News Note. Additionally, reduced costs can often be obtained when long-term or single-source contracts are signed with suppliers.

Companies should be aware of the suppliers available for needed goods and services. New suppliers should be investigated to determine whether they can provide needed items in the quantity, quality, and time desired. Comparing costs and finding new sources of supply can increase buying power and reduce costs. Buying in bulk is not a new or unique idea, but it is often not applied on an extended basis for related companies or enterprises. In a corporation, one division can take the responsibility for obtaining a supplier contract for items (such as computer disks) that are necessary to all divisions. The savings resulting from buying a combined

Major airlines are acutely aware of the need to control meal costs of domestic flights. Some companies have reduced costs by eliminating "presentation frills," such as lettuce leaves under vegetables; others serve sandwiches rather than hot meals. Less likely to be reduced are the costs of food and beverages in first-class cabins.

quantity appropriate for all divisions could offset the additional costs of shipping the disks to the divisions.

An organization may circumvent seasonal cost changes by postponing or advancing purchases of goods and services. However, such purchasing changes should not mean buying irresponsibly or incurring excessive carrying costs. As discussed later in this chapter, the concepts of economic order quantities, safety stock levels, materials requirements planning, and the JIT philosophy should be considered in making purchases.

Cost Avoidance and Reduction

cost avoidance
a process of finding acceptable alternatives to high-cost items and not spending money for unnecessary goods or services

Cost containment can prove very effective if it can be implemented. In some instances, cost containment may not be possible but cost avoidance may be. **Cost avoidance** means finding acceptable alternatives to high-cost items and not spending money for unnecessary goods or services. Avoiding one cost may require that an alternative, lower cost be incurred. For example, WestJet does not provide meals to travellers, in order to offer bargain-basement fares. This lack of meals is not a burden to travellers as the flights are all relatively short.

cost reduction
a process of lowering current costs, especially those in excess of necessary costs

Closely related to cost avoidance, **cost reduction** means lowering current costs. Management at many companies believes that cost reduction automatically means labour reduction. For example, Air Canada sees its bankruptcy as a means of reducing labour costs. If Air Canada is to provide jobs, employees must take lower wages and salaries. The following quote provides a more appropriate viewpoint:

> Cutting staff to cut costs is putting the cart before the horse. The only way to bring costs down is to restructure the work. This will then result in reducing the number of people needed to do the job, and far more drastically than even the most radical staff cutbacks could possibly accomplish. Indeed, a cost crunch should always be used as an opportunity to re-think and to re-design operations.[5]

Sometimes cutting costs by cutting people merely creates other problems. The people who are cut may have been performing a value-added activity, and by eliminating them, a company may reduce its ability to perform necessary and important tasks. To reduce costs, unnecessary or non-value-adding activities should be eliminated and the efficiency of value-adding activities should be improved through automation or improved procedures.

Organizations are beginning to view their personnel needs from a strategic staffing perspective. This outlook requires departments to analyze their personnel needs by considering long-term objectives and determining a specific combination of permanent and temporary or highly skilled and less-skilled employees that offers the best opportunity to meet those needs. Contract employees are used if there are time limits to the demand for a skill. If an organization's workload fluctuates substantially, temporary employees (temps) can be hired for peak periods. Temps are also being hired to work on special projects, provide expertise in a specific area, or fill in until the right full-time employee can be found for a particular position. Temps may cost more per hour than full-time workers, but total cost may be reduced because organizations do not have to pay for benefits. Using temporary employees provides a flexible staffing "cushion" that helps insulate the jobs of permanent, core employees. Nevertheless companies should be sensitive to the needs of employees when making decisions to replace permanent employees with temporary employees. Temporary positions do not meet the needs of those who prefer permanent positions.

A starting point for determining appropriate cost-reduction practices is to focus on the activities that are creating costs. As discussed in Chapter 6 on activity-based management, reducing or eliminating non-value-added activities will cause the associated costs to be reduced or eliminated. Carrier Corporation, the world's largest producer of air conditioning and heating products, has instituted an effective activity-based costing and management system that is used, in part, to highlight areas that increase product costs and need to be cut. Carrier uses that system to "quantify the benefits of redesigning plant layouts, using common parts, outsourcing, strengthening supplier and customer relationships, and developing alternative product designs."[6]

Organizations may also reduce costs by outsourcing specific activities or services rather than maintaining internal departments. Information technology, internal audit, legal, travel, and accounting are all prime candidates for outsourcing. As indicated in Chapter 1, however, companies must make certain that they are not outsourcing core competencies or competitive advantage activities. Both cost savings and higher quality can be advantages of outsourcing.

Implementing Cost Control

Managers may adopt the five-step method of implementing cost control shown in Exhibit 7-3. First, the types of costs incurred by an organization must be understood. Are the costs under consideration fixed or variable, product or period? What cost drivers affect those costs? Has management committed to incurring the costs for the long term or the short term? Second, the need for cost consciousness must be communicated to all employees for the control process to be effective. Employees must be aware of which costs need to be better controlled and why cost control is important to both the company and the employees themselves. Third, employees must be educated in cost control techniques, encouraged to provide ideas on how to control costs, and motivated by some type of incentive to embrace the concepts. The incentives may range from simple verbal recognition to monetary

EXHIBIT 7-3

Implementing Cost Control

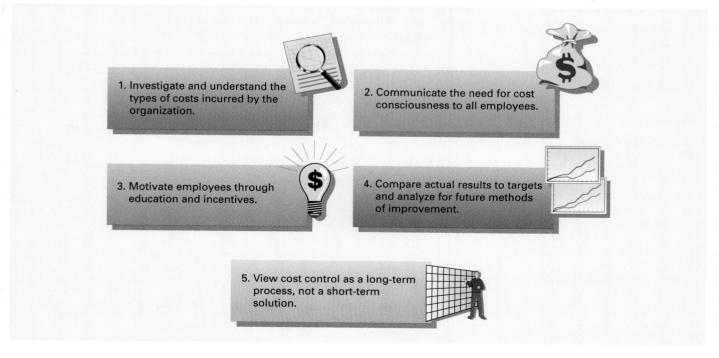

1. Investigate and understand the types of costs incurred by the organization.

2. Communicate the need for cost consciousness to all employees.

3. Motivate employees through education and incentives.

4. Compare actual results to targets and analyze for future methods of improvement.

5. View cost control as a long-term process, not a short-term solution.

rewards to time off with pay. Managers must also be flexible enough to allow for changes from the current method of operation. Fourth, reports must be generated indicating actual results, estimate-to-actual comparisons, and variances. These reports must be evaluated by management as to why costs were or were not controlled in the past. Such analysis may provide insightful information about cost drivers so that the activities causing costs may be better controlled in the future. And fifth, the cost control system should be viewed as a long-run process, not a short-run solution.

Following these five steps will provide an atmosphere conducive to controlling costs to the fullest extent possible as well as deriving the greatest benefit from the costs that are incurred. Expected future costs should be compared to expected benefits before cost incurrence takes place. Alternatively, future costs may be controlled based on information learned about past costs. Cost control should not cease at the end of a fiscal period or because costs were reduced or controlled during the current period.

LEARNING OBJECTIVE 2

How does a company determine from whom, how much, and when to order inventory?

ABC analysis
an inventory control method that separates items into three groups based on annual cost-to-volume usage; items having the highest dollar volume are referred to as A items, while C items represent the lowest dollar volume

MANAGING INVENTORY

To control costs, management needs to control its inventory outlays in a way that maximizes attention paid to the most important inventory items and minimizes attention paid to the least important items. Unit cost is commonly a factor in the degree of control that is maintained over an inventory item. As the unit cost increases, internal controls, such as access to inventory, are typically tightened, and a perpetual inventory system is more often used. Recognition of the appropriate cost–benefit relationships may result in an **ABC analysis** of inventory, which separates inventory into three groups based on annual cost-to-volume usage. Items having the highest dollar volume are referred to as A items, while C items represent the lowest dollar volume. All other inventory items are designated as B items. Exhibit 7-4 provides the results of a typical ABC inventory analysis: 20% of the inventory items account for 80% of the total inventory cost;[7] an additional 30% of the items, taken together with the first 20%, account for 90% of the cost; and the remaining 50% of the items account for the remaining 10% of the cost.

Once inventory items are categorized as A, B, or C, management can determine the best inventory control method for the items within each category. A-type inventory should require a perpetual inventory system. Such items are likely candi-

EXHIBIT 7-4

ABC Inventory Analysis

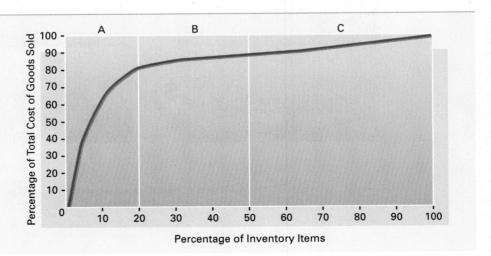

dates for purchasing techniques that minimize the funds tied up in inventory investment. The highest-level control procedures should be assigned to these items. Such a treatment reflects the financial accounting concept of materiality.

Controls on C-type inventory items are normally minimal because of the immateriality of the inventory cost. C-category items may justify only periodic inventory procedures and may use either a two-bin or a red-line system. Under a **two-bin system**, two containers (or stacks) of inventory are available for production needs. When it is necessary to begin using materials from the second bin, a purchase order is placed to refill the first bin. Having the additional container or stack of inventory on hand is considered reasonable because the dollar amount of investment for C-category items is insignificant. In a **red-line system**, a red line is painted on the inventory container at a designated reorder point. Both the two-bin and red-line systems require that estimates of production needs and receipt times from suppliers be fairly accurate.

For B-type items, the inventory system (perpetual or periodic) and the level of internal control depend on management judgment. Such judgment will be based on how crucial the item is to the production process, how quickly suppliers respond to orders, and whether the estimated benefits of increased controls are greater than the costs. Advances in technology, such as computers and bar coding, have made it easier and more cost beneficial to institute additional controls over inventory.

Costs Associated with Inventory

Most organizations engaging in a **conversion** process use both intangible and tangible inputs. For example, direct labour and other types of services are nonphysical and are supplied and consumed simultaneously. In contrast, raw materials are tangible and may be stockpiled for later use. Similarly, outputs of a manufacturing process may be stored until sold. The potential for physical items to be placed in or withdrawn from storage creates opportunities for managers to improve organizational effectiveness and efficiency relative to the quantities in which such items are purchased, produced, and stored.

Good inventory management relies largely on cost-minimizing strategies. As indicated in Exhibit 7-5 on page 390, there are three basic costs associated with inventory: (1) purchasing or production, (2) ordering or setup, and (3) carrying or not carrying goods in stock.

The **purchasing cost** of inventory is the quoted purchase price, minus any discounts allowed, plus shipping cost and insurance charges while the items are in transit. In a manufacturing company, **production cost** includes costs associated with buying direct materials, paying for direct labour, incurring traceable overhead, and absorbing allocated fixed overhead. Purchasing or production cost is recorded in Merchandise Inventory, Raw Materials Inventory, Work in Process Inventory, or Finished Goods Inventory.

The incremental, variable costs associated with preparing, receiving, and paying for an order are **ordering costs.** These costs include the cost of forms and a variety of clerical costs. Ordering costs are traditionally expensed as incurred. Under an activity-based costing system, however, these costs can be traced to the items ordered as an additional direct cost. Retailers incur ordering costs for all of their merchandise inventory. Manufacturers incur ordering costs for raw material purchases. If a manufacturer produces rather than orders a part, direct and indirect **setup costs** (rather than ordering costs) are incurred as equipment is readied for each new production run.

two-bin system
an inventory system in which two containers or stacks of inventory are available for production needs; when production begins to use materials in the second bin, a purchase order is placed to refill the first bin

red-line system
an inventory system in which a single container (or stack) of inventory is available for production needs, and a red line is painted on the inventory container (or the wall, for a stack) at a point deemed to be the reorder point

conversion
the transformation of organizational inputs into outputs

purchasing cost
the quoted purchase price minus any discounts allowed plus shipping charges

production cost
in a manufacturing company, includes costs associated with buying direct materials, paying for direct labour, incurring traceable overhead, and absorbing allocated fixed overhead

ordering costs
the variable costs associated with preparing, receiving, and paying for an order

setup costs
the direct and indirect labour costs of getting equipment ready for a new production run

EXHIBIT 7-5

Categories of Inventory Costs

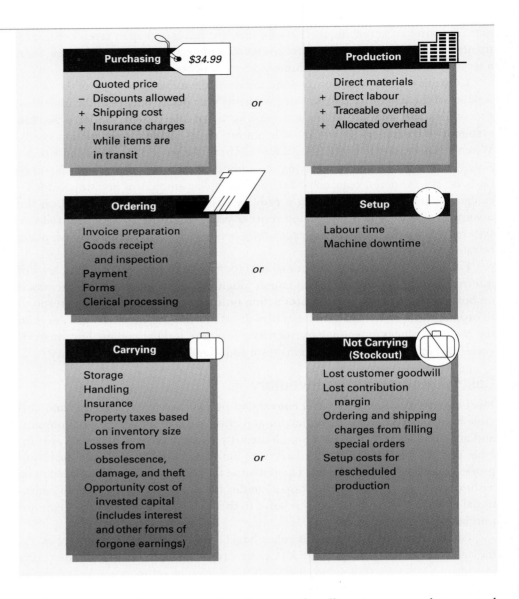

Inventory **carrying costs** consist of storage, handling, insurance charges, and property taxes based on inventory size. Because inventory is one of many organizational investments, it should be expected to earn a rate of return similar to other investments.[8] Carrying cost should include an opportunity cost for the amount invested in inventory. One additional opportunity cost that is often ignored is any possible loss that might result from inventory obsolescence or damage. Carrying costs can be estimated by use of information from various estimates, special studies, or other analytical techniques. Estimates of annual carrying cost in the range of 20% to 30% of inventory value are not unusual.

Although excess inventory generates costs, so can a fully depleted inventory. When a company does not have inventory available upon customer request, a stockout occurs. Stockout cost is not easily determinable or recordable. It is an opportunity cost that includes lost customer goodwill, lost contribution margin from not being able to fill a sale, and the ordering and shipping charges incurred from filling special orders.

All of the costs associated with inventory should be considered when purchasing decisions are made—and purchases should be made in reasonable quantities. The economic order quantity model is one technique that is often used to determine reasonable quantity. It is discussed later in this chapter.

Suppliers and Quantities

When buying inventory, a purchasing manager needs to make essentially three decisions—from whom, how much, and when. Each of these decisions depends in part on the relationship an organization has with its suppliers. In the past, the buyer–supplier relationship was generally viewed as adversarial; however, many companies are now viewing this relationship as a more cooperative, integrated partnership. Suppliers are stakeholders.

Which Supplier?

Traditionally, deciding from whom to buy was based primarily on price. A company found several firms that could provide the desired item and chose the firm offering the lowest price. However, the lowest-cost supplier in the short run is not necessarily the best supplier for the long run. The partnership approach views purchase cost in relation to quality and reliability, while taking a long-run perspective on the management of relationships with suppliers. Purchases are made from suppliers offering the most appropriate quality at the best overall price—and delivering in the most reliable manner—to prevent the necessity of having to return unfit goods, the creation of non-value-added paperwork, production delays, or the need to seek alternative suppliers.

Moving from the adversarial to the partnership view of buyer–supplier relations takes time, effort, and trust on the part of both entities. To accommodate such a partnership, changes must be made relative to contract agreements, quality, delivery, and conditions to communicate information openly.

In the traditional system, buyers would order large quantities of goods to obtain quantity discounts or to maximize usage of truck or other shipping container volumes. In contrast, in buyer–supplier partnership arrangements, order size is often considerably reduced and frequency of delivery increased. Long-term supplier contracts are negotiated, and then delivery reliability is monitored. Generally, suppliers missing a certain number of scheduled deliveries by more than a specified number of hours are dismissed. To comply with the need for frequent deliveries, it is desirable for vendors to be located close to the company, which helps to minimize both delivery time and shipping cost. Alternatively, overnight delivery services can be used. These services have recognized the critical nature of prompt delivery and have risen in importance in the business world. Managers of both buying and supplying companies are becoming well-versed in analyzing the cost–benefit relationship involved in using such services.

To build truly productive relationships, purchasing firms should help suppliers improve their processes to achieve reduced costs. Purchasing firms should also solicit information from suppliers about cost reduction possibilities related to new or existing products. Such an interchange of information and ideas requires that the partnership be built on a foundation of trust.

What Quantity?

After the supplier is selected, the firm must decide how many units to buy at a time. The objective is to buy in the most economical quantity possible, which requires consideration of the ordering and carrying costs of inventory. One tool used in this

economic order quantity
an estimate of the least costly number of units per order that would provide the optimal balance between ordering and carrying costs

decision process is the **economic order quantity** (EOQ) model. The EOQ model provides an estimate of the number of units per order that would achieve the optimal balance between ordering and carrying costs. The EOQ formula is

$$EOQ = \sqrt{(2QO \div C)}$$

where EOQ = economic order quantity in units
   Q = estimated quantity in units used per year
   O = estimated cost of placing one order
   C = estimated cost to carry one unit in stock for one year

The EOQ formula does not include purchasing cost, since that amount relates to "from whom to buy" rather than "how many to buy." Purchasing cost does not affect ordering and carrying costs, except to the extent that opportunity cost is calculated on the basis of cost.

In a manufacturing company, managers are concerned with "how many units to produce" in addition to "how many units (of a raw material) to buy." The EOQ formula can be modified to provide the appropriate number of units to manufacture in an economic production run. The economic production run quantity minimizes the total costs of setting up a production run and carrying a unit in stock for one year. In the economic production run formula, the terms of the EOQ equation are defined as manufacturing costs rather than purchasing costs:

$$\text{Economic production run} = \sqrt{(2QS \div C)}$$

where Q = estimated quantity in units produced per year
   S = estimated cost of setting up a production run
   C = estimated cost of carrying one unit in stock for one year

Assume that WPI purchases pulpwood for its production. The purchasing manager has found several suppliers who can continuously provide tonnes of the proper quality of pulpwood at a cost of $400 per tonne. Exhibit 7-6 provides information for use in calculating economic order quantity. The exhibit uses an estimate to show the total costs of purchasing 4,200 tonnes per year in various order sizes.

The EOQ model assumes that orders are filled exactly when needed, so when the order arrives, the inventory on hand is zero units. The average inventory size is half of the order size. The frequency with which orders must be placed depends on how many units are ordered each time. The total number of orders equals the total annual quantity of units needed divided by the size of the order.

Based on total costs, Exhibit 7-6 indicates that WPI's most economical order size is between 150 and 200 tonnes. The formula yields a value of 159 tonnes for the economic order quantity:

EXHIBIT 7-6

Yearly Purchasing Cost for Tonnes of Pulpwood

Quantity needed per year (Q) = 4,200 tonnes
Cost of ordering (O) = $30 per order
Cost of carrying (C) = $10 per tonnes

Size of order (tonnes)	50	100	150	200	300
Number of orders	84	42	28	21	140
Average inventory (tonnes)	25	50	75	100	150
Annual ordering cost	$2,520	$1,260	$ 840	$ 630	$ 420
Annual carrying cost	250	500	750	1,000	1,500
Total annual cost	$2,770	$1,760	$1,590	$1,630	$1,920

$$EOQ = \sqrt{(2QO \div C)}$$
$$= \sqrt{(2(4,200)(\$30) \div \$10)}$$
$$= 159 \text{ tonnes (rounded)}$$

The total annual cost to place and carry orders of 159 tonnes is $1,587, calculated as follows:

Number of orders (4,200 ÷ 159)	26.4	(rounded)
Average inventory (159 ÷ 2)	79.5	
Cost of ordering (26.4 × $30)	$ 792.0	
Cost of carrying (79.5 × $10)	$ 795.0	(rounded)
Total cost	$1,587.0	

Note again that this total cost does not include the $400 purchase cost per tonne.

Exhibit 7-7 shows graphically the costs relationships from the table in Exhibit 7-6.

The EOQ formula contains estimated values and may produce answers that are unrealistic. For example, it is not feasible to place an order that includes fractions of a tonne. And, WPI's supplier may only sell pulpwood in 10-tonne quantities. In that case, WPI will need to order 150 or 160 tonnes at a time. In most instances, small errors in estimating costs or rounding results do not have major effects on total cost. If the cost of ordering quantities close to the EOQ level is not significantly different from the cost of ordering at the EOQ level, some leeway is available in choosing the order size. Other factors, such as cash availability and storage space constraints, should also be considered.

As order size increases, the number of orders and the total annual ordering costs decline. At the same time, the total annual cost of carrying inventory increases because more units are being held in stock at any given point. Conversely, smaller orders reduce carrying costs but increase annual ordering costs.

EXHIBIT 7-7

Graphic Solution to Economic Order Size

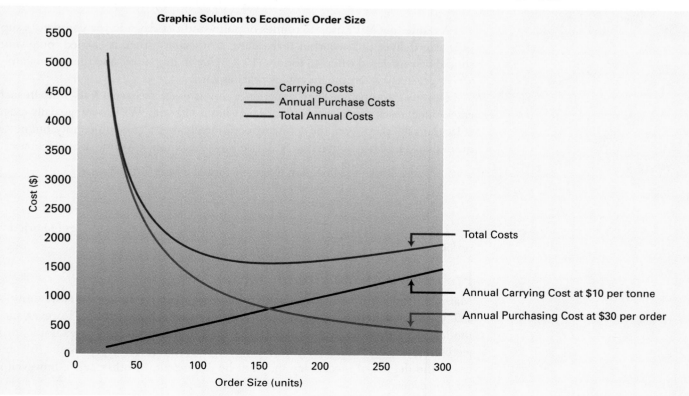

Companies are currently decreasing their order costs dramatically by using techniques such as electronic data interchange and open purchase ordering. A single purchase order, which expires at a set or determinable future date, is prepared to authorize a supplier to provide a large quantity of one or more specified items. The goods will then be requisitioned in smaller quantities as needed by the buyer over the extended future period.

Another development in this area involves carrying costs, which are increasing. Companies are using higher estimates of these costs in part because of a greater awareness of the high cost of non-value-added activities, such as move time and storage time for units that were purchased but not needed. As carrying costs rise, the economic order quantity falls. For example, if WPI's ordering and carrying costs were reversed and estimated at $10 and $30, respectively, the EOQ would be 53 tonnes of pulpwood.

When to Order?

order point
the inventory level that triggers the placement of an order

lead time
the time from the placement of an order to the arrival of the goods

safety stock
the quantity of inventory kept on hand by a company to compensate for potential fluctuations in usage or unusual delays in receiving orders

Although the EOQ model indicates how many units to order, managers are also concerned with the **order point**—the inventory level that triggers the placement of an order. Order point is based on usage, the amount of inventory used or sold each day; **lead time**, the time from order placement to order arrival; and **safety stock**, a quantity of inventory carried for protection against stockouts. The size of the safety stock for a particular item should be based on how crucial the item is to the business, the item's purchase cost, and the amount of uncertainty related to both usage and lead time. The optimal safety stock is the quantity that balances the cost of carrying with the cost of not carrying safety stock units.

When companies can project a constant figure for both usage and lead time, the order point is calculated as follows:

$$\text{Order point} = (\text{Daily usage} \times \text{Lead time}) + \text{Safety stock}$$

Assume that WPI uses 15 tonnes of pulpwood per day and the company's supplier can deliver pulpwood in three days. If no safety stock is carried, pulpwood should be reordered when 45 tonnes (15×3) are in inventory, and the order should arrive precisely when the inventory reaches zero.

However, companies often experience excess usage or excess lead time. In such cases, safety stock provides an inventory cushion. Although WPI's average daily usage is 15 tonnes of pulpwood, the company occasionally uses a greater quantity, but never more than 19 tonnes in one day. A simple way to estimate safety stock is as follows:

$$\begin{aligned} \text{Safety stock} &= (\text{Maximum usage} - \text{Normal usage}) \times \text{Lead time} \\ &= (19 - 15) \times 3 \\ &= 12 \text{ tonnes} \end{aligned}$$

Using this estimate, WPI would reorder pulpwood when 57 tonnes (45 original order point + 12 safety stock) were on hand.

Problems with the EOQ Model

Mathematical determination of economic order quantity and optimal quantity of safety stock will help a company control its investment in inventory. However, such models are only as valid as the estimates used in the formulas. For example, projecting costs such as lost customer goodwill may be extremely difficult. In some cases, the degree of inaccuracy may not be important; in other cases, however, it may be crucial.

The basic EOQ model determines what quantity of inventory to order. But there are at least three major problems associated with this model. First, identifying all the relevant inventory costs, especially carrying costs, is very difficult. Second, the model does not provide any direction for managers attempting to control the individual types of ordering and carrying costs. By considering only trade-offs between total ordering and total carrying costs, the EOQ model fails to lead managers to consider inventory management alternatives that might simultaneously reduce cost in both categories. Third, relationships among inventory items are ignored. For example, WPI might require 8 tonnes of pulpwood for each standard production run. If the EOQs for tonnes of pulpwood and the chemicals needed for each production run are computed independently, this interrelationship could be overlooked. WPI might find that, at a time when 96 tonnes of pulpwood are on hand (enough for 12 production runs), there are only enough chemicals on hand for three production runs. Computer techniques known as MRP and MRP II overcome this deficiency in the EOQ model by integrating interrelationships of units into the ordering process.

The most significant shortcoming of EOQ is the assumption that there is some optimal level of inventory. That assumption is contrary to the just-in-time approach to inventory, which assumes the optimal level of inventory to be no inventory. More will be said about just-in-time later in this chapter.

MATERIALS REQUIREMENTS PLANNING

LEARNING OBJECTIVE   3

What is materials requirements planning, and how does it affect costs?

MRP or **materials requirements planning** is a computer simulation system that was developed to answer the questions of what, how many, and when items are needed. MRP coordinates the future production output requirements with individual future production input needs using a master production schedule.

The master production schedule is developed from estimated sales information. Once projected sales and production for a product have been estimated, the MRP computer model accesses the product's bill of materials to determine all production components. Quantities needed are compared with current inventory balances. If purchases are necessary, the estimated lead time for each purchase is obtained from supplier information contained in an internal database. The model then generates a time-sequenced schedule for purchases and production component needs.

materials requirement planning
a computer simulation system that helps organizations plan by coordinating future production output requirements with individual future production input needs using a master production schedule

The master production schedule is integrated with the operations flow documents to project the workload for each work centre that would result from the master schedule. The workload is compared with the work centre's capacity to determine whether meeting the master schedule is feasible. Potential **bottlenecks,** or resource constraints, are identified so that changes in input factors, such as the quantity of a particular component, can be made. Then the MRP program is run again. This process is repeated until the schedule compensates for all potential bottlenecks in the production system.

bottleneck
resource constraint

A variation of the MRP system is known as **MRP II** or **manufacturing resource planning**. This fully integrated system plans production jobs using the usual MRP method and also calculates resource needs such as labour and machine hours. MRP II involves manufacturing, marketing, and finance in determining the master production schedule. Although manufacturing is primarily responsible for carrying out the master schedule, it is essential that appropriate levels of resource and sales support be available to make the plan work.

manufacturing resource planning
a fully integrated system that plans production jobs using the usual MRP method and also calculates resource needs such as labour and machine hours; involves manufacturing, marketing, and finance in determining the master production schedule

EXHIBIT 7-8

Push System of Production Control

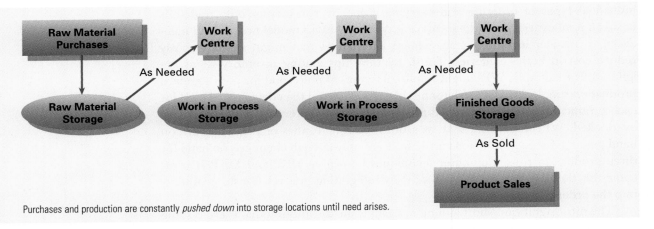

Purchases and production are constantly *pushed down* into storage locations until need arises.

push system
a production system in which work centres may purchase or produce inventory that is not currently needed because of lead time or economic order (production) quantity requirements; the excess inventory is stored until it is needed

The MRP models extend, rather than eliminate, the economic order quantity concept. EOQ indicates the most economical quantity to order at one time, and MRP indicates which items of inventory to order at what points in time. The EOQ and MRP models are considered **push systems** of production control because they may cause inventory that is not currently needed to be purchased or produced. Such inventory must be stored—that is, pushed into storage—until needed by a work centre. Exhibit 7-8 depicts the relationship of inventory to production processes in a traditional push production environment.

Many firms like WPI have achieved such significant benefits as reduced inventories, improved labour and space utilization, improved communications, and streamlined scheduling by using MRP and MRP II. In addition, companies report better customer service because of the elimination of erratic production and backorders. In contrast to the push system technology tools of EOQ, MRP and MRP II, just-in-time systems are based on a more recently emerging approach known as pull system technology.

LEARNING OBJECTIVE 4

What is JIT, and how does it affect costs?

JUST-IN-TIME SYSTEMS

Just-in-time (JIT) is a philosophy about when to do something. The *when* is "as needed" and the *something* is a production, purchasing, or delivery activity. The basic elements of the JIT philosophy are outlined in Exhibit 7-9. JIT tends to be used in larger organizations rather than small organizations because it works best when there are extensive repetitive operations. Small organizations tend to have one-off activities that cannot use JIT. In addition, regardless of the type of organization (retail, service, or manufacturing) in which it exists, a just-in-time system has three primary goals:

- Eliminate any production process or operation that does not add value to the product/service
- Continuously improve production/performance efficiency
- Reduce the total cost of production/performance while increasing quality

JIT manufacturing system
acquires components and produces inventory units only as they are needed, minimizes product defects, and reduces lead/setup times for acquisition and production

For example, a company using a **JIT manufacturing system** attempts to acquire components and to produce inventory units only as they are needed, to minimize product defects, and to reduce lead/setup times for acquisition and production.

- Inventory is a liability, not an asset; eliminate it to the extent possible.*
- Storage space is directly related to inventories; eliminate it in response to the elimination of inventories.
- Long lead times cause inventory buildup; keep lead times as short as possible by using frequent deliveries.
- Creative thinking doesn't cost anything; use it to find ways to reduce costs before making expenditures for additional resources.
- Quality is essential at all times; work to eliminate defects and scrap.
- Suppliers are essential to operations; establish and cultivate good relationships with them, including the use of long-term contracts.
- Employees often have the best knowledge of ways to improve operations; listen to them.
- Employees generally have more talents than are being used; train them to be multi-skilled and increase their productivity.
- Ways to improve operations are always available; constantly look for them, being certain to make fundamental changes rather than superficial ones.

*This paradoxical statement, that inventory is a liability, reflects the attitude that if a company is holding inventory for which there is no immediate demand or use, the company is unnecessarily incurring the carrying costs described in Exhibit 7-5. The statement also implies that there are creative ways of avoiding the costs of not carrying inventory, as described in Exhibit 7-5.

EXHIBIT 7-9
Elements of JIT Philosophy

Production was traditionally dictated by the need to smooth operating activity over time, which allowed a company to maintain a steady workforce and generate continuous machine use. However, smooth production often tends to build in buffer stocks of inventory and components. This process creates a just-in-case rather than a just-in-time scenario. It leads to work in process and finished goods inventories. Some of these inventories may never be needed.

In traditional systems, the various types of inventory—raw material, components, supplies, and work in process—were generally maintained at high enough levels to cover up for inefficiencies in acquisition or production. Exhibit 7-10 on page 398 depicts these inefficiencies or problems as rocks in a stream. The traditional philosophy is that the water level representing inventory should be kept high enough for the rocks (problems) to be deeply submerged, so that there will be smooth sailing in production activity. This technique is intended to solve the original problems, but it creates a new one. By covering up the problems, the excess inventory adds to the difficulty of making corrections. In other words, traditional or push systems result in excess inventories—with inherent storage and obsolescence costs—that create unnecessary or non-value-adding costs. The JIT manufacturing philosophy is to lower the inventory level, expose the problems, and eliminate those problems to the extent possible.

Just-in-time manufacturing has many names, including zero inventory production system (ZIPS), material as needed (MAN), and **kanban** (the Japanese word for *card*). The JIT system originated in Japan from the use of cards to control the flow of materials between work centres. In a JIT system, products are not produced until customers have demanded them; no manufacturing activity occurs unless the resulting product is needed by the next work centre in the production line. These factors make JIT a pull, rather than a push, system of production control.

In a **pull system** of production, parts are delivered or manufactured only as they are needed by the work centre for which they are intended. There are no storage areas to which unneeded work can be "pushed." Exhibit 7-11 on page 399 illustrates a pull system of production. Excess inventories do not occur and costs are reduced.

kanban
the Japanese word for *card*; another name for just-in-time manufacturing, which originated in Japan from the use of cards to control the flow of materials or units between work centres

pull system
a production system in which parts are delivered or manufactured only as they are needed

EXHIBIT 7-10

Traditional and JIT Production Philosophies

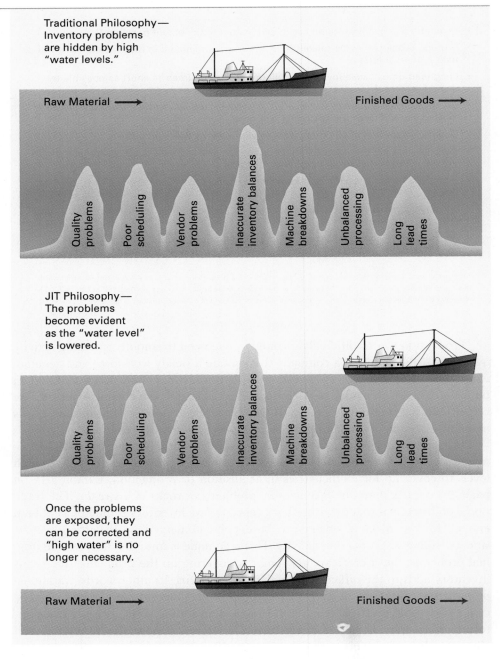

Traditional Philosophy— Inventory problems are hidden by high "water levels."

Raw Material ⟶   Finished Goods ⟶

Quality problems • Poor scheduling • Vendor problems • Inaccurate inventory balances • Machine breakdowns • Unbalanced processing • Long lead times

JIT Philosophy— The problems become evident as the "water level" is lowered.

Quality problems • Poor scheduling • Vendor problems • Inaccurate inventory balances • Machine breakdowns • Unbalanced processing • Long lead times

Once the problems are exposed, they can be corrected and "high water" is no longer necessary.

Raw Material ⟶   Finished Goods ⟶

Because JIT is a pull system, it depends on accurate market data, since a tight linkage is required between sales and production volume. Forecasted sales demand is the controlling production force. Once demand is estimated, the production schedule is set for an extended period (such as a month), and schedule changes should be minimal. Level scheduling creates a constant rate of use for component materials, labour, equipment, materials handling, maintenance, and support functions. Additionally, high-quality production processes are mandatory so that defects can be avoided. Slack time in the schedule is not treated as idle time. If workers are not needed for production activities, time is used for employee training, machine maintenance, and workplace organization.

JIT cannot be implemented overnight; Toyota took more than 20 years to develop its system and realize significant benefits from it. Although JIT techniques

EXHIBIT 7-11

Pull System of Production
Control

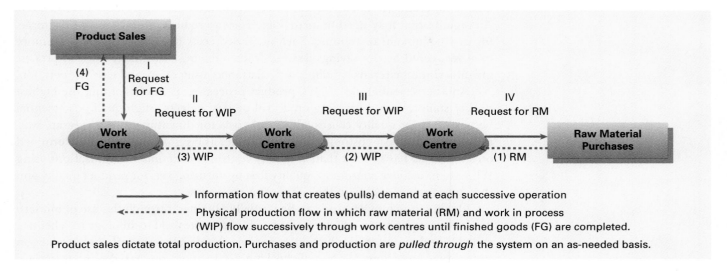

Information flow that creates (pulls) demand at each successive operation

Physical production flow in which raw material (RM) and work in process
(WIP) flow successively through work centres until finished goods (FG) are completed.

Product sales dictate total production. Purchases and production are *pulled through* the system on an as-needed basis.

are becoming better known and can be more quickly and easily implemented, the
most impressive benefits are normally reached only after the system has been operational for five to ten years. Exhibit 7-12 details some of the improvements experienced over a four-year period by *Oregon Cutting Systems* after implementing a JIT
program when such programs were beginning to gain popularity.

Any company that aims to achieve the JIT goals must change the majority of its
organizational functions. It must investigate the partnership-type purchasing
arrangements discussed earlier in the chapter. It must also address product design,
product processing, plant layout considerations, and employee empowerment.

EXHIBIT 7-12

Productivity Increases from JIT
at Oregon Cutting Systems

- Cut die change time from 6.5 hours to 1 minute and 40 seconds
- Cut space requirements by 40%
- Cut lead times from 21 days to 3 days
- Reduced floor space required for manufacturing between 30% and 40%
- Reduced setup time for a punch press from 3 hours to 4.5 minutes
- Reduced defects 80% with no increases in quality costs
- Reduced scrap, sort, and rework 50%
- Reduced work in process 85%
- Reduced manufacturing costs 35%
- Improved shipping productivity 90%
- Improved order turnaround time 10–14 days with a 75% order fill rate to 1–2 days
  with a 97% order fill rate
- Reduced product flow distance 94%
- Reduced lot sizes between 75% and 90%

Source: Republished with permission of the Institute of Management Accounting, from "Cutting Waste with JIT," Jack C. Bailes
and Ilene K. Kleinsorge, *Management Accounting,* May 1992; permission conveyed through Copyright Clearance Center. Inc.

Product Processing

In making processing improvements, one primary JIT consideration is to reduce machine setup time. Reducing setup time allows processing to shift more rapidly among different types of units, and makes the manufacturing process more flexible. An organization may need to incur some costs to reduce setup time—for example, for new equipment or training. Such increased costs have been found to be more than recovered by the savings derived from reducing downtime, work in process inventory, and materials handling, as well as increasing safety and ease of operation.

Another essential part of JIT product processing is implementing the highest quality standards and focusing on a goal of zero defects. High quality is essential because inferior quality causes additional costs for downtime, rework, scrap, warranty work, and lost customer goodwill. Under JIT systems, quality is determined on a continual basis rather than at quality control checkpoints. Organizations using JIT systems achieve continuous quality first by ensuring vendor product quality and then by ensuring quality in the conversion processes.

Quality in manufacturing can be partially obtained through the use of modern production equipment, which often relies on computerized technology to schedule, control, and monitor production processes. Some elements of the production system may be designed to be self-checking. In the most integrated systems, sophisticated computer programs monitor each process in the production stream and develop statistical data on the reliability of both components and processes. The data are then available for use in programs that design new products and processes, and in evaluating the reliability of components obtained from each internal and

INTERNATIONAL NEWS NOTE

Automatic Inventory Management System

Manufacturers have placed component purchasing at the top of their priority list in their efforts to reduce lead times, respond quickly to customers and their changing needs, improve quality, and increase efficiencies. The search for improved purchasing procedures has led to the development of the JIT II process, pioneered by Bose Corp.

In sales, purchasing, and material planning applications, the customer, planner, buyer, and supplier sales persons are replaced by an "in-plant" supplier employee who is empowered to issue customer purchase orders to his or her own organization. Supplier access and linkage to customer computers is also used. They also perform concurrent engineering with the customer engineering department from within the customer company. "Vendor managed inventory" and "automatic material replenishment" are other features of JIT II.

Rush Electronics Ltd. of Mississauga, Ontario, a components distributor, has put its own twist on JIT II. Called the R-Star system, Rush provides an effective way to routinely replace parts used in manufacturing with virtually no procurement cost for the transaction. Using the R-Star system, personnel can reduce inventory levels while eliminating stock-outs. Training time is almost zero.

The system uses a Kanban two-bin approach with bar-coded inventory bins. When one bin is empty, the bar code is simply scanned with a wireless bar code reader. After that, the R-Star system is fully automatic. The scanned data is collected and transmitted directly to the computer. An order is entered and shipping documents are prepared. Parts are picked from controlled and consigned inventory and shipped for delivery the following day. "For manufacturers, there's much more to the total expense of component procurement than just unit cost," says Rush Electronics president Kenneth Pulkonic. The R-Star JIT II system eliminates many of those hidden costs. It also fosters better working relationships because the distributor truly becomes a partner with the manufacturer. "When you're working with someone, you're on the same side of the table."

Source: "Rush Implements JIT II," *Canadian Electronics,* Vol. 14, Issue 1, February 1999. Reprinted by permission of *Canadian Electronics*.

external supplier. In the event that defective products are made, they should be promptly discovered and the problem that created them identified and corrected.

Often, the traditional cost accounting system "buries" quality control costs and costs of scrap in the standard cost of production. For instance, adding excess materials or labour time into the standard quantities creates a buried cost of quality. Such costs are often 10 to 30% of total production cost. Consider a company making a $10 product that has quality inspection and scrap costs of 10%, or $1 per unit. If that company's annual cost of goods sold is $10,000,000, its quality inspection and scrap costs are $1,000,000! When quality is controlled on an ongoing basis, costs of obtaining high quality may be significantly reduced. It is less costly in many manufacturing situations to avoid mistakes than to correct them.

Plant Layout

In an effective JIT system, the physical plant is arranged in a way that is conducive to the flow of goods and the organization of workers. Equipment is placed in a rational arrangement based on the materials flow. Such a layout reduces materials handling costs and the lead time required to get work in process from one point to another. Streamlined design allows people to see problems—such as excess inventory, product defects, equipment malfunctions, and out-of-place tools—more easily.

One way to minimize cycle time through the plant is to establish linear or U-shaped groupings of workers or machines, commonly referred to as manufacturing cells. A U-shaped manufacturing cell is depicted in Exhibit 7-13. These cells improve materials handling and flow, increase machine utilization rates, maximize communication among workers, and result in better quality control.

Manufacturing cells create an opportunity for workers to be cross-trained and thereby broaden their skills and deepen their workplace involvement. Training workers to be multiskilled is valid even in nonmanufacturing companies. For instance, USAA, a San Antonio, Texas, insurance and financial services company, consolidated its departments and trained its salespeople to handle every aspect of processing insurance policies after installing a huge network of automated equipment. The cost of training in such situations can be substantial, and workers often resent change. In the long run, however, employers have a more viable workforce, and workers seem to be more satisfied with their jobs. Additionally, companies may

EXHIBIT 7-13

Depiction of a Manufacturing Cell

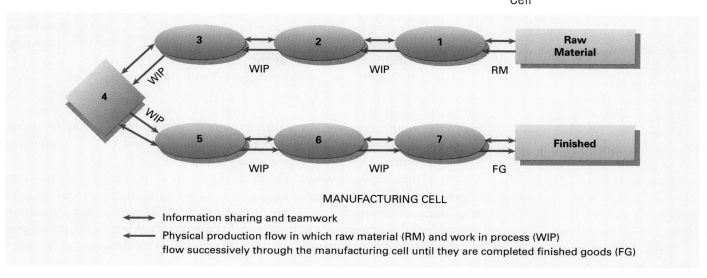

MANUFACTURING CELL

⟷ Information sharing and teamwork

⟵ Physical production flow in which raw material (RM) and work in process (WIP)
    flow successively through the manufacturing cell until they are completed finished goods (FG)

Having workers in linear groups means that there is less opportunity for backlogs to accumulate. Additionally, components or partially completed units do not have to be gathered in batches and moved to distant workstations within the plant.

find that workers, when they know more about the process as a whole, are better able to provide helpful suggestions about process improvement.

Employee Empowerment

An underlying feature of a just-in-time system and its emphasis on cross-training is the concept of employee **empowerment**. Employees can only be empowered if they have the abilities, tools, and training to perform tasks. They must be involved in organizational planning. Also, employees must trust management and be trusted by management. Given these factors, employees will be able to commit themselves to the pursuit of organizational goals and objectives. But before any employee empowerment can take place, the organization must be willing to invest resources in people and training activities.

empowerment
all practices that are designed to give workers the training, authority, and responsibility they need to manage their own jobs and make decisions about their work

Any business should recognize that the first condition of hiring and placement is to put the right people in the right jobs. Employees placed in jobs for which they do not have the appropriate skills are destined to fail. If workers do not have the necessary abilities when they are hired, the organization is responsible for making certain that they can acquire these abilities through training.

Training should not be limited to giving people basic competencies but should be an ongoing process designed to increase employees' knowledge and capabilities. Such training will improve both job quality and employee self-esteem. Employees who learn more are better able to perform their current tasks, analyze those tasks, and suggest methods for improvements. They are also better able to acquire new skills, and participate to a greater degree in organizational planning.

The organization must provide employees with the necessary tools—including equipment, information, and authority—to perform their jobs in a manner consistent with organizational objectives. Employees who use improperly maintained or ineffective equipment, who do not have the necessary problem-solving tools and information to investigate and correct problems, or who cannot effect solutions to identified problems are not empowered in their jobs.

At a minimum, involvement in organizational planning requires that employees be told of, and agree with, the business's basic strategy. However, true empowerment means that the company has flattened the organizational structure and pushed decision-making authority and responsibility down to the lowest reasonable level. Flatter structures are more flexible, allowing decisions to be made rapidly in response to need. When such structures exist, feedback must be provided to employees about their involvement and the impact of their decisions.

For empowerment to work effectively in an organization, there must be an atmosphere of trust among all employees at all levels. This element of empowerment is crucial and often difficult to obtain, because many organizations currently operate in an atmosphere of mistrust between managers and subordinates.[9] This mistrust creates a wide variety of fears: fear of making mistakes, fear of retaliation (including job loss), fear of being viewed as a troublemaker, fear of taking risks, fear of speaking out, and, very importantly, fear of change. Employees' fears can be eliminated only through development of mutual trust, which will allow the fears and their underlying causes to be confronted, analyzed, and resolved.

Overall, the just-in-time philosophy is more than a cost-cutting endeavour. It requires good human resource management and a dedication to teamwork. Exhibit 7-14 provides an action plan for implementing a JIT system.

It is important to note that just-in-time systems may not be appropriate for all types of companies. Companies whose raw materials or components are crucial to processing activities may be unable to afford the potential stockout cost of maintaining minimal inventories.

Finally, when there are unexpected occurrences, such as a rail strike, companies using a just-in-time system may face business closure or limited production for some time—even if they have arranged for alternative means of transport. We are currently seeing circumstances surrounding international conflict leading to long delays for motorists at the Canada–U.S. border. This makes JIT problematic (for example, for the automotive industry) because without predictable lead times, JIT cannot be effective.

The Two Most Important Relationships for JIT

Each organization tends to have a set of upstream suppliers and a set of downstream customers in its value creation chains. It is at the upstream and downstream interfaces of these relationships that real opportunities for improvement exist. By building improved cooperation, communication, and integration, these entities can treat each other as extensions of themselves. In so doing, they can enjoy gains in quality, output, and cost efficiency. Non-value-added activities can be reduced or eliminated and performance of value-added activities can be enhanced. Shared expertise and problem solving can be very beneficial. Products and services can be provided faster and with fewer defects, and activities can be performed more effectively and reliably with fewer deficiencies and less redundancy.

---

1. Determine how well products, materials, or services are delivered now.
2. Determine how customers define superior service, and set priorities accordingly.
3. Establish specific priorities for distribution (and possibly purchasing) functions to meet customer needs.
4. Collaborate with and educate managers and employees to refine objectives and to prepare for implementation of JIT.
5. Execute a pilot implementation project and evaluate its results.
6. Refine the JIT delivery program and execute it companywide.
7. Monitor progress, adjust objectives over time, and always strive for excellence.

Source: Gene R. Tyndall, "Just-in-Time Logistics: Added Value for Manufacturing Cost Management," *Journal of Cost Management*, Spring 1989, pp. 57–59. Reprinted by permission of Research Institute of America Group.

EXHIBIT 7-14

Seven Steps to Implement a JIT System

Consider the following opportunities for improvement between entities:

- Improved communication of requirements and specifications
- Greater clarity in requests for products or services
- Improved feedback regarding unsatisfactory products or services
- Improvements in planning, controlling, and problem solving
- Shared managerial and technical expertise, supervision, and training

All of the above can also be said for individuals and groups within an organization. Within the organization or work centre, employees have both an upstream supplier and a downstream customer who form the context within which work is accomplished. When employees see their internal suppliers and customers as extensions of themselves and work to exploit the opportunities just indicated, teamwork is significantly enhanced.

Backflush Costing

Accounting in a JIT system focuses on the plant's output to the customer.[10] Because each area depends on the previous area, any problems will quickly stop the production process. Daily accounting for the individual costs of production is no longer necessary; all costs should be at standard, since variations are observed and corrected almost immediately.

Further, since costs are more easily traced to their related output in a JIT system, fewer costs are arbitrarily allocated to products. Costs are incurred in specified cells on a per-hour or per-unit basis. Energy costs are direct to production in a comprehensive JIT system because there should be a minimum of downtime by machines or unplanned idle time for workers. Virtually the only costs still being allocated are costs associated with the structure (building depreciation, rent, taxes, and insurance) and machinery depreciation. By using more cost drivers, activity-based costing allocates manufacturing overhead costs to products more accurately than traditional cost accounting, which uses many fewer cost drivers.

Backflush costing is a streamlined cost accounting method that speeds up, simplifies, and reduces accounting effort in an environment that minimizes inventory balances, requires few allocations, uses standard costs, and has minimal variances from standard. During the period, this costing method records purchases of raw material and accumulates actual conversion costs. Then, either at completion of production or upon the sale of goods, an entry is made to allocate the total costs incurred to Cost of Goods Sold and to Finished Goods Inventory, using standard production costs.

Implementation of a just-in-time system can result in significant cost reductions and productivity improvements. But even within a single organization, not all inventories need to be managed according to a just-in-time philosophy. The costs and benefits of any inventory control system must be evaluated before management installs the system.

Exhibit 7-15 provides information on a product of the Bernard Company. This information is used to illustrate the journal entries for backflush costing. The company has a long-term contract with its supplier for raw material at $75 per unit, so there is no material price variance. Bernard's JIT inventory system has minimum inventories that remain constant from period to period. Beginning inventories for June are assumed to be zero.

Three alternatives are possible to the entries in Exhibit 7-15. First, if Bernard's production time was extremely short, the company might not journalize raw

backflush costing
a costing system that focuses on output and works backward through the system to allocate costs to cost of goods sold and inventory

Bernard Company's standard production cost per unit:

Raw material	$ 75
Conversion	184
Total cost	$259

No beginning inventories exist.

(1) Purchased $1,530,000 of raw material in June:

Raw and In Process Inventory	1,530,000	
Accounts Payable		1,530,000

Purchased material at standard cost under a long-term agreement with supplier.

(2) Incurred $3,687,000 of conversion costs in June:

Conversion Costs	3,687,000	
Various accounts		3,687,000

Record conversion costs. Various accounts include wages payable for direct and indirect labour, accumulated depreciation, supplies, etc.

(3) Completed 20,000 units of production in June:

Finished Goods (20,000 × $259)	5,180,000	
Raw and In Process Inventory (20,000 × $75)		1,500,000
Conversion Costs (20,000 × $184)		3,680,000

(4) Sold 19,800 units on account in June for $420:

(a) Cost of Goods Sold (19,800 × $259)	5,128,200	
Finished Goods		5,128,200
(b) Accounts Receivable (19,800 × $420)	8,316,000	
Sales		8,316,000

Ending Inventories:

Raw and In Process ($1,530,000 – $1,500,000)	$30,000
Finished Goods ($5,180,000 – $5,128,200)	51,800

In addition, there are underapplied conversion costs of $7,000 ($3,687,000 – $3,680,000).

EXHIBIT 7-15
Backflush Costing

INTERNATIONAL NEWS NOTE

Simplify or Computerize?

Should a company simplify operations or computerize? An example of each is provided.

Lantech Inc. chose to simplify. The Lantech plant is running on technology that could have been installed 40 years ago. And instead of computers, Lantech's managers use basic visual aids like cue cards (to indicate when to order new supplies) and tape (to indicate the direction of the production flow). Simplification has increased Lantech's productivity by almost 100% since the company scuttled its computerized system in 1992. Lantech changed production from a "hurry-up-and-wait pattern," in which inventory was transferred in batches from one part of the plant to another, into a method that consists of several production cells. Each of those cells is responsible for all the processes—sawing, welding, electrical wiring—once spread throughout the whole plant. The use of cells has allowed an increase in the attention given to each step, both because more people are involved and because the smaller line configuration has enabled each person to see what the others are doing. Inventory cards were placed on the bottoms of storage bins; when a card becomes visible, it is picked up and an order is faxed to the supplier. With the new system, Lantech makes one set of parts at a time, fabricating them as directed by actual orders rather than by projections.

Computerization has been selected by Dell Computer Corporation to make its inventories traceable and trackable throughout its entire logistical operations, even with outsourced activities. Executing a supply chain with full visibility gives Dell better information and a more flexible system. By producing custom products at a rapid pace, Dell receives payments from customers before it pays suppliers. Dell can do this only if there is a very short time lapse between receiving and shipping an order. Dell's customers are able to track their own order, from assembly and testing to shipment. The Dell system requires substantial investment in information technology. Every step needs to be connected (e.g., truck drivers report deliveries by wireless technology).

Sources: Erin Crawford, "The Best Way from Here to There," *Des Moines Business Record*, Vol. 17, Issue 12, March 19, 2001, pp. 12–13; Fred Hapgood, "Keeping It Simple," *Inc. Technology*, 1996, No. 1, pp. 66–72.

materials purchases until completion of production. In that case, entries (1) and (3) from Exhibit 7-15 could be combined as follows:

Raw and In Process Inventory	30,000	
Finished Goods	5,180,000	
Accounts Payable		1,530,000
Conversion Costs		3,680,000

If goods were immediately shipped to customers on completion, Bernard could use a second alternative, in which entries (3) and (4a) from Exhibit 7-15 could be combined in the following manner to complete and sell the goods:

Finished Goods	51,800	
Cost of Goods Sold	5,128,200	
Raw and In Process Inventory		1,500,000
Conversion Costs		3,680,000

The third alternative reflects the ultimate JIT system, in which only one entry is made to replace entries (1), (3), and (4a) in Exhibit 7-15. For Bernard, this entry would be:

Raw and In Process Inventory (minimal overpurchases)	30,000	
Finished Goods (minimal overproduction)	51,800	
Cost of Goods Sold	5,128,200	
Accounts Payable		1,530,000
Conversion Costs		3,680,000

Note that in all cases, entry (2) is not affected. All conversion costs must be recorded as incurred, or accrued at the end of a period, because of their effect on a variety of accounts.

LEARNING OBJECTIVE 5

What is life cycle costing?

LIFE CYCLE COSTING

The product life cycle is a significant consideration in executing an organization's planning and control functions regarding product costs and other costs. The stage a product has reached in its life cycle significantly affects sales volume, price, and costs. Both revenues and costs for a given product change as it advances through the development, introduction, growth, maturity, and harvest stages.

Total revenues are nonexistent during the development stage and commence during introduction. They typically rise during growth, level off in maturity, and decline during harvest. In contrast, costs are characteristically high during development and introduction and tend to stabilize as production becomes routine. Rigorous product development and design efforts are usually worthwhile because 80% to 90% of a product's life cycle cost is determined by decisions made before production begins.

Products and services, like people, go through a series of life cycle stages. It is not easy to determine how old a product must be before it moves from one stage to another. Some products, such as the hula hoop, come and go fairly quickly; others, such as Barbie and Ken dolls, have changed minimally and managed to remain popular products. Still other products, such as bell-bottoms and miniskirts, have been revitalized and have come back with renewed vigour. Services, too, change over time. For instance, 25 years ago personal financial planning and home health-care services were in their infancy, and long-distance bus service was beginning to decline in importance. Today, long-term care insurance is making its debut. It is difficult, if not impossible, to predict what services will be available in 2015.

Fashion trends seem to run through the product life cycle over and over again. However, changes do occur relative to colours, patterns, and fabric usage.

The stages of the product life cycle are development, introduction, growth, maturity, and harvest; relative sales levels for these stages are shown in Exhibit 7-16. Organizations must be aware of the life cycle stage at which each of their products has arrived, because the stage may have a tremendous impact on costs, sales, and pricing strategies.

Development Stage

If products are designed properly, they should require few engineering changes after being released to production. Each time an engineering change is made, one or more of the following activities occur, creating additional costs: the operations flow document must be reprinted, workers must relearn tasks, machine dies or setups must be changed, and parts currently ordered or in stock may be made obsolete. As indicated in Exhibit 7-17 on page 408, if cost and time to market are not to be affected significantly, any design changes must be made early in the process.

Products need to be designed to use the smallest number of parts, and parts should be standardized to the greatest extent possible. Consumers may appreciate some degree of variety, but a company can end up with too much of a good thing; for example, "at one point, Nissan had 300 different ashtrays in its cars."[11] Changes

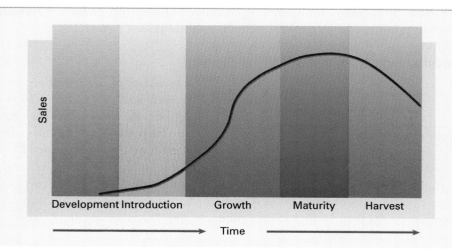

EXHIBIT 7-16
Product Life Cycle

EXHIBIT 7-17

Design Change Effects on Cost and Time to Market

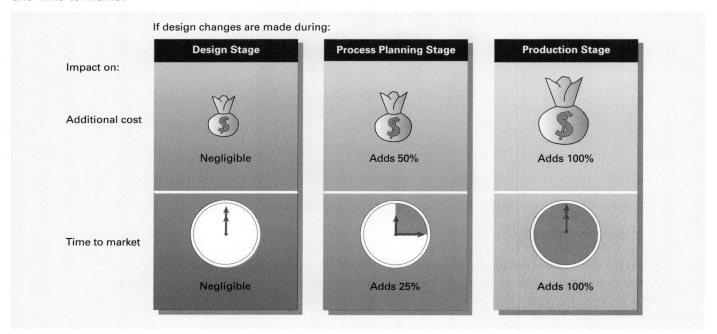

If design changes are made during:

	Design Stage	Process Planning Stage	Production Stage
Additional cost	Negligible	Adds 50%	Adds 100%
Time to market	Negligible	Adds 25%	Adds 100%

Impact on:

Source: Reprinted from the 1992 issue of *BusinessWeek/Reinventing America* by special permission. Copyright (1992) by The McGraw-Hill Companies.

can be made after original design, but any cost savings generated by such changes will be substantially less than if the changes had been made early in the design/development process.

Decisions made during the development stage are particularly important. They can affect product sales, design, production costs, and quality for the remainder of the product's life cycle.

Introduction Stage

Product introduction is essentially a startup phase. Sales are usually quite low, and selling prices often are set according to the market price of similar substitute goods or services, if such goods or services are available. Costs can be quite substantial in the introduction phase, however. Costs incurred during this phase are typically related to product design, market research, advertising, and promotion.

Growth, Maturity, and Harvest Stages

The growth stage begins when the product first breaks even. During the growth stage, the product has been accepted by the market, and profits begin to rise. Product quality also may improve during this stage because competitors may have improved on original production designs. Prices are fairly stable during this period because many substitutes exist or because consumers have become attached to the product and are willing to pay a particular price for it rather than buy a substitute.

In the maturity stage, sales begin to stabilize or slowly decline, and firms often compete on the basis of selling price. Costs are often at their lowest level during this period, so profits may be high. Some products, like Kool-Aid and Jell-O, seem to remain at this stage forever.

The harvest (decline) stage reflects waning sales. During the harvest stage, prices are often cut dramatically to stimulate business. As the name implies, management usually attempts to generate as much short-term profit and cash flow as possible at this stage.

Cost and Price Changes Over Life

Customers are concerned with obtaining a high-quality product or service for a price they perceive to be reasonable. Product prices change, however, over the product life cycle. Producers of goods and providers of service should be concerned with maximizing profits over a product's or service's life cycle because, to be profitable, the product or service must generate revenues in excess of its total (not single period-by-period) costs.

Because each stage of the product life cycle influences sales and costs differently, each requires its own expected cost focus. Then, as activities take place and plans are implemented, a monitoring system needs to be in place to capture sales and costs and compare them to an appropriately prepared expectation for each particular life cycle stage. Such a comparison provides feedback so that managers will have the information by which to direct activities to achieve desired results throughout each stage of the product life cycle.

Reducing time to market is merely one of many ways a company can reduce costs; other ways are listed in Exhibit 7-18. Getting products to market quickly and profitably requires a compromise between the advantages associated with speed of product innovation and superior product design. Rapid time to market may mean that a firm incurs costs associated with design flaws (such as the costs of future changes) that could have been avoided if more time had been allowed for the product's development. Also, if a flawed product is marketed, some costs will likely be incurred for returns, warranty work, or customer skepticism regarding the firm's reputation for product quality.

Another aspect of an organization's operating environment is supplier relations. Many companies that have formed long-term alliances with suppliers have found such relationships to be effective cost control mechanisms. For example, by involving suppliers early in the design and development stage of new products, a better design for manufacturability will be achieved and the likelihood of meeting target costs will be improved.

- Develop new production processes.
- Capture learning curve and experience effects.
- Increase capacity utilization.
- Focus factory arrangements to reduce coordination costs.
- Design for manufacturability to reduce assembly time, training costs, warranty costs, and required number of spare parts.
- Design for logistical support.
- Design for reliability.
- Design for maintainability.
- Adopt advanced manufacturing technologies to reduce inventory levels, production floor space, defects, rework, and quality costs.

Source: Adapted from Gerald I. Susman, "Product Life Cycle Management," *Journal of Cost Management*, Summer 1989, pp. 8–22. Reprinted by permission of Research Institute of America Group.

EXHIBIT 7-18

Actions to Substantially Reduce Product Costs and Improve Performance

target costing
a process of determining an allowable cost for a product or component that is inferred from projecting a market price for the product and subtracting a required profit margin

TARGET COSTING

Target costing, shown on the right-hand side of Exhibit 7-19, is a process of determining an allowable cost for a product or component that is inferred from projecting a market price for the product and subtracting a required profit margin. This method originated in Japan. As market price is the starting point in target costing, and market price equates to a customer's valuation of the value creation chain output, target costing is a customer-driven analysis. By subtracting the required profit margin from the estimated market price, the allowance for the total cost for research and development, product design, manufacturing, marketing, distribution, and customer service is determined.

In developing products to market, Western manufacturers have traditionally confined their approach to the following sequence: a product is designed, its costs are determined, and a selling price is set, based to some extent on the costs involved. If the market will not bear the resulting selling price, either the company does not make as much profit as it had hoped or it attempts to lower production costs. This process is illustrated on the left-hand side of Exhibit 7-19.

Let us consider a target costing example. Suppose a car assembler decides to introduce a sub-compact car to compete with the existing sub-compacts of the other automotive assemblers, domestic and imports. After careful consideration of the market and existing sub-compacts, a spot in the lineup and features are chosen that suggest a wholesale price of $14,000 to dealers. With the expected profit margin on sales of, say, 18%, this means all costs need to be $11,480 per unit ($14,000 × (1.00 − 0.18)). Thus, over the planned lifetime of the car, the total costs need to be $11,480 per unit. These total costs include all costs for research and development, product design, manufacturing, marketing, distribution, and customer service. To succeed in meeting the requirements of expected customers and the financial performance requirements of the organization, the proposed sub-compact needs to be produced for the target cost of $11,480. The profit margin is expected to be $2,520 (14,000 − 11,480 or 0.18 × 14,000).

The implied maximum, or target cost, is compared with the expected product cost. If the target cost is less than the expected cost, the organization has several alternatives. First, the product design or production process can be changed to reduce costs. Preparation of cost tables helps in determining how such adjustments can be made. These tables are databases that provide information about how using different input resources, manufacturing processes, and design specifications would affect product costs. Second, a less-than-desired profit margin can be accepted. Third, the organization can decide that it does not want to enter this particular product market at the current time because it cannot generate the profit margin it desires.

To reduce estimated costs, both production processes and production components can be examined. For those components that are produced in-house, outsourcing may be considered if the components can be purchased at a lower cost. For those parts that are purchased from vendors, negotiation with vendors may lead to price concessions; alternatively, vendors may collaborate in redesigning the product so that the cost of components or conversion processes can be reduced.

The degree to which target costing techniques are used is affected by the type of product being manufactured. As product cost and complexity increase and as the production stage of the life cycle is shortened because of changing consumer preferences, target costing becomes more important, because proper design can generate greater potential savings.

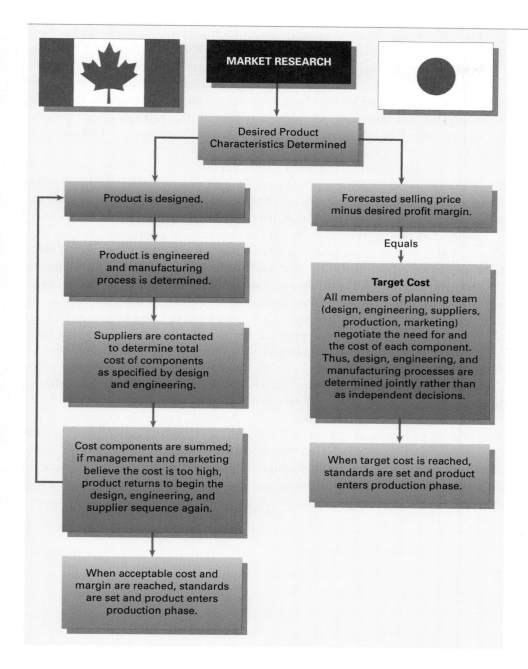

EXHIBIT 7-19
Developing Product Costs

Value Engineering

Value engineering works in tandem with a target costing system. For value
engineering to be applied, the total value (price) of the finished product must be
decomposed into the various functions of the product. Product functions are
the product/service design features that deliver value to the customer. Collectively,
the values of the individual functions equal the value of the product. To illustrate,
the value of an automobile can be decomposed into values for the following functions: basic transportation, air conditioning, power steering, power brakes, power
seats, safety equipment, towing capacity, warranty terms, fuel economy, sound
system, etc.

value engineering
a tool used to manage the relationship between product design,
product price, and target cost

Once the customer value associated with each function has been determined, the cost of each function is estimated. The cost of each function consists of the costs of buying or making the component parts, plus the costs of assembly and installation. With estimates of both the value and cost of each function in hand, managers can identify those functions that have poor value-to-cost relationships. It is these functions that will be subject to further scrutiny in the product design process because the object of value engineering is to improve the value-to-cost relationship so that the target profit can be realized.

By pushing the cost analysis down to the function level, the design and conversion processes required for individual product components can be scrutinized. For the accountant, determining the cost of individual functions can require application of advanced cost techniques such as activity-based costing and cost driver analysis.

Value engineering leads to exchanges of information among the firm, its vendors, and its customers. Customer input is necessary to determine the value of functions; vendors must be involved to determine the cost of purchased components, to generate ideas on alternative product and component designs, and to identify engineering constraints. Functions that cannot be delivered to the customer at an acceptable value-to-cost relationship, despite all efforts to lower cost, may be considered for elimination from the product. For supplier/customer firms that have long-term relationships, it is possible to develop more formal information systems that combine information.

The **survival triplet** in Exhibit 7-20 consists of three dimensions that define a product: cost/price (internal cost structure/external selling price), quality (conformity to specifications), and functionality (what it does).[12] In considering the adoption of generic strategies—cost leadership and differentiation—the survival triplet indicates that only products with acceptable values along each of the three dimensions stand a chance of continuing. The survival range for each dimension is defined by determining the minimum and maximum values that each dimension can have for the product to be successful. To survive, the company must operate competitively within those ranges.

survival triplet
the cost/price, quality, and functionality that products need to demonstrate in order to survive and prosper

EXHIBIT 7-20
The Survival Triplet

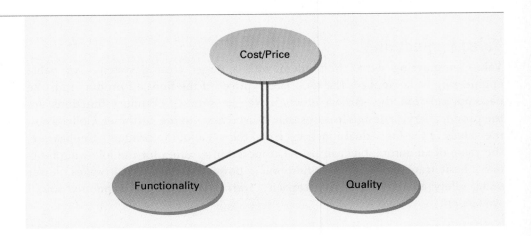

WestJet and Southwest Airlines

WestJet was modelled after Southwest Airlines, the most consistently profitable airline ever. Clive Beddoe, WestJet president and CEO, insists that WestJet's extraordinary performance is due to its corporate culture, "The entire environment is conducive to bringing out the best in people ... [it is] the culture that creates the passion to succeed."

WestJet gives workers a high degree of latitude to perform their jobs without interference. Standards and expectations are set, with employees determining how to meet those expectations.

For example, flight attendants are only asked to serve customers in a caring, positive, and cheerful manner, with the rest left to their discretion. The benefits of WestJet's approach to management are substantial. First, the enormous layer of supervision can be avoided. Second, there is a higher level of productivity per person. Third, employees share in the profits, which makes them responsive to cost control.

Beddoe admits that there is one thing that could spoil WestJet—unionized employees. In contrast to this anti-union attitude at WestJet, Southwest is unionized, and that has not impeded its success. Southwest has been successful because it invested in relationships, not only with frontline employees, but with its unions and supervisors. It makes you think, the most successful and best managed airline—Southwest—is not troubled by its unions. Union relationships need to be managed just like those with all other stakeholders.

With the announcement of Air Canada's bankruptcy on April 1, 2003, WestJet's strategy has been validated. However, a leaner, meaner Air Canada may be a more capable competitor for WestJet.

Sources: Peter Verburg, "Prepare for Takeoff," *Canadian Business,* Vol. 73, Issue 24, December 25, 2000, pp. 94–99; Jody Hoffer Gittell, "Investing in Relationships," *Harvard Business Review*, Vol. 79, Issue 6, June 2001, pp. 28+.

CHAPTER SUMMARY

Cost control is essential to an organization's long-run success. Effective cost control encompasses efforts before, during, and after a cost is incurred. Regardless of the type of cost involved, managers and other employees must exercise attitudes of cost consciousness to provide the best base for cost control. Cost consciousness reflects employees' predisposition toward cost understanding, cost containment, cost avoidance, and cost reduction.

Another type of cost control is the careful management of inventory. There are a number of available techniques. Classifying inventory into ABC categories allows management to establish controls over inventory items that are related to the cost and volume of inventory items. A-category items require good inventory controls and usually are accounted for using a perpetual inventory system. Two-bin and red-line systems are acceptable for C-category inventory items because of the limited financial investment that they involve.

Costs associated with inventory can be significant for any company, and sound business practices seek to limit the amounts of those costs. Inventory costs include the costs of purchasing, ordering, carrying, and not carrying inventory. The economic order quantity (EOQ) model determines the purchase order size that minimizes, in total, the costs of ordering and carrying inventory. (This model can also be adapted to find the most economical production run.)

The EOQ model ignores relationships among product components. To overcome this shortcoming, materials requirements planning (MRP) can be used to generate master production and time-sequenced purchasing schedules. Manufacturing resource planning (MRP II) implements MRP on a companywide basis and includes top management input. Both MRP models reflect a push system of production control dictated by delivery lead times and EOQ requirements. Purchased and produced goods must be stored until needed.

In contrast, a pull system of production control, such as just-in-time (JIT) manufacturing, involves the purchase or production of inventory only as needs arise. Storage is eliminated except for a minimal level of safety stock.

The JIT philosophy can be applied to some extent in any company having inventories. JIT requires that purchases be made in small quantities and that deliveries be frequent. Production lot sizes are minimized so that many different products can be made on a daily basis. Products are designed for quality, and component parts are standardized to the extent possible. Machine setup time is reduced so that production runs can easily be shifted between products. To eliminate the need for or buildup of buffer inventories between operations, plant layout emphasizes manufacturing cells, and the operating capabilities of all factory equipment are considered.

The product life cycle—development, introduction, growth, maturity, and harvest—provides opportunities to control costs. More control can be exercised in the development stage than at any other stage.

Other contexts for sharing information are applications of target costing and value engineering. These are specific tools that drive interorganizational information sharing in designing new products. These tools facilitate cost management across the value creation chain in the life cycle design stage. Other types of information often shared within a value creation chain are data on product cost, quality, technology, and research.

Cross-Functional Applications

Topic of Note	Discipline	Cross-Functional Applications
Economic Order Quantity (EOQ)	Purchasing	Most firms employ some variation of centralized purchasing to benefit from the savings of large-scale ordering. When technical specifications are beyond the purchasing manager's competence, the EOQ provides a basis to approach the requisitioning department for alternatives by making department personnel aware of the cost constraints. Some firms have established a policy limiting the access of technical sales people to company engineers in an attempt to avoid requisitions

(cont.)

Cross-Functional Applications

Topic of Note	Discipline	Cross-Functional Applications
		that can only be filled by one source. This widespread practice undermines the EOQ cost considerations for which a purchasing manager is responsible.
	Marketing Research	Marketers often project trends in customer purchasing behaviour to concentrate their sales and promotional efforts on the customer's reorder point. Information concerning fluctuations in customer EOQ may signal marketers to change their pricing policy or terms of trade. Intermittently, in-house marketing researchers may influence the EOQ of the company's production department by identifying a shift in product demand.
	Production	The space requirements of an excessive inventory or a prolonged holding period obscure problems such as defective units, deterioration, or obsolescence that may be identified too late to minimize losses or to take corrective action. This situation can result in inefficient production runs, excessive quality costs, and inflexibility in retooling (production changeovers). EOQ's emphasis on cost factors assists production managers, in a cooperative effort with centralized purchasing, to maintain inventories that support flexible decision making and minimize losses of all forms of inventory shrinkage.
Just-in-Time Inventory Management (JIT)	Software Design	The efficient use of JIT systems depends on a close working relationship between customers and their suppliers. Cooperation must be supported by an understanding of both the technical and commercial needs of all involved. Software designers use JIT models to establish technical specifications, usage rates, and delivery times in a common database that is sufficiently flexible to accommodate the requirements of everyone involved. This information-sharing arrangement between organizations is usually a monumental task for software designers.
	Taxation	Many U.S. states and some foreign nations charge a tax on inventories that is usually levied only on finished goods. JIT systems can minimize this tax burden by reducing inventories or delaying them in a subassembly status (work in process). Some governments have considered taxing inventories as value is added during processing (*ad valorum* tax). This form of taxation involves expensive administrative costs; however, if it is used, the JIT systems can provide a greater tax savings for tax managers.

(cont.)

Cross-Functional Applications

Topic of Note	Discipline	Cross-Functional Applications
	Quality Assurance/ Quality Control	QA/QC and safety engineers can discover waste, spoilage, and defective products in a much shorter time, which permits managers to take corrective action or at least minimize loss and liability related to inventory problems. Quality- and safety-conscious firms can experience a reduction in quality costs by adopting or improving the JIT system.
	Industrial Law Enforcement	Law enforcement agencies responsible for industrial espionage, pirating, and theft of inventory are more effective in reducing criminal activity when a JIT system is used. JIT systems usually have well-defined sourcing, product specifications, and handling conditions, which establish responsibility and reduce investigative costs. Criminal conspirators tend to avoid an efficient JIT system, in part because responsible employees at all levels are more aware of their activity in a lean inventory.
	Environmental and Regulatory Law	Firms that produce toxic or regulated substances have a mandated responsibility to control their products, from inputs to ultimate disposal. JIT systems assist both governmental regulators and a firm's compliance officers with identifying, reporting, and correcting any serious violations with minimal efforts.
	Financial Accounting	Recent regulatory proposals concerning income reporting and comprehensive income may abolish the practice of income smoothing by some firms with large inventories. Financial reporting for firms with a reliable JIT system can yield more accurate income and asset-evaluation information. With a lean inventory, cost flows are more predictable, which supports superior matching of cost of goods sold with sales. In addition, financial accounting guidelines usually overstate the value of inventory by understating the carrying costs. Financial management decisions involving cash flows will be enhanced by more accurate income and carrying cost information.

Supplementary Learning Objectives on the Web

W7-1: What is the impact of flexible manufacturing systems on production and on satisfying customers?

W7-2: Why does re-engineering cause radical changes in how firms execute processes?

W7-3: Why is throughput an important performance measure for organizations that apply the theory of constraints?

W7-4: Why is linear programming a valuable tool for managers?

Key Terms

ABC analysis (p. 388)
Backflush costing (p. 404)
Bottleneck (p. 395)
Carrying costs (p. 390)
Conversion (p. 389)
Cost avoidance (p. 386)
Cost behaviour (p. 381)
Cost consciousness (p. 381)
Cost containment (p. 384)
Cost control system (p. 380)
Cost reduction (p. 386)
Economic order quantity (p. 392)
Empowerment (p. 402)
Horizontal price fixing (p. 384)
JIT manufacturing system (p. 396)
Kanban (p. 397)
Lead time (p. 394)
Materials requirements planning
  (p. 395)

Manufacturing resource planning
  (p. 395)
Ordering costs (p. 389)
Order point (p. 394)
Price fixing (p. 383)
Production cost (p. 389)
Pull system (p. 397)
Purchasing cost (p. 389)
Push system (p. 396)
Red-line system (p. 389)
Safety stock (p. 394)
Setup costs (p. 389)
Survival triplet (p. 412)
Target costing (p. 410)
Two-bin system (p. 389)
Value engineering (p. 411)
Vertical price fixing (p. 384)

Solution Strategies

Economic Order Quantity

$$EOQ = \sqrt{(2QO \div C)}$$

where EOQ = economic order quantity in units
  Q = estimated quantity in units used per year
  O = estimated cost of placing one order
  C = estimated cost to carry one unit in stock for one year

Economic Production Run

$$EPR = \sqrt{(2QS \div C)}$$

where ERP = economic production run
  Q = estimated quantity in units produced per year
  S = estimated cost of setting up a production run
  C = estimated cost of carrying one unit in stock for one year

Order Point

Order point = (Daily usage × Lead time) + Safety time

DEMONSTRATION PROBLEM

Monica Pickles owns a large office supply store in the university section of London, Ontario. She wonders how many legal-sized writing pads to order at a time, when to place an order, and how many legal pads she should maintain as a safety stock. Upon analysis, she determines the following information:

Annual sales in units	10,400
Number of days the store is open	260
Average lead time in days to receive an order	3
Cost per order	$ 4
Cost of carrying one unit for one year	$0.10
Maximum lead time in days	5
Maximum daily sales in units	50

Required:

a.   Determine the economic order quantity.
b.   Determine the safety stock.
c.   Determine the reorder point.
d.   Determine the total ordering cost using the economic order quantity.
e.   Determine the total carrying cost using the economic order quantity.

Solution to Demonstration Problem

a. $EOQ = \sqrt{2(10,400)(\$4) \div \$0.10} = 912.14$ or 912
b   Safety stock = (Maximum lead time − Average lead time) (Maximum daily usage Average daily usage)
     Average daily usage = $10,400 \div 260 = 40$ units
     Safety stock = $(5 − 3)(50 − 40) = 20$ units
c.   Reorder point = (Average daily usage × Average lead time) + Safety stock
     Reorder point = $(40 \times 3) + 20 = 140$ units
d.   Total ordering cost = Cost per order × Number of orders
     Number of orders = $10,400 \div 912 = 11.4$ orders
     Total ordering cost = $\$4 \times 11.4 = \$45.60$
e.   Total carrying cost = Average inventory × Carrying cost per unit
     Average inventory = (EOQ ÷ 2) + Safety stock = $[(912 \div 2) + 20] = 476$
     Total carrying cost = $476 \times \$.10 = \$47.60$

End-of-Chapter Materials

SELF-TEST QUESTIONS

(SOLUTIONS APPEAR AT THE END OF THE CHAPTER.)

1. Which technique deals most explicitly with inventories?
    a. MRP
    b. TOC
    c. LP
    d. EOQ

2. Which of the following is least likely to be outsourced when controlling costs?
    a. Core activity
    b. Noncore activity
    c. Payroll
    d. Human resources

3. Which is not a step in constraining costs?
    a. Investigate and understand the types of costs incurred by the organization
    b. Reduce the available funding
    c. Communicate the need for cost consciousness to all employees

d. Compare actual results to targets and analyze for future methods of improvement

4. Which is not a life cycle stage?
    a. Development
    b. Introduction
    c. Exit
    d. Harvest

5. Which is not related to target costing?
    a. Assets
    b. Price
    c. Cost
    d. Profit margin

6. Value engineering is concerned with
    a. Actual input and actual output
    b. Planned output and actual input
    c. Actual output and planned output
    d. Product design and product price

7. C-category inventory items may justify the use of a:
    a. Just-in-time system
    b. Saving system
    c. Costing system
    d . Two-bin system

8. An EOQ model indicates
    a. What to order
    b. The order point
    c. Lead time
    d. Safety stock

9. How many bins does a kanban system have?
    a. 1
    b. 2
    c. 3
    d. 4

10. Backflush costing records product costs
    a. Before production
    b. With LIFO
    c. After production
    d. With FIFO

QUESTIONS

1. In cost control, at what points in time can control over an activity be exerted? Why are these points of cost control important?

2. Explain the meaning and significance of cost consciousness.

3. Why is on-the-job training an important component in the process of instilling cost consciousness within an organization?

4. What factors may cause costs to change from one period to another? Which of these are subject to cost containment and which are not? What creates the difference in controllability?

5. What options does a company have when its costs change because of higher prices from suppliers or from increased costs of complying with government regulations?

6. Compare and contrast general and specific price-level changes.

7. In an ABC analysis of inventory, what are the characteristics of the items that would be placed in each category?

8. List four costs included in each of the following categories: ordering inventory, carrying inventory, and not carrying inventory. How does incurring costs in one of these categories affect the costs in the other categories?

9. Describe some major considerations in deciding from whom to buy. How have the considerations changed over time?

10. In buyer–supplier relationships, why is it desirable for the supplier to be located geographically close to the buyer?

11. Assuming that all costs in the EOQ formula could be determined with absolute precision, discuss some reasons that a company might not buy at the economic order quantity amount.

12. Although MRP is based on EOQ and safety stock models, it overcomes an inherent deficiency in those models. What is this deficiency, and how does MRP overcome it?

13. Why is MRP said to be a push system?

14. What significant benefits have many firms achieved using MRP?

15. Why is it said that JIT views inventory as a liability rather than as an asset?

16. What are the primary goals of the JIT philosophy, and how does JIT attempt to achieve these goals?

17. Discuss the differences between push and pull inventory systems.

18. What is empowerment, and why does it frequently accompany the adoption of JIT?

19. "Philosophically, JIT is aimed at minimizing time, space, and energy." Discuss what you think was meant by the person making this statement.

20. Are MRP and JIT systems compatible? Explain your answer.

21. Why are decisions that are made during the development stage of a product so important?

22. Give three examples of industries in which time to market is critical. Give three examples of industries in which time to market is almost irrelevant. Discuss the reasons for importance or lack thereof in each industry.

23. Why is a product life cycle stage such an important consideration in managing production costs?

24. How do target costing and value engineering facilitate the exchange of information between firms in the same value creation chain?

25. As a decision-making structure, cross-functional teams are used extensively in business today. What advantages might be gained by organizing a cross-functional team to design a new product rather than delegating the entire design responsibility to the in-house engineering department?

EXERCISES

1. (LO 1) Below are various actions taken by management teams to control costs. For each item listed, indicate whether the action indicates an application of cost understanding, cost containment, cost avoidance, or cost reduction.

   a. A company cancelled its contract with an external firm that it used for training in computerized manufacturing methods. At the same time, the firm created an in-house training department. Even though the in-house training will be more expensive, management believes the extra cost to be justified because of the flexibility in scheduling training sessions.

   b. A municipality, faced with a 13% increase in health insurance premiums, raised the deductible on its coverage, and was able to keep health insurance costs at the prior year's level.

   c. Anticipating a rise in raw material prices, a manufacturing organization used forward contracts to acquire a year's supply of materials at the current prices.

   d. Because beef by-product costs had been rising over the past year, a dog food manufacturer increased the proportion of pork by-products relative to the content of beef by-products in the mix of its dog food.

   e. Because a small foreign country offered a 10-year income tax holiday for new businesses, a Canadian leather-goods manufacturer relocated its production facilities to that country.

   f. Because it had suffered large losses caused by currency fluctuations, a Canadian importer instituted a practice of hedging its currency translation risk.

   g. After the new union contract was signed, wage rates for highly skilled workers rose by 18%. As a result, a tool-and-die maker elected to automate three of its higher-volume production processes. This decision resulted in a cost savings of $1,400,000 over a period of 5 years.

2. (LO 1) You have just been appointed director of Youth Hotline, a not-for-profit organization that operates a phone bank for individuals experiencing emotional difficulties. The phones are staffed by qualified social workers and psychologists who are paid on an hourly basis. In your first week at Youth Hotline, you took the following actions:

   a. Increased the funding appropriation for advertising of the Hotline

   b. Exchanged the more expensive pushbutton, cream-coloured designer telephones for regular, pushbutton desk telephones

c. Eliminated the call-forwarding feature installed on all telephones since Youth Hotline will now be staffed 24 hours a day

d. Eliminated two paid clerical positions and replaced these individuals with volunteers

e. Ordered blank notepads for the counsellors to keep by their phones; the old notepads (stock now depleted) had the Youth Hotline logo and address printed on them

f. Negotiated a new contract with the telephone company. Youth Hotline will now pay a flat rate of $100 per month, regardless of the number of telephones installed by the Hotline. The previous contract charged the organization $10 for every telephone. At the time that contract was signed, Youth Hot Line only had ten telephones. However, with the increased staff, you plan to install at least five additional telephones

Required:

Indicate whether each of the actions represents cost understanding, cost containment, cost avoidance, or cost reduction. Some actions may have more than one implication; if they do, indicate the reason.

3. (LO 2, 3, 4) A business publication to which you subscribe has recently included a crossword puzzle listing the items on the right below. Your roommate has provided you with the terms listed on the left below, and has challenged you to match the numbered items on the right to the lettered items on the left:

a. Push system
b. ABC analysis
c. MRP
d. Lead time
e. Bottleneck
f. Two-bin system
g. Pull system
h. Setup cost
i. Kanban
j. Manufacturing cell

1. Generates an interrelated purchase order and production schedule
2. Time from placing an order to receiving the goods
3. U-shaped grouping of workers or machines
4. Any resource whose ability to process is less than the need for processing
5. Segregates inventory into three groups based on cost and volume
6. Inventory is acquired/produced no sooner than it is needed/sold
7. Inventory is produced and stored before it is sold
8. Direct and indirect labour costs of getting equipment ready for a production run
9. When it is necessary to begin using materials from the second bin, a purchase order is issued to refill the first bin
10. A system using cards to control the flow of material or units between work centres

4. (LO 2) Following is a list of techniques used to control inventories.
   a. Perpetual inventory system
   b. Daily inventory counts
   c. Monthly inventory counts
   d. Annual inventory count
   e. Limited access to storage areas
   f. Open-access display areas
   g. Red-line system
   h. Two-bin system
   i. Specific identification inventory method
   j. Weighted-average cost flow
   k. Rigorous, in-depth demand estimation (EOQ, lead time, order point, safety stock)

Required:
Management of the company for which you are working as an intern has asked you to indicate whether each of the items just listed would most likely be used for A-, B-, or C-type inventory items. More than one type of inventory item may be indicated for a given technique.

5. (LO 2) The president of a company for which you are consulting has requested that you help personnel managing inventory to classify each of the following items as a cost of ordering (O), carrying (C), or not carrying (N) inventory. Use N/A for items not fitting any of the categories.
   a.   Contribution margin lost on a sale because of a stockout
   b.   Spoilage of products in storage
   c.   Opportunity cost of capital invested in inventory
   d.   Inventory storage cost
   e.   Wages of staff in purchasing agent's office
   f.   Long-distance calls to vendor to get prices
   g.   Property tax on inventory
   h.   Freight-out on sales of inventory
   i.   Purchase order forms, receiving report forms, disbursement voucher forms
   j.   Insurance on warehouse and its inventory contents
   k.   Extra freight on rush orders necessitated by stockouts
   l.   Freight-in on special purchases/orders
   m.   Postage to send purchase orders
   n.   Handling costs for products on hand
   o.   Purchase price of products

6. (LO 2) Your best friend knows that you have taken a course in managerial accounting. He has a new business and has asked you to determine the carrying costs for an item costing $12, given the following per-unit cost information:

Shipping cost	$0.04
Storage cost	0.15
Handling cost	0.05
Production labour cost	0.95
Insurance	0.06
Import taxes (per unit)	0.29

7. (LO 2) In a job interview, you are given the following information as part of a qualifying test for the job. Rows (a) through (e) below represent five independent situations, each with a missing item of data.

	EOQ	(Q) Quantity Used per Year	(O) Ordering Cost	(C) Carrying Cost
a.	?	8,100	$ 1	$2
b.	40	?	$ 2	$4
c.	100	1,000	$15	?
d.	20	400	$ 5	?
e.	30	150	?	$3

Required:
Provide the missing numbers.

8. (LO 2) Archer Toy Company manufactures its Little Red wagon. Among the parts needed to manufacture each wagon are two axles and four wheels. These parts are purchased from external vendors. The annual ordering costs, carrying costs, and demand for each follow:

Component	Ordering Cost	Carrying Cost	Demand
Axles	$20	$0.50	2,000
Wheels	$36	$3.00	4,000

Required:
a.   Compute the EOQ for each component.
b.   Compute the average inventory level for each component assuming that no safety stock is carried.

c. Write a memo to management discussing any problems you perceive in managing the inventories of these two components. Also, suggest solutions to any problems you identify.

9. (LO 2) Jean Lefleur is a British Columbia salmon farmer. His fish eat approximately 7,300 kilograms of feed per year. On the average, 18 days go by from the time he places an order until the feed is delivered. It costs Jean $0.75 to place each order and $0.48 per kilogram for the annual carrying cost.
Required:
a. What is Jean's EOQ?
b. Assuming he holds no safety stock, calculate Jean's order point.
c. Assuming the lead time varies by three days, calculate a safety stock.
d. Assuming the average daily consumption per fish varies 10%, calculate a safety stock.
e. Using the information calculated in parts (c) and (d), determine a conservative order point.

PROBLEMS

1. (LO 1) Temporary or part-time employees are sometimes hired to
    a. Draw house plans for construction companies
    b. Make desserts for restaurants
    c. Perform legal research for law firms
    d. Prepare tax returns for CA firms
    e. Sell clothing in department stores during the Christmas season
    f. Serve as security guards
    g. Tailor men's suits for department stores
    h. Teach evening courses at universities
    i. Work as medical doctors in the emergency rooms of hospitals
    j. Write articles for monthly magazines
Required:
For each job listed, suggest potential advantages and disadvantages of using temporary or part-time employees from the perspective of the employer.

2. (LO 2) The following 20 items, along with unit costs and volumes of sales last year, are part of an ABC analysis of Andy's Diving Goods:

	Items	Unit Cost	Volume Sold
Flippers (pair):	Men's	$ 3.00	320
	Women's	2.50	210
	Children's	1.80	66
Masks:	Men's	4.00	280
	Women's	3.40	172
	Children's	2.80	40
Weight belts:	Men's	1.80	63
	Women's	1.70	46
	Children's	1.20	12
Snorkels		1.20	420
Air tanks		36.00	42
Meters and connections		42.00	36
Wet suits:	Men's	60.00	170
	Women's	52.00	102
	Children's	42.00	12
Weights:	Large	2.00	160
	Medium	1.50	180
	Small	1.25	64
Underwater watches		25.00	32
O-rings		0.25	120

Required:

a. Rearrange the items in descending order of magnitude according to the result of multiplying cost times volume. Use these headings: Items; Unit Cost; Volume Sold; and Cost × Volume.

b. Classify the items in three groups: A items (to include 20% of the total volume sold); B items (to include the next 30% of the total volume sold); and C items (to include the final 50% of the volume sold).

c. Recommend three techniques to control each group.

3. (LO 2) BetterMetalWorks has been evaluating its policies with respect to control of the costs of sheet metal, one of the firm's major component materials. The firm's controller has gathered the following financial data, which may be pertinent to controlling costs associated with the sheet metal:

Ordering Costs

Annual salary of purchasing department manager	$72,500
Depreciation of equipment in purchasing department	$45,300
Cost per order for purchasing department supplies	$ 0.95
Typical phone expense per order placed	$ 3.20
Monthly expense for heat and light in purchasing department	$ 900

Carrying Costs

Annual depreciation on material storage building	$35,000
Annual inventory insurance premium (per dollar of inventory value)	$ 0.15
Annual property tax on material storage building	$ 3,700
Obsolescence cost, per dollar of average annual inventory	$ 0.12
Annual salary of security officer assigned to the material storage building	$38,000

Required:

a. Which of the ordering costs would BetterMetalWorks' controller take into account in using the EOQ model? Explain.

b. Which of the carrying costs would BetterMetalWorks' controller take into account in using the EOQ model? Explain.

4. (LO 2) Fortress Construction Company's requirement for cement amounts to 80,000 bags per year. Cement costs $4 a bag; carrying cost is $6 per unit per year; and processing a purchase order costs $24. The lead time is 30 days.

Required:

a. Find the EOQ.

b. Calculate the total cost of ordering and carrying inventory for a period of one year.

c. Determine the order point.

d. How does total inventory cost change if the firm orders in a lot size of 4,000 units rather than the EOQ?

e. Why might the company prefer to order in a lot size of 4,000 units rather than the EOQ?

5. (LO 2) Each of the following independent cases has a missing amount.

	Case A	Case B	Case C	Case D	Case E
Order point	400	b	120	300	500
Daily usage	20	30	c	15	e
Lead time (days)	12	10	7	d	5
Safety stock	a	60	50	30	60

Required:

Supply the missing amounts for the lettered spaces.

6. (LO 4) Items (a) through (i) describe features of just-in-time systems. The descriptions labeled D, U, and T also relate to JIT systems. Indicate by letter which of the three categories applies to each item. More than one category may apply to an item.

   D—desired intermediate result of using JIT

   U—ultimate goal of JIT

   T—technique associated with JIT

   a. Reducing setup costs
   b. Reducing total cost of producing and carrying inventory
   c. Pulling purchases and production through the system based on sales demand
   d. Designing products to minimize design changes after production starts
   e. Monitoring quality on a continuous basis
   f. Using manufacturing cells
   g. Minimizing inventory stored
   h. Using backflush costing
   i. Having workers and machines continuously monitor quality during processing

7. (LO 4) The next table gives symbols for areas where changes occur as a result of the implementation of JIT. Categorize items (a) through (q) in the list that follows the table by associating the appropriate symbol with each item.

Symbol	Area of Change Related to Use of JIT
PSR&D	Purchasing, Supplier Relationships, and Distribution
PD	Product Design
PP	Production Processing
PL	Plant Layout
JP	JIT Philosophy
AI	Accounting Implications of JIT

   a. Management recognizes that employees often know best how to improve operations.
   b. Careful design minimizes the number of subsequent changes.
   c. The ideal is one vendor for each part or raw material.
   d. Setup time is reduced.
   e. Layout is intended to minimize production time.
   f. Long-term contracts are negotiated.
   g. Physical arrangement is conducive to a worker handling a greater number of tasks.
   h. Inventory is viewed as a liability.
   i. A single conversion account combines direct labour and overhead.
   j. Fewer costs need to be arbitrarily allocated.
   k. Workers and machines monitor quality during processing.
   l. U-shaped groupings of workers and machines are used.
   m. Many setup tasks are performed while machines are running.
   n. Layout makes the use of visual controls more effective.
   o. The plan is to use fewest number of parts (reduce product complexity).
   p. Creative thinking doesn't cost anything.
   q. As many parts as possible are standardized.

CASES

1. The following chart indicates where each part of the dollar that a student pays for a new college/university textbook goes.

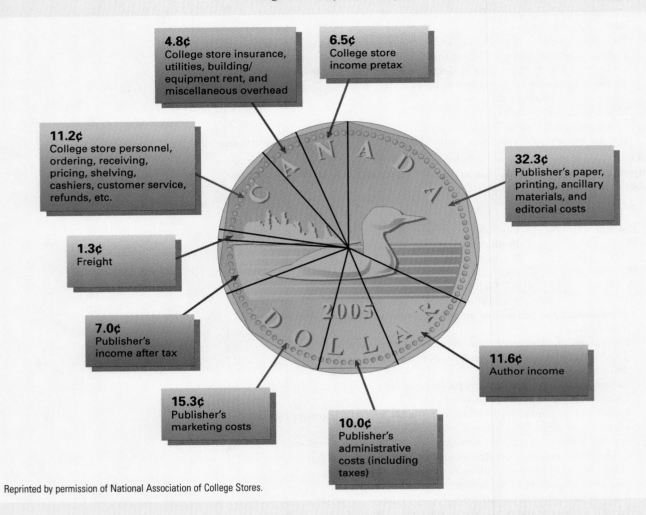

4.8¢
College store insurance, utilities, building/ equipment rent, and miscellaneous overhead

6.5¢
College store income pretax

11.2¢
College store personnel, ordering, receiving, pricing, shelving, cashiers, customer service, refunds, etc.

32.3¢
Publisher's paper, printing, ancillary materials, and editorial costs

1.3¢
Freight

7.0¢
Publisher's income after tax

11.6¢
Author income

15.3¢
Publisher's marketing costs

10.0¢
Publisher's administrative costs (including taxes)

Reprinted by permission of National Association of College Stores.

Students are frustrated with the cost of their textbooks, but most publishers would say that the selling prices have merely kept pace with inflation. Buying used books is an option, but publishers say that used books simply drive up the cost of future texts: if the publisher cannot sell as many of the new edition as are printed, the price is raised "to compensate for decreased sales volume, and the cycle starts again." Publishers also must cover the costs of many nonsaleable supplements that are requested by faculty such as instructor manuals, solutions manuals, transparency acetates, videos, and test banks (hard copy and electronic). Additionally, as the books become more elaborate—with multiple colours and photographs—costs also increase.

Required:

Write a paper that

a   Provides suggestions for ways the college/university bookstore could control costs
b. Provides suggestions for ways the publisher could control costs
c. Provides suggestions for ways students can legally control textbook expenditures (i.e., substantial reproduction of the text is illegal)
d. Discusses why college/university textbooks today are so different from college/university textbooks of 20 years ago. Are these differences cost-beneficial from your perspective?

2. John Holster, controller for ProCorp, Inc., has been examining all phases of ProCorp's manufacturing operations in order to reduce costs and improve efficiency. The reason for urgency is that the company's sales force has been complaining about lost sales caused by product stockouts, and the production people are unhappy about downtime caused by shortages of raw material. Holster believes the company may be losing as much as $220,000 in revenue as a result of these problems.

ProCorp manufactures only one product: boomerangs (trademarked "Boomers"). The single raw material used in making Boomers is plastic, with each Boomer requiring 0.5 kilograms of red plastic. ProCorp expects to manufacture 300,000 Boomers this year with a steady demand through the entire year. The ordering costs for clerical processing are $30 per order of plastic. There is a three-day delay between placement of an order and receipt of the inventory. The carrying costs for storage, handling, insurance, and interest are $0.72 per Boomer unit per year.

Required:
a. Discuss the general benefits of a well-managed inventory policy.
b. By using the economic order quantity formula, ProCorp, Inc. determined that the optimal economic order quantity is 2,500 kilograms of plastic, which will produce 5,000 units.
   i. Discuss how an increase in each of the following components will affect the economic order quantity; annual sales demand; ordering costs; and carrying costs for storage, handling, insurance, and interest.
   ii. Determine the number of times ProCorp will order plastic during the year.
c. ProCorp, Inc., while reviewing its safety stock policy, has determined that an appropriate safety stock is 1,250 kilograms of plastic, which will produce 2,500 units.
   i. Describe the factors that affect an appropriate safety stock level.
   ii. List the effects of maintaining an appropriate safety stock level on ProCorp's short-term and long-term profitability.
   iii. Identify the effect that a well-implemented just-in-time inventory procedure will have on safety stock level, and explain why it will have this effect.

(CMA adapted)

3. The management at Megafilters, Inc. has been discussing the possible implementation of a just-in-time (JIT) production system at its Manitoba plant, where oil filters and air filters for heavy construction equipment and large, off-road vehicles are manufactured. The Metal Stamping Department at the Manitoba plant has already instituted a JIT system for controlling raw materials inventory, but the remainder of the plant is still discussing how to proceed with the implementation of this concept. Some of the other department managers have grown increasingly cautious about the JIT process after hearing about the problems that have arisen in the Metal Stamping Department.

Robert Goertz, manager of the Manitoba plant, is a strong proponent of the JIT production system and recently made the following statement at a meeting of all departmental managers. "Just-in-time is often referred to as a management philosophy of doing business rather than a technique for improving efficiency on the plant floor. We will all have to make many changes in the way we think about our employees, our suppliers, and our customers if we are going to be successful in using just-in-time procedures. Rather than dwelling on some of the negative things you have heard from the Metal Stamping Department, I want each of you to prepare a list of things we can do to make a smooth transition to the just-in-time philosophy of management for the rest of the plant."

Required:
a. The just-in-time management philosophy emphasizes objectives for the general improvement of a production system. Describe several important objectives of this philosophy.
b. Discuss several actions that Megafilters, Inc., can take to ease the transition to a just-in-time production system at the Manitoba plant.
c. For the JIT production system to be successful, Megafilters, Inc., must establish appropriate relationships with its vendors, employees, and customers. Describe each of these three relationships.

(CMA adapted)

4. AgriCorp is a manufacturer of farm equipment that is sold by a network of distributors throughout Canada. A majority of the distributors are also repair centres for AgriCorp equipment and depend on AgriCorp's Service Division to provide a timely supply of spare parts.

In an effort to reduce the inventory costs incurred by the Service Division, Richard Bachman, division manager, implemented a just-in-time inventory program on June 1, 2004, the beginning of the company's fiscal year. Because JIT has been in place for a year, Bachman has asked the division controller, Janice Grady, to determine the effect the program has had on the Service Division's financial performance. Grady has been able to document the following results of JIT implementation:

a. The Service Division's average inventory declined from $550,000 to $150,000.
b. Projected annual insurance costs of $80,000 declined 60% because of the lower average inventory.
c. A leased 8,000-square-metre warehouse, previously used for raw material storage, was not used at all during the year. The division paid $11,200 annual rent for the warehouse and was able to sublet three-quarters of the building to several tenants at $2.50 per square metre, while the balance of the space remained idle.
d. Two warehouse employees whose services were no longer needed were transferred on June 1, 2004, to the Purchasing Department to assist in the coordination of the JIT program. The annual salary expense for these two employees totalled $38,000 and continued to be charged to the indirect labour portion of fixed overhead.
e. Despite the use of overtime to manufacture 7,500 spare parts, lost sales caused by stockouts totalled 3,800 spare parts. The overtime premium incurred amounted to $5.60 per part manufactured. The use of overtime to fill spare parts orders was immaterial prior to June 1, 2004.

Prior to the decision to implement the JIT inventory program, AgriCorp's Service Division had completed its 2004–2005 expected financial performance. The division's pro forma income statement, without any adjustments for JIT inventory, is presented next. AgriCorp's borrowing rate related to inventory is 9% after income taxes. All AgriCorp pro forma income statements are prepared using an effective tax rate of 40%.

Agricorp Service Division
Pro Forma Income Statement
for the Year Ending May 31, 2005

Sales (280,000 spare parts)		$ 6,160,000
Cost of goods sold		
Variable	$2,660,000	
Fixed	1,120,000	(3,780,000)
Gross profit		$ 2,380,000
Selling and administrative expense		
Variable	$ 700,000	
Fixed	555,000	(1,255,000)
Operating income		$ 1,125,000
Other income		75,000
Income before interest and taxes		$ 1,200,000
Interest expense		(150,000)
Income before income taxes		$ 1,050,000
Income taxes		(420,000)
Net income		$ 630,000

Required:
a. Calculate the after-tax cash savings (loss) for AgriCorp's Service Division that resulted during the 2004–2005 fiscal year from the adoption of the JIT program.
b. Identify and explain the factors, other than financial, that should be considered before a company implements a JIT program.

(CMA)

5. Peter Babic, president of the Newmarket Company (NMC), sat dejectedly in his chair after reviewing the year 2005 first-quarter financial report on one of the organization's core products: a standard, five-speed transmission (Product Number 2122) used in the heavy equipment industry in the manufacture of earth-moving equipment. Some of the information in the report follows:

Market Report, Product Number 2122, Quarter 1, 2005

Sales data:

Total sales (dollars) Quarter 1, 2005	$4,657,500
Total sales (units) Quarter 1, 2005	3,450
Total sales (dollars) Quarter 1, 2004	$6,405,000
Total sales (units) Quarter 1, 2004	4,200

Market data:

Industry unit sales, Quarter 1, 2005	40,000
Industry unit sales, Quarter 1, 2004	32,000
Industry average sales price, Quarter 1, 2005	$ 1,310
Industry average sales price, Quarter 1, 2004	$ 1,640

Profit data:

NMC average gross profit per unit, Quarter 1, 2005	$ 45
NMC average profit per unit, Quarter 1, 2004	$ 160
Industry average profit per unit, Quarter 1, 2005	$ 75
Industry average profit per unit, Quarter 1, 2004	$ 140

NMC's strategy for this transmission is to compete on the basis of price. NMC's transmission offers no features that allow it to be differentiated from those of major competitors and NMC's level of quality is similar to the average of the industry.

Also on Mr. Babic's desk was a report from his business intelligence unit. Mr. Babic underlined some key pieces of information from the report. The underlined items follow:

1. Commodity transmission components (nuts, bolts, etc.), which all major transmission producers acquire from specialty vendors, decreased in price by approximately 5% from January 2004 to January 2005.

2. Two major competitors moved their major assembly operations to China from the United States in early 2004. These competitors are believed to have the lowest unit production cost in the industry

3. A third major competitor ceased manufacture of major gear components and began outsourcing these parts from a Mexican firm in mid-2004. This firm increased its market share in 2004 from 10% to 14% after a major decrease in sales price.

4. NMC's production operations did not change in any material respect from 2004 to 2005.

5. NMC manufactures approximately 83% of the components used in the heavy industrial transmission. The industry norm is to make 57% of the components.

6. For the balance of 2005, industry experts agree that quarterly demand for the heavy industrial transmission will be even higher than the levels posted for the first quarter of 2005.

Required:

a. Examine the information as Mr. Babic does. Analyze the data that are given to identify as specifically as possible the problems that have led to NMC's loss of profit and market share in the heavy industrial transmission market.

b. Based on your analysis in part a, and the information given to Mr. Babic, suggest specific alternatives that Mr. Babic should consider to make his firm more competitive in the heavy industrial transmission market. Use concepts presented in the chapter as the basis of your recommendations.

ETHICS AND QUALITY DISCUSSIONS

1. Assume that you are in charge of a social service agency that provides counselling services to families on welfare. The agency's costs have been increasing with no corresponding increase in funding. In an effort to reduce some costs, you implement the following ideas:
   - Counsellors are empowered to make their own decisions about the legitimacy of all welfare claims.
   - To emphasize the concept of doing it right the first time, counsellors are told not to review processed claims at a later date.
   - To discourage out-of-control conditions, an upper and lower control limit of 5 minutes is set on a standard 15-minute time for consultations.

   Required:
   Discuss the ethics as well as the positive and negative effects of each of the ideas listed.

2. Canada is considering requiring immigrants to speak either English or French. Why? A government report states that this will reduce language-training costs and help ensure that the people will integrate into Canadian life. Many Canadians as well as immigrants want the proposal scrapped. (Note: The April 1, 1998, *Wall Street Journal* article "Canadians Clash over Cost of Diversity" may provide a useful starting point.)

   Required:
   a. What are the costs and benefits of diversity—within an organization or within a country?
   b. Who pays when immigrants do not speak the language of the country/province to which they are immigrating? How is payment made? Can you think of a methodology in which the costs of diversity could be passed to the immigrants?
   c. Why might such a language requirement be beneficial to immigrants?

3. In early 1998, Warner Bros. announced that it would cancel or postpone several high-profile movies. Warner Bros. management indicated that the company would begin making only about 20 movies per year rather than 30. Cost containment is the phrase of the moment, after some films' costs escalated dramatically. (Note: The April 23, 1998, *Wall Street Journal* article "Warner Bros. Cancels Films, Cuts Budgets" may provide a useful starting point.)

   Required:
   a. Discuss the relationship between movie cost and movie quality.
   b. Provide some reasons that film costs are almost consistently over the estimates.
   c. If you were part of the management team at Warner Bros., what cost containment techniques would you implement? Why?

4. A plant manager and her controller were discussing the plant's inventory control policies one day. The controller suggested that the plant's ordering policies needed revising. The controller argued that the revision was needed because of new technology that had been put in place in the plant's purchasing department. Among the changes were (1) installation of computerized inventory tracking; (2) installation of electronic data interchange capabilities, which would allow communications with the plant's major suppliers; and (3) installation of in-house facilities for electronic fund transfers.

   Required:
   a. As technology changes, why should managers update ordering policies for inventory?
   b. What would be the likely impact of the changes in this plant on the EOQ of material inputs?
   c. What experts should be invited to provide input into designing new policies for ordering materials?

5. *In 1994 Ford Motor Co. halted production at one of its assembly plants for compact sedans for one week because of a fuel-leakage problem with 28,500 of the cars.*

   Ford wanted to rush replacement fuel-tank assemblies to dealers and customers. Of the 28,500 affected cars, nearly 8,000 had been delivered to U.S. and Canadian customers. The shutdown was expected to cost Ford production of 6,400 cars. Ford hoped to recoup its lost production through additional overtime shifts at the plant.

This problem stemmed from a tricky weld near the fuel tank's filler pipe, Ford said. When the weld is improperly made, fuel can leak from the reinforcement on the fuel tank. Ford said it learned of the problem from its customers.

(Source: Oscar Suris, "Ford is Halting the Production of a New Line," *The Wall Street Journal*, October 18, 1994, p. A4.)

Required:

a. This story indicates one reason for making engineering changes. What are some other possible reasons for such changes?

b. Why would Ford elect to shut down assembly operations to correct the production flaw?

c. In what ways might a firm learn of the existence of production flaws? Why would a firm prefer to learn of such flaws from sources other than customers?

6. Laura Applegate is the production manager for the DeRigeur Company, located in a small town in Nova Scotia. DeRigeur is the only major employer in the community, which has substantial unemployment.

   Laura is in the process of trying to reduce costs through improved equipment and practices in the organization. Of the 150 employees at DeRigeur, approximately 80% have little formal education and have worked for the company for 15 years or more. Some—but not all—of these employees are close to retirement.

   In talking with the employees, Laura determines that most would require substantial training before they would be able to change from performing their current single-task production jobs to handling multifunctional tasks.

   A neighbouring county has a vocational–technical school that is educating many young people in the use of the new types of multitask equipment that could be used at DeRigeur. Laura has discussed the organization's plans with the head of the vocational–technical school, who has indicated that the school could easily provide a cadre of 150 well-trained employees within the next 10 months—approximately the time it will take the equipment to arrive and be installed.

   Laura is excited to hear this, because DeRigeur would not have to pay for training and would be able to hire new graduates at a slightly lower hourly wage because of their lack of experience. Her only difficulty is trying to determine how to remove the older workforce from the plant. She decides to institute a rigorous training program that would be intolerable for most of the less-educated employees.

Required:

a. Discuss the business sense of hiring graduates with the necessary skills rather than paying for on-location training.

b. Discuss the ethics of the plan to remove the current workforce.

c. Why should Laura and DeRigeur be concerned about the welfare of the current workforce if it makes good business sense to hire the graduates of the vocational–technical school?

(Adapted with permission of The Associated Press.)

7. Two potential impediments to the implementation of JIT and other quality-oriented production systems that require employee participation are union contracts and labour relations laws. In the case of labour unions, union officials are often suspicious of management actions taken in the name of quality improvement because employers have frequently used such quality initiatives as excuses to fire employees. This historical context of quality improvement has caused present-day mistrust between employees and managers. Implementation of genuine quality-enhancing programs is often met with suspicion by employees.

   Even so, labour and management are trying to cooperate in some firms for the sake of their mutual survival. For example, in 1999 an international newspaper organization worked out an agreement with its labour union that allowed the union to sign up an additional 10,000 of the company's employees. In exchange, the union agreed to certain changes to make the company more efficient. For example, in its Hamilton, Ontario, plant, the organization restructured the production line of 320 people into teams of approximately 15 workers.

   Some employees felt that the new agreement began a new age of trust and cooperation between their union and their employer; other workers were more suspicious of the new, cozy relationship between management and the union.

(Source: Adapted from Josh Lemieux, "Hopes Set on Levi Strauss, Union Pact," *Bryan-College Station [Texas] Eagle*, October 16, 1994, C3.)

Required:

a. Why might unionization constrain the successful implementation of quality-oriented programs in Canadian manufacturing plants?

b. What are the ethical obligations of management to workers in implementing quality programs?

c. What ethical obligations do employees bear in implementing new programs devised by managers?

COMMUNICATIONS ACTIVITIES

1. This chapter discusses numerous techniques for controlling costs (e.g., EOQ, MRP, JIT, life cycle costing, and target costing). The supplementary materials on the Web for Chapter 7 add four more techniques for controlling costs (e.g., flexible manufacturing, re-engineering, theory of constraints, and linear programming). However, are these techniques merely management fads? "Fads" will fizzle out, but substantive management "classics" will endure.

    "Fad concepts are easy to understand and communicate and tend to be framed with labels, buzzwords, lists, and acronyms.... Unlike most fads ... classics demand real organizational changes at significant cost and have lasting effects. Classics typically arise not from the writings of academics or consultants but emerge out of practitioner responses to economic, social, and competitive challenges."

    (Source: Danny Miller and Jon Hartwick, "Spotting Management Fads," *Harvard Business Review*, October 2002, p. 27.)

    Required:

    Assess the techniques discussed in this chapter (including the supplementary materials on the Web page) as to whether they are fads or classics.

2. Select an organization in your area or one about whose production processes you can find substantial information. Assume that you have been hired as a consultant to provide a plan for successfully implementing JIT in one of the organization's plants. Prepare a broad written plan for implementing JIT, being certain to address the following items: internal and external communications; possible engineering changes needed for new production arrangements and their impacts; number, quality, and location of suppliers and any changes needed in supplier arrangements; behavioural implications; and length of time horizon for systems implementation.

PROJECTS

1. With restrictive funding and increasing demand for service because of general population growth and the aging of the baby boomers, Canadian hospitals have faced great pressures in the last two decades. The hospitals have had to be innovative in surgical techniques and anesthesia to make operations faster, less invasive, and less drastic to increase efficiency. Now many operations that in the past required overnight hospitalization can be done in day surgery.

    Required:

    Advances in technology have drastically affected cost control efforts in the medical field. Discuss with a person you know in the medical field—doctor, nurse, etc.—these advances in technology and how they have affected costs. A two- or three-page report will be sufficient.

2. Customer satisfaction—what brings customers back to hotels—is directly related to hotel employee experience. Experienced employees are more capable of providing the requisite service. However, with high turnover in most hotels, employees tend to be inexperienced.

    Required:

    Divide your class into teams of five members. Each team should be assigned to research one prominent publicly traded organization in the hotel industry. Obtain copies of annual reports for each organization over the period 1992 to 2003. [Note: Many university libraries have these types of records on computerized databases.] For each organization in each year, determine how it sought to improve customer satisfaction and repeat business.

3. Find an organization in your area that adopted JIT. Discuss with a representative of the company the benefits that the company expected to derive from the system and the benefits that the company has actually realized thus far. Ask the representative to discuss the implementation plan, including any major problems that were encountered.

USING THE INTERNET

1. Use Google or another search engine to find two Canadian organizations in the retail industry that, during the last decade, have introduced cost-reduction programs. Compare the two cost-reduction programs as to particular cost focus, implementation plan, and success. Be sure to assess the assumptions about costs in each organization. For example, were costs considered to be the result of inefficiency, or were costs assumed to be the result of strategic choice and, thus, cost reduction was a strategic issue? Prepare a four- or five-page report.

2. Use Google or another search engine to obtain lists of organizations: 10 that use EOQ, 10 that use JIT, and 10 that use MRP or MRP II. How do these organizations differ, or in other words, what organizational characteristics led these organizations to choose EOQ, JIT, or MRP/MRP II?

SOLUTIONS TO SELF-TEST QUESTIONS

1. d, 2. a, 3. b, 4. c, 5. a, 6. d, 7. d, 8. b, 9. b, 10. c

ENDNOTES

1. Normally "budget" would have been used instead of "expectations." This could not be done as budgeting is introduced in Chapter 9.

2. www.opseu.org/research/cpitable1.htm

3. John Huey, "Waking Up to the New Economy," *Fortune,* June 27, 1994, p. 37.

4. "Air Canada Cuts Its Fuel Surcharge in Half as Jet Fuel Prices Fall," *The Canadian Press,* Tuesday, November 20, 2001.

5. Peter Drucker, "Permanent Cost Cutting," *The Wall Street Journal,* January 11, 1999, A8.

6. Dan. W. Swenson, "Managing Costs through Complexity Reduction at Carrier Corporation," *Management Accounting,* April 1998, pp. 20–21.

7. This is often called the 20/80 inventory rule (i.e., 20% of the inventory items account for 80% of the inventory costs).

8. The rate of return should be the weighted average cost of capital, which is discussed in Chapter 10.

9. Pam Withers, "Finders–Keepers: The Six Secrets of Attracting and Retaining Great Employees," *CMA Magazine,* Vol. 75, Issue 7, October 2001, pp. 24–26.

10. A company may wish to measure the output of each manufacturing cell or work centre rather than total output. Although this practice may reveal problems in a given area, it does not correlate with JIT philosophy, which emphasizes a team approach, plantwide attitude, and total cost picture.

11. Jacob M. Schlesinger, Michael Williams, and Craig Forman, "Japan Inc., Wracked by Recession, Takes Stock of Its Methods," *Wall Street Journal,* September 29, 1993, A4.

12. Robin Cooper and Regine Slagmulder, *Target Costing and Value Engineering,* Montvale, NJ: The IMA Foundation for Applied Research, Inc., 1997, pp. 5–6.

Chapter 8

LEARNING OBJECTIVES

After reading this chapter, you should be able to answer the following questions:

1 What constitutes relevance in a decision-making situation?

2 Why is a sunk cost not relevant in decision making but an opportunity cost is?

3 What are the relevant costs in equipment replacement decisions?

4 What relevant costs and qualitative factors exist in a make-or-buy situation?

5 How can management best utilize a scarce resource?

6 How does relevant costing relate to sales mix, special pricing, compensation changes, and advertising budget decisions?

7 How is product margin used to determine whether a product line should be retained or eliminated?

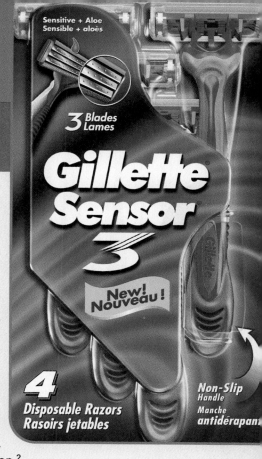

www.gillette.com

The Gillette Company

In 1905, GILLETTE opened a sales office in London and a factory in Paris, which were the beginning of today's global company. That year, King C. Gillette's portrait and signature debuted on razor blade packaging and quickly became the worldwide symbol of Gillette quality.

Gillette's manufacturing operations are conducted at facilities around the world, and its products are distributed through wholesalers, retailers, and agents in more than 200 countries and territories. Of the world's annual 20 billion razor blade sales, 33% are made by Gillette, even though most nondomestic markets have local manufacturers of double-edged blades.[1] In 2001, blades and razors accounted for $3.4 billion of Gillette's total sales of $8.96 billion.[2]

A key driver of Gillette's success has been a steady stream of new products. For every 15 product candidates that Gillette identifies, only one actually makes it into development. And, of those, only a third advance from development to eventually reach the market. The others are dropped or "shelved" because manufacturing costs are higher than the company would like. This is the major reason that Gillette has outpaced its competition for decades: the company has the ability to reduce manufacturing costs consistently while improving quality.[3]

In 1998, the company introduced the biggest shaving innovation in decades, the triple-bladed Mach3. Backed by an unprecedented advertising campaign, the Mach3 system quickly became a worldwide success.[4] The Gillette Company, on November 7, 2002, introduced Sensor 3, the only disposable razor with three independently spring-mounted Sensor® blades that adjust to the curves and contours of the skin. Gillette Sensor 3 provides overall the best shave of any disposable razor.[5] "Sensor 3 represents a significant breakthrough in disposable razor performance," said Peter K. Hoffman, president, Gillette Grooming Products. "It is one more example of our unwavering commitment to deliver the best shave possible for users of all types of wet shaving products."[6]

*G*illette has made numerous decisions about which products it will sell, the pricing of the products, and which product lines to eliminate. In addition, while the company would prefer universality in its products, it occasionally must adapt to a particular foreign market, since only approximately 71% of its sales come from the North American market. For instance, in some foreign markets, razors are selling well even though a razor could cost almost a month's pay. Many customers cannot afford to purchase replacement blades so the company has altered its packaging to make them affordable. In a business where even tenths of pennies are important, many such decisions must be based solely on monetary factors. The company commonly assesses the viability of its decisions using **relevant costs**, which are those costs that are pertinent to or logically associated with a specific problem or decision, and which differ between alternatives.

relevant cost
a cost that is pertinent to or logically associated with a specific problem or decision and that differs between alternatives

Gillette's business choices reflect a common type of decision: how to competently allocate available but limited organizational resources so that company goals and objectives are achieved. As indicated in the following quote, making decisions in today's business environment is not an easy task.

Decision making in the 1990s and beyond will be more of an art and less of a science. Not only is the world growing more complex and uncertain at a faster and faster pace, but the old decision-making models are failing, and we can expect their failure to accelerate as well.

If executives once imagined they could gather enough information to read the business environment like an open book, they have had to dim their hopes. The flow of information has swollen to such a flood that managers are in danger of drowning; extracting relevant data from the torrent is increasingly a daunting task.[7]

Accounting information can improve but not perfect management's understanding of the consequences of resource allocation decisions. To the extent that this information can reduce management's uncertainty about the economic facts, outcomes, and relationships involved in various courses of action, the information is valuable for decision-making purposes and necessary for conducting business.

As discussed in Chapter 3, many decisions are made on the basis of incremental analysis. Such analysis encompasses the concept of relevant costing, which allows managers to focus on pertinent facts and disregard extraneous information. This chapter illustrates the use of relevant costing in decisions about making or buying a product or part, allocating scarce resources, and determining the appropriate sales or production mix. Although these decisions are often viewed by managers as short-run, each decision also has significant long-run implications that must be considered.

LEARNING OBJECTIVE 1

What constitutes relevance in a decision-making situation?

THE CONCEPTS OF RELEVANCE AND RELEVANT COSTING

Managers routinely make decisions concerning alternatives that have been identified as feasible solutions to problems or feasible methods for the attainment of objectives. In doing so, they must weigh the relevant costs and benefits associated with each course of action and then determine the best course. Relevant costs are those costs that are pertinent to or logically associated with a specific problem or decision and that differ between alternatives.

Information is relevant when it logically relates to a decision about a future endeavour. Costs provide information, and different costs can be used for many different purposes. No single cost can be relevant in all decisions or to all managers. The challenge is to get specific information.

Accountants can assist managers in determining which costs are relevant to the objectives and decisions at hand. The challenge is to get the most specific information. To the extent possible and practical, **relevant costing** allows managers to focus on pertinent facts and disregard extraneous information by comparing the differential, incremental revenues and costs of alternative decisions. *Differential* refers to the different costs between or among the choices. *Incremental* means the additional or extra amount associated with some action. Thus, **incremental revenue** is the additional revenue resulting from a contemplated sale or provision of service. An **incremental cost** is the additional cost of producing or selling a contemplated additional quantity of output.

Success in strategic development and implementation requires that managers, in making decisions, are completely clear on what costs are relevant. They must be able to separate the relevant from the irrelevant to be effective in decision making.

Decision making is facilitated by an organization's having an ERP system. ERP systems with their rigorous handling of the recording and allocating of costs have more accurate costs. Similarly, the greater accuracy with recording revenues allows for more accurate revenue data. This greater accuracy means that relevance can be more precisely considered in an ERP environment.

Differential and, therefore, incremental costs are relevant costs. These costs may be variable or fixed. Two general rules for short-run decision making are that (1) most variable costs are relevant and (2) most fixed costs are not. The reasoning behind this rule is that, as sales or production volumes change, variable costs change but fixed costs do not. There are, however, some exceptions that must be acknowledged in the decision-making process.

For example, the direct material cost of a product is a relevant incremental variable cost in a decision to make each additional unit. In contrast, the fixed cost of the available production machinery would not be relevant to the production of each additional unit. However, the cost of buying new machinery is an incremental fixed cost relevant to the decision to produce a new product line or expand an existing one beyond the current relevant range.

Some relevant costs, such as sales commissions and the prime costs of production (direct material and direct labour), are easily identified and quantified. These factors are integral parts of the accounting system. Other factors (such as opportunity costs) may be relevant and quantifiable but are not recorded in the accounting system. (An **opportunity cost** represents the benefits forgone when one course of action is chosen over another. For example, by choosing to attend university, a student incurs an opportunity cost of the forgone earnings that could have been made by working at a paying job instead.) Such factors cannot be overlooked simply because they may be more difficult to obtain or may require the use of estimates.

A **sunk cost** is one that has already been incurred and cannot be changed regardless of the alternative selected. A sunk cost is not a relevant cost since it is a cost that will not be incurred in the future; it has already been incurred.

The difference between the incremental revenue and incremental cost of a particular alternative is the positive or negative incremental benefit of that course of action. When evaluating alternative courses of action, managers should select the alternative that provides the highest incremental benefit to the company. Such a comparison may superficially appear simple but often is not, because relevance is a concept that is inherently individual. For example, an investment proposal might provide a high rate of return for a company but might also create a future potential

relevant costing
a process that allows managers to focus on pertinent facts and disregard extraneous information by comparing, to the extent possible and practical, the differential, incremental revenues and incremental costs of alternative decisions

incremental revenue
the additional revenue resulting from a contemplated sale of a quantity of output

incremental cost
the additional cost of producing or selling a contemplated quantity of output

LEARNING OBJECTIVE 2

Why is a sunk cost not relevant in decision making but an opportunity cost is?

opportunity cost
the benefit forgone when one course of action is chosen over another

sunk cost
the historical or past cost that is associated with the acquisition of an asset or a resource

environmental hazard. One unit manager might view the potential hazard as very relevant, while another manager might minimize the relevance of that possibility. In some instances, all alternatives result in incremental losses, and managers must choose the one that creates the smallest incremental loss.

One alternative course of action often considered is defensive avoidance, or the "change nothing for the moment" option. Although other alternatives have certain incremental revenues and costs associated with them, the "change nothing" alternative represents current conditions. It may serve as a baseline against which all other alternatives can be measured. However, even the "change nothing" alternative may involve the risk of loss of competitive advantage. If a firm chooses this alternative while its competitors upgrade processes, that firm may incur the ultimate incremental loss—losing its market. Also, the opportunity costs associated with the status quo may result in less benefit than another alternative.

The "change nothing" alternative should be chosen only when it is perceived to be the best decision choice. Often, however, this alternative is selected only because it is easier than making changes. At other times, this selection is made because decision makers, lacking information, perceive uncertainty to be so great that they consider the risk of making a change to be greater than the risk of continuing the current course of action. When this condition exists, the results achieved from the "change nothing" alternative (current results) are thought to be more advantageous than the potential incremental benefit of any other alternative.

In some situations, such as those involving government regulations or mandates, a "change nothing" alternative does not truly exist. For example, if a company were polluting river water and a governmental regulatory agency issued an injunction against that company, it would be forced to correct the pollution problem (assuming it wished to continue in business). The company could, of course, delay installation of the pollution control devices at the risk of fines or closure, creating additional incremental cost effects that would have to be considered. Managers in this situation must make decisions using a "now-versus-later" attitude and may determine that now is better regardless of the cost.

Since a comprehensive evaluation of all alternative courses of action is part of rational management behaviour, the chosen course should be the one that will make the business and its stakeholders better off in the future. This means that managers must provide some mechanism for including all nonmonetary or inherently nonquantifiable considerations in the decision process. They can do that by attempting to quantify items or simply by making instinctive value judgments about nonmonetary benefits and costs.

To illustrate this point, consider the factors that should be evaluated when a labour-intensive company analyzes the labour savings that would result from replacing employees with robots or, as discussed in the following News Note, from changing locales. Company managers need to weigh potential future cost reductions and increases in productivity against possible short- and long-range negative public reaction toward the company because of the layoffs. Although public reactions are difficult to measure and quantify and may not be immediately noticeable, such reactions should still be factored into the decision. In addition, there may be very relevant but highly nonquantifiable costs resulting from ethical considerations, such as the moral obligations the firm has toward the displaced workers. Such costs must be estimated in a reasonable manner if the decision to replace workers is to be based on a truly valid analysis.

Where Is It Cheaper?

In a dramatic rethink of its corporate structure, Caltex moved its headquarters from Dallas to Singapore last year to be closer to its customers. It shifted Web site development to South Africa. And it set up the Manila accounting division before switching off the lights forever at the Dallas office early this year. "As technology and communications improve, we are scattering centers of excellence around the world," says William Pfluger, general manager of Caltex's Manila operation.

Caltex is on the cutting edge of a trend that is likely to revolutionize operations for the twenty-first century corporation. More and more service and professional jobs are shifting from high-cost Europe and the United States to developing countries.[8]

Phillips, founded in 1891, has moved production to countries with lower labour costs and has cut more than a fifth of the company's workforce since Kleisterlee [chief executive] took the helm in 2001.[9]

Levi Strauss & Co., whose jeans are an all-American symbol, said it is closing six U.S. plants and eliminating 3,600 jobs, or 22% of its workforce, as it moves away from the business of actually making the clothes it sells. "There is no question that we must move away from owned-and-operated plants in the U.S. to remain competitive in our industry," said Philip Marineau, chief executive officer. Contracting to outside manufacturers will enable the company to have a more flexible cost structure, protect its profit margins, and invest more in product development, marketing, and retailing, Mr. Marineau said.[10]

We can see much the same thing happening at Hornby's Hogwarts Express, a company that produces model train sets. The company has now outsourced all production to China. The chief executive said the decision to outsource all production to China meant that the group could sell products with "substantially better detail and authenticity" for the same cost. Hornby's site near Hong Kong employed 1,100 people for the same amount it cost to employ 500 people in the U.K.

"If we had not moved to China we may not have been in business now; our profits and market share were in decline," he said.[11]

RIS, which is in the midst of setting up its first offshore office, has about 360 staff and hopes to employ about 20 or 30 in Bucharest by the end of the year (2003) It's all about cost and global competition. A software developer in India or Romania might cost half to one eighth of what a Canadian-equivalent developer does. For a software or IT outsourcing company, most of its costs are labour, so the offshore savings can't be ignored. Now more than ever before it's easier and cheaper to just hire full-time employees halfway around the world in a place like Bangalore, India.[12]

The need for specificity in information depends on how important that information is relative to management objectives. If all other factors are equal, more precise information is given greater weight in the decision-making process. However, if information is important but qualitative and imprecise, management should find a way to estimate the impact such information may have on known monetary details and company profits.

Information can be based on past or present data but is relevant only if it relates to a future choice and creates a differential effect in regard to alternative choices. All managerial decisions are made to affect future events, so the information on which decisions are based should reflect future conditions. The future may be the short run (two hours from now or next month) or the long run (five years or more from now).[13]

Future costs are the only costs that can be avoided, and the longer into the future a decision's time horizon extends, the more costs are avoidable, controllable, and relevant. *Only information that has a bearing on future events is relevant in decision making.* But people too often forget this basic truth and try to make decisions using inappropriate data.

SUNK COSTS AND JOINT PROCESSES

One common error is trying to use a previously incurred, historical cost to make a current decision. Current costs (such as replacement or budgeted costs) are assumed to be accurate or reasonably accurate at the current time. As such, these costs represent relevant information and should be considered in the decision-making process. In contrast, historical costs incurred in the past to acquire an asset or a resource—called sunk costs—are not recoverable and cannot be changed, regardless of what current circumstances exist or what future course of action is taken. A current or future selling price may be present for an asset, but that is the result of current or future conditions and is not a recouping of a historical cost. The following discussion illustrates why sunk costs are not relevant costs.

Like Gillette, almost every company makes and sells a wide variety of products. Companies often must engage in multiple production processes to produce their products; for instance, Gillette could not manufacture its razors and Oral-B toothbrushes in the same manufacturing operation. However, it is possible for a single process to generate several different outputs simultaneously, as when Tyson Foods processes chickens to produce whole birds, parts, and "nuggets." Industries that produce multiple products from a single process include refineries, lumber mills, and food, chemical, and cosmetics manufacturers. A single process in which one product cannot be manufactured without others being produced is known as a **joint process.**

A company undertakes a joint production process to generate outputs known as **joint products**. Each type of joint product has substantial revenue-generating ability. In contrast, **by-products** and **scrap** are incidental outputs of a joint process. Both are saleable, but their sales values alone would not be enough for management to justify undertaking the joint process. By-products are viewed as having a higher sales value than scrap. A final output from a joint process is waste. **Waste** is a residual output that has no sales value. A normal amount of waste is considered a production cost that cannot be avoided.

A corn processing plant can be used to illustrate the types of outputs resulting from a joint process. Outputs may include corn on the cob and whole-kernel corn (joint products), partial corn kernels (by-products) used for cornmeal, inferior kernels (scrap) for sale to producers of animal food, and cobs (waste) that are discarded. Exhibit 8-1 shows the outputs of such a joint process.

The point at which the outputs of a joint process are first identifiable as individual products is called the **split-off point.** A joint process may have one or more split-off points, depending on the number and types of output produced. Output may be sold at the split-off point, if a market exists for products in that condition. Alternatively, some or all of the products may be processed further after exiting the joint process.

The costs incurred for materials, labour, and overhead during a joint process (up to the split-off point) are referred to as the **joint cost** of the production process. For companies to engage in a joint process, total revenues from sales of all resulting products should exceed the total costs of those products. The joint process results in a "basket" of products, and managers must be aware that some output from the joint process may require additional processing to make it saleable. However, after the joint process cost has been incurred, it is a sunk cost *regardless* of whether the output is saleable at the end of the joint process and *regardless* of how much the output may sell for.

joint process
a process in which one product cannot be manufactured without others being produced

joint products
two or more products that have relatively significant sales values and are not separately identifiable as individual products until the split-off point

by-products
products that have minor sales value as compared with the sales value of the major products and are not separately identifiable as individual products until they have become split-off

scrap
inputs that do not become part of the outputs but have very minor values

waste
inputs that do not become part of the output

split-off point
the point at which the outputs of a joint process are first identifiable as individual products

joint cost
the cost incurred, up to the split-off point, for material, labour, and overhead in a joint process

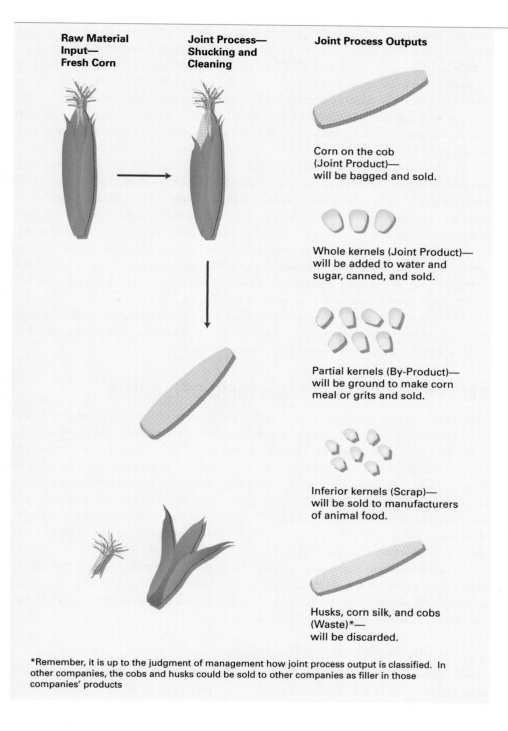

Raw Material Input— Fresh Corn

Joint Process— Shucking and Cleaning

Joint Process Outputs

Corn on the cob (Joint Product)— will be bagged and sold.

Whole kernels (Joint Product)— will be added to water and sugar, canned, and sold.

Partial kernels (By-Product)— will be ground to make corn meal or grits and sold.

Inferior kernels (Scrap)— will be sold to manufacturers of animal food.

Husks, corn silk, and cobs (Waste)*— will be discarded.

*Remember, it is up to the judgment of management how joint process output is classified. In other companies, the cobs and husks could be sold to other companies as filler in those companies' products

EXHIBIT 8-1

Illustration of Joint Process Output

If any of the joint process *outputs* are processed after the split-off point, additional costs will be incurred. Costs after split-off are assigned to the separate products for which those costs are incurred. Thus, management must consider the total joint costs plus any separate processing or selling costs it expects will be incurred before making the decision to commit resources to the joint process.

At the split-off point, the joint cost is allocated only to the joint products and not to any resulting by-products, scrap, or waste. The rationale for this allocation is that the joint products are the primary reason that management undertook production. Allocation may be made on the basis of a physical measure (such as kilograms or units) or a monetary measure (such as final sales value). Joint cost is a necessary and reasonable cost of producing the joint products and, thus, should be attached to those products for external financial statement purposes. However, the amount of joint cost allocated to the joint products is not relevant to decision making because once the joint process costs are incurred, they are historical and, therefore, sunk.

To illustrate, assume that a joint product has a selling price of $10 at split-off, but its selling price after further processing is $16. If the additional processing costs are less than $6 ($16 – $10), then the incremental revenue exceeds the incremental costs and additional processing should occur. Notice that the joint cost is not considered in this decision process. Once the products have reached the split-off point, the joint cost is a sunk cost. Additionally, the joint cost is a common cost of all joint products and is irrelevant to the decision to sell or process a particular joint output further. The only relevant items in the decision whether to sell or process further are the incremental costs after the split-off point.

The previous example illustrates the difference between relevant and irrelevant costs. The next section shows how the concepts of relevant costing are applied in making some common managerial decisions.

RELEVANT COSTS FOR SPECIFIC DECISIONS

Managers routinely make decisions on alternatives that have been identified as feasible solutions to problems or feasible methods for the attainment of objectives. In doing so, managers weigh the costs and benefits of alternative courses of action and determine which course is best. Incremental revenues, costs, and benefits of all courses of action are measured from a base that corresponds to current conditions. This statement means that managers must provide some mechanism for including the inherently nonquantifiable considerations. Inclusion can be made by attempting to quantify items or by simply making instinctive value judgments about nonmonetary benefits and costs.

When evaluating alternative courses of action, managers should select the alternative that provides the highest incremental benefit to the company. In some instances, all alternatives result in incremental losses, and managers must choose the one that creates the smallest incremental loss.

Equipment Replacement Decisions

LEARNING OBJECTIVE 3

What are the relevant costs in equipment replacement decisions?

Many business decision situations relate to assets. After an asset or resource is acquired, managers may find that the product produced or service performed by that asset is no longer marketable or that the asset is no longer adequate for the intended purposes, does not perform to expectations, or is not technologically current. Decisions must then be made whether to keep or dispose of the old asset and, if disposed, whether to replace it. Although asset acquisition decisions are covered in depth in Chapter 10, the following illustration provides an excellent starting point to introduce the concept of using relevant cost information for making asset replacement decisions.

Assume that Spiros Zeros purchases a computer system for $3,200 on December 28, 2004, from a company that is going out of business on December 31. Spiros expects the computer to last for his three years at law school and, after that

Keep the old or buy the new? What should Spiros do?

time, to have no salvage value. This computer will be referred to as the "old" computer. One week later, on January 4, 2005, Spiros notices an advertisement for a similar computer for $2,300 at one of the major electronics discount stores. This computer also has an estimated life of three years and no salvage value. This "new" computer will perform as well as the "old" computer and, in addition, has a larger hard drive memory for faster processing time. The new computer will save $300 per year in operating, maintenance, and repair costs over the old computer. Upon investigation, Spiros discovers that he can sell his week-old computer for only $2,200—the "going out of business" price had not been such a bargain, and he is unable to return it to the store since it no longer exists. Data on the old and new computers are shown in Exhibit 8-2.

Spiros has two options: (1) use the old computer or (2) sell the old computer and buy the new one. Exhibit 8-3 on page 444 presents the relevant costs Spiros should consider in making his asset replacement decision. As shown in the computations in Exhibit 8-3, the $3,200 purchase price of the old computer does not affect the decision process. This $3,200 was "gone forever" when Spiros bought the computer. However, if he sells the old computer, he will effectively be able to reduce the net cash outlay for the new computer to $100 because he will have $2,200 more than he has currently. Using either computer, Spiros will spend money over the next three years for operating costs, but he will spend $900 less using the new computer ($300 savings per year × 3 years).

The $1,000 difference between the $3,200 original cost and the $2,200 resale value is either a current period loss or, if he keeps the computer, future period depreciation. Thus, the $1,000 loss or its equivalent in depreciation charges is the

	Old Computer (Purchased December 28, 2004)	New Computer (Available on January 4, 2005)
Cost	$3,200	$2,300
Annual operating cost	1,200	900
Salvage value	0	0
Current resale value	2,200	Not applicable
Life in years	3	3

EXHIBIT 8-2

Spiros Zeros' Computer Information

EXHIBIT 8-3

Relevant Costs Related to
Spiros's Alternatives

Alternative 1: Use old computer		
Operating cost over life of old computer ($1,200 × 3 years)		$3,600
Alternative 2: Sell old computer and buy new		
Cost of new computer	$2,300	
Resale value of old computer	2,200	
Effective net outlay for new computer	$ 100	
Operating cost over life of new computer ($900 × 3 years)	2,700	
Total cost of new computer		2,800
Benefit from purchasing new computer		$ 800

same in magnitude whether Spiros disposes of the old computer and buys the new one or retains the old computer and uses it. This $1,000 cannot be avoided under either alternative; it will be either a loss or an expense. Since the amount is the same under both alternatives, it is not relevant to the decision process.

The relevant factors in deciding whether to purchase the new computer are

a. the cost of the new computer ($2,300)

b. the current resale value of the old computer ($2,200)

c. the annual savings of the new computer ($300) and the number of years (three) that the savings would be enjoyed

The common tendency is initially to believe that Spiros should not purchase the new computer because he will incur a $1,000 loss on an asset that he has only had for seven days. Even if Spiros received only $1,500 from its sale, the choice would have remained the same. In this case, he would save a total of $100 by buying the new computer and abandoning the old, as shown in the following computation:

Operating cost of old computer		$3,600
Cost of new computer:		
Purchase price ($2,300 – $1,500)	$ 800	
Operating cost	2,700	3,500
Savings by purchasing new computer		$ 100

Spiros must resign himself to accept the past as a fact and make new choices given his set of future alternatives.

Relevant costing techniques are also appropriate in make-or-buy decisions.

LEARNING OBJECTIVE 4

What relevant costs and qualitative factors exist in a make-or-buy situation?

outsource
use a source external to the company to provide a service or manufacture a needed product or component

make-or-buy decision
a decision that compares the cost of internally manufacturing a product component with the cost of purchasing it from outside suppliers or from another division at a specified price and, thus, attempts to assess the best uses of available facilities

RELEVANT COSTS ON MAKE-OR-BUY DECISIONS

A constant concern in manufacturing is whether components of the right quality will be available at the right time and at a reasonable price. Companies often assure the availability of a component by manufacturing it themselves. (In some cases, this decision may be made because the company is interested in embarking on a vertical integration path, in which one division or subsidiary can serve as a supplier to others within the same company.) Other companies prefer to **outsource,** or purchase some or all components from external parties. "Toyota makes only about 25% of its own parts."[14] Dell buys circuit boards, disk drives, and other modules—designed specifically for Dell—from outside manufacturers and assembles the computers in its own warehouses.[15] This type of **make-or-buy decision** should be made only after proper analysis. Managers should compare the cost of internally manufacturing a product component with the cost of purchasing it from outside suppliers (or from another division). They should also assess the best uses of the available

EXHIBIT 8-4

Make-or-Buy Considerations

Relevant Quantitative Factors

Incremental production costs for each unit
Unit cost of purchasing from outside supplier (price less any discounts available plus shipping)
Availability of production capacity to manufacture components
Opportunity costs of using facilities for production rather than for other purposes
Availability of storage space for units and raw materials

Relevant Qualitative Factors

Relative net advantage given uncertainty of estimates (costs, risks, and so forth)
Reliability of source(s) of supply
Ability to assure quality when units are purchased from outside
Nature of the work to be subcontracted (such as the importance of the part to the whole product)
Number of available suppliers
Impact on customers and markets
Future bargaining position with supplier(s)
Perceptions regarding possible future price changes
Perceptions about current product prices (Is the price appropriate or—as may be the case with international suppliers—is product dumping involved?)
Strategic and competitive importance of component to long-run organizational success

facilities. (Consideration of a "make" option implies that the company has the available capacity for that purpose.) Relevant information for a make-or-buy decision includes both quantitative and qualitative factors.

Exhibit 8-4 presents some of these quantitative and qualitative factors. Many of the quantitative factors (such as incremental production costs per unit and the purchase price quoted by the supplier) are known with a high degree of certainty. Other factors, such as the opportunity cost associated with production facilities, must be estimated. The qualitative factors should be evaluated by more than one individual so that personal biases do not cloud valid business judgments.

Exhibit 8-5 provides information about a motor for a ladies' electric shaver that is produced by Jabat Ltd., a company that produces a variety of health and beauty aids. The total cost to manufacture one motor is $5. The company can purchase motors from Chancellor Manufacturing Ltd. for $4.75 per unit. Jabat's accountant, Bradley Carleton, is trying to determine whether the company should make the motors or buy them from an outside supplier..

EXHIBIT 8-5

Make-or-Buy Cost Information

	Present Manufacturing Cost per Motor	Relevant Cost per Motor to Manufacture
Direct materials	$1.60	$1.60
Direct labour	2.00	2.00
Variable manufacturing overhead	0.80	0.80
Fixed manufacturing overhead[1]	0.60	0.20
Total unit cost	$5.00	$4.60
Quoted price from Chancellor Manufacturing Ltd.	$4.75	

[1] Of the $0.60 fixed manufacturing overhead, only $0.20 is directly linked to production of the motors. This amount is related to the production supervisor's salary and could be avoided if the firm chose not to produce shaver motors. The remaining $0.40 of fixed manufacturing overhead is an allocated indirect (common) cost that would continue even if shaver motor production ceased.

Relevant costs are those costs that are pertinent and avoidable, regardless of whether they are variable or fixed. In a make-or-buy decision, variable costs of production are relevant. Fixed production costs may be relevant if they can be avoided by discontinuance of production. Production of each shaver motor requires a cost outlay of $4.40 for materials, labour, and variable overhead. In addition, $0.20 of the fixed overhead is considered a relevant product cost because it specifically relates to the manufacture of motors. This $0.20 is an incremental cost, since it could be avoided if shaver motors were not produced. The remaining $0.40 of fixed overhead is not relevant to the decision of whether to make or buy the motors. This $0.40 is a common cost that cannot be associated with shaver motor production and is incurred because of general production activity. Because this portion of the fixed cost would continue under either alternative, it is not relevant.

The relevant cost for the "make" alternative is $4.60—the cost that would be avoided if the product were not made. This amount should be compared with the $4.75 price quoted by the supplier under the "buy" alternative. The $4.60 is the incremental cost of production, and the $4.75 is the incremental cost of purchasing. Based solely on the quantitative information, management should choose to manufacture the motors rather than buy them, since the company will save $0.15 on each motor produced rather than purchased.

The opportunity cost associated with the facilities being used by production may also be relevant in a make-or-buy alternative. Jabat's management must determine whether an alternative purpose exists for the facilities now being used to manufacture the motors. If a more profitable alternative is available, management should consider diverting the capacity to this alternative use.

For example, assume that Jabat Ltd. has an opportunity to rent the building now used to produce motors to an outside tenant for $176,000 per year. Jabat presently produces 800,000 motors annually. Thus, it incurs an opportunity cost of $0.22 per unit ($176,000 ÷ 800,000 motors) by using the facilities rather than renting them. There are two ways to treat this opportunity cost. Both methods provide the same selection decision.

First, the $0.22 per unit can be treated as a reduction in the purchase cost because the facilities can be rented only if the component is purchased. Second, $0.22 per unit can be added to the production cost, since the company is giving up this amount by choosing to make the component. (This treatment is more consistent with the definition of an opportunity cost.) The giving up of inflows is as much a cost as the incurrence of an outflow. Exhibit 8-6 shows these two treatments on a per-unit and a total cost basis. Under either format, the comparison indicates that there is a $0.07 per unit advantage to purchasing rather than producing.

Jabat Ltd.'s accountant should inform management that, based on the information shown in Exhibit 8-6, it is more economical to buy motors from Chancellor Manufacturing Ltd. for $4.75 than to manufacture them. Such information is the typical starting point of the decision process—determining whether an alternative satisfies the quantitative considerations associated with a problem. If it does, managers then use judgment to assess the qualitative aspects of the decision.

Assume that Jabat's purchasing agent recently read in *The Globe and Mail* that Chancellor Manufacturing Ltd. was in poor financial condition and was likely to file for bankruptcy. In this case, Jabat's management will probably decide to continue producing the motors rather than purchasing them from Chancellor. Even though quantitative analysis supports the purchase of the units, qualitative judgment suggests that this would not be a wise course of action, since the stability of the supplying source is questionable. If Jabat stops motor production and rents out its

EXHIBIT 8-6

Opportunity Cost in a Make-or-Buy Decision

Per Unit	I			II	
	Make	**Buy**	**or**	**Make**	**Buy**
Direct production costs	$4.60			$4.60	
Opportunity cost (revenue forgone)		(0.22)		0.22	
Purchase cost		$4.75			$4.75
Cost per motor	$4.60	$4.53		$4.82	$4.75

In Total	**Make**	**Buy**	**Difference in Favour of Purchasing**
Revenue from renting facility	$ 0	$ 176,000	$ 176,000
Direct cost for 800,000 motors	(3,680,000)[1]	(3,800,000)[2]	$(120,000)
Net (cost) or revenue	$(3,680,000)	$(3,624,000)	$ 56,000[3]

[1] $4.60 × 800,000

[2] $4.75 × 800,000

[3] The $56,000 represents the net purchase benefit of $0.07 per unit multiplied by the 800,000 units to be purchased during the year.

facilities and Chancellor Manufacturing, Ltd. goes bankrupt, Jabat could be faced with high start-up costs to revitalize its motor production process. This was essentially the situation faced by Stoneyfield Farm, a yogurt company. Stoneyfield Farm subcontracted its yogurt production and, one day, found its supplier bankrupt—creating an inability to fill customer orders. It took Stoneyfield two years to acquire the necessary production capacity and regain market strength.

These additional considerations also indicate that there are many potential long-run effects of a theoretically short-run decision. Control over product quality and on-time delivery are two other important factors in decisions to buy from suppliers. Outsourcing may appear on the surface to be the best answer to cost control; however, if contract manufacturers do not produce properly, it may be less expensive to acquire internal resources.

Outsourcing has dramatic long-term consequences. It involves an ongoing relationship with considerable complexity and business risk. Future business environments may bear little resemblance to those of today, possibly nullifying the benefits of outsourcing.

Outsourcing is not right for all organizations, nor is it a cure-all or a quick-fix solution to a long-term challenge, but it is a potentially beneficial strategy when used in the right situation.[16]

Some companies have taken a more long-range perspective of certain make-or-buy decisions. Gillette, for instance, took a very long-run perspective when it decided to manufacture razor blades internally rather than purchase them from outside suppliers. The company believed that there was a competitive advantage to be obtained by determining how to shape and strengthen the blade on internally designed laser welding equipment. This choice was apparently the right one: total razor and blade sales for Gillette have increased both in North America and worldwide.

Another example is that of IBM. IBM developed magneto-resistive (MR) disk-drive recording heads. MR heads can increase a disk drive's data-storage capacity by a factor of 10, but achieving that increase is not an easy feat. A drive maker cannot simply outsource these heads and then plug them into a conventionally designed product. The disk and dozens of other elements must be modified as the heads are incorporated. MR technology isn't understood well enough for engineers to specify to a supplier which attributes of the head are most critical. Also, engineers don't yet understand how changes in design affect manufacturability or how subtle changes in manufacturing methods affect performance. So IBM has to build these devices in-house.[17]

Make-or-buy decisions are not confined to manufacturing entities. Many service organizations must make the same kinds of choices. For example, accounting and law firms must decide whether to prepare and present in-house continuing education programs or rely on external sources such as professional organizations and consultants. Private schools must determine whether to own school buses or hire independent contractors. Doctors must investigate the relative merits of having blood drawn and tested in their offices or having this work done in separate lab facilities; considerations include cost, quality of results, and convenience to patients. These examples simply indicate that the term *make* in *make-or-buy* does not necessarily mean converting a raw material to a finished component; it can also mean providing an in-house service.

Make-or-buy decisions consider the opportunity costs associated with utilized facilities because these facilities are in limited supply. If capacity is occupied in one way, it cannot be used at the same time for another purpose. Limited capacity is only one type of scarce resource that managers need to consider when making decisions.

<table>
<tr><td>LEARNING OBJECTIVE</td><td>5</td></tr>
</table>

How can management best utilize a scarce resource?

scarce resources
resources that are available only in limited quantity; they create constraints on producing goods or providing services and may include money, machine hours, skilled labour hours, raw materials, and production capacity

RELEVANT COSTS IN SCARCE RESOURCE DECISIONS

Managers are frequently confronted with the short-run problem of making the best use of **scarce resources** that are essential to production activity but are available only in limited quantity. Scarce resources create constraints on producing goods or providing services.[18] These resources may include money, machine hours, skilled labour hours, raw materials, and production capacity. In the long run, management may desire and be able to obtain a greater abundance of a scarce resource, for example, by purchasing additional machines to increase availability of machine hours. However, in the short run, management must make the best current use of the scarce resources it has.

Determining the best use of a scarce resource requires that specific company objectives be recognized. If management's objective is to maximize company contribution margin and profits, the best use of a scarce resource is for the production and sale of the product that has the highest contribution margin per unit of the scarce resource. This strategy assumes that the company is faced with only one scarce resource.

Exhibit 8-7 presents information on the two products made by Reed Ltd. on its plastic moulding machines. Reed Ltd. has only 4,000 machine hours available per month to make plastic housings for either hair dryers or hot rollers or some combination of both of these. Demand is unlimited for both products. Assume there are no variable selling, general, or administrative costs related to either product.

The hair dryer's $30 unit selling price minus its $20 unit variable cost provides a contribution margin of $10 per unit. The hot rollers' contribution margin per unit is $13 ($24 − $11). Fixed overhead totals $320,000 and is allocated to products on a machine hour basis for purposes of inventory valuation. However, fixed overhead does not change with production levels within the relevant range and, therefore, is not a relevant cost for a decision on scarce resource mix.

Since fixed overhead per unit is not relevant in the present case, unit contribution margin rather than unit gross margin is the appropriate measure of profitability

	Hair Dryers	Hot Rollers
Selling price per unit (a)	$ 30	$ 24
Variable production cost per unit:		
Direct material	$ 6	$ 5
Direct labour	8	4
Variable overhead	6	2
Total variable cost per unit (b)	(20)	(11)
Unit contribution margin [(c) = (a) − (b)]	$ 10	$ 13
Units of output per machine hour (d)	80	40
Contribution margin per machine hour [(c) × (d)]	$800	$520

EXHIBIT 8-7

Reed Ltd. Product Information
Scarce Resource—Machine Hours

of the two products. Unit contribution margin is multiplied by the number of units of output per unit of the scarce resource (in this case, machine hours) to obtain the contribution margin per unit of scarce resource. The last line in Exhibit 8-7 shows contribution margin per machine hour of $800 ($10 × 80) for hair dryers compared with $520 ($13 × 40) for hot rollers. Hair dryers are the more profitable item for Reed Ltd. to produce.

At first, it would appear that hot rollers would be more profitable, since their $13 unit contribution margin is higher than the $10 unit contribution margin for hair dryers. However, since one hour of machine time produces twice as many hair dryers as hot rollers, a greater amount of contribution margin per hour of scarce resource is generated by the production of hair dryers. If Reed Ltd. wanted to achieve the highest possible profit, it would dedicate all machine time to the production of hair dryers. If all units produced were sold, this strategy would provide a total contribution margin of $3,200,000 per month ($800 per hour × 4,000 available hours).

For all of the above reasons, management may decide that some less profitable products are necessary components in the company's product mix. Production mix translates into sales mix on the revenue side. The next section addresses the issue of sales mix.

RELEVANT COSTS IN SALES MIX AND SALES PRICE DECISIONS

Management continuously strives to satisfy a variety of company goals such as maximization of company profit, improvement of relative market share, and generation of customer goodwill and loyalty. These goals are achieved through selling products or performing services. Regardless of whether the company is a retailer, manufacturer, or service organization, **sales mix** refers to "the relative combination of quantities of sales of the various products that make up the total sales of a company."[19] One way a company can achieve its goals is to manage its sales mix effectively.

Dell Computer is introducing complementary items to its core PC line to increase overall profits. In addition to printers and scanners, Dell is adding a micro-portable projector. "Nick Eades, Marketing Director at Dell Computer Corporation, says projectors are a logical complement to a notebook computer for presenters. 'Our goal with this product is to deliver the practicality and features our customers want at a great value. We've created a projector that not only addresses the needs of a broad spectrum of customers, but stands on its own as a strong entry into the market.'"[20]

LEARNING OBJECTIVE 6

How does relevant costing relate to sales mix, special pricing, compensation changes, and advertising budget decisions?

sales mix
the relative combination of quantities of sales of the various products that make up the total sales of a company

EXHIBIT 8-8

Abssy Corporation—Product Information

	Basic Scale		Deluxe Scale		Talking Scale	
Unit selling price		$100.00		$130.00		$150.00
Variable unit costs:						
Direct material	$ 15.00		$ 20.00		$ 36.00	
Direct labour	10.00		15.00		31.00	
Variable manufacturing overhead	3.00		7.00		17.00	
Total variable production cost	$ 28.00		$ 42.00		$ 84.00	
Variable selling expense[1]	10.00		13.00		15.00	
Total variable cost		(38.00)		(55.00)		(99.00)
Contribution margin per unit		$ 62.00		$ 75.00		$ 51.00

[1]The only variable selling expense is a sales commission, which is always 10% of unit selling price.

Some important factors affecting the appropriate sales mix of a company are product selling prices, salesforce compensation, and advertising expenditures. A change in one or all of these factors may cause a company's sales mix to shift. Abssy Corporation produces a line of bathroom scales—basic, deluxe, and talking. The data presented in Exhibit 8-8 above are used to illustrate the effects on sales mix relating to this line.

Sales Price Changes and Relative Profitability of Products

Managers must continuously monitor the selling prices of company products, in relation to each other as well as to competitors' prices. This process may provide information that causes management to change one or more selling prices. For example, if Abssy Corporation found that the talking scale sold better at the beginning of the year (after the holidays) than at other times, it might increase the sales price of this scale during this period. Factors that might influence price changes include fluctuations in demand, production distribution costs, economic conditions, and competition. Any shift in the selling price of one product in a multiproduct firm will normally cause a change in the sales mix of that firm because of the economic law of demand elasticity with respect to price.[21]

Abssy's management has set profit maximization as the primary corporate goal. This strategy does not necessarily mean selling as many units as possible of the product with the highest selling price and as few as possible of the products with lower selling prices. The product with the highest selling price per unit does not necessarily yield the highest contribution margin per unit or per unit of scarce resource. In Abssy Corporation's case, the talking scale yields the lowest unit con-

Each of Abssy Corporation's scales yields a different contribution margin.

Basic   Deluxe   Talking

tribution margin of the three products. The talking scale also requires more direct labour and machine time. Costs are high for direct labour and variable manufacturing overhead. Even making the simplistic assumption that no resources are scarce, it is more profit-beneficial to sell the deluxe scale than either the basic or talking scales, since a deluxe scale provides the highest unit contribution margin of the three products. Even a basic scale is more profitable than a talking scale because, although the basic scale has the lowest unit selling price, its unit contribution margin is greater than that of the talking scale.

If profit maximization is the company's goal, a product's sales volume and unit contribution margin should be considered. Total company contribution margin is equal to the combined contribution margins provided by all the products' sales. Exhibit 8-9 indicates the respective total contribution margins of Abssy's three types of bathroom scales. Although the basic scale does not have the highest unit contribution margin, it does generate the largest total product line contribution margin because of its sales volume. To maximize profits, Abssy's management must maximize total contribution margin rather than per-unit contribution margin.

The sales volume of a product or service is almost always intricately related to its selling price. When selling price is increased and demand is elastic with respect to price, demand for that product decreases.[22] Thus, if Abssy's management, in an attempt to increase profits, decides to raise the price of the basic scale to $120, there should be some decline in demand. Assume that consultation with marketing research personnel indicates that such a price increase would cause demand for the product to drop from 20,000 to 12,000 scales per period. Exhibit 8-10 shows the effect of this pricing decision on total contribution margin.

Even though the contribution margin per unit of the basic scale increased from $62 to $80, the total dollar contribution margin generated by sales of the product has declined because of the decrease in sales volume. This example assumes that

	Unit Contribution Margin (From Exhibit 8-8)	Current Sales Volume in Units	Total
Basic scale	$62	20,000	$1,240,000
Deluxe scale	75	13,000	975,000
Talking scale	51	8,000	408,000
Total contribution margin of product sales mix			$2,623,000

EXHIBIT 8-9

Relationship Between Contribution Margin and Sales Volume

	Unit Contribution Margin	New Sales Volume in Units	Total
Basic scale	$80.00[1]	12,000	$ 960,000
Deluxe scale	$75.00	13,000	975,000
Talking scale	$51.00	8,000	408,000
Total contribution margin of product sales mix			$2,343,000

[1]Calculated as:

New selling price	$120
Total variable production cost (from Exhibit 8-8)	(28)
Total variable selling expense (10% of selling price)	(12)
Contribution margin	$ 80

EXHIBIT 8-10

Relationship Between Sales Price and Demand

customers did not switch their purchases from the basic scale to other Abssy bathroom scales when the price of the basic scale was raised. Price increases normally cause customers to switch from a company's high-priced products to its lower-priced products or to a competitors' product. In this instance, switching within the company was ignored because the basic scale was the company's lowest-priced scale. It is *unlikely* that customers would stop buying the basic scale because of a $20 price increase and begin buying the deluxe scale (which costs even more)—but that situation could occur. Customers might believe that the difference in quality between the basic and deluxe scales is worth the extra $10 (rather than the $30) and make such a purchasing switch.

In making decisions to raise or lower prices, the relevant quantitative factors include (1) prospective or new contribution margin per unit of product, (2) both short-term and long-term changes in product demand and production volume caused by the price increase or decrease, and (3) best use of any scarce resources. Some relevant qualitative factors involved in decisions regarding price changes are (1) influence on customer goodwill, (2) customer product loyalty, and (3) competitors' reactions to the firm's new pricing structure.[23]

When deciding to change the prices of current products or to introduce new products that will compete with current products that may affect their sales volumes, managers need to be certain that their assumptions about consumer behaviour are rational. Comparisons are typically made against a "base case" scenario, which estimates how consumers will behave if no changes are made. Often companies implicitly assume that the base case is simply a continuation of the status quo, but this assumption ignores market trends and competitor behaviour. Using the wrong base case is typical of product launches in which the new product will likely erode the market for the company's existing product line.[24] Failure to diversify as product demand for current products and services wanes can be costly.

Mattel is building on its best-selling Barbie doll. Mattel will this year add pets and houses to the "What's Her Face" line of write-on, wipe-off dolls, and new baby dolls called Shining Stars that include materials to name and register them with the International Star Registry. Still, double-digit international Barbie sales and strong sales in the other girls' products pushed the division to an overall sales gain of 3%. In late 2002, the company introduced a line of women's accessories, including china and stationery sets designed with colours and patterns from vintage Barbie dresses and featuring more subtle Barbie images.[25]

Special Order Pricing

special order pricing
determining a sales price to charge for manufacturing or service jobs that are outside the company's normal production or service realm

In **special order pricing**, management must determine a sales price to charge for manufacturing or service jobs that are outside the company's normal production or service realm. Special order situations include jobs that require a bid, are taken during slack periods, or are manufactured to a particular buyer's specifications. Typically, the sales price quoted on a special order job should be high enough to cover the variable costs of the job and any incremental (additional) fixed costs caused by the job, and to generate a profit. Special order pricing requires knowledge of the relevant costs associated with the specific problem or decision at hand.

Abssy Corporation has been given the opportunity to bid on a special order for 1,000 deluxe scales. Company management wants to obtain the order as long as the additional business will provide a satisfactory contribution to profit. The company has machine and labour hours that are not currently being used (idle capacity), and raw materials can be obtained from the supplier. Also, Abssy Corporation has no immediate opportunity to use its current excess capacity in any other way, so opportunity cost is not a factor.

The information necessary to determine a bid price on the deluxe scale is presented in Exhibit 8-8 (page 450). Direct material, direct labour, and variable manufacturing overhead costs are relevant to setting the bid price because these variable production costs will be incurred for each additional deluxe scale manufactured. Although all variable costs are normally relevant to a special pricing decision, the variable selling expense is irrelevant in this instance because no sales commission will be paid on this sale.

Fixed production overhead and fixed selling and administrative expenses are not expected to increase because of this sale, so these expenses are not included in the pricing decision.

Using the available cost information, the relevant cost used to determine the bid price for the scale is $42 (direct material, direct labour, and variable manufacturing overhead). This cost is the minimum special order price at which the company should sell a deluxe scale. If the existing fixed costs have been covered by regular sales, any price set higher than $42 will provide the company with some profit.

Assume that Abssy Corporation is currently experiencing a $10,000 net loss. Company managers want to set a bid price that would cover the net loss generated by other sales and create a $3,000 before-tax profit. In this case, Abssy would spread the total $13,000 desired amount over the 1,000 deluxe scales at $13 per scale. This would give a bid price of $55 per scale ($42 variable cost + $13). However, any price above the $42 variable cost will contribute toward reducing the $10,000 loss.

In setting the bid price, management must decide how much profit it would consider to be reasonable on the special order. As another example, since Abssy's usual selling price for a deluxe scale is $130, each sale provides a normal contribution margin of $75 or approximately 58%. Setting the bid price for the special order at $66.36 would cover the variable production costs of $42 and provide a normal 58% contribution margin. This computation illustrates a simplistic cost-plus approach to pricing but ignores both product demand and market competition. Abssy Corporation's bid price should also reflect the latter considerations. In addition, company management should consider the effect that the special order will have on all company activities (purchasing, receiving, warehousing, and so forth) and whether these activities will create additional, unforeseen costs.

There are situations in which a company will depart from its typical price-setting routine. For example, a company may "low-ball" bid some jobs. A low-ball bid may only cover variable costs or it may be below such costs. The rationale behind making low-ball bids is to obtain the job in order to introduce company products or services to a particular market segment.

Special pricing of this nature may provide work for a period of time but cannot be continued for the long run. To remain in business, a company must set product or service selling prices to cover total variable costs, to cover an appropriate amount of fixed, selling, or administrative costs, and to provide a reasonable profit margin. An exception to this general rule, however, may occur when a company produces related or complementary products as can be seen in the following discussion.

At first Gillette gave away a razor and sold the blades. Adobe Systems was one of the first to realize that this model made sense in the digital world. Adobe gave away its basic Acrobat Reader software to better sell its high-margin creative tools, such as Acrobat Distiller. Adobe is now the second-largest North American PC-software company, with annual revenues exceeding $1.2 billion. Other companies quickly followed suit, including Oracle, which gives away its development tools to promote sales of its database software, and Sun Microsystems, which supplies Java for free and sells workstations and the Sun operating system.[26]

Special pricing concessions may also be justified when orders are of an unusual nature (because of the quantity, method of delivery, or packaging) or because the products are being tailor-made to customer specifications. Further, special pricing can be used when producing goods for a one-time job, such as an overseas order that will not affect domestic sales.

When setting a special order price, management must consider the qualitative issues as well as the quantitative ones. For instance, will a low bid price cause this customer (or others) to feel that a precedent has been established for future prices? Will the contribution margin on a bid set low enough to acquire the job earn an amount sufficient to justify the additional burdens placed on management or employees by this activity? How, if at all, will special order sales affect the company's normal sales? If the job is taking place during a period of low business activity (off-season or recession), is management willing to take the business at a lower contribution or profit margin simply to keep a trained workforce employed?

Compensation Changes

Many companies compensate their salespeople by paying a fixed commission rate on gross sales dollars. If Abssy Corporation uses this type of commission structure, sales personnel will be motivated to sell the talking scale, rather than the basic or deluxe scales. Emphasizing sales of the talking scale will not help the company achieve its profit maximization objective, however, since this scale provides the lowest unit contribution margin. If management wants to motivate salespeople to ensure that the company is able to achieve its profit maximization objective, a change in the commission compensation structure is needed.

The starting point for a change in the compensation structure is knowledge of the product contribution margin, which is equal to selling price minus total variable production (but not variable selling) costs. The per-unit product contribution margins of Abssy's line of scales are as follows:

	Selling Price	Total Variable Production Cost	Product Contribution Margin
Basic scale	$100	$28	$72
Deluxe scale	130	42	88
Talking scale	150	84	66

Abssy is considering a new policy of paying salespeople a commission of 20% on product contribution margin rather than 10% on sales price. This policy change should motivate sales personnel to sell more of the product that produces the highest commission for them, which, in turn, will shift the original sales mix toward sales of products most profitable to the company.

Exhibit 8-11 compares Abssy's total contribution margin based on the original sales mix and commission structure (repeated from Exhibit 8-9) with total contribution margin under the new assumed sales mix and commission structure. The new commission policy is beneficial for the company because it shifts the sales mix from the high-priced, low-contribution-margin talking scale toward the lower-priced but more profitable basic and deluxe scales.

Fixed costs are not considered in setting sales commissions. All sales and production volumes of the respective products are assumed to be within the relevant

EXHIBIT 8-11

Impact of Change in
Commission Structure

Old Policy—Commissions equal 10% of selling price

	Product Contribution Margin Before Commission	Commission	Contribution Margin After Commission	Total Old Volume	Contribution Margin
Basic scale	$72	$10 (0.1 × $100)	$62	20,000	$1,240,000
Deluxe scale	88	13 (0.1 × $130)	75	13,000	975,000
Talking scale	66	15 (0.1 × $150)	51	8,000	408,000
Total contribution margin for product sales					$2,623,000

New Policy—Commissions equal 20% of product contribution margin per unit

	Product Contribution Margin Before Commission	Commission	Contribution Margin After Commission	Total New Volume	Contribution Margin
Basic scale	$72	$14.40 (0.20 × $72)	$57.60	20,500	$1,180,800
Deluxe scale	88	17.60 (0.20 × $88)	70.40	17,000	1,196,800
Talking scale	66	13.20 (0.20 × $66)	52.80	3,500	184,800
Total contribution margin for product sales					$2,562,400

range of activity for the company. Therefore, regardless of a shift in activity levels, total fixed costs will remain constant.

For morale purposes, the sales personnel must be shown that the new commissions are expected to slightly exceed the total commissions under the original plan. These computations are shown in Exhibit 8-12. In this instance, the total volume is held constant at 41,000. Sales personnel should be made aware that attempts to increase sales of the basic and deluxe scales should be easier than attempts to increase sales of the talking scale, and such efforts will result in even higher total commissions and higher company income. The relationships should be stressed so that the sales personnel will work more effectively at accomplishing company profit objectives.

EXHIBIT 8-12

Total Effect of Changing Sales
Commissions

Original Plan

Product	Commission	Volume	Total Commission
Basic scale	$10.00	20,000	$200,000
Deluxe scale	13.00	13,000	169,000
Talking scale	15.00	8,000	120,000
Total		41,000	$489,000

New Plan

Product	Commission	Volume	Total Commission
Basic scale	$14.40	20,500	$295,200
Deluxe scale	17.60	17,000	299,200
Talking scale	13.20	3,500	46,200
Total		41,000	$640,600

Advertising Budget Changes

Another factor that may cause shifts in the sales mix involves either increasing the total company advertising budget or reallocating the budget among the products that the company sells. This discussion uses the original sales mix data for the line of scales of Abssy Corporation (Exhibit 8-8, page 450) and examines a proposed increase in the company's total advertising budget.

Abssy Corporation's advertising manager, Michael Baldwin, has proposed doubling the advertising budget from $30,000 to $60,000 per year. Baldwin thinks the increased advertising will result in the following additional unit sales during the coming year: basic, 200 scales; deluxe, 500 scales; and talking, 100 scales.

If the company spends the additional $30,000 for advertising, will the additional 800 units of sales raise profits? The original fixed costs as well as the contribution margin generated by the old sales level are irrelevant to the decision. The relevant items are the increased sales revenue, increased variable costs, and increased fixed cost—the incremental effects of the change. The difference between incremental revenues and incremental variable costs is the incremental contribution margin. The incremental contribution margin minus the incremental fixed cost is the incremental benefit (or loss) resulting from the decision.[27]

Exhibit 8-13 shows how the increased advertising expenditures are expected to affect contribution margin. The $55,000 of additional contribution margin far exceeds the $30,000 incremental cost for advertising, so Abssy Corporation should definitely increase its advertising budget by $30,000.

Increasing advertising may cause changes in the sales mix or the number of units sold. Sales can also be affected by opportunities that allow companies to obtain business at a sales price that differs from the normal price, such as the situations discussed earlier in this chapter.

EXHIBIT 8-13

Incremental Analysis of Increasing Advertising Cost

	Basic	Deluxe	Talking	Total
Increase in volume	200	500	100	800
Contribution margin per unit	$ 62	$ 75	$ 51	
Incremental contribution margin	$12,400	$37,500	$5,100	$55,000
Less: Incremental fixed cost of advertising				30,000
Incremental benefit of increased advertising expenditure				$25,000

LEARNING OBJECTIVE 7

How is product margin used to determine whether a product line should be retained or eliminated?

RELEVANT COSTS IN PRODUCT LINE DECISIONS

To facilitate performance evaluations, operating results in multiproduct environments are often presented in terms of separate product lines. In reviewing these disaggregated statements, managers must distinguish relevant from irrelevant information for each product line. If all costs (variable and fixed) are allocated to product lines, a product line or segment may be perceived to be operating at a loss when actually it is not. Such perceptions may be caused by the commingling of relevant and irrelevant information on the statements.

Exhibit 8-14 presents basic earnings information for the Men's Products Division of Cliff Taylor Ltd., which manufactures three product lines: Canadian Woods Shaving Creme, Yukon Gold Aftershave, and Prairie Cologne. The format of the information in the top half of the exhibit makes it appear that the shaving creme and aftershave lines are operating at a net loss ($16,500 and $5,250, respec-

EXHIBIT 8-14
Product Line Income Statements

	Shaving Creme	Aftershave	Cologne	Total
Sales	$150,000	$ 85,000	$380,000	$615,000
Total direct variable expenses	(87,500)	(55,250)	(228,000)	(370,750)
Total contribution margin	$ 62,500	$ 29,750	$152,000	$244,250
Total fixed expenses[1]	(79,000)	(35,000)	(77,000)	(191,000)
Net income (loss)	$(16,500)	$ (5,250)	$ 75,000	$ 53,250

[1] Fixed expenses:

	Shaving Creme	Aftershave	Cologne	Total
(a) Traceable fixed expenses[2]	$50,000	$32,000	$48,000	$130,000
(b) Nontraceable fixed expenses	9,000	1,000	6,000	16,000
(c) Allocated common costs	20,000	2,000	23,000	45,000
Total	$79,000	$35,000	$77,000	$191,000

[2] This cost will no longer exist if the product is dropped.

tively). Managers reviewing such results might reason that Taylor's Men's Product Division would be $21,750 ($16,500 + $5,250) more profitable if both of these products were eliminated. This conclusion may be premature, however, because of the mixture of relevant and irrelevant information in the income statement presentation. This problem results from the fact that all fixed expenses have been allocated to the individual product lines.

Fixed cost allocations are traditionally based on one or more measures that are presumed to provide an "equitable" division of costs. These measures might include the number of square metres of the manufacturing plant occupied by each product line, number of machine hours incurred for production of each product line, or number of employees directly associated with each product line. Regardless of the allocation base, allocations may force fixed costs into specific product line operating results even though the costs may not have actually been caused by the making or selling of that product line. This inequity results from the fact that most cost allocation schemes currently used by managers are arbitrary.

The detail in Exhibit 8-14 separates the Men's Products Division's fixed expenses into three categories: (1) those that could be avoided by elimination of the product line; (2) those that are directly associated with the product line but are unavoidable; and (3) those that are incurred for the division as a whole (common costs) and allocated to the individual product lines. The latter two categories are irrelevant to the question of whether to eliminate a product line.

An unavoidable cost will be shifted to another product line if the product line with which it is associated is eliminated. For example, the division has several senior employees who work in the shaving creme area. If that product line were eliminated, those employees would be transferred to the aftershave or cologne areas. Similarly, depreciation on factory equipment used to manufacture a specific product is an irrelevant cost in product line decisions. If the equipment were kept in service and used to produce other products, its depreciation expense would be unavoidable. However, if the equipment were sold, the selling price would be relevant because it would increase the marginal benefit of a decision to discontinue the product line.

As to common costs, they will be incurred regardless of which product lines are retained. One example of a common cost is the insurance premium on a manufacturing facility that houses all product lines.

If Taylor eliminated both shaving creme and aftershave, its total profit would decline by $10,250 [$12,500 + ($2,250)]. This amount represents the combined lost

product margin
the excess of a product's revenues over both its direct variable expenses and any avoidable fixed expenses related to the product; the amount remaining to cover unavoidable direct fixed expenses and common costs and then to provide profits

product margin of the two product lines as shown in Exhibit 8-15. Product margin represents the excess of revenues over direct variable costs and avoidable fixed costs. It is the amount remaining to cover unavoidable direct fixed costs and common costs and then to provide profits.[28] The product margin is the appropriate figure on which to base a decision to continue or eliminate a product, since that figure measures the product's ability to help cover indirect and unavoidable costs.

For the Men's Products Division, the decrease in total before-tax profit from eliminating both shaving creme and aftershave can be shown in the following alternative computations:

Current before-tax profit	$ 53,250
Increase in income due to elimination of aftershave product line (product margin)	2,250
Decrease in income due to elimination of shaving creme product line (product margin)	(12,500)
New before-tax income	$ 43,000

or

Product contribution margin of cologne line	$152,000
Minus avoidable fixed expenses of cologne line	(48,000)
Product margin of the cologne line	$104,000
Minus all remaining expenses shown on Exhibit 8-15 ($16,000 + $45,000)	(61,000)
Before-tax profit with one product line	$ 43,000

Based on the quantitative information in Exhibit 8-15, the Men's Products Division should eliminate only the aftershave line. That product line is generating a negative product margin and thus is not even covering its own costs. If that product line were eliminated, total divisional income would increase by $2,250, the amount of the negative product margin.

Before making decisions to discontinue a product line or sell off a segment, management should also carefully consider what it would take to turn that product line or division around. Some product lines (and even segments or divisions of companies) must be abandoned through either discontinuance or sale.

The News Note on page 459 discusses some actions taken by companies to improve their financial situation.

EXHIBIT 8-15

Product Line Income Statements

	Shaving Creme	Aftershave	Cologne	Total
Sales	$150,000	$ 85,000	$ 380,000	$ 615,000
Total direct variable cost	(87,500)	(55,250)	(228,000)	(370,750)
Product contribution margin	$ 62,500	$ 29,750	$ 152,000	$ 244,250
(1) Traceable fixed cost	(50,000)	(32,000)	(48,000)	(130,000)
Product margin	$ 12,500	$ (2,250)	$ 104,000	$ 114,250
(2) Nontraceable direct fixed cost (see Exhibit 8-14)				(16,000)
Product line operating results				$ 98,250
(3) Allocated common cost				(45,000)
Profit before tax				$ 53,250

Product Line Decisions

In March 2001, computer maker Gateway, Inc. closed its 10 Canadian stores and laid off 220 workers as the company moved to improve its finances in the wake of rapidly falling sales. For Gateway, its retail stores in Canada had a short lifespan. "The decision to close the Canadian stores was certainly part of our total analysis," [Gateway, Inc.'s regional vice president Judy] Quye said. "We have really gone back to a back-to-basics strategy in evaluating our individual locations and making each store efficient instead of focusing on new points of distribution," she said.[29]

In 1989, Dell Computer Corp. became the first computer producer to sell at "superstore" outlets; in July 1994, it was "the first to pull out as it abandoned its unprofitable retail efforts."[30] Dell Computer has decided to go retail once again only using a different model than it did earlier. Dell has opened in three Triangle malls to help reach more PC shoppers and encourage them to buy a Dell. Chris Bates, senior manager of Dell's Direct Store program, said the new kiosks will allow would-be customers a chance to touch and use the computers and accessories such as printers and scanners, and ask salespeople for advice. Then shoppers can go online and place an order. "The kiosks will allow us to bring the benefits of Dell's models to the customer," Bates said.[31]

As well in early November [2002], Dell opened three freestanding kiosks at shopping malls in Toronto. Shoppers can toy with Dell notebooks and PCs, as well as third-party *peripherals*. If they decide they're getting a Dell, sales associates (who work partly on *commission*) are on hand to help customers order their PC of choice via the Internet.

So does this mean Dell is ready to venture into retail? No way, says [Dell Canada's senior manager of product marketing David] Gair, who adds this is merely an extension of Dell's traditional phone and Internet selling approach. "The computers are still custom built to order—the sales are still online," he says. "It's just adding that face-to-face interaction."[32]

On the other hand, we see many companies looking at individual product line profits. Unilever has an enormous portfolio of some 1,800 brands, which it believes to be three-quarters too many. Their next strategic move will be to reduce the stable of brands. This will enable them to focus on their core brands. They have an A list and a B list. They are looking to cut a number of B list items. All non-profitable brands have quietly been dropped, such as the complementary range to Pears soap, or sold off, such as the Harmony brand.[33]

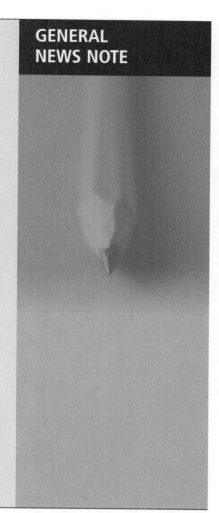

PRODUCT EXPANSION OR EXTENSION

The other decision relative to product lines is expansion or extension. Expansion refers to the introduction of totally new products. Extension refers to the introduction of "offshoots" of current products because the company decides that the market needs to be more highly segmented. The segmentation might focus on price, size, operating costs, or aesthetics issues; alternatively, extensions may be necessary to meet competitive pressures.

For example, a key driver of Gillette's success has been a steady stream of new products. Gillette launched the first twin-blade shaving system, the Trac II in 1971. In 1989, the Sensor shaving system debuted, with its automatically adjusting twin blades. Three years later, Gillette revolutionized female shaving with the Sensor for Women shaving system. Over the years, Gillette has added to its product lineup such leading brands as Right Guard deodorants, Foamy shave cream, Braun electric shavers, Oral-B manual toothbrushes, and Braun Oral-B power toothbrushes.[38] This shows that many of Gillette's products are extensions of existing products.

The Gillette Company

Gillette's chairman and CEO believes in rapid cycle time—getting there first with the highest-quality. Company profit margins increased nicely as customers began using expensive "shaving systems"—as Gillette calls reusable razors like Trac II, Atra, Atra Plus, and Sensor razors—rather than cheap disposable razors. "We don't sell a lot more units or raise prices from year to year, but we earn more from each customer."[34]

Over the years, the company has discontinued many product lines. Most recently the company sold off its stationery products business because it was pulling down its earnings.[35]

Whether deciding to introduce a new product, cut or raise a price in a market, or discontinue a product line, Gillette's management must understand the incremental costs and benefits of each alternative. Recognizing how the benefit of cutting fractions of a cent off a variable production cost is compounded when large volumes of that product are sold focuses management's attention on controlling costs.

In a speech on February 22, 2002, James M. Kilts, chairman and chief executive officer, said the company is now poised to start "realizing its goal to deliver consistent earnings growth that will result in top-tier performance over time." He went on to describe a number of strategic initiatives relating to the company's core businesses. He concluded his remarks by stating, "Over the next three years, we want Gillette to be the best investors can get. We believe that we have the assets—in our categories, our brands, our strategies and our people—to make this happen."[36]

Over the years, Gillette has had great success with applying a trade-up strategy to its blades and razors. Periodically, Gillette comes out with a new razor with added features. Then it uses marketing campaigns to convince consumers they should stop using their old razors and pay more for the new higher-priced product. The hope is, of course, that an UltraGrip or a Good News customer might trade up to a Sensor 3 and that, ultimately, a Sensor 3 customer might trade up to a Mach3Turbo.[37]

Incremental costs of expansions and extensions (other than the variable costs of the product) include market research, product and packaging development, product introduction, and advertising. Extensions have often been viewed as fairly low-cost endeavours especially if a company has excess capacity. However, sometimes unanticipated incremental costs of expansions and extensions (other than the variable costs of the product) become necessary; these costs include market research, product and packaging development, product introduction, and advertising.

CHAPTER SUMMARY

Management's task is to allocate its finite stock of resources effectively and efficiently to accomplish its chosen set of corporate goals and objectives. Managers should explain how requested information will be used so that accountants can make certain that relevant information is provided in an appropriate form. In this way, managers will have a reliable quantitative basis on which to analyze problems, compare viable solutions, and choose the best course of action.

For information to be relevant, it must (1) relate to the decision at hand, (2) be important to the decision, and (3) have a bearing on a future endeavour. Relevant costing compares the incremental, or additional, revenues and/or costs associated with alternative decisions.

Relevant information may be quantitative or qualitative. Variable costs are generally relevant to a decision; they are irrelevant only when they cannot be avoided under any possible alternative or when they do not differ between (or among) alternatives. Direct avoidable fixed costs are also relevant to decision making. Sometimes costs seem relevant when they actually are not. Examples of such irrelevant costs include sunk costs, arbitrarily allocated common costs, and nonincremental fixed costs that have been averaged on a per-unit basis.

Managers use relevant cost information to determine the incremental benefits of alternatives. One option often available is to "change nothing." This option, however, may be strategically risky if competitors gain advantage by upgrading their processes. After rigorous analysis of the quantifiable factors associated with each alternative, a manager must assess the merits and potential risks of the qualitative factors involved so that the best possible course of action is chosen.

Relevant costing is essential in many decision-making situations, including those related to further processing of a product, make-or-buy alternatives, scarce resource allocations, sales mix distributions, and retentions or eliminations of product lines. The following points are important to remember:

a. In deciding whether to engage in further processing of a product at split-off, management should ignore the total or allocated joint cost. The only relevant items are the incremental revenues and costs of processing further.

b. In a make-or-buy decision, management should include the opportunity costs associated with the make alternative; the buy alternative may provide an opportunity to make plant assets and personnel available for other purposes.

c. In a decision involving a single scarce resource, if the objective is to maximize company contribution margin and profits, then production and sales should be focused toward the product with the highest contribution margin per unit of the scarce resource.

d. Changes in selling prices and advertising normally affect a company's sales volume and sales mix, thus changing the company's total contribution margin. Special order prices may be set using variable costs as a starting point. Tying sales commissions to contribution margin will motivate salespeople to sell the products that are most beneficial to the company's profit picture.

e. In a product line decision, product lines should be evaluated on their product margins rather than on their income amounts. Product margin considers relevant direct costs and avoidable fixed expenses but excludes unavoidable fixed expenses and allocated common costs.

Quantitative analysis is short-range in perspective. Additional qualitative factors should be reviewed by management in each case. Some of these qualitative factors may have long-range planning and policy implications. Others may be short-range in nature. Managers must decide the relevance of individual factors based on experience, judgment, knowledge of economic theory, and logic.

Cross-Functional Applications

Topic of Note	Discipline	Cross-Functional Applications
Relevant Cost versus Irrelevant Cost	Accounting	Helps managers to focus on information that is important in decision making; it reinforces the idea that past costs are sunk costs. Accurate costs can improve appropriate product pricing, which must be supportable in cost-plus contracts and fair trade pricing.
	Economics	Is a form of the economic concept of marginal costing, which holds that rational decisions for short-run problems are made on the basis of marginal revenue versus marginal cost. Understanding the concept of relevant costs will help the decision maker avoid two common pitfalls: ignoring opportunity cost and not ignoring sunk costs. Decisions should be based on a comparison of incremental revenues versus incremental (relevant and opportunity) costs.
	Finance	Helps decision makers to evaluate major financial decisions about expansion or contraction of product lines.
	Management	Emphasizes the critical nature of differentiating among avoidable fixed, unavoidable fixed, and allocated common costs in making valid product decisions. It helps to differentiate between costs useful for short-run decisions and costs useful for long-run decisions. It helps in the allocation of scarce resources.
	Marketing	Helps to indicate the reasons behind basing sales commissions on contribution margin rather than on sales price; basing special prices on incremental costs to win business; and justifying additional advertising cost by comparing the increase in fixed costs with the incremental contribution generated by the advertising.

Key Terms

By-products (p. 440)
Incremental cost (p. 437)
Incremental revenue (p. 437)
Joint cost (p. 440)
Joint process (p. 440)
Joint products (p. 440)
Make-or-buy decision (p. 444)
Opportunity cost (p. 437)
Outsource (p. 444)
Product margin (p. 458)

Relevant cost (p. 436)
Relevant costing (p. 437)
Sales mix (p. 449)
Scarce resources (p. 448)
Scrap (p. 440)
Special order pricing (p. 452)
Split-off point (p. 440)
Sunk cost (p. 437)
Waste (p. 440)

Solution Strategies

General rule of decision making: choose the alternative that yields the greatest incremental benefit (or the smallest incremental loss).

> Incremental (additional) revenues
> − Incremental (additional) costs
> = Incremental benefit (positive or negative)

Relevant Costs

> Direct materials and direct labour
> Variable production overhead
> Variable selling expenses related to each alternative (may be greater or less than under the "change nothing" alternative)
> Avoidable fixed production overhead
> Avoidable fixed selling/administrative costs (if any)
> Opportunity cost of choosing some other alternative (can be viewed as either increasing one alternative's cost or reducing the cost of the other)

Single Scarce Resource

1. Determine the scarce resource.
2. Determine the production per unit of the scarce resource.
3. Determine the contribution margin (CM) per unit of the scarce resource.
4. Multiply units of production times CM per unit of the scarce resource to obtain total CM provided by the scarce resource. Production and sale of the product with the highest CM per unit of scarce resource will maximize profits.

> **Product Lines**
> Sales
> − Direct variable expenses
> = Contribution margin
> − Avoidable fixed expenses
> = Product margin*

* The decision to retain or eliminate a product line should be based on this line item.

DEMONSTRATION PROBLEMS

Problem 1

Mountifield Home Products is a firm that manufactures several types of high-quality home appliances. One of the company's product lines consists of electric coffeepots. The company produces three different models of coffeepots. Mountifield is presently considering a proposal from a supplier who wishes to supply the company with glass carafes for the coffeepots. The company currently produces all of the carafes it requires. Because customers have differing preferences, Mountifield now offers two alternative carafes for each coffeepot model (therefore, the company currently produces a total of six different types of carafes). The supplier has indicated it would produce three different types of carafes for each coffeepot model, thus expanding the variety of carafes that could be offered to the customer. This supplier would charge Mountifield $2.60 per carafe.

Mountifield produces its carafes along with all the other coffeepot components in its factory in Victoria, British Columbia. For the coming year, Mountifield has projected the costs of carafe production as follows (based on a projected volume of 100,000 units):

Direct materials	$ 75,000
Direct labour	65,000
Variable overhead	55,000
Fixed overhead	
Depreciation on equipment[1]	50,000
Property taxes on production space and equipment[2]	15,000
Factory supervision[3]	34,970
Total production costs	$294,970

[1]The equipment used to produce the carafes has no alternative use and no material market value.

[2]The space occupied by carafe production activities will remain idle if the company purchases rather than makes the carafes.

[3]The factory supervision cost reflects the salary of a production supervisor who oversees carafe production. This individual would be dismissed from the firm if carafe production ceased.

Required:

a. Determine the net advantage or disadvantage of purchasing rather than producing the carafes that are required for the coming year.
b. Determine the level of coffeepot production at which Mountifield would be indifferent between buying and producing the carafes. If the volume of production were expected to increase in the future, would the firm be more likely to make or buy?
c. For this part only, assume that the space presently occupied by carafe production could be leased to another firm for $45,000 per year. How would this affect the make-or-buy decision?
d. What other factors should the company take into account in determining whether it should make or buy the carafes?
e. Assume that Mountifield Home Products is currently experiencing a $25,000 loss from operations. The company has an opportunity to sell an additional 10,000 carafes to a foreign distributor. Mountifield has the capacity to produce the additional carafes and no opportunity costs are associated with the order. What is the minimum price per carafe that the company should charge for the special order? What price should the company charge if it wants to achieve a $5,000 net income?

Problem 2

Zippy Products Ltd. produces a line of dolls in three different qualities: economy, standard, and deluxe. The selling price, average variable cost, and market demand (in units) for each type of doll are shown below:

	Price	Average Variable Cost	Market Demand
Economy	$ 25.00	$12.00	100,000
Standard	40.00	21.00	80,000
Deluxe	100.00	72.00	50,000

Mr. Edward, the production manager, and Mr. Klauz, the sales manager, have determined that three possible production and sales plans are feasible for the coming year.

	Plan #1 Units	Plan #2 Units	Plan #3 Units
Economy	90,000	110,000	100,000
Standard	60,000	75,000	85,000
Deluxe	30,000	50,000	35,000
Fixed production and marketing costs	$1,500,000	$3,000,000	$2,000,000

In addition to the costs shown above, committed fixed costs related to this product line are $1,400,000, regardless of the level of production and sales.

Required:

a. Determine the most profitable alternative for the company from the three plans given.
b. The president, Ms. Zippora, after reviewing the results of part (a), suggests that gross margin per product should be calculated to see whether each of the products is covering its fixed costs. Respond briefly, but fully, to the president's suggestion.

Solutions to Demonstration Problems

Problem 1

a. Relevant costs to make 100,000 carafes:

Direct materials ($0.75 per unit)	$ 75,000
Direct labour ($0.65 per unit)	65,000
Variable overhead ($0.55 per unit)	55,000
Factory supervision	34,970
Total	$ 229,970
Cost to buy 100,000 × $2.60	(260,000)
Net advantage of in-house production	$ 30,030

Note that the only fixed cost that is relevant to the decision is the cost of factory supervision. The other fixed costs would be unaffected by the decision.

b. The total relevant cost to make the carafes can be expressed as $34,970 + $1.95X$, where X represents production volume. The item $34,970 is the relevant fixed cost and the item $1.95X$ represents the total relevant variable costs. The total relevant cost to buy the required carafes can be expressed as $2.60X$, where X represents production volume.

When the production cost equation is set equal to the purchase cost equation, the point of indifference can be found:
$2.60X = 1.95X + $34,970$
$0.65X = $34,970$
$X = 53,800$ units

As production volume goes up, so does the benefit of in-house production, because the average cost per unit will continually decline (due to the fixed cost element) and total cost rises only at a rate of $1.95 per unit rather than $2.60 per unit.

c. Referring to the solution to part (a), the net advantage of in-house production is $30,030. The possibility of renting the production space for $45,000 per year increases the cost of in-house production because an opportunity cost of $45,000 is incurred. Consequently, the balance shifts to favour the purchase of the carafes:

Original advantage of producing in-house	$ 30,030
Additional opportunity cost (lost rent)	(45,000)
Net cost of producing the carafes (or net advantage of purchasing)	$(14,970)

d. Among the additional factors that might be considered are the quality of the carafes produced relative to the quality of the carafes purchased, supplier reliability, number of competing suppliers, effect of the additional variety of carafes on customer demand, likelihood of supplier price increases in the future, and alternative (cost-reducing or income-generating) uses of the space currently utilized to produce carafes.

e. The minimum selling price per unit would be the $1.95 variable cost per unit. The price that would allow the company to make $5,000 would be $4.95 [($25,000 + $5,000) ÷ 10,000] = $3.00; $3.00 + $1.95 = $4.95.

Problem 2

a.

Production of	Plan #1	Plan #2	Plan #3
Economy	$ 1,170,000[1]	$ 1,300,000[4]	$ 1,300,000[7]
Standard	1,140,000[2]	1,425,000[5]	1,520,000[8]
Deluxe	840,000[3]	1,400,000[6]	980,000[9]
Total CM	$ 3,150,000	$ 4,125,000	$ 3,800,000
Less: Fixed Production & Mfg. Cost	$ 1,500,000	$ 3,000,000	$ 2,000,000
Committed Fixed Cost	1,400,000	1,400,000	1,400,000
Total Fixed Cost	$ 2,900,000	$ 4,400,000	$ 3,400,000
Net Income	$ 250,000	$ (275,000)	$ 400,000

[1] 90,000 × $13 [4] 100,000 × $13 [7] 100,000 × $13
[2] 60,000 × $19 [5] 75,000 × $19 [8] 80,000 × $19
[3] 30,000 × $28 [6] 50,000 × $28 [9] 35,000 × $28

Therefore, the most profitable alternative is Plan 3.

b. The problem with the president's suggestion is that it assumes that fixed costs can be attributed specifically to each of the three models. The problem information implies that the fixed costs are common to the line and thus not separable unless one uses an arbitrary application base. The relevant metric here would be to see whether each product has a positive contribution margin (which each has) and further, if information were given, whether there were any production constraints that would affect the relative contribution margin per constraining factor for each of the products.

End-of-Chapter Materials

SELF-TEST QUESTIONS

(SOLUTIONS APPEAR AT THE END OF THE CHAPTER.)

1. In an equipment replacement decision, which of the following is considered a relevant cost?
    a. Annual depreciation of the old equipment
    b. Write-off of the book value of the old equipment
    c. Book value of the old equipment
    d. Annual depreciation of the new equipment

2. Joint costs of the joint products are
    a. All costs necessary to prepare units for sale
    b. All costs following the split-off point
    c. All costs prior to the split-off point
    d. None of the above

3. If a firm is operating at full capacity, what costs must a minimum special order price cover?
    a. Variable and incremental fixed costs associated with the special order plus forgone contribution margin on regular units not produced
    b. Variable and fixed manufacturing costs associated with the special order
    c. Variable costs associated with the special order
    d. Variable and incremental fixed costs associated with the special order

4. Which of the following best defines relevant costs?
    a. Past costs that differ between alternatives
    b. Past costs that do not differ between alternatives
    c. Future costs that differ between alternatives
    d. Future costs that do not differ between alternatives

5. Under which of the following conditions should a joint product be sold at the split-off point and not processed further?
    a. If the selling price at the split-off point is greater than joint production costs allocated to the joint product
    b. If the selling price, after further processing, is less than the sum of the joint production costs allocated to the joint product and the incremental costs from further processing

c. If incremental costs from further processing are greater than the increase in selling price due to further processing
d. If incremental costs from further processing are greater than the joint production costs allocated to the joint product at the split-off point

6. In a make-or-buy decision, which costs are relevant?
    a. Fixed costs that can be avoided in the future if the decision is to buy
    b. Fixed costs that will not change regardless of the decision
    c. Direct material costs only
    d. Conversion costs only

(Self-Test Questions 5 and 6 reprinted from *Management Accounting examinations* published by the Certified General Accountants Association of Canada © CGA-Canada 2000, used by permission.)

7. Nowman Enterprises Ltd. is considering closing down Phyllis Shampoo, one of its divisions. The division presently has a contribution margin of $500,000. Overhead allocated to the division is $1,250,000, of which $125,000 cannot be eliminated. If this division were discontinued, by what amount would Nowman's pretax income increase?
    a. $125,000
    b. $500,000
    c. $625,000
    d. $750,000

8. Edmonton Industries Ltd. currently manufactures all component parts used in the manufacture of various tools. A steel handle is used in three different tools. The 2005 estimate for 40,000 handles has the following unit cost:

Direct material	$0.60
Direct labour	0.40
Variable overhead	0.10
Fixed overhead	0.20
Total unit cost	$1.30

Nickele Walker Corporation has offered to supply 40,000 handles to Edmonton Industries for $1.25 each, delivered. If Edmonton Industries currently has idle capacity that cannot be used, accepting the offer will:
a. Decrease the handle unit cost by $0.05

b . Increase the handle unit cost by $0.15
c. Decrease the handle unit cost by $0.15
d. Decrease the handle unit cost by $0.25
e. Increase the handle unit cost by $0.05

(Self-Test Questions 7 and 8 reprinted from *Management Accounting examinations* published by the Certified General Accountants Association of Canada © CGA-Canada 1999, used by permission.)

9. Sunk costs
   a. Are a substitute for opportunity costs
   b. In and of themselves are not relevant to decision making
   c. Are relevant to decision making

d. Are relevant to long-run decisions but not to short-run decisions
e. None of the above

(IMA adapted)

10. Opportunity costs are
    a. Not used for decision making
    b. The same as variable costs
    c. Equal to historical costs
    d. Always relevant to decision making
    e. None of the above

(IMA adapted)

QUESTIONS

1. What three characteristics must a cost possess to be relevant to a decision? Why are these characteristics important?

2. What is meant by the term *incremental* as it applies to costs and revenues?

3. Are future variable costs always relevant costs? Discuss the rationale for your answer.

4. What category of costs is often relevant in decision making, but is probably never directly recorded in a company's accounting records? Explain.

5. On November 13, 2005, Bill paid Jim $25 for a concert ticket that Jim had originally purchased for $50. On December 15, 2005, Ted offered Bill $30 for the ticket. Which of the costs mentioned are relevant in Bill's decision regarding whether to sell the ticket to Ted or attend the concert? What opportunity cost will Bill incur if he decides to attend the concert? Explain.

6. What is the "change nothing" alternative? Why is it not always a feasible alternative?

7. What term is used to describe historical costs? Are such costs relevant in making decisions? Explain.

8. What are joint products, and what is the split-off point? Once joint products have reached the split-off point, are joint costs relevant? Are joint costs relevant before joint products reach the split-off point? Explain.

9. In an asset replacement decision, which of the following costs would typically be relevant?
   a. The purchase cost of the new machine
   b. The purchase cost of the old machine
   c. The cost of electricity to run the old machine
   d. The cost of electricity to run the new machine
   e. The annual depreciation expense on the old machine

10. What are some qualitative factors that should be considered in make-or-buy decisions?

11. In a make-or-buy decision, could some of the fixed costs associated with the "make" option be relevant? Explain.

12. Evaluate the merit of the following statement: "In the long run, the only binding constraint on a firm's output is capital; in the short run, nearly any resource can be a binding constraint."

13. In production decisions that involve the allocation of a single scarce production resource among multiple products, which of the following is relevant? Explain the reasons for your answers.
    a. Sales demand for each product
    b. Sales price of each product
    c. Fixed production costs
    d. Variable selling costs for each product
    e. Variable production costs for each product

14. In allocating a scarce production resource in a multiproduct corporation whose goal is to maximize the total corporate contribution margin, why would management not simply produce the product that generates the highest contribution margin per unit?

15. In a multiproduct company, what is meant by the term *sales mix*?

16. What factors are most likely to be manipulated in managerial attempts to change a company's sales mix?

17. Why does the compensation structure for marketing personnel have a direct effect on the sales mix?

18. How are special prices set and when are they used?

19. In a special order decision, to avoid losing money on the order, the minimum selling price a company should charge is the sum of all the incremental costs of production and sales. Is this a true statement? Discuss the rationale for your answer.

20. In considering a special order that will enable a company to make use of currently idle capacity, which costs are likely to be relevant? Which costs are likely to be irrelevant?

21. Why are some direct fixed costs irrelevant to the decision to eliminate a product line?

22. What is product margin and how is it related to the decision to keep or eliminate a product line?

23. In the short run, which of the following must be non-negative in order for management to decide to retain a product line and why?
   a. Product line contribution margin
   b. Product line product margin
   c. Product line net income

EXERCISES

1. (LO 2; Process further) The Pana Canada Petro-Chemical Company uses a production process that generates joint products. The joint costs associated with the process are $30,000.

Product ID	Units of Output	Selling Price at Split-Off	Additional Processing Costs	Final Selling Price
AA	10,000	$1.00	$0.75	$1.50
BB	20,000	$0.50	$1.00	$3.00
CC	500	$0.75	$0.10	$0.90

Required:
   a. Compute the incremental revenue and incremental costs associated with further processing of each joint product.
   b. Compute the incremental profit generated from further processing of each joint product. Which of the joint products should be processed beyond the split-off point?

2. (LO 2; Process further) A certain joint process yields two joint products, A and B. The joint cost for June 2005 is $32,000. The sales value of the output at split-off is $86,000 for product A and $27,000 for product B. Management is trying to decide whether to process its products further. If the products are processed beyond split-off, the final sales value will be $100,000 for product A and $38,000 for product B. The additional costs of processing are expected to be $16,000 for A and $4,000 for B.
   Required:
   a. Should management process the products further? Show computations.
   b. Are any revenues and/or costs not relevant to the decision? If so, what are they and why are they not relevant?

3. (LO 2; Process further) Because of an increasing demand for Brady Company's Chow-Chow bottles, the company overproduced the product in both 2003 and 2004. In 2005, another company began to produce a much improved product that made Brady Company's product obsolete. In 2005, after the inventory was counted, Brady had

$50,604 worth of Chow-Chow bottles on hand. After considering many alternatives, it was determined that the company could sell the product for scrap for $6,850 or recycle it into another product. It will cost $12,500 to rework the product, and it will sell for $20,500. On top of this additional cost, salespeople will receive 3% of the selling price.

Required:

What should Brady Company do with the inventory of Chow-Chow bottles?

4. (LO 3; Cost identification) Managers at Harry's Mutt & Cutt are trying to decide whether they should keep their old dog grooming equipment or invest in new energy-efficient equipment. Some data on both groups of equipment follow:

	Old Equipment	New Equipment
Remaining life	5 years	5 years
Original cost	$12,000	$21,000
Accumulated depreciation	$ 4,000	$ 0
Annual cash operating costs	$ 7,000	$ 3,000
Current salvage value	$ 2,000	$21,000
Salvage value in 5 years	$ 0	$ 0

Required:

a. Identify any sunk costs listed above.
b. Identify any irrelevant (nondifferential) future costs.
c. Identify all relevant costs to the equipment replacement decision.
d. What are the opportunity costs associated with the alternative of keeping the old machine?
e. What is the incremental cost to purchase the new machine?

5. (LO 3; Incremental analysis) Two years ago, Roses R Us Flower Shop purchased a two-tonne delivery truck. Because of increases in fuel prices and the other high costs of operating this truck, the company is considering replacing this truck with a smaller, more efficient pickup. Data on the existing and proposed trucks follow:

	Old Truck	Proposed Truck
Remaining life	3 years	3 years
Original cost	$20,000	$10,000
Market value now	$ 5,000	$10,000
Salvage value in 3 years	$ 0	$ 0
Annual cash operating costs	$ 6,000	$ 4,500
Annual depreciation	$ 4,000	$ 3,333

Required:

a. What is the incremental cost of the proposed truck?
b. What are the incremental savings in annual operating costs?
c. What should the company do? Support your decision with calculations.

6. (LO 4; Make-or-buy) Seguin Company has been purchasing a component part from another company since it began operations five years ago. Seguin now has a steady demand for its product and feels it has the capacity to produce the component part itself. Last year Seguin purchased 120,000 units at a cost of $1.10 per unit and feels it will purchase 10% more this year at the same price. If Seguin produces this part, its costs will be:

Direct material	$	0.45
Direct labour	$	0.30
Variable overhead	$	0.20
Avoidable fixed manufacturing overhead	$33,000	

Required:

Should Seguin Company purchase this part or produce it in-house?

7. (LO 4; Make-or-buy) The Judy Poë Shoe Company manufactures various types of shoes for sports and recreational use. Several types of shoes require a built-in air pump. The company presently makes all of the air pumps it requires for production, however, management is evaluating an offer from The Ray Air Supply Company to

provide air pumps at a cost of $5 each. Poë's management has estimated that the variable production costs of the air pump amount to $3 per unit. The firm also estimates that it could avoid $50,000 per year in fixed costs if it purchased rather than produced the air pumps.

Required:

a.   If Poë requires 20,000 pumps per year, should it make them or buy them from Ray Air Supply Company?

b.   If Poë requires 30,000 pumps per year, should it make them or buy them?

c.   Assuming all other factors are equal, at what level of production would Poë be indifferent between making and buying the pumps? Show computations.

8. (LO 4; Make-or-buy) The Luste Corporation needs 100 rock crushers to use in its gravel production plant. An outside supplier has offered to sell the company the required crushers at a price of $4,000 per rock crusher. If the company does not manufacture the rock crushers, it can manufacture gravel grinders. The manufacture of gravel grinders would produce $6,000 of additional contribution margin. Costs for Luste Corporation to manufacture 100 rock crushers follow:

Direct material	$130,000
Direct labour	150,000
Variable overhead	72,000
Fixed overhead ($70,000 allocated and $50,000 direct)	120,000

Required:

a.   Identify the relevant out-of-pocket costs to produce the rock crushers.

b.   Identify any other relevant costs.

c.   Should Luste Corporation make the rock crushers or purchase them? Show computations.

9. (LO 5; Scarce resource) Because of a labour strike in the plant of its major competitor, Joe Kernen Tool Co. has found itself operating at peak capacity. The firm makes two electronic woodworking tools: sanders and drills. At this time the company can sell as many of either product as it can make. The firm's machines can only be run 90,000 hours per month. Data on each product follow:

	Sanders	Drills
Sales	$45	$28
Variable costs	30	19
Contribution margin	$15	$9
Machine hours required per unit	8	6

Fixed costs are $110,000 per month.

Required:

a.   How many of each product should the company make? Explain your answer.

b.   How much profit would the company expect to make based on your recommendation in part (a)?

10. (LO 5; Scarce resource) Merry Melodies manufactures holiday bells. The firm produces three types of bells: jingles, jangles, and tingalings. Because of political turmoil in Sangana, a critical raw material—bellinium—is in very short supply, thus restricting the number of bells the firm can produce. For the coming year, the firm will be able to purchase only 20,000 kilograms of bellinium (at a cost of $5 per kilogram). The firm needs to determine how to allocate the bellinium to maximize profits. The following information has been gathered for your consideration:

	Jingles	Jangles	Tingalings
Sales demand in units	200,000	300,000	100,000
Sales price per unit	$15.00	$10.00	$4.00
Bellinium cost per unit	$ 6.25	$ 5.00	$2.50
Direct labour cost per unit	$ 6.00	$ 3.00	$1.00
Variable overhead cost per unit	$ 2.00	$ 1.00	$0.25

Fixed production costs total $200,000 per year, fixed selling costs are $28,000, and there are no variable selling costs.

Required:

a. How should Merry Melodies allocate the bellinium?

b. Based on the optimal allocation, what is the company's projected contribution margin for the coming year?

11. (LO 6; Sales mix) Michelle Klauz's Hound Pound Ltd. provides two types of services to dog owners: grooming and training. All company personnel can perform either service equally well. To expand sales and market share, Michelle relies heavily on radio and billboard advertising. For fiscal 2005 advertising expense is expected to be very limited. Information on projected operations for 2005 follows:

	Grooming	Training
Projected billable hours for 2005	10,000	8,000
Revenue per billable hour	$ 15	$ 25
Variable cost of labour	$ 5	$ 10
Material cost per billable hour	$ 1	$ 2
Allocated fixed costs per year	$100,000	$90,000

Required:

a. What is Michelle's projected profit or loss for fiscal 2005?

b. If $1 spent on advertising could increase either grooming revenue or training revenue by $20, on which service should the advertising dollar be spent?

c. If $1 spent on advertising could increase grooming billable time or training billable time by one hour, on which service should the advertising dollar be spent?

12. (LO 6; Sales mix) Among many products made by the Baldwin Toy Company is a plastic tricycle. The company's projections for this product for 2005 follow:

Projected volume in units	100 000
Sales price per unit	$ 62
Variable production costs per unit	$ 42
Variable selling costs per unit	$ 8
Total fixed production costs	$500,000
Total fixed selling and administration costs	$200,000

Required:

a. Compute the projected profit to be earned on tricycle sales during fiscal 2005.

b. Corporate management estimates that unit volume could be increased by 15% if the sales price were decreased by $4. How would such a change affect the profit level projected in part (a)?

c. Rather than cutting the sales price, management is considering holding the sales price at the projected level and increasing advertising by $200,000. Such a change would increase expected volume by 20%. How would the level of profit under this alternative compare with the profit projected in part (a)?

13. (LO 6; Special order) Jus Simpson Company produces a plastic courtroom set that includes a judge's bench, witness stand, jury box, and 25 people. The set is sold to exclusive toy stores for $200. Plant capacity is 20,000 sets per year. Production costs are as follows:

Direct materials costs per set	$ 20
Direct labour cost per set	$ 30
Variable overhead cost per set	$ 40
Variable selling cost per set	$ 10
Fixed overhead cost per year	$1,100,000

A prominent Montreal store, which has not previously purchased from Jus Simpson Company, has approached the marketing manager about buying 5,000 sets for $170 each. No selling expenses would be incurred on this offer, but the Montreal store wants the set to include five plastic briefcases. This request means that Jus Simpson Company will incur an additional $2 cost per set. The company is currently selling 18,000 courtroom sets, so acceptance of this order would require that the company reject some of its current business.

Required:

a. What is the current operating income of Jus Simpson Company?

b. If the company accepted this offer, what would be its operating income? Should the company accept the offer?

c. If Jus Simpson Company were currently selling only 10,000 sets per year and wanted to earn $150,000 of income for the year, what selling price would the company have to quote the Montreal store?

14. (LO 7; Special order) The manufacturing capacity of the Chung Ltd. plants is 60,000 units of product per year. A summary of operations for the year ended December 31, 2005, is as follows:

Sales (36,000 units at $75 per unit)		$2,700,000
Variable manufacturing costs	$1,440,000	
Variable selling costs	180,000	(1,620,000)
Contribution margin		$1,080,000
Fixed costs		(990 000)
Operating income		$ 90,000

An offshore distributor has offered to buy 20,000 units at $60 per unit during 2006. Assume all costs (including variable selling expenses) will be at the 2005 level during fiscal 2006.

Required:
If Chung Ltd. accepts this offer and also sells as many units to regular customers as it did in 2005, what would be the total operating income for 2006? (Normal variable selling costs will be incurred on this order and all other transactions.)

15. (LO 6; Special order) Tim Russert Ltd. has been approached by a volume buyer with an offer to purchase 50,000 toy pianos at $21.50 per unit. Delivery must be made within 30 days and variable selling costs will be $1 per unit. The productive capacity of Russert is 320,000 pianos per month and 10,000 pianos are currently on hand. At the regular price, sales of 300,000 pianos are expected for this month. The sales manager believes that 40% of sales lost during this month could be recovered later in the year. Price and cost data of regular sales are as follows:

Selling price		$33
Variable costs		
Production	$18	
Selling	6	24
Contribution		$ 9

Required:
a. Determine whether Tim Russert Ltd. should accept or reject this special order.
b. To make no profit on this order, what price would have to be charged?
c. What other factors should be considered before accepting the order?

16. (LO 6; Special order) At the start of your employment with Deluxe Spa Products Inc., you are given the following income statements for the months of September and October 2005.

	September	October
Sales revenue	$100,000	$120,000
Costs	140,000	150,000
Net loss	$(40,000)	$(30,000)

You are able to obtain the following additional information:
i.   Each dollar of variable cost is made up of 40% direct materials, 35% direct labour, and 25% variable manufacturing overhead.
ii. Total fixed costs amount to $90,000.
iii. The selling price of each unit is $5.00.
iv. The capacity of the plant is 40,000 units per month.
A new customer is willing to purchase 20,000 units at $3.50/unit. During October, Deluxe Spa Products already received confirmed orders from its regular customers for November sales of 25,000 units at $5.00 per unit. Direct labour costs on the special order would be reduced by 5%, but additional insurance and administrative costs will result in an increase of $10,000 if the special order is accepted.

Required:
Should this special order be accepted?

17. (LO 7; Product line) Nick Newman encountered lots of problems when he tried to book acts into his Crimson Lights coffee shop. Having learned his way around the booking industry, he decided to open a celebrity booking company.

He registered the company under the name of Nick's Marketing Ltd. and began the business of hiring celebrities and marketing their services. The firm has three operating segments: rock and roll (R & R) entertainment, after-dinner speakers, and political action speakers. Projected income statements for the fourth quarter of this fiscal year follow:

	R & R	After-Dinner	Political
Sales	$ 600,000	$ 250,000	$ 300,000
Variable costs of professional service	(200,000)	(150,000)	(162,500)
Variable marketing costs	(100,000)	(37,500)	(50,000)
Direct fixed costs	(200,000)	(75,000)	(62,500)
Allocated fixed costs	(30,000)	(15,000)	(15,000)
Net income	$ 70,000	$ (27,500)	$ 10,000

Required:
a. Assuming that $35,000 of the direct fixed costs of the After-Dinner segment can be avoided if the segment is eliminated, what would be the effect of its elimination on Nick's overall net income?
b. Before the After-Dinner segment is eliminated, what qualitative factors should be considered?

18. (LO 7; Product line) The management at Erika Kane Company is currently contemplating the elimination of one of its products, Pimples, because this product is now showing a loss. An annual income statement follows:

Erika Kane Company
Income Statement
For Year Ended August 1, 2005
(In Thousands)

	Product			
	Wimples	**Pimples**	**Bimples**	**Total**
Sales	$ 2,200	$ 1,400	$ 1,800	$ 5,400
Variable cost of sales	(1,400)	(800)	(1,080)	(3,280)
Production contribution margin	$ 800	$ 600	$ 720	$ 2,120
Traceable fixed and variable				
marketing costs	$ 630	$ 525	$ 520	$ 1,675
Allocated fixed costs	90	80	105	275
Total fixed costs	$ 720	$ 605	$ 625	$ 1,950
Operating profit	$ 80	$ (5)	$ 95	$ 170

Required:
a. Should the management at Erika Kane Company management stop sales of Pimples? Support your answer with appropriate schedules.
b. How would the net income of the company be affected by the decision?

PROBLEMS

1. (LO 2; Process further) Shearer, Inc. produces two final products, C and D, from a joint process. Process 1 yields 400 units of intermediate product A and 600 units of intermediate product B. For this yield, a cost of $15,000 is incurred in process 1. The 400 units of product A are then sent to process 2. Joint costs of $16,000 are incurred in process 2 to produce 800 units of product C and 1,200 units of product D. The final sales price for products C and D are, respectively, $10 and $20.

Required:

Assuming the 400 units of intermediate product A could have been sold for $18,000, should this intermediate product have been processed further? Explain your answer.

2. (LO 2; Process further) Valentine Textiles Ltd. produces three products (pre-cut fabrics for hats, shirts, and pants) from a joint process. Rather than sell the products at the split-off point, the company can complete each product. Information related to these products is shown below:

	Hats	Shirts	Pants	Total
Number of units produced	5,000	8,000	3,000	16,000
Joint cost allocated	$ 56,250	$?	$?	$180,000
Sales value at split-off point	?	129,000	40,000	300,000
Additional costs of processing further	13,000	10,000	39,000	62,000
Sales value after all processing	150,000	134,000	105,000	389,000

Required:

a. As a management accountant, describe the process you may have used to determine the additional costs of processing further.

b. What sales value for hats at the split-off point would make the firm indifferent between completing the hats and selling pre-cut fabric for hats?

c. What amount of joint cost allocated to pre-cut shirts would make it economically infeasible to produce them?

d. What is the effect on the corporate profit of completing the pants rather than selling pre-cut fabric for pants?

3. (LO 2; Joint processing) The joint process at Losell Co. Ltd. produces three separate products. The current estimated average cost of one batch of joint inputs is $1,000. Each of the products—Aferon, Beteron, and Ceteron—can either be sold at the split-off point or processed further and then sold. After the joint process, each product is independently processed. The management of Losell Co. Ltd. has gathered the following information:

	Total	Variable Costs	Fixed But Avoidable With Shutdown of Process	Fixed, Not Avoidable With Shutdown of Process
Cost of joint process	$1,000	$600	$250	$150
Cost of separate process				
Aferon	40	30	8	2
Beteron	60	40	15	5
Ceteron	20	15	3	2

At the split-off point, Aferon can be sold for $450 or processed further at an incremental cost of $40 and then sold for $520.

At the split-off point, Beteron can be sold for $300 or processed further at an incremental cost of $60 and then sold for $350.

At the split-off point, Ceteron can be sold for $250 or processed further at an incremental cost of $20 and then sold for $265.

Required:

a. Advise the management of Losell whether they should sell the products at split-off, sell them in their fully processed form, discontinue production, or employ some other course of action.

b. There is an opportunity for Losell to modify the units that result from the separate process for Ceteron at an incremental cost of $140. These products (to be called Deteron) would be sold at a price of $400. Should Losell produce Deteron rather than Ceteron?

(Adapted by the author from *Management Accounting examinations,* published by the Certified General Accountant Association of Canada © CGA-Canada, 1995, used by permission.)

4. (LO 3; Asset replacement) The Funky Chicken Conglomerate offers products and services to various restaurants under a franchising arrangement. For operating purposes,

The Funky Chicken has three autonomous divisions: Steamed, Fried, and Barbecued. For fiscal 2005, the Steam Division has projected its net income at $1.2 million.

One of the Steamed Division's most important operations involves a water boiler that is used to steam the chickens. The division's management has recently asked its controller to prepare a comparative financial analysis of a new steam-generating technology with the existing boiler. The following information was presented by the controller to division management:

	Old Boiler	New Technology
Remaining life	8 years	8 years
Original cost	$ 3,000,000	$ 2,000,000
Market value now	$ 200,000	—
Operating costs	$ 400,000	$ 50,000
Salvage value in 8 years	$ 0	$ 0
Accumulated depreciation	$ 1,000,000	$ —

After allowing the Steamed Division manager to examine the previous information for a few moments, the division controller said, "As the financial information clearly indicates, we must invest in the new technology."

Required:

a. Identify the costs that are relevant to the Steamed Division's equipment replacement decision.

b. Do you agree with the controller's conclusions? Provide your own computations based only on relevant costs.

c. For this part only, assume that the cost of the new technology is unknown. What is the maximum amount that the division could pay for the new technology and be no worse off financially?

5. (LO 3; Asset replacement) Shepton Specialty Products Ltd. is a manufacturer of surgical instruments. Given the changes in surgical technology, Shepton has had to invest heavily in maintaining and upgrading its state-of-the-art product line. Shepton has become known for the high quality of its product and the reasonableness of its prices.

Shepton is currently evaluating the design and production of its neurosurgical line of products, to establish what the current quality costs are and how much it would cost to improve quality. Currently, the company has an expected spoilage rate in the neurosurgical line of one unit for every 200 units produced. Inspection of this product costs $2,000 per week plus $0.10 per unit. With the current inspection policy and production specifications, the company experiences a return and warranty claim of one unit for every 500 units produced. Such a return normally costs the company the cost of the replacement unit and creates the potential for lost customers. Shepton estimates that every warranty claim loses five unit sales for the company.

Shepton has looked at revamping its quality control system. Using a new computer-assisted design and manufacturing system (which can be leased for $200,000 per year) the company could reduce the spoilage rate to one unit for every 350 units produced and reduce variable inspection costs to $0.065 per unit. As well, product returns are expected to drop to one unit for every 900 units produced. Average unit cost for the neurosurgical line is shown below.

Shepton Specialty Products Ltd.
Neurosurgical Product Line
Average Unit Cost[1]
For the Year 2005

Material	$ 5.00
Labour	6.50
Variable manufacturing overhead	6.00
Fixed manufacturing overhead[2]	5.00
Total	$22.50

[1] Excludes inspection costs
[2] Based on estimated production of 5,000,000 good units of product in 2005.

The average selling price is $33 per unit and variable selling costs are 15% of the selling price.

Required:

Given Shepton's interest in quality control, determine whether the company should lease the computer system.

(Adapted by the author from *Management Accounting examinations,* published by the Certified General Accountant Association of Canada © CGA-Canada, 1993, used by permission.)

6. (LO 4; Make-or-buy) The New Sulyma Lighting Company manufactures various types of household light fixtures. Most of the light fixtures require 60-watt light bulbs. Historically, the company has produced its own light bulbs. The costs to produce a bulb (based on capacity operation of 3,000,000 bulbs per year) are as follows:

Direct materials	$0.10
Direct labour	0.05
Variable manufacturing overhead	0.01
Fixed manufacturing overhead	0.03
Total	$0.19

The fixed manufacturing overhead includes $60,000 of depreciation on equipment for which there is no alternative use and no external market value. The balance of the fixed manufacturing overhead pertains to the salary of the production supervisor. The production supervisor of the light bulb operation has a lifetime employment contract; she also has skills that could be used to displace another manager (the part-time supervisor of electrical cord production), who draws a salary of $15,000 per year but is due to retire from the company.

The M. Connor Electric Company has recently approached New Sulyma with an offer to supply all the light bulbs New Sulyma requires at a price of $0.18 per bulb. Anticipated sales demand for the coming year will be 2,000,000 bulbs.

Required:

a.   Identify the relevant costs in this make-or-buy decision.

b.   What is the total annual advantage or disadvantage (in dollars) of buying, rather than making, the bulbs?

c.   What qualitative factors should be taken into account in this make-or-buy decision?

d.   As an accountant, how would you obtain information about the employment contracts of factory managers?

e.   As the human resources manager, how might you respond to a suggestion by the accounting staff to fire the supervisor of electrical cord production?

7. (LO 4; Make-or-buy) Gomes Active Wear Corporation is a large clothing manufacturer. Profitability has gone down in the past few years, and after a bitter internal struggle, Gamon Gomes has been appointed the new CEO. Gomes' opinion is that the company can increase profitability by discontinuing the Distribution Department and hiring a trucking firm to transport the company's products to retail outlets. You have been given the task of determining whether he is correct. The following information (given in thousands) is available for the preceding fiscal year:

	Manufacturing	Packaging	Distribution	Total
Salaries and wages	$4,000	$ 500	$1,950	$ 6,450
Material	2,000	750	0	2,750
Office supplies	500	350	350	1,200
Occupancy costs	420	300	300	1,020
Selling and administrative expense	650	310	450	1,410
Depreciation	200	75	90	365
Total	$7,770	$2,285	$3,140	$13,195

Additional information:

• After a detailed review of personnel, management decides it can transfer the distribution supervisor (who earns a salary of $35,000), an assistant distribution supervisor (who earns a salary of $25,000), and six part-time labourers (who earn average wages of $15,000) to the Packaging Department to prepare goods for shipment.

- Owing to more stringent requirements imposed by trucking companies, an additional $100,000 will have to be spent annually for packaging materials.
- The space of the Distribution Department will be required by the Packaging Department for storage of goods prior to shipment.
- The cost of office supplies for the Packaging Department is expected to increase by $50,000.
- Insurance costs included in selling and administrative expenses are expected to decline by $50,000. Other administrative costs are expected to increase, because of the addition of three part-time staff members in Accounts Payable at an annual rate of $12,000 per employee and two additional part-time people in the Payroll Department at an annual salary of $15,000 each. In addition, management will need to add four part-time clerical positions at an annual rate of $10,000 each.
- A trucking company has offered to provide shipping for $2.5 million annually.
- None of the equipment that is presently in use in the Distribution Department has alternative applications or external market value.

Required:

a.   Prepare a statement setting forth in comparative form the costs of product distribution under the present arrangement and under the proposed change in operations. Determine the net savings or cost of accepting the proposal.

b.   Assuming the company is functionally organized (that is, Manufacturing, Packaging, Distribution, and Marketing currently all have separate managements), what concerns might these managers have in the restructuring that Gamon Gomes should address?

(IMA adapted)

8.   (LO 4; Make-or-buy) David Faber Inc. is a wholesale distributor supplying moderately priced sporting equipment to large chain stores. About 60% of Faber's products are purchased from other companies, while the rest are manufactured by Faber. The company's Plastics Department currently manufactures moulded fishing tackle boxes. Faber manufactures and sells 8,000 tackle boxes annually, making full use of its direct labour capacity at available workstations. Following are the selling price and costs associated with Faber's tackle boxes:

Selling price per box		$86.00
Costs per box:		
Moulded plastic	$ 8.00	
Hinges, latches, handle	9.00	
Direct labour ($15 per hour)	18.75	
Manufacturing overhead	12.50	
Selling and administrative costs	17.00	65.25
Profit per box		$20.75

Faber believes that the company could sell 12,000 tackle boxes if it had sufficient manufacturing capacity. The company has looked into the possibility of purchasing the tackle boxes for distribution. Mark Haines Products, a steady supplier of high-quality products, would be able to provide up to 9,000 tackle boxes per year at a price of $68 per box delivered to Faber's facility.

Joe Kernen, Faber's product manager, has suggested that the company could make better use of its Plastics Department by manufacturing skateboards. A market report indicates an expanding skateboard market and a need for additional suppliers. Kernen believes that Faber could sell 17,500 skateboards per year at $45 per skateboard. Manufacturing cost estimates follow:

Selling price per skateboard		$45 00
Costs per skateboard:		
Moulded plastic	$5.50	
Wheels, hardware	7.00	
Direct labour ($15 per hour)	7.50	
Manufacturing overhead	5 00	
Selling and administrative costs	9.00	34.00
Profit per skateboard		$11.00

In the Plastics Department, Faber uses direct labour as the application base for manufacturing overhead. This year, the Plastics Department has been allocated $50,000 of factorywide fixed manufacturing overhead. Every unit of product that Faber sells, whether purchased or manufactured, is allocated $6 of fixed overhead cost for distribution; this amount is included in the selling and administrative cost. Total selling and administrative costs for the purchased tackle boxes would be $10 per unit.

Required:

Using the data presented, determine which products David Faber, Inc., should manufacture and which it should purchase. Support your answer with appropriate calculations.

(IMA adapted)

9. (LO 5; Scarce resource) The Marta Stuart Bakery produces three types of cakes: birthday, wedding, and special occasion. The cakes are made from scratch and baked in a special cake oven. During the holiday season (roughly November 15 through January 15), total demand for the cakes exceeds the capacity of the cake oven. The cake oven is available for baking 690 hours per month, but because of the size of the cakes, it can bake only one cake at a time. Management must determine how to ration the oven time among the three types of cakes. Information on costs, sales prices, and product demand follows:

	Birthday Cakes	Wedding Cakes	Special Occasion Cakes
Required minutes of oven time per cake	10	80	18
Sales price	$ 25	$100	$40
Variable costs:			
Direct material	5	30	10
Direct labour	5	15	8
Variable overhead	2	5	4
Variable selling	3	12	5
Fixed costs (monthly):			
Manufacturing	$1,200		
Selling and administrative	800		

Required:

a. If demand is essentially unlimited for all three types of cakes during the holiday season, which cake or cakes should Marta Stuart bake during the holiday season? Why?

b. Based on your answer in part (a), how many cakes of each type will be produced? What is the projected level of monthly profit for the holiday season?

c. If you were the marketing manager for Marta Stuart, how would your marketing efforts differ between the holiday season and the rest of the year?

10. (LO 5; Scarce resource) Christina Kim has been studying the role of relevance in making decisions. She very badly wants to enter law school. She has decided that she may be able to employ the concepts she has learned to allocate her limited time to review for final exams. Allowing adequate time for meals and rest, she has estimated that she has 34 hours available to review for final exams. As a first step, she has determined that her goal should be to maximize her semester grade point average. Her grade point average is measured on a four-point scale where an A is worth four points, a B is worth three points, a C is worth two points, and a D is worth one point. She is currently enrolled in six courses. She has estimated, for each course, the review time that she must spend to maintain her existing semester grade (failure to invest this review time will result in the semester grade dropping by one letter) and the total time that she would have to study to actually raise her semester grade by one letter. The following table summarizes her estimates:

Course	Existing Grade	Review Time Required to Maintain Existing Grade	Total Review Time Required to Raise Grade by One Letter
Geology	B	4 hours	9 hours
Accounting	C	3 hours	7 hours
Chemistry	B	4 hours	9 hours
Marketing	B	4 hours	10 hours
Spanish	C	5 hours	12 hours
French	A	7 hours	N/A

Required:

a. Determine how Christina should allocate the time she spends reviewing for final exams to maximize her grade point average.

b. Based on your solution to part (a), what is Christina's expected grade point average for the semester?

c. What other factors should Christina consider in deciding how to allocate her time?

11. (LO 6; Sales mix) One year ago, Gary Bartlet gave up his position as the movie critic and sportswriter of the local paper and purchased the rights (under a five-year contract) to several concession stands at a local municipal football stadium. After analyzing the results of his first year of operations, Gary is somewhat disappointed. His two main products are "dogs" and "burgers." He had expected to sell about the same number of each product over the course of the year. However, his sales mix was approximately two-thirds dogs and one-third burgers. Gary feels this combination is less profitable than a balanced mix of dogs and burgers. He is now trying to determine how to improve profitability for the coming year and is considering strategies to improve the sales mix. His first year operations are summarized below:

Dogs:

Sales	(100,000 @ $1.50)	$150,000	
Less:	Direct materials	(40,000)	
	Direct labour	(15,000)	
	Fixed costs	(45 000)	
Net profit			$50,000

Burgers:

Sales	(50,000 @ $2.50)	$125,000	
Less:	Direct materials	(55,000)	
	Direct labour	(10,000)	
	Fixed costs	(15,000)	
Net profit			45,000
Total profit			$95,000

If Gary takes no action to improve profitability, he expects sales and expenses in the second year to mirror the first-year results. Gary is considering two alternative strategies to boost profitability.

Strategy 1:   Add point-of-sale advertising to boost burger sales. The estimated cost per year for such advertising would be $29,000. Gary estimates the advertising would decrease dog sales by 6,000 units and increase burger sales by 22,000 units.

Strategy 2:   Provide a sales commission to his employees. The commission would be paid at a rate of 10% of the product contribution margin (sales less variable production costs) generated on all sales. Gary estimates this strategy would increase dog sales by 10% and burger sales by 25%.

Required:

a. Determine what Gary should do: take no action, adopt strategy 1, or adopt strategy 2. (Show your supporting calculations.)

b. Assuming Gary decided to implement either of the new strategies, what behavioural concerns should he be prepared to address? Explain.

12. (LO 6; Special order) Nubo Manufacturing, Inc. is presently operating at 50% of practical capacity producing about 50,000 units annually of a patented electronic component. Nubo recently received an offer from a company in Yokohama, Japan, to purchase 30,000 components at $6.00 per unit, FOB Nubo's plant. Nubo has not previously sold components in Japan. Budgeted production costs for 50,000 and 80,000 units of output follow:

Units	50,000	80,000
Costs:		
Direct material	$ 75,000	$120,000
Direct labour	75,000	120,000
Manufacturing overhead	200,000	260,000
Total costs	$350,000	$500,000
Cost per unit	$ 7.00	$ 6.25

The sales manager thinks the order should be accepted, even if it results in a loss of $1.00 per unit, because he feels that the sale may build up future markets. The production manager does not wish to have the order accepted primarily because the order would show a loss of $0.25 per unit when computed on the new average unit cost. The treasurer has made a quick computation indicating that accepting the order will actually increase gross margin.

Required:

a. Explain what apparently caused the drop in cost from $7.00 per unit to $6.25 per unit when budgeted production increased from 50,000 to 80,000 units.

b. i. Explain whether (either or both) the production manager and the treasurer are reasoning correctly.

   ii. Explain why the conclusions of the production manager and the treasurer differ.

c. Explain why each of the following may affect the decision to accept or reject the special order.

   i. The likelihood of repeat special sales and/or all sales to be made at $6.00 per unit.

   ii. Whether the sales are made to customers operating in two separate, isolated markets or whether the sales are made to customers competing in the same market.

(IMA adapted)

13. (LO 6; Special order) Mark Haines Ltd. manufactures television cabinets for its own use and for sale to outsiders. Management expects that, during the third quarter of 2005 (the three months ending September 30, 2005), the plant will be operating at 80% of normal capacity. Because a higher utilization of plant capacity is desired, acceptance of a special order would be considered. The selling price of the cabinets to outside companies is $9.00. Cost data for the cabinets is as follows:

Raw materials	$2.50
Direct labour (0.5 hours at $6.00 per hour)	3.00
Overhead (0.25 machine hours at $4.00 per hour)	1.00
Total cost	$6.50

The following special order enquires are being discussed by management:

i. Kernen Ltd., a new customer, requires 25,000 cabinets to be shipped by October 1, 2005, at a price of $6.00 each. The cost data for this order would be similar to the existing structure except that it would require less expensive material. The cost of the raw materials for this order would amount to $2.25 per cabinet. It is estimated by management that the remaining costs, labour time, and machine time will be the same as the costs listed above.

ii. Bartiromo has submitted a special order to Haines Ltd. for 8,000 cabinets at $7.50 per cabinet. The cabinets would have to be shipped by October 1, 2005. However, the estimated unit costs of this cabinet are different from the usual costs and are as follows:

Raw materials	$3.25
Direct labour (0.5 hours at $6.00 per hour)	3.00
Overhead (0.25 hours at $4.00 per hour)	1.00
Total cost	$7.25

In addition Haines will incur $1,800 in additional set-up costs and will have to purchase a special device costing $2,600 to manufacture these cabinets. This device would be discarded once the special order is completed.

Haines Ltd.'s manufacturing capabilities are limited to the total machine hours available. The maximum plant capacity available under normal operating conditions is 87,000 machine hours per year or 7,250 machine hours per month. The budgeted fixed overhead for 2005 is $208,800. All manufacturing overhead costs are applied to production at the predetermined overhead rate of $4.00 per hour.

Haines Ltd. will have the entire third quarter to work on the special orders. It is not expected that any repeat business will be generated from either special order.

Required:

Should Haines Ltd. accept either special order? Justify your answer.

14. (LO 6; Special order) Jenny Fong's company makes and sells "Huggable Brown"—her famous stuffed puppy for young children. They are sold to department stores for $50. The capacity of the plant is 20,000 Huggables per year. Costs to make and sell each stuffed animal are as follows:

Direct materials	$ 5.50
Direct labour	7.00
Variable overhead	10.00
Fixed overhead	12.00
Variable selling expenses	3.00

An Australian import/export company has approached Jenny about buying 2,000 Huggables. Fong Company is currently making and selling 20,000 Huggables per year. The Australian firm wants its own label attached to each stuffed animal, which will raise costs by $0.50 each. No selling expenses would be incurred on this order. Jenny Fong feels she must make an extra $1 on each stuffed animal to accept the order.

Required:

a. What is the opportunity cost per unit of selling to the Australian firm?

b. What is the minimum selling price that Jenny should set?

c. Predict how much more operating profit Jenny will have if she accepts this order at the price specified in part (b).

d. Prove your answer to part (c) by providing operating profits without and with the new order.

15. (LO 6; Special order) Brittany Hodges Ltd. makes miniature holiday wax figurines, which are sold in gift shops. The selling price is $1.25 each. Brittany's costs are as follows:

Variable production cost per unit	$0.45
Fixed production cost per unit	0.15

Brittany pays her salespeople a 10% commission on all sales. Other period expenses are all fixed in total at $20,000 per year. Fenmores, a large department store, has asked Brittany to bid on providing 1,000 figurines for the Christmas season. Brittany Hodges Ltd. has sufficient unused capacity to fill the order and has already done sufficient business to be profitable for the year prior to the bid request.

Required:

a. What is the lowest bid price that would not result in a loss on this special order?

b. What price should Brittany bid to make a 10% profit on the order?

c. Accepting this order will increase fixed expenses by $200. What price should Brittany bid for the 1,000 figurines in order to earn 5% profit on the order?

16. (LO 7; Product line) Forrester Creations Ltd. is presently considering the elimination of one of its existing products (product C) because decreased sales have resulted in the product generating a loss. The following information is available for the most recent operating year:

	A	B	C
Units produced and sold	1,000	1,500	1,000
Sales price per unit	$ 2.00	$ 4.00	$ 2.10
Cost of goods sold:			
Material per unit	0.80	2.00	1.05
Labour per unit	0.30	0.75	0.80
Manufacturing overhead per unit	0.35	0.45	0.35
Selling and administrative expenses per unit:	0.15	0.30	0.20

The following information is also available:

i.   If product C were eliminated, the sales of products A and B would remain the same.

ii.   Variable manufacturing overhead is charged as follows: product A, $0.25 per unit; product B, $0.35 per unit; product C, $0.20 per unit.

iii. Variable selling and administrative expenses are charged as follows: product A, $0.10 per unit; product B, $0.20 per unit; product C, $0.15 per unit.

Required:

Prepare a schedule to help Forrester Creations Ltd.'s management decide whether to eliminate product C. What is your choice, and what are your reasons for this choice?

17.   (LO 7; Product line) Schonblum's Big Buckle, a western wear store, is considering dropping its line of boots, which is now showing a loss. The firm's accountant raised the issue and submitted the following operating statement, which is typical for recent operations:

	Shirts	Hats	Boots	Total
Revenue from sales	$110,000	$60,000	$35,000	$205,000
Cost of sales				
Raw material	$ 15,000	$22,000	$13,000	$ 50,000
Direct labour	27,000	10,000	10,000	47,000
Manufacturing overhead	13,000	8,500	7,000	28,500
	$ 55,000	$40,500	$30,000	$125,500
Gross margin on sales	$ 55,000	$19,500	$ 5,000	$ 79,500
Selling and administrative expenses	(30,000)	(9,700)	(8,000)	(47,700)
Operating profit (loss)	$ 25,000	$ 9,800	$ (3,000)	$ 31,800

That accountant is no longer employed by the firm, and the management team would like you to advise them on the issue that has been brought to light. You examine the costs and conclude the following:

- Variable costs include raw material, direct labour, and manufacturing overhead.
- Variable manufacturing overhead per product line is shirts, $6,000; hats, $4,250; boots, $3,500.
- Variable selling and administrative expenses are shirts, $16,000; hats, $5,000; boots, $6,000.
- Nonvariable costs include $14,750 manufacturing overhead and $20,700 selling and administrative expenses. These costs are allocated to the product lines.
- No fixed costs are avoidable if the boot line is dropped.

Required:

a.   Revise the operating statement so that it provides better information for the management team as it decides whether to continue or eliminate its line of western boots. Give your advice on the decision.

b.   As a marketing manager, what concerns that would not be obvious to an accountant might you have about eliminating a product line? Explain.

18.   (LO 3, 7; Purchase new equipment) You have been presented with the following income statements for three products that Karina Hope Ltd. produces. The production costs for all three products are similar. The fixed selling and administrative expenses are allocated on the basis of square metres occupied by the production of each product.

	A	B	C	D
Unit sales	5,000	250,000	62,500	317,500
Revenues	$46,250	$ 50,000	$28,750	$125,000
Cost of goods sold:				
Variable	$14,250	$ 17,500	$ 7,500	$ 39,250
Fixed	15,210	14,450	8,340	38,000
	$29,460	$ 31,950	$15,840	$ 77,250
Gross margin	$16,790	$ 18,050	$12,910	$ 47,750
Selling and administrative expenses:				
Variable	$13,500	$ 10,000	$ 4,000	$ 27,500
Fixed	10,290	5,050	3,910	19,250
Income before taxes	$(7,000)	$ 3,000	$ 5,000	$ 1,000

The president of the company is concerned about the loss incurred on product A and has been presented with two alternative courses of action. You have been requested to advise her on whether to

a.   Maintain the status quo,
b.   Go with Alternative I, or
c.   Go with Alternative II.

The following are Alternatives I and II.

Alternative I:

Purchase new machinery to manufacture product A, which would result in an immediate cash outlay of $100,000 and increase the fixed costs allocated to product A by $4,800 per year. This new machinery would result in the total variable expenses of product A being reduced to 55% of total revenues. No additional fixed costs would be allocated to products B and C.

Alternative II:

Stop manufacturing product A. Product C's sales would increase by 50%. The present machinery devoted to product A would be sold and after disposition costs the company would not have a gain or loss on disposal. This would reduce the fixed costs allocated to product A by $4,290. The remaining fixed costs allocated to product A include $5,000 rent expense paid per year to a leasing company. This space could be sublet to an outside party for $6,000 per year.

Required:

Advise the president which of the alternatives is best for the company.

19.   (LO 7; Product line) The Rochelle Gordon Paper Company produces three types of consumer products: sticky note pads, tablets, and custom stationery. The firm has become increasingly concerned about the profitability of the custom stationery line. A segmented income statement for the most recent quarter follows:

	Sticky Notes	Tablets	Custom Stationery
Sales	$ 800,000	$ 400,000	$ 1,000,000
Variable costs:			
Production	(200,000)	(150,000)	(550,000)
Selling	(150,000)	(100,000)	(200,000)
Fixed costs:			
Production	(160,000)	(80,000)	(300,000)
Selling	(200,000)	(60,000)	(180,000)
Net income	$ 90,000	$ 10,000	$ (230,000)

Because of the significance of the loss on custom stationery products, the company is considering the elimination of that product line. Of the fixed production costs, $400,000 are allocated to the product lines based on relative sales value; likewise, $250,000 of fixed selling expenses are allocated to the product lines based on relative sales value. All of the other fixed costs charged to each product line are direct and would be eliminated if the product line were dropped.

Required:
Recast the income statements in a format more meaningful for deciding whether the custom stationery product line should be eliminated. Based on the new income statements, determine whether any product line should be eliminated and discuss the rationale for your conclusion.

CASES

1. Spectra Classic Clothing is a retail organization that sells upscale clothing to professional women in Central Canada. Each year store managers, in consultation with their supervisors, establish financial goals. Actual performance is captured by a monthly reporting system.

    District A contains three stores. This district has historically been a very poor performer. Consequently, its supervisor has been searching for ways to improve the performance of her three stores. For May, the district supervisor has set performance goals with the managers of stores 1 and 2. Each of these managers will receive bonuses if certain performance measures are exceeded. The manager of store 3 has decided not to participate in the bonus scheme. The manager of store 1 will receive a bonus based on sales in excess of budgeted sales of $570,000, while the manager of store 2 will receive a bonus based on net income in excess of budgeted net income. The company's net income goal for each store is 12% of sales. The budgeted sales for store 2 are $530,000. Other pertinent data for May follow:

    - At store 1, sales were 40% of total district A sales, while sales at store 2 were 35% of total district A sales. The cost of goods sold at both stores was 42% of sales.
    - Variable selling expenses (sales commissions) were 6% of sales for all stores and districts.
    - Variable administrative expenses were 2.5% of sales for all stores and districts.
    - The maintenance cost includes janitorial and repair services and is a direct cost for each store. The store manager has complete control over this outlay, however, this cost should not be below 1% of sales.
    - Advertising is considered a direct cost for each store and is completely under the control of the store manager. Store 1 spent two-thirds of district A's total outlay for advertising, which was 10 times more than store 2 spent on advertising.
    - The rent expense at store 1 is 40% of district A's total, while store 2 incurs 30% of district A's total.
    - District A expenses are allocated to the stores based on sales.

    Required:
    a. Which store, store 1 or store 2, would appear to be generating the most profit under the new bonus scheme?
    b. Which store, store 1 or store 2, would appear to be generating the most revenue under the new bonus scheme?
    c. Why would store 1 be motivated to spend so much more on advertising than store 2?
    d. Which store manager has more incentive to spend money on regular maintenance? Explain.
    e. Which bonus scheme appears to offer more incentive to improve the profit performance of the district in the short term? In the long term?

    (CMA adapted)

2. Ping Zhang Products Ltd. makes three products from three different material inputs. A component on the production line is due for replacement. The machine can be produced in-house or purchased from another firm for $1,010,000. The following is the income statement for last year:

Sales	$ 6,210,000
Cost of goods sold	(5,047,500)
Selling and administrative expense	(270,000)
Operating profit	$ 892,500

Additional information:
- Plant capacity is 162,500 machine hours.
- The material inputs (X, Y, and Z) for products A, B, and C are as follows:

Product	Input (in units)		
	X	Y	Z
A	7	2	5
B	4	6	3
C	5	3	2

- Variable overhead is based on machine hours used and is applied at the rate of $12 per hour. Machine hours used for product A are 3.75 hours; for product B, 5 hours; and for product C, 1.875 hours.
- Per-unit costs for material inputs are as follows:

Input	Current Cost	Replacement Cost
X	$5	$6
Y	7	7
Z	3	5

- The requirements for the new machine in terms of materials are part X, 2,000 units; part Y, 2,000 units; and part Z, 1,000 units. In addition, the company will need to purchase materials totalling $150,000 to produce the machine.
- Sales for last year were product A, 10,000 units; product B, 15,000 units; and Product C, 5,000 units.
- Fixed production costs of $450,000 are allocated based on units produced.
- Direct labour hours for product A are 3 hours; for product B, 4 hours; and for product C, 2.5 hours.
- Selling and administrative expenses, fixed and variable, are allocated based on units sold. Fixed selling and administrative expenses are $150,000.
- The selling price for product A is $186; for product B; $248; and for product C, $126.
- If Ping Zhang builds the machine rather than buys it, construction will use 30% of the machine hour capacity. If building the machine and producing the three existing products exceeds total capacity, production of the product with the lowest contribution margin will be reduced.
- Constructing the machine will require 10,000 direct labour hours.
- Ping Zhang expects unit sales and contribution margins to remain constant throughout the year.

Required:
Should Ping Zhang Products Ltd. purchase the new machine or produce it in-house? (Defend your decision with calculations.)

3. Carlton Ltd. builds custom motor homes, which range in price from $100,000 to $400,000. For the past 25 years, the company's owner has determined the selling price of each vehicle by estimating the cost of materials, labour, and prorated overhead, and adding 25% to these estimated costs. For example, a recent price quotation was determined as follows:

Direct materials	$ 50,000
Direct labour	80,000
Overhead	20,000
Cost	$150,000
Plus 25%	37,500
Selling price	$187,500

Overhead is allocated to all orders at 25% of direct labour. The company has traditionally operated at 80% of full capacity. Occasionally, a customer would reject a price quote and, if the company were in a slack period, Carlton would often be willing to reduce the markup to as little as 10% over estimated costs. The average markup for the year is estimated to be 20%.

Carlton has recently completed a course on pricing with an emphasis on the contribution margin approach to pricing. He thinks that such an approach would be helpful in determining the selling prices of his custom vehicles.

Total overhead, which includes selling and administrative costs for the year, is estimated to be $1,500,000. Of this amount, $900,000 is fixed and the remainder is variable in direct proportion to direct labour.

Required:

a. Assume the customer in the example rejected the $187,500 bid and also rejected a $165,000 bid. The customer countered with a $150,000 offer.

   i. What is the difference in net income for the year (assuming no replacement offer) between accepting and rejecting the customer's offer?

   ii. What is the minimum selling price Carlton could have quoted the customer without reducing or increasing net income for the year?

b. What advantage does the contribution margin approach to pricing have over the approach Carlton is currently using?

c. What pitfalls are there, if any, to contribution pricing?

(CMA adapted)

4. Bush Industries Ltd. is a multiproduct company with several manufacturing plants. The Clinton Plant manufactures and distributes two household cleaning and polishing compounds, regular and heavy duty, under the Cleen-Brite label. The forecasted operating results for the first six months of 2005, when 100,000 cases of each compound are expected to be manufactured and sold, are presented in the following statement:

Cleen-Brite Compounds—Clinton Plant
Forecasted Results of Operations
For the Six-Month Period Ending June 30, 2005
(in Thousands)

	Regular	Heavy Duty	Total
Sales	$ 2,000	$ 3,000	$ 5,000
Cost of sales	(1,600)	(1,900)	(3,500)
Gross profit	$ 400	$ 1,100	$ 1,500
Selling and administrative expenses			
Variable	$ 400	$ 700	$ 1,100
Fixed*	240	360	600
Total selling and administrative expenses	$ 640	$ 1,060	$ 1,700
Income (loss) before taxes	$ (240)	$ 40	$ (200)

*The fixed selling and administrative expenses are allocated between the two products on the basis of dollar sales volume on the internal reports.

The regular compound sold for $20 per case and the heavy duty compound sold for $30 per case during the first six months of 2005. The manufacturing costs by case of product are presented in the following schedule:

	Cost Per Case	
	Regular	Heavy Duty
Raw materials	$ 7	$ 8
Direct labour	4	4
Variable manufacturing overhead	1	2
Fixed manufacturing overhead*	4	5
Total manufacturing cost	$16	$19
Variable selling and administrative costs	$ 4	$ 7

*Depreciation charges are 50% of the fixed manufacturing overhead of each product.

Each product is manufactured on a separate production line. Annual normal manufacturing capacity is 200,000 cases of each product. However, the plant is capable of producing 250,000 cases of regular compound and 350,000 cases of heavy duty compound annually.

The following schedule reflects the consensus of top management regarding the price/volume alternatives for the Cleen-Brite products for the last six months of 2005. These are essentially the same alternatives management had during the first six months of 2005.

Regular		Heavy Duty Compound	
Alternative Prices (per case)	Sales Volume (in cases)	Alternative Prices (per case)	Sales Volume (in cases)
$18	120,000	$25	175,000
20	100,000	27	140,000
21	90,000	30	100,000
22	80,000	32	55,000
23	50,000	35	35,000

Top management believes the loss for the first six months reflects a tight profit margin caused by intense competition. Management also believes that many companies will be forced out of this market by next year and profits should improve.

Required:

a. What unit selling price should Bush Industries Ltd. select for each of the Cleen-Brite compounds for the remaining six months of 2005? Support your answer with appropriate calculations.

b. Without considering your answer to part (a), assume that the optimum price/volume alternatives for the last six months are a selling price of $23 and volume level of 50,000 cases for the regular compound, and a selling price of $35 and volume of 35,000 cases for the heavy duty compound.

   i. Should Bush Industries Ltd. consider closing down its operations until 2006 to minimize its losses? Support your answer with appropriate calculations.

   ii. Identify and discuss the qualitative factors that should be considered in deciding whether the Clinton Plant should be closed down during the last six months of 2005. Who would general managers ask for the information necessary to assess these factors?

(CMA adapted)

5. Your client, Ocean Company, manufactures and sells three different products—Ex, Why, and Zee. Projected income statements by product line for the year ended December 31, 2005, are presented on the next page.

	Ex	Why	Zee	Total
Unit sales	10,000	500,000	125,000	635,000
Revenues	$ 925,000	$1,000,000	$575,000	$2,500,000
Variable cost of units sold	285,000	350,000	150,000	785,000
Fixed cost of units sold	304,200	289,000	166,800	760,000
Gross margin	$ 335,800	$ 361,000	$258,200	$ 955,000
Variable general and administrative (G&A) expenses	$ 270,000	$ 200,000	$ 80,000	$ 550,000
Fixed G&A expenses	125,800	136,000	78,200	340,000
Total expenses	$ 395,800	$ 336,000	$158,200	$ 890,000
Income (loss) before tax	$ (60,000)	$ 25,000	$100,000	$ 65,000

Production costs are similar for all three products. The fixed general and administrative expenses are allocated to products in proportion to revenues. The fixed cost of units sold is allocated to products by various allocation bases, such as square metres for factory rent and machine hours for repairs, etc.

Ocean management is concerned about the loss for product Ex and is considering two alternative courses of corrective action.

Alternative I:

Ocean would purchase some new machinery for the production of product Ex. This new machinery would involve an immediate cash outlay of $650,000. Management expects that the new machinery would reduce variable production costs so that total variable costs (cost of units sold and general and administrative expenses) for product Ex would be 52% of product Ex revenues. The new machinery would increase the total fixed costs allocated to product Ex to $480,000 per year. No additional fixed costs would be allocated to products Why or Zee.

Alternative II:

Ocean would discontinue the manufacture of product Ex. Selling prices of Why and Zee would remain constant. Management expects that product Zee production and revenues would increase by 50%. Some of the present machinery devoted to product Ex could be sold at scrap value, which would equal its removal costs. The removal of this machinery would reduce fixed costs allocated to product Ex by $30,000 per year. The remaining fixed costs allocated to product Ex include $155,000 of rent expense per year. The space previously used for product Ex can be rented to an outside organization for $157,500 per year.

Required:
Prepare a schedule analyzing the effects of alternatives A and B on projected total company income before tax.

(IMA adapted)

ETHICS AND QUALITY DISCUSSIONS

1. In Japan, the decision to stop production of a product or to close down a plant has different cost consequences than in North America. One principal difference is that Japanese managers are much less likely to fire workers who are displaced by an event such as a plant closing. Japanese managers simply try to move the displaced workers to active plants. However, this concept of permanent or lifetime employment can be awkward to manage when economic times become difficult and prudent financial management suggests that activities, including employment, be scaled back to cut costs. This is becoming more commonplace today.

Required:
Which companies in Japan no longer keep workers when the economy is slow? Go to the library or use the Internet to find the information.

2. Aspinall Computers Ltd. manufactures computers and all their components. The purchasing agent recently informed the company owner, Patrick Aspinall, that another company has offered to supply keyboards for Aspinall's computers at prices below the variable costs at which Aspinall can make them. Incredulous, Mr. Aspinall hired an industrial consultant to explain how the supplier could offer the keyboards at less than Aspinall's variable costs.

   The consultant explained that she suspected that the supplier was purchasing from countries that use low-paid individuals to work in its factories. These people are poverty stricken and will take such work at substandard wages. The purchasing agent and the plant manager feel that Aspinall should buy the keyboards from the supplier, as "no one can blame us for the supplier's hiring practices, and no one will even be able to show that we knew of those practices."

   Required:
   a. What are the ethical issues involved in this case?
   b. What are the advantages and disadvantages of buying from this competitor supplier?
   c. What do you think Mr. Aspinall should do, and why?

COMMUNICATIONS ACTIVITIES

1. Teddy Edwards and his friend Donald Thump visit several Las Vegas casinos over spring break to gamble. Donald disappears for the entire afternoon but returns to the hotel room around dinnertime looking haggard and dejected. Before Teddy gets a chance to speak, Donald says, "Look, pal, I've been shoving quarters in the same slot machine all afternoon. I've invested $300 in a machine, but I've run out of money. Please lend me $50 so I can get back to the casino. I've got that slot primed, and the odds are now in my favour to win a tonne of money."

   Required:
   Using concepts from this chapter, briefly describe how Teddy could inform his friend that the $300 should simply be forgotten.

2. The following costs are associated with a product line of Lapland Technologies, Inc. The costs reflect capacity-level production of 10,000 units per year.

Variable production costs	$15
Fixed production costs	13
Variable selling costs	22
Fixed selling and administrative costs	31

   Required:
   Prepare a presentation showing how time, relative to the stage of production, affects relevant costs for a product line. Begin with the point in time at which the above product line is in the planning stage. Then show how the set of relevant costs changes (1) after acquisition of the production facilities but before production commences and (2) after production is complete.

PROJECTS

1. Lawrence Chung is about to graduate from Private University. He is currently trying to decide whether he should stay at the university and obtain a master's degree or enter the job market with only a bachelor's degree. He has asked for your help and provided you with the following information:

Cost incurred for the bachelor's degree	$48,000
Out-of-pocket costs to get a master's degree	20,000
Estimated starting salary with BA	29,500
Estimated starting salary with MA	33,000
Estimated time to complete master's degree	2 years
Estimated time from the present to retirement	40 years

Required:

Prepare a classroom presentation in which you answer the following questions:

a.   Which of the previous factors are relevant in Lawrence's decision?

b.   What incremental costs must Lawrence incur to obtain the master's degree?

c.   What is Lawrence's best financial alternative?

2.   One of the major present trends is the movement of production facilities and production jobs from North America to developing nations. Hewlett-Packard is one of the firms that have set up operations outside North America. In moving certain operations to Malaysia, Hewlett-Packard obviously expected to cut costs.

Visit your library or use the Internet and read articles on the movement of North American production facilities to other countries. Write a report summarizing the major causes for such moves and express your opinion about the long-term effects of such moves on the North American economy and the global economy.

USING THE INTERNET

1.   To discover information about outsourcing when making a decision to make or buy, go to http://www.ecommerce-now.com/images/ecommerce-now/MakeorBuy.htm.

2.   The following site discusses the guidelines for the making or buying of bar code labels and provides tables to help calculate the costs to consider when making these kinds of decisions: http://www.aimglobal.org/technologies/barcode/makebuy.htm.

Required:

Write a note describing the methods which are described.

3.   The following advertisement appeared in the *Financial Post* on March 15, 2003:

OUTSOURCE YOUR WAREHOUSING NEEDS.

"We will receive your inventory, stock and storage. We will conduct QC and product re-work as necessary. We will ship your product as per purchase orders or release orders confirmed by you. We will follow up to ensure 100% of compliance and customer satisfaction. We will invoice you a flat monthly retainer, as a percentage of sales, and in some cases finance your inventory on a margin fee basis."

Go to www.onlinefufill.com and find out what this company has to offer a small business.

SOLUTIONS TO SELF-TEST QUESTIONS

1.   d

2.   c

3.   a

4.   c

5.   c

6.   a

7.   c:

Overhead that can be eliminated ($1,250,000 – $125,000)	$ 1,125,000
Less: Contribution margin	(500,000)
	$ 625,000

8.   b:

Differential Costs	Make	Buy
Purchasing		$1.25
Direct material	$0.60	
Direct labour	0.40	
Variable overhead	0.10	
Total	$1.10	$1.25

9.   b

10. e

ENDNOTES

1. Rita Koselka, "It's My Favourite Statistic," *Forbes*, September 12, 1994, pp. 172, 176.

2. *The Boston Globe*, November 8, 2002.

3. William H. Miller, "Gillette's Secret to Sharpness and The Gillette Advantage," *Industry Week*, January 3, 1994, pp. 26, 28.

4. Business Editors, "The Gillette Company Celebrates Its Centennial in 2001," *Business Wire*, New York, September 4, 2001.

5. Newstream.com Multimedia News for the 21st Century Newsroom (www.newstream.com/us/story).

6. Ibid.

7. Amitai Etzioni, "Humble Decision Making," *Harvard Business Review*, July–August 1989, p. 122.

8. Clifford and Kripalani, with Dawley in London, "Different Countries, Adjoining Cubicles," *Business Week*, New York, August 28, 2000.

9. Joost Akkermans, "Royal Philips Poised to Shed 1,600 Workers," Bloomberg News, *Toronto Star*, Friday, March 14, 2003.

10. "Levi Shuts Factories, Shifts Focus," *Globe and Mail* and Associated Press and Reuters News Agency, *The Globe and Mail*, Tuesday, April 9, 2002, p. B12.

11. "Harry Puts Hornby on Track; Scale of Success: Outsourcing Production to China Good Move," *Birmingham Post*, Birmingham U.K.; February 5, 2002.

12. Scott Adams, *Financial Post*, June 16, 2003.

13. Short-run decisions typically focus on a measure of accounting income that excludes some past costs, such as depreciation on old assets. Long-range decision analysis commonly uses cash flow as its decision criterion; this topic is covered in Chapter 10.

14. Alex Taylor III, "The Auto Industry Meets the New Economy," *Fortune*, September 5, 1994, p. 56.

15. Shawn Tully, "You'll Never Guess Who Really Makes ...," *Fortune*, October 3, 1994, p. 124.

16. "Outsourcing Information Systems," *Management Accounting Guideline 23*, Society of Management Accountants, Canada, 1994.

17. Clayton M. Christensen, *Business Week*; New York; August 28, 2000, pp. 180–181.

18. For additional information on theory of constraints and linear programming, see Web Chapter 7.

19. Institute of Management Accountants (formerly National Association of Accountants), *Statements on Management Accounting Number 2: Management Accounting Terminology* (Montvale, N.J.: National Association of Accountants, June 1, 1983), p. 94.

20. M2 Communications Ltd., "Dell Introduces New Micro-Portable Projector; Light, Bright, Affordable Projector Complements Dell's Notebook Computers," June 27, 2002.

21. The law of demand elasticity indicates how closely price and demand are related. Product demand is highly elastic if a small price reduction generates a large demand increase. If demand is less elastic, large price reductions are needed to bring about moderate sales volume increases.

22. Such a decline in demand generally does not occur when the product in question has no close substitute or is not a major expenditure in consumers' budgets.

23. Patrick Barwise, Paul R. Marsh, and Robin Wensley, "Must Finance and Strategy Clash?" *Harvard Business Review*, September–October 1989, p. 86.

24. In regard to this last item, consider what occurs when one airline raises or lowers its fares between cities. It typically does not take very long for all the other airlines flying that route to adjust their fares accordingly. Thus, competitive advantage often exists only for a short time. Another example of this is seen in the following news item. "On March 10, 2002, Delta announced that it would no longer pay commissions to travel

agents for booking flights. As a result, Air Canada stated that it will eliminate base commissions to travel agents for all tickets sold in Canada." (Keith McArthur, *Globe and Mail*, March 23, 2002, p. B3.)

25. Abigail Goldman, *The Los Angeles Times*, Los Angeles, California, February 28, 2002, page C1.

26. Richard Martin, "Business Strategy: The Razor's Edge," *The Industry Standard*, August 6, 2001.

27. This same type of incremental analysis is shown in Chapter 3 in relation to CVP computation.

28. It is assumed here that all common costs are fixed costs; this is not always the case. Some common costs are variable, such as costs of processing purchase orders and computer time-sharing expenses for payroll or other corporate functions.

29. "Gateway Computer Closes Canadian Stores; 220 Laid Off," *Sault Star*, March 31, 2001, Final Edition, p. C5.

30. Ibid.

31. Scott McCarnety, "Dell Computer Plans to Quit Retail Field and Refocus on Its Mail Order Business," *The Wall Street Journal*, July 12, 1994, p. A2.

32. Rasha Mourtadaa, "Dude, Touch My Dell," *Canadian Business*, November 25, 2002.

33. Imogen Matthews, "Unilever: Making It Happen in the Mass Market, *European Cosmetic Markets*, August 1, 1999.

34. William H. Miller, "Gillette's Secret to Sharpness," *Industry Week*, January 3, 1994, p. 26.

35. "Gillette Issues Warning; Says It May Shed Units," *New York Times*, October 22, 1999.

36. Business Editors, "Gillette CEO Outlines Business Progress, Describes Solid Start to Company Turnaround," *Business Wire*, New York, February 22, 2002.

37. *The Boston Globe*, November 8, 2002.

38. James M. Kilts, "The Gillette Company Celebrates Its Centennial in 2001," *Business Wire*, New York, September 4, 2001.

Chapter 9

The Budgeting Process

LEARNING OBJECTIVES

After reading this chapter, you should be able to answer the following questions:

1 What
is the importance of the budgeting process?

2 What
is the difference between strategic and tactical planning and how do these relate to the budgeting process?

3 What
are the benefits and disadvantages of imposed budgets and participatory budgets?

4 How
are budget variances computed and used to analyze differences between budgeted and actual revenues?

5 What
complicates the budgeting process in a multinational environment?

6 What
is the starting point of a master budget and how do the components relate to one another?

7 How
does traditional budgeting differ from zero-based budgeting?

8 What
are future perspectives for budgeting?

ON SITE

www.relconsult.com

REL Consultancy Group

REL CONSULTANCY GROUP is an international leader in delivering shareholder value from financial operations by the introduction of "best in class" processes and methods affecting the management of business assets.

"We [REL Consultancy Group] have a proven track record built up over 25 years of helping many of the world's leading companies to reduce working capital and increase cashflow whilst rigorously addressing cost efficiency, productivity and customer service. We are passionate about delivering value through quantified improvements and rapid paybacks, aligned closely to a client's strategic objectives."

REL's specialist consulting team is deployed worldwide. It is supported by extensive proprietary tools, techniques, and "best practice" processes developed from assignments conducted for more than 500 major organizations in more than 60 countries.[1]

For years, senior managers at REL Consultancy Group handled budgeting and revenue forecasting much the way most other companies do. As year-end approached, they would evaluate performance, set sales targets for the upcoming year, and then work to see that everyone met or exceeded the goals.

Unfortunately, the process didn't always produce the intended results.

"Invariably," recalls Stephen Payne, president of the London-based global management consulting firm, "one of the account directors would land a couple of good clients early in the year and make his annual budget well before the year closed. More often than not, he'd then take his foot off the gas and coast."

To make the budgeting process more timely and relevant, the firm embraced a more complex, albeit intuitive, approach to financial forecasting—the rolling budget. Rather than creating an annual financial forecast that remains static for the year, Payne and his colleagues now produce an 18-month budget and then update projections every month—in effect recalculating the whole budget. As the firm's actual sales figures come in each month, directors plug them into their forecasting model in place of what they had projected, then roll the budget forward one more month.[2]

*T*he annual budget is the financial plan to implement the organization's strategy for the next year. When that organization's environment is relatively stable, budgeting factors are fairly predictable and the budgeting process is less challenging than when environmental factors are highly uncertain. For many organizations some of the underlying budget assumptions, such as the severity of winter temperatures, are extremely unpredictable. In these situations, factors that can significantly affect the budget require an ongoing monitoring process as the year progresses. Although budgeting is important for all organizations, entities that have significant amounts of cash and other resources should prepare and use detailed budgets for both planning and control purposes.

Regardless of the type of endeavour in which you engage, it is necessary at some point to visualize the future, imagine what results you want to achieve, and determine the activities and resources required to achieve those results. Even individuals frequently must engage in budgeting. For example, Nicholas Sperry-Rand, who is a second-year student at Atkinson College, York University, has been invited to spend his spring vacation week at his roommate's home in Vancouver, British Columbia. Nicholas has only $180 available and asks his dad for supplemental money for the trip. His dad requires that Nicholas prepare a budget. Nicholas provides the following budgetary estimates for his proposed vacation:

Nicholas' Vacation Budget

Gasoline [(2,000 kilometres ÷ 25 kilometres per litre) × $1.30 per litre] ÷ 2 persons*	$ 52
Meals and lodging for the round trip [(10 meals @ $15) + (4 nights @ $50)]	350
Beach clothes, sunglasses, and suntan oil	40
Admissions, entertainment, and snacks	100
Total cost of trip	$ 542
Less the money Nicholas already has	(180)
Money needed from dad	$ 362

*Nicholas' roommate agrees to pay for half of the gasoline.

Fortunately for Nicholas, he had just received his midterm grades, and they were all favourable. He mailed his midterm grades and his budget request to his dad. By return mail, Nicholas received a cheque for $362 and a note from his parents congratulating him on his grades.

Most budgeting situations are more complex than the simplistic example just given. When the budgeting process requires the integration of large amounts of funds, people, and organizational units, budgets and budgetary results should be committed to paper or input to a computer. This is because of the human tendency to forget and the difficulty of mentally processing many facts and relationships at the same time.

Detailed plans that are monetarily enumerated are called budgets. They are the detailed quantification of targets for near-term choices of actions. Budgeting is not planning—it is the quantification of planning! Commitments defined in the budget are vital management tools to guide and evaluate short-term performance. The budget is, and should always be seen as, the commitment.[3]

This chapter not only describes some of the managerial aspects of **budgeting** but also covers quantitative aspects of the process and the preparation of a master budget.

budgeting
the process of determining a financial plan for future operations

PURPOSES OF BUDGETING

Planning is the cornerstone of effective management, strategic development, and implementation. One vital part of good planning is budgeting. During the planning process, managers attempt to agree on company goals and objectives and how to achieve them. Typically, goals are stated in abstract terms, while objectives are quantifiable for a period of time. Achievement of goals and objectives requires undertaking complex activities and providing diverse resources that, in turn, typically demand a formalized planning or budgeting process.

Planning should include qualitative narratives of goals, objectives, and means of accomplishment. However, if plans were limited to qualitative narratives, the process of comparing actual results to expectations would only allow generalizations, and trying to measure how well the organization met its specified objectives would be impossible. Therefore, management translates qualitative narratives into a quantitative format, or **budget**, which expresses an organization's commitment to planned activities and resource acquisition and use. "A budget is more than a forecast. A forecast is a prediction of what may happen and sometimes contains prescriptions for dealing with future events. A budget, on the other hand, involves a commitment to a forecast to make an agreed upon outcome happen."[4]

Budgeting is the process of devising a financial plan for future operations. Budgeting is a management task, not an accounting task. The accounting function simply assembles the information provided into a known and consistent format. Budgeting is an important part of an organization's planning and controlling processes.

A good budget is more than just a process of collecting and consolidating numbers; it's a map that can guide your company to competitive advantage. It's all about allocating resources to achieve your company's strategy and objectives, and providing a forum for making decisions related to those allocations. It ties all the pieces together, providing the goals and benchmarks against which to measure performance.[5]

Budgets can be used to indicate direction and priorities; measure individual, divisional, and corporate performance; encourage achievement and continuous improvement efforts; and identify areas of concern. The process itself can be performed in a variety of ways: top-down, bottom-up, or a combination of the two. The basics of the budgeting process are illustrated in the flow diagram in Exhibit 9-1 on page 498; the individual steps are discussed in this chapter.

Like any other planning activity, budgeting helps managers focus on one direction chosen from many future alternatives. Management generally defines the chosen path using some accounting measure of financial performance, such as net income, earnings per share, or sales level in dollars or units. Budgeting is the tool that managers use to successfully plan and manage operations and programs.[6] Such accounting-based measures provide specific quantitative criteria against which future performance (also recorded in accounting terms) can be compared. Budgets, then, are a type of standard, and variances from budget can be computed.

Budgeting can also help identify potential problems in achieving specified goals and objectives. For example, assume that a particular company has fiscal 2006 objectives of generating $55 million in revenues and $2.5 million of net income for the year. The budget might indicate that, based on current prices and expenses, such objectives cannot be attained. Managers could then brainstorm to find ways to increase revenues or reduce costs so that these objectives can be reached. By

budget
the quantitative expression of an organization's commitment to planned activities and resource acquisition and use

LEARNING OBJECTIVE 1

What is the importance of the budgeting process?

EXHIBIT 9-1

The Budgeting Process

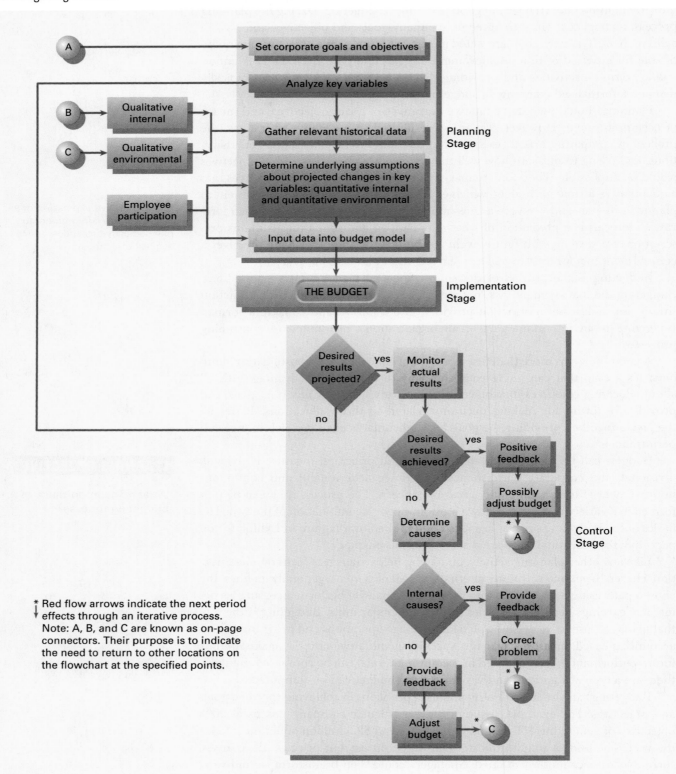

* Red flow arrows indicate the next period effects through an iterative process.
Note: A, B, and C are known as on-page connectors. Their purpose is to indicate the need to return to other locations on the flowchart at the specified points.

quantifying potential difficulties and making them visible, budgets can help stimulate managers to think of ways to overcome those difficulties.

A well-prepared budget as a means of implementing strategy can be an effective device to communicate objectives, constraints, and expectations to people throughout an organization. Such communication helps everyone understand exactly what is to be accomplished, how those accomplishments are to be achieved, and how resources are to be allocated. Decisions about resource allocations are made, in part, through a process of obtaining information, justifying requests, and negotiating compromises. Allowing managers to participate in the budgeting process motivates them and instills a feeling of teamwork. Employee participation is needed to effectively integrate necessary information from various sources as well as to obtain individual managerial commitment to the resulting budget.

The budget indicates the resource constraints under which managers must operate for the upcoming budget period. Thus, the budget becomes the basis for controlling activities and resource usage. Periodic budget-to-actual comparisons allow managers to determine how well they are doing and to assess how well they understand their operations.

While budgets are typically expressed in financial terms, the budgeting and planning processes are concerned with all organizational resources—raw materials inventory, supplies, personnel, and facilities. These processes can be viewed from a long-term or a short-term perspective.

Strategic and Tactical Planning

When managers plan on a long-term basis (5 to 10 years), they are engaged in **strategic planning**. This process is generally performed only by top-level management with the assistance of several key staff members. The result of the process is a statement of long-range goals for the organization and of the strategies and policies that will help in the achievement of those goals.

Expressing long-term goals first requires an acknowledgment of the organization's business. Sometimes, the obvious function is not the true function.

Strategic planning is not concerned with day-to-day operations, although the strategic plan will be the foundation on which short-term planning is based. Managers engaging in strategic planning should identify **key variables**, or critical factors believed potentially to be direct causes of the achievement or nonachievement of organizational goals and objectives. Key variables can be internal or external. Exhibit 9-2 on page 500 provides the results of one study about the external factors considered to be the most critical in determining the strategic plans of manufacturing companies. One conclusion from the survey was that a "firm's long-term success is dependent on the integration of the forces in its environment into its own planning process so that the firm *influences* its own destiny instead of constantly *reacting* to environmental forces."[7] Internal key variables are under the control of management, while external key variables are normally uncontrollable.

After key variables have been identified, information related to them can be gathered. Much of this information will be historical and qualitative and provides a useful starting point for tactical planning activities.

The process of determining the specific objectives and means by which strategic plans will be achieved is called **tactical** (or operational) **planning**. Although some tactical plans, such as corporate policy statements, exist for the long term and address repetitive situations, most tactical plans are short-term (1 to 18 months). Such short-term tactical plans are considered "single use" plans and have been developed to address a given set of circumstances or for a specific time frame.

EXHIBIT 9-2

External Factors to Include in Strategic Plans

Organizational Characteristics

- Market share
- Quality of products
- Discretionary cash flow/gross capital investment

Market and Consumer Behaviour

- Market segmentation
- Market size
- New market development
- Buyer loyalty

Industry Structure

- Rate of technological change in products or processes
- Degrees of product differentiation
- Industry price/cost structure
- Economies of scale

Supplier

- Major changes in availability of raw materials

Social, Economic, and Political

- GNP trend
- Interest rates
- Energy availability
- Government-established and legally enforceable regulations

Source: Republished with permission of the Institute of Management Accounting from "How U.S. Firms Conduct Strategic Planning," James F. Brown, Jr., *Management Accounting*, February 1986; permission conveyed through Copyright Clearance Center, Inc.

The annual budget is an example of a single use tactical plan. Although a budget's focus is on a 12-month period, intermediate (quarterly and monthly) plans should also be included for the budget to work effectively. Remember, at REL Consultancy Group, the budgets are reviewed and updated on a monthly basis.

A well-prepared budget "translates the strategic plans of the organization and [the company's] implementation programs into period-oriented operational guides to company activities."[8] Exhibit 9-3 illustrates the relationships among strategic planning, tactical planning, and budgeting.

Both strategic and tactical planning require that information regarding the economy, environment, technological developments, and available resources be incorporated into the setting of goals and objectives.

Once management has evaluated the operating environment and relevant product life cycles and has decided on the organization's strategic plan, budgeting activity should begin for future periods. The budgeting process requires carefully integrating a complex set of facts and projections with human relationships and attitudes. Therefore, no single system of budgeting is right for all organizations. However, it is recognized that there are basically two ways by which budgets can be derived: from the top down (**imposed budgets**) or from the bottom up (**participatory budgets**).

If employees pad, stuff, and under- or overforecast revenue during the budgetary process, then the budget isn't serving as the useful tool that it could. So how do you create a budget that motivates employees to achieve targets and doesn't get filed in the bottom of a drawer?

Some approaches to the budgetary process motivate employees to achieve targets, and others do the opposite. Many central planners think that they are in

LEARNING OBJECTIVE 3

What are the benefits and disadvantages of imposed budgets and participatory budgets?

imposed budget
a budget that is prepared by top management with little or no input from operating personnel, who are simply informed of the budget goals and constraints

participatory budget
a budget that has been developed through a process of joint decision making by top management and operating personnel

Who?	What?	How?	Why?
Top management	Strategic planning	Statement of organizational mission, goals, and strategies, long-range (5 to 10 years)	Establish a long-range vision of the organization and provide a sense of unity and commitment to specified purposes
Top and mid-management	Tactical planning	Statement of organizational objectives and operational plans, short-range (12 to 18 months)	Provide direction for the achievement of strategic plans; state strategic plans in terms that can be acted on; furnish a basis against which results can be measured
Top, mid-, and operational management	Budgeting	Quantitative and monetary statements that coordinate company activities for periods of 12 months or less	Allocate resources effectively and efficiently; indicate a commitment to objectives; provide a monetary control device

EXHIBIT 9-3

Relationships Among Planning Processes

charge and often act as police over the rest of the business, which creates resentment and results in an "us-and-them" attitude. If senior managers dictate the budget, operational personnel are alienated from ownership of the budget, and if a budget is implemented as a stick to use on managers, it will waste time, effort, and money.

The budget may be tossed into the bottom drawer and forgotten until next year: "We have satisfied the accountants this year, so let's get on with the real job. The result: Employees in operations then use their own guidelines to run the business, and the whole budget process has been an almost complete waste of time."[9]

For decades, budgets in governmental and not-for-profit organizations have had the primary goals of monetary control and fiscal responsibility. Business budgets originally maintained the same focus and were prepared by top management with little or no input from operating personnel. Such budgets were simply imposed on the operating personnel, who had to work within the budgeted figures and constraints. In such a budgeting environment, operating personnel may be given an opportunity to suggest changes to the budget, but such suggestions are not always seriously considered. As indicated in Exhibit 9-4 on page 502, imposed budgets are effective and provide some distinct advantages under certain circumstances; but they involve disadvantages as well.

Businesspeople slowly recognized the disadvantages of imposed budgets and the dissatisfaction they caused. Thus, participation at various management levels was introduced. From the standpoint of operational managers, participation can be viewed on a spectrum. At one end is the right to comment on budgets before their implementation; at the other is the ultimate right to set budgets. Neither end of the spectrum is quite appropriate. Simply giving managers the right to comment on the handed-down budget still reflects an imposed budgeting system, while giving each individual manager the right to set his or her own budget ignores the fact that cooperation and communication among areas are essential to the functioning of a cohesive organization.

A participatory budget is generally defined as one that has been developed through a process of joint decision making by top management and operating personnel. The degree to which lower-level operating management is allowed to

EXHIBIT 9-4

Imposed Budgets

Best Times to Use:
- In start-up organizations
- In extremely small businesses
- In times of economic crisis
- When operating managers lack budgetary skills or perspective
- When organizational units require precise coordination of efforts

Advantages of Imposed Budgets:
- Increase probability that the organization's strategic plans will be incorporated in planned activities
- Enhance coordination among divisional plans and objectives
- Use top management's knowledge of overall resource availability
- Reduce the possibility of input from inexperienced or uninformed lower-level employees
- Reduce the time frame for the budgeting process

Disadvantages of Imposed Budgets:
- May result in dissatisfaction, defensiveness, and low morale among individuals who must work under the budget
- Reduce the feeling of teamwork
- May limit the acceptance of the stated goals and objectives
- Limit the communication process between employees and management
- May create a view of the budget as a punitive device
- May result in unachievable budgets for international divisions if local operating and political environments are not adequately considered
- May stifle the initiative of lower-level managers

participate in budget development usually depends on two factors: top management's awareness of the advantages of the participation process and its confidence in those advantages. Both the advantages and disadvantages of participatory budgets are listed in Exhibit 9-5.

Managers may introduce **budget slack** (the intentional underestimation of revenues and/or overestimation of expenses) into the budgeting process. Slack, if it exists, is usually built into the budget during the participation process; it is not often found in imposed budgets. Having slack in the budget allows subordinate managers to achieve their objectives with less effort than if there were no slack. Budget slack creates problems because of the significant interaction of budgeting factors. If sales are understated, for example, problems can arise in the production, purchasing, and personnel areas.

To reduce the possibility of slack, management may wish to consider basing the budget on activities rather than costs. Activity-based budgets require an analysis of cost drivers and the relating of budget line items to activities performed. These budgets can be motivational to those who use them because they're easy to understand and department managers can see the changes flow through them. They are user oriented. Because they aren't bogged down in details and complex financial terms, simplified budgets will be used by department managers for strategic management and cost management activities rather than being filed and forgotten.

Activity-based budgeting is a new budget format whereby budget costs are arrayed according to the expected costs of activities rather than products, services, or resources.[10]

budget slack
the intentional underestimation of revenues and/or overestimation of expenses

EXHIBIT 9-5
Participatory Budgets

Best Times to Use:

- In well-established organizations
- In extremely large businesses
- In times of economic affluence
- When operating managers have strong budgetary skills and perspectives
- When organizational units are quite autonomous

Advantages of Participatory Budgets:

- Provide information from persons most familiar with the needs and constraints of organizational units
- Integrate knowledge that is diffused among various levels of management
- Lead to better morale and higher motivation
- Provide a means to develop fiscal responsibility and the budgetary skills of employees
- Develop a high degree of acceptance of and commitment to organizational goals and objectives by operating management
- Are generally more realistic
- Allow organizational units to coordinate with one another
- Allow subordinate managers to develop operational plans that conform to organizational goals and objectives
- Include specific resource requirements
- Blend overview of top management with operating details
- Provide a social contract that expresses expectations of top management and subordinates

Disadvantages of Participatory Budgets:

- Require significantly more time than imposed budgets
- Create a level of dissatisfaction with the process similar to that occurring under imposed budgets when the effects of managerial participation are negated by top-management changes
- Create an unachievable budget when managers are ambivalent or unqualified to participate
- May cause lower-level managers to introduce slack into the budget
- May support "empire building" by subordinates
- May start the process earlier in the year when there is more uncertainty about the future year

Some benefits of using activity-based budgets are discussed in the News Note on page 504.

Since the functions of operating personnel are affected by the budget and these individuals must work under the budget guidelines, input from the operating level is often invaluable in the planning process. Although there is no concrete evidence as to how well participatory budgeting works in all circumstances, such participation by operating managers also seems to create a higher commitment to the budget's success. To the extent that participation reduces the precarious aspect of projections by providing managers with a greater quantity and quality of information, it results in more accurate budgets.

The budgeting process, as mentioned, represents a continuum with imposed budgets on one end and participatory budgets on the other. Currently, most business budgets are prepared through a coordinated effort that includes input from operating personnel and revision by top management. In this manner, plans of

Activity-Based Budgeting Focuses on Work, Not Costs

A budget should be based on knowledge of how good the organization can be and should be. Developing an achievable budget is often difficult because most managers develop a budget on what they spend, not on what they do (activities) that consumes the budgeted costs.

Many organizations, such as Johnson & Johnson and Chrysler Corporation, are looking to their existing activity-based cost systems as the basis for re-engineering their budgeting process. Unlike conventional budgeting that focuses on resource cost, the re-engineered budget process should assume that the focus will centre on activities and business processes. Activity-based budgeting (ABB) is a process of planning and controlling the expected activities of an organization. ABB links work (activity) with the strategic cost, time, and quality objectives of the organization. ABB focuses on activities. Costs are determined after the activity workload is defined.

The following list compares traditional and activity-based budgeting:

Top 10 Weaknesses of Traditional Budgeting	Top 10 Advantages of Activity-Based Budgeting
1. Does not provide a common language that supports common sense.	1. Uses a common (verb + noun) activity language.
2. Focuses on costs, not quality or time.	2. Focuses on activity cost, time, and quality.
3. Focuses on input (costs), not output.	3. Focuses on activity input and output.
4. Does not link to the strategic plan.	4. Strategic goals are linked to the activity's cost, time, and quality.
5. Does not identify levels of service.	5. Focuses on required versus discretionary activity output.
6. Does not identify root causes of costs.	6. Aids in identifying the cost drivers of activities and processes.
7. Focuses on functions, not processes.	7. Focuses on functional activities and business processes.
8. Focuses on cuts, not continuous improvement.	8. Focuses on the unending improvement of activity output.
9. Does not identify work or workload.	9. Focuses on activity and output.
10. Does not identify or quantify waste.	10. Quantifies non-value-added activity costs.

Source: Tom Pryor, "The Budget Is Not the Best You Can Be," *Focus on ABM*, Winter 1993, pp. 1–2. www.icms.net/1993

managers at all levels can be considered. Top management first sets strategic objectives for lower-level management, then lower-level managers suggest and justify their operations' performance targets. Upper-level managers combine all component budgets, evaluate the overall results, and provide feedback on any needed changes to the lower-level managers.

Regardless of whether the process is top-down or bottom-up, management must review the completed budget before approving and implementing it. This process is necessary to determine (1) if the underlying assumptions on which the budget is based are reasonable and (2) if the budgeted results are acceptable and realistic. The budget may indicate that the results expected from the planned activities do not achieve the desired objectives. In this case, planned activities should be reconsidered and revised. The revision should guide the company toward the desired outcomes expressed during planning for the intermediate term.

THE BUDGETING PROCESS

The budget is normally prepared on an annual basis and detailed first by quarters and then by months within those quarters. At a minimum, budget preparation should begin two to three months before the period to be covered, but management must keep two things in mind: (1) participatory budget development will take longer than an imposed budget process; and (2) the larger and more complex the company is, the longer the budgeting process will take.

The speed of change in today's economy has generated a trend toward adopting continuous forecasting as part of the planning process.[11]

Some companies use a continuous (or rolling) budget, an ongoing 12-month budget that adds a new budget month (12 months into the future) as each current month expires. **Continuous budgets** make the planning process less sporadic and disruptive. Rather than "going into the budgeting period" at a specific point in time, managers are continuously involved in planning and budgeting. Continuous budgets also provide a longer-range focus so that no surprises occur at year-end. This is illustrated in the News Note below.

In the illustration shown in Exhibit 9-6 on page 506, management is working within the present one-month component of a full 12-month annual budget at any point in time.

The evolution of electronic spreadsheets has dramatically affected the budgeting process. Computerized spreadsheets allow companies to quickly and inexpensively examine "what if" scenarios and adjust interrelated budgets to reflect environmental or internal changes. These spreadsheets are also helpful to a company's ability to maintain a continuous budget. Once the set of budget headings, budget formulas, and current 12 months of budget figures have been tested and entered on a spreadsheet, each new month's figures can be developed as the month just concluded is deleted.

A good budget requires a substantial amount of time and effort from the persons engaged in preparing it. This process can be improved by the availability of an organizational **budget manual,** a detailed set of documents that provides

continuous budget
an ongoing 12-month budget that adds a new budget month (12 months into the future) as each current month expires

budget manual
a detailed set of documents that provides information and guidelines about the budgetary process

---

Using Continuous Budgeting

The Hon Company, the largest maker of mid-priced office furniture in the United States and Canada, has overcome obstacles of change through the use of a continuous three-month budget cycle. The budget has become the integral planning and control device for achieving two strategic objectives: ongoing new product and service development and rapid continuous improvement. The budget also serves as an important vehicle for ensuring that the corporate culture is unified in its understanding of—and commitment to—strategic objectives.

Managers at the Hon Company communicate and coordinate operating plans through a process called continuous quarterly budgeting. All departments work together to produce an updated four-quarter budget at the beginning of each quarter. Thus, a budget prepared for the third quarter of the year includes plans for the third and fourth quarters of the year and for the first two quarters of the next year. Each quarterly budget requires the next four quarters to be completely re-budgeted. By having a detailed quarterly budget that is up-to-date and comprehensive, managers and employees in all areas are prepared to deal with rapid change.[12]

GENERAL NEWS NOTE

EXHIBIT 9-6

Continuous Budget

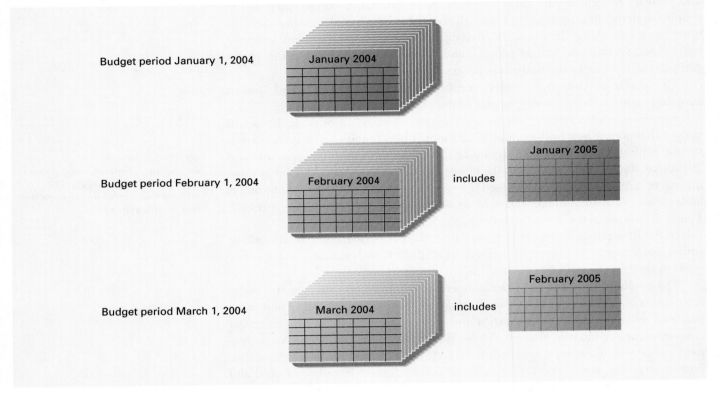

Budget period January 1, 2004   **January 2004**

Budget period February 1, 2004   **February 2004**   includes   **January 2005**

Budget period March 1, 2004   **March 2004**   includes   **February 2005**

information and guidelines about the budgetary process. The manual should include the following:

1. Statements of the budgeting purpose and its desired results
2. A listing of specific budgetary activities to be performed
3. A calendar of scheduled budgetary activities
4. Sample budget forms
5. Original, revised, and approved budgets

The *statements of budgeting purpose and desired results* communicate the reasons behind the process and should flow from general statements to specific details. An example of a general statement of budgeting purpose is: "The cash budget provides a basis for planning, reviewing, and controlling cash flows from and for various activities; this budget is essential to the preparation of a pro forma Cash Flow Statement." Specific statements regarding the cash budget could include references to minimum desired cash balances and periods of high cash needs. These needs are taken into consideration when the cash budget portion of the master budget is prepared.

Budgetary activities should be listed by job rather than by a person's name because the responsibility for actions should be delegated to whomever is holding each specific job when the manual is implemented. This section should indicate who has the final authority for revising and approving the budget. Budget approval may be delegated to a budget committee or to one or several members of top management.

The *budget calendar* coordinates the budgetary process and should include a timetable for all budgetary activities. The budget timetable is unique to each organization. The larger the organization, the more time will be needed to gather information, coordinate the information, identify weak points in the process or the budget itself, and take corrective action. The calendar should also indicate control points for the upcoming periods, when budget-to-actual comparisons will be made, and when and how feedback will be provided to managers responsible for operations.

Sample forms provide a means for consistent presentation of budget information by all individuals, making summarizations of information easier, quicker, and more effective. The sample forms should be understandable and could include standardized worksheets that allow managers to update historical information to arrive at budgetary figures. This section of the manual may also provide standard cost tables for items on which the organization has specific guidelines or policies. For example, in estimating employee fringe benefit costs, the company's rule of thumb may be 30% of base salary. Similarly, a company policy may set the daily meal allowance for salespersons at $50; therefore in estimating meal expenses for the future period, the sales manager would simply multiply total estimated travel days by $50.

The last section of the manual should include the original and revised budgets. It is helpful for future planning to understand how the revision process works and why changes were made. The final approved budget is known as the master budget. It is composed of many individual budgets and serves as a control document for budget-to-actual comparisons.

Implementation and Control

After a budget is prepared and accepted, it is implemented. Budget implementation means that the budget is now considered a standard against which performance can be measured. Managers operating under budget guidelines should be provided with copies of all appropriate budgets. These managers should also be informed that their performance will be evaluated by comparing actual results to budgeted amounts. Such evaluations should generally be made by budget category for specific periods of time.

Once the budget is implemented, the control phase begins. Control includes making actual-to-budget comparisons, determining variances, providing feedback to operating managers, investigating the causes of the variances, and taking any necessary corrective action. This control process indicates the cyclical nature of budgeting (see Exhibit 9-7 on page 508). Feedback (both positive and negative) is essential to the control process and must be provided in a timely manner to be useful.

SALES PRICE AND SALES VOLUME VARIANCES

LEARNING OBJECTIVE 4

How are budget variances computed and used to analyze differences between budgeted and actual revenues?

When actual-to-budget comparisons are made, managers are held accountable for the revenues (if any) and the costs in the operating areas over which they have authority and responsibility. Actual performance should be compared against budgeted performance to determine variances from expectations. In making such comparisons, however, management needs to be certain that it is considering results from a proper perspective.

For an operating area in which revenues are being generated (for example, sales for the Mercury Division of Ford Motor Company), comparisons should first be made on the revenue level to determine how closely projected revenues are being met. As discussed in Chapter 5 (standard costing), a total variance from standard can have both a price and a quantity element. Thus, revenue variance calculations should be made for both of these elements.

EXHIBIT 9-7

Nature of the Budgeting Process

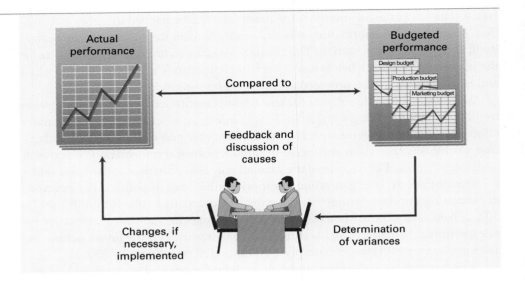

sales price variance
the difference between actual and
budgeted selling prices multiplied by
the actual number of units sold

sales volume variance
the difference between actual and
budgeted volumes multiplied by the
budgeted selling price

Calculating the difference between actual and budgeted selling prices and multiplying this number by the actual number of units sold will provide the **sales price variance**. This variance indicates the portion of the total variance that is related to a change in selling price. A variance is also created by the difference between actual and budgeted sales volumes; multiplying this difference by the budgeted selling price yields the **sales volume variance**. The sales variance model is as follows:[13]

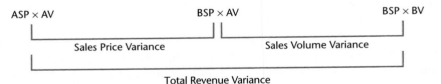

where ASP = Actual selling price
AV = Actual volume
BSP = Budgeted selling price
BV = Budgeted volume

To illustrate these computations, assume that the Maritime Lobsters (a fictitious minor-league hockey team) budget 2006 ticket sales at $70,000 per home game, which represents the sale of an estimated 10,000 tickets at $7. At July's first home game, actual gate ticket revenue was $66,000, creating a total unfavourable revenue variance of $4,000. To make a valid comparison, it is necessary to know that the $66,000 was composed of a volume of 12,000 tickets sold at a price of $5.50 each. Thus, the following variance calculations can be made:

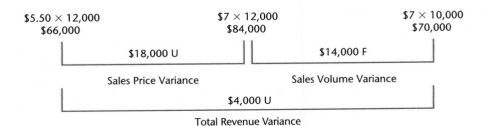

Team management should be pleased with the increased volume but displeased with the reduced selling price. Discussions with managers might indicate that this game was a special promotional game in which everyone received a $1.50 discount for bringing a can of food for charity. If these people enjoyed themselves and will return for future games, the unfavourable revenue variance may be eliminated in the future.

Analyzing Cost Variances

After revenue variances have been explained, managers can focus on analyzing cost variances. It is important that costs be analyzed in relation to the *actual* volume of sales rather than the *budgeted* volume of sales. Such analysis requires the use of flexible budgets and flexible budget formulas (i.e., looking at costs and revenues at different sales and production levels).

For example, assume that the Maritime Lobsters have a budget formula for selling expenses of $200 per game plus 5% of sales dollars. The original selling expense budget estimate for this game would have been $3,700 [$200 + 0.05 × (10,000 × $7.00)]. However, since the team only achieved an actual sales level of $66,000, the team should only expect selling expenses of $3,500 [$200 + 0.05($5.50 × 12,000)]. If actual selling expenses were $3,700, the team did not perform up to expectations and should recognize a $200 unfavourable variance for selling expenses. Comparing actual expenses to budgeted expenses that were calculated at a *different level of sales* will not provide valid information on how well costs were controlled during the period.

In addition to determining whether costs were controlled, managers need to analyze the ways in which money was spent. Spending analysis should focus on individual line items, not just totals, and on spending within categories. Oftentimes, money is spent simply because it is available for spending—not because there is a need for spending.

As with any variance computation, the reason for making income statement actual-to-budget comparisons is to determine why the actual results differed from those that were planned. To determine the underlying reasons for variances requires that comparisons be made as early as possible. Delaying variance computations until the end of a period may impede a manager's ability to detect and, therefore, control variance causes. Providing useful variance computations requires that an effective and prompt variance reporting system be maintained.

Management should also consider the effects that current changes in conditions may have on future operations and on the types and extent of future budgetary variances. Will increased sales today mean reduced sales in later periods? Could a current selling price reduction spur product demand sufficiently to increase revenues to total projected levels? Does the increased cost of a raw material make the use of an alternative, higher-quality material more cost beneficial? These are some of the possible questions that management needs to consider when making actual-to-budget comparisons.

Exhibit 9-8 on page 510 indicates some possible problems and causes of poor actual-to-budget performance. This exhibit is not intended to be a comprehensive list, and some factors may work together in performance problems. Once the causes of the performance deviations are known, management may wish to consider budget revisions.

EXHIBIT 9-8

Problems and Causes of Poor Performance

Problem	Possible Causes (or lack of consideration given to)
Sales significantly less than expected	Weakening economic conditions that reduced company product sales volume or necessitated a lower selling price
Direct materials cost significantly higher than expected	Inflation rate that caused direct materials cost to increase; use of higher quality materials
Compensation cost higher than expected	Changes in labour contract rates or increases in minimum wage law
Overhead cost higher than expected	Increased fringe benefit costs, insurance costs, or utility rates
Severe cash-flow difficulties	Declining collection patterns, increases in interest rates and costs, or weakened money supply
Selling expenses higher than expected	Advertising rates increased or media changes made (substituted TV spots for print advertising)
Interest cost higher than expected	Inflation, tightened money supply
Production not able to keep up with demand	Shortages of critical direct material or supplies

Budget Revisions

Arrangements cannot usually be made rapidly enough to revise the current month's budget. However, under certain circumstances and if it so desires, management may decide to revise future months' budgets. If actual performance is substantially less than what was expected, the budget may or may not be adjusted depending on the causes of the variances. If the causes are beyond the organization's control (such as when OPEC [Organization of Petroleum Exporting Countries] decides to decrease the supply of oil and oil prices increase dramatically), management may decide to revise budget estimates upward to reflect costs more realistically. If the causes are internal (sales staff simply is not selling the product), management may leave the budget in its original form so that the lack of operational control is visible in the comparisons.

If actual performance is substantially better than expected, budget alterations may be made. However, sometimes when positive results occur, management may decide not to alter the budget so that the positive performance is highlighted. Regardless of whether the budget is revised, managers should commend those responsible and communicate the effects of such performance to related departments. For example, if the sales force has been very effective and has sold significantly higher quantities of product than expected (at the expected selling price), the production and purchasing areas will need to be notified to increase the number of units manufactured and materials bought.

Performance Evaluation

One important reason that management must decide whether to revise is that the budget is often used to evaluate performance. When things do not turn out the way they were expected to, management must communicate to those people being evaluated how or if budget revisions will affect their performance evaluations. Although revised budgets may provide more accurate information, they also create a fluctuating measure against which people may be uncertain of their performance. Thus, if revised budgets are prepared, top management may want to compare performance to both the original and the revised budgets and then use multiple evaluation tools to judge the quality as well as the quantity of performance.

The possibility that operating managers may attempt to introduce budgetary slack into their budgets was mentioned earlier in the chapter. One way in which top management can try to reduce slack is to evaluate actual performance against budgeted performance through a bonus system. Operating managers would be rewarded with large bonuses for budgeting relatively high performance levels and achieving those levels. If performance is set at a low or minimal level, achievement of that performance is either not rewarded or only minimally rewarded.

In addition to including budget slack in the process, managers may play other "budget games." Budget games may be played by top management or by lower-level management; some of these games are discussed in Exhibit 9-9 on page 512.

These games exist because of human nature. If managers (either top-level or subordinate) are playing one or more of these games in the budgeting process, performance evaluations will become very ineffective, since many of the numbers become more sham, than real, projections. Company management often expects that good budgets will result simply because participating is allowed and encouraged. Good budgets result only from having responsible individuals involved in the process and from creating an atmosphere of sound interpersonal relationships. In other words, good budgeting relies heavily on trust among the parties involved.

If budgets are to be used in effectively evaluating performance, they should be challenging but achievable. The advantages of using achievable budget targets include the following:[14]

1. Managers' commitment to achieving the budget targets is increased because the managers will have little reason not to be able to meet the targets.
2. Managers' confidence remains high; achievement of the target is perceived as successful performance.
3. Organizational control costs decrease because there is less necessity to apply the management by exception principle when targets are achieved.
4. The risk of managers engaging in harmful short-term "income-management" practices (such as delaying maintenance or shifting sales between years) is reduced.
5. Effective managers are allowed greater operating flexibility because they may be able to accumulate some additional resources on the basis of good performance.
6. The corporation is somewhat protected against the costs of optimistic projections, such as overproduction and warehousing.
7. The predictability of corporate earnings is increased because the probability of target achievement is high.

The degree of "achievability" needed in budgets to obtain the previous seven benefits depends, of course, on the organization's stage of life, its environmental considerations (past performance, need for sales, types of products, and product life cycles), and its management personnel and their motivation levels.

Budgets are not the "be-all and end-all" managerial accounting technique. Budgets, if used properly, can provide significant benefits; if used improperly, they can cause serious organizational problems.

BUDGETING IN AN INTERNATIONAL BUSINESS

LEARNING OBJECTIVE 5

What complicates the budgeting process in a multinational environment?

Similar to many other business practices, the budgeting process and budget uses are unique to individual businesses. The budgeting process in a small, closely held company may be informal and, potentially, imposed on lower-level managers by

EXHIBIT 9-9

Budget Games

1. *The Dictator Game*
   This game is simply imposed budgeting. The budget is developed by top management and is handed down to lower levels with no room for discussion.

2. *The Father-Knows-Best Game*
   In this game, input is requested from lower-level managers but either is not used or is changed with no reasons provided. This game allows people to believe at first that they are important to the process, but they recognize in the end that they are not.

3. *The Do-What-You-Want (and Fail) Game*
   In this game, lower-level managers submit their own budgets, which are then used for performance evaluation purposes. Unfortunately, individual managers are not informed of the "big picture" and then at year-end fail to measure up because their budget figures were (a) too high and unachievable to begin with or (b) too low and not acceptable to begin with.

4. *The It's-Not-in-the-Budget Game*
   In this game, a manager submits a worthwhile project that is turned down because money is unavailable. Then, when the manager's performance level is low, he or she may be criticized for not justifying the project convincingly.

5. *The Cut-Everything-10% Game*
   This game is a favourite of all organizations. Rather than allowing managers to decide to cut certain expenditures and have the opportunity to justify why others need to be raised, the mandate is simply handed down. Managers get to figure out how to pay with what remains. A problem with this game, if played too often by top management, is that lower-level managers simply increase their budget requests by 10% and, therefore, are not disturbed by the reduction.

6. *The End-of-Year (or Spend-It-or-Lose-It) Game*
   Lower-level managers, recognizing that the end of the period is near, evaluate the remaining budget dollars per category and spend everything that is left. In this way, they can justify budget increases next year, because "I used everything I was budgeted for this year, and you know costs will increase."
   (The opposite of this game is played by top managers. Budget dollars that were not spent this period are lost, regardless of the reasons. This is a tough game when played with personnel budgets—a person not replaced is a position lost.)

7. *The It-Wasn't-My-Fault Game*
   The object of this game is for a manager to try to shift the blame for failure to meet the budget on someone or something else. This game probably allows for the most creativity. (Hint: The "economy" is always a good target because it's hard to prove or disprove.)

8. *The Accounting Change Game*
   This game requires a high degree of understanding of accounting rules but can work wonders on income statements. Unfortunately, you are only allowed one play for any given accounting change.

9. *The Sell-It-No-Matter-What Game*
   Managers who play this game are probably headed for a transfer and wanting to make a final name for themselves. They should be aware of CVP relationships; if the contribution margin is high and fixed costs are low, then increased volume will pad the bottom line substantially. But if the sales were accomplished using high-pressure techniques or by reducing quality, watch out for returns next period.

10. *The Build-a-Kingdom Game*
    This game allows managers to use budgets to create their own kingdoms. The larger the budget that can be obtained, the more "possessions" (equipment, personnel, etc.) the kingdom has. This game provides many opportunities to win friends by helping others maintain or increase their budget requests while extracting promises from those who help you maintain or increase your kingdom. However, these relationships can only work for a limited period of time before the kingdoms are in competition for the same budget dollars, and then war occurs.

top management. As the organization becomes more complex, so does the budgeting process. Lower-level managerial participation in the budgeting process may be more important. When an organization reaches multinational status, participatory budgeting is not simply desired; it becomes necessary for the effort to be effective.

The budgeting process differs among organizations and cultures. Budgets in Japanese firms are more flexible and short-run oriented than budgets in Western firms. The underlying rationale is that employees can better focus on near-term targets to ascertain that they comply with the organization's highly inflexible vision and strategic plan.

In a multinational environment, an organization faces an almost unlimited number of external variables that can affect the planning process, for example, the effects of foreign currency exchange rates, interest rates, inflation, inventory transfer price implications, and so forth. The risk may necessitate the preparation of separate budgets for each international market served in addition to a coordinated corporatewide budget. Budget preparation must incorporate a thorough understanding of local market conditions, including all known external forces and estimates of potential economic and market changes. Thus, each foreign operation's budget should also be supported by a comprehensive list of assumptions explaining how budget figures were derived.

Budgets are not only developed differently in different types of companies, but they are also used differently. In small organizations, the budget may be used simply as a basis against which actual results are compared and not as a control or managerial performance evaluation mechanism. As the business expands, the need for budgeting as a control and coordination tool arises because of interactions among multiple departments or organizational units. Managerial and employee performance may then be gauged against the budget and resulting comparisons may be used in a reward system.

In many circumstances, it is difficult to determine the underlying causes of budget variations because of the effects of noncontrollable factors such as competitive manoeuvres, economic conditions, and government regulations. In an international organization, the supporting list of assumptions is critical if the budget is to be used for control and evaluation purposes. Managers and employees should not be faulted for failing to achieve budget targets if the underlying causes reflect unforeseen, noncontrollable factors such as newly introduced governmental policies relating to import or export restrictions, exchange rate fluctuations, or market disturbances created by economic adjustments in a foreign country. Managers should, however, be held accountable for not taking advantage of new opportunities created by these same factors.

The News Note on page 514 discusses the differences between the budgeting process and budget usage in North America and Japan. This excerpt highlights the

INTERNATIONAL NEWS NOTE

Budgeting Purposes Are Not the Same Worldwide

Japanese planning and budgeting processes are very different from the typical North American practice. Japanese companies develop a vision that is relatively permanent. They also develop a strategic plan that, again, is relatively brief and revised infrequently. More importantly, Japanese companies develop what they call a midterm plan, which really is generated at only a very high level of the organization. It is relatively simple, containing such information as market share, sales, product costs, selling and administrative expenses, financing expenses, and inventory. It is revised periodically but never more than once a year.

The heart of Japanese companies' planning and budgeting is the six-month budget. Some companies tag onto it a rolling set of half-year projections that reach out several additional years. The six-month budget normally is prepared in no more than one month's time and often takes only two or three weeks.

The six-month budget is produced in a fashion similar to North American methods, with some top-down guidelines and a bottom-up estimate of achievable results. The finance and accounting staff plays a strong role in facilitation, working with senior management to communicate market realities and with line personnel to revise target costs. Even in the short two- to three-week cycle there may be several iterations of guideline delivery, budget preparation, and presentation.

The final budget is translated into target cost and productivity measures for the various groups. It is fair to say that the purpose to which Japanese companies put their plans and budgets is very different from North American companies. The primary purpose is to take a new look at the foreseeable future and to set short-run targets that are communicated clearly to the appropriate levels and groups of management so they can focus their efforts toward achieving them. Japanese companies spend virtually no time each month comparing actual results to budget and, more importantly, going through a lengthy, drawn-out process of explaining the causes of such variances. Rather, everyone is committed to achieving the targets that have been embodied into the six-month budgets.

Performance measurement and achievement of individual bonuses is another explanation for the different levels of detail generated by North American and Japanese companies in preparing annual budgets. In North America, managers' bonuses and salaries are related directly to how well they achieve their individual plans. Japanese companies, on the other hand, place little emphasis on meeting budget when evaluating individual performance and therefore do not require as detailed a budget or plan.

Source: Republished with permission of the Institute of Management Accounting, from "Management Accounting (and Other) Lessons from the Japanese," Robert A. Howell and Michiharu Sakurai, *Management Accounting*, December 1992; permission conveyed through Copyright Clearance Center, Inc.

fact that no single planning process is correct and that not only will differences exist among companies of different sizes, but also that multinationals domiciled in different countries will also have different perspectives.

THE MASTER BUDGET

master budget
the comprehensive set of all budgetary schedules and the pro forma financial statements of an organization

operating budget
a budget that is expressed in both units and dollars

financial budget
a budget that reflects the funds to be generated or used during the budget period; includes the cash and capital budgets and the projected or pro forma financial statements

From an accounting standpoint, the budgeting process culminates in the preparation of a **master budget,** which is a comprehensive set of an organization's budgetary schedules and pro forma (projected) financial statements. The master budget comprises both operating and financial budgets. **Operating budgets** are expressed in both units and dollars. When an operating budget is related to revenues, the units are those expected to be sold, and the dollars reflect selling prices. When an operating budget relates to expense items, the units are those expected to be used and the dollars reflect costs.

Monetary details from the operating budgets are aggregated in **financial budgets**, which reflect the funds to be generated or consumed during the budget period. Financial budgets include the company's cash and capital budgets as well as its pro forma financial statements. These budgets are the ultimate focal points for the firm's top management.

The master budget is prepared for a specific period and is static rather than flexible. It is static in that it is based on a single, most probable level of output demand. Expressing the budget on a single level of output is necessary to facilitate the many time-consuming financial arrangements that must be made before beginning operations for the budget period. Such arrangements include hiring an adequate number of people, obtaining needed production and/or storage space, obtaining suppliers, and confirming prices, delivery schedules, and quality of resources.

The output level of sales or service quantities selected for use in the preparation of the master budget affects all organizational components. It is essential that all the components interact in a coordinated manner. Exhibit 9-10 indicates the budgetary interrelationships among the primary departments of a manufacturing organization. A budget developed by one department is commonly an essential ingredient in developing another department's budget.

Exhibit 9-11 on page 516 presents an overview of the master budget preparation sequence and component budgets. It indicates the department responsible for each budget's preparation, and illustrates how the budgets relate to one another. The process begins with Sales Department estimates of the types, quantities, and timing of demand for products and services. This information is needed by both Production and Accounts Receivable. Production managers combine sales estimates with information from Purchasing, Human Resources, Operations, and Capital

LEARNING OBJECTIVE   6

What is the starting point of a master budget and how do the components relate to one another?

EXHIBIT 9-10

The Budgetary Process in a Manufacturing Organization

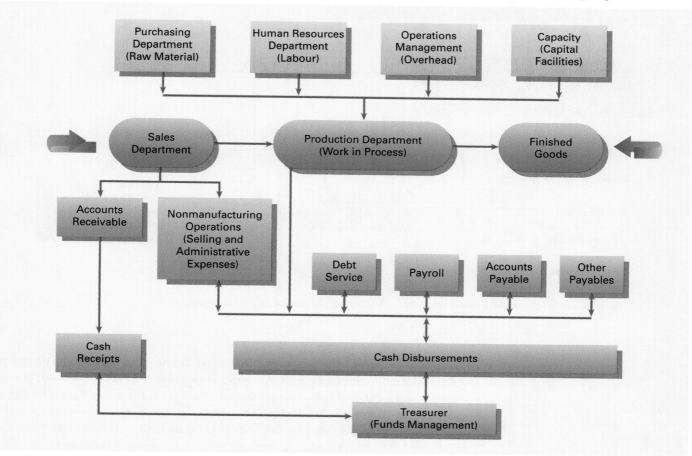

EXHIBIT 9-11

The Master Budget: An
Overview

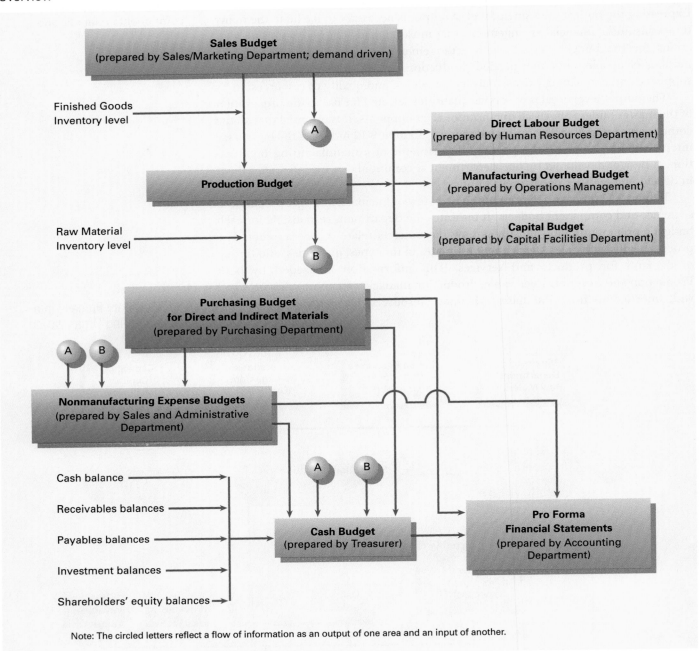

Note: The circled letters reflect a flow of information as an output of one area and an input of another.

Facilities to determine the types, quantities, and timing of products to be produced and transferred to finished goods. Accounts Receivable uses sales estimates, in conjunction with estimated collection patterns, to determine the amounts and timing of cash receipts. Cash receipts information is necessary for the treasurer to manage the organization's flow of funds properly. All areas create cash disbursements that must be matched with cash receipts so that cash is available when it is needed.

Note that certain information must flow back into a department in which it began. For example, the Sales Department must receive finished goods information to know if goods are in inventory (or can be produced to order) before selling products. The treasurer must continually receive input information on cash receipts and disbursements as well as provide output information to various organizational units on the availability of funds so that proper funds management can be maintained.

Assuming that top management is engaging in participatory budgeting, each department in the budgetary process either prepares its own budget or provides information for inclusion in a budget.

While the flow of information is visible in Exhibit 9-11, the quantitative and monetary implications are not. The remainder of the chapter reflects these implications through the preparation of a master budget.

THE MASTER BUDGET ILLUSTRATED

Triton Enterprises Inc. is used to illustrate the process of preparing a master budget for fiscal 2006. The company produces metal shut-off valves for use in the natural gas industry. The master budget is prepared for the entire year and then subdivided into quarterly and monthly periods. Triton Enterprises Inc.'s Marketing Division has estimated total sales for the year at 2,000,000 valves. While annual sales are detailed on a monthly basis, the Triton Enterprises Inc. illustration focuses only on the first-quarter budgets. The process of developing the master budget is the same regardless of whether the time frame is one year or one quarter.

The December 31, 2005, balance sheet presented in Exhibit 9-12 on page 518 provides account balances needed to prepare the master budget. The December 31 balances are really projections rather than actual figures because the budget process for 2006 must begin significantly before December 31, 2005. A company's budgetary time schedule depends on many factors, including its size and its degree of forecasting sophistication. Triton Enterprises Inc. starts its budgeting process in November 2005 when the sales forecast is received by either management or the *budget committee*. The **budget committee** reviews and approves, or makes adjustments to, the master budget and/or the budgets submitted from operational managers. This committee is usually composed of top management and the chief financial officer.

budget committee
a group, usually composed of top management and the chief financial officer, that reviews and approves or makes adjustments to the master budget and/or the budgets submitted from operational managers

Sales Budget

The sales budget is prepared in terms of both units and sales dollars. The selling price set for 2006 is $2.00 per valve. The price is the same for all sales territories and all customers. Monthly sales demand and revenue for the first five months of 2006 are shown in Exhibit 9-13 on page 518. Dollar sales figures are computed as sales quantities multiplied by the product selling price. April and May information is presented because it is needed to determine production information for the March budget. The "Total for Quarter" column reflects sales only for January, February, and March.

Production Budget

The production budget follows naturally from the sales budget and uses information regarding the type, quantity, and timing of units to be sold. Sales information is combined with information on beginning and ending inventories so that managers can schedule the necessary production.

Ending inventory policy (as to quantity of units) is generally specified by company management. Desired ending inventory is normally a function of the quantity

EXHIBIT 9-12

Triton Enterprises Inc. Balance Sheet

(projected) December 31, 2005

Assets		
Current Assets		
Cash		$ 5,090
Accounts Receivable	$ 168,000	
Less Allowance for Uncollectible Accounts	(2,400)	165,600
Inventories		
Direct Material (87,580 grams)	$ 17,516	
Finished Goods (15,400 units @ $1.26)	19,404	36,920
Total Current Assets		$207,610
Plant Assets		
Property, Plant, and Equipment	$ 540,000	
Less Accumulated Depreciation	(180,000)	360,000
Total Assets		$567,610
Liabilities and Shareholders' Equity		
Current Liabilities		
Accounts Payable	$ 80,000	
Dividends Payable (due 1/15/2006)	15,000	
Total Current Liabilities		$ 95,000
Shareholders' Equity		
Common Stock	$ 300,000	
Retained Earnings	172,610	472,610
Total Liabilities and Shareholders' Equity		$567,610

EXHIBIT 9-13

Sales Budget

(for the three months and quarter ending March 31, 2006)

	January	February	March	Total for Quarter	April	May
Sales in units	220,000	205,000	195,000	620,000	180,000	195,000
Sales in dollars	$440,000	$410,000	$390,000	$1,240,000	$360,000	$390,000

and timing of demand in the upcoming period together with the firm's production capacity and speed. Before making a decision about how much inventory to keep on hand, managers should consider the high costs of stockpiling inventory. Management may stipulate that ending inventory be a given percentage of the next period's projected sales. Other alternatives include maintaining a constant amount of inventory, building up inventory levels for future high-demand periods, and keeping inventory levels near zero under a just-in-time system. The decision about ending inventory levels affects whether a firm has constant production with varying inventory levels or variable production with constant inventory levels. And, as indicated in the following quote, the size of the inventory is also directly related to cash flow.

> Mismanagement of your company's inventory can create a financial hemorrhage that may cripple the business for life. Excessive inventory purchases, slow-moving inventory, and the inability to reorder in a timely fashion can all wreak havoc on your cash flow. Remember that inventory is "cash" sitting on your shelves without earning any interest. Actually, it may be one of your firm's largest expenditures, depending on the type of business and industry you are in.[15]

	January	February	March	Total
Sales in units (from Exhibit 9-13)	220,000	205,000	195,000	620,000
+ Desired ending inventory	14,350	13,650	12,600	12,600
Total needed	234,350	218,650	207,600	632,600
− Beginning inventory	(15,400)[1]	(14,350)	(13,650)	(15,400)
Units to be produced	218,950	204,300	193,950	617,200

[1] From Exhibit 9-12

Note: April's production would be 180,000 + 13,650 − 12,600 = 181,050

EXHIBIT 9-14

Production Budget

(for the three months and quarter ending March 31, 2006)

Demand for valves varies throughout the year, and Triton Enterprises Inc. carries very little inventory. Production time is short, so company management has a policy that Finished Goods Inventory need be only 7% of the next month's sales. Based on the ending inventory policy and the sales information from Exhibit 9-13, the production budget shown in Exhibit 9-14 is prepared.

The beginning inventory balance shown for January is the number of units on hand at December 31, 2005. This inventory figure is 15,400 units (from Exhibit 9-12), which represents 7% of January's estimated 220,000 units of sales. March's ending inventory balance is 7% of April's estimated 180,000 units of sales (from Exhibit 9-13). Triton Enterprises Inc. has no Work in Process Inventory because all units placed into production are fully completed each period.[16]

Direct Materials Purchases Budget

Direct materials are essential to production and must be purchased each period in sufficient quantities to meet production needs and to conform with the company's ending inventory policies. Triton Enterprises Inc.'s management has established that direct materials will be 10% of the following month's production needs. This inventory level is slightly higher than that of the finished goods because the lead time to acquire direct materials is somewhat longer and more uncertain than the production time to complete finished goods.

The direct materials purchases budget is first stated in whole units of finished products. It is subsequently converted to individual direct material component requirements. Production of each valve requires four grams of metal alloy. The quantity of material used in the valve gate and its cost are insignificant, so that item is treated as indirect material. Unit material cost has been estimated by the purchasing agent to be $0.20 per gram. The whole-unit and component purchases budgets for each month of the first quarter of 2006 are shown in Exhibit 9-15 on page 520. The beginning inventory for January is 10% of January production.

Given expected production, the Engineering and Human Resources Departments can work together to determine the necessary labour requirements for the factory, sales force, and office staff. Labour requirements are stated in total number of people, and number of specific types of people (skilled labourers, salespeople, clerical personnel), as well as production hours required of factory employees. Labour costs are computed based on items such as union labour contracts, minimum wage laws, fringe benefit costs, payroll taxes, and bonus arrangements. The various personnel amounts are shown, as appropriate, in either the direct labour budget, the manufacturing overhead budget, or the selling and administrative costs budget.

EXHIBIT 9-15

Materials Purchases Budget

(for the three months ending March 31, 2006)

	January	February	March
Units to be produced (from Exhibit 9-14)	218,950	204,300	193,950
+ Ending Inventory units (10% of next month's production)	20,430	19,395	18,105[1]
= Total whole unit quantities needed	239,380	223,695	212,055
− Beginning inventory units (10% of current production)	(21,895)[2]	(20,430)	(19,395)
= Purchases required in whole unit quantities	217,485	203,265	192,660
× Grams per unit	× 4	× 4	× 4
Total grams to be purchased	869,940	813,060	770,640
× Price per gram	× $0.20	× $0.20	× $0.20
Total cost of alloy	$ 173,988	$162,612	$154,128

[1] 10% of April's production (from Exhibit 9-14)
[2] Beginning inventory of Direct Material was 87,580 grams, or enough for 21,895 units (from Exhibit 9-12).

Direct Labour Budget

The management of Triton Enterprises Inc. has reviewed the staffing requirements and has developed the direct labour cost estimates shown in Exhibit 9-16 for the first quarter of 2006. Manufacturing direct labour costs are based on the standard hours of labour needed to produce the number of units shown in the production budget. The average wage rate shown in the exhibit includes both the basic direct labour payroll rate and the payroll taxes and fringe benefits related to direct labour. Taxes and fringe benefits usually add between 25% and 30% to the base labour cost. All compensation is paid in the month in which it is incurred.

Overhead Budget

Overhead is another production cost that must be estimated by management. Exhibit 9-17 presents Triton Enterprises Inc.'s monthly cost of each overhead item for the first quarter of 2006. The company has determined that machine hours are the best predictor of overhead costs.

In estimating overhead, all costs must be specified and mixed costs must be separated into their (a) fixed and (b) variable elements. Each overhead amount shown is calculated by use of the $y = a + bx$ formula for a mixed cost,[17] in which x is the number of units of activity (in this case, machine hours). For example, February maintenance cost is the fixed amount of $2,600 plus the variable portion ($5.80 × 200 estimated machine hours), or $2,600 + $1,160 = $3,760. Both the total cost and the cost net of depreciation are shown in the budget. The cost net of depreciation is the amount that is expected to be paid in cash during the month and will, therefore, affect the cash budget.

EXHIBIT 9-16

Direct Labour Budget

(for the three months ending March 31, 2006)

	January	February	March	Total
Units to be produced	218,950	204,300	193,950	617,200
× Standard hours per unit	× 0.022	× 0.022	× 0.022	× 0.022
Total hours allowed	4,816.90	4,494.60	4,266.90	13,578.40
× Average wage rate (including fringe benefits)	× $10	× 10	× $10	× $10
Direct labour cost (rounded)	$ 48,169	$ 44,946	$ 42,669	$ 135,784

			January	February	March	Total
Estimated Machine Hours (x) (given)			220	200	190	610
	Value of					
	Fixed Cost	**Variable Cost per Unit**				
Manufacturing Overhead Items:	(a)	(b)				
Non-cash item						
Depreciation	$14,000	$10.00	$16,200	$16,000	$15,900	$ 48,100
Cash items						
Indirect materials	—	$ 0.10	$ 22	$ 20	$ 19	$ 61
Indirect labour	$ 7,000	0.50	7,110	7,100	7,095	21,305
Utilities	3,000	1.60	3,352	3,320	3,304	9,976
Property taxes	5,000	—	5,000	5,000	5,000	15,000
Insurance	6,500	—	6,500	6,500	6,500	19,500
Maintenance	2,600	5.80	3,876	3,760	3,702	11,338
Total cash items	$24,100	$ 8.00	$25,860	$25,700	$25,620	$ 77,180
Total Cost (y)	$38,100	$18.00	$42,060	$41,700	$41,520	$125,280

EXHIBIT 9-17

Manufacturing Overhead Budget *(for the three months and quarter ending March 31, 2006)*

Selling and Administrative (S&A) Budget

Selling, general, and administrative expenses for each month can be predicted in the same manner as overhead costs. Exhibit 9-18 presents the selling and administrative budget. Note that sales figures rather than production levels are used as the measure of activity in preparing this budget. Triton's sales force consists of a manager with a monthly salary of $5,000 and four salespeople who receive $500 per month plus a 10% commission on sales. Administrative staff salaries total $18,000 per month.

Capital Budget

The budgets included in the master budget focus on the short-term or upcoming fiscal period. Managers, however, must also consider long-term needs in the area of

			January	February	March	Total
Predicted Unit Sales (from Exhibit 9-13)			220,000	205,000	195,000	620,000
	Value of					
	Fixed Cost	**Variable Cost per Unit**				
S&A Items:	(a)	(b)				
Non-cash item						
Depreciation	$ 3,800	—	$ 3,800	$ 3,800	$ 3,800	$ 11,400
Cash items						
Supplies	$ 350	$0.04	$ 9,150	$ 8,550	$ 8,150	$ 25,850
Utilities	200	—	200	200	200	600
Miscellaneous	500	—	500	500	500	1,500
Salaries:						
Sales manager	5,000	—	5,000	5,000	5,000	15,000
Salespeople	2,000	0.20	46,000	43,000	41,000	130,000
Administrative	18,000	—	18,000	18,000	18,000	54,000
Total cash items	$26,050	$0.24	$78,850	$75,250	$72,850	$226,950
Total Cost (y)	$29,850	$0.24	$82,650	$79,050	$76,650	$238,350

EXHIBIT 9-18

Selling and Administrative Budget *(for the three months and quarter ending March 31, 2006)*

capital budgeting
a process for evaluating proposed long-range projects or courses of future activity for the purpose of allocating limited resources to desirable projects

plant and equipment purchases. The process of assessing such needs and budgeting for the expenditures is called **capital budgeting**.[18] The capital budget is prepared separately from the master budget, but since expenditures are involved, capital budgeting does affect the master budgeting process. Sometimes the timing of current-year planned capital purchases is dependent on the extent to which actual revenues conform to budgetary revenues.

Corporate financial professionals should recognize that capital asset decisions are the most irrevocable long-range activities because they (1) involve significant corporate funding, (2) are the least flexible in terms of changing the strategic direction of the business, (3) are the least flexible for conversion into more liquid assets, (4) may geographically impact the long-term raw material supply capability as well as the long-term customer access of the business, and (5) involve decisions about assets that are unique to the company. Since the unique features of capital assets represent the source of a company's product individuality and position in the marketplace, capital decisions must support the company's strategic plans.[19]

As shown in Exhibit 9-19, the managers of Triton Enterprises Inc. have decided that only one capital purchase will be made in the first quarter of 2006. The company is planning to acquire a network of state-of-the-art computers to better control shop-floor activities. This network will cost $240,000 and will be purchased and placed into service at the beginning of January 2006. The company will pay for this acquisition at the end of February. Depreciation on this computer network is included in the overhead calculation in Exhibit 9-17. No other equipment will be sold or scrapped when the network is purchased.

Cash Budget

After all the preceding budgets have been developed, a cash budget can be constructed. The cash budget may be the most important schedule prepared during the budgeting process because, as indicated in the News Note below, without cash a company cannot survive. "Market growth cannot materialize, expansion will stagnate, capital expansion programs cannot occur, and R&D programs cannot be achieved without adequate cash flow."[20]

EXHIBIT 9-19

Capital Budget

(for the three months and quarter ending March 31, 2006)

	January	February	March	Total
Acquisitions:				
Computer network	$240,000	$ 0	$0	$240,000
Cash payments:				
Computer network	$ 0	$240,000	$0	$240,000

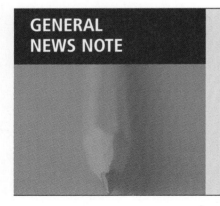

GENERAL NEWS NOTE

A Corporation's Oxygen is Its Cash

Any company, no matter how big or small, moves on cash, not profits. You can't pay bills with profits, only cash. You can't pay employees with profits, only cash. And when anyone asks you, "Did you make any profits?" all they probably want to know is whether you've got any cash.

Those may sound like extreme statements, but time and again I've heard managers complain, "If I'm making such big profits, why don't I have any money?" It doesn't matter whether your industry is high tech or low, smokestack or service. In the end, you need to have enough money to pay your obligations or you'll go out of business.

Source: An excerpt from "When Is There Cash in Cash Flow?" by James McNeill Stancill, *Harvard Business Review*, March–April 1987, p. 2.

The following model can be used to summarize cash receipts and disbursements in a manner that helps managers to devise appropriate financing measures to meet company needs.

Cash Budget Model

Beginning cash balance

\+   Cash receipts from collections

\=   Cash available for disbursements exclusive of financing

\−   Cash needed for disbursements

\=   Cash excess or deficiency (a)

\−   Minimum desired cash balance

\=   Cash (needed) or available for investment or repayment

Financing methods:

±   Borrow money (repay loans)

±   Issue (reacquire) capital stock

±   Sell (acquire) investments or plant assets

±   Receive (pay) interest or dividends

       Total impact (+ or −) of planned financing (b)

\=   Ending cash balance (c) = Cash excess (or deficiency) (a) ± Total impact of planned financing (b)

Cash budgets can be used to predict seasonal variances in any potential cash flow. Such predictions can indicate a need for short-term borrowing and a potential schedule of repayments. The cash budget may also show the possibility of surplus cash, which can be used for funds management, such as for investment. Cash budgets can be used to measure the performance of the accounts receivable and accounts payable departments by comparing actual to scheduled collections, payments, and discounts taken.

Cash Receipts and Accounts Receivable

Once sales revenues have been determined, managers translate that information into expected cash receipts through the use of an expected collection pattern. This pattern considers the actual collection patterns experienced in recent past periods and management's judgment about changes that could disturb current collection patterns. For example, changes that could weaken current collection patterns

Budgeting for cash collections at a movie theatre is less complicated than at many organizations. Ticket revenue is predominantly cash, with multi-tiered pricing for adults, children, students, and seniors. Thus, there are no cash discounts for prompt payment and no uncollectible accounts.

include recessionary conditions, increases in interest rates, or less strict credit-granting practices.

In specifying collection patterns, managers should recognize that different types of customers pay in different ways. Any sizable, unique category of clientele should be segregated. It is essential for companies to know their customers' payment patterns.

Triton Enterprises Inc. has two types of customers: 40% of the customers pay cash and receive a 2% discount; 60% of the customers purchase products on credit and have the following collection pattern—30% in the month of sale, 69% in the month following the sale, and 1% of credit sales are uncollectible. The collection pattern of Triton Enterprises Inc. is illustrated in Exhibit 9-20.

Using the sales budget, information on December 2005 sales, and the collection pattern, management can estimate cash receipts from sales during the first three months of 2006. The December sales amounted to $400,000. Management must have this sales information because collections for credit sales extend over two months, meaning that some collections from the December 2005 sales will occur in January 2006. Projected monthly collections for the first quarter of 2006 are shown in Exhibit 9-21. The individual calculations relate to the alternative collection patterns and corresponding percentages presented in Exhibit 9-20.

The December collection amounts can be reconciled to the December 31, 2005, balance sheet (Exhibit 9-12), which indicated an Accounts Receivable balance of $168,000. This amount appears in the collection schedule as follows:

January 2006 collections of December sales	$165,600
January 2006 estimate of December uncollectible accounts	2,400
December 31, 2005, Accounts Receivable balance	$168,000

The remaining monthly amounts are computed in the same manner. Note that the collection in the month after the sale is 69% of the original credit sale, and uncollectibles are 1% of the original credit sales, not of the remaining balance.

Once the schedule of cash collections is prepared, the balances of the Accounts Receivable and Allowance for Uncollectible Accounts can be projected. The T-accounts for Triton Enterprises Inc. are shown next and will be used in preparing the pro forma first-quarter 2006 financial statements. Note that the Allowance

EXHIBIT 9-20
Collection Pattern for Sales

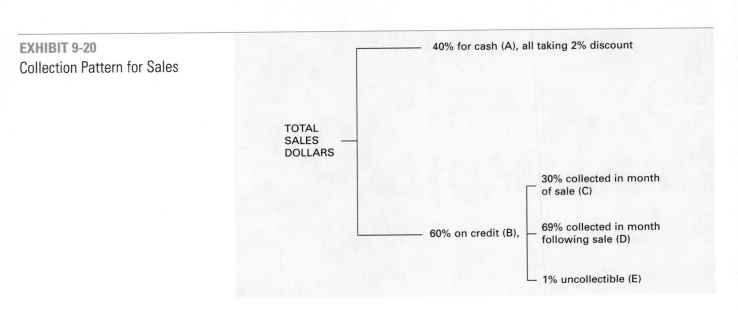

TOTAL SALES DOLLARS

40% for cash (A), all taking 2% discount

60% on credit (B),
- 30% collected in month of sale (C)
- 69% collected in month following sale (D)
- 1% uncollectible (E)

	January	February	March	Total
January				
Previous month's credit sales collected				
($400,000 × 60% × 69%)	$165,600			$ 165,600
Current month's cash sales				
($440,000 × 40%)[1]	172,480 N			172,480
Current month's credit sales collected				
($440,000 × 60% × 30%)	79,200			79,200
February				
Previous month's credit sales collected				
($440,000 × 60% × 69%)		$182,160		182,160
Current month's cash sales				
($410,000 × 40%)[1]		160,720 N		160,720
Current month's credit sales collected				
($410,000 × 60% × 30%)		73,800		73,800
March				
Previous month's credit sales collected				
($410,000 × 60% × 69%)			$169,740	169,740
Current month's cash sales				
($390,000 × 40%)[1]			152,880 N	152,880
Current month's credit sales collected				
($390,000 × 60% × 30%)			70,200	70,200
Totals	$417,280	$416,680	$392,820	$1,226,780

[1] The result multiplied by 98% yields the amount collected; the result multiplied by 2% yields the amount of the discount. "N" stands for "Net of discount."

Total discount = $9,920 [January $440,000 × 40% × 2% = $3,520; February $410,000 × 40% × 2% = $3,280; March $390,000 × 40% × 2% = $3,120]

Total amount uncollectible = $7,440 [January $440,000 × 60% × 1% = $2,640; February $410,000 × 60% × 1% = $2,460; March $390,000 × 60% × 1% = $2,340]

EXHIBIT 9-21

Cash Collections

(for the three months and quarter ending March 31, 2006)

account balance indicates that Triton Enterprises Inc. has not written off any accounts receivable since December 2005. The company may still believe that some of these accounts are collectible.

Accounts Receivable			
Dec. 31, 2005, Bal. (Ex. 9-12)	168,000	January collections (Ex 9-21)	417,280
January 2006 Sales (Ex. 9-13)	440,000	January discounts (Ex. 9-21)	3,520
February 2006 Sales (Ex. 9-13)	410,000	February collections (Ex. 9-21)	416,680
March 2006 Sales (Ex. 9-13)	390,000	February discounts (Ex. 9-21)	3,280
		March collections (Ex. 9-21)	392,820
		March discounts (Ex. 9-21)	3,120
March 31, 2005, Balance	171,300		

Allowance for Uncollectible Accounts		
	Dec. 31, 2005, Balance (Ex. 9-12)	2,400
	January estimate (Ex. 9-21)	2,640
	February estimate (Ex. 9-21)	2,460
	March estimate (Ex. 9-21)	2,340
	March 31, 2006, Balance	9,840

Cash Disbursements and Accounts Payable

Using the purchases information from Exhibit 9-15, management can prepare an estimated cash disbursements schedule for Accounts Payable. All purchases of

EXHIBIT 9-22

Cash Disbursements-Accounts Payable

(for the three months ending March 31, 2006)

	January	February	March	Discount
Payment for purchases of:				
December 2005 (from Exhibit 9-12)	$ 80,000			
January 2006 (from Exhibit 9-15)				
$173,988(40%)(98%)	68,203 N			$1,392
$173,988(60%)		$104,393		
February 2006 (from Exhibit 9-15)				
$162,612(40%)(98%)		63,744 N		1,301
$162,612(60%)			$ 97,567	
March 2006 (from Exhibit 9-15)				
$154,128(40%)(98%)			60,418 N	1,233
Total disbursements for Accounts Payable	$148,203	$168,137	$157,985	$3,926[1]

[1] Discounts taken: January [($173,988 × 0.40) × 0.02]; February [($162,612 × 0.40) × 0.02]; March [($154,128 × 0.40) × 0.02]
Note: "N" stands for "Net of discount." The total amount of gross purchases being paid for in the month of purchase is the sum of the net of discount payment plus the amount shown on the same line in the discount column.

direct material are made on account by Triton Enterprises Inc. The company pays for 40% of each month's purchases in the month of purchase, taking a 2% cash discount. The remaining 60% of each month's purchases are paid for in the month following the month of purchase; no discount is available for these payments.

Exhibit 9-22 presents the cash disbursements information related to purchases for the first quarter of 2006. The December 31, 2005, Accounts Payable balance of $80,000 reflected in Exhibit 9-12 represents the 60% remaining payment required for December purchases. This amount is also shown in Exhibit 9-22 as the first amount paid. (All amounts in this exhibit have been rounded to whole dollars.)

The Accounts Payable activity is summarized in the following T-account. The March 31 balance represents 60% of March purchases that will be paid during April.

Accounts Payable			
		Dec. 31, 2005, Balance (Ex. 9-12)	80,000
January payments (Ex. 9-22)	148,203	January purchases (Ex. 9-15)	173,988
January discounts taken (Ex. 9-22)	1,392		
February payments (Ex. 9-22)	168,137	February purchases (Ex. 9-15)	162,612
February discounts taken (Ex. 9-22)	1,301		
March payments (Ex. 9-22)	157,985	March purchases (Ex. 9-15)	154,128
March discounts taken (Ex. 9-22)	1,233		
		March 31, 2006, Balance	92,477

Using the cash budget model, the company uses the cash receipts and disbursements information to prepare the cash budget shown in Exhibit 9-23. The company has established $5,000 as its desired minimum cash balance. The primary reason for maintaining a minimum cash balance is the uncertainty associated with the budgeting process. If management had perfect certainty about cash inflows and outflows, there would be no need for this cash "cushion."

All borrowings by Triton Enterprises Inc. are assumed to take place in increments of $100 at the beginning of a month. All repayments and investments are made in $100 amounts and are assumed to occur at the end of a month. These assumptions are simplistic, since management would not actually borrow until the need for funds arose and would repay as quickly as possible so as to minimize interest expenditures. Interest on any company investments is assumed to be added to the company's bank account at the end of each month.

	January	February	March	Total
Beginning cash balance (Exhibit 9-12)	$ 5,090	$ 5,088	$ 5,002	$ 5,090
Cash collections (Exhibit 9-21)	417,280	416,680	392,820	1,226,780
Cash available exclusive of financing	$ 422,370	$ 421,768	$397,822	$1,231,870
Disbursements:				
Accounts payable (Exhibit 9-22)	$ 148,203	$ 168,137	$157,985	$ 474,325
Direct labour (Exhibit 9-16)	48,169	44,946	42,669	135,784
Overhead (Exhibit 9-17)[1]	25,860	25,700	25,620	77,180
S&A expenses (Exhibit 9-18)[1]	78,850	75,250	72,850	226,950
Total planned disbursements	$ 301,082	$ 314,033	$299,124	$ 914,239
Cash excess or (inadequacy)	$ 121,288	$ 107,735	$ 98,698	$ 317,631
Minimum cash balance desired	5,000	5,000	5,000	5,000
Cash available or (needed)	$ 116,288	$ 102,735	$ 93,698	$ 312,631
Financing:				
Borrow (repay)	$ 0	$ 35,800	$ (35,800)	$ 0
Issue (reacquire) stock	0	0	0	0
Liquidate (acquire) investments	(101,200)	101,200	(57,600)	(57,600)
Sell (pay for) plant assets (Exhibit 9-19)	0	(240,000)	0	(240,000)
Receive (pay) interest or dividends[2]	(15,000)	267	(239)	(14,972)
Total impact of planned financing	$(116,200)	$(102,733)	$ (93,639)	$ (312,572)
Ending cash balance	$ 5,088	$ 5,002	$ 5,059	$ 5,059

[1] These amounts are the net of depreciation figures.

[2] Dividends payable on the December 31, 2005, balance sheet were shown as being owed on January 15, 2006. Interest on investments is calculated assuming a 6% rate, and interest on borrowings is calculated assuming an 8% rate. Borrowings are made at the beginning of the month, and repayments or investments are made at the end of the month. For February, interest owed is $239 ($35,800 × 0.08 × 1/12) and interest received is $506 ($101,200 × 0.06 × 1/12). In March, interest owed is $239 ($35,800 × 0.08 × 1/12).

EXHIBIT 9-23

Cash Budget

(for the three months and quarter ending March 31, 2006)

Exhibit 9-23 indicates that Triton Enterprises Inc. has $121,288 in excess cash available in January. This excess not only meets the specified $5,000 minimum balance and the dividend payment requirement from the December 2005 balance sheet, but also gives the firm an opportunity to invest $101,200. In February, Triton Enterprises Inc. expects to have enough cash to meet its desired minimum cash balance but not enough to pay for the computer network purchased in January. The January investment must be liquidated and an additional $35,800 borrowed. Since the machine does not have to be paid for until the end of the month, the investment can continue to draw interest until that time. The borrowing has been assumed, however, to occur at the beginning of the month for consistency with the previously specified plan. Thus, Triton Enterprises Inc. earns interest on the investment but must pay interest on the borrowings for February. In March, there is enough cash available to meet budgeted disbursements, pay off the February borrowings, and make a $57,600 investment. Interest on borrowings and investments is calculated at the bottom of Exhibit 9-23. Any changes in interest rates will affect any future budget-to-actual comparisons.

Several things should be specially noted involving the total column in Exhibit 9-23. First, the beginning cash balance is not the total of the three months, but is the balance at January 1. Second, the monthly and quarterly minimum cash balance is $5,000, not $15,000. Last, the ending cash balance should be the same as what appears in the final month of the quarter. These figures (beginning, minimum, and ending cash balances), cash available exclusive of financing, cash excess or inadequacy, and cash available or needed are the only ones that are not summed across from the three-month information; all other figures are totals. These figures can be updated monthly; a spreadsheet program is very useful for this function.

Budgeted Financial Statements

The final step in the budgeting process is the development of budgeted or pro forma financial statements for the period. These statements reflect the results that will be achieved if the estimates and assumptions used for all previous budgets actually occur. Such statements allow management to determine whether the predicted results are acceptable for the period. If the predicted results are not acceptable, management has the opportunity to change and adjust items before beginning the period.

For example, if expected net income is not considered a reasonable amount, management may discuss raising selling prices or finding ways to decrease costs. Any specific changes considered by management may have related effects that must be included in the revised projections. For example, if selling prices are raised, volume may decrease. Alternatively, reductions in costs from using a lesser grade of materials could increase spoilage during production or the lower-quality product could cause a decline in demand. Computer spreadsheet programs are used to quickly and easily make the recalculations necessary from such changes in assumptions.

Cost of Goods Manufactured Statement

Before an income statement can be drafted, management must prepare a cost of goods manufactured statement, which is necessary to determine the cost of goods sold.[21] Using information from previous budgets, Triton Enterprises Inc.'s accountant has prepared the budgeted cost of goods manufactured statement shown in Exhibit 9-24. Since there were no beginning or ending work in process inventories, cost of goods manufactured is equal to the manufacturing costs of the period.

Income Statement

The projected income statement for Triton Enterprises Inc. for the first quarter of 2005 is presented in Exhibit 9-25. This statement uses much of the information previously developed in determining the revenues and expenses for the period.

EXHIBIT 9-24

Pro Forma Cost of Goods Manufactured Statement

(for the first quarter of 2006)

Cost of direct material used:	
Beginning balance of direct material (Exhibit 9-12)	$ 17,516
Purchases (net of $3,926 of discounts taken) (from Accounts Payable, p. 526)[1]	486,802
Total direct material available	$504,318
Ending balance of direct material (Note A)	(14,484)
Cost of direct material used	$489,834
Direct labour (Exhibit 9-16)	135,784
Manufacturing overhead (Exhibit 9-17)	125,280
Total costs to be accounted for	$750,898
Plus: Beginning work in process	0
	$750,898
Less: Ending work in process	0
Cost of goods manufactured	$750,898

Note A

Ending balance (Exhibit 9-15) in units	18,105
Grams of alloy per unit	× 4
Total grams needed	72,420
Price per gram	× $0.20
Ending balance	$14,484

[1] Total Purchases = $490,728 (Exhibit 9-15) [$173,988 + $162,612 + $154,128] minus Discounts $3,926 (Exhibit 9-22) = Net Purchases of $486,802.

Sales (Exhibit 9-13)		$1,240,000
Less: Sales discounts (from Accounts Receivable, p. 525)		(9,920)
Net sales		$1,230,080
Cost of goods sold:		
Finished goods—Dec. 31, 2005 (Exhibit 9-12)	$ 19,404	
Cost of goods manufactured (Exhibit 9-24)	750,898	
Cost of goods available for sale	$770,302	
Finished goods—March 31, 2006 (Note A)	(15,876)	(754,426)
Gross margin		$ 475,654
Expenses:		
Bad debts expense (Note B)	$ 7,440	
S&A expenses (Exhibit 9-18)	238,350	
Interest expense/income (net) (Exhibit 9-23)[1]	(28)	(245,762)
Income before income taxes		$ 229,892
Income taxes (assumed rate of 30%)		(68,968)
Net income (profit)		$ 160,924

[1] Interest Expense (net) [Feb. $239 + March $239 – Interest Income Feb. $506]

Note A

Beginning finished goods (Exhibit 9-12)		15,400
Production (Exhibit 9-14)		617,200
Units available for sale		632,600
Sales (Exhibit 9-13)		(620,000)
Ending finished goods (Exhibit 9-14)		12,600
Costs per unit:		
Direct material[1] (Exhibit 9-12)	$ 0.80	
Conversion (assumed) (Exhibit 9-12)	0.46	× $1.26
Cost of ending inventory		$ 15,876

Note B

Total sales	$1,240,000
× % credit sales	× 0.60
= Credit sales	$ 744,000
× % estimated uncollectible	× 0.01
= Estimated bad debts (from Exhibit 9-21)	$ 7,440

[1] [($17,516 ÷ 87,580 grams) × 4 grams per unit]

EXHIBIT 9-25

Pro Forma Income Statement *(for the first quarter of 2006)*

Balance Sheet

Upon completion of the income statement, Triton Enterprises Inc.'s accountant can prepare a pro forma March 31, 2005, balance sheet (Exhibit 9-26 on page 530). The letters in parentheses after some of the items in Exhibit 9-26 refer to the calculations shown at the bottom of the exhibit.

Cash Flow Statement

The information found on the income statement, balance sheet, and cash budget is used in preparing a cash flow statement (CFS). This statement is a principal internal, as well as external, report. The CFS explains the change in the cash balance by reflecting the company's inflows and outflows of cash. Such knowledge is useful in judging the company's ability to handle fixed cash outflow commitments, adapt to adverse changes in business conditions, and undertake new commitments. Further, because the cash flow statement identifies the relationships between net income and net cash flow from operations, it assists managers in judging the quality of the company's earnings.

While the cash budget is essential to current cash management, the budgeted CFS gives managers a more global view of cash flows by rearranging them into three distinct major activities: operating, investing, and financing. Such a rearrangement permits management to judge whether the specific anticipated

EXHIBIT 9-26

Pro Forma Balance Sheet

(March 31, 2005)

Assets

Current Assets		
Cash (Exhibit 9-23)		$ 5,059
Investments (Exhibit 9-23)		57,600
Accounts Receivable (p. 525)	$171,300	
Less Allowance for Uncollectibles (a)	(9,840)	161,460
Inventory		
Direct Materials (Exhibit 9-24, Note A)	$ 14,484	
Finished Goods (Exhibit 9-25, Note A)	15,876	30,360
Total Current Assets		$254,479
Plant Assets		
Property, Plant, and Equipment (b)	$780,000	
Less Accumulated Depreciation (c)	(239,500)	540,500
Total Assets		$794,979

Liabilities and Shareholders' Equity

Current Liabilities		
Accounts Payable (p. 526)		$ 92,477
Income Taxes Payable (Exhibit 9-25)		68,968
Total Current Liabilities		$161,445
Shareholders' Equity		
Common Stock	$300,000	
Retained Earnings (d)	333,534	633,534
Total Liabilities and Shareholders' Equity		$794,979

(a)	Beginning balance (Exhibit 9-12)	$ 2,400
	Additional allowance (Note B; Exhibit 9-25)	7,440
	Total	$ 9,840
(b)	Beginning balance (Exhibit 9-12)	$540,000
	Purchased network computer system (Exhibit 9-19)	240,000
	Ending balance	$780,000
(c)	Beginning balance (Exhibit 9-12)	$180,000
	Factory depreciation (Exhibit 9-17)	48,100
	S&A depreciation (Exhibit 9-18)	11,400
	Ending balance	$239,500
(d)	Beginning balance (Exhibit 9-12)	$172,610
	Net income (profit) (Exhibit 9-25)	160,924
	Ending balance	$333,534

flows are consistent with the company's strategic plans. In addition, the CFS incorporates a schedule or narrative about significant noncash transactions, such as an exchange of shares for land, which are ignored in the cash budget.

Under Section 1540 of the *CICA Handbook*, it is acceptable for external reporting to present the operating section of the cash flow statement on either a direct or an indirect basis. The direct basis uses pure cash flow information—cash collections and cash disbursements for operating activities. The indirect basis begins the operating section with net income and makes reconciling adjustments to derive cash flow from operations. Exhibit 9-27 provides a cash flow statement for Triton Enterprises Inc. using the information from the cash budget in Exhibit 9-23. Indirect presentation of the operating section uses the information from the income statement in Exhibit 9-25 and the balance sheets in Exhibits 9-12 and 9-26. This method appears at the bottom of Exhibit 9-27.

Both cash flow from operations and net income are necessary for long-run success in business. It appears that Triton Enterprises Inc. is performing well on both counts.

Operating Activities:
Cash collections:

From sales	$1,226,780	
From interest	28	$1,226,808

Cash payments:
For manufacturing costs:

Direct material	$474,325	
Direct labour	135,784	
Overhead	77,180	$ 687,289

For nonmanufacturing costs:

Salaries	$199,000	
Supplies	25,850	
Other S&A expenses	2,100	226,950
		(914,239)
Net cash inflow from operating activities		$ 312,569

Investing Activities:

Purchase of plant asset	$ (240,000)
Short-term investment	(57,600)
Net cash outflow from investing activities	(297,600)

Financing Activities:

Issuance of short-term note payable	$ 35,800
Repayment of short-term note payable	(35,800)
Payment of dividends (owed at Dec. 31, 2005)	(15,000)
Net cash outflow from financing activities	(15,000)
Net decrease in cash	$ (31)

Alternative (Indirect) Basis

Operating Activities:

Net income		$ 160,924
+ Depreciation ($48,100 + $11,400)[1]		59,500
+ Decrease in Accounts Receivable		
($165,600 – $161,460)	$ 4,140	
+ Decrease in Inventory ($36,920 – $30,360)	6,560	
+ Increase in Accounts Payable ($92,477 – $80,000)	12,477	
+ Increase in Taxes Payable	68,968	92,145
Net cash inflow from operating activities		$ 312,569

[1] Exhibits 9-17 and 9-18

EXHIBIT 9-27

Pro Forma Cash Flow Statement
(for the first quarter of 2006)

ZERO-BASED BUDGETING

Traditional budgeting is often limited in its usefulness as a control tool because poor budgeting techniques are often used. One such technique involves beginning with the prior year's funding levels and treating these as given and essential to operations. Decisions are then made about whether and by what percentage to incrementally raise existing **appropriations**, which represent maximum allowable expenditures. Such an approach has often resulted in what is known as the "creeping commitment syndrome," in which activities are funded without systematic annual regard for priorities or alternative means for accomplishing objectives.

To help eliminate the creeping commitment syndrome, **zero-based budgeting** (**ZBB**) was developed for the government. ZBB is a comprehensive budgeting process that systematically considers the priorities and alternatives for current and proposed activities relative to organizational objectives. Annual justification of programs and activities is required so that managers must rethink priorities within the context of agreed-upon objectives. Specifying that each operation be evaluated from a zero-cost base would be unrealistic and extreme, but ZBB does require that managers reevaluate all activities at the start of the budgeting process to make

LEARNING OBJECTIVE **7**

How does traditional budgeting differ from zero-based budgeting?

appropriation
a maximum allowable expenditure for a budget item

zero-based budgeting
a comprehensive budgeting process that systematically considers the priorities and alternatives for current and proposed activities in relation to organizational objectives

EXHIBIT 9-28

Differences Between Traditional Budgeting and Zero-Based Budgeting

Traditional Budgeting	Zero-Based Budgeting
Starts with last year's funding appropriation	Starts with a minimal (or zero) figure for funding
Focuses on money	Focuses on goals and objectives
Does not systematically consider alternatives to current operations	Directly examines alternative approaches to achieving similar results
Produces a single level of appropriation for an activity	Produces alternative levels of funding based on availability of funds and desired results

decisions about which activities should be continued, eliminated, or funded at a lower level. Differences between traditional budgeting and zero-based budgeting are shown in Exhibit 9-28.

Zero-based budgeting is applicable in all organizations, especially in the support and service areas, where nonmonetary measures of performance are available. ZBB does not, however, provide measures of efficiency, and it is difficult to implement because of the significant amount of effort necessary to investigate the causes of prior costs and justify the purposes of budgeted costs.

The ZBB process is based on organizational goals and objectives and involves three steps: (1) converting the company activities into decision packages, (2) ranking each decision package, and (3) allocating resources based on priorities. A decision package contains information about the activity: objectives and benefits, consequences of not funding, and necessary costs and staffing requirements. The decision packages are ranked and prioritized on the basis of need, costs, and benefits.

Zero-based budgeting is a rigorous exercise that demands considerable time and effort, as well as wholehearted commitment by the organization's personnel to make it work. An organization lacking the time, effort, and commitment needed should not attempt ZBB. An organization that can supply these three ingredients can use ZBB to become more effective in planning for and controlling costs. One of the major benefits of zero-based budgeting is that, in using it, managers focus on identifying non-value-added activities and work to reduce items that are unnecessary or ineffective expenses.

An organization considering ZBB should assess whether the benefits are worth the costs. Management may consider "zero-basing" certain segments of the company on a rotating basis over a period of years as an alternative to applying the approach to the entire firm annually.

LEARNING OBJECTIVE 8

What are future perspectives for budgeting?

THE IMPACT OF ENTERPRISE RESOURCE PLANNING SYSTEMS ON BUDGETING

This chapter is premised on the assumption that budgets are generally prepared for a year in advance and then divided into monthly budgets. Consequently, budgeting is developed to provide guidance to decision making during the year when financial reporting is not available. Then, at the end of each month, when the income statement is available, actual performance is compared to the expected performance in the budget to ascertain operational success.

A major assumption underlying budgeting is that the environment is relatively stable and that a budget for the month or year represents an agreement between the manager and the manager's superior. There is sufficient certainty in the environment that the manager can forecast what will likely happen in terms of customers and competitors, and comfortably commit to a level of performance.

Also, budgeting is premised on the assumption that feedback is not instantaneous. It takes time to process the information and to explain what has happened in financial terms. In the past the delay has been that financial performance is reported a few days or weeks after the end of the month. The result is that decision making is done in advance of the information on those decisions. Budgets help this situation by providing guidance for that decision making.

Budgeting has been a standard and acceptable management practice for U.S. manufacturing and retail firms since General Motors and DuPont introduced budgeting in the 1920s. The Hudson's Bay Company, as noted in Chapter 1, was using a form of budgeting before 1800. In recent years, despite the general and long-term acceptance of budgeting as an integral part of management, a movement has developed among many major firms to discontinue budgeting. The Beyond Budgeting Round Table (BBRT), a group of mostly large European firms, was formed in 1998 to discuss best practices to replace traditional budgeting.[22] Some of the BBRT's members include Anheuser Busch, Barclays Bank, Cadbury Schweppes, Mars Confectionery, Siemens, Standard Life, and Texas Instruments. The BBRT is seriously focused on eliminating or at least significantly changing the way budgeting is practised.

The BBRT has gathered information to make the case that budgeting—for example, as discussed in this chapter—is failing users:

- Few firms are satisfied with their budgeting processes. The BBRT cites recent surveys where 88%[23] and 66%[24] of chief financial officers were dissatisfied with their budgeting and planning processes.
- Far too much time is devoted to budgeting and too little time is spent on strategy. The BBRT cites research showing that 78% of the companies do not change their budgets with the fiscal cycle,[25] 60% of the organizations do not link their strategy to budgeting,[26] and 85% of management teams devote less than one hour per week to discussing strategy.
- Fixed assets are a small part of the market values of many firms. The BBRT notes that intangible assets such as brands and systems for dealing with customers and suppliers are often more valuable. Thus, budgeting for fixed assets and other balance sheet items becomes less important as the value of the company is contained in off balance sheet intangible assets.
- Budgeting is very expensive and often adds little value. The BBRT cites a study showing costs in terms of person years, which indicated that budgeting consumes a large part of the time of managers, especially senior managers.[27]

"The corporate planning and budgeting ritual is already the bane of managers everywhere. It's a cancer and it's in every blue-chip organization," states Mr. Hope, co-author of *Beyond Budgeting*. He is behind a movement that would scrap the annual budgeting process and replace it with a more adaptive, continuing process.

"In companies such as Enron, the rot began with fixed targets, extended to the hyped guidance for investment analysis, and ended with outright cheating to make the numbers add up," he says.

He makes the following recommendations:

- Replace annual budgets with constant rolling forecasts
- Get rid of the fixed numerical target
- Adopt a new vision that moves away from command-and-control direction from the top and "empowers" people to take ownership of processes and work to serve strategy and customers, not numbers

Mr. Hope argues that with his model, managers do not lose control, "in fact, they get more control—they get control over what's happening next." The average company, he says, spends four to five months on the annual planning of the budget, and the cost is onerous—Ford Motor Co. spends an estimated US$12 billion a year to do the numbers.[28]

After demonstrating the marginal benefit of budgeting in many organizations, the BBRT indicates some of the management innovations over the last few decades that have been put forth to address these shortcomings. Budgeting innovations include, for example, zero-based budgeting, activity-based budgeting, faster, cheaper, rolling budgets, and the balanced scorecard.

After reviewing the problems with traditional budgeting and examining what many of its member organizations have been doing to replace traditional budgeting, the BBRT made a recommendation. Specifically, they recommended that traditional budgeting be replaced with an alternative that includes the use of an enterprise resource planning system (ERP) that allows all parts of the organization to be tied together via information. The BBRT says that the IT system should be derived from and thus support business strategy, not the IT specialists. The operations should be managed in terms of activities rather than in terms of finances. With the activity and information orientation, the organization should be measured against its strategy—not in financial terms, but in operational terms from multiple

GENERAL NEWS NOTE

Companies Abandon Traditional Budgets to Boost Shareholder Value

The annual budget may be going the way of the dinosaur as companies introduce new and more accurate financial models capable of linking budgeting to overall corporate strategy according to results of a recent global Accenture/Cranfield School of Management study. The research also points to a correlation between companies modifying their budget processes and stock price performance.

"Companies are able to reduce their budget cycle time 30% to 40% by adopting approaches to the budget process that are more in concert with their overall strategic planning," says Herman Heynes, partner at Accenture's Financial and Performance Management practice and author of the study. The study, entitled "Driving Value Through Strategic Planning and Budgeting," concludes that among these new approaches are rolling budgets, and in some instances, elimination of budgets entirely.

"Our study indicates that the budget process is obsolete given today's economy, resulting in documents that are time consuming to produce, of little predictive value, subject to gamesmanship and, quite frankly, out of date by the time they're implemented," Heynes adds. "We found that companies are beginning to radically modify their budget processes and are thinking actively about approaches beyond budgeting."

Based on the findings of the study, corporations are moving away from preparing annual budgets towards reducing costs, improving forecasting and better managing investor expectations in order to reduce the risk of missed earnings targets and analyst downgrades. Emerging technology is providing corporations with the tools to modify their budget processes.

"Three themes clearly emerged in the study," says Professor Andy Neely, director of the Centre of Business Performance at Cranfield School of Management. "First companies can no longer justify the time and effort they invest in the budgeting process; second, budgets have to be much more responsive, enabling nearly real-time tracking; and third, management must understand that budgets cannot serve as both control and motivational devices. Companies that understand this and act on it are poised to enhance their credibility and performance."

For more information visit www.accenture.com

Source: *CMA Management*, February 2002, p. 9. Reprinted by permission of Accenture.

perspectives with a balanced scorecard (which is discussed in Chapter 13. Using the balanced scorecard, performance should be benchmarked (discussed in Chapters 11 and 13) against peers internally and externally.

If balanced scorecard and benchmarking (discussed in Chapters 11 and 13) are used to measure operational or physical performance, budgeting is not needed as the ERP systems can be used frequently to forecast the expected financial results to the end of the next month, quarter, or year. These rolling forecasts can be interpreted within the framework of a shareholder value model such as economic value-added (EVA), which is discussed in Chapter 13.

The BBRT-recommended replacement for budgeting is really the management of the organization in physical terms with standards or expectations that, if achieved, will yield the desired financial performance. This alternative is achievable if information is sufficiently extensive to manage in physical terms and if the organization periodically or frequently forecasts the performance.

CONCLUDING COMMENTS

Because of its fundamental importance in the budgeting process for implementing strategy, demand must be predicted as accurately and with as many details as possible. Sales forecasts must indicate type and quantity of products to be sold, geographic locations of the sales, types of buyers, and points in time at which the sales are to be made. Such detail is necessary because different products require different production and distribution facilities; different customers have different credit terms and payment schedules; and different seasons or months may necessitate different shipping schedules or methods.

Estimated sales demand has a pervasive impact on the master budget. To arrive at a valid prediction, managers use all the information available and may combine several estimation approaches. Combining prediction methods provides managers with corroboration of estimates, which reduces uncertainty. Some ways of estimating future demand are (1) asking sales personnel for a subjective consensus; (2) making simple extrapolations of past trends; (3) using market research; and (4) employing statistical and other mathematical models.

Sensitivity analysis is one modelling technique that can be used in assessing risk in the budgeting process. It is a means of determining the amount of change that must occur in one variable before a different decision is made. In preparing the master budget, for example, the variable under consideration might be selling price, advertising expense, grade of materials used in production, machine hours available, or maintenance expenditures. The technique identifies an "error" range for each of the various estimated values over which the budget will still provide a reasonably acceptable forecast. These repetitive computer simulations can be run after one or more factors has changed so that managers can review expected results under various circumstances.

After the master budget and all of its pro forma financial statements have been developed, they can and should be used for a variety of purposes. One common use of the master budget is to help the organization obtain bank loans. Banks also need to be kept informed after loans have been obtained. Additionally, management can use master budgets to monitor performance by comparing budgeted figures to actual results. Variances, as they occur, should be investigated so that the underlying causes can be determined.

Understanding the reasons for not meeting a budget can be useful in controlling future operations within the budget period, evaluating performance, and

What Happens If ... ?

The management accountant should take the initiative for making contingency planning an integral part of the planning and budgeting process. An effective response to a business reversal is not mere recognition of the problem. Rather, early warning signals should trigger implementation of a contingency plan that details the predetermined counter-measures required to avoid a crisis while maintaining the firm's financial integrity.

Preparation of a contingency plan starts with an analysis of the company's financial capacity for responding to and weathering various simulated adversities such as a sales decline caused by a general recession or a change in competitive position. These scenarios serve as the backdrop for designing the strategic manoeuvres needed to ensure the firm's survival at various levels of financial distress. The principal components of these strategies are

- An estimate of the uncommitted liquid reserves that would be readily available during a given emergency
- A program for reducing both controllable cash outflows and the level of investment in current assets and fixed assets
- A strategic plan that, in the event of a prolonged or irreparable misfortune, outlines the controlled liquidation of plant, equipment, or business units previously identified as expendable

Developing a contingency plan, through the combined efforts of the management accountant and top-level management, forces the latter to examine the extent to which resources are available, the strong interdependence of planning and control, and the delicate interrelationship between financial reserves and budgeted cash outflows.

Source: Republished with permission of the Institute of Management Accounting, from "Turnarounds: Lessons for the Management Accountant," Arthur R. DeThomas, William B. Fredenberger, and Monojit Ghosal, *Management Accounting*, July 1994; permission conveyed through Copyright Clearance Center, Inc.

budgeting more accurately in the future. Finally, management should be aware that forecasted sales and profits may not materialize, and factors beyond the business's control may create problems. In such instances, it is essential that management has made contingency plans, as discussed in the above News Note.

CHAPTER SUMMARY

An organization is an open system that must successfully adapt to its environment to survive and prosper. The firm's adaptation process and business strategy are influenced by its operating environment, which includes market structure, government regulation, and supply-and-demand relationships. There are four basic market structures: pure competition, monopolistic competition, monopoly, and oligopoly. New global markets are providing sales opportunities but these markets are also creating pricing and quality pressures for domestic firms. Numerous government regulations affect how business can be carried out.

Budgets may be imposed or participatory, but in either case top management is responsible for assuring that the budget is attainable and acceptable. The common budget period is one fiscal year, segmented for quarterly and monthly periods. Continuous budgets may be used to ensure an ongoing one-year planning cycle.

A budget is the primary basis and justification for financial operations in a firm. Implementing and administering a budget are parts of the coordination and control functions. A well-prepared budget provides the following benefits:

1. A detailed path for managers to follow to achieve organizational goals
2. Improved planning and decision making

REL Consultancy Group

For REL, the result was an always-current financial forecast that reflects not only the company's most recent monthly results but also any material changes to its business outlook or the economy. In addition, it provides fewer opportunities for account directors to ride the coattails of past performance.

"Now, even the guy who booked a million dollars' worth of business in one month can't sit still because 30 days later we're going to have an entirely new forecast," [president of the London-based global management consulting firm Stephen] Payne says, adding, "It's a dynamic process that makes a lot more sense."

Although traditional one-year budgets are still the norm at most companies large and small, many accountants argue that rolling budgets can be a far more useful tool. Unlike static budgets, they encourage managers to react more quickly to changing economic developments or business conditions. They discourage what is too often a fruitless focus on the past ("Why don't we meet our numbers?") in favour of a realistic focus on the future. And they produce forecasts that, over the near term, are never more than a few months old even when companies are rolling them forward on a quarterly basis—the more common approach—rather than REL's monthly basis.

Implementing a rolling budget involves more than going through the annual budgeting process four times a year instead of one. Because the time between budgets has been compressed, management must access and process information more quickly than it was able to do in the past. To do that, line managers must become more involved in the process and the company must embrace technology that will allow it to quickly capture and disseminate the raw data needed for decision making and forecasting.[29]

3. An allocation of resources among departments
4. A better understanding of key business variables
5. A means of employee participation and influence
6. A means to determine troublesome or hard-to-control cost areas
7. A recognition of departmental interrelationships
8. A means of responding more rapidly to changing economic conditions
9. A means by which managerial performance can be judged

Budget manuals may be used to assure that procedures are standardized and understood by all parties involved in the process. When budgets are used for performance evaluation, care should be taken that the budget is achievable and that managers understand the process by which they will be evaluated.

Actual operating results should be compared against budget figures to measure how effectively and efficiently organizational goals were met. Sales price and sales volume variances should be calculated before expense comparisons are made. Expense comparisons should be made based on the actual level of sales volume achieved rather than on budgeted volume. Regardless of whether variances are unfavourable or favourable, feedback to operating personnel is an important part of the budget process. Additionally, managers should recognize that budget games may be played and should strive to create a climate of mutual trust and respect to minimize or eliminate this counterproductive behaviour.

Planning is the process of setting goals and objectives and translating them into activities and resources required for their accomplishment within a specified time horizon. Budgeting is the quantification of a company's financial plans and activities. Budgets facilitate communication, coordination, and teamwork.

To use budgets for performance evaluation, care should be taken that the budget itself is achievable and that managers understand the process by which they will be evaluated. Recognize that budget games may be played and strive to minimize or eliminate their occurrence.

A master budget is a comprehensive set of projections (pro forma financial statements and their supporting schedules) for a specific budget period. It is composed of operating and financial budgets and is usually detailed by quarters and months.

Sales demand is the proper starting point for the master budget. Once sales demand is determined, managers forecast revenues, production, costs, and cash flows for the firm's activities for the upcoming period. These expectations reflect the firm's input and output of resources and are used in preparing the master budget.

When budgeting, managers need to remember that the various organizational departments interact with each other and the budget for one department may form the basis of or have an effect on the budgets in other departments. For example, the production department's production budget is predicated on sales demand provided by the sales department. The production budget then influences the purchasing department's budget as well as the treasurer's budgeting of cash flows and accounts payable management. Sales also affect cash flows and the selling and administrative expense budget.

Pro forma financial statements help managers determine if their plans will provide the desired results, in terms of both net income and cash flow. Inadequate results should cause a reevaluation of the objectives that have been set, and appropriate changes should be made.

Clearly, creating a budget is under attack. In addition to promoting gamesmanship among managers, key criticisms include the lack of linkage with firm strategy, and high cost and inefficiency. While the debate will continue to rage in both corporate boardrooms and academic circles, the reality is that the annual budget is not going to disappear any time soon.[30]

Cross-Functional Applications

Topic of Note	Discipline	Cross-Functional Applications
Operating Budget (OB)	Accounting	Integrating budgets and standards into the accounting system is necessary for capturing and reporting variances for cost control purposes.
		A master budget provides a basis against which actual accounting information can be compared and translates management's plans into quantitative and monetary information. The budgetary process organizes management's plans according to the accountant's chart of accounts so

(cont.)

Cross-Functional Applications

Topic of Note	Discipline	Cross-Functional Applications
		that plans can conform to the way in which financial statement results will be presented, thus allowing accounting to assist managers in performance evaluation.
	Marketing Research	Usually market research provides the most critical data for an OB. The selling price, expected sales volume, time of sale or seasonality, and selling-related expenses are projected by market researchers. If their data are reasonably accurate then cost of sales and overhead can be accurately predicted or locked in by contractual arrangements. Reciprocally, marketers must be guided in their research by operational constraints such as production limitations, which are communicated to them by the OB process.
	Production Management	In a highly competitive, consumer-driven marketplace often characterized by short and flexible production runs, a production manager must have OB information to plan the optimum use of productive resources. In addition to planning, the expectations of cost control are formally communicated to the production manager by the OB. Purchasing policies in both production and merchandising operations are dependent upon OB information.
	Operations Management	Since most administrative overhead costs can usually be well estimated, operating managers depend on OBs to establish responsibilities, performance criteria, and constraints. Any employee who has requested job-related travel expenses will appreciate the constraining capacity of OBs. In terms of strategic management, the OBs are critical in coordinating the efforts of the various strategic business units toward the overall objectives of the firm.
	Financial Management	Accurate OBs are necessary for financial planners to predict cash flows from operating activities, which are often the most important source and use of cash. Financial planners use this information to determine debt loads and repayment schedules for long-term financing as well as cash requirements or liquid investments over the short run. In the bigger strategic picture, OBs are a necessary input into decisions concerning the acquisition of plant, equipment, technology, and information.
Zero-Based Budgeting (ZBB)	Public Administration	ZBB in governmental organizations was a reaction to popular demand for more efficiency, change, and flexibility. Public planners regularly relied upon fixed estimates of a budget's dynamic margins (most changeable costs/activities) to project future requirements. ZBB processes require

(cont.)

Cross-Functional Applications

Topic of Note	Discipline	Cross-Functional Applications
		planners to justify non-dynamic costs/activities that are relevant to their mandated objectives. While ZBB requires more resources, it enhances efficiency and flexibility by making planners analyze each resource with respect to the changing environment.
	Operations	Operational researchers often have the resources to conceptualize a budget assisted by the ZBB processes, which are not available to a particular strategic business unit that is the object of the study. Problems and opportunities can be evaluated more objectively by a comparison of the researchers' ZBB budget with the unit's traditional budgetary process. This reconciliation process will reduce ZBB costs by targeting the units of greatest concern to management.
	Engineering	ZBB processes are necessary to guide engineers in their selection of new or alternative technologies where little prior experience exists. A new technology incorporated into an older system requires a top-down budgetary evaluation of the overall operation to conserve resources and maximize efficiency.
	Management	ZBB requires documentation of the decisions and attending costs associated with each planning unit in the organization. Top managers responsible for the overall goal congruence of the organization can review the ZBB documentation to establish priorities, discontinue activities, and slash costs. This review process assists managers in coordinating the activities and evaluating the benefits of the various planning units.

Key Terms

Appropriation (p. 531)
Budget (p. 497)
Budget committee (p. 517)
Budget manual (p. 505)
Budget slack (p. 502)
Budgeting (p. 496)
Capital budgeting (p. 522)
Continuous budget (p. 505)
Financial budget (p. 514)
Imposed budget (p. 500)

Key variable (p. 499)
Master budget (p. 514)
Operating budget (p. 514)
Participatory budget (p. 500)
Sales price variance (p. 508)
Sales volume variance (p. 508)
Strategic planning (p. 499)
Tactical planning (p. 499)
Zero-based budgeting (p. 531)

Solution Strategies

Budget Manual
Should include
1. Statements of the budgetary purpose and its desired results
2. A listing of specific budgetary activities to be performed
3. A calendar of scheduled budgetary activities
4. Sample budgetary forms
5. Original, revised, and approved budgets

Sales Budget
    Units of sales
$\times$ Selling price per unit
= Dollars of sales

Production Budget
    Units of sales
$+$ Units desired in ending inventory
$-$ Units in beginning inventory
= Units to be produced

Direct Materials Purchases Budget
    Units to be produced
$+$ Ending inventory in units
= Total whole unit quantities needed
$-$ Beginning inventory in units
= Purchases required in whole unit quantities
$\times$ Appropriate quantity measure of input material
= Quantity of input material needed
$\times$ Price per unit measure of input quantity
= Cost of purchases

Direct Labour Budget
    Direct labour hours required for production
$\times$ Wages per hour
= Cost of direct labour compensation

Overhead Budget
    Predicted activity base
$\times$ VOH rate per unit of activity
= Total variable overhead cost
$+$ Fixed overhead cost
= Total overhead cost

Selling and Administrative Budget
    Predicted sales dollars (or other variable measure)
$\times$ Variable selling and administrative rate per dollar (or other variable measure)
= Total variable selling and administrative cost
$+$ Fixed selling and administrative cost
= Total selling and administrative cost

Schedule of Cash Collections (for sales on account)

Dollars of credit sales for month
$\times$ Percent collection for month of sale
= Credit to Accounts Receivable for month's sales
− Sales discounts allowed and taken
= Receipts for current month's sales
+ Current month's cash receipts for prior months' sales
= Cash receipts for current month

Schedule of Cash Payments (for purchases on account)

Total cost of purchases
$\times$ Percent payment for current purchases
= Debit to Accounts Payable for month's purchases
− Purchase discounts taken
= Cash payments for current month's purchases
+ Current month's payments for prior months' purchases
= Cash payments for Accounts Payable for current month

Cash Budget

Beginning cash balance
+ Cash receipts
= Cash available for disbursements
− Cash needed for disbursements:
　　Cash payments for Accounts Payable for month
　　Cost of compensation
　　Total cost of overhead less depreciation
　　Total selling general and administrative cost less depreciation
= Cash excess or deficiency ←
− Minimum desired cash balance
= Cash needed or available for investment or financing

= Cash excess or deficiency ←
+ Various financing amounts
= Ending cash balance

Revenue Variances

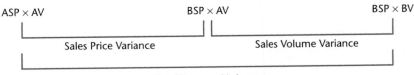

where ASP = actual selling price
　　AV = actual volume
　　BSP = budgeted selling price
　　BV = budgeted volume

DEMONSTRATION PROBLEM

The balance sheet of Janet David Cosmetics Ltd. at April 30, 2005, includes the following:

Cash	$ 25,000 debit
Accounts Receivable	100,800 debit
Allowance for Uncollectible Accounts	2,240 credit
Merchandise Inventory	21,000 debit

Raphael David, the company CEO, has designated $25,000 as the firm's monthly minimum cash balance. Other information about the firm follows:

- Revenues of $280,000 and $336,000 are expected for May and June, respectively. All goods are sold on account.
- The collection pattern for Accounts Receivable is 55% in the month of sale, 44% in the month following the sale, and 1% uncollectible.
- Cost of Goods Sold approximates 60% of sales revenue.
- Management's desired ending balance of Merchandise Inventory is 10% of that month's budgeted sales.
- All Accounts Payable are for inventory and are paid in the month of purchase.
- Other monthly expenses are $37,800, which includes $2,800 of depreciation but does not include bad debt expense.
- Borrowings or investments can only be made in $5,000 amounts. Interest will be paid at the rate of 10% per year; interest will be earned at the rate of 8% per year.

Required:

a. Forecast the May cash collections.
b. Forecast the May and June cost of purchases.
c. Prepare the cash budget for May including the effects of financing (borrowing or investing).

Solution to Demonstration Problem

a.

May Collections

From April ($100,800 − $2,240)	$ 98,560
From May ($280,000 × 0.55)	154,000
Total	$252,560

b.

	May	June
Sales	$280,000	$336,000
Cost of goods (60%)	$168,000	$201,600
Add: Desired ending inventory balance	16,800	20,160
Total purchases	$184,800	$221,760
Less: Beginning inventory balance	(21,000)	(16,800)
Cost of purchases	$163,800	$204,960

c.

May Cash Budget

Beginning cash balance		$ 25,000
May collections		252,560
Total cash available before financing		$277,560
Disbursements:		
Purchases of merchandise	$163,800	
Other monthly expenses		
($37,800 − $2,800)	35,000	
Total disbursements		(198,800)
Cash excess (a)		$ 78,760
Less: Minimum cash balance desired		(25,000) $ 25,000
Cash available		$ 53,760
Financing: Acquire investment (b)		(50,000) 3,760
Ending cash balance (c); (c = a − b)		$ 28,760

End-of-Chapter Materials

SELF-TEST QUESTIONS

(SOLUTIONS APPEAR AT THE END OF THE CHAPTER.)

1. Orion Corporation is preparing a cash budget for the six months beginning January 1, 2005. Shown below is the company's historical collection pattern:

   65% collected in month of sale
   20% collected in the first month after sale
   10% collected in the second month after sale
    4% collected in the third month after sale
    1% uncollectible

   Budgeted credit sales for the period are as follows:

   January, $160,000; February, $185,000; March, $190,000; April, $170,000.

   The estimated total cash collections during April from accounts receivable would be
   a. $154,900
   b. $167,000
   c. $171,666
   d. $173,400
   e. $176,200

Use the following information to answer Questions 2 and 3.

Stephen Klauz Ltd. manufactures an animated rabbit with moving parts and a built-in voice box. Projected sales in units for the next five months are as follows:

Month	Projected Sales in Units
January	30,000
February	36,000
March	33,000
April	40,000
May	29,000

Each rabbit requires basic materials that Klauz purchases from a single supplier at $3.50 per rabbit. Voice boxes are purchased from another supplier for $1.00 each. Assembly labour cost is $2.00 per rabbit and variable overhead cost is $0.50 per rabbit.

Fixed manufacturing overhead applicable to rabbit production is $12,000 per month. Klauz's policy is to manufacture 1.5 times the coming month's projected sales every **other** month (i.e., odd-numbered months) starting with January for February sales, and to manufacture 0.5 times the coming month's projected sales in alternate months. This allows Klauz to allocate limited manufacturing resources to other products as needed during the even-numbered months.

2. The unit production budget for animated rabbits for January is
   a. 45,000 units
   b. 16,500 units
   c. 54,000 units
   d. 14,500 units
   e. 60,000 units

3. The dollar production budget for animated rabbits for February is
   a. $327,000
   b. $390,000
   c. $113,500
   d. $127,500
   e. $432,000

Use the following information to answer Questions 4 to 8.

The Craig Wesley Company has been accumulating operating data in order to prepare an annual profit plan. Details regarding Wesley's sales for the first six months of the coming year are as follows:

Estimated Monthly Sales		Type of Monthly Sale	
January	$600,000	Cash sales	20%
February	650,000	Credit sales	80%
March	700,000		
April	625,000		
May	720,000		
June	800,000		

Collection Pattern for Credit Sales

Month of sale	30%
One month following sale	40%
Second month following sale	25%

Wesley's cost of goods sold average 40% of the sales value. Wesley's objective is to maintain a target inventory equal to 30% of the next month's sales. Purchases of merchandise for resale are paid for in the month following the sale.

The variable operating expenses (other than cost of goods sold) for Wesley are 10% of sales and are paid for in the month following the sale. The annual fixed operating expenses are presented below. All of these are incurred uniformly throughout the year and paid monthly except for insurance and property taxes. Insurance is paid quarterly in January, April, July, and October. Property taxes are paid twice a year in April and October.

Annual Fixed Operating Costs

Advertising	$720,000
Depreciation	420,000
Insurance	180,000
Property taxes	240,000
Salaries	1,080,000

4. The amount of cash collected in March for Wesley Company from the sales made during March will be
   a. $140,000
   b. $210,000
   c. $308,000
   d. $350,000
   e. $636,000

5. Wesley Company's total cash receipts for the month of April will be
   a. $504,000
   b. $629,000
   c. $653,000
   d. $665,400
   e. $755,000

6. The purchases of merchandise that Wesley Company will need to make during February will be
   a. $254,000
   b. $260,000
   c. $266,000
   d. $275,000
   e. $344,000

7. The amount for cost of goods sold that will appear on Wesley Company's pro forma income statement for the month of February will be
   a. $195,000
   b. $254,000
   c. $266,000

d. $260,000
e. $272,000

8. The total cash disbursements that Wesley Company will make for the operating expenses (expenses other than cost of goods sold) during the month of April will be
   a. $255,000
   b. $290,000
   c. $377,500
   d. $385,000
   e. $420,000

9. Which one of the following tasks should be done first when developing a comprehensive budget for a manufacturing company?
   a. Determination of the advertising budget
   b. Development of a sales budget
   c. Development of the capital budget
   d. Determination of equipment acquisitions
   e. Preparation of a pro forma income statement

10. Which one of the following is the last schedule to be prepared in the normal budget preparation process?
    a. Cash budget
    b. Cost of goods sold budget
    c. Direct labour budget
    d. Manufacturing overhead budget
    e. Selling expense budget

(Self-Test Questions 1–10 are IMA adapted.)

QUESTIONS

1. Why is budgeting important? Discuss the reasons why it may be more important in some organizations than in others.

2. Briefly describe the basic budgeting process. Which steps do you consider to be the most critical?

3. How do goals and objectives differ? Give three examples in which a goal could be quantifiable.

4. Explain how strategic and tactical planning differ.

5. When are imposed budgets appropriate? Why?

6. Why do most organizations use participatory budgets? Discuss the disadvantages of using such budgets.

7. Define *budget slack*. Why does it occur, and what might be done to reduce or eliminate it?

8. What does the sales price variance measure? What does the sales volume variance measure? Collectively, what do the sales price and sales volume variances explain?

9. Why should cost variances be based on actual volume of sales rather than budgeted volume of sales?

10. If a given manager fails to achieve his or her budget target, does this necessarily indicate that the manager has performed poorly? Explain.

11. What is a continuous budget? Why would a company use a continuous budget?

12. List the sections of a budget manual and briefly explain the role of each section.

13. Why is it important to put organizational plans in written form?

14   How are operating and financial budgets different? How are they related?

15.   Why is the master budget said to be a static budget? Why is it necessary for the master budget to be static?

16.   Why must the beginning of the budget year balance sheet be estimated? Why is it needed in the master budget process?

17.   Why is the sales budget the first of the operating budgets prepared?

18.   Explain the purposes of the production budget. How is this budget influenced by the firm's inventory policies?

19.   What are the primary inputs in the determination of the purchases budget?

20.   What source documents would likely be used to compile a direct labour budget?

21.   Why is it necessary to separate overhead costs into variable and fixed components to determine the budget for overhead costs?

22.   Even though the capital budget is not a component of the master budget, how may it influence the preparation of the master budget?

23.   Explain the importance of the cash budget.

24.   How are cash collections from sales determined? What part do cash collections play in the budgeting process?

25.   How do a firm's credit terms for credit sales affect the pattern for cash collections? Why would a firm give a discount for early payment?

26.   Why would a firm wish to maintain a minimum cash balance?

27.   Why are pro forma statements included in the master budget?

28.   Since a cash budget is included in the master budget, why is a budgeted cash flow statement also included?

29.   What is the relationship between the budgeted cash flow statement and the budgeted balance sheet?

30.   Give some examples of items included in the financing section of a cash flow statement and their cash flow effects.

31.   Why would it be desirable to prepare the master budget using a spreadsheet program and link the individual budgets?

32.   List the schedules and statements that make up the master budget in the sequence in which they would normally be prepared. If two or more schedules can be prepared simultaneously, so indicate.

33.   What is zero-based budgeting? Why do you think it began in the governmental sector rather than in the business sector?

34.   What is the name of the group that is pursuing the elimination of budgets, or seriously trying to change the way in which budgeting is practised?

35.   What are some examples of how budgeting has failed its users?

EXERCISES

1. (LO 1, 3, 4, 7; Terminology) Match the numbered item on the right with the lettered term on the left.

a. Budget committee
b. Sales price variance
c. Budgeting
d. Sales volume variance
e. Imposed budget
f. Budget
g. Participatory budget
h. Appropriation
i. Zero-based budgeting

1. Developed through joint decision making by top managers and operating personnel
2. A quantitative expression of commitment to planned activities and resource acquisition and use
3. A difference between actual and budgeted revenues caused by selling a different number of units than budgeted
4. Prepared by top managers with little or no input from operating personnel
5. Reviews, adjusts, and approves the master budget and/or budgets submitted by operational managers
6. A difference between budgeted and actual sales caused by a difference between actual and budgeted sales price
7. Developing a quantitative plan in financial terms to satisfy company goals and objectives
8. Systematically (re)considers current or proposed activities in light of priorities and alternatives for achievement of organizational goals and objectives
9. Maximum allowable expenditure for an item in the budget

2. (LO 3; Imposed versus participatory budgets) Top management has asked for your assistance in trying to determine the advantages of imposed and participatory budgets and has suggested a number of goals it would like to achieve in whatever type of budget it might choose. Indicate whether each of the following is an advantage of an imposed budget (AI), an advantage of a participatory budget (AP), or neither (N).
a. Develop fiscal responsibility and budgetary skills of operating personnel
b. Blend overview of top management with operating details
c. Reduce budgeting to entering data into a computer program
d. Increase chances that strategic plans will be incorporated into planned activities
e. Allow operating managers to take over the budgeting process completely
f. Incorporate top management's knowledge of overall resource availability
g. Produce more realistic budgets
h. Improve morale and motivation
i. Encourage operating managers to establish the long-run company goals
j. Incorporate inputs from persons most familiar with the needs and constraints of organizational units

3. (LO 4; Sales variances) West Wing Company budgeted sales of 200,000 units at a $40 unit selling price for 2005. In early 2006, the company president, Jeb Bartlett, asked you why budgeted revenue had not been achieved. Investigation revealed the following:

Actual sales volume	206,000
Actual average sales price	$38

Required:
Analyze the facts given and provide an explanation for the president.

4. (LO 4; Sales variances) As sales manager of Cliff Taylor Dairies, you have been asked by the company owner why sales of milk are below budget. A review of the budget reveals that revenue was expected to be $42,000, based on expected sales of 420,000 litres at $0.10 per litre. Inspection of the records shows that 430,000 litres were actually sold at $0.09 per litre.
Required:
Analyze sales and explain what happened.

5. (LO 4; Sales variances) Judith Poë Training Ltd. delivers two-day statistical process control seminars for manufacturing workers. The fee for each program amounts to $4,000. Last year Judith presented 30 seminars, and she budgeted a 20% increase in programs for the current year. At the end of the current year, she is disappointed that her actual revenue is only $136,500. She presented 39 programs during the year. She is puzzled by this and wants answers to the following:
Required:
a.   What was her expected revenue for the current year?
b.   Why was the budgeted revenue not achieved?

6. (LO 6; Production budget) Mary Jane Bok Company has budgeted its third-quarter unit sales for 2006 as follows:

July	8,000
August	10,000
September	11,000

The company desires an ending inventory equal to 8% of budgeted sales of the following month. October's sales are expected to be 12,000 units.
Required:
As manager of production prepare a third-quarter production budget by month and in total.

7. (LO 6; Production budget) Alison Ground Electronics has projected quarterly sales of electric motors for the year 2006 as follows:

First quarter	200,000
Second quarter	150,000
Third quarter	250,000
Fourth quarter	180,000

The firm expects to begin fiscal 2006 with 80,000 motors. Desired ending balances are to be 40% of the subsequent quarter's sales. Sales in the first quarter of 2006 are expected to be 220,000 motors.
Required:
a.   Prepare a production budget by quarter and in total for the year 2006.
b.   Explain how the firm might benefit by reducing the level of finished goods inventories carried.

8. (LO 6; Purchases budget) Shearer Flippers Ltd. expects to sell 15,200 pairs of swim flippers during June. Two kilograms of rubber are required to make each pair. The company's June 1 opening inventory includes 3,300 pairs of flippers and 10,200 kilograms of rubber. The company wishes to end June with 7,200 pairs of flippers and 16,000 kilograms of rubber. Because flippers can be made very quickly from heated rubber, the firm does not maintain any work in process inventory.
Required:
How much rubber should Shearer Flippers Ltd. budget to buy for June?

9. (LO 7; Purchases budget) Lawrence Chung Metals Ltd. expects to sell 74,000 units of its major product in April 2006. Each unit requires two kilograms of material A and five kilograms of material B. Material A costs $4.80 per kilogram, and material B costs $2.10 per kilogram. Expected beginning and ending inventories are as follows:

	April 1	April 30
Finished goods (units)	4,000	6,300
Material A (kilograms)	4,000	4,900
Material B (kilograms)	6,100	6,000

Required:

a. How many kilograms of material A does Lawrence Chung Metals Ltd. plan to purchase in April? What is the expected cost of those purchases?

b. How many kilograms of material B does Lawrence Chung Metals Ltd. plan to purchase in April? What is the expected cost of those purchases?

c. Briefly describe how improved raw materials inventory management could reduce the level of raw materials inventories carried.

10. (LO 6; Mixed overhead cost budget) Rochelle Gordon Inc. wants to estimate the cost of manufacturing overhead in the master budget. Overhead is a mixed cost with the following flexible budget formula: $y = \$320,000 + \$14.25x$, where x represents machine hours. The fixed overhead includes $35,000 of depreciation.

Required:

a. Calculate the overhead cost assuming Rochelle Gordon Inc. plans to incur 12,000 machine hours for the coming year.

b. Determine how much cash will be spent for overhead if the company incurs the 12,000 machine hours.

11. (LO 6; Cash collections) Forrest Creations Ltd. is experiencing difficulty in estimating cash collections for the second quarter of 2006 and has asked you, its consultant, for help. Inspection of records and documents reveals the following sales information:

February	March	April	May	June
$252,000	$232,000	$248,000	$292,000	$272,000

Analysis of past collection patterns has helped management to develop the following information:

- 30% of each month's sales are for cash, with no discount.
- Of the credit sales, 50% are collected in the month of sale; all customers paying during this time are given a 2% discount.
- 40% of credit sales are collected in the month following the sale.
- 10% of credit sales are collected in the second month after the sale. Bad debts are negligible and should be ignored.
- Forrest Creations Ltd.'s Accounts Receivable balance at April 1 is estimated at $98,840.

Required:

a. Prepare a schedule of cash received from sales for each month in the second quarter (April to June 2006).

b. Calculate the Accounts Receivable balance at the end of the second quarter.

12. (LO 6; Cash collections) Joanne Steinman Consulting Ltd.'s records revealed an Accounts Receivable balance of $194,000 at June 1, 2006. Analysis shows that $140,000 of this balance remains from May billings. June billings are expected to be $210,000. The company's pattern of collections is 30% in the month of billing for services, 40% in the month following the service, 29% in the second month following the service, and 1% uncollectible. No write-off of bad debts has been made for April or May billings.

Required:

a. What were the April billings?

b. What amount of the May billings is expected to be uncollectible?

c. What are the projected cash collections in June?

d. Prepare a brief report to Joanne Steinman's managers describing how they might change their credit policies to collect credit sales sooner.

e. What types of information should be gathered before making a decision to change a credit policy?

13. (LO 6; Cash collections) Wilf Blitzer Inc. expects sales of $400,000, $300,000, and $360,000 for January, February, and March, respectively. Blitzer has determined the following collection profile from its sales, all of which are on account:

Collections from:

Current month's sales	22%
Prior month's sales	60%
Second month after sale	14%
Uncollectible accounts	4%

A bank loan is due in March, so Blitzer's managers want you, their accountant, to be sure that they have done a good job of predicting collections.

Required:

a.   How much cash can Blitzer expect to collect in March?

b.   Write a brief report to Blitzer's managers describing actions they might take to reduce the level of uncollectible accounts.

14. (LO 6; Cash payments) Dan Ondrack Tennis Ltd. is trying to budget the November 2006 cash payments for Accounts Payable. Management believes that, of a given month's purchases, 40% are paid in the month of purchase, and a 2% discount is given on one-half of what is paid in that month. The remaining 60% are paid in the following month. Expected unit purchases for October and November of 2006 are 91,200 and 68,300, respectively. The cost per unit is $3.80. As Ondrack's consultant, you have been asked to provide the following answers.

Required:

a.   What are expected cash payments for purchases on account in November?

b.   If Ondrack expects a temporary cash shortage in November, what actions might managers take with respect to its creditors to address the cash shortage?

15. (LO 6; Cash budget) Bold Enterprises Ltd. expects to begin fiscal 2006 with a cash balance of $10,000. Cash collections from sales on account are expected to be $468,600. The firm wants to maintain a minimum cash balance of $4,000. Cash disbursements are projected as follows:

Notes payable payment	$ 45,600
Interest on notes payable	4,200
Purchase of computer system	14,800
Payments on account for operating costs and purchases	90,000
Direct labour payments	100,000
Overhead payments	127,000
Selling and administrative payments	93,000

Required:

As assistant to Bold Enterprises' financial vice-president, you have been asked to prepare the 2006 cash budget in good form.

16. (LO 6; Cost of goods manufactured statement) Maria Bartiromo Supplies Ltd. is trying to complete preparation of its 2006 master budget. The firm provides you, its management accountant, with the following expected data:

Work in Process Inventory—January 1	$ 9,200
Work in Process Inventory—December 31	3,300
Direct Material Inventory—January 1	2,300
Direct Material Inventory—December 31	5,200
Purchases of direct material—from purchases budget	287,700
Direct labour—from human resources compensation budget	106,700
Manufacturing overhead—from manufacturing overhead budget	115,500

Required:

Prepare a pro forma cost of goods manufactured statement.

17. (LO 7; Theory) Describe some alternative procedures to budgeting where control is exercised but the inherent bureaucracy of traditional budgeting is eliminated.

PROBLEMS

1. (LO 3; Causes of poor performance) Match the numbered possible causes on the right with the lettered problems on the left in assessing poor performance (more than one numbered cause may be appropriately matched with a problem, and a cause can be used more than once).

    a. Compensation cost higher than expected
    b. Sales volume less than expected
    c. Severe cash flow difficulties
    d. Overhead cost higher than expected
    e. Production cannot keep up with demand
    f. Selling expense higher than expected
    g. Direct materials cost higher than expected
    h. Interest cost higher than expected

    1. Shortage in supply of direct materials was greater than expected
    2. Increased rate for fringe benefits, insurance, or utilities
    3. Increase in labour contract rates or minimum wage law
    4. Recessionary economic conditions
    5. Inflation
    6. Declining collection patterns
    7. Operations are at a maximum capacity
    8. Advertising rates increased

2. (LO 3; Budget games) Match the numbered descriptions on the right with the lettered name of budget games on the left.

    Name of Game

    a. It-Wasn't-My-Fault
    b. It's-Not-in-the-Budget
    c. The Accounting Change
    d. Build-a-Kingdom
    e. Sell-It-No-Matter-What
    f. The Dictator
    g. Father-Knows-Best
    h. Cut-Everything-10-Percent
    i. Spend-It-or-Lose-It
    j. Do-What-You-Want

    Description

    1. Trying to increase the bottom line without regard to reducing customer satisfaction and subsequent sales returns
    2. Imposed budgeting with no room for discussion
    3. Mandated across-the-board cuts without opportunity to justify selected increases and decreases
    4. Inputs by operating personnel are encouraged but subsequently ignored
    5. Worthwhile projects are rejected, and manager is later blamed for low performance because the project was not adequately justified
    6. Changing accounting methods to influence calculated net income
    7. Shifting blame for failure to achieve budget to someone else or something else
    8. Pushing for larger budgets to gain power
    9. Withholding support information; allowing a subordinate manager to undertake budgetary projects that are probably destined to fail
    10. Spending everything left at end of period in a budget so that next period's budget will not be reduced

3. (LO 4; Budget-to-actual comparison) Seinfeld does wedding photography on weekends. He had been charging $225 for a complete album, and his costs averaged $78 each. He believed he could book 30 weddings in 2005, and on that basis he prepared the following budget:

Revenue (30 × $225)	$6,750
Costs (30 × $78)	2,340
Projected profits	$4,410

In 2005, Seinfeld was contemplating his results and was disappointed that his profits were only $4,256. He asks for your help in understanding the shortfall. Review of his journal shows that his fee averaged $218 per wedding and that his costs averaged $85. Seinfeld photographed 32 weddings in 2005.

Required:
Explain to Seinfeld why he made less than he budgeted.

4. (LO 4; Sales variances) Deluxe Spa Products Ltd. employs a budgeting system to aid in organizational planning and control. At the end of the period, actual results are compared against budgeted amounts. The company's actual and budgeted data for 2006 appear below:

Unit sales	Budgeted	Actual
Product A	24,000	20,000
Product B	16,000	30,000
Dollar sales		
Product A	$96,000	$85,000
Product B	48,000	75,000
Cost of sales (all variable)		
Product A	$48,000	$50,000
Product B	32,000	60,000

Required:
a. Compute the budgeted gross margin for each product.
b. Compute the actual gross margin for each product.
c. Compute the sales variances for each product.
d. Why do the sales volume and price variances not explain the entire difference between budgeted and actual gross margin for both products?

5. (LO 4; Sales variances) Wayne Greatsky Sporting Goods manufactures two products: pucks and shoulder pads. For fiscal 2006, the firm budgeted the following:

	Pucks	Shoulder Pads
Sales	$800,000	$1,200,000
Unit sales price	$ 40	$ 30

At the end of 2006, managers were informed of the following:
i. Actual sales of pucks were 21,000 units. The price variance for pucks was $63,000 unfavourable.
ii. Actual sales of shoulder pads generated revenue of $1,120,000 and a volume variance of $240,000 unfavourable

Required:
a. Compute the budgeted sales volume for each product.
b. Compute the volume variance for 2006 for pucks.
c. Compute the price variance for 2006 for shoulder pads.
d. Summarize the difference between budgeted and actual sales for 2006.

6. (LO 4; sales variances) William Wong manages the marketing department at Festive Figurines Limited. He is evaluated based on his ability to meet budgeted revenues. For May 2005, his revenue budget was as follows:

	Price per Unit	Unit Sales
Daniel Boone	$240	1,600
Funny Bunny	130	2,150
Barbie Doll	160	4,200

The actual sales generated by the marketing department in May were as follows:

	Price per Unit	Total Sales Dollars
Daniel Boone	$230	$391,000
Funny Bunny	140	282,800
Barbie Doll	150	622,500

Required:

a. For May 2005, compute the sales price variance for Festive Figurines for each product.

b. For May 2005, compute the sales volume variance for Festive Figurines.

c. Assuming that the variances you computed in parts (a) and (b) are controllable by William Wong, discuss what actions he may have taken to cause actual results to deviate from budgeted results.

7. (LO 6; Production and purchases budgets) During November 2005, the following forecasted sales figures were presented to the management of Mark Haines Manufacturing Ltd.

	January	February	March	Total	April
Sales in units	36,000	32,000	30,000	98,000	28,000

The following are estimates of finished units and direct material in kilograms at various times:

	December 31, 2004	January 1, 2005	February 28, 2005	March 31, 2005
Finished units	9,000	8,000	7,500	7,000
Direct material M	6,750	6,000	5,625	5,250
Direct material N	4,500	4,000	3,750	3,500
Direct material O	9,000	8,000	7,500	7,000

The production process requires three kilograms of material M, two kilograms of material N, and four kilograms of material O. You have just been hired as chief accountant and have been assigned to address the following company needs:

Required:

a. Prepare a monthly production and purchases budget for the first quarter of fiscal 2005 (January–March).

b. The company is considering the installation of new production equipment before fiscal 2005. Such equipment would largely replace the current labour-intensive production system. Write a memo to corporate management explaining why new production equipment could affect the production and purchases budgets.

c. If new production equipment is installed, who should be consulted to determine the new material requirements per unit?

8. (LO 6; Production purchases, direct labour and overhead budgets) Lilly Simon Reliable Tools Ltd. makes two products: saws and hammers. Estimated production needs for a unit of each product follow:

	Saws	Hammers
Steel (in kilograms)	2	4
Wood (in board feet)	0.5	0.2
Direct labour (in hours)	2	4
Machine hours	0.5	3

Overhead is applied to production at the rate of $16 per machine hour. The estimated sales by product for 2006 are:

	Saws	Hammers
Sales (in units)	40,000	15,000

The estimated beginning and required ending inventories for 2006 are

	Beginning	Ending
Steel (kilograms)	1,000	700
Wood (board feet)	400	300
Saws (units)	400	320
Hammers (units)	600	450

Lilly Simon, company president, has been preoccupied with astrology interests and has asked you, her company accountant, to assist her by addressing the following:

Required:
a. Prepare the following budgets: production, purchases, direct labour hours (only), and overhead.
b. What evidence exists to support the argument that this company uses modern methods to manage inventories of material and products?

9. (LO 6; Estimates of various items) Lloyd Robertson Mercantile Ltd. expects its June 2006 Cost of Goods Sold to be $420,000. Included in this amount is $24,000 of fixed overhead. Total variable cost approximates 70% of sales. Lloyd Robertson's gross margin percentage averages 35% of sales, and net income averages 15% of sales. Depreciation is $7,000 per month. All other expenses and purchases are paid 60% in the month incurred and 40% in the following month. Lloyd Robertson purchases only enough goods to satisfy sales of any given month.

Required:
a. Estimate Lloyd Robertson's expected June sales.
b. Estimate Lloyd Robertson's expected variable selling and administrative costs for June.
c. How much are Lloyd Robertson's total expected fixed costs for June?
d. Lloyd Robertson Mercantile Ltd. normally collects 75% of its sales in the month of sale and 25% in the following month. Estimate cash collections and cash payments in June related only to June transactions.

10. (LO 6; Multiple budgets) Dale Eisen Furniture Co. makes bookcases. Sales quantities, sales dollars, and cash collections for the first quarter of 2006 are as follows:

	January	February	March	Total
Quantity (units)	6,400	5,200	7,400	19,000
Revenue	$73,600	$59,800	$85,100	$218,500
Collections	$76,200	$61,300	$81,100	$218,600

The December 31, 2005, estimated balance sheet contains the following balances: Cash, $18,320; Direct Material Inventory, $8,230; Finished Goods Inventory, $23,200; and Accounts Payable, $5,800. The Direct Material Inventory balance represents 2,000 kilograms of scrap iron and 3,200 bookcase bases. Finished Goods Inventory consists of 4,220 bookcases.

Each bookcase requires two kilograms of scrap iron, which costs $2 per kilogram. Bookcase bases are purchased from a local lumber mill at a cost of $1.80 per unit. Beginning in 2006, management wants the ending balance of Direct Material Inventory to equal 25% of the following month's production requirements. Management also wants the ending balance of Finished Goods Inventory to equal 20% of the next month's sales. Sales for April and May are expected to be 8,000 bookcases per month.

The payment pattern for purchases is 75% in the month of purchase with a 1% discount. The remainder is paid in the next month with no discount.

Direct labour is budgeted at $0.70 per bookcase and out-of-pocket plant overhead runs $24,000 per month plus $1.30 per bookcase. Total monthly out-of-pocket period costs run $13,600 plus 10% of sales revenue. All out-of-pocket costs are paid in the month of incurrence, with the exception of material purchases, as discussed earlier. Management wants a minimum cash balance of $15,000. The company has a policy of borrowing funds in multiples of $1,000 at the beginning of a month and repaying borrowed funds in multiples of $1,000 plus interest at the end of a month at the rate of 12% per year.

The president, Dale Eisen, has asked you, a newly hired staff accountant, to prepare the following items.

Required:
a. Monthly production budget for the first quarter of 2006
b. Monthly direct material purchases budget for the first quarter of 2006
c. Monthly schedule of cash payments for purchases for the first quarter of 2006
d. Combined payments schedule for manufacturing overhead and period costs on a monthly basis for the first quarter of 2006
e. Cash budget for each month and in total for the first quarter of 2006
f. Assume that you, as the new staff accountant, will be assigned to work on the materials purchasing budget. With whom are you likely to confirm the credit policies of the firm's vendors? Explain.

11. (LO 6; Cash budget) Margaret Connor Wholesale Appliances Ltd.'s April 30, 2006, balance sheet follows:

Assets		**Liabilities and Shareholders' Equity**		
Cash	$ 40,000	Accounts payable	$272,000	
Accounts receivable (net of		Total liabilities	$272,000	
$3,800 allowance for bad debts)	144,400			
Inventory	108,000			
Plant assets (net of $40,000		**Shareholders' Equity**		
of accumulated depreciation)	320,000	Common stock	120,000	
		Retained earnings	220,400	340,400
		Total liabilities and		
Total assets	$612,400	shareholders' equity		$612,400

Other information about the company follows:
- The company wants a minimum cash balance of $40,000.
- Revenues of $360,000 and $480,000 are expected for May and June 2006, respectively.
- The collection pattern is 60% in the month of sale, 38% in the next month, and 2% uncollectible.
- Cost of goods sold is 75% of sales.
- Purchases each month are 60% of the current month's sales and 40% of the following month's sales. All purchases are paid for in the month following the purchase.
- Other monthly expenses total $48,000. This amount includes $2,000 of depreciation but does not include bad debts expense.

Required:
a. May cash collections
b. May 31 inventory balance
c. May 31 retained earnings balance
d. May cash budget, including the amount available for investment or to be borrowed during May
e. Why would the firm want to maintain a minimum cash balance of $40,000? Who would set such a policy?

12. (LO 6; Cash collections and payments) Jay Leno Jokes-for-Blokes is a wholesale distributor of joke books and humorous magazines. The company is preparing its budget for the first three months of 2006. At the end of 2005, the following balances are estimated:

Accounts Receivable	$188,280
Inventory	52,875
Accounts Payable[1]	41,700
Other Payables	7,120

[1]for inventory purchases

Management has agreed on the following guidelines in preparing the budget:

Collections
- Credit sales are billed on the last day of each month.
- Cash customers and credit customers who pay by the 10th of the month after billing are allowed a 1% discount.
- 10% of sales are for cash. Of the credit sales, 10% are received within the discount period; another 40% are received during the rest of the month after billing; 40% are received in the second month after billing; and 10% are received in the third month after billing.

Payments
- 40% of purchases are paid for in the month of purchase. The rest are paid in the next month.
- Of the operating expenses incurred, 60% are paid in the month incurred and the remainder is paid in the next month.

Other Operating Statistics
- All sales are made at 200% of cost.
- Desired ending inventory is set at 75% of the following month's Cost of Goods Sold.
- Actual and projected sales are estimated at

October	$122,000
November	128,000
December	133,000
January	141,000
February	139,000
March	124,000
April	127,000

Selling and administrative expenses run 10% of sales plus $6,000 monthly. Included in the monthly selling and administrative expenses are $1,500 of depreciation.

Required:
a. Determine total monthly cash receipts for the first quarter.
b. Determine monthly purchases for the first quarter.
c. Determine monthly cash disbursements for the first quarter.

13. (LO 6; Cash budget and pro forma income statement) Baldwin's Fresh Fruit Stand purchases, wholesales, and retails fresh fruits and vegetables. Company estimates reveal the following for the first three fiscal months of 2006:

	Purchases	Wholesale Sales
June	$66,000	$102,000
July	58,000	92,000
August	79,600	116,000

Management expects that May 2006 purchases and sales will be $80,000 and $120,000, respectively. The company usually pays 60% of any month's purchases in the month of purchase and takes an average 2% discount. The remaining amount is paid in the following month with no discount. Other monthly payments for expenses run $24,000 plus 12% of sales. Depreciation is $4,000 per month. The company wishes to maintain a minimum cash balance of $28,000 and expects to start May with $36,000 cash.

All retail sales are for cash and all wholesale transactions are on credit. Overall, experience indicates the following expected collection pattern for sales: 25% in the month of sale, 60% in the month after the sale, and 15% in the second month after the sale. The company has no debt other than what is currently owed for purchases on account.

Required:

a. Calculate the July 31 balances for Accounts Receivable and Accounts Payable.
b. Calculate the cash collections expected in August.
c. Calculate the expected total cash disbursements in August.
d. Present a cash budget for August. Assume management wants no more cash on hand at August 31 than the minimum cash balance desired.
e. Prepare an income statement for August. Assume an average gross margin percentage of 40%. Ignore income taxes.
f. Explain how and why inventory management must be different for perishable commodities than for nonperishable commodities.

14. (LO 6; Pro forma income statement/balance sheet) The projected January 31, 2006, balance sheet for Lawrence Rubber Co. follows (all dollar amounts are in thousands):

Assets

Cash	$ 16,000
Accounts Receivable (net of allowance for	
uncollectible accounts of $4,000)	76,000
Inventory	32,000
Property, Plant, and Equipment (net)	70,000
Total Assets	$194,000

Liabilities and Shareholders' Equity

Accounts Payable	$165,000
Common Stock	100,000
Retained Earnings (deficit)	(71,000)
Total Liabilities and Shareholders' Equity	$194,000

Additional information:
Sales are budgeted as follows:

February	$220,000
March	240,000

Collections are expected to be 60% in the month of sale, 38% in the next month, and 2% uncollectible.

The company's gross margin is projected at 25% of sales. Purchases each month are 75% of the next month's projected sales, and these are paid in full in the following month.

Other expenses for each month, paid in cash, are expected to be $31,000. Monthly depreciation is $10,000.

Required:

a. Prepare a pro forma income statement for February.
b. Prepare a pro forma balance sheet for February.
c. Describe any special problems this company may encounter because of its weak balance sheet. As a management accountant, recommend actions that the firm might take to improve the balance sheet.

15. (LO 6; Cash budget) The Josh Lyman Co. began operations in January of 2004. The information below pertains to the operations of Lyman for the three months from January to March (that is, the first quarter, Q1) of 2005.

Expenses for Quarter 1

Depreciation	$40,000
Manufacturing overhead	10,000
Income taxes	15,000
Payroll	30,000
Selling costs (Commission: 2% of sales)	8,000
Administrative costs	10,000

Costs are assumed to be incurred evenly throughout the year with the exception of the following:

- Depreciation is taken on new assets starting in the quarter subsequent to the quarter purchased.
- Income taxes are payable in half-yearly installments, on the first day of each six-month period, based on last year's actual tax expense of $30,000.

Other information:

i.   Sales (made evenly throughout the quarter)

    Q1, actual $400,000
    Q2, forecast   400,000
    Q3, forecast   800,000

Collection from sales are as follows: 50% in the quarter of the sale; 45% in the quarter following; 5% uncollectible.

ii.   Purchases (made evenly throughout the quarter)

    Q1, actual $200,000
    Q2   ?

Note that merchandise purchased during a quarter would equal inventory to meet the current quarter's sales demands plus 25% of the next quarter's forecasted sales. The gross margin ratio is constant at 60%.

Cash payments for purchases are as follows: 50% in the quarter of purchase; 50% in the quarter thereafter.

iii. The company purchased capital equipment in the amount of $100,000 in February 2006. The estimated useful life of this equipment is 10 years; estimated scrap value is $0. Dividends of $20,000 are declared on the last day of each quarter, to be paid at the end of the following month. Cash in the bank at the end of Q1 equals $25,000.

Required:

a. Prepare a cash budget for Lyman for Q2 of 2006. Show all your supporting calculations.

b. List three advantages of budgeting.

(Adapted by the author from *Management Accounting examinations,* published by the Certified General Accountants Association of Canada © CGA-Canada, 2000, used by permission.)

16. (LO 6; Comprehensive) Reed Associates Ltd. makes an environmentally friendly artificial fireplace log. You have been asked to prepare the company's 2005 master budget and have been provided with the following:

a.   The following projected December 31, 2004, balances are:

Assets

Cash		$ 4,330
Accounts Receivable		8,450
Direct Material Inventory (2,046 kilograms)		409
Finished Goods Inventory (1,200 logs)		2,808
Plant and Equipment	$220,000	
Less: Accumulated Depreciation	(57,700)	162,300
Total Assets		$178,297

Liabilities and Shareholders' Equity

Accounts Payable	$ 1,109	
Note Payable	20,000	
Total Liabilities		$ 21,109
Common Stock	$100,000	
Retained Earnings	57,188	157,188
Total Liabilities and Shareholders' Equity		$178,297

b.   Each log requires the following standards for direct material and labour:

3.3 kilograms of material mix at $0.20
    (0.3 kilograms is discarded as waste) $0.66
2 minutes of labour time; direct labour
    averages $14.40 per hour   0.48

Each finished log requires three minutes of machine time. Variable overhead is applied at the rate of $12 per hour of machine time. Annual fixed production overhead of $42,000 is applied based on an expected annual production capacity of 70,000 logs. The total fixed manufacturing overhead comprises the following:

Salaries	$26,000
Insurance	1,800
Fixed portion of utilities	5,300
Depreciation	8,900

Fixed overhead is incurred evenly throughout the year.

c. Expected sales in units for the first five months of 2005 are:

January	6,000
February	9,000
March	6,500
April	5,900
May	5,100

Reed Associates grants no discounts, and all sales are on credit at $6 per log. The company's collection pattern is 80% in the month of sale, 15% in the month following the sale, and 5% in the second month following the sale. The Accounts Receivable balance in the balance sheet represents amounts remaining due from November sales of $33,000 and December sales of $34,000.

d. Reed Associates completes all production each day. The desired ending balance of Direct Material Inventory is 10% of the amount needed to satisfy the next month's production for finished goods. The desired ending balance in Finished Goods Inventory is 20% of the next month's sales.

e. Purchases are paid 70% in the month of purchase and 30% in the month following the purchase. No discounts are taken. The note payable has a 12% interest rate, and the interest is paid at the end of each month. The $20,000 balance of the principal on the note is due on March 31, 2005.

f. Reed Associates' minimum desired cash balance is $4,000. The firm may borrow at the beginning of a month and repay at the end of the month in $500 increments. Interest on these short-term loans, if any, is payable monthly at a 14% rate. Investments and investment liquidations are made only in $500 amounts at the end of a month. Investments earn 12% per year, collected monthly at month's end.

g. Period (selling and administrative) expenses, paid as incurred, run $9,000 per month plus 1% of revenue. Direct labour and overhead are paid as incurred.

h. The company accrues income taxes at a 40% rate. A quarterly tax installment will be paid on April 15, 2005.

Required:
Prepare master budget schedules on a monthly basis for the first quarter of 2005 and pro forma financial statements at the end of the first quarter. (Round all numbers in the schedules and pro forma statements to the nearest whole dollar.)

CASES

1. Your Canadian-based consumer electronics firm, CanadaExcel, is in the process of establishing a video camera assembly plant in Malaysia. The manager of the Malaysian plant is to have responsibility for the following: sourcing materials (about 60% of materials will be acquired from outside the company and the other 40% will be acquired from internal plants located in Canada and Mexico); hiring, training, and supervising workers; controlling operating costs; meeting a production schedule that is based on projected sales; and maintaining production quality. Completed units will be shipped to internal marketing divisions located in North America.

Required:
Place yourself in the position of the controller of CanadaExcel. It is your job to incorporate the operating plans for the Malaysian assembly plant into the company's formal budget. Describe, in general terms, what information you would need to acquire to develop the budget for the Malaysian operation and where you would expect to acquire such information. Further, describe any significant decisions that you would be

responsible for making in compiling the budget. What problems and concerns might you have in getting the required information on the Malaysian operations? How might you handle these problems and concerns?

2. The Spudas Agency, a division of General Service Industries, offers consulting services to clients for a fee. The corporate management at General Service is pleased with the performance of the Spudas Agency for the first nine months of the current year and has recommended that the division manager of the Spudas Agency, Karina TenVeldhuis, submit a revised forecast for the remaining quarter, as the division has exceeded the annual year-to-date plan by 20% of operating income. An unexpected increase in billed hour volume over the original plan is the main reason for this gain in income. The original operating budget for the first three quarters for the Spudas Agency is as follows:

2005–2006 Operating Budget

	1st Quarter	2nd Quarter	3rd Quarter	Total
Revenue:				
Consulting fees				
Management consulting	$315,000	$315,000	$315,000	$ 945,000
IT consulting	421,875	421,875	421,875	1,265,625
Total	$736,875	$736,875	$736,875	$2,210,625
Other revenue	10,000	10,000	10,000	30,000
Total	$746,875	$746,875	$746,875	$2,240,625
Expenses:				
Consultant salaries	$386,750	$386,750	$386,750	$1,160,250
Travel and entertainment	45,625	45,625	45,625	136,875
General and administration	100,000	100,000	100,000	300,000
Depreciation	40,000	40,000	40,000	120,000
Corporate allocation	50,000	50,000	50,000	150,000
Total	$622,375	$622,375	$622,375	$1,867,125
Operating income	$124,500	$124,500	$124,500	$ 373,500

When comparing the actuals for the first three quarters against the original plan, TenVeldhuis analyzed the variances. Her revised forecast for the fourth quarter will reflect the following information:

- The division currently has 25 consultants on staff—10 for management consulting and 15 for IT consulting—and has hired 3 additional management consultants to start work at the beginning of the fourth quarter in order to meet the increased client demand.
- The hourly billing rate for consulting revenues is acceptable in the market and will remain at $90 per hour for each management consultant and $75 per hour for each IT consultant. However, owing to the favourable increase in billing hour volume, the hours for each consultant will be increased by 50 hours per quarter. New employees are as capable as current employees and will be billed at the current rates.
- The budgeted annual salaries and actual annual salaries, paid monthly, are the same at $50,000 for a management consultant and 8% less for an IT consultant. Corporate management has approved a merit increase of 10% at the beginning of the fourth quarter for all 25 existing consultants, while the new consultants will be compensated at the planned rate.
- The planned salary expense includes a provision for employee fringe benefits amounting to 30% of the annual salaries; however, the improvement of some corporatewide employee programs will increase the fringe benefit allocation to 40%.
- The original plan assumes a fixed hourly rate for travel and other related expenses for each billing hour of consulting. These expenses are not reimbursed by the client, and the previously determined hourly rate has proved to be adequate to cover these costs.
- Other revenues are derived from temporary rentals and interest income and remain unchanged for the fourth quarter.

- Administrative expenses have been favourable at 7% below the plan; this 7% savings on fourth-quarter expenses will be reflected in the revised plan.
- Depreciation for office equipment and microcomputers will stay constant at the projected straight-line rate.
- Because of the favourable experience for the first three quarters and the division's increased ability to absorb costs, the corporate management at General Service Industries has increased the corporate expense allocation by 50%.

Required:

a. Prepare a revised operating budget for the fourth quarter for the Spudas Agency, which TenVeldhuis will present to General Service Industries. Be sure to furnish supporting calculations for all revised revenue and expense amounts.

b. Discuss the reasons why an organization would prepare a revised forecast.

(CMA adapted)

3. Katsya Corporation, a rapidly expanding crossbow distributor to retail outlets, is in the process of formulating plans for 2006. Lisa Katsya, the director of marketing, has completed her 2006 forecast and is confident that sales estimates will be met or exceeded. The following sales figures show the growth expected and will provide the planning basis for other corporate departments.

Month	Forecasted Sales	Month	Forecasted Sales
January	$1,800,000	July	$3,000,000
February	2,000,000	August	3,000,000
March	1,800,000	September	3,200,000
April	2,200,000	October	3,200,000
May	2,500,000	November	3,000,000
June	2,800,000	December	3,400,000

Sandie Rinoldo, the assistant controller, has been given the responsibility for formulating the cash flow projection, a critical element during a period of rapid expansion. The following information will be used in preparing the cash analysis:

- Katsya Corporation has experienced an excellent record in accounts receivable collections and expects this trend to continue. The company collects 60% of billings in the month after the sale and 40% in the second month after the sale. Uncollectible accounts are insignificant and should not be considered in the analysis.
- The purchase of crossbows is Katsya's largest expenditure; the cost of these items equals 50% of sales. The company receives 60% of the crossbows one month prior to sale and 40% during the month of sale.
- Prior experience shows that 80% of accounts payable are paid by Katsya one month after receipt of the purchased crossbows, and the remaining 20% are paid the second month after receipt.
- Hourly wages, including fringe benefits, are a function of sales volume and are equal to 20% of the current month's sales. These wages are paid in the month incurred.
- Administrative expenses are projected to be $2,640,000 for 2006. All of these expenses are incurred uniformly throughout the year except the property taxes. Property taxes are paid in four equal installments in the last month of each quarter. The composition of the expenses is:

Salaries	$ 480,000
Promotion	660,000
Property taxes	240,000
Insurance	360,000
Utilities	300,000
Depreciation	600,000
Total	$2,640,000

- Income tax payments are made by Katsya in the first month of each quarter based on income for the prior quarter. Katsya's income tax rate is 40%. Katsya's net income for the first quarter of 2006 is projected to be $612,000.

- Katsya has a corporate policy of maintaining an end-of-month cash balance of $100,000. Cash is invested or borrowed monthly, as necessary, to maintain this balance.
- Katsya uses a calendar year reporting period.

Required:

a. Prepare a pro forma schedule of cash receipts and disbursements for Katsya Corporation, by month, for the second quarter of 2006. Be sure that all receipts, disbursements, and borrowing/investing amounts are presented on a monthly basis. Ignore the interest expense and/or interest income associated with the borrowing/investing activities.

b. Discuss why cash budgeting is particularly important for a rapidly expanding company such as Katsya Corporation.

c. Do monthly cash budgets ignore the pattern of cash flows within the month? Explain.

(CMA adapted)

4. Quinn Management Education Inc. (QME) is a nonprofit organization that sponsors a wide variety of management seminars throughout western Canada. In addition, it is heavily involved in research into improved methods of teaching and motivating college administrators. The seminar activity is largely supported by fees and the research program by membership dues.

QME operates on a calendar year basis and is in the process of finalizing the budget for 2006. The following information has been taken from approved plans, which are still tentative at this time:

Seminar Program

Revenue—The scheduled number of programs should produce $12,000,000 of revenue for the year. Each program is budgeted to produce the same amount of revenue as the others. The revenue is collected during the month the program is offered. The programs are scheduled during the basic academic year and are not held during June, July, August, or December. In each of the first five months of the year 12% of the revenue is generated, and the remainder is distributed evenly during September, October, and November.

Direct expenses—The seminar expenses are made up of three types:
- Instructors' fees are paid at the rate of 70% of seminar revenue in the month following the seminar. The instructors are considered independent contractors and are not eligible for QME employee benefits.
- Facilities fees total $5,600,000 for the year. Fees are the same for all programs and are paid in the months the programs are given.
- Annual promotional costs of $1,000,000 are spent equally in all months except June and July, when there is no promotional effort.

Research Program

Research grants—The research program has a large number of projects nearing completion. The other main research activity this year includes feasibility studies for new projects to be started in 2006. The total grant expense of $3,000,000 for 2006 is expected to be paid out at the rate of $500,000 per month during the first six months of the year.

Salaries and Other QME Expenses

Office lease—Annual amount of $240,000 paid monthly at the beginning of each month.
General administrative expenses—$1,500,000 annually or $125,000 per month; these are paid in cash as incurred.
Depreciation expense—$240,000 per year.
General QME promotion—Annual cost of $600,000, paid monthly.

Salaries and benefits—

Number of Employees	Annual Cash Salary	Total Annual Salaries
1	$50,000	$ 50,000
3	40,000	120,000
4	30,000	120,000
15	25,000	375,000
5	15,000	75,000
22	10,000	220,000
50		$960,000

Employee benefits amount to $240,000, or 25% of annual salaries. Except for the pension contribution, the benefits are paid as salaries are paid. The annual pension payment of $24,000, based on 2.5% of total annual salaries, is due on April 15, 2006.

Other Information

Membership income—QME has 100,000 members, and each pays an annual fee of $100. The fee for the calendar year is invoiced in late June. The collection schedule is as follows: July, 60%; August, 30%; September, 5%; and October, 5%.

Capital expenditures—The capital expenditures program calls for a total of $510,000 in cash payments to be spread evenly over the first five months of 2006.

Cash and temporary investments—At January 1, 2006, these are estimated at $750,000.

Required:

a. Budget of the annual cash receipts and disbursements for 2006

b. Cash budget for QME Inc. for January 2006

(CMA adapted)

5. London Corporation manufactures and sells extended keyboard units to be used with microcomputers. Elizabeth Windsor, budget analyst, coordinated the preparation of the annual budget for the year ending August 31, 2006. The budget was based on the prior year's sales and production activity. The pro forma statements of income, cost of goods manufactured, and cost of goods sold schedule are as follows:

London Corporation
Pro Forma Statement of Income
For the Year Ended August 31, 2006
($000 omitted)

Net sales		$ 25,550
Cost of goods sold		(16,565)
Gross profit		$ 8,985
Operating expenses		
Marketing	$3,200	
Selling and administrative	2,000	(5,200)
Income from operations before income taxes		$ 3,785

London Corporation
Pro Forma Cost of Goods Manufactured Statement
For the Year Ended August 31, 2006
($000 omitted)

Direct material:		
Direct materials inventory, September 1, 2005	$ 1,200	
Plus: Purchases of direct material	11,400	
Direct materials available for use	$12,600	
Less: Direct materials inventory, August 31, 2006	1,480	
Direct materials used		$11,120
Direct labour		980
Manufacturing overhead		
Indirect materials	$ 1,112	
General manufacturing overhead	2,800	3,912
Cost of goods manufactured		$16,012

London Corporation
Pro Forma Cost of Goods Sold Schedule
For the Year Ended August 31, 2006
($000 omitted)

Finished goods inventory, September 1, 2005	$ 930
Plus: Cost of goods manufactured	16,012
Goods available for sale	$16,942
Less: Finished goods inventory, August 31, 2006	377
Cost of goods sold	$16,565

On December 10, 2005, Elizabeth Windsor met with Philip Mountbatten, vice president of finance, to discuss the first quarter's results (the period September 1 to November 30, 2005). After their discussion, Mountbatten directed Windsor to reflect the following changes to the budget assumptions in revised pro forma statements.

- The estimated production in units for the fiscal year should be revised from 140,000 to 145,000 units, with the balance of production being scheduled in equal segments over the last months of the year. The actual first quarter's production was 25,000 units.
- The planned inventory for finished goods of 3,300 units at the end of the fiscal year remains unchanged and will be valued at the average manufacturing cost for the year. The finished goods inventory of 9,300 units on September 1, 2005, had dropped to 9,000 units by November 30, 2005.
- Due to a new labour agreement, the labour rate will increase 8% effective June 1, 2006, the beginning of the fourth quarter, instead of the previously anticipated effective date of September 1, 2006, the beginning of the next fiscal year. The assumptions remain unchanged for direct material inventory at 16,000 units for beginning inventory and 18,500 units for ending inventory. Direct material inventory is valued on a first-in, first-out basis. One unit of direct material is needed for each keyboard produced. During the first quarter, direct material for 27,500 units of output was purchased for $2,200,000. Although direct material will be purchased evenly for the last nine months, the cost of the direct material will increase by 5% on March 1, 2006, the beginning of the third quarter.
- Indirect material costs will continue to be projected at 10% of the cost of direct material consumed.
- One-half of general manufacturing overhead and all of the marketing and general and administrative expenses are considered fixed.

Required:

a. Based on the revised data presented, calculate London Corporation's projected sales for the year ending August 31, 2006, in (1) number of units to be sold and (2) dollar volume of net sales.

b. Prepare the pro forma schedule of cost of goods sold for the year ending August 31, 2006.

c. In light of the fact that management is aware that certain changes (price change for materials and rate increase for labour) are forthcoming, what actions might management take to exploit the changes?

d. For each budgetary change mentioned, identify the source or sources of information Philip Mountbatten might have used to become aware of the change.

(CMA adapted)

6. Chrétien Manufacturing, a division of Trudeau Corporation, produces and sells a variety of leather goods to both wholesalers and retail outlets. Four months ago, Trudeau sent a team from its Internal Audit Department to Chrétien to perform a routine review of operations. A portion of the audit report presented to Trudeau on the operations of Chrétien is presented below.

Observation

Departmental budgets are not being utilized at Chrétien. Currently, the division does not have the automated systems capability to produce budget analyses at the departmental level. Traditionally, the plant has been controlled through a total plant concept rather than a departmental approach to cost control. Given present business conditions, this approach may no longer be the optimum control process. Increased competition in the marketplace, declining profits, deteriorating margins, and increased costs have combined to necessitate an aggressive approach to cost reduction. Based on experience at other Trudeau plants, we believe that Chrétien would benefit from the development and use of departmental budgets for all functions.

Recommendation

We recommend that Chrétien establish a management objective to develop and utilize flexible departmental expense budgets for all departments. Resources and systems development efforts should be devoted to this objective as they become available. We suggest, as an interim step, that an operating budget be employed on a monthly basis. Operating targets for both direct labour and indirect labour expense should be established for each manufacturing department monthly. Departmental managers should track performance and explain deviations from targets as part of the regular agenda at the weekly production meetings.

Preliminary Management Response

Chrétien will develop and utilize a flexible departmental budget system. In the interim, work has begun to establish daily, month-to-date, and annual targets for direct and indirect labour for the manufacturing departments. These targets include efficiency objectives, overtime objectives, and indirect labour usage objectives based on volume and product mix.

Prior to making the Preliminary Management Response presented in the audit report, the president of Chrétien announced to the departmental managers that the company was planning to accept the audit recommendation to implement a departmental budgeting system. The managers were asked for suggestions on implementation procedures and were encouraged to raise any questions they might have about the budget system.

Required:

a. Describe the benefits, other than better cost control, that are likely to accrue to Chrétien Manufacturing from the implementation of departmental budgeting.

b. Discuss the behavioural impact that the introduction of departmental budgeting is likely to have on Chrétien Manufacturing's
   i. departmental managers
   ii. production workers

c. Describe several steps that Chrétien Manufacturing should take in order to gain maximum acceptance of the new departmental budgeting system.

7. Yue Li is the chief financial officer of Artech Corporation, a manufacturer and distributor of electronic security devices primarily suited for residential applications. Li is currently in the process of preparing the 2005 annual budget and implementing an incentive plan to reward the performance of key personnel. The final operating plans will then be presented to the board of directors for approval.

Li is aware that 2005 may be a very difficult year due to announced price increases to major customers. Artech's president has put pressure on management to achieve the current year's earnings per share amounts. Li is, therefore, considering introducing zero-based budgeting in order to bring costs in line with revenue expectations.

Ping Jiang, Artech's manufacturing director, is attempting to convince Li to build "budgetary slack" into the operating budget. Jiang contends that productivity is burdened by an abnormal amount of product design changes and small lot size production orders that incur costly set-up times.

Required:

a. Explain at least three advantages and at least three disadvantages of budgetary slack from the point of view of Artech Corporation's management group as a whole.

b. Describe how zero-based budgeting could be advantageous to Artech Corporation's overall budget process.

8. On December 5, 2001, SAP AG, the giant German software company, announced a new functionality that would "allow more comprehensive processing and interpretation of key performance and financial data to further streamline the planning processes and provide a closed-loop strategic enterprise management process beyond budgeting."

Required:

Based on what you have learned in the first nine chapters of this textbook, how would you expect SAP to replace traditional budgeting?

ETHICS AND QUALITY DISCUSSIONS

1. Assume that you are a top manager in an advertising firm with eight regional locations. Alex McKay is the manager in charge of the Calgary office.

In 2004, Alex worked diligently with her staff to create an optimal 2005 budget for her office; she believed the amounts for revenues and expenses were forecasted as precisely as they could be. When you received her 2005 budget, you immediately increased her expected revenues 15% and reduced all expense categories by 10%. You informed her that you believed her office was capable of dealing with both adjustments. Near the end of 2005, it was obvious that Alex's office would probably come in about 12% below the increased budget in regard to revenues and almost exactly equal to her original estimates in regard to costs.

Although 2005 has not ended, Alex needs to prepare the 2006 budget. She again elicits substantial information from her staff and prepares a detailed budget. Before sending it to you, however, she reduces revenues by 20% and increases costs by 15% in each category.

Required:

a. What justifications might you have had for changing Alex's 2005 budget? What ethical considerations are involved in your decision to change her budget without consulting her after asking for her input?

b. Why would Alex have sent a less accurate forecast for 2006 than she did for 2005? What ethical considerations are involved in her decision to make the budget misstatements?

c. Since advertising firms do not manufacture products, what effects would Alex's understatement of her revenues have on other offices of the firm?

2. Williams Ltd., a manufacturer of infant furniture and carriages, is in the initial stages of preparing the annual budget for 2005. Isabel Branyah has recently joined Williams' accounting staff and is interested in learning as much as possible about the company's budgeting process. During a recent lunch with Marianne Misters, sales manager, and Michael Baldwin, production manager, Branyah initiated the following conversation:

Branyah: "Since I'm new around here and am going to be involved with the preparation of the annual budget, I'd be interested to learn how the two of you estimate sales and production numbers."

Misters: "We start out very methodically by looking at recent history, discussing what we know about current accounts, potential customers, and the general state of consumer spending. Then we add that usual dose of intuition to come up with the best forecast we can."

Baldwin: "I usually take the sales projections as the basis for my projections. Of course, we have to make an estimate of what this year's closing inventories will be, which is sometimes difficult."

Branyah: "Why does that present a problem? There must have been an estimate of closing inventories in the budget for the current year."

Baldwin: "Those numbers aren't always reliable, since Misters makes some adjustments to the sales numbers before passing them on to me."

Branyah: "What kind of adjustments?"

Misters: "Well, we don't want to fall short of the sales projections, so we generally give ourselves a little breathing room by lowering the initial sales projection anywhere from 5% to 10%."

Baldwin: "So, you can see why this year's budget is not a very reliable starting point. We always have to adjust the projected production rates as the year progresses and, of course, this changes the ending inventory estimates. By the way, we make similar adjustments to expenses by adding at least 10% to the estimates. I think everyone around here does the same thing."

Required:

a.   Misters and Baldwin have described the use of budgetary slack.

    i.   Explain why Misters and Baldwin behave in this manner, and describe the benefits they expect to realize from the use of budgetary slack.

    ii.   Explain how the use of budgetary slack can adversely affect Misters and Baldwin.

b.   As a management accountant, Isabel Branyah believes that the behaviour described by Misters and Baldwin may be unethical and that she may have an obligation not to support this behaviour. Explain why the use of budgetary slack may be unethical.

(CMA)

3.   Many managers believe that if all amounts in their budgets are not spent during a period, they will lose all allocations in future periods and little or no recognition will result from cost savings. The following figure indicates results of a survey of IMA members about the motivating factors behind budgeting issues:

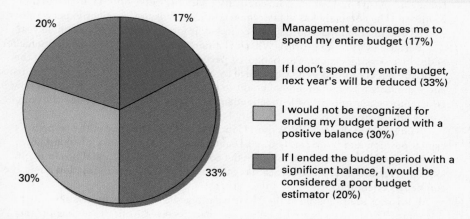

Management encourages me to spend my entire budget (17%)

If I don't spend my entire budget, next year's will be reduced (33%)

I would not be recognized for ending my budget period with a positive balance (30%)

If I ended the budget period with a significant balance, I would be considered a poor budget estimator (20%)

Required:

Discuss the behavioural and ethical issues involved in a "spend it or lose it" attitude. Include in your discussion the issue of negotiating budget allocation requests before the beginning of the period.

4.   Phyllis Abbott is the manager of budgets for a medium-sized diversified financial services organization that uses a PeopleSoft ERP system. Annually she reviews and consolidates the budgets for all operating divisions and subsidiaries with those of the corporate departments to produce the consolidated budget that is reviewed and approved by the executive committee consisting of the senior managers. The last step is for the consolidated budget to be approved by the board of directors in late November in order for it to be implemented on January 1 when the next fiscal year begins.

    To do her job properly, Phyllis familiarizes herself with all budget details in order to avoid errors. In the end, she understands the assumptions and premises behind each number. For example, she reviews the growth and yield assumption for each loan portfolio. She also understands each one-time expense in the corporate departments.

    One budgeted outlay in the treasury department for $135 million attracted Phyllis' attention. The treasurer said the board of directors budgeted the money for the purchase of the outstanding shares held by minority shareholders of a 90% owned trust company subsidiary. A 20% premium would be paid for the shares. The expected acquisition date was four months away.

Recognizing a sure investment, Phyllis acquired 10,000 shares of the subsidiary in the month before the acquisition date.

Required:

Comment on Phyllis' actions in acquiring the shares.

COMMUNICATIONS ACTIVITIES

1. Over the past 20 years, the legal profession has been characterized by its fixation on hourly billing. By basing revenues on hours of time worked and materials consumed, law firms have had very predictable revenue streams. However, for their clients, the hourly billing system means very unpredictable costs and no guarantee of either the quality of the service or the outcome of litigation. Before the 1970s, most legal work performed was billed on a fixed fee basis.

   Required:
   a. How does billing based on time spent promote inefficiency?
   b. What budgeting advantage does a fixed fee billing arrangement offer clients?
   c. In general, how does a billing arrangement affect the ability of a supplier to predict revenues and a customer to predict costs?

2. Wilson Container, a privately held firm founded in the early '90s, specializes in the packaging of toys and games. The company's administrative officers are located in Montreal. The company has many regional offices. Wilson Container expects sales to exceed $25 million next year and the company is forecasting a very profitable year.

   Because of its rapid growth, Wilson Container has had ongoing requirements for additional working capital. The bank that participated in the initial financing of the company has continued to be supportive by arranging for additional long-range loans and extending a $3 million line of credit to the company. However, the bank is now reluctant to enter into a new loan agreement and has declined to increase the company's line of credit.

   The board of directors of Wilson Container is concerned about the company's capital position and has recently hired Dan Ondrack as treasurer of the company. Ondrack has been directed to improve the company's working capital position. Since joining Wilson Container, Ondrack has gathered the following information about the company's operations.

   • All invoices are prepared at the Montreal office during the last week of each month. These invoices are based on sales data received from the regional plants. All sales are made on a credit basis, and payment terms are net 30 days.
   • Customers' cheques are sent to the Montreal office for processing and are deposited in the bank at 3:00 each afternoon. Approximately 1.5 days are required to process and deposit a cheque once it is received at the Montreal office.
   • The collection effort on past-due accounts is haphazard and consists entirely of phone calls made by the controller when time allows. The company does not charge interest on past-due accounts.
   • Wilson Container has a strict credit policy, but it is not applied evenly. Because sales are made from all five locations, credit is often approved and extended by the individual making the sale.
   • Each of Wilson Container's regional plants has its own bank account for disbursements, which include payroll, inventory purchases, and repair and maintenance of equipment. These accounts are replenished by wire transfer of funds from the Montreal office.
   • Because each plant controls its own disbursements, payment procedures are not standardized. Some locations take advantage of vendor discounts, while others pay in 30 days.
   • Wilson Container has yet to develop inventory policies and procedures. Each plant does its own purchasing and maintains its own inventory records. New toys and games are continually being developed to keep up with changing tastes, and Wilson Container must keep pace. Therefore, new items are frequently added to inventories.

Wilson Container's board of directors is concerned about the company's working capital position; however, board members do not wish to make a public offering to raise cash unless it becomes absolutely necessary.

Required:

a. Discuss how Dan Ondrack could improve Wilson Container's working capital position by addressing the following areas of cash management:
   i. Acceleration of cash receipts
   ii. Deceleration of cash disbursements
   iii. Generation of cash

b. Describe how Wilson Container's cash management might differ between a period of high interest rates and a period of low interest rates.

3. SteelCo is a medium-sized company in the steel fabrication industry with six divisions located in different geographical sectors of the country. Considerable autonomy in operational management is permitted in the divisions, due in part to the distance between corporate headquarters in Hamilton and five of the six divisions.

   Corporate management establishes divisional budgets using prior year data adjusted for industry and economic changes expected for the coming year. Budgets are prepared by year and by quarter, with top management attempting to recognize problems unique to each division in the divisional budget-setting process. Once the year's divisional budgets are set by corporate management, they cannot be modified by division management.

   The budget for calendar year 2005 projects total corporate net income before taxes of $3,750,000 for the year, including $937,500 for the first quarter. Results of first-quarter operations presented to corporate management in early April showed corporate net income of $865,000, which was $72,500 below the projected net income for the quarter. The Halifax Division operated at 4.5% above its projected divisional net income, while the other five divisions showed net incomes with variances ranging from 1.5% to 22% below budgeted net income.

   Corporate managers are concerned with the first-quarter results because they believed strongly that differences between divisions had been recognized. An entire day in late November of last year had been spent presenting and explaining the corporate and divisional budgets to the division mangers and their division controllers. A mid-April meeting of corporate and division management had generated unusual candor. All five other division managers cited reasons why first-quarter results in their respective divisions represented effective management and was the best that could be expected. Corporate management remained unconvinced and informed division managers that "results would be brought into line with the budget by the end of the second quarter."

   Required:

   a. Identify and explain the major disadvantages in the procedures employed by SteelCo's corporate management in preparing and implementing the divisional budgets.

   b. Discuss the behavioural problems that may arise from requiring division managers to meet the quarterly budgeted net income figures as well as the annual budgeted net income.

   c. Describe how you, as a high-level corporate manager at SteelCo, would attempt to evaluate the reasons offered by the divisional managers for their poor performance.

4. Discuss the contents, need for, and advantages of a budget manual.

5. Discuss what is likely to occur in a large firm that decides not to prepare an annual budget.

6. Successful business organizations appear to be those that have clearly defined long-range goals and a well-planned strategy to reach those goals. These successful organizations understand the markets in which they do business as well as their internal strengths and weaknesses. These organizations take advantage of this knowledge to grow (through internal development or acquisitions) in a consistent and disciplined manner.

   Required:

   a. Discuss the need for long-range goals for business organizations.

   b. Discuss how long-range goals are set.

c. Define the concepts of strategic planning and management control. Discuss how they relate to each other and contribute to the progress toward the attainment of long-range goals.

7. Lymar Products is a divisionalized corporation in the agribusiness industry with its corporate headquarters in Calgary. The Research and Development (R&D) Division is located in central Canada and is responsible for all of the corporation's seed, fertilizer, and insecticide research and development. R&D is conducted primarily for the benefit of Lymar's other operating divisions. The R&D Division conducts research for outside firms when such research does not interfere with the division's regular work or does not represent work that is directly competitive with Lymar's interests.

Lymar's annual budget preparation begins approximately five months before the beginning of the next fiscal year. Each division manager is responsible for developing the budget for his or her division within the guidelines provided by corporate headquarters. Once the annual budget procedure is completed and the budget is accepted and approved, the division managers have complete authority to operate within the limits prescribed by the budget.

The budget procedures apply to the R&D Division. However, because this division does work for other Lymar divisions and for the corporate office, careful coordination between the R&D Division and the other units is needed to construct a good budget for the R&D Division. Further, the costs associated with the contract research require special consideration by Lymar's management. In the past, there has been good cooperation that has resulted in sound budget practices.

R&D's management has always presented well-documented budgets for both the internal and external contract research. When the submitted budget has been changed, the revisions are the result of review, discussion, and agreement between R&D's management and corporate management.

Staff travel is a major item included in R&D's budget. Some 25 to 35 trips are made annually to corporate headquarters for meetings by R&D's employees. In addition, the division's technical staff make trips related to their research projects and are expected to attend professional meetings and seminars. These trips have always been detailed in a supporting schedule presented with the annual budget.

Lymar's performance for the current year is considered reasonable in light of current and expected future poor economic conditions, but corporate management has become extremely cost conscious. Divisions have been directed to cut down on any unnecessary spending. A specific new directive has been issued stating that any travel in excess of $500 must now be approved in advance by corporate headquarters. In addition, once a division's total dollar amount budgeted for travel has been spent, no budget overruns will be allowed. This directive is effective immediately, and corporate management has indicated that it will continue to be in effect for at least the next two years.

The R&D manager is concerned because this directive appears to represent a change in budget policy. Now, travel that was thought already approved because it was included in the annual budget must be reapproved before each trip. In addition, some scheduled trips that were previously approved may have to be cancelled because travel funds are likely to run out before the end of the year. R&D staff members have already had to make five special trips to corporate headquarters that were not included in the current year's budget.

The new directive will probably increase costs. The approval process may delay the purchase of airline tickets, thus reducing the opportunity to obtain the lowest fares. Further, there will be a major increase in paperwork for the R&D Division because virtually every trip exceeds the $500 limit.

Required:

a. The directive requiring the approval of all travel in excess of $500 could have far-reaching efforts for Lymar Products.
   i. Explain how this directive could affect the entire budget process, especially the validity of the annual budget.
   ii. Explain what effect this directive is likely to have on the care with which divisions prepare their annual travel budgets in the future.

b.   Explain what effect the directive on reapproval of travel costs is likely to have on the morale and motivation of the division manager and research staff of the R&D Division.

(CMA adapted)

PROJECTS

1.   Assume that you and two or three of your classmates are part of top management in one of the following types of organizations: a major automotive manufacturer, a major airline, a major advertising agency, or a major hospital. Obtain several current annual reports (if available) from a particular company of your choice, perform some library or Internet research, and do some creative thinking to prepare a research paper that answers the following questions about that company.
     a.   What should this type of company take into account when preparing yearly budgeting documents?
     b.   What are the differences in planning and budgeting in the different industries listed above?

2.   Assume that it is the first day of your managerial accounting class and your instructor has just been introduced. Following the introduction, the instructor indicates that it is time to prepare a "class budget" for the semester. The lecturer passes out the course outline that describes the material (and a weekly work schedule) to be covered during the semester. The outline also contains the following information:

Course Objectives

We have three primary objectives. They are to gain a fundamental understanding of and the ability to communicate to others the (1) technical aspects of managerial accounting; (2) role of accountants in organizations; and (3) behavioural implications of accounting information.

Use of Class Time

_____

Performance Evaluation

_____

You immediately note that the last two categories are blank. The instructor believes in a "participative" course plan. Your task is to complete the outline and submit it to your instructor for approval. In completing the outline, be mindful of the course objectives and remember that you are helping to establish the standard by which you will be evaluated.

3.   Prepare budgets for the illustrations in the chapter, using Microsoft® Excel®.

USING THE INTERNET

1.   Go to www.cbsc.org/osbw.
     Click on English.
     Click on Planning Fundamentals.
     Click on Preparing a Cash Flow Forecast.

     Answer the following:
     a.   Why should you prepare a cash flow forecast?
     b.   How do you get started?
     c.   How do you make the best use of your cash flow?
     d.   How do you design a cash flow worksheet?

2. Find out more about REL Consultancy Group, the company discussed in this chapter's On Site and Site Analysis sections.

    Go to www.relconsult.com.
    a. Click on the sidebars to answer the following:
        i.   Using REL Consultancy Group's benchmarking model, how do companies you have selected benchmark with each other?
        ii. What services does the company offer?
        iii. Who are the major clients of the firm?
    b. Click on "In The News." Read the article "Budgets on a Roll" and prepare a summary of the information in the article.

3. In the 1990s the "beyond budgeting" movement was born and gained momentum. It was assisted by enterprise resource planning systems such as those made by SAP and PeopleSoft and the general expansion of information technology into all aspects of our organizations and lives. Use the Internet to assess the development of beyond budgeting since the summer of 2002, when the section on beyond budgeting was written for this textbook. Is "beyond budgeting" being used in more or fewer organizations? Has it been successful? How has it changed? Is it still a radical notion? Do this assignment in groups of three, and prepare a report of four or five pages.

SOLUTIONS TO SELF-TEST QUESTIONS

1. d:

From April	$110,500
From March	38,000
From February	18,500
From January	6,400
Total	$173,400

2. c: $36,000 \times 1.5 = 54,000$

3. d: Production $= (16,500 \times \text{Variable cost}) + \$12,000$
    $= (16,500 \times \$7.00) + \$12,000 = \$127,500$

4. c: $700,000 \times 0.80 = \$560,000 \times 0.30 = \$168,000 + \$140,000 = \$308,000$

5. b:

$625,000 \times 80\% = \$500,000 \times 0.30$	$150,000
Cash $= \$625,000 \times 20\%$	125,000
Feb. $= \$650,000 \times 80\% \times 25\%$	130,000
March $= \$700,000 \times 80\% \times 40\%$	224,000
Total	$629,000

6. c: $(\$650,000 \times 0.40) - (\$650,000 \times 0.30 \times 0.40) + (\$700,000 \times 0.40 \times 0.30)$
    $= \$260,000 - \$78,000 + \$84,000 = \$266,000$

7. d: $\$650,000 \times 0.40 = \$260,000$

8. d: $\$70,000 + \$60,000 + \$45,000 + \$120,000 + \$90,000 = \$385,000$

    Variable operation (10% of March sales) $\$700,000 \times 0.10 = \$70,000$
    Advertising $= \$720,000 \div 12 = \$60,000$
    Insurance $= \$180,000 \div 4 = \$45,000$
    Taxes $= \$240,000 \div 2 = \$120,000$
    Salaries $= \$1,080,000 \div 12 = \$90,000$
    (Depreciation is not a cash disbursement)

9. b

10. a

ENDNOTES

1. REL Consultancy Group Web site (www.relconsult.com).

2. Randy Myers, "Budgets on a Roll," *Journal of Accountancy*, New York, December 2001, pp. 41–46.

3. R.E. Grisold, "How to Link Strategic Planning with Budgeting," *CMA Magazine*, July–August 1995, pp. 21–23.

4. Neil C. Churchill, "Budget Choice: Planning vs. Control," *Harvard Business Review*, July–August 1984, p. 150.

5. Kathryn Jehle, "Budgeting as a Competitive Advantage," *Strategic Finance*, Montvale, October 1999, pp. 54–57.

6. Diane Contino, "Budget Training: It's Overdue," *Nursing Management*, Chicago, August 2001.

7. James F. Brown, Jr., "How US Firms Conduct Strategic Planning," *Management Accounting*, February 1986, p. 55.

8. Neil C. Churchill, "Budget Choice: Planning vs. Control," *Harvard Business Review*, July–August 1984, p. 151.

9. Bruce R. Neumann, "Streamline Budgeting in the New Millennium," *Strategic Finance*, December 2001.

10. Ibid., pp. 44–49.

11. Phil Montgomery, "Effective Rolling Forecasts," *Strategic Finance*, Montvale, February 2002, pp. 41–44.

12. Ralph Drtina, Steve Hoeger, and John Schaub, "Continuous Budgeting at The Hon Company," *Management Accounting*, Montvale, January 1996.

13. These computations assume the company sells a single product. If the company sells multiple products, another variance will exist called the sales mix variance. This variance explains the change in budgeted revenue caused by selling a mix of products different from the expected. Sales mix is discussed in Chapter 3 on cost–volume–profit analysis. Sales mix variance computations require information on the estimated percentage of total expected sales for each product.

14. Kenneth A. Merchant, "How Challenging Should Profit Budget Targets Be?" *Management Accounting*, November 1990, pp. 46–48. Published by the Institute of Management Accountants, Montvale, NJ.

15. Leslie N. Masonson, ed., *Cash Management Performance Report*, Boston: Warren, Gorham & Lamont, January 1991, p. 1.

16. Most manufacturing entities do not produce only whole units during the period. Normally, partially completed beginning and ending in-process inventories exist. Consideration of partially completed inventories is covered in Chapter 4.

17. This concept was discussed in Chapter 2.

18. Chapter 10 covers the concepts and techniques of capital budgeting.

19. Henry R. Migliore and Douglas E. McCracken, "Tie Your Capital Budget to Your Strategic Plan," *Strategic Finance*, Montvale, June 2001.

20. Cosmo S. Trapani, "Six Critical Areas in the Budgeting Process," *Management Accounting*, November 1982, p. 54.

21. The cost of goods manufactured statement is discussed in Chapter 2.

22. Jeremy Hope and Robin Fraser, *Beyond Budgeting, White Paper*, Beyond Budgeting Round Table, CAM-I Europe, May 2001.

23. Russ Banham, "Revolution in Planning," *CFO Magazine*, August 1999.

24. Cathy Lazere, "Altogether Now," *CFO Magazine*, February 1998.

25. "Corporate Strategic Planning Suffers from Inefficiencies," Hackett Benchmarking PR Newswire, October 25, 1999.

26. Robert S. Kaplan and David P. Norton, *The Strategy Focused Organization*, Harvard Business School Press, 2001, p. 274.

27. Benchmarking Solutions, http://www.thgi.com/ppfax.htm

28. Gordon Pitts, "The Root of All Corprate Evil? The Budget," *The Globe and Mail, Canadian Business,* Saturday, 20 September 2003, p. 135.

29. Randy Myers, "Budgets on a Roll," *Journal of Accountancy*, New York, December 2001, pp. 41–46. Copyright © 2001 by the American Institute of Certified Public Accountants, Inc. Opinions of the authors are their own and do not necessarily reflect policies of the AICPA. Reprinted with permission.

30. Michael Senyshen, "Spreadsheet Superheroes," *CGA Magazine*, September–October 2002, pp. 24–30.

Chapter 10

Capital Asset Selection and Capital Budgeting

LEARNING OBJECTIVES

After reading this chapter, you should be able to answer the following questions:

1 How
do managers choose which capital projects to fund?

2 Why
do most capital budgeting methods rely on analyses of cash flows?

3 What
are the differences among payback period, the net present value method, profitability index, and internal rate of return?

4 How
do the underlying assumptions and limitations of each capital project evaluation method affect its use?

5 Why
are quality management, training, and research and development controlled largely by capital budget analyses?

6 Why
do managers occasionally need to quantify qualitative information in making capital budgeting decisions?

7 Why
are environmental issues becoming an increasingly important influence on the capital budget?

8 How
and why should management conduct a post-investment audit of a capital project?

9 How
does ERP impact capital budgeting?

10 What
calculations are necessary to control for the time value of money? (Appendix 10A)

11 How
is the accounting rate of return for a project determined? (Appendix 10B)

12 How
does capital cost allowance affect cash flows? (Appendix 10C)

www.petro-canada.ca

Petro-Canada

PETRO-CANADA is a major integrated Canadian oil company with two main operating sectors, Upstream and Downstream. Capitalizing on an exceptional business environment, Petro-Canada achieved record earnings of $1,024 million in fiscal 2002. The return on equity improved to 18.3 percent from 18.1 percent in 2001. Revenues increased from $5 billion in 1998 to $9.9 billion in 2002.

During fiscal 2000 the company established a clear game plan for performance improvement and growth, based on a sharp strategic focus, disciplined execution, and strong financial and organizational capacity. In 2000 the company began development of extensive oil sands leases with a start on construction of the first *in situ* production project.

Fiscal 2002 saw increased production from the Hibernia oil field. The Terra Nova oil field came up to full production in early 2002. The Oil Sands business expects strong growth from an integrated strategy that will produce and refine bitumen to finished products. Significant production increments are expected over the coming years, from both the Syncrude expansion and the *in situ* bitumen developments. The downstream business delivered strong results in spite of a difficult business environment of rising crude prices and weak margins. Maximizing plant reliability, high-grading the lubricant sales mix and growing sales while reducing operating costs are key elements of the drive toward first quartile performance.

Petro-Canada had an increase in retail fuel sales growth that outpaced the industry as a whole and a remarkable 30 percent increase in nonpetroleum sales at retail convenience stores.

Mr. Ron Brenneman, chief executive officer, knows that the future of Petro-Canada depends on obtaining and investing capital in projects that will generate cash and profits in years to come. He says "Our [Petro-Canada's] goal is to create shareholder value over the long term by maintaining a profitable base business and capitalizing on our superb opportunities for growth, delivering results through disciplined execution."[1]

SOURCE: Adapted by permission of Petro-Canada.

*A*ll firms, Petro-Canada included, must determine which investment opportunities to pursue from a virtually unlimited list of potential projects. The investment choices ultimately made by Petro-Canada managers will be reflected in the company's capital budget. Making investment decisions is one of the most important tasks managers must undertake; the ultimate success or failure of these decisions will be reflected in profits of future periods.

Organizational strategies include investments in physical or nonphysical assets that have uncertain future paybacks. This chapter provides the management tools for assessing the profitability of long-term strategic investments.

Investments are made in short-term working capital assets such as inventory and in long-term capital assets that are used to generate future revenues or cost savings. *Capital assets* provide production, distribution, or service capabilities lasting more than one year. Capital assets may be tangible, such as machinery and buildings, or intangible, such as capital leases and patents. And, as the News Note on page 577 indicates, expenditures that are not normally treated as capital assets should perhaps be treated as such when making decisions. It makes an argument for what should be included as a capital item.

The investment in capital assets often coincides with the execution of major strategies, such as development of new product lines or acquisitions of other companies. Capital investments are also associated with major management initiatives to improve competitive position, such as raising product or service quality through the acquisition of new technology. Other capital investments are made to maintain and support existing operations, such as replacing a worn-out delivery truck with a new van. Capital asset acquisition decisions involve long-term commitments of large amounts of money.

Making the most economically beneficial investments within resource constraints is critical to the organization's long-range well-being. Capital budgeting techniques are designed to enhance management's success in making capital investment decisions.

This chapter presents four methods used to analyze capital projects: payback period, net present value, profitability index, and internal rate of return. The role of the capital budget in managing quality, employee training, and research and development is discussed. Also covered in the chapter are some complexities of acquiring automated equipment, control of environmental costs, the need to include qualitative information in decision making, and the desirability of post-investment audits. In Appendix 10A are elementary concepts for measuring the time value of money. The accounting rate of return measure is discussed in Appendix 10B, and taxation and its effects on cash flows with respect to capital budgeting are covered in Appendix 10C.

capital asset
an asset used to generate revenues or cost savings by providing production, distribution, or service capabilities for more than one year

THE INVESTMENT DECISION

Capital budgeting is the process of evaluating long-range investment proposals for the purpose of allocating limited resources effectively and efficiently. The future activities, commonly referred to as **projects**, typically include the purchase, installation, and operation of a capital asset. Management must identify the investments that best support the firm as it works to fulfill its goals and objectives. This process requires answers to the following four basic questions:

1. Is the activity worth the investment?
2. Which assets can be used for the activity?
3. Of the suitable assets, which are the best investments?
4. Which of the best investments should the company choose?

capital budgeting
the process of evaluating long-range investment proposals for the purpose of allocating limited resources effectively and efficiently

project
a future activity, such as the purchase, installation, and operation of a capital asset

GENERAL NEWS NOTE

Advertising: Capital or Ordinary Expenditure?

Should the decision to commit funds to an advertising campaign be treated as a business expense and rationed as a component of a single year's working capital expenditure; or should advertising expenditures be analyzed as an investment with multiperiod effects utilizing a capital budgeting decision framework?[2]

For advertising to be financially effective, the message must be retained by the market audience for some period of time. Many studies have shown that advertising information is typically retained by consumers at various levels in memory. It therefore is possible to apply capital budgeting techniques to evaluate whether or not the advertising expenditures represent rational, or value maximizing, behaviour.[3]

So far as is known, no corporation puts advertising in its capital budget, but maybe it belongs there. Several parties say so.

- The stock market says it belongs there. It says the benefits derived from promotional outlays are just as capitalizable as the tangible assets that the bookkeeper does capitalize.
- Corporation presidents say it belongs there, especially when they evoke investments in advertising to justify poor current operating profits.
- New entrants into an industry say it belongs there. They say it by including the promotional outlays required to build brand-acceptance as an integral part of the total investment required to break into a business.
- Antitrust economists say it belongs there. They say it by viewing brand acceptance built up by promotion, is just as substantial a barrier to entry as the investment required in buildings and machinery.[4]

Is the Activity Worth the Required Investment?

LEARNING OBJECTIVE 1

How do managers choose which capital projects to fund?

Companies acquire assets that have value relative to specific organizational activities. For example, oil companies acquire pipelines to move their products to large markets economically. Before making decisions to acquire assets, company management must be certain that the activity for which the assets will be needed is worth the required investment.

Pipelines are valuable capital assets for oil companies. These snake-like networks wind over water or fields of snow and ice to move oil, gas, and other refined products from drilling sites to processing or distribution points.

Management initially measures an activity's worth by monetary cost–benefit analysis. If an activity's financial benefits exceed its costs, the activity is, to that extent, considered worthwhile. In some cases, however, benefits cannot be measured in terms of money. In other cases, it is known in advance that the financial benefits will not exceed the costs. An activity meeting either of these criteria may still be judged worthwhile for some qualitative reasons.

For instance, an oil company may invest in advanced systems in its downstream (retail) operations to sell gasoline. Rather than requiring the customer to pay a cashier for gasoline purchases, the customer can simply use the automated equipment to scan a credit or debit card. The result is lower labour costs for the oil company and greater convenience for the customer. Oil company management may not be able to measure the monetary benefits of the automated equipment objectively but may believe that it is worth the cost because it provides access to a specific market segment. Another example is a rural hospital that invests in a kidney dialysis machine although there are only a few kidney patients in the area. Hospital administrators may believe the goodwill generated by such an acquisition justifies the cost. If an activity is deemed worthwhile, the question of cost may become secondary.

Which Assets Can Be Used for the Activity?

Selecting the assets for conducting the intended activity is closely related to assessing the activity's worth. As with many managerial decisions, part of the decision process is a comparison of costs and benefits. Management must estimate the cost of the proposed investment to determine if the activity should be pursued. Managers should gather monetary and nonmonetary information about each available and suitable asset. As shown in Exhibit 10-1, this information includes initial cost, estimated life and salvage value, raw material and labour requirements, operating costs (both fixed and variable), output capability, service availability and cost, maintenance expectations, and revenues to be generated (if any).

Of the Suitable Assets, Which Are the Best Investments?

In judging the acceptability of capital projects, managers should recognize that there are two types of capital budgeting decisions: screening and preference. A **screening decision** indicates whether a capital project is desirable based on some previously established minimum criterion or criteria. If the project does not meet the minimum standards, it is excluded from further consideration. Once unacceptable projects have been screened out, a **preference decision** is made in which the remaining projects are ranked based on their contributions to the achievement of company objectives.

Many companies set up ranking categories such as those shown in Exhibit 10-2 on page 580. Projects are first screened and placed into an appropriate category. Within each category, projects are ranked according to some established criterion or criteria. Resources are then allocated to projects in a top-to-bottom fashion. Management's goal should be to fund those projects that, within budget constraints, will maximize shareholder wealth over the long run.

A company may use one set of techniques to screen projects as to acceptability and another set to rank the projects in order of preference. The method of choosing techniques to be used for screening and ranking varies among companies. Additionally, most large companies have committees to discuss, evaluate, and

screening decision
a judgment regarding the desirability of a capital project based on some previously established minimum criterion or criteria

preference decision
a judgment regarding how projects are to be ranked based on their impact on the achievement of company objectives

EXHIBIT 10-1
Capital Investment Information

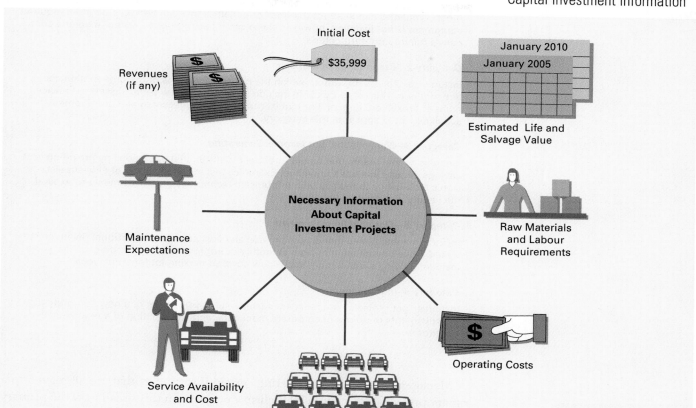

approve capital projects. In small companies, the owner–managers may simply decide on capital projects.

Which of the Best Investments Should the Company Choose?

Although many worthwhile investments exist, resources at any given time are limited. Therefore, after choosing the best asset for each activity, management must decide which activities and assets to fund. Investment projects may be classified as mutually exclusive, independent, or mutually inclusive.

Mutually exclusive projects are alternative projects that perform the same basic task. When one project is selected from the group, all others will be rejected, as they would provide unneeded or redundant capability. Asset replacement decisions are mutually exclusive projects. If the company keeps the old asset, it will not buy the new one; if the new one is purchased, the old one will be sold.

Other potential investments are **independent projects** in that they have no specific bearing on one another. For instance, acquiring a microcomputer system is not related to purchasing an automated teller machine. Each project is analyzed and accepted or rejected on its own merits. Although limited resources may preclude the acquisition of all acceptable projects, these projects are not mutually exclusive.

mutually exclusive projects
a set of proposed investments for which there is a group of available candidates that all perform essentially the same function or meet the same objective; from this group, one is chosen and all others are rejected

independent project
an investment project that has no specific bearing on any other investment project

EXHIBIT 10-2

Ranking Categories for Capital Projects

Category 1—Required by Legislation

Includes items such as safety equipment and environmental protection equipment. Most companies can ill afford the fines or penalties that can be assessed if the required equipment is not installed; however, these capital acquisitions may not meet the company's minimum return criteria.

Category 2—Essential to Operations

Includes capital assets without which the primary functions of the organization could not continue. This category could include purchases of new capital assets or replacement of broken equipment. For high-technology firms, research and development activities would appear in this category.

Category 3—Nonessential but Income Generating

Includes capital assets that would improve organizational operations by providing cost savings or supplements to revenue. Examples include acquisitions of efficient electronic technology to replace labour-intensive technology and investments to expand the variety of a product line.

Category 4—Optional Improvements

Includes capital assets that do not provide any cost savings or additional revenues but would make operations run more smoothly or improve working conditions. Examples include building a break room and a new covered parking lot for employees.

Category 5—Miscellaneous

Includes "pet projects" of managers such as the development of a new corporate logo, improvements to offices of corporate managers, and construction of a new executive washroom.

---

mutually inclusive projects
a set of proposed investments that are all related to a primary project; when the primary project is chosen, all related investments are also selected

Management may be considering certain investments that are all related to a primary project, or are **mutually inclusive projects.** In this situation, if the primary project is chosen, all related projects are also selected. Alternatively, rejection of the primary project requires rejection of the other related projects. For instance, Petro-Canada expects to spend a record $2.6 billion in 2003 on capital projects but has warned that $415 million earmarked for the start of two oilsands projects that would eventually be worth $5.25 billion remains unclear because of the Kyoto Accord.[5]

Exhibit 10-3 shows a typical investment decision process. To assure that capital funds are invested in the best projects available, managers must carefully evaluate

---

EXHIBIT 10-3

Typical Investment Decision Process

Deciding on a New Delivery System—What Is Involved?

1. Is the activity worth the investment? Yes, the costs of the current product delivery system are causing a decline in profits even as product sales in the area are growing at a rate of 10% per year.
2. Which assets can be used for the activity? *Traditional freight modes*: purchase trucks or railroad tankers. *Other available technology*: lease a pipeline or build a pipeline.
3. Which assets are the best investments? Compare all relevant information and choose the best asset candidate from the alternatives. Because the alternatives are mutually exclusive, only one method can be selected. Assume construction of a new pipeline is the preferred alternative.
4. Which investment should the company make? Compare the best asset candidate to the current method of product delivery. This is a mutually exclusive project decision that requires selection of only one delivery mode. Based on an analysis of relevant costs and revenues, either the present delivery contract with the independent freight company will be maintained or the pipeline will be constructed.

Conclusion: Building a new pipeline will result in substantial cost savings over the next 50 years. This alternative is selected.

all projects and decide which ones represent the most effective and efficient uses of resources—a difficult determination. The evaluation process should consider and rank projects based on business activity priorities, project risk, and project cash flows.

Corporate financial professionals should recognize that capital asset decisions are the most irrevocable long-range activities because they (a) involve significant corporate funding, (b) are the least flexible in terms of changing the strategic direction of the business, (c) are the least flexible for conversion into more liquid assets, (d) may geographically impact the long-term raw material supply capability of the business, (e) may geographically impact the business's long-term customer access, and (f) involve decisions about assets that are unique to the company. Since the unique features of capital assets represent the source of a company's product individuality and position in the marketplace, capital decisions must support the company's strategic plans.[6]

CASH FLOWS

LEARNING OBJECTIVE 2

Why do most capital budgeting methods rely on analyses of cash flows?

A strategic investment is expected to earn some type of return. The amount of the return allows analysts to equate diverse investments, such as oil exploration projects, an investment in marketable securities (bonds or shares), and an investment in an operating asset (refinery). In each case, money is spent and money—in the form of future revenues, cash dividends, or cash generated from use—is returned (it is hoped). Information on the cash generated from asset use is not available from the income statement because it reflects accrual-based revenues and expenses—not all of which may currently be realized as cash. It is the expected cash return on investments that drives individuals and firms to purchase capital assets. Consequently, it is the cash expenditures and cash receipts associated with potential capital assets that are the major focus of investment analysis.

Cash flows are cash receipts and cash disbursements that arise from the purchase, operation, and disposition of capital assets. Cash receipts include project revenues that have been earned and collected, savings generated by reduced project operating costs, and inflows from the asset's sale and release of working capital at the end of the asset's useful life. Cash disbursements include expenditures to acquire the asset, additional working capital investments, and amounts paid for related operating costs.

cash flow
the receipt or disbursement of cash

Interest is a cash flow created by the method used to finance a project and should not be considered in project evaluation. The funding of projects is a financing, not an investing, decision; cash flows of the two types of decisions should not be combined. A **financing decision** is a judgment regarding how funds will be raised to make an acquisition. Financing is based on the entity's ability to issue and service debt and equity securities. In contrast, **investing decisions** are judgments about which assets will be acquired by an entity to achieve its stated objectives. Company management must justify the acquisition and use of an asset before justifying the method of financing that asset.

financing decision
a judgment regarding how funds will be obtained to make an acquisition

investing decision
a judgment regarding which assets an entity will acquire to achieve its stated objectives

Cash flows from a capital project are received and paid at different times in a project's life. Within each period, some cash flows occur at the beginning (for example, a payment on a leased asset) and some at the end (for example, a payment on a mortgaged asset). Although many cash flows occur during the period, analysts simplify reality by assuming that flows occur either at the beginning or the end of the period during which they actually occur. Assumed end-of-period cash flows include inflows provided by contribution margins from product sales and outflows for repair expenditures and property taxes on the capital asset.

A distinction must be made between cash flows representing a return of capital and those representing a return on capital. A **return of capital** is the recovery of the original investment, while a **return on capital** represents income. The return on capital is computed for each period of the investment's life and is equal to the interest included in the receipt or payment. The usual period of analysis is a year. An investment makes a company better off only when, over the life of the investment, it produces cash inflows greater than the investment made plus the cost of the investment capital.

The calculation of cash flows is illustrated by the following example. Canada Oil Ltd. is considering purchasing a fleet of trucks to move jet fuel from the refinery to a pipeline terminal located 64 kilometres from the refinery. Currently the jet fuel is transported by an independent truck freight company. Data relating to the project appear in Exhibit 10-4. This detailed information can be simplified into two basic cash flows: a net negative flow representing the acquisition of the new equipment and a net positive flow representing the net annual cost savings from reduced operating expenses. The savings provided by the new trucks do not represent new cash flows into the company (as would occur with the sale of a product, for example). The savings do, however, represent a decrease in cash outflows—an equally beneficial situation.

Note that depreciation is excluded in these cash flow computations. In Canada, financial accounting depreciation is not allowable for tax purposes; **Capital Cost Allowance (CCA)** as set out in the *Income Tax Act* is used. Neither depreciation nor Capital Cost Allowance is a cash flow item. Capital Cost Allowance is important in capital budgeting only to the extent that it reduces the amount of taxable income and thus reduces the amount of taxes that will be payable. Income taxes and the related capital cost allowance effect are important elements in capital budgeting analysis, but they add unnecessary complexities at this point. These elements are discussed in Appendix 10C.

One helpful tool for analyzing cash flows is a **timeline**, which illustrates the timing of expected cash receipts and payments. On a timeline, cash inflows are shown as positive amounts and cash outflows are shown as negative amounts. The following timeline represents the cash flows from Canada Oil Ltd.'s truck fleet purchase. Information related to this purchase is presented in Exhibit 10-4. Although individual cash flows can be shown in a timeline, it is easier to use net cash flows. Thus, only two types of cash flows are shown: the net negative flow for the acquisition and the net positive flow produced each year by the cash operating savings. The equal annual cash flows are called an annuity. The data are shown in thousands of dollars.

Time:	t_0	t_1	t_2	t_3	t_4	t_5	t_6
Amount:	−$2,400	+$600	+$600	+$600	+$600	+$600	+$1,300

On a timeline, the acquisition date is time point 0 (t_0). Each year thereafter is a period. Periods only serve to separate the times at which flows occur; nothing is presumed to happen during a period. Thus, for example, the net savings provided by the truck fleet purchase each year are shown as occurring at the end of, rather than during, the time period. A less conservative assumption would show the cash flows occurring at the beginning of the period. In period 6, the salvage value of $700,000 is included with the cash operating savings of $600,000 to create a total cash inflow of $1,300,000.

return of capital
recovery of the original investment

return on capital
income equals the discount rate times an investment amount

Capital Cost Allowance
tax depreciation

timeline
illustration of the timing of expected cash receipts and payments; cash inflows are shown as positive amounts and cash outflows are shown as negative amounts

Purchase price of 20 trucks, trailers, and equipment	$ 1,800,000
Cost of custom modifications	600,000
Total cash acquisition cost	$ 2,400,000
Annual cash cost of hiring freight company to move product	$ 3,200,000
Annual cash operating costs of company-owned fleet	(2,600,000)
Annual cash operating savings	$ 600,000

Expected life of the truck fleet is six years. At the end of the sixth year, the trucks are expected to have a salvage (residual) value of $700,000.

EXHIBIT 10-4

Truck Fleet Acquisition Decision

PAYBACK PERIOD

The information on the timing of net cash flows is an input to a simple and often used capital budgeting analysis technique called **payback period**. This method provides a measure of the time it will take a project's cash inflows to equal the original investment. At the end of the payback period, a company has recouped its investment.

In one sense, payback period measures a dimension of project risk by focusing on timing of cash flows. The assumption is that the longer it takes to recover the initial investment, the greater is the project's risk, because cash flows in the more distant future are more uncertain than near-term cash flows. Another reason for concern about long payback periods relates to capital reinvestment. The faster capital is returned from an investment, the more rapidly it can be invested in other projects.

When a project provides an **annuity** cash inflow, the payback period equals the investment cost divided by the amount of the projected annuity inflow. The payback period for Canada Oil Ltd.'s truck fleet is four years ($2,400,000 ÷ $600,000).

To determine the payback period for a project having unequal cash inflows, it is necessary to accumulate the projected cash flows until the original investment is recovered. For instance, consider a project costing $58,000 and providing the following cash flows over its life:

Year	Amount
1	$12,000
2	18,000
3	22,000
4	24,000
5	16,000
6	5,000

A yearly cumulative total of the above inflows is prepared:

Year	Amount	Cumulative Total
1	$12,000	$12,000
2	18,000	30,000
3	22,000	52,000
4	24,000	76,000
5	16,000	92,000
6	5,000	97,000

At the end of the first three years, $52,000 has been received, and $6,000 more is needed to recover the original $58,000 investment. If the $24,000 inflow in the fourth year is assumed to occur evenly throughout the year, it should take 25%

LEARNING OBJECTIVE 3

What are the differences among payback period, the net present value method, profitability index, and internal rate of return?

payback period
the time required to recoup the original investment in a project through its cash flows

annuity
a series of equal cash flows occurring at equal time intervals

($6,000 ÷ $24,000) of the fourth year to recover the rest of the original investment, giving a payback period for this project of three years and three months.

Company management typically sets a maximum acceptable payback period as part of its evaluation of capital projects. Different categories of capital projects may have different payback criteria. For example, research and development projects may have a required payback of 12 years, but equipment replacement projects may have a required payback of five years. Most companies use payback period as only one of several ways of judging an investment project—usually as a screening technique. Normally, after being found acceptable in terms of payback period, a project is subjected to evaluation by another capital budgeting technique. This second evaluation is performed because the payback period method ignores three important considerations: inflows occurring after the payback period has been reached, the company's desired rate of return, and the time value of money. These issues are incorporated into the decision process by use of discounted future cash flow values.

DISCOUNTED CASH FLOW METHODS

Money has a time value because interest is paid or received on funds.[7] For example, $1,000 received today has greater value than the same sum received one year from today, because that money can be invested at an interest rate that will cause it to accumulate to more than $1,000 by the end of one year. This fact encourages the use of discounted cash flow techniques in most capital budgeting situations.

discounting
the process of removing the portion of a future cash flow that represents interest, thereby reducing that flow to a present value amount

present value
the amount that a future cash flow is worth currently, given a specified rate of interest

Discounting future cash flows means reducing them to their present values by removing the portion that represents interest. This imputed interest amount is based on two considerations: the timing of receipts or payments, and the assumed interest rate. After discounting, all future values are stated in a common base of current dollars, or **present values (PVs)**. The future value of a cash flow will exceed the present value of the cash flow because the future value includes the interest component. All other factors being equal, the future value grows larger as both time and interest rate increase. Using present values of future cash flows occurring at different points in time allows managers to view all project amounts in common terms (present values). Cash flows occurring at the beginning of a project are already stated at their present values and do not need to be discounted.

Because current expenditures such as initial project investment are undiscounted in the capital budgeting process, it is extremely important for managers to obtain the best possible information about these cash flows. Next, the amounts and timing of future cash inflows and outflows must be carefully estimated. Managers need to consider all future cash flows—those that are obvious and those that might be hidden. Companies installing computer systems, for example, find that the highest costs are those that are not readily apparent: supplies, support, training, maintenance, and opportunity costs.

discount rate
the rate of return on capital investments required by the company; the rate of return used in present value computations

cost of capital
the weighted average rate that reflects the costs of the various sources of funds making up a firm's debt and equity structure

To discount the future cash flows appropriately, managers must estimate the rate of return on capital required by the company. This rate of return is called the **discount rate** and is used to determine the imputed interest portion of future cash receipts and expenditures. The discount rate should equal or exceed the company's **cost of capital (COC)**, which is the weighted average rate for the costs of the various sources of funds (debt and stock) that a firm's capital structure comprises.[8] For example, a company with a COC of 10% pays an annual average rate of 10% on each capital dollar to finance investment projects. To determine if a capital project is a worthwhile investment, this company should generally use a minimum rate of 10% to discount the project's future cash flows.

The Japanese are reputed to reject discounted cash flow (DCF) as an investment appraisal method. Instead, investments are assessed on their payback, which indicates when cash will become available for the next stage of development. Japanese companies look sideways at their competitors in order to assess investment necessity rather than forwards through the DCF telescope to assess investment desirability. This is argued to be a superior method of appraising investment in new technology.[9]

Three discounted cash flow techniques are the net present value method, the profitability index, and the internal rate of return. These methods are discussed and illustrated in the following subsections.

Net Present Value Method

The **net present value method** uses discounted cash flows to compare the rate of return on a project to the desired rate of return (discount rate). A discount rate may be selected that is unique to categories of projects because different types of projects may be viewed dissimilarly by management; and the discount rate may be adjusted up or down to compensate for unique underlying factors in alternative investment projects.

For instance, managers in multinational organizations may use cost of capital as the discount rate for domestic projects but use a higher rate for international investments. The higher rate compensates for the greater risks involved in those projects; greater risks may be associated with factors such as foreign exchange fluctuations and political instability. Managers may also raise or lower the discount rate to compensate for qualitative factors. For instance, an investment in high-technology equipment that would provide a strategic advantage over competitors might be discounted at a rate lower than the COC. This lower rate would provide higher present values for the cash flows and make it easier for such a project to be selected as a viable candidate for funding.

The NPV of a project is estimated by forecasting the project's annual cash flows during its expected life, discounting them back to the present at a risk-adjusted rate, then subtracting the initial start-up capital expenditure. Thus, a project's **net present value (NPV)** is the difference between the present values of all of the project's cash inflows and cash outflows.

The data provided in Exhibit 10-4 are used to illustrate the computation of net present value; the calculations are shown in Exhibit 10-5 on page 586. First, net present value is computed using a 10% rate and then recomputed based on a 14% rate.

The truck fleet acquisition project generates a positive net present value regardless of whether the 10% or 14% discount rate is used and thus is acceptable under either rate. NPV represents the net cash benefit or cost to a company acquiring and using the investment asset. Applying this criterion, whenever the NPV is zero or greater, the project is acceptable on a quantitative basis. If the NPV is zero, the actual rate of return on the project is equal to the desired rate of return. If the NPV is positive, the actual rate is greater than the desired rate. If NPV is negative, the actual rate of return is less than the desired rate of return. If all estimates are correct, the truck fleet acquisition being considered by Canada Oil Ltd. will provide a return of over 14%. The exact rate of return is not determined by the net present value method unless the NPV happens to be exactly equal to zero.

Exhibit 10-5 demonstrates that when the discount rate is set to 14%, a different NPV results than when 10% is selected as the discount rate. As the discount rate

net present value method
an investment evaluation technique that uses discounted cash flow to determine if the rate of return on a project is equal to, higher than, or lower than the desired rate of return

net present value
the difference between the present values of all of the project's cash inflows and cash outflows

EXHIBIT 10-5

Canada Oil Ltd.'s Fleet Acquisition Decision

Cash Flow Timeline

Time:	t_0	t_1	t_2	t_3	t_4	t_5	t_6
Amount:	−$2,400	+$600	+$600	+$600	+$600	+$600	+$1,300

NPV Calculation (assuming a 10% discount rate)

(1)	(2)	(3)	(4)	(5) = (3) × (4)
Description	Time	Cash Flow Amount	Discount[1] Factor	Present Value
Investment	t_0	$(2,400,000)	1.0000[2]	$(2,400,000)
Cash savings	$t_1 - t_5$	600,000	3.7908[3]	2,274,480
Cash savings & salvage	t_6	1,300,000	0.5645[4]	733,850
Net present value				$ 608,330

NPV Calculation (assuming a 14% discount rate)

(1)	(2)	(3)	(4)	(5) = (3) × (4)
Description	Time	Cash Flow Amount	Discount[1] Factor	Present Value
Investment	t_0	$(2,400,000)	1.0000[2]	$(2,400,000)
Cash savings	$t_1 - t_5$	600,000	3.4331[3]	2,059,860
Cash savings & salvage	t_6	1,300,000	0.4556[4]	592,280
Net present value				$ 252,140

[1] The factors used to compute the net present values are obtained from the present value tables provided in Appendix B at the end of the text.
[2] The discount factor of 1.000 indicates that no discounting occurs with respect to cash flows made at the start of a project.
[3] The annual cash savings for years 1 through 5 are treated as an annuity because the annual cash flow is identical for these years. In the first example, the discount factor is for a 10% rate; in the second example, the discount factor is for a 14% rate.
[4] The discount factor is for a single cash flow occurring in the sixth period. In the first example, the discount factor is based on a 10% rate and in the second example, the discount factor is based on a 14% rate.

---

rises, the NPV decreases; as the discount rate decreases, the NPV rises. Thus, each unique discount rate generates a unique NPV.[10]

The NPV is also sensitive to other assumptions made. Changes in the estimated amounts or timing of cash inflows and outflows affect the net present value of a project. The effects on the NPV of cash flow changes depend on the nature of the changes themselves. For example, decreasing the estimate of cash outflows causes NPV to increase; reducing the stream of the cash inflows causes NPV to decrease. When amounts and timing of cash flows change in conjunction with one another, it is impossible to predict the effects of the changes without calculating the results.

Although the net present value method does not provide the expected rate of return on a project, unless the computed NPV equals zero, it does provide information on how the actual rate compares with the desired rate. This information allows managers to eliminate from consideration any projects on which the rates of return are less than the desired rate.

The NPV method can be used to select the best project when choosing among investments that can perform the same task or achieve the same objective. However, when making investment comparisons, managers must use the same project life span for all projects under consideration. This is necessary because the funds released from a shorter-lived project can be used for another investment, which will generate additional dollars of revenues and create additional dollars of costs.[11]

Further, NPV should not be used to compare independent investment projects that do not have approximately the same original asset cost. Such comparisons favour projects having higher net present values over those with lower net present values without regard to uneven amounts of capital invested in the projects. Logically, companies should invest in projects that produce the highest return per investment dollar.

Profitability Index

Projects with different costs can be compared by use of a variation of the NPV method known as the profitability index (PI). The **profitability index (PI)** is a ratio of the present value of all cash flows occurring after time period 0 to the time period 0 net investment. The PI is calculated as follows:

profitability index
a ratio that compares the present value of net cash inflows with the present value of the net investment

$$\text{PI} = \text{Present value of net future cash flows} \div \text{Net investment}$$

Using a 10% discount rate, the PI of the truck fleet acquisition project of Canada Oil Ltd. is approximately 1.25, calculated as \$3,008,330 (\$2,274,480 + \$733,850) divided by \$2,400,000. The present value of the net future cash inflows is equal to the net present value of \$608,330 plus the investment cost of \$2,400,000.

An NPV of \$0 is the equivalent of a PI of 1. Accordingly, the general rule for project acceptability when the profitability index is used is that the PI should be equal to or greater than 1.00. Such a PI indicates that the present value of the expected net cash inflows is equal to or greater than the investment cost. Thus, Canada Oil Ltd. would consider the fleet acquisition an acceptable project.

The present value of the net future cash flows represents an output measure of the project's worth. This amount equals the cash benefit provided by the project, or the present value of future cash inflows minus the present value of future cash outflows. The present value of the investment represents an input measure of the project's cost. By relating these two measures, the profitability index gauges the firm's efficiency at using its capital. The higher the index, the more efficient are the firm's capital investments.

In some instances, the NPV and PI methods provide different conclusions as to the relative ranking of projects. For example, the NPV of Project A may be higher than the NPV of Project B, but the PI for Project B may be greater than that for Project A. In such a case, either of the following two conditions must exist for the PI to provide better information than the NPV. First, the projects must be mutually exclusive. Accepting one project must require rejecting the other. This condition would be met if, for example, Canada Oil Ltd. were considering the purchase of a truck fleet from alternative suppliers such as GM or Ford. Alternatively, the availability of investment funds must be limited. If Canada Oil Ltd.'s total capital budget is constrained by the availability of capital, buying the truck fleet might preclude investment in another project such as acquiring new refinery equipment.

Like the net present value method, the profitability index does not indicate an investment's expected rate of return. This measure is provided by the project's internal rate of return.

Internal Rate of Return

A project's **internal rate of return (IRR)** is its expected rate of return. The IRR is the discount rate that causes the NPV of a project to equal zero. This relationship can also be expressed as the discount rate that causes the present value of all cash

internal rate of return
the discount rate at which the present value of the cash inflows minus the present value of the cash outflows equals zero

inflows to equal the present value of all cash outflows. This relationship is shown in the following formula:

NPV = −Investment + PV of cash inflows − PV of other cash outflows
        0 = −Investment + [Cash inflows × Discount factor] − [Cash outflows ×
                Discount factor]

In evaluating a capital project, managers have information about the investment amount, cash inflows, and cash outflows. Thus, the only missing items in the formula are the discount factors that identify the specific discount rate (IRR).

When all cash flows after time period 0 compose an annuity, the NPV formula can be restated as follows:

NPV = −Investment + PV of annuity
        0 = −Investment + (Annuity cash flow × Discount factor)

Determining the internal rate of return involves substituting known amounts (investment and annuity) into the formula, rearranging terms, and solving for the unknown (the discount factor).

NPV = −Investment + (Annuity × Discount factor)
        0 = −Investment + (Annuity × Discount factor)
Investment = (Annuity × Discount factor)
Investment ÷ Annuity = Discount factor

The solution yields a discount factor for the number of annuity periods of project life at the internal rate of return. Tracing this factor in an appropriate PV table to its associated interest rate provides the internal rate of return.

To illustrate, consider a possible project that will cost $30,000 (initial investment) and produce annual net cash inflows of $4,600 for eight years. Assume there are no other cash flows. These values are substituted into the NPV equation, which is then solved for the present value factor.

NPV = −Investment + (Annuity × Discount factor)
        0 = −$30,000 + ($4,600 × Discount factor)
$30,000 = ($4,600 × Discount factor)
$30,000 ÷ $4,600 = Discount factor
6.5217 = Discount factor

The table of present values of an ordinary annuity (Table 2, Appendix B at the back of the text) will provide the internal rate of return. In the table, find the row representing the project's life (in this case, eight periods). Look across the row for the 6.5217 discount factor yielded by the equation. The IRR (or its approximation) is the rate at the top of the column containing the factor. The 6.5217 factor on row 8 falls between the discount factors for 4% (6.7327) and 5% (6.4632). Interpolation, a computer program, or a programmable calculator gives 4.78% as the IRR for this project, if all assumed project information holds true.[12]

When a project does not have equal annual cash flows, finding the IRR involves an iterative trial-and-error process. An initial estimate is made of a rate believed to be close to the IRR, and the NPV is computed. If the resulting NPV is negative, a lower rate is estimated, and the NPV is computed again. If the NPV is positive, a higher rate is tried. This process is continued until the net present value equals zero, at which time the internal rate of return has been found.

Because the NPV was found to be positive using a discount rate of 14% (from Exhibit 10-5), the next iteration uses a discount rate of 18%. The calculations follow.

NPV = −Investment + (PV of cash inflows) − (PV of cash outflows)
   = −$2,400,000 + ($600,000 × 3.1272) + ($1,300,000 × 0.3704) − $0
   = −$2,400,000 + $1,876,320 + $481,520 − $0
   = −$42,160

Because using 18% produces a negative NPV, the IRR must be between 18% and 14%. Because the NPV found using 18% as the discount rate is very close to $0, the IRR is much closer to 18% than it is to 14%. The next iteration uses 17% as the discount rate.

NPV = −$2,400,000 + ($600,000 × 3.1994) + ($1,300,000 × 0.3898) − $0
   = −$2,400,000 + $1,919,640 + $506,740 − $0
   = $26,380

The IRR is between 17% and 18%.

EXHIBIT 10-6

Trial-and-Error Determination of IRR for Canada Oil Ltd. Truck Fleet Investment

Exhibit 10-6 uses data given in Exhibit 10-5 for Canada Oil Ltd. to demonstrate this process. The truck fleet acquisition was shown to have an expected rate of return of more than 14% (since discounting at that rate resulted in a positive NPV). Exhibit 10-6 indicates a first estimate of 18% as the IRR for this project, but the NPV is negative at this discount rate. A second estimate of 17% is made, resulting in a positive NPV. Thus, the internal rate of return falls between 17% and 18%.

Once the IRR on a project is known, it is compared with the company's discount rate or a preestablished **hurdle rate**. A company's hurdle rate is the rate of return deemed by management to be the lowest acceptable return on investment. This rate should be at least equal to the cost of capital. It is typically the discount rate used in computing net present value amounts.

hurdle rate
the rate of return deemed by management to be the lowest acceptable return on investment

If a project's IRR is equal to or greater than the hurdle rate, the project is considered to be an acceptable investment. The higher the internal rate of return, the more financially attractive is the investment proposal. In choosing among alternative investments, however, managers cannot look solely at the internal rates of return on projects. The rate does not reflect the dollars involved. An investor would normally rather have a 10% return on $1,000 than a 100% return on $10!

ASSUMPTIONS AND LIMITATIONS OF METHODS

LEARNING OBJECTIVE 4

How do the underlying assumptions and limitations of each capital project evaluation method affect its use?

Each capital budgeting technique has its own underlying assumptions and limitations; these are summarized in Exhibit 10-7 on page 590. To derive the most success from the capital budgeting process, managers should understand the basic similarities and differences of the various methods and use several techniques to evaluate a project.

All of the methods share two limitations: (1) they do not consider management preferences about the pattern of cash flows, and (2) they use a single, deterministic measure of cash flow amounts rather than ranges of cash flow values based on probabilities. Management can compensate for the first limitation by subjectively favouring projects whose cash flow profiles better suit organizational preferences, assuming other project factors are equal. The second limitation can be overcome by use of probability estimates of cash flows. These estimates can be input into a computer program to determine a distribution of cash flows for each method under various conditions of uncertainty.

The previous examples of capital budgeting analysis have all ignored one major influence—taxation and its effects on cash flows. This topic is covered in Appendix 10C.

EXHIBIT 10-7

Selected Assumptions and
Limitations of Capital Budgeting
Methods

Assumptions	Limitations
Payback	
Speed of investment recovery is the key consideration	Basic method treats cash flows and project life deterministically without explicit consideration of probabilities
Timing and size of cash flows are accurately predicted	Ignores time value of money
Risk (uncertainty) is lower for a shorter payback project	Cash flow pattern preferences are not explicitly recognized
Ignores cash flows after payback	
Net Present Value	
Discount rate used is valid	Basic method treats cash flows and project life deterministically without explicit consideration of probabilities
Timing and size of cash flows are accurately predicted	
Life of project is accurately predicted	NPV does not measure expected rates of return on projects being compared
If the shorter-lived of two projects is selected, the proceeds of that project will continue to earn the discount rate of return through the theoretical completion of the longer-lived project	Cash flow pattern preferences are not explicitly recognized
	IRR of project is not reflected
Profitability Index	
Same as NPV	Same as NPV
Size of PV of net inflows relative to size of PV of investment measures efficient use of capital	Gives a relative answer but does not reflect dollars of NPV
Internal Rate of Return	
Hurdle rate used is valid	Does not reflect dollars of NPV
Timing and size of cash flows are accurately predicted	Basic method treats cash flows and project life deterministically without explicit consideration of probabilities
Life of project is accurately predicted	
If the shorter-lived of two projects is selected, the proceeds of that project will continue to earn the IRR through the theoretical completion of the longer-lived project	Cash flow pattern preferences are not explicitly recognized
	It is possible to calculate multiple rates of return on the same project
Projects are ranked for funding based on IRR rather than dollar size	
Accounting Rate of Return	
(presented in Appendix 10B)	
Effect on company accounting earnings relative to average investment in a project is a key consideration	Ignores cash flows
	Ignores time value of money
Size and timing of investment cost, project life, salvage value, and increases in earnings can be accurately predicted	Treats earnings and project life deterministically without explicit consideration of probabilities

INVESTING TO MANAGE QUALITY COSTS, TRAINING, AND RESEARCH AND DEVELOPMENT

Many important responsibilities of managers are directly or indirectly achieved by effective management of the capital budget. One such area of responsibility is quality management. In Chapter 7, control of quality was discussed in terms of managing four related costs: internal failure, external failure, appraisal, and prevention. Total quality cost is the sum of costs in these four categories. It is argued that management of quality costs requires analysis of tradeoffs among the categories. Specifically, spending greater amounts for prevention and appraisal are likely to lead to reductions in both failure cost categories.

Prevention and appraisal costs are both partly managed in the capital budget. For example, quality problems can be prevented by acquiring more sophisticated manufacturing technology and by training workers to use manufacturing techniques that reduce errors. Statistical quality controls can be applied to monitor operations and determine when acceptable error tolerances are exceeded.

Quality issues are rarely considered in isolation in capital budgeting decisions. In fact, quality may be a secondary issue in some capital budgeting decisions. To illustrate how quality considerations can be impounded in capital budget analysis, assume that Ace Lighting Company produces several products—one of which is a security light. Data for the security light follow.

Expected sales volume by future budget year follows:

Year	Sales Volume
2004 (t_1)	25,000
2005 (t_2)	40,000
2006 (t_3)	50,000
2007 (t_4)	20,000

By the end of 2007, the life cycle of the security light will be over. During the remaining life cycle of the product, assuming no changes in production methods are made, the unit production costs are expected to be as follows:

Direct labour	$ 9
Direct material	8
Variable overhead	7
Total variable production costs[13]	$24

Company management is evaluating the possibility of installing automated equipment that would reduce the cost of direct labour from $9 to $5 per unit. The equipment would cause variable overhead to increase by $1 per unit; no other costs or revenues would be affected (ignoring quality costs). Thus, variable cost would decrease by a net amount of $3 per unit. The estimated acquisition cost of the new equipment is $330,000 and it would be installed at the start of fiscal 2004. The timeline of cash flows for the project follows:

t_0	t_1	t_2	t_3	t_4
−$330,000	$75,000	$120,000	$150,000	$60,000

Assuming the company's cost of capital is 10%, the pretax NPV of the project is shown next.

Description	Time	Cash Flow	Discount Factor	Present Value
Investment	t_0	$(330,000)	1.0000	$(330,000)
Cash savings	t_1	75,000	0.9091	68,183
Cash savings	t_2	120,000	0.8265	99,180
Cash savings	t_3	150,000	0.7513	112,695
Cash savings	t_4	60,000	0.6830	40,980
Net Present Value				$ (8,962)

Based on the NPV, the project is unacceptable. However, assume that the new technology would generate many fewer defective products than the existing manual conversion process, and that the company inspects each light upon completion for defects. To simplify the example, assume any defective product produced is identified in the process of inspection; there are no external defects. Defective lights are scrapped because it is not economical to rework them. Under the manual production process, defects are produced at a rate of 2% of units sold. With the advanced technology, defects are estimated to be only 0.25% of units sold. The following table shows the potential savings in quality defect costs:

Year	Cost Savings
2004	$24 \times 25,000 \times (0.02 - 0.0025) = \$10,500$
2005	$24 \times 40,000 \times (0.02 - 0.0025) = \$16,800$
2006	$24 \times 50,000 \times (0.02 - 0.0025) = \$21,000$
2007	$24 \times 20,000 \times (0.02 - 0.0025) = \$ 8,400$

The timeline of revised cash flows for the project follows:

	t_0	t_1	t_2	t_3	t_4
Investment	-$330,000				
Labour savings		$75,000	$120,000	$150,000	$60,000
Quality cost savings		10,500	16,800	21,000	8,400
Total cash flow	-$330,000	$85,500	$136,800	$171,000	$68,400

Considering the quality cost savings, together with the labour savings, a new NPV can be calculated:

Description	Time	Cash Flow	Discount Factor	Present Value
Investment	t_0	$(330,000)	1.0000	$(330,000)
Cash savings	t_1	85,500	0.9091	77,728
Cash savings	t_2	136,800	0.8265	113,065
Cash savings	t_3	171,000	0.7513	128,472
Cash savings	t_4	68,400	0.6830	46,717
Net Present Value				$ 35,982

By considering the quality costs, the NPV of the proposed project has been increased dramatically. The project is now acceptable. If this example were expanded, many additional quality costs could be considered in the NPV framework. For example, external failure costs can be considered, such as warranty expense, customer returns, and loss of reputation. Savings from reducing inspections could also be considered.

Training costs also should be examined in the capital budget using discounted cash flow analysis. Much like investment in new equipment, training costs are incurred in the present to generate future benefits. Because the benefits of training can persist for the entire tenure of an employee, it is proper to regard training benefits as multi-period. Along with acquisition of advanced technology, providing training to employees is a fundamental tool to improve quality.

Like investment in new technology, investment in training results in an increase in prevention costs in the present, to be offset by future decreases in other quality

Learning something from a textbook is sometimes no substitute for on-the-job training. Investment in teaching employees how to do their jobs more effectively and efficiently pays off through higher quality products and fewer defects.

cost categories. Particularly, decreases in external and internal failure costs should result from effective training expenditures.

Although quality is certainly an important dimension of organizational performance that is partly managed by the capital budget, the capital budget may be even more important for managing research and development activities.

Managing Research and Development

Another major area of managerial responsibility that ties directly to capital budgeting is evaluation of research and development projects. Research and development (R&D) activities are necessary to generate the innovative products and services that will provide future revenues. As competition in the global market intensifies, the pressure to manage R&D activities effectively increases.

Because many firms competing in a given market today have developed effective R&D programs, the life cycles of many products have decreased. The reduction in life cycle is caused by one competitor introducing to the market a new product that is soon made obsolete by the new product introduction of a second competitor. Once an innovative product reaches the market, competitors can respond more quickly with products that meet or exceed the quality and features of the "innovative" product.

Sustainable success of a business's operations is product innovation. How effectively a business designs and executes its supply chain to support new product introduction will go a long way in determining its overall business success. Over the last 10 years, companies that have focused on redesigning their core business processes have achieved considerable improvements in performance. New product introduction places particular demands on the supply chain. In the race to be first to market with a new product, each week of delay can mean millions of dollars of lost revenue and profit.[14]

In this competitive game whose outcome depends on the pace of introducing new products, the generation of future profits critically depends on effective capital budget analysis. Research and development requires a commitment of cash and other resources in the present to reap cash inflows from sales of products in the future. Like all other capital projects, research and development activities should be managed using discounted cash flow techniques that relate the future cash inflows to the current outflows. Furthermore, the analysis must consider the fact that life cycles are likely to get shorter over time, requiring firms to recapture their investments quickly if new products are to be profitable. Although the strategy of the firm is the major driver of R&D, capital budget analysis is the major control tool.

In addition to R&D, the acquisition of high-tech assets that are related to quality initiatives, product life-cycle management, and new product development has a large role in determining the success of businesses today.

HIGH-TECH INVESTMENTS AND QUALITATIVE CONSIDERATIONS

One area of business investment in which uncertainty is extremely prevalent is that of high-technology equipment. Some of the most pressing investment decisions currently facing American companies are those related to the purchase of automated and robotic equipment.

High-technology equipment generally requires massive monetary investment. Justification of such equipment must include the numerous advantages from these investments, including significantly reduced labour costs, increased quality and quantity of production, shortened processing time, and increased utility and maintenance costs. Thus, significant thought should be given to the investment's tangible benefits (such as increased output) and intangible benefits (such as increased customer satisfaction with the quality of products). The grid shown in Exhibit 10-9 identifies some of the quantifiable and nonquantifiable benefits of high-tech capital equipment and their association with the short-term financial and long-term strategic objectives of the organization. As indicated in the News Note on page 595, many companies find high-tech projects (including investments in information technology) to be difficult to analyze quantitatively.

EXHIBIT 10-9

Characteristics of High-Technology Capital Projects

	Quantifiable	Nonquantifiable
Financial (shorter-term)	Material cost reduction Labour savings Inventory reduction Scrap/waste reduction Increased capacity	Setup reduction Elimination of non-value-added activities (moves; inspections) Reduced manufacturing lead time Reduced administration cycle time Increased plant safety
Strategic (longer-term)	Increased flexibility Improved quality Increased market share due to new product/innovation Price premiums due to shorter lead times	Improved employee morale Improved work environment Ability to attract better employees Perceived technology leadership Regulatory requirements met

Source: Chris Koepfer, "To Buy or Not to Buy—A New Look at Justifying Capital Equipment," *Modern Machine Shop*, November 1992, p. 72. Reprinted by permission of *Modern Machine Shop*, Gardner Publications Inc.

Measuring Up

GENERAL NEWS NOTE

Every CFO and accounting professional can do it in their sleep. Calculating a project's Return on Investment (ROI) is just part of "Business 101." When you ask accounting professionals if they require it for new Information Technology (IT) projects, the answer is yes—well, sort of. Evaluating the potential return on the investment in an IT project can be straightforward—at least in theory. When a CIO shows that a new system will cut costs and pay for itself after a couple of years, or that it will significantly improve efficiency at a reasonable price, top executives usually sign up and give them the green light. This is especially true of the more tactical IT projects, such as new applications that cut order-processing costs, or reduce production costs. But in other cases, some IT initiatives have become so important that companies are either not evaluating them with an ROI, or they're looking for new ways to measure ROI to take into account a project's strategic value.

Wait a minute! You mean there is somebody out there in our organization spending money (and sometimes a lot of it) on IT projects and there is no payback analysis? How can this be? It's quite simple. IT projects can be justified for a number of reasons without ever having considered the calculation of a ROI.

Tangible benefits are the ones that are easy to identify and quantify. They include the typical advantages like lowering head count, reducing inventory, or reduced processing costs. However, quantifying an intangible benefit like customer satisfaction or closing the books faster can be tough. And then there are the "strategic" benefits like increased market share that can be downright confusing. It takes more than the traditional set of flashcards to assemble the ROI for today's IT projects. It requires a new business view that the IT project is really its own business venture and that it requires its own set of books. That means building a careful plan with specific definitions, and then managing your project to that plan. If the project calls for intangible or strategic benefits, the plan should identify specifically what will be required to achieve that benefit. By valuing those activities, you are now on your way to gathering the data to perform the ROI analysis.

It's easy to measure the ROI of an IT application that reduces your back-office processing costs, more so than one that improves your customer's satisfaction. But as you struggle to come up with new ROI metrics that measure the ROI of IT projects, you will also need to take into account another key aspect of nearly all new IT E-business initiatives—cross-functional projects. The investments that you will need to make will come from different organizational buckets. Don't get tangled up in looking at the project as "just another IT project." In the emerging arena of E-business, any new ROI metric you develop must be flexible enough to adapt as your company's E-business ROI metrics need to reflect the traditional long-term vision of ROI.

Source: Reprinted from an article appearing in the March 2000 issue of *CMA Management* magazine by Preston Cameron, with permission of Certified Management Accountants of Canada.

Considerations in High-Tech Investment Analysis

LEARNING OBJECTIVE 6

Why do managers occasionally need to quantify qualitative information in making capital budgeting decisions?

Managers making decisions about investments in automated equipment or equipment that enhances product or process quality should make their capital budgeting analyses carefully. First, the discount or hurdle rate used should be chosen very thoughtfully. Although interest rates are fairly low at this time, managers often still set hurdle or discount rates between 12% and 14%. Such high rates severely penalize capital investments (such as flexible manufacturing systems) that require high initial investments and may take many years to achieve payback.

Second, both the quantitative and qualitative benefits to be provided by all capital expenditures need to be considered, especially high-tech ones. In making investment decisions, because of the difficulty in determining their worth, management has often assigned a zero dollar value to benefits such as reduced product development time, shortened delivery time, and improved competitive position. Some managers do attempt to quantify these qualitative factors in their analyses.

Robotic equipment can perform tasks much more rapidly and with higher quality than humans often can. Although quantifying some of the benefits of using automated technology may be difficult, not to do so is to ignore a very large part of why the equipment is being considered for purchase—hardly a rational attitude!

Quantifying every benefit is important because it overcomes the main excuse managers have for making investments without an evaluation.

A third item to consider in regard to high-tech investments is that such projects are not "free-standing." Many high-tech investments are interrelated, integrated parts of a whole and should not be viewed as individual projects. The benefits of the "bundled" project are greater than the benefits that would accrue from the individual elements. Consider that after General Motors made a multibillion-dollar investment in robots in the 1980s, the company failed to reengineer factories so the robots could be used to their full potential to produce "different models and innovative designs by the car lot. [Instead, the company simply] wound up using the robots as an inflexible substitute for labour."[15]

Finally, consideration should be given to the opportunity cost of not acquiring automated equipment. The opportunity cost of nonautomation refers to the competitive disadvantage a company will experience when its competitors acquire such equipment and experience the qualitative benefits mentioned earlier.

In making capital budgeting decisions, managers should quantify all benefits and costs that can be quantified with any reasonable degree of accuracy. Managers can also attempt to quantify the qualitative benefits using probabilities. The probabilities can be included in calculations of the investment's net present value or internal rate of return. Alternatively, management can simply make subjective evaluations of nonquantifiable items to make certain that those items are properly weighted in the decision model.

The hottest high-tech investments being made by manufacturers are flexible manufacturing systems (FMS) that use computer systems to produce numerous high-quality customized products at very low per-unit costs.

An example of such an investment can be found at SPM Tech of Brampton, Ontario. It is a sophisticated flexible manufacturing system that is boosting productivity at a small but fast-growing custom precision sheet metal fabricating shop. Central to the flexible manufacturing system is MARS technology from Amada Canada. This versatile system enables the company to take on virtually any job—

including high-volume production work. MARS can perform four operations at the same time, unattended: unloading sheet metal, punching, loading for the next job, and loading or unloading a pallet at the rear.

SPM's purchase of the system was only the third MARS bought in Canada. The first two went to shops in Quebec.

SPM co-owner Rodney Maltais says MARS reduces labour inputs and boosts efficiency without sacrificing quality or profitability. "MARS eliminates a lot of movement. It makes our productivity more reliable. For example, you know it will take three minutes to get material unloaded, and that someone won't spend 10 minutes doing it because they can't find the material."[16]

An FMS is not inexpensive, but the investment can pay for itself through increased sales at higher prices as well as lower costs.

Another area of growing importance to firms is the influence of their operations on the environment. The effect of operations on the environment can have substantial impacts on future costs. These effects can be partly controlled by capital budgeting decisions.

INVESTING TO MANAGE ENVIRONMENTAL COSTS

LEARNING OBJECTIVE   **7**

Why are environmental issues becoming an increasingly important influence on the capital budget?

The impact of organizations on the environment is becoming more of a concern to governments, citizens, investors, and businesses. Accountants are increasingly concerned with both measuring business performance with regard to environmental issues and managing environmental costs. In the future, investors are likely to evaluate a company's environmental track record, as well as financial record, in making investment decisions.

Management of environmental costs requires that environmental issues be considered in every aspect of operations. For example, environmental effects are related to the amount of scrap and by-products produced in manufacturing operations, the materials selected for product components (are they recyclable or not), the actions of suppliers who produce necessary inputs, and habits of customers in consuming and disposing of products and packaging. In short, environmental issues span the entire value chain. The following quote summarizes some of the major issues in managing environmental costs.

> Another dimension is added to the cost of a product: accounting for the future disposal cost of products produced now and in the past. North American companies will likely be held responsible for the ultimate reuse, remanufacturing, recycling, or proper disposal of the products they produce. To account for the effect of product take-back on product costing and capital investment, companies need to improve their identification and tracking of current and future environmental costs. A common hurdle is that current environmental expenditures often concern production completed decades ago. Through improved measurement and reporting of environmental impacts and the impacts related to product take-back, management accountants can dramatically improve management decision making and corporate profitability.[17]

The News Note on page 598 bears this out.

Petro-Canada, in its 2002 annual report, notes the following: "In 2002 we invested $318 million in environmental programs, including $90 million for operating expenses and $228 million in capital expenditures for facility upgrades. We expect environmental costs to remain high, as we prepare to meet new federal

GENERAL
NEWS NOTE

The Environment

An entirely different approach to environmental accounting is used by an oil and gas company in western Canada. In this company, environmental restoration cost estimates are included in the conservation–reclamation plan required by the provincial government when applying for the multi-year production permit. The costs, based on engineering estimates, are projected over the life of the project.

Total projected costs are amortized over the estimated number of barrels of oil. Environmental costs are then charged against income each year, based upon the number of barrels produced, with a corresponding long-term liability recognized in the balance sheet. Remedial expenditures in any particular year reduce this liability. The estimates are reviewed periodically, so that adjustment can be made in light of changes to cost projections, technology, and estimates of recoverable oil.

Although minimizing the impact of operations on the environment may be a reasonable goal, it must be remembered that some impact on the environment is unavoidable. For example, energy must be consumed to manufacture products; similarly, materials must be consumed as goods are produced. With no energy and material consumption, no goods can be manufactured.

In the management of environmental costs, accountants must analyze environmental dimensions of investment decisions. In the capital investment area, accountants can help managers by including quality and environmental benefits in the analysis. If a proposed project is more energy efficient or produces less pollution than an alternative, those factors should be included in the analysis. The financial data should include any cost savings from lower energy usage. If the company must control pollution, the financial impact should be recognized.

Source: Vanessa Magness, "Environmental Accounting in Canada," *CMA Magazine*, 71 (1), February 1997, pp. 15–18. For more information on this concept, see Frances Cairncross, *Costing the Earth*, Boston: Harvard Business School Press, 1992, p. 26; Harold P. Roth and Carl E. Keller, Jr., "Quality, Profits, and the Environment: Diverse Goals or Common Objectives?" *Management Accounting*, July 1997, pp. 50–55.

environmental limits for sulphur in gasoline, future fuel reformation issues, and tighter standards for oil and gas production."[18] The cost as a result of the Kyoto Protocol is yet to be determined.

On September 4, 2003, Petro-Canada announced that it will close its Oakville, Ontario, refinery by the end of fiscal 2004. Petro-Canada chief executive Ron Brenneman said, "We would have put some C$250 million to C$300M into Oakville to enable the facility to meet the new specifications for ultra low sulphur gasoline and diesel. Those new environmental standards are important for better air quality, but it did not make sense for us [Petro-Canada] to pour that kind of money into a small disadvantaged facility."[19]

In the management of environmental costs are embedded other topical managerial concerns discussed in this chapter: managing quality, research and development, and technology acquisition. Although the relationship between quality costs and environmental costs is not fully understood, many cases can be cited suggesting that quality and environmental costs are highly related. For example, it is easy to grasp that the reduction in scrap and waste production (quality improvements) serves to reduce environmental costs and concerns (waste disposal).

Through research and development, new products and production processes are identified, and new materials are developed. The design of new products influences (1) the types and quantities of materials to be produced, (2) the types and quantities of waste, scrap, and by-products to be produced, (3) the amount of energy to be consumed in the production process, and (4) the potential for gathering and recycling the products when they reach obsolescence.

Technology acquisition also has many impacts on the environment. For instance, technology affects energy consumption and conservation; environmental emissions; the quantity, types, and characteristics of future obsolete equipment (for instance, whether the equipment is made of materials that can be recycled); the rate of defective output produced; the quantities of scrap, waste, and by-products produced; and the nature and extent of support activities necessary to keep the technology operating.

After the capital budget has been prepared, it can be used as a control tool. The actual success of approved capital projects can be compared to the calculations made in the evaluation process. This is the role of a post-investment audit.

POST-INVESTMENT AUDIT

After a capital investment has been made, information on actual project results can be gathered and compared against expected results. This comparison, which is referred to as a **post-investment audit**, is also a means of assessing strategic success. This process is intended "to accomplish at least four primary objectives: serve as an important financial control mechanism, provide information for future capital expenditure decisions, remove certain psychological and/or political impediments usually associated with asset control and abandonment, and have a psychological impact on those proposing capital investments."[20]

The pressing need to invest capital wisely prompts the central financial office of most companies to anticipate, predict, and control the financial impacts of proposed operations improvement projects.

Follow-up, however, contains a deadly trap. Assessing actual numerical values for the cost and benefit items used for the original cost justification misses the point. Using the same methodology to trace actual costs and benefits that were used for the original projections also misses the point.[21]

Management should make the decision about when to have the post-investment audit. In cases where significant learning or training is necessary, start-up costs of the first year may not be appropriate indicators of future costs. Such projects should be given a chance to stabilize before the project audit is made. Once the project is stabilized, actual information about the costs and benefits of the project can be gathered and extrapolated to future periods. Such extrapolations allow the cash flows for the full life of the asset to be considered. Actual-to-expected cash flow comparisons should be made using the technique or techniques originally used to determine project acceptance, but such comparisons are not enough. Management should take action to find the causes of any adverse differences and the means, if possible, of remedying them.

As the size of capital expenditures increases, post-investment audits become more crucial. Although an audit cannot change a past investment decision, it can be used to pinpoint areas of operations that are not in line with expectations so that problems can be corrected at an early stage. Also, an audit will help managers evaluate the accuracy of the original cost/benefit predictions. Project sponsors may have been biased in favour of their projects. As a result, their forecasts of future revenues, cost savings, or expenses may have been overly optimistic. Individuals who provided unrealistic estimates should be required to explain all major differences. Furthermore, knowing that post-investment audits will be made may cause project sponsors to provide more realistic cash flow forecasts for capital requests in the future.

LEARNING OBJECTIVE 8

How and why should management conduct a post-investment audit of a capital project?

post-investment audit
a comparison of expected and actual project results after a capital investment

Performing a post-investment audit is not easy, for several reasons. First, actual information may be in a form different from that of the original estimates. Second, some project benefits may be difficult to quantify. Third, project returns vary considerably over time, so results gathered at one point in time may not be representative of the project. But regardless of the difficulties involved, post-investment audits provide managers with information that can help them to make better capital investment decisions in the future.

Capital Budgeting with Enterprise Resource Planning Systems

In organizations without enterprise resource planning (ERP) systems, capital budgeting analysis, as discussed in this chapter, considers all revenues and costs that are affected by the capital project for the foreseeable future. These revenue and cost items are placed on a spreadsheet for the expected life of the investment, and the net present value, internal rate of return, and/or payback are calculated. The project is accepted if it is economically viable relative to the available funds. Often, accepted projects are post-audited to determine whether they were as profitable as expected.

The approach to capital budgeting discussed in this chapter—or, in other words, pre-ERP capital budgeting—is *ad hoc* as there are no solid links between the data items on the spreadsheet and what has or may happen in the future at the organization. Pre-ERP capital budgeting focuses on the expected impact on the income statement and the balance sheet completely independently of the information systems of the organization.

Capital budgeting can be done differently in organizations with functioning ERP systems because of the integration of all subsystems. ERP systems, with their common unified data warehouses, are able to integrate, for example, financial transactions, activities in ABC and ABM subsystems, budgets and plans, and performance measures such as customer satisfaction or an entire balanced scorecard.

ERP systems impact capital budgeting at three stages: (1) the capital project preparation and approval stage, (2) the operational stage, and (3) the post-audit stage.

During the first stage, an ERP system will allow the revenue and cost items to be linked to actual activities. For example, if some of the costs are labour, the actual model for labour used in manufacturing a product will be accessed and improvements in labour productivity due to the new asset will be modelled. Modelling allows alternative approaches or variants to be tested and understood. Similarly, if there is a change in material usage, this will be modelled. ERP systems, in effect, allow capital projects to be modelled as mini independent businesses (i.e., investment centres, which are discussed in Chapter 11). These models are used to analyze the projects. For the second stage, the models can be accessed after the capital project is implemented to ascertain on an ongoing basis whether the assumptions were validated. Similarly, for the third stage, at or near the end of the capital project, the models can be accessed to do a post-audit to determine the success of the project and to provide feedback on the capital budgeting process.

The opportunity to plan a capital project from component activities up to the impact on the income statement and balance sheet is the main advantage of ERP systems. Capital projects are generally part of the internal processes of an organization. To understand and control a project, it is necessary to have a suborganizational form that is specific to the project and that is appropriately linked to all other organizational units involved. To be successful, project goals must be precisely described and the project activities to be performed must be structured. A project is structured in two ways: hierarchically and functionally. Hierarchically structured means that the involved divisions, departments, and units must be specified in order to collect costs and revenues. Functionally structured means that processes and activities must be specified.

Hyperion Activity Based Management (HABM) is software from Hyperion Solution Corporation that can be used with various ERP systems—SAP, PeopleSoft, Oracle, etc.—to undertake various analyses including capital budgeting. For capital budgeting projects, HABM can readily determine costs and profitability from actual activities performed and resources consumed.

In addition to capital budgeting, HABM, with its modelling applications, allows managers to evaluate proposed initiatives and new product ideas, and even complete business scenarios. HABM works by moving data from an ERP data warehouse to a separate analyses program and database (i.e., the Hyperion Essbase OLAP server). This allows HABM to combine operational and financial models with each other and with other sources, and make the results accessible to a large number of end users.

SITE ANALYSIS

Petro-Canada

Ron Brenneman, chief executive officer, knows that to ensure his firm remains as one of the leaders in the industry requires a great commitment to investing in growth opportunities. Capital spending levels have increased and fiscal 2003 will drive forward with a strategic plan aimed at achieving the full potential of the company's five core businesses.

Petro-Canada's capital expenditure budget for 2003 is $2.575 million, up 38 percent from expenditures of $1.861 million in fiscal 2002. It plans to spend $2.045 million on upstream work, $500 million on downstream activities, and $30 million on other projects. The capital budget will also continue to advance oil sands development as well.

Ron Brenneman is very excited about the future for Petro-Canada. He feels the company has accomplished a great deal during the past year (2002) and stresses that there is much more potential to realize. He says, "As we move through 2003, I am confident that we will continue on that path." The company has excellent assets, superb growth opportunities, financial strength, and a skilled, dedicated workforce.[22]

More success is in reach.

APPENDIX 10A

Time Value of Money

LEARNING OBJECTIVE 10

What calculations are necessary to control for the time value of money?

future value
the amount to which one or more sums of money invested at a specified interest rate will grow over a specified number of time periods

simple interest
interest calculated as a percentage of only the original investment, or principal amount

compound interest
interest earned in prior periods is added to the original investment so that, in each successive period, interest is earned on both principal and interest

compounding period
the time from one interest computation to the next

The time value of money can be discussed in relation to its future or its present value. **Future value (FV)** refers to the amount to which a sum of money invested at a specified interest rate will grow over a specified number of time periods. Present value (PV) is the amount that a future cash flow is worth currently, given a specified rate of interest. Thus, future and present values depend on three things: (1) amount of the cash flow, (2) rate of interest, and (3) timing of the cash flow. Only present values are discussed in this appendix, since they are most relevant to the types of management decisions discussed in this text.

In computing future and present values, simple or compound interest may be used. **Simple interest** is calculated as a percentage of the original investment, or principal amount, only.[23] With **compound interest**, interest earned in prior periods is added to the original investment so that, in each successive period, interest is earned on both principal and interest. The time from one interest computation to the next is called the **compounding period**. The more often interest is compounded, the higher is the actual rate of interest being received, relative to the stated rate. The following discussion assumes compound interest, since most transactions use this method.

Interest rates are typically stated for an annual period. If compounding occurs more often, the annual interest rate must be divided by the number of compounding periods per year to get the interest rate per compounding period. The number of years multiplied by the number of compounding periods per year provides the total number of interest periods. For example, if 14% interest is to be received each year for five years and the compounding period is semiannual, the rate per compounding period is 7% (14% ÷ 2), and the total number of interest periods is 10 (5 years × 2).

Present Value of a Single Cash Flow

Assume that Christina Kim knows that her bank pays interest at 4% per year compounded semiannually. Christina wants to have $1,126 in three years and wants to know what amount she must invest now to realize that sum. A table of factors for the present value of $1 (Table 1 in Appendix B at the end of the text) for a variety of i and n values can be used to solve this problem:

$$PV = FV \text{ (discount factor for } i \text{ and } n\text{)}$$

where PV = present value of a future amount
  FV = future value of a current investment
  i = interest rate per compounding period
  n = total number of compounding periods

The discount factor is obtained from Table 1 using the known interest rate of 2% and the six discount periods. Substituting known values into the formula gives the following:

$$PV = \$1,126 \, (0.8880) = \$1,000 \text{ (rounded)}$$

The rate of return used in present value computations is called the discount rate. In capital budgeting, future amounts normally need to be converted to present values. The process of discounting is merely the reverse of the process of compounding.

Present Value of an Annuity

An annuity is a series of equal cash flows. In an **ordinary annuity** (such as bond interest), the first cash flow occurs at the end of the first period. In contrast, the cash flows from an **annuity due** occur at the beginning of a period. A lease payment made at the beginning of the month for the upcoming month is one cash flow of an annuity due. Each equal cash flow of an annuity is called a **rent**.

To illustrate the computation of the present value of an annuity, consider the following situation. A donor is planning to give your university a charitable contribution of $5,000 at the end of each of the next five years. The university would prefer to have the money now to invest in a project that will earn 6% compounded annually. The donor is willing to give the university a lump sum amount now but refuses to give the entire $25,000. University administrators need to know what amount represents the current equivalent of the $5,000 per year cash flow in the future. The following timeline presents the situation:

Time	0	1	2	3	4	5
Future Value		$5,000	$5,000	$5,000	$5,000	$5,000
Present Value	?	(using the desired 6% interest rate)				

The present value of each single cash flow can be found by use of the 6% discount factors from Table 1 in Appendix B as follows:

PV of first receipt	$5,000 (0.9434)	$ 4,717
PV of second receipt	$5,000 (0.8900)	4,450
PV of third receipt	$5,000 (0.8396)	4,198
PV of fourth receipt	$5,000 (0.7921)	3,961
PV of fifth receipt	$5,000 (0.7473)	3,737
Total present value		$21,063

The present value factor for an ordinary annuity can be determined by addition of the present value factors for all periods having a future cash flow. Alternatively, Table 2 in Appendix B provides factors for the present value of an ordinary annuity at various interest rates and time periods. From this table, the factor of 4.2124 can be obtained. Multiplying by $5,000 yields the same result as above (absent any rounding errors).

If this had been an annuity due problem, the ordinary annuity discount factors could have been converted to annuity due discount factors. Using one less time period and adding 1.000 to the annuity discount factor given would achieve this conversion. For example, assume that the donor wanted to give the university $5,000 per year for five years, beginning immediately. The following timeline reflects the cash flows, and the calculation of the present value (using 6% and four periods) is also given.

Time	0	1	2	3	4
Future Value	$5,000	$5,000	$5,000	$5,000	$5,000

Present Value   ?   (assuming a 6% interest rate)

PV = $5,000 (1 + 3.4651) = $22,326

ordinary annuity
an annuity in which each cash flow occurs at the end of the period

annuity due
an annuity in which each cash flow occurs at the beginning of the period

rent
each equal cash flow of an annuity

APPENDIX 10B

Accounting Rate of Return

How is the accounting rate of return for a project determined?

accounting rate of return
the rate of accounting earnings obtained on an average capital investment (or initial investment) over a project's life

The **accounting rate of return (ARR)** measures the expected rate of earnings on the average capital investment over a project's life. This evaluation method uses the projected net income amount shown on accrual-based financial statements and is a return on investment formula for a single project. It is the one evaluation technique that is not based on cash flows. The formula to compute the accounting rate of return is:

$$\text{ARR} = \text{Average annual income from project} \div \text{Average investment in project (or initial investment)}$$

Average annual net income is net of depreciation. Project investment includes original cost and project support costs, such as those needed for working capital items (for example, inventory). Investment, salvage value, and working capital released at the end of the project's life are summed and divided by 2 to obtain the average investment.[24]

To illustrate the computation of the accounting rate of return, consider information for a piece of equipment being analyzed by Canada Oil Ltd. Data on the potential investment are as follows:

Beginning investment	
Initial cost of equipment	$400,000
Additional working capital needed for the project	140,000
	$540,000
Return at end of project	
Salvage value of equipment at the end of 10 years	$40,000
Working capital released at the end of 10 years	140,000
	$180,000
Return over life of project	
Average incremental company profits after taxes	$ 88,000

Applying the formula for the accounting rate of return using the average investment gives

$$\text{ARR} = \$88,000 \div [(\$540,000 + \$180,000) \div 2]$$
$$= \$88,000 \div \$360,000 = 24.4\%$$

The project's 24.4% ARR can be compared with a preestablished hurdle rate set by management. This hurdle rate will most likely not be the same as the desired discount rate, since the data used in calculating the accounting rate of return are not cash flow data. Management may set the ARR hurdle rate at a higher level than the discount rate because the method does not account for the time value of money. In addition, the 24.4% accounting rate of return for this project should be compared with ARRs on other investment projects being considered by Canada Oil Ltd. to determine which projects have the highest accounting rates of return.

APPENDIX 10C

The Effect of Taxation on Cash Flows

Income taxes are a significant aspect of the business world. Tax planning is a central part of management planning and overall business profitability. Managers should give thorough consideration to the tax implications of all company decisions. In evaluating capital projects, managers should use after-tax cash flows to determine the projects' acceptability. It is only the amount of cash that remains after paying taxes that is available for management's use.

LEARNING OBJECTIVE 12

How does capital cost allowance affect cash flows?

Treatment of Depreciation for Tax Purposes

Depreciation is calculated yearly under GAAP to represent the benefits accrued to a business for using fixed assets for that period. Financial accounting uses useful life as the basis of the write-off of a capital expenditure, while the tax system might be based on legal life or fiscal policy. In Canada, for tax purposes, depreciation is not a deductible expense. In its place, the *Income Tax Act* allows for the deduction of Capital Cost Allowance (CCA) using rates set by the government. For tax purposes, assets are assigned to a class along with other similar assets. The calculation of CCA is similar to that for the declining balance method (a constant rate is applied to a declining value). Like interest on debt, Capital Cost Allowance on capital assets is deductible in computing taxable income. As taxable income decreases, so do the taxes that must be paid; thus, cash flow is affected. (See Exhibit 10-8 for examples of various classes of assets and their CCA rate.)

EXHIBIT 10-8

Classes of Assets for Tangible Capital Property

Classes for some of the more common assets are contained in the following list:

Class		
Class 1	4%	Most buildings or other structures, including component parts such as electrical wiring and fixtures, plumbing, heating and central air conditioning, acquired after 1987
Class 3	5%	Buildings or other structures, including component parts acquired before 1988 and limited costs of an addition or alteration made after 1988
Class 8	20%	Miscellaneous tangible capital property, such as furniture and fixtures and outdoor advertising signs (bought after 1987), and machinery or equipment, such as photocopiers, refrigeration equipment, telephones and tools costing $200 or more, not included in another class (i.e., general default class for tangible capital property)
Class 9	25%	Aircraft, including furniture or equipment attached to the aircraft, and spare parts
Class 10	30%	Automotive equipment, such as automobiles (except taxis and those used in a daily rental business), vans, trucks, tractors, wagons, and trailers, and general-purpose electronic data processing equipment with its systems software
Class 10.1	30%	A passenger vehicle with a cost in excess of the limit prescribed for paragraph 13(7)(g) (i.e., $30,000 if acquired after 2000)
Class 12	100%	Tools, instruments and kitchen utensils costing less than $200; linen, uniforms, dies, jigs or moulds; rental video cassettes; computer software
Class 13	100%	Leasehold interest
Class 14	100%	Patent,[1] franchise, concession or licence for a limited period
Class 17	8%	Roads, parking lots, sidewalks, airplane runways, storage areas, or similar surface construction
Class 39	25%	Property used in manufacturing or processing acquired after 1987 and before February 26, 1992

[1] Regulation 1103(2h) provides that taxpayers may elect not to use Class 44 for such patents, in which case the property will be classified in Class 14.[25]

tax shield
the amount of the reduction of taxable income provided by Capital Cost Allowance

Continuously profitable businesses generally find it advantageous to claim Capital Cost Allowance (CCA) deductions as rapidly as permitted by tax law. The rate stated in the *Income Tax Act* is the maximum rate that can be claimed in a year. Companies may, however, claim less than the maximum rate allowable by the *Income Tax Act*. As noted earlier, Capital Cost Allowance (CCA), like its accounting counterpart depreciation, is not a cash flow item. Companies neither pay nor receive any funds for Capital Cost Allowance. However, by reducing the amount of taxable income, Capital Cost Allowance becomes a **tax shield** for revenues. The amount of the tax shield depends on the rules and regulations set out in the *Income Tax Act*. The tax shield produces a tax benefit equal to the capital cost allowance amount multiplied by the tax rate.

The concepts of tax shield and tax benefits are illustrated on the following income statements. The tax rate is assumed to be 38%.

No Capital Cost Allowance Deduction		Capital Cost Allowance Deduction	
Sales	$1,100,000	Sales	$1,100,000
Cost of goods sold	(450,000)	Cost of goods sold	(450,000)
Gross margin	$ 650,000	Gross margin	$ 650,000
Expenses other than		Expenses other than	
Capital Cost Allowance	(150,000)	Capital Cost Allowance	(150,000)
Capital Cost Allowance	0	Capital Cost Allowance	(200,000)
Income before income taxes	$ 500,000	Income before income taxes	$ 300,000
Provision for taxes	190,000	Provision for taxes	114,000
Net income	$ 310,000	Net income	$ 186,000

The tax shield is the capital cost allowance amount of $200,000. The tax benefit is $76,000 ($200,000 × 38%), or the difference between $190,000 of tax expense on the first income statement and $114,000 of tax expense on the second income statement. Since taxes are reduced by $76,000, less cash must be paid out, and the pattern of cash flows is improved. Income tax laws regarding Capital Cost Allowance are subject to periodic revision. In analyzing capital investments, managers should be sure to use the most current capital cost allowance regulations to calculate cash flows from projects as capital cost allowance has a major impact on after-tax-cash flows. The higher the tax benefits are, the higher the net present value over the life of the investment project.

Even when managers use the most current tax regulations in evaluating a capital project, rules may change, and the expected Capital Cost Allowance rate may not be available by the time the investment is actually made and the asset is placed into service. Such changes can dramatically affect the timing of projected after-tax cash flows.

Changes may also occur in the tax rate structure. Rate changes are relatively unpredictable. A reduction in the tax rate lowers the tax benefit provided by the Capital Cost Allowance tax shield because the cash flow impact is lessened. Tax rate changes can, of course, cause actual outcomes to vary from expected outcomes.

Further Discussion—Capital Cost Allowance

The *Income Tax Act* states that in the year of purchase the asset is subject to the half-year rule—this means that the amount of the CCA that can be claimed is reduced to one-half the amount in the year of acquisition. The impact of this rule is that the amount of CCA that is claimed in the first year is lower and the amounts claimed in future years are increased. When additions and disposals of assets are made in any year, it is the excess of acquisition costs over disposal amounts that is subject to the half-year rule.

Pools of Assets

For tax purposes, most assets owned by businesses are grouped into classes or pools of assets (see Exhibit 10-8 on page 605 for examples of these classes). This may not be the case for financial reporting purposes. Grouping of assets allows for the removal and addition of assets without claiming losses or gains on disposition of any assets for taxation purposes. **Canada Customs and Revenue Agency (CCRA)** assumes that until the last asset in the pool is disposed of, there will not be any calculation of losses or gains. If the last asset in the pool is disposed of and if the amount received is less than the remaining book value or "undepreciated capital cost" (UCC), a terminal loss for the amount of the difference can be deducted as an expense. If the amount received is greater than the undepreciated capital cost, the amount must be claimed as an income producing item called "**Recaptured CCA.**"

The impact of pooling is to blend the "inaccuracies" of the CCA calculations over long periods of time. As new assets are acquired, their cost is blended into the UCC of the pool and the amount of cash received on disposal is removed from the pool.

If an asset sells for more than its original cost, at any time, a capital gain occurs. The maximum amount that can be used to reduce the UCC balance is the original cost. If the disposal value exceeds the original cost, a capital gain occurs. The regulations, circa 2003, say that 50% of all such capital gains are taxable at the corporation's marginal tax rate.

During the first year of any corporation's existence, the amount of CCA that can be claimed is limited to that portion of the first year during which the firm was in existence. If the company started operations on July 1, it could only claim three months of CCA.

Further regulations require that all assets must be used during the year to produce goods and/or services in order for any CCA to be claimed. The rules, circa 2003, state that acquiring a machine on December 15, 2003, would not allow the firm to deduct any CCA during 2003 unless it was used to produce goods prior to the close of business on December 31, 2003.

Disposal of Assets

The total value of the proceeds of the sale is deducted at the lesser of the capital cost or the proceeds of disposition prior to the calculation of the capital cost allowance amount for the year. A terminal loss is recognized in the year of disposition when the proceeds of disposition are less than the undepreciated capital cost and there are no assets remaining in the class. This means that the assets in the class have been under-depreciated relative to their disposal value.

Illustration of After-Tax Cash Flows in Capital Budgeting

Canada Oil Ltd. is considering the purchase of an advanced computerized system to monitor its pipeline flows. The system would allow an increase in through-puts and reduce operating costs and the potential for undetected leaks. Information about this investment is given in Exhibit 10-9 on page 608. Cash flows of the project would represent only a small part of Canada Oil Ltd.'s total cash flows. However, the effect of the project on the company's total tax liability must be estimated and included in the project analysis.

Canada Customs and Revenue Agency
the federal government body that collects income taxes; formerly known as Revenue Canada

recapture
occurs when all assets in a class are sold and the proceeds exceed the undepreciated capital cost of the class; the excess is subject to tax

EXHIBIT 10-9

Advanced Pipeline Monitoring
System Data

Estimated life	8 years
Cost	$640,000
Salvage value	$ 60,000
Estimated additional annual revenue	$80,000
Estimated annual operating cost savings	25,000
Net operating cash flow (NOCF)	$105,000
Tax rate for Canada Oil Ltd.	38%
Discount rate and hurdle rate for IRR	12%
Minimum payback period	5 years
Capital Cost Allowance rate (class 10)	30%

The incremental income tax each year is added to the other cash outflows in a capital budgeting project. The amount of incremental, net after-tax cash flows can be estimated for the project described in Exhibit 10-9 as follows.

Calculation of Yearly CCA

Year	UCC	CCA
1	$640,000	$96,000[1]
2	544,000	163,200
3	380,800	114,240
4	266,560	79,968
5	186,592	55,978
6	130,614	39,184
7	91,430	27,429
8	64,001	19,200[2]

[1] In year of acquisition the asset is subject to the half-year rule [($640,000 × 0.30) ÷ 2]
[2] At end of year 8, UCC = $44,801 ($64,001 − $19,200). Since the proceeds of the sale are $60,000, then $15,199 ($60,000–$44,801) is subject to recapture. This recapture amount is subject to taxes in the amount of $2,888.

The net after-tax cash flows from the advanced pipeline monitoring system are as follows:

Year	A CCA	B Tax Benefit From CCA (A × Tax Rate)	C Net of Tax Cash Inflows (NOCF) (1 – Tax Rate)	D Net After-Tax Cash Inflows (B + C)
1	$96,000	$36,480	$65,100	$101,580
2	163,200	62,016	65,100	127,116
3	114,240	43,411	65,100	108,511
4	79,968	30,388	65,100	95,488
5	55,978	21,272	65,100	86,372
6	39,184	14,890	65,100	79,990
7	27,429	10,423	65,100	75,523
8	19,200	7,296	65,100	129,508[1]
				$804,088

[1] [After-tax cash operating flows + (Salvage – Taxes on recapture amount)]

The net after-tax cash flow time line is:

Time	t_0	t_1	t_2	t_3	t_4	t_5	t_6	t_7	t_8
Net Operating Cash Flows		$101,580	$127,116	$108,511	$95,488	$86,372	$79,990	$75,523	$ 72,396
Other Cash Flows	($640,000)								57,112[1]
Total Cash Flows	($640,000)	$101,580	$127,116	$108,511	$95,488	$86,372	$79,990	$75,523	$129,508

[1] Subject to recapture (Salvage − UCC), which is ($60,000 − $44,801) × 0.50 = $7,600. Recapture is subject to taxation at 38%, which amounts to $7,600 × 0.38 = $2,888 in taxes to be paid. Therefore, the increase in cash flow from salvage amounts to $57,112 ($60,000 − $2,888).

The net present value of the investment is calculated as follows using a discount (hurdle) rate of 12%:

Description	Time	After-Tax Cash Flow	Discount Factor	Present Value
Investment	t_0	$(640,000)	1.0000	$(640,000)
Net After-Tax Cash Flow	t_1	101,580	0.8929	90,701
	t_2	127,116	0.7972	101,337
	t_3	108,511	0.7118	77,238
	t_4	95,488	0.6355	60,683
	t_5	86,372	0.5674	49,007
	t_6	79,990	0.5066	40,523
	t_7	75,523	0.4524	34,167
	t_8	72,396	0.4039	29,241
Salvage	t_8	57,112[1]	0.4039	23,068
Net Present Value				$(134,035)

[1]$60,000 − $2,888 = $57,112

Note that the after-tax cash flow for the investment is identical to the pretax amount because no tax deduction is allowed for that expenditure. This amount is expensed for tax purposes through CCA over the eight years that it will be used.

Since the NPV is negative, the computerized monitoring system will earn a rate lower than the 12% discount rate. The project is not acceptable based on the NPV criterion.

Alternative Solution

This problem can be completed using the following formulas:
Step One—Calculate the present value of the tax shield.

$$PV = [Cdt \div (d + k)] \times [(1 + 0.5k) \div (1 + k)]$$

where
C = the capital cost of the asset added to the pool
d = CCA rate
t = the firm's marginal income tax rate
k = the cost of capital

$[(1 + 0.5k) \div (1 + k)]$ = the correction factor for the half-year rule

$[\$640,000 \times 0.30 \times 0.38] \div (0.30 + 0.12) \times [1 + (0.5 \times 0.12)] \div (1 + 0.12)$
= ($72,960 ÷ 0.42) × 0.94643
= $173,714.28 × 0.94643
= $164,408.40

Step Two—Calculate the present value of the salvage value received at the end of year 8.

$$\$60,000 \times 0.4039 = \$24,234$$

Step Three—The CCA tax shield will be reduced because the total value of the pool will be smaller. The CCA tax shield formula must be adjusted by deducting the present value of the tax shield in year 8 when the asset is disposed of.

Where S = Undepreciated Capital Cost (Salvage value)

$$[S^1 dt \div (d + k)] \times [1 \div (1 + k)^n]$$
$$[(\$44{,}801 \times 0.30 \times 0.38) \div (0.30 + 0.12)] \times (1 \div 2.4760)$$
$$= \$4{,}911.26$$

$^1S = \$64{,}001 - \$19{,}200$

Step Four—The present value of the after-tax cash flow from the sale of the equipment at the end of its life

$$= (\$60{,}000 - \$44{,}801)(0.50) \times 0.38 \times 0.4039$$
$$= \$1{,}166.39$$

Using the numbers created by the formulas, the result can be reconciled as follows:

Present value of cash operating flows $65,100 × 4.9676	$323,391.00
Present value of tax shield (from Step 1)	164,408.00
Present value of salvage (from Step 2)	24,234.00
Less: Present value of lost tax savings (Step 3)	4,911.00
Present value of recapture (Step 4)	1,166.00
Original Cash Outlay	640,000.00
	$134,044.00*

* Difference due to rounding

Profitability Index

The PI for the investment is determined as follows:

$$\text{PI} = \text{Present value of net future cash flows} \div \text{Net investment}$$
$$= (\text{NPV} + \text{Investment}) \div \text{Present value of investment}$$
$$= \$(134{,}044) \div \$640{,}000$$
$$= 0.21$$

This result is less than 1.00; thus, the investment earns less than the 12% discount rate.

Internal Rate of Return

The internal rate of return for the system must be less than 12% because there is a negative NPV based on a 12% discount rate. Because the cash flows are not even each year, a trial-and-error approach to determining the IRR must be used. Trial and error attempts show the IRR is about 5.3%. This is proven in the NPV calculations that follow, which are based on a 5% discount rate. The NPV of $13,015 is relatively near $0. The IRR, when used as the discount rate, would cause the NPV to be exactly zero.

Description	Time	After-Tax Cash Flow	Discount Factor	Present Value
Investment	t_0	$(640,000)	1.0000	$(640,000)
Net After-Tax Cash Flow	t_1	101,580	0.9524	96,745
	t_2	127,116	0.9070	115,294
	t_3	108,511	0.8638	93,732
	t_4	95,488	0.8227	78,558
	t_5	86,372	0.7835	67,672
	t_6	79,990	0.7462	59,689
	t_7	75,523	0.7107	53,674
	t_8	72,396	0.6768	48,998
Residual	t_8	57,112	0.6768	38,653
Net Present Value				$ 13,015

Payback Period

The after-tax payback period is found as follows:

Year	Net After-Tax Cash Inflows	Cumulative Total
1	$101,580	$101,580
2	127,116	228,696
3	108,511	337,207
4	95,488	432,695
5	86,372	519,067
6	79,990	599,057
7	75,523	674,580
8	72,396	746,976

It should take about six years plus approximately 54% of the seventh year [($640,000 − $599,057) ÷ $75,523] to recover the initial $640,000. The payback period, then, is approximately six years and six months. Because the company's maximum acceptable payback period is five years, the payback period on this project is unacceptable.

Based solely on quantitative investment criteria, each of the previous techniques indicates that purchasing the computerized pipeline monitoring system is not a viable investment for Canada Oil Ltd. However, the company should consider whether any financial costs or benefits have been omitted before concluding that the project is unacceptable. Additionally, any qualitative benefits of this project, such as a reduced likelihood of undetected leaks, should be considered.

CHAPTER SUMMARY

The capital budget is a key tool in implementing management strategies. The capital budget is also a key control tool for managing quality, employee training, and research and development.

Capital budgeting, as an integral part of strategic formulation, is the process of evaluating long-range projects involving the acquisition, operation, and disposition of one or more capital assets. Management should select investment projects that will help the organization achieve its objectives, provide a reasonable rate of return on invested capital, and help maximize shareholder wealth. The company must determine whether the activities in which it wishes to engage are worth an investment and which assets can be used for those activities. Then decisions must be made about the best investments to accept from those available.

A study of firms of different sizes showed the following financial analysis techniques being used for the appraisal of major investments.[26]

	Firm Sizes		
	Small %	Medium %	Large %
Method			
Payback	71	75	66
Accounting Rate of Return	62	50	55
Internal Rate of Return	76	83	84
Net Present Value	62	79	97

The most common capital budgeting evaluation techniques are payback period, net present value (NPV), profitability index (PI), and internal rate of return (IRR). NPV, PI, and IRR are discounted cash flow methods. The minimum rate at which the discount rate should be set is the cost of capital, but setting this rate requires management judgment based on the amount of capital employed and the risk involved.

Tax depreciation, known as the Capital Cost Allowance (CCA), and changes in tax rates affect after-tax cash flows. CCA, although not a cash flow, provides a tax shield for revenues. For the best results, discounted cash flow methods should use after-tax cash flows. The tax rates and allowable CCA rates used in analyzing an investment may not be the ones in effect when the project is implemented. Such changes can cause the actual NPV and IRR amounts to differ significantly from those originally estimated on the project.

Each capital project evaluation technique is based on certain assumptions and, therefore, has certain limitations. To compensate for these limitations, many managers subject capital projects to more than one evaluation technique.

Today, successfully competing in global markets requires firms to manage product quality effectively. Consumers demand high quality and the capital budget is a primary tool for developing quality improvements. Research and development activities are also controlled by the capital budget. The success of these activities will determine the flows of future revenues and cash from new products.

Installation of high-technology equipment is one type of capital investment currently being considered by many company managers. Such equipment can significantly reduce labour cost, increase quality and quantity of production, and shorten throughput time. However, investments of this type are often not justifiable under traditional capital budgeting evaluation techniques because the payback period is long and many of the benefits are nonquantifiable.

Firms are becoming more sophisticated in managing their impact on the environment. Alternatives in materials, production technology, delivery methods, and product packaging methods can be used to manage environmental impacts. In turn, decisions involving these variables are largely managed in the capital budgeting process.

After a capital project is accepted and implemented, a post-investment audit should be undertaken to compare actual with expected results. The audit will help managers identify and correct any problems that may exist, evaluate the accuracy of estimates used for the original investment decision, and help improve the forecasts of future investment projects.

Cross-Functional Applications

Topic of Note	Discipline	Cross-Functional Applications
Capital Budgeting	Finance	Capital budgeting is the paramount tool used by financial managers to analyze and predict profitability, cash flows, and the demand for financial resources in the future. Various alternatives among debt and equity financing can be evaluated by capital budgeting to arrange a minimum cost/capital blend. Timing is everything in finance because it determines discounted net cash flow. Capital budgets give financial decision makers the time perspective they require for optimum planning.
	Taxation	Few capital acquisition decisions can be made without consideration of the serviceable life of the asset. Tax planners use capital budgets to advise management on long-term strategies to minimize taxes and exploit exclusions, deductions, and exemptions.
	Economics	Any change in one of the factors of production (land, labour, capital, entrepreneurship, or information) will affect all others. Capital budgets assist economists in planning an optimum production function based on utility preference concepts. Evaluating tradeoffs between capital-intensive and labour-intensive production methods illustrates an economic decision based on capital budgeting information.
	Engineering	The selection of technologies is often the responsibility of engineers. Capital budgets give engineers a financial perspective on their decisions concerning alternative technologies to employ in production processes.
	Contract Law	Capital budgets are the basis for capital leases and operating leases. Lease agreement negotiations determine the cost of leasing, the term of the lease, and the residual or buy-out value. In addition, indefinite contracts such as stop loss agreements are frequently referenced to the capital budgetary requirements of the buyer.

(cont.)

Cross-Functional Applications

Topic of Note	Discipline	Cross-Functional Applications
	Financial Accounting	Acquisition of capital assets has implications for future levels of cash flows, income, assets, and liabilities. Financial accounting is responsible for reporting these various effects in a manner that is consistent with generally accepted accounting principles.
Time Value of Money	Finance	Alternative investments or financing arrangements can be evaluated in terms of discounted net cash flows. All financing terms that agree upon some future payments must adjust absolute dollar values to present values. Long-term liabilities such as pension funds, bonds, or mortgages represent future cash payouts that must also be adjusted for present cash value. This concept permits a more realistic valuation of long-lived assets, investments, and long-term liabilities.
	Human Resource Management	Employers bear tremendous risks in providing employees with future pension benefits. A reasonable assumption concerning the growth rate of an investment in today's capital markets could appear to be exaggerated in future recessionary periods, causing insufficient funding of benefits.
	Economics/Actuarial Science	Financial and managerial accounting are very dependent upon assumptions made by economists and actuaries. Actuaries supply projections dealing with risks such as mortality or casualty. Economists often integrate the impact of inflation or foreign currency exchange rates with the time value concept to yield a projection of overall economic value in the future.

Key Terms

Accounting rate of return (p. 604)
Annuity (p. 583)
Annuity due (p. 603)
Canada Customs and Revenue Agency (p. 607)
Capital asset (p. 576)
Capital budgeting (p. 576)
Capital Cost Allowance (p. 582)
Cash flow (p. 581)
Compound interest (p. 602)
Compounding period (p. 602)
Cost of capital (p. 584)

Discount rate (p. 584)
Discounting (p. 584)
Financing decision (p. 581)
Future value (p. 602)
Hurdle rate (p. 589)
Independent project (p. 579)
Internal rate of return (p. 587)
Investing decision (p. 581)
Mutually exclusive projects (p. 579)
Mutually inclusive projects (p. 580)
Net present value (p. 585)
Net present value method (p. 585)

Ordinary annuity (p. 603)
Payback period (p. 583)
Post-investment audit (p. 599)
Preference decision (p. 578)
Present value (p. 584)
Profitability index (p. 587)
Project (p. 576)
Recapture (p. 607)

Rent (p. 603)
Return of capital (p. 582)
Return on capital (p. 582)
Screening decision (p. 578)
Simple interest (p. 602)
Tax shield (of CCA) (p. 606)
Timeline (p. 582)

Solution Strategies

Prepare a timeline to illustrate all moments in time when cash flows are expected to occur. Use the cost of capital rate as the discount rate to determine PV.

Payback Period

1. For projects with equal annual cash flows:

   Payback period = Investment ÷ Annuity amount

2. For projects with unequal annual cash flows:
   Sum the annual cash flows until investment is reached to find payback period. *If payback period is equal to or less than a preestablished maximum number of years, the project is acceptable.*

Net Present Value

	Current investment (always valued at a factor of 1.0000)
+	PV of future cash inflows or cost savings
−	PV of future cash outflows
=	NPV

If NPV is equal to or greater than zero, the project is returning a rate equal to or greater than the discount rate. The project is acceptable.

Profitability Index

+	PV of future cash inflows or cost savings
−	PV of future cash outflows
=	PV of net future cash flows
PI =	(PV of net future cash flows) ÷ PV of investment

If PI is 1.00 or greater, the project is returning a rate equal to or greater than the discount rate. The project is acceptable.

Internal Rate of Return

1. For projects with equal annual cash flows:

   Discount factor = Investment ÷ Annuity amount

   In a table, find the discount factor (or the one closest to it) on the row for the appropriate number of periods. The percentage at the top of the column where this factor is found will approximate the IRR.

2. For projects with unequal annual cash flows:
Estimate the rate provided by the project; compute the NPV. If the NPV is positive (negative), try a higher (lower) rate. Repeat this process until the NPV is zero. *Compare IRR with the discount rate or preestablished hurdle rate. If the IRR is equal to or greater than that rate, the project is acceptable.*

Accounting Rate of Return

ARR = Average annual income from project ÷ Average investment in project (or Initial investment)

The average annual income is net of depreciation.
The average investment = (Initial investment + Return at end of project) ÷ 2

Compare calculated ARR to hurdle ARR. If calculated ARR is equal to or greater than that rate, the project is acceptable.

Tax Benefit of Capital Cost Allowance

When calculating the after-tax cash flows, it must be remembered that the use of Capital Cost Allowance reduces the amount of taxes. Depreciation cannot be used for the calculation of taxes.

When the asset is disposed of, the proceeds of disposition are removed from the pool of assets and thus future CCA claims will be diminished. Again there are tax consequences relating to the disposal. If the disposed asset is the last asset in the class and the disposal amount is greater than the UCC amount, the excess up to the original cost is called recapture and is subject to taxation.

Basic Concepts of Capital Budgeting Techniques

	NPV	PI	IRR	Payback	ARR
Uses time value of money?	Yes	Yes	Yes	No	No
Provides a rate of return?	No	No	Yes	No	Yes
Uses cash flows?	Yes	Yes	Yes	Yes	No
Considers returns throughout life of project?	Yes	Yes	Yes	No	Yes
Discount rate used in calculation?	Yes	Yes	No*	No	No

*Discount rate is not used in the calculation, but it may be used as the hurdle rate.

DEMONSTRATION PROBLEM

John Stewart's Custom Printing Ltd. is considering the purchase of specialized equipment. The equipment is expected to cost $125,000, have a useful life of five years, and have a salvage value of $30,000 at the end of its useful life. The CCA rate for this special equipment is 30%. The company's tax rate is 34%, and its cost of capital is 8%. The equipment is expected to generate the following cash savings and cash expenses:

Year	Cash Savings	Cash Expenses
1	$40,000	$ 5,000
2	55,000	5,000
3	60,000	10,000
4	50,000	5,000
5	40,000	3,000

Required:

a. Prepare a timeline presenting the after-tax operating cash flows.

b. Determine the following on an after-tax basis:
   i. Payback period
   ii. Net present value
   iii. Profitability index

Solution to Demonstration Problem

a. Calculation of Yearly CCA (30%)

Year	UCC	CCA
1	$125,000	$18,750[1]
2	106,250	31,875
3	74,375	22,313
4	52,062	15,619
5	36,443	10,933[2]

[1] In the year of acquisition, the asset is subject to the half-year rule [($125,000 × 0.30) ÷ 2]

[2] At the end of year 5, UCC = $25,510 ($36,443 − $10,933). Since the proceeds of the sale are $30,000, then $4,490 ($30,000 − $25,510) is subject to recapture. This recapture amount is subject to taxes in the amount of $763 [($4,490 × 0.34) ÷ 2].

The net after-tax cash flows from this purchase are as follows:

Year	(1) Pre-tax Cash Flow	(2) CCA	(3) = (1) − (2) Taxable Income	(4) = (3)(0.34) Tax	(5) = (1) − (4) Net After-Tax Cash Inflows
1	$35,000	$18,750	$16,250	$5,525	$ 29,475
2	50,000	31,875	18,125	6,163	43,837
3	50,000	22,313	27,687	9,414	40,586
4	45,000	15,619	29,381	9,990	35,010
5	37,000	10,933	26,067	8,863	28,137
5 Salvage					29,237[1]
					$206,282

[1] Salvage − Taxes on recapture amount ($30,000 − $763).

The net after-tax cash flow timeline is:

t_0	t_1	t_2	t_3	t_4	t_5
$(125,000)	$10,725	$11,962	$18,273	$19,391	$57,374*

* $28,137 + $29,237

b.
   i. Payback Period

Year	Net Cash Flow	Cumulative Cash Flow
1	$29,475	$ 29,475
2	43,837	73,312
3	40,586	114,168

Payback = 3 years + ($10,832 ÷ $35,010)
       = 3 years + 30% of the next year (3 years and almost 4 months)

   ii. Net Present Value:

Description	Time	Cash Flow After-Tax	Discount Factor	Present Value
Investment	Year 0	$(125,000)	1.0000	$(125,000)
Cash inflow	Year 1	29,475	0.9259	27,291
Cash inflow	Year 2	43,837	0.8573	37,581
Cash inflow	Year 3	40,586	0.7938	32,217
Cash inflow	Year 4	35,010	0.7350	25,732
Cash inflow	Year 5	57,374[1]	0.6806	39,049
NPV				$36,870

[1] $28,137 + 29,237

   iii. Profitability Index:
       Profitability index = $36,870 ÷ $125,000 = 0.30

End-of-Chapter Materials

SELF-TEST QUESTIONS

(SOLUTIONS APPEAR AT THE END OF THE CHAPTER.)

Use the following information to answer Questions 1 and 2.

Sue Herrara Ltd. is reviewing an investment proposal. The initial cost as well as other related data for each year are presented in the schedule below. All cash flows are assumed to take place at the end of the year. The salvage value of the investment at the end of each year is equal to its net book value, and there will be no salvage value at the end of the investment's life.

Investment Proposal

Year	Initial Cost and Book Value	Annual Net After-Tax Cash Flows	Net Income
0	$105,000	$ 0	$ 0
1	70,000	50,000	15,000
2	42,000	45,000	17,000
3	21,000	40,000	19,000
4	7,000	35,000	21,000
5	0	30,000	23,000

Herrara uses a 24% after-tax target rate of return for new investment proposals.

1. The traditional payback period for the investment proposal is
   a. 0.875 years
   b. 1.933 years
   c. 2.25 years
   d. more than 5 years
   e. some period other than those given above

   (IMA adapted)

2. The accounting rate of return for the investment proposal over its life using the *initial* value of the investment is
   a. 36.2%
   b. 18.1%
   c. 28.1%
   d. 38.1%
   e. 24.0%

   (IMA adapted)

3. A series of equal cash flows per period in which each cash flow occurs at the beginning of the period is called a(n):
   a. rent
   b. ordinary annuity
   c. annuity due
   d. none of the above

4. The time value of money is ignored by
   a. the accounting rate of return method
   b. the internal rate of return method

   c. both of the above
   d. none of the above

5. When ranking two mutually exclusive investments with different initial amounts, management should give first priority to the project
   a. that generates cash flows for the longer period of time
   b. whose net after-tax flows equal the initial investment
   c. that has the greater accounting rate of return
   d. whose cash flows vary the least
   e. that has the greater profitability index

6. The Net Present Value (NPV) method and the Internal Rate of Return (IRR) method are used to analyze capital expenditures. The IRR method (as contrasted with the NPV method)
   a. is considered inferior because it fails to calculate compounded interest rates
   b. incorporates the time value of money while the NPV method does not
   c. almost always gives a different result than the NPV method as to the acceptability of a given proposal
   d. assumes that the rate of return on the reinvestment of the cash proceeds is at the indicated rate of return of the project analyzed rather than at the discount rate used
   e. is preferred in practice because it is able to handle multiple desired hurdle rates, which is impossible with the NPV method

7. A company is considering the replacement of some old research equipment with new equipment that should save $8,000 per year in net cash operating costs. The estimated economic life of the new equipment is 12 years and will cost $25,000. What is the payback period?
   a. 2.5 years
   b. 3 years
   c. 3.1 years
   d. 8.3 years

8. The internal rate of return for a project can be determined
   a. only if the project's profitability index is greater than one
   b. by finding the discount rate that yields a net present value of zero
   c. only if the project cash flows are equal each year
   d. none of the above

9. A company has invested $55,000 in a new machine. Management expects to receive net cash flows of $12,000 per year over the next 8 years. What is the investment's payback period?
   a. 4 years
   b. 4.3 years

c. 4.6 years

d. 5 years

10. Once the internal rate of return on a project is known, it is compared to the:

a. tax rate

b. discount rate or hurdle rate

c. net present value of the project

d. tax shield

(Self-Test Questions 7 and 9 are reprinted from *Management Accounting examinations* published by the Certified General Accountants Association of Canada © CGA-Canada, 1999 (#7) and 2000 (#9) used by permission.)

QUESTIONS

1. What is a capital asset? How is it distinguished from other assets?

2. What is the objective of capital budgeting? Why is this objective an important business consideration?

3. Discuss some reasons why managers might use different techniques to screen projects and to evaluate project preferences.

4. In the capital budgeting context, what are mutually exclusive projects? Give three examples.

5. In the capital budgeting context, what are independent projects? Give three examples.

6. Of the capital budgeting techniques discussed in the chapter, which ones consider the time value of money? How does discounting account for the time value of money?

7. Why do the capital budgeting methods that consider the time value of money use only cash flows rather than accrual-based accounting numbers?

8. What is the distinction between a return on capital and a return of capital?

9. What is a timeline, and how does it aid the evaluation of capital projects?

10. What is the difference between an annuity and an ordinary cash flow?

11. What does the payback period of a project represent? Why is the payback method commonly used in conjunction with other methods rather than as a stand-alone evaluation measure?

12. How is an interest rate selected for discounting the cash flows associated with a project?

13. When using the NPV method, how does one determine whether the actual rate of return on a project is greater than or less than the discount rate?

14. If a project's net present value is zero, what can be said about the internal rate of return on the project? Discuss the reasoning behind your answer.

15. Relative to the NPV method, what is the primary strength of the profitability index method of evaluating capital projects?

16. In general, how does one estimate the internal rate of return on a potential project?

17. What are the major weaknesses unique to the internal rate of return method of project evaluation?

18. Why is the management of quality costs a role served by the capital budget?

19. Why is the control of research and development activities a function of capital budget analysis?

20. Why are high-technology projects often rejected when their evaluation relies on traditional capital budgeting techniques?

21. Why are environmental issues increasingly evaluated in capital budget analyses?

22. Why is it important to perform a post-investment audit?

23. What is a profitability index? How is it used in capital budgeting?

24. Define internal rate of return. How is it different from net present value?

25. If the net present value of an investment is zero, does this mean that no profit will be earned from the investment?

26. What factors affect the present value of a sum of $1 to be received at some point in the future? (Appendix 10A)

27. Which method of evaluating capital projects uses accrual accounting information rather than cash flows? How does net income differ from net cash flows? (Appendix 10B)

28. What characteristic of the accounting rate of return method makes it unique among the techniques discussed in this chapter? (Appendix 10B)

29. How does depreciation expense, which is an accounting expense rather than a cash flow, become relevant in the capital budgeting analysis when the effects of income taxes are considered? (Appendix 10C)

30. If all other factors are equal, which of the following changes will increase the present value of the CCA tax shield? (Appendix 10C)
    a. An increase in the tax rate
    b. An increase in the discount rate

EXERCISES

1. (LO 3; Payback) The city manager of Regina is considering two mutually exclusive investment proposals for the city's water utility. Both proposals, A and B, promise cash inflows of $40,000 per year based on an investment of $120,000. Expected useful lives are as follows:

Proposal	Life
A	3.5 years
B	4.5 years

   Required:
   a. Compute the payback period for each alternative. Based on the payback criterion, which of the alternatives is preferred?
   b. How does this exercise demonstrate a need to use a second evaluation technique when the payback technique is used?

2. (LO 3; Payback) Barrigan's Department Store is considering a new product line, a flower booth. The new product line would require an investment of $60,000 in equipment and fixtures and $40,000 for working capital. Company managers expect the following pattern of net cash inflows from the flower booth over the life of the investment.

Year	Amount
1	$22,000
2	28,000
3	32,000
4	36,000
5	30,000
6	28,000
7	24,000

   Required:
   a. Compute the payback period for the proposed flower booth. If the company requires a four-year payback on its investments, should it invest in the new product line? Explain.
   b. As the financial specialist on the capital project evaluation team, would you recommend that any other capital project evaluation methods be applied before making an investment decision? Explain.

3. (LO 3; NPV, timeline) A plumbing supply company is considering the purchase of some building equipment costing $300,000. The equipment is expected to have a life of five years with no salvage value. Cash inflows are expected to be $125,000 per year for the first two years, and $40,000 for the next three years. The company uses a discount rate of 10% to evaluate capital projects.
   Required:
   Prepare a timeline showing all cash flows, and compute the net present value of the equipment investment. Ignore taxes.

4. (LO 3; NPV, timeline) Don Brean is faced with two investment alternatives. In one case, he can invest $50,000 with an expected return of $6,000 per year for the next six years. At the end of the sixth year, the investment can be sold for $50,000.
   Alternatively, he can purchase some equipment for $50,000 that will provide him with revenues of $15,000 a year for four years and $5,000 a year for two more years. No salvage value is expected at the end of the sixth year.
   Required:
   a. Prepare a timeline for each project showing all associated cash flows.
   b. Assuming his discount rate is 12%, compute the net present value of the alternative investments. Ignore taxes.
   c. Is either investment acceptable? Explain. Which investment is preferred? Explain.

5. (LO 3; NPV, payback) The managers of Crimson Lights, a regional restaurant chain, are evaluating the feasibility of purchasing the rights to serve Old Days ice cream, a popular regional brand. The rights would give the firm exclusive licence to market the ice cream in a four-province area for a period of six years. According to estimates by the company's marketing staff, the licence would increase net annual cash receipts by $630,000 in each of the six years.
   Required:
   a. Assuming the company's cost of capital is 10%, what is the most it would pay for the marketing rights? Ignore taxes.
   b. Based on your answer in part (a), compute the payback period.
   c. As the marketing manager of the company, what additional concerns might you have about purchasing the franchise rights?

6. (LO 3; PI) Lawrence Booth Rapids Technology Company is considering developing a new product. The product would require an additional investment of $360,000. The product would have a life of 10 years with no residual value. Managers expect the new product to generate net annual increases in cash flows of $62,000 per year for each of the 10 years. The company uses a 9% required rate of return for evaluating capital projects.
   Required:
   a. Compute the profitability index of the product investment. Ignore taxes.
   b. Should the company invest in the new product?
   c. What is the minimum acceptable value for the profitability index for an investment to be acceptable?

7. (LO 3; PI, IRR) Gina Roma Food Products Company plans to buy a new vending machine at a fully installed cost of $55,475. The company estimates that the machine will have a life of six years. Net annual cash inflows are estimated to be $12,000. No salvage value is expected at the end of the sixth year.
   Required:
   a. Assuming the company's discount rate is 12%, compute the profitability index. Ignore taxes.
   b. Calculate the internal rate of return for this project. If the company's cost of capital is 12%, is this an acceptable investment? Explain.

8. (LO 3; IRR) Ashley Tax Services is considering the purchase of a new computer. One vendor is offering a system at a price of $90,000. The vendor claims Ashley could save $15,000 annually for 10 years over what she would spend using the current computer system. No salvage value is expected on the system at the end of its useful life. The firm's cost of capital and discount rate are 10%.

Required:

a. Calculate the internal rate of return for the computer system. Does this indicate that it is an acceptable investment? Ignore taxes.

b. Should the company purchase the system? As a management accountant, how would you confirm the claims made by the vendor regarding the amount of annual cost savings?

9. (LO 5; Managing research and development) Hill Components Company manufactures a variety of parts and components used in the manufacture of automobiles. Over the past five years, since 2000 the company has been losing customers because its competitors have been introducing innovative products at a faster pace than Hill. Hill has also found that many of the new products it has introduced in the past three years have generated lower sales than expected. As a result of the problems Hill has been experiencing, profits have dropped by 75% from their levels of five years ago.

Required:

As an accounting consultant who understands the role that the capital budget can play in managing research and development, prepare a brief written report for Harold Hill, president of the company. In your report, explain how the development of a rigorous capital budgeting system could be used to improve profitability.

10. (LO 10; PV) On January 1, 2005, GW Corporation invested funds in a note that will mature on December 31, 2007. The controller determined that the firm would earn 12% interest (compounded annually) on this investment.

Required:

If the maturity value of the investment is $1,200,000, how much did the company invest?

11. (LO 10; PV) Assume that you recently purchased a new car and paid $6,000 down and financed the balance on an installment credit plan. According to the credit agreement, you will pay $400 per month for a period of 48 months.

Required:

If the credit agreement were based on a monthly interest rate of 1%, what was the cost of the car?

12. (LO 11; ARR) The large securities firm of Jack Sheriton & Co. is considering an investment in 100 new personal notebook computers with internal modems and CD ROM drives. The new computers would be used by floor traders to track their daily transactions and positions in each security. The cost of the new computers would be $340,000, and they would have an expected life of five years. The company would depreciate the computers using the straight-line method. At the end of their lives, the computers would be donated to local charities. The computers would increase the company's annual net cash flows by $82,000 for each of the five years.

Required:

Compute the accounting rate of return on the computer investment using the average value of the investment. (Ignore income taxes.)

13. (LO 3, 10, 11; All methods) Hill Top Garden Supply Co. is considering purchasing a new fertilizer blender. The equipment would cost $300,000 and produce annual cost savings of $50,000. The equipment is expected to last 10 years and have no salvage value. The company's discount rate is 10%. Calculate the following relative to this investment. (Ignore taxes.)

Required:

a. Net present value
b. Profitability index
c. Internal rate of return
d. Payback period
e. Accounting rate of return

14. (LO 12; CCA, cross-functional management) Spectra Solutions Ltd. is a software firm specializing in applications related to manufacturing technology. The firm is presently considering an investment in a new computer system to aid in management of its software development. The computer would cost $1,500,000. For tax purposes, the computer is class 10 with a CCA rate of 30%. No salvage value is expected to be realized. The company's cost of capital is 10%, and its tax rate is 50%. (Additional assets are in this class.)

Required:

Compute the present value of the CCA tax shield.

15. (LO 3, 12; NPV; CCA) A company presently sells 50,000 units a year at a price of $140 per unit. These units are produced using a machine that was purchased three years ago at a cost of $800,000. Its current book value is $500,000, while its market is only $375,000. The machine is expected to last another five years, after which there will be no salvage value. The following are the production costs per unit:

Direct materials (10 grams @ $2.80 per gram)	$ 28.00
Direct labour (3 hours @ $12 per hour)	36.00
Variable overhead (3 hours @ $4 per hour)*	12.00
Fixed overhead (3 hours @ $12 per hour)*	36.00
Total production costs per unit	$112.00

*Based on annual activity of 150,000 direct labour hours. Variable and fixed overhead are allocated based on the number of labour hours.

The company expects the following changes next year:

- The selling price will decrease by 10% due to the new cost strategy adopted by the president of the company.
- The direct labour rate will increase by 5%.
- Sales are expected to increase to 55,000 units, which is still below the full capacity of the facilities.

Management is considering replacing the old machine with a new one at the beginning of next year, which would cost $1,000,000. The expected useful life of the new machine is five years with a salvage value of $425,000 at that time. The new machine's capital cost allowance rate is 20%. By using the new machine, management expects to reduce variable direct labour to 2.8 hours per unit. The company has a minimum desired after-tax rate of return of 14% and a tax rate of 40%. The company plans to replace the new machine with an asset in the same class.

Required:

a. Calculate the contribution margin cash flows associated with the machine replacement decision for next year.

b. Using the net present value method, determine whether or not the company should invest in the new machine, and state your conclusions.

PROBLEMS

1. (LO 3; NPV, PI) Central Warehousing provides storage services for industrial firms. Usual items stored include records, inventory, and waste items. The company is evaluating more efficient methods of moving inventory items into and out of storage areas. One vendor has proposed to sell Central Warehousing a conveyor system that would offer high-speed routing of inventory items. The required equipment would have an initial cost of $2,500,000 including installation. The vendor has indicated that the machinery would have an expected life of 7 years, with an estimated salvage value of $200,000. Estimates of the annual labour savings as well as the additional costs associated with the operation of the new equipment are as follows:

	Annual Amounts
Labour cost savings (14 workers)	$465,000
Maintenance costs	20,000
Property taxes	14,000
Insurance costs	22,000

Required:

a. Assuming the company's cost of capital is 9%, compute the NPV of the investment in the conveyor equipment. Ignore taxes.

b. Based on the NPV, should the company invest in the new machinery?

c. Compute the profitability index for this potential investment. Ignore taxes.

d. What other factors should the company consider in evaluating this investment?

e. How would the quality of the company's services likely be affected by the new equipment? How could these effects be considered in the analysis?

2. (LO 3; Timeline, payback, NPV) Managers of Green River Variety store are considering leasing a building next to their Edmonton, Alberta store to stock additional merchandise for travellers and tourists. The owner of the building has offered an eight-year lease. Green River managers anticipate that upfront repairs and improvements costing $120,000 would be necessary to make the building suitable for their purposes. Although more inventory would be required to stock the additional space, the company already owns the necessary inventory and has it stored in their central warehouse. Annual incremental fixed costs (including the cost of the lease) of the facility are expected to be as follows:

Year	Amount
1	$7,400
2	9,600
3	9,600
4	9,600
5	9,900
6	9,900
7	9,900
8	9,900

Managers estimate that annual revenues could be increased by $150,000 from the additional merchandise sales. The firm's contribution margin is typically 22% of sales. At the end of the lease, Green River would not be entitled to any payment for improvements made to the building. The firm uses a 10% discount rate.

Required:
a. Construct a timeline for the building lease.
b. Determine the payback period.
c. Calculate the net present value of the project. (Ignore taxes.) Is the project acceptable based on the NPV criterion? Explain.

3. (LO 3; NPV) Ondrack Steelworks manufactures running gears for various types of automobile trailers. One of its main manufacturing processes involves bending sheet metal into various shapes. At the current time, this process is performed manually by a staff of 10 workers. The company is considering mechanizing this process with a computer-driven bending machine. The machine would cost $1,200,000 and would be operated by a single person. It would have an estimated life of 10 years and a salvage value of $50,000 at the end of its life. Following are estimates of the annual labour savings as well as the additional costs associated with the operation of the new machine:

Annual labour cost savings (10 workers)	$260,000
Wages of bending machine operator	50,000
Annual maintenance costs	22,000
Annual property taxes	14,000
Annual insurance costs	14,000

Required:
a. Assuming the company's cost of capital is 12%, compute the net present value of the investment in the computer-driven bending machine. (Ignore taxes.)
b. Based on the NPV, should the company invest in the new machine?
c. How could the quality of operations be affected by this decision? What specific types of quality-related costs should be considered in the decision?
d. Why would you want the human resources director to be involved in this capital budgeting decision?

4. (LO 3; Uncertainty) The Harizanov Materials Company provides materials to construction companies to build roads and bridges. The company has been searching for a location at which to mine gravel for a new major road project.

The owner of one location is willing to allow the company to mine all the gravel it needs for the road project, provided the firm reclaims the land (which essentially involves building a road and a small lake and planting trees) after the road project is completed. The firm would also be required to post a $2,000,000 damage deposit, which would be refunded (without interest) at the end of the reclamation. The road project is expected to last three years, and the reclamation of the mining location would require an additional year. To evaluate the feasibility of this offer, the company has estimated cash expenses and cash income under a pessimistic and an optimistic scenario.

	Pessimistic	Optimistic
Costs to relocate mining equipment	$200,000	$200,000
Damage deposit	2,000,000	2,000,000
Year 1 gravel sales	4,000,000	4,400,000
Year 2 gravel sales	4,000,000	4,400,000
Year 3 gravel sales	6,000,000	7,000,000
Costs of reclamation (year 4)	1,000,000	700,000
Annual fixed cash expenses	800,000	800,000
Annual variable expenses	75% of sales	70% of sales

The annual fixed and variable expenses would be incurred only in years 1 through 3, when the mine is operational.

Required:

a. Assuming the company's cost of capital is 11%, compute the net present value under both alternatives. Ignore taxes.

b. Suppose the company estimates that the probability of the pessimistic scenario occurring is .3 and the probability of the optimistic scenario occurring is .7. What should the company do? [Hint: Weight the NPV of each scenario by its probability.]

5. (LO 3, 11, 12; comprehensive) Paul Williams Investigations Ltd. is evaluating the purchase of a computer system. The company purchasing agent, Marleanna Evans, advised the owner, Paul Williams, that the system would generate $13,000 of cash savings each year for four years. At the end of that time, the system would have no salvage value because of technological obsolescence. The purchasing agent also estimated that cash operating and maintenance costs would be $1,500 annually. The company's tax rate is 40%. The asset is class 10 and the CCA rate is 30%. The initial cost of the system would be $36,000. The company owns additional assets in this class.

Required:

a. Determine the annual after-tax cash flows from the project.

b. Determine the after-tax payback period for the project.

c. Determine the after-tax accounting rate of return for the project.

6. (LO 3, 11, 12; payback; ARR, CCA, comprehensive) Vicky Newman Auction operates an auction market for cattle. The company is considering the purchase of a new computerized scale to weigh cattle. The equipment selected would cost $150,000 and would have a life of eight years and an estimated salvage value of $20,000. This is a class 10 asset and is subject to a CCA rate of 30%. The company has no other assets in this class. The corporate tax rate is 53%. Additional business generated by installation of the new scale would increase annual net cash inflows on a before-tax basis by $40,000. Annual cash maintenance costs would amount to $4,000. The company requires that the cost of the investment be recouped in less than five years and that the investment produce an accounting rate of return of at least 16%.

Required:

a. Compute the after-tax payback period and the after-tax accounting rate of return for this piece of equipment.

b. Quantitatively, is this piece of equipment an acceptable investment? Why or why not?

c. Regardless of your answer to part (b), what other factors relating to this purchase should be considered?

7. (LO 7; Environmental costs) Poë Chemical Ltd. produces chemicals that are used in commercial applications. One popular product, a chemical solvent, has among its required materials two very caustic acids, A and B. These acids are a very serious environmental hazard if not disposed of properly. For every tonne of chemical produced, 500 litres of Acid A and 300 litres of Acid B are required. Because of inefficiencies in the present production process, 40 litres of Acid A and 20 litres of Acid B remain as waste for each tonne of chemical manufactured. Because of impurities in the waste

acids, they cannot be used in the production of future batches of the product. The company incurs a cost of $2 per litre to dispose of waste acid produced.

Recently, the company has become aware of new technology that reduces the quantity of waste acids produced. This technology would generate only 10 litres of Acid A and 5 litres of Acid B as waste from each tonne of chemical manufactured. Corporate management has estimated that the new technology could be acquired and installed at a cost of $500,000. The technology would have a life expectancy of 6 years. The new technology would not otherwise affect the cost of producing the chemical solvent. No existing machinery would be sold if the new technology were acquired.

Required:
a. Assume Poë Chemical's cost of capital is 9%, and the company produces 750 tonnes of the chemical solvent annually. What is the net present value of the new technology? (Ignore taxes.)
b. Discuss any other factors that should be weighed in the decision to acquire the new technology.

8. (LO 3, 12; NPV, CCA) Eric Forrester, president of Forrester Creations Ltd., asked his accountant to evaluate a proposal to buy a new press that would cost $104,000. The purchase would be made at the beginning of the company's fiscal year. The press would have an estimated life of 8 years and no salvage value at the end of its life. Forrester's accountant, Sheila Carter, estimated that the press would save $38,000 annually in operating costs. The firm uses a discount rate of 8% and has a tax rate of 50%. The asset is considered to be class 39 with a CCA rate of 40% and the company owns additional assets in this class.

Required:
a. Calculate the net present value of the press.
b. What discount rate would cause the NPV to equal zero? What is this discount rate called?

9. (LO 3, 12; NPV, CCA) Ms. Kate Roberts manages the Canadian division of Basic Black Industries. Kate Roberts is presently contemplating an investment in a new fruit processing technology. The new technology is superior to existing technology because it reduces waste and spoilage. However, several years of experience will be required to understand and utilize the technology fully. The following are financial characteristics of the investment.

Initial cost	$2,500,000
Net annual increase in cash revenues	
Year 1	250,000
Year 2	500,000
Year 3	650,000
Year 4	2,000,000
Year 5	1,800,000

The technology will have a five-year life with no salvage value. The company's cost of capital is 10% and its income tax rate is 50%. This asset is class 10 and is subject to a CCA rate of 30%. The company has additional assets in this class.

Required:
a. Compute the after-tax NPV of the potential investment.
b. Based on the NPV, will Kate Roberts invest in the project?
c. Based on your computations in part (b), will Ms. Roberts want to invest in the new project? Explain.

10. (LO 3, 12; comprehensive) The Brady Chowder House is considering adding a new product line. The line would consist of several different glass chowder bowls and would require the following investment:

Production equipment	$ 600,000
Working capital	300,000
Marketing equipment and displays	150,000
Total	$1,050,000

The production and marketing equipment and the marketing displays could be sold for a total of $25,000 at the end of 10 years. For CCA purposes, this equipment is considered to be class 43, which has a 30% CCA rate. The company owns additional assets in this class. Following are the expected operating cash receipts and cash expenses by year for the proposed product line:

	Cash Receipts	**Cash Expenses**
Year 1	$120,000	$150,000
Year 2	240,000	150,000
Year 3	300,000	155,000
Year 4	360,000	205,000
Year 5	450,000	200,000
Years 6–10	540,000	245,000

The company's tax rate is 40%, and its cost of capital is 7%.

Required:

a. Compute the after-tax net present value and profitability index for the proposed investment.

b. Compute the after-tax payback for the proposed investment.

c. Based on the NPV and PI, should the investment be made?

11. (LO 3, 12; comprehensive, CCA) Allan White Fashions Ltd. manufactures high-quality products from armadillo skins. Currently the company relies on a system of carts and pallets to move materials among workstations. The company is now considering the installation of a robotic conveyor system to move the materials. Some of the financial characteristics of the proposed investment follow:

Required initial investment (class 8, 20%)	$1,800,000
Net annual savings in cash operating costs	$ 310,000
Annual depreciation expense	$ 120,000
Expected salvage value	$ 0
Expected life	15 years

The company's income tax rate is 50%. (The company owns additional assets in class 8.)

Required:

a. To the nearest whole percentage point, compute the internal rate of return on the investment in the conveyor system.

b. If its cost of capital is 11%, should the company invest in the conveyor system? Are there any qualitative factors that might need to be considered?

c. Compute the after-tax payback period for the investment.

12. (LO 11; ARR) Fashion Tanning is a tanning business that operates 25 tanning booths. The company's president, Angelica Ambatali, is presently considering the installation of computer-controlled tanning equipment. The major benefit of the computer-controlled machinery is that it consumes less electricity and requires less maintenance and oversight. Furthermore, the equipment can be centrally monitored. The installation of 10 computer-controlled machines would allow the firm to scrap 10 existing tanning machines that have no market value. The following financial information summarizes the prospective investment:

Initial cost of the equipment and software	$140,000
Annual depreciation	$ 28,000
Annual labour savings	$ 32,000
Expected salvage value in 5 years	$ 0
Expected life of the computerized machines	5 years

Required:

a. Compute the accounting rate of return on this investment. If Ms. Ambatali requires that projects generate an accounting rate of return of 12% or greater, is the project acceptable from a quantitative perspective? Ignore taxes.

b. Based on your knowledge of computerized equipment, do you think Ms. Ambatali has captured all of the relevant costs and benefits associated with the installation of the computerized equipment? Explain.

c. How could the new equipment impact the quality of services delivered to customers?

13. (LO 3, 11; Comprehensive) The management of Booth Manufacturing Company is evaluating a proposal to purchase a new drill press as a replacement for a less efficient piece of similar equipment, which would then be sold. The cost of the new drill press, including delivery and installation, is $87,500. If the equipment is purchased, Booth will incur $2,500 of costs to remove the present equipment and revamp service facilities. The present equipment has a book value of $25,000 and a remaining useful life of 10 years. The present market value is also $25,000.

Management has provided you with the following comparisons:

	Present Equipment	New Equipment
Annual production in units	200,000	250,000
Revenue from each unit	$0.15	$0.15
Annual costs:		
Labour	$ 15,000	$ 12,500
Depreciation (10% of asset book value or cost)	2,500	8,750
Other cash operating costs	24,000	10,000

The company uses a 14% discount rate in evaluating capital projects and expects the cost of capital projects to be recouped within 5 years. Both the existing and new equipment are expected to have a negligible salvage value at the end of 10 years. Calculate the following. (Ignore taxes.)

Required:
a. Net present value of the new equipment.
b. Payback period for the new equipment.
c. Accounting rate of return for the new equipment. Assume the company's hurdle rate is 14%.

14. (LO 3, 12; NPV, CCA) Supplix Textile Inc. is considering replacing its weaving machine acquired 2 years ago at a cost of $28,000. This machine is still in good condition but management wants more flexibility and lower manufacturing costs. The actual market value of the machine is $3,500.

A manufacturer is offering a new weaving machine at a price of $40,000. The machine would last 10 years if management invested $2,000 at the end of year 4 and $3,000 at the end of year 7. The investments in year 4 and year 7 should be considered as expenses. The new machine has an expected salvage value of $7,000.

With the new machine, management estimates an important decrease in the manufacturing costs:

	Old Weaving Machine	New Weaving Machine
Annual production (in units)	500,000	500,000
Annual expenses:		
Direct labour	$12,500	$7,900
Machinery costs	4,000	3,400
Receiving and inspection	1,000	1,200
Depreciation	5,600	4,000

The capital cost allocation rate is 20% for this machine. There are other assets in the CCA class at the end of year 10. Supplix has a minimum desired after-tax rate of return of 14% and a tax rate of 40%.

Required:
Use the net present value method to determine whether or not Supplix should buy the new weaving machine, and state your conclusion.

(Adapted by the author from *Management Accounting examinations,* published by the Certified General Accountants Association of Canada © CGA-Canada, 2000, used by permission.)

CASES

1. The board of directors of the Toronto Hospital is attempting to decide whether to purchase or lease a CAT scanner. The cost of the equipment is $500,000, and its estimated useful life is 7 years. The lease period is only 5 years, so the lease would have to be

renewed for the additional 2 years. The renewal rate is 10% of the original lease rate of $100,000 per year.

All costs of operating the CAT scanner are the same under both alternatives. Therefore, they are not relevant to this decision. In addition, all revenues (except those generated by the Provincial Health Plan reimbursements) are the same under both alternatives. The Provincial Health Plan reimbursement is based on either the amount of depreciation or the amount of the lease payment. Provincial Health Plan patients are assumed to use the CAT scanner 30% of the time, and the Provincial Plan will reimburse that percentage of equipment cost. Equipment cost is defined in the Provincial Health Plan reimbursement policy as annual straight-line depreciation or out-of-pocket lease payments. Toronto Hospital has a discount rate of 8%.

Required:

a. Assume that the CAT scanner will have no salvage value if it is purchased. Lease payments and Provincial Health Plan reimbursements occur at the end of each year. What is the net present value of the purchase alternative? The lease alternative? Should the board purchase or lease the CAT scanner?

b. Assume that the CAT scanner will have no salvage value if it is purchased. Lease payments are made at the beginning of the year, and Provincial Health Plan reimbursements occur at the end of the year. What is the net present value of each alternative? Should the board purchase or lease the CAT scanner?

c. Assume that the CAT scanner will have a 5% salvage value if it is purchased. Lease payments and Provincial Health Plan reimbursements occur at the end of each year. What is the net present value of each alternative? Should the board purchase or lease the CAT scanner?

2. Da Limo is a limousine service operating in Montreal, Quebec. The owner is considering the purchase of 5 new white stretch limos at a cost of $75,000 each. Each limo will have a useful life of 5 years and a salvage value of $15,000. Estimated revenues and operating costs for each limo are as follows:

Rental Fees

| First 2 years | $150 per hour; 20 hours per week for 52 weeks |
| Next 3 years | $100 per hour; 15 hours per week for 52 weeks |

Operating Costs

Driver's annual salary	$12,000 (increases $1,000 each year)
Uniform	$200 (at the beginning of the first, third, and fifth years)
Annual insurance	$5,000 each year; annual rate decreases for age are offset by annual increases in premium rates (paid at the beginning of each year)

Annual fees:

Personalized licence plate and inspection	$100 (paid at the beginning of each year)
Annual gas and oil	$36,850 (increases 10% each year of use)
Annual repairs and maintenance	$10,000 (increases 10% each year of use)
Major repairs at the end of the third year	$2,000
Tires at end of second and fourth years	$400

(Ignore income taxes in answering the following questions.)

Required:

a. Determine the net cash flows for each year of the 5-year period.

b. Assuming a 14% discount rate, what is the net present value? Is the purchase quantitatively acceptable?

c. Assuming a 16% discount rate, what is the net present value? Is the purchase quantitatively acceptable?

d. What other factors should Da Limo's owner consider before acquiring the limos, assuming a positive net present value?

3. The Consumer Products Company is considering an investment in a new product line: a high-tech frisbee boomerang. To make the product, the company would need to acquire additional production equipment with an investment of $1,000,000. Assume a single asset in this class. The equipment would have an expected life of 6 years, at which time it would have a disposal value of $100,000. The company would also need to invest $200,000 in additional working capital (primarily to support an increase in Accounts Receivable).

Over the 6-year life of the equipment, the company projects the following sales volume:

	Sales Volume
Year 1	200,000 units
Year 2	300,000 units
Year 3	400,000 units
Year 4	300,000 units
Year 5	200,000 units
Year 6	200,000 units

The company has set the sales price for the new product at $2.75 for all years and estimates that all variable costs would be $1.30 per unit. Fixed cash expenses are projected at $125,000 per year. For tax purposes, the CCA rate on equipment is 30%. For financial accounting purposes, the equipment would be depreciated based on the straight-line method over 6 years.

The company's marginal tax rate is expected to remain at the current rate of 53% for the foreseeable future. To evaluate projects of this type the company uses a hurdle rate of 8% (its cost of capital).

Required:
a. Compute the after-tax NPV of the proposed project. Based on the NPV, is the project acceptable?
b. Compute the profitability index.
c. Compute the payback period for the proposed project.
d. Without computing the IRR, determine whether the IRR is greater than the discount rate.

ETHICS AND QUALITY DISCUSSIONS

1. Heidi Swenson, the plant manager of the St. Catharines plant of the Nordtvedt Manufacturing Company, has submitted a capital budgeting proposal for a new CAD/CAM system for her plant. She is excited about the acquisition, as it meets the plant's needs almost perfectly and she has received approval from the home office. However, in reading the local newspaper this morning, Heidi is surprised to discover that Nordtvedt's purchasing agent happens to be the sister of the vendor of the CAD/CAM system.

Nordtvedt Manufacturing has a strict policy that prohibits purchasing from relatives. If this relationship comes to light, the purchasing agent could be fired, and Heidi might not get the system that, in her judgment, is best for the plant. The purchasing agent's last name is different from her brother's, and it is unlikely that a connection will be made. Heidi is concerned about what to do—abide by the policy or acquire the necessary system at the reasonable price quoted by the vendor.

Required:
a. Why would a company have a policy of this nature?
b. What are the ethical conflicts in this situation?
c. What are the potential risks for Heidi? For the company?
d. What do you recommend, and why?

2. The Denise Russell Corporation has operations in more than two dozen countries. Russell's headquarters are in Vancouver, British Columbia, and company executives frequently travel to visit Russell's foreign and domestic operations.

Russell owns two business jets with international range and six smaller aircraft for shorter flights. Company policy is to assign aircraft to trips based on cost minimization, but the practice is to assign aircraft based on the organizational rank of the traveller. Russell offers its aircraft for short-term lease or for charter by other organizations whenever Russell employees do not plan to use the aircraft. Russell surveys the market often to keep its lease and charter rates competitive.

Mark Haines, Russell's vice president of finance, claims that a third business jet can be justified financially. However, some people in the controller's office think the real reason for a third business jet is that people outranking Haines keep the two business jets busy. Thus, Haines usually must travel in the smaller aircraft.

The third business jet would cost $11 million. A capital expenditure of this magnitude requires a formal proposal with projected cash flows and net present value computations using Russell's minimum required rate of return. If Russell's president and finance committee approve the proposal, it will be submitted to the full board. The board has final approval on capital expenditures exceeding $5 million and has established a policy of rejecting any discretionary proposal that has a negative net present value.

Haines asks Maria Bartiromo, the assistant corporate controller, to prepare a proposal on a third business jet. Bartiromo gathers the following information:
- Acquisition cost of the jet, including instrumentation and interior furnishings
- Operating cost of the jet for company use
- Projected avoidable commercial airfare and other avoidable costs from company use of the plane
- Projected value of executive time saved by using the third business jet
- Projected contribution margin from incremental lease and charter activity
- Estimated resale value of the jet
- Estimated income tax effects of the proposal

When Haines reviews Bartiromo's completed proposal and sees the large negative net present value figure, he returns the proposal to Bartiromo and insists that she has made an error in her calculations.

Feeling some pressure, Bartiromo checks her computations and finds no errors. However, Haines' message is clear. Bartiromo discards her projections and estimates and replaces them with figures that have only a remote chance of actually occurring but are more favourable to the proposal. For example, she uses first-class airfares to refigure the avoidable commercial airfare costs, even though the company policy is to fly coach. She finds revising the proposal to be distressing.

The revised proposal still has a negative net present value. Haines' anger is evident as he tells Bartiromo to revise the proposal again and to start with a $100,000 positive net present value and work backward to compute supporting estimates and projections.

Required:

a. Explain whether Maria Bartiromo's revision of the proposal was in violation of the Standards of Ethical Conduct for Management Accountants.

b. Was Mark Haines ethical in asking Bartiromo to revise the proposal? Explain your answer.

c. What elements of the projection and estimation process would be compromised in preparing an analysis for which a preconceived result is sought?

d. Identify specific controls over the capital budgeting process that Russell Corporation could implement to prevent unethical behaviour on the part of the vice president of finance.

3. Lloyd Robertson was reprimanded by the home office for recommending a pollution abatement project because the project did not meet the standard financial criterion of a 10% rate of return. However, Robertson had concluded that the $60,000 piece of equipment was necessary to prevent small amounts of arsenic from seeping into the city's water system. No warnings had been issued to the company.

Required:

a. Discuss the company requirement of a 10% rate of return on all projects.

b. What might be the ultimate consequence to Robertson's company if it fails to prevent arsenic seepage into the groundwater system?

c. How should (or can) Robertson justify the purchase of the equipment to the home office?

COMMUNICATIONS ACTIVITIES

1. Soap Suds Linen Supply Company provides laundered items to various commercial and service establishments in a large city. Soap Suds is scheduled to acquire new cleaning equipment in mid-2005 that should provide some operating efficiencies. The new equipment would enable Soap Suds to increase the volume of laundry that it handles without any increase in labour costs. In addition, the estimated maintenance costs in terms of kilograms of laundry would be reduced slightly with the new equipment.

   The new equipment was justified not only on the basis of reduced cost but also on the basis of an expected increase in demand starting in late 2005. However, since the original forecast was prepared, several potential new customers have either delayed or discontinued their own expansion plans in the market area that is serviced by Soap Suds. The most recent forecast indicates that no great increase in demand can be expected until late 2006 or early 2007.

   Required:
   Identify and explain the factors that Soap Suds Linen Supply Company should consider in deciding whether to delay the investment in the new cleaning equipment. In your presentation, distinguish between those factors that tend to indicate that the investment should be made as scheduled versus those that tend to indicate that the investment should be delayed.

   (CMA)

2. David Rosenberg Ltd. has formal policies and procedures to screen and ultimately approve capital projects. Proposed capital projects are classified as one of the following types:
   - Expansion requiring new plant and equipment
   - Expansion by replacement of present equipment with more productive equipment
   - Replacement of old equipment with new equipment of similar quality

   All expansion projects and replacement projects that will cost more than $50,000 must be submitted to the top management capital investment committee for approval. The investment committee evaluates proposed projects considering the costs and benefits outlined in the supporting proposal and the long-range effects on the company.

   The projected revenue and/or expense effects of the projects, once operational, are included in the proposal. Once a project is accepted, the committee approves an expenditure budget for the project from its inception until it becomes operational. The expenditures required each year for the expansions or replacements are also incorporated into Rosenberg's annual budget procedure. The budgeted revenue and/or cost effects of the projects, for the periods in which they become operational, are incorporated into the 5-year forecast.

   David Rosenberg Ltd. does not have a procedure for evaluating projects once they have been implemented and become operational. The vice president of finance, Jason Rosenberg, has recommended that the company establish a post-investment audit program to evaluate its capital expenditure projects.

   Required:
   a. Discuss the benefits a company could derive from a post-investment audit program for capital expenditure projects.
   b. Discuss the practical difficulties in collecting and accumulating information that would be used to evaluate a capital project once it becomes operational.

PROJECTS

1. Invite to class the executive who is responsible for computer systems at your university. Ask the individual to explain to the class
   a. What factors are considered in evaluating the need for new computer systems
   b. How new computer systems are financially justified

c. How a selection is made among competing computer vendors

2. Assume that you are employed by a large wholesaler of automobile replacement parts. Your firm provides parts to more than 3,000 retailers in Canada, the United States, Mexico, Europe, and Asia. The firm is now considering the acquisition of a new parts management system that would allow major retailers to have an on-line link to the firm for their inventory purchasing and inventory management. The system is compatible with the point-of-sale inventory management systems used by many retailers. Some major benefits of the system include faster response to orders from retailers, reduced travel costs for salespeople, and reduced paper costs and other transaction costs associated with sales orders.

   Divide your class into four groups (groups may be formed based on the natural interest of the students): management, marketing, finance, and accounting. Have each group prepare a five-minute oral presentation outlining the contribution that each functional area could make to the evaluation of the proposed inventory management system. After each group has made its presentation, discuss areas of redundancy and any gaps in coverage of relevant areas.

USING THE INTERNET

1. Capital Investment Analysis—Find a local business (such as a copy shop) that rents time on computers for an hourly rate. Determine the hourly rate. Next, determine the price of a mid-range computer at www.micron.com. Combine this information and perform a capital budgeting analysis. Assume that a computer will be used 35 hours per semester for the next three years. Also assume that the minimum rate of return is 10%. Use the tables in Appendix B at the back of the textbook in performing your analysis. (Hint: Use the appropriate present value factor for 5% compounded for six semiannual periods.)

   Does your analysis support purchasing the computer?

2. Go to http://teachmefinance.com. This Web site reviews the concepts taught in the chapter.

3. Go to www.Investopedia.com. In the search area, click on "Dictionary" and find definitions for the capital budgeting techniques mentioned in the chapter.

4. Go to www.ExcelEverywhere.com. At this site, create an ROI calculator.

SOLUTIONS TO SELF-TEST QUESTIONS

1. c: It will take 2.25 years assuming that the inflows occur evenly throughout the year. ($50,000 + $45,000 + $10,000)

2. b: 18.1% Average annual income ÷ original investment
    $19,000 ÷ $105,000.

3. c

4. a

5. e

6. d

7. c: $25,000 ÷ $8,000 = 3.1 years

8. b

9. c: $55,000 ÷ $12,000 = 4.6 years

10. b

ENDNOTES

1. Adapted from Petro-Canada Annual Report 2002.

2. Margan P. Miles, "The Financial Implications of Advertising as an Investment," *Journal of Advertising Research*, 36(4), July 1996, pp. 43–52.

3. Ibid, part 2.

4. Joel Dean, "Does Advertising Belong in the Capital Budget?" *Marketing Management*, Volume 3, No. 2, 1994, pp. 52–56.

5. Tony Seskus, "Petro-Canada Expects Record Capital Spending," *Financial Post*, November 30, 2002.

6. Anonymous, *Oil & Gas Journal*, 98(41), October 9, 2000, p. 9.

7. Time value of money and present value computations are reviewed in Appendix 10A. These concepts are essential to your understanding of the rest of the chapter; be certain that they are clear to you before continuing.

8. Some managers believe the discount rate should reflect the opportunity cost of capital, which is the highest rate of return that could be earned by using capital for the most attractive alternative project available. Using the opportunity cost of capital to discount project cash flows reflects the benefits that could have been realized from the forgone opportunity. Use of this rate has theoretical merit, but its application is generally not feasible. Therefore, most companies use the overall cost of capital as the discount rate. The computations involved in calculating the cost of capital are covered in finance textbooks and are beyond the scope of this text.

9. David E. Tyrrall, "Discounted Cash Flow: Rational Calculation or Psychological Crutch?" *Management Accounting*, February 1998, London.

10. Under some circumstances, a project may have more than one discount rate that will generate the same NPV. However, this rarely occurs and is associated with projects that have large cash outflows at both the beginning and end of the project.

11. If the alternative projects' lives are not equal, they are treated for computational purposes as if they were. For example, if Canada Oil Limited could purchase or lease the truck fleet, but the required lease has a life of three years while the purchase alternative has a six-year life, managers could compare the two alternatives either by using only three years of cash flows on the purchase alternative or by assuming that another lease could be executed at the end of the first lease. For the latter assumption, managers would make appropriate estimates relating to any cash flows that varied from the first and second lease agreements. Computer packages are available that can quickly do "what if" (or sensitivity) analysis for such scenarios.

12. Interpolation is the process of finding a term between two other terms in a series. The difference in the NPVs at 4% and 5% is $2,479 [$1,941 − (−$538)]. The interpolation process gives the following computation: Actual rate = 4% + [($1,941 ÷ $2,479)(1.0)] = 4% + (0.78)(1.0) = 4.78% (rounded). The 1.0 represents the 1% difference between the 4% and 5% rates.

13. Fixed costs are ignored in the example because they are not relevant to the decision.

14. "How To Support New Product Introductions," *Supply Chain Management Review*, 5(4), July 2001, pp. 36–42.

15. Rob Norton, "A New Tool to Help Managers," *Fortune*, May 30, 1994, p. 140.

16. Cummings-Chris, "FMS Pushes Fab Shop Forward," *Canadian Machinery and Metalworking*, V93(2), March 1998.

17. Marc J. Epstein, "Accounting for Product Take-Back," *Management Accounting*, August 1996, pp. 29–33.

18. Petro-Canada Annual Report, 2002.

19. Reuters News. September 3, 2003.

20. Lawrence A. Gordon and Mary D. Myers, "Postauditing Capital Projects," *Management Accounting*, January 1991, p. 39.

21. Ed Heard, "Cost Justification: Getting More Bank for Your Investment Bucks," *IT Solutions*, 28(6), June 1996, pp. 32–34, 36+.

22. Adapted from Petro-Canada Annual Report, 2002.

23. Interest can be earned or owed, received or paid. To simplify the discussion, the topic of interest is viewed only from the inflow standpoint.

24. Sometimes initial cost rather than average investment is used as the denominator in the ARR equation. This form of the equation ignores the return of funds at the end of the project's life and therefore provides a more conservative return estimate.

25. Beam, Laiken, and Barnett, *Federal Taxation in Canada*, CCH Canadian, 2003, pp. 253–254

26. G. Arnold and P. I. Hatzopoulos, "The Theory–Practice Gap in Capital Budgeting: Evidence from the United Kingdom," *Journal of Business Finance & Accounting*, 27(5) & (6), June/July 2000.

Chapter 11

Responsibility Accounting and Transfer Pricing in Decentralized Operations

LEARNING OBJECTIVES

After reading this chapter, you should be able to answer the following questions:

1 When
are decentralized operations appropriate?

2 How
does responsibility accounting relate to decentralization?

3 What
are the differences among the four types of responsibility centres?

4 What
is suboptimization and what are its effects?

5 How and why
are transfer prices for products used in organizations?

6 What
are the differences among the various definitions of product cost for transfer pricing?

7 How and why
are transfer prices for services used in organizations?

ON SITE

www.cn.ca

Centralized or Decentralized Management?

Rather than swinging toward either extreme—centralize or decentralize—the pendulum seems to have settled somewhere in between for **CANADIAN NATIONAL RAILWAY (CN)**. A debate in the railroad industry has been over whether management should be highly centralized or decentralized. Over the years, both concepts have been in vogue. More recently, technology allowed railroads to build huge centralized dispatching centres to handle all dispatching, crew management, maintenance scheduling, and everything else involved in operating the railroad. Decentralization is back in vogue as carriers strive to generate new business and to adapt to changing market conditions. Those that have them are not scrapping the investment in centralized dispatch centres, but they are blending more decentralized management with centralized planning. In 1999 CN announced a broad restructuring in preparation for its pending merger with Illinois Central Railway. The new management structure included five regional divisions with local decision-making authority and responsibility for meeting service and financial goals. The five divisional managers report to senior executives in CN's Montreal headquarters, who will continue to make broad strategic, financial, marketing, and operational decisions as CN, the first major North American railway system. CN sees the divisions as a way to serve small- and medium-size customers. Knowledge of local conditions and needs assists in building confidence with customers. CN operates in a highly disciplined system as far as the trip plan is concerned. All divisional dispatch offices cooperate or interact among themselves to ensure the success of trip plans that involve more than one division. Ninety percent of decisions are made in the planning process. The other 10% involves line operations, grade crossings incidents, and similar issues. Disciplined service allows CN to give the local managers the authority to act.

SOURCES: Canadian National Railway, *Annual Reports*, 1999, 2000; Lawrence H. Kaufman, "Centralized or Decentralized Management?" *Railway Age*, August 2000, Vol. 201 Issue 8, pp. 47–53.

*M*any large companies expand over the years until their corporate structures are so cumbersome that they hinder, rather than help, achievement of organizational goals and objectives. In such cases, top managers often decide to change those structures so the companies can more effectively use their resources and their employees' talents. Each organization's structure evolves as its goals, technology, and employees change. For many companies, the progression goes from highly centralized to highly decentralized. The degree of centralization reflects a chain of command, authority and responsibility relationships, and decision-making capabilities. The structure affects the management accounting practices used by the organization. This chapter discusses the extent to which top managers delegate authority to subordinate managers and the reporting systems and management accounting practices that can be used to communicate managerial responsibility. In addition, since many decentralized organizations exchange goods and services internally, the concept of transfer pricing among organizational units is discussed.

LEARNING OBJECTIVE **1**

When are decentralized operations appropriate?

centralization
an organizational strategy in which top management makes most decisions and controls most activities of the organizational units from the company's central headquarters

decentralization
the downward delegation by top management of authority and decision making to the individuals who are closest to internal processes and customers

DECENTRALIZATION

The degree to which authority is retained by top management (**centralization**) or released from top management and passed to lower managerial levels (**decentralization**) can be viewed in terms of a continuum. In a completely centralized firm, a single individual, usually the company owner or president, performs all decision making and retains full authority and responsibility for that organization's activities. In contrast, a purely decentralized organization has virtually no central authority, and each subunit acts as a totally independent entity. Either of these extremes represents a clearly undesirable arrangement. In the totally centralized company, the single individual may not have enough expertise or information to make decisions in all areas. In the totally decentralized firm, subunits may act in ways that are not consistent with the goals of the total organization. Factors associated with pure centralization and pure decentralization are presented in Exhibit 11-1. Most businesses—regardless of national domicile—fall somewhere between the extremes at a point dictated by practical necessity or by management design.

While almost every organization is decentralized to some degree, quantifying the extent of decentralization may not be possible. Some subunits may have more autonomy than others. In addition to top management philosophy, decentralization depends on the type of organizational unit. For example, a unit, segment, or division that operates in a turbulent environment and must respond quickly to new and unanticipated problems is likely to be a prime candidate for decentralization.

Top management must also consider the subunit managers' personalities and perceived abilities. Managers in decentralized environments must be goal-oriented, assertive, decisive, and creative. While these employee traits are always desirable, they are essential for decentralized company managers. In decentralized companies, managers must also be willing to accept the authority delegated by top management and to be judged based on the outcomes of the decisions that they make. Some subunit managers may be either reluctant or unable to accept this authority or responsibility. Therefore, a company may allow some units to be highly decentralized, while others are only minimally decentralized. Since managerial behaviours change and managers are replaced, supervisors should periodically reassess their decisions about a unit's extent of decentralization.

Decentralization does not necessarily mean that a unit manager has the authority to make all decisions concerning that unit. Top management selectively

Factor	Continuum		
	Pure Centralization		*Pure Decentralization*
Age of firm	Young	⟶	Mature
Size of firm	Small	⟶	Large
Stage of product development	Stable	⟶	Growing
Growth rate of firm	Slow	⟶	Rapid
Expected impact of incorrect decisions on profits	High	⟶	Low
Top management's confidence in subordinates	Low	⟶	High
Historical degree of control in firm	Tight	⟶	Moderate or loose
Use of technology	Low	⟶	High
Rate of change in the firm's market	Slow	⟶	Rapid

EXHIBIT 11-1

Continuum of Authority in Organizational Structures

determines what types of authority to delegate and what types to withhold. For example, many large, diversified companies want decentralization with centralized reporting and control. They achieve this goal in part by establishing coordinated accounting methods and by retaining certain functions at headquarters. Treasury and legal work are often provided by headquarters, sometimes through free-standing service centres whose output is charged to the various decentralized units. In addition, purchasing is frequently consolidated for efficiency, effectiveness, and coordination.

Like any management technique, decentralization has advantages and disadvantages. These pros and cons are summarized in Exhibit 11-2 and are discussed in the following sections.

Advantages of Decentralization

Decentralization has many personnel advantages. Managers have both the need and the opportunity to develop their leadership qualities, creative problem-solving abilities, and decision-making skills. Decentralized units provide excellent settings for training personnel and for screening aspiring managers for promotion. Managers can be judged on job performance and on the results of their units relative

EXHIBIT 11-2

Advantages and Disadvantages of Decentralization

Advantages

- Helps top management recognize and develop managerial talent
- Allows managerial performance to be comparatively evaluated
- Often leads to greater job satisfaction
- Makes the accomplishment of organizational goals and objectives easier
- Allows the use of management by exception

Disadvantages

- May result in a lack of goal congruence or suboptimization
- Requires more effective communication abilities
- May create personnel difficulties upon introduction
- Can be extremely expensive
- Requires accepting inappropriate decisions as it is a training ground

to units headed by other managers; such comparisons can encourage a healthy level of organizational competition. Decentralization also often leads to greater job satisfaction for managers because it provides for job enrichment and gives a feeling of increased importance to the organization. Employees are given more challenging and responsible work that provides greater opportunities for advancement.

In addition to the personnel benefits, decentralization is generally more effective than centralization in accomplishing organizational goals and objectives. The decentralized unit manager has more knowledge of the local operating environment than top management, which leads to (1) reduction in decision-making time, (2) minimization of difficulties resulting from attempts to communicate problems and instructions through an organizational chain of command, and (3) quicker perceptions of environmental changes. Thus, the manager of a decentralized unit is not only in closest contact with daily operations but also is charged with making decisions about those operations.

A decentralized structure also allows implementation of the **management by exception** principle. Top management, when reviewing divisional reports, can address issues that are out of the ordinary rather than dealing with operations that are proceeding according to plans.

An alternative to either centralization or decentralization is **outsourcing.** By outsourcing, decisions do not need to be made on centralizing or decentralizing. All decisions are made by the supplier or vendor when outsourcing is pursued. Outsourcing was examined in Chapter 1 and is further discussed in the accompanying News Note.

management by exception
a technique in which managers set upper and lower limits of tolerance for deviations and investigate only deviations that fall outside those tolerance ranges

outsourcing
the contracting with outside manufacturers or vendors for necessary goods or services rather than producing the goods or performing services in-house

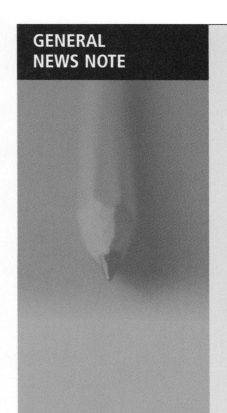

GENERAL NEWS NOTE

Reimbursing Time Inc. Journalists

Time Inc.'s worldwide network of journalists routinely overcomes all sorts of hurdles to report on newsworthy events for *People, Fortune, Sports Illustrated,* and the company's flagship magazine, *Time,* along with many other well-known Time Inc. publications. But when it came time to log travel and expenses, those very same journalists faced hurdles of a more frustrating nature.

Time Inc. always had a review and audit process for T & E (travel and entertainment) but it was decentralized. Each publication kept its own records, adding another layer of frustration to the process. Time Inc.'s reporters accessed a petty cash window to get their travel expenses up front. This solution offered little incentive for staff to file reports after their travel, making the reconciliation process a challenge.

Time Inc. learned from benchmarking studies that its cost of tracking travel and expenses was above the average. "We knew we had to consolidate the T & E reporting structure and eliminate travel advances, and we were investigating 'best practices' for all of finance and accounting," Donna Stuermer says. "It quickly became obvious that we could streamline the T & E part of the process by outsourcing the work."

Now, Time Inc. uses Gelco Information Network's outsource expense management solution that allows travelers to report expenses immediately and gives three-day turnaround on expenses, directly depositing expense reimbursements into staff's personal accounts. Gelco also pays the corporate card expenses automatically. "Our people are happy now because they get their money quickly. And we're pleased that the cost of managing T & E and reimbursing travelers dropped by more than 50% since implementation," Stuermer says.

Source: Republished with permission of the Institute of Management Accounting, from "T & E Expense: To Outsource or Not?," Shimon Avish, *Management Accounting* September 1997; permission conveyed through Copyright Clearance Center, Inc.

Disadvantages of Decentralization

Not all aspects of a decentralized structure are positive. For instance, authority and responsibility for making decisions may be divided among too many individuals, which can result in a lack of *goal congruence* among the organizational units. (**Goal congruence** exists when the personal and organizational goals of decision makers throughout a firm are consistent and mutually supportive.) In a decentralized company, unit managers are essentially competing with one another since the results of unit activities are compared. Unit managers may make decisions that positively affect their own units but are detrimental to other organizational units or to the whole company. This process results in suboptimization, which is discussed later in the chapter.

goal congruence
a condition that exists when the personal and organizational goals of decision makers throughout the firm are consistent and mutually supportive

A decentralized organization requires more effective methods of communicating plans, activities, and achievements because decision making is removed from the central office. Top management has delegated the authority to make decisions to unit managers but still retains the ultimate responsibility to corporate ownership for the effects of those decisions. Thus, to determine whether operations are progressing toward established goals, top management must be continuously aware of events occurring at lower levels. If decentralization gets totally out of control, top management must be willing to step in and take action.

Some employees may be disturbed when top management attempts to introduce decentralization policies. Employees may be asked to do too much too soon or without enough training. Furthermore, some top managers have difficulty relinquishing control or are unwilling or unable to delegate effectively.

A final disadvantage of decentralization is that it may be extremely expensive. In a large company, it is unlikely that all subordinate managers have equally good decision-making skills. Thus, the first cost is for training lower-level managers to make better decisions. Second, there is the potential cost of poor decisions. Decentralization implies the willingness of top management to let subordinates make some mistakes, but says ABB's Percy Barnevik, "You have to accept a fair share of mistakes. I tell my people that if we make 100 decisions and 70 turn out to be right, that's good enough. I'd rather be roughly right and fast than exactly right and slow."[1] This philosophy is reiterated in the following quote:

> Decentralization of authority in itself has ethical consequences. It absolutely requires trust and latitude for error. The inability to monitor the performance especially when measurement of results is the only surveillance of executives assigned to tasks their superiors cannot know in detail results inexorably in delegation. The leaders of a corporation are accustomed to reliance upon the business acumen of ... managers, whose results they watch with a practiced eye. Those concerned with the maintenance of the ethical standards of the corporation are dependent just as much on the ethical judgment and moral character of the managers to whom authority is delegated. Beyond keeping our fingers crossed, what do we do?[2]

Another cost of decentralization relates to developing and operating a more sophisticated planning and reporting system. Since top management delegates decision-making authority but retains ultimate responsibility for decision outcomes, a reporting system must be implemented that will provide top management with the ability to measure the overall accountability of the subunits. This reporting system is known as a responsibility accounting system.

Decentralization can also create a duplication of activities that can be quite expensive in terms of both time and money. For example, it is not unusual for an organization to recentralize, in part to unify its resources for greater efficiency and effectiveness.[3]

Responsibility Accounting Systems

Responsibility accounting refers to an accounting system that provides information to top management about the performance of an organizational unit. As decentralization became more prevalent in the business environment, responsibility accounting systems evolved from the increased need to communicate operating results through the managerial hierarchy.

A responsibility accounting system produces **responsibility reports** to assist each successively higher level of management in evaluating the performances of its subordinate managers and their respective organizational units. These reports reflect the revenues and/or costs under the control of a specific unit manager. Any revenues or costs that are not under the control of a specific unit manager should not be shown on his or her responsibility reports. For example, a portion of straight-line depreciation on the company headquarters building may be allocated to the Sales Department. Because the manager of the Sales Department has no control over this cost, it should not be included on the responsibility report of the Sales Department manager. Much of the information communicated on these reports is monetary, although other data may be included. Examples include proportion of deliveries made on time, number of defects generated by production for the month, and tonnes of waste produced during the month.

The number of responsibility reports routinely issued for a decentralized unit depends on how much influence that unit's manager has on the unit's day-to-day operations and costs. If a manager strongly influences all operations and costs of a unit, one report will suffice for both the manager and the unit. Normally, however, some costs are not controlled—or are only partially or indirectly controlled—by the unit manager. In such instances, the responsibility report takes one of two forms. First, a single report can be issued that shows all costs incurred in the unit, separately classified as either controllable or uncontrollable by the manager. Alternatively, separate reports can be prepared for the manager and the unit. The manager's report includes only costs under his or her control, while the unit's report includes all costs.

A responsibility accounting system is the linchpin in making decentralization work effectively. The responsibility reports about unit performance are primarily tailored to fit the planning, controlling, and decision-making needs of subordinate managers. Top managers review these reports to evaluate the efficiency and effectiveness of each unit and each manager.

One purpose of a responsibility accounting system is to "secure control at the point where costs are incurred instead of assigning them all to products and processes remote from the point of incurrence."[4] This purpose agrees with the concepts of standard costing and activity-based costing. In standard costing, variances are traced to the person (or machine) responsible for the variance; for example, the material purchase price variance can generally be traced to the purchasing agent. Activity-based costing attempts to trace as many costs as possible to the activities that caused the costs rather than using highly aggregated allocation techniques.

Control procedures are implemented for the following three reasons:

1. Managers attempt to cause actual operating results to conform to planned results. This conformity is known as **effectiveness**.

2. Managers attempt to cause, at a minimum, the standard output to be produced from the actual input costs incurred. This conformity is known as **efficiency**.

3. Managers need to ensure, to the extent possible, a reasonable utilization of plant and equipment. Utilization is primarily affected by product or service demand. At higher volumes of activity or utilization, fixed capacity costs can be spread over more units, resulting in a lower unit cost. However, demand for the product or service must first be generated before the benefits of spreading the overhead can be realized. Otherwise output is produced that creates holding costs that burden the company.

Responsibility accounting implies that subordinate managers accept the authority given to them by top management and helps them in conducting the five basic control functions shown in Exhibit 11-3. Budgets are used to officially communicate output expectations (sales, production, and so forth) and, through budget appropriations, to delegate the authority to spend. Ideally, subunit managers

efficiency
the degree to which the relationship between outputs and inputs is satisfactory; performance of a task to produce the best outcome at the lowest cost from the resources used

EXHIBIT 11-3
Basic Steps in a Control Process

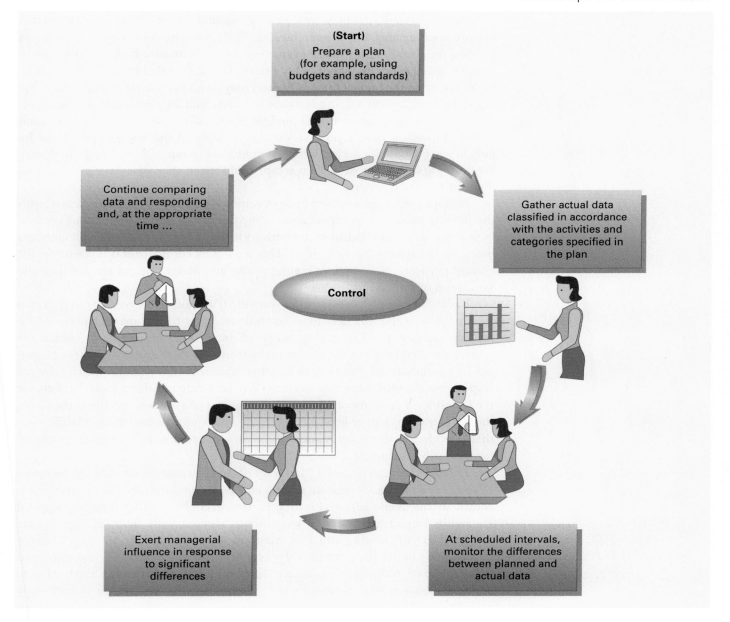

negotiate budgets and standards for their units with top management for the coming year. Involvement in the budgeting process is essential for motivating those whose performance will be evaluated on budget-to-actual comparisons.

The responsibility accounting system should be designed so that actual data are captured in conformity with budgetary accounts. During the year, the accounting system records and summarizes data for each organizational unit. Operating reports comparing actual account balances with budgeted, standard, or target amounts are prepared periodically and issued to managers. Because of day-to-day contact with operations, managers should be aware of any significant variances before they are reported, identify variance causes, and attempt to correct causes of the problems. Top managers, on the other hand, may not know about operational variances until they receive responsibility reports. By the time top management receives the reports, problems causing the variances should have been corrected, or subordinate managers should be able to explain why the problems were not or could not be resolved.

The responsibility reports received by top management may compare actual performance against the master budget. Such a comparison can be viewed as yielding an overall performance evaluation, since the master budget reflects management's expectations about sales prices, volume, and mix, as well as costs. However, using the budget for comparison may be inappropriate in some cases. For example, if the budget has an allowance for scrap built into the materials usage estimate, comparing results with the budget figure fails to support a focus on total quality. In such a case, a positive variance relative to the budget should not be judged as favourable performance if significant scrap still is being produced. Establishing a target goal of zero scrap would mean that any variance would be identified as unfavourable.

Perhaps a more appropriate form of responsibility report is that associated with the flexible budget. This report form compares actual information about controllable items (revenues and/or costs) both with the master budget and with amounts based on the achieved activity level. This secondary comparison is more useful for control purposes, since both operating results and budget figures are based on the same level of activity.

Regardless of the comparisons provided, responsibility reports reflect the upward flow of information from operational units to top management. These reports indicate the broadening scope of managerial responsibility. Managers receive detailed information on the performance of their immediate areas of control and summary information on all other organizational units for which they are responsible. Summarizing results causes a pyramiding of information. Reports for the lowest-level units are highly detailed, while reports are less specific at the top of the organization. Upper-level managers desiring information more specific than that provided in summary reports can review the responsibility reports prepared for their subordinates.

Exhibit 11-4 illustrates the March set of performance reports for the Generics Division of Heinrick Chemicals, a fictional Dutch conglomerate. All information is shown in the home office currency of Dutch Guilders (Hfl). The Mixing and Preparing Department's actual costs are compared with those in the flexible budget. Data for Mixing and Preparing are then aggregated with data of other departments under the control of the production vice president. These combined data are shown in the middle section of Exhibit 11-4. In a like manner, the total costs of the production vice president's area of responsibility are combined with other costs for which the company president is responsible and are shown in the top section of Exhibit 11-4.

Variances should be individually itemized in lower-level performance reports so that the manager under whose supervision those variances occurred has the detail needed to take appropriate corrective action. Under the management by exception principle, major deviations from expectations are highlighted in the subordinate manager's reporting section to assist upper-level managers in making decisions about when to become involved in the subordinate's operations. If no significant deviations exist, top management is free to devote its attention to other matters. In addition, such detailed variance analysis alerts operating managers to items they may need to explain to superiors.

In addition to the monetary information shown in Exhibit 11-4, many responsibility accounting systems are now providing information on critical nonmonetary measures of the period's activity. Some examples are shown in Exhibit 11-5 on page 646. Many of these measures are equally useful for manufacturing and service

EXHIBIT 11-4

Generics Division March 2004 Performance Reports

President's Performance Report

	Actual Results	Flexible Budget	Variance Over (Under)
Administrative Office—President	Hfl 267,200	Hfl 264,000	Hfl 3,200
Financial Vice President	313,200	316,600	(3,400)
Production Vice President	1,105,200	1,103,800	1,400
Sales Vice President	368,800	366,000	2,800
Totals	Hfl 2,054,400	Hfl 2,050,400	Hfl 4,000

Production Vice President's Performance Report

	Actual Results	Flexible Budget	Variance Over (Under)
Administrative Office—VP	Hfl 243,000	Hfl 240,000	Hfl 3,000
Inspect, Polish, and Package	112,600	113,400	(800)
Finishing	168,000	169,600	(1,600)
Mixing and Preparing	581,600	580,800	800
Totals	Hfl 1,105,200	Hfl 1,103,800	Hfl 1,400

Mixing and Preparing Manager's Performance Report

	Actual Results	Flexible Budget	Variance Over (Under)
Direct Material	Hfl 163,400	Hfl 166,400	Hfl (3,000)
Direct Labour	255,200	253,000	2,200
Supplies	24,600	23,400	1,200
Indirect Labour	59,600	58,600	1,000
Power	50,200	52,200	(2,000)
Repairs and Maintenance	17,200	16,200	1,000
Other	11,400	11,000	400
Totals	Hfl 581,600	Hfl 580,800	Hfl 800

EXHIBIT 11-5

Nonmonetary Information for
Responsibility Reports

- Departmental/divisional throughput
- Number of defects (by product, product line, supplier)
- Number of orders backlogged (by date, quantity, cost, and selling price)
- Number of customer complaints (by type and product); method of complaint resolution
- Percentage of orders delivered on time
- Manufacturing (or service) cycle efficiency
- Percentage of reduction of non-value-added time from previous reporting period (broken down by idle time, storage time, quality control time)
- Number of employee suggestions considered significant and practical
- Number of employee suggestions implemented
- Number of unplanned production interruptions
- Number of schedule changes
- Number of engineering change orders; percentage change from previous period
- Number of safety violations; percentage change from previous period
- Number of days of employee absences; percentage change from previous period

organizations and can be used along with basic financial measurements in judging performance.

The performance reports of each management layer are reviewed and evaluated by all successive layers of management. Managers are likely to be more careful and alert in controlling operations knowing that the reports generated by the responsibility accounting system reveal financial accomplishments and problems. Thus, in addition to providing a means for control, responsibility reports can motivate managers to influence operations in ways that will reflect positive performance.

The focus of responsibility accounting is people. The people emphasized are the managers responsible for an organizational unit such as a department, division, or geographic region. The subunit under the control of a manager is called a responsibility centre.

LEARNING OBJECTIVE 3

What are the differences among the four types of responsibility centres?

responsibility centre
the cost object under the control of a manager; in the case of a decentralized company, the cost object is an organizational unit such as a division, department, or geographical region

cost centre
an organizational unit in which the manager has the authority only to incur costs and is specifically evaluated on the basis of how well costs are controlled

TYPES OF RESPONSIBILITY CENTRES

Responsibility accounting systems identify, measure, and report on the performance of people who control the activities of responsibility centres. There are four types of **responsibility centres**, based on the manager's scope of authority and type of financial responsibility: cost, revenue, profit, and investment. They are illustrated in Exhibit 11-6 and discussed in the following sections.

Cost Centres

In a **cost centre**, the manager has the authority only to incur costs and is specifically evaluated on the basis of how well costs are controlled. In many cost centres, no revenues are generated because the unit does not engage in any revenue-producing activity. For example, the placement centre in a university may be a cost centre, since it does not charge for the use of its services but does incur costs.

In some cost centres, the costs may be difficult to control because there are many drivers. The cost of healthcare in Canada is an example of an entity with multiple cost drivers, as noted in the News Note. In other instances, revenues may be associated with a particular subunit, but they either are not under the manager's control or are not effectively measurable. The first type of situation exists in a gov-

Cost centre—manager is responsible for cost containment.

Revenue centre—manager is responsible for revenue generation.

EXHIBIT 11-6

Types of Responsibility Centres

Profit centre—manager is responsible for profit (both revenue generation and cost containment).

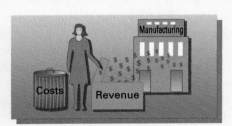

Investment centre—manager is responsible for return on asset base.

ernmental agency that is provided a specific proration of sales tax dollars but has no authority to levy or collect the related taxes. The second situation could exist in discretionary cost centres, such as a marketing research or a research and development department, in which the outputs (revenues or benefits generated from the cost inputs) are not easily measured.[5] In these situations, revenues should not be included in the manager's responsibility accounting report.

In the traditional manufacturing environment, a standard costing system is generally used, and variances are reported and analyzed. In such an environment, the highest priority in a cost centre is often the minimization of unfavourable cost variances. Top management may often concentrate only on the unfavourable variances occurring in a cost centre and ignore the efficient performance indicated by favourable variances. For example, referring back to Exhibit 11-4 on page 645, the production vice president of the Generics Division of Heinrick Chemicals might focus only on the unfavourable material and power variances for the Mixing and Preparing Department while disregarding the favourable variances for the other

What Drives the Cost of Healthcare

INTERNATIONAL NEWS NOTE

The costs of healthcare are driven by numerous factors. Clinical decisions drive supply side costs; clinical activity is also implicated, along with patient demand, in determining demand side costs. A reason, which may explain the higher cost of healthcare in Canada, is that the system incorporates a financial incentive to treat, as their clinicians are paid on a fee-for-service basis. Thus, on the supply side, Canadian doctors are more likely to order more services per patient and to offer more specialist care at a lower level of treatment (for example, specialists in Canada offer their services to patients outside of the hospitals). The greater supply of healthcare in Canada raises expectations of the patients and impacts on demand so that, for example, second opinions are more easily obtained in Canada than in the U.K. or the U.S.

Source: Ron Eden, Sue Llewellyn, and Douglas Paton, "Benchmarking on Costs in Healthcare," *Management Accounting: Magazine for Chartered Management Accountants*, March 1998, Vol. 76, Issue 3, pp. 28–30.

costs of production. Significant favourable variances should not be ignored if the management by exception principle is to be applied appropriately. Using this principle, all variances—both favourable and unfavourable—that fall outside the preestablished limits for normal deviations should be investigated.

In the Heinrick Chemicals example, Gottfried Menchen, the manager of the Mixing and Preparing Department, should have determined the causes of the variances before filing the report. For instance, it is possible that substandard material was purchased and caused excessive usage. If this is the case, the purchasing agent, not Mr. Menchen, should be held accountable for the variance. Other possible causes for the unfavourable material variance include increased material prices, excess waste, or some combination of all these causes. Only additional inquiry or investigation can determine whether that variance could have been controlled by Menchen. Similarly, the power variance may have resulted from an increase in utility costs.

The favourable direct labour variance should also be analyzed. Mr. Menchen may have used inexperienced personnel who were being paid lower rates. Such a situation might explain both the favourable direct labour variance and, to some extent, the unfavourable direct material variance (because the workers were less skilled and may have overused material). Alternatively, the people working in the Mixing and Preparing Department could simply have been very efficient this period. In this case, Menchen would compliment and reward the efficient employees and might also consider incorporating the improvement as a revised time standard.

Revenue Centres

revenue centre
an organizational unit in which the manager is accountable only for the generation of revenues and has no control over selling prices or budgeted costs

A **revenue centre** is strictly defined as an organizational unit whose manager is accountable only for the generation of revenues and has no control over setting selling prices or budgeting costs. In many retail stores, the individual sales departments are considered independent units and managers are evaluated based on the total revenues generated by their departments. Departmental managers, though, may not be given the authority to change selling prices to affect volume, and they often do not participate in the budgeting process. Thus, the departmental managers may have no impact on costs. In general, however, few pure revenue centres exist.

Managers of revenue centres are typically responsible for revenues and also are involved in planning and control related to some, but not necessarily all, of the centre's costs. Thus, a more appropriate term for this organizational unit is a "revenue and limited cost centre." For example, a sales manager who is responsible for the sales revenues generated in her territory may additionally be accountable for controlling the mileage and other travel-related expenses of her sales staff. She may not, however, be able to influence the types of cars her sales staff obtain, because automobiles are acquired on a fleetwide basis by top management.

Salaries, if directly traceable, are often a cost responsibility of a revenue centre manager. This situation reflects the traditional retail environment in which each sales clerk is assigned to a specific department and is only allowed to check out customers who want to purchase that department's merchandise. Most stores have found such a checkout situation to be detrimental to business, because customers are forced to wait for the appropriate clerk. Clerks in many stores are now allowed to assist all customers with all types of merchandise. Such a change in policy converts what was a traceable departmental cost into an indirect cost. Stores carrying high-cost, high-selling-price merchandise normally retain the traditional system.

Individual departments in a large retail store may be treated as cost or revenue centres by the store manager, while the store itself may be treated as a profit or investment centre by corporate headquarters. Such designations reflect the degree of control a manager has over selling prices, costs, and plant assets.

Managers of such departments are thus able to trace sales salaries as a direct departmental cost.

In analyzing variances from budget, managers in a revenue centre need to consider three possible causes: sales price differences, sales mix differences, and volume differences. A model is expanded below to illustrate the effect of a difference in product sales mix from that which was budgeted.

Actual Price ×	Standard Price ×	Standard Price ×	Standard Price ×
Actual Mix ×	Actual Mix ×	Standard Mix ×	Standard Mix ×
Actual Volume	Actual Volume	Actual Volume	Budgeted Volume

Price Variance   Mix Variance   Volume Variance

Exhibit 11-7 on page 650 presents the revenue statistics and variance computations for the Canadian Sales Division of Heinrick Chemicals for June 2004. The Canadian Sales Division is a wholesaler that sells to retail chains in lot sizes of 1,000 units each. Inspection of the results reveals that (1) prices increased (except for hunger suppressants), causing an overall favourable price variance; (2) the actual mix included more of the lower-priced products (vitamins and facial cream) than the standard mix, causing an overall unfavourable mix variance; and (3) the number of lots sold (6,100) was greater than the number of lots budgeted (6,000), causing a favourable volume variance. The Canadian Sales Division's manager is to be commended for good performance.

EXHIBIT 11-7

Variances for a Revenue Centre

Budget	Lots	Lot Price	Revenue	Standard Mix for Budgeted Volume
Vitamins (V)	3,000	$1,400	$4,200,000	3,000 ÷ 6,000 = 50.0%
Hunger suppressant (H)	2,000	1,600	3,200,000	2,000 ÷ 6,000 = 33.3%
Facial cream (F)	1,000	1,100	1,100,000	1,000 ÷ 6,000 = 16.7%
Totals	6,000		$8,500,000	100.0%
Actual Mix for Actual Volume				
Vitamins	3,200	$1,500	$4,800,000	
Hunger suppressant	1,800	1,600	2,880,000	
Facial cream	1,100	1,200	1,320,000	
Totals	6,100		$9,000,000	
Standard Mix for Actual Volume				
Vitamins	(6,100 × .500) = 3,050			
Hunger suppressant	(6,100 × .333) = 2,031			
Facial cream	(6,100 × .167) = 1,019			

	Actual Price × Actual Mix × Actual Volume	Standard Price × Actual Mix × Actual Volume	Standard Price × Standard Mix × Actual Volume	Standard Price × Standard Mix × Budgeted Volume
V	$1,500(3,200) = $4,800,000	$1,400(3,200) = $4,480,000	$1,400(3,050) = $4,270,000	$1,400(3,000) = $4,200,000
H	$1,600(1,800) = 2,880,000	$1,600(1,800) = 2,880,000	$1,600(2,031) = 3,249,600	$1,600(2,000) = 3,200,000
F	$1,200(1,100) = 1,320,000	$1,100(1,100) = 1,210,000	$1,100(1,019) = 1,120,900	$1,100(1,000) = 1,100,000
Totals	$9,000,000	$8,570,000	$8,640,500	$8,500,000

	$430,000 F		$70,500 U		$140,500 F	
	Price Variance		Mix Variance		Volume Variance	

$500,000 F

Total Revenue Variance

Profit Centres

profit centre
an organizational unit in which the manager is responsible for generating revenues and planning and controlling all expenses

In **profit centres**, managers are responsible for generating revenues and for planning and controlling all expenses. A profit centre manager's goal is to maximize the centre's net income. Profit centres should be independent organizational units whose managers have the authority to obtain resources at the most economical prices and to sell products at prices that will maximize revenue. If managers do not have complete authority to buy and sell at objectively determined costs and prices, it is difficult to make a meaningful evaluation of the profit centre.

Profit centres are not always manufacturing divisions or branches of retail stores. A dental clinic may view each department (Cleaning, X-Ray, Tooth and Gum Restoration, and Crown Fabrication) as a profit centre, and a university may view certain educational divisions as profit centres (undergraduate education, non-degree-seeking night school, and graduate divisions).

To illustrate the variance computations for a profit centre, assume that Heinrick Chemicals uses 18-wheel trucks to deliver products throughout Western Europe and each truck is considered a profit centre. The budgeted and actual revenues and

	Master Budget	Actual	Variance	
Delivery revenues	F 180,000	F186,000	F 6,000	F
Variable costs:				
Direct labour	F 4,500	F 4,600	F 100	U
Gas and oil	37,800	39,050	1,250	U
Variable overhead	7,740	7,850	110	U
Total	F 50,040	F 51,500	F 1,460	U
Contribution margin	F 129,960	F134,500	F 4,540	F
Fixed overhead—controllable	(38,400)	(38,000)	400	F
Segment margin—controllable	F 91,560	F 96,500	F 4,940	F
Fixed overhead—not controllable				
by profit centre manager	(27,000)	(29,250)	(2,250)	U
Profit centre income	F 64,560	F 67,250	F 2,690	F

EXHIBIT 11-8

Profit Centre Master Budget Comparisons for August 2004

expenses for "Tour de France," a truck for which Claudette Harfleur is responsible, are shown in Exhibit 11-8. The profit centre should be judged on the F67,250 of profit centre income (in Franch francs—F), but Harfleur should be judged on the controllable margin of F96,500. Harfleur should point out that her delivery revenues were greater than budgeted because she drove more kilometres than budgeted. Thus, using the master budget as a basis for comparison, it is natural that unfavourable variances would exist for all of the variable costs.

The comparison of actual results to a flexible budget at the actual activity level shown in Exhibit 11-9 on page 652 provides better information for assessing cost control within the profit centre. Harfleur did a good job controlling the costs of her profit centre; the problem area is related to the noncontrollable fixed overhead. She should investigate the causes for the F2,250 unfavourable variance. Then she and her manager can discuss any ideas she may have for addressing those causes. It is also possible that the budgeted figure for the noncontrollable fixed overhead is inappropriate because of cost increases for some or all of the items composing that fixed overhead pool.

Investment Centres

An **investment centre** is an organizational unit in which the manager is responsible for generating revenues, planning and controlling costs, and acquiring, using, and

investment centre
an organizational unit in which the manager is responsible for generating revenues, planning and controlling costs, and acquiring, disposing of, and using plant assets to earn the highest feasible rate of return on the investment base

The establishment of a national call centre at Canadian Tire has helped to streamline operations, both internally and externally.

EXHIBIT 11-9

Profit Centre Flexible Budget
Comparisons for August 2004

	Flexible Budget	Actual	Variance
Delivery revenues	F 186,000	F186,000	F 0
Variable costs:			
Direct labour	F 4,650	F 4,600	F 50 F
Gas and oil	39,060	39,50	10 F
Variable overhead	7,998	7,850	148 F
Total	F 51,708	F 51,500	F 208 F
Contribution margin	F 134,292	F134,500	F 208 F
Fixed overhead—controllable	(38,400)	(38,000)	400 F
Segment margin—controllable	F 95,892	F 96,500	F 608 F
Fixed overhead—not controllable			
by profit centre manager	(27,000)	(29,250)	(2,250) U
Profit centre income	F 68,892	F 67,250	F 1,642 U

disposing of plant assets. The manager performs each of these activities with the aim of earning the highest feasible rate of return on the investment base. Many investment centres are independent, freestanding divisions or subsidiaries of a firm. This independence allows investment centre managers the opportunity to make decisions about all matters affecting their organizational units and to be judged on the outcomes of those decisions.

Assume that Walker Pharmaceuticals (a subsidiary of Heinrick Chemicals) is an investment centre headed by Henri LeBaron. The 2004 income statement for the company (in Swiss francs—Fr) is as follows:

Sales	Fr1,613,200
Variable expenses	900,000
Contribution margin	Fr 713,200
Fixed expenses	490,000
Net income	Fr 223,200

LeBaron has the authority to set selling prices, incur costs, and acquire and dispose of plant assets. The plant has an asset base of Fr2,480,000; and thus, the rate of return on assets for the year was 9% (Fr223,200 ÷ Fr2,480,000). In evaluating the performance of Walker Pharmaceuticals, top management would compare this rate of return with the rates desired by Heinrick Chemicals' management and with the rates of other investment centres in the company. Rate of return and other performance measures for responsibility centres are treated in greater depth in Chapter 13.

SUBOPTIMIZATION

Because of their closeness to daily divisional activities, responsibility centre managers should have more current and detailed knowledge about sales prices, costs, and other market information than does top management. Managers of profit and investment centres are encouraged, to the extent possible, to operate those subunits as separate economic entities while making certain that they exist to achieve goals consistent with those of the larger organization of which they are part.

Regardless of size, type of ownership, or product or service being sold, one basic goal for any business is to generate profits. For other organizations, such as charities and governmental entities, the ultimate financial goal may be to break even. The ultimate goal will be achieved through the satisfaction of organizational

Turn a Cost Centre into a Profit Centre—A Report

At Canadian Tire, we felt our national call centre would inevitably become more efficient and profitable if we established a system that puts the customer at the centre of the transaction. Our company puts special emphasis on creating customers for life. In our stores, there are customer service buttons throughout the aisles, and video kiosks or other customer service aids to make shopping easy. We wanted to bring the same level of customer care to our call centre.

Much of our call centre activity grew out of CTAL, a wholly owned subsidiary providing proprietary credit card services to Canadian Tire customers. CTAL services all transactions for Canadian Tire's four million credit card holders. It also offers a variety of financial products such as insurance, an emergency roadside assistance auto club, and telecommunications products, as well as administering Canadian Tire's credit card-based customer loyalty reward programs. With 800 employees in its call centre, CTAL is, in effect, the central point of nonretail contact for customers. We handle more than 15 million calls per year, covering more than 200 different types of transactions.

About a year ago, we decided to improve the efficiency, responsiveness, and revenue capability of our call centres. Our primary goal was to create a customer-focused environment that would enable us to understand customer behaviour and needs, offer timely introduction of new services, and enhance existing services to meet changing customer expectations. We took a look at our operations and saw too many independent call centres. It seemed that every time we introduced a new product or service, we set up a new call centre, resulting in a network of more than 20 call centres. Our first goal was to reduce this to 10. Through cross-training and expanded knowledge, we enabled customer service agents to handle a wider variety of requests. We streamlined operations, hoping to make it possible for customers to reach the right representative 95% of the time. We expected to improve internal operations by eliminating (1) multiple processes for similar tasks, (2) multiple system logins, (3) multiple non-integrated databases, and (4) complex customized environments that make it difficult to quickly introduce new products or services.

To determine the success of our effort, we created key metrics around reduced customer transfer rates and customer satisfaction, customer service levels, and product introduction lead times. For example, in the beginning, our customers were reaching the right representative about 70% of the time. We began a systematic effort to reduce transfer rates. Through cross-training and consolidating the number of call centres, we have been able to reduce transfers by 50%. However, our long-term goal is to further reduce transfers by an additional 50%.

In our initial phase, we achieved significant returns through training. To make further gains, however, we decided to implement a next-generation solution—to combine information from different data sources into a single application. Integrating telephony equipment with desktop applications would allow customer service representatives to match customer information with calls.

In the year since we began, we have cut our transfer rate in half and learned a number of valuable lessons. Perhaps most important is to strike a delicate balance between organizational changes and technology purchases.

Source: Mary Turner and Gavin Welbourn, "Turn a Cost Centre into a Profit Centre," *Communications News*, October 1998, Vol. 35, Issue 10, p. 69. Reprinted by permission of *Communications News*.

critical success factors—those items that are so important that, without them, the organization would cease to exist. Most organizations would consider quality, customer service, efficiency, cost control, and responsiveness to change as five critical success factors. If all of these factors are managed properly, the organization should be financially successful. If they are not, sooner or later the organization will fail. All members of the organization—especially managers—should work toward the same basic objectives if the critical success factors are to be satisfied. Losing sight of the overall organizational goals while working to achieve a separate responsibility centre's conflicting goal will result in *suboptimization*.

LEARNING OBJECTIVE   4

What is suboptimization and what are its effects?

suboptimization
a situation in which unit managers make decisions that positively affect their own unit but that are detrimental to other organizational units or to the company as a whole

Suboptimization exists when individual managers pursue goals and objectives that are in their own and/or their segments' particular interests rather than in the company's best interest. Because managers of profit and investment centres have great flexibility in regard to financial decisions, these managers must remember that their operations are integral parts of the entire corporate structure. Thus, actions of these organizational units should be in the best long-run interest of both the unit and its parent organization. Unit managers should be aware of and accept the need for goal congruence throughout the organization.

For suboptimization to be limited or minimized, top management must be aware of it and must develop ways to avoid it. One way managers can limit suboptimization is by communicating corporate goals to all organizational units. Exhibit 11-10 depicts other ways of limiting suboptimization as stairsteps to the achievement of corporate goals. These steps are in no hierarchical order. If any steps are missing, however, the climb toward corporate goals and objectives becomes more difficult for divisional managers.

Companies may define their organizational units in various ways based on management accountability for one or more income-producing factors—costs,

EXHIBIT 11-10

Performance Measures to Limit Suboptimization

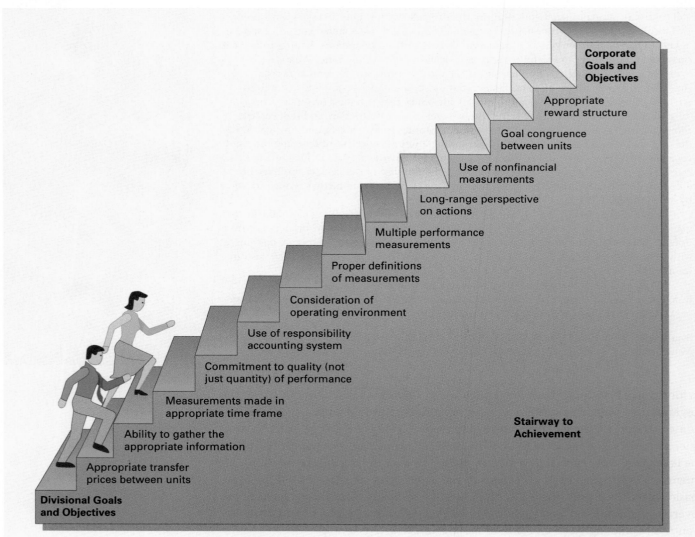

Corporate Goals and Objectives

Appropriate reward structure

Goal congruence between units

Use of nonfinancial measurements

Long-range perspective on actions

Multiple performance measurements

Proper definitions of measurements

Consideration of operating environment

Use of responsibility accounting system

Commitment to quality (not just quantity) of performance

Measurements made in appropriate time frame

Ability to gather the appropriate information

Appropriate transfer prices between units

Divisional Goals and Objectives

Stairway to Achievement

revenues, and/or assets. To properly evaluate the accomplishments of segments and their managers, a company, such as Teva Pharmaceutical Industries, will often set a price at which to transfer goods or services between segments. Such prices can help measure a selling segment's revenue and a buying segment's costs.

TRANSFER PRICING

How and why are transfer prices for products used in organizations?

Responsibility centres often provide goods or services to other company segments. These transfers require that a **transfer price** (or charge-back system) be established to account for the flow of these goods or services within the company. A transfer price is an internal charge established for the exchange of goods or services between organizational units of the same company. Internal company transfers should be presented on external financial statements at the producing segment's costs. Thus, if transfers are sold at an amount other than cost, the intersegment profit, expense, and/or revenue must be removed from the accounts for external financial reporting.

transfer price
an internal charge established for the exchange of goods and services between organizational units of the same company

Intracompany transfers should be made only if they are in the best interest of the whole organization. If both the buying and selling managers have the authority to negotiate the transfer price, the following general rules create the limits of the transfer pricing model:[6]

- The maximum transfer price should be no greater than the lowest market price at which the buying segment can acquire the goods or services externally.
- The minimum transfer price should be no less than the sum of the selling segment's incremental production costs plus the opportunity cost of the facilities used. Incremental cost refers to the additional cost of producing a contemplated quantity of output, which generally means variable costs of production. Examples of opportunity cost include forgone contribution margin on alternative products not made and rent on the facilities that would otherwise be available if the company were not making the product that is the subject of the transfer price analysis.

Companies often sell components between divisions using transfer prices. Determination of a transfer price for these door stampings can be made on the basis of unit cost or market value, or it could result from negotiation between divisional managers.

The difference between this model's upper and lower limits is the corporate profit (or savings) generated by producing internally rather than buying externally. The transfer price acts to "divide the corporate profit" between the buying and selling segments. From the company's perspective, any transfer price set between these two limits is generally considered appropriate. If the market price is less than the internal incremental cost, it may be concluded that the competition is significantly more efficient than the firm at making a specific product. In this case, management should consider either discontinuing production of that product or finding ways to make it more efficiently and competitively.

To illustrate use of this model, assume that product K is made by Division A of Heinrick Chemicals Company. Product K has per unit incremental production and opportunity costs of $8 and $5, respectively. The $5 opportunity cost represents the forgone unit contribution margin on a similar product the company would otherwise make. If Division A were to sell product K to Division B, the minimum transfer price would be $13. The same product is available from external suppliers for $11. Heinrick Chemicals' management has two choices. First, it can have Division A stop making product K and, instead, have Division B buy it from the external suppliers. This decision is reasonable since, compared with those suppliers, Division A does not appear to be cost efficient in its production activities. Stopping production would release the facilities for other, more profitable purposes. Alternatively, management could insist that Division A improve its efficiency and reduce the cost of making product K. Either choice would benefit the company as a whole.

After the transfer price range limits have been determined, management may consider understandability in choosing a price within the range. Managers should be able to comprehend how a transfer price was set and how it will affect their divisions' profits. Most transfer prices are cost-based, market-based, or arrived at through a process of negotiation.

Assume that the Sussex Division (managed by Mr. Henry Higgins) of Heinrick Chemicals manufactures the basic compounds needed to formulate its antioxidant pill for the Montbatton Pharmaceutical Sales Territory (managed by Ms. Julie Pickering). The managers are attempting to establish a transfer price for each lot-size of 1,000 bottles. Sussex Division data (shown in Exhibit 11-11) are used to illustrate various transfer pricing approaches. Note that Sussex Division is capable of supplying all external and internal production needs.

Canadian tax reform could affect transfer prices, if the U.S. lead is followed. The U.S. Senate Finance Committee recently approved a bill that would treat U.S. companies domiciled in tax havens, like Bermuda, as U.S. firms for tax purposes unless they do a meaningful amount of business in their new host country.[7] An example would be a small appliance made in a low-tax country where the domiciled U.S. subsidiary pays $5 for it, only to sell the appliance for $50, to its U.S. parent, which sells it to Wal-Mart for $55. The $45 in income is taxed at a low rate, while the $5 is taxed at the higher U.S. rates. The U.S. Senate Finance Committee wants the entire $50 in profit to be taxed at the higher U.S. rates.

LEARNING OBJECTIVE 6

What are the differences among the various definitions of product cost for transfer pricing?

Cost-Based Transfer Prices

Because of its emphasis on cost, the cost-based method of establishing a transfer price would seem to be logical and appropriate. There are, however, numerous ways to compute cost. Product cost is defined as including direct material, direct labour, variable production overhead, and fixed production overhead. This definition reflects the concept of absorption, or full, costing. In contrast, variable costing

Standard production cost per lot:		
Direct material (DM)	$160	
Direct labour (DL)	48	
Variable overhead (VOH)	72	
Variable selling and administrative	8	
Total variable costs		$288
Fixed overhead (FOH)*	$ 78	
Fixed selling and administrative*	10	88
Total costs		$376
Normal mark-up on variable cost (50%)		144
List selling price		$520

Estimated annual production: 400,000 lots
Estimated sales to outside entities: 150,000 lots
Estimated intracompany transfers: 250,000 lots

*Fixed costs are allocated to all lots produced based on estimated annual production.

EXHIBIT 11-11

Standard Cost and Other Information about Antioxidant Pills

includes only those cost components that change in relationship to volume (direct material, direct labour, and variable production overhead) in product cost. Variable costing treats fixed production overhead as a period expense. If cost is to be used as the basis for setting a transfer price, a definition of *cost* must first be agreed on by the managers engaging in the intracompany transfer.

The absorption cost for a 1,000-bottle lot is $358 ($160 DM + $48 DL + $72 VOH + $78 FOH). A transfer price equal to absorption cost provides a contribution toward covering the selling division's fixed production overhead. Such a transfer price does not produce the same amount of income that would be generated if the transferring division sold the goods externally, but it does provide for coverage of all production costs.

A transfer price for a lot size of bottles of antioxidant pills based on variable cost is either $280 or $288. The difference depends on whether variable cost is defined as variable production cost or total variable cost. Using either of these costs as the transfer price will not give Mr. Higgins much incentive to transfer the antioxidant pills internally. Fixed costs of Sussex Division would not be reduced by selling internally and no contribution margin would be generated by the transfers to help cover these fixed expenses.

One final difficulty with using a cost-based transfer price is whether an actual or standard cost should be used. If actual costs are used, inefficiencies in production may not be corrected, since their cost will simply be covered by the buying division. But, if standard costs are used, and savings are effected over standard costs, the buying division will be "paying" more than actual cost for the goods.

Market-Based Transfer Prices

To avoid the problems involved in defining cost, some companies simply use a market price approach to setting transfer prices. Market price is believed to be an objective measure of value and simulates the selling price that would exist if the segments were independent companies. If a selling division is operating efficiently relative to its competition, it should ordinarily be able to show a profit when transferring products or services at market prices. An efficiently operating buying division should not be troubled by a market-based transfer price. After all, that is what would have to be paid for the goods or services if the alternative of buying internally did not exist.

Transfer Pricing in the Canadian Oil Industry

The Canadian oil industry has been the subject of several debates with respect to charges of transfer pricing. On the basis of a large data set, which includes all oil shipments into the U.S. and Canada from 1974–84, the direct test of manipulation transfer pricing, based on actual company behaviour, is performed. Through regression analysis it emerges that the six largest Canadian affiliates of multinational corporations paid crude oil import prices that were generally equal to or lower than prices of third-party transactions for a country in a given year. This is a fairly robust result, which highlights the existence of manipulative transfer pricing. In the present case, the practice was beneficial to Canada.

Source: Jean-Thomas Bernard and Eric Genest-LaPlante, "Transfer Pricing by the Canadian Oil Industry: A Company Analysis," *Applied Economics Letters*, No. 3, 1996, pp. 333–340.

Still, several problems may exist with using market prices for intracompany transfers. The first problem is that transfers may involve products that have no exact counterpart in the external market. Second, market price may not be entirely appropriate because of internal cost savings arising from reductions in bad debts, packaging, advertising, and delivery expenditures. Third, difficulties can arise in setting a transfer price when the market is depressed because of a temporary reduction in demand for the product. Should the current depressed price be used as the transfer price, or should the expected long-run market price be used? Last, a question exists as to what is the "right" market price to use. Different prices are quoted and different discounts and credit terms are allowed to different buyers. Thus, it may not be possible to determine the most appropriate market price to charge.

NEGOTIATED TRANSFER PRICES

negotiated transfer prices
an intracompany charge for goods or services that has been set through a process of negotiation between the selling and purchasing unit managers

Because of the problems associated with both cost-based and market-based prices, **negotiated transfer prices** are often set through a process of bargaining between the selling and purchasing unit managers. Such prices are normally below the external sales price of the selling unit, above that unit's incremental costs plus opportunity cost, and below the market purchase price for the buying unit. A negotiated price meeting these specifications falls within the range limits of the transfer pricing model.

A negotiated transfer price for the Sussex Division of Heinrick Chemicals would be less than the $520 list selling price or the Montbatton Pharmaceutical Sales Division's buying price, if lower. The price would also be set greater than the $288 incremental (variable) costs. If some of the variable selling costs could be eliminated, the incremental cost would be even less. If Sussex Division could not sell any additional lots of antioxidant pills externally or downsize its facilities, there would be no opportunity cost involved. If neither of these conditions existed, an opportunity cost would have to be determined. This could increase total costs to as much as the $520 list selling price, if all lots could be sold externally.

Authority to negotiate a transfer price implies that division managers have the autonomy to sell or buy products externally if internal negotiations fail. To encourage cooperation between the transferring divisions, top management may consider allowing each party to set a different transfer price.

Dual Pricing

dual pricing arrangement
a transfer price method that allows a selling division to record the transfer of goods or services at a market-based or negotiated price and a buying division to record the transfer at a cost-based amount

Since a transfer price is used to satisfy internal managerial objectives, a **dual pricing arrangement** can be used that allows different transfer prices for the selling and the buying segments. The selling division records the transfer of goods or services at a market or negotiated market price, which provides a profit for that division. The buying division records the transfer at a cost-based amount, which provides a minimal cost for that division. Dual transfer pricing gives managers the most relevant information for decision making and performance evaluation.

Choosing the Appropriate Transfer Price

The final determination of which transfer pricing system to use should reflect the circumstances of the organizational units, as well as corporate goals. No one method of setting a transfer price is best in all instances. Exhibit 11-12 provides the results of a transfer pricing survey of Canadian multinational corporations (MNC) and indicates that transfer pricing is a major concern, especially for income tax reasons. An amazing 95% of the Canadian respondents reported that they had been investigated by the Canada Customs and Revenue Agency (CCRA), thus suggesting that multinational corporations and other companies should set transfer prices to approximate market prices. Regardless of what method is used, a thoughtfully set transfer price will provide the following advantages:

- A means of encouraging what is best for the organization as a whole
- An appropriate basis for the calculation and evaluation of segment performance
- The rational acquisition or use of goods and services between corporate divisions
- The flexibility to respond to changes in demand or market conditions
- A means of motivating managers in decentralized operations

Setting a reasonable transfer price is not an easy task. Everyone involved in the process must be aware of the positive and negative aspects of each type of transfer price and be responsive to suggestions of change if the need is indicated.

Transfer Prices for Service Departments

Setting transfer prices for products moving between one organizational unit and another is a well-established practice. Instituting transfer prices for services is a less common technique but an effective one for some types of service departments. Examples of services for which transfer prices may be used include computer services, secretarial services, legal services, and maintenance services. If management is

LEARNING OBJECTIVE 7

How and why are transfer prices for services used in organizations?

- 68% of Canadian parent respondents believe that transfer pricing is very important to their group at present, and 64% think it will be a major international tax issue for them over the next two years.

- 20 out of 25 Canadian subsidiary respondents report undergoing a transfer pricing examination; 84% expect they will be subject to a transfer pricing examination in the next two years.

- 84% of our Canadian subsidiary respondents reported that they have prepared transfer pricing documentation in accordance with the tax rules in their country.

- 56% of Canadian parent respondents placed a high priority on an integrated global approach.

- 28% of Canadian parent respondents include transfer pricing as a part of their corporate strategic planning.

- 28% of Canadian parent respondents have considered the transfer pricing related issues to e-commerce.

- For Canadian subsidiary respondents that hold intellectual property, 25% charge for tax purposes only and another 40% charge for management and tax purposes.

Source: "Transfer Pricing: 2001 Global Survey," Ernst & Young. Permission to use copyrighted material granted by Ernst & Young LLP.

EXHIBIT 11-12

Survey of Canadian Transfer Pricing Methods

considering setting a transfer price for a service department, the questions in Exhibit 11-13 should first be answered. The exhibit also presents some suggestions as to how the transfer price should be set. All the questions should be considered simultaneously and the suggestions combined to form a reasonable transfer price.

A department planning to use transfer prices for services must decide on a capacity level for use in price development. This decision is equivalent to that made in setting a predetermined overhead rate. For example, a service department may use expected annual capacity or practical capacity. If expected annual capacity is chosen, the transfer price per unit of service will be higher than if practical capacity is chosen. If the service department uses expected annual capacity and performs more services than expected, a favourable volume variance will arise.[8] Users will not necessarily benefit from reduced charges, because the transfer price is not normally changed. Use of practical capacity will, on the other hand, create a lower price. It might also encourage more internal services use and generate ideas as to how to use the additional capacity to fill outside needs. In addition, if the practical capacity level is not achieved, an unfavourable volume variance is noted, and the opportunity cost of underutilization is clearly identifiable.

In developing transfer prices for services, general costs must be allocated to the various departments equitably, and the underlying reason for cost incurrence must be determined. Transfer prices are useful when service departments provide distinct, measurable benefits to other areas or provide services having a specific cause-and-effect relationship. Transfer prices in these circumstances can provide certain advantages (see Exhibit 11-14) to the organization in both the revenue-producing and service departments.

EXHIBIT 11-13

Setting a Transfer Price for Services

	If Response Is:	
Questions	**Yes**	**No**
Is the service department to be considered a "money maker"?	Set transfer price using market-based, negotiated, or dual pricing.	Set transfer price using cost-based prices.
Does a user department have significant control over the quantity and quality of service used?	Use a base that reflects total quantity of activity of the service department.	Transfer prices are not particularly useful.
Do opportunities exist to use external services rather than internal services?	Use a base that reflects the typical manner in which external purchases are made.	Set transfer price by negotiation or upper level management; use a base that reflects the quantity of activity of the service department.
Is there a reasonable alternative (or surrogate) measure of service benefits provided to users?	Use a base representing total volume of alternative measures produced by the service department.	Transfer prices are not particularly useful.
Are the services provided of a recurring nature?	Use a fixed price for each service used.	Use a price that reflects the degree of use, constrained by whether the user can bear the cost.
Are all services provided of a similar nature?	Use a fixed price based on a single factor of use.	Use a price that reflects the degree of use, constrained by whether user can bear the cost.
Are the services performed typically expensive?	Use market-based or negotiated prices, constrained by whether the user can bear the cost. The base may be more complex than typical.	Use cost-based or negotiated prices. The base should be easy to understand and to compute.

	User Departments	**Provider Departments**
User involvement	Because they are being charged for services, user departments may suggest ways in which provider departments can improve services.	Because they are charging for the services they are providing, provider departments may become more aware of the needs of their users and seek to develop services that are more beneficial to user departments.
Cost consciousness	Because they are being charged for services, user departments may restrict usage to those services that are necessary and cost beneficial.	Because they are charging for the services they are providing, provider departments must be able to justify the prices charged and, thus, may maintain more control over costs.
Performance evaluations	Because control over amount of services used exists, user departments can include costs in performance evaluations.	Because transfer prices can generate "revenues" for their departments, provider department managers have more ways to evaluate departmental performance.

First, transfer prices can encourage more involvement between the user and service departments. Users are more likely to suggest ways for the service department to improve its performance, since improved performance could result in lower transfer prices. Service departments are more likely to interact with users to find out the specific types of services that are needed and to eliminate or reduce those that are not cost beneficial.

Second, use of a transfer price for services should cause managers to be more cost conscious. Managers of user departments should attempt to eliminate waste. For example, if an MIS Department charged recipients in other departments for the number of reports received, managers would be less likely to request reports simply to be "on the receiving list," as sometimes occurs. For managers of the service departments, cost consciousness is directed at monitoring the cost to provide services. If excessive costs are incurred, a reasonable transfer price may not cover costs or a high transfer price may not be justifiable to users.

Last, transfer prices can provide information useful in evaluating managerial performance. Responsibility reports for user departments show a service department cost related to the quantity of actual services used. User department managers should be able to justify what services were used during the period. Transfer prices allow service departments to be treated as money-making operations rather than simply cost-generating operations. Responsibility reports of these departments indicate the transfer prices charged and the costs of providing services. Thus, these managers can be held accountable for cost control and profitability. The cost effectiveness of the provider department can then be determined and compared with the cost of outsourcing.

Although transfer prices for services can be effective tools, they do have certain disadvantages. First, there can be, and often is, disagreement among unit managers as to how the transfer price should be set. Second, implementing transfer prices in the accounting system requires additional organizational costs and employee time.

Third, transfer prices may not work equally well for all types of service departments. Service departments that do not provide measurable benefits or cannot show a distinct cause-and-effect relationship between cost incurrence and service use by other departments should not use transfer prices. Finally, depending on how the transfer price is set, a transfer price may cause dysfunctional behaviour among the organizational units; for example, certain services may be underutilized or overutilized. A company should weigh the advantages and disadvantages of using transfer prices before deciding whether a transfer pricing system would enhance or detract from organizational effectiveness and efficiency.

TRANSFER PRICING IN A MULTINATIONAL SETTING

Because of the differences in tax systems, customs duties, freight and insurance costs, import/export regulations, and foreign exchange controls, setting transfer prices for products and services becomes extremely difficult when the company is engaged in multinational operations. In addition, as shown in Exhibit 11-15, the internal and external objectives of transfer pricing in multinational companies (MNCs) differ.

Because of these differences, there is no simple way to determine transfer prices in MNCs. Multinational companies may use one transfer price when a product is sent to or received from one country and a totally different transfer price for the same product when it is sent to or received from another. However, some guidelines as to transfer pricing should be set by the company and followed on a consistent basis. For example, a company should not price transfers to nondomestic subsidiaries in a way that would send the majority of costs to a subsidiary in the country with the highest tax rate unless that pricing method was reasonable and equitable to all subsidiaries. The general test of reasonableness is that transfer prices should reflect unbiased, or "arm's-length," transactions.

As indicated in the News Note, MNC transfer prices are now being carefully scrutinized by tax authorities in both the home and host countries because such prices determine which country taxes the income from the transfer. The Government of Canada is concerned about both Canadian multinationals operating in low-tax countries and foreign companies operating in Canada. The Government of Canada believes that, in both situations, companies could avoid paying Canadian corporate income taxes by using misleading or inaccurate transfer

EXHIBIT 11-15

Multinational Company Transfer Pricing Objectives

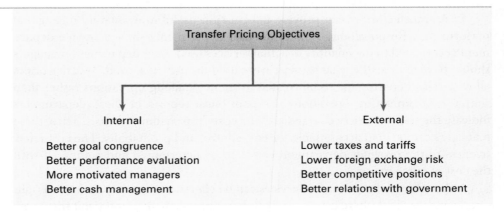

Source: Republished with permission of the Institute of Management Accounting, from "Guidelines for CEOs in Transfer Pricing Policies," Wagdy M. Abdallah, *Management Accounting*, September 1998; permission conveyed through Copyright Clearance Center, Inc.

Advanced Pricing Agreement Procedures

INTERNATIONAL NEWS NOTE

Much of Canada's trade is carried on in other countries by multinational corporations (MNC). Since such transactions are not conducted at arm's length, transfer pricing has become an important tax issue. This becomes a problem when the transfer price is deliberately set lower (or higher) than the arm's length market rate. This practice is quite common, as MNCs can use various transfer pricing strategies to minimize their worldwide tax liabilities. To counteract these strategies, government taxation authorities in different countries have developed a number of approaches to limit an MNC's ability to avoid taxation and to ensure taxes are not disproportionately levied across countries. This has resulted in disputes that can be costly and time consuming to resolve, especially when several countries are involved.

In order to alleviate some of these problems, several countries—including Australia, Canada, Germany, Italy, Japan, New Zealand, the United Kingdom, and the United States—have implemented, or are in the process of implementing, advance pricing agreement (APA) procedures. An APA is an agreement between a corporation and a country's taxation authority. It outlines the methodology to be used in pricing goods and services between the taxpayer corporation and its related parties. An APA can be unilateral (between the taxpayer and the taxation authority in its country of residence), bilateral, or multilateral (involving the taxpayer and two or more relevant taxation authorities).

Generally, it is expected that because an APA is based on a pre-approved inter-company transfer pricing method—as opposed to a particular transfer price—it should reduce the possibility of a pricing dispute arising between the company and the tax authority at some point in the future. This should provide certainty to a corporation that it will not have to deal with costly and disruptive disputes with the Canada Customs and Revenue Agency (CCRA) often years after a transaction has taken place. In addition, an APA should reassure CCRA, as the applicant is bound by the agreement not to manipulate transfer prices to its advantage.

CCRA states in IC94-4 that the purpose of introducing APAs is "to promote voluntary compliance by assuring taxpayers that the TPMs (transfer pricing methodologies) they use to establish transfer prices are acceptable." Because compliance is voluntary, a Canadian corporation interested in an APA must take the initiative to contact the head office or district office of CCRA.

Source: Alexander M.G. Gelardi and Sophia Y.L. Wong, "New Solution to Transfer Pricing Problems," *CGA Magazine*, January 1996, pp. 48–52+.

pricing. Thus, the Canada Customs and Revenue Agency may be quick to investigate Canadian subsidiaries that operate in low-tax countries or areas and suddenly show unusually high profits. If foreign companies charge their Canadian subsidiaries higher prices than what they would charge subsidiaries in their home country, Canadian taxable income (and thus the tax base) will decline—which may also bring about a CCRA review.

As mentioned in Chapter 1, transfers among nations are becoming easier because of trade arrangements such as the European Union, the North American Free Trade Zone, and the General Agreement on Tariffs and Trade and the World Trade Organization. These arrangements should help reduce the significance of transfer price manipulations through the harmonization of tax structures and reductions in import/export fees, tariffs, and capital movement restrictions.

CHAPTER SUMMARY

Centralization refers to a concentration of management control at high organizational levels, while decentralization refers to the downward delegation of decision-making authority to subunit managers. Thus, a decentralized organization comprises operational units led by managers who have some autonomy in decision making. The degree to which a company is decentralized depends on top

CN's Service Plan

Within CN's decentralized structure, there is a service plan. Each division is accountable for its own business performance, including operational responsibility for yards, terminals, switching and facilities; maintenance of infrastructure and equipment; and account sales. From the customer's perspective, quality service means having the railway car, in good condition, at the shipping dock when promised, and getting the car with the shipment intact to the destination on time, at a price. Within the service plan, CN operates its network like a conveyor belt. Precise scheduling enables CN to evenly space trains, which results in smooth yard operations, reduces transit times and dramatically improves its ability to deliver service at a competitive price.

CN uses an electronic catalogue that provides exact transit times, to the hour, dock to dock, for more than 3,600 routings. This is CN major service. Each account manager, in a division, uses a laptop computer to review the product catalogue with customers, providing information such as origin and destination, specific routing options and transit times for each option, to help them choose the routing that best fits their needs. Account managers can even add cars to certain trains to meet customer requirements.

Efficiencies brought about by the service plan have allowed CN to reduce its locomotive and railcar fleets by 650 and 12,700 units, respectively. These improvements in asset use contributed to the best operating ratio among North American Class 1 railways in 1999. The success of the decentralized structure was recognized by the railway industry. In 2002, Hunter Harrison, executive vice president and chief operating officer of CN, was named 2002 Railroader of the Year by the railway industry magazine *Railway Age* for his leadership in designing and implementing the scheduled services at CN. The citation for the award said,

> We chose Hunter Harrison for a ... range of reasons. First and foremost, we believe he's quite possibly the best operating man in the railroad industry today. He's set a benchmark for Class I's with CN's highly successful scheduled railroad. Other carriers are following CN's example by implementing some form of scheduled operations of their own.

"There's a lot of expense and cultural issues in moving people," Harrison says. "In the old days, dispatcher offices were wherever a crew change point was. They were face-to-face. We lost some of that with centralization." In today's CN, divisions are effectively profit centres. "The network is sacred," Harrison says. "They have to comply with network rules, but they're given a great deal of autonomy in dealing with local customers and situations."

Sources: Canadian National Railway, Annual Reports, 1999, 2000; Lawrence H. Kaufman, "Centralized or Decentralized Management?" *Railway Age*, August 2000, Vol. 201, Issue 8, pp. 47–53; RailroadInfo.com

management's philosophy and the unit managers' abilities to perform independently. Decentralization provides the opportunity for managers to develop leadership qualities, creative problem-solving abilities, and decision-making skills. It also lets the individual most closely in tune with the operational unit and its immediate environment make the decisions for that unit, and reduces the time spent in communicating and making decisions.

In a decentralized structure, subunit managers are evaluated in part by use of responsibility reports. Responsibility reports reflect the upward flow of information from each decentralized unit to the top of the organization. Managers receive information regarding the activities under their immediate control and under the control of their direct subordinates. The information is successively aggregated, and the reports allow the application of the management by exception principle.

Responsibility centres are classified as cost, revenue, profit, or investment. Each classification reflects the degree of authority managers have for financial items within their subunits. The type of responsibility centre also affects the kind of performance measurements that can be used for the centre and its manager.

Transfer prices are intracompany charges for goods or services exchanged between segments of a company. Product transfer prices are typically cost-based, market-based, or negotiated. A dual pricing system that assigns different transfer prices to the buying and selling units may also be used. Management should promote a transfer pricing system that is in the best interest of the whole company, motivates managers to strive for segment effectiveness and efficiency, and is practical.

Setting transfer prices in multinational enterprises is a complex process because of the differences that exist in tax structures, import/export regulations, customs duties, and other factors associated with international subsidiaries and divisions. A valid transfer price for a multinational firm is one that achieves economic benefit for the entire company and generates support from the domestic and international managers utilizing the system.

Supplementary Learning Objectives on the Web

W11-1 What is the minimum or general transfer-pricing rule?
W11-2 What is the impact of capacity on the transfer price?

Cross-Functional Applications

Topic of Note	Discipline	Cross-Functional Applications
Transfer Pricing	Marketing	A strategic business unit may have an option to sell its output without further processing to an outside customer or to another unit within the firm. In the absence of top management guidelines for internal purchasing, the producing unit must consider the transfer price in relation to the current market value when making both production and sales decisions. If the marketing department of the producing unit is evaluated as a revenue centre, then its motive would be selling price optimization. Consider the same unit as an investment centre, and the producing unit could be more flexible in its pricing policy. Transfer pricing often has other nonfinancial objectives to a marketer, such as the predictability of future business, order size, price stability, and convenience.
	Taxation	The sales tax on producer goods accrues at the point of consumption. Transfer pricing guides firms involved in international business

(cont.)

Cross-Functional Applications

Topic of Note	Discipline	Cross-Functional Applications
		operations in minimizing the sales tax in broadly diversified organizations. In addition, fluctuating foreign currency exchange rates and taxation policies must be factored into transfer pricing. In any particular business environment, income taxes may be minimized by a high transfer price and sales/consumption taxes can be maximized. A tax manager must influence transfer pricing decisions.
	Organization Theory	The top management of vertically integrated organizations must consider the impact of transfer pricing on the performance evaluation of their various divisions. A blanket policy such as variable cost-based transfer pricing could minimize the segment margin of the producing division and perhaps exaggerate the contribution of the consumer unit in overall financial performance. Even at full costing or market price costing, a distortion of true performance can occur because frequently in-house transactions have a lower administrative cost than outsourcing.
	Operations Research	Researchers often use transfer pricing as a "shadow price" in mathematical models and computer simulations of optimum performance in productive capacity, sales, and profitability. Suboptimization models can be designed to compensate an autonomous division for accepting less profitability, based upon transfer pricing imposed on it by strategic planning.
	Engineering	Shared information and technological resources usually reduce design, manufacturing, and packaging costs. The formation of transfer pricing is heavily influenced by such synergies as engineering specifications and standards, as well as the ultimate use for the product. This synergy is often extended to vital customers; however, the overall costs are usually less in-house. Transfer pricing policies set a guideline for engineers in both the design of a product and the convenience of manufacturing it.
	Legal Services	Contract negotiators and legal service reviewers must consider transfer pricing when they involve their divisions in sales/purchase agreements. In practice a transfer price is negotiated with contingent terms, such as price or quantity fluctuations, continued relationships, and services to the buyer. Negotiators and attorneys must be aware of the contingencies that influence any particular transfer price to design an agreement that gives a manager maximum flexibility for future decisions in an ever-changing business environment.
Responsibility Reporting	Marketing Management	A product or product line is frequently a strategic business unit (SBU) within the larger marketing department; or, occasionally, a firm is organized around product divisions. Responsibility reporting communicates the operating results of product SBUs and their management upward in the organization. Upper-level management can focus its

(cont.)

Cross-Functional Applications

Topic of Note	Discipline	Cross-Functional Applications
		attention on extraordinary performance evaluations, which often suggest a strength, weakness, opportunity, or threat for a particular SBU. A surge or slide in the expected sales performance of a product could be the result of an internal strength/weakness or some external opportunity/threat. The responsible product manager must prepare a report for his or her superiors describing the nature of the sales variance.
	Production Management	Complex engineering projects are often organized along a matrix management system. A project manager is responsible for moving a particular product through functional departments for processing. Disagreement frequently occurs between project and departmental managers because their objectives may conflict. Responsibility reporting assists top managers in resolving the friction inherent in matrix management by subordinating the performance of various projects or units to the strategic plan. A department manager may be called upon to use highly specialized employees in a lower technical capacity or at overtime rates because a project's performance could have strategic priority over containment of departmental cost. In this situation, the responsibility reports are a tool to implement strategic planning.
	Contract Law	Large government projects, such as weapon systems for the defence department, frequently use cost-plus contracting arrangements to assure suppliers of a profit margin in the uncertainty of high research and development investments. After decades of profiteering on unrestrained cost, defence contractors have been constrained by performance-measuring guidelines, established by the Department of Defence, termed cost accounting standards. This situation is unique in that responsibility reporting is made to a consumer entity above top management for approval. For example, extraordinary material costs or unusual handling by a contractor's purchasing department could invoke Department of Defence auditors to reduce the cost basis of the responsible department.
	Human Services Administration	Both public and private support for human services is often linked to the responsibility reports of individual administrators. Responsibility reporting in human services is usually linked to the behavioural results of the recipients as opposed to the predominately financial performance measurement used in commerce. Social welfare administrators may be funded on job placements for welfare recipients. In an attempt to shoulder the burden of social responsibility, many businesses have adopted similar responsibility reporting criteria, such as the recruitment, hiring, and job training of the socially dependent.

Key Terms

Centralization (p. 638)

Cost centre (p. 646)

Decentralization (p. 638)

Dual pricing arrangement (p. 658)

Effectiveness (p. 642)

Efficiency (p. 643)

Goal congruence (p. 641)

Investment centre (p. 651)

Management by exception (p. 640)

Negotiated transfer prices (p. 658)

Outsourcing (p. 640)

Profit centre (p. 650)

Responsibility accounting (p. 642)

Responsibility centre (p. 646)

Responsibility reports (p. 642)

Revenue centre (p. 648)

Suboptimization (p. 654)

Transfer price (p. 655)

Solution Strategies

Transfer Prices (Cost-based, market-based, negotiated, dual)

Assuming both managers have the authority to negotiate transfer price:

Upper Limit: Lowest price available from external suppliers

Feasible region for setting a reasonable transfer price

Lower Limit: Incremental costs of producing and selling the transferred goods or services plus the opportunity cost for the facilities used

DEMONSTRATION PROBLEM

Jorgensen Company of Sweden makes duck callers. The firm's annual revenue is SKr14,000,000 (SKr is the symbol for the krona, the currency unit in Sweden). Johan Ericsen, the firm's controller, devised a new budgetary system. Annual budget figures are divided into 12 equal monthly amounts for monthly performance evaluations. Greta Thommasen, vice president of production, was distressed when she reviewed the following responsibility report for the Forming and Polishing Department for March 2004:

Forming and Polishing Department—Responsibility Report
For the Month Ended March 31, 2004

	Actual	Budget	Variance Over (Under)
Volume in units	3,822	3,600	222
Variable production costs:			
Direct material	SKr119,250	SKr115,200	SKr 4,050
Direct labour	140,650	133,200	7,450
Variable overhead	168,170	159,840	8,330
Total	SKr428,070	SKr408,240	SKr19,830
Fixed production costs:			
Depreciation	SKr 7,200	SKr 7,200	SKr 0
Indirect labour	15,840	16,000	(160)
Insurance	1,150	1,150	0
Taxes	1,440	1,440	0
Other	4,930	4,460	470
Total	SKr 30,560	SKr 30,250	SKr 310
Corporate costs:			
Quality assurance staff	SKr 17,890	SKr 11,520	SKr 6,370
Selling and general	19,560	17,280	2,280
Total	SKr 37,450	SKr 28,800	SKr 8,650
Total costs	SKr496,080	SKr467,290	SKr28,790

Required:

a. Discuss the weaknesses in the report.
b. Revise the report to reduce or eliminate the weaknesses.
c. Variances greater than 10% of budget are considered to be significant enough to be investigated. Identify these.
(IMA adapted)

Solution to Demonstration Problem

a. There are two major deficiencies in the report:
   1. Responsibility reports for a cost centre should compare actual costs with flexible budget costs. The report presented compares actual costs with static budget costs (which were estimated for 3,600 units, while actual production was 3,822 units). Costs measured at two different activity levels are not comparable for control or evaluation purposes.
   2. The report presented includes corporate costs that are not within the control of the Forming and Polishing Department manager. Some of the fixed production costs are also probably not controllable by the manager of this cost centre, although the problem does not provide enough information to address this concern.

b.

Forming and Polishing Department—Responsibility Report
For the Month Ended March 31, 2004

Volume in units	Actual (3,822)		Budget (3,822)		Variance
	Per unit	**Total**	**Per unit**	**Total**	**Over (Under)**
Variable production costs:					
Direct material	SKr 31.20	SKr 119,250	SKr 32.00	SKr 122,304	SKr (3,054)
Direct labour	36.80	140,650	37.00	141,414	(764)
Variable overhead	44.00	168,170	44.40	169,697	(1,527)
Total	SKr 112.00	SKr 428,070	SKr 113.40	SKr 433,415	SKr (5,345)
Fixed production costs:					
Depreciation		SKr 7,200		SKr 7,200	SKr 0
Indirect labour		15,840		16,000	(160)
Insurance		1,150		1,150	0
Taxes		1,440		1,440	0
Other		4,930		4,460	470
Total		SKr 30,560		SKr 30,250	SKr 310
Total production costs		SKr 458,630		SKr 463,665	SKr (5,035)

c. Only the "other" cost category reflects a variance exceeding 10% of budget. Note that the revised report provides a more realistic and a more favourable view of performance than does the original report.

End-of-Chapter Materials

SELF-TEST QUESTIONS

(SOLUTIONS APPEAR AT THE END OF THE CHAPTER.)

1. Decentralization works best in organizations with all of the following attributes except
   a. Young
   b. Growing
   c. Large
   d. Top management has high confidence in subordinates

2. Which of the following is a disadvantage of decentralization?
   a. Helps top management recognize and develop managerial talent
   b. Requires more effective communication abilities
   c. Often leads to job satisfaction
   d. Allows the use of management by exception

3. Centralization works best in organizations with all of the following attributes except
   a. High use of technology
   b. Young
   c. Small
   d. Slow growth rate

4. Responsibility accounting
   a. Ensures that managers are responsible
   b. Means that a firm uses budgets and plans
   c. Is another word for flexible budgeting
   d. Assists management in evaluating subordinate performance

5. The steps of the control process include all of the following except
   a. Prepare a plan
   b. Gather actual data
   c. Demand performance from subordinates
   d. Monitor the differences between planned and actual data

6. Responsibility centres include the following
   a. Cost centres
   b. Revenue centres
   c. Investment centres
   d. All of the above

7. Suboptimization exists when
   a. Optimization is not known
   b. Individual managers pursue goals that are not the organization's goals
   c. Individual managers pursue the company's goals
   d. Companies are unable to define their optimal goals

8. Transfer prices can be all of the following except
   a. Cost-based
   b. Revenue-based
   c. Market-based
   d. Negotiated

9. In setting transfer prices with multinational firms, the following should occur
   a. Transfer prices should be minimized
   b. Transfer prices should be maximized
   c. Transfer prices should reflect non-arm's length transactions
   d. Transfer prices should reflect arm's-length transactions

10. Which is not an advantage of transfer prices for services?
    a. Suggest ways in which provider departments cannot improve services
    b. Suggest ways in which provider departments can improve services
    c. User departments may restrict usage
    d. User departments can include costs in performance evaluation

QUESTIONS

1. Differentiate decision-making authority between centrally organized and decentrally organized companies.

2. Would a very young company or a large mature company be more likely to employ decentralized management? Explain.

3. Why do the personality traits of subunit managers affect the success of efforts to decentralize decision making?

4. Some organizational activities are more likely to be decentralized than others. What activities are most likely to be decentralized? Least likely? Why?

5. Top managers at Worldwide Manufacturing Company are pondering the possibility of decentralizing control of all foreign operating divisions. The firm has traditionally maintained very tight central control over these operations. What major costs of decentralization should Worldwide's top managers consider in making their decision?

6. What is a responsibility accounting system? What is its role in a decentralized firm?

7. Why is a segment manager's performance evaluated separately from the segment's performance?

8. Describe the four types of responsibility centres. For each type, how can performance be measured?

9. How are variances used by managers in controlling the organization?

10. How is the philosophy of management by exception employed in responsibility accounting systems?

11. Describe how suboptimization is related to the performance measures that are used to evaluate segment managers and segment performance.

12. Is managerial performance always evaluated solely on financial measures? Explain.

13. What is a transfer price? What role does a transfer price play in a decentralized company?

14. What are the high and low limits of transfer prices, and why do these limits exist?

15. A company is considering the use of a cost-based transfer price. What argument favours the use of standard, rather than actual, cost?

16. What practical problems may interfere with the use of a market-based transfer price?

17. What is dual pricing? What is the intended effect of dual pricing on the reported performance of each division affected by the dual price?

18. How can service departments use transfer prices, and what advantages do transfer prices have over cost allocation methods?

19. Explain why determining transfer prices may be more complex in a multinational setting than in a domestic setting.

20. Why do provincial, federal, and foreign taxing authorities scrutinize transfer price determination in multinational companies?

EXERCISES

1. (LO 1, 2, 3, 4, 6) Your roommate has asked you for help in matching each of the lettered items on the left with the number of the appropriate item on the right.

a. Suboptimization	1. Decisions in this type of company are made by division managers
b. Dual pricing arrangement	
c. Centralized organization	2. Manager is primarily responsible for generating revenues, controlling costs, and managing assets
d. Goal congruence	
e. Profit centre	3. Manager is primarily responsible for controlling operating costs
f. Decentralized organization	
g. Cost centre	4. The process of making decisions that may not be in the best interest of the entire firm
h. Investment centre	
i. Responsibility centre	5. Price charged to buying division differs from price paid to selling division
j. Revenue centre	
	6. Organizational and personal goals are consistent
	7. Manager is responsible for revenue generation and operating cost control
	8. Manager is primarily responsible for revenue generation
	9. The organizational cost object under the control of a manager
	10. Decisions in this type of company are generally made by top management

2. (LO 1, 2) Each of the following independent descriptions characterizes some trait of an organization. You have become involved in the formation of a new company and are considering how to structure it.

Required:

For each description below, you have been asked by your investor group to indicate whether the firm would be more likely to adopt a centralized (C) or decentralized (D) control structure.

a. The firm has just been established.
b. A bad decision would have disastrous consequences for the company.
c. The firm is growing very rapidly.
d. The entrepreneurial CEO is the firm's founder and wants to maintain involvement in all aspects of the business.
e. The firm's operations span the globe. Many of the foreign divisions have operations that are very sensitive to volatility in local economic conditions.
f. Top management expresses sincere doubts about the capability of lower-level managers to make sound economic decisions.

3. (LO 1) The local chapter of the Chamber of Commerce has invited you to give an after-dinner speech on selecting an appropriate organizational structure. A friend of yours has suggested a number of issues that might be considered in choosing between a centralized organization and a decentralized one. However, before he can discuss these issues with you, he gets lost in cyberspace and refuses to be disturbed.

Required:

Since your talk is tonight, you need to decide whether each of the following might be a potential advantage (A) of decentralization, a disadvantage (D) of decentralization, or neither (N).

a. Promotion of goal congruence
b. Support of training in decision making
c. Development of leadership qualities
d. Complication of communication process
e. Cost of developing planning and reporting systems
f. Placement of decision maker closer (in time and place) to problem
g. Speed of decisions
h. Use of management by exception principle by top management
i. Greater job satisfaction
j. Delegation of ultimate responsibility

4. (LO 2) The Tool and Die Department of Metro Manufacturing is structured as a cost centre. Below are selected budget and actual costs of the department for 2006:

	Planning Budget	Actual	Flexible Budget
Professional labour	$900,000	$925,000	$1,000,317
Supplies	14,000	15,200	16,200
Materials	114,000	119,350	117,200
Energy	26,000	29,300	32,100
Quality control	172,600	172,000	195,100
Depreciation	250,000	250,000	250,000
Software amortization	90,000	103,000	90,000

Metro has a policy of investigating any variance that differs from the expected amount for the actual level of operations by 5% or more.

Required:

The company accountant has become ill and the CEO has enlisted you to address the following:

a. Which budget amount, planning or flexible, reflects the expected level of cost occurrence for the actual level of operations?
b. Based on your answer in part (a), compute variances for each cost category.
c. Which variances should be investigated further?
d. Which favourable variances, if any, might be of great concern to management? Explain.

5. (LO 3) Namer Industries produces and sells a stainless steel surgical knife. The Marketing Department is evaluated based on a comparison of achieved revenues with budgeted revenues. For 2005, the company projected sales to be 410,000 units at an average price of $42. The company actually sold 425,000 knives at an average price of $39.50.

Required:

The Marketing Department manager is upset and has enlisted your help in trying to understand the revenue shortfall.
   a. Compute the revenue price and volume variances for 2005.
   b. The president of Namer is curious as to why you didn't compute a sales mix variance. Write a brief memo explaining to her why a sales mix variance is inappropriate for her company.
   c. Based on your computations in part (a), can you determine whether profits were above or below the budget level? Explain.

6. (LO 3) The Sales Department of the Aqua Store is responsible for sales of two principal products: flippers and masks. For August 2005, the Sales Department's actual and budgeted sales were as follows:

| | **Flippers** | | **Masks** | |
	Dollars	*Units*	*Dollars*	*Units*
Budgeted sales	$20,000	4,000	$80,000	4,000
Actual sales	18,000	3,000	69,000	3,000

Required:

The sales manager for the Aqua Store is your friend and has asked you to help her with the following.
   a. For August 2005, compute the price variance for the Sales Department of the Aqua Store.
   b. Compute the volume variance for the Sales Department for August 2005.
   c. Compute the sales mix variance for the Sales Department for August 2005.
   d. Explain why you would expect a relatively minor sales mix variance for this company even when substantial variances may arise for sales volume and price.

7. (LO 3) Fine Leather Products Inc. manufactures two products: women's shoes and baseball gloves. For 2005, the firm budgeted the following:

	Shoes	**Baseball gloves**
Sales	$800,000	$1,800,000
Unit sales price	$ 40	$ 30

At the end of 2005, managers were informed that total actual sales amounted to 70,000 units and totalled $2,700,000. Shoe sales for the year amounted to 30,000 units at an average price of $35.

Required:
   a. Compute the total revenue variance for 2005.
   b. Compute the price variance for 2005.
   c. Compute the sales mix variance for 2005.
   d. Compute the sales volume variance for 2005.

8. (LO 3) Cascade Inns evaluates its inns and innkeepers based on a comparison of actual profit with budgeted profit. A budgeted 2005 income statement for the Cascade Inn in Saskatoon follows:

Revenues		$ 2,650,000
Cost of services provided:		
Direct labour	$265,000	
Supplies	53,000	
Variable overhead	318,000	(636,000)
Contribution margin		$ 2,014,000
Fixed overhead—controllable		(320,000)
Controllable segment margin		$ 1,694,000
Fixed overhead—not controllable by segment manager		(1,220,000)
Profit centre income		$ 474,000

For 2005, actual revenues generated were $2,900,000. Actual variable costs were direct labour, 12% of revenues; supplies, 3% of revenues; variable overhead, 14% of revenues. Controllable fixed costs amounted to $330,000, and other fixed overhead costs amounted to $1,425,000.

Required:

a. Prepare an actual income statement for 2005.

b. Compute revenue and cost variances for 2005.

c. Evaluate the performance of the manager of the Cascade Inn for 2005.

d. Evaluate the performance of the Cascade Inn for 2005.

9. (LO 5) The Accessory Division, an autonomous segment (profit centre) of All-Canadian Motors, is considering what price to charge for transfers of water pumps to the Large Truck Division of the company. The following data on production cost per water pump have been gathered:

Direct materials	$20.40
Direct labour	4.20
Variable overhead	12.60
Fixed overhead	10.80
Total	$48.00

The Accessory Division sells the water pumps to external buyers for $63. Managers of the Large Truck Division have received external offers to provide comparable water pumps ranging from $55 at one company to $73 at another.

Required:

Top management has engaged you for help in developing a transfer price for these water pumps.

a. Determine the upper and lower limits for the transfer price between the Accessory Division and the Large Truck Division.

b. What is the transfer price if it is equal to full production cost?

c. What is the transfer price if it is equal to variable production cost?

d. Why would the Accessory Division be reluctant to transfer goods at a price equal to variable cost?

10. (LO 5) Bridgeport Corporation has several operating divisions. The Motor Division manufactures motors for ceiling fans and other appliances. The Fan Division manufactures ceiling fans and several other products that require a motor similar to the one produced by the Motor Division. The Motor Division sells 90% of its output externally and transfers the other 10% to the Fan Division. Bridgeport Corporation makes all internal transfers at market price. The Motor Division's cost and revenue structure follows:

Sales price per motor	$75
Variable manufacturing costs	37
Fixed manufacturing costs	14
Variable selling and administration	2
Fixed selling and administration	5

Both per-unit fixed cost computations are based on an expected capacity of 200,000 units.

Required:

As a student intern assigned to Bridgeport's finance office, you have been asked to address the following items.

a. From the perspective of Bridgeport Corporation, what is the variable cost of producing and selling a fan motor?

b. What is the variable cost of a fan motor from the perspective of the Fan Division?

c. Under what circumstances would it be desirable for the Fan Division to know the true variable cost of an electric fan motor?

11. (LO 5) Among other products, the Office Supplies Division of Upscale Artifacts Company produces small plastic cases. Of its output, 40% is sold to the Garden Division of Upscale Artifacts Company, and the rest is sold to external parties. All internal transfers occur at a fixed price of $1.25 per unit. Office Supplies Division's expected results for 2005 are shown next.

	Internal	**External**
Sales (150,000 units)	$ 75,000	$ 135,000
Costs:		
Variable	(30,000)	(45,000)
Fixed	(36,000)	(54,000)
Gross profit	$ 9,000	$ 36,000

Office Supplies Division has received an external offer that would enable it to sell, at $1.40 per unit, all the units now scheduled to be sold internally. To accommodate this sale, Garden Division would have to purchase its units externally for $1.70 per unit.

Required:

The two division managers have come to you, the firm's chief accountant, with the following questions.

a. By what amount will Office Supplies Division's gross profit change if it accepts the offer from the external party?

b. By what amount will Garden Division's gross profit change if Office Supplies Division accepts the offer from the external party?

c. Assume Office Supplies Division negotiates a transfer price with Garden Division of $1.40 per unit. However, the additional gross profit (relative to the normal internal sales price) generated for Office Supplies Division by this transfer price will be split between Office Supplies Division and Garden Division. What will be the actual transfer price for each unit after this sharing of profit takes place?

d. How could a dual pricing system be used to provide incentive for an internal transfer in this situation?

12. (LO 5) Accessories Division produces a speaker set that is sold to Stereo Division at the market price of $90. Accessories Division does not sell any speakers externally. Annual production and sales are 40,000 sets. The cost of production for a speaker set is shown below:

Variable production costs	$55
General fixed overhead ($12 per hour; 1 hour for production time)	12
Direct fixed overhead ($320,000 ÷ 40,000)	8
Unit cost	$75
Variable shipping expenses	4
Total unit cost	$79

General fixed overhead is composed of some allocated production costs relating to the building and the production activities. Discontinuation of speaker production would save Accessories Division $40,000 in annual direct fixed overhead. Accessories Division's management has asked you to address the following items.

Required:

a. Determine the incremental cost of producing one speaker set.

b. Assume Accessories Division is operating at full capacity. What is the appropriate unit cost to be used to set a minimum transfer price for selling speaker sets to Stereo Division? Why is this cost most appropriate?

13. (LO 7) A friend of yours has asked you whether, in relation to using transfer prices for service department costs, each of the following conditions might be a potential advantage (A), a potential disadvantage (D), or neither (N):

a. Can make a service department into a profit centre

b. May reduce goal congruence

c. Can make users and providers more cost conscious

d. Can increase disagreements about how transfer prices should be set

e. Can put all service departments on an equal footing

f. Can cause certain services to be underutilized or overutilized

g. Can improve ability to evaluate performance

h. Can increase communication about what additional services are needed and which can be reduced or eliminated

i. Requires additional cost and employee time commitment

14. (LO 7) The computer operation of Brown Legal Services is in the process of developing a transfer price for its services. Capacity is defined by the computer operation in minutes of computer time. Expected annual capacity for 2006 is 600,000 minutes, and full capacity is 800,000 minutes. Costs of the computer area for 2006 are expected to total $720,000.

Required:
a. What is the transfer price if it is based on expected annual capacity?
b. What is the transfer price if it is based on full capacity?
c. Assume the actual cost of operating the computer area in 2006 is $745,000. What is the total variance of that department? What are some possible causes of that variance?

PROBLEMS

1. (LO 2) Metropolitan Engineering Associates was suffering from a decline in profit because of competitive pressures. One of its responses to declining profitability was to establish a responsibility accounting system. One of the responsibility centres established was the Electrical Engineering Division. This division is treated as a cost centre for control purposes. In 2006, the first year after responsibility accounting was put in place, the responsibility report for the Electrical Engineering Division contained the following comparisons:

	Budgeted	Actual	Variance
Variable costs:			
Professional labour	$1,000,000	$ 940,000	$60,000 F
Travel	50,000	40,000	10,000 F
Supplies	100,000	90,000	10,000 F
Fixed costs:			
Professional labour	400,000	405,000	(5,000) U
Facilities cost	250,000	265,000	(15,000) U
Insurance	80,000	78,000	2,000 F
Totals	$1,880,000	$1,818,000	$62,000 F

For 2006, the Electrical Engineering Division projected that it would generate $2,000,000 of revenues; it actually generated $1,800,000. The company has consulted with you for help in understanding what is happening. You decide to address the items that follow.

Required:
a. What are the major weaknesses in the responsibility report above?
b. Recast the responsibility report in a more meaningful format for cost control evaluation.
c. Metropolitan Engineering Associates utilizes a management by exception philosophy. Using the report prepared in part (b), which costs are likely to receive additional evaluation? Explain.
d. In most organizations, who would you expect to be involved in establishing policies on which variances should be investigated? Explain.

2. (LO 3, 4) On January 1, 2005, Tom Clark was promoted to the position of production manager in Seattle Seafood Company. The firm purchases raw fish, cooks and processes it, and then cans it in single-portion containers. The canned fish is sold to several wholesalers specializing in providing food to school lunch programs in the Northwest region of the United States and certain areas in Canada. All processing is conducted in the firm's highly automated plant in Parksville, British Columbia. Performance of the production manager is evaluated on the basis of a comparison of actual costs with standard costs. Only costs that are controllable by the production

manager are included in the comparison (all are variable). The cost of fish is noncontrollable. Standard costs per kilogram of canned fish for 2005 were set as follows:

Direct labour	$0.50
Repairs	0.10
Maintenance	0.60
Indirect labour	0.10
Power	0.20

For 2005, the company purchased 2,500,000 kilograms of fish and canned 1,500,000 kilograms. There were no beginning or ending inventories of raw, in-process, or canned fish. Actual 2005 costs were:

Direct labour	$600,000
Repairs	160,000
Maintenance	650,000
Indirect labour	155,000
Power	315,000

Required:

As the chief managerial accountant for the company, you have been asked to address the following.

a. Prepare a performance report for Tom Clark for 2005.

b. Evaluate Tom Clark's performance based on your report.

c. Tom feels that his 2005 performance is so good that he should be considered for immediate promotion to the position of vice president of operations. Do you agree? Defend your answer.

d. Should additional performance measures (other than standard cost variances) be added to evaluate the production manager's performance? If so, identify the measures you would recommend.

3. (LO 3) Nancy Padgett is a production supervisor at the West Vancouver plant of Alberta Steelworks, which manufactures steel bridge guards. As plant production supervisor, Ms. Padgett is evaluated based on her ability to meet standard production costs. The standard costs to produce a one-metre section of bridge guard are given below:

Metal		$12.00
Galvanizing ($10 per litre)		2.00
Direct labour ($15 per hour)		3.00
Overhead		
Welding supplies	$0.90	
Utilities	1.10	
Indirect labour	0.80	
Machine maintenance/repairs	0.40	
Equipment depreciation	2.20	
Miscellaneous	0.80	6.20
Total		$23.20

In October 2005, the West Vancouver plant produced 35,000 metres of bridge guards. During October, the plant incurred the following costs:

Metal		$507,500
Galvanizing ($9.40 per litre)		65,800
Direct labour ($14.90 per hour)		104,300
Overhead		
Welding supplies	$34,900	
Utilities	38,300	
Indirect labour	25,500	
Machine maintenance/repairs	21,200	
Equipment depreciation	77,000	
Miscellaneous	29,500	226,400
Total		$904,000

Required:

a. For October 2005, management has requested that you compute the variance for each production cost category in the West Vancouver plant.

b. Based on the variances computed in part (a), management has asked you to evaluate the performance of Nancy Padgett. Which variances might deserve closer scrutiny by top management? Explain.

4. (LO 3) David Leno manages the Sales Department at PEI Electric Supply. He is evaluated based on his ability to meet budgeted revenues. He has asked for your help in several ways listed below. For May 2005, Mr. Leno's revenue budget was as follows:

	Price per Unit	Unit Sales
Floor lamps	$107	960
Hanging lamps	55	2,800
Ceiling fixtures	75	4,240

The actual sales generated by Mr. Leno's department in May were as follows:

	Price per Unit	Total Sales in Dollars
Floor lamps	$115	$ 93,150
Hanging lamps	50	207,000
Ceiling fixtures	78	315,900

Required:

a. For May 2005, compute the revenue price variance in the Sales Department at PEI Electric Supply.

b. For May 2005, compute the revenue mix variance in the Sales Department at PEI Electric Supply.

c. For May 2005, compute the revenue volume variance in the Sales Department at PEI Electric Supply.

d. Based on your answers to parts (a), (b), and (c), evaluate the performance of Mr. Leno.

e. Assume you are Mr. Leno's supervisor. Why might you want to consider giving Mr. Leno the authority to set the salary and commission structure for the salespersons?

5. (LO 3) Beth Jackson, the head of the accounting department at Red River College, has felt increasing pressure to raise external monies to compensate for dwindling provincial financial support. Accordingly, in early January 2005, she conceived the idea of offering a three-day accounting workshop in income taxation for local accountants. She asked Jim Thomas, a tenured tax professor, to supervise the planning for the seminar, which was to be held in late March 2006. In early February, Professor Thomas presented Jackson with the following budgetary plan:

Revenues ($800 per participant)		$ 80,000
Expenses:		
Speakers ($1,000 each)	$10,000	
Rent on facilities	7,200	
Advertising	4,200	
Meals and lodging	36,000	
Departmental overhead allocation	7,000	(64,400)
Profit		$ 15,600

Explanation of budget items: The facilities rent of $7,200 is a fixed rental to be paid to a local hotel for use of its meeting rooms. The advertising is also a fixed budgeted cost. Meals expense is budgeted at $10 per person per meal (a total of nine meals are to be provided for each participant); lodging is budgeted at the rate of $90 per participant per night. The departmental overhead includes a specific charge for supplies costing $20 for each participant as well as a general allocation of $5,000 for use of departmental secretarial resources. After reviewing the budget, Jackson gave Thomas approval to proceed with the seminar.

Required:

As Dr. Jackson's assistant, you have been asked to address several issues presented below.

a. Recast the income statement above in a segment income statement format.

b. Assume the actual financial results of the seminar were as follows:

Revenues (120 participants)		$ 77,000
Expenses:		
Speakers ($1,550 each)	$ 15,500	
Rent on facilities	8,400	
Advertising	5,800	
Meals and lodging	43,200	
Departmental overhead allocation	7,400	(80,300)
Loss		$ (3,300)

Explanation of actual results: Because sign ups were running below expectations, the seminar fee was reduced from $800 to $600 for late enrollees, and the advertising expense was increased. These changes caused the number of participants to be larger than expected, so a larger meeting room had to be rented from the local hotel. In budgeting for the speakers, Professor Thomas neglected to include airfare, which averaged $500 per speaker. Recast the actual results in a segment income statement format.

c. Compute variances between the budgeted segment income statement and the actual segment income statement. Identify and discuss the factors that are primarily responsible for the difference between the budgeted profit and the actual loss on the tax seminar.

d. Evaluate Professor Thomas's management of the tax seminar.

6. (LO 5, 6) Better Homes Products' Canadian operations are organized into two divisions: West and East. West Division sells a component that could be used by East Division in making one of the company's principal products. East Division has obtained three price quotations from external suppliers for the component: $154, $138, and $143. Examination of West Division's accounting records pertaining to the production of the component reveals the following costs: direct materials, $56; direct labour, $44; variable overhead, $18; and fixed overhead, $25.

Required:

As the chief accountant, you have been directed by the CEO to determine the following.

a. What savings (or profits) would be available to Better Homes Products if East Division bought the component internally rather than externally?

b. What would the transfer price be if the two divisions agreed to split the total company savings evenly between them?

c. Assuming dual transfer pricing is used, set the maximum realistic price for West Division and the minimum realistic price for East Division.

7. (LO 5, 6) Two of the divisions of Heavy-Duty Equipment Company are the Motor Division and the Dragline Division. The Motor Division produces motors that are used by both the Dragline Division and a variety of external industrial customers.

For external sales, sales orders are generally produced in 100-unit lots. Based on this typical lot size, the cost per motor is as follows:

Variable production costs	$2,100
Fixed manufacturing overhead	900
Variable selling expenses	300
Fixed selling expenses	420
Fixed general and administrative expenses	640
Total unit cost	$4,360

Motor Division normally has earned a profit margin of 20% on internal sales but has set the external selling price at $5,400. Because a significant number of sales are being made internally, Motor Division managers have now decided that $5,400 is the appropriate price to use for all future transfers to the Dragline Division. Previous transfers have been based on full cost plus the stipulated per-unit profit.

When the managers in Dragline Division hear of this change in the transfer price, they become very upset since the change will have a major negative impact on Dragline's net income. Because of competition, corporate management has asked Motor Division to lower its sales price and consider reducing the transfer price. At the same time, Dragline Division management has asked to be allowed to buy motors externally. Bill Bird, Dragline's president, has gathered the following price information in order to help the two divisional managers negotiate an equitable transfer price:

Current external sales price	$5,400
Total variable production cost plus 20% profit margin ($2,100 × 1.2)	2,520
Total production cost plus 20% profit margin ($3,000 × 1.2)	3,600
Unit bid price from external supplier (if motors are purchased in 100-unit lots)	4,800

Required:

Mr. Bird is a former classmate of yours and has asked you to help him analyze the following matters:

a. Discuss advantages and disadvantages of each of the above transfer prices to the selling and buying divisions and to Heavy-Duty Equipment Company. Explain what circumstances would make each of the alternative prices the most appropriate choice.

b. If Motor Division can sell all of its production externally at $5,400 per unit, what is the appropriate transfer price and why?

8. (LO 4, 5) The Accessories Division of Johnson Power Sources manufactures a starter with the following standard costs:

Direct materials	$10
Direct labour	60
Overhead	30
Total unit cost	$100

The standard direct labour rate is $30 per hour, and overhead is assigned at 50% of the direct labour rate. Normal direct labour hours are 20,000, and the overhead rate is $5 variable and $10 fixed per direct labour hour.

The starters sell for $150, and the Accessories Division is currently operating at a level of about 16,000 direct labour hours for the year. Transfers in Johnson Power Sources are normally made at market price, although the divisional managers are permitted to negotiate a mutually agreed upon transfer price.

The Motor Division currently purchases 2,000 starters annually from the Accessories Division at the market price. The divisional manager of the Motor Division can purchase the starters from a foreign supplier for $140. Since she is free to select a supplier, she has indicated that she would like to negotiate a new transfer price with the Accessories Division. The manager of the Accessories Division believes that the foreign supplier is attempting to "buy in" by selling the starters at what he considers an excessively low price.

Required:

As vice president of finance for Johnson Power Sources, your expertise has been requested in the following matters.

a. From the viewpoint of the firm, should the Motor Division purchase the starters internally or externally? Show calculations and explain.

b. From the viewpoint of the Motor Division, should the starters be purchased internally or externally? Show calculations and explain.

c. Assume that the Accessories Division is presently operating at capacity and could sell the starters that it now sells to the Motor Division to external buyers at its usual price. From the viewpoint of the firm, should the Motor Division purchase the starters internally or externally? Show calculations and explain.

d. If you were the marketing manager of the Motor Division, what concerns might you have regarding the decision to buy internally or externally?

9. (LO 5, 6) Irresistible Scents Ltd. manufactures a line of perfume. The manufacturing process is basically a series of mixing operations involving the addition of certain aromatic and colouring ingredients. The finished products are packaged in company-produced glass bottles and packed in cases containing six bottles.

Management feels that the sale of its product is heavily influenced by the appearance of the bottle and has, therefore, devoted considerable managerial effort to the bottle production process. This has resulted in the development of certain unique processes in which management takes considerable pride.

The two areas (perfume production and bottle manufacturing) have evolved almost independently over the years; in fact, rivalry has developed between management personnel about which division is more important to Irresistible Scents. This attitude was probably intensified when the bottle manufacturing plant was purchased intact 10 years ago. No real interchange of management personnel or ideas (except at the top corporate level) has taken place.

Since the Bottle Division was acquired, its entire production has been absorbed by the Perfume Division. Each area is considered a separate profit centre and evaluated as such. As the new corporate controller, you are responsible for the definition of a proper transfer price to use between the bottle production profit centre and the packaging profit centre. At your request, the general manager of the Bottle Division has asked certain other bottle manufacturers to quote a price for the quantities and sizes demanded by the Perfume Division. These competitive prices for cases of six bottles each are as follows:

Volume	Total Price	Price per Case
2,000,000 cases	$ 8,000,000	$4.00
4,000,000 cases	14,000,000	3.50
6,000,000 cases	20,000,000	3.33

A cost analysis of the internal bottle plant indicates that it can produce bottles at these costs:

Volume	Total Price	Price per Case
2,000,000 cases	$ 6,400,000	$3.20
4,000,000 cases	10,400,000	2.60
6,000,000 cases	14,400,000	2.40

The above analysis represents fixed costs of $2,400,000 and variable costs of $2 per case.

These figures have given rise to considerable corporate discussion about the proper value to use in the transfer of bottles to the Perfume Division. This interest is heightened because a significant portion of a division manager's income is an incentive bonus based on profit centre results.

The Perfume Division has the following costs in addition to the bottle costs:

Volume	Total Cost	Cost per Case
2,000,000 cases	$32,800,000	$16.40
4,000,000 cases	64,800,000	16.20
6,000,000 cases	96,780,000	16.13

Market Research has furnished you with the following price–demand relationships for the finished product:

Sales Volume	Total Sales Revenue	Sales Price per Case
2,000,000 cases	$ 51,000,000	$25.50
4,000,000 cases	91,200,000	22.80
6,000,000 cases	127,800,000	21.30

Required:

a. Irresistible Scents has used market-based transfer prices in the past. Using the current market prices and costs, and assuming a volume of 6,000,000 cases, calculate the income for the Bottle Division, the Perfume Division, and Irresistible Scents Ltd.

b. The 6,000,000-case production and sales level is the most profitable volume for which of the following: the Bottle Division, the Perfume Division, or Irresistible Scents Ltd.? Explain your answer.

c. As the corporate controller, answer the following question posed by the president of Irresistible Scents Ltd.: "Why have we structured the bottle operation as a separate division?"

(CMA adapted)

10. (LO 5, 6) Madison Decorative Floors operates with 10 profit centres. Company policy requires all transfers between corporate units to be made at fair market price. Tile Division has been asked to produce 10,000 standard tiles for Consumer Products Division. Tile Division is operating at full capacity and could otherwise sell any output it produces externally. This order represents 10% of the division's capacity, stated in terms of machine hours. Tile Division has quoted a $3.50 price per unit, but Consumer Products Division has found an external company that will make the tiles for $2.80. Since corporate policy states that external market prices must be used, Tile Division will be required to sell the units at $2.80. Tile Division's total variable cost for this specific type of tile is $2.20.

You have just graduated with a business degree, and your dad owns Madison Decorative Floors. He has asked you to help him with the following matters.

Required:

a. What amount of contribution margin will Tile Division earn at the originally quoted price? At the externally quoted price?

b. What effect does the use of the externally quoted purchase price of $2.80 have on Madison Decorative Floors' net income?

c. Some of the time that would be required to produce Consumer Products Division's order could be used instead to produce a special order for an outside company. Discuss how Tile Division management should make the choice between producing the order for Consumer Products Division and producing the outside company's order. What factors should be considered?

d. Should market price always be used to set a transfer price between organizational units? If so, discuss why. If not, discuss why not and when it is appropriate.

11. (LO 5, 6) Industrial Solutions Inc. has several regional divisions, which often purchase from each other. The company is fully decentralized, with divisions buying from and selling to each other or in outside markets. Conveyor Systems Division purchases most of its needs for hydraulic pumps from Hydraulic Division. The managers of these two divisions are currently negotiating a transfer price for the hydraulic pumps for next year. Hydraulic Division prepared the following financial information for negotiating purposes:

Costs of hydraulic pumps as manufactured by Hydraulic Division:

Direct material costs	$120
Direct labour costs	40
Variable overhead costs	30
Fixed overhead costs	50
Fixed selling expenses	30
Fixed administrative expenses	20
Total	$290

Hydraulic Division is currently operating at 70% of its capacity. It is the policy of the division to target a net income to sales ratio of 20%.

The current market price for hydraulic pumps is $260 each. Recently, there has been a drop in price for such products because of industry advances in production technology.

Required:

Answer each of the following questions independently.

a. If Hydraulic Division desires to achieve its goal of a net income to sales ratio of 20%, what should be the transfer price of pumps?

b. If Hydraulic Division wants to maximize its income, what transfer price would you recommend that it offer to the Conveyor Systems Division?

c. What is the price that you believe should be charged by Hydraulic Division if overall company profit is to be maximized?

(CMA adapted)

12. (LO 5, 6) CanElectric is a decentralized company with divisions throughout Canada. Each division has its own sales force and production facilities and is operated autonomously as either a profit or an investment centre. Switch Division has just been awarded a contract for a product that uses a component that is manufactured by Wire

Division as well as by outside suppliers. Switch Division uses a cost figure of $3.80 for the component in preparing the bid for the new product. This cost figure was supplied by Wire Division in response to Switch Division's request for the average variable cost of the component.

Wire Division has an active sales force that is continually soliciting new customers. Its regular selling price for the component needed by Switch Division for the new product is $6.50. Sales of the component are expected to increase. Wire Division management has associated the following costs with the component:

Standard variable manufacturing cost	$3.20
Standard variable selling and distribution expenses	0.60
Standard fixed manufacturing cost	1.20
Total	$5.00

The two divisions have been unable to agree on a transfer price for the component. Corporate management has never established a transfer price because no interdivisional transactions have ever occurred. The following suggestions have been made for the transfer price.
- Regular selling price
- Regular selling price less variable selling and distribution expenses
- Standard manufacturing cost plus 15%
- Standard variable manufacturing cost plus 20%

Required:
a. Compute each of the suggested transfer prices.
b. Discuss the effect each of the transfer prices might have on Wire Division management's attitude toward intracompany business.
c. Is the negotiation of a price between Switch Division and Wire Division a satisfactory method for solving the transfer price problem? Explain your answer.
d. Should the corporate management of CanElectric become involved in this transfer controversy? Explain your answer.

(CMA adapted)

CASES

1. Family Resorts, Inc. is a holding company for several vacation hotels in the Maritimes and Northern Ontario. The firm originally purchased several old inns, restored the buildings, and upgraded the recreational facilities. The inns have been well received by vacationing families, as many services are provided that accommodate children and afford parents time for themselves. Since the completion of the restorations 10 years ago, the company has been profitable.

    Family Resorts has just concluded its annual meeting of regional and district managers. This meeting is held each November to review the results of the previous season and to help the managers prepare for the upcoming year. Prior to the meeting, the managers submitted proposed budgets for their districts or regions as appropriate. These budgets have been reviewed and consolidated into an annual operating budget for the entire company. The 2005 budget has been presented at the meeting and accepted by the managers.

    To evaluate the performance of its managers, Family Resorts uses responsibility accounting. Therefore, the preparation of the budget is given close attention at headquarters. If major changes need to be made to the budgets submitted by the managers, all affected parties are consulted before the changes are incorporated. The following two pages are from the budget booklet that all managers received at the meeting.

Family Resorts, Inc.
Responsibility Summary
($000 omitted)

Reporting Unit: Family Resorts
Responsible Person: President

Maritimes	$ 605
Northern Ontario	365
Unallocated costs	(160)
Income before taxes	$ 810

Reporting Unit: Northern Ontario
Responsible Person: Regional Manager

Region A	$ 200
Region B	140
Region C	105
Unallocated costs	(80)
Total contribution	$ 365

Reporting Unit: Region C
Responsible Person: District Manager

Harbour Inn	$ 80
Camden Country Inn	60
Unallocated costs	(35)
Total contribution	$105

Reporting Unit: Harbour Inn
Responsible Person: Innkeeper

Revenue	$ 600
Controllable costs	(455)
Allocated costs	(65)
Total contribution	$ 80

The budget for Family Resorts, Inc. follows.

Family Resorts, Inc.
Condensed Operation Budget—Maritime/Northern Ontario Districts
For the Year Ending December 31, 2005
($000 omitted)

	Family Resorts	Maritimes	Northern Ontario	Unallo-cated[1]	Region A	Region B	Region C	Unallo-cated[2]	Harbor	Camden Country
Net sales	$ 7,900	$4,200	$3,700		$1,400	$1,200	$1,100		$600	$500
Cost of sales	(4,530)	(2,310)	(2,220)	____	(840)	(720)	(660)	____	(360)	(300)
Gross margin	$ 3,370	$1,890	$1,480	____	$ 560	$ 480	$ 440	____	$240	$200
Controllable expenses										
Supervisory expenses	$ 240	$ 130	$ 110		$ 35	$ 30	$ 45	$ 10	$ 20	$ 15
Training expenses	160	80	80		30	25	25		15	10
Advertising expenses	500	280	220	$ 50	55	60	55	15	20	20
Repairs and maintenance	480	225	255		90	85	80		40	40
Total controllable expenses	$(1,380)	$ (715)	$ (665)	$(50)	$ (210)	$ (200)	$ (205)	$(25)	$(95)	$ (85)
Controllable contribution	$ 1,990	$1,175	$ 815	$(50)	$ 350	$ 280	$ 235	$(25)	$145	$115
Expenses controlled by others										
Depreciation	$ 520	$ 300	$ 220	$ 30	$ 70	$ 60	$ 60	$ 10	$ 30	$ 20
Property taxes	200	120	80		30	30	20		10	10
Insurance	300	150	150		50	50	50		25	25
Total expenses controlled by others	$(1,020)	$ (570)	$ (450)	$(30)	$ (150)	$ (140)	$ (130)	$(10)	$ (65)	$ (55)
Total contribution	$ 970	$ 605	$ 365	$(80)	$ 200	$ 140	$ 105	$(35)	$ 80	$ 60
Unallocated costs[3]	(160)									
Income before taxes	$ 810									

[1]Unallocated expenses include a regional advertising campaign and equipment used by the regional manager.
[2]Unallocated expenses include a portion of the district manager's salary, district promotion costs, and district manager's car.
[3]Unallocated costs include taxes on undeveloped real estate, headquarters expense, legal, and audit fees.

Required:
a. Responsibility accounting has been used effectively by many companies, both large and small.
   i. Define responsibility accounting.
   ii. Discuss the benefits that accrue to a company using responsibility accounting.
   iii. Describe the advantages of responsibility accounting for the managers of a firm.
b. The budget of Family Resorts, Inc. was accepted by the regional and district managers. Based on the facts presented, evaluate the budget process employed by Family Resorts by addressing the following:
   i. What features of the budget preparation process are likely to result in the managers adopting and supporting the budget process?
   ii. What recommendations, if any, could be made to the budget preparers to improve the budget process? Explain your answer.

(CMA)

2. Pittsburgh–Walsh Company (PWC) is a manufacturing company whose product line consists of lighting fixtures and electronic timing devices. The Lighting Fixtures Division assembles units for the upscale and midrange markets. The Electronic

Timing Devices Division manufactures instrument panels that allow electronic systems to be activated and deactivated at scheduled times for both efficiency and safety purposes. Both divisions operate in the same manufacturing facility and share production equipment.

PWC's budget for the year ending December 31, 2005, was prepared on a business segment basis under the following guidelines:
- Variable expenses are directly assigned to the incurring division.
- Fixed overhead expenses are directly assigned to the incurring division.
- Common fixed expenses are allocated to the divisions on the basis of units produced, which bear a close relationship to direct labour. Included in common fixed expenses are costs of the corporate staff, legal expenses, taxes, staff marketing, and advertising.
- The production plan is for 8,000 upscale fixtures, 22,000 midrange fixtures, and 20,000 electronic timing devices.

Pittsburgh–Walsh Company
Budget for the Year Ending December 31, 2005
(amounts in thousands)

| | Lighting Fixtures | | Electronic | |
	Upscale	Midrange	Timing Devices	Totals
Sales	$1,440	$770	$800	$3,010
Variable expenses				
Cost of goods sold	(720)	(439)	(320)	(1,479)
Selling and administrative	(170)	(60)	(60)	(290)
Contribution margin	$ 550	$271	$420	$1,241
Fixed overhead expenses	(140)	(80)	(80)	(300)
Segment margin	$ 410	$191	$340	$941
Common fixed expenses				
Overhead	(48)	(132)	(120)	(300)
Selling and administrative	(11)	(31)	(28)	(70)
Net income (loss)	$ 351	$ 28	$192	$ 571

PWC established a bonus plan for division management that requires meeting the budget's planned net income by product line, with a bonus increment if the division exceeds the planned product line net income by 10% or more.

Shortly before the year began, the CEO, Jack Parkow, had a heart attack and subsequently retired. After reviewing the 2005 budget, the new CEO, Joe Kelly, decided to close the lighting fixtures midrange product line by the end of the first quarter and use the available production capacity to increase the remaining two product lines. The marketing staff advised that electronic timing devices could grow by 40% with increased direct sales support. Increases above that level and increasing sales of upscale lighting fixtures would require expanded advertising expenditures to increase consumer awareness of PWC as an electronics and upscale lighting fixture company. Kelly approved the increased sales support and advertising expenditures to achieve the revised plan. Kelly advised the divisions that for bonus purposes, the original product line net income objectives must be met, but he did allow the Lighting Fixtures Division to combine the net income objectives for both product lines for bonus purposes.

Prior to the close of the fiscal year, the division controllers were furnished with preliminary actual data for review and adjustment, as appropriate. These following preliminary year-end data reflect the revised units of production amounting to 12,000 upscale fixtures, 4,000 midrange fixtures, and 30,000 electronic timing devices.

Pittsburgh–Walsh Company
Preliminary Actuals
for the Year Ending December 31, 2005
(amounts in thousands)

| | Lighting Fixtures | | Electronic | |
	Upscale	Midrange	Timing Devices	Totals
Sales	$2,160	$140	$1,200	$3,500
Variable expenses				
Cost of goods sold	(1,080)	(80)	(480)	(1,640)
Selling and administrative	(260)	(11)	(96)	(367)
Contribution margin	$ 820	$ 49	$ 624	$1,493
Fixed overhead expenses	(140)	(14)	(80)	(234)
Segment margin	$ 680	$ 35	$ 544	$1,259
Common fixed expenses				
Overhead	(78)	(27)	(195)	(300)
Selling and administrative	(60)	(20)	(150)	(230)
Net income (loss)	$ 542	$ (12)	$ 199	$ 729

The controller of the Lighting Fixtures Division, anticipating a similar bonus plan for 2006, is contemplating postponing the recognition of some revenues until next year because the sales are not yet final, and advancing into the current year some expenditures that will be applicable to the first quarter of 2006. The corporation would meet its annual plan, and the division would exceed the 10% incremental bonus plateau in the year 2005 despite the postponed revenues and advanced expenses contemplated.

Required:

a. i.   Outline the benefits that an organization realizes from segment reporting.
   ii. Evaluate segment reporting on a variable cost basis versus an absorption cost basis.

b. i.   Segment reporting can be developed based on different criteria. What criteria must be present for division management to accept being evaluated on a segment basis?
   ii. Why would the managers of the Electronic Timing Devices Division be unhappy with the current reporting, and how should the reporting be revised to gain their acceptance?

c.   Are the adjustments contemplated by the controller of the Lighting Fixtures Division unethical? Explain.

(CMA)

3. Golf course maintenance at the Westlake Country Club is managed by the greenskeeper and treated as a cost centre. Performance measurement is based on a comparison of the budgeted amounts with the actual expenses for the year. The following statement has been prepared by the bookkeeper of the club.

Westlake Country Club
Golf Course Expenses
For the Year Ended December 31, 2005

	Budgeted Amount	Actual Expense	Variance
Payroll and payroll taxes	$54,000	$54,500	$ (500)
Sand and gravel	300	500	(200)
Topsoil	1,000	800	200
Fertilizer	5,000	8,500	(3,500)
Fungicide	1,000	1,400	(400)
Grass seed	800	300	500
Parts	2,500	1,800	700
Petroleum products	1,800	3,100	(1,300)
Golf equipment	500	100	400
Uniforms	300	0	300
Training	300	0	300
Equipment rental	2,500	250	2,250
Utilities	3,000	5,100	(2,100)
Depreciation	5,000	5,000	0
Total	$78,000	$81,350	$(3,350)

The budget for the golf course is prepared by the greens committee and Mr. Jim Wallace, the greenskeeper. The budget is approved by the board of directors of the club and is used in evaluating the performance of Mr. Wallace at the end of the year. As a part of this evaluation, the following conversation takes place between Mr. Driver, the president of the club, and Mr. Wallace:

Mr. Driver: Jim, you should realize that the golf course budget represents the best judgments of the greens committee and the board of directors as to how resources should be used on the golf course. It is my opinion that differences between each budgeted amount and the expense incurred should be minor if you operate the course as directed by the committee with the approval of the board. The only items on this report where I view the differences as insignificant are payroll and depreciation. In many areas—such as fertilizer, petroleum products, and utilities—you significantly exceeded the budgeted amounts. To cover up these excesses, you failed to carry out our wishes concerning golf equipment and uniforms, and I can't explain the problem with equipment rental. I have received several complaints from our members about the condition of our markers and ball washers and the appearance of the help on the course. I now see how this is reflected in this report. Besides that, we have had many complaints as to the condition of the course.

Mr. Wallace: My understanding has been that I am to run the golf course and try to remain within the total budget. I can explain all of the differences that show up on this report. The cost of fertilizer, fungicide, petroleum products, and utilities went up significantly this year. Because of this, we only put out a minimum of fertilizer. It was either this or incur a significant budget overrun. The late summer was very dry, which required excessive pumping, and this added to the increased utility cost.

Mr. Driver: Jim, you're telling me that the budget did not allow for any price increases, but I know this is not the case.

Mr. Wallace: I know price increases were built into the budget, but they in no way covered the actual increases for the year. No one could have anticipated the short supply of fertilizer and fungicide that existed this year.

Mr. Driver: You should have limited your expenditures for these items to the amounts in the budget, and you should have bought the new uniforms and golf equipment and started some of the reseeding that was included in your budget.

Mr. Wallace: In my opinion, I did the best job possible to maintain the course, given the economic and weather conditions during the year. These things cannot be anticipated in preparing a budget. I must use my professional judgment in some of these matters. In addition, concerning the depreciation, I have nothing to do with it! It just shows up at the end of each year.

Mr. Driver: I am not sure that helps the situation.

Required:

a. Explain how Mr. Driver and Mr. Wallace differ in the way that they interpret the budget and in the way they believe Mr. Wallace's performance is to be evaluated.

b. Prepare a report suggesting how the differences you identified in part (a) can be reconciled.

c. Do you see any problems with the treatment of depreciation in the budget? Explain.

d. Who should evaluate Mr. Wallace's performance: the greens committee or the board of directors? Explain.

4. The Advertising Department of Ace Wholesale Sporting Goods is evaluated as a cost centre. The fiscal year for the company ends on July 30, and divisional managers are evaluated on their ability to operate within their budgets. For the last several years, the Advertising Department has run out of office supplies in June, and the advertising manager has made a vigorous attempt to control the volume of mail leaving the department.

During these year-end periods, office equipment is not repaired, photo supplies run short, the signing of advertising and printing contracts is postponed, and all travel is eliminated. Because of these shortages, sales personnel and manufacturers' representatives frequently complain of inadequate service during these year-end periods. Several employees in the Advertising Department have observed that this condition is being encountered earlier each year. Some employees have been known to stockpile office supplies during the year so that they can function at the year's end.

Required:

a. Describe the probable causes of the problems in the Advertising Department.

b. Write a memo to the Advertising Department manager suggesting several means by which some of these problems can be corrected.

c. How could advice from an expert in human behaviour be used to deal with the games that are being played with the budget?

ETHICS AND QUALITY DISCUSSIONS

1. The British Columbia Division is one of several divisions of North American Products. The divisional manager has a high degree of autonomy in operating the division. British Columbia Division's management staff consists of a division controller, a division sales manager, and a division production manager, all reporting to the division manager. The division manager reports to the executive vice president at corporate headquarters, while the division controller has a functional reporting relationship to the corporate controller.

The members of the management staff of the British Columbia Division have developed good working relationships with each other over the past several years. Regularly scheduled staff meetings are held, and most of the management process is carried out through daily contact among the members of the staff.

An important staff meeting is held each September. At the meeting, management makes decisions required to finalize the annual budget to be submitted to corporate headquarters for the coming calendar year. The fourth-quarter plans are finalized, and the current year's forecasted results are reviewed prior to completion of the budget for the coming year.

For the first time in recent years, the budgeted amounts of the British Columbia Division for the coming year (2006) show no growth and lower profits than the forecast for the current year. A review of the coming year's plans has not uncovered any alternatives that could improve the sales and profits. This unusual situation is of concern to the division manager because he has developed a reputation for producing growing profits. In addition, growth and profits affect the division manager's performance evaluation and annual bonus.

During the meeting in September 2005, the division manager stated that he would like to see some of the profits shifted from 2005 to 2006. He has heard that another company shifted profits, and believes that the following actions were used to accomplish this objective.

- Shipments made to customers in the last two weeks of December were not billed until January.
- The sales force was instructed to encourage customers to specify January delivery rather than December wherever possible.
- Abnormally generous amounts were used to establish accruals for warranties, bad debts, and other expenses.
- Raw materials for which title had passed and that were in transit at the end of December were recorded as purchased in December; however, the raw materials were not included in the year-end inventory.
- Sales on account for the last day of December were not recorded until the first business day of January.
- The cleaning and painting of the exterior of the plant was rescheduled to be completed in the current year rather than in the coming year as planned.

The dollar amounts involved in these actions were material and would be material for the British Columbia Division if similar actions were taken. The division manager asks the division controller whether profits would be shifted from 2005 to 2006 if actions similar to these were carried out at the British Columbia Division.

Required:

a.   For each of the enumerated items, indicate whether there would be a shift of profit from 2005 to 2006.

b.   How could the described manipulations of the responsibility accounting system adversely affect the quality of work performed in the division?

c.   Comment on the ethics of accelerating or delaying transactions in order to manipulate the level of profit reported by a division.

2. A large Canadian corporation participates in a highly competitive industry. To meet this competition and achieve profit goals, the company has chosen the decentralized form of organization. Each manager of a decentralized investment centre is measured on the basis of profit contribution, market penetration, and return on investment. Failure to meet the objectives established by corporate management for these measures is unacceptable and usually results in demotion or dismissal of an investment centre manager.

An anonymous survey of managers in the company has revealed that the managers feel pressure to compromise their personal ethical standards to achieve corporate objectives. For example, at certain plant locations there is pressure to reduce quality control to a level that cannot assure that all unsafe products will be rejected. Also, sales personnel are encouraged to use questionable sales tactics to obtain orders, including gifts and other incentives to purchasing agents.

The chief executive officer is disturbed by the survey findings. In his opinion, such behaviour cannot be condoned by the company. He concludes that the company should do something about this problem.

Required:

a.   Discuss what might be causing the ethical problems described.

b.   Outline a program that could be instituted by the company to help reduce the pressures on managers to compromise personal ethical standards in their work.

(CMA)

3. Egret and Swan are partners in an accounting firm. Egret runs the tax practice and is both a CA and a CMA. Swan is in charge of the management consulting area; his background is in information systems and statistics. Egret and Swan used to be good friends; but since his divorce, Egret believes that everyone is out to take him for everything possible. In addition to their salaries, Egret and Swan receive (1) a bonus based on the profits of their respective practice areas and (2) a share of total profits after expenses. The tax practice has consistently shown higher profits than the consulting area, although consulting revenues are growing and costs are remaining fairly constant.

Recently, Swan asked for some help regarding several of his client engagements in tax matters. Egret also needed some computer assistance from Swan's area. Therefore, they agreed to establish a transfer price for such assistance. The transfer price was to be the cost of service provided. At the end of the year, the tax area showed a very large profit while the consulting area's increase was not so substantial, even though several new clients had been acquired. Egret spent his bonus on a trip to the island of St. Thomas and felt much better when he returned after three weeks. He hoped the following year would be even more profitable, since he was using absorption (full) cost as the basis for transferring his assistance to consulting and Swan was using variable cost as the basis for transferring his assistance to tax.

Required:

a.   Do you think it is necessary to inform the uninformed about the differences in how things can be defined in accounting? You do not need to limit this discussion to cost-based transfer prices.

b.   Is Egret being unethical in the distribution of profits with Swan? Discuss.

c.   Is Egret being illegal in the distribution of profits with Swan? Discuss.

d.   The assistance being rendered between the two areas is similar to a product, since both areas produce revenues. Suggest an equitable way to determine a transfer price for the firm, and discuss how your transfer price would affect the bonuses earned by Egret and Swan.

4.   The Robinson Company has several plants, one of which produces military equipment for the federal government. Many of the contracts are negotiated by use of cost plus a specified markup. Some of the other plants have been only marginally profitable, and the home office has engaged a consultant, Mr. Slick, to meet with top management. At the meeting, Slick observes that the company isn't using some of the more "creative" accounting techniques to shift costs toward the plant serving the federal government and away from the marginally profitable plants. He notes that "transfer pricing and service department allocations involve a lot of subjectivity, and there is plenty of room to stack the deck and let the taxpayer foot the bill. Taxpayers will never know, and even if the government suspects, it can't prove motive if we document the procedures with contrived business jargon." One of the staff states that "this would be a way to get back some of those exorbitant income taxes we have had to pay all these years." The company president ends the meeting and asks for some time to consider the matter.

Required:

a.   What is the purpose of setting transfer prices and making service department allocations?

b.   Can or should transfer prices and service department allocations be used to shift income from one plant to another? If so, under what conditions?

c.   Do you think that what the consultant is suggesting is legal? Ethical? Ever been done? Discuss your reasoning for each answer.

5.   Klein Corp. is a diversified manufacturing company with corporate headquarters in Kitchener, Ontario. The three operating divisions are the Aerospace Division, the Ceramic Products Division, and the Glass Products Division. Much of the manufacturing activity of the Aerospace Division is related to work performed for the American space program under negotiated contracts.

Klein Corp. headquarters provides general administrative support and computer services to each of the three operating divisions. The computer services are provided by an application service provider (ASP) located in Kitchener. The division's networks are connected to the ASP by dedicated data lines. The cost of general administration may be allocated to negotiated defence contracts. Further, the standards provide that, in situations in which computer services are provided by corporate headquarters, the actual costs (fixed and variable) of operating the computer department may be allocated to another division based on a reasonable measure of computer usage.

The general managers of the three divisions are evaluated based on the before-tax performance of the divisions. The November 2005 performance evaluation reports (in millions of dollars) for each division is presented next.

	Aerospace Division	Ceramic Products Division	Glass Products Division
Sales	$23.0	$15.0	$55.0
Cost of goods sold	(13.0)	(7.0)	(38.0)
Gross profit	$10.0	$ 8.0	$17.0
Selling and administrative:			
Division selling and administration costs	$ 5.0	$ 5.0	$ 8.0
Corporate general administration costs	1.0	–	–
Corporate computing	1.0	–	–
Total	$ (7.0)	$ (5.0)	$ (8.0)
Profit before taxes	$ 3.0	$ 3.0	$ 9.0

If they are not charged for computing services, the operating divisions may not make the most cost-effective use of the resources of the Computer Systems Department of Klein Corp.

Required:
Outline and discuss a method for charging the operating divisions for use of computer services that would promote cost consciousness on the part of the operating divisions and operating efficiency by the Computer Systems Department.

(CMA adapted)

COMMUNICATIONS ACTIVITIES

1. Traditionally, if an organization wanted to expand, there were two routes it could take: organic expansion or acquisition. With organic expansion, the organization built new assets; with acquisition, the proprietary assets were purchased. Another route—called "leveraged growth"—is increasingly being used. It is premised on "mobilization of resources supplied by many organizations operating at many levels of the value chain." Leveraged growth is broader and less restricted than outsourcing; it includes the coordination or orchestration of all activities, or multiple outsourcing, in a value creation chain.

    (Source: John Hagell III, "Leveraged Growth: Expanding Sales Without Sacrificing Profits," *Harvard Business Review*, October 2002, pp. 68–77.)
    Required:
    Discuss how you would impose responsibility accounting with leveraged growth.

2. "Improving corporate governance is one of the hottest topics in boardrooms, regulatory commissions, and business newsrooms around the world. Reasons for this stem from a variety of problems that surfaced in the 1990s, such as well-publicized business failures that have been related to inadequate governance structures, including Bre-X, Livent, and YBM, and questions about the adequacy of management in organizations like Air Canada, Moore, and Nortel.... Continuing concerns about improving corporate governance have also been voiced in such reports as the influential Crystal Report On Executive Compensation by analyst Graef Crystal, which debates whether boards act in the best interests of shareholders, particularly in the area of setting executive compensation. ... Statements expressed by securities regulators, such as David Brown, chair of the Ontario Securities Commission (OSC), suggesting that external auditors are increasingly becoming advocates for their clients instead of impartial arbitrators of financial statement disclosure fairness are also influencing decisions pertaining to corporate accountability."

    (Source: Reprinted from an article appearing in the February 2002 issue of *CMA Management* magazine by Anthony A. Atkinson and Steven Salterio, with permission of Certified Management Accountants of Canada.)

Required:
Discuss how you would ensure an organization pursues good corporate governance practices.

PROJECTS

1. Assume that the organization you work for has just purchased a fleet of cars from a major automobile producer. The cars are to be made available to the six autonomous divisions in your organization for business use by a variety of personnel. Each division has authority to either use these automobiles or make outside arrangements for its transportation needs. Your job is to determine an effective transfer pricing scheme under the two conditions below.

   a. Demand from the divisions far exceeds the size of the fleet. Thus, you need to devise a transfer pricing scheme that will ration the cars to the divisions. The pricing scheme you develop should allow for recovery of all costs to acquire and operate the fleet.

   b. The divisions demonstrate little interest in using the central fleet. Accordingly, you need to devise a transfer pricing scheme that will encourage the divisions to use the fleet rather than vehicles acquired from outside the firm. In this case, all costs of operating the fleet must be covered, but it is not necessary for the original cost of the vehicles to be fully recovered.

2. You are involved in the development of a new health food business that is to compete in major metropolitan areas of North America. The business will open 100 retail stores per year for the next several years. Your job is to develop a responsibility accounting system to evaluate the performance of the store managers in each retail store. The firm will centralize the financing, purchasing, and accounting functions to obtain economies of scale. Nearly all other decisions will be made locally.

   Your primary concern is with identifying the most important issues to be considered in the design of the responsibility accounting system. You are not concerned with operational details. For example, one major issue might be behavioural issues (such as manipulating accounting measures) that could occur within the control system.

   You are to prepare a written report of these major issues to present to your business colleagues. You might consider working with two or three other class members as a team. Each team should devise its own method for apportioning the work among team members. If teams are used, one report that integrates the work of all members should be prepared for each team.

USING THE INTERNET

1. Organizations continuously move between centralization and decentralization as mentioned in the On Site on page 637 that discussed Canadian National Railway. Organizations frequently centralize during bad times to reduce costs and decentralize during good times to expand customer sales or service. Use the Internet to survey the business periodicals to gather information on organizations that are pursuing centralization and those that are pursuing decentralization. Classify the reasons for centralizing and the reasons for decentralizing.

2. To understand the importance of transfer pricing in multinational companies, it is helpful to know the nature and extent of intracompany transfers. Conduct an Internet search with Google or another search engine on multinational transfers and transfer pricing. Based on this search, write a report documenting the kinds of services, technology, and products that are the subject of intracompany transfers. Also, discuss any findings on the factors that affect the selection of the transfer pricing scheme.

SOLUTIONS TO SELF-TEST QUESTIONS

1. a, 2. b, 3. a, 4. d, 5. c, 6. d, 7. b, 8. b, 9. d, 10. a

ENDNOTES

1. William Taylor, "The Logic of Global Business: An Interview with ABB's Percy Barnevik," *Harvard Business Review*, March–April 1991, p. 101.

2. Kenneth R. Andrews, ed., *Ethics in Practice: Managing the Moral Corporation*, Boston: Harvard Business School Press, 1989, p. 7.

3 Matt Murray, "After Long Overhaul, Banc One Now Faces Pressure to Perform," *The Wall Street Journal*, March 10, 1998, pp. A1, A10.

4. W. W. Cooper and Yuri Ijiri, eds., *Kohler's Dictionary for Accountants*, Englewood Cliffs, N.J.: Prentice-Hall, 1983, pp. 43–45.

5. Discretionary costs were discussed in Chapter 8.

6. These rules are more difficult to implement when the selling division is in a captive relationship and is not able to sell its products outside the corporate entity. In such situations, opportunity cost must be estimated to give the selling division an incentive to transfer products.

7. Ian Karleff, "Tax Haven Earnings at Risk?" *National Post*, August 9, 2002, p. 1N+.

8. Volume variances are covered in Chapter 5, on standard costing.

Chapter 12

Cost Management and Performance Measurement Systems

LEARNING OBJECTIVES

After reading this chapter, you should be able to answer the following questions:

1 What
is a cost management system?

2 What
is a performance measurement system?

3 What
are the four stages of cost management and performance measurement systems?

4 How
do enterprise resource planning systems integrate cost management and performance measurement systems?

5 How
has Wal-Mart's enterprise resource planning system contributed to its outstanding success?

6 How
do the internal and external operating environments impact cost management and performance measurement systems?

7 What
three groups of elements affect the design of cost management and performance measurement systems, and how are these elements used?

8 How
is gap analysis used in the implementation of cost management and performance measurement systems?

www.nbc.ca

The National Bank of Canada: Controlling the Cost of Plastic

Cost management systems should do more than count costs. They should help direct and implement strategy—especially in the fiercely competitive arena of credit card services. Cost management systems need to address not only how they can support decisions on strategic opportunities but also how they influence behaviour to minimize strategic threats. The Credit Card Services division of the **NATIONAL BANK OF CANADA** demonstrates how cost management systems can be used to support strategy, and cautions management accountants to be vigilant in guarding against the incongruities that this brings.

The cost management system developed by the National Bank's Credit Card Services department estimates costs and profits on a product basis. Although the system uses a two-stage activity approach, it is in fact much older than the popular ABC [activity-based costing] in the late 1980s. An important feature of this system is that it allocates fully loaded costs to all products. All costs are initially assigned to one of 39 activity centres and then for each activity, the variable that best describes cost behaviour is used to allocate costs to products. For example, some costs are assigned according to the number of cards outstanding, other costs are assigned according to the number of cards in active use, and other costs are assigned based on the level of bad debts.

The approach used at the National Bank has several important control features. The first relates to the decision to use an activity base on the full cost model. Conventional wisdom would recommend that a marginal cost analysis would be most appropriate for making decisions about individual products. Yet on the other hand, a marginal analysis may fail to address the cumulative effects of individual decisions, and can inadvertently portray some products as significantly more profitable than they really are. Since a large part of the costs are step-fixed, some new products will add revenue but little supplementary cost, while others will tip the balance in the other direction by adding more fixed costs such as personnel, telephone lines, or floor space than their proportionate weight. The risk brought by the ABC system is that in charging fully absorbed costs to products, the bank may lose key information on the effects of an individual decision. So to compensate, the bank must find a way to ensure that the behaviourally based numbers do not lead to poor decisions.

For the National Bank, the ABC model is not the only cost management tool employed for managing product profitability. In evaluating significant new product proposals (those that require senior management approval) accounting managers at the National Bank use a second, direct cost model. This model is considered in conjunction with the first, but the analysis is not shared with operational managers. Therefore, the control system is constructed to balance the long-term and short-term needs of the organization. By fully allocating costs to products, the system forces managers to consider the long-term effects of the ensemble of products on the resources of the bank. However the second direct cost evaluation allows management to regard the effects of an individual new product on the short-term consumption of resources.

SOURCE: Reprinted from an article appearing in the July/August 1999 issue of *CMA Management* magazine by Alexander Mersereau, with permission of Certified Management Accountants of Canada.

The National Bank provides an example of where cost control, or more precisely cost management, must be considered in a systematic manner rather than ad hoc. In the previous chapters, you were provided with numerous ad hoc techniques for controlling costs: strategy and value creation chain (Chapter 1); terminology (Chapter 2); an explanation of cost behaviours (Chapter 3); process costing and other approaches (Chapter 4); standards (Chapter 5); activity-based management (Chapter 6); various cost control techniques (Chapter 7); relevant costs (Chapter 8); budgeting (Chapter 9); capital budgeting (Chapter 10); and responsibility accounting (Chapter 11). Chapter 12 puts these techniques together as a cost management system, which is primarily concerned with managing and controlling the cost of activities. Relatedly, this chapter introduces a system for managing the performance of the activities that go into the creation of value. Then, a model of the stages through which organizations evolve in developing cost management and performance measurement systems is discussed. The highest level is when enterprise resource planning systems incorporate both cost management and performance measurement. The enterprise resource planning system of Wal-Mart is then described, as an example of the leader in integrating cost management and performance measurement. This chapter also discusses how the life cycle of products and services and other factors affect cost management and performance measurement systems.

LEARNING OBJECTIVE 1

What is a cost management system?

cost management system
a set of formal methods developed for controlling an organization's cost-generating activities relative to its goals and objectives

COST MANAGEMENT SYSTEM

A **cost management system (CMS)** is a set of formal methods developed for controlling the costs of an organization's activities in its value creation chain relative to its goals and objectives. A CMS is not merely a system for minimizing the costs incurred by an organization. Instead, it should help an organization to obtain maximum benefits from incurring costs. More specifically, a CMS should help managers

- identify the cost of resources consumed in performing significant activities of the organization
- determine the efficiency and effectiveness of the activities performed
- identify and evaluate new activities that can improve the future performance of the organization
- accomplish the three previous objectives in an environment characterized by changing technology[1]

The information generated from the CMS should integrate and benefit all functional areas of the entity. As shown in Exhibit 12-1, the CMS should "improve the quality, content, relevance, and timing of cost information that managers use for decision making."[2]

By crossing all functional areas (not simply accounting), a cost management system can be viewed as having five primary goals: (1) to develop reasonably accurate product/service costs; (2) to assess product/service profitability over the entire

EXHIBIT 12-1

A Functionally Integrated Cost Management System

Source: Robert McIlhattan, "The Path to Total Cost Management," *Emerging Practices in Cost Management*, p. 178, Warren, Gorham and Lamont. ©2003 Thomson/RIA, All rights reserved.

life of the product/service; (3) to improve understanding of internal processes and activities; (4) to control costs; and (5) to allow the pursuit of organizational strategies.

First and foremost, a CMS should provide the means to develop reasonably accurate product and/or service costs. Thus, the system must be designed to gather information in a manner that allows costs to be traced to products and services. It is not necessary that the system be "the most accurate one, but one which matches benefits of additional accuracy with expenses of achieving additional accuracy. The best system will report approximate, but inaccurate, product costs, with the degree of approximation determined by the organization's competitive, product, and process environment."[3] Traceability has been made easier by improved information technology, such as bar coding and the Internet.

The product/service costs generated by the CMS are the input to managerial processes. These costs are used to plan, prepare financial statements, assess individual products/services and period profitability, establish prices for outputs, and create a basis for performance measurement. If the input costs accumulated and assigned by the CMS are not reasonably accurate, the information output of the CMS will be inappropriate for control and decision-making purposes.

Although product/service profitability may be calculated periodically as a requirement for external reporting, the financial accounting system does not reflect life-cycle information. The CMS should provide information about the life-cycle cost of a product or service. Without life-cycle information, managers will not have a basis to relate costs incurred in one stage of the life cycle to costs and profitability of other stages. For example, managers may not recognize that increasing investment in the development and design stage of the life cycle could provide significant rewards in later stages by minimizing potential future costs caused by design, environmental pollution, or product recall. Further, if development/design cost is not traced to the related product or service, managers may not be able to recognize organizational investment "disasters." Finally, companies should take a long-term view and determine cost based on life-cycle relationships (rather than period-by-period relationships) among prices, profit margins, and costs.

Lastly, to maintain a competitive position in an industry, an organization must generate information necessary to determine present and future costs regarding its organizational strategies. As discussed in Chapter 1, strategy is the set of long-term plans that provide the link between an organization's goals and objectives and the costs of activities actually conducted by the organization. In the current global market, organizations must be certain that such a linkage exists. Information provided by a CMS allows managers to perform strategic analyses on such issues as determining core competencies and managing organizational resources from a cost–benefit perspective, assessing the positive and negative financial and non-financial factors of investment and operational plans, and engaging in employee empowerment by utilizing new management techniques such as those discussed in Chapters 6 and 7. Thus, the cost management system is essential to the generation of information for effective resource management.

Designing a Cost Management System

Because a CMS is concerned with costs, it has been founded in part on accounting information. All accounting information is generated from one accounting system and one set of accounts. Although existing technology would allow companies to design different accounting systems for different purposes, most companies still rely on a single system to supply all accounting information. Historically, most accounting systems have been focused on providing information for financial accounting purposes, and their informational outputs must be adapted to meet most internal management requirements.

An activity-based costing (ABC) system is an alternative approach that can gather accurate cost information on products and customers. As noted in Chapter 6, ABC is an accounting information system that identifies the various activities performed in an organization and collects costs on the basis of the underlying nature and extent of the activities. ABC has been described as "an economic map of the organization's expenses and profitability based on organizational activities."[4] The concern of ABC is with determining and documenting the activities being undertaken by the organization's resources. With this activity information the costs are calculated for performing activities and processes. ABC also ascertains the activity requirements for producing the organization's products, services, and customers.

Four steps have been identified in developing an ABC system:
1. Develop the activity dictionary or list of activities.
2. Determine how much the organization is spending on each of its activities.
3. Identify the organization's products, services, and customers.
4. Select activity cost drivers that link activity costs to the organization's products, services, and customers.[5]

To be an economic map, an ABC system must, as Step 1, identify the activities being performed by the indirect or overhead costs. For example, the indirect costs related to supervision or ordering parts must be allocated to activities, and the costs of those activities will subsequently be allocated to products, services, and customers. After more than a decade of experience with implementing ABC systems, standard activity dictionaries have been developed that provide a template for determining the appropriate activity classification for nearly all overhead activities. For example, a set of activities for a purchasing function might include (1) develop specifications and obtain a list of potential vendors; (2) send specifications to prospective vendors and request quotes from them; and (3) review submitted quotes against specifications and award order. Activity dictionaries can vary, containing from as few as 10 activities to hundreds of activities and more, with more activities being related to size and complexity of the organization and the desire for detailed costs.

Step 2 is to attach indirect costs to activities. In effect, this involves attaching the respective indirect costs to the respective activity in the activity dictionary. For example, if the purchasing department has eight activities, the second step would be allocation of the total cost of the purchasing department to each of the activities. The allocation method may be based on asking employees where they spend their work time in percentage terms, by observing where they spend their time, etc.

Step 3 is to identify the activities' products, services, and customers. Products, services, and customers are the intended result of incurring indirect costs for activities. The indirect costs are first allocated to products and services, and then the same costs are allocated to the customers of those products and services.

Finally, in Step 4, the linkages between the activity costs in Step 2 and the products, services, and customers in Step 3 are made with what is called activity cost drivers. Cost drivers are what drive the activity costs in making the products and services for the customers. Activity drivers require substantial judgment. There is no single, obvious, and precise driver for every type of activity cost.

Three generic types of activity drivers form a framework for determining appropriate drivers: transaction, duration, and intensity.[6] Transaction drivers count how often an activity is done (e.g., number of truck tires inspected). Duration

Software Standardizes Claim Costs

INTERNATIONAL NEWS NOTE

Each year Canadian and U.S. "insureds" are involved in millions of automobile accidents. The cost to repair these vehicles tops an eye-popping nine billion dollars more than the combined net incomes of Microsoft, Sears, and Disney. Not surprisingly, automobile insurance companies in Canada and the U.S. are seeking tools to better allocate their resources to control costs and better manage their business. One increasingly popular method is a software information management system that allows insurance claims executives to monitor the performance, productivity, and compliance of their in-house and external adjusters. Standard or customized reports can instantly show up to 114 data elements—including parts usage, labour costs, and estimator productivity—while providing regular updates on industry average claim costs.

A growing number of insurers across North America are utilizing Advanced Information Management (AIM) software from San Diego-based Mitchell International to manage costs and gauge against up-to-date industry standards. The latest release provides information from a variety of Canadian and U.S. insurers updated monthly on disk.

Fred Spicer, a leader in the claims office at Royal & SunAlliance Canada, has been using AIM for over a year. He says the cost management software helps isolate costs to better optimize his operation. "Before AIM, we used to get paper reports from our appraisers with the information we wanted," he says. "The reports weren't great, they were too modelled and had too much information. [However, for] automobile appraisers ... analyzing information is not their forte."

Spicer says the cost management software has been useful in reviewing adjuster appraisals. Royal & SunAlliance does not use it directly to evaluate their own in-house people, but could to identify individuals not complying with company appraisal standards. "If you are using AIM to manage your people and the quality of their work ... that can save a company money," Spicer says. "And in theory, every dollar you don't spend allows you to keep your premiums lower and remain more competitive in the market."

Source: Michael Andrews, *Canadian Underwriter*, Vol. 67, Issue 1, January 2000, p. 70. Reprinted by permission of *Canadian Underwriter* Magazine.

drivers represent the amount of time required for the activity (e.g., four hours to inspect a completed diesel motor). Intensity drivers charge directly for the time required for the activity (e.g., the cost to patent the truck transmission was $125,900, which included all legal fees plus out-of-pocket disbursements). To be an effective driver, the change in the driver level must be highly related or, more specifically, correlated with the costs of the activities.

<table>
<tr><td>**LEARNING OBJECTIVE   2**</td></tr>
</table>

What is a performance measurement system?

performance measurement system a major set of financial and, particularly, nonfinancial performance measures for evaluating the performance of a manager, activity, or organizational unit

PERFORMANCE MEASUREMENT SYSTEM

A **performance measurement system** provides economic feedback to managers and operators about process efficiency and effectiveness.[7] ABC systems reveal the activities that must be undertaken to effectively produce products and services. Greater awareness of activities leads to the explicit management of the detailed activities, which is often called activity-based management. This requires nonfinancial information for feedback on activities, which allows for modification in the way activities are carried out in order to improve performance.

A performance measurement system should help managers and operators to comprehend business processes and organizational activities. Only by understanding how an activity is accomplished in terms of nonfinancial performance measures, and the reasons for performance variation, can managers make cost–benefit improvements in products and services. Managers desiring to implement new technology such as installing robotic assembly lines must identify the costs and benefits that will flow from such actions; these assessments can be made only if the managers understand how processes and activities affect the value creation chain.

Cost management systems are not sufficient. Knowing the costs is important and necessary, but managers need to know on an ongoing basis—hourly or at least daily—the efficiency and effectiveness of the performance of activities. Only by efficiently and effectively undertaking all activities can Canadian organizations be competitive in the global market. Activities can be controlled only when the activity is known and its performance monitored against reasonable expectations or standards. The information generated from a performance measurement system should also help managers measure and evaluate human and equipment performance and assess future decision alternatives. Financial and, particularly, nonfinancial measurements captured at different organizational levels can be combined and used for different purposes.

Lastly, to maintain a competitive position in an industry, an organization must generate performance information necessary to define and implement its strategies. Information provided by a performance measurement system allows managers to understand how well activities are being done. A performance measurement system for reporting on activity accomplishments complements a CMS, which reports on the cost of activities. Thus, a performance measurement system is essential to the generation of information for effective resource management.

The activities that an organization undertakes should contribute to creating value for customers. The success of an organization in creating value for customers can be ascertained by evaluating or measuring the performance or success in carrying out the activities that create value for customers. The implementation of an ABC system is often an important step in understanding activities. The managing of activities to create customer value or activity-based management is equally important.

Streamlining Operations and Improving Services with ABM

Activity-based management tools empowered the Borough of East York (now part of the city of Toronto) with information to reduce costs and increase efficiency. The challenge to the government sector is to find ways to eliminate service duplication, increase efficiencies and reduce costs without reducing the quality of service to taxpayers. To accomplish this, the Borough looked for a new method to effectively analyze service provision. The Borough's staff realized the critical need of properly understanding the real costs of each action inherent in each service, and the need to see how different activities interacted with each other. This awareness led the staff to consider using tools such as activity-based costing (ABC) and activity-based management (ABM). The staff knew its activity-based approach should integrate operational, financial, and strategic information that could deliver sound management solutions and informed strategies. Additionally, the Province of Ontario's decision to implement benchmarking further reinforced this decision.

In April of 1996, the Borough established an ABM pilot project. The project modelled 70 different activities involved in providing water and sewer service, such as private drain investigations, pump station operations, and repairing water-main breaks. This modelling exercise entailed a process model consisting of demands, activities, and resources. At the end of the pilot project, the staff identified a number of inefficiencies in the system. These inefficiencies also revealed the potential for process improvements, cost recovery, and the ability to make better decisions in the future. The Borough's first pilot project revealed a tremendous amount of valuable information that led the staff to recommend that the Borough council implement ABM for all of its services.

Additionally, the staff selected and implemented a process-based system that could identify real costs of activities, rather than costs by department. The modelling project broke down each activity into its many elements—from the cost of labour to investigate a drain to materials and cost of operating a vehicle. This was assisted by having its ABM software program—NetProphet by Sapling Corporation—play out "what-if" scenarios. These scenarios tested the sensitivity of the model to changes in the Borough's service mix and volumes, changes in programs offered, changes in cycle times, changes in costs of outputs, and changes in availability of resources.

Source: Reprinted from an article appearing in the October 1997 issue of *CMA Management* magazine by Gay Gooderham, with permission of Certified Management Accountants of Canada.

GENERAL NEWS NOTE

FOUR STAGES OF COST MANAGEMENT AND PERFORMANCE MEASUREMENT SYSTEMS

LEARNING OBJECTIVE 3

What are the four stages of cost management and performance measurement systems?

Four stages have been identified for evolution of cost and performance measurement systems.[8]

Stage I:	Inadequate for financial reporting
Stage II:	Financial reporting-driven
Stage III:	Customized, managerially relevant, standalone
Stage IV:	Integrated cost management, financial reporting, and performance measurement

This sequence of systems or progression in the development of cost and performance measurement systems is premised on the belief that it is most elementary for organizations to accurately report product and other costs for external reporting purposes specified by law. Only after that can organizations develop cost management and performance measurement systems.

Stage I Systems

These relatively simple organizations of the first stage have cost systems that are inadequate for financial reporting. They are not able to record costs accurately and they do not have the means to accurately allocate overhead costs to products and services. Although these systems often exist in new organizations, they also exist in mature organizations that continue to use what is presently called legacy systems. Stage I systems have five characteristics that are consequences of the inability to accurately record and allocate costs:

1. Extensive amounts of time and resources needed to consolidate different reporting entities within the company and to close the books each accounting period
2. Unexpected variances at the end of each accounting period when physical inventories are reconciled
3. Large writedowns of inventory after internal and external audits
4. Many postclosing adjusting entries to financial accounts
5. A general lack of integrity and auditability of the system

Stage II Systems

Organizations with Stage II systems are able to meet financial reporting requirements and to collect costs accurately by responsibility centres (but not by activities and business processes). In other words, they are adequate for valuing inventory for financial reporting purposes and for preparing periodic financial reports. However, these systems produce highly distorted product costs because traditional allocation systems are used instead of ABC (see Chapter 6 for a discussion), and relatedly they have nonexistent or highly distorted customer costs and performance feedback that is too late, too aggregated, and too financial.

Stage II systems are able, shortly after the end of an accounting period, to prepare complete financial statements that require minimal postclosing adjustments. Product or service costing with Stage II systems reports individual product or service costs with the same simple and aggregate methods used for external financial reporting, to value inventory, and to measure cost of goods sold. The problems with Stage II are

- The inability to estimate the cost of activities and business processes, and therefore the cost and profitability of products, services, and customers
- The inability to provide useful feedback to improve business processes

These deficiencies are a result of the financial reporting system that is being used for both product costing and performance measurement. Financial reporting systems, although appropriate for external reporting, do not operate at the activity level, which is necessary for accurate costing and performance measurement. Consequently, Stage II systems do not provide adequate information to managers for planning, decision making, and control.

Stage III Systems

When organizations operate at Stage III, they have all of the necessary systems, but the systems are freestanding rather than integrated. Freestanding systems lead to confusion because of inconsistent assessments among the three systems, which are

1. A traditional but well-functioning financial reporting system capable of basic accounting and transaction-capturing functions, such as preparing monthly and quarterly financial statements for external stakeholders
2. One or more activity-based costing systems that use data from the financial reporting and other systems to measure the costs of organizational units, customers, products, services, processes, and activities

3. Performance measurement systems of various types that provide front-line workers and their superiors with timely, accurate information—financial and nonfinancial—on the efficiency and effectiveness of activities and processes.

These Stage III organizations are often those with satisfactory Stage II financial reporting systems for accurately reporting to external stakeholders. These financial reporting systems are augmented by one or more ad hoc activity-based costing system to provide accurate cost information and are further augmented by one or more ad hoc performance measurement systems.

Stage IV Systems

Rather than separate systems for financial reporting, cost management, and performance measurement, Stage IV organizations have ABC and performance measurement systems that are integrated. Consequently, no fundamental conflict exists between the product costs from the ABC system and the external requirements for financial reporting. The ABC cost drivers are used for assigning overhead costs for both internal decision making and external financial reporting. Any allocations (i.e., nonmanufacturing costs) that do not comply with GAAP, regulatory requirements, or tax rules can be eliminated for external financial reporting. Simple attribute fields for activities can identify these noninventoriable costs for the system to eliminate them from product costs in inventory accounts.

The transition to Stage IV systems is generally facilitated by the installation of enterprise resource planning (ERP) systems that were discussed in Chapter 1. SAP, PeopleSoft, Great Plains, and Oracle are examples of organizations that provide ERP systems.

ENTERPRISE RESOURCE PLANNING SYSTEMS

Implementing an **enterprise resource planning (ERP)** system is a major undertaking. An ERP system has a common database or data warehouse that integrates all systems for all parts of the organization, including, for example, financial, manufacturing, sales, inventory, and human resources. By linking all systems with a data warehouse, an ERP system allows an organization to manage its activities holistically. An ERP is able to include not just the parts of an organization but also its suppliers and customers. Consequently, an ERP system is able to integrate financial reporting, cost management, and performance measurement along with all other systems in an organization.

Implementation of an ERP system is a major challenge for all organizations. ERP systems consist of relatively rigid sets of software for processing transactions and information. In implementing an ERP system, there is minimal customization of the software to meet the organization's requirements. Standard software is less prone to errors, and with a shortage of skilled programmers, it is economically more viable to adjust the organization to the software than vice versa. Thus, instead of customizing software, the organization must change its business processes. This is called **business process redesign.** There are three basic approaches for ERP business process redesign.[9]

- First, change all processes to achieve the ideal set of business processes. With these changes, there may be difficulties with implementing an ERP system as the new processes may be inconsistent with ERP system requirements.
- Second, accept the ERP design. This allows for fast implementation—and the saving of time, human energy, and money—because issues regarding process

LEARNING OBJECTIVE 4

How do enterprise resource planning systems integrate cost management and performance measurement systems?

enterprise resource planning
a fully integrated, full-service suite of software with a common database that can be used to plan and control resources across an entire organization

business process redesign
when an organization changes its business processes

GENERAL NEWS NOTE

Reaping the Promise of Enterprise Resource Systems

Organizations initiating ERP projects rated their cost management systems significantly higher than did non-ERP organizations. Surveys by the U.S. IMA's Cost Management Member Interest Group showed that organizations with ERP systems have almost twice as many cost allocation bases (9.6) on average than non-ERP organizations (5.8). With far more cost-driver information available, ERP systems enable a greater variety of allocation bases to be used. Pillowtex, for example, previously used plantwide overhead rates spread evenly by department. Now with its ERP system providing access to information by activity, the company's accountants can do a better job of allocating specific overhead to different cost objects, such as customers, according to Allan Pedersen, a Pillowtex division controller.

Another benefit of ERP systems is that activity-based costing (ABC) is finding a new home within ERP systems at many companies. Partnership agreements between major ERP vendors and ABC software developers now exist, such as the one between SAP and ABC Technologies. These alliances may help ABC proponents overcome some of the traditional problems such as lack of top management buy-in and infrequent updates.

The IMA surveys found that 41% of organizations using ABC systems have initiated ERP projects while 48% of organizations considering ABC have initiated ERP projects. These results suggest that many organizations consider ABC and ERP mutually beneficial but have found the need to implement them one at a time. At Hammond Group, a manufacturer of lead chemicals and battery oxides, ABC is a standalone system. The company's decision to initiate an ERP project using Oracle software was made independent of the ABC system—mainly for competitive reasons. Competitors were "kicking us in the teeth," says John McCarthy, financial project manager at Hammond Group. "No matter how we allocated costs, we needed to lower overhead." While ABC helps Hammond see that overhead, sales and administration costs are too high, the ERP system is required to become more efficient in handling transaction costs.

Energy Northwest, an electric utility in Richland, Washington, installed an Indus Passport ERP system in 1993. This system ran the company's complex operations including work management, document control, accounts payable, inventory, and purchasing. Indus had a strategic alliance with PeopleSoft, and in 1997, Energy Northwest installed PeopleSoft modules for payroll, human resources and benefits, and time and labour tracking. Later it added PeopleSoft modules for general ledger, budgets, and asset management. "We didn't need asset management right away, so we limited the scope of our initial implementation to only those modules we needed immediately," says Chad Bartram, Energy Northwest's supervisor of business planning and finance. The benefits of Energy Northwest's new ERP system are beginning to accrue. In accounting and financial reporting, analysts get more and better data quicker, which is helping accountants produce better and more complex analyses such as what-if scenarios showing how different allocation methods impact various business units. The functional staff now develops its own reports online rather than having to request special reports from the information services staff. Before the ERP implementation, Energy Northwest had seven systems analysts. Now it has three and a half full-time employees who maintain the system. "We've been able to survive without all the technical support," Bartram notes.

Source: Republished with permission of *Strategic Finance,* from "Reaping the Promise of Enterprise Resource Systems," Kip R. Krumwiede and Win G. Jordan, *Strategic Finance,* October 2000; permission conveyed through Copyright Clearance Center, Inc.

redesign are avoided. Generally, with this approach the disadvantage is the lack of flexibility; business processes that use the ERP vendor's design might not be sufficiently appropriate for the organization.

- Third, redesign with the ERP system in mind. This approach is often called "ERP design by default." The advantage of this approach is that for most processes the plain ERP system is adequate. For those few cases where customized software is crucial, the extra cost needs to be incurred.

The third approach, i.e., "(t)he path of least resistence is usually to meet [the ERP system] halfway and not to try to change the software to meet the organization's vision completely, but rather to accept a speedy implementation of 85 to 90 percent of [the] vision and get on with the business of doing business."

The re-engineering of business processes in conjunction with ERP would involve the elimination of technical and organizational bottlenecks, the improvement in quality of information, the replacement of out-of-date processes and activities, the integration of processes, and the reduction in standalone systems and interfaces.[10] Generally, process redesign is pursued before and after the ERP implementation. **Process re-engineering** (which involves more dramatic changes than process redesign) would need to be done prior to ERP implementation. The elimination of non-value-adding work and the automation of low-valuing work will allow employees to undertake truly value-adding work and to dramatically increase productive capacity. There are some common themes for process redesign:

- Forgetting about old business practices
- Organizing around continuous business processes aimed at getting products and services to customers
- Applying increasingly sophisticated information technology[11]

process re-engineering
process innovation and redesign aimed at finding and implementing radical changes in how things are made or how tasks are performed to achieve substantial cost, service, or time reductions

To be effective, an ERP system will contain an extensive **chart of accounts** or codes for accurate recording and tracking of activities and costs. The coding incorporates stable entities of a business, such as divisions, plants, stores, and warehouses. At a lower level there are codes for functions such as finance, production, sales, marketing, and materials management. There are also the traditional financial account codes such as assets, liabilities, revenues, and expenses, and the central ERP feature of coding processes, activities, and sub-activities.

chart of accounts
the list of all codes for recording transactions

There must be consistency of coding among all entities of an organization in order for all parts to relate to one another. In addition, by coding to the activity and sub-activity levels for entire organizations, the reach of ABC can be expanded via assigning business and corporate-level expenses to activities, as well as assigning brand, product line, and channel support costs. Direct costs are easy to assign to activities; indirect costs are more difficult but once they have been analyzed, it is easier to see how these indirect costs can be traced to activities with cause-and-effect relationships of activity cost drivers to cost objects such as products, services, and customers.

An important characteristic of an ERP system is the coding of activities that allows activity costs to be used to construct ABC for products and services as well as for periodic reporting. The same activity-based costs of an ERP system can be used for financial reporting to external parties. The ABC costs relevant for financial reporting are assigned according to GAAP. For example, manufacturing overhead can be assigned to products and then to the cost of goods sold or inventory. Nonmanufacturing overhead can be assigned as period costs. ABC costs would include marketing overhead, which could not be assigned to products. With ABC, the marketing overhead would be allocated with the relevant cost driver, but with financial accounting the marketing costs would be accumulated functionally as a period cost.

Beginning January 1, 2005, global electronic commerce associations are recommending that retailers use 14-digit bar codes that accompany the UPC (universal product code).[12] Currently, North American goods have a 12-digit code and 13- or 14-digit codes are used elsewhere. With the existing 12-digit bar code in Canada, the first six digits identify the manufacturer, the next five identify the item, and the last is a check for ensuring correct scanning.

When an organization has an ERP system, it can access daily expenses for activities and processes as well as daily quantities for activity cost drivers. This daily access to information on activity costs and activity drivers is much more efficient than pre-ERP systems, with which businesses often waited a month for the needed information. This feedback relates to costs and also to the cost of operations. Accordingly, ERP activity-based information is the basis of cost management and performance measurement—both are based on the activities that are done to create organizational value. Frequent information or feedback on costs and drivers of those costs facilitates learning, which makes for improved performance and decision making.

As the ERP system incorporates activities in terms of quantities of resources, including labour, a record of resource use is maintained. Therefore, performance can be measured in physical terms and compared to standards, which allows for the production of variances. This performance measurement at the activity level serves as a feedback system on efficiency and effectiveness. The confusion of monetary measures is erased, and what is actually happening with the conversion of resources into goods and services can be seen. Performance measurement deals with demand, the success in meeting that demand, delays, defects, backlogs, outputs, defects, etc. More specifically, using the example of a courier company, a performance measure would be "percent of time when the parcels arrived when promised." In contrast, ABC would be concerned with the average cost—based on all variable and fixed costs—of delivering a parcel.

Performance measurement and ABC are complementary. ABC determines the cost of activities in dollar terms. ABC also allows the costs of activities to be compared intra- and interorganizationally. When activity costs exceed expectations, the changes that need to be made involve resource utilization and performance measurement.

LEARNING OBJECTIVE 5

How has Wal-Mart's enterprise resource planning system contributed to its outstanding success?

WAL-MART'S ENTERPRISE RESOURCE PLANNING SYSTEM

Wal-Mart is now the world's largest company. At $220 billion in sales, Wal-Mart is an outstanding example of a successful retail strategy. Basically, the strategy is to offer customers everyday low prices on a broad assortment of merchandise, which is supported with a focus on store-level execution, rigid expense control, logistics superiority, and a corporate culture that emphasizes personal responsibility.[13] Wal-Mart's competitive advantage came from converging product lines or departments, and then establishing various store types to pursue its growth objectives. Sam Walton, who started with a single 16,000-square-foot store with 22 departments in Rogers, Arkansas, in 1962,[14] developed Wal-Mart into the world's largest retailer, whose store types now include:[15]

- *Wal-Mart Stores*: The national discount retailer offers a wide variety of general merchandise out of 36 departments that include family apparel, health and beauty aids, household needs, electronics, toys, fabrics and crafts, lawn and garden, jewellery, and shoes.
- *SuperStores*: The growing demand for one-stop shopping led to Wal-Mart's decision in 1988 to open a full-line grocery department in many of its new stores. These Superstores generally include 36 departments and from 100,000 to 210,000 square feet of retail space. A 109,000-square-foot format that includes innovative features has been particularly popular in recent years.[16]

Shattering ERP Misconceptions

For most finance people, the reality of moving enterprise resource planning (ERP) applications to an outsourced, Web-based environment is lost in a fog of misconceptions. "How can I control it if it's off-site?" is one of the most popular refrains among executives considering the application service provider (ASP) model. In fact most ERP-as-ASP solutions blend product and service offerings as well as Web and non-Web architectures, and provide little or no drop off in control compared with on-site platforms.

Chief financial officers (CFOs) considering hybrid solutions must correct common misconceptions about ASP solutions and evaluate the value proposition of moving toward an ERP system accessed over the Internet. Then, they can better determine how to expand the ERP footprint within their organization and decide whether that solution should have one or both feet on the Web.

They have many choices. Under the most basic level of ASP service, a company chooses a service provider to run its applications, house and run its IT equipment and provide continuous access to the software—a "ping, power and pipe" arrangement. At the other end of the spectrum, "the highest level is when the [ASP] partner purchases all of the equipment, puts the company's applications on it, answers all help desk and tech support calls, and makes all the changes to the application," notes Pete Koltis, an Andersen partner based in Miami. Most of the ERP-via-ASP arrangements are closer to the basic end of the spectrum and require the client company's IT personnel to write any custom reports finance executives need. Koltis says that large ERP software vendors like PeopleSoft and Oracle would rather establish standard, "vanilla" environments that their clients can customize.

Another twist on the ASP model is when a company serves as its own host. Some businesses do not use an external service provider at all but, rather than installing ERP software on every end-user's desktop, provide access to the applications via the Internet or an intranet. This approach lets IT departments centrally manage the software, and the only application end users need on their desktop is a Web browser.

Managing Misconceptions

As CFOs evaluate the array of potential ERP solutions, one myth they must address is the idea that a hosted ERP system must be all-Web or have no Web capabilities. A new breed of accounting applications, called "loosely coupled," offer a mix of locally installed products with services delivered over the Internet. Evidence of such loose couplings appears in recent ERP software releases. And the three largest ERP vendors have all added, or recently enhanced, consulting services.

Many companies that continue to invest in traditional accounting solutions have begun to use Web-based services to optimize their systems. "We have no doubt that we're moving to a Web-based ERP," notes Jean Braaten, financial reporting director of Hirsh Industries in Des Moines, Iowa, "but we're not there quite yet." Instead, the consumer durables manufacturer invested in an offline upgrade to its SAP suite while asking Web-based consultants to help it get the most out of the new version.

Similarly prevalent—but false—is the notion that companies must give up control and sacrifice security to use the ASP model. Kyle Lambert, vice president of information solutions for Portland, Ore.-based John I. Haas Inc., the largest domestic grower of hops, recently implemented Oracle's Web-based version 11i. "One of the concerns we heard was 'How are we going to manage systems and software that aren't on-site?'" he says. "Is that going to be secure, and what level of access will we have to those systems and to those boxes?" These questions came mainly from the user community and non-IT executives. "It was a curious statement for them to make because most of them had never seen the boxes in the first place," he adds. "It was truly a perception issue."

Haas' CFO, to whom Lambert reports, previously used a wide-area network (WAN) to access the company's ERP system. "He had always used remote services," Lambert adds. "My staff is located primarily in Yakima, Washington, supporting a number of sites remotely. When I put it in those sorts of contexts, he and other executives became much more comfortable with the concept."

Source: Eric Krell, "Shattering ERP Misconceptions," *Business Finance*, February 2002, pp. 25–26. Reprinted by permission of *Business Finance* magazine, www.bf.mag.com

GENERAL NEWS NOTE

- *Sam's Clubs*: These members-only warehouse or volume sales outlets have approximately 3,500 different items appealing to local businesses. Merchandise is typically in larger institutional sizes or multipacks of like or assorted items, and includes a complete line of food products and frozen foods, janitorial products, tires, batteries, auto supplies, computers and equipment, etc.
- *Neighborhood Market*: At 42,000 to 55,000 square feet, these stores offer about 28,000 items that include groceries, pharmaceuticals, and general merchandise.
- *International*: Since 1991, Wal-Mart has established more than 1,000 outlets in nine countries. For example, Wal-Mart is already the largest retailer in Canada and Mexico.[17]
- *walmart.com*: The business of selling to customers was brought to the Internet store, which has yet to become a significant part of operations.
- *Specialty Divisions*: These include Tire & Lube Express, Wal-Mart Pharmacy, Wal-Mart Vacations (cruises, vacation packages, car rental and hotel discounts, select theme park tickets), and Wal-Mart's Used Fixture Auctions (allows for the resale of fixtures for reuse in another location).

Outsourcing has contributed to Wal-Mart's success. Private brands have been avoided. With outsourcing, Wal-Mart differentiates itself by reaching back into the value creation chain to influence the goods it acquires, in effect by forcing suppliers to adhere to Wal-Mart's performance and cost expectations, as implied in the following quote:

> Suppliers are treated as part of the family, once they have proved their worth. Nervous newcomers are shown to "the row," a long corridor of drab rooms, each adorned with a notice explaining that Wal-Mart buyers do not accept bribes. It is like a scene from a bazaar: sweaters spill out of suitcases and haggling over prices continues all day. Angel Burgos, from Puerto Rico, wants to sell computers to Wal-Mart: "We were grapes," he sighs, "but now we are raisins. They suck you dry." ... Proven suppliers, though, feel differently. Through Wal-Mart's proprietary systems, they are given full and free access to real-time data on how their products are selling, store by store. By sharing information that other retailers jealously guard, Wal-Mart allows suppliers to plan production runs earlier and so offer better prices. Procter & Gamble's $6 billion-a-year business with Wal-Mart is so important that the maker of Crest toothpaste has a 150-strong Bentonville office dedicated to it. Andy Jett, a director there, says Europe's retailers are still blind to the competitive edge that partnering with suppliers gives Wal-Mart. "Wal-Mart treats suppliers as extensions of its company. All retailers will eventually work this way," he predicts.[18]

Wal-Mart's use of ERP has contributed to its success as one of the world's leading retailers.

In Canada, Wal-Mart has outsourced logistics and distribution to the U.K.-based Tibbet & Britten, one of the world's 10 largest logistic and supply chain management organizations.

Part of Wal-Mart's success has come from its use of information technology. Low-cost information has been used to link the manufacturers with the stores with minimal inventory in transit and no excess inventory in stores. Even in the late 1980s and early 1990s, Wal-Mart's systems logged every item sold, automatically kept warehouses informed of the merchandise to be ordered, and directed the flow of goods not only to the stores but also to the proper shelves.[19] A related benefit from the low-cost information was Wal-Mart's early adoption of uniform product code (UPC) technology, which is used for point-of-sale electronic scanning for keeping accurate track of product movement.

Wal-Mart's information system, "Retail Link," is an ERP system plus a supply chain management (SCM) system, which integrates its electronic data interchange (EDI) network with an extranet used by Wal-Mart buyers and some 10,000 suppliers to gather and disseminate information about sales and inventory levels in every store.[20] Retail Link allows the world's largest organization to be managed, to grow, and to prosper. It allows Wal-Mart and its suppliers to make decisions to optimize the acquisition and sale of merchandise, to control its suppliers, to manage multiple product lines, and to manage stores around the world

McKinsey Global Institute (MGI), the research arm of the McKinsey consulting organization, found that Wal-Mart directly and indirectly caused the bulk of U.S. retail trade productivity, which contributed to 0.31 percentage points of the 1.33-percentage-point total growth in the U.S. economy from 1987 to 1999.[21] Wal-Mart maintained a significant productivity advantage over other general merchandiser retailers. Market share for Wal-Mart was 9% in 1987, 27% in 1995, and 30% in 1999. The authors of the MGI report attribute Wal-Mart's success to the improvement in the organization of functions and tasks through enablement by information technology, which is epitomized by Retail Link. Four improvements in Wal-Mart's organization of functions and tasks were noted by MGI:

- The more extensive use of cross-docking and better flow of goods/palleting to maximize in-store labour efficiency, which was enabled by "sScan" or other electronic supply chain management tools
- The use of forecasting tools to better align staffing levels with demand
- The redefining of store responsibilities and cross-training employees through the pooling of labour across aisles and organization of tasks such as price changes on a functional rather than departmental level
- The improvement of productivity measurement and utilization rates at check-out

The MGI authors note that the first two sources are possible because of information technology. The third and fourth sources are the result of continual process improvement and managerial innovation. Furthermore, the authors estimate that information technology contributed approximately one-half of the growth in Wal-Mart's productivity improvement.

CRITICAL FACTORS IN COST MANAGEMENT AND PERFORMANCE MEASUREMENT SYSTEM DESIGN

LEARNING OBJECTIVE 6

How do the internal and external operating environments impact cost management and performance measurement systems?

Cost management and performance measurement systems are necessary to determine product or service costs, to manage a business, to meet customer expectations, and to meet external reporting requirements. In designing or improving cost

Suddenly, It All Makes Sense

Are your hottest products and most valuable customers bleeding you dry? Thanks to activity-based costing, the horrible truth can no longer be hidden.

Few developments could cause executives ulcers so much as the discovery that they do not know what it costs to make their own products. But that is exactly the realization dawning in corporate finance departments across the country. Activity-based costing is unveiling the awful truth. ABC is a relatively new system of assigning overheads to a company's products or services by separating out the numerous tasks that turn knowledge and materials into cash in the bank. The grim reality is that many products—and customers—are unprofitable, with costs of up to 20 times more than revenues.

A costing conundrum of this scale becomes a management problem. For strategic, regulatory or just plain public relations reasons, most companies cannot afford simply to drop great numbers of customers and products. That's why some managers look at ABC as only the first step in a process of activity-based management, which means determining that certain products and customers cost more than first thought. They identify key factors for success, set benchmarks and decide whether to fix unprofitable processes through continuous improvement and total quality management or re-engineer the processes altogether. Either way, it is a critical voyage of corporate self-discovery. "An activity-based costing study tells you things you never knew before," says Bob Walker, director in corporate performance at Bell Canada. "In cases such as that, you are going to want to alter the way you do business."

Source: John Southerst, "Suddenly, It All Makes Sense," *Canadian Business*, March 1994, Vol. 67 Issue 3, pp. 39–41. Reprinted by permission of John Southerst.

management and performance systems, managers and accountants must be attuned to the unique characteristics of their organizations.

Effective cost management and performance measurement systems successfully implement the strategies of their organization and, consequently, achieve their organizations' goals and objectives. Generic cost management and performance measurement systems cannot be pulled off the shelf and applied to any organization. Each organization warrants to some extent custom-tailored cost management and performance measurement systems. Some overriding factors critical to designing these systems are described in the following sections.

Organizational Form, Structure, and Culture

organizational form
the nature of the legal entity created for a business enterprise

An entity's legal nature reflects its **organizational form**. Selecting the organizational form is one of the most important decisions made by business owners because that choice affects the costs of raising capital, of operating the business (including taxation issues), and, possibly, of litigating. In recent years, organizational form alternatives have increased remarkably. Partnerships and limited liability forms are still available, along with the increasingly prevalent use of outsourcing, which reduces the actual size of the organization but not what it can accomplish through other partnering arrangements.

Once the organizational form is selected, top managers are responsible for creating a structure that is best suited to achieving the organization's goals and objectives. Top managers make judgments about how to organize subunits or outsource, and the extent to which authority will be decentralized. Although the current competitive environment is conducive to a high degree of decentralization, top managers usually retain authority over operations that can be performed more efficiently at a central location. For example, financing, personnel, and certain accounting functions may be maintained at headquarters rather than being delegated to organizational subunits.

In designing the organizational structure, top managers normally will try to group subunits either geographically or by similar missions or natural product clusters. These aggregation processes provide effective cost management because of proximity or similarity of units under a single manager's control. Relatedly, senior management must decide what to do internally and what to outsource. As a general rule, the organization should only outsource noncore activities and should handle the core or strategically important activities internally. The extent to which organizations decentralize also determines who will be accountable for cost management and performance measurement. These systems must provide relevant and timely information to the people who are making decisions that have cost and performance implications.

An entity's culture also plays an important role in designing cost management and performance measurement systems. To illustrate the effect of organizational culture on the cost management system, consider Syncrude Canada, an oil producer based in Fort McMurray, Alberta. For Syncrude, the cost of extracting oil from the sand to which it is chemically bound has been and remains one of the main risks that must be managed, and this must be considered when reducing costs.[22] To instill a culture of risk management along with cost control, all Syncrude employees are given a laminated card that lists five questions: (1) Why am I doing this task at all? (2) What could go wrong? (3) How could it affect others or me? (4) How likely is it to happen? (5) What can I do about it? In such a culture, the requirements of cost management and performance measurement systems have to be constrained by risk considerations.

Organizational Mission and Critical Success Factors

Knowledge of the organization's mission is a key consideration in the design of cost management and performance measurement systems. The mission provides a long-term goal toward which the organization wishes to move. If the organization's mission is unknown, it does not matter what information is generated by the cost management and performance measurement systems—or any other information system. The mission suggests the type of information that will be important for cost management and performance measurement.

Clarification of mission can be served by identifying the organization's **critical success factors**, which are dimensions of operations that are so important to an organization's survival that, with poor performance in these areas, the entity would cease to exist. Most organizations would consider timeliness, quality, customer service, efficiency and cost control, and responsiveness to be critical success factors. Once managers have gained consensus on the organization's critical success factors, the cost management and performance measurement systems can be designed to (1) gather information related to measurement of those items and (2) generate output about those critical success factors in forms that are useful to interested parties such as top managers.

In Chapter 1, we discussed two generic strategies: differentiation and cost leadership. For an organization pursuing a differential strategy, critical success factors would focus on how the products or services are achieving differentiation. Similarly, for organizations pursuing cost leadership, the critical success factors would need to identify that the organization was in effect the low-cost producer in its markets.

critical success factor
an item that is so important to an organization that, without it, the organization would fail; timeliness, quality, customer service, efficiency and cost control, and responsiveness to change are five basic critical success factors

INTERNATIONAL NEWS NOTE

Organizations Are Advised to Locate in Low-Tax Jurisdictions

Multinational enterprises are abandoning their traditional organizational structures in favour of arrangements organized by economic functions rather than by legal entities. A comprehensive analysis is needed for an entrepreneurial entity in a lower-tax jurisdiction to oversee the development, production, and sale of goods in Canada. The various tax and non-tax issues associated with the location, design, and operation of the entrepreneurial entity must be carefully assessed. Several possible approaches a multinational enterprise might employ to distribute tangible goods into Canada when departing from a full-fledged Canadian distribution model are available. These distribution approaches are distinguished primarily by how they avoid the creation of a Canadian agency permanent establishment for the entrepreneurial entity. Considerations relevant to selecting the optimal distribution approach under this new business model include avoiding controlled foreign corporation rules applicable to the multinational enterprise in its home country, establishing appropriate and defensible transfer pricing for the lower reward earned by the Canadian subsidiary, and minimizing any negative commodity tax implications of the conversion.

Source: Marc Darmo and Steve Dunk, "Rethinking the Canadian Inbound Business Model: Part 1," *Canadian Tax Journal*, Vol. 49, Issue 1, 2001, pp. 148–81.

LEARNING OBJECTIVE 7

What three groups of elements affect the design of cost management and performance measurement systems, and how are these elements used?

ELEMENTS OF COST MANAGEMENT AND PERFORMANCE MEASUREMENT SYSTEMS

Cost management and performance measurement systems comprise a set of three primary elements: motivational, informational, and reporting. These elements are detailed in Exhibit 12-2. Managers develop cost management and performance measurement systems by selecting appropriate items from each of the three categories of elements. The selected elements must be consistent with the strategies and missions of the subunits. The purpose in selecting individual control elements (see Chapter 1) is to successfully implement the organization's strategies that have been formulated for the overall organization and individual subunits.

Motivational Elements

Cost and performance measurements should be selected to be consistent with organizational goals and objectives, and to drive managers toward designated achieve-

EXHIBIT 12-2

Cost Management and Performance Measurement System Elements

Motivational Elements
- Performance measurements
- Reward structure
- Support of organizational mission and competitive strategy

Informational Elements
- Support of budgeting process
- Emphasis on product life cycle
- Differentiation of value-added and non-value-added activities
- Support of target costing
- Focus on cost control
- Assessment of core competencies and support of decision making

Reporting Elements
- Preparation of financial statements
- Provision of details for responsibility accounting system

ments. These measurements may be quantitative or nonquantitative, financial or nonfinancial, and short-term or long-term. For example, if a subunit is expected to generate a specified annual profit amount, the established performance measure is quantitative, financial, and short-term. A longer-term performance measure would be the change in profit over a five- to ten-year period.

The cost management and performance measurement systems should be designed to encourage managers to act in the best interest of the organization and its subunits, and in support of the organizational mission and competitive strategies. Once defined, the criteria used for cost management and performance measurement should be linked to the organizational incentive system because, typically, "You get what you measure." Establishing a performance–reward linkage assures that managers will be rewarded in line with the quality of their organizational and subunit decisions, and thereby, for their contributions to achieving the organizational mission.

In addition, different forms of rewards have different incentive effects and can reflect different time orientations. In general, longer-term incentives encourage managers to be more long term-oriented in their decisions, and short-term incentives encourage managers to be focused on the near future. To illustrate, cash is the most obvious reward for short-term performance. All managers receive some compensation in cash so they may pay ordinary living expenses. However, once a manager receives a cash reward, its value is not dependent on future performance. In contrast, a stock option that is not exercisable until a future time encourages a manager to be concerned about long-term performance. The ultimate value of the stock option is determined in the future when it is exercised, rather than on the date it is received.

Rewards for top management may consist of both short-term and long-term incentives. Normally, a major incentive is performance-based pay that is tied to the organization's stock price. The rewards for subunit managers should be based on the specific subunit's mission. Managers of subunits charged with a growth-of-organization mission should receive long-term incentives. These managers need to be concerned about long-term success and be willing to make short-term sacrifices for long-term gains. Alternatively, managers of subunits charged with a cash-generation mission must be more oriented to the short term. These subunits are expected to produce as much cash and profit as possible from their operations. Accordingly, incentives should be in place to encourage managers in these subunits to have a short-term focus in decision making.

Managers will evaluate decision alternatives based on how the outcomes may impact the specified performance (measurement and reward) criteria. Because higher performance equates to a larger reward, the cost management and performance measurement systems must have specified performance measuring sticks and provide measurement information to the appropriate individuals for evaluation purposes. Performance is meaningful only in a comparative or relative sense. Typically, current performance is assessed relative to past or expected performance.

Informational Elements

An organization's ERP system (or accounting function for smaller organizations) is expected to support the planning, controlling, performance evaluation, and decision-making functions. All of these roles converge in a system designed for cost management and performance measurement.

Relative to the planning role, the cost management and performance measurement systems should provide a sound foundation for the budgeting process. Budgets provide both a specification of expected achievement and a benchmark against which to compare actual performance. Cost management and performance measurement systems, like a traditional cost accounting system, should provide the financial information needed for budget preparation. But in addition, well-designed cost management and performance measurement systems help identify the factors that cause costs and performance to be incurred so that more useful simulations of alternative scenarios can be made. The same systems can highlight any activities in the budgeting process that provide no tangible benefits so that these activities can be reduced or eliminated and, thus, reduce the time needed for budget preparation. "By reducing the length of the budgeting cycle and making the process more efficient, the informational benefit of semiannual or quarterly budgeting may become practical."[23]

As a competitive advantage becomes more and more difficult to maintain, organizations must place greater emphasis on management of the product life cycle. Organizations often use innovative tools—such as target costing, which was first developed by the Japanese—to provide information relevant to assessing their competitive positions. As discussed earlier, most actions available to managers to control costs are concentrated in the earliest part of the product life cycle. Accordingly, information relevant to managing costs must be focused on decisions made during that time—that information will be provided by a well-designed and integrated cost management and performance measurement system.

The life cycle of many products will shorten as organizations become more adept at duplicating (without pirating) their competitors' offerings. In this type of environment, organizations will be forced to squeeze cash from their older and more mature products to support new product development. Additionally, a greater emphasis will be placed on an organization's ability to adapt to changing competitive conditions. Flexibility will be an important organizational attribute and will cause managers to change the emphasis of control systems, as shown in Exhibit 12-3.

To provide information relevant to product design and development, the cost management and performance measurement systems must relate resource consumption and cost to alternative product and process designs. In addition, managers will be more concerned about investing in research and development or acquiring new technology. Such decisions will need to be analyzed relative to effects

EXHIBIT 12-3

Shift in Control Emphasis in Future Competitive Environment

	From	To
Strategic Focus	Achieving financial results: sales, costs, and profits	Achieving critical success factors: low cost, high quality, sales mix variety, on-time delivery, and high capacity usage
Product Sales	Submitting bids and taking orders	Developing partnerships and creating sales opportunities
Budgeting	Developing annual plans	Ongoing planning and frequent budget revisions
Culture	Meeting project expectations	Learning and improving upon processes

Source: Reprinted by permission of the publisher: Ralph E. Drtina and Gary A. Monetti, "Controlling Flexible Business Strategies," *Journal of Cost Management*, Fall 1995, pp. 43–49; © 1995 by Warren Gorham and Lamont of RIA.

on an organization's future cost structure, long-range competitive benefits, and organizational cash flow. Then, consideration must be given to the level of flexibility the organization will maintain if short-run changes create new competitive challenges or opportunities.

The information required to support decisions depends on the unique situational factors of the organization and its subunits. The cost management and performance measurement systems must allow the decision maker to evaluate how alternative decision choices would impact the items that are used to measure and evaluate the decision maker's performance.

Reporting Elements

The reporting elements of cost management and performance measurement systems refer to methods of providing information to persons in evaluative roles. First and foremost, the cost management and performance measurement systems must be effective in generating fundamental external financial statement information including inventory valuation and cost of goods sold. This information will not necessarily be used for internal planning, control, performance evaluation, or decision-making purposes. If the feeder systems to the cost management and performance measurement systems have been appropriately integrated and the systems have been designed to minimize informational distortions, however, generating both external and internal product or service costs will not be difficult.

In addition to financial statement valuations, the reporting elements of the cost management and performance measurement systems must address the internal needs of a **responsibility accounting system**. These systems provide information to top management about the performance of organizational subunits and their managers.[24] For each subunit, the responsibility accounting system separately tracks costs and, if appropriate, revenues.

responsibility accounting system
a system that provides information to top management about segment or subunit performance

Performance reports are useful only to the extent that the actual performance can be compared to a meaningful baseline of expected performance. Expected performance can be denoted in financial terms (such as budgetary figures) or in nonfinancial terms (such as customer satisfaction measures, capacity utilization, and research and development activities). By comparing actual and expected performance information generated from the cost management and performance measurement systems, top managers are able to determine which managers and subunits exceeded, met, or failed to meet expectations. This information can then be linked to managerial decisions about performance rewards.

The movement toward decentralization and outsourcing has increased the importance of an effective reporting system. With decentralization and outsourcing, top managers must depend on the reporting system to keep all organizational subunits striving to achieve their subunit missions and organizational goals and objectives. Cost management and performance measurement systems are not designed to cut costs; they exist to ensure that a satisfactory outcome is realized from the incurrence of costs and activities. Accordingly, cost management and performance measurement begin with an understanding that different costs and activities are incurred for different purposes. Some costs and activities are incurred to yield immediate benefit; others are expected to yield a benefit in the near or distant future.

Only by linking cost to activities and activities to strategies can the benefits of cost incurrence be understood. Thus, a starting point in achieving effective cost management and performance measurement is sorting organizational activities according to their strategic roles. This logic suggests that organizational management is made easier by dividing operations into subunits. By so doing, top managers can assign responsibility and accountability for distinct subunit missions to a particular manager. In turn, by creating the correct incentives for each subunit manager, top management will have set the stage for each subunit manager to act in the best interest of the overall organization. This linkage focuses the attention of a specific subunit manager on a set of costs and activities that uniquely relate to the subunit's organizational mission.

For subunit managers to be effective in managing costs and performance, each must be provided with relevant information. As the natures and time horizons of decisions made by managers vary across subunits, each manager requires unique information. Additionally, a manager needs to know how each alternative decision is likely to impact his or her performance.

A reporting system provides a comparison of expected to actual costs and performance for each manager. This comparison is the basis for distinguishing strong from weak or unacceptable performance. The comparison is also a basis for determining the relative rewards (bonus pay, stock options, etc.) of each manager. The better the performance, the greater the reward that is earned. Accordingly, the reporting system provides motivation for subunit managers to act in the best interest of the organization so that their rewards are maximized.

LEARNING OBJECTIVE 8

How is gap analysis used in the implementation of cost management and performance measurement systems?

IMPLEMENTING COST MANAGEMENT AND PERFORMANCE MEASUREMENT SYSTEMS

Because most businesses have a cost management system and some form of performance measurement system in place, cost management and performance measurement system design and implementation issues typically relate to modifications of existing cost management systems. Often this involves the implementation of an ERP system. Once the organization and its subunits have been assessed and the structure of the cost management and performance measurement systems determined, the current system(s) should be evaluated. A gap analysis is necessary to compare the information needed to the information that is currently available, or how well desired outputs coincide with current outputs. Any difference represents

EXHIBIT 12-4

Designing Cost Management and Performance Measurement Systems

Analyze
- Organizational form and structure
- Organizational mission and critical success factors
- Operating (including suppliers) and competitive environment and strategies

Determine desired outputs of the cost management and performance measurement systems to support.
- Motivational elements
- Informational elements
- Reporting elements

Perform gap analysis between desired output and output of current cost management and performance measurement systems.
- Prioritize differences
- Develop and deploy key improvements to the cost management and performance measurement systems

Assess gap reduction generated by improvements

a gap to be overcome. Exhibit 12-4 demonstrates how gap analysis is used to design changes in the cost management and performance measurement systems or an ERP system.

In many situations, eliminating all system gaps is impossible in the short term, potentially because of software or hardware capability or availability. Methods of reducing or eliminating the gaps, including all related technical requirements and changes to existing feeder systems, should be specified in detail. These details should be expressed, qualitatively and quantitatively, in terms of costs and benefits. Cost management and performance measurement systems are never finished. They require continuous improvement to reflect ongoing organizational and environmental changes.

The National Bank of Canada: Head Office Costs

An even more significant challenge for the cost management system at the National Bank of Canada comes from the fact that it represents a way of analyzing programs that is not common in a bank. Other bank divisions account for costs mainly by function and therefore the notion of fully loaded product costing can put the service in conflict with the bank's overall accounting system and the assumptions that arise from it. If a difference occurs in the bank's cost allocation systems and an extra charge is transferred without appropriate justification to the card service, such a move might have no or limited behavioural effects on other departments who maintain more conventional accounting systems. But the strategic cost management system of the card services department could have transferred these extra charges directly to products; and the weight of such a charge not related to cost behaviour can significantly upset the product decision mechanism.

The strategic cost management system is able to play two important roles in avoiding this outcome. First, because of the integral use of the system in modelling cost behaviour, card services division managers are able to see the negative effects of such a downloading on their division. Secondly, managers are able to use the data from the system to explain to head office the dysfunctional action. The result is that the card service department is able to identify those costs that legitimately belonged to the department and to avoid the downloading of those that did not. Thus the integrity of the cost system was retained.

For many people, cost management simply means a vigilant regard for costs in all areas. However if such an approach was acceptable in more stable economic times, organizations today must manage cost reduction more strategically. This means, among other things, designing cost estimation systems to both influence behaviour and aid decision making. An important challenge for management accountants who work with these systems is managing the trade-offs arising from having a cost management system with multiple purposes. They must develop support mechanisms to ensure that behavioural and decisional goals do not collide. And they must be capable to defend the system against well-intentioned but destructive events that threaten the integrity of the system.

Source: Reprinted from an article appearing in the July/August 1999 issue of *CMA Management* magazine by Alexander Mersereau, with permission of Certified Management Accountants of Canada.

In the event of limited resources, top management must prioritize the differences as to which gap issues to address and in which order. As systems implementations proceed, management should assess the effectiveness of the improvements and evaluate the need for other improvements. Once the cost management and performance measurement systems have been established, previously identified gaps may become irrelevant or may rise in priority. It is only through continuous improvement efforts that the cost management and performance measurement systems will provide an ongoing, viable network of information to users. It should be remembered that an ERP system provides the best opportunity for integrated cost management and performance measurement systems.

CHAPTER SUMMARY

Managerial accountants provide information for managers' planning, controlling, performance-evaluation, and decision-making needs. Cost management and performance measurement systems are parts of an organization's overall control system. Cost management and performance measurement systems exist to guide organizations to achievement of their goals and objectives by implementing plans and strategies. These systems serve multiple purposes: develop product costs, assess product/service profitability, improve understanding of how processes affect costs, facilitate cost control, measure performance, and implement organizational strategies. ERP systems such as SAP, PeopleSoft, and J.D. Power provide integrated cost management and performance measurement systems.

Three factors that should be taken into account in designing cost management and performance measurement systems are the organizational form, structure, and culture; organizational mission and critical success factors; and the competitive environment. Cost management and performance measurement systems must be designed using elements from three groups of management control tools: motivational, informational, and reporting elements. The selected elements of the systems should be consistent with the missions of the individual subunits.

The motivational elements provide managers with the incentive to take the actions that are in the best interests of their subunits and the overall organization. Managers are motivated to do the right thing when their rewards are linked to the quality of decisions they make on behalf of the organization and their specific subunits.

The informational elements provide relevant data that are useful in measuring the performance of managers and their subunits and in making managerial decisions. To compete in the global environment, organizations need a variety of informational techniques to assess their relative competitive positions. The reporting elements provide information regarding managerial performance. A responsibility accounting system provides information to top management about the performance of an organizational subunit and its manager. The information provided by the reporting elements is the basis for rewarding managers.

Gap analysis is the key to identifying differences, or gaps, between the ideal cost management and performance measurement systems and the existing systems. By prioritizing the order in which gaps are to be closed, managers can proceed in an orderly manner with updating the cost management and performance measurement systems. Because business processes are constantly evolving, the cost management and performance measurement systems must be continuously evaluated and updated so that they are able to provide the information and motivation required by managers.

Cross-Functional Applications

Topic of Note	Discipline	Cross-Functional Applications
Product Costs	Marketing	Marketers use product costs to determine a product's competitiveness in the marketplace. A product cost is necessary to design the marketing strategies, especially pricing, research, and distribution strategies.
	Financial Accounting	Product costs are necessary to determine cost of goods sold and project gross margins as well as inventories. Most organizations project their financial statements into the future for planning purposes. These are called "pro forma" financial statements.
	Engineering	Reduction of product costs through innovative technology and less expensive material and processes is a major goal of industrial engineers. In addition, improvement of a product's features, attributes, and benefits is constrained by consideration of product cost. Engineers' efforts to improve a product's utility and competitiveness are ultimately constrained by those same considerations.
	Microeconomics	Product costs are a primary determinant of selling price. Certain products are sensitive to a change in selling price, causing the market to find a ready substitute product when the selling price exceeds some limit; this is a condition known as "elasticity."
Period Costs	Microeconomics	When a cost cannot be traced as a factor of production into a product, then it is associated with the period of time in which the product was produced or sold. The value-added concept of product cost can never explain the total cost of producing a product for sale. Therefore, an accounting period is used as a second parameter of total cost.
	Financial Accounting	All costs of operating a business except for those associated with providing a product are termed operating costs and are often subdivided into general, administrative, and selling expenses. These operating costs appear on the income statement as a deduction from gross

(cont.)

Cross-Functional Applications

Topic of Note	Discipline	Cross-Functional Applications
		margin if they are associated with the organization's main line of business, or as other expenses if they are related to a secondary line of business in which the organization engages.
	Marketing	"Distribution costs in marketing" is usually a loosely defined term for all costs necessary to position a product for sale, excluding the cost of the product itself. Distribution costs are usually quoted as a percentage of the sales dollar, although many of these costs are controllable by marketing managers.
Cost Behaviour—Fixed, Variable	Business Law	Management attempts to stabilize cost behaviour through contractual arrangements, thus locking in certain aspects of the cost structure. Future costs that are not predictable are limited by contingency contracts, which relate future costs to some fixed event.
	Engineering	Engineers often project cost behaviour based upon the inputs into the manufacturing process—such as material specifications, power consumption, and efficiency of the process. This approach depends more on the physical measurements of the factors of production to determine cost than does traditional accounting. However, when new or unproven processes are being evaluated, this method is indispensable. Also, it could be coordinated with the more traditional approaches once the organization has some baseline experience with the new process.
	Management	Management is attempting to mitigate the trend in many organizations toward a greater relative fixed cost component by sharing those costs with willing suppliers or customers. The key term in management is "cooperative." Advertising can be thought of as a committed fixed cost. Cooperative advertising could spread the burden among the supplier, the organization offering the product for sale, and even some other organizations with complementary products.

Key Terms

Business process redesign (p. 705)
Chart of accounts (p. 707)
Cost management system (p. 698)
Critical success factor (p. 713)
Enterprise resource planning
   (p. 705)

Organizational form (p. 712)
Performance measurement system
   (p. 702)
Process re-engineering (p. 707)
Responsibility accounting system
   (p. 717)

End-of-Chapter Materials

SELF-TEST QUESTIONS

(SOLUTIONS APPEAR AT THE END OF THE CHAPTER.)

1. Which of the following is not a stage of cost management and performance measurement systems?
   a. Inadequate for financial reporting
   b. Financial reporting driven
   c. Customized, managerially relevant, standalone
   d. Wal-Mart ERP

2. A cost management system and a performance measurement system are
   a. Complements
   b. Substitutes
   c. Part of a financial accounting system
   d. Stage II systems

3. Which of the following is incorrect regarding Stage IV systems?
   a. ABC is included
   b. Cost management and performance measurement systems are integrated
   c. GAAP statements are prepared
   d. PeopleSoft would not be included

4. What allows an ERP system to tie all types of information together?
   a. Cost management systems
   b. Performance measurement systems
   c. Financial accounting systems
   d. Codes

5. What is used by Wal-Mart to track products that are purchased and sold?
   a. JIT
   b. Uniform product codes
   c. Fields
   d. Rows

6. What is not a theme for process redesign?
   a. Forgetting about old business practices
   b. Organizing around continuous business processes aimed at getting products and services to customers
   c. Applying increasingly sophisticated information technology
   d. Reducing costs

7. Which is not one of the basic approaches for business process redesign when implementing an ERP system?
   a. Re-engineer all processes to achieve an ideal set of business processes
   b. Accept the ERP design
   c. Redesign with the ERP system in mind
   d. Implement a cost management system

8. Which of the following are dimensions of operations that are so important to an organization's survival that with poor performance in these areas the entity would cease to exist?
   a. Cost management systems
   b. Performance measurement systems
   c. Critical success factors
   d. Relational databases

9. What are not elements of cost management and performance measurement systems?
   a. Motivational elements
   b. Informational elements
   c. Reporting elements
   d. Financial numbers

10. In assessing the effectiveness of cost management and performance measurement systems, what kind of analysis is done?
    a. Gap
    b. ERP
    c. Accounting
    d. Financial

QUESTIONS

1. How can a cost management system help managers?

2. What are the five primary goals of a cost management system?

3. Identify examples of useful information that could be provided to a cost management system by each of the functional areas shown in Exhibit 12-1.

4. Identify examples of useful information that could be provided to a performance measurement system by each of the functional areas shown in Exhibit 12-1.

5. Why would management be willing to accept "inaccurate" costs from the cost management system? What sacrifices would be necessary to obtain "accurate" costs?

6. What are examples of costs that a cost management system might treat differently for internal and external purposes? Why would these treatments be appropriate?

7. Why would an organization have multiple control systems in place?

8. What is a performance measurement system?

9. Why is a performance measurement system necessary if an organization has a cost management system?

10. How does a performance measurement system help an organization remain competitive?

11. What are the four stages of cost management and performance measurement systems? Be sure to describe each stage.

12. Compare Stage III and Stage IV in regard to the use of enterprise resource planning systems. In which of these stages is there the greatest integration?

13. What are some brands of enterprise resource planning systems?

14. Discuss the database used with enterprise resource planning systems.

15. What are the three basic approaches for enterprise resource planning system business process redesign?

16. What is a chart of accounts? How is a chart of accounts used with an ERP system?

17. What is Wal-Mart's information system called? What does it do?

18. What were the four improvements in Wal-Mart's organization of functions and tasks?

19. In designing the organizational structure, senior managers will try to group subunits. How will they tend to do this grouping?

20. What classification of factors is important in designing performance measurement systems? What is that one term that describes these factors?

21. What is the most important—motivational, informational, or reporting elements—in designing cost management and performance measurement systems?

22. How will controls have to change in the future if competition, as expected, increases in intensity?

23. What is gap analysis? How is gap analysis used in updating cost management or performance measurement systems?

24. Name and describe the four steps for designing a cost management and performance measurement systems.

25. What kind of organizations implement ERP systems?

EXERCISES

1. (LO 1, 2, 3, 4, 5, 8) Match each lettered item in the left-hand column with a numbered item in the right-hand column.

   a. Cost management system
   b. Performance measurement system
   c. Stage II system
   d. Stage III system
   e. Business process redesign
   f. Process re-engineering
   g. Retail Link
   h. Critical success factor
   i. Gap analysis
   j. Stage IV system

   1. Wal-Mart's information system (i.e., its enterprise resource planning and supply chain management systems)
   2. Comparison between what exists and what is desirable
   3. Dimensions of operations that must be accomplished for the organization to survive
   4. Financial reporting driven
   5. Integrated cost management, financial reporting, and performance measurement
   6. Customized, managerially relevant, standalone
   7. A formal set of methods for providing feedback about activity or process efficiency
   8. Modest or minor changes to an organization's activities and processes
   9. A formal set of methods for controlling the costs of an organization's activities
   10. Major changes to an organization's activities and processes

2. (LO 1, 2, 3) The following words or phrases describe or are associated with one of the stages of cost management and performance measurement systems. Categorize them as "I" for Stage I, "II" for Stage II, "III" for Stage III, and "IV" for Stage IV.
   a. Extensive amounts of time needed to consolidate different reporting entities and to close the books each period
   b. All necessary systems, albeit with inconsistency
   c. Existence of an ERP system
   d. No conflict among the three systems
   e. Not able to record costs accurately
   f. Simple organization
   g. Financial reporting supplemented by *ad hoc* ABC and performance measurement systems
   h. Financial reporting used for both product costing and performance measurement
   i. Adequate for valuing inventory for financial reporting purposes, but no more
   j. Completely integrated financial reporting, cost management, and performance measurement
   k. All necessary systems—but freestanding
   l. Able to meet financial reporting requirements, but not able to collect costs accurately by responsibility centre
   m. Traditional cost allocation methods used rather than ABC
   n. Legacy systems

3. (LO 4) Beside each of the following, indicate where the word or phrase refers to business process redesign (BPR) or process re-engineering (PRE)
   a. Accept 80% to 90% of the vision
   b. Forget old business practices
   c. Eliminate technical and organizational bottlenecks
   d. Organize around continuous businesses aimed at getting products and services to customers

  e. Apply increasingly sophisticated information technology
  f. Drastic changes
  g. Accept the ERP design, thus minimal changes
  h. Change all processes to achieve an ideal
  i. Design process with the ERP system in mind

4. (LO 1) Prepare a brief report on how cost management information can (a) help and (b) hinder an organization's progress toward its mission and objectives.

5. (LO 1) In groups of four or five students, develop an activity dictionary for the specific organization where one member of the group worked or works. The organizational subject should be the part of the organization where the student worked or works, and not the entire organization. For example, if the student worked for McDonald's in serving customers, then the subject should be order taking, order preparation, change making, order delivering, etc., activities. Generally, the work of an employee can be classified into six to eight meaningful activities.

6. (LO 2) Assume that you are an accountant who is considering employment with one of two organizations. The first organization is a fast-growing technology organization. Its sales are $500 million per year, with annual sales projected to grow at a rate of 22% over the next five years. The other organization is in a mature industry in which approximately 12 organizations are fiercely competing to maintain market share and profitability. This organization has annual sales of $2 billion. Prepare a brief report in which you discuss how your job focus and daily activities would likely vary between the two organizations.

7. (LO 2) Performance measurement systems are expected to provide information on the efficiency and effectiveness of operations sufficiently frequently as to allow adjustments to correct shortcomings. For the deli counter of a large grocery store, specify a performance measurement system.

8. (LO 3) Form groups of three or four students to discuss the types of documents and information you would expect to be produced by a Stage I organization. How frequently would this information be produced?

9. (LO 3) Form groups of three or four students to discuss the types of documents and information you would expect to be produced by a Stage II organization. How frequently would this information be produced?

10. (LO 3) Form groups of three or four students to discuss the types of documents and information you would expect to be produced by a Stage III organization. How frequently would this information be produced?

11. (LO 3) Form groups of three or four students to discuss the types of documents and information you would expect to be produced by a Stage IV organization. How frequently would this information be produced?

12. (LO 4) What systems would you expect to be integrated with an ERP system? How does an ERP system facilitate reconciliation among different systems?

13. (LO 4) What is a chart of accounts? Why is it important for an ERP system?

14. (LO 4, 5) Wal-Mart is the world's largest retailer and easily argued to be the world's most successful retailer. How does Retail Link contribute to Wal-Mart's success?

15. (LO 5, 6) In this text, Wal-Mart and Dell Computer have been used as examples of organizations that have pioneered value creation chains that have set the standards for their respective competitors. Specify two or three critical success factors for Wal-Mart. Do the same for Dell Computer.

16. (LO 7) If you were responsible for organizing a major sporting event, such as the Winter Olympics or Commonwealth Games, you would clearly have some systems for cost management and performance measurement. How would you build support for these systems?

17. (LO 7) An operation such as provincial driver testing has a very explicit and clear mission or mandate, and requires a substantial number of different activities replicated over many sites across a province to carry out that mission. For example, there are various tests and each test has different components that must be offered in the

province. What information obtained from a performance measurement system would you use to ascertain whether driver testing is being done efficiently and effectively?

18. (LO 7, 8) Form groups of four or five students. Select one student who has worked for an organization where there was a cost management or performance measurement system, however crude. Ask the student to describe the system. The other members are to describe an ideal system and do a gap analysis. Smaller units are preferable to larger units or an entire organization.

CASES

1. Flatland Metals Co. produces steel products for a variety of customers. One division of the company is Residential Products Division. This division was created in the late 1940s; its principal products since that time have been galvanized steel components used in garage door installations. The division has been continuously profitable since 1950 and in 2005 generated profits of $10 million on sales of $300 million.

   However, over the past 10 years, growth in the division has been slow; profitability has become stagnant, and few new products have been developed, as the garage door components market has matured. The president of the company, John Stamp, has asked his senior staff to evaluate the operations of the Residential Products Division and to make recommendations for changes that would improve its operations. The staff uncovered the following facts:

   a. Jolene Green, aged 53, has been president of the division for the past 15 years.
   b. Ms. Green receives a compensation package that includes a salary of $175,000 annually plus a cash bonus based on achievement of the budgeted level of annual profit.
   c. Growth in sales in the residential metal products industry has averaged 12% annually over the past decade. Most of the growth has occurred in ornamental products used in residential privacy fencing.
   d. Nationally, the division's market share in the overall residential metal products industry has dropped from 12% to 7% during the past 10 years, and it has dropped from 40% to 25% for garage door components.
   e. The division maintains its own information systems. The systems in use today are mostly the same systems that were in place 15 years ago; however, some of the manual systems have been computerized (e.g., payroll, accounts payable, accounting).
   f. The division has no customer service department. A small sales staff solicits and takes orders by phone from national distribution chains.
   g. The major intradivision communication tool is the annual operating budget. No formal statements have been prepared in the division regarding strategies, mission, values, goals, or objectives, or identifying core competencies or critical success factors.

   Required:
   You have been hired as a consultant for the Residential Products Division. Given the introductory paragraphs, prepare a report in which you identify the major problems in the Residential Products Division regarding cost management and performance measurement, and develop recommendations to address the problems you have identified.

2. You are the manager of management accounting for one of Canada's largest trucking firms, Nanton Trucking International Limited. The mission of Nanton is to provide shipment services for products and parts for manufacturers and retailers interprovincially and between Canada and the United States. All shipments are based on medium- and long-term contracts, and revenues are based on weight, volume, and distance. The company has excellent financial accounting and logistics systems. Success is measured by achievement on contract and the profitability of those contracts.

   The controller, to whom you report, recently talked to you about an article she read in a management accounting magazine that reported on a survey. It was reported that the best-run organizations are 200% more likely to obtain business-critical information. Specifically, organizations that make decisions strictly based on financial numbers (45% of the organizations studied) were at a disadvantage to those using non-financial performance measures. Moreover, the most successful firms were constantly monitoring performance and making changes. They did not wait for the annual budgeting and planning exercise.

The controller then asked you whether Nanton had nonfinancial performance measures; you both knew the answer to be "no." She then asked you to propose how to introduce nonfinancial performance measures to Nanton. (Adapted from Kathy Williams, "Is Your Planning a Continuous Process?" *Strategic Finance*, July 2002, pp. 17+.)

Required:

a.   Adhere to the controller's request to provide a proposal on how nonfinancial performance measures can be introduced to Nanton. Be specific and provide explicit examples of the relevant types of measures.

b.   Suggest how Nanton could introduce cost management and performance measurement systems, and the advantages of those systems.

3   Garment manufacturer VF Corporation is using wireless technology to redesign its information systems to integrate its factory processes seamlessly with its global supply chain.[25] VF, a $5 billion manufacturer of apparel such as Lee and Wrangler jeans and Vanity Fair Lingerie, was planning to install wireless LANs in 200 manufacturing plants to tie automated manufacturing systems into its ERP system. VF expects the wireless devices to cut time-to-market for new designs by 20%. The organization expects to develop direct and strong ties with retailers such as Wal-Mart into the new system to provide VF with the information to respond quickly to the fashion whims of consumers.

Required:

How should VF proceed with this wireless proposal to integrate its ERP with the requirements of customers?

ETHICS AND QUALITY DISCUSSIONS

1.   Some people may view an organization's culture as a mechanism to eliminate diversity in the workplace. Is it ethical to attract and retain only individuals who accept an organization's culture and value system? In responding, be sure to discuss the positive and negative aspects of conformity as part of organizational culture.

2.   The underlying assumption with a cost management system is to reduce costs, not just once, but continuously. Organizations such as Wal-Mart, Dell Computer, and Intel have become successful by constantly reducing costs. However, there is also a negative relationship between cost and quality (i.e., as costs are cut, quality suffers). How can you have constantly declining costs without declining quality? In responding, be sure to use the value creation chain in your argument.

3.   Naomi Klein, in her book *No Logo*, observed,

> ... the "part-time" classification is often more a technicality than a reality, with retail employees keeping their part-timers just below the forty-hour legal cutoff for full-time—Laurie Bonang, for instance, clocks between thirty-five and thirty-nine hours a week at Starbucks. For all intents and purposes, she has the duties of a full-time employee, but under forty hours the company does not have to pay overtime or guarantee full-time hours. Other chains are equally creative.

Klein then mentions the practices of Wal-Mart and GAP in employing part-time employees rather than full-time employees.

Required:

Evaluate the extensive use of part-time employees from the perspective of part-time employees and also from the perspective of the shareholders of these organizations.

4.   Stage IV of cost management and performance measurement systems is described as integrated cost management, financial reporting, and performance systems using an enterprise resource planning system. Recently, we have read in the financial press about organizations such as WorldCom and Enron, which have manipulated their

financial statements to the detriment of shareholders. It is unclear whether such delinquent organizations have a Stage IV cost management and performance measurement system, but if they did, what would be the consequences of misleading or fraudulent financial reporting on cost management and performance measurement? There could be an impact as cost management and performance measurement are integrated with financial reporting.

COMMUNICATIONS ACTIVITIES

1. Leonard D. Schaeffer, the chairman and CEO of a major health organization, reports that during the course of his 30-year career he practised three leadership styles: the autocrat, the participative leader, and the reformer. Schaeffer claims that the autocrat style is most appropriate in turnaround situations. Participative leadership works best, according to Schaeffer, when "the development of goals, budgets, and strategies is strictly controlled from the top while staff is given free rein to meet those goals, as long as they stay on budget." Schaeffer says reformers demonstrate what is possible while defying convention and making the world a better place.

   (Source: Leonard D. Schaeffer, "The Leadership Journey," *Harvard Business Review*, October 2002, pp. 42–47.)
   Required:
   If you were Mr. Schaeffer, what leadership approach would you expect a vice president and chief information officer (CIO) to use in implementing a Stage IV cost management and performance measurement system? How would you facilitate this leadership style on the part of the CIO?

2. It has been surmised by Bazerman, Loewenstein, and Moore that the recent auditor problems (such as Andersen with Enron) were not due to inherent auditor corruption but caused by unconscious bias. They noted that psychological research shows "that our desires powerfully influence the way we interpret information, even when we're trying to be objective and impartial. When we are motivated to reach a particular conclusion, we usually do." Three structural aspects of accounting provide opportunities for biases.
   - *Ambiguity.* Bias thrives where information can be interpreted in different ways
   - *Attachment.* When there are strong business reasons to accomplish what the client wants, bias can occur.
   - *Approval.* Self-serving biases become even stronger when people are endorsing others' biased judgments.
   Three aspects of human nature can amplify unconscious biases:
   - *Familiarity.* People are more willing to harm strangers.
   - *Discounting.* People are more responsive to immediate consequences than delayed ones.
   - *Escalation.* People will conceal or explain away minor indiscretions or oversights, sometimes without realization, and over time these oversights tend to become larger and even seriously wrong.

   (Source: Max Bazerman, George Loewenstein, and Don A. Moore, "Why Good Accountants Do Bad Audits," *Harvard Business Review*, November 2002, pp. 96–102.)
   Required:
   Although the above finding related to external auditors, discuss how unconscious bias can occur with cost management and performance measurement systems, and how it can be minimized.

PROJECTS

1. Study the annual reports for McDonald's, Royal Bank, Stelco, ATCO, and the Hudson's Bay Company to determine their stages regarding cost management and performance measurement systems. The stages are: I, inadequate for financial reporting; II, financial reporting driven; III, customized, managerially relevant, stand-

alone; and IV, integrated cost management and financial reporting. Write one to two pages on each company.

2. Sobey's attempted to implement an ERP (i.e., SAP) system that was unsuccessful and was eventually terminated. Based on its annual report and other publicly available information, why was the implementation unsuccessful? What is Sobey's doing as an alternative? One or two pages will be sufficient.

USING THE INTERNET

1. Many organizations have implemented ERP systems. More recently, ERP systems have been implemented in conjunction with Web systems. For SAP, these "Webified" ERP systems are called MySAP. Use Google or another search engine to identify five organizations that have implemented MySAP and determine the rationales for those implementations. Your report should be five or six pages in length.

2. There are also many organizations that decide not to implement MySAP and stay with their earlier versions of SAP software. Use Google or another search engine to identify why organizations are delaying the implementation of MySAP. Your report should be two or three pages in length.

SOLUTIONS TO SELF-TEST QUESTIONS

1. d, 2. a, 3. d, 4. d, 5. b, 6. d, 7. d, 8. c, 9. d, 10. a

ENDNOTES

1. Callie Berliner and James A. Brimson, eds., *Cost Management for Today's Advanced Manufacturing*, Boston: Harvard Business School Press, 1988, p. 10.

2. Steven C. Schnoebelen, "Integrating an Advanced Cost Management System into Operating Systems (Part 2)," *Journal of Cost Management*, Spring 1993, p. 60.

3. Robin Cooper and Robert S. Kaplan, *The Design of Cost Management Systems*, Englewood Cliffs, N.J.: Prentice-Hall, 1991, p. 4.

4. Ibid., p. 79.

5. Ibid., pp. 85–99.

6. Ibid., pp. 95–98.

7. Robert S. Kaplan and Robin Cooper, *Cost and Effect: Using Integrated Cost Systems to Drive Profitability and Performance*, Boston: Harvard Business School Press, 1998, p. 2. Note that this outstanding book was used extensively for parts of this chapter.

8. Ibid., pp. 11–27.

9. Grant Norris, Ian Wright, James R. Hurley, John Dunleavy, and Alison Gibson, *SAP: An Executive's Comprehensive Guide*, New York: Wiley, 1998, pp. 84–86.

10. Subba Rao Siriginidi, "Enterprise Resource Planning in Re-engineering Business," *Business Process Management Journal*, Vol. 6, Issue 5, 2000. p. 377

11. Op. cit., Norris et al., p. 128.

12. Marina Strauss, "Big Chains Set for Globalization 14-Digit Bar Code," *The Globe and Mail*, August 19, 2002.

13. Mike Troy, "The Super Growth Leaders—Wal-Mart: Global Dominance Puts Half Trillion in Sight," *DSN Retailing Today*, December 10, 2001, pp. 17–18+.

14. Sandra S. Vance and Roy V. Scott, *Wal-Mart: A History of Sam Walton's Retail Phenomenon*, New York: Twayne Publishers, 1994, pp. 43–44.

15. These descriptions are based on information from the Wal-Mart homepage, http://www.walmartstores.com/wmstores/wms

16. Mike Troy, "Wal-Mart Fills in Markets with 'One-oh-Nine' Footprint," *DSN Retailing Today*, Vol. 39, Issue 17, September 4, 2000, pp. 3, 46.

17. "Business Around the World; Wal-Mart," *The Economist*, Vol. 361, Issue 8251, December 8, 2001, pp. 55–57.

18. Ibid.

19. Op. cit., Vance and Scott, pp. 92–93.

20. Barry Janoff, "High-Tech Knowledge," *Progressive Grocer*, December 2000, pp. 45–48.

21. McKinsey Global Institute, *U.S. Productivity Growth 1995–2001: Understanding the Contribution of Information Technology Relative to Other Factors*, October 2001, Chapter 4, sector case studies—retail trade.

22. Gavon Souter, Managing Risk Adds Value," *Business Insurance*, October 30, 2000, Vol. 34, Issue 44, pp. 22–23.

23. Ibid.

24. Responsibility accounting concepts are discussed in detail in Chapter 13.

25. Bob Brewin, "Garment Maker Donning Wireless," *Computerworld*, September 11, 2000, pp. 1, 16.

Chapter 13

Measuring and Rewarding Performance

LEARNING OBJECTIVES

After reading this chapter, you should be able to answer the following questions:

1 Why should organizations use multiple performance measures to assess performance?

2 How are return on investment (ROI) and residual income (RI) similar and different?

3 Why has economic value added (EVA) become a popular performance measure?

4 Why are nonfinancial measures important to evaluating performance?

5 How are activity-based costing concepts related to performance measurement?

6 Why is it more difficult to measure performance in multinational firms than in solely domestic companies?

7 How should employee rewards, including compensation, and performance be linked?

8 How do expatriate reward systems differ from those for domestic operations?

www.managementmag.com

Various Approaches to Performance Measurement

In the early 1990s, managers, academics, and consultants proposed new systems of strategic performance measurement defined as measurement systems that simultaneously reflected, supported, and evaluated strategy. They posed the question "how can managers choose measures, financial and non-financial, that will guide them in delivering consistent value for the enterprise over the course of months and years?"

From the results of a research project conducted in 1990 with 12 companies, Robert Kaplan, of Harvard Business School, and David Norton, of Renaissance Worldwide, answered that question in their article introducing the balanced scorecard. One of the most significant contributions of the Kaplan and Norton model was to stress that executives should use the measures to translate vision and strategy into concrete directions for action by people throughout the organization. In their later work, Kaplan and Norton showed managers how to use the balanced scorecard as a strategic management system. Instead of the measures in the balanced scorecard being a wish list for continuous improvement, they prescribe a plan for strategic execution.

Meanwhile, in Sweden, at Skandia Group, a team led by Leif Edvinsson, corporate director of intellectual capital, operated under the belief that to succeed as an insurer, the company had to build value through "intellectual capital." That is, to deliver reliable financial results, Skandia had to build and leverage the value of intangible assets like solid customer relationships and unique computer software. In 1990, Skandia pioneered new ways to value intellectual capital and created measures for managing a firm that relies on intellectual capital to build value. Skandia created a balanced scorecard called the "navigator," separating corporate performance into five categories, or "focuses": financial, customer, human, process, and renewal and development As with the Kaplan and Norton model, performance in the latter four contribute to financial performance. Edvinsson, like Kaplan and Norton, stressed the importance of learning and renewal as a root source of financial results.

At about the same time, other organizations were experimenting with a third approach to the balanced scorecard. In Canada, at the Bank of Montreal, a team led by Robert Wells, the vice president of finance, believed that success required the bank to recognize and manage its relationships with its key stakeholder groups. In the Bank of Montreal's case, these included shareholders (who required a target return on invested capital), customers (who wanted good service and competitive rates), employees (who wanted good working environments and competitive pay), and communities (who wanted the bank to provide social leadership in their communities).

The stakeholder approach conceives of the set of relationships between the organization and its stakeholders as an articulated set (or nexus) of explicit and implicit contracts. Each of these contracts specifies what the organization expects to receive from and give to each stakeholder group in exchange for that group's continued contribution toward the organization's pursuit of its objectives. For example, employees might demand competitive wages, good working conditions, and an appropriate management style in return for the application

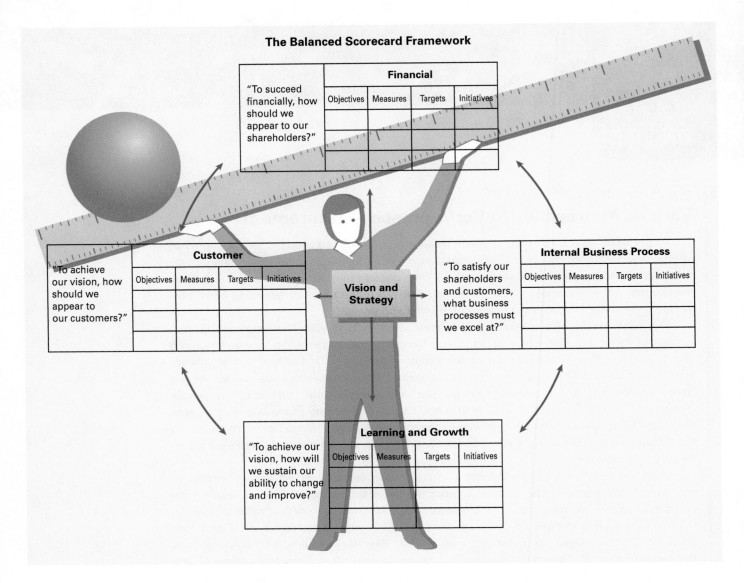

The Balanced Scorecard Framework

Financial

"To succeed financially, how should we appear to our shareholders?"

Objectives	Measures	Targets	Initiatives

Customer

"To achieve our vision, how should we appear to our customers?"

Objectives	Measures	Targets	Initiatives

Vision and Strategy

Internal Business Process

"To satisfy our shareholders and customers, what business processes must we excel at?"

Objectives	Measures	Targets	Initiatives

Learning and Growth

"To achieve our vision, how will we sustain our ability to change and improve?"

Objectives	Measures	Targets	Initiatives

of their effort, skill, and knowledge in making decisions that advance the organization's objectives. The role of performance measurement is to monitor the give and take expressed or implied by each of these contracts.

SOURCE: Reprinted from an article appearing in the September 2000 issue of *CMA Management* magazine by Anthony A. Atkinson and Marc Epstein, with permission of Certified Management Accountants of Canada.

This chapter covers two related sets of topics. First, performance measurement is discussed in the context of the balanced scorecard and more conventional monetary indicators, such as cash flows, return on investment, and residual income. The more innovative nonmonetary and monetary performance measures that are needed by world-class, customer-driven companies are also addressed. Second, a variety of employee rewards that might be used by an organization seeking to balance short-run and long-run interests are presented, along with discussion of the related topics for performance enhancement.

MEASURING ORGANIZATIONAL AND EMPLOYEE PERFORMANCE

LEARNING OBJECTIVE 1

Why should organizations use multiple performance measures to assess performance?

As indicated in previous chapters, people must have benchmarks against which to compare their accomplishments in order to evaluate performance. A benchmark can be monetary, such as a target level of economic value added (EVA), or nonmonetary, such as product defect rate or market share. Whatever measures are used, the following four general rules for performance measurement are appropriate:

- Measures that assess progress toward organizational goals and objectives should be established.
- Persons being evaluated should have some input in developing the performance measurements and should be aware of them.
- Persons being evaluated should have the appropriate skills and be provided the necessary equipment, information, and authority to be successful under the measurement system.
- Feedback relative to performance should be provided in a timely and useful manner.

In selecting performance measures, missions of specific subunits must be considered. For example, objectives established for newly formed divisions are likely described in terms of sales growth, market share, research and development success, or rate of new product introductions. For these divisions, the use of profit measures to assess performance is inappropriate. Alternatively, objectives for mature divisions can be couched in terms of profits and cash flows; hence, profit measures are appropriate for evaluating the relative success of mature divisions.

Multiple performance measures can be used to evaluate the success of any activity—even Winterlude in Ottawa. The city could evaluate the success of this festivity by measures that include visitor spending, hotel occupancy rates, and tonnes of garbage cleaned up.

As organizations have a variety of goals and objectives, some of which are related to product life cycle issues, it is unlikely that a single measure or even several measures of the same type will effectively assess organizational progress toward all of those goals and objectives. A primary goal is, by necessity, to be financially solvent. As solvency is determined by the relationship between cash inflows and cash outflows, cash flow is often used as a performance measure. If the organization is profit oriented, a goal of the firm is to provide a satisfactory return to shareholders. This requirement is satisfied by generating a net income considered by the owners to be sufficient, relative to the assets (capital) invested. Accordingly, some measurement of income is used by virtually all businesses to assess performance.

Although financial measures provide necessary indications of performance, they do not address some of the new issues of competitive reality essential to business survival in a global economy. Many companies have established goals relative to customer satisfaction rates, product defect rates, lead time to market, and environmental social responsibility. Such goals are not measured directly by income. Companies producing inferior goods, delivering late, abusing the environment, or, in general, making customers dissatisfied will lose market share and, eventually, be forced out of business. Nonfinancial performance measures can be developed that indicate progress (or lack thereof) toward achievement of the important, long-run critical success factors of world-class companies. As the following quote indicates, selecting performance measures is a crucial organizational decision because the performance measures will determine how, and on what bases, managers and other employees focus their time and attention.

> Performance measures are usually used to track progress towards [a] target. Often the measures become a surrogate for the target itself. When we turn our attention to what gets measured, and only what gets measured, we may overlook avenues of investigation that offer far greater opportunities to achieve [the target].[1]

Nonfinancial indicators are, in effect, surrogate measures of financial performance.

Financial and nonfinancial performance measures can be combined to provide a comprehensive portrayal of organizational and managerial performance. Exhibit 13-1 illustrates a balanced scorecard that ultimately links all aspects of performance to the company's strategies. The balanced scorecard is defined as a performance measurement conceptualization that translates an organization's strategy into clear objectives, measures, targets, and initiatives organized by the four perspectives: financial, customer, business processes, and human resources. The balanced scorecard provides a set of financial and nonfinancial measures that encompasses both internal and external perspectives. Think of the balanced scorecard as the dials and indicators in an airplane cockpit. For the complex task of navigating and flying an airplane, pilots need detailed information about many aspects of the flight. They need information on fuel, air speed, altitude, bearing, destination, and other indicators that summarize the current and predicted environment. Reliance on one instrument can be fatal.

It is estimated that a balanced scorecard should have 15 to 25 measures that support a company's strategy and are linked together in the form of cause-and-effect hypothesis statements. Forming these linkages encourages a company to specify how investments in human resources will drive continuous process improvements, increasing customer satisfaction and financial prosperity.

What would a balanced scorecard look like for Dell? Peter Brewer, an authority on balanced scorecards, has some suggestions for a balanced scorecard for Dell. Brewer uses Dell's mission statement to create a balanced scorecard.[2] Dell's mission

EXHIBIT 13-1

Performance Measurement
"Balanced Scorecard"

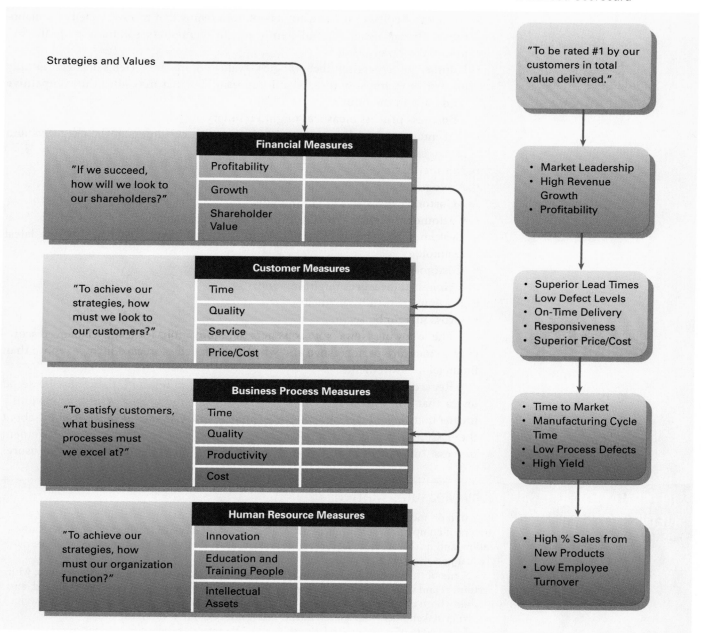

Source: Reprinted by permission of the publisher: Lawrence S. Maisel, "Performance Measurement: The Balanced Scorecard Approach," *Journal of Cost Management*, Summer 1992, p. 50; © 1992 by Warren Gorham and Lamont of RIA.

statement, which appears on its Web site, is "to be the most successful computer company in the world at delivering the best customer experience in markets we serve." From an understanding of Dell and deductive logic, Brewer suggests that the following might be the four balanced scorecard perspectives.

Human resources measures might include:

- Training dollars spent per full-time equivalent by customer segment to ensure that well-educated business segment managers provide state-of-the-art advice to customers
- Number of collaborative customer-solution teams that motivate Dell to collaborate with its customers and jointly create technology solutions to fulfill any unmet customer needs
- Number of emerging technologies evaluated inspires Dell's leaders to stay abreast of technology threats and opportunities that may alter the competitive landscape in the future

Business process measures might include:

- Percentage of total hours spent in contact with customers at the executive and managerial levels
- Number of customer-initiated product innovations
- Average customer idea ramp-up time

Customer measures might include:

- Customer perception of customized response capability
- Customer perception of stability and first-to-market capability with the latest technology
- Customer retention

Financial measures might include:

- Revenue growth by segment
- Gross margin by segment

The following News Note considers the motivations for using a balanced scorecard to measure performance and why the balanced scorecard includes more than financial measurements.

Regardless of which performance measures are selected, they must be set at levels that will encourage employees to do their best. Such a notion obviously means that individuals who will be evaluated by those measures must know about them. Communication of information is essential in any performance measurement process. Individuals must know about and understand the performance measures

---

INTERNATIONAL NEWS NOTE

Why Measures Matter

Research on more than 3,000 companies in North America has shown that the strongest drivers of competitive achievement are the intangibles, especially intellectual property, innovation, and quality. If these factors are important, then they should be measured, because "[w]hat gets measured gets done."

Some of the most important intangible assets a company can have are relationships, with customers and with employees. Employee loyalty and customer loyalty are closely linked, and retaining both is essential for success. Both are stakeholders; and there is no conflict between satisfying stakeholders and shareholders. You cannot do one without the other.

The quality of important relationships must therefore be reflected in a performance measurement framework, often called a scorecard, because of the sporting analogy. Remember, "If you aren't keeping score, then you're only practising."

A rich performance framework does not mean just picking a few nonfinancial measures to stand alongside the financial measures. Measures not only reflect strategy, they are also used for process control, so naturally they must be based on an analysis of the company's processes, as well as an understanding of how these processes are supported by knowledge and relationships.

Source: Thomas G. McWeeney, "Linking Resources to Planning and Performance Measurement," *Public Manager*, Fall 1997, pp. 35–36.

to be used so that they can make a conscious choice to perform or not perform in a manner consistent with the measurement system. Withholding information about measures will keep employees from performing at their highest level of potential, will be frustrating for them, and will not support feelings of mutual respect and cooperation. In addition, participation in devising performance measures captures the attention of those persons being evaluated and results in a social contract between participants and evaluators. Performance measures should also promote harmonious operations among organizational units. The effects of suboptimization can then be minimized because all employees will be working toward the same goals.

Managers must place individuals in appropriate jobs, because employees who are put in jobs for which they are unsuited are destined to fail. Assuming employees possess basic competencies, they must be given the appropriate tools—including equipment, information, authority, training, and support—to perform their jobs in a manner consistent with the measurement process. Competent individuals or teams of workers having the necessary job tools can be held responsible for their performance. If these tools are unavailable, people cannot be expected to accomplish their tasks.

Employee performance should be monitored and feedback provided on a continuous basis. Positive feedback encourages employees to continue favourable behaviours, while negative feedback creates awareness of problems so that employees can respond with different behaviours.

FINANCIAL PERFORMANCE MEASUREMENTS FOR MANAGERS

LEARNING OBJECTIVE **2**

How are return on investment (ROI) and residual income (RI) similar and different?

Attempts to use financial measures to evaluate higher-level managerial performance must consider the type of responsibility centre over which the manager has control. If a manager is responsible for only one monetary item (such as in a cost or revenue centre), performance measurements are limited to those relevant to that single monetary measure. Alternatively, profit and investment centre managers are responsible for their centres' revenues and expenses. Given this greater accountability, a greater number of financial measures can be used to evaluate performance.

Cash Flow

Use of accrual-based segment margin or income as a performance measure may divert management's attention from two critical issues—the size and the direction of cash flows. Profit and investment centre managers know that continuous liquidity is essential for their entities to succeed. Thus, another important performance measure is cash flow. The cash flow statement highlights the cash impacts of the three primary categories of business activities: operating, investing, and financing. A cash-based portrayal of operations helps managers to judge an entity's ability to meet current fixed cash outflow commitments, undertake new commitments, and adapt to adverse changes in business conditions. Also, by identifying relationships between segment margin (or net income) and net cash flow from operations, the cash flow statement assists managers in judging the quality of the entity's earnings.

Like segment margin and income, cash flow can be manipulated and relates to the short run rather than the long run. But, as pointed out earlier, adequate cash flow is essential to business success. Inadequate cash flow may indicate poor judgment and decision making on the part of the entity's manager. A variety of financial ratios that include cash flow information—such as the current ratio, acid test ratio, and number of days' collections in accounts receivable—can help managers conduct their functions efficiently and effectively.

Return on Investment

return on investment
a ratio that relates income generated by the investment centre to the resources (or asset base) used to produce that income

Because they are responsible for generating revenues, controlling costs, and acquiring, using, and disposing of assets, investment centre managers can be evaluated using return on investment. **Return on investment (ROI)** is a ratio that relates income generated by an entity to the resources (or the asset base) used to produce that income. The return on investment formula is:

$$ROI = Income \div Assets\ invested$$

Before the ROI formula can be used effectively, the numerator and denominator must be specifically defined. In Exhibit 13-2 there are questions relative to these definitions—and the answers to and rationale for each, assuming that the entity being measured is an investment centre. The answers would be different if ROI were being calculated for an entire company. The ROI formula can be used to evaluate individual investment centres, as well as to make intracompany, intercompany, and industry comparisons, if managers making these comparisons are aware of and allow for any differences in the entities' characteristics and accounting methods.

EXHIBIT 13-2
ROI Definitional Questions and Answers

Question	Preferable Answer	Rationale
Is income defined as segment margin or operating income?	Segment margin	This amount includes only elements controllable by the investment centre manager.
Is income defined on a before-tax or after-tax basis?	Before-tax basis	Investment centres are not taxed separately; if they were, the tax would probably be a different amount.
Is income defined on a before-interest or after-interest basis?	Before-interest basis	Interest rates are generally negotiated based on the company's (not the investment centre's) creditworthiness; if the centre had to borrow funds as an independent entity, the rate might be different.
Should assets be defined as • total assets utilized, • total assets available for use, or • net assets (equity)?	Total assets available for use	The investment centre manager is responsible for all assets, even idle ones.
Should plant assets be included in the asset denominator at • original costs, • depreciated book values, or • current values?	Current values	These values measure the opportunity cost of using the assets.
Should beginning, ending, or average assets be used?	Average assets	Periodic income relates to assets used during the entire period.

Exhibit 13-3 uses data for the Richmond Machine Company to illustrate ROI computations. The company has three product-line divisions: Machinery, Materials Handling, and Tools. All of the divisions are operated as separate investment centres.

To provide useful information about individual factors that compose the rate of return, the ROI formula can be restated in terms of profit margin and asset turnover. **Profit margin** is the ratio of income to sales; it indicates what proportion of each sales dollar is not used for expenses and so becomes profit. **Asset turnover**, which is calculated as sales divided by assets, shows the sales dollars generated by each dollar of assets and measures asset productivity. The ROI formula restated in terms of profit margin and asset turnover is called the **Du Pont model**:

$$ROI = Profit\ margin \times Asset\ turnover$$

As with the original ROI formula, terms must be specifically defined before the formula can be used for comparative or evaluative purposes. This model provides refined information about organizational improvement opportunities. Profit margin can be used to indicate management's efficiency as shown in the relation between sales and expenses. Asset turnover can be used to judge the effectiveness of asset use relative to revenue production. Calculations based on the Richmond Machine Company information are given in Exhibit 13-4 on page 742. Income and asset base are defined as segment margin and total historical cost. Thus, these computations provide the same answers as those given in Exhibit 13-3.

With the profit margin and asset turnover ratios computed for each division, the division's performance can be evaluated relative to benchmark ratios. The benchmark ratios could be expectations of performance for each division, industry performance levels, or similar ratios for specific competitors. Because the three divisions compete in different industries, it would not be appropriate to compare one internal division's performance to the performance of the others.

profit margin
the ratio of income to sales

asset turnover
a ratio that measures asset productivity; it is the number of sales dollars generated by each dollar of assets during a specific period

Du Pont model
ROI = Profit margin × Asset turnover

EXHIBIT 13-3

Richmond Machine Company Divisional ROI Computation

	Machinery	Materials Handling	Tools	Total
Revenues	$ 6,000,000	$ 967,400	$ 1,771,000	$ 8,738,400
Direct costs:				
Variable	(2,100,000)	(387,000)	(815,500)	(3,302,500)
Fixed (avoidable)	(1,100,000)	(120,000)	(302,000)	(1,522,000)
Segment margin	$ 2,800,000	$ 460,400	$ 653,500	$ 3,913,900
Unavoidable fixed and allocated costs	(725,000)	(92,400)	(153,000)	(970,400)
Operating income	$ 2,075,000	$ 368,000	$ 500,500	$ 2,943,500
Taxes (34%)	(705,500)	(125,120)	(170,170)	(1,000,790)
Net income	$ 1,369,500	$ 242,880	$ 330,330	$ 1,942,710
Current assets	$ 110,000	$ 42,000	$ 90,000	
Plant assets	11,422,000	995,000	8,825,000	
Total asset cost	$ 11,532,000	$ 1,037,000	$ 8,915,000	
Accumulated depreciation	(1,750,000)	(123,000)	(4,568,000)	
Asset book value	$ 9,782,000	$ 914,000	$ 4,347,000	
Liabilities	(4,205,000)	(117,000)	(927,000)	
Net assets	$ 5,577,000	$ 797,000	$ 3,420,000	
ROI: Segment margin	$ 2,800,000	$ 460,400	$ 653,500	
÷ Assets invested*	÷$ 11,532,000	÷$ 1,037,000	÷$ 8,915,000	
= Return on investment	24.3%	44.4%	7.3%	

*Although use of current values would have been preferable, Richmond Machine Company found these values difficult to obtain and had more confidence in the original cost of the assets used.

EXHIBIT 13-4

Richmond Machine Company
Du Pont Model ROI
Computations

ROI = Profit Margin × Asset Turnover

= (Income ÷ Sales) × (Sales ÷ Assets)

Machinery:
ROI = ($2,800,000 ÷ $6,000,000) × ($6,000,000 ÷ $11,532,000)

= .467 × .520 = 24.3%

Materials Handling:
ROI = ($460,400 ÷ $967,400) × ($967,400 ÷ $1,037,000)

= .476 × .933 = 44.4%

Tools:
ROI = ($653,500 ÷ $1,771,000) × ($1,771,000 ÷ $8,915,000)

= .369 × .199 = 7.3%

ROI is affected by management decisions involving sales prices, volume and mix of products sold, expenses, and capital asset acquisitions and dispositions. Return on investment may be increased through various management actions, including (1) raising sales prices, if demand will not be impaired; (2) decreasing expenses; and (3) decreasing dollars invested in assets, especially if those assets are no longer productive. Thus, actions to improve performance should be taken only after all the interrelationships that determine ROI have been considered. A change in one of the component elements can affect many of the others. For instance, a selling price increase can reduce sales volume if demand is elastic with respect to price.

Assessments of whether profit margin, asset turnover, and return on investment are favourable or unfavourable can be made only by comparison of actual results for each component. Valid bases of comparison include expected results, prior results, and results of similar entities. Many companies establish target rates of return either for the company or for each division. These rates are based on the nature of the industry or market in which the company or division operates. Favourable results should mean rewards for investment centre managers.

Unfavourable rates of return should be viewed as managerial opportunities for improvement. Factors used in the computation should be analyzed for more detailed information. For example, if asset turnover is low, additional analyses can be made of inventory turnover, accounts receivable turnover, machine capacity level experienced, and other rate-of-utilization measures. Such efforts should help indicate the causes of the problems so that adjustments can be made. Another measure related to return on investment is the residual income of an investment centre.

Residual Income

residual income
the profit earned that exceeds an amount "charged" for funds committed to a responsibility centre

Residual income (RI) is the profit earned that exceeds an amount "charged" for funds committed to an investment centre. The amount charged for funds is equal to a management-specified target rate of return multiplied by the assets used by the division. The rate can be changed periodically to reflect market rate fluctuations or to compensate for risk. The residual income computation is:

Residual income = Income − (Target rate × Asset base)

Perhaps the most significant advantage of residual income over return on investment is that residual income provides a dollar figure of performance rather than a percentage. It is always to a company's advantage to obtain new assets if the assets will earn an amount greater than the cost of the additional investment. Expansion, or additional investments in assets, can occur in an investment centre as long as positive residual income is expected on the additional investment.

Residual income can be calculated for each investment centre of Richmond Machine Company. The company has established 12% as the target rate of return on total historical cost of assets invested and continues to define income as segment margin. Calculations are shown in Exhibit 13-5. The residual income measures provide a clear indication of the relative contributions of the three divisions to the profit of the company. Although the Machinery and Materials Handling divisions are contributing substantial profits to the company, the profit of the Tools Division is insufficient to cover the required return on capital.

Limitations of Return on Investment and Residual Income

When used to measure investment centre performance, return on investment and residual income have certain limitations (see Exhibit 13-6 on page 744) that must be considered by managers.

Item 1 problems are common to most accounting-based measurements. However, use of ROI or RI in the new global environment can lead to the significant problems listed in Item 2. For example, intangible assets such as patents are significant keys to competing successfully today. The market values of such assets may differ very substantially from the assets' book values. Furthermore, some intangible assets may simply be ignored by traditional accounting methods, and therefore will be ignored by the analysis. A reputation for high-quality output and a high level of customer loyalty are examples of such assets.

Additionally, ROI and RI are short-term performance measures; consequently, they are better measures of performance for mature divisions than for high-growth divisions. For divisions that have opportunities for high rates of growth, the ROI and RI measures punish managers who currently invest in assets that do not generate returns until future periods.

economic value added
EVA = After-tax income − (Cost of capital % × Capital invested)

ECONOMIC VALUE ADDED

Perhaps the most popular trend in performance measurement is the development of measures intended to align the interests of common shareholders and managers more directly. Leading this trend is corporate adoption of the measure known as **economic value added (EVA).** Conceptually similar to RI, EVA is a measure of the

LEARNING OBJECTIVE 3

Why has economic value added (EVA) become a popular performance measure?

EXHIBIT 13-5

Richmond Machine Company Residual Income Calculations

Residual income = Income − (Target rate × Asset base)

Machinery:
RI = $2,800,000 − [0.12($11,532,000)] = $2,800,000 − $1,383,840 = $1,416,160

Materials Handling:
RI = $460,400 − [0.12($1,037,000)] = $460,400 − $124,440 = $335,960

Tools:
RI = $653,500 − [0.12($8,915,000)] = $653,500 − $1,069,800 = $(416,300)

EXHIBIT 13-6

Limitations of ROI and RI

1. **Problems related to income**
   - Income can be manipulated on a short-term basis by accelerating or delaying the recognition of income and expenses.
   - Because income depends on accounting methods selected, all investment centres must use the same methods if comparisons are to be made.
   - Accrual-based income reflects neither the cash flow patterns nor the time value of money, and these performance dimensions are generally important.

2. **Problems related to the asset base**
   - Some asset investment values are difficult to measure or assign to investment centres, while some other values, such as research and development, are not capitalized.
   - Current managers may be evaluated on decisions over which they had no control, such as decisions by previous managers to acquire some of the assets included in the division's investment base.
   - Inflation causes investment book values to be understated unless they are price-level adjusted.

3. **ROI and RI reflect investment centre performance without regard to companywide objectives, which can result in suboptimization.**

income produced above the cost of capital. The major distinction between RI and EVA is that the target rate of return for EVA is applied to the capital invested in the division or firm as opposed to the market value or book value of book assets, which is the measure used for RI. Furthermore, because only after-tax profits are available to shareholders, EVA is calculated based on after-tax income:

$$\text{EVA} = \text{After-tax income} - (\text{Cost of capital \%} \times \text{Capital invested})$$

Capital invested is defined as the market value of total equity and interest-bearing debt. *Cost of capital* is the weighted-average cost of capital, introduced in Chapter 10. For reasons mentioned earlier, the market value of invested capital can differ considerably from the book or market value of booked assets. As this difference increases, so do the relative benefits of using EVA rather than RI as a performance measure.

It is not uncommon from time to time for the market value of a firm to be significantly higher than the book value of the firm. Accordingly, RI, which is based on a target rate of return applied to the book value of assets, is likely to indicate much better performance than EVA. This point is demonstrated in Exhibit 13-7. Because the invested capital of Richmond Machine Company far exceeds its book value of assets, the firm's performance measured by EVA is well below the performance measured by RI. The News Note highlights the practicality of the EVA measure.

Despite the growing popularity of the EVA measure, it cannot measure all dimensions of performance, and it is a short-term measure of performance. Accordingly, the EVA measure can discourage investment in long-term projects because such investments drive up the amount of invested capital immediately but increase after-tax profits only at some point in the future. The result is a near-term decrease in EVA. Thus, EVA should be supplemented with longer-term financial performance measures and with nonfinancial performance measures, especially for growth-oriented organizational subunits.

Invested capital	$45,000,000
Book value of assets	26,484,000*
Required return	12%
Net income (sum of divisions' net incomes from Exhibit 13-3)	$1,942,710

RI = Income − (Target rate × Asset base)
  = $1,942,710 − (0.12 × $26,484,000) = $(1,235,370)

EVA = After-tax income − (Cost of capital % × Capital invested)
  = $1,942,710 − (0.12 × $45,000,000) = $(3,457,290)

*Book value of assets is equal to the sum of asset costs for each of the company's three divisions, as given in Exhibit 13-3 ($11,532,000 + $1,037,000 + $8,915,000) plus an assumed amount of $5,000,000 of corporate assets that are not associated with any of the three divisions.

EXHIBIT 13-7

Comparison of RI and EVA for Richmond Machine Company

EVA and Canadian Banks

GENERAL NEWS NOTE

The Canadian Imperial Bank of Commerce and Royal Bank of Canada are the most undervalued of the Big Five banks, analyst Robert Wessel of National Bank Financial says in a news report. Royal Bank's shares are undervalued by about 6%, while Canadian Imperial Bank of Canada shares are trading about 10% below their deserved market price, Mr. Wessel concluded. Royal Bank ranked number one given its undervalued stock and ability to create value "now and in the future," he said. To arrive at that conclusion, Mr. Wessel used the "economic value added" (EVA) method of evaluating the "implied" share prices of the banks compared with their current market values, instead of employing typical metrics such as earnings per share or return on equity.

In simple terms, the EVA approach measures the cash generated by a bank against the cash it has invested in the business. EVA is the value created by a business over a specified period of time, which drives "market value added" (MVA), the value created above the invested capital. As Mr. Wessel pointed out, this method of evaluating banks is poignant given the key importance of capital allocation in the banking sector and the large number of non-cash charges typically included in a bank's income statement.

Royal Bank is by far the most profitable bank on an EVA basis, Mr. Wessel found. Royal has a "disciplined approach to capital management" and has been the most consistent performer with only one negative EVA quarter in the past three years. Based on Royal Bank's current share price of $48.92, it may be undervalued by about $3.

The Canadian Imperial Bank of Commerce's share price "does not reflect improved performance and magnitude of [the bank's] turnaround," Mr. Wessel concluded. The bank posted a strong turnaround in 2000, compared with "dismal" results in the previous two years, he added. Improved operating performance and merchant banking gains, which offset the bank's heavy investment in retail electronic bank Amicus Financial, prompted the significant improvement.

By comparison, Bank of Nova Scotia is fairly valued, Mr. Wessel said. "[The Bank of Nova Scotia] is a consistent EVA performer despite underperforming Latin American investments," he argued, aided by strict expense control and a disciplined approach to acquisitions. The bank ranking could improve once these investments begin generating stronger returns. Bank of Montreal and Toronto-Dominion Bank are overvalued, Mr. Wessel said, significantly in the case of the Toronto-Dominion Bank. Much of the Toronto-Dominion Bank's growth between 1998 and 1999 was driven by discount brokerage TD Waterhouse, which is now struggling amid downtrodden equity markets.

Source: Keith Kalawsky, "[Canadian Imperial Bank of Commerce], Royal Bank Most Undervalued, Analyst Says," *Financial Post (National Post)*, December 15, 2001, p. FP6. Reprinted by permission of *National Post*.

Why are nonfinancial measures important to evaluating performance?

NONFINANCIAL PERFORMANCE MEASURES

The previous two sections discussed the financial measures of the balanced score-card. This section discusses nonfinancial performance measures, which include the other three parts of the balanced scorecard: customer measures, business process measures, and human resource measures. This section also expands on the sections in Chapter 12, particularly performance measurement. The earlier chapter dealt with the system details of nonfinancial performance measurement, whereas this section deals more with content of nonfinancial performance measures.

Customarily, performance evaluations have been conducted based almost solely on financial results. But top management, in maintaining such a narrow focus, is similar to a hockey player who, in hopes of playing well, concentrates solely on the scoreboard. Both the financial measures and game score reflect the results of past decisions. Success also requires that considerable attention be placed on the individual actions for effective competitiveness—not just the summary performance measure, the score. A hockey player must focus on skating, hitting, passing, and shooting. A company must focus on performing well in activities such as customer service, product development, manufacturing, marketing, and delivery. For a company to improve, its performance measurements must specifically track the causes and occurrences of these activities.

Thus, a progressively designed performance measurement system should encompass both financial and nonfinancial measures, especially those that track factors necessary for world-class status. **Nonfinancial performance measures (NFPMs)** include statistics for activities such as on-time delivery, manufacturing cycle time, set-up time, defect rate, number of unplanned production interruptions, and customer returns. NFPMs have two distinct advantages over financial performance measures:

nonfinancial performance measures statistics on activities such as on-time delivery, manufacturing cycle time, set-up time, defect rate, number of unplanned production interruptions, and customer returns

- Nonfinancial indicators directly measure an entity's performance in the activities that create shareholder wealth, such as manufacturing and delivering quality goods and services and providing service for the customer.
- As they measure productive activity directly, nonfinancial measures may better predict the direction of future cash flows. For example, the long-term financial viability of some industries rests largely on their ability to keep promises of improved product quality at a competitive price.

The performance pyramid depicted in Exhibit 13-8 indicates some financial and nonfinancial measures needed at various organizational levels and for various purposes. Also included are measures that can help in assessing both short-term and long-term organizational considerations.

Selection of Nonfinancial Measures

The set of nonfinancial performance measures that can be used is quite large because it is limited only by the imaginations of the persons establishing the system. Before establishing the measurement system, though, management should strive to identify the firm's critical success factors. A company's critical success factors may include quality, customer satisfaction, manufacturing efficiency and effectiveness, technical excellence, and rapid response to market demands.

For each success factor chosen, management should target a few attributes of each relevant NFPM for continuous improvement. These attributes should include both short-run and long-run measures to steer organizational activities properly. For instance, a short-range success measure for quality is the number of customer com-

EXHIBIT 13-8
The Performance Pyramid

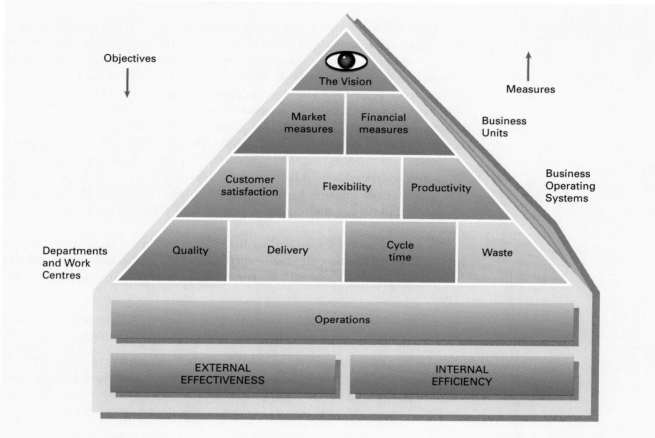

Source: C.J. McNair, Richard L. Lynch, and Kelvin F. Cross, "Do Financial and Nonfinancial Measures of Performance Have to Agree?" *Management Accounting* (November 1990), p. 30, Figure 1. Adapted with permission of the Institute of Management Accountants, Montvale, N.J., USA, www.imanet.org

plaints in the current period. A long-range success measure for quality is the number of patents obtained to improve the quality of the company's products.

The nonfinancial measures selected for the performance evaluation system can be qualitative or quantitative. Qualitative measures are often subjective; for example, simple low-to-high rankings may be assigned for job skills, such as knowledge, quality of work, and need for supervision. Although such measures provide useful information, performance should also be compared against a quantifiable standard.

Quantitative performance measures are more effective in creating employee receptiveness and compliance, because such measures provide a defined target at which to aim. These measures must be systematically captured and compared with predetermined standards to assess performance.

Establishment of Comparison Bases

After performance measures have been chosen, managers should establish acceptable performance levels by providing bases against which actual measurement data can be compared. These benchmarks can be developed internally (for example, based on a high-performing division) or can be determined from external sources, such as other companies, regardless of whether they are within the company's industry.

In each area in which a performance measurement is to be made, employees must agree (1) to accept specific responsibility for performance and (2) to be evaluated. A system for monitoring and reporting comparative performance levels should be established at appropriate intervals, as shown in Exhibit 13-9. The exhibit reflects a responsibility hierarchy of performance standards, with the broader issues addressed by higher levels of management and the more immediate issues addressed by lower-level employees. Note also that the lower-level measures are monitored more frequently (continuously, daily, or weekly) while the upper-level measures are investigated less frequently (monthly, quarterly, and annually). Measures addressed by middle-level employees (in Exhibit 13-9, the plant manager) are intermediate linkages between the lower-level and upper-level performance measures and require monitoring at intermediate points in time (weekly, monthly, and annually).

A general model for measuring the relative success of an activity compares a numerator representing number of successes with a logical and valid denominator representing total activity volume. For example, market share can be measured as follows:

$$\text{Market share} = \text{Number of units sold by specific firm} \times \text{Total units sold in the industry}$$

Assume an internal division sold 9,000 units during a period in which 48,000 units were sold by all the participants in the industry. The division's market share is 18.75% (9,000 ÷ 48,000). If a competitive benchmark for market share has been set at 20%, success will be evaluated as close to, but slightly below, the mark.

Throughput

synchronous management
all endeavours that help an organization achieve its goals

throughput
the rate at which a company generates cash from selling products and services to customers

All endeavours undertaken to help an organization achieve its goals are considered to be **synchronous management** techniques. The intent behind synchronous management is to increase throughput, while reducing inventory and operating expenses. Throughput is a valuable indicator of performance that is gaining wide acceptability. Throughput can be measured in either financial or nonfinancial terms. Defined in nonfinancial terms, **throughput** refers to the number of good units produced and sold by an organization within a time period. An important aspect of this definition is that the company must sell the units and not simply produce them for inventory stockpiles. A primary goal of a profit-oriented organization is to make money, and inventory must be sold for profits to be achieved. Throughput can also refer to the number of services requested, performed, and delivered in a period.

One useful way to measure performance is to determine the extent to which the company is meeting its goal of making money by having rapid and high-quality throughput. Throughput, as mentioned, simply reflects how many good units are produced and sold for each available processing hour. Throughput can also be viewed as a set of component elements, as the Du Pont model, presented earlier, includes components of return on investment. Components of throughput include manufacturing cycle efficiency, process productivity, and process quality yield.

EXHIBIT 13-9

Performance Measurement Factors and Timetables

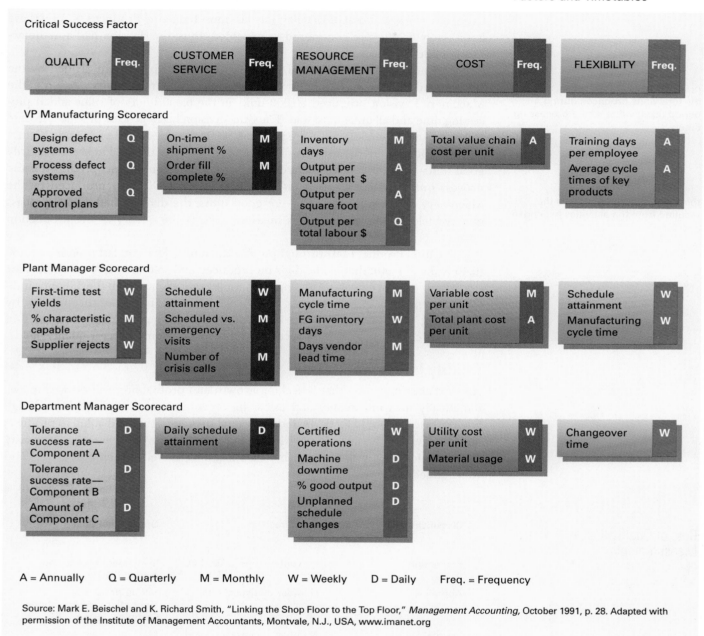

Critical Success Factor

| QUALITY | Freq. | CUSTOMER SERVICE | Freq. | RESOURCE MANAGEMENT | Freq. | COST | Freq. | FLEXIBILITY | Freq. |

VP Manufacturing Scorecard

Design defect systems	Q	On-time shipment %	M	Inventory days	M	Total value chain cost per unit	A	Training days per employee	A
Process defect systems	Q	Order fill complete %	M	Output per equipment $	A			Average cycle times of key products	A
Approved control plans	Q			Output per square foot	A				
				Output per total labour $	Q				

Plant Manager Scorecard

First-time test yields	W	Schedule attainment	W	Manufacturing cycle time	M	Variable cost per unit	M	Schedule attainment	W
% characteristic capable	M	Scheduled vs. emergency visits	M	FG inventory days	W	Total plant cost per unit	A	Manufacturing cycle time	W
Supplier rejects	W	Number of crisis calls	M	Days vendor lead time	M				

Department Manager Scorecard

Tolerance success rate— Component A	D	Daily schedule attainment	D	Certified operations	W	Utility cost per unit	W	Changeover time	W
Tolerance success rate— Component B	D			Machine downtime	D	Material usage	W		
Amount of Component C	D			% good output	D				
				Unplanned schedule changes	D				

A = Annually   Q = Quarterly   M = Monthly   W = Weekly   D = Daily   Freq. = Frequency

Source: Mark E. Beischel and K. Richard Smith, "Linking the Shop Floor to the Top Floor," *Management Accounting,* October 1991, p. 28. Adapted with permission of the Institute of Management Accountants, Montvale, N.J., USA, www.imanet.org

Throughput = Manufacturing cycle efficiency × Process productivity × Process quality yield

or

[Good units × Total time] = [Value-added processing time ÷ Total time] × [Total units ÷ Value-added processing time] × [Good Units ÷ Total Units]

The manufacturing cycle efficiency is the proportion of total processing time from beginning of production to completion, or service performance that is value-added. This time relates to activities that increase the product's worth to the customer. For instance, assume that the Machinery Division of Richmond Machine Company worked a total of 15,000 hours last month making Product L007. Of these hours, only 6,000 were considered value-added; thus, the division had a manufacturing cycle efficiency of 40%.

process productivity
the total units produced during a period using value-added processing time

Total units started, completed, and sold during the period are divided by the value-added processing time to determine **process productivity**. Assume the Machinery Division produced 30,000 units in the 6,000 hours of value-added processing time and all units were sold. Thus, the division had a process productivity rate of 5.0, meaning that 5.0 units were produced in each value-added processing hour.

process quality yield
the proportion of good units that resulted from the activities expended

But not all units started, completed, and sold during the period are necessarily good units—some may be defective. The proportion of good units produced is the **process quality yield**. Thus, if only 27,000 of the 30,000 units produced by the Machinery Division last month were good units, the division had a 90% process quality yield for the period. This measure reflects the quality of the production process.

The total Product L007 throughput for Machinery Division last month was 1.80 ($0.40 \times 5.0 \times 0.90$); that is, the division produced and sold only 1.80 good units for every hour of total actual processing time—quite a difference from the 5.0 units indicated as process productivity! The division could increase throughput by decreasing non-value-added activities, increasing total production and sales of units, decreasing the per-unit processing time, or increasing process quality yield.

Quality Indicators

A world-class company that is seeking growth and profitability will do well to systematically measure quality and assess its organizational cost of quality (COQ). Such measures should focus on and be related to actions that add value to products and services for the customer. Exhibit 13-10 presents several examples of quality indicators for each of the four quality classifications, as well as their cost drivers and value-added status.

EXHIBIT 13–10

Cost of Quality (COQ) Measurements

Classifications	Measure	Operational Cost Drivers
Prevention	Prevention cost ÷ Total COQ	Investment in reducing overall COQ operations
Appraisal	Number of inspections	Set-up frequency Tight tolerance operations Complex design
Internal failure	Number of pieces rejected	Machine reliability Tooling age or condition Design error Operator error
External failure	Number of customer complaints	Order entry errors Incorrect assembly instructions Product failure Operator error

Source: Reprinted by permission of the publisher: Michael R. Ostrenga, "Return on Investment through the Cost of Quality," *Journal of Cost Management*, Summer 1991, p. 43; © 1991 by Warren Gorham and Lamont of RIA.

The only value-added COQ category presented in Exhibit 13-10 is prevention, which eliminates defects from products consumed by consumers. As they cannot be added to products, appraisal costs add no customer value. Internal and external failures add no value for anyone; they simply create unnecessary correction costs that make total costs higher for both the company and the customer. These failure costs are the result of poor quality.

A firm can drive down the costs of appraisal, internal failure, and external failure by investing in prevention. Many prevention measures involve one-time costs that improve quality now and long into the future. Some prevention measures are fairly inexpensive. Such measures are often suggested by the employees engaged in the process. Suggestion programs can be effective in pointing out opportunities for continuous improvement that will benefit employees, customers, and the firm and its owners.

ACTIVITY-BASED COSTING AND PERFORMANCE MEASUREMENT

LEARNING OBJECTIVE **5**

How are activity-based costing concepts related to performance measurement?

Choosing appropriate nonfinancial performance measures can significantly help a company focus on activities that create costs. By controlling these activities, the company can more effectively control costs and improve processes.

Activity-based costing is concerned with reducing non-value-added activities to increase throughput. Traditional performance measurements in accounting are filled with factors that contribute to non-value-added activities. Material and labour standards often include factors for waste and idle time. Predetermined overhead rates are based on estimates of expected capacity usage rather than full capacity usage. Inventories are produced to meet budget expectations rather than sales demand. Detailed explanations of how to treat spoiled and defective unit costs are provided in organizational accounting procedures. Exhibit 13-11 on page 752 provides some traditional performance indicators and some potential suboptimizing results they may encourage.

If companies are to move toward world-class operations, non-value-added activities must be removed from performance evaluation measurements and value-added activities must be substituted. For example, when a performance measurement is the cost of defective units produced during a period, the original assumption is that management is expecting defects to occur and will accept some stated or implied defect cost. Instead, when the performance benchmark is zero defects, the assumption is that no defects will occur. It seems reasonable that managers would strive harder to eliminate defects under the second measurement than under the first.

As activity-based costing focuses on actions that add value from a customer's viewpoint, this accounting method stresses external performance measurements. Customers define good performance as that which equals or exceeds their expectations as to quality, cost, and delivery. Companies that cannot measure up will find themselves without customers and without a need for financial measures of performance. In this regard, nonfinancial measures are more effective because they can be designed to monitor the characteristics desired by external parties rather than internal financial goals.

Knowing that performance is to be judged according to some external criteria of success should cause companies to begin implementing concepts such as just-in-time inventory and total quality management. The common themes of these

EXHIBIT 13-11

Traditional Performance
Measurements and Results

Measurement	Action	Result
Purchase price variance	Purchasing increases order quantity to get lower price and ignores quality and speed of delivery	Excess inventory; increased carrying cost; suppliers with the best quality and delivery are overlooked
	Purchasing acquires inferior quality materials to generate positive price variances	Production quality suffers and customers receive inferior goods
Machine utilization percentage	Supervisor requires employees to produce more than daily unit requirements to maximize machine utilization percentage	Excess inventory; wrong inventory
Scrap built into standard cost	Supervisor takes no action if there is no variance (from the lax standard)	Inflated standard; scrap threshold built in
Overhead rate based on expected capacity	Supervisor overproduces WIP or FG to have a favourable fixed overhead volume variance	Excess inventory
Responsibility centre reporting	Management focus is on responsibility centres instead of activities	Missed cost reduction opportunities because common activities among responsibility centres are overlooked

concepts are to make the organization, its products, and its processes better and to lower costs to provide better value.

Although some performance measurements, such as zero defects, can be implemented anywhere, companies operating in a multinational environment face more complex issues than do companies operating only in a domestic setting. Thus, multinational companies need to consider some additional factors relative to performance measurement and evaluation.

LEARNING OBJECTIVE 6

Why is it more difficult to measure performance in multinational firms than in solely domestic companies?

PERFORMANCE EVALUATION IN MULTINATIONAL SETTINGS

Operating overseas business units is more complex than operating domestic units. In attempting to compare multinational organizational units, differences among cultures and economies are as important as differences in accounting standards and reporting practices. CEOs in Japan take long-term views and make decisions accordingly, whereas Canadian and U.S. CEOs are very short-term oriented and cater to the stock markets. This attitude allows Japanese companies to concentrate on long-run, rather than short-run, business decisions.

The investment base needed to create a given type of organizational unit may differ substantially in different countries. For example, because of the exchange rate and legal costs, it is significantly more expensive for a company to open a Japanese subsidiary than an Indonesian one. If performance measures are based on a concept such as residual income, the Japanese unit will be placed at a distinct disadvantage because of its large investment base. However, the parent company may believe that the possibility of future joint ventures with Japanese organizations—

which the parent has specified as a primary corporate goal—justifies the larger investment. The company may wish to handle the discrepancy in investment bases by assigning a lower target rate to compute residual income for the Japanese subsidiary. Such a differential is appropriate because of the lower political, financial, and economic risks.

Income comparisons between multinational units may be invalid because of important differences in trade tariffs, income tax rates, currency fluctuations, and possible restrictions on the transfer of goods or currency. Income earned by a multinational unit may also be affected by conditions totally outside its control, such as government protection of local companies, government aid in some countries, and varying wage rates resulting from differing standards of living, levels of industrial development, or quantities of socialized services. If the multinational subunit adopts the local country's accounting practices, differences in international standards can make income comparisons among units difficult and inconvenient even after the statements have been translated to a single currency basis.

The diverse economic, legal/political, and tax structures of countries have affected the development and practice of accounting. The International Accounting Standards Committee is working to achieve harmonization of accounting standards. However, many of the standards issued to date by this organization reflect compromise positions, allow for a significant number of alternatives, and rely on voluntary compliance. Additionally, as discussed in Chapter 11, managers may be able to transfer goods between segments at prices that minimize profits or tariffs in locations where taxes are high by shifting profits or cost values to more advantageous climates. These transfers must, of course, be made within the constraints of legal, moral, and social responsibility.

Recently, many Western firms have stepped up their investments in China. These firms are struggling with measurement and reward structures that result in efficient operations and retention of managerial talent. In hiring local managers, firms are finding that they must nurture loyalty, or talented individuals will be attracted to rival firms. Thus, measurement of performance must be partly based on the goal of retaining highly qualified local talent.

Given all these difficulties in monitoring the performance of their nondomestic investment centres, companies should use multiple measures that consider both the short run and the long run. Firms should establish flexible systems of measuring profit performance for those units. Such systems should recognize that differences in sales volume, accounting standards, economic conditions, and risk may be outside the control of an international subunit's manager. In such cases, nonfinancial, qualitative factors may become significantly more useful than monetary ones. Performance evaluations can include measures such as market share increases, quality improvements (reduction of defects), establishment of just-in-time inventory systems with the related reduction in working capital, and new product development.

The use of measures that limit suboptimization of resources is vital to the proper management of multinational responsibility centres. No single system is appropriate for all companies or, perhaps, even for all responsibility centres within the same company. The measurement of performance is the measurement of people. Since each person is unique and has multiple facets, the performance measurement system must reflect these individual differences. Once the measurement system is established, people are generally concerned about the way in which that system will affect their personal rewards or compensation.

How should employee rewards, including compensation, and performance be linked?

compensation strategy
a foundation for the compensation plan that addresses the role compensation should play in the organization

RELATING COMPENSATION AND PERFORMANCE

A company should compensate employees in a manner that motivates them to act in ways that result in the company's effectively and efficiently achieving its goals. A rational compensation plan ties its component elements—organizational goals, performance measurements, and employee rewards—together in a cohesive package. The relations and interactions among these elements are shown in Exhibit 13-12.

In this model, strategic organizational goals are determined by the board of directors (the governing body representing shareholder interests) and top management. From these strategic goals, the organization's critical success factors are identified, and operational targets are defined. For example, operational targets could include specified annual net income, unit sales of a specific product, quality measures, customer service measures, or costs.

The board of directors and top management must also decide on a **compensation strategy** for the organization. This strategy should provide a foundation for the compensation plan by addressing the role compensation should play in the organization. The compensation strategy should be made known to everyone, from the board of directors to the lowest-level worker. In an era of cost competitiveness, automatic cost-of-living adjustments and annual pay raises are being reduced or eliminated. Compensation plans need to encourage greater levels of employee performance and loyalty, while lowering overall costs and raising profits. Plans of this kind reflect a pay-for-performance strategy that encourages behaviour essential to achieving organizational goals and maximizing shareholder value.

EXHIBIT 13-12
Plan–Performance–Reward Model

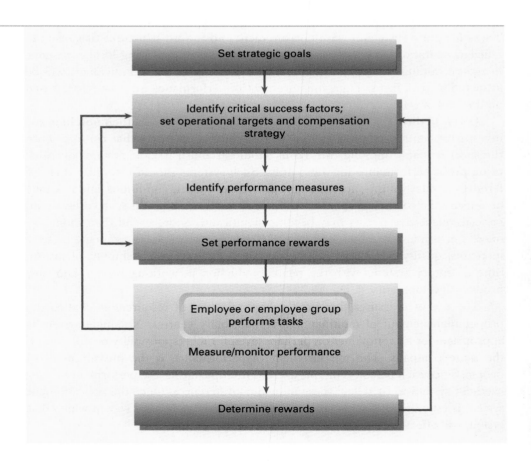

Pay-for-Performance Plans

Recall that what gets measured gets employees' attention—especially when compensation is involved. Therefore, in structuring a pay-for-performance plan, it is crucial that the defined performance measures be highly correlated with the organization's operational targets. Otherwise, suboptimization may occur and workers can earn incentive pay even though broader organizational objectives are not achieved.

Tying an organization's pay-for-performance plan to goals established in the strategic planning phase is the first step to motivating employees to focus on productivity improvement. The entire package of decisions regarding performance measurements can be referred to as a performance management system, depicted in Exhibit 13-13. When employees meet improvement objectives, rewards follow, and organizational results—such as growth in market share, faster throughput, and greater profits—can be expected. Reevaluating the performance measurement linkages with the satisfaction of corporate goals completes the cycle.

Traditionally, performance measures have focused on short-run profits without giving adequate attention to long-run performance. If done properly, pay-for-performance criteria should encourage employees to adopt a long-run perspective. To encourage a long-range perspective, many top executives receive a significant portion of their compensation in the form of stock or stock options, and this can

EXHIBIT 13-13

Performance Management System

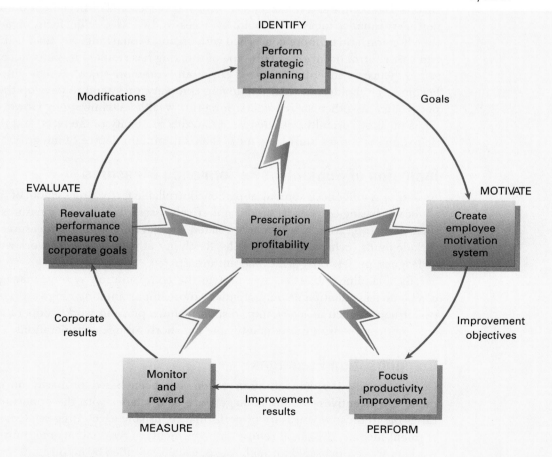

Source: Dan J. Seidner and Glenn Kieckhaefer, "Using Performance Measurement Systems to Create Gainsharing Programs," (Grant Thornton) *Manufacturing Issues,* Summer 1990, p. 9. Reprinted by permission of Grant Thornton LLP.

work well if the executives are committed to the organization for the long term. If the executives are short-term oriented, they can manipulate the performance of their organization, exercise their options, or sell their shares before the share price falls. This negative aspect has been seen with such firms as Nortel, Enron, and WorldCom.

Since many companies have shifted from evaluating workers by observing their inputs to evaluating them based on their outputs, new problems have been created in the pay-for-performance relationship for workers as well as managers. Earlier chapters have stressed the importance of evaluating managers and workers only on the basis of controllable factors. Regrettably, most performance measures tend to capture results that are a function of both controllable and noncontrollable factors.

Actual performance results from worker effort, worker skill, and random effects. Random effects include performance measurement error, problems or efficiencies created by co-workers or adjacent workstations, illness, and weather-related production problems. Once actual performance has been measured, it is impossible in many instances to determine the contributions of controllable and noncontrollable factors to the achieved performance. Consequently, the worker bears the risk that a less-than-desirable outcome may result from an uncontrollable cause. Management should seek to identify performance measures that minimize this risk.

At the basic worker level, performance measures should be specific and should usually focus on cost or quality control. At higher organizational levels, the critical success factors under a manager's control and responsibility become more important. Performance measures should, by necessity, be less specific, focus on a longer time horizon, and be more concerned with organizational longevity than with short-run cost control or income. This type of thinking has resulted in shifts in compensation plans to include shares of corporate common stock. When employees become shareholders in their employing company, they tend to develop the same perspective as other shareholders: long-run wealth maximization. However, the plans must be carefully designed to obtain this mutuality of interests, and the participating executives must have more than a minimum degree of integrity.

Inclusion of Subjective Performance Measures

As output is influenced somewhat by noncontrollable factors, one school of thought advocates basing compensation on subjectively assessed intangible measures rather than more objective, performance-related measures. Subjective measures could include items such as leadership skills, flexibility, attitude, ability to work well with colleagues, professional pride, and enthusiasm.

By including subjective measures in the compensation system, management can blend less quantifiable but potentially more important long-range aspects of job performance—such as leadership, responsiveness, pride in work, cooperativeness, and enthusiasm—with more quantifiable but shorter-range considerations.

Compensation Packages

Conventionally, the compensation system has been based primarily on current monetary incentives. Middle managers are paid salaries with the opportunity for raises based on some measure of performance, usually accounting-related, such as segment income, divisional return on investment, or residual income. Lower-level workers are compensated through wages, usually specified by union contract or tied to the minimum wage law, based on the number of hours worked or production level achieved; current or year-end bonuses may be given when performance is above some specified quantitative measure. If provided, worker performance bonuses usually amount to a fairly small sum or percentage of wages. Significant incentive pay is usually limited to top management, and possibly the sales force, regardless of the levels of employees who may have contributed to increased profits. The reason for linking top management pay to incentives such as earnings and common share performance pay is that there is a direct relation. Lower level employees have little control over earnings and common share performance.

As with performance measures, an employee's organizational level and current compensation should affect the types of rewards chosen. Individuals at different levels of employment typically view monetary rewards differently because of the relationship of pay to standard of living. Using relative pay scales is essential to recognizing the value of this difference. At lower employee levels, more incentives should be monetary and short-term; at higher levels, more incentives should be nonmonetary and long-term. The system should, though, include some nonmonetary and long-term incentives for lower-level employees and some monetary and short-term incentives for top management. Such a two-faceted compensation system provides lower-paid people with tangible rewards that directly enhance their lifestyles—more money—but also provides rewards (such as stock options) that cause them to take a long-run "ownership" view of the organization. In turn, top managers, who are well paid by most standards, would receive more rewards (stock and stock options) that should cause them to be more concerned about the organization's long-term well-being rather than short-term personal gains.

Another consideration in designing compensation packages is to balance the incentives provided for both groups, or teams, and individuals. In automated production systems, workers function more by indirectly monitoring and controlling machinery and are, therefore, less directly involved in hands-on production. Additionally, evolving organizational and managerial philosophies, such as total quality management and implementation of quality circles, have stressed group performance and the performance of work in teams.

Incentive plans for small groups and individuals are often virtually interchangeable. As the group grows larger, incentives must be in place for both the group and the individual. Group incentives are necessary to encourage cooperation among workers. However, if only group incentives are offered, the incentive compensation system may be ineffective because the reward for individual effort goes to the group. The larger the group size, the smaller the individual's share of the group reward becomes. Eventually, individual workers will be encouraged to take a free ride on the group. This situation occurs when individuals perceive their proportional shares of the group reward as insufficient to compensate for their efforts.

A recent study found that two-thirds of surveyed companies use quantifiable measures of team effectiveness in addition to measures of individual effectiveness.[3] The study also found that subjective, qualitative measures are frequently used to assess the performance of individuals in teams, such as level of cooperation and level of participation in teams.

In addition to various forms of monetary compensation, workers may be motivated by nonfinancial factors. Although all employees value and require money to satisfy basic human needs, other human needs are not necessarily fulfilled with monetary wealth. Employees generally desire some compensation that is not monetary in nature but that satisfies the higher-order social needs of humans. For example, workers and managers are typically more productive in environments in which they believe their efforts to be appreciated. Simple gestures such as

Rewards for performance do not always have to be monetary. Sometimes, tokens of appreciation convey an equally satisfying acknowledgement for a job performed well.

compliments and small awards can be used by superiors to formally recognize contributions of subordinates. Allowing subordinates to participate in decisions affecting their own welfare and the welfare of the firm also contributes to making employment socially fulfilling. Such efforts provide assurance to employees that they are serving a productive role in the firm and that superiors are attentive to and appreciative of employee contributions.

Care must also be taken that a company's compensation strategy does not result in suppressing creativity, innovation, risk taking, and proactive assumption and conduct of job responsibilities. If monetary rewards can be withheld when failure occurs, employees who are otherwise industrious and cooperative might avoid taking actions or making proposals that could fail. Fear of failure can be reduced if management creates an atmosphere of employee empowerment in which failure is accepted as part of the progression toward continuous improvement.

Organizational compensation packages must be developed that blend organizational goals with monetary and nonmonetary employee rewards. Only if there is a perception of equity across the contributions and entitlements of labour, management, and capital will the organization be capable of achieving the efficiency to compete in global markets.

LEARNING OBJECTIVE 8

How do expatriate reward systems differ from those for domestic operations?

GLOBAL COMPENSATION

With international operations increasing, plans that compensate expatriate employees and managers on a fair and equitable basis must be developed. Expatriates are parent-company and third-country nationals assigned to a foreign subsidiary or foreign nationals assigned to the parent company. Placing employees

A New Compensation Base

According to a July 2001 survey by Hay Group, 84% of companies offering stock option programs said they had no plans to amend their program. The survey also found that flexible pay has become prevalent across hierarchical levels in both public and private sector organizations. Last year, in the private sector, 89% of senior management, 82% of middle management, 65% of technical and support staff, and 46% of blue collar workers qualified for annual bonus programs based on productivity gains and profit sharing.

Source: Gerard Berube, "A New Compensation Base," *CA Magazine*, Vol. 135, Issue 1, January–February 2002, p. 6.

GENERAL NEWS NOTE

in foreign countries requires careful consideration of compensation. What is thought to be a fair and reasonable compensation package in one setting may not be fair and reasonable in another.

Expatriates' compensation packages must reflect labour market factors, cost-of-living considerations, and currency fluctuations, as well as tax consequences. Since expatriates have a variety of financial requirements, these individuals may be paid in the currency of the country where they have been relocated, or in their home currency, or a combination of both. An expatriate's base salary and fringe benefits should typically reflect what he or she would have been paid domestically. This base should then be adjusted for reasonable cost-of-living factors. These factors may be obvious, such as needs similar to those that would exist in the home country (transportation, shelter, clothing, and food), or the need to be compensated for a spouse's loss of employment; or they may be less apparent, such as a need to hire someone in the home country to care for young children or to manage an investment portfolio.

Price-level adjustment clauses are often included in the compensation arrangement to mitigate any local currency inflation or deflation. Regardless of the currency makeup of the pay package, the fringe benefit portion related to retirement must be tied to the home country and should be paid in that currency. These adjustments can be very expensive. For example, Douglas R. Stanton, a Hong Kong-

When employees go to other countries to live and work, their compensation needs to reflect lifestyle differences. For instance, the street vendors and outdoor cafés in Switzerland are moderately priced alternatives to the stores and restaurants in Canadian cities.

based partner for the consulting firm Towers Perrin Inc., says he knows of one company whose expatriate general manager collects compensation equal to a quarter of the firm's revenue in China.[4]

Income taxes are important in expatriates' compensation packages because such individuals may be required to pay taxes in the local country, the home

Implementing the Balanced Scorecard

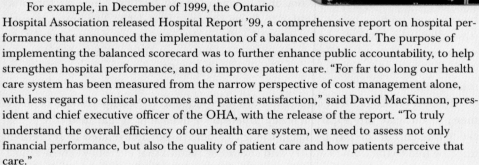

As the balanced scorecard affects perspectives, rewards, and relationships in organizations, managers must take into account not only organizational structure and systems when implementing the balanced scorecard; they must consider their organization's history, management style, and culture. The approach to implementation that suits one organization will not always suit the next. This is especially true of nonprofit organizations, whose missions vary dramatically.

For example, in December of 1999, the Ontario Hospital Association released Hospital Report '99, a comprehensive report on hospital performance that announced the implementation of a balanced scorecard. The purpose of implementing the balanced scorecard was to further enhance public accountability, to help strengthen hospital performance, and to improve patient care. "For far too long our health care system has been measured from the narrow perspective of cost management alone, with less regard to clinical outcomes and patient satisfaction," said David MacKinnon, president and chief executive officer of the OHA, with the release of the report. "To truly understand the overall efficiency of our health care system, we need to assess not only financial performance, but also the quality of patient care and how patients perceive that care."

The scorecard developed by the OHA measures and reports on the following areas: financial performance; patient satisfaction; clinical use and outcomes (how hospitals deal with some of the most common conditions requiring hospital care); and system integration and change. The last area includes the hospitals' efforts to invest in the future by improving linkages with other providers of care, investing in better information for decision making, and improving coordination of care. The release of this report was followed immediately by strong complaints raised by Mark Ortlieb, president of the Service Employees International Union Local 204, which represents over 10,000 nurses, support staff, and housekeeping workers in hospitals across South Central Ontario. Mr. Ortlieb claimed that the report was prepared without the input of those directly involved in patient care and was, therefore, both an incomplete and a potentially biased picture of the state of affairs in health care. Mr. Ortlieb concluded, "If the OHA were really interested in improving the quality of care it should have asked the people who provide the care."

Whether Mr. Ortlieb's comments are fair or even accurate, the issue remains that implementing a balanced scorecard without the input and participation of those who implement the organization's strategies and plans will doom the balanced scorecard to being a source of controversy rather than an integrating and focussing force in the organization.

Source: Reprinted from an article appearing in the September 2000 issue of *CMA Management* magazine by Anthony A. Atkinson and Marc Epstein, with permission of Certified Management Accountants of Canada.

country, or both. Some countries, such as the United States and Great Britain, exempt expatriates from taxation on a specified amount of income earned in a foreign country. If a tax treaty exists and local taxes are paid on the balance of the nonexempt income of an expatriate, those taxes may be credited against the expatriate's home-nation income taxes.

In conclusion, tying the compensation system to performance measurement is essential because everyone in business recognizes that what gets measured and rewarded is what gets accomplished. Businesses must focus their reward structures to motivate employees to succeed at all activities that will create shareholder and personal value. In this highly competitive age, the new paradigm of success is to provide high-quality products and services at a reasonable price while generating a reasonable profit margin.

CHAPTER SUMMARY

Performance measures should assess progress toward goals and objectives and should be accepted by those being evaluated. Using multiple measures of the firm's critical success factors is more effective than using a single performance measure. Divisional profits and cash flow are frequently used financial performance measures.

Two other significant financial measures of performance are return on investment and residual income. Return on investment is computed as segment margin, or net income, divided by invested assets. Residual income is the amount of segment margin, or net income, in excess of an amount calculated by use of a preestablished "interest charge" on the asset base. Both ROI and RI provide important information about the efficiency and effectiveness of managers. Neither should be used alone, however, and their inherent limitations, including the fact that they can be manipulated because of their basis in accounting, should be considered.

One of the most popular, evolving performance measures is economic value added (EVA). EVA is superior to other short-term financial performance measures because of its close linkage to stockholders' interests. EVA is measured as the difference between net income for a period and the dollar cost of invested capital for a period.

Financial measures can be effectively coupled with nonfinancial measures to provide a more complete and useful picture of performance. One useful nonfinancial measure is throughput—the nondefective goods or services started, finished, and sold by an organization during a period. When throughput is increased, the company goal of making money is enhanced. Various quality measures have also gained prominence as companies begin to compete more heavily in the global marketplace. These measures focus on activities that add value for the customer.

Performance measures may be more difficult to establish for multinational units than for domestic units because of differences in taxes, tariffs, currency exchange rates, and transfer restrictions. Because of such differences, top management may wish to consider extending the use of qualitative performance measures.

Customarily, compensation systems have often been based solely on individual performance and short-run financial results. Because of operational changes and shifts in managerial philosophies, performance measurements and their related rewards now encompass group success, nonfinancial performance attributes, and long-run considerations. Companies also need to recognize that some top managers' compensation grossly exceeds pay to ordinary workers. Such excesses can be counterproductive, causing a demoralizing effect within the firm, and ultimately, failure to maximize long-term shareholder wealth. Thus, it is important that the compensation strategy and system are in harmony with the performance measurement system and that together they serve to assure fairness, effectiveness, and efficiency in an organization.

Cross-Functional Applications

Topic of Note	Discipline	Cross-Functional Applications
Financial Performance Measurements (FPMs)	Financial Management	FPMs such as return on investment (ROI), return on assets (ROA), residual income (RI), and economic value added (EVA) establish performance expectations and guide investment decisions. Creditors and investors evaluate firms in terms of stock prices, income generation, cash flows, and dividend payouts. FPMs give financial managers a relatively standardized benchmark to compare alternative investment opportunities and to examine such opportunities from the perspective of creditors and investors.
	Management	Senior-level managers use FPMs to measure performance of investment centres. The performance of operating managers, and the rewards provided to them, are linked to FPMs such as ROI, RI, and EVA. Increasingly, the use of FPMs is complemented by selected nonfinancial performance measures to assess other dimensions of performance such as quality, customer service, and safety.
	Labour and Industrial Relations	In some large multinational firms, union leaders hold positions on boards of directors. Union leaders want to be assured that union members receive an appropriate share of the financial benefits that are generated by corporate operations. Many unionized firms have negotiated labour agreements with unions to tie pension fund contributions or profit-sharing provisions to FPMs.
	Financial Analysis	Financial analysts, inside and outside the firm, can provide valuable insights about the financial health of a company by comparing the FPMs of a firm to those of firms in the same industry or to industrial averages. These comparisons may expose problems and opportunities that require further research by management.

(cont.)

Cross-Functional Applications

Topic of Note	Discipline	Cross-Functional Applications
		Sometimes firms use different accounting methods, and these differences can make comparisons more difficult for analysts.
	Research and Development (R&D)	The evaluation of R&D managers must be based on FPMs that are long-term oriented. For example, net present value (NPV) and internal rate of return (IRR) are appropriate measures because they are capable of capturing the multiple-period costs and benefits of R&D projects.
Nonfinancial Performance Measures (NFPMs)	Sales Management	NFPMs provide sales managers with standards and objectives necessary to coordinate their contributions to the overall corporate strategic plan. Exceptional salespeople are often defined in terms of narrow departmental objectives such as recruitment of new business or achievement of sales quotas. Rewards are provided to salespeople based on the achieved level of performance.
	Production/Operations Management	Production managers' decisions concerning quality, delivery time, machine usage, inventory holdings, and scrap and waste management are often guided by NFPMs.
	Economics	Economists regularly incorporate NFPMs in both macro- and microeconomic modelling. Productivity improvement is a frequent example.
	Human Resource Management (HR)	HR managers are guided by NFPMs in decisions concerning the training, evaluation, and motivation of employees. Although individual departments set technical standards for employment decisions, HR is responsible for meeting external legal standards and internal ethical standards in such decisions. There are many demographic dimensions to diversity: age, gender, race, geographic location, educational level, and income level. Each of these demographic factors can affect the demand for existing and potential products. Having a diverse employee base allows a firm

(cont.)

Cross-Functional Applications

Topic of Note	Discipline	Cross-Functional Applications
		to develop better strategies for marketing consumer products to markets with a specific demographic profile by using such approaches as market segmentation, product differentiation, custom packaging, and targeted promotion.

Recently, legal issues and social responsibilities have dominated use of HR resources for other purposes, such as screening and promotion decisions. For example, maintaining compliance with affirmative action rules and other nondiscrimination provisions has been a heavy burden for HR departments. |
	Service Operations	NFPMs enhance financial performance measurements in applying concepts of responsibility accounting. To illustrate the use of NFPMs in a service organization, consider their use in a typical university. NFPMs for faculty include new program development, contributions to research and teaching, and service to the community.
	Labour and Industrial Relations	Management's negotiations with labour unions often pivot on nonfinancial performance dimensions such as a ratio of employees to machines, safety, and quality of employee performance. In a manufacturing setting, machine output may be dictated by a labour agreement rather than the technical capacity of the machine.
	Management	Programs of provincial and federal governments to increase diversity in employment throughout the economy have led to employment equity hiring. Universities also have employment equity programs to increase the number of women and visible minority faculty members.

Supplementary Learning Objectives on the Web

W13-1 What is open-book management and why does its adoption require changes in accounting methods and practices?

W13-2 Why are operations of many firms becoming more diverse, and how does the increasing diversity affect the roles of the firms' accounting system?

Key Terms

Asset turnover (p. 741)
Compensation strategy (p. 754)
Du Pont model (p. 741)
Economic value added (p. 743)
Nonfinancial performance measure (p. 746)
Process productivity (p. 750)

Process quality yield (p. 750)
Profit margin (p. 741)
Residual income p. 742)
Return on investment (p. 740)
Synchronous management (p. 748)
Throughput (p. 748)

Solution Strategies

Performance Measurements for Responsibility Centres

- Profit Centre

    Budgeted divisional profits
− Actual divisional profits
= Variances (consider materiality)

    Cash inflows
− Cash outflows
= Net cash flow (adequate for operations?)

- Investment Centre

    Budgeted investment centre profits
− Actual investment centre profits
= Variances (consider materiality)

    Cash inflows
− Cash outflows
= Net cash flow (adequate for operations?)

$$\text{Return on Investment} = \text{Income} \div \text{Assets Invested (high enough rate?)}$$

Du Pont model:

$$\text{ROI} = \text{Profit margin} \times \text{Asset turnover}$$
$$= (\text{Income} \div \text{Sales}) \times (\text{Sales} \div \text{Assets})$$
$$\text{(high enough rate?)}$$
$$\text{RI} = \text{Income} - (\text{Target rate} \times \text{Asset base})$$

or

$$\text{RI} = \text{Asset base} \times (\text{ROI} - \text{Target rate})$$
$$\text{(positive or negative? high enough amount?)}$$
$$\text{EVA} = \text{After-tax income} - (\text{Cost of capital \%} \times \text{Capital invested})$$
$$\text{(positive or negative? high enough amount?)}$$

Measuring Throughput

$$\text{Throughput} = \text{Manufacturing cycle efficiency} \times \text{Process productivity} \times \text{Process quality yield}$$

or

$$[\text{Good units} \div \text{Total time}] = [\text{Value-added processing time} \div \text{Total time}] \times [\text{Total units} \div \text{Value-added processing time}] \times [\text{Good units} \div \text{Total units}]$$

Designing a Reward System

It is impossible to design a generic incentive model that would be effective across a variety of firms. However, affirmative answers to the following questions provide guidance as to the applicability of a proposed incentive and reward plan for a particular organization.

1. Will the organizational and subunit objectives be achieved if the proposed compensation structure is implemented?
2. Is the proposed structure consistent with the organizational design, culture, and management philosophy?
3. Are there reasonable and objective performance measures that are good surrogates for the organizational objectives?
4. Are factors beyond employee/group control minimized under the performance measures of the proposed compensation structure?
5. Are there minimal opportunities for employees to manipulate the performance measurements tied to the proposed compensation structure?
6. In light of the interests of managers, workers, and shareholders, is the proposed reward structure fair and does it encourage and promote ethical behaviour?
7. Is the proposed reward structure arranged to take advantage of potential employee/employer tax benefits?
8. Does the proposed reward structure promote harmony between employee groups?
9. Is there an adequate balance between group and individual incentives?

DEMONSTRATION PROBLEM

Meltzer Wholesaling sells a broad line of clothing goods to specialty retail and department stores. For last year, the company's Canadian Division had the following performance targets:

Asset turnover	1.8
Profit margin	8%
Target rate of return on investments for EVA, RI	10%
Income tax rate	25%

Actual information concerning the performance of the Canadian Division for last year follows:

Total assets at beginning of year	$ 4,800,000
Total assets at end of year	7,200,000
Total invested capital (annual average)	11,000,000
Sales	12,000,000
Variable operating costs	5,000,000
Direct fixed costs	6,280,000
Allocated common costs	800,000

Required:

1. For the Canadian Division of Meltzer Wholesaling, compute the segment margin and average assets for the year.
2. Based on segment income and average assets, compute the actual profit margin, asset turnover, and ROI.
3. Evaluate the ROI performance of the Canadian Division.
4. Using your answers from Question 2, compute the Canadian Division's residual income using segment margin.
5. Compute the EVA of the Canadian Division using net income. Why are EVA and RI levels different?
6. Based on the data given in the problem, discuss why ROI, EVA and RI may be inappropriate measures of performance for the Canadian Division.

Solution to Demonstration Problem

1.

Sales	$12,000,000
Variable costs	(5,000,000)
Direct fixed costs	(6,280,000)
Segment margin	$ 720,000

Average assets = ($4,800,000 + $7,200,000) ÷ 2 = $ 6,000,000

2. Profit margin = $\dfrac{\$720{,}000}{\$12{,}000{,}000} = 6\%$

   Asset turnover = $\dfrac{\$12{,}000{,}000}{\$6{,}000{,}000} = 2$

   ROI = 6% × 2 = 12%

3. The target ROI for the division was 8% × 1.8 = 14.4%. The division generated an ROI of only 12%. Thus, the division did not achieve its target rate of return. The poor performance resulted from the division's failure to achieve the target profit margin. Even though the asset turnover target was exceeded, the ROI fell below the target level because the profit margin was 2% below its target level.

4. RI = $720,000 − (0.10 × $6,000,000)
      = $720,000 − $600,000 = $120,000

5. After-tax income = Segment margin − Taxes
      = $720,000 − ($720,000 × 0.25) = $540,000
   EVA = $540,000 − (0.10 × $11,000,000) = $(560,000)

   EVA and RI differ for two reasons. First, RI is based on segment margin, rather than after-tax income; second, RI is based on the book value of investment while EVA is based on the market value of investment.

6. As discussed in the chapter, ROI, RI, and EVA are measures of short-term performance. These measures may be particularly inappropriate for divisions that have long-term missions, such as growth. In this case, the relatively large growth in assets of the Canadian Division from the beginning to the end of the period may indicate that this division is oriented to growth. If so, the ROI and RI measures will provide an incentive contrary to the growth mission.

End-of-Chapter Materials

SELF-TEST QUESTIONS

(SOLUTIONS APPEAR AT THE END OF THE CHAPTER.)

1. Organizations have multiple performance measures for all the following reasons except
   a. They have a variety of goals and objectives
   b. They are big
   c. Their products have life cycles
   d. Financial performance measures are not comprehensive

2. The balanced scorecard is best described as
   a. A performance measurement conceptualization that translates an organization's strategy into clear objectives, measures, targets, and initiatives organized by the four perspectives.
   b. An intracompany charge for goods or services that has been through a process of negotiations between the selling and purchasing unit managers.
   c. The set of basic assumptions about the organization, its goals, and its business practices; describes an organization's norms in internal and external, as well as formal and informal, transactions.
   d. A listing of all tasks necessary to make a unit of product or perform a service and the time allowed for each operation

3. Which is the definition of return on investment?
   a. Assets invested ÷ Income
   b. Profit margin ÷ Asset turnover
   c. Asset turnover ÷ Profit margin
   d. Income ÷ Assets invested

4. The Du Pont model is calculated with
   a. Assets invested ÷ Income
   b. Profit margin × Asset turnover
   c. Asset turnover ÷ Profit margin
   d. Income ÷ Assets invested

5. Residual income is calculated with
   a. After-tax income – (Cost of capital % × Capital invested)
   b. Income – (Cost of capital % × Asset base)
   c. Income – (Cost of capital % × Capital invested)
   d. Income – (Target rate × Asset base)

6. Which is a limitation of ROI and RI?
   a. Income can be manipulated on a short-run basis by accelerating or delaying the recognition of income and expenses
   b. Accrual-based income reflects neither the cash flow pattern nor the time value of money, and these performance dimensions are generally important
   c. Some asset investment values are difficult to measure or assign to investment centres, while some other values, such as research and development, are not capitalized
   d. All of the above

7. Which of the following is out of sequence when going from the top to the bottom of the performance pyramid?
   a. Vision
   b. Operations
   c. Market measures, financial measures
   d. Customer satisfaction, flexibility, productivity

8. Throughput is the product of which of the following?
   a. Manufacturing cycle efficiency, process productivity, and process quality yield
   b. Manufacturing cycle efficiency, process productivity
   c. Process productivity, process quality yield
   d. Manufacturing cycle efficiency, process quality yield

9. Of the following cost of quality measures, which relates to appraisal?
   a. Prevention ÷ Total cost of quality
   b. Number of inspections
   c. Number of pieces rejected
   d. Number of customer complaints

10. Which one of the following is not a traditional performance measure?
    a. Purchase price variance
    b. Machine utilization percentage
    c. Customer satisfaction scores
    d. Responsibility centre reporting

QUESTIONS

1. What basic rules should be observed in selecting benchmarks for evaluating managers' performance?

2. Should performance measures be financial, nonfinancial, or both? Justify your answer.

3. What message is conveyed by the phrase "managers devote their attention to activities that get measured"?

4. What are the two primary financial requirements for the success of a profit or investment centre? Why are these important?

5. What is the major difference between a profit centre and an investment centre? How does this difference create a need for different financial performance measures in these two types of centres?

6. Discuss the most appropriate definition of the term "assets invested" in computing return on investment.

7. What is residual income and how is it used to measure divisional performance? How is it similar to and different from the return on investment measure?

8. Describe the circumstances in which use of ROI would likely create a suboptimization problem. Under what circumstances would use of this measure be less likely to create a suboptimization problem?

9. How is economic value added computed? Why is the measure potentially superior to residual income?

10. Modular Office Systems manufactures movable partitions for commercial offices. Recently, the company has become much more concerned about reducing the number of flaws in its completed products. Identify some performance measures that the company could use to monitor the effectiveness of its efforts to improve product quality.

11. What is captured by a throughput measure? Why is throughput defined on the basis of goods sold rather than goods produced?

12. Why is prevention the only value-added cost of quality category?

13. How can activity-based costing concepts be used in designing performance measures?

14. Why is the design of performance measures a more complex task in multinational companies than in single-country operations?

15. To be effective, why must firms link the compensation system to the performance measurement structure?

16. Why is it desirable to have chief executives (as well as other managers) own stock in their companies?

17. What special considerations bear on designing pay plans for expatriates?

EXERCISES

1. (LO 1, 2, 3) Match the numbered definitions with the lettered terms. Definitions may be used more than once or not at all.

a. Throughput	1. A parent-company worker in a foreign subsidiary
b. Economic value added	2. A measure of asset productivity
c. Synchronous management	3. A method of computing ROI as the product of two separate ratios
d. Residual income	4 All endeavours that help an organization achieve its goal
e. Compensation strategy	5 After-tax profits minus a charge for cost of invested capital
f. Expatriate	6. Profits that exceed a normal return on assets
g. Du Pont model	7. A ratio of income to sales
h. Asset turnover	8. A ratio of good units to total units
i. Profit margin	9. A plan for determining the role of compensation in an organization
j. Process quality yield	10. The total good output completed and sold within an operating period

2. (LO 2) Johnson Wholesale Supply of Newmarket comprises three autonomous divisions. Data for each division for the year 2003 follow:

Division	1	2	3
Segment income	$20,000	$ 225,000	$ 150,000
Asset investment	80,000	1,500,000	1,500,000

Compute the return on investment in each division.

3. (LO 2) The managers of Hong Kong Industries are evaluating the use of ROI to measure performance. The managers have gathered the following information for their most recent operating period.

Average assets invested	$ 3,600,000
Revenues	14,400,000
Expenses	13,004,000

Required:
a. Calculate profit margin.
b. Calculate asset turnover.
c. Calculate return on investment using your answers to parts (a) and (b).

4   (LO 2) For the most recent fiscal year, the Pullman Division of Modern Luggage generated an asset turnover ratio of 5 and a profit margin (as measured by the segment margin) ratio of 4% on sales of $4,000,000.
Required:
Compute:
a. Average assets employed by Pullman Division
b. Segment margin
c. ROI

5. (LO 2) Your managerial accounting class has been assigned a case, but the professor has provided only partial information. You have been told that a division of a company has an ROI of 12.5%, average total assets of $3,400,000, and total direct expenses of $1,275,000.

Required:

You have been asked to do the following:
a. Determine segment income.
b. Determine total revenues.
c. Determine asset turnover.
d. Determine profit margin.
e. Prove that ROI is 12.5% from the amounts calculated in parts (a) to (d).

6. (LO 2) Leduc Law, Inc., has a target rate of return of 14% for its Criminal Law Division. For 2005, the Criminal Law Division generated gross fees of $10,000,000 on average assets of $5,000,000. The Criminal Law Division's variable costs were 35% of sales and fixed costs were $3,750,000.

Required:

For 2005, compute the Division's
a. Residual income
b. Profit margin
c. Asset turnover
d. Return on investment

7. (LO 2) North and South Divisions of Western Financial Corp. reported the following data for 2005 (in thousands):

	North Division	**South Division**
Segment income	$ 30,000	$ 68,000
Investment	180,000	290,000

Required:
a. Assuming the firm charges each division 12% of the capital invested, determine the residual income for each division.
b. Based on the preceding information, which division is more successful? Explain.

8. (LO 2) Sarnia Chemical comprises two divisions. Following is some financial information about each of these divisions.

	Industrial Products	**Consumer Products**
Sales	$4,800,000	$ 8,400,000
Total variable cost	1,200,000	5,460,000
Total fixed cost	2,800,000	1,250,000
Average assets invested	4,000,000	10,000,000

Required:
a. What is each division's residual income if the company has established a 14% target rate of return on invested assets?
b. Which division is more successful? Explain.
c. What would be each division's residual income if its sales increased by 10% and no other changes occurred? Which division would be more successful if such a sales change occurred? Explain.
d. Explain why the answers to parts (b) and (c) differed or did not differ.

9. (LO 3) Chancellor Environmental Services Co. relies on the EVA measure to evaluate the performance of certain segment managers. The target rate of return on invested capital for all segments is 16%. One subsidiary, Water Systems, generated after-tax income of $1,800,000 for the year just ended. For the same period, the invested capital in the subsidiary was $12,000,000.

Required:

Compute the EVA of Water Systems.

10. (LO 3) Stealth Technology Corporation has a required rate of return of 12% on invested capital. The firm's Laser Division generated an EVA of $4,000,000 last year. The amount of capital invested in Laser Division is $38,000,000.
    Required:
    a. How much after-tax income was generated by Laser Division last year?
    b. As the controller of Stealth Technology Corporation, how could you determine the level of capital investment for a particular division?

11. (LO 3) Mary Jenks is a division manager of Nova Scotia Pneumatic. She is presently evaluating a potential new investment that has the following characteristics:

Capital investment required	$8,000,000

    Net annual increase in after-tax divisional income:

Year 1	800,000
Year 2	800,000
Year 3	1,160,000
Year 4	2,900,000
Year 5	2,700,000

    Ms. Jenks is evaluated and compensated based on the amount of EVA her division generates. More precisely, she receives an annual salary of $350,000 plus a bonus equal to 12% of divisional EVA. Nova Scotia Pneumatic has a required rate of return of 13%.
    a. Compute the effect of the new investment on the level of divisional EVA for years 1 through 5.
    b. Determine the effect of the new project on Ms. Jenks's compensation for each of the five years.
    c. Based on your computations in part (b), will Ms. Jenks want to invest in the new project? Explain.
    d. As the CEO of Nova Scotia Pneumatic, would you prefer that Ms. Jenks invest or not invest in the project?
    e. What nonfinancial performance measures could be used to supplement EVA as a performance measure that would serve to make Ms. Jenks more long-term oriented?

12. (LO 4) The Waterloo Wave is a chain of microbreweries. The company evaluates its store managers on the basis of both financial and nonfinancial performance measures. One of the nonfinancial measures used is throughput. The following data pertain to the company's store in Moncton. The unit of measurement is litres.

Units started into production	360,000
Total good units completed	270,000
Total hours of value-added processing time	180,000
Total hours	240,000

    Required:
    a. What was the manufacturing cycle efficiency?
    b. What was the process productivity of the store?
    c. What was the process quality yield of the store?
    d. What was the total throughput per hour?
    e. As the production manager of the Waterloo Wave, how could you use the information on the component ratios of throughput to increase performance?

13. (LO 4) For each of the following nonfinancial performance measures, indicate whether the measure captures performance in terms of quality (Q), customer service (CS), resource management (RM), or flexibility (F), and discuss the rationale for your answer.
    a. First-time-through rejection rate
    b. Percent on-time shipments
    c. Manufacturing cycle time
    d. Percent good output
    e. Percent of units meeting design tolerance
    f. Output per labour dollar
    g. Number of crisis calls
    h. Changeover time
    i. Machine downtime
    j. Supplier rejects

14. (LO 4) For the past three years, the highest divisional ROI within Lumar Corporation has been generated by the Winch Division, a very high-tech manufacturing division. The segment income and ROI for each year appear below. Lumar Corporation has specified a growth mission for the Winch Division.

	2004	2005	2006
Segment income (thousands)	$200,000	$195,000	$193,500
ROI	20%	23%	27%

Required:
a. Why do you think the Winch Division has been so successful as measured by its ROI?
b. As controller of Lumar Corporation, what change or changes would you recommend to control the continued escalation in the ROI?
c. Assume that Lumar Corporation operates in a very competitive industry and its strategy is based on maintaining market share by delivering the best customer service in the industry. What nonfinancial performance measures could be used to capture Lumar's performance?

15. (LO 2) Explain how each of the following items will affect the asset turnover ratio of a corporate division if asset amounts are determined by their net book values.
a. A new labour contract is negotiated that reduces labour costs by 10%.
b. Unused assets are carried on the books. These assets could be sold.
c. Obsolete inventory is carried on the books.
d. Uncollectible accounts receivable are carried on the books.
e. The rate of depreciation on plant and equipment is increased.
f. Fixed costs allocated to the division drop by 4%.

16. (LO 4) Managers must be able to deliver both positive and negative feedback to employees. The method of delivering such feedback is often as important as the message in terms of its impact on the affected employee. Discuss how, as a manager, you would deliver critical comments to an employee whose performance is unsatisfactory. How would you deliver feedback to an employee whose performance is superlative?

17. (LO 1 to 6) You have recently been appointed as the chief executive officer (CEO) of a medium-sized, decentralized, national, multiproduct manufacturing and marketing corporation, which employs over 6,000 people. Although revenues have remained constant over the last five years, net income has decreased by over 50% in this period. As a result of this decline in profitability, the share price has decreased 60%.

Required:
Identify five management accounting techniques or tools that you will instruct your staff to investigate. For each technique or tool identified, explain what specific benefits you hope to realize. Note that to state that profitability will improve is too general; rather you should explain how the technique leads to this improvement. Be thoughtful and practical in your discussions and be mindful of the type of company of which you are CEO.

Reprinted from *Management Accounting examinations* published by the Certified General Accountants Association of Canada © CGA-Canada, 1999, used by permission.

PROBLEMS

1. (LO 4, 6) Western Division of the Raymond Fabrics Co. produces and markets floor covering products to wholesalers in British Columbia, Alberta, Saskatchewan, and Manitoba. The manager of Western Division is Kara Forrester. Raymond Fabrics evaluates all of its division managers on the basis of a comparison of budgeted profit to actual profit achieved. The profit measure used is pretax income. For 2005, the budgeted income for Raymond Fabrics is as shown next.

Sales	$12,000,000
Variable costs	(8,400,000)
Contribution margin	$ 3,600,000
Fixed costs	(2,400,000)
Segment income	$ 1,200,000

At the end of 2005, the actual results for Western Division were determined. Those results follow.

Sales	$13,000,000
Variable costs	(9,750,000)
Contribution margin	$ 3,250,000
Fixed costs	(2,410,000)
Segment income	$ 840,000

Required:

a. Assume that you are the controller of Raymond Fabrics. Based on the preceding information, evaluate the performance of the Western Division. What was the principal reason for the poor profit performance?

b. Explain how complete income statements provide a better basis to evaluate the profit performance of a manager than mere comparisons of the bottom lines of the budgeted and actual income statements.

c. Given your answer to part (a), describe some nonfinancial performance measures that could be used by the manager of the Western Division in a strategy to improve divisional profit performance in the next year.

2. (LO 2) Complete Solutions Inc. manufactures various production equipment. Corporate management has examined industry-level data and determined the following industry norms for producers of material handling systems:

Asset turnover	1.6 times
Profit margin	8%

The actual 2005 results for the company's Material Handling Division are summarized below:

Total assets at year-end 2004	$ 9,600,000
Total assets at year-end 2005	12,800,000
Sales	13,440,000
Operating expenses	12,499,200

Required:

a. For 2005, how did the Material Handling Division perform relative to industry norms?

b. As the divisional manager of Material Handling, how would you use the comparison in part (a) to improve performance in the division?

3. (LO 2) Johnson, First Star, and Nolan Bay are three companies that operate in the retail clothing industry. Some information on each of these companies for 2005 follows:

	Johnson	First Star	Nolan Bay
Average total assets	$ 6,300,000	$ 5,400,000	$ 7,200,000
Revenues	12,600,000	16,200,000	14,400,000
Expenses	11,340,000	15,228,000	12,420,000

Required:

a. For each company, calculate profit margin, asset turnover, and return on investment.

b. As an investment analyst, you are going to recommend that stock in one of these companies be purchased by your clients. Which of these companies would you recommend? Why?

c. Do the ratios indicate how any of the companies could improve their performance? How?

4. (LO 2) The 2005 income statement for the Aurora Division of Industrial Services Corp. follows.

Sales	$ 3,200,000
Variable expenses	(1,600,000)
Contribution margin	$ 1,600,000
Fixed expenses	(800,000)
Segment income	$ 800,000

Assets at the beginning of 2005 for Aurora Division were $3,600,000. Because of various capital investments during the year, the division ended 2005 with $4,400,000 of assets. Overall, Industrial Services Corp. experienced a 15% return on investment for 2005. It is company policy to award year-end bonuses to the managers whose divisions show the highest ROIs.

The chief operating officer of Aurora is investigating a new product line for the division. The new line is expected to show the following approximate annual results: sales, $400,000; variable expenses, $200,000; and fixed expenses, $100,000. The product line would require a $620,000 average first-year investment in plant assets.

Required:

a.   What was Aurora's 2005 ROI?

b.   What is the expected ROI on the new product line?

c.   If Aurora had invested in the new product line in 2005 and the expected results had occurred, what would have been the division's ROI?

d.   Is the Aurora Division manager likely to want to add the new product line? Would the president of Industrial Services Corp. want Aurora to add the new product line? Discuss the rationale of each of the individuals.

5. (LO 2) The numbers (1–9) in the following table identify missing data for three divisions of Big Creek Industries.

	Package Division	Transport Division	Storage Division
Sales	$2,000,000	$16,000,000	$8,000,000
Segment income	$ 400,000	(4)	$1,000,000
Profit margin	(1)	15%	(7)
Asset turnover	(2)	1.4	(8)
Average assets	(3)	(5)	$4,000,000
Return on investment	10%	(6)	(9)

Required:

a.   Determine the values for each of the missing items.

b.   Identify the area where each division's performance is weakest and strongest relative to the other divisions.

6. (LO 2) Stolzer Wholesaling sells a broad line of clothing to specialty retail and department stores. For 2005, the company's Canadian Division had the following performance targets:

Asset turnover	1.5 times
Profit margin	8%

Actual information concerning the performance of the Canadian Division in 2005 follows:

Total assets at year-end 2004	$2,400,000
Total assets at year-end 2005	3,600,000
Sales for 2005	6,000,000
Operating expenses for 2005	5,640,000

Required:

a.   For 2005, what was the Canadian Division's target objective for ROI? Show calculations.

b.   For 2005, did the Canadian Division achieve its target objectives for ROI, asset turnover, and profit margin?

c.   Where, as indicated by the performance measures, are the areas that are most in need of improved performance?

d.   If the company has an overall target return of 13%, what was the Canadian Division's residual income for 2005?

7. (LO 2, 5) The following are transactions affecting a specific division within a multiple-division company. Indicate whether each described transaction would increase (IN),

decrease (D), have no effect (N) on, or have an indeterminate effect (I) on each of the following measures: asset turnover, profit margin, ROI, and RI for the present fiscal year. Each transaction is independent.

Required:

a. The division writes down an inventory of obsolete finished goods through the cost of goods sold expense account. The journal entry is

Cost of Goods Sold	40,000	
Finished Goods Inventory		40,000

b. A special overseas order is accepted. The sales price for this order is well below the normal sales price but is sufficient to cover all costs traceable to this order.

c. A piece of equipment is sold for $70,000. The equipment's original cost was $400,000. At the time of sale, the book value of the equipment was $60,000. The sale of the equipment has no effect on product sales.

d. The division fires its research and development manager. The manager will not be replaced during the current fiscal year.

e. The company raises its target rate of return for this division from 12% to 14%.

f. At mid-year, the divisional manager decides to increase scheduled annual production by 2,000 units. This decision has no effect on scheduled sales.

g. Also at mid-year, the division manager spends an additional $150,000 on advertising. Sales immediately increase.

h. The divisional manager replaces a labour-intensive operation with machine technology. This action has no effect on sales, but total annual expenses of the operation are expected to decline by 12%.

8. (LO 2) The Canadian Yacht Company evaluates the performance of its two division managers using an ROI formula. For the forthcoming period, divisional estimates of relevant measures are:

	Pleasure	Commercial	Total Company
Sales	$12,000,000	$48,000,000	$60,000,000
Expenses	10,800,000	42,000,000	52,800,000
Divisional assets	10,000,000	30,000,000	40,000,000

The managers of both operating divisions have the authority to make decisions regarding new investments. The manager of Pleasure Crafts is contemplating an investment in an additional asset that would generate an ROI of 14%, and the manager of Commercial Crafts is considering an investment in an additional asset that would generate an ROI of 18%.

Required:

a. Compute the projected ROI for each division disregarding the contemplated new investments.

b. Based on your answer in part (a), which of the managers is likely to actually invest in the asset under consideration?

c. Are the outcomes of the investment decisions in part (b) likely to be consistent with overall corporate goals? Explain.

d. If the company evaluated the division managers' performances using a residual income measure with a target return of 17%, would the outcomes of the investment decisions be different from those described in part (b)? Explain.

9. (LO 3) You are a division manager of Luxwood Design Co. Your performance as a division manager is evaluated primarily on one measure: after-tax divisional segment income less the cost of capital invested in divisional assets. For existing operations in your division, projections for 2006 follow:

Sales	$ 40,000,000
Expenses	(35,000,000)
Segment income	$ 5,000,000
Taxes	(1,500,000)
After-tax segment income	$ 3,500,000

The invested capital of the division is $25,000,000, the required return on capital is 12%, and the tax rate is 30%.

At this moment, you are evaluating an investment in a new product line that would, according to your projections, increase 2006 pretax segment income by $400,000. The cost of the investment has not yet been determined.

Required:

a.   Ignoring the new investment, what is your projected EVA for 2006?

b.   In light of your answer in part (a), what is the maximum amount that you would be willing to invest in the new product line?

c.   Assuming the new product line would require an investment of $1,100,000, what would be the revised projected EVA for your division in 2006 if the investment were made?

10. (LO 4) Bangor Spool Co. has historically evaluated divisional performance exclusively on financial measures. Top managers have become increasingly concerned with this approach to performance evaluation and are now actively seeking alternative measures. Specifically, they wish to focus on activities that generate value for customers. One promising measure is throughput. To experiment with the annual throughput measure, management has gathered the following historical information on one of its larger operating divisions:

Units started into production	200,000
Total good units completed	130,000
Total hours of value-added processing time	80,000
Total hours	120,000

Required:

a.   What is the manufacturing cycle efficiency?

b.   What is the process productivity of the division?

c.   What is the process quality yield of the division?

d.   Based on your answers to parts (a), (b), and (c), what is the total throughput per hour?

e.   Which of the previous measures—part (a), (b), or (c)—reflects the possible existence of a production bottleneck? Why?

f.   Which of the previous measures—part (a), (b), or (c)—reflects potentially poor quality in the production process as measured by the number of defective units? Why?

11. (LO 2) Fruta Division, one of the investment centres of Wholesale Fruits Inc., had net operating income in 2004 of $360,000. The average assets employed by Fruta during 2004 were $1,800,000. In January of 2005, the division manager of the Fruta Division retired after 15 years to start a bookkeeping business. The chief executive officer (CEO) of Wholesale Fruits appointed you as the new division manager of Fruta. After assuming your new position, you discovered that most of Fruta's manufacturing equipment needed to be replaced. You also found out that at the end of 2004, the previous division manager had disposed of some of the plant and equipment. In order to increase efficiency, you made a large investment to replace the obsolete equipment and to update the facilities. In 2005, on a total of $4,000,000 of average assets employed, the division reported net operating income of $735,000.

The CEO of Wholesale Fruits uses return on investment (ROI) to evaluate the performance of his division managers. He feels that your performance in running Fruta is not as good as the previous manager's since the 2005 ROI is much lower than it was in 2004.

Required:

a.   Calculate the ROI for Fruta in 2004 and 2005.

b.   You feel quite strongly that you have done a much better job than the previous manager and suggest to the CEO that he should consider residual income (RI) as an alternative performance measure. Wholesale Fruits' minimum required rate of return is 16%. Calculate the RI for Fruta in 2004 and 2005. If RI were used by the CEO, whose performance would be better?

c.   Explain and justify the lower ROI in 2005 compared to that in 2004.

d.   You find out that in 2004 the previous manager was presented with an investment opportunity that would have required a $500,000 investment and that would have provided net operating income of $90,000. Explain fully why the previous manager refused to undertake this investment.

e.   You had convinced the CEO that RI is a better performance measure than ROI. However, the CEO recently found out that one of your competitors had a net operating income of $5,000,000 on a total of $25,000,000 in average assets employed during 2005. As a result, the CEO is still unhappy with your 2005 performance. Using the same minimum required rate of return as Wholesale Fruits, calculate the RI of this competitor. How are you going to respond to the CEO's criticisms?

Reprinted from *Management Accounting examinations* published by the Certified General Accountants Association of Canada © CGA-Canada, 1999, used by permission.

CASES

1. Raddington Industries produces tool and die machinery for manufacturers. The company expanded vertically in 2001 by acquiring one of its suppliers of alloy steel plates, Reigis Steel Company. In order to manage the two separate businesses, the operations of Reigis are reported separately as an investment centre.

Raddington monitors its divisions on the basis of both unit contribution and return on average investment (ROI), with investment defined as average operating assets employed. Management bonuses are determined based on ROI. All investments in operating assets are expected to earn a minimum return of 11% before income taxes.

Reigis's cost of goods sold is considered to be entirely variable, while the division's administrative expenses are not dependent on volume. Selling expenses are a mixed cost with 40% attributed to sales volume. Reigis's ROI has ranged from 11.8% to 14.7% since 2001. During the fiscal year ended November 30, 2005, Reigis contemplated a capital acquisition with an estimated ROI of 11.5%; however, division management decided that the investment would decrease Reigis's overall ROI.

The 2005 operating statement for Reigis follows. The division's operating assets employed were $15,750,000 at November 30, 2005, a 5% increase over the 2004 yearend balance.

Reigis Steel Division
Operating Statement
For the Year Ended November 30, 2005
($000 Omitted)

Sales revenue		$ 25,000
Less expenses:		
Cost of goods sold	$16,500	
Administrative expenses	3,955	
Selling expenses	2,700	(23,155)
Operating income before taxes		$ 1,845

Required:
a.   Calculate the unit contribution for Reigis Steel Division if 1,484,000 units were produced and sold during the year ended November 30, 2005.
b.   Calculate the following performance measures for 2005 for the Reigis Steel Division:
   i.   Pretax return on average investment in operating assets employed (ROI)
   ii. Residual income calculated on the basis of average operating assets employed
c.   Explain why the management of the Reigis Steel Division would have been more likely to accept the contemplated capital acquisition if residual income rather than ROI was used as a performance measure.
d.   The Reigis Steel Division is a separate investment centre within Raddington Industries. Identify several items that Reigis should control if it is to be evaluated fairly by either the ROI or residual income performance measure.

(CMA)

2. Northstar Offroad Co. (NOC), a subsidiary of Allston Automotive, manufactures go-carts and other recreational vehicles. Family recreational centres that feature go-cart tracks, miniature golf, batting cages, and arcades have increased in popularity. As a result, NOC has been receiving some pressure from Allston Automotive top management to diversify into some of these other recreational areas. Recreational Leasing Inc. (RLI), one of the largest firms that leases arcade games to family recreation centres, is looking for a friendly buyer. Allston Automotive management believes that RLI's assets could be acquired for an investment of $3.2 million and has strongly urged Bill Grieco, division manager of NOC, to consider acquiring RLI.

Grieco has reviewed RLI's financial statements with his controller, Marie Donnelly, and they believe that the acquisition may not be in NOC's best interests. "If we decide not to do this, the Allston Automotive people are not going to be happy," said Grieco. "If we could convince them to base our bonuses on something other than return on investment, maybe this acquisition would look more attractive. How would we do if the bonuses were based on residual income using the company's 15% cost of capital?"

Allston Automotive has traditionally evaluated all of its divisions on the basis of return on investment, which is defined as the ratio of operating income to total assets; the desired rate of return for each is 20%. The management team of any division reporting an annual increase in the return on investment is automatically eligible for a bonus. The management of divisions reporting a decline in the return on investment must provide convincing explanations for the decline to be eligible for a bonus, and this bonus is limited to 50% of the average bonus paid to divisions reporting an increase.

Presented below are condensed financial statements for both NOC and RLI for the fiscal year ended May 31, 2005.

	NOC	RLI
Sales revenue	$10,500,000	
Leasing revenue		$2,800,000
Variable expenses	(7,000,000)	(1,000,000)
Fixed expenses	(1,500,000)	(1,200,000)
Operating income	$2,000,0000	$ 600,000
Current assets	$ 2,300,000	$1,900,000
Long-term assets	5,700,000	1,100,000
Total assets	$ 8,000,000	$3,000,000
Current liabilities	$ 1,400,000	$ 850,000
Long-term liabilities	3,800,000	1,200,000
Shareholders' equity	2,800,000	950,000
Total liabilities and shareholders' equity	$ 8,000,000	$3,000,000

Required:

a.   Under the present bonus system, how would the acquisition of RLI affect Grieco's bonus expectations?

b.   If Grieco's suggestion to use residual income as the evaluation criterion is accepted, how would acquisition of RLI affect Grieco's bonus expectations?

c.   Given the present bonus arrangement, is it fair for Allston Automotive management to expect Grieco to acquire RLI?

d.   Is the present bonus system consistent with Allston Automotive's goal of expansion of NOC into new recreational products?

3. Major Currency, the controller of Altoma Meat Products, has become increasingly disillusioned with the company's system of evaluating the performance of profit centres and their managers. The present system focuses on a comparison of budgeted to actual income from operations. Major's concern with the current system is the ease with which the measured income from operations can be manipulated by profit centre managers. The basic business of Altoma Meat Products consists of purchasing live hogs and cattle, slaughtering the animals, and then selling the various meat products and by-products to regional wholesalers and large retail chains. Most sales are made on credit, and all live animals are purchased for cash. The profit centres consist of geographical segments of Altoma Meat Products, and all profit centre segments conduct

both production and sales activities within their geographical territories. Following is a typical quarterly income statement for a profit centre, which appears in the responsibility report for the profit centre:

Sales	$ 5,000,000
Cost of goods sold	(3,000,000)
Gross profit	$ 2,000,000
Selling and administrative expenses	(1,500,000)
Income from operations	$ 500,000

Major has suggested to top management that the company replace the accrual income evaluation measure *income from operations* with a measure called *cash flow from operations*. He says that this measure will be less susceptible to manipulation by profit centre managers. To defend his position, he compiles a cash flow income statement for the same profit centre:

Cash receipts from customers	$ 4,400,000
Cash payments for production labour, livestock, and overhead	(3,200,000)
Cash payments for selling and administrative activities	(800,000)
Cash flow from operations	$ 400,000

Required:

a. If Major is correct about profit centre managers' manipulating the income measure, where are manipulations likely taking place?

b. Is the proposed cash flow measure less subject to manipulation than the income measure? Explain.

c. Could manipulation be reduced if both cash flow and income measures were utilized? Explain.

d. Do the cash and income measures reveal different information about profit centre performance? Explain.

e. Could the existing income statement be used more effectively in evaluating performance? Explain.

4. Western Chemical Group. is a multinational firm that markets a variety of chemicals for industrial uses. One of the many autonomous divisions is the North America Petro-Chemical Division (NAPCD). The manager of NAPCD, Karyn Kravitz, was recently overheard discussing a vexing problem with her controller, William Michaels. The topic of discussion was whether the division should replace its existing chemical-handling equipment with newer technology that is safer, more efficient, and cheaper to operate.

According to an analysis by Mr. Michaels, the cost savings over the life of the new technology would pay for the initial cost of the technology several times over. However, Ms. Kravitz remained reluctant to invest. Her most fundamental concern involved the disposition of the old processing equipment. Because the existing equipment has been in use for only two years, it has a very high book value relative to its current market value. Ms. Kravitz noted that if the new technology were not purchased, the division would expect a segment income of $4 million for the year. However, if the new technology were purchased, the old equipment would have to be sold, and the division could probably sell it for only $1.2 million. This equipment had an original cost of $8 million, and $1.5 million in depreciation has been recorded. Thus, a book loss of $5.3 million ($6.5 million – $1.2 million) would be recorded on the sale.

Ms. Kravitz' boss, Jim Heitz, is the president of the Western Chemical Group, and his compensation is based almost exclusively on the amount of ROI generated by his group, which includes NAPCD. After thoroughly analyzing the facts, Ms. Kravitz concluded, "The people in the Western Chemical Group will swallow their dentures if we book a $5.3 million loss."

Required:

a. Why is Ms. Kravitz concerned about the book loss on disposal of the old technology in her division?

b. What weaknesses in Western Chemical Group's performance pay plan are apparently causing Ms. Kravitz to avoid an investment that meets all of the normal criteria for acceptability (ignoring the ROI effect)?

ETHICS AND QUALITY DISCUSSIONS

1. "A typical executive is in his mid-40s, frequently travels on business, says he values self-respect, and is very likely to commit financial fraud. That, anyway, is the conclusion of four business school professors, whose study on fraud was published in a recent issue of the *Journal of Business Ethics*.

    After getting nearly 400 people (more than 85 percent of them men) over the past seven years to play the role of a fictional executive named Todd Folger, the professors found that 47 percent of the top executives, 41 percent of the controllers, and 76 percent of the graduate-level business students surveyed were willing to commit fraud by understating write-offs that cut into their companies' profits."

    (Source: Dawn Blalock, "Study Shows Many Execs Are Quick to Write Off Ethics," *The Wall Street Journal*, March 16, 1996, pp. C1, C13.)
    Required:
    a. What creates the incentive for managers to understate write-offs?
    b. How does the use of accounting as a performance measurement system of managers affect the objectivity of accounting information?
    c. What are the ethical obligations of accountants in dealing with managers who desire to manipulate accounting information for their personal benefit?

2. In a survey published in 1990, 649 managers responded to a questionnaire and provided their opinion as to the ethical acceptability of manipulating accounting earnings to achieve higher managerial compensation. One of the questions dealt with the acceptability of changing a sales practice to pull some of next year's sales into the current year so that reported current earnings can be pushed up. The results of the survey indicated that about 43% of the respondents felt this practice was ethically acceptable, 44% felt the practice was ethically questionable, and 13% felt the practice was ethically unacceptable.

    Other results of the survey indicate that the managers considered large manipulations more unethical than small manipulations and income-increasing manipulations more ethically unacceptable than income-decreasing manipulations.

    (Source: Based on William J. Bruns and Kenneth A. Merchant, "The Dangerous Morality of Managing Earnings," *Management Accounting*, August 1990, pp. 22–25.)
    Required:
    a. If managers can manipulate earnings to effect changes in their pay, is this a weakness in the pay-for-performance plan? Explain.
    b. In your view, does the materiality of a manipulation partly determine the extent to which the manipulation is ethically acceptable?
    c. Describe any circumstances in which you believe manipulation would be ethically acceptable and provide justification for your decision.

COMMUNICATIONS ACTIVITIES

1. "The work force of many Canadian organizations, particularly those located in the metropolitan areas, is often jokingly referred to as "the United Nations," since they employ so many new Canadians. Consequently, people trained in Canada and people trained overseas often work side-by-side on project teams. This diversity of experience and thoughts can be double-edged sword.... Diversity brings a wider range of potential solutions to complex technical and/or organizational problems ..."

    (Source: Lionel Laroche, "Teaming Up," *CMA Magazine*, April 2001, pp. 22–25.)
    Required:
    Discuss the advantages of diverse groups in the workplace.

2. In order to survive, organizations must innovate. Peter Drucker says, "How much of innovation is inspiration, and how much is hard work? If it's mainly the former, then the management's role is limited: Hire the right people, and get out of the way. If it's the latter, management must play a more vigorous role: Establish the right roles and processes, set clear goals and relevant measures, and review progress at every level."

(Source: Peter Drucker, "The Discipline of Innovation," *Harvard Business Review*, August 2002, pp. 95–102. [Reprinted from 1985.])

Required:

Discuss how innovation would be measured and rewarded for both (1) innovation as inspiration and (2) innovation as managed.

PROJECTS

1. The textbook discusses the importance of delivering both positive and negative feedback to employees. The method of delivering such feedback is often as important as the nature of the feedback in terms of its impact on the affected employee. Invite a high-level manager from a local organization to address your class on methods he uses to deliver feedback to employees. Use the methods as a basis for class discussion about desired and undesirable ways to give feedback.

2. Develop teams of three or four students to investigate the quality control practices at a local service organization. In preparing for the field trips, teams should read "Quality Isn't Just for Widgets," by Michael Arndt, in *Business Week*, July 22, 2002, pp. 72–73. Arndt says that the "Six Sigma" approach to quality control started with Motorola's manufacturing area, but now it is spreading to service organizations and the service parts of manufacturing firms. Be sure to ask,
   - How do you ensure that service quality is maintained and improved upon?
   - Provide examples of your quality improvement practices.
   - What measures do you use for measuring quality?
   - Do your quality improvement practices lead to reduced need for personnel, capital spending, inventory, or overhead—and if so, how?

   Prepare a three- or four-page report on your field trip.

3. Five critical dimensions need to be in place for performance measurement to be effective, according to Omar Aguilar of Gunn Partners, quoted in Kathy Williams, "New Developments in Performance Measurement," *Strategic Finance*, April 2002, pp. 19–22:
   - *Strategic planning.* Create a strategic business plan and objectives that can be cascaded down through the organization and help every division, unit, department, and individual set and pursue the right priorities.
   - *Performance measurement.* Establish key metrics that tell management at every level whether the goals of the plan are being realized and, if not, where and by what degree they are falling short.
   - *Integrated business planning.* Design and integrate processes—operational planning, budgeting, and forecasting—that create value and align efforts rather than simply police and keep score.
   - *Management reporting.* Provide concise, timely information that helps management see what needs to be done and how to do it.
   - *Organizational culture and reward systems.* Create a culture that energizes employees and inspires them to work together to achieve the company's strategic objectives and develop systems that reward them for their success.

   Required:

   In groups of three or four, select a significant performance measure for a major well-known firm, and then explain in a four- or five-page paper how these five points relate to the performance measure.

USING THE INTERNET

1. BCE, previously known as Bell Canada, has been a long-term supplier of telephone services in central Canada. In recent years, it made a number of investments in an attempt to pursue a "convergence" strategy. In groups of three, use the Internet to understand what BCE meant by convergence, what it did to pursue convergence, and the eventual result. Also, track the stock market value of BCE from before its "convergence play" until the present date. Prepare a five-to-six-page report on your findings and your conclusion about the efficacy of the convergence strategy.

2. The September 10, 2002, issue of *The Globe and Mail* announced that John Roth, the previous CEO of Nortel, sold his remaining shares in the telecommunications equipment maker on August 1 for $1.55. In groups of three, use the Internet to determine when and for what prices Mr. Roth previously sold shares he received as part of remuneration. For the period beginning in 1997, when Mr. Roth became CEO, assess the trend of Nortel share prices and earnings per share, and the efficacy of shares and options for aligning the objectives of senior managers and shareholders. The report should be four or five pages in length.

3. Individually, or as a group, visit *The Globe and Mail's* Web page, and examine its Report on Business section for its annual study of the Top 50 Companies to Work For in Canada. If you do not have online access to *The Globe and Mail,* you may have access to the printed version in your library. Identify the practices that would be the most appealing to you.

SOLUTIONS TO SELF-TEST QUESTIONS

1. b, 2. a, 3. d, 4. b, 5. d, 6. d, 7. b, 8 a, 9. b, 10. c

ENDNOTES

1. Gay Gooderham and Jennifer La Trobe, "Measures Must Motivate," *Cost and Measurement,* October 1997, p. 52.

2. Peter Brewer, "Putting Strategy into the Balanced Scorecard," *Strategic Finance,* January 2002, pp. 44–52.

3. Jac Fitz-Enz, "Measuring Team Effectiveness," *HR Focus,* August 1997, p. 55.

4. Bob Hagerty, "Executive Pay (A Special Report)—Asian Scramble: Multinationals in China Hope Lucrative Compensation Packages Can Attract Local Executives They Desperately Need," *Wall Street Journal,* April 10, 1997, p. R12.

Appendix A

Using the Ethics Discussion Questions

There are few more difficult issues facing business graduates or people in the business world today than those pertaining to ethical dilemmas. Some of these situations are specifically covered by professional codes of conduct; others reflect the differences among what is ethical, what is legal, and what is professionally accepted. Most traditional coverage of ethics in accounting courses focuses on the teachings of the various professional codes of ethics. Although learning about codes of ethics is important, an ability to make ethical choices can be greatly enhanced by presenting cases involving questionable breaches of proper conduct in the myriad of everyday business transactions. By covering such situations, instructors have an opportunity to make a significant contribution to their students' success and well-being in the area of day-to-day ethics.

The text provides a series of end-of-chapter situations that can be used to give students practice in recognizing ethical issues and opportunities to develop appropriate responses. Some questions address what appear to be fairly innocuous issues (such as where to place expenses on an income statement); others address mainstream environmental and ethical matters (such as the handling of environmentally destructive waste materials). Both types of situations have important underlying ethical conflicts, however, and require a logical thought process to arrive at the most ethical solution rather than simply *rationalizing* any solution chosen. Students need to recognize that it may be easy to make an unethical decision when the stakes are not very high; when the stakes increase, the pattern of unethical decision making may already be in place and difficult to change. If minor ethical decisions can be analyzed and resolved ethically, major decisions are more likely to be addressed in a thoughtful and ethical manner.

It is important that students be prepared, while they are in school, for ethical conflicts with which they may be confronted in the workplace. An essential part of such preparation is developing the *ability to recognize* ethical problems before they become realities and learning how, when, and to whom to respond to such problems. The purpose of a managerial accounting course is not to provide a philosophy lecture, but it is an opportunity to provide students with an awareness of some major ethical theories and problem-solving models before being asked to analyze and resolve ethical conflict situations. Thus, the following information may be useful to both the instructor teaching this course and the students taking it.

Ethics can be viewed and taught at two levels: (1) as a set of general theories and (2) as a set of specific principles.

ETHICS AS A SET OF THEORIES

Viewing ethics as a set of general theories allows people to learn the background used in developing specific principles and, therefore, be able to develop their own principles or guidelines when confronted with unique situations in which the existing principles seem to have no relevance. This type of teaching is usually performed in philosophy courses, but some of the basic theories can be briefly defined and illustrated at this point. Although these are not the only ethical theories that exist, they do provide a foundation from which to begin ethical discussions.

Utilitarianism

This theory holds that the primary method of determining what is right or ethical is the usefulness of an action or a policy in producing other actions or experiences that people value. It emphasizes the consequences that an action has on all the people directly and/or indirectly affected by that action. This theory reflects a societal viewpoint of the "greatest good for the greatest number." (Utilitarianism is a type of cost–benefit analysis.)

Although this theory may provide extremely valid ethical decisions, in practice it is highly unworkable in its theoretical state. This model would require determining *all* possible solutions to a dilemma, determining *all* possible stakeholders for each solution, determining *all* the costs and benefits of *each* solution to *each* stakeholder, summing such costs and benefits, and choosing the decision that maximized the benefits of the most stakeholders. Thus, when utilitarianism is applied as a model of ethical decision making, certain shortcuts are normally taken, such as considering only certain types of stakeholders or solutions within a certain type of framework. When such shortcuts are taken, however, the decision maker should occasionally review them to make sure that such simplifications have not automatically ignored important constituencies, reference points, interests, or values.

Categorical Imperatives

This set of rules requires that a person act on the premise that whatever he or she does would become a universal law. Categorical imperatives form the basis of duties that are considered inherently right. Actions are inherently right or wrong, regardless of any positive or negative consequences resulting from those actions. Thus, the model emphasizes treating all persons equally and as the person acting would like to be treated as well as emphasizing a respect for individuals and their freedoms. (Categorical imperatives reflect a "Do unto others as you would have them do unto you" concept.)

Theory of Rights

This theory asserts that people have some fundamental rights that must be respected in all decisions. Rights advocates suggest that there are liberty and welfare rights for all persons. Liberty rights have primarily been embedded in the *Canadian Charter of Rights and Freedoms*, and include:
* Fundamental freedoms
* Democratic rights
* Mobility rights
* Legal rights
* Equality rights

- Official languages of Canada, and
- Minority language education rights

Welfare rights reflect the rights of all people to some minimum standard of living; these rights typically have fallen into the realm of governmental or corporate social responsibilities.

Theory of Justice

This theory requires that people make decisions based on equity, fairness, and impartiality. This theory requires that people who are similar be treated in a similar manner and allows people who are different in a *relevant* way to be treated differently. Relevant ways affecting when people can be treated differently cannot relate to arbitrary characteristics; differences must be related to the task that is to be performed or differences in people's needs. In using the theory of justice, a decision maker must be careful to make certain that the characteristic(s) on which he or she is making the distinction is (are) relevant and not discriminatory.

ETHICS AS A SET OF PRINCIPLES

Teaching ethics as a set of specific principles provides individuals with a means to answer concrete, problem-oriented situations. This method is typically how ethics is treated in an auditing course or in discussions of codes of ethics.

In looking at ethics as a set of principles, one must distinguish between ethics and legality. Ethics can be viewed as a nonjurisdictional system of moral rights. It represents the moral rights that people have regardless of where or when they live, whether these rights are legally recognized or not. Legality merely refers to what is permissible under the law in a particular society. Sometimes society may condone an act as legal because of the surrounding circumstances even though the act itself may be viewed as unethical. (For example, it is unethical to kill another human being, but society may make it legal to do so under certain situations.) Legitimizing a "wrong" act because of circumstances does not make that act any more moral.

MAKING ETHICAL DECISIONS

In making ethical decisions, a person must first have the sensitivity to recognize that an ethical dilemma exists and must exert the self-control to attempt to resolve it. This conflict may be at the personal, organizational, or societal level. All feasible alternatives should be considered along with their influencing factors such as values, laws, resource constraints, pressures, and cultural mores. *Once all ramifications are considered and the decision maker selects an alternative using whatever theories or processes he or she chooses, the decision maker must also be willing to accept the outcomes from and responsibility for that choice.* An individual acts as an autonomous agent when he or she acts on the basis of principles that have been consciously evaluated and accepted by the individual as the correct principles to direct behavior; individuals cannot be considered autonomous when they act based on principles that have been imposed from the outside (through peer pressure or by some authority) or that have been internalized as a matter of mere habit.

The making of ethical choices is not a science; it is subjective and cannot be resolved from a societal point of view. Different individuals will always have different viewpoints as to what is ethical and what is the proper decision for an ethical dilemma. The challenge is to create a means for students to foresee potential problems, recognize they have an obligation to derive internal and personal criteria by which to resolve such dilemmas, and accept personal, organizational, societal, and legal determinations as to the ethical or unethical nature of solutions chosen when (or if) those solutions are made public.

Appendix B

Present and Future Value Tables

TABLE 1   PRESENT VALUE OF $1

Period	1.00%	2.00%	3.00%	4.00%	5.00%	6.00%	7.00%	8.00%	9.00%	9.50%	10.00%	10.50%	11.00%
1	0.9901	0.9804	0.9709	0.9615	0.9524	0.9434	0.9346	0.9259	0.9174	0.9132	0.9091	0.9050	0.9009
2	0.9803	0.9612	0.9426	0.9246	0.9070	0.8900	0.8734	0.8573	0.8417	0.8340	0.8265	0.8190	0.8116
3	0.9706	0.9423	0.9151	0.8890	0.8638	0.8396	0.8163	0.7938	0.7722	0.7617	0.7513	0.7412	0.7312
4	0.9610	0.9239	0.8885	0.8548	0.8227	0.7921	0.7629	0.7350	0.7084	0.6956	0.6830	0.6707	0.6587
5	0.9515	0.9057	0.8626	0.8219	0.7835	0.7473	0.7130	0.6806	0.6499	0.6352	0.6209	0.6070	0.5935
6	0.9421	0.8880	0.8375	0.7903	0.7462	0.7050	0.6663	0.6302	0.5963	0.5801	0.5645	0.5493	0.5346
7	0.9327	0.8706	0.8131	0.7599	0.7107	0.6651	0.6228	0.5835	0.5470	0.5298	0.5132	0.4971	0.4817
8	0.9235	0.8535	0.7894	0.7307	0.6768	0.6274	0.5820	0.5403	0.5019	0.4838	0.4665	0.4499	0.4339
9	0.9143	0.8368	0.7664	0.7026	0.6446	0.5919	0.5439	0.5003	0.4604	0.4419	0.4241	0.4071	0.3909
10	0.9053	0.8204	0.7441	0.6756	0.6139	0.5584	0.5084	0.4632	0.4224	0.4035	0.3855	0.3685	0.3522
11	0.8963	0.8043	0.7224	0.6496	0.5847	0.5268	0.4751	0.4289	0.3875	0.3685	0.3505	0.3334	0.3173
12	0.8875	0.7885	0.7014	0.6246	0.5568	0.4970	0.4440	0.3971	0.3555	0.3365	0.3186	0.3018	0.2858
13	0.8787	0.7730	0.6810	0.6006	0.5303	0.4688	0.4150	0.3677	0.3262	0.3073	0.2897	0.2731	0.2575
14	0.8700	0.7579	0.6611	0.5775	0.5051	0.4423	0.3878	0.3405	0.2993	0.2807	0.2633	0.2471	0.2320
15	0.8614	0.7430	0.6419	0.5553	0.4810	0.4173	0.3625	0.3152	0.2745	0.2563	0.2394	0.2237	0.2090
16	0.8528	0.7285	0.6232	0.5339	0.4581	0.3937	0.3387	0.2919	0.2519	0.2341	0.2176	0.2024	0.1883
17	0.8444	0.7142	0.6050	0.5134	0.4363	0.3714	0.3166	0.2703	0.2311	0.2138	0.1978	0.1832	0.1696
18	0.8360	0.7002	0.5874	0.4936	0.4155	0.3503	0.2959	0.2503	0.2120	0.1952	0.1799	0.1658	0.1528
19	0.8277	0.6864	0.5703	0.4746	0.3957	0.3305	0.2765	0.2317	0.1945	0.1783	0.1635	0.1500	0.1377
20	0.8195	0.6730	0.5537	0.4564	0.3769	0.3118	0.2584	0.2146	0.1784	0.1628	0.1486	0.1358	0.1240
21	0.8114	0.6598	0.5376	0.4388	0.3589	0.2942	0.2415	0.1987	0.1637	0.1487	0.1351	0.1229	0.1117
22	0.8034	0.6468	0.5219	0.4220	0.3419	0.2775	0.2257	0.1839	0.1502	0.1358	0.1229	0.1112	0.1007
23	0.7954	0.6342	0.5067	0.4057	0.3256	0.2618	0.2110	0.1703	0.1378	0.1240	0.1117	0.1006	0.0907
24	0.7876	0.6217	0.4919	0.3901	0.3101	0.2470	0.1972	0.1577	0.1264	0.1133	0.1015	0.0911	0.0817
25	0.7798	0.6095	0.4776	0.3751	0.2953	0.2330	0.1843	0.1460	0.1160	0.1034	0.0923	0.0824	0.0736
26	0.7721	0.5976	0.4637	0.3607	0.2812	0.2198	0.1722	0.1352	0.1064	0.0945	0.0839	0.0746	0.0663
27	0.7644	0.5859	0.4502	0.3468	0.2679	0.2074	0.1609	0.1252	0.0976	0.0863	0.0763	0.0675	0.0597
28	0.7568	0.5744	0.4371	0.3335	0.2551	0.1956	0.1504	0.1159	0.0896	0.0788	0.0693	0.0611	0.0538
29	0.7493	0.5631	0.4244	0.3207	0.2430	0.1846	0.1406	0.1073	0.0822	0.0719	0.0630	0.0553	0.0485
30	0.7419	0.5521	0.4120	0.3083	0.2314	0.1741	0.1314	0.0994	0.0754	0.0657	0.0573	0.0500	0.0437
31	0.7346	0.5413	0.4000	0.2965	0.2204	0.1643	0.1228	0.0920	0.0692	0.0600	0.0521	0.0453	0.0394
32	0.7273	0.5306	0.3883	0.2851	0.2099	0.1550	0.1147	0.0852	0.0634	0.0058	0.0474	0.0410	0.0355
33	0.7201	0.5202	0.3770	0.2741	0.1999	0.1462	0.1072	0.0789	0.0582	0.0500	0.0431	0.0371	0.0319
34	0.7130	0.5100	0.3660	0.2636	0.1904	0.1379	0.1002	0.0731	0.0534	0.0457	0.0391	0.0336	0.0288
35	0.7059	0.5000	0.3554	0.2534	0.1813	0.1301	0.0937	0.0676	0.0490	0.0417	0.0356	0.0304	0.0259
36	0.6989	0.4902	0.3450	0.2437	0.1727	0.1227	0.0875	0.0626	0.0449	0.0381	0.0324	0.0275	0.0234
37	0.6920	0.4806	0.3350	0.2343	0.1644	0.1158	0.0818	0.0580	0.0412	0.0348	0.0294	0.0249	0.0210
38	0.6852	0.4712	0.3252	0.2253	0.1566	0.1092	0.0765	0.0537	0.0378	0.0318	0.0267	0.0225	0.0190
39	0.6784	0.4620	0.3158	0.2166	0.1492	0.1031	0.0715	0.0497	0.0347	0.0290	0.0243	0.0204	0.0171
40	0.6717	0.4529	0.3066	0.2083	0.1421	0.0972	0.0668	0.0460	0.0318	0.0265	0.0221	0.0184	0.0154
41	0.6650	0.4440	0.2976	0.2003	0.1353	0.0917	0.0624	0.0426	0.0292	0.0242	0.0201	0.0167	0.0139
42	0.6584	0.4353	0.2890	0.1926	0.1288	0.0865	0.0583	0.0395	0.0268	0.0221	0.0183	0.0151	0.0125
43	0.6519	0.4268	0.2805	0.1852	0.1227	0.0816	0.0545	0.0365	0.0246	0.0202	0.0166	0.0137	0.0113
44	0.6455	0.4184	0.2724	0.1781	0.1169	0.0770	0.0510	0.0338	0.0226	0.0184	0.0151	0.0124	0.0101
45	0.6391	0.4102	0.2644	0.1712	0.1113	0.0727	0.0476	0.0313	0.0207	0.0168	0.0137	0.0112	0.0091
46	0.6327	0.4022	0.2567	0.1646	0.1060	0.0685	0.0445	0.0290	0.0190	0.0154	0.0125	0.0101	0.0082
47	0.6265	0.3943	0.2493	0.1583	0.1010	0.0647	0.0416	0.0269	0.0174	0.0141	0.0113	0.0092	0.0074
48	0.6203	0.3865	0.2420	0.1522	0.0961	0.0610	0.0389	0.0249	0.0160	0.0128	0.0103	0.0083	0.0067
49	0.6141	0.3790	0.2350	0.1463	0.0916	0.0576	0.0363	0.0230	0.0147	0.0117	0.0094	0.0075	0.0060
50	0.6080	0.3715	0.2281	0.1407	0.0872	0.0543	0.0340	0.0213	0.0135	0.0107	0.0085	0.0068	0.0054

11.50%	12.00%	12.50%	13.00%	13.50%	14.00%	14.50%	15.00%	15.50%	16.00%	17.00%	18.00%	19.00%	20.00%
0.8969	0.8929	0.8889	0.8850	0.8811	0.8772	0.8734	0.8696	0.8658	0.8621	0.8547	0.8475	0.8403	0.8333
0.8044	0.7972	0.7901	0.7832	0.7763	0.7695	0.7628	0.7561	0.7496	0.7432	0.7305	0.7182	0.7062	0.6944
0.7214	0.7118	0.7023	0.6931	0.6839	0.6750	0.6662	0.6575	0.6490	0.6407	0.6244	0.6086	0.5934	0.5787
0.6470	0.6355	0.6243	0.6133	0.6026	0.5921	0.5818	0.5718	0.5619	0.5523	0.5337	0.5158	0.4987	0.4823
0.5803	0.5674	0.5549	0.5428	0.5309	0.5194	0.5081	0.4972	0.4865	0.4761	0.4561	0.4371	0.4191	0.4019
0.5204	0.5066	0.4933	0.4803	0.4678	0.4556	0.4438	0.4323	0.4212	0.4104	0.3898	0.3704	0.3521	0.3349
0.4667	0.4524	0.4385	0.4251	0.4121	0.3996	0.3876	0.3759	0.3647	0.3538	0.3332	0.3139	0.2959	0.2791
0.4186	0.4039	0.3897	0.3762	0.3631	0.3506	0.3385	0.3269	0.3158	0.3050	0.2848	0.2660	0.2487	0.2326
0.3754	0.3606	0.3464	0.3329	0.3199	0.3075	0.2956	0.2843	0.2734	0.2630	0.2434	0.2255	0.2090	0.1938
0.3367	0.3220	0.3080	0.2946	0.2819	0.2697	0.2582	0.2472	0.2367	0.2267	0.2080	0.1911	0.1756	0.1615
0.3020	0.2875	0.2737	0.2607	0.2483	0.2366	0.2255	0.2149	0.2049	0.1954	0.1778	0.1619	0.1476	0.1346
0.2708	0.2567	0.2433	0.2307	0.2188	0.2076	0.1969	0.1869	0.1774	0.1685	0.1520	0.1372	0.1240	0.1122
0.2429	0.2292	0.2163	0.2042	0.1928	0.1821	0.1720	0.1625	0.1536	0.1452	0.1299	0.1163	0.1042	0.0935
0.2179	0.2046	0.1923	0.1807	0.1699	0.1597	0.1502	0.1413	0.1330	0.1252	0.1110	0.0986	0.0876	0.0779
0.1954	0.1827	0.1709	0.1599	0.1496	0.1401	0.1312	0.1229	0.1152	0.1079	0.0949	0.0835	0.0736	0.0649
0.1752	0.1631	0.1519	0.1415	0.1319	0.1229	0.1146	0.1069	0.0997	0.0930	0.0811	0.0708	0.0618	0.0541
0.1572	0.1456	0.1350	0.1252	0.1162	0.1078	0.1001	0.0929	0.0863	0.0802	0.0693	0.0600	0.0520	0.0451
0.1410	0.1300	0.1200	0.1108	0.1024	0.0946	0.0874	0.0808	0.0747	0.0691	0.0593	0.0508	0.0437	0.0376
0.1264	0.1161	0.1067	0.0981	0.0902	0.0830	0.0763	0.0703	0.0647	0.0596	0.0506	0.0431	0.0367	0.0313
0.1134	0.1037	0.0948	0.0868	0.0795	0.0728	0.0667	0.0611	0.0560	0.0514	0.0433	0.0365	0.0308	0.0261
0.1017	0.0926	0.0843	0.0768	0.0700	0.0638	0.0582	0.0531	0.0485	0.0443	0.0370	0.0309	0.0259	0.0217
0.0912	0.0826	0.0749	0.0680	0.0617	0.0560	0.0509	0.0462	0.0420	0.0382	0.0316	0.0262	0.0218	0.0181
0.0818	0.0738	0.0666	0.0601	0.0543	0.0491	0.0444	0.0402	0.0364	0.0329	0.0270	0.0222	0.0183	0.0151
0.0734	0.0659	0.0592	0.0532	0.0479	0.0431	0.0388	0.0349	0.0315	0.0284	0.0231	0.0188	0.0154	0.0126
0.0658	0.0588	0.0526	0.0471	0.0422	0.0378	0.0339	0.0304	0.0273	0.0245	0.0197	0.0160	0.0129	0.0105
0.0590	0.0525	0.0468	0.0417	0.0372	0.0332	0.0296	0.0264	0.0236	0.0211	0.0169	0.0135	0.0109	0.0087
0.0529	0.0469	0.0416	0.0369	0.0327	0.0291	0.0258	0.0230	0.0204	0.0182	0.0144	0.0115	0.0091	0.0073
0.0475	0.0419	0.0370	0.0326	0.0289	0.0255	0.0226	0.0200	0.0177	0.0157	0.0123	0.0097	0.0077	0.0061
0.0426	0.0374	0.0329	0.0289	0.0254	0.0224	0.0197	0.0174	0.0153	0.0135	0.0105	0.0082	0.0064	0.0051
0.0382	0.0334	0.0292	0.0256	0.0224	0.0196	0.0172	0.0151	0.0133	0.0117	0.0090	0.0070	0.0054	0.0042
0.0342	0.0298	0.0260	0.0226	0.0197	0.0172	0.0150	0.0131	0.0115	0.0100	0.0077	0.0059	0.0046	0.0035
0.0307	0.0266	0.0231	0.0200	0.0174	0.0151	0.0131	0.0114	0.0099	0.0087	0.0066	0.0050	0.0038	0.0029
0.0275	0.0238	0.0205	0.0177	0.0153	0.0133	0.0115	0.0099	0.0086	0.0075	0.0056	0.0043	0.0032	0.0024
0.0247	0.0212	0.0182	0.0157	0.0135	0.0116	0.0100	0.0088	0.0075	0.0064	0.0048	0.0036	0.0027	0.0020
0.0222	0.0189	0.0162	0.0139	0.0119	0.0102	0.0088	0.0075	0.0065	0.0056	0.0041	0.0031	0.0023	0.0017
0.0199	0.0169	0.0144	0.0123	0.0105	0.0089	0.0076	0.0065	0.0056	0.0048	0.0035	0.0026	0.0019	0.0014
0.0178	0.0151	0.0128	0.0109	0.0092	0.0078	0.0067	0.0057	0.0048	0.0041	0.0030	0.0022	0.0016	0.0012
0.0160	0.0135	0.0114	0.0096	0.0081	0.0069	0.0058	0.0049	0.0042	0.0036	0.0026	0.0019	0.0014	0.0010
0.0143	0.0120	0.0101	0.0085	0.0072	0.0060	0.0051	0.0043	0.0036	0.0031	0.0022	0.0016	0.0011	0.0008
0.0129	0.0108	0.0090	0.0075	0.0063	0.0053	0.0044	0.0037	0.0031	0.0026	0.0019	0.0013	0.0010	0.0007
0.0115	0.0096	0.0080	0.0067	0.0056	0.0046	0.0039	0.0033	0.0027	0.0023	0.0016	0.0011	0.0008	0.0006
0.0103	0.0086	0.0077	0.0059	0.0049	0.0041	0.0034	0.0028	0.0024	0.0020	0.0014	0.0010	0.0007	0.0005
0.0093	0.0077	0.0063	0.0052	0.0043	0.0036	0.0030	0.0025	0.0020	0.0017	0.0012	0.0008	0.0006	0.0004
0.0083	0.0068	0.0056	0.0046	0.0038	0.0031	0.0026	0.0021	0.0018	0.0015	0.0010	0.0007	0.0005	0.0003
0.0075	0.0061	0.0050	0.0041	0.0034	0.0028	0.0023	0.0019	0.0015	0.0013	0.0009	0.0006	0.0004	0.0003
0.0067	0.0054	0.0044	0.0036	0.0030	0.0024	0.0020	0.0016	0.0013	0.0011	0.0007	0.0005	0.0003	0.0002
0.0060	0.0049	0.0039	0.0032	0.0026	0.0021	0.0017	0.0014	0.0011	0.0009	0.0006	0.0004	0.0003	0.0002
0.0054	0.0043	0.0035	0.0028	0.0023	0.0019	0.0015	0.0012	0.0010	0.0008	0.0005	0.0004	0.0002	0.0002
0.0048	0.0039	0.0031	0.0025	0.0020	0.0016	0.0013	0.0011	0.0009	0.0007	0.0005	0.0003	0.0002	0.0001
0.0043	0.0035	0.0028	0.0022	0.0018	0.0014	0.0012	0.0009	0.0007	0.0006	0.0004	0.0003	0.0002	0.0001

TABLE 2   PRESENT VALUE OF AN ORDINARY ANNUITY OF $1

Period	1.00%	2.00%	3.00%	4.00%	5.00%	6.00%	7.00%	8.00%	9.00%	9.50%	10.00%	10.50%	11.00%
1	0.9901	0.9804	0.9709	0.9615	0.0524	0.9434	0.9346	0.9259	0.9174	0.9132	0.9091	0.9050	0.9009
2	1.9704	1.9416	1.9135	1.8861	1.8594	1.8334	1.8080	1.7833	1.7591	1.7473	1.7355	1.7240	1.7125
3	2.9410	2.8839	2.8286	2.7751	2.7233	2.6730	2.6243	2.5771	2.5313	2.5089	2.4869	2.4651	2.4437
4	3.9020	3.8077	3.7171	3.6299	3.5460	3.4651	3.3872	3.3121	3.2397	3.2045	3.1699	3.1359	3.1025
5	4.8534	4.7135	4.5797	4.4518	4.3295	4.2124	4.1002	3.9927	3.8897	3.8397	3.7908	3.7429	3.6959
6	5.7955	5.6014	5.4172	5.2421	5.0757	4.9173	4.7665	4.6229	4.4859	4.4198	4.3553	4.2922	4.2305
7	6.7282	6.4720	6.2303	6.0021	5.7864	5.5824	5.3893	5.2064	5.0330	4.9496	4.8684	4.7893	4.7122
8	7.6517	7.3255	7.0197	6.7327	6.4632	6.2098	5.9713	5.7466	5.5348	5.4334	5.3349	5.2392	5.1461
9	8.5660	8.1622	7.7861	7.4353	7.1078	6.8017	6.5152	6.2469	5.9953	5.8753	5.7590	5.6463	5.5371
10	9.4713	8.9826	8.5302	8.1109	7.7217	7.3601	7.0236	6.7101	6.4177	6.2788	6.1446	6.0148	5.8892
11	10.3676	9.7869	9.2526	8.7605	8.3064	7.8869	7.4987	7.1390	6.8052	6.6473	6.4951	6.3482	6.2065
12	11.2551	10.5753	9.9540	9.3851	8.8633	8.3838	7.9427	7.5361	7.1607	6.9838	6.8137	6.6500	6.4924
13	12.1337	11.3484	10.6350	9.9857	9.3936	8.8527	8.3577	7.9038	7.4869	7.2912	7.1034	6.9230	6.7499
14	13.0037	12.1063	11.2961	10.5631	9.8986	9.2950	8.7455	8.2442	7.7862	7.5719	7.3667	7.1702	6.9819
15	13.8651	12.8493	11.9379	11.1184	10.3797	9.7123	9.1079	8.5595	8.0607	7.8282	7.6061	7.3938	7.1909
16	14.7179	13.5777	12.5611	11.6523	10.8378	10.1059	9.4467	8.8514	8.3126	8.0623	7.8237	7.5962	7.3792
17	15.5623	14.2919	13.1661	12.1657	11.2741	10.4773	9.7632	9.1216	8.5436	8.2760	8.0216	7.7794	7.5488
18	16.3983	14.9920	13.7535	12.6593	11.6896	10.8276	10.0591	9.3719	8.7556	8.4713	8.2014	7.9452	7.7016
19	17.2260	15.6785	14.3238	13.1339	12.0853	11.1581	10.3356	9.6036	8.9501	8.6496	8.3649	8.0952	7.8393
20	18.0456	16.3514	14.8775	13.5903	12.4622	11.4699	10.5940	9.8182	9.1286	8.8124	8.5136	8.2309	7.9633
21	18.8570	17.0112	15.4150	14.0292	12.8212	11.7641	10.8355	10.0168	9.2922	8.9611	8.6487	8.3538	8.0751
22	19.6604	17.6581	15.9369	14.4511	13.1630	12.0416	11.0612	10.2007	9.4424	9.0969	8.7715	8.4649	8.1757
23	20.4558	18.2922	16.4436	14.8568	13.4886	12.3034	11.2722	10.3711	9.5802	9.2209	8.8832	8.5656	8.2664
24	21.2434	18.9139	16.9355	15.2470	13.7986	12.5504	11.4693	10.5288	9.7066	9.3342	8.9847	8.6566	8.3481
25	22.0232	19.5235	17.4132	15.6221	14.0939	12.7834	11.6536	10.6748	9.8226	9.4376	9.0770	8.7390	8.4217
26	22.7952	20.1210	17.8768	15.9828	14.3752	13.0032	11.8258	10.8100	9.9290	9.5320	9.1610	8.8136	8.4881
27	23.5596	20.7069	18.3270	16.3296	14.6430	13.2105	11.9867	10.9352	10.0266	9.6183	9.2372	8.8811	8.5478
28	24.3164	21.2813	18.7641	16.6631	14.8981	13.4062	12.1371	11.0511	10.1161	9.6971	9.3066	8.9422	8.6016
29	25.0658	21.8444	19.1885	16.9837	15.1411	13.5907	12.2777	11.1584	10.1983	9.7690	9.3696	8.9974	8.6501
30	25.8077	22.3965	19.6004	17.2920	15.3725	13.7648	12.4090	11.2578	10.2737	9.8347	9.4269	9.0474	8.6938
31	26.5423	22.9377	20.0004	17.5885	15.5928	13.9291	12.5318	11.3498	10.3428	9.8947	9.4790	9.0927	8.7332
32	27.2696	23.4683	20.3888	17.8736	15.8027	14.0840	12.6466	11.4350	10.4062	9.9495	9.5264	9.1337	8.7686
33	27.9897	23.9886	20.7658	18.1477	16.0026	14.2302	12.7538	11.5139	10.4664	9.9996	9.5694	9.1707	8.8005
34	28.7027	24.4986	21.1318	18.4112	16.1929	14.3681	12.8540	11.5869	10.5178	10.0453	9.6086	9.2043	8.8293
35	29.4086	24.9986	21.4872	18.6646	16.3742	14.4983	12.9477	11.6546	10.5668	10.0870	9.6442	9.2347	8.8552
36	30.1075	25.4888	21.8323	18.9083	16.5469	14.6210	13.0352	11.7172	10.6118	10.1251	9.6765	9.2621	8.8786
37	30.7995	25.9695	22.1672	19.1426	16.7113	14.7368	13.1170	11.7752	10.6530	10.1599	9.7059	9.2870	8.8996
38	31.4847	26.4406	22.4925	19.3679	16.8679	14.8460	13.1935	11.8289	10.6908	10.1917	9.7327	9.3095	8.9186
39	32.1630	26.9026	22.8082	19.5845	17.0170	14.9491	13.2649	11.8786	10.7255	10.2207	9.7570	9.3299	8.9357
40	32.8347	27.3555	23.1148	19.7928	17.1591	15.0463	13.3317	11.9246	10.7574	10.2473	9.7791	9.3483	8.9511
41	33.4997	27.7995	23.4124	19.9931	17.2944	15.1380	13.3941	11.9672	10.7866	10.2715	9.7991	9.3650	8.9649
42	34.1581	28.2348	23.7014	20.1856	17.4232	15.2245	13.4525	12.0067	10.8134	10.2936	9.8174	9.3801	8.9774
43	34.8100	28.6616	23.9819	20.3708	17.5459	15.3062	13.5070	12.0432	10.8380	10.3138	9.8340	9.3937	8.9887
44	35.4555	29.0800	24.2543	20.5488	17.6628	15.3832	13.5579	12.0771	10.8605	10.3322	9.8491	9.4061	8.9988
45	36.0945	29.4902	24.5187	20.7200	17.7741	15.4558	13.6055	12.1084	10.8812	10.3490	9.8628	9.4163	9.0079
46	36.7272	29.8923	24.7755	20.8847	17.8801	15.5244	13.6500	12.1374	10.9002	10.3644	9.8753	9.4274	9.0161
47	37.3537	30.2866	25.0247	21.0429	17.9810	15.5890	13.6916	12.1643	10.9176	10.3785	9.8866	9.4366	9.0236
48	37.9740	30.6731	25.2667	21.1951	18.0772	15.6500	13.7305	12.1891	10.9336	10.3913	9.8969	9.4449	9.0302
49	38.5881	31.0521	25.5017	21.3415	18.1687	15.7076	13.7668	12.2122	10.9482	10.4030	9.9063	9.4524	9.0362
50	39.1961	31.4236	25.7298	21.4822	18.2559	15.7619	13.8008	12.2335	10.9617	10.4137	9.9148	9.4591	9.0417

11.50%	12.00%	12.50%	13.00%	13.50%	14.00%	14.50%	15.00%	15.50%	16.00%	17.00%	18.00%	19.00%	20.00%
0.8969	0.8929	0.8889	0.8850	0.8811	0.8772	0.8734	0.8696	0.8658	0.8621	0.8547	0.8475	0.8403	0.8333
1.7012	1.6901	1.6790	1.6681	1.6573	1.6467	1.6361	1.6257	1.6154	1.6052	1.5852	1.5656	1.5465	1.5278
2.4226	2.4018	2.3813	2.3612	2.3413	2.3216	2.3023	2.2832	2.2644	2.2459	2.2096	2.1743	2.1399	2.1065
3.0696	3.0374	3.0056	2.9745	2.9438	2.9137	2.8841	2.8850	2.8263	2.7982	2.7432	2.6901	2.6386	2.5887
3.6499	3.6048	3.5606	3.5172	3.4747	3.4331	3.3922	3.3522	3.3129	3.2743	3.1994	3.1272	3.0576	2.9906
4.1703	4.1114	4.0538	3.9976	3.9425	3.8887	3.8360	3.7845	3.7341	3.6847	3.5892	3.4976	3.4098	3.3255
4.6370	4.5638	4.4923	4.4226	4.3546	4.2883	4.2236	4.1604	4.0988	4.0386	3.9224	3.8115	3.7057	3.6046
5.0556	4.9676	4.8821	4.7988	4.7177	4.6389	4.5621	4.4873	4.4145	4.3436	4.2072	4.0776	3.9544	3.8372
5.4311	5.3283	5.2285	5.1317	5.0377	4.9464	4.8577	4.7716	4.6879	4.6065	4.4506	4.3030	4.1633	4.0310
5.7678	5.6502	5.5364	5.4262	5.3195	5.2161	5.1159	5.0188	4.9246	4.8332	4.6586	4.4941	4.3389	4.1925
6.0698	5.9377	5.8102	5.6869	5.5679	5.4527	5.3414	5.2337	5.1295	5.0286	4.8364	4.6560	4.4865	4.3271
6.3406	6.1944	6.0535	5.9177	5.7867	5.6603	5.5383	5.4206	5.3069	5.1971	4.9884	4.7932	4.6105	4.4392
6.5835	6.4236	6.2698	6.1218	5.9794	5.8424	5.7103	5.5832	5.4606	5.3423	5.1183	4.9095	4.7147	4.5327
6.8013	6.6282	6.4620	6.3025	6.1493	6.0021	5.8606	5.7245	5.5936	5.4675	5.2293	5.0081	4.8023	4.6106
6.9967	6.8109	6.6329	6.4624	6.2989	6.1422	5.9918	5.8474	5.7087	5.5755	5.3242	5.0916	4.8759	4.6755
7.1719	6.9740	6.7848	6.6039	6.4308	6.2651	6.1063	5.9542	5.8084	5.6685	5.4053	5.1624	4.9377	4.7296
7.3291	7.1196	6.9198	6.7291	6.5469	6.3729	6.2064	6.0472	5.8947	5.7487	5.4746	5.2223	4.9897	4.7746
7.4700	7.2497	7.0398	6.8399	6.6493	6.4674	6.2938	6.1280	5.9695	5.8179	5.5339	5.2732	5.0333	4.8122
7.5964	7.3658	7.1465	6.9380	6.7395	6.5504	6.3701	6.1982	6.0342	5.8775	5.5845	5.3162	5.0700	4.8435
7.7098	7.4694	7.2414	7.0248	6.8189	6.6231	6.4368	6.2593	6.0902	5.9288	5.6278	5.3528	5.1009	4.8696
7.8115	7.5620	7.3257	7.1016	6.8889	6.6870	6.4950	6.3125	6.1387	5.9731	5.6648	5.3837	5.1268	4.8913
7.9027	7.6447	7.4006	7.1695	6.9506	6.7429	6.5459	6.3587	6.1807	6.0113	5.6964	5.4099	5.1486	4.9094
7.9845	7.7184	7.4672	7.2297	7.0049	6.7921	6.5903	6.3988	6.2170	6.0443	5.7234	5.4321	5.1669	4.9245
8.0578	7.7843	7.5264	7.2829	7.0528	6.8351	6.6291	6.4338	6.2485	6.0726	5.7465	5.4510	5.1822	4.9371
8.1236	7.8431	7.5790	7.3300	7.0950	6.8729	6.6629	6.4642	6.2758	6.0971	5.7662	5.4669	5.1952	4.9476
8.1826	7.8957	7.6258	7.3717	7.1321	6.9061	6.6925	6.4906	6.2994	6.1182	5.7831	5.4804	5.2060	4.9563
8.2355	7.9426	7.6674	7.4086	7.1649	6.9352	6.7184	6.5135	6.3198	6.1364	5.7975	5.4919	5.2151	4.9636
8.2830	7.9844	7.7043	7.4412	7.1937	6.9607	6.7409	6.5335	6.3375	6.1520	5.8099	5.5016	5.2228	4.9697
8.3255	8.0218	7.7372	7.4701	7.2191	6.9830	6.7606	6.5509	6.3528	6.1656	5.8204	5.5098	5.2292	4.9747
8.3637	8.0552	7.7664	7.4957	7.2415	7.0027	6.7779	6.5660	6.3661	6.1772	5.8294	5.5168	5.2347	4.9789
8.3980	8.0850	7.7923	7.5183	7.2613	7.0199	6.7929	6.5791	6.3776	6.1872	5.8371	5.5227	5.2392	4.9825
8.4287	8.1116	7.8154	7.5383	7.2786	7.0350	6.8060	6.5905	6.3875	6.1959	5.8437	5.5277	5.2430	4.9854
8.4562	8.1354	7.8359	7.5560	7.2940	7.0482	6.8175	6.6005	6.3961	6.2034	5.8493	5.5320	5.2463	4.9878
8.4809	8.1566	7.8542	7.5717	7.3075	7.0599	6.8275	6.6091	6.4035	6.2098	5.8541	5.5356	5.2490	4.9898
8.5030	8.1755	7.8704	7.5856	7.3193	7.0701	6.8362	6.6166	6.4100	6.2153	5.8582	5.5386	5.2512	4.9930
8.5229	8.1924	7.8848	7.5979	7.3298	7.0790	6.8439	6.6231	6.4156	6.2201	5.8617	5.5412	5.2531	4.9930
8.5407	8.2075	7.8976	7.6087	7.3390	7.0868	6.8505	6.6288	6.4204	6.2242	5.8647	5.5434	5.2547	4.9941
8.5567	8.2210	7.9090	7.6183	7.3472	7.0937	6.8564	6.6338	6.4246	6.2278	5.8673	5.5453	5.2561	4.9951
8.5710	8.2330	7.9191	7.6268	7.3543	7.0998	6.8615	6.6381	6.4282	6.2309	5.8695	5.5468	5.2572	4.9959
8.5839	8.2438	7.9281	7.6344	7.3607	7.1050	6.8659	6.6418	6.4314	6.2335	5.8713	5.5482	5.2582	4.9966
8.5954	8.2534	7.9361	7.6410	7.3662	7.1097	6.8698	6.6450	6.4341	6.2358	5.8729	5.5493	5.2590	4.9972
8.6058	8.2619	7.9432	7.6469	7.3711	7.1138	6.8732	6.6479	6.4364	6.2377	5.8743	5.5502	5.2596	4.9976
8.6150	8.2696	7.9495	7.6522	7.3754	7.1173	6.8761	6.6503	6.4385	6.2394	5.8755	5.5511	5.2602	4.9980
8.6233	8.2764	7.9551	7.6568	7.3792	7.1205	6.8787	6.6524	6.4402	6.2409	5.8765	5.5517	5.2607	4.9984
8.6308	8.2825	7.9601	7.6609	7.3826	7.1232	6.8810	6.6543	6.4418	6.2421	5.8773	5.5523	5.2611	4.9986
8.6375	8.2880	7.9645	7.6645	7.3855	7.1256	6.8830	6.6559	6.4431	6.2432	5.8781	5.5528	5.2614	4.9989
8.6435	8.2928	7.9685	7.6677	7.3881	7.1277	6.8847	6.6573	6.4442	6.2442	5.8787	5.5532	5.2617	4.9991
8.6489	8.2972	7.9720	7.6705	7.3904	7.1296	6.8862	6.6585	6.4452	6.2450	5.8792	5.5536	5.2619	4.9992
8.6537	8.3010	7.9751	7.6730	7.3925	7.1312	6.8875	6.6596	6.4461	6.2457	5.8797	5.5539	5.2621	4.9993
8.6580	8.3045	7.9779	7.6752	7.3942	7.1327	6.8886	6.6605	6.4468	6.2463	5.8801	5.5541	5.2623	4.9995

TABLE 3 FUTURE VALUE OF $1

Period	3.00%	4.00%	5.00%	6.00%	7.00%	8.00%	9.00%	10.00%	11.00%	12.00%	13.00%	14.00%	15.00%
1	1.0300	1.0400	1.0500	1.0600	1.0700	1.0800	1.0900	1.1000	1.1100	1.1200	1.1300	1.1400	1.1500
2	1.0609	1.0816	1.1025	1.1236	1.1449	1.1664	1.1881	1.2100	1.2321	1.2544	1.2769	1.2996	1.3225
3	1.0927	1.1249	1.1576	1.1910	1.2250	1.2597	1.2950	1.3310	1.3676	1.4049	1.4429	1.4815	1.5209
4	1.1255	1.1699	1.2155	1.2625	1.3108	1.3605	1.4116	1.4641	1.5181	1.5735	1.6305	1.6890	1.7490
5	1.1593	1.2167	1.2763	1.3382	1.4026	1.4693	1.5386	1.6105	1.6851	1.7623	1.8424	1.9254	2.0114
6	1.1941	1.2653	1.3401	1.4185	1.5007	1.5869	1.6771	1.7716	1.8704	1.9738	2.0820	2.1950	2.3131
7	1.2299	1.3159	1.4071	1.5036	1.6058	1.7138	1.8280	1.9487	2.0762	2.2107	2.3526	2.5023	2.6600
8	1.2668	1.3686	1.4775	1.5938	1.7182	1.8509	1.9926	2.1436	2.3045	2.4760	2.6584	2.8526	3.0590
9	1.3048	1.4233	1.5513	1.6895	1.8385	1.9990	2.1719	2.3579	2.5580	2.7731	3.0040	3.2519	3.5179
10	1.3439	1.4802	1.6289	1.7908	1.9672	2.1589	2.3674	2.5937	2.8394	3.1058	3.3946	3.7072	4.0456
11	1.3842	1.5395	1.7103	1.8983	2.1049	2.3316	2.5804	2.8531	3.1518	3.4785	3.8359	4.2262	4.6524
12	1.4258	1.6010	1.7959	2.0122	2.2522	2.5182	2.8127	3.1384	3.4985	3.8960	4.3345	4.8179	5.3503
13	1.4685	1.6651	1.8856	2.1329	2.4098	2.7196	3.0658	3.4523	3.8833	4.3635	4.8980	5.4924	6.1528
14	1.5126	1.7317	1.9799	2.2609	2.5785	2.9372	3.3417	3.7975	4.3104	4.8871	5.5348	6.2613	7.0757
15	1.5580	1.8009	2.0789	2.3966	2.7590	3.1722	3.6425	4.1772	4.7846	5.4736	6.2543	7.1379	8.1371
16	1.6047	1.8730	2.1829	2.5404	2.9522	3.4259	3.9703	4.5950	5.3109	6.1304	7.0673	8.1372	9.3576
17	1.6528	1.9479	2.2920	2.6928	3.1588	3.7000	4.3276	5.0545	5.8951	6.8660	7.9861	9.2765	10.7613
18	1.7024	2.0258	2.4066	2.8543	3.3799	3.9960	4.7171	5.5599	6.5436	7.6900	9.0243	10.5752	12.3755
19	1.7535	2.1068	2.5270	3.0256	3.6165	4.3157	5.1417	6.1159	7.2633	8.6128	10.1974	12.0557	14.2318
20	1.8061	2.1911	2.6533	3.2071	3.8697	4.6610	5.6044	6.7275	8.0623	9.6463	11.5231	13.7435	16.3665

TABLE 4 FUTURE VALUE OF AN ORDINARY ANNUITY OF $1

Period	3.00%	4.00%	5.00%	6.00%	7.00%	8.00%	9.00%	10.00%	11.00%	12.00%	13.00%	14.00%	15.00%
1	1.0000	1.0000	1.0000	1.0000	1.0000	1.0000	1.0000	1.0000	1.0000	1.0000	1.0000	1.0000	1.0000
2	2.0300	2.0400	2.0500	2.0600	2.0700	2.0800	2.0900	2.1000	2.1100	2.1200	2.1300	2.1400	2.1500
3	3.0909	3.1216	3.1525	3.1836	3.2149	3.2464	3.2781	3.3100	3.3421	3.3744	3.4069	3.4396	3.4725
4	4.1836	4.2465	4.3101	4.3746	4.4399	4.5061	4.5731	4.6410	4.7097	4.7793	4.8498	4.9211	4.9934
5	5.3091	5.4163	5.5256	5.6371	5.7507	5.8666	5.9847	6.1051	6.2278	6.3528	6.4803	6.6101	6.7424
6	6.4684	6.6330	6.8019	6.9753	7.1533	7.3359	7.5233	7.7156	7.9129	8.1152	8.3227	8.5355	7.7537
7	7.6625	7.8983	8.1420	8.3938	8.6540	8.9228	9.2004	9.4872	9.7833	10.0890	10.4047	10.7305	11.0668
8	8.8923	9.2142	9.5491	9.8975	10.2598	10.6366	11.0285	11.4359	11.8594	12.2997	12.7573	13.2328	13.7268
9	10.1591	10.5828	11.0266	11.4913	11.9780	12.4876	13.0210	13.5795	14.1640	14.7757	15.4157	16.0853	16.7858
10	11.4639	12.0061	12.5779	13.1808	13.8164	14.4866	15.1929	15.9374	16.7220	17.5487	18.4197	19.3373	20.3037
11	12.8078	13.4864	14.2068	14.9716	15.7836	16.6455	17.5603	18.5312	19.5614	20.6546	21.8143	23.0445	24.3493
12	14.1920	15.0258	15.9171	16.8699	17.8885	18.9771	20.1407	21.3843	22.7132	24.1331	25.6502	27.2707	29.0017
13	15.6178	16.6268	17.7130	18.8821	20.1406	21.4953	22.9534	24.5227	26.2116	28.0291	29.9847	32.0887	34.3519
14	17.0863	18.2919	19.5986	21.0151	22.5505	24.2149	26.0192	27.9750	30.0949	32.3926	34.8827	37.5811	40.5047
15	18.5989	20.0236	21.5786	23.2760	25.1290	27.1521	29.3609	31.7725	34.4054	37.2797	40.4175	43.8424	47.5804
16	20.1569	21.8245	23.6575	25.6725	27.8881	30.3243	33.0034	35.9497	39.1899	42.7533	46.6717	50.9804	55.7175
17	21.7616	23.6975	25.8404	28.2129	30.8402	33.7502	36.9737	40.5447	44.5008	48.8837	53.7391	59.1176	65.0751
18	23.4144	25.6454	28.1324	30.9057	33.9990	37.4502	41.3013	45.5992	50.3959	55.7497	61.7251	68.3941	75.8364
19	25.1169	27.6712	30.5390	33.7600	37.3790	41.4463	46.0185	51.1591	56.9395	63.4397	70.7494	78.9692	88.2118
20	26.8704	29.7781	33.0660	36.7856	40.9955	45.7620	51.1601	57.2750	64.2028	72.0524	80.9468	91.0249	102.4436

(Numbers in parentheses refer to the chapter(s) containing the main discussion of the term.)

A

ABC analysis an inventory control method that separates items into three groups based on annual cost-to-volume usage; items having the highest dollar volume are referred to as A items, while C items represent the lowest dollar volume (7)

Abnormal spoilage units lost in production due to circumstances not inherent in the manufacturing process; these losses are not expected under normal, efficient operating conditions and are accounted for as period costs (4)

Absorption costing a cost accumulation method that treats the costs of all manufacturing components (direct materials, direct labour, variable overhead, and fixed overhead) as inventoriable or product costs; also known as full costing (3)

Accepted quality level a predetermined level of acceptability (4)

Accounting rate of return the rate of accounting earnings obtained on an average capital investment (or initial investment) over a project's life (10)

Activity a repetitive action, movement, or work sequence performed to fulfill a business function (1, 6)

Activity-based costing an accounting information system that identifies the various activities performed in an organization and collects costs on the basis of the underlying nature and extent of those activities (6)

Activity-based management a discipline that focuses on how the activities performed during the production/performance process can improve the value received by a customer and the profit achieved by providing this value (6)

Activity centre a segment of the production or service process for which management wants a separate report of the costs of activities performed (6)

Activity cost driver a measure of the demands placed on activities and, thus, the resources consumed by products and services; often indicates an activity's output (6)

Allocate assign indirect or overhead costs based on the use of a cost driver, a predictor, or an arbitrary method (2)

Annuity a series of equal cash flows occurring at equal time intervals (10)

Annuity due an annuity in which each cash flow occurs at the beginning of the period (10)

Applied overhead the amount of overhead assigned to Work in Process Inventory as a result of the occurrence of the activity that was used to develop the application rate; the result of mul-

tiplying the quantity of actual activity by the predetermined rate (2)

Appropriation a maximum allowable expenditure for a budget item (9)

Asset turnover a ratio that measures asset productivity; it is the number of sales dollars generated by each dollar of assets during a specific period (13)

Authority the right (usually by virtue of position or rank) to use resources to accomplish a task or achieve an objective; can be delegated or assigned to others (1)

B

Backflush costing a costing system that focuses on output and works backward through the system to allocate costs to cost of goods sold and inventory (7)

Batch-level cost a cost that is created by a group of similar things made, handled, or processed at a single time (6)

Bill of materials a document that contains information about product material components, their specifications (including quality), and the quantities needed for production (5)

Bottleneck resource constraint (7)

Breakeven graph a graphical depiction of the relationships among revenues, variable costs, fixed costs, and profits (or losses) (3)

Breakeven point that level of activity, in units or dollars, at which total revenues equal total costs (3)

Budget the quantitative expression of an organization's commitment to planned activities and resource acquisition and use (9)

Budget committee a group, usually composed of top management and the chief financial officer, that reviews and approves or makes adjustments to the master budget and/or the budgets submitted from operational managers (9)

Budgeting the process of determining a financial plan for future operations (9)

Budget manual a detailed set of documents that provides information and guidelines about the budgetary process (9)

Budget slack the intentional underestimation of revenues and/or overestimation of expenses (9)

Business process redesign when an organization changes its business processes (12)

Business process reengineering process innovation and redesign aimed at finding and implementing radical changes in how things are made or how tasks are performed to achieve substantial cost, service, or time reductions (6)

Business-value-added activity an activity that is necessary for the operation of a business but for which a customer would not want to pay (6)

By-products products that have minor sales value as compared with the sales value of the major products and are not separately identifiable as individual products until they have become split-off (8)

C

Canada Customs and Revenue Agency the federal government body that collects income taxes; formerly known as Revenue Canada (10)

Capacity a measure of production volume or of some other cost driver related to plant production capability during a period (2)

Capital asset an asset used to generate revenues or cost savings by providing production, distribution, or service capabilities for more than one year (10)

Capital budgeting a process for evaluating proposed long-range projects or courses of future activity for the purpose of allocating limited resources to desirable projects (9, 10)

Capital Cost Allowance tax depreciation (10)

Carrying costs the (variable) costs of carrying one unit of inventory in stock for one year; consist of storage, handling, insurance charges, property taxes based on inventory size, possible losses from obsolescence or the like, and opportunity cost (7)

Cash flow the receipt or disbursement of cash (10)

Centralization an organizational structure in which top management makes most decisions and controls most activities of the organizational units from the organization's central headquarters (1, 11)

Chart of accounts the list of all codes for recording transactions (12)

Compensation strategy a foundation for the compensation plan that addresses the role compensation should play in the organization (13)

Compounding period the time from one interest computation to the next (10)

Compound interest interest earned in prior periods is added to the original investment so that, in each successive period, interest is earned on both principal and interest (10)

Concurrent engineering see *simultaneous engineering* (6)

Constraint a restriction on management's pursuit of its objective (Web 7)

Continuous budget an ongoing 12-month budget that adds a new budget month (12 months into the future) as each current month expires (9)

Continuous loss reductions that occur uniformly during processing (4)

Contribution margin selling price per unit minus all variable production, selling, and administrative costs per unit (3)

Contribution margin ratio contribution margin divided by revenue; indicates what proportion of selling price remains after variable costs have been covered (3)

Control exertion of managerial influence on operations so that they will conform to plans (1)

Conversion the transformation of organizational inputs into outputs (7)

Conversion cost the sum of direct labour and manufacturing overhead that is directly or indirectly necessary for transforming direct (raw) materials and purchased parts into a saleable finished product (2)

Core competency any critical function or activity in which one organization has a higher proficiency than its competitors; the roots of competitiveness and competitive advantage (1)

Correlation a statistical measure of the strength of the relationship between two variables (2)

Cost a monetary measure of the resources given up to acquire a good or service (2)

Cost accounting tools and methods applied to determine the cost of making products or performing services (1)

Cost avoidance a process of finding acceptable alternatives to high-cost items and not spending money for unnecessary goods or services (7)

Cost behaviour the manner in which a cost responds to a change in a related level of activity (2, 7)

Cost centre an organizational unit in which the manager has the authority only to incur costs and is specifically evaluated on the basis of how well costs are controlled (11)

Cost consciousness an organizationwide employee attitude toward cost understanding, cost containment, cost avoidance, and cost reduction (7)

Cost containment the process of attempting, to the extent possible, to minimize period-by-period increases in per-unit variable and total fixed costs (7)

Cost control system a logical structure of formal and informal activities designed to influence costs and to enable management to analyze and evaluate how well expenditures were managed during a period (7)

Cost driver a factor that has a direct cause–effect relationship to a cost (2)

Cost leadership a competitive strategy in which an organization becomes the low-cost producer/provider and is thus able to charge low prices that emphasize cost efficiencies (1)

Cost management system a set of formal methods developed for controlling an organization's cost-generating activities relative to its goals and objectives (12)

Cost object anything to which costs attach or are related (2)

Cost of capital the weighted average rate that reflects the costs of the various sources of funds making up a firm's debt and equity structure (10)

Cost of goods manufactured the total manufacturing costs attached to units produced during an accounting period (2)

Cost of goods manufactured statement the total cost of the goods that were completed and transferred to Finished Goods Inventory during the period (2)

Cost of goods sold the cost of the products or services sold during the period (2)

Cost of production report a document used in a process costing system; details all manufacturing quantities and costs, shows the computation of cost per equivalent unit of production (EUP), and indicates the cost assignment to goods produced during the period (4)

Cost-plus job a job being billed at cost plus a specified profit margin (4)

Cost reduction a process of lowering current costs, especially those in excess of necessary costs (7)

Cost–volume–profit analysis the process of examining the relationships among revenues, costs, and profits for a relevant range of activity and for a particular time period (3)

Critical success factor an item that is so important to an organization that, without it, the organization would fail; timeliness, quality, customer service, efficiency and cost control, and responsiveness to change are five basic critical success factors (12)

Cycle time the time from when a customer places an order to the time that the product or service is delivered or, using a full life-cycle approach, the time from the conceptualization of a product or service to the time the product or service is delivered to the market/customer (6)

D

Decentralization the downward delegation by top management of authority and decision making to the individuals who are closest to internal processes and customers (1, 11)

Defective unit see *spoilage* (4)

Degree of operating leverage a measure of how a percentage change in sales will affect profits; calculated at a specified sales level as contribution margin divided by income before tax (3)

Dependent variable an unknown variable that is to be predicted by use of one or more independent variables (2)

Differentiation a competitive strategy in which an organization distinguishes its products or services from those of competitors by adding enough value (including quality and/or features) that customers are willing to pay a higher price (1)

Direct cost a cost that is clearly, conveniently, and economically traceable to a particular cost object (2)

Direct costing see *variable costing* (3)

Direct labour the time spent by individuals who work specifically on manufacturing a product or performing a service and whose efforts are conveniently and economically traceable to that product or service; can also be viewed as the cost of the direct labour time (2)

Direct material a readily identifiable, physical part of a product that is clearly, conveniently, and economically traceable to that product (2)

Discounting the process of removing the portion of a future cash flow that represents interest, thereby reducing that flow to a present value amount (10)

Discount rate the rate of return on capital investments required by the company; the rate of return used in present value computations (10)

Dual pricing arrangement a transfer price method that allows a selling division to record the transfer of goods or services at a market-based or negotiated price and a buying division to record the transfer at a cost-based amount (11)

Du Pont model ROI = Profit margin $\times$ Asset turnover (13)

E

Economic order quantity an estimate of the least costly number of units per order that would provide the optimal balance between ordering and carrying costs (7)

Economic value added EVA = After-tax income − (Cost of capital % $\times$ Capital invested) (13)

Effectiveness a measure of how well the firm's objectives and goals were achieved; it involves comparing actual output results with desired results (11)

Employee time sheet (time ticket) a source document that indicates, for each employee, what jobs were worked on during the day and for what amounts of time (4)

Empowerment all practices that are designed to give workers the training, authority, and responsibility they need to manage their own jobs and make decisions about their work (1, 7)

Enterprise resource planning a fully integrated, full-service suite of software with a common database that can be used to plan and control resources across an entire organization (12)

Environmental constraint any limitation on strategy caused by external cultural, fiscal (such as taxation structures), legal/regulatory, or political situations or by competitive market structures; tends to have long-run rather than short-run effects (1)

Equivalent units of production an approximation of the number of whole units of output that could have been produced during a period from the actual effort expended during that period (4)

Ethical standards norms that represent beliefs about moral and immoral behaviours; norms for individual conduct in making decisions and engaging in business transactions (1)

Expected annual capacity a short-run concept representing the anticipated level of activity for the upcoming year (2)

Expected standard a standard that reflects what is actually expected to occur in a future period (5)

F

Facility-level cost see *organizational-level cost* (6)

FIFO method a method of process costing that computes an average cost per equivalent unit of production using only current production and current cost information; units and costs in beginning inventory are accounted for separately (4)

Financial accounting generation of accounting information for external reporting (1)

Financial budget a budget that reflects the funds to be generated or used during the budget period; includes the cash and capital budgets and the projected or pro forma financial statements (9)

Financing decision a judgment regarding how funds will be obtained to make an acquisition (10)

Fixed cost a cost that remains constant in total within a specified range of activity (2)

Fixed overhead spending variance the difference between actual and budgeted (planned) fixed overhead (5)

Functional classification a grouping of costs incurred for the same basic purpose (3)

Future value the amount to which one or more sums of money invested at a specified interest rate will grow over a specified number of time periods (10)

G

Goal a desired result or condition that is expressed in qualitative terms (1)

Goal congruence a condition that exists when the personal and organizational goals of decision makers throughout the firm are consistent and mutually supportive (11)

H

High–low method a technique for separating mixed costs that uses actual observations of a total cost at the highest and lowest levels of activity and calculates the change in both activity and cost; the levels chosen must be within the relevant range (2)

Horizontal price fixing the practice by which competitors attempt to regulate prices through an agreement or conspiracy (7)

Hurdle rate the rate of return deemed by management to be the lowest acceptable return on investment (10)

I

Ideal capacity see *theoretical capacity* (2)

Idle time storage time and time spent waiting at a production operation for processing (6)

Imposed budget a budget that is prepared by top management with little or no input from operating personnel, who are simply informed of the budget goals and constraints (9)

Incremental analysis a technique used in decision analysis that compares alternatives by focusing on the differences in their projected revenues and costs (3)

Incremental cost the additional cost of producing or selling a contemplated quantity of output (8)

Incremental revenue the additional revenue resulting from a contemplated sale of a quantity of output (8)

Independent project an investment project that has no specific bearing on any other investment project (10)

Independent variable a variable that, when changed, will cause consistent, observable changes in another variable; a variable used as the basis of predicting the value of a dependent variable (2)

Indirect cost a cost that cannot be clearly traced to a particular cost object (2)

Inspection time the time taken to perform quality control (6)

Internal rate of return the discount rate at which the present value of the cash inflows minus the present value of the cash outflows equals zero (10)

Investing decision a judgment regarding which assets an entity will acquire to achieve its stated objectives (10)

Investment centre an organizational unit in which the manager is responsible for generating revenues, planning and controlling costs, and acquiring, disposing of, and using plant assets to earn the highest feasible rate of return on the investment base (11)

J

Job a single unit or group of like units identifiable as being produced to distinct customer specifications (4)

Job order costing system a product costing method used by entities that produce limited quantities of custom-made goods or services that conform to specifications designated by the purchaser (4)

Job order cost sheet a source document that provides virtually all the financial information about a particular job; the set of all job order cost sheets for uncompleted jobs composes the Work in Process Inventory subsidiary ledger (4)

Joint cost the cost incurred, up to the split-off point, for material, labour, and overhead in a joint process (8)

Joint process a process in which one product cannot be manufactured without others being produced (8)

Joint products two or more products that have relatively significant sales values and are not separately identifiable as individual products until the split-off point (8)

Just-in-time a philosophy about when to do something; the *when* is "as needed" and the *something* is a production, purchasing, or delivery activity; the idea that inventory is manufactured (or purchased) only as the need arises or in time to be sold or used (5)

Just-in-time manufacturing system acquires components and produces inventory units only as they are needed, minimizes product defects, and reduces lead/setup times for acquisition and production (7)

K

Kanban the Japanese word for *card*; another name for just-in-time manufacturing, which originated in Japan from the use of cards to control the flow of materials or units between work centres (7)

Key variable a critical factor believed to be a direct cause of the achievement or nonachievement of organizational goals and objectives; can be internal or external (9)

L

Labour efficiency variance the difference between the number of actual direct labour hours worked and the standard hours allowed for the actual output multiplied by the standard labour rate per hour (5)

Labour rate variance the difference between the total actual direct labour wages for the period and the standard rate for all hours actually worked during the period (5)

Lead time the time from the placement of an order to the arrival of the goods (7)

Least-squares regression analysis a statistical technique for mathematically determining the cost line of a mixed cost that best fits the data set by considering all representative data points; allows the user to investigate the relationship between or among dependent and independent variables (2)

Long-term variable cost a cost that has traditionally been viewed as fixed but that will actually react to some significant change in activity; also referred to as a step fixed cost (6)

M

Make-or-buy decision a decision that compares the cost of internally manufacturing a product component with the cost of purchasing it from outside suppliers or from another division at a specified price and, thus, attempts to assess the best uses of available facilities (8)

Management accounting the gathering and application of information used to plan, make decisions, evaluate performance, and control an organization (1)

Management by exception a technique in which managers set upper and lower limits of tolerance for deviations and investigate only deviations that fall outside those tolerance ranges (5, 11)

Manufacturing cycle efficiency value-added production time divided by total cycle time; provides a measure of processing efficiency (6)

Manufacturing resource planning a fully integrated system that plans production jobs using the usual MRP method and also calculates resource needs such as labour and machine hours; involves manufacturing, marketing, and finance in determining the master production schedule (7)

Margin of safety the excess of the estimated (budgeted) or actual sales of a company over its breakeven point; can be calculated in units or sales dollars, or as a percentage (3)

Mass customization the relatively low-cost mass production of products to the unique specifications of individual customers; requires the use of flexible manufacturing systems (6)

Master budget the comprehensive set of all budgetary schedules and the pro forma financial statements of an organization (9)

Material price variance the amount of money spent below (F for favourable) or above (U for unfavourable) the standard price for the quantity of materials purchased (5)

Material quantity variance the cost saved (F) or expended (U) because of the difference between the actual quantity of material used and the standard quantity of material allowed for the goods produced or services rendered during the period (5)

Materials requirements planning a computer simulation system that helps organizations plan by coordinating future production output requirements with individual future production input needs using a master production schedule (7)

Materials requisition form a source document that indicates the types and quantities of materials to be placed into production or used in performing a service; causes materials and their costs to be released from the raw materials warehouse and sent to Work in Process Inventory (4)

Method of neglect a method of treating spoiled units in the schedule calculating equivalent units (4)

Mixed cost a cost that has both a variable and a fixed component; it does not fluctuate in direct proportion to changes in activity, nor does it remain constant with changes in activity (2)

Multiple regression regression analysis using two or more independent variables (2)

Mutually exclusive projects a set of proposed investments for which there is a group of available candidates that all perform essentially the same function or meet the same objective; from this group, one is chosen and all others are rejected (10)

Mutually inclusive projects a set of proposed investments that are all related to a primary project; when the primary project is chosen, all related investments are also selected (10)

N

Negotiated transfer prices an intracompany charge for goods or services that has been set through a process of negotiation between the selling and purchasing unit managers (11)

Net present value the difference between the present values of all of the project's cash inflows and cash outflows (10)

Net present value method an investment evaluation technique that uses discounted cash flow to determine if the rate of return on a project is equal to, higher than, or lower than the desired rate of return (10)

Nonfinancial performance measures statistics on activities such as on-time delivery, manufacturing cycle time, set-up time, defect rate, number of unplanned production interruptions, and customer returns (13)

Non-value-added activity an activity that increases the time spent on a product or service but does not increase its value or worth to the customer (6)

Normal capacity a firm's long-run average activity (over five to ten years), which gives effect to historical and estimated future production levels and to cyclical and seasonal fluctuations (2)

Normal spoilage units lost due to the nature of the manufacturing process; such losses are unavoidable and represent a product cost (4)

O

Objective a quantitatively expressed result that can be achieved during a preestablished period or by a specified date; should logically measure progress in achieving goals (1)

Objective function the mathematical equation stating the objective in an LP problem—either to maximize or to minimize some measure of performance (Web 7)

Open-book management a philosophy about increasing a firm' s performance by involving all workers and by ensuring that all workers have access to operational and financial information necessary to achieving performance improvements (Web 13)

Operating budget a budget that is expressed in both units and dollars (9)

Operating leverage a factor that reflects the relationship of a company's variable and fixed costs; measures the change in profits expected to result from a specified percentage change in sales (3)

Operations flow document a listing of all tasks necessary to make a unit of product or perform a service and the time allowed for each operation (5)

Opportunity cost the benefit forgone when one course of action is chosen over another (8)

Ordering costs the variable costs associated with preparing, receiving, and paying for an order (7)

Order point the inventory level that triggers the placement of an order (7)

Ordinary annuity an annuity in which each cash flow occurs at the end of the period (10)

Organizational culture the set of basic assumptions about the organization, its goals, and its business practices; describes an

organization's norms in internal and external, as well as formal and informal, transactions (1)

Organizational form the nature of the legal entity created for a business enterprise (12)

Organizational-level cost a cost incurred to support ongoing operations, which in turn provide available facilities (6)

Organizational structure the way in which authority and responsibility for making decisions is distributed in an organization (1)

Outlier a nonrepresentative point that falls outside of the relevant range of activity or that is a distortion of normal costs within the relevant range (2)

Outsourcing contracting with outside manufacturers or vendors for necessary goods or services rather than producing the goods or performing the services in-house (1, 8, 11)

Overapplied overhead overhead applied to Work in Process Inventory that is greater than actual overhead incurred for a period (2)

Overhead the expenses of a business such as rent, insurance, and utilities consumed in the production of a product or consumed in the supplying of a service (2)

P

Participatory budget a budget that has been developed through a process of joint decision making by top management and operating personnel (9)

Payback period the time required to recoup the original investment in a project through its cash flows (10)

Performance measurement system a major set of financial and, particularly, nonfinancial performance measures for evaluating the performance of a manager, activity, or organizational unit (12)

Period cost a cost that is incurred during an accounting period to support the activities of the company; the cost of resources consumed during the period (2)

Post-investment audit a comparison of expected and actual project results after a capital investment (10)

Practical capacity the activity level that could be achieved during normal working hours given unused capacity and ongoing, regular operating interruptions, such as holidays, downtime, and start-up time (2)

Practical standards standards that can be reached or slightly exceeded approximately 60% to 70% of the time with reasonable effort by workers (5)

Predetermined overhead rate a budgeted constant charge per unit of activity used to assign overhead costs to production or services (2)

Predictor an activity measure that is accompanied by a consistent, observable change in a cost item (2)

Preference decision a judgment regarding how projects are to be ranked based on their impact on the achievement of company objectives (10)

Present value the amount that a future cash flow is worth currently, given a specified rate of interest (10)

Price fixing a practice by which firms conspire to set a product's price at a specified level (7)

Price variance the difference between what was paid and what should have been paid for inputs during the period (5)

Prime cost the total cost of direct materials and direct labour; so called because these costs are most convincingly associated with and traceable to a specific product (2)

Process costing a method of accumulating and assigning costs to units of production in companies that make large quantities of homogeneous products (4)

Process costing system a product costing system used by companies that produce large amounts of homogeneous products through a continuous production flow (4)

Process-level cost see *product-level cost* (6)

Process map a flowchart or diagram that indicates every step in making a product or providing a service (6)

Process productivity the total units produced during a period using value-added processing time (13)

Process quality yield the proportion of good units that resulted from the activities expended (13)

Process re-engineering process innovation and redesign aimed at finding and implementing radical changes in how things are made or how tasks are performed to achieve substantial cost, service, or time reductions (12)

Product complexity the number of components in a product or the number of processes or operations through which a product flows (6)

Product cost a cost associated with making or acquiring inventory or providing a service (2)

Production cost in a manufacturing company, includes costs associated with buying direct materials, paying for direct labour, incurring traceable overhead, and absorbing allocated fixed overhead (7)

Product-level cost a cost created by the need to implement or support a specific product (6)

Product margin the excess of a product's revenues over both its direct variable expenses and any avoidable fixed expenses related to the product; the amount remaining to cover unavoidable direct fixed expenses and common costs and then to provide profits (8)

Product variety the number of different types of products produced (6)

Profitability index a ratio that compares the present value of net cash inflows with the present value of the net investment (10)

Profit centre an organizational unit in which the manager is responsible for generating revenues and planning and controlling all expenses (11)

Profit margin the ratio of income to sales (13)

Profit–volume graph a graphical presentation of the profit or loss associated with each level of sales (3)

Project a future activity, such as the purchase, installation, and operation of a capital asset (10)

Pull system a production system in which parts are delivered or manufactured only as they are needed (7)

Purchasing cost the quoted purchase price minus any discounts allowed plus shipping charges (7)

Push system a production system in which work centres may purchase or produce inventory that is not currently needed because of lead time or economic order (production) quantity requirements; the excess inventory is stored until it is needed (7)

Q

Quantity variance the difference between the quantity of actual inputs and the standard quantity of inputs for the actual output of the period multiplied by a standard price or rate (5)

R

Recapture occurs when all assets in a class are sold and the proceeds exceed the undepreciated capital cost of the class; the excess is subject to tax (10)

Red-line system an inventory system in which a single container (or stack) of inventory is available for production needs, and a red line is painted on the inventory container (or the wall, for a stack) at a point deemed to be the reorder point (7)

Regression analysis a statistical procedure used to determine and measure a predictive relationship between one dependent variable and one or more other variables (2)

Regression line a line that represents the cost formula for a set of cost observations fit to those observations in a mathematically determined manner (2)

Relevant cost a cost that is pertinent to or logically associated with a specific problem or decision and that differs between alternatives (8)

Relevant costing a process that allows managers to focus on pertinent facts and disregard extraneous information by comparing, to the extent possible and practical, the differential, incremental revenues and incremental costs of alternative decisions (8)

Relevant range the specified range of activity over which a variable cost remains constant per unit and a fixed cost remains fixed in total (2)

Rent each equal cash flow of an annuity (10)

Residual income the profit earned that exceeds an amount "charged" for funds committed to a responsibility centre (13)

Responsibility the obligation to accomplish a task or achieve an objective; cannot be delegated to others (1)

Responsibility accounting an accounting system that provides information to top management about segment or sub-unit performance (11, 12)

Responsibility centre the cost object under the control of a manager; in the case of a decentralized company, the cost object is an organizational unit such as a division, department, or geographical region (11)

Responsibility reports reflect the revenues and/or costs under the control of a specific unit manager (11)

Return of capital recovery of the original investment (10)

Return on capital income equals the discount rate times an investment amount (10)

Return on investment a ratio that relates income generated by the investment centre to the resources (or asset base) used to produce that income (13)

Revenue centre an organizational unit in which the manager is accountable only for the generation of revenues and has no control over selling prices or budgeted costs (11)

S

Safety stock the quantity of inventory kept on hand by a company to compensate for potential fluctuations in usage or unusual delays in receiving orders (7)

Sales mix the relative combination of quantities of sales of the various products that make up the total sales of a company (8)

Sales price variance the difference between actual and budgeted selling prices multiplied by the actual number of units sold (9)

Sales volume variance the difference between actual and budgeted volumes multiplied by the budgeted selling price (9)

Scarce resources resources that are available only in limited quantity; they create constraints on producing goods or providing services and may include money, machine hours, skilled labour hours, raw materials, and production capacity (8)

Scrap inputs that do not become part of the outputs but have very minor values (8)

Screening decision a judgment regarding the desirability of a capital project based on some previously established minimum criterion or criteria (10)

Service variety the number of different types of services provided (6)

Setup costs the direct and indirect labour costs of getting equipment ready for a new production run (7)

Simple interest interest calculated as a percentage of only the original investment, or principal amount (10)

Simple regression regression analysis using only one independent variable to predict the dependent variable (2)

Simultaneous engineering an integrated approach in which all primary functions and personnel contributing to a product's origination and production are involved continuously from the beginning of a project (6)

Special order pricing determining a sales price to charge for manufacturing or service jobs that are outside the company's normal production or service realm (8)

Split-off point the point at which the outputs of a joint process are first identifiable as individual products (8)

Spoilage unit of product with imperfections that cannot be corrected in an economical way (4)

Spoiled unit see *spoilage* (4)

Standard cost a budgeted or estimated cost to manufacture a single unit of product or perform a single service (5)

Standard cost card a document that summarizes the direct materials and direct labour standard quantities and prices needed to complete one unit of product as well as the overhead allocation bases and rates (5)

Standard costing system a product costing method using unit norms for production costs (5)

Standard quantity allowed a measure of quantity that translates the actual output achieved into the standard input quantity that should have been used to achieve that output (5)

Standards benchmarks or norms against which actual results may be compared (5)

Step cost a variable or fixed cost that shifts upward or downward when activity changes by a certain interval or step (2)

Strategic alliance an agreement involving two or more firms with complementary core competencies to jointly contribute to the value creation chain (1)

Strategic planning the process of developing a statement of long-range (5 to 10 years) goals for the organization and defining the strategies and policies that will help the organization achieve those goals (9)

Strategy a long-term dynamic plan that fulfills organizational goals and objectives through satisfaction of customer needs or wants within the company's acknowledged operating markets (1)

Suboptimization a situation in which unit managers make decisions that positively affect their own unit but that are detrimental to other organizational units or to the company as a whole (11)

Sunk cost the historical or past cost that is associated with the acquisition of an asset or a resource (8)

Survival triplet the cost/price, quality, and functionality that products or services need to demonstrate in order to survive and prosper (7)

Synchronous management all endeavours that help an organization achieve its goals (13)

T

Tactical planning the process of determining the specific objectives and means by which strategic plans will be achieved; are short-term (1 to 18 months), single use plans that have been developed to address a given set of circumstances or for a specific time frame (9)

Target costing a process of determining an allowable cost for a product or component that is inferred from projecting a market price for the product and subtracting a required profit margin (7)

Tax shield (of CCA) the amount of the reduction of taxable income provided by Capital Cost Allowance (10)

Theoretical capacity the estimated absolute maximum potential production activity that could occur in a production facility during a specific time frame (2)

Theoretical standards standards that allow for no inefficiencies of any type; encompass the highest level of rigour and do not allow for normal operating delays or human limitations such as fatigue, boredom, or misunderstanding (5)

Theory of constraints a management philosophy about focusing attention on the constraints (sometimes called bottlenecks) that limit organizational achievements such as maximization of profits (Web 7)

Throughput the rate at which a company generates cash from selling products and services to customers (13)

Throughput accounting the operational use of throughput, assets, and operational expenses to measure performance (Web 7)

Timeline illustration of the timing of expected cash receipts and payments; cash inflows are shown as positive amounts and cash outflows are shown as negative amounts (10)

Total contribution margin revenue minus all variable costs regardless of the area of incurrence (production or nonproduction) (3)

Total cost to account for the balance in Work in Process Inventory at the beginning of the period plus all current costs for direct material, direct labour, and overhead (4)

Total quality management (TQM) a philosophy for organizational management and organizational change that seeks ever-increasing quality (5)

Total units to account for total whole or partial physical units for which the department is responsible during the current period; beginning WIP inventory units plus units started (4)

Transfer price an internal charge established for the exchange of goods and services between organizational units of the same company (11)

Transfer time the time it takes to move products or components from one place to another (move time) (6)

Two-bin system an inventory system in which two containers or stacks of inventory are available for production needs; when

production begins to use materials in the second bin, a purchase order is placed to refill the first bin (7)

U

Underapplied overhead overhead applied to Work in Process Inventory that is less than actual overhead incurred for a period (2)

Unit-level cost a cost created by the production or acquisition of a single unit of production or the delivery of a single unit of service (6)

Units started and completed the total units completed during the period minus the units in beginning inventory; alternatively, units started minus units in ending inventory (4)

V

Value-added activity an activity that increases the worth of a product or service to the customer and for which the customer is willing to pay (6)

Value-added processing time the time it takes to perform the functions necessary to manufacture a product (6)

Value-added service time the time it takes to perform all necessary service functions for a customer (6)

Value chart a visual representation of the value-added and non-value-added activities and the time spent in all of these activities from the beginning to the end of a process (6)

Value creation chain the set of processes and activities that convert inputs into products and services that have value to the organization's customers (1)

Value engineering a tool used to manage the relationship between product design, product price, and target cost (7)

Variable cost a cost that varies in total in direct proportion to changes in activity (2)

Variable costing a cost accumulation method that includes only variable production costs (direct materials, direct labour, and variable manufacturing overhead) as product or inventoriable costs and treats fixed overhead as a period cost; also known as direct costing (3)

Variable cost ratio 100% minus the CM ratio; represents the variable cost proportion of each revenue dollar (3)

Variable overhead efficiency variance the difference between budgeted (planned) variable overhead at actual input activity and budgeted variable overhead at standard input activity allowed (5)

Variable overhead spending variance the difference between actual variable overhead and budgeted (planned) variable overhead based on actual input (5)

Variance any difference between actual and standard costs or quantities (5)

Variance analysis the process of categorizing the nature (favourable or unfavourable) of the differences between standard and actual costs and seeking the reasons for those differences (5)

Vertical integration the extent to which the value creation chain resides within a single firm (1)

Vertical price fixing collusion between producing businesses and their distributors to control the prices at which their products may be sold to consumers (7)

Volume variance the difference between budgeted (planned) and applied fixed overhead (5)

W

Waste inputs that do not become part of the output (8)

Weighted average method a method of process costing that computes an average cost per equivalent unit of production; combines beginning inventory units with current production and beginning inventory costs with current costs to compute that average (4)

Z

Zero-based budgeting a comprehensive budgeting process that systematically considers the priorities and alternatives for current and proposed activities in relation to organizational objectives (9)